CONNECT PLUS FEATURES

Lecture Videos

Edmonds' Connect Plus Accounting Lecture Videos, new to this edition, teach each chapter's core learning objectives and concepts through an engaging, hands-on presentation, bringing the text content to life. The videos have been developed by the author team and have the touch and feel of a live lecture, as opposed to a canned presentation. Paired with self assessment questions, students can learn at their own pace. Harnessing the full power of technology to truly engage and appeal to all learning styles, the lecture videos are ideal in all class formats—online, face-to-face, flipped, and hybrid.

End-of-Chapter Material

McGraw-Hill Education redesigned the student interface for our end-of-chapter assessment content. The new interface provides improved answer acceptance to reduce students' frustration with formatting issues (such as rounding), and, for select questions, provides an expanded table that guides students through the process of solving the problem. Many questions have been redesigned to more fully test students' mastery of the content.

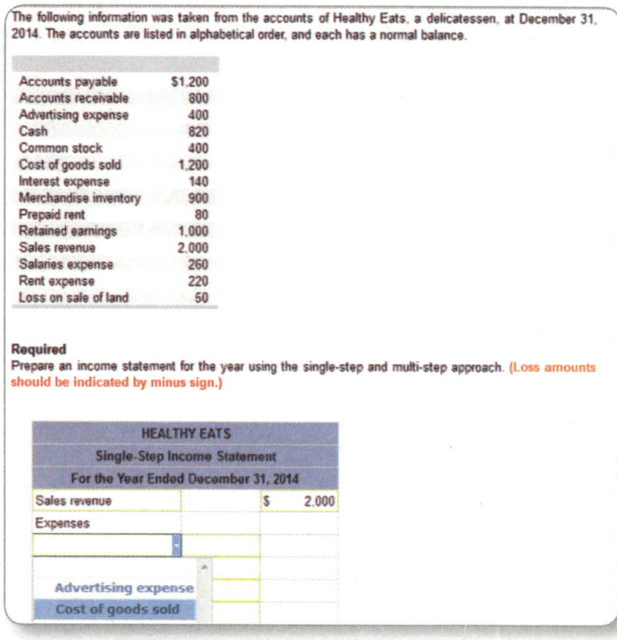
The following information was taken from the accounts of Healthy Eats, a delicatessen, at December 31, 2014. The accounts are listed in alphabetical order, and each has a normal balance.

Accounts payable	$1,200
Accounts receivable	800
Advertising expense	400
Cash	820
Common stock	400
Cost of goods sold	1,200
Interest expense	140
Merchandise inventory	900
Prepaid rent	80
Retained earnings	1,000
Sales revenue	2,000
Salaries expense	260
Rent expense	220
Loss on sale of land	50

Required

Prepare an income statement for the year using the single-step and multi-step approach. (Loss amounts should be indicated by minus sign.)

HEALTHY EATS		
Single-Step Income Statement		
For the Year Ended December 31, 2014		
Sales revenue		$ 2,000
Expenses		
Advertising expense		
Cost of goods sold		

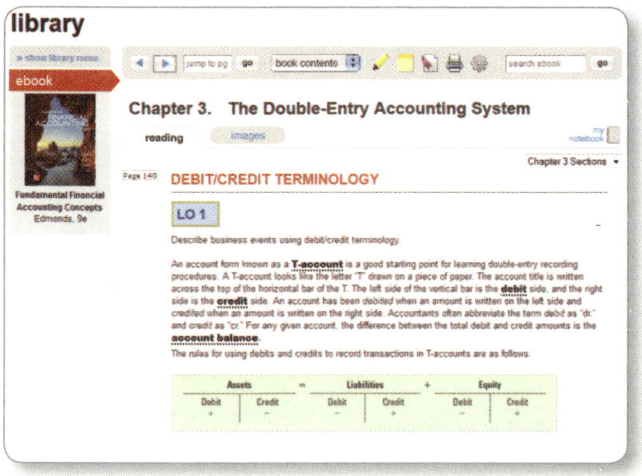
library

» show library menu

ebook

jump to pg go book contents search ebook go

Fundamental Financial Accounting Concepts Edmonds, 9e

Chapter 3. The Double-Entry Accounting System

reading images my notebook

Chapter 3 Sections

Page 140

DEBIT/CREDIT TERMINOLOGY

LO 1

Describe business events using debit/credit terminology.

An account form known as a **T-account** is a good starting point for learning double-entry recording procedures. A T-account looks like the letter "T" drawn on a piece of paper. The account title is written across the top of the horizontal bar of the T. The left side of the vertical bar is the **debit** side, and the right side is the **credit** side. An account has been *debited* when an amount is written on the left side and *credited* when an amount is written on the right side. Accountants often abbreviate the term *debit* as "dr." and *credit* as "cr." For any given account, the difference between the total debit and credit amounts is the **account balance**.

The rules for using debits and credits to record transactions in T-accounts are as follows.

Assets		=	Liabilities		+	Equity	
Debit +	Credit −		Debit −	Credit +		Debit −	Credit +

eBook

Connect Plus includes a media-rich eBook that allows you to share your notes with your students. Your students can insert and review their own notes, highlight the text, search for specific information, and interact with media resources. Using an eBook with Connect Plus gives your students a complete digital solution that allows them to access their materials from any computer.

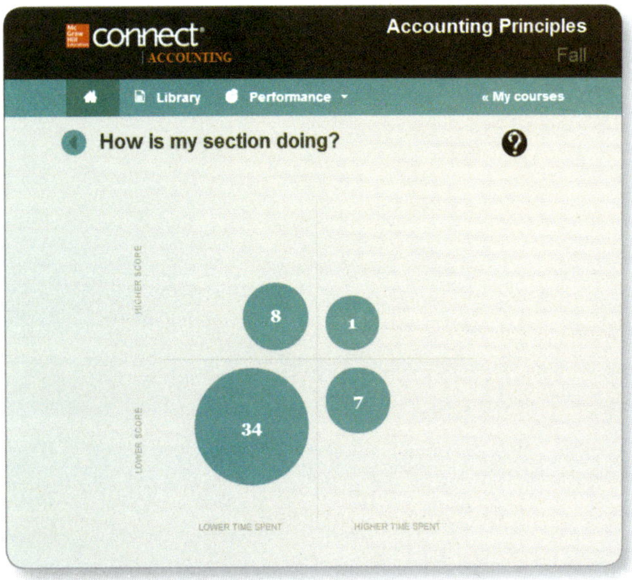

Connect Insight

The first and only analytics tool of its kind, Connect Insight is a series of visual data displays that are each framed by an intuitive question and provide at-a-glance information regarding how an instructor's class is performing. Connect Insight is available through Connect or Connect Plus titles.

EASY TO USE

Learning Management System Integration

McGraw-Hill Campus is a one-stop teaching and learning experience available to use with any learning management system. McGraw-Hill Campus provides single sign-on to faculty and students for all McGraw-Hill material and technology from within the school website. McGraw-Hill Campus also allows instructors instant access to all supplements and teaching materials for all McGraw-Hill products.

Blackboard users also benefit from McGraw-Hill's industry-leading integration, providing single sign-on to access all Connect Plus assignments and automatic feeding of assignment results to the Blackboard grade book.

The Best of Both Worlds

POWERFUL REPORTING

Connect Plus generates comprehensive reports and graphs that provide instructors with an instant view of the performance of individual students, a specific section, or multiple sections. Since all content is mapped to learning objectives, Connect Plus reporting is ideal for accreditation or other administrative documentation.

ninth edition

Fundamental Financial Accounting Concepts

Thomas P. Edmonds
University of Alabama–Birmingham

Christopher T. Edmonds
University of Alabama–Birmingham

Frances M. McNair
Mississippi State University

Philip R. Olds
Virginia Commonwealth University

Mc Graw Hill Education

FUNDAMENTAL FINANCIAL ACCOUNTING CONCEPTS, NINTH EDITION

This book is printed on acid-free paper.

1 2 3 4 5 6 7 8 9 0 DOW/DOW 1 0 9 8 7 6 5

ISBN 978-0-07-802590-7
MHID 0-07-802590-7

Senior Vice President, Products & Markets: *Kurt L. Strand*
Vice President, General Manager, Products & Markets: *Marty Lange*
Vice President, Content Design & Delivery: *Kimberly Meriwether David*
Managing Director: *Tim Vertovec*
Marketing Director: *Brad Parkins*
Senior Brand Manager: *Natalie King*
Director, Product Development: *Rose Koos*
Director of Digital Content: *Patricia Plumb*
Lead Product Developer: *Ann Torbert*
Product Developer: *Danielle Andries*
Marketing Manager: *Kathleen Klehr*
Digital Product Developer: *Kevin Moran*
Digital Product Analyst: *Xin Lin*
Director, Content Design & Delivery: *Linda Avenarius*
Program Manager: *Daryl Horrocks*
Content Project Managers: *Pat Frederickson* and *Angela Norris*
Buyer: *Carol A. Bielski*
Design: *Debra Kubiak*
Content Licensing Specialists: *Keri Johnson* and *Ann Marie Jannette*
Cover Image: *©Piriya Photography/Getty Images*
Compositor: *Aptara®, Inc.*
Printer: *R. R. Donnelley*

Library of Congress Cataloging-in-Publication Data

Edmonds, Thomas P.
Fundamental financial accounting concepts / Thomas P. Edmonds, University of Alabama-Birmingham, Christopher T. Edmonds, University of Alabama-Birmingham, Frances M. McNair, Mississippi State University, Philip R. Olds, Virginia Commonwealth University. – Ninth Edition.
pages cm
ISBN 978-0-07-802590-7 (alk. paper) – ISBN 0-07-802590-7 (alk. paper)
1. Accounting. I. Edmonds, Christopher T. II. McNair, Frances M., 1945–
III. Olds, Philip R. IV. Title.
HF5636.E36 2014
657–dc23

2014033592

www.mhhe.com

This book is dedicated to our students, whose questions have so frequently caused us to reevaluate our method of presentation that they have, in fact, become major contributors to the development of this text.

NOTE FROM THE AUTHORS

connect plus+ ACCOUNTING

LECTURE VIDEOS: A SEA CHANGE IN INSTRUCTIONAL METHODOLOGY

We are excited to announce the availability of instructional videos that explain the content associated with every learning objective introduced throughout the text. ***These videos have been developed by a member of the author team and are available when assigned through McGraw-Hill Connect Plus Accounting.*** They have the touch and feel of a live lecture as opposed to a canned PowerPoint presentation. The benefits are enormous. Videos allow students to pause for contemplation and note-taking. They permit students to repeat difficult concepts or fast-forward through content they have mastered. In other words, videos enable self-paced learning. No longer is the lecture too fast for some and too slow for others. Now the lecture satisfies the needs of each individual student.

Many accounting educators have taught in professional exam prep courses that make extensive use of video lectures. Now you can bring that prep course learning approach into your everyday classroom. You can use the videos we provide to transform the traditional classroom from a passive listening exercise into an active learning experience. Here are some examples of how you can use instructional videos to improve the classroom environment.

• Flip courses

Instructional videos enable instructors to flip the traditional teaching model. Specifically, instead of providing a lecture in class and then assigning homework, ***flip courses*** deliver the lecture at home and use the classroom as a place for students to work problems and ask questions. The teacher's function moves from lecturer to coach and tutor. Without a requirement to deliver a lecture, the instructor is free to tutor students in small groups or individually. Instruction becomes more focused and individualized. Indeed, when coupled with *Connect*® technology, instructors can obtain real-time feedback that allows them to identify and approach specific students who are having difficulty without disturbing those students who are able to digest the material independently.

• Competency-based learning courses

Video instruction enables the implementation of a competency-based grading system. Since learning is self-paced, grades can be assigned on the basis of how deep students go into the content as opposed to an averaging approach. For example, content could be divided into modules. Grades could be assigned based on the number of modules completed successfully. Weaker students could repeat lower-level modules, while stronger students move on to more advanced topics. When you are no longer forced to move students through your class in a lock-step fashion, the potential for improving the learning environment is virtually limitless.

There are many different competency-based models that can be applied to introductory accounting. At this point, our objective is to introduce the general possibilities for improving learning. If you are interested in developing a specific competency-based approach for your classroom, you can speak directly with a member of the author team who has used videos in a variety of settings (contact information is provided on the following page). Standardized lesson plans that can be adapted for use in your individual classroom are available upon request.

• Mass section courses

Many schools deliver live lectures to mass section classes. Students then break into small groups that are led by teaching assistants or adjunct faculty. While this approach is cost-effective, it frequently results in dissatisfaction. Students often find it difficult to see and hear in large lecture halls. Also, the lecture must be set at an average pace which by its nature is too fast for many students and too slow for others. Prerecorded video lectures resolve these issues. They enable students to study the lecture before class. They can then bring questions about the lecture to the breakout sessions. Since videos eliminate the need for mass lectures, there is more time for students to meet in small groups where they are able to receive more individualized attention.

• Distance learning courses

One of the fastest-growing markets in higher education today is Internet-based courses. Many students struggle with these courses. Generally, they would prefer to learn from a lecture but due to timing or location are unable to attend class. Prerecorded video lectures solve this problem by allowing students to access lectures on demand. Until now, the only way to provide video coverage was for the instructor to make personal recordings. Anyone who has tried this knows it is a time-consuming activity. We offer a standardized turnkey course that is composed of prerecorded instructional videos, self-assessment quizzes, and instructor-generated evaluative exams. The instructor simply selects the learning objectives to be covered. There is no simpler way to develop a distance learning course.

• Supplement your traditional lecture-based course

You do not have to change the way you teach your class to reap many of the benefits available from video instruction. Students who have to miss class or who have trouble comprehending certain concepts can benefit from watching video lectures. Also, many students who attend class will be able to build confidence by watching videos that reinforce the concepts presented in class. Since the videos are tied directly to the learning objectives, you can develop a specific plan for students who are struggling with specific topics. Alternatively, you may offer video instruction to enable advanced students to cover additional topics.

These are only a few opportunities made possible by video lectures. If you would like to discuss these or other possible applications, please contact Chris Edmonds at **cedmonds@gmail.com**.

ABOUT THE AUTHORS

Thomas P. Edmonds

Thomas P. Edmonds, Ph.D., is Professor Emeritus in the Department of Accounting at the University of Alabama at Birmingham (UAB). He has been actively involved in teaching accounting principles throughout his academic career. Dr. Edmonds has coordinated the accounting principles courses at the University of Houston and UAB. He has taught introductory accounting in mass sections and in distance learning programs. He has received five prestigious teaching awards, including the Alabama Society of CPAs Outstanding Educator Award, the UAB President's Excellence in Teaching Award, and the distinguished Ellen Gregg Ingalls Award for excellence in classroom teaching. He has written numerous articles that have appeared in many publications, including *Issues in Accounting,* the *Journal of Accounting Education, Advances in Accounting Education, Accounting Education: A Journal of Theory, Practice and Research,* the *Accounting Review, Advances in Accounting,* the *Journal of Accountancy, Management Accounting,* the *Journal of Commercial Bank Lending,* the *Banker's Magazine,* and the *Journal of Accounting, Auditing, and Finance.* Dr. Edmonds has served as a member of the editorial board for *Advances in Accounting: Teaching and Curriculum Innovations* and *Issues in Accounting Education.* He has published five textbooks, five practice problems (including two computerized problems), and a variety of supplemental materials including study guides, work papers, and solutions manuals. Dr. Edmonds's writing is influenced by a wide range of business experience. He is a successful entrepreneur. He has worked as a management accountant for Refrigerated Transport, a trucking company. Dr. Edmonds also worked in the not-for-profit sector as a commercial lending officer for the Federal Home Loan Bank. In addition, he has acted as a consultant to major corporations, including First City Bank of Houston (now Citi Bank), AmSouth Bank in Birmingham (now Regions Bank), Texaco, and Cortland Chemicals. Dr. Edmonds began his academic training at Young Harris Community College in Young Harris, Georgia. He received a B.B.A. degree with a major in finance from Georgia State University in Atlanta, Georgia. He obtained an M.B.A. degree with a concentration in finance from St. Mary's University in San Antonio, Texas. His Ph.D. degree with a major in accounting was awarded by Georgia State University. Dr. Edmonds's work experience and academic training have enabled him to bring a unique user perspective to this textbook.

Christopher T. Edmonds

Christopher T. Edmonds is an Assistant Professor of Accounting at the University of Alabama at Birmingham (UAB). His focus is on new teaching pedagogies such as "flipping the classroom," competency learning, and online education. In his classes, students watch lectures at home and come to class to work with others and practice skills. Although early in his career, Dr. Edmonds has received multiple teaching awards and published several articles in the area of accounting education. He has written articles that appeared in *Issues in Accounting Education*, *Advances in Accounting Education*, *AIS Educators Journal*, and *Advances in Accounting.*

Frances M. McNair

Frances M. McNair holds the KPMG Peat Marwick Professorship in Accounting at Mississippi State University (MSU). She has been involved in teaching principles of accounting for the past 20 years and currently serves as the coordinator for the principles of accounting courses at MSU. Dr. McNair was selected by the Mississippi Society of CPAS as outstanding educator for 2014. She joined the MSU faculty in 1987 after receiving her Ph.D. from the University of Mississippi. The author of various articles that have appeared in the *Journal of Accountancy, Management Accounting, Business and Professional Ethics Journal, The Practical Accountant, Taxes,* and other publications, she also coauthored the book *The Tax Practitioner* with Dr. Denzil Causey. Dr. McNair is currently serving on committees of the American Taxation Association, the American Accounting Association, and the Institute of Management Accountants as well as numerous School of Accountancy and MSU committees.

Philip R. Olds

Professor Olds is Associate Professor of Accounting at Virginia Commonwealth University (VCU). He serves as the coordinator of the introduction to accounting courses at VCU. Professor Olds received his A.S. degree from Brunswick Junior College in Brunswick, Georgia (now Costal Georgia Community College). He received a B.B.A. in accounting from Georgia Southern College (now Georgia Southern University) and his M.P.A. and Ph.D. degrees are from Georgia State University. After graduating from Georgia Southern, he worked as an auditor with the U.S. Department of Labor in Atlanta, Georgia. A former CPA in Virginia, Professor Olds has published articles in various professional journals and presented papers at national and regional conferences. He also served as the faculty adviser to the VCU chapter of Beta Alpha Psi for five years. In 1989, he was recognized with an Outstanding Faculty Vice-President Award by the national Beta Alpha Psi organization. Professor Olds has received both the Distinguished Teaching Award and the Distinguished Service Award from the VCU School of Business.

WHAT WE DID TO MAKE IT BETTER

As discussed in the "Note from the Authors" this text has been revised to include video lectures that provide coverage of all of the learning objectives included in the text. These videos have been developed by a member of the author team and have the touch and feel of a live lecture as opposed to a canned PowerPoint presentation. The videos provide unparalleled opportunities for instructional innovation including the development of flip courses, distance learning courses, and competency-based teaching. The videos can also be used in traditional courses to help students who need additional instruction. For example, students who are unable to keep up in class or who have to miss class now have a video lecture that can be used to catch up. The videos can be assigned to individual students or to the class as a whole through McGraw-Hill *Connect Plus*. The instructor has complete control over student access to video content and the accompanying self-assessment quizzes.

Specific chapter changes:

Chapter 1 An Introduction to Accounting

- Added video lectures and self-assessment quizzes for each learning objective.
- Organized coverage of the statement of cash flows into a separate learning objective.
- Revised coverage of the closing process. Developed a modular approach that allows you to skip coverage of the subject or to place greater emphasis on the topic depending on your preference.
- Revised the *Curious Accountant* feature using new high-profile companies and products.
- Updated *Focus on International Issues* textbox with new high-profile companies.
- New *Reality Bytes* content.
- Updated real-world financial statements in *The Financial Analyst* content.
- Updated exercises, problems, and cases.

Chapter 2 Accounting for Accruals and Deferrals

- Added video lectures and self-assessment quizzes for each learning objective.
- Revised learning objectives and content to more equally distribute material between Sections 1 and 2.
- Revised content to highlight the relationship between the initial transaction and the associated adjusting entries for supplies, prepaid items, and unearned revenues. The revised content also eliminated redundancies and improved clarity.
- Revised the *Curious Accountant* feature using new high-profile companies and products.
- New *Reality Bytes* content.
- Reorganized exercises and problems to match the sequence of learning objectives as presented in the chapter.
- Updated exercises, problems, and cases.

Chapter 3 The Double-Entry Accounting System

- Added video lectures and self-assessment quizzes for each learning objective.
- Revised the *Curious Accountant* feature using new high-profile companies and products.
- Updated industry ratios and other real-world data in *The Financial Analyst* content.
- Updated exercises, problems, and cases.

Chapter 4 Accounting for Merchandising Businesses

- Added video lectures and self-assessment quizzes for each learning objective.
- Combined the learning objective associated with gains and losses with the learning objective related to the multistep income statement. Also, combined the learning objective associated with inventory shrinkage with the learning objective related to transportation cost, cash discounts, and purchase returns and allowances. Related content was moved to appropriate parts of the chapter.
- New *Reality Bytes* content.
- Updated real-world financial statements associated with *The Curious Accountant* content.
- Reorganized exercises and problems to match the sequence of learning objectives as presented in the chapter.
- Updated exercises, problems, and cases.

Chapter 5 Accounting for Inventories

- Added video lectures and self-assessment quizzes for each learning objective.
- Revised the *Curious Accountant* feature using new high-profile companies and products.
- Updated *Focus on International Issues* content.
- Updated industry ratios and other real-world data in *The Financial Analyst* content.
- Updated exercises, problems, and cases.

Chapter 6 Internal Control and Accounting for Cash

- Added video lectures and self-assessment quizzes for each learning objective.
- New *Curious Accountant* content.
- New *Reality Bytes* content.
- Updated exercises, problems, and cases.

Chapter 7 Accounting for Receivables

- Added video lectures and self-assessment quizzes for each learning objective.
- Updated *Curious Accountant* content.
- Combined the learning objective associated with the introduction of the allowance method with the learning objective related to estimating uncollectible accounts expense using the percent of revenue method. Related content was rewritten.

- Created a separate learning objective for aging of accounts receivable.
- New *Reality Bytes* content.
- Updated industry ratios and other real-world data in *The Financial Analyst* content.
- Updated exercises, problems, and cases.

Chapter 8 Accounting for Long-Term Operational Assets

- Added video lectures and self-assessment quizzes for each learning objective.
- New *Curious Accountant* content.
- Created separate learning objectives for straight-line, double-declining-balance, and units-of-production depreciation methods. Also, created separate learning objectives for identifying and determining the cost of intangible assets versus recognizing amortization expense.
- Created a separate learning objective for aging of accounts receivable.
- Updated *Reality Bytes* content.
- Updated industry ratios and other real-world data in *The Financial Analyst* content.
- Updated exercises, problems, and cases.

Chapter 9 Accounting for Current Liabilities and Payroll

- Added video lectures and self-assessment quizzes for each learning objective.
- Updated *Curious Accountant* content.
- Updated *Reality Bytes* content.
- Updated industry ratios and other real-world data in *The Financial Analyst* content.
- Updated exercises, problems, and cases.

Chapter 10 Accounting for Long-Term Debt

- Added video lectures and self-assessment quizzes for each learning objective.
- Created separate learning objectives for the treatment of bond discounts and premiums under both the straight-line and the effective interest rate methods of amortization.
- New *Curious Accountant* content.
- Updated *Reality Bytes* content.
- Updated industry ratios and other real-world data in *The Financial Analyst* content.
- Updated exercises, problems, and cases.

Chapter 11 Proprietorships, Partnerships, and Corporations

- Added video lectures and self-assessment quizzes for each learning objective.
- Created separate learning objectives for the treatment of bond discounts and premiums under both the straight-line and the effective interest rate methods of amortization.
- Revised the *Curious Accountant* feature using new high-profile companies and products.
- New *Reality Bytes* content.
- Updated *Focus on International Issues* content.
- Updated real-world data in *The Financial Analyst* content.
- Updated exercises, problems, and cases.

Chapter 12 Statement of Cash Flows

- Added video lectures and self-assessment quizzes for each learning objective.
- New *Curious Accountant* content.
- New *Reality Bytes* content.
- Updated real-world data in *The Financial Analyst* content.
- Updated exercises, problems, and cases.

Chapter 13 Financial Statement Analysis (Available online in the *Connect* Library)

- Added video lectures and self-assessment quizzes for each learning objective.
- Revised learning objectives.
- New *Curious Accountant* content.
- Reorganized exercises and problems to match the sequence of learning objectives as presented in the chapter.
- Updated exercises, problems, and cases.

HOW DOES THE BOOK

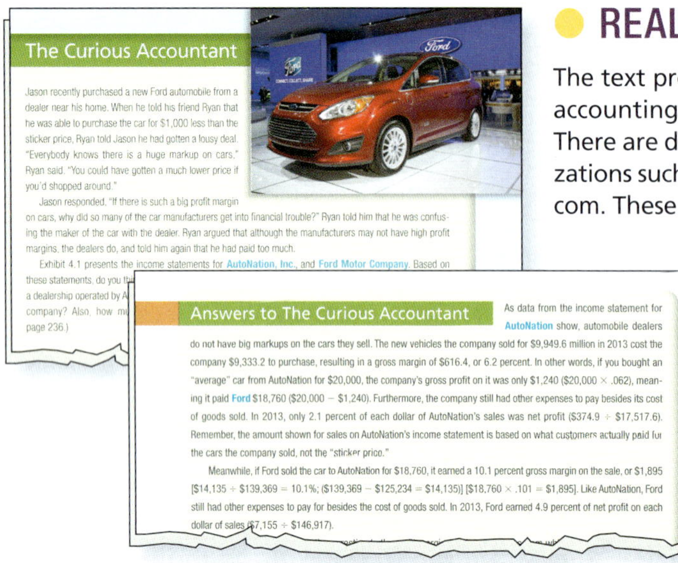

REAL-WORLD EXAMPLES

The text provides a variety of real-world examples of financial accounting as an essential part of the management process. There are descriptions of accounting practices from real organizations such as Coca-Cola, Enron, General Motors, and Amazon.com. These companies are highlighted in blue in the text.

THE CURIOUS ACCOUNTANT

Each chapter opens with a short vignette. These pose a question about a real-world accounting issue related to the topic of the chapter. The answer to the question appears in a separate sidebar a few pages further into the chapter.

FOCUS ON INTERNATIONAL ISSUES

These boxed inserts expose students to IFRS and other international issues in accounting.

THE FINANCIAL ANALYST

Financial statement analysis is highlighted in each chapter under this heading.

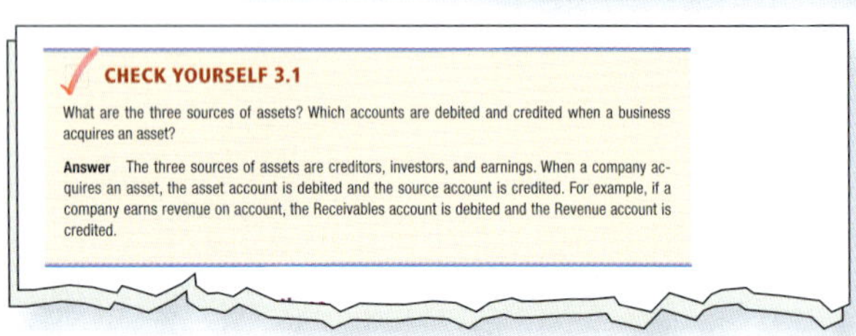

CHECK YOURSELF

These short question/answer features occur at the end of each main topic and ask students to stop and think about the material just covered. The answer follows to provide immediate feedback before students go on to a new topic.

REALITY BYTES

This feature expands on the topics by showing how companies use the concepts discussed in the chapter to make real-world business decisions.

MOTIVATE STUDENTS?

ANNUAL REPORTS

The 2013 annual report for Target Corporation is shown in Appendix B.

Business Application Problems related to the annual report are included at the end of each chapter.

A financial statement analysis project for the annual report is located in Appendix D. Also, a general purpose annual report project is included for instructors to assign for any company.

APPENDIX B

PORTION OF THE FORM 10-K FOR TARGET CORPORATION

This appendix contains a portion of the Form 10-K for the Target Corporation that was filed with the Securities and Exchange Commission on March 14, 2014. The document included in this appendix is Target's annual report, which was included *as a part* of its complete Form 10-K for the company's fiscal year ended February 1, 2014. Throughout this text this is referred to as the company's 2013 fiscal year.

This document is included for illustrative purposes, and it is intended to be used for educational purposes only. It should not be used for making investment decisions. Target Corporation's complete Form 10-K may be obtained from the SEC's EDGAR website, using the procedures explained in Appendix A. The Form 10-K may also be found on Target's website under "Investor Relations." From this page, click on the "SEC Filings" tab and scroll to locate the appropriate 10-K report.

UNITED STATES
SECURITIES AND EXCHANGE COMMISSION
Washington, D.C. 20549

FORM 10-K

(Mark One)

[X] ANNUAL REPORT PURSUANT TO SECTION 13 OR 15(d) OF THE SECURITIES EXCHANGE ACT OF 1934

For the fiscal year ended February 1, 2014

OR

[ ] TRANSITION REPORT PURSUANT TO SECTION 13 OR 15(d) OF THE SECURITIES EXCHANGE ACT OF 1934

For the transition period from to

Commission file number 1-6049

CHAPTER FOCUS COMPANY

Each chapter introduces important managerial accounting topics within the context of a realistic company. Students see the impact of managerial accounting decisions on the company as they work through the chapter. When the Focus Company is presented in the chapter, its logo is shown so the students see its application to the text topics.

Name and Type of Company Used as Main Chapter Example

Chapter Title	Company Used as Main Chapter Example	Company Logo	Type of Company
1. An Introduction to Accounting	Rustic Camp Sites		Rents land
2. Accounting for Accruals and Deferrals	Cato Consultants		Provides training services
3. The Double-Entry Accounting System	Collins Brokerage Services, Inc.		Investment consulting firm
4. Accounting for Merchandising Businesses	June's Plant Shop		Sells gardening supplies
5. Accounting for Inventories	The Mountain Bike Company		Sells bicycles
6. Internal Control and Accounting for Cash	Green Shades Resorts, Inc.		Rents resort facilities
7. Accounting for Receivables	Allen's Tutoring Services		Provides tutoring services
8. Accounting for Long-Term Operational Assets	Dryden Enterprises		Van rental company
9. Accounting for Current Liabilities and Payroll	Herrera Supply Company		Supply company
10. Accounting for Long-Term Debt	Mason Company		Leases land
11. Proprietorships, Partnerships, and Corporations	Nelson Incorporated		Software development company
12. Statement of Cash Flows	New South Corporation		Retail gift shop

A LOOK BACK/A LOOK FORWARD

Students need a roadmap to make sense of where the chapter topics fit into the "whole" picture. A Look Back reviews the chapter materials and a Look Forward introduces students to what is to come.

A Look Back <<

Merchandising companies earn profits by selling inventory at prices that are higher than the cost paid for the goods. Merchandising companies include *retail companies* (companies that sell goods to the final consumer) and *wholesale companies* (companies that sell to other merchandising companies). The products sold by merchandising companies are called *inventory.* The costs to purchase inventory, to receive it, and to ready it for

>> A Look Forward

To this point, the text has explained the basic accounting cycle for service and merchandising businesses. Future chapters more closely address specific accounting issues. For example, in Chapter 5 you will learn how to deal with inventory items that are purchased at differing prices. Other chapters will discuss a variety of specific practices that are widely used by real-world companies.

HOW ARE CHAPTER CONCEPTS

Regardless of the instructional approach, there is no shortcut to learning accounting. Students must practice to master basic accounting concepts. The text includes a prodigious supply of practice materials and exercises and problems.

SELF-STUDY REVIEW PROBLEM

A step-by-step audio-narrated series of slides is available in the Connect library.

Academy Sales Company (ASC) started the 2016 accounting period with the balances given in the financial statements model shown below. During 2016 ASC experienced the following business events.

1. Purchased $16,000 of merchandise inventory on account, terms 2/10, n/30.
2. The goods that were purchased in Event 1 were delivered FOB shipping point. Freight costs of $600 were paid in cash by the responsible party.
3. Returned $500 of goods purchased in Event 1.

4a. Recorded the cash discount on the goods purchased in Event 1.
4b. Paid the balance due on the account payable within the discount period.
5a. Recognized $21,000 of cash revenue from the sale of merchandise.
5b. Recognized $15,000 of cost of goods sold.

6. The merchandise in Event 5a was sold to customers FOB destination. Freight costs of $950 were paid in cash by the responsible party.
7. Paid cash of $4,000 for selling and administrative expenses.
8. Sold the land for $5,600 cash.

PROBLEMS—SERIES A

connect plus+ ACCOUNTING ***All applicable Problems in Series A are available with McGraw-Hill's Connect Plus Accounting.***

Problem 7-17A ***Accounting for uncollectible accounts: two cycles using the percent of revenue allowance method*** LO 7-1

The following transactions apply to Jova Company for 2016, the first year of operation:

1. Issued $10,000 of common stock for cash.
2. Recognized $210,000 of service revenue earned on account.
3. Collected $162,000 from accounts receivable.
4. Paid $125,000 cash for operating expenses.
5. Adjusted the accounts to recognize uncollectible accounts expense. Jova uses the allowance method of accounting for uncollectible accounts and estimates that uncollectible accounts expense will be 1 percent of sales on account.

The following transactions apply to Jova for 2017:

1. Recognized $320,000 of service revenue on account.
2. Collected $335,000 from accounts receivable.
3. Determined that $2,150 of the accounts receivable were uncollectible and wrote them off.
4. Collected $800 of an account that had previously been written off.
5. Paid $205,000 cash for operating expenses.
6. Adjusted the accounts to recognize uncollectible accounts expense for 2017. Jova estimates uncollectible accounts expense will be 0.5 percent of sales on account.

Required

Complete the following requirements for 2016 and 2017. Complete all requirements for 2016 prior to beginning the requirements for 2017.

a. Identify the type of each transaction (asset source, asset use, asset exchange, or claims exchange).
b. Show the effect of each transaction on the elements of the financial statements, using a horizontal statements model like the one shown here. Use + for increase, − for decrease, and NA

CHECK FIGURES
c. Ending Accounts Receivable, 2016: $48,000
d. Net Income, 2017: $113,400

"The self-study problems and supplements on the web are very useful for students."

BARRY BUCHOFF,
TOWSON UNIVERSITY

"Exercises and problems are great and provide a variety as well as multiple examples for students to practice."

PATRICIA BANCROFT,
BRIDGEWATER STATE UNIVERSITY

SELF-STUDY REVIEW PROBLEM

These example problems include a detailed, worked-out solution and provide support for students before they work problems on their own. These review problems are included in an animated audio presentation in the *Connect* Library.

EXERCISE SERIES A & B AND PROBLEM SERIES A & B

There are two sets of problems and exercises, Series A and B. Instructors can assign one set for homework and another set for classwork.

• Check Figures

The figures provide key answers for selected problems.

• Excel

Many problems can be solved using the Excel™ templates available in the *Connect* Library. A logo appears in the margins next to these problems.

REINFORCED?

ANALYZE, THINK, COMMUNICATE (ATC)

Each chapter includes an innovative section entitled Analyze, Think, Communicate (ATC). This section offers Business Applications Cases, Group Assignments, Real-World Cases, Writing Assignments, Ethical Dilemma Problems, Research Assignments, and Spreadsheet Assignments.

We use logos to help students identify the type of question being asked.

- Target Corporation • Target Corp.
- • Group Work
- • Excel
- • Real World Company
- • Ethics
- • Research
- • Writing

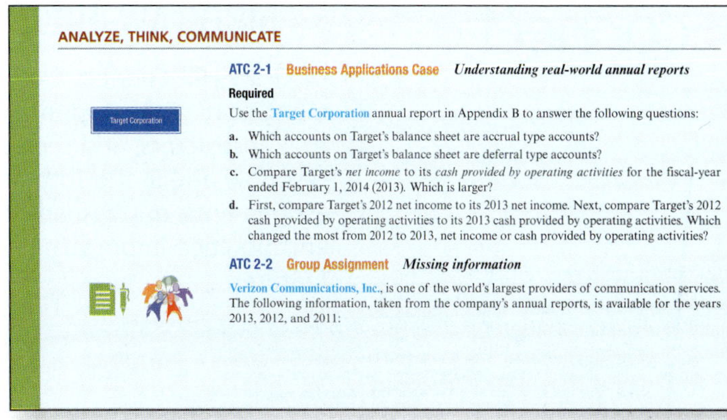

ANALYZE, THINK, COMMUNICATE

ATC 2-1 Business Applications Case *Understanding real-world annual reports*

Required

Use the Target Corporation annual report in Appendix B to answer the following questions:

a. Which accounts on Target's balance sheet are accrual type accounts?
b. Which accounts on Target's balance sheet are deferral type accounts?
c. Compare Target's *net income* to its *cash provided by operating activities* for the fiscal-year ended February 1, 2014 (2013). Which is larger?
d. First, compare Target's 2012 net income to its 2013 net income. Next, compare Target's 2012 cash provided by operating activities to its 2013 cash provided by operating activities. Which changed the most from 2012 to 2013, net income or cash provided by operating activities?

ATC 2-2 Group Assignment *Missing information*

Verizon Communications, Inc., is one of the world's largest providers of communication services. The following information, taken from the company's annual reports, is available for the years 2013, 2012, and 2011:

COMPREHENSIVE PROBLEM

Beginning in Chapter 1, a comprehensive problem builds in each successive chapter, with the ending account balances in one chapter becoming the beginning account balances in the next chapter.

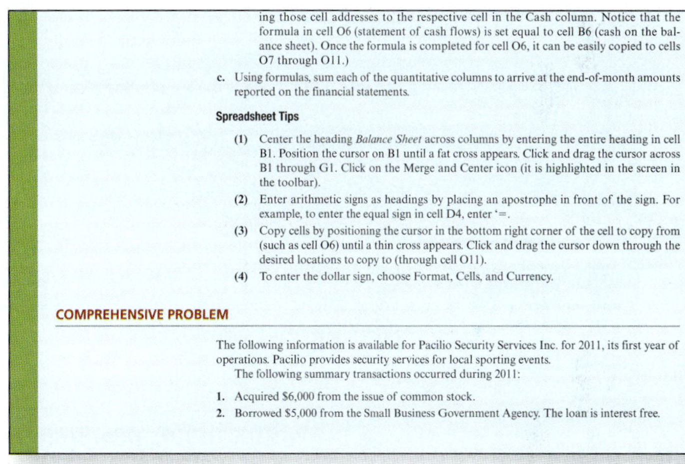

ing those cell addresses to the respective cell in the Cash column. Notice that the formula in cell O6 (statement of cash flows) is set equal to cell B6 (cash on the balance sheet). Once the formula is completed for cell O6, it can be easily copied to cells O7 through O11.)

c. Using formulas, sum each of the quantitative columns to arrive at the end-of-month amounts reported on the financial statements.

Spreadsheet Tips

(1) Center the heading *Balance Sheet* across columns by entering the entire heading in cell B1. Position the cursor on B1 until a fat cross appears. Click and drag the cursor across B1 through G1. Click on the Merge and Center icon (it is highlighted in the screen in the toolbar).
(2) Enter arithmetic signs as headings by placing an apostrophe in front of the sign. For example, to enter the equal sign in cell D4, enter '=.
(3) Copy cells by positioning the cursor in the bottom right corner of the cell to copy from (such as cell O6) until a thin cross appears. Click and drag the cursor down through the desired locations to copy to (through cell O11).
(4) To enter the dollar sign, choose Format, Cells, and Currency.

COMPREHENSIVE PROBLEM

The following information is available for Pacilio Security Services Inc. for 2011, its first year of operations. Pacilio provides security services for local sporting events.

The following summary transactions occurred during 2011:

1. Acquired $6,000 from the issue of common stock.
2. Borrowed $5,000 from the Small Business Government Agency. The loan is interest free.

MASTERING EXCEL AND USING EXCEL

The Excel applications are used to make students comfortable with this analytical tool and to show its use in accounting.

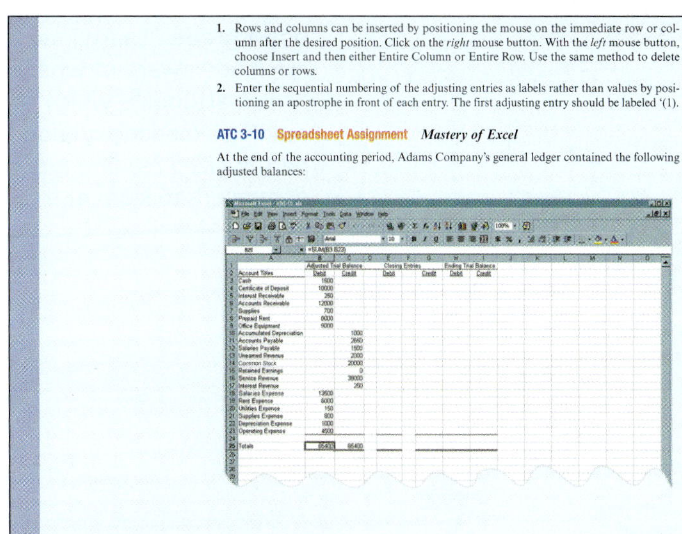

1. Rows and columns can be inserted by positioning the mouse on the immediate row or column after the desired position. Click on the *right* mouse button. With the *left* mouse button, choose Insert and then either Entire Column or Entire Row. Use the same method to delete columns or rows.
2. Enter the sequential numbering of the adjusting entries as labels rather than values by positioning an apostrophe in front of each entry. The first adjusting entry should be labeled '(1).

ATC 3-10 Spreadsheet Assignment *Mastery of Excel*

At the end of the accounting period, Adams Company's general ledger contained the following adjusted balances:

"Lots of good exercises and problems at the end of each chapter with A and B choices."

CAROL SHAVER,
LOUISIANA TECH UNIVERSITY

"I love the spreadsheet assignments and the comprehensive problems at the end of each chapter. I love the check figures that are available on some of the problems."

JANE GARVIN,
IVY TECH COMMUNITY COLLEGE

HOW CAN TECHNOLOGY HELP

MCGRAW-HILL *CONNECT PLUS ACCOUNTING*

McGraw-Hill *Connect Plus Accounting* is a digital teaching and learning environment that gives students the means to better connect with their coursework, their instructors, and the important concepts that they will need to know for success now and in the future. With *Connect Plus Accounting*, instructors can deliver assignments, quizzes, and tests easily online. Students can review course material and practice important skills. *Connect Plus Accounting* provides the following features:

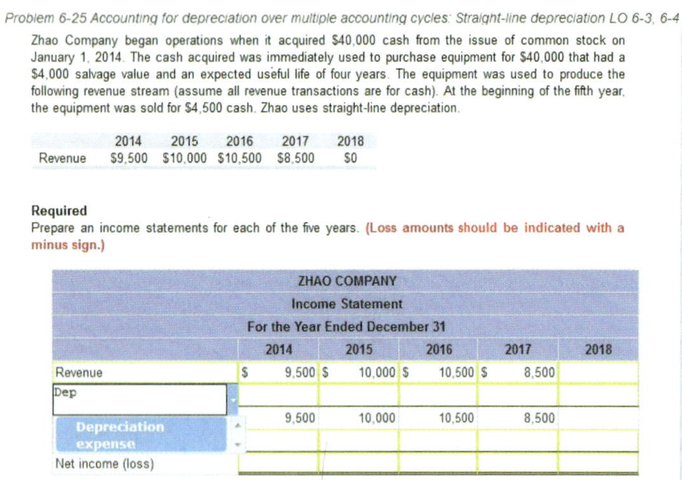

- SmartBook and LearnSmart.
- Auto-graded Online Homework.
- An integrated media-rich eBook, allowing for anytime, anywhere access to the textbook.
- Dynamic links between the problems or questions you assign to your students and the location in the eBook where that concept is covered.
- A powerful search function to pinpoint and connect key concepts to review.

In short, *Connect Plus Accounting* offers students powerful tools and features that optimize their time and energy, enabling them to focus on learning.

For more information about *Connect Plus Accounting*, go to **www.connect.mheducation.com,** or contact your local McGraw-Hill Higher Education representative.

• SmartBook, powered by LearnSmart

LearnSmart® is the market-leading adaptive study resource that is proven to strengthen memory recall, increase class retention, and boost grades. LearnSmart allows students to study more efficiently because they are made aware of what they know and don't know.

SmartBook®, which is powered by LearnSmart, is the first and only adaptive reading experience designed to change the way students read and learn. It creates a personalized reading experience by highlighting the most impactful concepts a student needs to learn at that moment in time. As a student engages with SmartBook, the reading experience continuously adapts by highlighting content based on what the student knows and doesn't know. This ensures that the focus is on the content he or she needs to learn, while simultaneously promoting long-term retention of material.

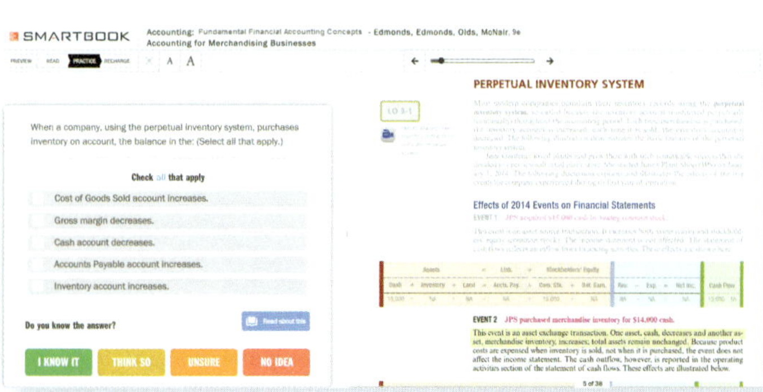

Use SmartBook's real-time reports to quickly identify the concepts that require more attention from individual students—or the entire class. The end result? Students are more engaged with course content, can better prioritize their time, and come to class ready to participate.

IMPROVE STUDENT SUCCESS?

• Online assignments

Connect Plus Accounting helps students learn more efficiently by providing feedback and practice material when they need it, where they need it. *Connect Plus* grades homework automatically and gives immediate feedback on any questions students may have missed. Our assignable, gradable end-of-chapter content includes a general journal application that looks and feels like what you would find in a general ledger software package. Also, select questions have been redesigned to test students' knowledge more fully. They now include tables for students to work through rather than requiring that all calculations be done offline.

• Lecture videos

One or more lecture videos are available for every learning objective introduced throughout the text. The videos have been developed by a member of the author team and have the touch and feel of a live lecture. The videos are accompanied by a set of self-assessment quizzes. Students can watch the videos and then test themselves to determine if they understand the material presented in the video. Students can repeat the process, switching back and forth between the video and self-assessment quizzes, until they are satisfied that they understand the material.

"The Lecture Videos are outstanding for online courses and as a tutorial for face-to-face presentation."

PHILIP LITTLE, COASTAL CAROLINA UNIVERSITY

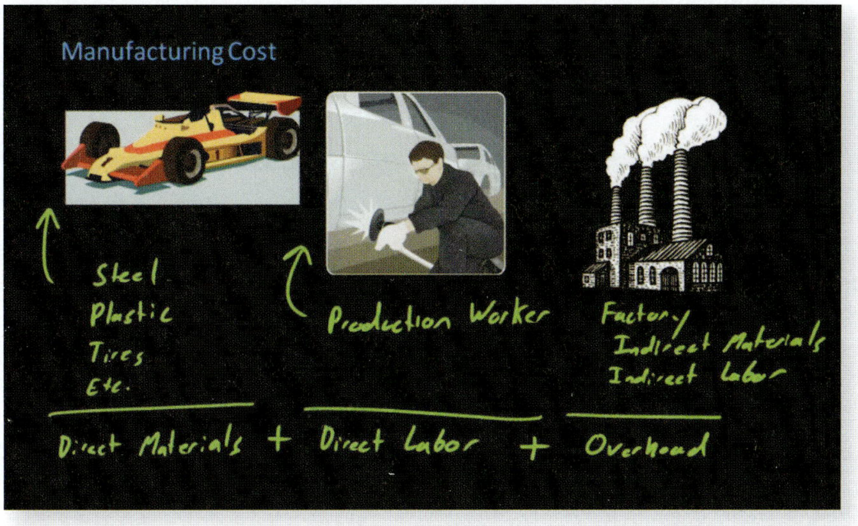

• Student Resource Library

The *Connect Plus Accounting* Student Resources give students access to additional resources such as recorded lectures, online practice materials, an eBook, and more.

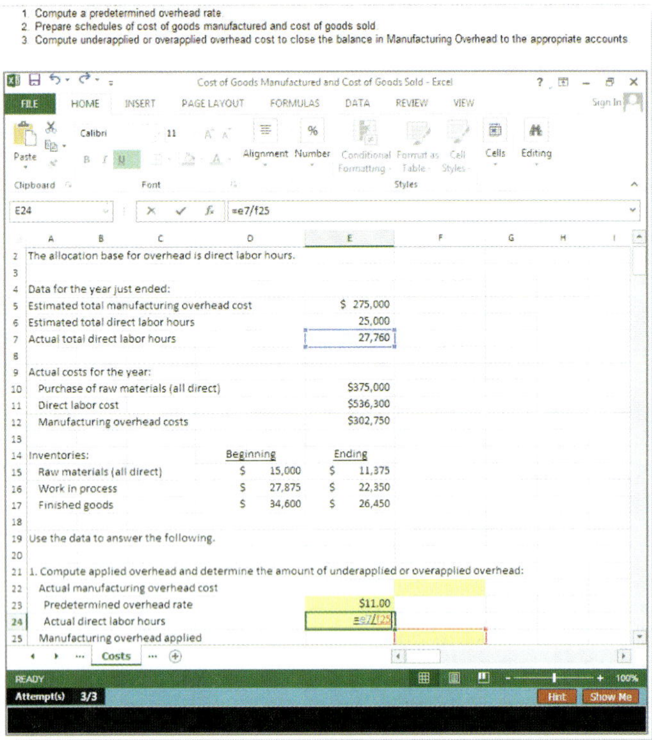

• Excel simulations

Simulated Excel questions, assignable within *Connect Plus Accounting*, allow students to practice their Excel skills—such as basic formulas and formatting—within the content of financial accounting. These questions feature animated, narrated Help and Show Me tutorials (when enabled), as well as automatic feedback and grading for both students and professors.

MCGRAW-HILL *CONNECT PLUS ACCOUNTING* FEATURES

Connect Plus Accounting offers powerful tools, resources, and features to make managing assignments easier, so faculty can spend more time teaching.

Simple Assignment Management and Smart Grading With *Connect Plus Accounting*, students can engage with their coursework anytime, anywhere, making the learning process more accessible and efficient.

- Create and deliver assignments easily with selectable end-of-chapter questions and test bank items.
- Have assignments scored automatically, giving students immediate feedback on their work and comparisons with correct answers.
- Access and review each response; manually change grades or leave comments for students to review.
- Reinforce classroom concepts with practice assignments, instant quizzes, and exams.

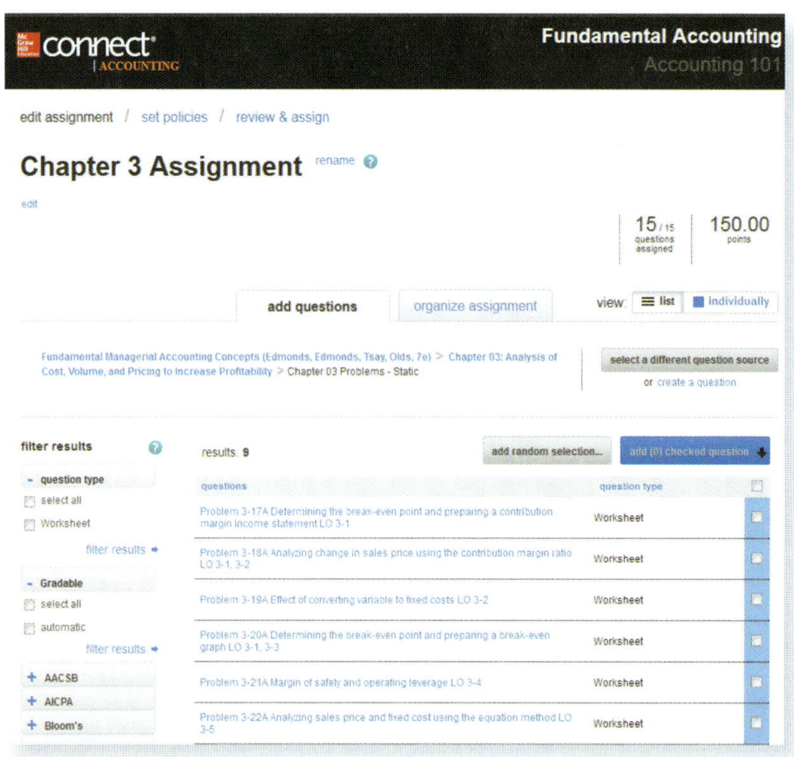

• Powerful Instructor and Student Reports

Connect Plus Accounting keeps instructors informed about how each student, section, and class is performing, allowing for more productive use of lecture and office hours. The reports tab enables you to:

- View scored work immediately and track individual or group performance with assignment and grade reports.
- Access an instant view of student or class performance relative to learning objectives.
- Collect data and generate reports required by many accreditation organizations, such as AACSB and AICPA.

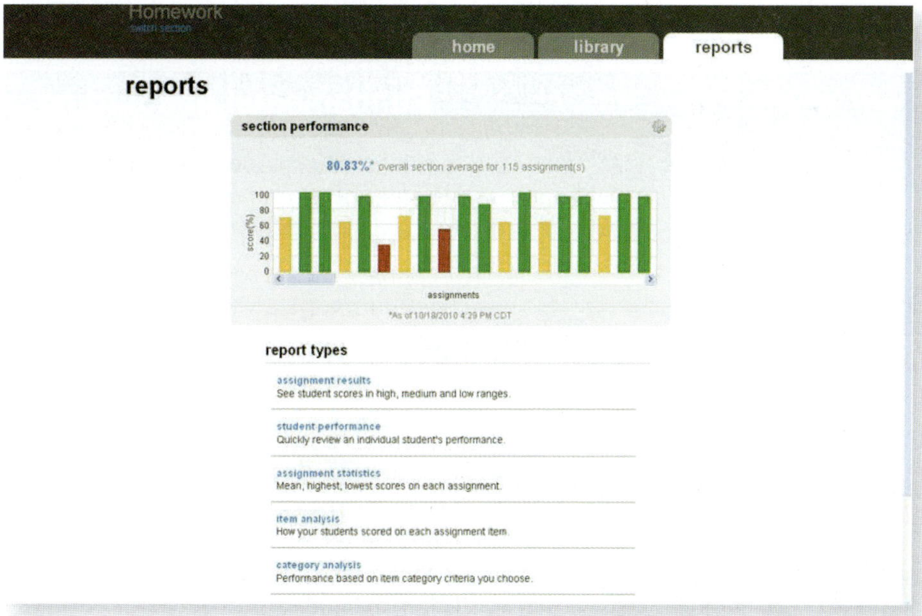

• Connect Insight

The first and only analytics tool of its kind, Connect Insight™ is a series of visual data displays—each framed by an intuitive question—to provide at-a-glance information regarding how your class is doing.

Connect Insight™ provides an at-a-glance analysis on five key insights, available at a moment's notice from your tablet device.

- How are my students doing?
- How is my section doing?
- How is this student doing?
- How are my assignments doing?
- How is this assignment going?

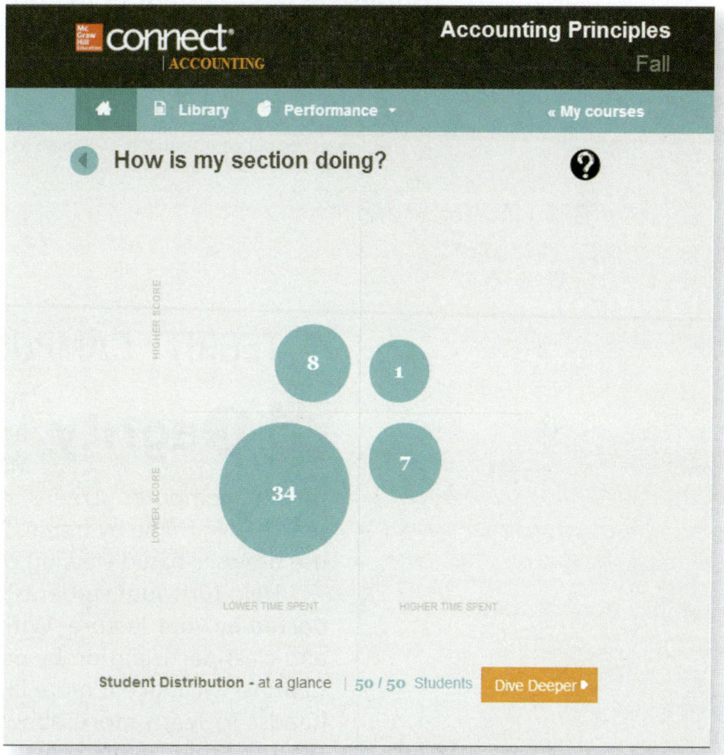

- **Instructor Library**

The *Connect Plus Accounting* Instructor Library is your repository for additional resources to improve student engagement in and out of class. You can select and use any asset that enhances your lecture. The *Connect Plus Accounting* Instructor Library includes access to:

- Solutions Manual
- Instructor's Manual
- Test Bank
- Instructor PowerPoint® slides
- Media-rich eBook

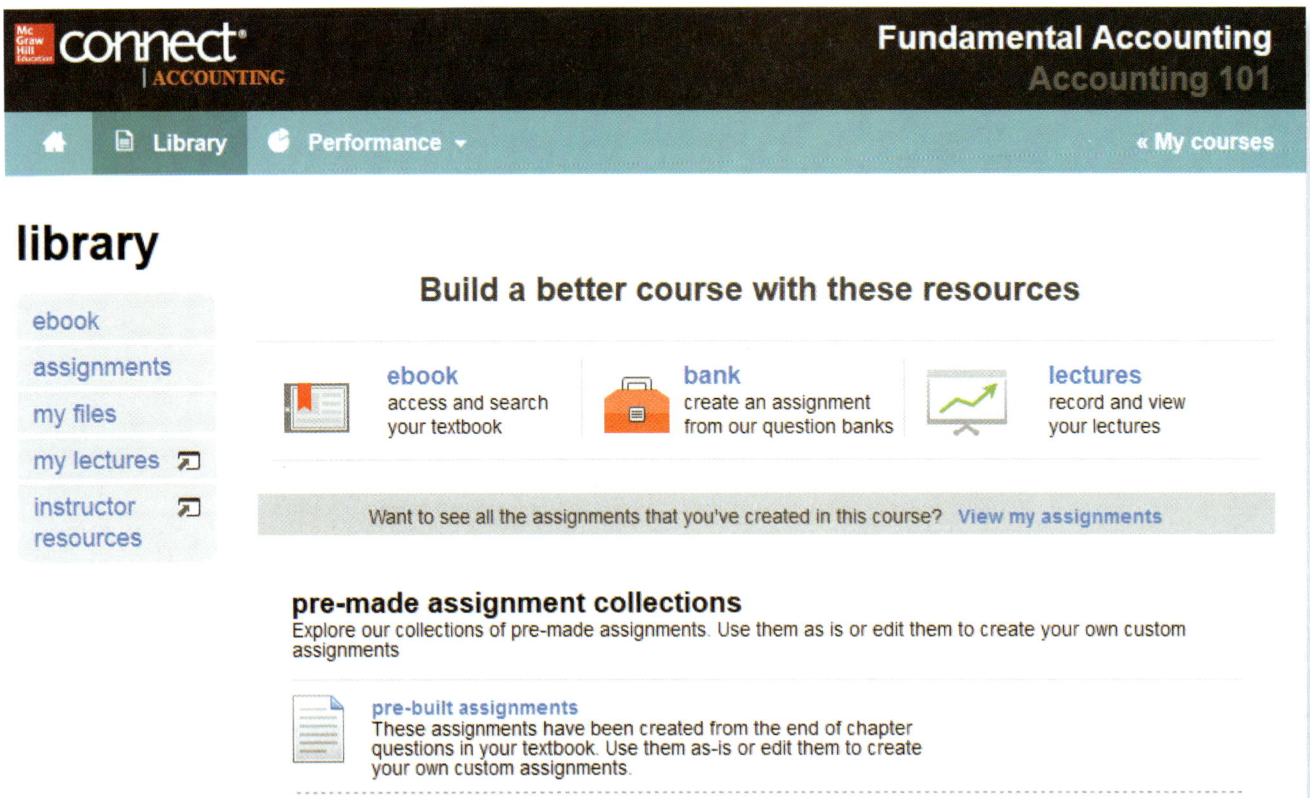

TEGRITY CAMPUS: LECTURES 24/7

Tegrity Campus, is a service that makes class time available 24/7 by automatically capturing every lecture. With a simple one-click start-and-stop process, you capture all computer screens and corresponding audio in a format that is easily searchable, frame by frame. Students can replay any part of any class with easy-to-use browser-based viewing on a PC, Mac, or other mobile device.

Help turn your students' study time into learning moments immediately supported by your lecture. With Tegrity Campus, you also increase intent listening and class participation by easing students' concerns about note-taking. Lecture Capture will make it more likely you will see students' faces, not the tops of their heads. To learn more about Tegrity, watch a 2-minute Flash demo at **http://tegritycampus.mhhe.com.**

• McGraw-Hill Campus

McGraw-Hill Campus™ is a new one-stop teaching and learning experience available to users of any learning management system. This institutional service allows faculty and students to enjoy single sign-on (SSO) access to all McGraw-Hill Higher Education materials, including the award-winning McGraw-Hill *Connect Plus* platform, from directly within the institution's website. To learn more about MH Campus, visit **http://mhcampus.mhhe.com.**

• Custom Publishing through Create

McGraw-Hill Create™ is a new, self-service website that allows instructors to create custom course materials by drawing upon McGraw-Hill's comprehensive, cross-disciplinary content. Instructors can add their own content quickly and easily and tap into other rights-secured third-party sources as well, then arrange the content in a way that makes the most sense for their course. Instructors can even personalize their book with the course name and information and choose the best format for their students—color print, black-and-white print, or an eBook.

Through Create, instructors can

- Select and arrange the content in a way that makes the most sense for their course.
- Combine material from different sources and even upload their own content.
- Choose the best format for their students—print or eBook.
- Edit and update their course materials as often as they like.

Begin creating now at **www.mcgrawhillcreate.com**.

• McGraw-Hill Customer Experience Group Contact Information

At McGraw-Hill, we understand that getting the most from new technology can be challenging. That's why our services don't stop after you purchase our products. You can contact our Product Specialists 24 hours a day to get product training online. Or you can search the knowledge bank of Frequently Asked Questions on our support website. For Customer Support, call **800-331-5094,** or visit **www.mhhe.com/support.** One of our Technical Support Analysts will be able to assist you in a timely fashion.

SUPPLEMENTS FOR INSTRUCTORS

Assurance of Learning Ready

Many educational institutions today are focused on the notion of *assurance of learning*, an important element of many accreditation standards. *Fundamental Financial Accounting Concepts 9e* is designed specifically to support your assurance of learning initiatives with a simple, yet powerful, solution.

Each chapter in the book begins with a list of numbered learning objectives, which appear throughout the chapter as well as in the end-of-chapter assignments. Every Test Bank question for *Fundamental Financial Accounting Concepts* maps to a specific chapter learning objective in the textbook. Each Test Bank question also identifies topic area, level of difficulty, Bloom's Taxonomy level, and AICPA and AACSB skill area. You can use our Test Bank software, *EZ Test Online*, or *Connect Plus Accounting* to easily search for learning objectives that directly relate to the learning objectives for your course. You can then use the reporting features of *EZ Test* to aggregate student results in similar fashion, making the collection and presentation of Assurance of Learning data simple and easy.

AACSB Statement

McGraw-Hill/Irwin is a proud corporate member of AACSB International. Understanding the importance and value of AACSB accreditation, *Fundamental Financial Accounting Concepts 9e* recognizes the curricula guidelines detailed in the AACSB standards for business accreditation by connecting selected questions in the text and the Test Bank to the general knowledge and skill guidelines in the revised AACSB standards.

The statements contained in *Fundamental Financial Accounting Concepts 9e* are provided only as a guide for the users of this textbook. The AACSB leaves content coverage and assessment within the purview of individual schools, the mission of the school, and the faculty. While *Fundamental Financial Accounting Concepts 9e* and the teaching package make no claim of any specific AACSB qualification or evaluation, we have, within the text and test bank, labeled selected questions according to the eight general knowledge and skill areas.

McGraw-Hill's *Connect Plus Accounting*

Connect Plus Accounting offers a number of powerful tools and features to make managing your classroom easier. *Connect Plus Accounting* with Edmonds 9e offers enhanced features and technology to help both you and your students make the most of your time inside and outside the classroom. See page 000 for more details.

EZ Test Online

This test bank in Word format contains multiple-choice questions, essay questions, and short problems. Each test item is coded for level of difficulty, learning objective, AACSB and AICPA skill area, and Bloom's Taxonomy level.

McGraw-Hill's EZ Test Online is a flexible and easy-to-use electronic testing program that allows instructors to create tests from book-specific items. EZ Test Online accommodates a wide range of question types and allows instructors to add their own questions. Multiple versions of the test can be created and any test can be exported for use with course management systems such as BlackBoard/WebCT. EZ Test Online gives instructors a place to easily administer exams and quizzes online. The program is available for Windows and Macintosh environments.

SUPPLEMENTS FOR STUDENTS

McGraw-Hill *Connect Plus Accounting*

McGraw-Hill *Connect Plus Accounting* helps prepare you for your future by enabling faster learning, more efficient studying, and higher retention of knowledge. *Connect Plus Accounting* includes access to a searchable, integrated online version of the text, and much more.

CourseSmart

Learn Smart. Choose Smart.

CourseSmart is a way for faculty to find and review eTextbooks. It's also a great option for students who are interested in accessing their course materials digitally and saving money. CourseSmart offers thousands of the most commonly adopted textbooks across hundreds of courses from a wide variety of higher education publishers. With the CourseSmart eTextbook, students can save up to 45 percent off the cost of a print book, reduce their impact on the environment, and access powerful Web tools for learning. CourseSmart is an online eTextbook, which means users access and view their textbook online when connected to the Internet. Students can also print sections of the book for maximum portability. CourseSmart eTextbooks are available in one standard online reader with full text search, notes and highlighting, and e-mail tools for sharing notes between classmates. For more information on CourseSmart, go to **www.coursesmart.com**.

Study Guide

ISBN-10: 1259296784 ISBN-13: 9781259296789

This proactive guide incorporates many of the accounting skills essential to student success. Each chapter contains a review and explanation of the chapter's learning objectives, as well as multiple-choice problems and short exercises. Unique to this Study Guide is a series of articulation problems that require students to indicate how accounting events affect the elements of financial statements. Now available through McGraw-Hill *Create*.

Working Papers

ISBN-10: 1259296792 ISBN-13: 9781259296796

This study aid contains forms that help students organize their solutions to homework exercises and problems. Now available through McGraw-Hill *Create*.

Excel Templates

These templates allow students to develop spreadsheet skills to solve selected assignments identified by an icon in the end-of-chapter material.

ACKNOWLEDGMENTS

Our grateful appreciation is extended to those who reviewed previous editions:

Special thanks to the talented people who prepared the supplements. These take a great deal of time and effort to write and we appreciate their efforts. Molly Brown of James Madison University prepared the Test Bank, Instructor's Manual, and PowerPoints. Jack Terry developed the Excel Templates. Ilene Leopold Persoff of Long Island University accuracy checked the Test Bank, Instructor's Manual, and PowerPoints. We also thank our text accuracy checkers Ilene Leopold Persoff of Long Island University—Post Campus and Kristine Palmer of Longwood University. A special thanks to Linda Bell of Park University for her contribution to the Financial Statement Analysis material that appears in Appendix D.

We extend our sincere appreciation to Tim Vertovec, James Heine, Diane Nowaczyk, Pat Fredrickson, Danielle Andries, Kathleen Klehr, and Carol Bielski. We deeply appreciate the long hours that you committed to the formation of a high-quality text.

• Thomas P. Edmonds • Christopher T. Edmonds • Frances M. McNair • Philip R. Olds

---

We would like to express our appreciation to the people who have provided assistance in the development of this textbook.

We express our sincere thanks to the following individuals who provided extensive reviews for the current and previous editions:

Reviewers

Stacey Adams, *Antelope Valley College*
Charles Richard Aldridge, *Western Kentucky University*
Mary Allen, *Boise State University*
Sheila Ammons, *Austin Community College*
Susan Anderson, *Appalachian State University*
Marie Archambault, *Marshall University*
Kashi Balachandran, *Stern School, New York University*
Patricia Bancroft, *Bridgewater State University*
Debra Barbeau, *Southern Illinois University-Carbondale*
Charles Baril, *James Madison University*
Beryl Barkman, *University of Massachusetts-Dartmouth*
Cheryl Bartlett, *Albuquerque TVI Community College*
Ira Bates, *Florida A&M University*
Jim Bates, *Mountain Empire Community College*
Deborah Beard, *Southeast Missouri State University*
Judy Beebe, *Western Oregon University*
Linda Bell, *William Jewell College*
Judy Benish, *Fox Valley Tech*
Debbie Benson, *Kennesaw State University*
J. Lawrence Bergin, *Winona State University*
Wilbur Berry, *Jacksonville State University*
Eddy Birrer, *Gonzaga University*
Nancy Bledsoe, *Millsaps College*
Amy Bourne, *Oregon State University*
Cendy Boyd, *Northeast Louisiana State*
Lindsey Boyer, *Central Piedmont Community College*
Arthur Boyett, *Francis Marion University*
Cassie Bradley, *Troy State University*
Rodger Brannan, *University of Minnesota, Duluth*
Roscoe Eugene Bryson, *University of Alabama in Huntsville*
Connie Buchanan, *Southwest Texas Junior College*
Barry Buchoff, *Towson University*
Georgia Buckles, *Manchester Community College*
Radie Bunn, *Southwest Missouri State University*
Jackie Burke, *Hofstra University*
Gregory Bushong, *Wright State University*
Sandra Byrd, *Missouri State University*
Judith Cadle, *Tarleton State University*
James Cahsell, *Miami University*
Scott Cairns, *Shippensburg College*

Mark Camma, *Atlantic Cape Community College*
Elizabeth Cannata, *Johnson & Wales University*
Eric Carlsen, *Kean University*
Frederic J. Carlson, *LeTourneau University*
Joan Carroll, *SUNY-College at Oswego*
Valrie Chambers, *Texas A&M University, Corpus Christi*
Bruce Chase, *Radford University*
Alan Cherry, *Loyola Marymount University*
Bea Chiang, *College of New Jersey*
Ginger Clark, *University of Cincinnati*
Paul Clikeman, *University of Richmond*
Ronald Colley, *State University of West Georgia*
Cheryl Corke, *Genesse Community College*
Samantha Cox, *Wake Technical Community College*
William Cress, *University of Wisconsin-La Cross*
Kathy Crusto-Way, *Tarrant County College Southeast*
Sue Cullers, *Tarleton State University*
Jill D'Aquila, *Iona College*
Wagih Dafashy, *College of William & Mary*
Laura DeLaune, *Louisiana State University*
Guenther Dermanelian, *Johnson & Wales University*
Robert Derstine, *Villanova University*
Walter Doehring, *Genesee Community College*
George Dow, *Valencia Community College*
Lola Dudley, *Eastern Illinois University*
Melanie Earls, *Mississippi State University*
Catherine Eason, *Queens University of Charlotte*
Alan Eastman, *Indiana University of Pennsylvania*
M. J. Edwards, *Adirondack Community College*
Susan Eldridge, *University of Nebraska, Omaha*
Terry Elliott, *Morehead State University*
Tom English, *Boise State University*
Denise English, *Boise State University*
Ruth Epps, *Virginia Commonwealth University*
Caroline Falconetti, *Nassau Community College*
John Farlin, *Ohio Dominican University*
Philip Fink, *University of Toledo*
David Fordham, *James Madison University*
Lou Fowler, *Missouri Western State College*
Ken Fowler, *San Jose State University*
Peter Frischmann, *Idaho State University*
Ralph Fritzsch, *Midwestern State University*
Mark Fronke, *Cerritos College*
Ross Fuerman, *Suffolk University*
Mary Anne Gaffney, *Temple University*
David Ganz, *University of Missouri-Saint Louis*
Michael Garner, *Salisbury State University*
Jane Garvin, *Ivy Tech Community College*
William T. Geary, *College of William and Mary*
Lucille Genduso, *Nova Southeastern University*
Frank Gersich, *Gustavus Adolphus College*
Daniel Gibbons, *Waubonsee Community College*
Claudia Gilbertson, *North Hennepin Community College*
Frank Giove, *Niagara University*
Lorraine Glasscock, *University of North Alabama*
Diane Glowacki, *Tarrant County College*
John Gould, *Western Carolina University*
Joseph Guardino, *Kingsborough Community College*
Jeffry Haber, *Iona College*
Abo-El-Yazeed Habib, *Minnesota State University, Mankato*
Larry Hagler, *East Carolina University*
Penny Hanes, *Virginia Tech University*
Deborah Hanks, *Cardinal Stritch University*
Leon Hanouille, *Syracuse University*
Coby Harmon, *University of California, Santa Barbara*
Judith Harris, *Nova Southeastern University*
Phillip Harsha, *Southwest Missouri State University*
Charles Hart, *Copiah-Lincoln Community College*
Paul Haugen, *Wisconsin Indianhead Technical College*
Thomas Hayes, *University of Louisiana, Monroe*
Inez Heal, *Youngstown State University*
Kenneth Hiltebeitel, *Villanova*
Nitham Hindi, *Shippensburg College*
Jan Holmes, *Louisiana State University*
Bambi Hora, *University of Central Oklahoma*
M. A. Houston, *Wright State University*
Susan Hughes, *Butler University*
Kurt Hull, *California State University, Los Angeles*
Karen Hull, *Kansas Wesleyan University*
Richard Hulme, *California State Polytechnic University-Pomona*
Gary Todd Jackson, *Northeastern State University*
Sharon Jackson, *Samford University*
Agatha Jeffers, *Montclair State University*
Scott Jerris, *San Francisco State University*
Pamela Jones, *Mississippi State University*

David Juriga, *Saint Louis Community College*
Shelley Stall Kane, *Wake Technical Community College*
Khondkar Karim, *Monmouth University*
Cindi Khanlarian, *University of North Carolina Greensboro*
Bonita Kramer, *Montana State University*
Nathan Kranowski, *Radford University*
Leah Kratz, *Eastern Mennonite University*
Joan Lacher, *Nassau Community College*
Steven LaFave, *Augsburg College*
Helen LaFrancois, *University of Massachusetts-Dartmouth*
Ellen Landgraf, *Loyola University, Chicago*
Robert Landry, *Massasoit Community College*
Joseph Larkin, *Saint Joseph's University*
Laurie Larson, *Valencia Community College*
William Lathen, *Boise State University*
Doug Laufer, *Metropolitan State College of Denver*
Daniel Law, *Gonzaga University*
David Law, *Youngstown State University*
Marilynn Leathart, *John Carroll University*
Patsy Lee, *University of Texas, Arlington*
June Li, *University of Minnesota, Duluth*
William Link, *University of Missouri-Saint Louis*
Philip Little, *Coastal Carolina University*
Larry Logan, *University of Massachusetts-Dartmouth*
Patricia Lopez, *Valencia Community College*
Angelo Luciano, *Columbia College—Chicago*
James Lukawitz, *University of Memphis*
Catherine Lumbattis, *Southern Illinois University-Carbondale*
Nancy Lynch, *West Virginia University*
Mary MacAusland, *Reading Area Community College*
Mostafa Maksy, *Northeastern Illinois University*
Mary Manktelow, *James Madison University*
Joseph Marcheggiani, *Butler University*
Herb Martin, *Hope College*
Elizabeth Matz, *University of Pittsburgh, Bradford*
Alan Mayer-Sommer, *Georgetown University*
Lynn Mazzola, *Nassau Community College*
Ruth Ann McEwen, *Suffolk University*
Dwight McIntyre, *Clemson University*
Dawn McKinley, *William Rainey Harper College*
Shaen McMurtrie, *Northern Oklahoma College*
Nancy Meade, *Radford University*
Trini Melcher, *California State University, San Marcos*
Sara Melendy, *Gonzaga University*
Pam Meyer, *University of Louisiana, Lafayette*
R. L. C. Miller, *California State University, Fullerton*
Elizabeth Minbiole, *Northwood University*
Susan Minke, *Indiana University-Purdue University, Ft. Wayne*
George Minmier, *University of Memphis*
Cheryl Mitchem, *Virginia State University*
Patrick Montgomery, *University of Wisconsin, Platteville*
Lu Montondon, *Southwest Texas State University*
Gerald Motl, *Xavier University*
Elizabeth Mulig, *Columbus State University*
Steve Muller, *Valencia Community College*
Steven Muller, *Valencia Community College*
Carol Murphy, *Quinsigamond Community College*
Irvin Nelson, *Utah State University*
Bruce Neumann, *University of Colorado, Denver*
Christine Noel, *Colorado State University—Pueblo*
Tim Nygaard, *Madisonville Community College*
Ron O'Brien, *Fayetteville Technical Community College*
Brian O'Doherty, *East Carolina University*
Bruce Oliver, *Rochester Institute of Technology*
Joseph Onyeocha, *South Carolina State University*
Ashton Oravetz, *Tyler Junior College*
Stephen Owusu-Ansah, *University of Texas, Pan American*
Lawrence Ozzello, *University of Wisconsin-Eau Claire*
Eileen Peacock, *Oakland University*
Kathy Perdue, *DeVry Institute of Technology at Decatur*
Viola Persia, *SUNY Stony Brook*
Jack Peterson, *Utah State University*
Thomas Phillips, Jr., *Louisiana Tech University*
Cynthia Phipps, *Lake Land College*
Ronald Pierno, *Florida State University*
Cathy Pitts, *Highline Community College*
Atul Rai, *Wichita State University*
Mary Raven, *Mount Mary College*
Thomas Rearick, *Indiana University*
Craig Reeder, *Florida A&M University*
Jane Reimers, *Florida State University*
Ann Rich, *Quinnipiac University*
Laura Rickett, *Kent State University*
Michael Riordan, *James Madison University*
Patricia Robinson, *Johnson and Wales University*
Luther Ross, *Central Piedmont Community College*
Pamela Rouse, *Butler University*
Ann Rowell, *Central Piedmont Community College*
Ken Ruby, *Idaho State University*
Nadine Russell
P. N. Saksena, *Indiana University, South Bend*
Nancy Schneider, *Lynchburg College*
Henry Schulman, *Grossmont College*

Jeffrey Schwartz, *Montgomery College*

Joanne Segovia, *Minnesota State University, Moorhead*

Cindy Seipel, *New Mexico State University*

Suzanne Sevalstad, *University of Nevada-Las Vegas*

Kim Shaughnessy, *James Madison University*

Carol Shaver, *Louisiana Tech University*

John Shaver, *Louisiana Tech University*

Lewis Shaw, *Suffolk University*

Mary Sheil, *Kennesaw State University*

Eileen Shifflett, *James Madison University*

Nathan Slavin, *Hofstra University*

Talitha Smith, *Auburn University*

Jill Smith, *Idaho State University*

Sondra Smith, *University of West Georgia*

Nancy Snow, *University of Toledo*

Paul E. Solomon

Mary Soroko, *St. Cloud State University*

Linda Specht, *Trinity University*

John Sperry, *Virginia Commonwealth University*

Barbara Squires, *Corning Community College*

Vic Stanton, *University of California Berkeley*

Paul Steinbart, *Saint Louis University-Saint Louis*

Scott Steinkamp, *College of Lake County*

Tim Stephens, *DeVry Institute of Technology at Addison*

Mary Stevens, *University of Texas-El Paso*

Sue Stickland, *University of Texas, Arlington*

Leonard Stokes, *Siena College*

Ronald Strittmater, *North Hennepin Community College*

Gloria Stuart, *Georgia Southern University*

Janice Swanson, *Southern Oregon University*

James Swayze, *University of Nevada, Las Vegas*

Ellen Sweatt, *Georgia Perimeter College*

Jan Sweeney, *Baruch College CUNY*

Rasoul Taghizadeh, *Lexington Community College*

Bill Talbot, *Montgomery College*

Maurice Tassin, *Louisiana Tech University*

Kerri Tassin, *Missouri State University*

Steve Teeter, *Utah Valley State College*

Kim Temme, *Maryville University*

Peter Theuri, *Northern Kentucky University*

James Thompson, *Oklahoma City University*

Ada Till, *Prairie View A&M University*

Karen Turner, *University of Northern Colorado*

Suneel Udpa, *St. Mary's College of California*

Donna Ulmer, *St. Louis Community College, Meramec*

Denise Dickins Veitch, *Florida Atlantic University*

George Violette, *University of Southern Maine*

Beth Vogel, *Mount Mary College*

Sharon Walters, *Morehead State University*

Andrea Weickgenannt, *Northern Kentucky University*

J. D. Weinhold, *Concordia College*

Judith Welch, *University of Central Florida*

T. Sterling Wetzel, *Oklahoma State University, Stillwater*

Thomas Whalen, *Suffolk University*

Thomas Whitacre, *University of South Carolina*

Jennifer Wilbanks, *State Fair Community College*

Macil C. Wilkie, Jr., *Grambling State University*

Marvin Williams, *University of Houston*

Stephen Willits, *Bucknell University*

Marie Winks, *Lynchburg College*

Kenneth Winter, *University of Wisconsin-La Cross*

Alan Winters, *Clemson University*

Gail Wright, *Bryant University*

Marjorie Yuschak, *Rutgers University*

Judith Zander, *Grossmont College*

Haiwen Zhang, *University of Minnesota*

Ping Zhon, *Baruch College*

Focus Group Participants

Mark Anderson, *University of Texas at Dallas*

Brenda Benson, *Blinn College*

Anna Marie Boulware, *St. Charles Community College*

Norris Dorsey, *California State University, Northridge*

Caroline Falconetti, *Nassau Community College*

Judith Harris, *Nova Southeastern University*

Carol Hutchinson, *AB Tech*

Douglas Larson, *Salem State College*

Joseph Lupino, *St. Mary's College of California*

Al Nagy, *John Carroll University*

Ron Pierno, *Florida State University*

Linda Poulson, *Elon University*

Atul Rai, *Wichita State University*

Gayle Richardson, *Bakersfield College*

Dwight Riley, *Richland College*

Megan Schaupp, *West Virginia University—Morgantown*

Rex Schildhouse, *Miramar College*

Virginia Smith, *Saint Mary's College of California*

Warren Smock, *Ivy Tech Community College*

Kathy Sobieralski, *University of Maryland, University College*

Rasoul Taghizadeh, *Bluegrass Community and Technical College*

LaVerne Thomas-Vertrees, *St. Louis Community College*

Al Wallace, *Owensboro Community & Technical College*

BRIEF CONTENTS

CONTENTS

Chapter 2 Accounting for Accruals and Deferrals 70

Chapter 3 The Double-Entry Accounting System 146

Chapter 5 Accounting for Inventories 274

Chapter 6 Internal Control and Accounting for Cash 318

Gulfstream

Chapter 8 Accounting for Long-Term Operational Assets 420

Chapter 9 Accounting for Current Liabilities and Payroll 480

Chapter 10 Accounting for Long-Term Debt 538

Chapter 11 Proprietorships, Partnerships, and Corporations 596

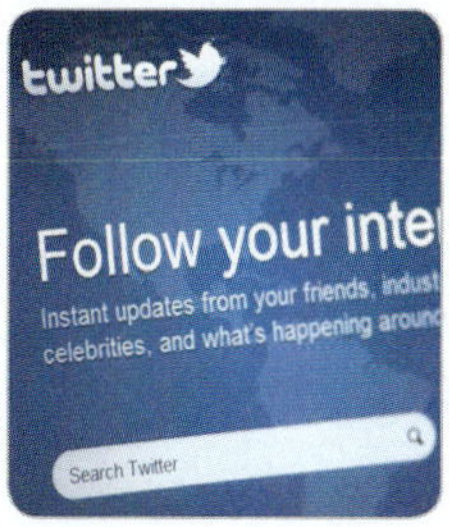

Chapter 12 Statement of Cash Flows 644

Chapter 13 Financial Statement Analysis (Available online in the *Connect* Library) 13-0

Fundamental Financial Accounting Concepts

CHAPTER 1

An Introduction to Accounting

LEARNING OBJECTIVES

After you have mastered the material in this chapter, you will be able to:

SECTION 1: COLLECTING AND ORGANIZING INFORMATION

LO 1-1 Explain the role of accounting in society.

LO 1-2 Construct an accounting equation and show how business events affect the equation.

LO 1-3 Interpret information shown in an accounting equation.

LO 1-4 Classify business events as asset source, use, or exchange transactions.

SECTION 2: REPORTING INFORMATION

LO 1-5 Prepare an income statement, a statement of changes in stockholders' equity, and a balance sheet.

LO 1-6 Prepare a statement of cash flows.

LO 1-7 Explain the closing process.

LO 1-8 Record business events using a horizontal financial statements model.

Video lectures and accompanying self-assessment quizzes are available for all learning objectives through McGraw-Hill Connect® Plus Accounting.

The Curious Accountant

Who owns **McDonald's**? Who owns the **American Red Cross** (ARC)? Many people and organizations other than owners are interested in the operations of McDonald's and the ARC. These parties are called ***stakeholders***. Among others, they include lenders, employees, suppliers, customers, benefactors, research institutions, local governments, flood victims, lawyers, bankers, financial analysts, and government agencies such as the Internal Revenue Service and the Securities and Exchange Commission. Organizations communicate information to stakeholders through ***financial reports***.

How do you think the financial reports of McDonald's differ from those of the ARC? (Answer on page 11.)

SECTION 1:

COLLECTING AND ORGANIZING INFORMATION

Why should you study accounting? You should study accounting because it can help you succeed in business. Businesses use accounting to keep score. Imagine trying to play football without knowing how many points a touchdown is worth. Like sports, business is competitive. If you do not know how to keep score, you are not likely to succeed.

Accounting is an information system that reports on the economic activities and financial condition of a business or other organization. Do not underestimate the importance of accounting information. If you had information that enabled you to predict business success, you could become a very wealthy Wall Street investor. Communicating economic information is so important that accounting is frequently called the *language of business.*

ROLE OF ACCOUNTING IN SOCIETY

LO 1-1

Explain the role of accounting in society.

How should society allocate its resources? Should we spend more to harvest food or cure disease? Should we build computers or cars? Should we invest money in IBM or General Motors? Accounting provides information that helps answer such questions.

Using Free Markets to Set Resource Priorities

Suppose you want to start a business. You may have heard "you have to have money to make money." In fact, you will need more than just money to start and operate a business. You will likely need such resources as equipment, land, materials, and employees. If you do not have these resources, how can you get them? In the United States, you compete for resources in open markets.

A **market** is a group of people or entities organized to exchange items of value. The market for business resources involves three distinct participants: consumers, conversion agents, and resource owners. *Consumers* use resources. Resources are frequently not in a form consumers want. For example, nature provides trees but consumers want furniture. *Conversion agents* (businesses) transform resources such as trees into desirable products such as furniture. *Resource owners* control the distribution of resources to conversion agents. Thus resource owners provide resources (inputs) to conversion agents who provide goods and services (outputs) to consumers.

For example, a home builder (conversion agent) transforms labor and materials (inputs) into houses (output) that consumers use. The transformation adds value to the inputs, creating outputs worth more than the sum of the inputs. For example, a house that required $220,000 of materials and labor to build could have a market value of $250,000.

Common terms for the added value created in the transformation process include **profit, income, or earnings.** Accountants measure the added value as the difference between the cost of a product or service and the selling price of that product or service. The profit on the house described above is $30,000, the difference between its $220,000 cost and $250,000 market value.

Conversion agents who successfully and efficiently (at low cost) satisfy consumer preferences are rewarded with high earnings. These earnings are shared with resource owners, so conversion agents who exhibit high earnings potential are more likely to compete successfully for resources.

Return to the original question. How can you get the resources you need to start a business? You must go to open markets and convince resource owners that you can produce profits. Exhibit 1.1 illustrates the market trilogy involved in resource allocation.

The specific resources businesses commonly use to satisfy consumer demand are financial resources, physical resources, and labor resources.

Financial Resources

Businesses (conversion agents) need **financial resources** (money) to get started and to operate. *Investors* and *creditors* provide financial resources.

- **Investors** provide financial resources in exchange for ownership interests in businesses. Owners expect businesses to return to them a share of the business, including a portion of earned income.
- **Creditors** lend financial resources to businesses. Instead of a share of the business, creditors expect the businesses to repay borrowed resources plus a specified fee called **interest.**

EXHIBIT 1.1

Market Trilogy in Resource Allocation

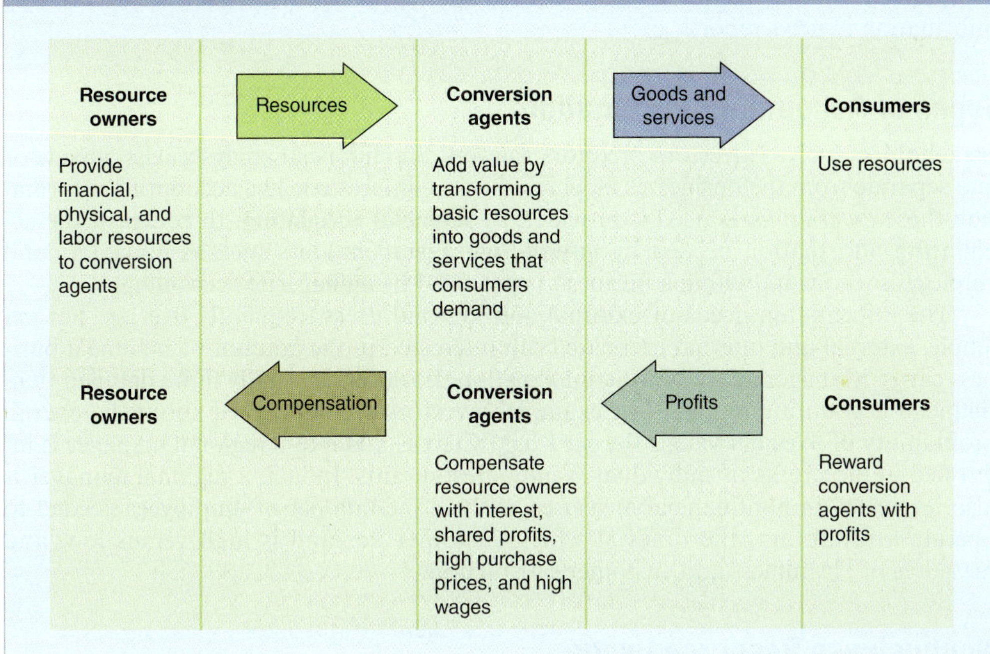

Investors and creditors prefer to provide financial resources to businesses with high earnings potential because such companies are better able to share profits and make interest payments. Profitable businesses are also less likely to experience bankruptcy.

Physical Resources

In their most primitive form, **physical resources** are natural resources. Physical resources often move through numerous stages of transformation. For example, standing timber may be successively transformed into harvested logs, raw lumber, and finished furniture. Owners of physical resources seek to sell those resources to businesses with high earnings potential because profitable businesses are able to pay higher prices and make repeat purchases.

Labor Resources

Labor resources include both intellectual and physical labor. Like other resource providers, workers prefer businesses that have high income potential because these businesses are able to pay higher wages and offer continued employment.

Accounting Provides Information

How do providers of financial, physical, and labor resources identify conversion agents (businesses) with high profit potential? Investors, creditors, and workers rely heavily on accounting information to evaluate which businesses are worthy of receiving resources. In addition, other people and organizations have an interest in accounting information about businesses. The many **users** of accounting information are commonly called **stakeholders.** Stakeholders include resource providers, financial analysts, brokers, attorneys, government regulators, and news reporters.

The link between conversion agents (businesses) and those stakeholders who provide resources is direct: businesses pay resource providers. Resource providers use accounting information to identify companies with high earnings potential because those companies are more likely to return higher profits, make interest payments, repay debt, pay higher prices, and provide stable, high-paying employment.

The link between conversion agents and other stakeholders is indirect. Financial analysts, brokers, and attorneys may use accounting information when advising their clients. Government agencies may use accounting information to assess companies' compliance with income tax laws and other regulations. Reporters may use accounting information in news reports.

Types of Accounting Information

Stakeholders such as investors, creditors, lawyers, and financial analysts exist outside of and separate from the businesses in which they are interested. The accounting information these *external users* need is provided by **financial accounting.** In contrast, the accounting information needed by *internal users,* stakeholders such as managers and employees who work within a business, is provided by **managerial accounting.**

The information needs of external and internal users frequently overlap. For example, external and internal users are both interested in the amount of income a business earns. Managerial accounting information, however, is usually more detailed than financial accounting reports. For example, investors are concerned about the overall profitability of **Wendy's** versus **Burger King**; whereas a Wendy's regional manager is interested in the profits of individual Wendy's restaurants. In fact, a regional manager is also interested in nonfinancial measures, such as the number of employees needed to operate a restaurant, the times at which customer demand is high versus low, and measures of cleanliness and customer satisfaction.

Nonbusiness Resource Usage

The U.S. economy is not purely market based. Factors other than profitability often influence resource allocation priorities. For example, governments allocate resources for national defense, to redistribute wealth, or to protect the environment. Foundations, religious groups, the Peace Corps, and other benevolent organizations prioritize resource usage based on humanitarian concerns.

Organizations that are not motivated by profit are called **not-for-profit entities** (also called *nonprofit* or *nonbusiness organizations*). Stakeholders interested in nonprofit organizations also need accounting information. Accounting systems measure the cost of the goods and services not-for-profit organizations provide, the efficiency and effectiveness of the organizations' operations, and the ability of the organizations to continue to provide goods and services. This information serves a host of stakeholders, including taxpayers, contributors, lenders, suppliers, employees, managers, financial analysts, attorneys, and beneficiaries.

The focus of accounting, therefore, is to provide information that is useful to a variety of business and nonbusiness user groups for decision making. The different types of accounting information and the stakeholders that commonly use the information are summarized in Exhibit 1.2.

Careers in Accounting

An accounting career can take you to the top of the business world. In a recent *Forbes* article Jeffery Sanders reveals that a significantly higher percentage of Fortune 500 CEOs advance from financial backgrounds than any other discipline. Sanders notes that large companies prefer CEOs who understand the financial ramifications of business decisions.

What do accountants do? Accountants identify, record, analyze, and communicate information about the economic events that affect organizations. They may work in either public accounting or private accounting.

Public Accounting

You are probably familiar with the acronym CPA. CPA stands for certified *public* accountant. Public accountants provide services to various clients. They are usually

EXHIBIT 1.2

Accounting as Information Provider

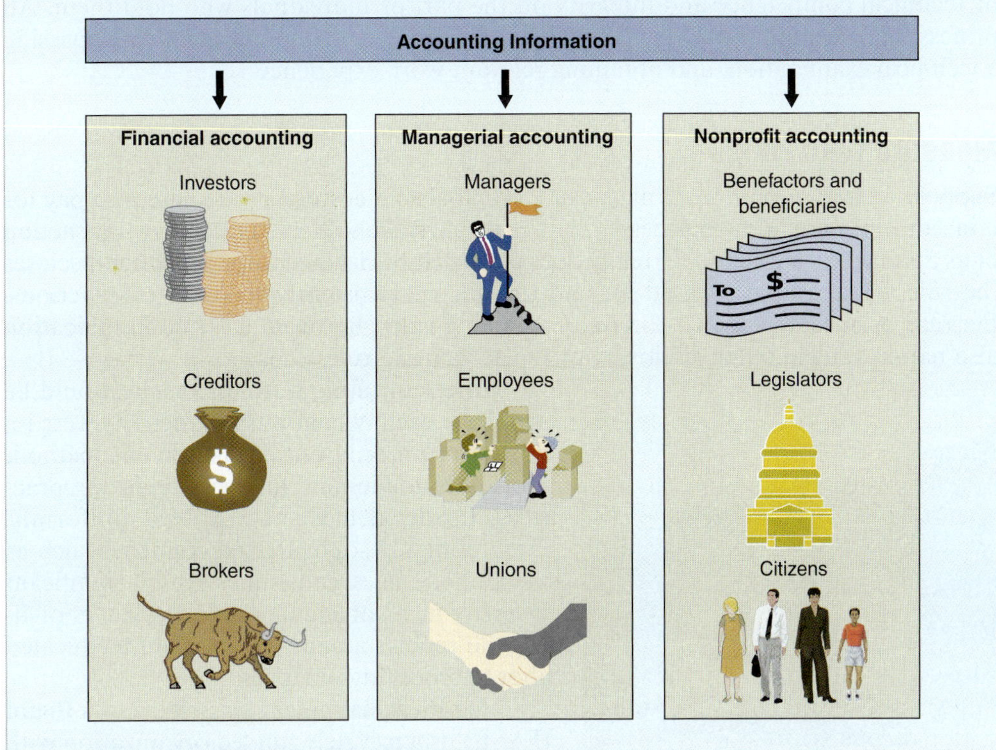

paid a fee that varies depending on the service provided. Services typically offered by public accountants include (1) audit services, (2) tax services, and (3) consulting services.

- *Audit services* involve examining a company's accounting records in order to issue an opinion about whether the company's financial statements conform to generally accepted accounting principles. The auditor's opinion adds credibility to the statements, which are prepared by the company's management.
- *Tax services* include both determining the amount of tax due and tax planning to help companies minimize tax expense.
- *Consulting services* cover a wide range of activities that include everything from installing sophisticated computerized accounting systems to providing personal financial advice.

All public accountants are not certified. Each state government, as well as Washington, DC, and four U.S. territories, establish certification requirements applicable in that jurisdiction. Although the requirements vary from jurisdiction to jurisdiction, CPA candidates normally must have a college education, pass a demanding technical examination, and obtain work experience relevant to practicing public accounting.

Private Accounting

Accountants employed in the private sector usually work for a specific company or nonprofit organization. Private sector accountants perform a wide variety of functions for their employers. Their duties include classifying and recording transactions, billing customers and collecting amounts due, ordering merchandise, paying suppliers, preparing and analyzing financial statements, developing budgets, measuring costs, assessing performance, and making decisions.

Private accountants may earn any of several professional certifications. For example, the Institute of Management Accountants issues the *Certified Management Accounting* (*CMA*) designation. The Institute of Internal Auditors issues the *Certified Internal Auditor* (*CIA*) designation. These designations are widely recognized indicators of technical competence and integrity on the part of individuals who hold them. All professional accounting certifications call for meeting education requirements, passing a technical examination, and obtaining relevant work experience.

Measurement Rules

Suppose a store sells an MP3 player in December to a customer who agrees to pay for it in January. Should the business *recognize* (report) the sale as a December transaction or as a January transaction? It really does not matter as long as the storeowner discloses the rule the decision is based on and applies it consistently to other transactions. Because businesses may use different reporting rules, however, clear communication also requires full and fair disclosure of the accounting rules chosen.

Communicating business results would be simpler if each type of business activity were reported using only one measurement method. World economies and financial reporting practices, however, have not evolved uniformly. Even in highly sophisticated countries such as the United States, companies exhibit significant diversity in reporting methods. Providers of financial reports assume that users are educated about accounting practices.

The **Financial Accounting Standards Board (FASB)**[1] is a privately funded organization with the primary authority for establishing accounting standards in the United States. The measurement rules established by the FASB are called **generally accepted accounting principles (GAAP).** Financial reports issued to the public must follow GAAP. This textbook introduces these principles so you will be able to understand business activity reported by companies in the United States.

Companies are not required to follow GAAP when preparing *management accounting* reports. Although there is considerable overlap between financial and managerial accounting, managers are free to construct internal reports in whatever fashion best suits the effective operation of their companies.

Reporting Entities

Think of accountants in the same way you would think of news reporters. A news reporter gathers and discloses information about some person, place, or thing. Likewise, an accountant gathers and discloses financial information about specific people or businesses. The people or businesses accountants report on are called **reporting entities.** When studying accounting you should think of yourself as the accountant. Your first step is to identify the person or business on which you are reporting. This is not always as easy as it may seem. To illustrate, consider the following scenario.

[1]The FASB consists of seven full-time members appointed by the supporting organization, the Financial Accounting Foundation (FAF). The FAF membership is intended to represent the broad spectrum of individuals and institutions that have an interest in accounting and financial reporting. FAF members include representatives of the accounting profession, industry, financial institutions, the government, and the investing public.

FOCUS ON INTERNATIONAL ISSUES

IS THERE GLOBAL GAAP?

As explained in this chapter, accounting is a measurement and communication discipline based on rules referred to as *generally accepted accounting principles (GAAP).* The rules described in this text are based on GAAP used in the United States, but what rules do the rest of the world use? Is there a global GAAP, or does each country establish its own unique GAAP?

Until recently, each country developed its own unique GAAP. Global companies were required to prepare multiple sets of financial statements to satisfy each country's GAAP. The use of multiple accounting standards across the globe made comparing company performance difficult and expensive. To address the need for a common set of financial standards, the International Accounting Standards Committee was formed in 1973. The committee was reorganized as the **International Accounting Standards Board (IASB)** in 2001. The IASB issues **International Financial Reporting Standards (IFRS),** which are rapidly gaining support worldwide. In 2005, companies in the countries who were members of the European Union were required to use the IFRS as established by the IASB, which is headquartered in London. Today, over 100 countries require or permit companies to prepare their financial statements using IFRS.

As of 2014, most of the major economic countries have switched from their local GAAP to IFRS. One notable exception is the United States, but even here, the Securities and Exchange Commission announced in 2008 that it was seriously considering adopting rules that would allow our companies to use either GAAP or IFRS. Although not finalized when this book was being prepared, many accountants in the United States believe this will occur. Additionally, there is an active process in place to reduce the differences between IFRS and U.S. GAAP.

There are many similarities between the IASB and the FASB. Both the FASB and the IASB are required to include members with a variety of backgrounds, including auditors, users of financial information, academics, and so forth. Also, both groups primarily require that their members work full-time for their respective boards; they cannot serve on the board while being compensated by another organization. (The IASB does allow up to three of its members to be part-time.) Members of each board serve five-year terms and can be reappointed once. The funds to support both boards, and the large organizations that support them, are obtained from a variety of sources, including selling publications and private contributions. To help maintain independence of the board's members, fund-raising is performed by separate sets of trustees.

Despite their similarities, there are significant differences between the IASB and the FASB. One of these relates to size and geographic diversity. The FASB has only seven members, all from the United States. The IASB has sixteen members, and these must include at least four from Asia, four from Europe, four from North America, one from Africa, and one from South America.

Not only is the structure of the standards-setting boards different but the standards and principles they establish may also differ significantly. In this chapter, you will learn that GAAP employs the *historical cost concept.* This means that the assets of most U.S. companies are shown on the balance sheet at the amount for which they were purchased. For example, land that has a market value of millions of dollars may be shown on Ford's financial statements with a value of only a few hundred thousand dollars. This occurs because GAAP requires Ford to show the land at its cost rather than its market value. In contrast, IFRS permits companies to show market values on their financial statements. This means that the exact same assets may show radically different values if the statements are prepared under IFRS rather than GAAP.

Throughout this text, where appropriate, we will note the differences between U.S. GAAP and IFRS. However, by the time you graduate, it is likely that among the major industrialized nations, there will be a global GAAP.

Jason Winston recently started a business. During the first few days of operation, Mr. Winston transferred cash from his personal account into a business account for a company he named Winston Enterprises. Mr. Winston's brother, George, invested cash in Winston Enterprises for which he received an ownership interest in the company. Winston Enterprises borrowed cash from First Federal Bank. Winston Enterprises paid cash to purchase a building from Commercial Properties, Inc. Winston Enterprises earned cash revenues from its customers and paid its employees cash for salaries expense.

How many reporting entities are described in this scenario? Assuming all of the customers are counted as a single entity and all of the employees are counted as a single entity, there are a total of seven entities named in the scenario. These entities include: (1) Jason Winston, (2) Winston Enterprises, (3) George Winston, (4) First Federal

Bank, (5) Commercial Properties, Inc., (6) the customers, and (7) the employees. A separate set of accounting records would be maintained for each entity.

Your ability to learn accounting will be greatly influenced by how you approach the entity concept. Based on your everyday experiences you likely think from the perspective of a customer. In contrast, this text is written from the perspective of a business entity. These opposing perspectives dramatically affect how you view business events. For example, as a customer you consider a sales discount a great bargain. The view is different from the perspective of the business granting the discount. A sales discount means an item did not sell at the expected price. To move the item, the business had to accept less money than it originally planned to receive. From this perspective, a sales discount is not a good thing. To understand accounting, train yourself to interpret transactions from the perspective of a business rather than a consumer. Each time you encounter an accounting event ask yourself, how does this affect the business?

CHECK YOURSELF 1.1

In a recent business transaction, land was exchanged for cash. Did the amount of cash increase or decrease?

Answer The answer depends on the reporting entity to which the question pertains. One entity sold land. The other entity bought land. For the entity that sold land, cash increased. For the entity that bought land, cash decreased.

ELEMENTS OF FINANCIAL STATEMENTS

The individuals and organizations that need information about a business are called *stakeholders.* Stakeholders include owners, lenders, government agencies, employees, news reporters, and others. Businesses communicate information to stakeholders through four financial statements:[2] (1) an income statement, (2) a statement of changes in equity, (3) a balance sheet, and (4) a statement of cash flows.

The information reported in **financial statements** is organized into ten categories known as **elements.** Eight financial statement elements are discussed in this chapter: assets, liabilities, equity, contributed capital, revenue, expenses, distributions, and net income. The other two elements, gains and losses, are discussed in a later chapter. In practice, the business world uses various titles to identify several of the financial statement elements. For example, businesspeople use net income, net *earnings,* and net *profit* interchangeably to describe the same element. Contributed capital may be called *common stock* and equity may be called *stockholders' equity, owner's capital,* and *partners' equity.* Furthermore, the transfer of assets from a business to its owners may be called *distributions, withdrawals,* or *dividends.* Think of accounting as a language. Different terms can describe the same business event. Detailed definitions of the elements and their placement on financial statements will be discussed in the following sections of the chapter.

Using Accounts to Gather Information

Detailed information about the elements is maintained in records commonly called **accounts.** For example, information regarding the element *assets* may be organized in separate accounts for cash, equipment, buildings, land, and so forth. The types and

[2]In practice these statements have alternate names. For example, the income statement may be called *results of operations* or *statement of earnings.* The balance sheet is sometimes called the *statement of financial position.* The statement of changes in equity might be called *statement of capital* or *statement of stockholders' equity.* Since the Financial Accounting Standards Board (FASB) called for the title *statement of cash flows,* companies do not use alternate names for that statement.

Answers to The Curious Accountant

Anyone who owns stock in **McDonald's** owns a part of the company. McDonald's has many owners. In contrast, nobody actually owns the **American Red Cross** (ARC). The ARC has a board of directors that is responsible for overseeing its operations, but the board is not its owner.

Ultimately, the purpose of a business entity is to increase the wealth of its owners. To this end, it "spends money to make money." The expense that McDonald's incurs for advertising is a cost incurred in the hope that it will generate revenues when it sells hamburgers. The financial statements of a business show, among other things, whether and how the company made a profit during the current year. For example, McDonald's income statements show how much expense was incurred from "food and paper" costs versus from "payroll and employee benefits."

The ARC is a not-for-profit entity. It operates to provide services to society at large, not to make a profit. It cannot increase the wealth of its owners, because it has no owners. When the ARC spends money to assist flood victims, it does not spend this money in the expectation that it will generate revenues. The revenues of the ARC come from contributors who wish to support efforts related to helping disaster victims. Because the ARC does not spend money to make money, it has no reason to prepare an *income statement* like that of McDonald's. The ARC's statement of activities shows how much revenue was received from contributions versus from "investment income."

Not-for-profit entities do prepare financial statements that are similar in appearance to those of commercial enterprises. The financial statements of not-for-profit entities are called the *statement of financial position,* the *statement of activities,* and the *cash flow statement.*

number of accounts used by a business depends on the information needs of its stakeholders. Some businesses provide very detailed information; others report highly summarized information. The more detail desired, the greater number of accounts needed. Think of accounts like the notebooks students keep for their classes. Some students keep detailed notes about every class they take in a separate notebook. Other students keep only the key points for all of their classes in a single notebook. Similarly, some businesses use more accounts than other businesses.

Diversity also exists regarding the names used for various accounts. For example, employee pay may be called salaries, wages, commissions, and so forth. Do not become frustrated with the diversity of terms used in accounting. Remember, accounting is a language. The same word can have different meanings. Similarly, different words can be used to describe the same phenomenon. The more you study and use accounting, the more familiar it will become to you.

Accounting Equation

LO 1-2

Construct an accounting equation and show how business events affect the equation.

You have probably heard the adage "you have to have money to make money." Indeed, you usually need a lot more than just money. For example, **Carmike Cinemas, Inc.**, uses buildings, seating, screens, projection equipment, vending machines, cash registers, and so on in order to make money from ticket sales. The resources a business uses to make money are called **assets.** So, where do businesses get assets? There are three distinct sources.

First, a business can borrow assets from creditors. Usually a business acquires cash from creditors and then uses the cash to purchase the assets it needs to conduct its operations. When a business receives cash from creditors it accepts an obligation to return the cash to the creditors at some future date. In accounting terms, the obligations a business has to its creditors are called **liabilities.**

The second source of assets is investors. When a business acquires assets from investors it commits to keep the assets safe and to use the assets in a manner that benefits the investors. The business also grants the investor an ownership interest in the business, thereby allowing the investor (owner) to share in the profits generated by the business. The specific commitments made to the investors are described in certificates called **common stock.** In accounting terms investors are called **stockholders.** Further, the business's commitment to the stockholders is called **stockholders' equity.**

The third source of assets is operations. Businesses use assets in order to produce higher amounts of other assets. For example, Best Buy may sell a TV that cost the company \$500 for \$600. The \$100 difference between the sales price and the cost of the TV results in an increase in Best Buy's total assets. This explains how operations can be a source of assets. Of course operations may also result in a decrease in assets. If Best Buy has to discount the sales price of the TV to \$450 in order to sell it, the company's total assets decrease by \$50.

Net increases in assets generated from operations are commonly called *earnings* or *income*. Net decreases in assets caused by operations are called *losses*. As a result of their ownership status, the stockholders reap the benefits and suffer the sacrifices that a business experiences from its operations. A business may distribute all or part of the assets generated through operations to the shareholders. The distribution of assets generated through earnings is called a *dividend*.

Notice that paying dividends is an option—not a legal requirement. Instead of paying dividends, a business may retain the assets it generates through operations. If a business retains the assets, it commits to use those assets for the benefit of the stockholders. This increase in the business's commitments to its stockholders is normally called **retained earnings.** Also, note that earnings that have been retained in the past can be used to pay dividends in the future. However, a company that does not have current or prior retained earnings cannot pay dividends.

As a result of providing assets to a business, the creditors and investors are entitled to make potential **claims**[3] on the assets owned by the business. The relationship between a business's assets and the claims on its assets is frequently expressed in an equality called the **accounting equation.** Based on the relationships described above, the accounting equation can be developed as follows:

Assets = Claims

Assets = Liabilities + Stockholders' equity

Assets = Liabilities + Common stock + Retained earnings

CHECK YOURSELF 1.2

Gupta Company has \$250,000 of assets, \$60,000 of liabilities, and \$90,000 of common stock. What percentage of the assets was provided by retained earnings?

Answer First, using algebra, determine the dollar amount of retained earnings:
Assets = Liabilities + Common stock + Retained earnings
Retained earnings = Assets − Liabilities − Common stock
Retained earnings = \$250,000 − \$60,000 − \$90,000
Retained earnings = \$100,000
Second, determine the percentage:
Percentage of assets provided by retained earnings = Retained earnings/Total assets
Percentage of assets provided by retained earnings = \$100,000/\$250,000 = 40%

[3]A claim is a legal action to obtain money, property, or the enforcement of a right against another party.

RECORDING BUSINESS EVENTS UNDER THE ACCOUNTING EQUATION

An **accounting event** is an economic occurrence that changes an enterprise's assets, liabilities, or stockholders' equity. A **transaction** is a particular kind of event that involves transferring something of value between two entities. Examples of transactions include acquiring assets from owners, borrowing money from creditors, and purchasing or selling goods and services. The following section of the text explains how several different types of accounting events affect a company's accounting equation.

Asset Source Transactions

As previously mentioned, businesses obtain assets (resources) from three sources. They acquire assets from owners (stockholders); they borrow assets from creditors; and they earn assets through profitable operations. Asset source transactions increase total assets and total claims. A more detailed discussion of the effects of asset source transactions is provided below:

EVENT 1 **Rustic Camp Sites (RCS) was formed on January 1, 2016, when it acquired $120,000 cash from issuing common stock.**

When RCS issued stock, it received cash and gave each investor (owner) a stock certificate as a receipt. Since this transaction provided $120,000 of assets (cash) to the business, it is an **asset source transaction.** It increases the business's assets (cash) and its stockholders' equity (common stock).

	Assets			=	Liab.	+	Stockholders' Equity		
	Cash	+	Land	=	N. Pay.	+	Com. Stk.	+	Ret. Earn.
Acquired cash through stock issue	120,000	+	NA	=	NA	+	120,000	+	NA

Notice the elements have been divided into accounts. For example, the element *assets* is divided into a Cash account and a Land account. Do not be concerned if some of these account titles are unfamiliar. They will be explained as new transactions are presented. Recall that the number of accounts a company uses depends on the nature of its business and the level of detail management needs to operate the business. For example, **Sears** would have an account called Cost of Goods Sold although **GEICO Insurance** would not. Why? Because Sears sells goods (merchandise) but GEICO does not.

Also, notice that a stock issue transaction affects the accounting equation in two places, both under an asset (cash) and also under the source of that asset (common stock). All transactions affect the accounting equation in at least two places. It is from this practice that the **double-entry bookkeeping** system derives its name.

EVENT 2 **RCS acquired an additional $400,000 of cash by borrowing from a creditor.**

This transaction is also an *asset source transaction.* It increases assets (cash) and liabilities (notes payable). The account title Notes Payable is used because the borrower (RCS) is required to issue a promissory note to the creditor (a bank). A promissory note describes, among other things, the amount of interest RCS will pay and for how long it will borrow the money.[4] The effect of the borrowing transaction on the accounting equation is indicated below.

	Assets			=	Liab.	+	Stockholders' Equity		
	Cash	+	Land	=	N. Pay.	+	Com. Stk.	+	Ret. Earn.
Acquired cash by issuing note	400,000	+	NA	+	400,000	+	NA	+	NA

Asset Exchange Transactions

Businesses frequently trade one asset for another asset. In such cases, the amount of one asset decreases and the amount of the other asset increases. Total assets are unaffected by asset exchange transactions. Event 3 is an asset exchange transaction.

EVENT 3 **RCS paid $500,000 cash to purchase land.**

This asset exchange transaction reduces the asset account Cash and increases the asset account Land. The amount of total assets is not affected. An **asset exchange transaction** simply reflects changes in the composition of assets. In this case, the company traded cash for land. The amount of cash decreased by $500,000 and the amount of land increased by the same amount.

	Assets			=	Liab.	+	Stockholders' Equity		
	Cash	+	Land	=	N. Pay.	+	Com. Stk.	+	Ret. Earn.
Paid cash to buy land	(500,000)	+	500,000	=	NA	+	NA	+	NA

Another Asset Source Transaction

EVENT 4 **RCS obtained $85,000 cash by leasing camp sites to customers.**

The *economic benefit* a company derives from providing goods and services to its customers is called **revenue**. In this example the economic benefit is an increase in the asset cash. Businesses may receive other benefits that will be discussed later. However, at this point we will limit our definition of revenue to being *an increase in assets* that results from providing goods and services to customers. For this event the increase in the asset account Cash is balanced by an increase in the equity account Revenue. The effects on the accounting equation are as follows:

	Assets			=	Liab.	+	Stockholders' Equity			
	Cash	+	Land	=	N. Pay.	+	Com. Stk.	+	Ret. Earn.	Acct. Title
Acquired cash by earning revenue	85,000	+	NA	=	NA	+	NA	+	85,000	Revenue

Note carefully that the $85,000 shown in the retained earnings column is *not* in the Retained Earnings account. It is in the Revenue account. It will be transferred to the Retained Earnings account at the end of the accounting period. Transferring the Revenue account balance to the Retained Earnings account is part of a process called *closing the accounts.*

[4]For simplicity, the computation of interest is ignored in this chapter. Interest computation is discussed in the appendix to Chapter 2 and in subsequent chapters.

Asset Use Transactions

Businesses use assets for a variety of purposes. For example, assets may be used to pay off liabilities or they may be transferred to owners. Assets may also be used in the process of generating earnings. All **asset use transactions** decrease the total amount of assets and the total amount of claims on assets (liabilities or stockholders' equity).

EVENT 5 RCS paid $50,000 cash for operating expenses such as salaries, rent, and interest. RCS could establish a separate account for each type of expense. However, the management team does not currently desire this level of detail. Remember, the number of accounts a business uses depends on the level of information managers need to make decisions.

An economic sacrifice a business incurs in the process of generating revenue is called an **expense.** In this example, the economic sacrifice is a decrease in the asset Cash. While expenses may result in other types of sacrifice, at this point we will limit our definition of expense to being a *use of assets* that is necessary to generate revenue. For this event the decrease in the asset account is balanced by a decrease in the amount of stockholders' equity (retained earnings). The effects on the accounting equation are as follows:

	Assets			=	Liab.	+	Stockholders' Equity			
	Cash	+	Land	=	N. Pay.	+	Com. Stk.	+	Ret. Earn.	Acct. Title
Used cash to pay expenses	(50,000)	+	NA	=	NA	+	NA	+	(50,000)	Expense

Like revenues, expenses are not recorded directly into the Retained Earnings account. The $50,000 of expense is recorded in the Expense account. It will be transferred to the Retained Earnings account at the end of the accounting period as part of the closing process. The current balance in the Retained Earnings account is zero.

EVENT 6 RCS paid $4,000 in cash dividends to its owners.

To this point operating RCS has caused the amount of total assets to increase by $35,000 ($85,000 of revenue − $50,000 of operating expenses). Since the owners bear the risk and reap the rewards of operating the business, the $35,000 increase in assets benefits them. RCS can use the additional assets to grow the business or the company can transfer the earned assets to the owners. If a business transfers some or all of its earned assets to owners, the transfer is called a **dividend.** The $4,000 dividend paid by RCS reduces the asset account Cash and the amount of stockholders' equity (retained earnings). The effects on the accounting equation are as follows:

	Assets			=	Liab.	+	Stockholders' Equity			
	Cash	+	Land	=	N. Pay.	+	Com. Stk.	+	Ret. Earn.	Acct. Title
Used cash to pay dividends	(4,000)	+	NA	=	NA	+	NA	+	(4,000)	Dividends

Like revenues and expenses, dividends are not recorded directly into the Retained Earnings account. The $4,000 dividend is recorded in the Dividends account. It will be transferred to retained earnings at the end of the accounting period as part of the closing process. The current balance in the Retained Earnings account is zero.

EVENT 7 The land that RCS paid $500,000 to purchase had an appraised market value of $525,000 on December 31, 2016.

Although the appraised value of the land is higher than the original cost, RCS will not increase the amount recorded in its accounting records above the land's $500,000 historical cost. In general, accountants do not recognize changes in market value. The

historical cost concept requires that most assets be reported at the amount paid for them (their historical cost) regardless of increases in market value.

Surely investors would rather know what an asset is worth instead of how much it originally cost. So why do accountants maintain records and report financial information based on historical cost? Accountants rely heavily on verification. Information is considered to be more useful if it can be independently verified. For example, two people looking at the legal documents associated with RCS's land purchase will both conclude that RCS paid $500,000 for the land. That historical cost is a verifiable fact. The appraised value, in contrast, is an opinion. Even two persons who are experienced appraisers are not likely to come up with the same amount for the land's market value. Accountants do not report market values in financial statements because such values are not reliable.

There are exceptions to the application of the historical cost rule. When market value can be clearly established, GAAP not only permits but requires its use. For example, securities that are traded on the New York Stock Exchange must be shown at market value rather than historical cost. We will discuss other notable exceptions to the historical cost principle later in the text. However, as a general rule you should assume that assets shown in a company's financial statements are valued at historical cost.

Summary of Transactions

The complete collection of a company's accounts is called the **general ledger.** A summary of the accounting events and the general ledger accounts is shown in Exhibit 1.3. The Revenue, Expense, and Dividend account data appear in the retained earnings column. These account titles are shown immediately to the right of the dollar amounts listed in the retained earnings column.

EXHIBIT 1.3

Accounting Events

1. RCS issued common stock, acquiring $120,000 cash from its owners.
2. RCS borrowed $400,000 cash.
3. RCS paid $500,000 cash to purchase land.
4. RCS received $85,000 cash from earning revenue.
5. RCS paid $50,000 cash for expenses.
6. RCS paid dividends of $4,000 cash to the owners.
7. The land that RCS paid $500,000 to purchase had an appraised market value of $525,000 on December 31, 2016.

General Ledger Accounts Organized under the Accounting Equation

	Assets			=	Liabilities	+	Stockholders' Equity			
Event No.	Cash	+	Land	=	Notes Payable	+	Common Stock	+	Retained Earnings	Other Account Titles
Beg. bal.	0		0		0		0		0	
1.	120,000						120,000			
2.	400,000				400,000					
3.	(500,000)		500,000							
4.	85,000								85,000	Revenue
5.	(50,000)								(50,000)	Expense
6.	(4,000)								(4,000)	Dividend
7.	NA		NA		NA		NA		NA	
	51,000	+	500,000	=	400,000	+	120,000	+	31,000	

INTERPRETING INFORMATION SHOWN IN THE ACCOUNTING EQUATION

Before showing how financial information is reported to stakeholders, we highlight some interesting features of the accounting equation.

LO 1-3

Interpret information shown in an accounting equation.

The Left versus the Right Side of the Accounting Equation

To illustrate the relationship between the left and right sides of the accounting equation, assume Educate Inc. begins an accounting period with balances shown in the following accounting equation:

Assets	=	Liabilities	+	Common Stock	+	Retained Earnings
2,000	=	1,200	+	500	+	300

Now assume that Educate Inc. uses all of its cash to purchase land. Immediately after this purchase, the company's accounting equation is as follows:

Assets			=	Liabilities	+	Common Stock	+	Retained Earnings
Cash		Land						
0	+	2,000	=	1,200	+	500	+	300

At this point the company has zero cash. This highlights the fact that the amounts in liabilities, common stock, and retained earnings do not represent cash. Instead they represent the original sources of the company's assets. Indeed, the right side of the accounting equation could be expressed as percentages instead of dollars. Specifically, the equation could be written as follows:

Assets			=	Liabilities	+	Common Stock	+	Retained Earnings
Cash		Land						
0	+	2,000	=	60%	+	25%	+	15%

This equation shows that 60 percent of Educate's assets came from creditors, 25 percent came from owners, and 15 percent from prior period earnings. However, this does not explain what has happened to the company's assets since they were acquired. Specifically, the right side of the equation does not show that the company acquired cash and then used the cash to purchase land. The right side identifies the sources of assets, not their composition.

Cash and Retained Earnings

While the amount of retained earnings does not represent the amount of cash a company has on hand, it does limit the amount of cash that can be used to pay dividends. To illustrate, assume Creative Associates begins an accounting period with balances shown in the following accounting equation:

Assets			=	Liabilities	+	Common Stock	+	Retained Earnings
Cash		Land						
400	+	1,900	=	700	+	1,000	+	600

Given that the company has $600 in retained earnings, can the company pay a $500 cash dividend? The answer is no. Remember, there is no cash in retained earnings. The only cash the company has is listed on the left side of the equation. In this case, the maximum cash dividend that can be paid is $400 because that is all the cash the company has. Suppose Creative Associates decides it no longer needs the land and sells it for $1,900 cash. After this event, the accounting equation appears as follows:

Assets			=	Liabilities	+	Common Stock	+	Retained Earnings
Cash		Land						
2,300	+	0	=	700	+	1,000	+	600

Given that Creative Associates now has $2,300 in cash, can the company pay a $700 dividend? The answer is no. Based on the information in the accounting equation, Creative Associates has retained only $600 of its earnings. Since dividends are a distribution of assets that were generated through earnings, the maximum dividend Creative can distribute at this time is $600. In summary, the payment of dividends is limited by both the amount of cash and the amount of retained earnings. In other words, to pay a cash dividend a company must have both cash and retained earnings.

Business Liquidations Resulting from Net Losses

If a business ceases to operate, its remaining assets are sold and the sale proceeds are returned to the creditors and investors through a process called business **liquidation**. Creditors have priority in business liquidations. This means the business uses its assets first to settle the obligations to the creditors. Any assets remaining after the creditors have been paid are then distributed to the investors.

To illustrate, assume Cruz Company was started on January 1, Year 1, when it acquired $200 cash from creditors and $100 cash from investors. Equation 1 shows Cruz's financial position immediately after these events.

EQUATION 1

Assets	=	Liabilities	+	Common Stock	+	Retained Earnings
300	=	200	+	100	+	0

Assume Cruz had a net operating loss of $75 during Year 1. At the beginning of Year 2, Cruz's accounting equation is as follows:

Assets	=	Liabilities	+	Common Stock	+	Retained Earnings
225	=	200	+	100	+	(75)

If Cruz is forced to liquidate at this point, the creditors would receive $200 and the owners (investors) would receive only $25.

Return to the original scenario shown in Equation 1 where Cruz acquires $200 cash from creditors and $100 cash from investors. Now suppose instead of experiencing a $75 loss Cruz experiences a $120 loss. In this scenario, Cruz's accounting equation at the beginning of Year 2 is as follows:

Assets	=	Liabilities	+	Common Stock	+	Retained Earnings
180	=	200	+	100	+	(120)

If Cruz is forced to liquidate at this point, the investors would receive zero and the creditors would receive only $180 even though the business owes them $200. Simply stated, Cruz cannot distribute assets that it does not have. This case shows that creditors as well as investors are at risk of losing some or all of the resources they provide to businesses. However, creditors are at lesser risk because they are first in line to receive assets in case of liquidation.

In practice, the relationships between creditors and investors are determined by complex legal documents that may conflict with the general conditions described above. We will discuss some of these exceptions in later chapters.

Business Liquidations Resulting from the Mismanagement of Assets

It is interesting to note that even profitable companies can be forced to liquidate. To illustrate, assume Bandera Company acquires $300 cash from creditors and $500 cash from investors and earns $200 of net income during its first year of operations. Also assume Bandera pays $950 to purchase land. Based on these events, Bandera would have the following accounting equation at the beginning of its second year of operation:

Assets			=	Liabilities	+	Common Stock	+	Retained Earnings
Cash		Land						
50	+	950	=	300	+	500	+	200

At this point, if the liabilities come due and the creditors demand payment, Bandera could be forced into bankruptcy. Assuming the land could not be sold immediately, Bandera has only $50 cash available to settle a $300 debt. A company must properly manage its assets as well as its liabilities and stockholders' equity in order to remain a going concern.

The **going concern** doctrine assumes that a business is able to continue its operations into the foreseeable future. Many procedures and practices used by accountants are based on a going concern assumption. If a company's going concern status becomes uncertain, accountants are required to notify creditors and investors.

Two Views of the Right Side of the Accounting Equation

Another important point to recognize is that there are two views of the right side of the accounting equation. One view is that the right side shows the sources of assets. Clearly, when a company borrows money from a bank the business receives an asset, cash. Therefore, we say creditors are a source of assets. However, borrowing money creates an obligation for the business to return the amount borrowed to creditors. Thus, we can view the liabilities of a company as its obligations to return assets to its creditors. In summary, liabilities can be viewed as sources of assets or, alternatively, as obligations of the business.

Similarly, a business may acquire assets from its owners by issuing stock or it may earn assets through its operations. Therefore, common stock and retained earnings can be viewed as sources of assets. However, the business has a **stewardship** function, which means that it has a duty to protect and use the assets for the benefit of the owners. As a result, common stock and retained earnings can be viewed as sources of assets or, alternatively, as commitments to the investors. In summary, the right side of the accounting equation can be viewed either as sources of assets or as the obligations and commitments of the business.

RECAP: TYPES OF TRANSACTIONS

LO 1-4

Classify business events as asset source, use, or exchange transactions.

The transactions described above have each been classified into one of three categories: (1) asset source transactions; (2) asset exchange transactions; and (3) asset use transactions. A fourth category, claims exchange transactions, is introduced in a later chapter. In summary:

- ***Asset source transactions*** increase the total amount of assets and increase the total amount of claims. In its first year of operation, RCS acquired assets from three sources: first, from owners (Event 1); next, by borrowing (Event 2); and finally, through earnings activities (Event 4).
- ***Asset exchange transactions*** decrease one asset and increase another asset. The total amount of assets is unchanged by asset exchange transactions. RCS experienced one asset exchange transaction; it used cash to purchase land (Event 3).
- ***Asset use transactions*** decrease the total amount of assets and the total amount of claims. RCS used assets to pay expenses (Event 5) and to pay dividends (Event 6).

As you proceed through this text, practice classifying transactions into one of the four categories. Businesses engage in thousands of transactions every day. It is far more effective to learn how to classify the transactions into meaningful categories than to attempt to memorize the effects of thousands of transactions.

The Curious Accountant

The RCS case includes only seven business events, one of which is not recognized in the ledger accounts. These events are assumed to have taken place over the course of a year. In contrast, real-world companies engage in thousands, even millions, of transactions in a single day. For example, think of the number of sales events **Kroger** processes in a day or how many tickets **American Airlines** sells. Presenting this many events in accounting equation format would produce such a volume of data that users would be overwhelmed with details. To facilitate communication, accountants summarize and organize the transaction data into reports called *financial statements.* This section discusses the information contained in financial statements and explains how they are prepared. While the RCS illustration contains only a few transactions, the financial statements prepared for this company contain the same basic content as those of much larger companies.

SECTION 2:

REPORTING INFORMATION

As indicated earlier, accounting information is normally presented to external users in four general-purpose financial statements. The information in the ledger accounts is used to prepare these financial statements. The data in the ledger accounts in Exhibit 1.3 are color coded to help you understand the source of information in the financial statements. The numbers in *green* are used in the *statement of cash flows.* The numbers in *red* are used to prepare the *balance sheet.* Finally, the numbers in *blue* are used to prepare the *income statement.* The numbers reported in the statement of changes in stockholders' equity have not been color coded because they appear in more than one statement. The next section explains how the information in the accounts is presented in financial statements.

PREPARING FINANCIAL STATEMENTS

Section 1 of this chapter focused on how accountants collect information about business events. Section 2 focuses on how that information is *reported* to stakeholders. Information is normally reported annually in four financial statements including the (1) income statement, (2) statement of changes in stockholders' equity, (3) balance sheet, and (4) statement of cash flows. To illustrate the reporting process we return to the Rustic Camp Sites example summarized in Exhibit 1.3. You should reacquaint yourself with this exhibit before reading about the statements that are shown in Exhibit 1.4.

LO 1-5

Prepare an income statement, a statement of changes in stockholders' equity, and a balance sheet.

Income Statement and the Matching Concept

The **income statement** matches revenue (benefits) with the expenses (sacrifices) that were incurred to generate the revenue. If revenues exceed expenses, the difference is called **net income**. If expenses are greater than revenues, the difference is called **net loss**. The practice of pairing revenues with expenses on the income statement is called the **matching concept**.

The income statement in Exhibit 1.4 shows that RCS earned $85,000 of revenue and incurred $50,000 of expenses resulting in net income of $35,000. Using our definition of revenue as increases in assets and expenses as decreases in assets, we can conclude that the net income figure of $35,000 represents an increase in the total amount of RCS's assets.[5]

Observe the phrase *For the Year Ended December 31, 2016*, in the heading of the income statement. The income statement is a report about the company's operations that occurred over a span of time called the **accounting period**. While accounting periods of one year are normal for external financial reporting, income can be measured weekly, monthly, quarterly, semiannually, or using any other desired time period. Accordingly, the terminology used to describe the date should clearly indicate the time period covered by the statement.

[5]The definitions for revenue and expense are expanded in subsequent chapters as additional relationships among the elements of financial statements are introduced.

EXHIBIT 1.4 Financial Statements

RUSTIC CAMP SITES
Income Statement
For the Year Ended December 31, 2016

Rental revenue (*asset increases*)		$85,000
Operating expenses (*asset decreases*)		(50,000)
Net income		$35,000

RUSTIC CAMP SITES
Statement of Changes in Stockholders' Equity
For the Year Ended December 31, 2016

Beginning common stock	$ 0	
Plus: common stock issued	120,000	
Ending common stock		$120,000
Beginning retained earnings	0	
Plus: Net income	35,000	
Less: Dividends	(4,000)	
Ending retained earnings		31,000
Total stockholders' equity		$151,000

RUSTIC CAMP SITES
Balance Sheet
As of December 31, 2016

Assets		
Cash	$ 51,000	
Land	500,000	
Total assets		$551,000
Liabilities		
Notes payable		$400,000
Stockholders' equity		
Common stock	$120,000	
Retained earnings	31,000	
Total stockholders' equity		151,000
Total liabilities and stockholders' equity		$551,000

RUSTIC CAMP SITES
Statement of Cash Flows
For the Year Ended December 31, 2016

Cash flows from operating activities:		
Cash receipts from revenue	$ 85,000	
Cash payments for expenses	(50,000)	
Net cash flow from operating activities		$ 35,000
Cash flows from investing activities:		
Cash payments to purchase land		(500,000)
Cash flows from financing activities:		
Cash receipts from borrowing funds	400,000	
Cash receipts from issuing common stock	120,000	
Cash payments for dividends	(4,000)	
Net cash flow from financing activities		516,000
Net increase in cash		51,000
Plus: beginning cash balance		0
Ending cash balance		$ 51,000

Notice that the cash RCS paid to its stockholders is not reported as an expense on the income statement because the dividends were not incurred for the purpose of generating revenue. For example, a company pays employees so that they will work to produce revenue. Since the salary payment was made for the purpose of producing revenue, it is called an expense. In contrast, a business pays dividends to reward stockholders for the investment they made in the business. The stockholders are not being paid to produce revenue. A business first determines how much income it has earned and then decides how much of that income it will distribute to reward stockholders. The portion of earnings (income) distributed to owners is called a dividend. In summary, dividends are paid after the amount of income is determined. Therefore, dividends are not included on the income statement.

CHECK YOURSELF 1.3

Mahoney, Inc., was started when it issued common stock to its owners for $300,000. During its first year of operation Mahoney received $523,000 cash for services provided to customers. Mahoney paid employees $233,000 cash. Advertising costs paid in cash amounted to $102,000. Other cash operating expenses amounted to $124,000. Finally, Mahoney paid a $25,000 cash dividend to its stockholders. What amount of net income would Mahoney's report on its earnings statement?

Answer The amount of net income is $64,000 ($523,000 Revenue − $233,000 Salary Expense − $102,000 Advertising Expense − $124,000 Other Operating Expenses). The cash received from issuing stock is not revenue because it was not acquired from earnings activities. In other words, Mahoney did not work (perform services) for this money; it was contributed by owners of the business. The dividends are not expenses because the decrease in cash was not incurred for the purpose of generating revenue. Instead, the dividends represent a transfer of wealth to the owners.

Statement of Changes in Stockholders' Equity

The **statement of changes in stockholders' equity** shown in Exhibit 1.4 explains the effects of transactions on stockholders' equity during the accounting period. It starts with the beginning balance in the common stock account. In the case of RCS, the beginning balance in the common stock account is zero because the company did not exist before the 2016 accounting period. The $120,000 of stock issued during the accounting period is added to the beginning balance to determine the ending balance in the common stock account.

In addition to reporting the changes in common stock, the statement describes the changes in retained earnings for the accounting period. RCS had no beginning balance in retained earnings. During the period, the company earned $35,000 and paid $4,000 in dividends to the stockholders, producing an ending retained earnings balance of $31,000 ($0 + $35,000 − $4,000). Since equity consists of common stock and retained earnings, the ending total equity balance is $151,000 ($120,000 + $31,000). This statement is also dated with the phrase *For the Year Ended December 31, 2016,* because it describes what happened to stockholders' equity only for the 2016 accounting period.

Balance Sheet

The **balance sheet** draws its name from the accounting equation. Total assets balance with (equal) liabilities plus stockholders' equity. The 2016 balance sheet for RCS is shown in Exhibit 1.4. In this case, total assets equal total liabilities plus stockholders' equity ($551,000 = $400,000 + $151,000).

The order in which assets are shown in the balance sheet is important. Assets are displayed in the balance sheet based on their level of liquidity. Financial **liquidity** is measured by how fast an asset can be converted to cash. Since in the normal course of business inventory can be sold for cash quicker than land can be sold, inventory is considered to be more liquid than land. On the balance sheet the most liquid asset, cash, is listed first, and the remaining assets are listed in the order of how rapidly they are normally converted into cash.

Observe carefully that the balance sheet is dated with the phrase *As of December 31, 2016*, indicating that it describes the company's financial condition at a specific *point in time*. To distinguish between *span of time* versus *point in time* statements, it may be helpful to draw a parallel to how income is reported for individuals. Most people think of income in annual terms. For example, when you start work your salary will be stated in terms of how much you will earn per year. For budgeting purposes you may also consider how much income you earn per month or per week. As these examples suggest, income is always measured in relation to some *span of time*. In contrast, the amount of your assets and liabilities is cumulative. For example, the amount of cash you own today (at this specific *point in time*) is equal to all of the cash you have collected minus all of the cash you have disbursed throughout your entire life.

For financial reporting purposes the income statement, statement of changes in stockholders' equity, and the statement of cash flows provide information about events that occurred over some *span of time*. In contrast, the balance sheet provides information about conditions that exist at a specific *point in time*.

CHECK YOURSELF 1.4

To gain a clear understanding of the balance sheet, try to create one that describes your personal financial condition. First list your assets, then your liabilities. Determine the amount of your equity by subtracting your liabilities from your assets.

Answer Answers for this exercise will vary depending on the particular assets and liabilities each student identifies. Common student assets include automobiles, computers, stereos, TVs, phones, MP3 players, clothes, and textbooks. Common student liabilities include car loans, mortgages, student loans, and credit card debt. The difference between the assets and the liabilities is the equity.

Statement of Cash Flows

LO 1-6

Prepare a statement of cash flows.

The **statement of cash flows** explains how a company obtained and used *cash* during the accounting period. Receipts of cash are called *cash inflows,* and payments are *cash outflows.* The statement classifies cash receipts (inflows) and payments (outflows) into three categories: financing activities, investing activities, and operating activities.

Businesses normally start with an idea. Implementing the idea usually requires cash. For example, suppose you decide to start an apartment rental business. First, you would need cash to finance acquiring the apartments. Acquiring cash to start a business is a financing activity. **Financing activities** include obtaining cash (inflow) from owners or paying cash (outflow) to owners (dividends). Financing activities also include borrowing cash (inflow) from creditors and repaying the principal (outflow) to creditors. In contrast, interest paid to creditors is an expense, and therefore, the associated cash flow is reported in the operating activities section of the statement of cash flows.

After obtaining cash from financing activities, you would invest the money by building or buying apartments. **Investing activities** involve paying cash (outflow) to purchase long-term assets or receiving cash (inflow) from selling long-term assets. Long-term assets are normally used for more than one year. Cash outflows to purchase land or cash inflows from selling a building are examples of investing activities.

After investing in the productive assets (apartments), you would engage in operating activities. **Operating activities** involve receiving cash (inflow) from revenue and paying cash (outflow) for expenses. Note that cash spent to purchase short-term assets such as office supplies is reported in the operating activities section because the office supplies would likely be used (expensed) within a single accounting period.

The primary cash inflows and outflows related to the types of business activity introduced in this chapter are summarized in Exhibit 1.5. The exhibit will be expanded as additional types of events are introduced in subsequent chapters.

The statement of cash flows for Rustic Camp Sites in Exhibit 1.4 shows that the amount of cash increased by $51,000 during the year. The beginning balance in the Cash account was zero; adding the $51,000 increase to the beginning balance results in a $51,000 ending balance. Notice that the $51,000 ending cash balance on the statement of cash flows is the same as the amount of cash reported in the asset section on the December 31 year-end balance sheet.

The statement of cash flows in Exhibit 1.4 is dated with the phrase *For the Year Ended December 31, 2016*. Specifically, this statement of cash flows explains what caused the balance in the Cash account to increase by $51,000 during the 2016 accounting period. The next statement of cash flows will explain what happens to the Cash account during the 2017 accounting period and so on with subsequent accounting periods.

EXHIBIT 1.5

Classification Scheme for Statement of Cash Flows

Cash flows from operating activities:
Cash receipts (inflows) from customers
Cash payments (outflows) to suppliers

Cash flows from investing activities:
Cash receipts (inflows) from the sale of long-term assets
Cash payments (outflows) for the purchase of long-term assets

Cash flows from financing activities:
Cash receipts (inflows) from borrowing funds
Cash receipts (inflows) from issuing common stock
Cash payments (outflows) to repay borrowed funds
Cash payments (outflows) for dividends

In summary, the balance sheet shows the amounts that exist in the accounts at the end of each accounting period, while the income statement, the statement of changes in stockholders' equity, and the statement of cash flows explain what caused the account balances to change from one accounting period to the next. To reflect these differences, balance sheets are dated with a phrase that begins with "As of" while the other statements are dated with a phrase that begins with "For the Period Ended."

Take note that information in one statement may relate to information in another statement. For example, the amount of net income reported on the income statement also appears on the statement of changes in stockholders' equity. Accountants use the term **articulation** to describe the interrelationships among the various elements of the financial statements. The key articulated relationships in RCS's financial statements are highlighted with the arrows shown in Exhibit 1.4.

CHECK YOURSELF 1.5

Classify each of the following cash flows as an operating activity, investing activity, or financing activity.

1. Acquired cash from owners.
2. Borrowed cash from creditors.
3. Paid cash to purchase land.
4. Earned cash revenue.
5. Paid cash for salary expenses.
6. Paid cash dividend.
7. Paid cash for interest.

Answer (1) financing activity; (2) financing activity; (3) investing activity; (4) operating activity; (5) operating activity; (6) financing activity; (7) operating activity.

The Closing Process

LO 1-7

Explain the closing process.

In practice the information about revenues, expenses, and dividends is *not* recorded directly into the Retained Earnings account. Instead information is recorded in separate Revenue, Expense, and Dividend accounts during the accounting period. Keeping the income and dividend accounts separate permits the capture of information that pertains to a specific accounting period. This information is needed to prepare the income statement and the statement of changes in equity. At the end of the accounting period, after the statements are prepared, the information is transferred from the separate accounts to the Retained Earnings account.

The process of transferring information from the revenue, expense, and dividend accounts to the Retained Earnings account is called **closing**. Since the Revenue, Expense, and Dividend information is held in the accounts temporarily, these accounts are called **temporary accounts**. At the beginning of each new accounting period, the temporary accounts have zero balances. In contrast, the Retained Earnings account balance carries forward from one accounting period to the next. Since this account is not closed, it is called a **permanent account**. Exhibit 1.6 shows a summary of Rustic Camp Sites's 2016 transaction data and the before-closing general ledger account balances.

EXHIBIT 1.6

Summary of 2016 Accounting Events and Before-Closing Account Balances

Accounting Events

1. Collected $120,000 cash from issue of common stock.
2. Borrowed $400,000 cash.
3. Paid $500,000 cash to purchase land.
4. Received $85,000 cash from earning revenue.
5. Paid $50,000 cash for expenses.
6. Paid $4,000 cash dividend to stockholders.
7. Land that cost $500,000 has a market value of $525,000.

General Ledger Accounts Before Closing

Assets	=	Liabilities	+	Stockholders' Equity		
Asset Accounts	=	Liability Accounts	+	Permanent Equity Accounts	+	Temporary Equity Accounts

Asset Accounts

Cash	
Bal.	0
(1)	120,000
(2)	400,000
(3)	(500,000)
(4)	85,000
(5)	(50,000)
(6)	(4,000)
Bal.	51,000

Land	
Bal.	0
(3)	500,000
Bal.	500,000

Liability Accounts

Notes Payable	
Bal.	0
(2)	400,000
Bal.	400,000

Permanent Equity Accounts

Common Stock	
Bal.	0
(1)	120,000
Bal.	120,000

Retained Earnings	
Bal.	0

Temporary Equity Accounts

Revenue	
Bal.	0
(4)	85,000
Bal.	85,000

Expense	
Bal.	0
(5)	(50,000)
Bal.	(50,000)

Dividend	
Bal.	0
(6)	(4,000)
Bal.	(4,000)

At the end of the accounting period, after the financial statements have been prepared, the temporary accounts will be closed as follows.

Cl. 1 Close the Revenue account to the Retained Earnings account.

Assets	=	Liabilities	+	Stockholders' Equity		
Asset Accounts	=	Liability Accounts	+	Permanent Equity Accounts	+	Temporary Equity Accounts
NA		NA		Retained Earnings 85,000		Revenue (85,000)

Cl. 2 Close the Expense account to the Retained Earnings account.

Assets	=	Liabilities	+	Stockholders' Equity		
Asset Accounts	=	Liability Accounts	+	Permanent Equity Accounts	+	Temporary Equity Accounts
NA		NA		Retained Earnings (50,000)		Expense 50,000

Cl. 3 Close the Dividends account to the Retained Earnings account.

Assets	=	Liabilities	+	Stockholders' Equity		
Asset Accounts	=	Liability Accounts	+	Permanent Equity Accounts	+	Temporary Equity Accounts
NA		NA		Retained Earnings (4,000)		Dividends 4,000

After posting the closing entries to the ledger accounts, the balance in the Retained Earnings account will be $31,000 and the balances in the Revenue, Expense, and Dividend accounts will be zero. A summary of the closing entries and the after-closing general ledger account balances are shown in Exhibit 1.7. The ending account balances for the 2016 accounting

EXHIBIT 1.7

Summary of the 2016 Closing Entries and the After-Closing Account Balances

Closing Entries

Cl. 1 Close the Revenue account to the Retained Earnings account.
Cl. 2 Close the Expense account to the Retained Earnings account.
Cl. 3 Close the Dividends account to the Retained Earnings account.

General Ledger Accounts After Closing

Assets	=	Liabilities	+	Stockholders' Equity		
Asset Accounts	=	Liability Accounts	+	Permanent Equity Accounts	+	Temporary Equity Accounts

Asset Accounts

Cash	
Bal.	0
(1)	120,000
(2)	400,000
(3)	(500,000)
(4)	85,000
(5)	(50,000)
(6)	(4,000)
Bal.	51,000

Land	
Bal.	0
(3)	500,000
Bal.	500,000

Liability Accounts

Notes Payable	
Bal.	0
(2)	400,000
Bal.	400,000

Permanent Equity Accounts

Common Stock	
Bal.	0
(1)	120,000
Bal.	120,000

Retained Earnings	
Bal.	0
Cl. 1	85,000
Cl. 2	(50,000)
Cl. 3	(4,000)
Bal.	31,000

Temporary Equity Accounts

Revenue	
Bal.	0
(4)	85,000
Bal.	85,000
Cl. 1	(85,000)
Bal.	0

Expense	
Bal.	0
(5)	(50,000)
Bal.	(50,000)
Cl. 2	50,000
Bal.	0

Dividend	
Bal.	0
(6)	(4,000)
Bal.	(4,000)
Cl. 3	4,000
Bal.	0

period will become the beginning account balances for the 2017 accounting period. Since the Revenue, Expense, and Dividend accounts will open with a zero balance, they are ready for the collection of information that applies exclusively to the 2017 accounting period.

CHECK YOURSELF 1.6

After closing on December 31, 2016, Walston Company had $4,600 of assets, $2,000 of liabilities, and $700 of common stock. During January of 2017, Walston earned $750 of revenue and incurred $300 of expense. Walston closes its books each year on December 31.

1. Determine the balance in the Retained Earnings account as of December 31, 2016.
2. Determine the balance in the Retained Earnings account as of January 1, 2017.
3. Determine the balance in the Retained Earnings account as of January 31, 2017.

Answer

1. Assets = Liabilities + Common Stock + Retained Earnings

   $4,600 = $2,000 + $700 + Retained Earnings

   Retained Earnings = $1,900
2. The balance in the Retained Earnings account on January 1, 2017, is the same as it was on December 31, 2016. This year's ending balance becomes next year's beginning balance. Therefore, the balance in the Retained Earnings account on January 1, 2017, is $1,900.
3. The balance in the Retained Earnings account on January 31, 2017, is still $1,900. The revenue earned and expenses incurred during January are not recorded in the Retained Earnings account. Instead, they are recorded in the 2017 temporary equity accounts. Balances in these temporary accounts will be closed to retained earnings at the end of the accounting period (December 31, 2017).

THE HORIZONTAL FINANCIAL STATEMENTS MODEL

LO 1-8

Record business events using a horizontal financial statements model.

Financial statements are the scorecard for business activity. If you want to succeed in business, you must know how your business decisions affect your company's financial statements. This text uses a **horizontal statements model** to help you understand how business events affect financial statements. This model shows a set of financial statements horizontally across a single page of paper. The balance sheet is displayed first, adjacent to the income statement, and then the statement of cash flows. Because the effects of equity transactions can be analyzed by referring to certain balance sheet columns, and because of limited space, the statement of changes in stockholders' equity is not shown in the horizontal statements model.

The model frequently uses abbreviations. For example, activity classifications in the statement of cash flows are identified using OA for operating activities, IA for investing activities, and FA for financing activities. NC designates the net change in cash. The statements model uses "NA" when an account is not affected by an event. The background of the *balance sheet* is red, the *income statement* is blue, and the *statement of cash flows* is green. To demonstrate the usefulness of the horizontal statements model, we use it to display the seven accounting events that RCS experienced during its first year of operation (2016).

1. RCS acquired $120,000 cash from the issuance of common stock.
2. RCS borrowed $400,000 cash.
3. RCS paid $500,000 cash to purchase land.
4. RCS received $85,000 cash from earning revenue.
5. RCS paid $50,000 cash for expenses.
6. RCS paid $4,000 of cash dividends to the owners.
7. The market value of the land owned by RCS was appraised at $525,000 on December 31, 2016.

	Balance Sheet									Income Statement						
	Assets			=	Liab.	+	Stockholders' Equity									
Event No.	Cash	+	Land	=	N. Pay.	+	Com. Stk.	+	Ret. Earn.	Rev.	−	Exp.	=	Net Inc.	Statement of Cash Flows	
Beg. bal.	0	+	0	=	0	+	0	+	0	0	−	0	=	0	NA	
1.	120,000	+	NA	=	NA	+	120,000	+	NA	NA	−	NA	=	NA	120,000	FA
2.	400,000	+	NA	=	400,000	+	NA	+	NA	NA	−	NA	=	NA	400,000	FA
3.	(500,000)	+	500,000	=	NA	+	NA	+	NA	NA	−	NA	=	NA	(500,000)	IA
4.	85,000	+	NA	=	NA	+	NA	+	85,000	85,000	−	NA	=	85,000	85,000	OA
5.	(50,000)	+	NA	=	NA	+	NA	+	(50,000)	NA	−	50,000	=	(50,000)	(50,000)	OA
6.	(4,000)	+	NA	=	NA	+	NA	+	(4,000)	NA	−	NA	=	NA	(4,000)	FA
7.	NA	+	NA	=	NA	+	NA	+	NA	NA	−	NA	=	NA	NA	
Totals	51,000	+	500,000	=	400,000	+	120,000	+	31,000	85,000	−	50,000	=	35,000	51,000	NC

Recognize that statements models are learning tools. Because they are helpful in understanding how accounting events affect financial statements, they are used extensively in this book. However, the models omit many of the details used in published financial statements. For example, the horizontal model shows only a partial set of statements. Also, since the statements are presented in aggregate, the description of dates (i.e., "as of" versus "for the period ended") does not distinguish periodic from cumulative data.

THE FINANCIAL ANALYST

This section of each chapter introduces topics related to analyzing real-world financial reports. We focus first on the types of businesses that operate in the real world. We also discuss the annual report that is used to communicate information to stakeholders.

Real-World Financial Reports

As previously indicated, organizations exist in many different forms, including *business* entities and *not-for-profit* entities. Business entities are typically service, merchandising, or manufacturing companies. **Service businesses,** which include doctors, attorneys, accountants, dry cleaners, and housekeepers, provide services to their customers. **Merchandising businesses,** sometimes called *retail* or *wholesale companies,* sell goods to customers that other entities make. **Manufacturing businesses** make the goods that they sell to their customers.

Some business operations include combinations of these three categories. For example, an automotive repair shop might change oil (service function), sell parts such as oil filters (retail function), and rebuild engines (manufacturing function). The nature of the reporting entity affects the form and content of the information reported in an entity's financial statements. For example, governmental entities provide statements of activities while business entities provide income statements. Similarly, income statements of retail companies show an expense item called *cost of goods sold,* but service companies that do not sell goods have no such item in their income statements. You should expect some diversity when reviewing real-world financial statements.

Throughout this book we usually present income statements that end with "Net income." Due to an accounting rule that became effective at the end of 2009, income statements of large, real-world companies often appear to have three lines for net income. The partial income statements for Merck & Company, a large pharmaceutical company, shown in Exhibit 1.8, illustrate this issue. Notice that the third line from the bottom of the statement is called "Net income." However, "Net income attributable to noncontrolling interest" is subtracted from this first net income to arrive at "Net income attributable to Merck & Co., Inc." The illustrations in this text always assume that there is no net income attributable to noncontrolling interests; therefore, our examples simply end with the term "Net income."

EXHIBIT 1.8 Real-World Financial Reporting

MERCK & CO., INC., AND SUBSIDIARIES
Consolidated Statement of Income (partial)
Years Ended December 31
($ in millions except per share amounts)

	2013	2012	2011
Sales	$44,033	$47,267	$48,047
Costs, expenses, and other			
Materials and production	16,954	16,446	16,871
Marketing and administrative	11,911	12,776	13,733
Research and development	7,503	8,168	8,467
Restructuring costs	1,709	664	1,306
Equity income from affiliates	(404)	(642)	(610)
Other (income) expense, net	815	1,116	946
	38,488	38,528	40,713
Income before taxes	5,545	8,739	7,334
Taxes on income	1,028	2,440	942
Net income	4,517	6,299	6,392
Less: Net income attributable to noncontrolling interests	113	131	120
Net income attributable to Merck & Co., Inc.	$ 4,404	$ 6,168	$ 6,272

Some real-world companies with complex operations report information related to *comprehensive income.* Comprehensive income is determined by adding or subtracting certain items to or from net income. A description of the items used to determine comprehensive income is complex and beyond the scope of this course. Even so, the reader should be aware that, as of 2011, companies that must report comprehensive income may do so in one of two ways. First, comprehensive income items can be added to the bottom of the primary statement of earnings. Alternatively, a separate statement showing the determination of comprehensive income can be presented immediately following the primary statement of earnings. If a company chooses to report comprehensive income in a separate statement, the company's annual report will contain five financial statements. This text limits coverage to the four financial statements that traditionally appear in real-world annual reports. The statement of comprehensive income is not covered.

Annual Report for Target Corporation

Organizations normally provide information, including financial statements, to *stakeholders* yearly in a document known as an **annual report.** The annual report for Target Corporation is referred to in some of the end-of-chapter assignments, and it is worth your while to review it as an example of a real-world annual report. This report can be found online at http://investors.target.com. On the webpage that appears, under the "Investors" link, click on "sec filings." Next, under "filter by form type," select "Annual filings" and then select the most recent "10-k" form from the list that appears. The pdf format is the easiest to work with. This report includes the company's financial

REALITY BYTES

Many people find flying to be boring, especially if they have to travel frequently for business. Additionally, it is often not possible to stay connected to one's business while in the air, as airlines currently prohibit the use of mobile phones. (Although the Federal Communications Commission has recently begun to consider allowing in-flight cell phone use, this is not likely to happen soon–if ever.) This is where **Gogo, Inc.**, enters the airplane.

In August of 2008 Gogo began offering travelers the opportunity to use Wi-Fi devices while flying. Today its service is available on more than 6,000 aircraft in the United States. On June 20, 2013, the company's stock became available to the public in an "initial public offering," usually referred to as an IPO. The stock is traded on the NASDAQ exchange. The IPO price of the company's stock was $17.00 per share, and only six months later it was selling for $24.08, an increase of 42 percent! The obvious question, once you look at the details, is why? The company has reported a net loss every quarter it has been in business. In fact, it lost more money in 2013 than it did in 2012, and it lost more in 2012 than it did in 2011. Clearly, investors' primary focus was not on past earnings.

Investors frequently use more information than just what is reported in a company's annual report. The annual report focuses on historical data, but investors are more interested in the future than the past. The historical information contained in the annual report is important because the past is frequently a strong predictor of what will occur in the future, but it does not provide a complete picture of a company's prospects.

A new company that has never earned a profit, like Gogo, may have an idea that is so innovative that investors rush to buy its stock, even though they believe it will be a few years before the company has positive earnings. Although Gogo has consistently reported losses in the past, it has become the leading provider of in-flight Internet connectivity. In new technology industries, history has shown that being first, and being the biggest, often gives a company a big advantage in the long run. Investors and creditors may also be motivated by nonfinancial considerations such as social consciousness, humanitarian concerns, or personal preferences. People who buy stock in the **Green Bay Packers**, the only publically traded NFL team, are motivated by team spirit, not profit.

While accounting information is very important, it is only part of the information pool that investors and creditors use to make decisions.

statements (see pages 35–39 of the 2013 annual report). Immediately following the statements are a set of notes that provide additional details about the items described in the statements (see pages 40–64 of the 2013 annual report). The annual report contains the *auditors' report,* which is discussed in Chapter 6. Annual reports also include written commentary describing management's assessment of significant events that affected the company during the reporting period. This commentary is called *management's discussion and analysis* (MD&A).

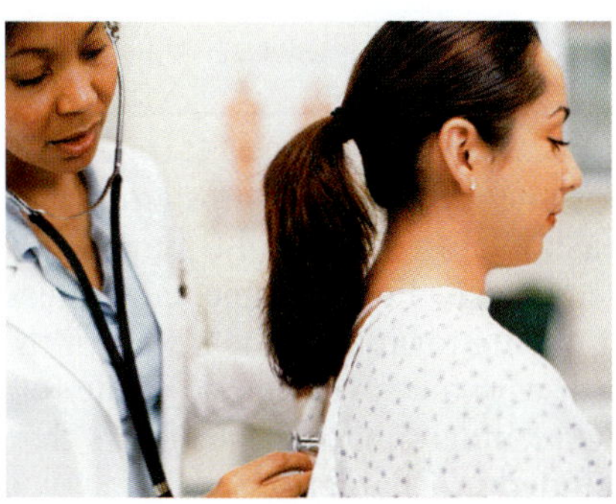

The U.S. Securities and Exchange Commission (SEC) requires public companies to file an annual report in a document known as a 10-K. The SEC is discussed in more detail later. Even though the annual report is usually flashier (contains more color and pictures) than the 10-K, the 10-K is normally more comprehensive with respect to content. As a result, the 10-K report frequently substitutes for the annual report, but the annual report cannot substitute for the 10-K. In an effort to reduce costs, many companies now use the 10-K report as their annual report.

Special Terms in Real-World Reports

The financial statements of real-world companies include numerous items relating to advanced topics that are not covered in introductory accounting textbooks, especially the first chapter of an introductory accounting textbook. Do not, however, be discouraged from browsing through real-world annual reports. You will significantly enhance your learning if you look at many annual reports and attempt to identify as many items as you can. As your accounting knowledge grows, you will likely experience increased interest in real-world financial reports and the businesses they describe.

We encourage you to look for annual reports in the library or ask your employer for a copy of your company's report. The Internet is another excellent source for obtaining annual reports. Most companies provide links to their annual reports on their home pages. Look for links labeled "About the company" or "Investor relations" or other phrases that logically lead to the company's financial reports. The best way to learn accounting is to use it. Accounting is the language of business. Learning the language will serve you well in almost any area of business that you pursue.

A Look Back

This chapter introduced the role of accounting in society and business: to provide information helpful to operating and evaluating the performance of organizations. Accounting is a measurement discipline. To communicate effectively, users of accounting must agree on the rules of measurement. *Generally accepted accounting principles (GAAP)* constitute the rules used by the accounting profession in the United States to govern financial reporting. GAAP is a work in progress that continues to evolve.

This chapter discussed eight elements of financial statements: *assets, liabilities, equity, common stock (contributed capital), revenue, expenses, dividends (distributions),* and *net income.* The elements represent broad classifications reported on financial statements. Four basic financial statements appear in the reports of public companies: the *balance sheet,* the *income statement,* the *statement of changes in stockholders' equity,* and the *statement of cash flows.* The chapter discussed the form and content of each statement as well as the interrelationships among the statements.

This chapter introduced a *horizontal financial statements model* as a tool to help you understand how business events affect a set of financial statements. This model is used throughout the text. You should carefully study this model before proceeding to Chapter 2.

A Look Forward

To keep matters as simple as possible and to focus on the interrelationships among financial statements, this chapter considered only cash events. Obviously, many real-world events do not involve an immediate exchange of cash. For example, customers use telephone service throughout the month without paying for it until the next month. Such phone usage represents an expense in one month with a cash exchange in the following month. Events such as this are called *accruals.* Understanding the effects that accrual events have on the financial statements is included in Chapter 2.

Video lectures and accompanying self-assessment quizzes are available for all learning objectives through McGraw-Hill Connect® Plus Accounting.

SELF-STUDY REVIEW PROBLEM

This problem extends the Rustic Camp Sites illustration shown in the main body of Chapter 1. The 2016 after-closing account balances shown in Exhibit 1.7 become the beginning balances for the 2017 accounting period illustrated in this problem.

During 2017 Rustic Camp Sites experienced the following transactions.

1. RCS acquired $32,000 cash by issuing common stock.
2. RCS received $116,000 cash for providing services to customers (leasing camp sites).
3. RCS paid $13,000 cash for salaries expense.
4. RCS paid a $9,000 cash dividend to the owners.
5. RCS sold land that had cost $200,000 for $200,000 cash.
6. RCS paid $49,000 cash for other operating expenses.

Required

a. Record the transaction data in an accounting equation like the one below. The 2017 beginning balances have been drawn from the 2016 ending balances (see Exhibit 1.7). The Revenue, Expense, and Dividend accounts have zero beginning balances because these accounts are designed to capture revenue, expense, and dividend events only for the 2017 accounting period. When recording revenue, expense, and dividend transactions, provide the title of the equity account affected by the transaction in the column titled "Account Titles." Otherwise, write "NA" in the "Account Titles" column to indicate that the transaction does not affect revenue, expense, or dividend accounts. The first transaction is shown as an example.

	Assets				Liabilities		Stockholders' Equity				
	Cash	+	Land	=	Notes Pay.	+	Com. Stk.	+	Ret. Earn.	+	Account
Beg. Bal	51,000	+	500,000	=	400,000	+	120,000	+	31,000	+	Titles
Event No. 1	32,000	+	NA	=	NA	+	32,000	+	NA	+	NA

b. Identify each event as an asset source, use, or exchange transaction.

c. Use the information in the accounting equation to prepare an income statement, a statement of changes in stockholders' equity, and a balance sheet.

d. Create a statement of cash flows. (*Hint*: It may be helpful to review each of the six transactions and classify the impact on cash flow as being an operating, investing, or financing activity before attempting to create the statement.)

e. As of December 31, 2017, can RCS pay a $100,000 cash dividend? What is the maximum dividend the company can pay?

f. As of December 31, 2017, what percent of total assets were acquired from the owners of the business?

g. Could RCS be forced into bankruptcy if the note payable is due on January 1, 2018?

h. Show how each of the six events affects the financial statements by recording the effects of each event in a financial statements model like the one shown below. In the Statement of Cash Flows column, classify the cash flows as operating activities (OA), investing activities

	Balance Sheet									Income Statement					
	Assets			=	Liab.	+	Stockholders' Equity								
Event No.	Cash	+	Land	=	N. Pay.	+	Com. Stk.	+	Ret. Earn.	Rev.	−	Exp.	=	Net Inc.	Statement of Cash Flows
Beg. bal.	51,000	+	500,000	=	400,000	+	120,000	+	31,000	NA	−	NA	=	NA	NA

(IA), or financing activities (FA). The beginning balances have been recorded as an example. They are the ending balances shown on RCS's December 31, 2016, financial statements illustrated in the chapter. Note that the revenue and expense accounts have a zero beginning balance. Amounts in these accounts apply only to a single accounting period.

Solution

a.

	Assets				Liabilities		Stockholders' Equity				Account Titles
	Cash	**+**	**Land**	**=**	**Notes Pay.**	**+**	**Com. Stk.**	**+**	**Ret. Earn.**	**+**	
Beg. Bal	**51,000**	**+**	**500,000**	**=**	**400,000**	**+**	**120,000**	**+**	**31,000**	**+**	
Event No.											
1	32,000	+	NA	=	NA	+	32,000	+	NA	+	NA
2	116,000	+	NA	=	NA	+	NA	+	116,000	+	Revenue
3	(13,000)	+	NA	=	NA	+	NA	+	(13,000)	+	Salary Expense
4	(9,000)	+	NA	=	NA	+	NA	+	(9,000)	+	Dividend
5	200,000	+	(200,000)	=	NA	+	NA	+	NA	+	NA
6	(49,000)	+	NA	=	NA	+	NA	+	(49,000)	+	Other Expenses
Totals*	328,000	+	300,000	=	400,000	+	152,000	+	76,000	+	

*Totals represent amounts before the accounts have been closed.

b.

1. RCS acquired $32,000 cash by issuing common stock. – ASSET SOURCE
2. RCS received $116,000 cash for providing services to customers. – ASSET SOURCE
3. RCS paid $13,000 cash for salaries expense. – ASSET USE
4. RCS paid a $9,000 cash dividend to the owners. – ASSET USE
5. RCS sold land that had cost $200,000 for $200,000 cash. – ASSET EXCHANGE
6. RCS paid $49,000 cash for other operating expenses. – ASSET USE

c.

RUSTIC CAMP SITES
Income Statement
For the Year Ended December 31, 2017

Revenue	$116,000
Salary Expense	(13,000)
Other Expenses	(49,000)
Net Income	$ 54,000

RUSTIC CAMP SITES
Statement of Changes in Stockholders' Equity
For the Year Ended December 31, 2017

Beginning Common Stock	$120,000	
Plus: Stock Issued	32,000	
Ending Common Stock		$152,000
Beginning Retained Earnings	31,000	
Plus: Net Income	54,000	
Minus: Dividend	(9,000)	
Ending Retained Earnings		76,000
Total Stockholders' Equity		$228,000

RUSTIC[illegible] Balanc[illegible] As of December[illegible]		
Assets		
Cash	$328,000	
Land	300,000	
Total Assets		
Liabilities		
Notes Payable	400,000	
Total Liabilities		
Stockholders' Equity		
Common Stock	152,000	
Retained Earnings	76,000	
Total Stockholders' Equity		228,000
Total Liabilities and Stockholders' Equity		$628,000

d.

1. RCS acquired $32,000 cash by issuing common stock. – FINANCING ACTIVITY
2. RCS received $116,000 cash for providing services to customers. – OPERATING ACTIVITY
3. RCS paid $13,000 cash for salaries expense. – OPERATING ACTIVITY
4. RCS paid a $9,000 cash dividend to the owners. – FINANCING ACTIVITY
5. RCS sold land that had cost $200,000 for $200,000 cash. – INVESTING ACTIVITY
6. RCS paid $49,000 cash for other operating expenses. – OPERATING ACTIVITY

RUSTIC CAMP SITES Statement of Cash Flows For the Year Ended December 31, 2017		
Cash Flows from Operating Activities:		
Cash Receipts from Customers	$116,000	
Cash Payments for Salary Expense	(13,000)	
Cash Payments for Other Expenses	(49,000)	
Net Cash Flow from Operating Activities		$ 54,000
Net Cash Flow from Investing Activities		
Cash Receipt from Sale of Land		200,000
Net Cash Flow from Financing Activities		
Cash Receipt from Stock Issue	32,000	
Cash Payment for Dividend	(9,000)	
Net Cash Flow from Financing Activities		23,000
Net Change in Cash		277,000
Plus: Beginning Cash Balance		51,000
Ending Cash Balance		$328,000

e. RCS cannot pay a $100,000 cash dividend as of December 31, 2017. The maximum dividend the company can pay on this date is $78,000 because dividend payments are restricted by the amount of total retained earnings.

f. RCS acquired $152,000 of assets from owners ($120,000 stock issue in 2016 and a $32,000 stock issue in 2017). Total assets as of December 31, 2017, amount to $628,000 ($328,000 cash + $300,000 land). Accordingly, 24.2 percent of assets ($152,000 common stock ÷ $628,000 total assets) were acquired from owners.

that date the note payable is to repay the debt. In practice iabilities. Most debt is simply unds through new borrowing.

ent		
	Net Inc.	Statement of Cash Flows
	NA	NA
	NA	32,000 FA
	116,000	116,000 OA
	(13,000)	(13,000) OA
	NA	(9,000) FA
	NA	200,000 IA
	(49,000)	(49,000) OA
	54,000	277,000 NC*

QUESTIONS

1. Explain the term *stakeholder.* Distinguish between stakeholders with a direct versus an indirect interest in the companies that issue financial reports.
2. Why is accounting called the *language of business*?
3. What is the primary mechanism used to allocate resources in the United States?
4. In a business context, what does the term *market* mean?
5. What market trilogy components are involved in the process of transforming resources into finished products?
6. Give an example of a financial resource, a physical resource, and a labor resource.
7. What type of income or profit does an investor expect to receive in exchange for providing financial resources to a business? What type of income does a creditor expect from providing financial resources to an organization or business?
8. How do financial and managerial accounting differ?

9. Describe a not-for-profit or nonprofit enterprise. What is the motivation for this type of entity?
10. What are the U.S. rules of accounting information measurement called?
11. Explain how a career in public accounting differs from a career in private accounting.
12. Distinguish between elements of financial statements and accounts.
13. What role do assets play in business profitability?
14. To whom do the assets of a business belong?
15. Describe the differences between creditors and investors.
16. Name the accounting term used to describe a business's obligations to creditors.
17. What is the accounting equation? Describe each of its three components.
18. Who ultimately bears the risk and collects the rewards associated with operating a business?
19. What does a *double-entry bookkeeping system* mean?
20. Discuss the two views of the right side of the accounting equation.
21. If a company has $2,000 cash, $1,200 liabilities, and $800 retained earnings, can it pay a dividend of $1,000?
22. How does acquiring capital from owners affect the accounting equation?
23. What is the difference between assets that are acquired by issuing common stock and those that are acquired using retained earnings?
24. How does earning revenue affect the accounting equation?
25. What are the three primary sources of assets?
26. What is the source of retained earnings?
27. How does distributing assets (paying dividends) to owners affect the accounting equation?
28. What are the similarities and differences between dividends and expenses?
29. What four general-purpose financial statements do business enterprises use?
30. Which of the general-purpose financial statements provides information about the enterprise at a specific designated date?
31. What causes a net loss?
32. What is a business liquidation?
33. What is the going concern doctrine?
34. Explain the matching concept.
35. What three categories of cash receipts and cash payments do businesses report on the statement of cash flows? Explain the types of cash flows reported in each category.
36. How are asset accounts usually arranged in the balance sheet?
37. Discuss the term *articulation* as it relates to financial statements.
38. How do temporary accounts differ from permanent accounts? Name three temporary accounts. Is retained earnings a temporary or a permanent account?
39. Why are temporary accounts closed at the end of the accounting period?
40. What is the historical cost concept and how does it relate to verifiability?
41. Identify the three types of accounting transactions discussed in this chapter. Provide an example of each type of transaction, and explain how it affects the accounting equation.
42. What type of information does a business typically include in its annual report?
43. What is U.S. GAAP? What is IFRS?

MULTIPLE-CHOICE QUESTIONS

Multiple-choice questions are available in the Connect library.

EXERCISES—SERIES A

All applicable Exercises in Series A are available with McGraw-Hill's Connect Plus Accounting.

SECTION 1

Exercise 1-1A *The role of accounting in society*

LO 1-1

Free economies use open markets to allocate resources.

Required

Identify the three participants in a free business market. Write a brief memo explaining how these participants interact to ensure that goods and services are distributed in a manner that satisfies consumers. Your memo should include answers to the following questions: If you work as a public accountant, what role would you play in the allocation of resources? Which professional certification would be most appropriate to your career?

Exercise 1-2A *Careers in accounting*

LO 1-1

While public and private accounting overlap, various professional certifications are designed to attest to competency for specific areas of interest.

Required

a. Name the most common professional certification held by public accountants. Describe the general requirements for attaining this certification.

b. Name two types of professional certification, other than CPA, held by private accountants. Describe the general requirements for attaining these certifications.

LO 1-1

Exercise 1-3A *Identifying the reporting entities*

Karen White helped organize a charity fund to help cover the medical expenses of a friend of hers who was seriously injured in a bicycle accident. The fund was named Vicky Hill Recovery Fund (VHRF). Karen contributed $1,000 of her own money to the fund. The $1,000 was paid to WKUX, a local radio station that designed and played an advertising campaign to educate the public as to the need for help. The campaign resulted in the collection of $20,000 cash. VHRF paid $12,000 to Mercy Hospital to cover Vicky's outstanding hospital cost. The remaining $8,000 was contributed to the National Cyclist Fund.

Required

Identify the entities that were mentioned in the scenario and explain what happened to the cash accounts of each entity that you identify.

LO 1-2

Exercise 1-4A *Missing information in the accounting equation*

Required

Calculate the missing amounts in the following table.

					Stockholders' Equity		
Company	**Assets**	=	**Liabilities**	+	**Company Stock**	+	**Retained Earnings**
A	$?		$25,000		48,000		$50,000
B	40,000		?		7,000		30,000
C	75,000		15,000		?		42,000
D	125,000		45,000		60,000		?

LO 1-2

Exercise 1-5A *Effect of events on the accounting equation*

Olive Enterprises experienced the following events during 2016:

1. Acquired cash from the issue of common stock.
2. Paid cash to reduce the principal on a bank note.
3. Sold land for cash at an amount equal to its cost.
4. Provided services to clients for cash.
5. Paid utilities expenses with cash.
6. Paid a cash dividend to the stockholders.

Required

Explain how each of the events would affect the accounting equation by writing the letter I for increase, the letter D for decrease, and NA for does not affect under each of the components of the accounting equation. The first event is shown as an example.

					Stockholders' Equity		
Event Number	**Assets**	=	**Liabilities**	+	**Common Stock**	+	**Retained Earnings**
1	I		NA		I		NA

Exercise 1-6A *Effect of transactions on general ledger accounts* LO 1-2

At the beginning of 2016, Better Corp.'s accounting records had the following general ledger accounts and balances.

BETTER CORP. Accounting Equation									
Event	Assets		=	Liabilities	+	Stockholders' Equity		Acct. Titles for RE
	Cash	Land		Notes Payable		Common Stock	Retained Earnings	
Balance 1/1/2016	10,000	20,000		12,000		7,000	11,000	

Better Corp. completed the following transactions during 2016:

1. Purchased land for $5,000 cash.
2. Acquired $25,000 cash from the issue of common stock.
3. Received $75,000 cash for providing services to customers.
4. Paid cash operating expenses of $42,000.
5. Borrowed $10,000 cash from the bank.
6. Paid a $5,000 cash dividend to the stockholders.
7. Determined that the market value of the land purchased in event 1 is $35,000.

Required

a. Record the transactions in the appropriate general ledger accounts. Record the amounts of revenue, expense, and dividends in the Retained Earnings column. Provide the appropriate titles for these accounts in the last column of the table.

b. As of December 31, 2016, determine the total amount of assets, liabilities, and stockholders' equity and present this information in the form of an accounting equation.

c. What is the amount of total assets, liabilities, and stockholders' equity as of January 1, 2017?

Exercise 1-7A *Missing information and recording events* LO 1-2

As of December 31, 2016, Moss Company had total cash of $195,000, notes payable of $90,500, and common stock of $84,500. During 2017, Moss earned $42,000 of cash revenue, paid $24,000 for cash expenses, and paid a $3,000 cash dividend to the stockholders.

Required

a. Determine the amount of retained earnings as of December 31, 2016.

b. Create an accounting equation and record the beginning account balances under the appropriate elements.

c. Record the revenue, expense, and dividend events under the appropriate elements of the accounting equation created in Requirement *b*.

d. Prove the equality of the accounting equation as of December 31, 2017.

e. Identify the beginning and ending balances in the Cash and Common Stock accounts. Explain why the beginning and ending balances in the Cash account are different but the beginning and ending balances in the Common Stock account remain the same.

Exercise 1-8A *Account titles and the accounting equation* LO 1-2

The following account titles were drawn from the general ledger of Holt Food Supplies, Incorporated (HFSI): Computers, Operating Expenses, Rent Revenue, Building, Cash, Notes Payable, Land, Utilities Payable, Utilities Expense, Trucks, Gasoline Expense, Retained Earnings, Supplies, Accounts Payable, Office Furniture, Salaries Expense, Common Stock, Service Revenue, Interest Expense, Dividends, Supplies Expense.

Required

a. Create an accounting equation using the elements assets, liabilities, and stockholders' equity. List each account title under the element of the accounting equation to which it belongs.

b. Will all businesses have the same number of accounts? Explain your answer.

LO 1-3

Exercise 1-9A *Components of the accounting equation*

Jones Enterprises was started when it acquired $6,000 cash from creditors and $10,000 from owners. The company immediately purchased land that cost $12,000.

Required

a. Record the events under an accounting equation.

b. After all events have been recorded, Jones's obligations to creditors represent what percent of total assets?

c. After all events have been recorded, Jones's stockholders' equity represents what percent of total assets?

d. Assume the debt is due. Given that Jones has $10,000 in stockholders' equity, can the company repay the creditors at this point? Why or why not?

LO 1-3

Exercise 1-10A *Components of the accounting equation*

	Assets	=	Liabilities	+	Common Stock	+	Retained Earnings
Allen	$10,000	=	$7,500	+	$2,000	+	$ 500
White	$12,000	=	$3,000	+	$7,200	+	$1,800

Required

a. Based on this information alone, can you determine whether White can pay a $2,000 cash dividend? Why or why not?

b. Reconstruct the accounting equation for each company using percentages on the right side of the equation instead of dollar values. Which company is more financially stable? Why?

c. Assume Allen incurs a $3,500 operating loss. The remaining assets are sold for the value shown on the books, and the cash proceeds are distributed to the creditors and investors. How much money will be paid to creditors and how much will be paid to investors?

d. Assume White incurs a $3,500 operating loss. The remaining assets are sold for the value shown on the books, and the cash proceeds are distributed to the creditors and investors. How much money will be paid to creditors and how much will be paid to investors?

LO 1-3

Exercise 1-11A *Differences between interest and dividends*

The following account balances were drawn from the financial records of Kent Company (KC) as of January 1, 2016. Assets, $35,000; Liabilities, $6,000; Common Stock, $12,000; and Retained Earnings, $17,000. KC has agreed to pay the creditors $400 of interest per year. Further, KC agrees that for the 2016 fiscal year any annual earnings remaining after the interest charges will be paid out as dividends to the owners.

Required

a. Assuming KC earns a profit of $1,600 before recognition of interest expense during 2016, determine the amount of interest and dividends paid.

b. Assuming KC earns a profit of $900 before recognition of interest expense during 2016, determine the amount of interest and dividends paid.

c. Assuming KC earns a profit of $300 before recognition of interest expense during 2016, determine the amount of interest and dividends paid.

LO 1-3

Exercise 1-12A *Distribution in a business liquidation*

Assume that Harris Company acquires $3,600 cash from creditors and $4,200 cash from investors.

Required

a. Explain the primary differences between investors and creditors.

b. If Harris has net income of $2,000 and then liquidates, what amount of cash will the creditors receive? What amount of cash will the investors receive?

c. If Harris has a net loss of $2,000 cash and then liquidates, what amount of cash will the creditors receive? What amount of cash will the investors receive?

d. If Harris has a net loss of $4,900 cash and then liquidates, what amount of cash will the creditors receive? What amount of cash will the investors receive?

Exercise 1-13A *Classifying events as asset source, use, or exchange* LO 1-4

Nevada Company experienced the following events during its first year of operations:

1. Acquired an additional $1,000 cash from the issue of common stock.
2. Paid $2,400 cash for utilities expense.
3. Paid a $1,500 cash dividend to the stockholders.
4. Provided additional services for $6,000 cash.
5. Purchased additional land for $2,500 cash.
6. The market value of the land was determined to be $24,000 at the end of the accounting period.
7. Acquired $16,000 cash from the issue of common stock.
8. Paid $3,500 cash for salary expense.
9. Borrowed $10,000 cash from New South Bank.
10. Paid $6,000 cash to purchase land.
11. Provided boarding services for $10,500 cash.

Required

Classify each event as an asset source, use, or exchange transaction or as not applicable.

EXERCISES—SERIES A

Exercise 1-14A *Missing information for determining net income* LO 1-3, 1-5

The December 31, 2016, balance sheet for Deen Company showed total stockholders' equity of $156,000. Total stockholders' equity increased by $65,000 between December 31, 2016, and December 31, 2017. During 2017 Deen Company acquired $20,000 cash from the issue of common stock. Deen Company paid a $5,000 cash dividend to the stockholders during 2017.

Required

Determine the amount of net income or loss Deen reported on its 2017 income statement. (*Hint:* Remember that stock issues, net income, and dividends all change total stockholders' equity.)

Exercise 1-15A *Preparing an income statement and a balance sheet* LO 1-5

Majka Company was started on January 1, 2016. During 2016, the company experienced the following three accounting events: (1) earned cash revenues of $28,600, (2) paid cash expenses of $13,200, and (3) paid a $1,500 cash dividend to its stockholders. These were the only events that affected the company during 2016.

Required

a. Create an accounting equation and record the effects of each accounting event under the appropriate general ledger account headings.

b. Prepare an income statement, statement of changes in stockholders' equity, and a balance sheet dated December 31, 2016, for Majka Company.

c. Explain why the income statement uses different terminology to date the income statement than is used to date the balance sheet.

LO 1-3, 1-5

Exercise 1-16A *Historical cost versus market value*

Sung Company purchased land in April 2010 at a cost of $500,000. The estimated market value of the land is $800,000 as of December 31, 2016. Sung purchased marketable equity securities (bought the common stock of a company that is independent of Sung) in May 2010 at a cost of $340,000. These securities have a market value of $360,000 as of December 31, 2016. Generally accepted accounting principles requires that the land be shown on the December 31, 2016, balance sheet at $500,000, while the marketable equity securities are required to be reported at $360,000.

Required

Write a brief memo that explains the contradiction regarding why GAAP requires Sung to report historical cost with respect to the land versus market value with respect to the marketable securities. This answer may require speculation on your part. Use your knowledge about the historical cost and verifiability to formulate a logical response.

LO 1-6

Exercise 1-17A *Statement of cash flows*

On January 1, 2016, Moore, a fast-food company, had a balance in its Cash account of $45,800. During the 2016 accounting period, the company had (1) net cash inflow from operating activities of $24,800, (2) net cash outflow for investing activities of $16,000, and (3) net cash outflow from financing activities of $6,800.

Required

a. Prepare a statement of cash flows.

b. Provide a reasonable explanation as to what may have caused the net cash inflow from operating activities.

c. Provide a reasonable explanation as to what may have caused the net cash outflow from investing activities.

d. Provide a reasonable explanation as to what may have caused the net cash outflow from financing activities.

LO 1-6

Exercise 1-18A *Prepare a statement of cash flows*

All-Star Automotive Company experienced the following accounting events during 2016:

1. Performed services for $25,000 cash.
2. Purchased land for $6,000 cash.
3. Hired an accountant to keep the books.
4. Received $50,000 cash from the issue of common stock.
5. Borrowed $5,000 cash from State Bank.
6. Paid $14,000 cash for salary expense.
7. Sold land for $9,000 cash.
8. Paid $10,000 cash on the loan from State Bank.
9. Paid $2,800 cash for utilities expense.
10. Paid a cash dividend of $5,000 to the stockholders.

Required

a. Indicate how each of the events would be classified on the statement of cash flows as operating activities (OA), investing activities (IA), financing activities (FA), or not applicable (NA).

b. Prepare a statement of cash flows. Assume All-Star Automotive had a beginning cash balance of $9,000.

LO 1-3, 1-5, 1-6

Exercise 1-19A *Preparing financial statements*

Dakota Company experienced the following events during 2016.

1. Acquired $30,000 cash from the issue of common stock.
2. Paid $12,000 cash to purchase land.
3. Borrowed $10,000 cash.

4. Provided services for $20,000 cash.
5. Paid $1,000 cash for utilities expense.
6. Paid $15,000 cash for other operating expenses.
7. Paid a $2,000 cash dividend to the stockholders.
8. Determined that the market value of the land purchased in Event 2 is now $12,700.

Required

a. The January 1, 2016, general ledger account balances are shown in the following accounting equation. Record the eight events in the appropriate general ledger accounts. Record the amounts of revenue, expense, and dividends in the Retained Earnings column. Provide the appropriate titles for these accounts in the last column of the table. The first event is shown as an example.

DAKOTA COMPANY
Accounting Equation

Event	Assets		=	Liabilities	+	Stockholders' Equity		Acct. Titles for RE
	Cash	Land		Notes Payable		Common Stock	Retained Earnings	
Balance 1/1/2016	2,000	12,000		0		6,000	8,000	
1.	30,000					30,000		

b. Prepare an income statement, statement of changes in equity, year-end balance sheet, and statement of cash flows for the 2016 accounting period.
c. Determine the percentage of assets that were provided by retained earnings. How much cash is in the retained earnings account?

Exercise 1-20A *Relating accounting events to entities* LO 1-4, 1-6

Riley Company paid $60,000 cash to purchase land from Smally Company. Smally originally paid $60,000 for the land.

Required

a. Was this event an asset source, use, or exchange transaction for Riley Company?
b. Was this event an asset source, use, or exchange transaction for Smally Company?
c. Was the cash flow an operating, investing, or financing activity on Riley Company's 2016 statement of cash flows?
d. Was the cash flow an operating, investing, or financing activity on Smally Company's 2016 statement of cash flows?

Exercise 1-21A *Preparing financial statements—retained earnings emphasis* LO 1-3, 1-4, 1-5, 1-6

On January 1, 2016, the following information was drawn from the accounting records of Carter Company: cash of $800; land of $3,500; notes payable of $600; and common stock of $1,000.

Required

a. Determine the amount of retained earnings as of January 1, 2016.
b. After looking at the amount of retained earnings, the chief executive officer (CEO) wants to pay a $1,000 cash dividend to the stockholders. Can the company pay this dividend? Why or why not?
c. As of January 1, 2016, what percent of the assets were acquired from creditors?
d. As of January 1, 2016, what percent of the assets were acquired from investors?
e. As of January 1, 2016, what percent of the assets were acquired from retained earnings?
f. Create an accounting equation using percentages instead of dollar amounts on the right side of the equation.

g. During 2016, Carter Company earned cash revenue of $1,800, paid cash expenses of $1,200, and paid a cash dividend of $500. Prepare an income statement, statement of changes in stockholders' equity, a balance sheet, and a statement of cash flows dated December 31, 2016. (*Hint:* It is helpful to record these events under an accounting equation before preparing the statements.)

h. Comment on the terminology used to date each statement.

i. An appraiser determines that as of December 31, 2016, the market value of the land is $4,200. How will this fact change the financial statements?

j. What is the balance in the Revenue account on January 1, 2017?

LO 1-5, 1-6

Exercise 1-22A *Preparing financial statements—cash flow emphasis*

As of January 1, 2016, Room Designs Inc. had a balance of $9,900 in Cash, $3,500 in Common Stock, and $6,400 in Retained Earnings. These were the only accounts with balances in the ledger on January 1, 2016. Further analysis of the company's cash account indicated that during the 2016 accounting period, the company had (1) net cash inflow from operating activities of $9,800, (2) net cash outflow for investing activities of $16,500, and (3) net cash inflow from financing activities of $11,000. All revenue and expense events were cash events. The following accounts and balances represent the general ledger of Room Designs Inc. as of December 31, 2016, before closing.

ROOM DESIGNS.
General Ledger

Assets	=	Liabilities	+	Stockholders' Equity	
Cash		Notes Payable		Common Stock	Revenue
Bal. 14,200		Bal. 9,000		Bal. 7,500	Bal. 18,100
Land				Retained Earnings	Expenses
Bal. 16,500				Bal. 6,400	Bal. 8,300
					Dividends
					Bal. 2,000

Required

a. Assume that the net cash inflow from financing activities of $11,000 was caused by three events. Based on the information above, identify these events and determine the cash flow associated with each event.

b. What did the company purchase that resulted in the cash outflow from investing activities?

c. Prepare an income statement, statement of changes in stockholders' equity, balance sheet, and statement of cash flows.

LO 1-7

Exercise 1-23A *Retained earnings and the closing process*

As of December 31, 2016, Flowers Company had total assets of $130,000, total liabilities of $50,000, and common stock of $70,000. The company's 2016 income statement contained revenue of $30,000 and expenses of $18,000. The 2016 statement of changes in stockholders' equity stated that $3,000 of dividends were paid to investors.

Required

a. Determine the before-closing balance in the Retained Earnings account on December 31, 2016.

b. Determine the after-closing balance in the Retained Earnings account on December 31, 2016.

c. Determine the before-closing balances in the Revenue, Expense, and Dividend accounts on December 31, 2016.

d. Determine the after-closing balances in the Revenue, Expense, and Dividend accounts on December 31, 2016.

e. Explain the difference between common stock and retained earnings.

f. On January 1, 2017, Flowers Company raised $30,000 by issuing additional common stock. Immediately after the additional capital was raised. Flowers reported total equity of $110,000. Are the stockholders of Flowers in a better financial position than they were on December 31, 2016?

Exercise 1-24A *The closing process*

LO 1-7

Sammy's Pizza opened on January 1, 2016. Sammy's reported the following for cash revenues and cash expenses for the years 2016 to 2018:

	Cash Revenues	Cash Expenses
2016	$20,000	$11,000
2017	$30,000	$14,000
2018	$40,000	$22,000

Required

a. What would Sammy's Pizza report for net income and retained earnings for the years 2016, 2017, and 2018?

b. Explain the difference between net income and retained earnings.

c. Assume that Sammy's Pizza paid a $5,000 dividend to stockholders in 2017. What would Sammy's Pizza report for net income and retained earnings for 2017 and 2018?

Exercise 1-25A *Retained earnings and the closing process*

LO 1-7

Critz Company was started on January 1, 2016. During the month of January, Critz earned $7,500 of revenue and incurred $4,800 of expenses. During the remainder of 2016, Critz earned $86,000 and incurred $51,000 of expenses. Critz closes its books on December 31 of each year.

Required

a. Determine the balance in the Retained Earnings account as of January 31, 2016.

b. Determine the balance in the Revenue and Expense accounts as of January 31, 2016.

c. Determine the balance in the Retained Earnings account as of December 31, 2016, before closing.

d. Determine the balances in the Revenue and Expense accounts as of December 31, 2016, before closing.

e. Determine the balance in the Retained Earnings account as of January 1, 2017.

f. Determine the balance in the Revenue and Expense accounts as of January 1, 2017.

Exercise 1-26A *Types of transactions and the horizontal statements model*

LO 1-4, 1-8

The Candle Shop experienced the following events during its first year of operations, 2016:

1. Acquired cash by issuing common stock.
2. Paid a cash dividend to the stockholders.
3. Paid cash for operating expenses.
4. Borrowed cash from a bank.
5. Provided services and collected cash.
6. Purchased land with cash.
7. Determined that the market value of the land is higher than the historical cost.

Required

a. Indicate whether each event is an asset source, use, or exchange transaction.

b. Use a horizontal statements model to show how each event affects the balance sheet, income statement, and statement of cash flows. Indicate whether the event increases (I), decreases (D), or does not affect (NA) each element of the financial statements. Also, in the Statement of Cash Flows column, classify the cash flows as operating activities (OA), investing activities (IA), or financing activities (FA). The first transaction is shown as an example.

Event No.	Balance Sheet									Income Statement					Statement of Cash Flows
	Cash	+	Land	=	N. Pay	+	C. Stock.	+	Ret. Ear.	Rev.	−	Exp.	=	Net Inc.	
1.	I	+	NA	=	NA	+	I	+	NA	NA	−	NA	=	NA	I FA

LO IFRS

Exercise 1-27A *International Financial Reporting Standards*

Indigo Fabrics Inc. is a U.S.-based company that develops its financial statements under GAAP. The total amount of the company's assets shown on its December 31, 2017, balance sheet was approximately $225 million. The president of Indigo is considering the possibility of relocating the company to a country that practices accounting under IFRS. The president has hired an international accounting firm to determine what the company's statements would look like if they were prepared under IFRS. One striking difference is that under IFRS the assets shown on the balance sheet would be valued at approximately $275 million.

Required

a. Would Indigo Fabrics's assets really be worth $50 million more if it moves its headquarters?

b. Discuss the underlying conceptual differences between U.S. GAAP and IFRS that cause the difference in the reported asset values.

SECTIONS 1 AND 2

PROBLEMS—SERIES A

connect plus+ ACCOUNTING *All applicable Problems in Series A are available with McGraw-Hill's Connect Plus Accounting.*

LO 1-1

Problem 1-28A *Accounting's role in not-for-profits*

Beverly Moore is struggling to pass her introductory accounting course. Beverly is intelligent but she likes to party. Studying is a low priority for Beverly. When one of her friends tells her that she is going to have trouble in business if she doesn't learn accounting, Beverly responds that she doesn't plan to go into business. She says that she is arts-oriented and plans someday to be a director of a museum. She is in the school of business to develop her social skills, not her quantitative skills. Beverly says she won't have to worry about accounting, since museums are not intended to make a profit.

Required

a. Write a brief memo explaining whether you agree or disagree with Beverly's position regarding accounting and not-for-profit organizations.

b. Distinguish between financial accounting and managerial accounting.

c. Identify some of the stakeholders of not-for-profit institutions that would expect to receive financial accounting reports.

d. Identify some of the stakeholders of not-for-profit institutions that would expect to receive managerial accounting reports.

LO 1-1

CHECK FIGURE

1. Entities mentioned: Bob Wilder and Wilder Co.

Problem 1-29A *Accounting entities*

The following business scenarios are independent from one another:

1. Bob Wilder starts a business by transferring $10,000 from his personal checking account into a checking account for his business, Wilder Co.
2. A business that Sam Pace owns earns $4,600 of cash revenue from customers.

3. Jim Sneed borrows $30,000 from the National Bank and uses the money to purchase a car from Iuka Ford.
4. OZ Company pays its five employees $2,500 each to cover their salaries.
5. Gil Roberts loans his son Jim $5,000 cash.
6. Gane, Inc., paid $100,000 cash to purchase land from Atlanta Land Co.
7. Rob Moore and Gil Thomas form the MT partnership by contributing $20,000 each from their personal bank accounts to a partnership bank account.
8. Stephen Woo pays cash to purchase $5,000 of common stock that is issued by Izzard, Inc.
9. Natural Stone pays a $5,000 cash dividend to each of its seven shareholders.
10. Billows, Inc., borrowed $5,000,000 from the National Bank.

Required

a. For each scenario, create a list of all of the entities that are mentioned in the description.
b. Describe what happens to the cash account of each entity that you identified in Requirement *a*.

Problem 1-30A *Classifying events as asset source, use, or exchange* LO 1-4

The following unrelated events are typical of those experienced by business entities:

1. Acquire cash by issuing common stock.
2. Pay other operating supplies expense.
3. Agree to represent a client in an IRS audit and to receive payment when the audit is complete.
4. Receive cash from customers for services rendered.
5. Pay employee salaries with cash.
6. Pay back a bank loan with cash.
7. Pay interest to a bank with cash.
8. Transfer cash from a checking account to a money market account.
9. Sell land for cash at its original cost.
10. Pay a cash dividend to stockholders.
11. Learn that a financial analyst determined the company's price-earnings ratio to be 26.
12. Borrow cash from the local bank.
13. Pay office supplies expense.
14. Make plans to purchase office equipment.
15. Trade a used car for a computer with the same value.

Required

Identify each of the events as an asset source, use, or exchange transaction. If an event would not be recorded under generally accepted accounting principles, identify it as not applicable (NA). Also indicate for each event whether total assets would increase, decrease, or remain unchanged. Organize your answer according to the following table. The first event is shown in the table as an example.

Event No.	Type of Event	Effect on Total Assets
1	Asset source	Increase

Problem 1-31A *Relating titles and accounts to financial statements* LO 1-5, 1-6

Required

Identify the financial statements on which each of the following items (titles, date descriptions, and accounts) appears by placing a check mark in the appropriate column. If an item appears on more than one statement, place a check mark in every applicable column.

Item	Income Statement	Statement of Changes in Stockholders' Equity	Balance Sheet	Statement of Cash Flows
Financing activities				
Ending common stock				
Interest expense				
As of (date)				
Land				
Beginning cash balance				
Notes payable				
Beginning common stock				
Service revenue				
Utility expense				
Stock issue				
Operating activities				
For the period ended (date)				
Net income				
Investing activities				
Net loss				
Ending cash balance				
Salary expense				
Consulting revenue				
Dividends				

LO 1-2, 1-3, 1-5, 1-6, 1-7

Problem 1-32A *Preparing financial statements for two complete accounting cycles*

CHECK FIGURES

a. Net Income 2016: $13,000

b. Retained Earnings 2017: $33,500

Mark's Consulting experienced the following transactions for 2016, its first year of operations, and 2017. *Assume that all transactions involve the receipt or payment of cash.*

Transactions for 2016

1. Acquired $20,000 by issuing common stock.
2. Received $35,000 for providing services to customers.
3. Borrowed $25,000 cash from creditors.
4. Paid expenses amounting to $22,000.
5. Purchased land for $30,000 cash.

Transactions for 2017

Beginning account balances for 2017 are:

Cash	$28,000
Land	30,000
Notes payable	25,000
Common stock	20,000
Retained earnings	13,000

1. Acquired an additional $24,000 from the issue of common stock.
2. Received $95,000 for providing services in 2017.
3. Paid $15,000 to reduce notes payable.
4. Paid expenses amounting to $71,500.
5. Paid a $3,000 dividend to the stockholders.
6. Determined that the market value of the land is $47,000.

Required

a. Write an accounting equation, and record the effects of each accounting event under the appropriate headings for each year. Record the amounts of revenue, expense, and dividends in the Retained Earnings column. Provide appropriate titles for these accounts in the last column of the table.
b. Prepare an income statement, statement of changes in stockholders' equity, year-end balance sheet, and statement of cash flows for each year.
c. Determine the amount of cash that is in the Retained Earnings account at the end of 2016 and 2017.
d. Compare the information provided by the income statement with the information provided by the statement of cash flows. Point out similarities and differences.
e. Determine the balance in the Retained Earnings account immediately after Event 2 in 2016 and in 2017 are recorded.

Problem 1-33A *Interrelationships among financial statements*

LO 1-2, 1-3, 1-5, 1-6, 1-7

CHECK FIGURE
a. Net Income: $9,550
Total Assets: $38,550

Pratt Corp. started the accounting period with $30,000 of assets, $12,000 of liabilities, and $5,000 of retained earnings. During the period, the Retained Earnings account increased by $7,550. The bookkeeper reported that Pratt paid cash expenses of $26,000 and paid a $2,000 cash dividend to stockholders, but she could not find a record of the amount of cash that Pratt received for performing services. Pratt also paid $3,000 cash to reduce the liability owed to a bank, and the business acquired $4,000 of additional cash from the issue of common stock.

Required

a. Prepare an income statement, statement of changes in stockholders' equity, period-end balance sheet, and statement of cash flows for the 2016 accounting period. (*Hint:* Determine the amount of beginning retained earnings before considering the effects of the current period events. It also might help to record all events under an accounting equation before preparing the statements.)
b. Determine the percentage of total assets that were provided by creditors, investors, and earnings.
c. Determine the balance in the Revenue, Expense, and Dividends accounts as of January 1, 2017.

Problem 1-34A *Recording events in a horizontal statements model*

LO 1-2, 1-3, 1-4, 1-5, 1-6, 1-7, 1-8

CHECK FIGURES
a. Net Income: $23,000
e. Net Cash Flow from Operating Activities: $23,000

Maben Company was started on January 1, 2016, and experienced the following events during its first year of operation:

1. Acquired $30,000 cash from the issue of common stock.
2. Borrowed $40,000 cash from National Bank.
3. Earned cash revenues of $48,000 for performing services.
4. Paid cash expenses of $25,000.
5. Paid a $1,000 cash dividend to the stockholders.
6. Acquired an additional $20,000 cash from the issue of common stock.
7. Paid $10,000 cash to reduce the principal balance of the bank note.
8. Paid $53,000 cash to purchase land.
9. Determined that the market value of the land is $75,000.

Required

a. Record the preceding transactions in the horizontal statements model. Also, in the Cash Flows column, classify the cash flows as operating activities (OA), investing activities (IA), or financing activities (FA). The first event is shown as an example.

Event No.	Balance Sheet									Income Statement					Statement of Cash Flows
	Cash	+	Land	=	N. Pay	+	C. Stock.	+	Ret. Ear.	Rev.	−	Exp.	=	Net Inc.	
1.	30,000	+	NA	=	NA	+	30,000	+	NA	NA	−	NA	=	NA	30,000 FA

b. Determine the amount of total assets that Maben would report on the December 31, 2016, balance sheet.

c. Identify the asset source transactions and related amounts for 2016.

d. Determine the net income that Maben would report on the 2016 income statement. Explain why dividends do not appear on the income statement.

e. Determine the net cash flows from operating activities, financing activities, and investing activities that Maben would report on the 2016 statement of cash flows.

f. Determine the percentage of assets that were provided by investors, creditors, and earnings.

g. What is the balance in the Retained Earnings account immediately after Event 3 is recorded?

MULTIPLE-CHOICE QUESTIONS

Multiple-choice questions are available in the Connect library.

EXERCISES—SERIES B

LO 1-1

Exercise 1-1B *The role of accounting in society*

Resource owners provide three types of resources to conversion agents that transform the resources into products or services that satisfy consumer demands.

Required

Identify the three types of resources. Write a brief memo explaining how resource owners select the particular conversion agents to which they will provide resources. Your memo should include answers to the following questions: If you work as a private accountant, what role would you play in the allocation of resources? Which professional certification would be most appropriate for your career?

LO 1-1

Exercise 1-2B *Careers in accounting*

Accounting is commonly divided into two sectors. One sector is called public accounting. The other sector is called private accounting.

Required

a. Identify three areas of service provided by public accountants.

b. Describe the common duties performed by private accountants.

LO 1-1

Exercise 1-3B *Identifying the reporting entities*

Ray Steen recently started a business. During the first few days of operation, Mr. Steen transferred $100,000 from his personal account into a business account for a company he named Steen Enterprises. Steen Enterprises borrowed $60,000 from First Bank. Mr. Steen's father-in-law, Stan Rhoades, invested $75,000 into the business for which he received a 25 percent ownership interest. Steen Enterprises purchased a building from Zoro Realty Company. The building cost $150,000 cash. Steen Enterprises earned $56,000 in revenue from the company's customers and paid its employees $31,000 for salaries expense.

Required

Identify the entities that were mentioned in the scenario and explain what happened to the cash accounts of each entity that you identify.

Exercise 1-4B *Missing information in the accounting equation*

LO 1-2

Required

Calculate the missing amounts in the following table.

					Stockholders' Equity		
Company	**Assets**	**=**	**Liabilities**	**+**	**Company Stock**	**+**	**Retained Earnings**
A	$?		$30,000		$ 50,000		$62,000
B	50,000		?		10,000		25,000
C	85,000		20,000		?		40,000
D	215,000		60,000		100,000		?

Exercise 1-5B *Effect of events on the accounting equation*

LO 1-2

Morrison Co. experienced the following events during 2016:

1. Acquired cash from the issue of common stock.
2. Borrowed cash.
3. Collected cash from providing services.
4. Purchased land with cash.
5. Paid operating expenses with cash.
6. Paid a cash dividend to the stockholders.

Required

Explain how each of these events affect the accounting equation by writing the letter I for increase, the letter D for decrease, and NA for does not affect under each of the components of the accounting equation. The first event is shown as an example.

					Stockholders' Equity		
Event Number	**Assets**	**=**	**Liabilities**	**+**	**Common Stock**	**+**	**Retained Earnings**
1	I		NA		I		NA

Exercise 1-6B *Effect of transactions on general ledger accounts*

LO 1-2

At the beginning of 2016, Master Corp.'s accounting records had the following general ledger accounts and balances.

MASTER CORP.
Accounting Equation

Event	Assets		=	Liabilities	+	Stockholders' Equity		Acct. Titles for RE
	Cash	Land		Notes Payable		Common Stock	Retained Earnings	
Balance 1/1/2016	20,000	50,000		35,000		25,000	10,000	

Master Corp. completed the following transactions during 2016:

1. Purchased land for $12,000 cash.
2. Acquired $20,000 cash from the issue of common stock.
3. Received $50,000 cash for providing services to customers.
4. Paid cash operating expenses of $42,000.
5. Borrowed $20,000 cash from the bank.
6. Paid a $2,000 cash dividend to the stockholders.
7. Determined that the market value of the land purchased in event 1 is $70,000.

Required

a. Record the transactions in the appropriate general ledger accounts. Record the amounts of revenue, expense, and dividends in the Retained Earnings column. Provide the appropriate titles for these accounts in the last column of the table.

b. As of December 31, 2016, determine the total amount of assets, liabilities, and stockholders' equity and present this information in the form of an accounting equation.

c. What is the amount of total assets, liabilities, and stockholders' equity as of January 1, 2017?

LO 1-2

Exercise 1-7B *Missing information and recording events*

As of December 31, 2016, Dunn Company had total cash of $156,000, notes payable of $85,600, and common stock of $52,400. During 2017, Dunn earned $36,000 of cash revenue, paid $20,000 for cash expenses, and paid a $3,000 cash dividend to the stockholders.

Required

a. Determine the amount of retained earnings as of December 31, 2016.

b. Create an accounting equation and record the beginning account balances under the appropriate elements.

c. Record the revenue, expense, and dividend events under the appropriate elements of the accounting equation created in Requirement *b*.

d. Prove the equality of the accounting equation as of December 31, 2017.

e. Identify the beginning and ending balances in the Cash and Common Stock accounts. Explain why the beginning and ending balances in the Cash account are different, but the beginning and ending balances in the Common Stock account remain the same.

LO 1-2

Exercise 1-8B *Account titles and the accounting equation*

The following account titles were drawn from the general ledger of Pest Control, Incorporated (PCI): Cash, Notes Payable, Land, Accounts Payable, Office Furniture, Salaries Expense, Common Stock, Service Revenue, Interest Expense, Utilities Payable, Utilities Expense, Trucks, Supplies, Operating Expenses, Rent Revenue, Computers, Building, Supplies Expense, Gasoline Expense, Retained Earnings, Dividends.

Required

a. Create an accounting equation using the elements assets, liabilities, and stockholders' equity. List each account title under the element of the accounting equation to which it belongs.

b. Will all businesses have the same number of accounts? Explain your answer.

LO 1-3

Exercise 1-9B *Components of the accounting equation*

Lewis Enterprises was started when it acquired $4,000 cash from creditors and $6,000 from owners. The company immediately purchased land that cost $9,000.

Required

a. Record the events under an accounting equation.

b. After all events have been recorded, Lewis's obligations to creditors represents what percent of total assets?

c. After all events have been recorded, Lewis's stockholders' equity represents what percent of total assets?

d. Assume the debt is due. Given that Lewis has $6,000 in stockholders' equity, can the company repay the creditors at this point? Why or why not?

Exercise 1-10B *Components of the accounting equation* LO 1-3

The financial condition of White Inc. is expressed in the following accounting equation:

Assets	=	Liabilities	+	Common stock	+	Retained earnings
$800 Cash + $9,200 Land	=	$7,000	+	$2,000	+	$1,000

Required

a. Are dividends paid to creditors or investors? Explain why.

b. How much cash is in the Retained Earnings account?

c. Determine the maximum dividend White can pay.

d. If the obligation to creditors is due, can White repay the loan? Why or why not?

e. Suppose the land sinks into the sea as a result of an earthquake and a resulting tsunami. The business is then liquidated. How much cash will creditors receive? How much cash will investors receive? (Assume there are no legal fees or other costs of liquidation.)

Exercise 1-11B *Differences between interest and dividends* LO 1-3

The following account balances were drawn from the financial records of Barnes Company (BC) as of January 1, 2016: Assets, $14,000; Liabilities, $4,000; Common Stock, $7,000; and Retained Earnings, $3,000. BC has agreed to pay the creditors $400 of interest per year. Further, BC agrees that for the 2016 fiscal year any annual earnings remaining after the interest charges will be paid out as dividends to the owners.

Required

a. Assuming BC earns a before interest expense recognition profit of $900 during 2016, determine the amount of interest and dividends paid.

b. Assuming BC earns a before interest expense recognition profit of $500 during 2016, determine the amount of interest and dividends paid.

c. Assuming BC earns a before interest expense recognition profit of $100 during 2016, determine the amount of interest and dividends paid.

Exercise 1-12B *Distribution in a business liquidation* LO 1-3

Assume that Clayton Company acquires $1,200 cash from creditors and $1,700 cash from investors.

Required

a. Explain the primary differences between investors and creditors.

b. If Clayton has net income of $800 and then liquidates, what amount of cash will the creditors receive? What amount of cash will the investors receive?

c. If Clayton has a net loss of $800 cash and then liquidates, what amount of cash will the creditors receive? What amount of cash will the investors receive?

d. If Clayton has a net loss of $1,900 cash and then liquidates, what amount of cash will the creditors receive? What amount of cash will the investors receive?

Exercise 1-13B *Classifying events as asset source, use, or exchange* LO 1-4

Trip's Business Services experienced the following events during its first year of operations:

1. Acquired $20,000 cash from the issue of common stock.
2. Borrowed $12,000 cash from First Bank.
3. Paid $5,000 cash to purchase land.
4. Received $25,000 cash for providing boarding services.
5. Acquired an additional $5,000 cash from the issue of common stock.
6. Purchased additional land for $4,000 cash.

7. Paid \$10,000 cash for salary expense.
8. Signed a contract to provide additional services in the future.
9. Paid \$1,200 cash for rent expense.
10. Paid a \$1,000 cash dividend to the stockholders.
11. Determined the market value of the land to be \$18,000 at the end of the accounting period.

Required

Classify each event as an asset source, use, or exchange transaction or as not applicable (NA).

SECTION 2

EXERCISES—SERIES B

LO 1-3, 1-5

Exercise 1-14B *Missing information for determining net income*

The December 31, 2016, balance sheet for James Company showed total stockholders' equity of \$156,000. Total stockholders' equity increased by \$65,000 between December 31, 2016, and December 31, 2017. During 2017 James Company acquired \$20,000 cash from the issue of common stock. James Company paid a \$5,000 cash dividend to the stockholders during 2017.

Required

Determine the amount of net income or loss James Company reported on its 2017 income statement. (*Hint:* Remember that stock issues, net income, and dividends all change total stockholders' equity.)

LO 1-5

Exercise 1-15B *Preparing an income statement and a balance sheet*

Petre Company was started on January 1, 2016. During 2016, the company experienced the following three accounting events: (1) earned cash revenues of \$14,500, (2) paid cash expenses of \$9,200, and (3) paid a \$500 cash dividend to its stockholders. These were the only events that affected the company during 2016.

Required

a. Create an accounting equation and record the effects of each accounting event under the appropriate general ledger account headings.
b. Prepare an income statement, statement of changes in stockholders' equity, and a balance sheet dated December 31, 2016, for Petre Company.
c. Explain why the income statement uses different terminology to date the income statement than is used to date the balance sheet.

LO 1-5

Exercise 1-16B *Historical cost versus market value*

Lakeside, Inc., purchased land in January 2009 at a cost of \$250,000. The estimated market value of the land is \$425,000 as of December 31, 2016.

Required

a. Name the December 31, 2016, financial statement(s) on which the land will be shown.
b. At what dollar amount will the land be shown in the financial statement(s)?
c. Name the key concept that will be used in determining the dollar amount that will be reported for land that is shown in the financial statement(s).

LO 1-6

Exercise 1-17B *Statement of cash flows*

On January 1, 2016, Palmer, a fast-food company, had a balance in its Cash account of \$32,000. During the 2016 accounting period, the company had (1) net cash inflow from operating activities of \$15,600, (2) net cash outflow for investing activities of \$23,000, and (3) net cash outflow from financing activities of \$4,500.

Required

a. Prepare a statement of cash flows.
b. Provide a reasonable explanation as to what may have caused the net cash inflow from operating activities.

c. Provide a reasonable explanation as to what may have caused the net cash outflow from investing activities.

d. Provide a reasonable explanation as to what may have caused the net cash outflow from financing activities.

Exercise 1-18B *Prepare a statement of cash flows*

LO 1-6

National Service Company experienced the following accounting events during 2016:

1. Paid $4,000 cash for salary expense.
2. Borrowed $8,000 cash from State Bank.
3. Received $30,000 cash from the issue of common stock.
4. Purchased land for $8,000 cash.
5. Performed services for $14,000 cash.
6. Paid $4,200 cash for utilities expense.
7. Sold land for $7,000 cash.
8. Paid a cash dividend of $1,000 to the stockholders.
9. Hired an accountant to keep the books.
10. Paid $3,000 cash on the loan from State Bank.

Required

a. Indicate how each of the events would be classified on the statement of cash flows as operating activities (OA), investing activities (IA), financing activities (FA), or not applicable (NA).

b. Prepare a statement of cash flows for 2016. Assume National Service had a beginning cash balance of $9,000 on January 1, 2016.

Exercise 1-19B *Preparing financial statements*

LO 1-3, 1-5, 1-6

Tennessee Company experienced the following events during 2016.

1. Acquired $50,000 cash from the issue of common stock.
2. Paid $15,000 cash to purchase land.
3. Borrowed $25,000 cash.
4. Provided services for $60,000 cash.
5. Paid $12,000 cash for rent expense.
6. Paid $22,000 cash for other operating expenses.
7. Paid a $5,000 cash dividend to the stockholders.
8. Determined that the market value of the land purchased in Event 2 is now $16,500.

Required

a. The January 1, 2016, general ledger account balances are shown in the following accounting equation. Record the eight events in the appropriate general ledger accounts. Record the amounts of revenue, expense, and dividends in the Retained Earnings column. Provide the appropriate titles for these accounts in the last column of the table. The first event is shown as an example.

TENNESSEE COMPANY
Accounting Equation

Event	Assets		=	Liabilities	+	Stockholders' Equity		Acct. Titles for RE
	Cash	Land		Notes Payable		Common Stock	Retained Earnings	
Balance 1/1/2016	15,000	10,000		0		20,000	5,000	
1.	50,000					50,000		

b. Prepare an income statement, statement of changes in equity, year-end balance sheet, and statement of cash flows for the 2016 accounting period.

c. Determine the percentage of assets that were provided by retained earnings. How much cash is in the retained earnings account?

LO 1-4, 1-6

Exercise 1-20B *Relating accounting events to entities*

Arnett Company was started in 2016 when it acquired $30,000 cash by issuing common stock to Dan Arnett.

Required

a. Was this event an asset source, use, or exchange transaction for Arnett Company?

b. Was this event an asset source, use, or exchange transaction for Dan Arnett?

c. Was the cash flow an operating, investing, or financing activity on Arnett Company's 2016 statement of cash flows?

d. Was the cash flow an operating, investing, or financing activity on Dan Arnett's 2016 statement of cash flows?

LO 1-3, 1-4, 1-5, 1-6

Exercise 1-21B *Preparing financial statements—retained earnings emphasis*

On January 1, 2016, the following information was drawn from the accounting records of Zeke Company: cash of $200; land of $1,800; notes payable of $600; and common stock of $1,000.

Required

a. Determine the amount of retained earnings as of January 1, 2016.

b. After looking at the amount of retained earnings, the chief executive officer (CEO) wants to pay a $300 cash dividend to the stockholders. Can the company pay this dividend? Why or why not?

c. As of January 1, 2016, what percent of the assets were acquired from creditors?

d. As of January 1, 2016, what percent of the assets were acquired from investors?

e. As of January 1, 2016, what percent of the assets were acquired from retained earnings?

f. Create an accounting equation using percentages instead of dollar amounts on the right side of the equation.

g. During 2016, Zeke Company earned cash revenue of $500, paid cash expenses of $300, and paid a cash dividend of $50. Prepare an income statement, statement of changes in stockholders' equity, a balance sheet, and a statement of cash flows dated December 31, 2016. (*Hint:* It is helpful to record these events under an accounting equation before preparing the statements.)

h. Comment on the terminology used to date each statement.

i. An appraiser determines that as of December 31, 2016, the market value of the land is $2,000. How will this fact change the financial statements?

j. What is the balance in the Revenue account on January 1, 2017?

LO 1-5, 1-6

Exercise 1-22B *Preparing financial statements—cash flow emphasis*

As of January 1, 2016, Shundra Inc. had a balance of $4,500 in Cash, $2,500 in Common Stock, and $2,000 in Retained Earnings. These were the only accounts with balances in the ledger on January 1, 2016. Further analysis of the company's cash account indicated that during the 2016 accounting period, the company had (1) net cash inflow from operating activities of $5,100, (2) net cash outflow for investing activities of $13,000, and (3) net cash inflow from financing activities of $7,600. All revenue and expense events were cash events. The following accounts and balances represent the general ledger of Shundra Inc. as of December 31, 2016, before closing.

SHUNDRA INC.
General Ledger

Assets		=	Liabilities		+	Stockholders' Equity			
Cash			**Notes Payable**			**Common Stock**		**Revenue**	
Bal.	4,200		Bal.	3,000		Bal.	8,000	Bal.	9,900
Land						**Retained Earnings**		**Expenses**	
Bal.	13,000					Bal.	2,000	Bal.	4,800
								Dividends	
								Bal.	900

Required

a. Assume that the net cash inflow from financing activities of $7,600 was caused by three events. Based on the information above, identify these events and determine the cash flow associated with each event.

b. What did the company purchase that resulted in the cash outflow from investing activities?

c. Prepare an income statement, statement of changes in stockholders' equity, balance sheet, and statement of cash flows.

Exercise 1-23B *Retained earnings and the closing process* LO 1-7

As of December 31, 2016, Big Horn Company had total assets of $100,000, total liabilities of $30,000, and common stock of $50,000. The company's 2016 income statement contained revenue of $16,000 and expenses of $11,000. The 2016 statement of changes in stockholders' equity stated that $2,000 of dividends were paid to investors.

Required

a. Determine the before-closing balance in the Retained Earnings account on December 31, 2016.

b. Determine the after-closing balance in the Retained Earnings account on December 31, 2016.

c. Determine the before-closing balances in the Revenue, Expense, and Dividend accounts on December 31, 2016.

d. Determine the after-closing balances in the Revenue, Expense, and Dividend accounts on December 31, 2016.

e. Explain the difference between common stock and retained earnings.

f. On January 1, 2017, Big Horn Company raised $40,000 by issuing additional common stock. Immediately after the additional capital was raised. Big Horn reported total equity of $110,000. Are the stockholders of Big Horn in a better financial position than they were on December 31, 2016?

Exercise 1-24B *The closing process* LO 1-7

Pam's Crafts opened on January 1, 2016. Pam's reported the following for cash revenues and cash expenses for the years 2016 to 2018:

	Cash Revenues	Cash Expenses
2016	$40,000	$21,000
2017	$50,000	$32,000
2018	$70,000	$48,000

Required

a. What would Pam's Crafts report for net income and retained earnings for the years 2016, 2017, and 2018?

b. Explain the difference between net income and retained earnings.

c. Assume that Pam's Crafts paid a $6,000 dividend to stockholders in 2017. What would Pam's Crafts report for net income and retained earnings for 2017 and 2018?

LO 1-7

Exercise 1-25B *Retained earnings and the closing process*

Carr Company was started on January 1, 2016. During the month of January, Carr earned $4,600 of revenue and incurred $3,000 of expenses. During the remainder of 2016, Carr earned $52,000 and incurred $42,000 of expenses. Carr closes its books on December 31 of each year.

Required

a. Determine the balance in the Retained Earnings account as of January 31, 2016.

b. Determine the balance in the Revenue and Expense accounts as of January 31, 2016.

c. Determine the balance in the Retained Earnings account as of December 31, 2016, before closing.

d. Determine the balances in the Revenue and Expense accounts as of December 31, 2016, before closing.

e. Determine the balance in the Retained Earnings account as of January 1, 2017.

f. Determine the balance in the Revenue and Expense accounts as of January 1, 2017.

LO 1-4, 1-8

Exercise 1-26B *Types of transactions and the horizontal statements model*

Pet Partners experienced the following events during its first year of operations, 2016:

1. Acquired cash by issuing common stock.
2. Borrowed cash from a bank.
3. Signed a contract to provide services in the future.
4. Purchased land with cash.
5. Paid cash for operating expenses.
6. Paid a cash dividend to the stockholders.
7. Determined that the market value of the land is higher than the historical cost.

Required

a. Indicate whether each event is an asset source, use, or exchange transaction.

b. Use a horizontal statements model to show how each event affects the balance sheet, income statement, and statement of cash flows. Indicate whether the event increases (I), decreases (D), or does not affect (NA) each element of the financial statements. Also, in the Statement of Cash Flows column, classify the cash flows as operating activities (OA), investing activities (IA), or financing activities (FA). The first transaction is shown as an example.

Event No.	Balance Sheet									Income Statement					Statement of Cash Flows
	Cash	+	Land	=	N. Pay	+	C. Stock.	+	Ret. Ear.	Rev.	−	Exp.	=	Net Inc.	
1.	I	+	NA	=	NA	+	I	+	NA	NA	−	NA	=	NA	I FA

LO IFRS

Exercise 1-27B *International Financial Reporting Standards*

Corrugated Boxes Inc. is a U.S.–based company that develops its financial statements under GAAP. The total amount of the company's assets shown on its December 31, 2016, balance sheet was approximately $305 million. The president of Corrugated is considering the possibility of relocating the company to a country that practices accounting under IFRS. The president has hired an international accounting firm to determine what the company's statements would look like if they were prepared under IFRS. One striking difference is that under IFRS the assets shown on the balance sheet would be valued at approximately $345 million.

Required

a. Would Corrugated Boxes' assets really be worth $40 million more if it moves its headquarters?
b. Discuss the underlying conceptual differences between U.S. GAAP and IFRS that cause the difference in the reported asset values.

PROBLEMS—SERIES B

Problem 1-28B *Applying GAAP to financial reporting* LO 1-1

Jan Perkins is a business consultant. She analyzed the business processes of one of her clients, Diamond Companies, in November 2016. She prepared a report containing her recommendation for changes in some of the company's business practices. She presented Diamond with the report in December 2016. Jan guarantees that her clients will save money by following her advice. She does not collect for the services she provides until the client is satisfied with the results of her work. In this case she received cash payment from Diamond in February 2017.

Required

a. Define the acronym GAAP.
b. Assume that Jan's accountant tells her that GAAP permits Jan to recognize the revenue from Diamond in either 2016 or 2017. What GAAP rule would justify reporting the same event in two different ways? Write a brief memo explaining the logic behind this rule.
c. If Jan were keeping records for managerial reporting purposes, would she be bound by GAAP rules? Write a brief memo to explain how GAAP applies to financial versus managerial reporting.

Problem 1-29B *Accounting entities* LO 1-1

The following business scenarios are independent from one another:

1. Chris Hann purchased an automobile from Classic Auto Sales for $10,000.
2. Sal Pearl loaned $15,000 to the business in which he is a stockholder.
3. First State Bank paid interest to Strong Co. on a certificate of deposit that Strong Co. has invested at First State Bank.
4. Cindy's Restaurant paid the current utility bill of $135 to Midwest Utilities.
5. Sun Corp. borrowed $50,000 from City National Bank and used the funds to purchase land from Carriage Realty.
6. Sue Wang purchased $10,000 of common stock of International Sales Corporation from the corporation.
7. Chris Gordon loaned $6,000 cash to his daughter.
8. Motor Service Co. earned $20,000 in cash revenue.
9. Poy Imports paid $4,000 for salaries to each of its four employees.
10. Borg Inc. paid a cash dividend of $4,000 to its sole shareholder, Mark Borg.

Required

a. For each scenario, create a list of all of the entities that are mentioned in the description.
b. Describe what happens to the cash account of each entity that you identified in Requirement *a.*

Problem 1-30B *Classifying events as asset source, use, or exchange* LO 1-4

The following unrelated events are typical of those experienced by business entities:

1. Pay cash for operating expenses.
2. Pay an office manager's salary with cash.
3. Receive cash for services that have been performed.
4. Pay cash for utilities expense.
5. Acquire land by accepting a liability (financing the purchase).
6. Pay cash to purchase a new office building.
7. Discuss plans for a new office building with an architect.

8. Repay part of a bank loan.
9. Acquire cash by issuing common stock.
10. Purchase land with cash.
11. Purchase equipment with cash.
12. Pay monthly rent on an office building.
13. Hire a new office manager.
14. Borrow cash from a bank.
15. Pay a cash dividend to stockholders.

Required

Identify each of the events as an asset source, use, or exchange transaction. If an event would not be recorded under generally accepted accounting principles, identify it as not applicable (NA). Also indicate for each event whether total assets would increase, decrease, or remain unchanged. Organize your answer according to the following table. The first event is shown in the table as an example.

Event No.	Type of Event	Effect on Total Assets
1	Asset use	Decrease

LO 1-5, 1-6

Problem 1-31B *Relating titles and accounts to financial statements*

Required

Identify the financial statements on which each of the following items (titles, date descriptions, and accounts) appears by placing a check mark in the appropriate column. If an item appears on more than one statement, place a check mark in every applicable column.

Item	Income Statement	Statement of Changes in Stockholders' Equity	Balance Sheet	Statement of Cash Flows
For the period ended (date)				
Net income				
Investing activities				
Net loss				
Ending cash balance				
Salary expense				
Consulting revenue				
Dividends				
Financing activities				
Ending common stock				
Interest expense				
As of (date)				
Land				
Beginning cash balance				
Notes payable				
Beginning common stock				
Service revenue				
Utility expense				
Stock issue				
Operating activities				

Problem 1-32B ***Preparing financial statements for two complete accounting cycles*** **LO 1-2, 1-3, 1-5, 1-6, 1-7**

Marco's Consulting experienced the following transactions for 2016, its first year of operations, and 2017. *Assume that all transactions involve the receipt or payment of cash.*

Transactions for 2016

1. Acquired $50,000 by issuing common stock.
2. Received $100,000 cash for providing services to customers.
3. Borrowed $15,000 cash from creditors.
4. Paid expenses amounting to $60,000.
5. Purchased land for $40,000 cash.

Transactions for 2017

Beginning account balances for 2017 are:

Cash	$65,000
Land	40,000
Notes payable	15,000
Common stock	50,000
Retained earnings	40,000

1. Acquired an additional $20,000 from the issue of common stock.
2. Received $130,000 for providing services.
3. Paid $10,000 to creditors to reduce loan.
4. Paid expenses amounting to $75,000.
5. Paid a $15,000 dividend to the stockholders.
6. Determined that the market value of the land is $50,000.

Required

a. Write an accounting equation, and record the effects of each accounting event under the appropriate headings for each year. Record the amounts of revenue, expense, and dividends in the Retained Earnings column. Provide appropriate titles for these accounts in the last column of the table.

b. Prepare an income statement, statement of changes in stockholders' equity, year-end balance sheet, and statement of cash flows for each year.

c. Determine the amount of cash that is in the Retained Earnings account at the end of 2016 and 2017.

d. Examine the balance sheets for the two years. How did assets change from 2016 to 2017?

e. Determine the balance in the Retained Earnings account immediately after Event 2 in 2016 and in 2017 are recorded.

Problem 1-33B ***Interrelationships among financial statements*** **LO 1-2, 1-3, 1-5, 1-6, 1-7**

Pearson Enterprises started the 2016 accounting period with $75,000 of assets (all cash), $15,000 of liabilities, and $25,000 of common stock. During the year, Pearson earned cash revenues of $46,000, paid cash expenses of $26,000, and paid a cash dividend to stockholders of $5,000. Pearson also acquired $15,000 of additional cash from the sale of common stock and paid $10,000 cash to reduce the liability owed to a bank.

Required

a. Prepare an income statement, statement of changes in stockholders' equity, period-end balance sheet, and statement of cash flows for the 2016 accounting period. (*Hint:* Determine the amount of beginning retained earnings before considering the effects of the current period events. It also might help to record all events under an accounting equation before preparing the statements.)

b. Determine the percentage of total assets that were provided by creditors, investors, and earnings.

c. Determine the balance in the Revenue, Expense, and Dividends accounts as of January 1, 2017.

LO 1-2, 1-3, 1-4, 1-5, 1-6, 1-7, 1-8

Problem 1-34B *Recording events in a horizontal statements model*

Daley Company was started on January 1, 2016, and experienced the following events during its first year of operation:

1. Acquired $52,000 cash from the issue of common stock.
2. Borrowed $20,000 cash from National Bank.
3. Earned cash revenues of $42,000 for performing services.
4. Paid cash expenses of $23,000.
5. Paid a $6,000 cash dividend to the stockholders.
6. Acquired an additional $10,000 cash from the issue of common stock.
7. Paid $10,000 cash to reduce the principal balance of the bank note.
8. Paid $45,000 cash to purchase land.
9. Determined that the market value of the land is $55,000.

Required

a. Record the preceding transactions in the horizontal statements model. Also, in the Statement of Cash Flows column, classify the cash flows as operating activities (OA), investing activities (IA), or financing activities (FA). The first event is shown as an example.

Event No.	Balance Sheet									Income Statement					Statement of Cash Flows
	Cash	+	Land	=	N. Pay	+	C. Stock.	+	Ret. Ear.	Rev.	−	Exp.	=	Net Inc.	
1.	52,000	+	NA	=	NA	+	52,000	+	NA	NA	−	NA	=	NA	52,000 FA

b. Determine the amount of total assets that Daley would report on the December 31, 2016, balance sheet.

c. Identify the asset source transactions and related amounts for 2016.

d. Determine the net income that Daley would report on the 2016 income statement. Explain why dividends do not appear on the income statement.

e. Determine the net cash flows from operating activities, financing activities, and investing activities that Daley would report on the 2016 statement of cash flows.

f. Determine the percentage of assets that were provided by investors, creditors, and earnings.

g. What is the balance in the Retained Earnings account immediately after Event 3 is recorded?

ANALYZE, THINK, COMMUNICATE

ATC 1-1 Business Applications Case *Understanding real-world annual reports*

Required

Target Corporation

Use the Target Corporation's annual report in Appendix B to answer the following questions.

a. What was Target's net income for 2013 (the year ended February 1, 2014)?

b. Did Target's net income increase or decrease from 2012 to 2013? By how much?

c. What was Target's accounting equation for 2013?

d. Which of the following had the largest percentage change from 2012 to 2013: sales, cost of sales, or selling, general, and administrative expenses? Show all computations.

ATC 1-2 Group Assignment *Missing information*

The following selected financial information is available for Best, Inc. Amounts are in millions of dollars.

Income Statements	2019	2018	2017	2016
Revenue	$ 860	$1,520	$ (a)	$1,200
Cost and expenses	(a)	(a)	(2,400)	(860)
Income from continuing operations	(b)	450	320	(a)
Unusual items	-0-	175	(b)	(b)
Net income	$ 20	$ (b)	$ 175	$ 300
Balance Sheets				
Assets				
Cash and marketable securities	$ 350	$1,720	$ (c)	$ 940
Other assets	1,900	(c)	2,500	(c)
Total assets	2,250	$2,900	$ (d)	$3,500
Liabilities	$ (c)	$ (d)	$ 1,001	$ (d)
Stockholders' equity				
Common stock	880	720	(e)	800
Retained earnings	(d)	(e)	800	(e)
Total stockholders' equity	1,520	1,345	(f)	2,200
Total liabilities and stockholders' equity	$2,250	$ (f)	$ 3,250	$3,500

Required

a. Divide the class into groups of four or five students each. Organize the groups into four sections. Assign Task 1 to the first section of groups, Task 2 to the second section, Task 3 to the third section, and Task 4 to the fourth section.

Group Tasks

(1) Fill in the missing information for 2016.

(2) Fill in the missing information for 2017.

(3) Fill in the missing information for 2018.

(4) Fill in the missing information for 2019.

b. Each section should select two representatives. One representative is to put the financial statements assigned to that section on the board, underlining the missing amounts. The second representative is to explain to the class how the missing amounts were determined.

c. Each section should list events that could have caused the unusual items category on the income statement.

ATC 1-3 Real-World Case *Classifying cash flow activities at five companies*

The following cash transactions occurred in five real-world companies:

1. In 2013, Delta Airlines purchased 44 new airplanes for $1 billion.
2. Google, Inc., paid $3.2 billion to purchase Nest Labs in January 2014.
3. American Electric Power, Inc., borrowed $251 million using notes payable during the third quarter of 2013.
4. Vail Resorts, Inc., collected $1.1 billion in cash sales during its 2013 fiscal year.
5. On September 19, 2013, The Home Depot, Inc., paid $577 million of dividends.
6. In its 2013 fiscal year Nike, Inc., completed the sale of its Cole Haan and Umbro subsidiaries, receiving $786 million in cash.

Required

Determine if each of the above transactions should be classified as an *operating, investing,* or *financing* activity. Also, identify the amount of each cash flow and whether it was an *inflow* or an *outflow*.

ATC 1-4 Business Applications Case *Forecasting from financial reports*

The following information was drawn from the annual report of Sierra Home Builders (SHB).

	For the Years	
	2016	**2017**
IIncome Statement		
Revenues	$800,000	$960,000
Operating expenses	640,000	768,000
Income from continuing operations	160,000	192,000
*Extraordinary item—lottery win		72,000
Net income	$160,000	$264,000
Balance Sheet		
Assets	$1,161,000	$1,161,000
Liabilities	$ 264,000	$ -
Stockholders' equity:		
Common stock	501,000	501,000
Retained earnings	396,000	660,000
Total liabilities and stockholders' equity	$1,161,000	$1,161,000

*By definition, extraordinary items are not likely to recur in the future.

Required

a. Compute the percentage of growth in net income from 2016 to 2017. Can stockholders expect a similar increase between 2017 and 2018?

b. Assuming that SHB collected $264,000 cash from earnings (i.e., net income), explain how this money was spent in 2017.

c. Assuming that SHB experiences the same percentage of growth from 2017 to 2018 as it did from 2016 to 2017, determine the amount of income from continuing operations that the owners can expect to see on the 2018 income statement.

d. During 2018, SHB experienced a $60,000 loss due to storm damage (note that this would be shown as an extraordinary loss on the income statement). Liabilities and common stock were unchanged from 2017 to 2018. Use the information that you computed in Requirement *c* plus the additional information provided in the previous two sentences to prepare an income statement and balance sheet as of December 31, 2018.

ATC 1-5 Writing Assignment *Elements of financial statements defined*

Sam and his sister Blair both attend the state university. As a reward for their successful completion of the past year (Sam had a 3.2 GPA in business, and Blair had a 3.7 GPA in art), their father gave each of them 100 shares of The Walt Disney Company stock. They have just received their first annual report. Blair does not understand what the information means and has asked Sam to explain it to her. Sam is currently taking an accounting course, and she knows he will understand the financial statements.

Required

Assume that you are Sam. Write Blair a memo explaining the following financial statement items to her. In your explanation, describe each of the two financial statements and explain the financial information each contains. Also define each of the elements listed for each financial statement and explain what it means.

Balance Sheets
Assets
Liabilities
Stockholders' equity
Income Statements
Revenue
Expense
Net income

ATC 1-6 Ethical Dilemma *Loyalty versus the bottom line*

Assume that Kevin has been working for you for five years. He has had an excellent work history and has received generous pay raises in response. The raises have been so generous that Kevin is quite overpaid for the job he is required to perform. Unfortunately, he is not qualified to take on other, more responsible jobs available within the company. A recent job applicant is willing to accept a salary $5,000 per year less than the amount currently being paid to Kevin. The applicant is well qualified to take over Kevin's duties and has a very positive attitude. The following financial statements were reported by your company at the close of its most recent accounting period.

Required

a. Reconstruct the financial statements (shown below), assuming that Kevin was replaced at the beginning of the most recent accounting period. Both Kevin and his replacement are paid in cash. No other changes are to be considered.

b. Discuss the short- and long-term ramifications of replacing Kevin. There are no right answers. However, assume that you are required to make a decision. Use your judgment and common sense to support your choice.

Financial Statements

Income Statements		
Revenue		$ 57,000
Expense		(45,000)
Net income		$ 12,000
Statement of Changes in Stockholders' Equity		
Beginning common stock	$20,000	
Plus: stock issued	5,000	
Ending common stock		$ 25,000
Beginning retained earnings	50,000	
Net income	12,000	
Dividends	(2,000)	
Ending retained earnings		60,000
Total stockholders' equity		$ 85,000

continued

Balance Sheet		
Assets		
Cash		$85,000
Equity		
Common stock		$25,000
Retained earnings		60,000
Total stockholders' equity		$85,000
Statement of Cash Flows		
Operating activities		
Inflow from customers	$ 57,000	
Outflow to suppliers expenses	(45,000)	
Net inflow from operations		$12,000
Investing activities		0
Financing activities		
Inflow from stock issue	5,000	
Outflow for dividends	(2,000)	
Net inflow from financing activities		3,000
Net change in cash		15,000
Plus: beginning cash balance		70,000
Ending cash balance		$85,000

ATC 1-7 Research Assignment *Finding real-world accounting information*

This chapter introduced the basic four financial statements companies use annually to keep their stakeholders informed of their accomplishments and financial situation. Complete the requirements below using the most recent (20xx) financial statements available on the Sonic Drive-In's website. Obtain the statements on the Internet by following the steps below. (The formatting of the company's website may have changed since these instructions were written.)

1. Go to www.sonicdrivein.com.
2. Click on the "Corporate" link at the bottom of the page. (Most companies have a link titled "Investors relations" that leads to their financial statements; Sonic uses "Corporate'" instead.)
3. Click on the "INVESTORS" link at the top of the page.
4. Click on the "*20xx Annual Report*" link at the lower left side of the page.
5. Go to the company's financial statements that begin around page 30 of the annual report.

Required

a. What was the company's *net income* in each of the last 3 years?
b. What amount of total *assets* did the company have at the end of the most recent year?
c. How much *retained earnings* did the company have at the end of the most recent year?
d. For the most recent year, what was the company's *cash flow from operating activities, cash flow from investing activities*, and *cash flow from financing activities*?

ATC 1-8 Spreadsheet Assignment *Using Excel*

The financial statements for Simple Company are reported here using an Excel spreadsheet.

Required

Recreate the financial statements using your own Excel spreadsheet.

a. For each number with an arrow by it, enter a formula in that particular cell address to solve for the number shown. (Do not enter the arrow.)

b. When complete, print the spreadsheet with formulas rather than absolute numbers.

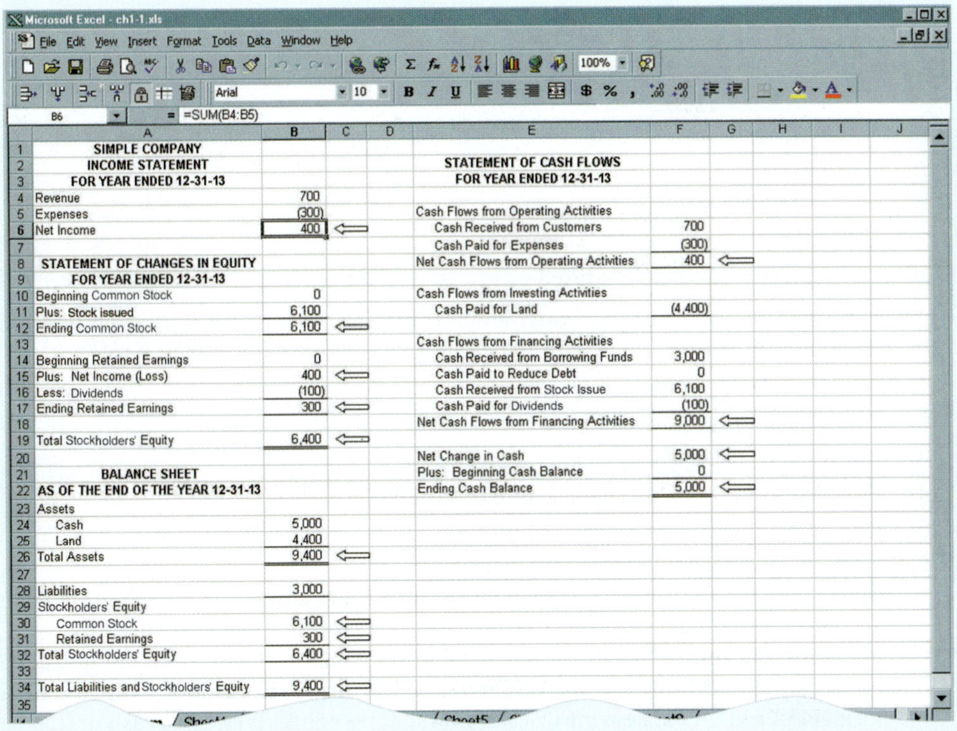

Microsoft Excel - ch1-1.xls

B6 = =SUM(B4:B5)

	A	B	C	D	E	F	G
1	SIMPLE COMPANY						
2	INCOME STATEMENT				STATEMENT OF CASH FLOWS		
3	FOR YEAR ENDED 12-31-13				FOR YEAR ENDED 12-31-13		
4	Revenue	700					
5	Expenses	(300)			Cash Flows from Operating Activities		
6	Net Income	400	⇐		Cash Received from Customers	700	
7					Cash Paid for Expenses	(300)	
8	STATEMENT OF CHANGES IN EQUITY				Net Cash Flows from Operating Activities	400	⇐
9	FOR YEAR ENDED 12-31-13						
10	Beginning Common Stock	0			Cash Flows from Investing Activities		
11	Plus: Stock issued	6,100			Cash Paid for Land	(4,400)	
12	Ending Common Stock	6,100	⇐				
13					Cash Flows from Financing Activities		
14	Beginning Retained Earnings	0			Cash Received from Borrowing Funds	3,000	
15	Plus: Net Income (Loss)	400	⇐		Cash Paid to Reduce Debt	0	
16	Less: Dividends	(100)			Cash Received from Stock Issue	6,100	
17	Ending Retained Earnings	300	⇐		Cash Paid for Dividends	(100)	
18					Net Cash Flows from Financing Activities	9,000	⇐
19	Total Stockholders' Equity	6,400	⇐				
20					Net Change in Cash	5,000	⇐
21	BALANCE SHEET				Plus: Beginning Cash Balance	0	
22	AS OF THE END OF THE YEAR 12-31-13				Ending Cash Balance	5,000	⇐
23	Assets						
24	Cash	5,000					
25	Land	4,400					
26	Total Assets	9,400	⇐				
27							
28	Liabilities	3,000					
29	Stockholders' Equity						
30	Common Stock	6,100	⇐				
31	Retained Earnings	300	⇐				
32	Total Stockholders' Equity	6,400	⇐				
33							
34	Total Liabilities and Stockholders' Equity	9,400	⇐				
35							

Spreadsheet Tips

(1) Widen a column by positioning the cursor on the vertical line between two column headings until cross-hairs appear. Either double click to automatically widen, or click and drag the crosshair to the desired width.

(2) Negative numbers can be parenthesized by choosing Format and then Cells. Under Number, choose Custom and under Type, choose the first option containing parentheses.

(3) The SUM function is one way to add a series of numbers. For example, the formula for net income in cell B6 is SUM(B4:B5).

(4) Single and double lines can be drawn using the Borders icon.

(5) Print a spreadsheet on one page by choosing File, Page Setup, and Fit to 1.

(6) Print without gridlines by choosing File, Page Setup, and Sheet and uncheck Gridlines. Another option is to choose Tools and Options and uncheck Gridlines.

(7) Print formulas by choosing Tools, Options, and Formulas.

ATC 1-9 Spreadsheet Assignment *Mastering Excel*

Required

a. Enter the following headings for the horizontal statements model onto a blank spreadsheet.

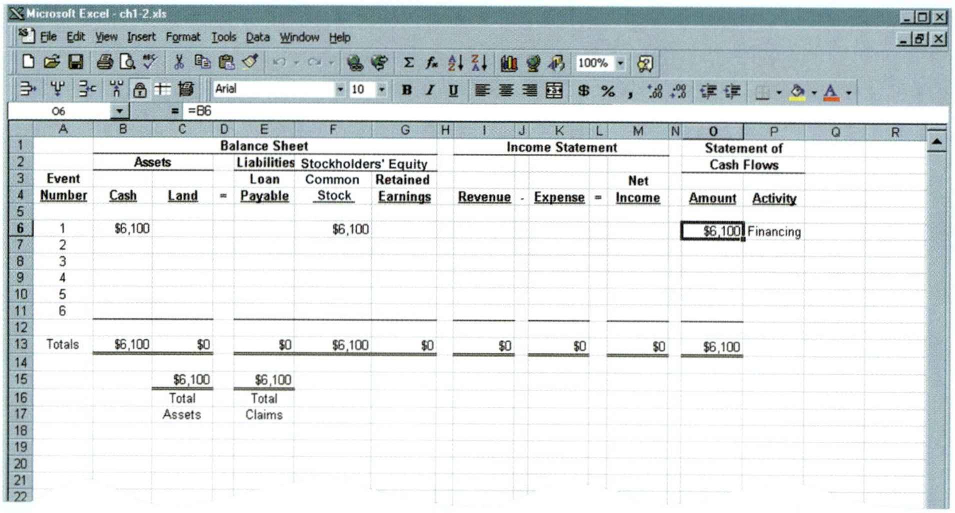

Event Number	Cash	Land	=	Loan Payable	Common Stock	Retained Earnings	Revenue	-	Expense	=	Net Income	Amount	Activity
1	$6,100				$6,100							$6,100	Financing
2													
3													
4													
5													
6													
Totals	$6,100	$0		$0	$6,100	$0	$0		$0		$0	$6,100	
		$6,100 Total Assets		$6,100 Total Claims									

b. Under the appropriate headings, record the effects of each of the following accounting events for the first month of operations. The first event has been recorded as an example.

(1) Acquired $6,100 from the issue of common stock.

(2) Paid $4,400 to purchase land.

(3) Borrowed $3,000 cash.

(4) Provided services to customers and received $700 in cash.

(5) Paid $300 for expenses.

(6) Paid a $100 dividend to the stockholders.

(*Note:* The amounts on the statement of cash flows can be referenced to the Cash account on the balance sheet. In other words, recording the cash amounts twice is not necessary. Instead, enter formulas in the Statement of Cash Flows column equating those cell addresses to the respective cell in the Cash column. Notice that the formula in cell O6 (statement of cash flows) is set equal to cell B6 (cash on the balance sheet). Once the formula is completed for cell O6, it can be easily copied to cells O7 through O11.)

c. Using formulas, sum each of the quantitative columns to arrive at the end-of-month amounts reported on the financial statements.

Spreadsheet Tips

(1) Center the heading *Balance Sheet* across columns by entering the entire heading in cell B1. Position the cursor on B1 until a fat cross appears. Click and drag the cursor across B1 through G1. Click on the Merge and Center icon (it is highlighted in the screen in the toolbar).

(2) Enter arithmetic signs as headings by placing an apostrophe in front of the sign. For example, to enter the equal sign in cell D4, enter '=.

(3) Copy cells by positioning the cursor in the bottom right corner of the cell to copy from (such as cell O6) until a thin cross appears. Click and drag the cursor down through the desired locations to copy to (through cell O11).

(4) To enter the dollar sign, choose Format, Cells, and Currency.

COMPREHENSIVE PROBLEM

The following information is available for Pacilio Security Services Inc. for 2011, its first year of operations. Pacilio provides security services for local sporting events.

The following summary transactions occurred during 2011:

1. Acquired $6,000 from the issue of common stock.
2. Borrowed $5,000 from the Small Business Government Agency. The loan is interest free.

3. Performed security services at local sporting events during the year for $9,000 cash.
4. Paid salaries expense of $3,000 for the year.
5. Purchased land for $4,000.
6. Paid other operating expenses of $2,000 for the year.
7. Paid a cash dividend to the shareholders of $2,500.
8. The market value of the land was determined to be $4,500 at December 31, 2011.

Required

a. Record the above transactions in an accounting equation. Provide the appropriate account titles for the amounts shown in the Retained Earnings column.

b. Prepare an income statement, statement of changes in stockholders' equity, balance sheet, and statement of cash flows for 2011.

CHAPTER 2

Accounting for Accruals and Deferrals

LEARNING OBJECTIVES

After you have mastered the material in this chapter, you will be able to:

SECTION 1: SHOW HOW ACCRUALS AFFECT FINANCIAL STATEMENTS

LO 2-1 Show how receivables affect financial statements.

LO 2-2 Show how payables affect financial statements.

LO 2-3 Prepare financial statements that include accruals.

LO 2-4 Explain the accounting cycle, including adjustments and the closing process.

SECTION 2: SHOW HOW DEFERRALS AFFECT FINANCIAL STATEMENTS

LO 2-5 Show how accounting for supplies affects financial statements.

LO 2-6 Show how accounting for prepaid items affects financial statements.

LO 2-7 Show how accounting for unearned revenues affects financial statements.

LO 2-8 Prepare financial statements that include deferrals.

LO 2-9 Classify accounting events into one of four categories.

LO 2-10 Discuss the primary components of corporate governance.

APPENDIX

LO 2-11 Compute depreciation expense and show how it affects financial statements.

LO 2-12 Compute interest expense and show how it affects financial statements.

Video lectures and accompanying self-assessment quizzes are available for all learning objectives through McGraw-Hill Connect® Plus Accounting.

SECTION 1:

ACCOUNTING FOR ACCRUALS

Users of financial statements must distinguish between the terms *recognition* and *realization.* **Recognition** means formally *reporting* an economic item or event in the financial statements. **Realization** refers to collecting money, generally from the sale of products or services. Companies may recognize (report) revenue in the income statement in a different accounting period from the period in which they collect the cash related to the revenue. Furthermore, companies frequently make cash payments for expenses in accounting periods other than the periods in which the expenses are recognized in the income statement.

To illustrate, assume Johnson Company provides services to customers in 2016 but collects cash for those services in 2017. In this case, realization occurs in 2017. When should Johnson recognize the services revenue?

Users of *cash basis* accounting recognize (report) revenues and expenses in the period in which cash is collected or paid. Under cash basis accounting, Johnson would recognize the revenue in 2017 when it collects the cash. In contrast, users of **accrual accounting** recognize revenues and expenses in the period in which they occur, regardless of when cash is collected or paid. Under accrual accounting, Johnson would recognize the revenue in 2016 (the period in which it performed the services) even though it doe s not collect (realize) the cash until 2017.

Accrual accounting is required by generally accepted accounting principles. Virtually all major companies operating in the United States use it. Its two distinguishing features are called *accruals* and *deferrals.*

- The term **accrual** describes a revenue or an expense event that is recognized *before* cash is exchanged. Johnson's recognition of revenue in 2016 related to cash realized in 2017 is an example of an accrual.
- The term **deferral** describes a revenue or an expense event that is recognized *after* cash has been exchanged. Suppose Johnson pays cash in 2016 to purchase office supplies it uses in 2017. In this case the cash payment occurs in 2016 although supplies expense is recognized in 2017. This is an example of a deferral.

The Curious Accountant

On September 15, 2016, Rachael Gross purchased a subscription to *Fitness* magazine for her sister's birthday. She paid $12 for a one-year subscription to the **Meredith Corporation**, the company that publishes *Fitness, American Baby, Better Homes and Gardens, The Ladies Home Journal,* and several other magazines. The company also owns 12 television stations. Rachael's sister will receive her first issue of the magazine in October.

How should Meredith Corporation account for the receipt of this cash? How would this event be reported on its December 31, 2016, financial statements? (Answer on page 92.)

ACCRUAL ACCOUNTING

LO 2-1

Show how receivables affect financial statements.

This section of the text describes seven events experienced by Cato Consultants, a training services company that uses accrual accounting. Recall that in a double-entry accounting system every event affects at least two ledger accounts. At the end of the accounting period the information that has been collected in the ledger accounts is used to prepare financial statements. We analyze the events in this chapter by first identifying the two accounts affected by each event. Next we show how the changes in the two accounts affect the accounting equation. Finally, we show how the event affects the financial statements.

EVENT 1 **Cato Consultants was started on January 1, 2016, when it acquired $5,000 cash by issuing common stock.**

This event increases the company's asset account (cash) and its stockholders' equity account (common stock). The effects of this event on the accounting equation are shown here:

Assets	=	Liabilities	+	Stockholders' Equity
Cash				Common Stock
5,000	=	NA	+	5,000

The issue of stock for cash is an **asset source transaction.** On the balance sheet assets and stockholders' equity increase. The transaction does not affect the income statement. Since the company is being financed by acquiring cash from the owners, the cash inflow is classified as a financing activity (FA). These effects are shown in the following financial statements model:

Balance Sheet							Income Statement					Statement of Cash Flows
Assets	=	Liab.	+	C. Stk.	+	R. Earn.	Rev.	−	Exp.	=	Net Inc.	
5,000	=	NA	+	5,000	+	NA	NA	−	NA	=	NA	5,000 FA

Accounting for Accounts Receivable

EVENT 2 **During 2016 Cato Consultants provided $84,000 of consulting services to its clients. Cato has completed the work and sent bills to the clients, but has not yet collected any cash. This type of transaction is frequently described as providing services *on account*.**

Accrual accounting requires companies to recognize revenue in the period in which the work is done regardless of when cash is collected. In this case, revenue is recognized in 2016 even though cash has not been realized (collected). Recall that revenue is an economic benefit (an increase in assets) that results from providing goods and services to customers. The specific asset that increases is called **Accounts Receivable.** The balance in Accounts Receivable represents the amount of cash the company expects to collect in the future. The effects on the accounting equation are as follows:

Assets	=	Liabilities	+	Stockholders' Equity
Accounts Receivable				Revenue
84,000	=	NA	+	84,000

Since the revenue recognition causes assets (accounts receivable) to increase, it is classified as an asset source transaction. On the balance sheet assets and stockholders' equity increase. The increase in revenue increases net income and ultimately retained earnings. The collection of cash will be realized in the future. Since cash was not collected or paid, the statement of cash flows is not affected for this event. The effects on the financial statements are shown in the following financial statements model:

Balance Sheet								Income Statement					Statement of Cash Flows
Assets	=	Liab.	+	C. Stk.	+	R. Earn.		Rev.	−	Exp.	=	Net Inc.	
84,000	=	NA	+	NA	+	84,000		84,000	−	NA	=	84,000	NA

EVENT 3 **Cato collected $60,000 cash from customers in partial settlement of its accounts receivable.**

This event causes one asset account (cash) to increase and another asset account (accounts receivable) to decrease. The effect of the collection of receivables on the accounting equation is as follows:

Assets		=	Liabilities	+	Stockholders' Equity
Cash	Accounts Receivable				
60,000	(60,000)	=	NA	+	NA

The collection of an account receivable is an **asset exchange transaction.** The amount of total assets is not affected. Notice that the company does not recognize revenue when the cash is collected. Remember that the revenue was recognized when the work was done (see Event 2). Revenue would be double counted if it were recognized again when the cash is collected. Accordingly, this event does not affect the income statement. Since the cash collection was derived from normal business operations, it is classified as an operating activity (OA). The effects on the financial statements are shown in the following financial statements model:

Balance Sheet								Income Statement					Statement of Cash Flows
Assets	=	Liab.	+	C. Stk.	+	R. Earn.		Rev.	−	Exp.	=	Net Inc.	
NA	=	NA	+	NA	+	NA		NA	−	NA	=	NA	60,000 OA

Other Events

EVENT 4 **Cato paid an instructor a $10,000 cash salary for teaching courses.**

This event causes a decrease in the asset account Cash. Recognizing salary expense causes a corresponding decrease in stockholders' equity. The effects on the accounting equation are as follows:

Assets	=	Liabilities	+	Stockholders' Equity
Cash				Salary Expense
(10,000)	=	NA	+	(10,000)

Cash payment for salary expense is an **asset use transaction**. On the balance sheet assets and stockholders' equity decrease. Recognizing the expense decreases net income on the income statement and ultimately retained earnings on the balance sheet. Since Cato paid cash for a normal operating expense, the statement of cash flows reflects a cash outflow from operating activities (OA). The effects on the financial statements are shown in the following financial statements model:

Balance Sheet							Income Statement					Statement of Cash Flows
Assets	=	Liab.	+	C. Stk.	+	R. Earn.	Rev.	−	Exp.	=	Net Inc.	
(10,000)	=	NA	+	NA	+	(10,000)	NA	−	10,000	=	(10,000)	(10,000) OA

EVENT 5 **Cato paid $2,000 cash for advertising costs. The advertisements appeared in 2016.**

The event causes the asset account Cash to decrease. Recognizing advertising expense causes a corresponding decrease in stockholders' equity. The effects on the accounting equation are as follows:

Assets	=	Liabilities	+	Stockholders' Equity
Cash				Advertising Expense
(2000)	=	NA	+	(2,000)

The cash payment for advertising expense is an asset use transaction. On the balance sheet assets and stockholders' equity decrease. Recognizing the expense decreases net income on the income statement and ultimately retained earnings on the balance sheet. Since Cato paid cash for a normal operating expense, the statement of cash flows reflects a cash outflow from operating activities. The effects on the financial statements are as follows:

Balance Sheet							Income Statement					Statement of Cash Flows
Assets	=	Liab.	+	C. Stk.	+	R. Earn.	Rev.	−	Exp.	=	Net Inc.	
(2,000)	=	NA	+	NA	+	(2,000)	NA	−	2,000	=	(2,000)	(2,000) OA

LO 2-2

Show how payables affect financial statements.

Accounting for Accrued Salary Expense (Year-End Adjusting Entry)

Accrual accounting requires that companies recognize expenses in the period in which they are incurred regardless of when cash is paid. As a result, expenses may be recognized before cash is paid. For example, Cato must recognize an expense for all of the work its employees performed in 2016 even if the employees are not paid until 2017. Expenses that are recognized before cash is paid are called **accrued expenses**. The accounting for Event 6 illustrates the effect of recognizing accrued salary expense.

EVENT 6 At the end of 2016 Cato recorded accrued salary expense of $6,000. The salary expense is for courses the instructor taught in 2016. However, Cato will not pay the instructor cash until 2017.

As of December 31, 2016, Cato has an unrecorded salary expense. Also on this date, Cato has an unrecorded liability. In other words, on December 31, 2016, Cato has an obligation to pay the instructor $6,000 in 2017. Accordingly, Cato must update its ledger account balances prior to using them to prepare the financial statements. The entry required to update the account balances is called an **adjusting entry**. The effect of the adjustment for accrued salary expense on the accounting equation is as follows:

Assets	=	Liabilities	+	Stockholders' Equity
Cash		Salaries payable		Salary Expense
NA	=	6,000	+	(6,000)

Recognizing accrued expense is a **claims exchange transaction.** The claims of creditors increase and the claims of stockholders decrease. Total claims remain unchanged. Specifically, the liability account **Salaries Payable** increases. The balance in the Salaries Payable account represents the amount of cash the company is obligated to pay the instructor in the future. Also, recognizing salary expense decreases net income and ultimately retained earnings. Since cash was not paid or collected, there is no impact on the statement of cash flows. The effect of recognizing accrued salary expense on the financial statements is as follows:

Balance Sheet									Income Statement					Statement of Cash Flows
Assets	=	Liab.	+	C. Stk.	+	R. Earn.			Rev.	−	Exp.	=	Net Inc.	
NA	=	6,000	+	NA	+	(6,000)			NA	−	6,000	=	(6,000)	NA

Expenses were previously defined as assets consumed in the process of generating revenue. However, in this case Cato's adjusting entry to recognize accrued salaries expense is not directly related to the use of assets. Instead of a decrease in assets, Cato recorded an increase in liabilities (salaries payable). *An* **expense** *can therefore be more broadly defined as an economic sacrifice (a decrease in assets or an increase in liabilities) resulting from operating activities undertaken to generate revenue.*

Also, be careful not to confuse liabilities with expenses. Although liabilities may increase when a company recognizes expenses, liabilities are *not* expenses. Liabilities are obligations. They can arise from acquiring assets as well as recognizing expenses. For example, when a business borrows money from a bank, it recognizes an increase in assets (cash) and liabilities (notes payable). However, in this case the increase in liabilities is not related to the recognition of expenses.

EVENT 7 During 2016 Cato signed contracts for $42,000 of consulting services to be performed in 2017.

The $42,000 for consulting services to be performed in 2017 is not recognized in the 2016 financial statements. Revenue is recognized for work actually completed, not work expected to be completed. This event does not affect any of the financial statements.

CHECK YOURSELF 2.1

During 2016, Anwar Company earned $345,000 of revenue on account and collected $320,000 cash from accounts receivable. Anwar paid cash expenses of $300,000 and cash dividends of $12,000. Determine the amount of net income Anwar should report on the 2016 income statement and the amount of cash flow from operating activities Anwar should report on the 2016 statement of cash flows.

Answer Net income is $45,000 ($345,000 revenue − $300,000 expenses). The cash flow from operating activities is $20,000, the amount of revenue collected in cash from customers (accounts receivable) minus the cash paid for expenses ($320,000 − $300,000). Dividend payments are classified as financing activities and do not affect the determination of either net income or cash flow from operating activities.

Summary of Events and General Ledger

The previous section of this chapter described seven events Cato Consultants experienced during the 2016 accounting period. These events and their effects on the accounting equation and the associated general ledger accounts are shown in Exhibit 2.1. Since the balances in the accounts reflect the company's financial condition immediately after the adjusting entry has been recorded, they are called the *adjusted ledger account* balances. The information in these accounts is used to prepare the financial statements.

Vertical Statements Model

LO 2-3

Prepare financial statements that include accruals.

The financial statements for Cato Consultants' 2016 accounting period are represented in a vertical statements model in Exhibit 2.2. A vertical statements model arranges a set of financial statement information vertically on a single page. Like horizontal statements models, vertical statements models are learning tools. They illustrate interrelationships among financial statements. The models do not, however, portray the full, formal presentation formats companies use in published financial statements. For example, statements models may use summarized formats with abbreviated titles and dates. As you read the following explanations of each financial statement, trace the color-coded financial data from Exhibit 2.1 to Exhibit 2.2.

Income Statement

The income statement reflects accrual accounting. Recall that accrual accounting recognizes revenue in the accounting period in which it is earned even when the associated cash is collected (realized) in a subsequent accounting period. In this case, the 2016 income statement shows $84,000 of consulting revenue even though Cato has received only $60,000 cash from its customers in 2016. Similarly, expenses include all sacrifices incurred to produce revenue regardless of whether cash has been paid. In this case, the 2016 income statement includes $6,000 of salary expense even though Cato will not pay cash for these expenses until 2017. These accrual reporting practices will cause differences between the amount of *net income* shown on the income statement and the amount of *cash flow from operating activities* shown on the statement of cash flows. Detailed comparisons are shown later.

Statement of Changes in Stockholders' Equity

The statement of changes in stockholders' equity explains the change in the amount of stockholders' equity that occurred during the 2016 accounting period. In this case total stockholders' equity increased from a beginning balance of zero to an ending balance of $71,000. The issue of stock explains $5,000 of the increase. The remaining $66,000 was caused by earnings.

EXHIBIT 2.1

Cato Consultants, Summary of Events and General Ledger

Panel 1 Transaction Data for 2016

1	Cato Consultants acquired $5,000 cash by issuing common stock.
2	Cato provided $84,000 of consulting services on account.
3	Cato collected $60,000 cash from customers in partial settlement of its accounts receivable.
4	Cato paid $10,000 cash for salary expense.
5	Cato paid $2,000 cash for 2016 advertising costs.
6	Cato recognized $6,000 of accrued salary expense.
7	Cato signed contracts for $42,000 of consulting services to be performed in 2017.

Panel 2 Accounting Equation

	Assets			=	Liabilities	+	Stockholders' Equity			
Event No.	**Cash**	**+**	**Accounts Receivable**	**=**	**Salaries Payable**	**+**	**Common Stock**	**+**	**Retained Earnings**	**Other Account Titles**
Beg. bal.	0		0		0		0		0	
1	5,000						5,000			
2			84,000						84,000	Consulting revenue
3	60,000		(60,000)							
4	(10,000)								(10,000)	Salary expense
5	(2,000)								(2,000)	Advertising expense
6					6,000				(6,000)	Salary Expense
End bal.	53,000	+	24,000	=	6,000	+	5,000	+	66,000	

Panel 3 General Ledger Accounts

Assets = Liabilities + Stockholders' Equity

Assets

Cash

Bal.	0
(1)	5,000
(3)	60,000
(4)	(10,000)
(5)	(2,000)
Bal.	(53,000)

Accounts Receivable

(2)	84,000
(3)	(60,000)
Bal.	24,000

Liabilities

Salaries Payable

(6) Adj.	6,000
Bal.	6,000

Stockholders' Equity

Common Stock

Bal.	0
(1)	5,000
Bal.	5,000

Retained Earnings

Bal.	0

Consulting Revenue

(2)	84,000
Bal.	84,000

Salary Expense

(4)	(10,000)
(6) Adj.	(6,000)
Bal.	(16,000)

Advertising Expense

(5)	(2,000)
Bal.	(2,000)

Balance Sheet

The balance sheet discloses an entity's assets, liabilities, and stockholders' equity at a particular point in time. As of December 31, 2016, Cato Consultants had total assets of $77,000 ($53,000 cash + $24,000 accounts receivable). These assets are equal to the obligations and commitments Cato has to its creditors and investors. Specifically, Cato has a $6,000 obligation (liability) to creditors, with the remaining $71,000 of assets available to support commitments (stockholders' equity) to stockholders.

EXHIBIT 2.2 Vertical Statements Model

CATO CONSULTANTS
Financial Statements*
Income Statement
For the Year Ended December 31, 2016

Consulting revenue		$84,000
Salary expense		(16,000)
Advertising expense		(2,000)
Net income		$66,000

Statement of Changes in Stockholders' Equity
For the Year Ended December 31, 2016

Beginning common stock	$ 0	
Plus: Common stock issued	5,000	
Ending common stock		$ 5,000
Beginning retained earnings	0	
Plus: Net income	66,000	
Less: Dividends	0	
Ending retained earnings		66,000
Total stockholders' equity		$71,000

Balance Sheet
As of December 31, 2016

Assets		
Cash	$53,000	
Accounts receivable	24,000	
Total assets		$77,000
Liabilities		
Salaries payable		$ 6,000
Stockholders' equity		
Common stock	$ 5,000	
Retained earnings	66,000	
Total stockholders' equity		71,000
Total liabilities and stockholders' equity		$77,000

Statement of Cash Flows
For the Year Ended December 31, 2016

Cash flows from operating activities		
Cash receipts from customers	$60,000	
Cash payment for salary expense	(10,000)	
Cash payment for advertising expense	(2,000)	
Net cash flow from operating activities		$48,000
Cash flow from investing activities		0
Cash flows from financing activities		
Cash receipt from issuing common stock	5,000	
Net cash flow from financing activities		5,000
Net change in cash		53,000
Plus: Beginning cash balance		0
Ending cash balance		$53,000

*In real-world annual reports, financial statements are normally presented separately with appropriate descriptions of the date to indicate whether the statement applies to the entire accounting period or a specific point in time.

Statement of Cash Flows

The statement of cash flows explains the change in cash from the beginning to the end of the accounting period. It can be prepared by analyzing the Cash account. Since Cato Consultants was established in 2016, its beginning cash balance was zero. By the end of the year, the cash balance was $53,000. The statement of cash flows explains this increase. The Cash account increased because Cato collected $60,000 from customers and decreased because Cato paid $12,000 for expenses. As a result, Cato's net cash inflow from operating activities was $48,000. Also, the business acquired $5,000 cash through the financing activity of issuing common stock, for a cumulative cash increase of $53,000 ($48,000 + $5,000) during 2016.

Comparing Cash Flow from Operating Activities with Net Income

The amount of net income measured using accrual accounting differs from the amount of cash flow from operating activities. For Cato Consulting in 2016, the differences are summarized below.

	Accrual Accounting	Cash Flow
Consulting revenue	$84,000	$60,000
Salary expense	(16,000)	(10,000)
Advertising expense	(2,000)	(2,000)
Net income	$66,000	$48,000

Many students begin their first accounting class with the misconception that revenue and expense items are cash equivalents. The Cato illustration demonstrates that a company may recognize a revenue or expense without a corresponding cash collection or payment in the same accounting period.

The Closing Process

LO 2-4

Explain the accounting cycle, including adjustments and the closing process.

Recall that the temporary accounts (revenue, expense, and dividends) are closed prior to the start of the next accounting cycle. Exhibit 2.3 shows the 2016 closing entries and the after-closing general ledger account balances. To reinforce your understanding of the closing process you should trace the closing entries to the ledger accounts.

After the 2016 year-end closing the Consulting Revenue and Salary Expense accounts have a zero balance. These temporary accounts are now ready to capture the revenue and expense information for the 2017 accounting period. At the end of 2017 they will be closed again. This process will continue for every accounting cycle throughout the life of the business. In other words, the revenue and expense accounts hold information temporarily (for a single accounting period), thereby facilitating the preparation of the annual statements. While not included in this illustration, the Dividend account has these same temporary properties. Notice that after closing, the balance in the Retained Earnings account is equal to the amount shown in the year-end balance sheet. This equality affirms the fact that all temporary accounts have been closed correctly.

Steps in an Accounting Cycle

An accounting cycle, which is represented graphically in Exhibit 2.4, involves several steps. The four steps identified to this point are (1) recording transactions; (2) adjusting the accounts; (3) preparing financial statements; and (4) closing the temporary accounts. The first step occurs continually throughout the accounting period. Steps 2, 3, and 4 normally occur at the end of the accounting period.

The Matching Concept

Cash basis accounting can distort reported net income because it sometimes fails to match expenses with the revenues they produce. To illustrate, consider the $6,000 of accrued salary expense that Cato Consultants recognized at the end of 2016. The instructor's teaching produced revenue in 2016. If Cato waited until 2017 (when it paid the instructor) to

EXHIBIT 2.3

Cato Corporation, 2016 Closing Process

Panel 1 Closing Entries

C1 Transfers the balance from the Consulting Revenue account to the Retained Earnings account.
C2 Transfers the balance from the Salary Expense account to the Retained Earnings account.
C3 Transfers the balance from the Advertising Expense account to the Retained Earnings account.

Panel 2 General Ledger Accounts after Closing

Assets = Liabilities + Permanent Equity + Temporary Equity

Assets

Cash	
Bal.	0
(1)	5,000
(3)	60,000
(4)	(10,000)
(5)	(2,000)
Bal.	(53,000)

Accounts Receivable	
(2)	84,000
(3)	(60,000)
Bal.	24,000

Liabilities

Salaries Payable	
(6) Adj.	6,000
Bal.	6,000

Permanent Equity

Common Stock	
Bal.	0
(1)	5,000
Bal.	5,000

Retained Earnings	
Bal.	0
Cl. 1	84,000
Cl. 2	(16,000)
Cl. 3	(2,000)
Bal.	66,000

Temporary Equity

Consulting Revenue	
(2)	84,000
Bal.	84,000
Cl.1	(84,000)
Bal.	0

Salary Expense	
(4)	(10,000)
(6) Adj.	(6,000)
Bal.	(16,000)
Cl. 2	16,000
Bal.	0

Advertising Expense	
(5)	(2,000)
Bal.	(2,000)
Cl. 3	2,000
Bal.	0

EXHIBIT 2.4

The Accounting Cycle

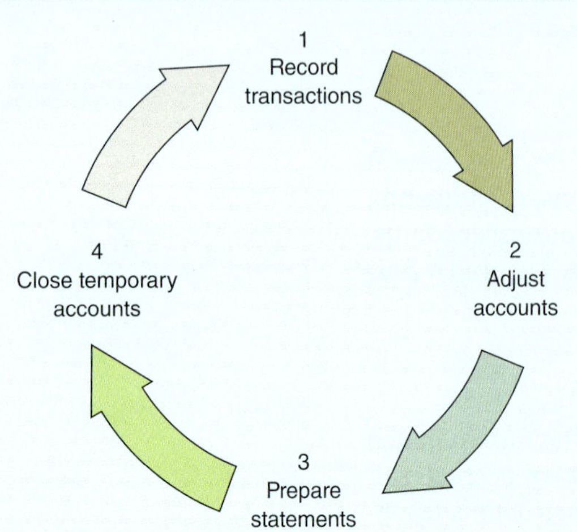

recognize $6,000 of the total $16,000 salary expense, then $6,000 of the expense would not be matched with the revenue it generated. By using accrual accounting, Cato recognized all the salary expense in the same accounting period in which the consulting revenue was recognized. A primary goal of accrual accounting is to appropriately match expenses with revenues, the **matching concept.**

Appropriately matching expenses with revenues can be difficult even when using accrual accounting. For example, consider Cato's advertising expense. Money spent on advertising may generate revenue in future accounting periods as well as in the current period. A prospective customer could save an advertising brochure for several years before calling Cato for training services. It is difficult to know when and to what extent advertising produces revenue. When the connection between an expense and the corresponding revenue is vague, accountants commonly match the expense with the period in which it is incurred. Cato matched (recognized) the entire $2,000 of advertising cost with the 2016 accounting period even though some of that cost might generate revenue in future accounting periods. Expenses that are matched with the period in which they are incurred are frequently called **period costs.**

Matching is not perfect. Although it would be more accurate to match expenses with revenues than with periods, there is sometimes no obvious direct connection between expenses and revenue. Accountants must exercise judgment to select the accounting period in which to recognize revenues and expenses. The concept of conservatism influences such judgment calls.

The Conservatism Principle

When faced with a recognition dilemma, **conservatism** guides accountants to select the alternative that produces the lowest amount of net income. In uncertain circumstances, accountants tend to delay revenue recognition and accelerate expense recognition. The conservatism principle holds that it is better to understate net income than to overstate it. If subsequent developments suggest that net income should have been higher, investors will respond more favorably than if they learn it was really lower. This practice explains why Cato recognized all of the advertising cost as expense in 2016 even though some of that cost may generate revenue in future accounting periods.

SECTION 2:

ACCOUNTING FOR DEFERRALS

As previously discussed, cash may be exchanged before revenue or expense is recognized. In this case the business defers recognition. This section introduces three common deferrals.

SECOND ACCOUNTING CYCLE

The effects of Cato Consultants's 2017 events are as follows:

EVENT 1 **Cato pays \$6,000 to the instructor to settle the salaries payable obligation.**

Cash payments to creditors are asset use transactions. When Cato pays the instructor, both the asset account Cash and the liability account Salaries Payable decrease. The effects on the accounting equation are as follows:

Assets	=	Liabilities	+	Stockholders' Equity
Cash		Salaries Payable		
(6,000)	=	(6,000)	+	NA

The event is an asset use transaction. It does not affect the income statement. The salary expense was recognized in 2016 when the instructor taught the classes. Since the cash was paid for salaries of employees that operate the business, the cash outflow is classified as an operating activity. The effects on the financial statements are shown in the following financial statements model.

Balance Sheet									Income Statement					Statement of Cash Flows
Assets	=	Liab.	+	C. Stk.	+	R. Earn.			Rev.	−	Exp.	=	Net Inc.	
(6,000)	=	(6,000)	+	NA	+	NA			NA	−	NA	=	NA	(6,000) OA

Accounting for Supplies Purchase

EVENT 2 **Cato purchases $800 of supplies on account.**

LO 2-5

Show how accounting for supplies affects financial statements.

The purchase of supplies on account is an asset source transaction. The asset account Supplies and the liability account Accounts Payable increase. The effects of this transaction on the accounting equation are shown here:

Assets	=	Liabilities	+	Stockholders' Equity
Supplies		Accounts Payable		
800	=	800	+	NA

Note that this event does not affect the income statement. Expense recognition is deferred until the supplies are used. Also, the statement of cash flows is not affected because the company did not spend cash to purchase the supplies. These effects are shown in the following financial statements model:

Balance Sheet									Income Statement					Statement of Cash Flows
Assets	=	Liab.	+	C. Stk.	+	R. Earn.			Rev.	−	Exp.	=	Net Inc.	
800	=	800	+	NA	+	NA			NA	−	NA	=	NA	NA

Year-End Adjustment

ADJ.1 **After determining through a physical count that it has $150 of unused supplies on hand as of December 31, Cato recognizes supplies expense.**

If a company were to attempt to record supplies expense each time a pencil, piece of paper, envelope, or other supply item were used, the cost of such tedious recordkeeping would far outweigh its benefits. Instead, accountants transfer to expense the total cost of all supplies used during the entire accounting period in a single year-end adjusting entry. The cost of supplies used is determined as follows:

Beginning balance of supplies	0
Plus: Supplies purchases	800
Supplies available for use	800
Less: Ending balance of supplies	(150)
Supplies used	650

Recognizing Cato's supplies expense is an asset use transaction. The asset account Supplies and the stockholders' equity account Retained Earnings decrease. The effects of this transaction on the accounting equation are shown here:

Assets	=	Liabilities	+	Stockholders' Equity
Supplies				Supplies Expense
(650)	=	NA	+	(650)

The recognition of supplies expense would cause the amount of net income shown on the income statement to decrease. Since the expense recognition did not involve the payment of cash, the statement of cash flows is not affected.

Balance Sheet									Income Statement					Statement of Cash Flows
Assets	=	Liab.	+	C. Stk.	+	R. Earn.			Rev.	−	Exp.	=	Net Inc.	
(650)	=	NA	+	NA	+	(650)			NA	−	650	=	(650)	NA

CHECK YOURSELF 2.2

Treadmore Company started the 2016 accounting period with $580 of supplies on hand. During 2016 the company paid cash to purchase $2,200 of supplies. A physical count of supplies indicated that there were $420 of supplies on hand at the end of 2016. Treadmore pays cash for supplies at the time they are purchased. Based on this information alone, determine the amount of supplies expense to be recognized on the income statement and the amount of cash flow to be shown in the operating activities section of the statement of cash flows.

Answer The amount of supplies expense recognized on the income statement is the amount of supplies that were used during the accounting period. This amount is computed below:

$580 Beginning balance + $2,200 Supplies purchases = $2,780 Supplies available for use
$2,780 Supplies available for use − $420 Ending supplies balance = $2,360 Supplies used

The cash flow from operating activities is the amount of cash paid for supplies during the accounting period. In this case, Treadmore paid $2,200 cash to purchase supplies. This amount would be shown as a cash outflow.

Accounting for Prepaid Items

EVENT 3 **On March 1, Cato pays $12,000 cash to lease office space for one year beginning immediately.**

LO 2-6

Show how accounting for prepaid items affects financial statements.

Accrual accounting draws a distinction between the terms cost and expense. A **cost** might be either an asset or an expense. If a company has already consumed a purchased resource in the process of earning revenue, the cost of the resource is an expense. For example, companies normally pay for electricity the month after using it. The cost of electric utilities is therefore usually recorded as an expense. In contrast, if a company purchases a resource it will use in the future to generate revenue, the cost of the resource represents an asset. Accountants record such a cost in an asset account and defer recognizing an expense until the resource has been used to produce revenue. Deferring the expense recognition provides more accurate matching of revenues and expenses.

The cost of the office space described in Event 3 is an asset. It is recorded in the asset account Prepaid Rent. Cato expects to benefit from incurring this cost by using the office to generate revenue over the next 12 months. Expense recognition is deferred until Cato actually uses the office space to help generate revenue. Other commonly deferred expenses include prepaid insurance and prepaid taxes. As these titles imply, deferred expenses are frequently called **prepaid items**. Exhibit 2.5 illustrates the relationship between costs, assets, and expenses.

EXHIBIT 2.5

Relationship between Costs, Assets, and Expenses

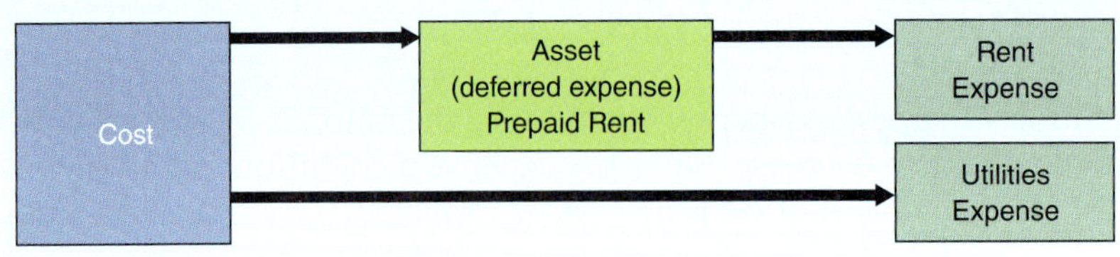

Purchasing prepaid rent is an asset exchange transaction. The asset account Cash decreases and the asset account Prepaid Rent increases. The effect on the accounting equation is as follows:

Assets		=	Liabilities	+	Stockholders' Equity
Cash	Prepaid Rent				
(12,000)	12,000	=	NA	+	NA

This is an asset exchange event. The amount of total assets is not affected. Note that this event does not affect the income statement. Expense recognition is deferred until the office space is used. Since the cash outflow was incurred to purchase prepaid rent (a short-term asset) that will be used to operate the business, it is classified as an operating activity on the statement of cash flows. The effects of this transaction on the financial statements are shown here:

Balance Sheet								Income Statement					Statement of Cash Flows
Assets	=	Liab.	+	C. Stk.	+	R. Earn.		Rev.	−	Exp.	=	Net Inc.	
NA	=	NA	+	NA	+	NA		NA	−	NA	=	NA	(12,000) OA

Year-End Adjustment

ADJ.2 Cato recognizes rent expense for the office space used during the 2017 accounting period.

At the end of 2017 Cato is required to expense the amount of office space that has been used. Recall that Cato paid $12,000 on March 1, 2017, to rent office space for one year (see Event 3). The portion of the lease cost that represents using office space from March 1 through December 31 is computed as follows:

$12,000 Cost of annual lease ÷ 12 Months = $1,000 Cost per month

$1,000 Cost per month × 10 Months used = $10,000 Rent expense

Recognizing the rent expense decreases the asset account Prepaid Rent and the amount of stockholders' equity. The effects on the accounting equation are as follows:

Assets	=	Liabilities	+	Stockholders' Equity
Prepaid Rent				Rent Expense
(10,000)	=	NA	+	(10,000)

The expense reduces net income shown on the income statement and ultimately the amount of stockholders' equity (retained earnings) shown on the balance sheet. The statement of cash flows is not affected. Recall that the cash flow effect was recorded in Event 3. The effects on the financial statements are as follows:

Balance Sheet									Income Statement					Statement of Cash Flows
Assets	=	Liab.	+	C. Stk.	+	R. Earn.			Rev.	−	Exp.	=	Net Inc.	
(10,000)	=	NA	+	NA	+	(10,000)			NA	−	10,000	=	(10,000)	NA

Note that while $12,000 cash was paid for rent, only $10,000 of that amount is recognized as an expense in 2017. The deferral of the additional $2,000 causes a difference between the amounts of cash flow from operating activities versus the amount of net income reported in 2017.

CHECK YOURSELF 2.3

Rujoub Inc. paid $18,000 cash for one year of insurance coverage that began on November 1, 2016. Based on this information alone, determine the cash flow from operating activities that Rujoub would report on the 2016 and 2017 statements of cash flows. Also, determine the amount of insurance expense Rujoub would report on the 2016 income statement and the amount of prepaid insurance (an asset) that Rujoub would report on the December 31, 2016, balance sheet.

Answer Since Rujoub paid all of the cash in 2016, the 2016 statement of cash flows would report an $18,000 cash outflow from operating activities. The 2017 statement of cash flows would report zero cash flow from operating activities. The expense would be recognized in the periods in which the insurance is used. In this case, insurance expense is recognized at the rate of $1,500 per month ($18,000 ÷ 12 months). Rujoub used two months of insurance coverage in 2016 and therefore would report $3,000 (2 months × $1,500) of insurance expense on the 2016 income statement. Rujoub would report a $15,000 (10 months × $1,500) asset, prepaid insurance, on the December 31, 2016, balance sheet. The $15,000 of prepaid insurance would be recognized as insurance expense in 2017 when the insurance coverage is used.

Accounting for Receipt of Unearned Revenue

EVENT 4 Cato receives $18,000 cash in advance from Westberry Company for consulting services Cato agrees to perform over a one-year period beginning June 1, 2017.

Cato must defer (delay) recognizing any revenue until it performs the consulting services (does the work) for Westberry. From Cato's point of view, the deferred revenue is a liability because Cato is obligated to perform services in the future. The liability is called **unearned revenue**. The asset account Cash and the liability account Unearned Revenue both increase. The effects on the accounting equation are shown as follows:

LO 2-7

Show how accounting for unearned revenues affects financial statements.

Assets	=	Liabilities	+	Stockholders' Equity
Cash		Unearned Revenue		
18,000	=	18,000	+	NA

The cash receipt is an asset source transaction. Collecting the cash has no effect on the income statement. The revenue will be reported on the income statement after Cato performs the services. The statement of cash flows reflects a cash inflow from operating activities. The effects of this transaction on the financial statements are shown here:

Balance Sheet								Income Statement					Statement of Cash Flows
Assets	=	Liab.	+	C. Stk.	+	R. Earn.		Rev.	−	Exp.	=	Net Inc.	
18,000	=	18,000	+	NA	+	NA		NA	−	NA	=	NA	18,000 OA

Year-End Adjustment

ADJ. 3 Cato recognizes the portion of the unearned revenue it earned during the accounting period.

The $18,000 cash advance requires Cato to provide consulting services from June 1, 2017, to May 31, 2018. By December 31, Cato has earned 7 months (June 1 through December 31) of the revenue related to this contract. Rather than recording the revenue continuously as the consulting services are being performed, Cato can simply recognize the amount earned in a single adjustment to the accounting records *at the end of the accounting period*. The amount of the adjustment is computed as follows:

$18,000 ÷ 12 months = $1,500 revenue earned per month

$1,500 × 7 months = $10,500 revenue to be recognized in 2017

The adjusting entry moves $10,500 from the liability Unearned Revenue account to the Consulting Revenue account. The effects on the accounting equation are as follows:

Assets	=	Liabilities	+	Stockholders' Equity
		Unearned Revenue		Consulting Revenue
NA	=	(10,500)	+	10,500

This adjusting entry is a claims exchange event. Assets are not affected. On the balance sheet the liabilities decrease and stockholders' equity (retained earnings) increases. Cash flow is not affected by the adjustment. Recall that the impact on cash occurred previously when Cato received the cash from Westberry in Event 4. The effects of this transaction on the financial statements are as follows:

Balance Sheet								Income Statement					Statement of Cash Flows
Assets	=	Liab.	+	C. Stk.	+	R. Earn.		Rev.	−	Exp.	=	Net Inc.	
NA	=	(10,500)	+	NA	+	10,500		10,500	−	NA	=	10,500	NA

Recall that revenue was previously defined as an economic benefit a company obtains by providing customers with goods and services. In this case the economic benefit is a decrease in the liability account Unearned Revenue. **Revenue** can therefore be more precisely defined as *an increase in assets or a decrease in liabilities that a company obtains by providing customers with goods or services.*

CHECK YOURSELF 2.4

Sanderson & Associates received a $24,000 cash advance as a retainer to provide legal services to a client. The contract called for Sanderson to render services during a one-year period beginning October 1, 2016. Based on this information alone, determine the cash flow from operating activities Sanderson would report on the 2016 and 2017 statements of cash flows. Also determine the amount of revenue Sanderson would report on the 2016 and 2017 income statements.

Answer Since Sanderson collected all of the cash in 2016, the 2016 statement of cash flows would report a $24,000 cash inflow from operating activities. The 2017 statement of cash flows would report zero cash flow from operating activities. Revenue is recognized in the period in which it is earned. In this case revenue is earned at the rate of $2,000 per month ($24,000 ÷ 12 months = $2,000 per month). Sanderson rendered services for three months in 2016 and nine months in 2017. Sanderson would report $6,000 (3 months × $2,000) of revenue on the 2016 income statement and $18,000 (9 months × $2,000) of revenue on the 2017 income statement.

Other 2017 Events

Cato also experienced the events described below during 2017. The effects of these types of events on the accounting equation and the financial statements have been covered in previous sections of Chapters 1 and 2 and will not be repeated here. However the transaction data have been recorded in the general ledger accounts shown in Exhibit 2.6. To confirm your understanding you should trace each transaction to the appropriate ledger accounts. The information in the ledger accounts has been labeled with the event or adjusting entry number to simplify the tracing process.

EVENT 5 **provided $96,400 of consulting services on account.**

EVENT 6 **collected $105,000 cash from customers as partial settlement of accounts receivable.**

EVENT 7 **paid $32,000 cash for salary expense.**

EVENT 8 **incurred $21,000 of other operating expenses on account.**

EVENT 9 **paid $18,200 in partial settlement of accounts payable.**

EVENT 10 **paid $79,500 to purchase land it planned to use in the future as a building site for its home office.**

EVENT 11 **paid $21,000 in cash dividends to its stockholders.**

EVENT 12 **acquired $2,000 cash from issuing additional shares of common stock.**

ADJ. 4 **recognized $4,000 of accrued salary expense.**

Summary of Events and General Ledger

The twelve events and four adjusting entries Cato Consultants experienced during 2017 are summarized in Exhibit 2.6. Recall that all adjustments are made at the end of the accounting period so that all account balances are updated prior to their use in preparing the financial statements. Notice that the 2017 beginning balances shown in the general ledger accounts are derived from the 2016 ending balances shown in Exhibit 2.3. Likewise, the 2017 ending balances will become the 2018 beginning balances. However, the Revenue, Expense, and Dividend account balances do not carry forward because they are designed to capture transaction data for a single accounting period. Therefore, the balances in these accounts are transferred to the Retained Earnings account at the end of the accounting period through the closing process. Prior to closing, the balances in the ledger accounts shown in Exhibit 2.6 are used to prepare the 2017 financial statements shown in Exhibit 2.7.

EXHIBIT 2.6

Ledger Accounts with 2017 Transaction Data

1. Cato paid $6,000 to the instructor to settle the salaries payable obligation.
2. Cato purchased $800 of supplies on account.
3. On March 1, Cato paid $12,000 cash to lease office space for one year.
4. Cato received $18,000 cash in advance from Westberry Company for consulting services to be performed for one year beginning June 1.
5. Cato provided $96,400 of consulting services on account.
6. Cato collected $105,000 cash from customers as partial settlement of accounts receivable.
7. Cato paid $32,000 cash for salary expense.
8. Cato incurred $21,000 of other operating expenses on account.
9. Cato paid $18,200 in partial settlement of accounts payable.
10. Cato paid $79,500 to purchase land it planned to use in the future as a building site for its home office.
11. Cato paid $21,000 in cash dividends to its stockholders.
12. Cato acquired $2,000 cash from issuing additional shares of common stock.

The year-end adjustments are:

Adj. 1 After determining through a physical count that it had $150 of unused supplies on hand as of December 31, Cato recognized supplies expense.

Adj. 2 Cato recognized rent expense for the office space used during the accounting period.

Adj. 3 Cato recognized the portion of the unearned revenue it earned during the accounting period.

Adj. 4 Cato recognized $4,000 of accrued salary expense.

Assets = Liabilities + Stockholders' Equity

Assets

Cash	
Bal.	53,000
(1)	(6,000)
(3)	(12,000)
(4)	18,000
(6)	105,000
(7)	(32,000)
(9)	(18,200)
(10)	(79,500)
(11)	(21,000)
(12)	2,000
Bal.	9,300

Accounts Receivable	
Bal.	24,000
(5)	96,400
(6)	(105,000)
Bal.	15,400

Supplies	
Bal.	0
(2)	800
Adj. 1	(650)
Bal.	150

Prepaid Rent	
Bal.	0
(3)	12,000
Adj. 2	(10,000)
Bal.	2,000

Land	
Bal.	0
(10)	79,500
Bal.	79,500

Liabilities

Accounts Payable	
Bal.	0
(2)	800
(8)	21,000
(9)	(18,200)
Bal.	3,600

Unearned Revenue	
Bal.	0
(4)	18,000
Adj. 3	(10,500)
Bal.	7,500

Salaries Payable	
Bal.	6,000
(1)	(6,000)
Adj. 4	4,000
Bal.	4,000

Stockholders' Equity

Common Stock	
Bal.	5,000
(12)	2,000
Bal.	7,000

Retained Earnings	
Bal.	66,000

Dividends	
Bal.	0
(11)	(21,000)
Bal.	(21,000)

Consulting Revenue	
Bal.	0
(5)	96,400
Adj. 3	10,500
Bal.	106,900

Other Operating Expenses	
Bal.	0
(8)	(21,000)
Bal.	(21,000)

Salary Expense	
Bal.	0
(7)	(32,000)
Adj. 4	(4,000)
Bal.	(36,000)

Rent Expense	
Bal.	0
Adj. 2	(10,000)
Bal.	(10,000)

Supplies Expense	
Bal.	0
Adj. 1	(650)
Bal.	(650)

EXHIBIT 2.7 Vertical Statements Model

CATO CONSULTANTS
Financial Statements
Income Statements
For the Years Ended December 31

	2016	2017
Consulting revenue	$84,000	$106,900
Operating expenses	(18,000)	(67,650)
Net income	$66,000	$ 39,250

Statements of Changes in Stockholders' Equity
For the Years Ended December 31

	2016	2017
Beginning common stock	$ 0	$ 5,000
Plus: Common stock issued	5,000	2,000
Ending common stock	5,000	7,000
Beginning retained earnings	0	66,000
Plus: Net income	66,000	39,250
Less: Dividends	0	(21,000)
Ending retained earnings	66,000	84,250
Total stockholders' equity	$71,000	$ 91,250

Balance Sheets
As of December 31

	2016	2017
Assets		
Cash	$53,000	$ 9,300
Accounts receivable	24,000	15,400
Supplies	0	150
Prepaid rent	0	2,000
Land	0	79,500
Total assets	$77,000	$106,350
Liabilities		
Accounts payable	$ 0	$ 3,600
Unearned revenue	0	7,500
Salaries payable	6,000	4,000
Total liabilities	6,000	15,100
Stockholders' equity		
Common stock	5,000	7,000
Retained earnings	66,000	84,250
Total stockholders' equity	71,000	91,250
Total liabilities and stockholders' equity	$77,000	$106,350

continued

EXHIBIT 2.7 *Concluded*

Statements of Cash Flows
For the Years Ended December 31

	2016	2017
Cash Flows from Operating Activities		
Cash receipts from customers	$60,000	$123,000
Cash payments for operating expenses	(12,000)	(68,200)
Net cash flow from operating activities	48,000	54,800
Cash Flows from Investing Activities		
Cash payment to purchase land	0	(79,500)
Cash Flows from Financing Activities		
Cash receipts from issuing common stock	5,000	2,000
Cash payments for dividends	0	(21,000)
Net cash flow from financing activities	5,000	(19,000)
Net change in cash	53,000	(43,700)
Plus: Beginning cash balance	0	53,000
Ending cash balance	$53,000	$ 9,300

Vertical Statements Model

LO 2-8

Prepare financial statements that include deferrals.

Financial statement users obtain helpful insights by analyzing company trends over multiple accounting cycles. Exhibit 2.7 presents for Cato Consultants a multicycle **vertical statements model** of 2016 and 2017 accounting data. To conserve space, we have combined all the expenses for each year into single amounts labeled "Operating Expenses," determined as follows:

	2016	2017
Other operating expenses	$ 0	$21,000
Salary expense	16,000	36,000
Rent expense	0	10,000
Advertising expense	2,000	0
Supplies expense	0	650
Total operating expenses	$18,000	$67,650

Similarly, we combined the cash payments for operating expenses on the statement of cash flows as follows:

	2016	2017
Supplies and other operating expenses	$ 0	$18,200*
Salary expense	10,000	38,000
Rent expense	0	12,000
Advertising expense	2,000	0
Total cash payments for operating expenses	$12,000	$68,200

*Amount paid in partial settlement of accounts payable

Recall that the level of detail reported in financial statements depends on user information needs. Most real-world companies combine many account balances together to report highly summarized totals under each financial statement caption. Before reading further, trace the remaining financial statement items from the ledger accounts in Exhibit 2.6 to where they are reported in Exhibit 2.7.

The vertical statements model in Exhibit 2.7 shows significant interrelationships among the financial statements. For each year, trace the amount of net income from the income statement to the statement of changes in stockholders' equity. Next, trace the ending balances of common stock and retained earnings reported on the statement of changes in stockholders' equity to the stockholders' equity section of the balance sheet. Also, confirm that the amount of cash reported on the balance sheet equals the ending cash balance on the statement of cash flows.

Other relationships connect the two accounting periods. For example, trace the ending retained earnings balance from the 2016 statement of stockholders' equity to the beginning retained earnings balance on the 2017 statement of stockholders' equity. Also, trace the ending cash balance on the 2016 statement of cash flows to the beginning cash balance on the 2017 statement of cash flows. Finally, confirm that the change in cash between the 2016 and 2017 balance sheets ($53,000 − $9,300 = $43,700 decrease) agrees with the net change in cash reported on the 2016 statement of cash flows.

Closing for the 2017 Accounting Period

At the end of the 2017 accounting period the Revenue, Expense, and Dividend accounts would be closed to the Retained Earnings Account. After the closing entries are posted, the balance in the Retained Earnings account is $84,250, which is equal to the amount of retained earnings shown on the 2017 balance sheet. The after-closing balances in the Revenue, Expense, and Dividend accounts will be zero, which makes them ready to capture information that pertains only to the 2018 accounting period.

REALITY BYTES

WHY DID THAT BIG EXPENSE CAUSE THE STOCK PRICE TO RISE?

If you follow business news, which you should if you are a business major, you have probably heard about a company reporting a big write-off of assets, sometimes called a "special charge." Such an announcement sends a signal to readers that the company's earnings will decrease as a result of the write-off. However, in many cases, this seemingly bad news does not cause the company's stock price to fall; in fact, it sometimes causes it to increase. Why?

There are at least a couple of reasons for this seeming contradiction. First, while write-offs do decrease earnings, they often do not decrease the companies' cash flows, and cash flow is at least as important to investors as earnings. Consider the following August 6, 2012, announcement from Johnson & Johnson (J&J), the large pharmaceutical company: "The Company expects to record an after-tax, non-cash special item related to in-process research and development consisting of a net charge to earnings of between $300 and $400 million in the third quarter of 2012 related to the discontinuation of the phase 3 clinical development of bapineuzumab IV . . . " The next day the price of the company's stock rose slightly. By the end of the year, J&J had recorded special charges totaling $3.5 billion, but $2.1 billion of these did not decrease cash flows in 2012, as the assets written off had been purchased in prior years. Despite this bad news, J&J's stock price rose 6.4 percent during 2012.

The second reason that writing off assets can have a positive effect on a company's stock price is because extra expenses that are recognized today may mean there will be less expenses recognized in the future; thus, future earnings will be higher than they otherwise would have been. This subject will be explained further in later chapters, but keep in mind that investors are more interested in the future than they are in the past, so lower current earnings that lead to higher future earnings is often viewed as good news.

So, when you hear a company make a big announcement about its business, always ask yourself two questions: How does this event affect cash flows? And, how will this event affect future earnings?

Answers to The Curious Accountant

Because the Meredith Corporation receives cash from customers before actually sending any magazines to them, the company has not earned any revenue when it receives the cash. Meredith has a liability called *unearned revenue.* If Meredith closed its books on December 31, then $3 of Rachael's subscription would be recognized as revenue in 2016. The remaining $9 would appear on the balance sheet as a liability.

Meredith actually ends its accounting year on June 30 each year. The actual June 30, 2013, balance sheet for the company is presented in Exhibit 2.8. The liability for unearned revenue was $355.2 million ($191.4 + $163.8)—which represented about 27.6 percent of total liabilities!

Will Meredith need cash to pay these subscription liabilities? Not exactly. The liabilities will not be paid directly with cash. Instead, they will be satisfied by providing magazines to the subscribers. However, Meredith will need cash to pay for producing and distributing the magazines supplied to the customers. Even so, the amount of cash required to provide magazines will probably differ significantly from the amount of unearned revenues. In most cases, subscription fees do not cover the cost of producing and distributing magazines. By collecting significant amounts of advertising revenue, publishers can provide magazines to customers at prices well below the cost of publication. The amount of unearned revenue is not likely to coincide with the amount of cash needed to cover the cost of satisfying the company's obligation to produce and distribute magazines. Even though the association between unearned revenues and the cost of providing magazines to customers is not direct, a knowledgeable financial analyst can use the information to make estimates of future cash flows and revenue recognition.

EXHIBIT 2.8 Balance Sheet for Meredith Corporation

MEREDITH CORPORATION AND SUBSIDIARIES
Consolidated Balance Sheets
As of June 30 (amounts in thousands)

	2013	2012
Assets		
Current assets		
Cash and cash equivalents	$ 27,674	$ 25,820
Accounts receivable		
(net of allowances of $10,559 in 2013 and $13,436 in 2012)	232,305	215,526
Inventories	28,386	22,559
Current portion of subscription acquisition costs	97,982	75,446
Current portion of broadcast rights	2,831	3,408
Other current assets	18,514	16,677
Total current assets	407,692	359,436
Property, plant, and equipment		
Land	20,318	19,517
Buildings and improvements	131,653	129,688
Machinery and equipment	295,476	290,866
Leasehold improvements	14,815	14,816
Construction in progress	1,993	384
Total property, plant, and equipment	464,255	455,271
Less accumulated depreciation	(277,938)	(260,967)
Net property, plant, and equipment	186,317	194,304

continued

EXHIBIT 2.8 *Concluded*

MEREDITH CORPORATION AND SUBSIDIARIES
Consolidated Balance Sheets
As of June 30 (amounts in thousands)

	2013	2012
Subscription acquisition costs	99,433	75,368
Broadcast rights	3,634	943
Other assets	69,848	66,858
Intangible assets, net	584,281	586,263
Goodwill	788,854	733,127
Total assets	$2,140,059	$2,016,299
Liabilities and Shareholders' Equity		
Current liabilities		
Current portion of long-term debt	$ 50,000	$ 105,000
Current portion of long-term broadcast rights payable	4,089	6,752
Accounts payable	78,458	72,911
Accrued expenses		
Compensation and benefits	56,030	52,402
Distribution expenses	12,505	12,029
Other taxes and expenses	64,141	52,640
Total accrued expenses	132,676	117,071
Current portion of unearned subscription revenues	**191,448**	**180,852**
Total current liabilities	456,671	482,586
Long-term debt	300,000	275,000
Long-term broadcast rights payable	5,096	3,695
Unearned subscription revenues	**163,809**	**141,408**
Deferred income taxes	247,487	204,054
Other noncurrent liabilities	112,700	112,111
Total liabilities	1,285,763	1,218,854
Shareholders' equity		
Series preferred stock, par value $1 per share	–	–
Common stock, par value $1 per share	36,242	35,791
Class B stock, par value $1 per share, convertible to common stock	8,324	8,716
Additional paid-in capital	50,170	53,275
Retained earnings	775,901	722,778
Accumulated other comprehensive income (loss)	(16,341)	(23,115)
Total shareholders' equity	854,296	797,445
Total liabilities and shareholders' equity	$2,140,059	$2,016,299

TRANSACTION CLASSIFICATION

LO 2-9

Classify accounting events into one of four categories.

Chapters 1 and 2 introduced four types of transactions. Although businesses engage in an infinite number of different transactions, all transactions fall into one of four types. By learning to identify transactions by type, you can understand how unfamiliar events affect financial statements. The four types of transactions are

1. *Asset source transactions:* An asset account increases, and a corresponding claims account increases.
2. *Asset use transactions:* An asset account decreases, and a corresponding claims account decreases.
3. *Asset exchange transactions:* One asset account increases, and another asset account decreases.
4. *Claims exchange transactions:* One claims account increases, and another claims account decreases.

CORPORATE GOVERNANCE

THE FINANCIAL ANALYST

Corporate governance is the set of relationships between the board of directors, management, shareholders, auditors, and other stakeholders that determine how a company is operated. Clearly, financial analysts are keenly interested in these relationships. This section discusses the key components of corporate governance.

Importance of Ethics

LO 2-10

Discuss the primary components of corporate governance.

The accountant's role in society requires trust and credibility. Accounting information is worthless if the accountant is not trustworthy. Similarly, tax and consulting advice is useless if it comes from an incompetent person. The high ethical standards required by the profession state "a certified public accountant assumes an obligation of self-discipline above and beyond requirements of laws and regulations." The **American Institute of Certified Public Accountants** (AICPA) requires its members to comply with the **Code of Professional Conduct.** The preface of the Code includes six Principles of Professional Conduct that are summarized in Exhibit 2.9. The importance of ethical conduct is universally recognized across a broad spectrum of accounting organizations. The Institute of Management Accountants requires its members to follow a set of Standards of Ethical Conduct. The Institute of Internal Auditors also requires its members to subscribe to the organization's Code of Ethics.

EXHIBIT 2.9

Principles of Professional Conduct: AICPA Code of Professional Conduct

Responsibilities Principle
In carrying out their responsibilities as professionals, members should exercise sensitive professional and moral judgments in all their activities.

The Public Interest Principle
Members should accept the obligation to act in a way that will serve the public interest, honor the public trust, and demonstrate commitment to professionalism.

Integrity Principle
To maintain and broaden public confidence, members should perform all professional responsibilities with the highest sense of integrity.

Objectivity and Independence Principle
A member should maintain objectivity and be free of conflicts of interest in discharging professional responsibilities. A member in public practice should be independent in fact and appearance when providing auditing and other attestation services.

Due Care Principle
A member should observe the profession's technical and ethical standards, strive continually to improve competence and the quality of services, and discharge professional responsibility to the best of the member's ability.

Scope and Nature of Services Principle
A member in public practice should observe the Principles of the Code of Professional Conduct in determining the scope and nature of services to be provided.

Sarbanes-Oxley Act

Credible financial reporting relies on a system of checks and balances. Corporate management is responsible for preparing financial reports while outside, independent accountants (CPAs) audit the reports. The massive surprise bankruptcies of Enron in late

2001 and WorldCom several months later suggested major audit failures on the part of the independent auditors. An audit failure means a company's auditor does not detect, or fails to report, that the company's financial reports are not in compliance with GAAP. The audit failures at Enron, WorldCom, and others prompted Congress to pass the Sarbanes-Oxley Act (SOX).

Prior to SOX, independent auditors often provided nonaudit services, such as installing computer systems, for their audit clients. The fees they earned for these services sometimes greatly exceeded the fees charged for the audit itself. This practice had been questioned prior to the audit failures at Enron and WorldCom. Critics felt the independent audit firm was subject to pressure from the company to conduct a less rigorous audit or risk losing lucrative nonaudit work. To strengthen the audit function, SOX included the following provisions:

- Prior to the enactment of SOX, independent auditors were self-regulated by the membership of the American Institute of Certified Public Accountants and by state boards of accountancy. Beyond self-regulation, SOX established the Public Company Accounting Oversight Board (PCAOB) to regulate accounting professionals that audit the financial statements of public companies.
- Independent auditors must register with the PCAOB or cease all participation in public company audits and abide by the board's pronouncements.
- The PCAOB has the responsibility to conduct inspections of registered firms. To ensure enforcement, the board has a full range of sanctions at its disposal, including suspension or revocation of registration, censure, and significant fines.
- To reduce the likelihood of conflicts of interest, SOX prohibits all registered public accounting firms from providing audit clients, contemporaneously with the audit, certain nonaudit services, including internal audit outsourcing, financial-information-system design and implementation services, and expert services.
- SOX provides significant corporate governance reforms regarding audit committees and their relationship to the auditor, making the audit committee responsible for the appointment, compensation, and oversight of the issuer's auditor.

Other provisions of SOX clarify the legal responsibility that company management has for a company's financial reports. The company's chief executive officer (CEO) and chief financial officer (CFO) must certify in writing that they have reviewed the financial reports being issued and that the reports present fairly the company's financial status. An executive who falsely certifies the company's financial reports is subject to a fine up to $5 million and imprisonment up to 20 years.

Common Features of Criminal and Ethical Misconduct

Unfortunately, it takes more than a code of conduct to stop fraud. People frequently engage in activities that they know are unethical or even criminal. The auditing profession has identified three elements that are typically present when fraud occurs, including:

1. The availability of an opportunity.
2. The existence of some form of pressure leading to an incentive.
3. The capacity to rationalize.

The three elements are frequently arranged in the shape of a triangle as shown in Exhibit 2.10.

Opportunity is shown at the top of the triangle because without opportunity fraud could not exist. The most effective way to reduce opportunities for ethical or criminal misconduct is to implement an effective set of internal controls. **Internal controls** are policies and procedures that a business implements to reduce opportunities for fraud and to assure that its objectives will be accomplished. Specific controls are tailored to meet the individual needs of particular businesses. For example, banks use elaborate vaults to protect cash and safety deposit boxes, but universities have little use for this

EXHIBIT 2.10

The Fraud Triangle

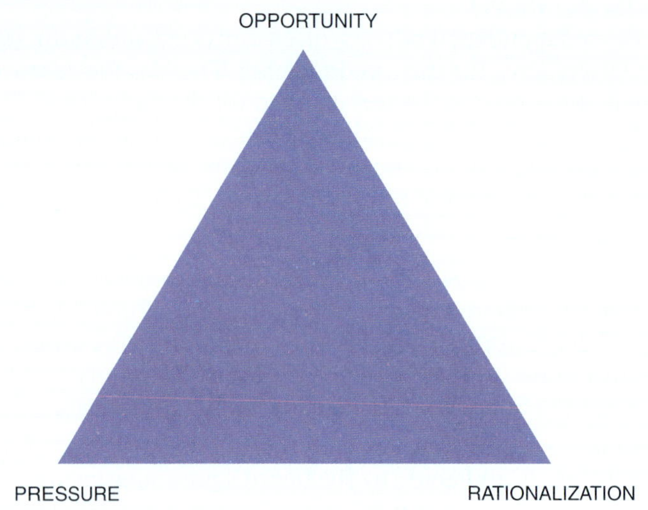

type of equipment. Even so, many of the same procedures are used by a wide variety of businesses. The internal control policies and procedures that have gained widespread acceptance are discussed in a subsequent chapter.

Only a few employees turn to the dark side even when internal control is weak and opportunities abound. So, what causes one person to commit fraud and another to remain honest? The second element of the fraud triangle recognizes **pressure** as a key ingredient of misconduct. A manager who is told "either make the numbers or you are fired" is more likely to cheat than one who is told to "tell it like it is." Pressure can come from a variety of sources, including:

- Personal vices such as drug addiction, gambling, and promiscuity.
- Intimidation from superiors.
- Personal debt from credit cards, consumer and mortgage loans, or poor investments.
- Family expectations to provide a standard of living that is beyond one's capabilities.
- Business failure caused by poor decision making or temporary factors such as a poor economy.
- Loyalty or trying to be agreeable.

The third and final element of the fraud triangle is **rationalization.** Few individuals think of themselves as evil. They develop rationalizations to justify their misconduct. Common rationalizations include the following:

- Everybody does it.
- They are not paying me enough. I'm only taking what I deserve.
- I'm only borrowing the money. I'll pay it back.
- The company can afford it. Look what they are paying the officers.
- I'm taking what my family needs to live like everyone else.

Most people are able to resist pressure and the tendency to rationalize ethical or legal misconduct. However, some people will yield to temptation. What can accountants do to protect themselves and their companies from unscrupulous characters? The answer lies in personal integrity. The best indicator of personal integrity is past performance. Accordingly, companies must exercise due care in performing appropriate background investigations before hiring people to fill positions of trust.

Ethical misconduct is a serious offense in the accounting profession. A single mistake can destroy an accounting career. If you commit a white-collar crime, you normally lose the opportunity to hold a white-collar job. Second chances are rarely granted; it is extremely important that you learn how to recognize and avoid the common features of ethical misconduct. To help you prepare for the real-world situations you are likely to encounter, we include ethical dilemmas in the end-of-chapter materials. When working with these dilemmas, try to identify the (1) opportunity, (2) pressure, and (3) rationalization associated with the particular ethical situation described. If you are not an ethical person, accounting is not the career for you.

A Look Back <<

This chapter introduced the *accrual accounting* concept. Accrual accounting causes the amount of revenues and expenses reported on the income statement to differ significantly from the amount of cash flow from operating activities reported on the statement of cash flows because of timing differences. These differences are readily apparent when relevant events are recorded in a horizontal financial statements model. To review, study the following transactions and the corresponding statements model. Set up a statements model on a piece of paper and try to record the effects of each event before reading the explanation.

Events

1. Provided $600 of services on account.
2. Collected $400 cash from accounts receivable.
3. Accrued $350 of salary expense.
4. Paid $225 cash in partial settlement of salaries payable.

Event No.	Balance Sheet							Income Statement					Statement of Cash Flows
	Cash	+	Accts. Rec.	=	Sal. Pay.	+	Ret. Earn.	Rev.	–	Exp.	=	Net Inc.	
1	NA	+	600	=	NA	+	600	600	–	NA	=	600	NA
2	400	+	(400)	=	NA	+	NA	NA	–	NA	=	NA	400 OA
3	NA	+	NA	=	350	+	(350)	NA	–	350	=	(350)	NA
4	(225)	+	NA	=	(225)	+	NA	NA	–	NA	=	NA	(225) OA
Totals	175	+	200	=	125	+	250	600	–	350	=	250	175 NC

Notice the $250 of net income differs from the $175 cash flow from operating activities. The entries in the statements model demonstrate the reasons for the difference. Although $600 of revenue is recognized, only $400 of cash was collected. The remaining $200 will be collected in the future and is currently shown on the balance sheet as Accounts Receivable. Also, although $350 of salary expense is recognized, only $225 was paid in cash. The remaining $125 will be paid in the future. This obligation is shown as Salaries Payable on the balance sheet. Study these relationships carefully to develop a clear understanding of how accrual accounting affects financial reporting.

Also, the definitions of revenue and expense have been expanded. The complete definitions of these two elements are as follows:

1. **Revenue:** Revenue is the *economic benefit* derived from operating the business. Its recognition is accompanied by an increase in assets or a decrease in liabilities resulting from providing products or services to customers.

2. **Expense:** An expense is an *economic sacrifice* incurred in the process of generating revenue. Its recognition is accompanied by a decrease in assets or an increase in liabilities resulting from consuming assets and services in an effort to produce revenue.

Finally, this chapter introduced the issues surrounding corporate governance. Codes of ethics, the relevant provisions of Sarbanes-Oxley, and the fraud triangle are discussed.

>> A Look Forward

To this point, we have used plus and minus signs to illustrate the effects of business events on financial statements. In real businesses, so many transactions occur that recording them with simple mathematical notations is impractical. In practice, accountants usually maintain records using a system of rules known as *double-entry bookkeeping.* Chapter 3 introduces the basic components of this bookkeeping system. You will learn how to record business events using a debit/credit format. You will be introduced to ledgers, journals, and trial balances. When you finish Chapter 3, you will have a clear understanding of how accountants maintain records of business activity.

APPENDIX

Companies frequently purchase assets that are used for several years. These assets are frequently called long-term assets. Also, companies incur liabilities that require the computation of interest. Accounting for these issues is introduced in this appendix. A more detailed discussion of these subjects will be included in subsequent chapters.

Accounting Events for 2016

Assume that on January 1, 2016, Libby Company had beginning balances of $43,000 in its Cash and Retained Earnings accounts. During 2016 Libby experienced the following transactions:

EVENT 1 **On January 1, 2016, Libby paid $43,000 cash to purchase a forklift.**

Libby expected to rent the forklift to its customers during the coming four years and then to sell the used forklift for $3,000. The expected period of use is commonly called the **useful life.** The amount Libby expects to receive from the sale of the asset at the end of its useful life is called the **salvage value.**

The purchase of the forklift is an asset exchange transaction. The balance in the Cash account decreases and the balance in a new asset account called Forklift increases. The purchase does not affect the income statement. Since the asset has a long-term useful life, the cash outflow necessary to buy the asset is an investing activity. The effects of the purchase on the financial statements are shown here:

Assets			=	Liab.	+	Equity						
Cash	+	Forklift	=				Rev.	−	Exp.	=	Net Inc.	Cash Flow
(43,000)	+	43,000	=	NA	+	NA	NA	−	NA	=	NA	(43,000) IA

EVENT 2 **On February 1, 2016, Libby borrowed $5,000 cash from the State Bank.**

As evidence of the debt, Libby issues a promissory note that describes the company's obligations to the bank. The note stipulates a one-year term and an annual interest rate of 6 percent. Issuing the note is an asset source transaction. The asset account Cash increases and a new liability account called Notes Payable increases. The income statement is not affected. The statement of cash flows shows a $5,000 cash inflow from financing activities. The effects on the financial statements are shown here:

Assets			=	Liab.	+	Equity						Cash Flow
Cash	+	Forklift	=	Note Payable			Rev.	−	Exp.	=	Net Inc.	Cash Flow
5,000	+	NA	=	5,000	+	NA	NA	−	NA	=	NA	5,000 FA

EVENT 3 **During 2016 Libby earned $16,000 cash by renting the forklift to its customers.**

The effects of this event on the financial statements are shown here:

Assets			=	Liab.	+	Equity						
Cash	+	Forklift	=			Retained Earnings	Rev.	−	Exp.	=	Net Inc.	Cash Flow
16,000	+	NA	=	NA	+	16,000	16,000	−	NA	=	16,000	16,000 OA

EVENT 4 **On December 31, 2016, Libby adjusts its accounts to recognize the expense of using the forklift during 2016.**

LO 2-11

Compute depreciation expense and show how it affects financial statements.

To measure the net economic benefit of running the business, Libby must estimate how much of the cost of the forklift it used in the process of earning revenue. Recall that the forklift has a four-year useful life and a $3,000 salvage value. Since the salvage value is expected to be recovered at the end of the forklift's useful life, only $40,000 ($43,000 cost − $3,000 salvage) worth of the forklift is ultimately expected to be used. Assuming the forklift is used evenly over its four-year life, it is logical to allocate an equal amount of the $40,000 to expense each year the forklift is used. The allocation is computed as follows:

(Asset cost − Salvage value)/Useful life = Depreciation expense
($43,000 − $3,000) / 4 years = $10,000 per year

As indicated above, the portion of the cost that represents the use of the asset is commonly called **depreciation expense.** The method of computing the depreciation expense that is described above is called **straight-line depreciation.** Recognizing depreciation expense is an asset use transaction. Assets and equity decrease. On the income statement, expenses increase and net income decreases. There are no cash flow consequences. Recall that the cash outflow occurred at the time the asset was purchased. There is no cash flow when the expense is recognized. The effects on the financial statements are shown here:

Assets			=	Liab.	+	Equity						
Cash	+	Book Value of Forklift	=			Retained Earnings	Rev.	−	Exp.	=	Net Inc.	Cash Flow
NA	+	(10,000)	=	NA	+	(10,000)	NA	−	10,000	=	(10,000)	NA

The asset account, Forklift, is not decreased directly. Instead, the asset reduction is recorded in a contra asset account called Accumulated Depreciation. This approach is used because it increases the usefulness of the information. The book value of the asset is the difference between the balances in the Forklift account and the related Accumulated Depreciation account as follows:

Forklift	$43,000
Accumulated Depreciation	(10,000)
Book Value	$33,000

The book value may also be called the **carrying value.** On the balance sheet the book value of the asset is added to the other asset account balances to determine the total amount of assets.

Depreciation expense is recognized each year the forklift is used. Like other expense accounts, the Depreciation Expense account is a temporary account that is closed to retained earnings at the end of each accounting cycle. In other words, each year $10,000 is recognized in the Depreciation Expense account and then closed to the Retained Earnings account. In this case, the Depreciation Expense account will be $10,000 each year.

In contrast, the Accumulated Depreciation account is a permanent account. As its name implies, the total amount in the Accumulated Depreciation account increases (accumulates) each time depreciation expense is recognized. For example, at the end of 2017, Libby will recognize $10,000 of depreciation expense and the balance in the Accumulated Depreciation account will increase to $20,000. At the end of 2018, Libby will recognize $10,000 of depreciation expense and the balance in the Accumulated Depreciation account will increase to $30,000, and so on.

EVENT 5 On December 31, 2016, Libby adjusts its books to recognize the amount of interest expense incurred during 2016.

LO 2-12

Compute interest expense and show how it affects financial statements.

Recall that Libby borrowed $5,000 on February 1, 2016. As a result, Libby owes the bank interest for the eleven months the loan was outstanding during the year. The accrued interest is $275 ($5,000 × .06 × 11/12). The adjusting entry is a claims exchange event. The liability account Interest Payable increases, and the equity account Retained Earnings decreases. The income statement would report interest expense. However, there is no effect on cash flow because the actual cash payment for interest will be made on the maturity date in 2017. The effects on the financial statements are shown here:

Assets			=	Liab.	+	Equity						
Cash	+	Forklift	=	Interest Payable	+	Retained Earnings	Rev.	−	Exp.	=	Net Inc.	Cash Flow
NA	+	NA	=	275	+	(275)	NA	−	275	=	(275)	NA

The events experienced by Libby during 2016 are summarized in Exhibit 2.11.

EXHIBIT 2.11

Transaction Data Recorded in Accounts

		Assets			=	Liabilities			+	Equity	
Event No.		Cash	+	Forklift	=	Notes Payable	+	Interest Payable	+	Retained Earnings	
Beg. bal.		43,000		0		0		0		43,000	
1	Purchase forklift	(43,000)		43,000							
2	Borrowed cash	5,000				5,000					
3	Recognize revenue	16,000								16,000	Revenue
4	Recognize depreciation			(10,000)						(10,000)	Depreciation Expense
5	Accrued interest							275		(275)	Interest Expense
End bal.		21,000	+	33,000	=	5,000	+	275	+	48,725	

Accounting Events for 2017

Libby would record three journal entries on January 31, 2017 (the maturity date). The first entry recognizes $25 ($5,000 × .06 × 1/12) of interest expense that accrued in 2017 for the month of January. The effects on the financial statements are shown here:

Assets			=	Liab.	+	Equity						
Cash	+	Forklift	=	Interest Payable	+	Retained Earnings	Rev.	−	Exp.	=	Net Inc.	Cash Flow
NA	+	NA	=	25	+	(25)	NA	−	25	=	(25)	NA

The second entry records Libby's cash payment for interest payable. This entry is an asset use transaction that reduces both the Cash and Interest Payable accounts for the total amount of interest due, $300. The interest payment includes the eleven months interest accrued in 2016 and one month accrued in 2017 ($275 + $25 = $300). There is no effect on the income statement because Libby recognized the interest expense previously. The statement of cash flows would report a $300 cash outflow from operating activities. The effects on the financial statements are shown here:

Assets			=	Liab.	+	Equity						
Cash	+	Forklift	=	Interest Payable			Rev.	−	Exp.	=	Net Inc.	Cash Flow
(300)	+	NA	=	(300)	+	NA	NA	−	NA	=	NA	(300) OA

The third entry on January 31, 2016, reflects repaying the principal. This entry is an asset use transaction. The Cash account and the Notes Payable account each decrease by $5,000. There is no effect on the income statement. The statement of cash flows would show a $5,000 cash outflow from financing activities. The effects on the financial statements are shown here:

Assets			=	Liab.	+	Equity						
Cash	+	Forklift	=	Note Payable			Rev.	−	Exp.	=	Net Inc.	Cash Flow
(5,000)	+	NA	=	(5,000)	+	NA	NA	−	NA	=	NA	(5,000) FA

Libby's balance sheets, income statements, and statements of cash flows for 2016 and 2017 are shown in Exhibit 2.12. The statements assume revenue for 2017 is also $16,000 cash and the company made the appropriate adjusting entry to recognize depreciation expense.

EXHIBIT 2.12 Financial Statements

LIBBY COMPANY
Financial Statements
December 31, 2016 and 2017

	2016	2017
Income Statements		
Revenue	$16,000	$16,000
Depreciation expense	(10,000)	(10,000)
Interest expense	(275)	(25)
Net income	$ 5,725	$ 5,975

continued

EXHIBIT 2.12 *Concluded*

Balance Sheets

	2016	2017
Assets		
Cash	$21,000	$31,700
Forklift less accumulated depreciation	33,000	23,000
Total Assets	$54,000	$54,700
Liabilities		
Notes Payable	$ 5,000	$ 0
Interest Payable	275	0
Total Liabilities	5,275	0
Stockholders' Equity		
Retained Earnings	48,725	54,700
Total Liab. and Stockholders' Equity	$54,000	$54,700

Statements of Cash Flows

	2016	2017
Cash flows from operations activities		
Inflow from customers	$16,000	$16,000
Cash flow from investing activities		
Outflow to purchase forklift	(43,000)	0
Cash flows from financing activities		
Inflow (outflow) from issue of note	5,000	(5,000)
Outflow for interest	0	(300)
Net change in cash	(22,000)	10,700
Plus beginning cash balance	43,000	21,000
Ending cash balance	$21,000	$31,700

Video lectures and accompanying self-assessment quizzes are available for all learning objectives through McGraw-Hill Connect® Plus Accounting.

SELF-STUDY REVIEW PROBLEM

Gifford Company experienced the following accounting events during 2016:

1. Started operations on January 1 when it acquired $20,000 cash by issuing common stock.
2. Earned $18,000 of revenue on account.
3. On March 1 collected $36,000 cash as an advance for services to be performed in the future.
4. Paid cash operating expenses of $17,000.
5. Paid a $2,700 cash dividend to stockholders.
6. On December 31, 2016, adjusted the books to recognize the revenue earned by providing services related to the advance described in Event 3. The contract required Gifford to provide services for a one-year period starting March 1.
7. Collected $15,000 cash from accounts receivable.

Gifford Company experienced the following accounting events during 2017:

1. Recognized $38,000 of cash revenue.
2. On April 1 paid $12,000 cash for an insurance policy that provides coverage for one year beginning immediately.
3. Collected $2,000 cash from accounts receivable.
4. Paid cash operating expenses of $21,000.

5. Paid a $5,000 cash dividend to stockholders.
6. On December 31, 2017, adjusted the books to recognize the remaining revenue earned by providing services related to the advance described in Event 3 of 2016.
7. On December 31, 2017, Gifford adjusted the books to recognize the amount of the insurance policy used during 2017.

Required

a. Record the events in a financial statements model like the following one. The first event is recorded as an example.

Event No.	Assets			= Liab.	+ Stockholders' Equity					
	Cash	+ Accts. Rec.	+ Prep. Ins.	= Unearn. Rev.	+ Com. Stk.	+ Ret. Earn.	Rev.	− Exp.	= Net Inc.	Cash Flow
1	20,000	+ NA	+ NA	= NA	+ 20,000	+ NA	NA	− NA	= NA	20,000 FA

b. What amount of revenue would Gifford report on the 2016 income statement?
c. What amount of cash flow from customers would Gifford report on the 2016 statement of cash flows?
d. What amount of unearned revenue would Gifford report on the 2016 and 2017 year-end balance sheets?
e. What are the 2017 opening balances for the revenue and expense accounts?
f. What amount of total assets would Gifford report on the December 31, 2016, balance sheet?
g. What obligations and commitments would Gifford report on the December 31, 2017, balance sheet?

Solution to Requirement a

The financial statements model follows:

Event No.	Assets			= Liab.	+ Stockholders' Equity					
	Cash	+ Accts. Rec.	+ Prep. Ins.	= Unearn. Rev.	+ Com. Stk.	+ Ret. Earn.	Rev.	− Exp.	= Net Inc.	Cash Flow
2016										
1	20,000	+ NA	+ NA	= NA	+ 20,000	+ NA	NA	− NA	= NA	20,000 FA
2	NA	+ 18,000	+ NA	= NA	+ NA	+ 18,000	18,000	− NA	= 18,000	NA
3	36,000	+ NA	+ NA	= 36,000	+ NA	+ NA	NA	− NA	= NA	36,000 OA
4	(17,000)	+ NA	+ NA	= NA	+ NA	+ (17,000)	NA	− 17,000	= (17,000)	(17,000) OA
5	(2,700)	+ NA	+ NA	= NA	+ NA	+ (2,700)	NA	− NA	= NA	(2,700) FA
6*	NA	+ NA	+ NA	= (30,000)	+ NA	+ 30,000	30,000	− NA	= 30,000	NA
7	15,000	+ (15,000)	+ NA	= NA	+ NA	+ NA	NA	− NA	= NA	15,000 OA
Bal.	51,300	+ 3,000	+ NA	= 6,000	+ 20,000	+ 28,300	48,000	− 17,000	= 31,000	51,300 NC
	Asset, liability, and equity account balances carry forward						Rev. & exp. accts. are closed			
2017										
Bal.	51,300	+ 3,000	+ NA	= 6,000	+ 20,000	+ 28,300	NA	− NA	= NA	NA
1	38,000	+ NA	+ NA	= NA	+ NA	+ 38,000	38,000	− NA	= 38,000	38,000 OA
2	(12,000)	+ NA	+ 12,000	= NA	+ NA	+ NA	NA	− NA	= NA	(12,000) OA
3	2,000	+ (2,000)	+ NA	= NA	+ NA	+ NA	NA	− NA	= NA	2,000 OA
4	(21,000)	+ NA	+ NA	= NA	+ NA	+ (21,000)	NA	− 21,000	= (21,000)	(21,000) OA
5	(5,000)	+ NA	+ NA	= NA	+ NA	+ (5,000)	NA	− NA	= NA	(5,000) FA
6*	NA	+ NA	+ NA	= (6,000)	+ NA	+ 6,000	6,000	− NA	= 6,000	NA
7†	NA	+ NA	+ (9,000)	= NA	+ NA	+ (9,000)	NA	− 9,000	= (9,000)	NA
Bal.	53,300	+ 1,000	+ 3,000	= 0	+ 20,000	+ 37,300	44,000	− 30,000	= 14,000	2,000 NC

*Revenue is earned at the rate of $3,000 ($36,000 ÷ 12 months) per month. Revenue recognized in 2016 is $30,000 ($3,000 × 10 months). Revenue recognized in 2017 is $6,000 ($3,000 × 2 months).

†Rent expense is incurred at the rate of $1,000 ($12,000 ÷ 12 months) per month. Rent expense recognized in 2017 is $9,000 ($1,000 × 9 months).

Solutions to Requirements b–g

b. Gifford would report \$48,000 of revenue in 2016 (\$18,000 revenue on account plus \$30,000 of the \$36,000 of unearned revenue).

c. The cash inflow from customers in 2016 is \$51,000 (\$36,000 when the unearned revenue was received plus \$15,000 collection of accounts receivable).

d. The December 31, 2016, balance sheet will report \$6,000 of unearned revenue, which is the amount of the cash advance less the amount of revenue recognized in 2016 (\$36,000 − \$30,000). The December 31, 2017, unearned revenue balance is zero.

e. Since revenue and expense accounts are closed at the end of each accounting period, the beginning balances in these accounts are always zero.

f. Assets on the December 31, 2016, balance sheet are \$54,300 [Gifford's cash at year-end plus the balance in accounts receivable (\$51,300 + \$3,000)].

g. Since all unearned revenue would be recognized before the financial statements were prepared at the end of 2017, there would be no liabilities on the 2017 balance sheet. In this case, all of the assets are committed to the investors.

KEY TERMS

Accounts Receivable 73
Accrual 71
Accrual accounting 71
Accrued expenses 75
Adjusting entry 75
American Institute of Certified Public Accountants (AICPA) 94
Asset exchange transaction 73
Asset source transaction 72
Asset use transaction 74
Carrying value 100
Claims exchange transaction 75
Code of Professional Conduct 94
Conservatism 81
Cost 83
Deferral 71
Depreciation expense 99
Expense 75
Internal controls 95
Matching concept 80
Opportunity 95
Period costs 80
Prepaid items 83
Pressure 96
Rationalization 96
Realization 71
Recognition 71
Revenue 86
Salaries Payable 75
Salvage value 98
Straight-line depreciation 99
Unearned revenue 85
Useful life 98
Vertical statements model 90

QUESTIONS

1. What does accrual accounting attempt to accomplish?
2. Define *recognition.* How is it independent of collecting or paying cash?
3. What does the term *deferral* mean?
4. If cash is collected in advance of performing services, when is the associated revenue recognized?
5. What does the term *asset source transaction* mean?
6. What effect does the issue of common stock have on the accounting equation?
7. How does the recognition of revenue on account (accounts receivable) affect the income statement compared to its effect on the statement of cash flows?
8. Give an example of an asset source transaction. What is the effect of this transaction on the accounting equation?
9. When is revenue recognized under accrual accounting?
10. Give an example of an asset exchange transaction. What is the effect of this transaction on the accounting equation?
11. What is the effect on the right side of the accounting equation when cash is collected in advance of performing services?
12. What does the term *unearned revenue* mean?
13. What effect does expense recognition have on the accounting equation?
14. What does the term *claims exchange transaction* mean?
15. What type of transaction is a cash payment to creditors? How does this type of transaction affect the accounting equation?
16. When are expenses recognized under accrual accounting?
17. Why may net cash flow from operating activities on the cash flow statement be different from the amount of net income reported on the income statement?
18. What is the relationship between the income statement and changes in assets and liabilities?
19. How does net income affect the stockholders' claims on the business's assets?
20. What is the difference between a cost and an expense?
21. When does a cost become an expense? Do all costs become expenses?
22. How and when is the cost of the *supplies used* recognized in an accounting period?
23. What does the term *expense* mean?
24. What does the term *revenue* mean?
25. What is the purpose of the statement of changes in stockholders' equity?
26. What is the main purpose of the balance sheet?
27. Why is the balance sheet dated *as of* a specific date when the income statement, statement of changes in stockholders' equity, and statement of cash flows are dated with the phrase *for the period ended*?
28. In what order are assets listed on the balance sheet?
29. What does the statement of cash flows explain?
30. What does the term *adjusting entry* mean? Give an example.
31. What types of accounts are closed at the end of the accounting period? Why is it necessary to close these accounts?
32. Give several examples of period costs.

33. Give an example of a cost that can be directly matched with the revenue produced by an accounting firm from preparing a tax return.

34. List and describe the four stages of the accounting cycle discussed in Chapter 2.

MULTIPLE-CHOICE QUESTIONS

Multiple-choice questions are available in the Connect library.

EXERCISES—SERIES A

All applicable Exercises in Series A are available with McGraw-Hill's Connect Plus Accounting.

Where applicable in all exercises, round computations to the nearest dollar.

Exercise 2-1A *Effect of collecting accounts receivable on the accounting equation and financial statements*

LO 2-1, 2-3

Holloway Company earned $18,000 of service revenue on account during 2016. The company collected $14,000 cash from accounts receivable during 2016.

Required

Based on this information alone, determine the following for Holloway Company. (*Hint:* Record the events in general ledger accounts under an accounting equation before satisfying the requirements.)

a. The balance of the accounts receivable that would be reported on the December 31, 2016, balance sheet.

b. The amount of net income that would be reported on the 2016 income statement.

c. The amount of net cash flow from operating activities that would be reported on the 2016 statement of cash flows.

d. The amount of retained earnings that would be reported on the 2016 balance sheet.

e. Why are the answers to Requirements *b* and *c* different?

Exercise 2-2A *Effect of accrued expenses on the accounting equation and financial statements*

LO 2-2, 2-3

During 2016, Chung Corporation earned $8,000 of cash revenue and accrued $5,000 of salaries expense.

Required

(*Hint:* Record the events in general ledger accounts under an accounting equation before satisfying the requirements.) Based on this information alone:

a. Prepare the December 31, 2016, balance sheet.

b. Determine the amount of net income that Chung would report on the 2016 income statement.

c. Determine the amount of net cash flow from operating activities that Chung would report on the 2016 statement of cash flows.

d. Why are the answers to Requirements *b* and *c* different?

Exercise 2-3A *Effect of accruals on the financial statements*

LO 2-1, 2-2, 2-3

Milea Inc. experienced the following events in 2016, its first year of operations:

1. Received $20,000 cash from the issue of common stock.
2. Performed services on account for $56,000.
3. Paid the utility expense of $2,500.
4. Collected $48,000 of the accounts receivable.
5. Recorded $10,000 of accrued salaries at the end of the year.
6. Paid a $2,000 cash dividend to the stockholders.

Required

a. Record the events in general ledger accounts under an accounting equation. In the last column of the table, provide appropriate account titles for the Retained Earnings amounts. The first transaction has been recorded as an example.

MILEA INC. General Ledger Accounts									
Event	Assets		=	Liabilities	+	Stockholders' Equity		Acct. Titles for Ret. Earn.
	Cash	Accounts Receivable		Salaries Payable		Common Stock	Retained Earnings	
1.	20,000					20,000		

b. Prepare the income statement, statement of changes in stockholders' equity, balance sheet, and statement of cash flows for the 2016 accounting period.

c. Why is the amount of net income different from the amount of net cash flow from operating activities?

LO 2-1, 2-2, 2-3

Exercise 2-4A *Effect of accounts receivable and accounts payable transactions on financial statements*

The following events apply to Lewis and Harper, a public accounting firm, for the 2016 accounting period:

1. Performed $70,000 of services for clients on account.
2. Performed $40,000 of services for cash.
3. Incurred $36,000 of other operating expenses on account.
4. Paid $10,000 cash to an employee for salary.
5. Collected $47,000 cash from accounts receivable.
6. Paid $16,000 cash on accounts payable.
7. Paid a $8,000 cash dividend to the stockholders.
8. Accrued salaries were $2,000 at the end of 2016.

Required

a. Show the effects of the events on the financial statements using a horizontal statements model like the following one. In the Cash Flow column, use OA to designate operating activity, IA for investment activity, FA for financing activity, and NC for net change in cash. Use NA to indicate the element is not affected by the event. The first event is recorded as an example.

Event No.	Assets			=	Liabilities			+	Equity						
	Cash	+	Accts. Rec.	=	Accts. Pay	+	Sal. Pay	+	Ret. Earn.	Rev.	−	Exp.	=	Net Inc.	Cash Flow
1.	NA	+	70,000	=	NA	+	NA	+	70,000	70,000	−	NA	=	70,000	NA

b. What is the amount of total assets at the end of 2016?

c. What is the balance of accounts receivable at the end of 2016?

d. What is the balance of accounts payable at the end of 2016?

e. What is the difference between accounts receivable and accounts payable?

f. What is net income for 2016?

g. What is the amount of net cash flow from operating activities for 2016?

LO 2-3

Exercise 2-5A *Missing information related to accruals*

Castile Inc. had a beginning balance of $4,000 in its Accounts Receivable account. The ending balance of Accounts Receivable was $4,500. During the period, Castile recognized $68,000 of revenue on account. Castile's Salaries Payable account has a beginning balance of $2,600 and an ending balance of $1,500. During the period, the company recognized $46,000 of accrued salary expense.

Required

a. Based on the information provided, determine the amount of net income.

b. Based on the information provided, determine the amount of net cash flow from operating activities.

Exercise 2-6A *Effect of accruals on the financial statements* LO 2-3

Cordell Inc. experienced the following events in 2016, its first year of operation:

1. Received $40,000 cash from the issue of common stock.
2. Performed services on account for $82,000.
3. Paid a $6,000 cash dividend to the stockholders.
4. Collected $76,000 of the accounts receivable.
5. Paid $53,000 cash for other operating expenses.
6. Performed services for $19,000 cash.
7. Recognized $3,500 of accrued utilities expense at the end of the year.

Required

a. Identify the events that result in revenue or expense recognition.

b. Based on your response to Requirement *a*, determine the amount of net income reported on the 2016 income statement.

c. Identify the events that affect the statement of cash flows.

d. Based on your response to Requirement *c*, determine the amount of cash flow from operating activities reported on the 2016 statement of cash flows.

e. What is the before- and after-closing balance in the Service Revenue account? What other accounts would be closed at the end of the accounting cycle?

f. What is the balance of the Retained Earnings account that appears on the 2016 balance sheet?

Exercise 2-7A *Net income versus changes in cash* LO 2-3

In 2016, Lee Inc. billed its customers $62,000 for services performed. The company collected $51,000 of the amount billed. Lee incurred $39,000 of other operating expenses on account. Lee paid $31,000 of the accounts payable. Lee acquired $40,000 cash from the issue of common stock. The company invested $21,000 cash in the purchase of land.

Required

(*Hint:* Identify the six events described in the paragraph and record them in general ledger accounts under an accounting equation before attempting to answer the questions.) Use the preceding information to answer the following questions:

a. What amount of revenue will Lee report on the 2016 income statement?

b. What amount of cash flow from revenue will be reported on the statement of cash flows?

c. What is the net income for the period?

d. What is the net cash flow from operating activities for the period?

e. Why is the amount of net income different from the net cash flow from operating activities for the period?

f. What is the amount of net cash flow from investing activities?

g. What is the amount of net cash flow from financing activities?

h. What amounts of total assets, liabilities, and equity will be reported on the year-end balance sheet?

Exercise 2-8A *Closing entries* LO 2-4

Love Company's accounting records show an after-closing balance of $42,100 in its Retained Earnings account on December 31, 2016. During the 2016 accounting cycle, Love earned $19,400 of revenue, incurred $9,800 of expense, and paid $500 of dividends. Revenues and expenses were recognized evenly throughout the accounting period.

Required

a. Determine the balance in the Retained Earnings account as of January 1, 2017.

b. Determine the balance in the temporary accounts as of January 1, 2016.

c. Determine the after-closing balance in the Retained Earnings account as of December 31, 2015.

d. Determine the balance in the Retained Earnings account as of June 30, 2016.

LO 2-4

Exercise 2-9A *Closing the accounts*

The following information was drawn from the accounting records of Wyckoff Company as of December 31, 2016, before the temporary accounts had been closed. The Cash balance was $3,600, and Notes Payable amounted to $4,000. The company had revenues of $7,500 and expenses of $3,400. The company's Land account had a $8,000 balance. Dividends amounted to $1,000. There was $2,000 of common stock issued.

Required

a. Identify which accounts would be classified as permanent and which accounts would be classified as temporary.

b. Assuming that Wyckoff's beginning balance (as of January 1, 2016) in the Retained Earnings account was $2,500, determine its balance after the temporary accounts were closed at the end of 2016.

c. What amount of net income would Wyckoff Company report on its 2016 income statement?

d. Explain why the amount of net income differs from the amount of the ending Retained Earnings balance.

e. What are the balances in the revenue, expense, and dividend accounts on January 1, 2017?

LO 2-4

Exercise 2-10A *Closing accounts and the accounting cycle*

Required

a. Identify which of the following accounts are temporary (will be closed to Retained Earnings at the end of the year) and which are permanent:

(1) Other Operating Expenses
(2) Utilities Expense
(3) Retained Earnings
(4) Salaries Expense
(5) Land
(6) Dividends
(7) Service Revenue
(8) Cash
(9) Salaries Payable
(10) Common Stock

b. List and explain the four stages of the accounting cycle. Which stage must be first? Which stage is last?

LO 2-4

Exercise 2-11A *Matching concept*

Companies make sacrifices known as *expenses* to obtain benefits called *revenues.* The accurate measurement of net income requires that expenses be matched with revenues. In some circumstances, matching a particular expense directly with revenue is difficult or impossible. In these circumstances, the expense is matched with the period in which it is incurred.

Required

a. Identify an expense that could be matched directly with revenue.

b. Identify a period expense that would be difficult to match with revenue. Explain why.

EXERCISES—SERIES A

Exercise 2-12A *Supplies and the financial statements model*

LO 2-5

Pizza Express Inc. began the 2016 accounting period with \$2,500 cash, \$1,400 of common stock, and \$1,100 of retained earnings. Pizza Express was affected by the following accounting events during 2016:

1. Purchased \$3,600 of supplies on account.
2. Earned and collected \$12,300 of cash revenue.
3. Paid \$2,700 cash on accounts payable.
4. Adjusted the records to reflect the use of supplies. A physical count indicated that \$250 of supplies was still on hand on December 31, 2016.

Required

a. Show the effects of the events on the financial statements using a horizontal statements model like the following one. In the Cash Flows column, use OA to designate operating activity, IA for investing activity, FA for financing activity, and NC for net change in cash. Use NA to indicate accounts not affected by the event. The beginning balances are entered in the following example:

Event No.	Assets			=	Liab.	+	Stockholders' Equity								Cash Flows
	Cash	+	Supplies	=	Accts. Pay	+	Com. Stk	+	Ret. Earn.	Rev.	−	Exp.	=	Net Inc.	Cash Flows
Beg. bal.	2,500	+	0	=	0	+	1,400	+	1,100	0	−	0	=	0	0

b. Explain the difference between the amount of net income and amount of net cash flow from operating activities.

Exercise 2-13A *Supplies on financial statements*

LO 2-5, 2-8

Yard Professionals Inc. experienced the following events in 2016, its first year of operation:

1. Performed services for \$35,000 cash.
2. Purchased \$6,000 of supplies on account.
3. A physical count on December 31, 2016, found that there was \$1,800 of supplies on hand.

Required

Based on this information alone:

a. Record the events under an accounting equation.

b. Prepare an income statement, balance sheet, and statement of cash flows for the 2016 accounting period.

c. What is the balance in the Supplies account as of January 1, 2017?

d. What is the balance in the Supplies Expense account as of January 1, 2017?

Exercise 2-14A *Distinguishing between an expense and a cost*

LO 2-5, 2-6

Charlene Rose tells you that accountants where she works are real hair splitters. For example, they make a big issue over the difference between a cost and an expense. She says the two terms mean the same thing to her.

Required

a. Explain to Charlene the difference between a cost and expense from an accountant's perspective.

b. Explain whether each of the following events produces an assets or an expense:

(1) Purchased a building for cash.

(2) Paid cash to purchase supplies.

(3) Used supplies on hand to produce revenue.
(4) Paid cash in advance for insurance.
(5) Recognized accrued salaries.

LO 2-6

Exercise 2-15A *Prepaid items on financial statements*

Life, Inc., experienced the following events in 2016, its first year of operation:

1. Performed counseling services for $36,000 cash.
2. On February 1, 2016, paid $18,000 cash to rent office space for the coming year.
3. Adjusted the accounts to reflect the amount of rent used during the year.

Required

Based on this information alone:

a. Record the events under an accounting equation.
b. Prepare an income statement, balance sheet, and statement of cash flows for the 2016 accounting period.
c. Ignoring all other future events, what is the amount of rent expense that would be recognized in 2017?

LO 2-6, 2-8

Exercise 2-16A *Effect of an error on financial statements*

On April 1, 2016, Maine Corporation paid $18,000 cash in advance for a one-year lease on an office building. Assume that Maine records the prepaid rent as an asset and that the books are closed on December 31.

Required

a. Show the payment for the one-year lease and the related adjusting entry to recognize rent expense in the accounting equation.
b. Assume that Maine Corporation failed to record the adjusting entry to reflect using the office building. How would the error affect the company's 2016 income statement and balance sheet?

LO 2-7

Exercise 2-17A *Unearned items on financial statements*

Yard Designs (YD) experienced the following events in 2016, its first year of operation:

1. On October 1, 2016, YD collected $54,000 for consulting services it agreed to provide during the coming year.
2. Adjusted the accounts to reflect the amount of consulting service revenue recognized in 2016.

Required

Based on this information alone,

a. Record the events under an accounting equation.
b. Prepare an income statement, balance sheet, and statement of cash flows for the 2016 accounting period.
c. Ignoring all other future events, what is the amount of service revenue that would be recognized in 2017?

LO 2-7

Exercise 2-18A *Unearned revenue defined as a liability*

Lan, an accounting major, and Pat, a marketing major, are watching a *Matlock* rerun on late-night TV. Of course, there is a murder and the suspect wants to hire Matlock as the defense attorney. Matlock will take the case but requires an advance payment of $150,000. Pat remarks that Matlock has earned a cool $150,000 without lifting a finger. Lan tells Pat that Matlock has not earned anything but has a $150,000 liability. Pat asks, "How can that be?"

Required

Assume you are Lan. Explain to Pat why Matlock has a liability and when Matlock would actually earn the $150,000.

Exercise 2-19A *Supplies, unearned revenue, and the financial statements model* LO 2-5, 2-7

Hart, Attorney at Law, experienced the following transactions in 2016, the first year of operations:

1. Accepted $36,000 on April 1, 2016, as a retainer for services to be performed evenly over the next 12 months.
2. Performed legal services for cash of $54,000.
3. Purchased $2,800 of office supplies on account.
4. Paid $2,400 of the amount due on accounts payable.
5. Paid a cash dividend to the stockholders of $5,000.
6. Paid cash for operating expenses of $31,000.
7. Determined that at the end of the accounting period $200 of office supplies remained on hand.
8. On December 31, 2016, recognized the revenue that had been earned for services performed in accordance with Transaction 1.

Required

Show the effects of the events on the financial statements using a horizontal statements model like the following one. In the Cash Flows column, use the initials OA to designate operating activity, IA for investing activity, FA for financing activity, and NC for net change in cash. Use NA to indicate accounts not affected by the event. The first event has been recorded as an example.

Event	Assets			=	Liabilities			+	Stk. Equity						
No.	Cash	+	Supplies	=	Accts. Pay	+	Unearn. Rev.	+	Ret. Earn.	Rev.	−	Exp.	=	Net Inc.	Cash Flow
1.	36,000	+	NA	=	NA	+	36,000	+	NA	NA	−	NA	=	NA	36,000 OA

Exercise 2-20A *Unearned revenue and the financial statements model* LO 2-7

Clark Bell started a personal financial planning business when he accepted $36,000 cash as advance payment for managing the financial assets of a large estate. Bell agreed to manage the estate for a one-year period beginning June 1, 2016.

Required

a. Show the effects of the advance payment and revenue recognition on the 2016 financial statements using a horizontal statements model like the following one. In the Cash Flows column, use OA to designate operating activity, IA for investing activity, FA for financing activity, and NC for net change in cash. Use NA if the account is not affected.

Event	Assets	=	Liab.	+	Stockholders' Equity	Rev.	−	Exp.	=	Net Inc.	Cash Flows
	Cash	=	Unearn. Rev.	+	Ret. Earn.						

b. How much revenue would Bell recognize on the 2017 income statement?

c. What is the amount of cash flow from operating activities in 2017?

Exercise 2-21A *Prepaid vs. unearned, the entity concept* LO 2-6, 2-7

On October 1, 2016, Josh Smith, attorney, accepted an $10,800 cash advance from his client, James Company, for services to be performed over the next six months.

Required

a. Record the deferral and the related December 31, 2016, adjustment for Josh Smith in an accounting equation.

b. Record the deferral and the related December 31, 2016, adjustment for James Company in an accounting equation.

LO 2-1, 2-2, 2-5, 2-6, 2-7

Exercise 2-22A *Identifying deferral and accrual events*

Required

Identify each of the following events as an accrual, a deferral, or neither:

a. Paid cash in advance for a one-year insurance policy.
b. Paid cash to settle an account payable.
c. Collected accounts receivable.
d. Paid cash for current salaries expense.
e. Paid cash to purchase supplies.
f. Provided services on account.
g. Provided services and collected cash.
h. Paid cash to purchase land.
i. Recognized accrued salaries at the end of the accounting period.
j. Paid a cash dividend to the stockholders.
k. Recognized accrued interest revenue at the end of the period.
l. Collected cash for services to be provided in the future.

LO 2-1, 2-2, 2-4, 2-5, 2-6

Exercise 2-23A *Revenue and expense recognition*

Required

a. Describe an expense recognition event that results in an increase in liabilities.
b. Describe an expense recognition event that results in a decrease in assets.
c. Describe a revenue recognition event that results in a decrease in liabilities.
d. Describe a revenue recognition event that results in an increase in assets.

LO 2-5, 2-6, 2-7

Exercise 2-24A *Adjusting the accounts*

Norell Inc. experienced the following accounting events during its 2016 accounting period:

1. Recognized revenue on account.
2. Issued common stock.
3. Paid cash to purchase supplies.
4. Collected a cash advance for services that will be provided during the coming year.
5. Paid a cash dividend to the stockholders.
6. Paid cash for an insurance policy that provides coverage during the next year.
7. Collected cash from accounts receivable.
8. Paid cash for operating expenses.
9. Paid cash to settle an account payable.
10. Paid cash to purchase land.

Required

a. Identify the events that would require a year-end adjusting entry.
b. Are adjusting or closing entries recorded first? Why?

LO 2-7, 2-8

Exercise 2-25A *Classifying events on the statement of cash flows*

The following transactions pertain to the operations of Ewing Company for 2016:

1. Acquired $30,000 cash from the issue of common stock.
2. Provided $65,000 of services on account.
3. Paid $22,000 cash on accounts payable.
4. Performed services for $8,000 cash.
5. Collected $51,000 cash from accounts receivable.
6. Incurred $37,000 of operating expenses on account.
7. Paid $6,500 cash for one year's rent in advance.
8. Paid a $4,000 cash dividend to the stockholders.

9. Paid $1,200 cash for supplies to be used in the future.
10. Recognized $3,100 of accrued salaries expense.

Required

a. Classify the cash flows from these transactions as operating activities (OA), investing activities (IA), or financing activities (FA). Use NA for transactions that do not affect the statement of cash flows.
b. Prepare a statement of cash flows. (There is no beginning cash balance.)

Exercise 2-26A *Relationship of accounts to financial statements* LO 2-8

Required

Identify whether each of the following items would appear on the income statement (IS), statement of changes in stockholders' equity (SE), balance sheet (BS), or statement of cash flows (CF). Some items may appear on more than one statement; if so, identify all applicable statements. If an item would not appear on any financial statement, label it NA.

CHECK FIGURES
a. BS
z. CF

a. Supplies
b. Cash Flow from Financing Activities
c. "As of" Date Notation
d. Ending Retained Earnings
e. Net Income
f. Dividends
g. Net Change in Cash
h. "For the Period Ended"
i. Land
j. Ending Common Stock
k. Salaries Expense
l. Prepaid Rent
m. Accounts Payable
n. Total Assets
o. Salaries Payable
p. Insurance Expense
q. Notes Payable
r. Accounts Receivable
s. Interest Receivable
t. Interest Revenue
u. Rent Expense
v. Price/Earnings Ratio
w. Taxes Payable
x. Unearned Revenue
y. Service Revenue
z. Cash Flow from Investing Activities
aa. Consulting Revenue
bb. Utilities Expense
cc. Ending Common Stock
dd. Total Liabilities
ee. Operating Cycle
ff. Cash Flow from Operating Activities
gg. Operating Expenses
hh. Supplies Expense
ii. Beginning Retained Earnings
jj. Beginning Common Stock
kk. Prepaid Insurance
ll. Salary Expense
mm. Beginning Cash Balance
nn. Ending Cash Balance

Exercise 2-27A *Effect of accounting events on the income statement and statement of cash flows* LO 2-8

Required

Explain how each of the following events or series of events and the related adjusting entry will affect the amount of *net income* and the amount of *cash flow from operating activities* reported on the year-end financial statements. Identify the direction of change (increase, decrease, or NA) and the amount of the change. Organize your answers according to the following table. The first event is recorded as an example. If an event does not have a related adjusting entry, record only the effects of the event.

	Net Income		Cash Flows from Operating Activities	
Event/ Adjustment	Direction of Change	Amount of Change	Direction of Change	Amount of Change
a	NA	NA	Decrease	$9,000
Adj	Decrease	$2,250	NA	NA

a. Paid $9,000 cash on October 1 to purchase a one-year insurance policy.
b. Purchased $2,000 of supplies on account. Paid $500 cash on accounts payable. The ending balance in the Supplies account, after adjustment, was $300.
c. Provided services for $10,000 cash.
d. Collected $2,400 in advance for services to be performed in the future. The contract called for services to start on May 1 and to continue for one year.
e. Accrued salaries amounting to $5,600.
f. Sold land that cost $3,000 for $3,000 cash.
g. Acquired $15,000 cash from the issue of common stock.
h. Earned $12,000 of revenue on account. Collected $8,000 cash from accounts receivable.
i. Paid cash operating expenses of $4,500.

LO 2-8, 2-9

Exercise 2-28A *Transactions that affect the elements of financial statements*

Required

Give an example of a transaction that will do the following:
a. Increase an asset and increase equity (asset source event).
b. Decrease an asset and decrease equity (asset use event).
c. Increase an asset and decrease another asset (asset exchange event).
d. Decrease a liability and increase equity (claims exchange event).
e. Increase a liability and decrease equity (claims exchange event).
f. Increase an asset and increase a liability (asset source event).
g. Decrease an asset and decrease a liability (asset use event).

LO 2-9

Exercise 2-29A *Identifying source, use, and exchange transactions*

Required

Indicate whether each of the following transactions is an asset source (AS), asset use (AU), asset exchange (AE), or claims exchange (CE) transaction.
a. Acquired cash from the issue of stock.
b. Paid a cash dividend to the stockholders.
c. Paid cash on accounts payable.
d. Incurred other operating expenses on account.
e. Paid cash for rent expense.
f. Performed services for cash.
g. Performed services for clients on account.
h. Collected cash from accounts receivable.
i. Received cash for services to be performed in the future.
j. Purchased land with cash.

LO 2-9

Exercise 2-30A *Identifying asset source, use, and exchange transactions*

Required

a. Name an asset use transaction that will *not* affect the income statement.
b. Name an asset exchange transaction that will affect the statement of cash flows.
c. Name an asset source transaction that will *not* affect the income statement.
d. Name an asset source transaction that will *not* affect the statement of cash flows.
e. Name an asset source transaction that will affect the income statement.

LO 2-8, 2-9

Exercise 2-31A *Identifying transaction type and effect on the financial statements*

Required

Identify whether each of the following transactions is an asset source (AS), asset use (AU), asset exchange (AE), or claims exchange (CE). Also show the effects of the events on the financial statements using the horizontal statements model. Indicate whether the event increases (I), decreases (D), or does not affect (NA) each element of the financial statements. In the Cash Flows column, designate the cash flows as operating activities (OA), investing activities (IA), or financing activities (FA). The first two transactions have been recorded as examples.

						Stockholders' Equity								
Event	Type of Event	Assets	=	Liabilities	+	Common Stock	+	Retained Earnings	Rev.	−	Exp.	=	Net Inc.	Cash Flows
a	AS	I		NA		NA		I	I		NA		I	I OA
b	AS	I		I		NA		NA	NA		NA		NA	NA

a. Provided services and collected cash.
b. Purchased supplies on account to be used in the future.
c. Paid cash in advance for one year's rent.
d. Paid cash to purchase land.
e. Paid a cash dividend to the stockholders.
f. Received cash from the issue of common stock.
g. Paid cash on accounts payable.
h. Collected cash from accounts receivable.
i. Received cash advance for services to be provided in the future.
j. Incurred other operating expenses on account.
k. Performed services on account.
l. Adjusted books to reflect the amount of prepaid rent expired during the period.
m. Paid cash for operating expenses.
n. Adjusted the books to record the supplies used during the period.
o. Recorded accrued salaries.
p. Paid cash for salaries accrued at the end of a prior period.
q. Recorded accrued interest revenue earned at the end of the accounting period.

Exercise 2-32A *Ethical conduct*

LO 2-10

Required

Name and provide a brief explanation of the six Principles of Professional Conduct of the AICPA Code of Professional Conduct.

Exercise 2-33A *Effect of depreciation on the accounting equation and financial statements (Appendix)*

LO 2-11

The following events apply to Tracey's Restaurant for the 2016 fiscal year:

1. Started the company when it acquired $21,000 cash from the issue of common stock.
2. Purchased a new cooktop that cost $22,000 cash.
3. Earned $32,000 in cash revenue.
4. Paid $16,000 cash for salaries expense.
5. Paid $7,000 cash for operating expenses.
6. Adjusted the records to reflect the use of the cooktop. The cooktop, purchased on January 1, 2016, has an expected useful life of five years and an estimated salvage value of $2,000. Use straight-line depreciation. The adjusting entry was made as of December 31, 2016.

Required

a. Write an accounting equation and record the effects of each accounting event under the appropriate general ledger account headings.
b. What amount of depreciation expense would Tracey's report on the 2017 income statement?
c. What amount of accumulated depreciation would Tracey's report on the December 31, 2017, balance sheet?
d. Would the cash flow from operating activities be affected by depreciation in 2017?

LO 2-11

Exercise 2-34A *Depreciation affecting multiple cycles (Appendix)*

On January 1, 2016, Your Ride Inc. paid $36,000 cash to purchase a taxi cab. The taxi had a four-year useful life and a $4,000 salvage value.

Required

a. Determine the amount of depreciation expense that would appear on the 2016 and 2017 income statements.

b. Determine the amount of accumulated depreciation that would appear on the 2016 and 2017 balance sheets.

c. Explain how the purchase of equipment would affect the 2016 and 2017 statements of cash flows.

LO 2-12

Exercise 2-35A *Effects of recognizing accrued interest on financial statements (Appendix)*

Ben Bradley started Bradley Company on January 1, 2016. The company experienced the following events during its first year of operation:

1. Earned $2,000 of cash revenue for performing services.
2. Borrowed $8,000 cash from the bank.
3. Adjusted the accounting records to recognize accrued interest expense on the bank note. The note, issued on August 1, 2016, had a one-year term and a 6 percent annual interest rate.

Required

a. What is the amount of interest expense in 2016?

b. What amount of cash was paid for interest in 2016?

c. Use a horizontal statements model to show how each event affects the balance sheet, income statement, and statement of cash flows. Indicate whether the event increases (I), decreases (D), or does not affect (NA) each element of the financial statements. Also, in the Cash Flows column, designate the cash flows as operating activities (OA), investing activities (IA), or financing activities (FA). The first transaction has been recorded as an example.

Event No.	Balance Sheet									Income Statement					Statement of Cash Flows
	Cash	=	Note Pay.	+	Int. Pay.	+	C. Stk.	+	Ret. Earn.	Rev.	−	Exp.	=	Net Inc.	
1	I	=	NA	+	NA	+	NA	+	I	I	−	NA	=	I	I OA

LO 2-12

Exercise 2-36A *Recognizing accrued interest revenue (Appendix)*

Leach Company invested $80,000 in a certificate of deposit on June 1, 2016. The certificate had a 2 percent annual rate of interest and a one-year term to maturity.

Required

a. What amount of interest revenue will Leach recognize for the year ending December 31, 2016?

b. Show how the December 31, 2016, adjusting entry to recognize the accrued interest revenue affects the accounting equation.

c. What amount of cash will Leach collect for interest revenue in 2016?

d. What is the amount of interest receivable as of December 31, 2016?

e. What amount of cash will Leach collect for interest revenue in 2017, assuming it does not renew the CD?

f. What amount of interest revenue will Leach recognize in 2017, assuming it does not renew the CD?

g. What is the amount of interest receivable as of December 31, 2017, assuming it does not renew the CD?

PROBLEMS—SERIES A

Problem 2-37A *Effect of adjusting entries on the accounting equation*

LO 2-4

CHECK FIGURE

d. adjustment amount: $4,000

Required

Each of the following independent events requires a year-end adjusting entry. Show how each event and its related adjusting entry affect the accounting equation. Assume a December 31 closing date. The first event is recorded as an example.

	Total Assets					Stockholders' Equity		
Event/ Adjustment	Cash	+	Other Assets	=	Liabilities	+	Common Stock	+	Retained Earnings
a	−4,800		+4,800		NA		NA		NA
Adj.	NA		−1,200		NA		NA		−1,200

a. Paid $4,800 cash in advance on October 1 for a one-year insurance policy.

b. Received an $3,600 cash advance for a contract to provide services in the future. The contract required a one-year commitment, starting April 1.

c. Purchased $1,200 of supplies on account. At year's end, $175 of supplies remained on hand.

d. Paid $9,600 cash in advance on August 1 for a one-year lease on office space.

Problem 2-38A *Closing the accounts*

LO 2-4

CHECK FIGURES

Net Income: $3,100

Ending Retained Earnings: $15,300

The following selected accounts and account balances were taken from the records of Nowell Company. Except as otherwise indicated, all balances are as of December 31, 2016, before the closing entries were recorded.

Consulting revenue	$18,200
Cash	35,600
Cash received from common stock issued during 2016	6,000
Travel expense	2,100
Dividends	4,000
Cash flow from investing activities	5,200
Rent expense	3,500
Payment to reduce debt principal	10,000
Retained earnings, January 1, 2016	16,200
Salary expense	7,200
Cash flow from operating activities	2,600
Common stock, December 31, 2016	16,000
Other operating expenses	2,300

Required

a. Prepare the income statement Nowell would include in its 2016 annual report.

b. Identify the accounts that should be closed to the Retained Earnings account.

c. Determine the Retained Earnings account balance at December 31, 2016. Identify the reasons for the difference between net income and the ending balance in Retained Earnings.

d. What are the balances in the Revenue, Expense, and Dividend accounts on January 1, 2017? Explain.

Problem 2-39A *Recording events in a horizontal statements model*

LO 2-8

CHECK FIGURES

Net Income: $12,300

Ending Cash Balance: $19,000

The following events pertain to Super Cleaning Company:

1. Acquired $10,000 cash from the issue of common stock.
2. Provided $15,000 of services on account.

3. Provided services for $5,000 cash.
4. Received $2,800 cash in advance for services to be performed in the future.
5. Collected $12,200 cash from the account receivable created in Event 2.
6. Paid $1,900 for cash expenses.
7. Performed $1,400 of the services agreed to in Event 4.
8. Incurred $3,600 of expenses on account.
9. Paid $4,800 cash in advance for one-year contract to rent office space.
10. Paid $2,800 cash on the account payable created in Event 8.
11. Paid a $1,500 cash dividend to the stockholders.
12. Recognized rent expense for nine months' use of office space acquired in Event 9.

Required

Show the effects of the events on the financial statements using a horizontal statements model like the following one. In the Cash Flows column, use the letters OA to designate operating activity, IA for investing activity, FA for financing activity, and NC for net change in cash. Use NA to indicate accounts not affected by the event. The first event is recorded as an example.

Event No.	Assets					=	Liabilities			+	Stockholders' Equity			Rev.	–	Exp.	=	Net Inc.	Cash Flows
	Cash	+	Accts. Rec.	+	Prep. Rent	=	Accts. Pay.	+	Unearn. Rev.	+	Common Stock	+	Ret. Earn.						
1	10,000	+	NA	+	NA	=	NA	+	NA	+	10,000	+	NA	NA	–	NA	=	NA	10,000 FA

LO 2-8

Problem 2-40A *Effect of events on financial statements*

CHECK FIGURES
b. $36,000
h. $(15,000)

Waddell Company had the following balances in its accounting records as of December 31, 2015:

Assets		Liabilities and Equity	
Cash	$35,000	Accounts Payable	$ 7,500
Accounts Receivable	9,000	Common Stock	40,000
Land	51,000	Retained Earnings	47,500
Total	$95,000	Total	$95,000

The following accounting events apply to Waddell Company's 2016 fiscal year:

Jan. 1 Acquired $20,000 cash from the issue of common stock.
Feb. 1 Paid $6,000 cash in advance for a one-year lease for office space.
Mar. 1 Paid a $2,000 cash dividend to the stockholders.
April 1 Purchased additional land that cost $15,000 cash.
May 1 Made a cash payment on accounts payable of $5,500.
July 1 Received $9,600 cash in advance as a retainer for services to be performed monthly over the coming year.
Sept. 1 Sold land for $30,000 cash that had originally cost $30,000.
Oct. 1 Purchased $2,500 of supplies on account.
Dec. 31 Earned $58,000 of service revenue on account during the year.
31 Received cash collections from accounts receivable amounting to $46,000.
31 Incurred other operating expenses on account during the year that amounted to $28,000.
31 Recognized accrued salaries expense of $6,500.
31 Had $50 of supplies on hand at the end of the period.
31 The land purchased on April 1 had a market value of $20,000.
31 Recognized $500 of accrued interest revenue.

Required

Based on the preceding information, answer the following questions for Waddell Company. All questions pertain to the 2016 financial statements. (*Hint:* Enter items in general ledger accounts under the accounting equation before answering the questions.)

a. Based on the preceding transactions, identify two additional adjustments and describe them.
b. What amount would Waddell report for land on the balance sheet?
c. What amount of net cash flow from operating activities would be reported on the statement of cash flows?
d. What amount of rent expense would be reported on the income statement?
e. What amount of total liabilities would be reported on the balance sheet?
f. What amount of supplies expense would be reported on the income statement?
g. What amount of unearned revenue would be reported on the balance sheet?
h. What amount of net cash flow from investing activities would be reported on the statement of cash flows?
i. What amount of total expenses would be reported on the income statement?
j. What amount of service revenue would be reported on the income statement?
k. What amount of cash flows from financing activities would be reported on the statement of cash flows?
l. What amount of net income would be reported on the income statement?
m. What amount of retained earnings would be reported on the balance sheet?

Problem 2-41A *Identifying and arranging elements on financial statements*

LO 2-8

CHECK FIGURES
Total Assets $93,200
Net Income $18,500

The following accounts and balances were drawn from the records of Barker Company at December 31, 2016:

Supplies	$ 1,000	Beginning retained earnings	$ 9,300
Cash flow from investing act.	(5,200)	Cash flow from financing act.	(5,000)
Prepaid insurance	1,200	Rent expense	2,500
Service revenue	65,200	Dividends	3,000
Other operating expenses	41,000	Cash	48,000
Supplies expense	1,100	Accounts receivable	14,200
Insurance expense	2,100	Prepaid rent	4,800
Beginning common stock	40,000	Unearned revenue	6,400
Cash flow from operating act.	15,600	Land	24,000
Common stock issued	5,000	Accounts payable	17,000

Required

Use the accounts and balances from Barker Company to construct an income statement, statement of changes in stockholders' equity, balance sheet, and statement of cash flows (show only totals for each activity on the statement of cash flows).

Problem 2-42A *Missing information in financial statements*

LO 2-8

Required

Fill in the blanks (indicated by the alphabetic letters in parentheses) in the following financial statements. Assume the company started operations January 1, 2016, and all transactions involve cash.

	For the Years		
	2016	2017	2018
Income Statements			
Revenue	$ 700	$ 1,300	$ 2,000
Expense	(a)	(700)	(1,300)
Net income	$ 200	$ (m)	$ 700

continued

Statements of Changes in Stockholders' Equity			
Beginning common stock	$ 0	$ (n)	$ 6,000
Plus: Common stock issued	5,000	1,000	2,000
Ending common stock	5,000	6,000	(t)
Beginning retained earnings	0	100	200
Plus: Net income	(b)	(o)	700
Less: Dividends	(c)	(500)	(300)
Ending retained earnings	100	(p)	600
Total stockholders' equity	$ (d)	$ 6,200	$ 8,600
Balance Sheets			
Assets			
Cash	$ (e)	$ (q)	$ (u)
Land	0	(r)	8,000
Total assets	$ (f)	$11,200	$10,600
Liabilities	$ (g)	$ 5,000	$ 2,000
Stockholders' equity			
Common stock	(h)	(s)	8,000
Retained earnings	(i)	200	600
Total stockholders' equity	(j)	6,200	8,600
Total liabilities and stockholders' equity	$8,100	$11,200	$10,600
Statements of Cash Flows			
Cash flows from operating activities			
Cash receipts from customers	$ (k)	$ 1,300	$ (v)
Cash payments for expenses	(l)	(700)	(w)
Net cash flows from operating activities	200	600	700
Cash flows from investing activities			
Cash payments for land	0	(8,000)	0
Cash flows from financing activities			
Cash receipts from loan	3,000	3,000	0
Cash payments to reduce debt	0	(1,000)	(x)
Cash receipts from stock issue	5,000	1,000	(y)
Cash payments for dividends	(100)	(500)	(z)
Net cash flows from financing activities	7,900	2,500	(1,300)
Net change in cash	8,100	(4,900)	(600)
Plus: Beginning cash balance	0	8,100	3,200
Ending cash balance	$8,100	$ 3,200	$ 2,600

LO 2-8, 2-9

CHECK FIGURES

Net Income, 2016: $2,400

Net Income, 2017: $9,150

Problem 2-43A *Events for two complete accounting cycles*

Alcorn Service Company was formed on January 1, 2016.

Events Affecting the 2016 Accounting Period

1. Acquired $20,000 cash from the issue of common stock.
2. Purchased $800 of supplies on account.
3. Purchased land that cost $14,000 cash.
4. Paid $800 cash to settle accounts payable created in Event 2.
5. Recognized revenue on account of $10,500.
6. Paid $3,800 cash for other operating expenses.
7. Collected $7,000 cash from accounts receivable.

Information for 2016 Adjusting Entries

8. Recognized accrued salaries of $3,600 on December 31, 2016.
9. Had $100 of supplies on hand at the end of the accounting period.

Events Affecting the 2017 Accounting Period

1. Acquired $15,000 cash from the issue of common stock.
2. Paid $3,600 cash to settle the salaries payable obligation.
3. Paid $9,000 cash in advance to lease office space.
4. Sold the land that cost $14,000 for $14,000 cash.
5. Received $6,000 cash in advance for services to be performed in the future.
6. Purchased $2,400 of supplies on account during the year.
7. Provided services on account of $24,500.
8. Collected $12,600 cash from accounts receivable.
9. Paid a cash dividend of $2,000 to the stockholders.
10. Paid other operating expenses of $2,850.

Information for 2017 Adjusting Entries

11. The advance payment for rental of the office space (see Event 3) was made on March 1 for a one-year term.
12. The cash advance for services to be provided in the future was collected on October 1 (see Event 5). The one-year contract started on October 1.
13. Had $300 of supplies remaining on hand at the end of the period.
14. Recognized accrued salaries of $4,800 at the end of the accounting period.
15. Recognized $500 of accrued interest revenue.

Required

a. Identify each event affecting the 2016 and 2017 accounting periods as asset source (AS), asset use (AU), asset exchange (AE), or claims exchange (CE). Record the effects of each event under the appropriate general ledger account headings of the accounting equation.

b. Prepare an income statement, statement of changes in stockholders' equity, balance sheet, and statement of cash flows for 2016 and 2017, using the vertical statements model.

Problem 2-44A *Ethics*

LO 2-10

Pete Chalance is an accountant with a shady past. Suffice it to say that he owes some very unsavory characters a lot of money. Despite his past, Pete works hard at keeping up a strong professional image. He is a manager at Smith and Associates, a fast-growing CPA firm. Pete is highly regarded around the office because he is a strong producer of client revenue. Indeed, on several occasions he exceeded his authority in establishing prices with clients. This is typically a partner's job but who could criticize Pete, who is most certainly bringing in the business. Indeed, Pete is so good that he is able to pull off the following scheme. He bills clients at inflated rates and then reports the ordinary rate to his accounting firm. Say, for example, the normal charge for a job is $2,500. Pete will smooth talk the client, then charge him $3,000. He reports the normal charge of $2,500 to his firm and keeps the extra $500 for himself. He knows it isn't exactly right because his firm gets its regular charges and the client willingly pays for the services rendered. He thinks to himself, as he pockets his ill-gotten gains, who is getting hurt anyway?

Required

The text discusses three common features (conditions) that motivate ethical misconduct. Identify and explain each of the three features as they appear in the above scenario.

Problem 2-45A *Effect of events on financial statements (Appendix)*

LO 2-6, 2-10, 2-11

Porser Company had the following balances in its accounting records as of December 31, 2016:

Assets		Claims	
Cash	$26,000	Accounts payable	$ 5,000
Accounts receivable	9,000	Common stock	28,000
Land	42,000	Retained earnings	44,000
Total	$77,000	Total	$77,000

The following accounting events apply to Porser Company's 2017 fiscal year:

Jan.	1	Acquired $15,000 cash from the issue of common stock.
	1	Purchased a truck that cost $22,000 and had a $2,000 salvage value and a four-year useful life.
Feb.	1	Borrowed $12,000 by issuing a note that had a 9 percent annual interest rate and a one-year term.
	1	Paid $3,000 cash in advance for a one-year lease for office space.
Mar.	1	Paid a $2,000 cash dividend to the stockholders.
April	1	Purchased land that cost $28,000 cash.
May	1	Made a cash payment on accounts payable of $4,000.
July	1	Received $5,400 cash in advance as a retainer for services to be performed monthly over the next 12 months.
Sept.	1	Sold land for $42,000 that originally cost $42,000.
Oct.	1	Purchased $5,000 of supplies on account.
Nov.	1	Purchased a one-year $50,000 certificate of deposit that paid a 6 percent annual rate of interest.
Dec.	31	Earned $42,000 of service revenue on account during the year.
	31	Received cash collections from accounts receivable amounting to $40,000.
	31	Incurred other operating expenses on account during the year that amounted to $6,000.
	31	Incurred accrued salaries expense of $5,200.
	31	Had $200 of supplies on hand at the end of the period.

Required

Based on the preceding information, answer the following questions. All questions pertain to the 2017 financial statements. (*Hint:* Enter items in general ledger accounts under the accounting equation before answering the questions.)

a. Based on the preceding transaction, identify five additional adjustments and describe them.
b. What amount of interest expense would Porser report on the income statement?
c. What amount of net cash flow from operating activities would Porser report on the statement of cash flows?
d. What amount of rent expense would Porser report on the income statement?
e. What amount of total liabilities would Porser report on the balance sheet?
f. What amount of supplies expense would Porser report on the income statement?
g. What amount of unearned revenue would Porser report on the balance sheet?
h. What amount of net cash flow from investing activities would Porser report on the statement of cash flows?
i. What amount of interest payable would Porser report on the balance sheet?
j. What amount of total expenses would Porser report on the income statement?
k. What amount of retained earnings would Porser report on the balance sheet?
l. What amount of service revenues would Porser report on the income statement?
m. What amount of cash flows from financing activities would Porser report on the statement of cash flows?
n. What amount of net income would Porser report on the income statement?

MULTIPLE-CHOICE QUESTIONS

Multiple-choice questions are available in the Connect library.

EXERCISES—SERIES B

Where applicable in all exercises, round computations to the nearest dollar.

LO 2-1, 2-3

Exercise 2-1B ***Effect of collecting accounts receivable on the accounting equation and financial statements***

Smith Company earned $12,000 of service revenue on account during 2016. The company collected $9,800 cash from accounts receivable during 2016.

Required

Based on this information alone, determine the following for Smith Company. (*Hint:* Record the events in general ledger accounts under an accounting equation before satisfying the requirements.)

a. The balance of the accounts receivable that Smith would report on the December 31, 2016, balance sheet.

b. The amount of net income that Smith would report on the 2016 income statement.

c. The amount of net cash flow from operating activities that would be reported on the 2016 statement of cash flows.

d. The amount of retained earnings that would be reported on the 2016 balance sheet.

e. Why are the answers to Requirements *b* and *c* different?

Exercise 2-2B *Effect of accrued expenses on the accounting equation and financial statements*

LO 2-2, 2-3

During 2016, Star Corporation earned $5,000 of cash revenue and accrued $3,000 of salaries expense.

Required

(*Hint:* Record the events in general ledger accounts under an accounting equation before satisfying the requirements.) Based on this information alone:

a. Prepare the December 31, 2016, balance sheet.

b. Determine the amount of net income that Star would report on the 2016 income statement.

c. Determine the amount of net cash flow from operating activities that Star would report on the 2016 statement of cash flows.

d. Why are the answers to Requirements *b* and *c* different?

Exercise 2-3B *Effect of accruals on the financial statements*

LO 2-1, 2-2, 2-3

Talley Inc. experienced the following events in 2016, in its first year of operation:

1. Received $20,000 cash from the issue of common stock.
2. Performed services on account for $38,000.
3. Paid the utility expense of $2,500.
4. Collected $21,000 of the accounts receivable.
5. Recorded $15,000 of accrued salaries at the end of the year.
6. Paid a $2,000 cash dividend to the shareholders.

Required

a. Record the events in general ledger accounts under an accounting equation. In the last column of the table, provide appropriate account titles for the Retained Earnings amounts. The first transaction has been recorded as an example.

TALLEY INC.
General Ledger Accounts

Event	Assets		=	Liabilities	+	Stockholders' Equity		Acct. Titles for Ret. Earn.
	Cash	Accounts Receivable		Salaries Payable		Common Stock	Retained Earnings	
1.	20,000					20,000		

b. Prepare the income statement, statement of changes in stockholders' equity, balance sheet, and statement of cash flows for the 2016 accounting period.

c. Why is the amount of net income different from the amount of net cash flow from operating activities?

LO 2-1, 2-2, 2-3

Exercise 2-4B *Effect of accounts receivable and accounts payable transactions on financial statements*

The following events apply to Parker and Moates, a public accounting firm, for the 2016 accounting period:

1. Performed $96,000 of services for clients on account.
2. Performed $65,000 of services for cash.
3. Incurred $45,000 of other operating expenses on account.
4. Paid $26,000 cash to an employee for salary.
5. Collected $70,000 cash from accounts receivable.
6. Paid $38,000 cash on accounts payable.
7. Paid a $10,000 cash dividend to the stockholders.
8. Accrued salaries were $3,000 at the end of 2016.

Required

a. Show the effects of the events on the financial statements using a horizontal statements model like the following one. In the Cash Flow column, use OA to designate operating activity, IA for investment activity, FA for financing activity, and NC for net change in cash. Use NA to indicate the element is not affected by the event. The first event is recorded as an example.

Event No.	Assets			=	Liabilities			+	Equity						
	Cash	+	Accts. Rec.	=	Accts. Pay	+	Sal. Pay	+	Ret. Earn.	Rev.	−	Exp.	=	Net Inc.	Cash Flow
1	NA	+	96,000	=	NA	+	NA	+	96,000	96,000	−	NA	=	96,000	NA

b. What is the amount of total assets at the end of 2016?
c. What is the balance of accounts receivable at the end of 2016?
d. What is the balance of accounts payable at the end of 2016?
e. What is the difference between accounts receivable and accounts payable?
f. What is net income for 2016?
g. What is the amount of net cash flow from operating activities for 2016?

LO 2-3

Exercise 2-5B *Missing information related to accruals*

Graphic Design Inc. had a beginning balance of $2,000 in its Accounts Receivable account. The ending balance of Accounts Receivable was $2,400. During the period, Graphic Design recognized $40,000 of revenue on account. The Salaries Payable account has a beginning balance of $1,300 and an ending balance of $900. During the period, the company recognized $35,000 of accrued salary expense.

Required

a. Based on the information provided, determine the amount of net income.
b. Based on the information provided, determine the amount of net cash flow from operating activities.

LO 2-3

Exercise 2-6B *Effect of accruals on the financial statements*

Rosewood Inc. experienced the following events in 2016, its first year of operation:

1. Received $50,000 cash from the issue of common stock.
2. Performed services on account for $67,000.
3. Paid a $5,000 cash dividend to the stockholders.
4. Collected $45,000 of the accounts receivable.
5. Paid $49,000 cash for other operating expenses.
6. Performed services for $10,000 cash.
7. Recognized $2,000 of accrued utilities expense at the end of the year.

Required

a. Identify the events that result in revenue or expense recognition.

b. Based on your response to Requirement *a*, determine the amount of net income reported on the 2016 income statement.

c. Identify the events that affect the statement of cash flows.

d. Based on your response to Requirement *c*, determine the amount of cash flow from operating activities reported on the 2016 statement of cash flows.

e. What is the before- and after-closing balance in the Service Revenue account? What other accounts would be closed at the end of the accounting cycle?

f. What is the balance of the Retained Earnings account that appears on the 2016 balance sheet?

Exercise 2-7B *Net income versus changes in cash* LO 2-3

In 2016, Hall Inc. billed its customers $62,000 for services performed. The company collected $51,000 of the amount billed. Hall incurred $39,000 of other operating expenses on account. Hall paid $31,000 of the accounts payable. Hall acquired $40,000 cash from the issue of common stock. The company invested $21,000 cash in the purchase of land.

Required

(*Hint:* Identify the six events described in the paragraph and record them in general ledger accounts under an accounting equation before attempting to answer the questions.) Use the preceding information to answer the following questions:

a. What amount of revenue will be reported on the 2016 income statement?

b. What amount of cash flow from revenue will be reported on the statement of cash flows?

c. What is the net income for the period?

d. What is the net cash flow from operating activities for the period?

e. Why is the amount of net income different from the net cash flow from operating activities for the period?

f. What is the amount of net cash flow from investing activities?

g. What is the amount of net cash flow from financing activities?

h. What amounts of total assets, liabilities, and equity will be reported on the year-end balance sheet?

Exercise 2-8B *Closing entries* LO 2-4

Beatty Company's accounting records show an after-closing balance of $19,400 in its Retained Earnings account on December 31, 2016. During the 2016 accounting cycle, Beatty earned $15,100 of revenue, incurred $9,200 of expense, and paid $1,500 of dividends. Revenues and expenses were recognized evenly throughout the accounting period.

Required

a. Determine the balance in the Retained Earnings account as of January 1, 2017.

b. Determine the balance in the temporary accounts as of January 1, 2016.

c. Determine the after-closing balance in the Retained Earnings account as of December 31, 2015.

d. Determine the balance in the Retained Earnings account as of June 30, 2016.

Exercise 2-9B *Closing the accounts* LO 2-4

The following information was drawn from the accounting records of Earles Company as of December 31, 2016, before the temporary accounts had been closed. The Cash balance was $6,000, and Notes Payable amounted to $3,000. The company had revenues of $7,000 and expenses of $4,200. The company's Land account had a $4,000 balance. Dividends amounted to $1,000. There was $2,000 of common stock issued.

Required

a. Identify which accounts would be classified as permanent and which accounts would be classified as temporary.

b. Assuming that Earles's beginning balance (as of January 1, 2016) in the Retained Earnings account was $5,200, determine its balance after the temporary accounts were closed at the end of 2016.

c. What amount of net income would Earles Company report on its 2016 income statement?

d. Explain why the amount of net income differs from the amount of the ending Retained Earnings balance.

e. What are the balances in the revenue, expense, and dividend accounts on January 1, 2017?

LO 2-4

Exercise 2-10B *Closing accounts and the accounting cycle*

Required

a. Identify which of the following accounts are temporary (will be closed to Retained Earnings at the end of the year) and which are permanent:

(1) Service Revenue
(2) Dividends
(3) Common Stock
(4) Notes Payable
(5) Cash
(6) Rent Expense
(7) Accounts Receivable
(8) Utilities Expense
(9) Prepaid Insurance
(10) Retained Earnings

b. Sam bragged that he had five years of accounting experience. Susan disagreed, responding, "No. You have had one year of accounting experience five times." Explain what Susan meant. (*Hint:* Refer to the accounting cycle.)

LO 2-4

Exercise 2-11B *Matching concept*

Companies make sacrifices known as *expenses* to obtain benefits called *revenues.* The accurate measurement of net income requires that expenses be matched with revenues. In some circumstances, matching a particular expense directly with revenue is difficult or impossible. In these circumstances, the expense is matched with the period in which it is incurred.

Required

Distinguish the following items that could be matched directly with revenues from the items that would be classified as period expenses:

a. Sales commissions paid to employees.
b. Advertising expense.
c. Supplies.
d. The cost of land that has been sold.

EXERCISES—SERIES B

SECTION 2

LO 2-5

Exercise 2-12B *Supplies and the financial statements model*

Handy Andy Inc. began the 2016 accounting period with $9,000 cash, $5,000 of common stock, and $4,000 of retained earnings. Handy Andy was affected by the following accounting events during 2016:

1. Purchased $9,500 of operating expenses supplies on account.
2. Earned and collected $32,500 of cash revenue.
3. Paid $7,200 cash on accounts payable.
4. Adjusted the records to reflect the use of supplies. A physical count indicated that $1,700 of supplies was still on hand on December 31, 2016.

Required

a. Show the effects of the events on the financial statements using a horizontal statements model like the following one. In the Cash Flows column, use OA to designate operating activity, IA for investing activity, FA for financing activity, and NC for net change in cash. Use NA to indicate accounts not affected by the event. The beginning balances are entered in the following example:

Event No.	Assets			=	Liab.	+	Stockholders' Equity								
	Cash	+	Supplies	=	Accts. Pay.	+	Com. Stk.	+	Ret. Earn.	Rev.	−	Exp.	=	Net Inc.	Cash Flows
Beg. bal.	9,000	+	0	=	0	+	5,000	+	4,000	0	−	0	=	0	0

b. Explain the difference between the amount of net income and amount of net cash flow from operating activities.

Exercise 2-13B *Supplies on financial statements* LO 2-5, 2-8

Janitorial Professionals Inc. experienced the following events in 2016, its first year of operation:

1. Performed services for $20,000 cash.
2. Purchased $4,000 of supplies on account.
3. A physical count on December 31, 2016, found that there was $1,000 of supplies on hand.

Required

Based on this information alone:

a. Record the events under an accounting equation.
b. Prepare an income statement, balance sheet, and statement of cash flows for the 2016 accounting period.
c. What is the balance in the Supplies account as of January 1, 2017?
d. What is the balance in the Supplies Expense account as of January 1, 2017?

Exercise 2-14B *Asset versus expense* LO 2-5, 2-6

A cost can be either an asset or an expense.

Required

a. Distinguish between a cost that is an asset and a cost that is an expense.
b. List three costs that are assets.
c. List three costs that are expenses.

Exercise 2-15B *Prepaid items on financial statements* LO 2-6

Forestry Services Inc. experienced the following events in 2016, its first year of operation:

1. Performed counseling services for $18,000 cash.
2. On February 1, 2016, paid $12,000 cash to rent office space for the coming year.
3. Adjusted the accounts to reflect the amount of rent used during the year.

Required

Based on this information alone:

a. Record the events under an accounting equation.
b. Prepare an income statement, balance sheet, and statement of cash flows for the 2016 accounting period.
c. Ignoring all other future events, what is the amount of rent expense that would be recognized in 2017?

LO 2-6, 2-8

Exercise 2-16B *Effect of an error on financial statements*

On June 1, 2016, Ark Corporation paid $8,400 to purchase a 24-month insurance policy. Assume that Ark records the purchase as an asset and that the books are closed on December 31.

Required

a. Show the purchase of the insurance policy and the related adjusting entry to recognize insurance expense in the accounting equation.

b. Assume that Ark Corporation failed to record the adjusting entry to reflect the expiration of insurance. How would the error affect the company's 2016 income statement and balance sheet?

LO 2-7

Exercise 2-17B *Unearned items on financial statements*

Interior Design Consultants (IDC) experienced the following events in 2016, its first year of operation:

1. On October 1, 2016, IDC collected $24,000 for consulting services it agreed to provide during the coming year.
2. Adjusted the accounts to reflect the amount of consulting service revenue recognized in 2016.

Required

Based on this information alone:

a. Record the events under an accounting equation.

b. Prepare an income statement, balance sheet, and statement of cash flows for the 2016 accounting period.

c. Ignoring all other future events, what is the amount of service revenue that would be recognized in 2017?

LO 2-7

Exercise 2-18B *Unearned revenue defined as a liability*

Jake Lewis received $800 in advance for tutoring fees when he agreed to help Laura Dalton with her introductory accounting course. Upon receiving the cash, Jake mentioned that he would have to record the transaction as a liability on his books. Laura asked, "Why a liability? You don't owe me any money, do you?"

Required

Respond to Laura's question regarding Jake's liability.

LO 2-5, 2-7

Exercise 2-19B *Supplies, unearned revenue, and the financial statements model*

Warren, Attorney at Law, experienced the following transactions in 2016, the first year of operations:

1. Purchased $1,500 of office supplies on account.
2. Accepted $36,000 on February 1, 2016, as a retainer for services to be performed evenly over the next 12 months.
3. Performed legal services for cash of $84,000.
4. Paid cash for salaries expense of $32,000.
5. Paid a cash dividend to the stockholders of $8,000.
6. Paid $1,200 of the amount due on accounts payable.
7. Determined that at the end of the accounting period, $150 of office supplies remained on hand.
8. On December 31, 2016, recognized the revenue that had been earned for services performed in accordance with Transaction 2.

Required

Show the effects of the events on the financial statements using a horizontal statements model like the following one. In the Cash Flow column, use the initials OA to designate operating activity, IA for investing activity, FA for financing activity, and NC for net change in cash. Use NA to indicate accounts not affected by the event. The first event has been recorded as an example.

Event No.	Assets			=	Liabilities			+	Stk. Equity						
	Cash	+	Supplies	=	Accts. Pay.	+	Unearn. Rev.	+	Ret. Earn.	Rev.	–	Exp.	=	Net Inc.	Cash Flow
1	NA	+	1,500	=	1,500	+	NA	+	NA	NA	–	NA	=	NA	NA

Exercise 2-20B *Unearned revenue and the financial statements model*

LO 2-7

Brandon Baily started a personal financial planning business when he accepted $120,000 cash as advance payment for managing the financial assets of a large estate. Baily agreed to manage the estate for a one-year period beginning May 1, 2016.

Required

a. Show the effects of the advance payment and revenue recognition on the 2016 financial statements using a horizontal statements model like the following one. In the Cash Flows column, use OA to designate operating activity, IA for investing activity, FA for financing activity, and NC for net change in cash. Use NA if the account is not affected.

Event	Assets	=	Liab.	+	Stockholders' Equity	Rev.	–	Exp.	=	Net Inc.	Cash Flows
	Cash	=	Unearn. Rev.	+	Ret. Earn.						

b. How much revenue would Baily recognize on the 2017 income statement?

c. What is the amount of cash flow from operating activities in 2017?

Exercise 2-21B *Prepaid vs. unearned, the entity concept*

LO 2-6, 2-7

On October 1, 2016, Stokes Company paid Eastport Rentals $4,800 for a 12-month lease on warehouse space.

Required

a. Record the deferral and the related December 31, 2016, adjustment for Stokes Company in the accounting equation.

b. Record the deferral and the related December 31, 2016, adjustment for Eastport Rentals in the accounting equation.

Exercise 2-22B *Identifying deferral and accrual events*

LO 2-1, 2-2, 2-5, 2-6, 2-7

Required

Identify each of the following events as an accrual, deferral, or neither:

a. Incurred other operating expenses on account.

b. Recorded expense for salaries owed to employees at the end of the accounting period.

c. Paid a cash dividend to the stockholders.

d. Paid cash to purchase supplies to be used over the next several months.

e. Paid cash to purchase land.

f. Provided services on account.

g. Collected accounts receivable.

h. Paid one year's rent in advance.

i. Paid cash for utilities expense.

j. Collected $2,400 in advance for services to be performed over the next 12 months.

k. Recorded interest revenue earned for the period.

LO 2-1, 2-2, 2-5, 2-6, 2-7

Exercise 2-23B *Revenue and expense recognition*

Required

a. Describe a revenue recognition event that results in an increase in assets.
b. Describe a revenue recognition event that results in a decrease in liabilities.
c. Describe an expense recognition event that results in an increase in liabilities.
d. Describe an expense recognition event that results in a decrease in assets.

LO 2-5, 2-6, 2-7

Exercise 2-24B *Adjusting the accounts*

Patal Inc. experienced the following accounting events during its 2016 accounting period:

1. Paid cash to settle an account payable.
2. Collected a cash advance for services that will be provided during the coming year.
3. Paid a cash dividend to the stockholders.
4. Paid cash for a one-year lease to rent office space.
5. Collected cash from accounts receivable.
6. Recognized cash revenue.
7. Issued common stock.
8. Paid cash to purchase land.
9. Paid cash to purchase supplies.
10. Recognized operating expenses on account.

Required

a. Identify the events that would require a year-end adjusting entry.
b. Are adjusting or closing entries recorded first? Why?

LO 2-8

Exercise 2-25B *Classifying events on the statement of cash flows*

The following transactions pertain to the operations of Blair Company for 2016:

1. Acquired $30,000 cash from the issue of common stock.
2. Performed services for $12,000 cash.
3. Paid a $7,200 cash advance for a one-year contract to rent equipment.
4. Recognized $15,000 of accrued salary expense.
5. Accepted a $21,000 cash advance for services to be performed in the future.
6. Provided $60,000 of services on account.
7. Incurred $28,000 of other operating expenses on account.
8. Collected $51,000 cash from accounts receivable.
9. Paid a $5,000 cash dividend to the stockholders.
10. Paid $22,000 cash on accounts payable.

Required

a. Classify the cash flows from these transactions as operating activities (OA), investing activities (IA), or financing activities (FA). Use NA for transactions that do not affect the statement of cash flows.
b. Prepare a statement of cash flows. (There is no beginning cash balance.)

LO 2-8

Exercise 2-26B *Relationship of accounts to financial statements*

Required

Identify whether each of the following items would appear on the income statement (IS), statement of changes in stockholders' equity (SE), balance sheet (BS), or statement of cash flows (CF). Some items may appear on more than one statement; if so, identify all applicable statements. If an item would not appear on any financial statement, label it NA.

a. Consulting Revenue
b. Market Value of Land
c. Supplies Expense
d. Salaries Payable
e. Notes Payable
f. Ending Common Stock
g. Beginning Cash Balance
h. Prepaid Rent
i. Net Change in Cash
j. Land
k. Operating Expenses
l. Total Liabilities
m. "As of" Date Notation
n. Salaries Expense
o. Net Income
p. Service Revenue
q. Cash Flow from Operating Activities
r. Operating Income
s. Interest Receivable
t. Interest Revenue
u. Rent Expense
v. Salary Expense
w. Total Stockholders' Equity
x. Unearned Revenue
y. Cash Flow from Investing Activities
z. Insurance Expense
aa. Ending Retained Earnings
bb. Interest Revenue
cc. Supplies
dd. Beginning Retained Earnings
ee. Utilities Payable
ff. Cash Flow from Financing Activities
gg. Accounts Receivable
hh. Prepaid Insurance
ii. Ending Cash Balance
jj. Utilities Expense
kk. Accounts Payable
ll. Beginning Common Stock
mm. Dividends
nn. Total Assets

Exercise 2-27B *Effect of accounting events on the income statement and statement of cash flows*

LO 2-8

Required

Explain how each of the following events or series of events and the related adjusting entry will affect the amount of *net income* and the amount of *cash flow from operating activities* reported on the year-end financial statements. Identify the direction of change (increase, decrease, or NA) and the amount of the change. Organize your answers according to the following table. The first event is recorded as an example. If an event does not have a related adjusting entry, record only the effects of the event.

	Net Income		Cash Flows from Operating Activities	
Event	Direction of Change	Amount of Change	Direction of Change	Amount of Change
a	NA	NA	NA	NA

a. Acquired $60,000 cash from the issue of common stock.
b. Earned $20,000 of revenue on account. Collected $15,000 cash from accounts receivable.
c. Paid $4,800 cash on October 1 to purchase a one-year insurance policy.
d. Collected $12,000 in advance for services to be performed in the future. The contract called for services to start on August 1 and to continue for one year.
e. Accrued salaries amounting to $5,000.
f. Sold land that cost $15,000 for $15,000 cash.
g. Provided services for $9,200 cash.
h. Purchased $2,000 of supplies on account. Paid $1,500 cash on accounts payable. The ending balance in the Supplies account, after adjustment, was $800.
i. Paid cash for other operating expenses of $2,200.

LO 2-9

Exercise 2-28B *Transactions that affect the elements of financial statements*

Required

Give an example of a transaction that will

a. Increase an asset and decrease another asset (asset exchange event).
b. Increase an asset and increase a liability (asset source event).
c. Decrease an asset and decrease a liability (asset use event).
d. Decrease an asset and decrease equity (asset use event).
e. Increase a liability and decrease equity (claims exchange event).
f. Increase an asset and increase equity (asset source event).
g. Decrease a liability and increase equity (claims exchange event).

LO 2-9

Exercise 2-29B *Identifying source, use, and exchange transactions*

Required

Indicate whether each of the following transactions is an asset source (AS), asset use (AU), asset exchange (AE), or claims exchange (CE) transaction:

a. Performed services for clients on account.
b. Paid cash for salary expense.
c. Acquired cash from the issue of common stock.
d. Incurred other operating expenses on account.
e. Performed services for cash.
f. Paid cash on accounts payable.
g. Collected cash from accounts receivable.
h. Paid a cash dividend to the stockholders.
i. Received cash for services to be performed in the future.
j. Purchased land with cash.

LO 2-9

Exercise 2-30B *Identifying asset source, use, and exchange transactions*

Required

a. Name an asset use transaction that will affect the income statement.
b. Name an asset use transaction that will *not* affect the income statement.
c. Name an asset exchange transaction that will *not* affect the statement of cash flows.
d. Name an asset exchange transaction that will affect the statement of cash flows.
e. Name an asset source transaction that will *not* affect the income statement.

LO 2-8, 2-9

Exercise 2-31B *Identifying transaction type and effect on the financial statements*

Required

Identify whether each of the following transactions is an asset source (AS), asset use (AU), asset exchange (AE), or claims exchange (CE). Also show the effects of the events on the financial statements using the horizontal statements model. Indicate whether the event increases (I), decreases (D), or does not affect (NA) each element of the financial statements. In the Cash Flows column, designate the cash flows as operating activities (OA), investing activities (IA), or financing activities (FA). The first two transactions have been recorded as examples.

Event	Type of Event	Assets	=	Liabilities	+	Stockholders' Equity: Common Stock	+	Stockholders' Equity: Retained Earnings	Rev.	−	Exp.	=	Net Inc.	Cash Flows
a	AE	I/D		NA		NA		NA	NA		NA		NA	D IA
b	AS	I		NA		I		NA	NA		NA		NA	I FA

a. Purchased land for cash.
b. Acquired cash from the issue of common stock.
c. Collected cash from accounts receivable.
d. Paid cash for operating expenses.
e. Recorded accrued salaries.
f. Purchased supplies on account.
g. Performed services on account.
h. Paid cash in advance for rent on office space.
i. Adjusted the books to record supplies used during the period.
j. Performed services for cash.
k. Paid cash for salaries accrued at the end of a prior period.
l. Paid a cash dividend to the stockholders.
m. Adjusted books to reflect the amount of prepaid rent expired during the period.
n. Incurred operating expenses on account.
o. Paid cash on accounts payable.
p. Received cash advance for services to be provided in the future.
q. Recorded accrued interest revenue earned at the end of the accounting period.

Exercise 2-32B *Ethical conduct*

LO 2-10

An October 31, 2012, news release from Hewlett-Packard Company (HP) included the following:

> *HP recorded a non-cash charge for the impairment of goodwill and intangible assets within its Software segment of approximately $8.8 billion in the fourth quarter of its 2012 fiscal year. The majority of this impairment charge is linked to serious accounting improprieties, disclosure failures and outright misrepresentations at Autonomy Corporation that occurred prior to HP's acquisition of Autonomy and the associated impact of those improprieties, failures and misrepresentations on the expected future financial performance of the Autonomy business over the long-term.*

Required

Comment on the provisions of SOX that pertain to intentional misrepresentation and describe the maximum penalty that CFO could face.

Exercise 2-33B *Effect of depreciation on the accounting equation and financial statements (Appendix)*

LO 2-11

The following events apply to Highland Grill for the 2016 fiscal year:

1. Started the company when it acquired $40,000 cash by issuing common stock.
2. Purchased a new stove that cost $24,000 cash.
3. Earned $21,000 in cash revenue.
4. Paid $3,500 of cash for salaries expense.
5. Adjusted the records to reflect the use of the stove. Purchased on January 1, 2016, the stove has an expected useful life of four years and an estimated salvage value of $4,000. Use straight-line depreciation. The adjusting entry was made as of December 31, 2016.

Required

a. Write an accounting equation and record the effects of each accounting event under the appropriate general ledger account headings.
b. Prepare a balance sheet and a statement of cash flows for the 2016 accounting period.
c. What is the net income for 2016?
d. What is the amount of depreciation expense Highland Grill would report on the 2017 income statement?
e. What amount of accumulated depreciation would Highland Grill report on the December 31, 2017, balance sheet?
f. Would the cash flow from operating activities be affected by depreciation in 2017?

LO 2-11

Exercise 2-34B *Depreciation affecting multiple cycles (Appendix)*

On January 1, 2016, Yallow Cab Inc. paid $29,000 cash to purchase a taxi cab. The taxi had a three-year useful life and a $5,000 salvage value.

Required

a. Determine the amount of depreciation expense that would appear on the 2016 and 2017 income statements.

b. Determine the amount of accumulated depreciation that would appear on the 2016 and 2017 balance sheets.

c. Explain how the purchase of equipment would affect the 2016 and 2017 statements of cash flows.

LO 2-12

Exercise 2-35B *Effects of recognizing accrued interest on financial statements (Appendix)*

Carry Connelly started Connelly Company on January 1, 2016. The company experienced the following events during its first year of operation:

1. Earned $6,200 of cash revenue.
2. Borrowed $10,000 cash from the bank.
3. Adjusted the accounting records to recognize accrued interest expense on the bank note. The note, issued on September 1, 2016, had a one-year term and a 9 percent annual interest rate.

Required

a. What is the amount of interest payable at December 31, 2016?

b. What is the amount of interest expense in 2016?

c. What is the amount of interest paid in 2016?

d. Use a horizontal statements model to show how each event affects the balance sheet, income statement, and statement of cash flows. Indicate whether the event increases (I) decreases (D), or does not affect (NA) each element of the financial statements. Also, in the Cash Flows column, designate the cash flows as operating activities (OA), investing activities (IA), or financing activities (FA). The first transaction has been recorded as an example.

Event No.	Balance Sheet									Income Statement					Statement of Cash Flows
	Cash	=	Note Pay.	+	Int. Pay.	+	C. Stk.	+	Ret. Earn.	Rev.	−	Exp.	=	Net Inc.	
1	I	=	NA	+	NA	+	NA	+	I	I	−	NA	=	I	I OA

LO 2-12

Exercise 2-36B *Recognizing accrued interest revenue (Appendix)*

California Company invested $120,000 in a certificate of deposit on August 1, 2016. The certificate had a 3 percent annual rate of interest and a one-year term to maturity.

Required

a. What amount of interest revenue will California recognize for the year ending December 31, 2016?

b. Show how the December 31, 2016, adjusting entry to recognize the accrued interest revenue affects the accounting equation.

c. What amount of cash will California collect for interest revenue in 2016?

d. What is the amount of interest receivable as of December 31, 2016?

e. What amount of cash will California collect for interest revenue in 2017, assuming it does not renew the CD?

f. What amount of interest revenue will California recognize in 2017, assuming it does not renew the CD?

g. What is the amount of interest receivable as of December 31, 2017, assuming it does not renew the CD?

PROBLEMS—SERIES B

Problem 2-37B *Effect of adjusting entries on the accounting equation*

LO 2-4

CHECK FIGURE
b. adjustment amount: $2,200

Required

Each of the following independent events requires a year-end adjusting entry. Show how each event and its related adjusting entry affect the accounting equation. Assume a December 31 closing date. The first event is recorded as an example.

	Total Assets					Stockholders' Equity		
Event/ Adjustment	Cash	+	Other Assets	=	Liabilities	+	Common Stock	+	Retained Earnings
a	−6,000		+6,000		NA		NA		NA
Adj.	NA		−4,500		NA		NA		−4,500

a. Paid $6,000 cash in advance on April 1 for a one-year insurance policy.
b. Purchased $2,400 of supplies on account. At year's end, $200 of supplies remained on hand.
c. Paid $7,200 cash in advance on March 1 for a one-year lease on office space.
d. Received an $18,000 cash advance for a contract to provide services in the future. The contract required a one-year commitment starting September 1.

Problem 2-38B *Closing the accounts*

LO 2-4

The following selected accounts and account balances were taken from the records of Wages Company. Except as otherwise indicated, all balances are as of December 31, 2016, before the closing entries were recorded.

Cash received from common stock issued during 2016	$4,500
Cash	10,500
Revenue	18,000
Salary expense	13,000
Cash flow from operating activities	4,500
Notes payable	6,000
Utility expense	1,800
Dividends	1,000
Cash flow from financing activities	5,000
Rent expense	1,600
Land	25,000
Retained earnings, January 1, 2016	19,700
Common stock, December 31, 2016	20,000

Required

a. Prepare the income statement Wages would include in its 2016 annual report.
b. Identify the accounts that should be closed to the Retained Earnings account.
c. Determine the Retained Earnings account balance at December 31, 2016. Identify the reasons for the difference between net income and the ending balance in Retained Earnings.
d. What are the balances in the Revenue, Expense, and Dividend accounts on January 1, 2017? Explain.

Problem 2-39B *Recording events in a horizontal statements model*

LO 2-8

The following events pertain to Weaver Cleaning Company:

1. Acquired $15,000 cash from the issue of common stock.
2. Provided services for $6,000 cash.
3. Provided $18,000 of services on account.
4. Collected $11,000 cash from the account receivable created in Event 3.
5. Paid $1,400 cash to purchase supplies.

6. Had $100 of supplies on hand at the end of the accounting period.
7. Received $3,600 cash in advance for services to be performed in the future.
8. Performed one-half of the services agreed to in Event 7.
9. Paid $6,500 for salaries expense.
10. Incurred $2,800 of other operating expenses on account.
11. Paid $2,100 cash on the account payable created in Event 10.
12. Paid a $1,000 cash dividend to the stockholders.

Required

Show the effects of the events on the financial statements using a horizontal statements model like the following one. In the Cash Flows column, use the letters OA to designate operating activity, IA for investing activity, FA for financing activity, and NC for net change in cash. Use NA to indicate accounts not affected by the event. The first event is recorded as an example.

	Assets					=	Liabilities			+	Stockholders' Equity								
Event No.	Cash	+	Accts. Rec.	+	Supp.	=	Accts. Pay.	+	Unearn. Rev.	+	Com. Stk.	+	Ret. Earn.	Rev.	−	Exp.	=	Net Inc.	Cash Flows
1	15,000	+	NA	+	NA	=	NA	+	NA	+	15,000	+	NA	NA	−	NA	=	NA	15,000 FA

LO 2-8

Problem 2-40B *Effect of events on financial statements*

Gossett Company had the following balances in its accounting records as of December 31, 2015:

Assets		Liabilities and Equity	
Cash	$ 60,000	Accounts Payable	$ 32,000
Accounts Receivable	45,000	Common Stock	60,000
Land	35,000	Retained Earnings	48,000
Totals	$140,000		$140,000

The following accounting events apply to Gossett for 2016:

Jan. 1	Acquired an additional $30,000 cash from the issue of common stock.
April 1	Paid $7,200 cash in advance for a one-year lease for office space.
June 1	Paid a $5,000 cash dividend to the stockholders.
July 1	Purchased additional land that cost $40,000 cash.
Aug. 1	Made a cash payment on accounts payable of $21,000.
Sept. 1	Received $9,600 cash in advance as a retainer for services to be performed monthly during the next eight months.
Sept. 30	Sold land for $20,000 cash that had originally cost $20,000.
Oct. 1	Purchased $1,200 of supplies on account.
Dec. 31	Earned $75,000 of service revenue on account during the year.
31	Received $62,000 cash collections from accounts receivable.
31	Incurred $27,000 other operating expenses on account during the year.
31	Recognized accrued salaries expense of $18,000.
31	Had $100 of supplies on hand at the end of the period.
31	The land purchased on July 1 had a market value of $56,000.
31	Recognized $120 of accrued interest revenue.

Required

Based on the preceding information for Gossett Company answer the following questions. All questions pertain to the 2016 financial statements. (*Hint:* Record the events in general ledger accounts under an accounting equation before answering the questions.)

a. What two additional adjusting entries need to be made at the end of the year?
b. What amount would be reported for land on the balance sheet?
c. What amount of net cash flow from operating activities would be reported on the statement of cash flows?

d. What amount of rent expense would be reported on the income statement?

e. What amount of total liabilities would be reported on the balance sheet?

f. What amount of supplies expense would be reported on the income statement?

g. What amount of unearned revenue would be reported on the balance sheet?

h. What amount of net cash flow from investing activities would be reported on the statement of cash flows?

i. What amount of total expenses would be reported on the income statement?

j. What total amount of service revenue would be reported on the income statement?

k. What amount of cash flows from financing activities would be reported on the statement of cash flows?

l. What amount of net income would be reported on the income statement?

m. What amount of retained earnings would be reported on the balance sheet?

Problem 2-41B *Identifying and arranging elements on financial statements*

LO 2-8

The following accounts and balances were drawn from the records of Shearer Company at December 31, 2016:

Cash	$22,100	Accounts receivable	$21,000
Land	43,000	Cash flow from operating act.	8,600
Insurance expense	2,500	Beginning retained earnings	47,200
Dividends	5,000	Beginning common stock	5,500
Prepaid insurance	3,500	Service revenue	86,000
Accounts payable	15,000	Cash flow from financing act.	9,000
Supplies	2,100	Ending common stock	14,500
Supplies expense	1,000	Cash flow from investing act.	(6,000)
Rent expense	3,500	Other operating expenses	59,000

Required

Use the accounts and balances from Shearer Company to construct an income statement, statement of changes in stockholders' equity, balance sheet, and statement of cash flows (show only totals for each activity on the statement of cash flows).

Problem 2-42B *Missing information in financial statements*

LO 2-8

Required

Fill in the blanks (indicated by the alphabetic letters in parentheses) in the following financial statements. Assume the company started operations January 1, 2016, and all transactions involve cash.

	For the Years		
	2016	2017	2018
Income Statements			
Revenue	$ 400	$ 500	$ 800
Expense	(250)	(l)	(425)
Net income	$ (a)	$ 100	$ 375
Statement of Changes in Stockholders' Equity			
Beginning common stock	$ 0	$ (m)	$9,100
Plus: Common stock issued	(b)	1,100	310
Ending common stock	$8,000	9,100	(s)
Beginning retained earnings	0	25	75
Plus: Net income	(c)	100	375
Less: Dividends	(d)	(50)	(150)
Ending retained earnings	25	(n)	300
Total stockholders' equity	$ (e)	$9,175	$ (t)

continued

Balance Sheets			
Assets			
Cash	$ (f)	$ (o)	$ (u)
Land	0	(p)	2,500
Total assets	$11,000	$11,650	$10,550
Liabilities	$ (g)	$ (q)	$ 840
Stockholders' equity			
Common stock	(h)	(r)	9,410
Retained earnings	(i)	75	300
Total stockholders' equity	8,025	9,175	9,710
Total liabilities and stockholders' equity	$11,000	$11,650	$10,550

Statements of Cash Flows			
Cash flows from operating activities			
Cash receipts from customers	$ (j)	$ 500	$ (v)
Cash payments for expenses	(k)	(400)	(w)
Net cash flows from operating activities	150	100	375
Cash flows from investing activities			
Cash payments for land	0	(5,000)	0
Cash receipt from sale of land	0	0	2,500
Net cash flows from investing activities	0	(5,000)	2,500
Cash flows from financing activities			
Cash receipts from borrowed funds	2,975	0	0
Cash payments to reduce debt	0	(500)	(x)
Cash receipts from stock issue	8,000	1,100	(y)
Cash payments for dividends	(125)	(50)	(z)
Net cash flows from financing activities	10,850	550	(1,475)
Net change in cash	11,000	(4,350)	1,400
Plus: Beginning cash balance	0	11,000	6,650
Ending cash balance	$11,000	$ 6,650	$ 8,050

LO 2-8, 2-9

Problem 2-43B *Events for two complete accounting cycles*

Iowa Service Company was formed on January 1, 2016.

Events Affecting the 2016 Accounting Period

1. Acquired cash of $60,000 from the issue of common stock.
2. Purchased $1,200 of supplies on account.
3. Purchased land that cost $18,000 cash.
4. Paid $800 cash to settle accounts payable created in Event 2.
5. Recognized revenue on account of $42,000.
6. Paid $21,000 cash for other operating expenses.
7. Collected $38,000 cash from accounts receivable.

Information for 2016 Adjusting Entries

8. Recognized accrued salaries of $3,200 on December 31, 2016.
9. Had $200 of supplies on hand at the end of the accounting period.

Events Affecting the 2017 Accounting Period

1. Acquired an additional $20,000 cash from the issue of common stock.
2. Paid $3,200 cash to settle the salaries payable obligation.
3. Paid $3,600 cash in advance for a lease on office facilities.
4. Sold land that had cost $15,000 for $15,000 cash.

5. Received $4,800 cash in advance for services to be performed in the future.
6. Purchased $1,000 of supplies on account during the year.
7. Provided services on account of $32,000.
8. Collected $33,000 cash from accounts receivable.
9. Paid a cash dividend of $5,000 to the stockholders.
10. Paid other operating expenses of $19,500.

Information for 2017 Adjusting Entries

11. The advance payment for rental of the office facilities (see Event 3) was made on March 1 for a one-year lease term.
12. The cash advance for services to be provided in the future was collected on October 1 (see Event 5). The one-year contract started October 1.
13. Had $300 of supplies on hand at the end of the period.
14. Recognized accrued salaries of $3,900 at the end of the accounting period.
15. Recognized $400 of accrued interest revenue.

Required

a. Identify each event affecting the 2016 and 2017 accounting periods as asset source (AS), asset use (AU), asset exchange (AE), or claims exchange (CE). Record the effects of each event under the appropriate general ledger account headings of the accounting equation.

b. Prepare an income statement, statement of changes in stockholders' equity, balance sheet, and statement of cash flows for 2016 and 2017, using the vertical statements model.

Problem 2-44B *Ethics*

LO 2-10

Raula Kato discovered a material reporting error in the accounting records of Sampoon, Inc. (SI), during the annual audit. The error was so significant that it will certainly have an adverse effect on the price of the client's stock which is actively traded on the western stock exchange. After talking to his close friend, and president of SI, Kato agreed to withhold the information until the president had time to sell his SI stock. Kato leaked the information to his parents so that they could sell their shares of stock as well. The reporting matter was a relatively complex issue that involved recently issued reporting standards. Kato told himself that if he were caught he would simply plead ignorance. He would simply say that he did not have time to keep up with the rapidly changing standards and he would be off the hook.

Required

a. Write a memo that identifies specific principles of the AICPA Code of Professional Conduct that were violated by Kato.

b. Would pleading ignorance relieve Kato from his audit responsibilities?

Problem 2-45B *Effect of events on financial statements (Appendix)*

LO 2-1, 2-2, 2-3, 2-4, 2-5, 2-6, 2-11, 2-12

Oaks Company had the following balances in its accounting records as of December 31, 2016:

Assets		Claims	
Cash	$ 61,000	Accounts payable	$ 25,000
Accounts receivable	45,000	Common stock	90,000
Land	27,000	Retained earnings	18,000
Totals	$133,000		$133,000

The following accounting events apply to Oaks's 2017 fiscal year:

Jan. 1 Acquired an additional $70,000 cash from the issue of common stock.

1 Purchased a delivery van that cost $26,000 and that had an $7,000 salvage value and a five-year useful life.

Mar. 1 Borrowed $21,000 by issuing a note that had an 8 percent annual interest rate and a one-year term.

April	1	Paid $6,600 cash in advance for a one-year lease for office space.
June	1	Paid a $3,000 cash dividend to the stockholders.
July	1	Purchased land that cost $25,000 cash.
Aug.	1	Made a cash payment on accounts payable of $13,000.
Sept.	1	Received $8,400 cash in advance as a retainer for services to be performed monthly during the next eight months.
Oct.	1	Purchased $900 of supplies on account.
Nov.	1	Purchased a one-year $30,000 certificate of deposit that paid a 4 percent annual rate of interest.
Dec.	31	Earned $80,000 of service revenue on account during the year.
	31	Received $56,000 cash collections from accounts receivable.
	31	Incurred $16,000 other operating expenses on account during the year.
	31	Incurred accrued salaries expense of $5,000.
	31	Had $250 of supplies on hand at the end of the period.

Required

Based on the preceding information, answer the following questions. All questions pertain to the 2017 financial statements. (*Hint:* Record the events in general ledger accounts under an accounting equation before answering the questions.)

a. What additional five adjusting entries are required at the end of the year?

b. What amount of interest expense would Oaks report on the income statement?

c. What amount of net cash flow from operating activities would Oaks report on the statement of cash flows?

d. What amount of rent expense would Oaks report on the income statement?

e. What amount of total liabilities would Oaks report on the balance sheet?

f. What amount of supplies expense would Oaks report on the income statement?

g. What amount of unearned revenue would Oaks report on the balance sheet?

h. What amount of net cash flow from investing activities would Oaks report on the statement of cash flows?

i. What amount of interest payable would Oaks report on the balance sheet?

j. What amount of total expenses would Oaks report on the income statement?

k. What amount of retained earnings would Oaks report on the balance sheet?

l. What total amount of service revenues would Oaks report on the income statement?

m. What amount of cash flows from financing activities would Oaks report on the statement of cash flows?

n. What amount of net income would Oaks report on the income statement?

ANALYZE, THINK, COMMUNICATE

ATC 2-1 Business Applications Case *Understanding real-world annual reports*

Required

Target Corporation

Use the Target Corporation annual report in Appendix B to answer the following questions:

a. Which accounts on Target's balance sheet are accrual type accounts?

b. Which accounts on Target's balance sheet are deferral type accounts?

c. Compare Target's *net income* to its *cash provided by operating activities* for the fiscal-year ended February 1, 2014 (2013). Which is larger?

d. First, compare Target's 2012 net income to its 2013 net income. Next, compare Target's 2012 cash provided by operating activities to its 2013 cash provided by operating activities. Which changed the most from 2012 to 2013, net income or cash provided by operating activities?

ATC 2-2 Group Assignment *Missing information*

Verizon Communications, Inc., is one of the world's largest providers of communication services. The following information, taken from the company's annual reports, is available for the years 2013, 2012, and 2011:

	2013	2012	2011
Revenues	$120,550	$115,846	$110,875
Operating expenses	88,582	102,686	97,995

In 2010, Verizon's operating income was $14,645. Operating income is a subcategory of net income.

Required

a. Divide the class into groups of four or five students. Organize the groups into three sections. Assign each section of groups the financial data for one of the preceding accounting periods.

Group Tasks

(1) Determine the amount of net income for the year assigned.

(2) How does the result in item 1 above affect the retained earnings of the company?

(3) Compute the percentage growth rate for each year.

(4) Have representatives from each section put the income statement for their respective year on the board.

Class Discussion

b. Have the class discuss the trend in revenue and net income.

ATC 2-3 Business Application Case *Analyzing earnings information using real-world data*

The following data are based on information in the 2013 annual report of Cracker Barrel Old Country Store. As of September 30, 2013, Cracker Barrel operated 624 restaurants and gift shops in 42 states. Dollar amounts are in thousands.

	2013	2012
Assets	$1,388,306	$1,418,992
Liabilities	904,280	1,036,317
Stockholders' equity	484,026	382,675
Revenues	2,644,630	2,434,435
Expenses	2,527,365	2,331,354
Dividends	53,515	26,915
Retained earnings at end of 2011		$ 298,757

Required

a. Calculate the company's net income and retained earnings for 2012 and 2013.

b. Which increased (or decreased) by the greatest percentage amount: revenues or net income? Show your computations.

c. For each year, calculate the company's net income as a percentage of its revenues. Show your computations.

d. Did the company perform better in 2012 or 2013? Explain your answer.

ATC 2-4 Business Application Case *Analyzing cash flow information using real-world data*

The following data are based on information in the 2013 annual report of Buffalo Wild Wings, Inc. As of December 29, 2013, there were 993 Buffalo Wild Wings restaurants. The parent company owned 434 restaurants and 559 were franchised. Dollar amounts are in thousands.

	2013	2012
Assets	$ 705,728	$ 591,087
Liabilities	239,920	207,715
Stockholders' equity	465,808	383,372
Revenues	1,266,719	1,040,530
Expenses	1,195,165	983,255
Cash flows from operating activities	179,360	145,188
Cash flows from investing activities	(145,741)	(142,753)
Cash flows from financing activities	3,039	(1,588)
Cash balance at the beginning of 2012 was $20,530		

Required

a. Calculate the company's net change in cash for 2012 and 2013.

b. Calculate the company's ending cash balance for 2012 and 2013.

c. Notice that cash flows from investing activities were negative for each year. Do you think this represents something positive or negative about the company? Explain your answer.

ATC 2-5 Business Application Case *Analyzing earnings information at two real-world companies*

The following data are based on information in the 2013 annual reports of Aéropostale, Inc., and American Eagle Outfitters, Inc. Dollar amounts are in thousands.

Aéropostale, Inc. is a retailer of casual apparel and accessories, targeting 14- to 17-year-old young women and young men. As of February 2, 2013, it operated 1,006 stores in 50 states Puerto Rico, and Canada.

American Eagle Outfitters, Inc., is a retailer of clothing and accessories, targeting 15- to 25-year-old customers. As of February 2, 2013, it operated 1,044 American Eagle Outfitters stores in the United States, Puerto Rico, and Canada.

	Aéropostale	American Eagle Outfitters
Assets	$ 740,844	$1,756,053
Liabilities	330,480	534,866
Stockholders' equity	410,364	1,221,187
Revenues	2,386,178	3,475,802
Expenses	2,351,255	3,243,694
Dividends	-	414,301
Retained earnings at end of 2012	459,279	1,771,464

Required

a. Calculate each company's net income and retained earnings for 2013.

b. For each company, calculate its net earnings as a percentage of its revenues. Show your computations.

c. Which company performed better in 2013? Explain your answer.

ATC 2-6 Business Application Case *Analyzing cash flow information at two real-world companies*

The following data are based on information in the 2013 annual reports of H&R Block, Inc., and Intuit, Inc. Dollar amounts are in thousands.

H&R Block, Inc., has subsidiaries that provide tax, investment, retail banking, accounting, and business consulting services and products in the United States, Canada, and Australia. For the fiscal year ended April 30, 2013, the company prepared approximately 25.4 million tax returns.

Intuit, Inc., is the company that sells the popular tax preparation software called Turbo Tax along with its other major product, QuickBooks. In the fiscal year ended July 31, 2013, its products were used by more than 45 million customers.

	H&R Block	Intuit
Assets	$4,537,779	$5,486,000
Liabilities	3,274,232	1,955,000
Stockholders' equity	1,263,547	3,531,000
Revenues	2,905,943	4,171,000
Expenses	2,471,995	3,313,000
Cash flows from operating activities	497,108	1,366,000
Cash flows from investing activities	(110,937)	(485,000)
Cash flows from financing activities	(584,541)	(262,000)
Cash balance at the beginning of 2013	1,944,334	393,000

Required

a. Calculate each company's net income and net change in cash for 2013.

b. Calculate each company's ending cash balance for 2013.

c. Notice that cash flows from investing activities were negative for both companies. Do you think this represents something positive or negative about the companies? Write a brief explanation of your answer.

d. Notice that cash flows from financing activities were negative for both companies. Write a brief explanation as to what might have caused this.

ATC 2-7 Ethical Dilemma *What is a little deceit among friends?*

Glenn's Cleaning Services Company is experiencing cash flow problems and needs a loan. Glenn has a friend who is willing to lend him the money he needs provided she can be convinced that he will be able to repay the debt. Glenn has assured his friend that his business is viable, but his friend has asked to see the company's financial statements. Glenn's accountant produced the following financial statements:

Income Statement	
Service Revenue	$ 38,000
Operating Expenses	(70,000)
Net Loss	$(32,000)

Balance Sheet	
Assets	$85,000
Liabilities	$35,000
Stockholders' Equity	
Common Stock	82,000
Retained Earnings	(32,000)
Total Liabilities and Stockholders' Equity	$85,000

Glenn made the following adjustments to these statements before showing them to his friend. He recorded $82,000 of revenue on account from Barrymore Manufacturing Company for a contract to clean its headquarters office building that was still being negotiated for the next month. Barrymore had scheduled a meeting to sign a contract the following week, so Glenn was sure that he would get the job. Barrymore was a reputable company, and Glenn was confident that he could ultimately collect the $82,000. Also, he subtracted $30,000 of accrued salaries expense and the corresponding liability. He reasoned that since he had not paid the employees, he had not incurred any expense.

Required

a. Reconstruct the income statement and balance sheet as they would appear after Glenn's adjustments. Comment on the accuracy of the adjusted financial statements.

b. Suppose you are Glenn and the $30,000 you owe your employees is due next week. If you are unable to pay them, they will quit and the business will go bankrupt. You are sure you will be able to repay your friend when your employees perform the $82,000 of services for Barrymore and you collect the cash. However, your friend is risk averse and is not likely to make the loan based on the financial statements your accountant prepared. Would you make the changes that Glenn made to get the loan and thereby save your company? Defend your position with a rational explanation.

c. Discuss the elements of the fraud triangle as they apply to Glenn's decision to change the financial statements to reflect more favorable results.

ATC 2-8 Research Assignment *Identifying accruals and deferrals at Netflix, Inc.*

This chapter defined and discussed accrual and deferral transactions. Complete the requirements below using the most recent financial statements available on the Internet for Netflix, Inc. Obtain the statements by following the steps below. (Be aware that the formatting of the company's website may have changed since these instructions were written.)

1. Go to www.netflix.com.
2. Click on "Investor Relations," which is at the bottom of the page in very small print.
3. Click on the "Annual Reports and Proxies" link at the left side of the page.
4. Click on the "20xxAnnual Report." Use the .pdf version of the annual report.
5. Find the company's balance sheet and complete the requirements below. In recent years this has been shown toward the end of the Form 10-K section of the company's annual report, around page 50. The "Index" near the beginning of the report can help you locate the financial statements.

Required

a. Make a list of all the accounts on the balance sheet that you believe are accrual type accounts.

b. Make a list of all the accounts on the balance sheet that you believe are deferral type accounts.

ATC 2-9 Spreadsheet Assignment *Using Excel*

Required

a. Refer to Problem 2-41A. Use an Excel spreadsheet to construct the required financial statements. To complete Requirement *b*, use formulas where normal arithmetic calculations are made within the financial statements (in particular the statement of changes in stockholders' equity).

b. It is interesting to speculate about what would happen if certain operating results change for better or worse. After completing Requirement *a*, change certain account balances for each of the following independent operating adjustments. After each adjustment, notice how the financial statements would differ if the change in operations were to occur. After noting the effect of each adjustment, return the data to the original amounts in Problem 2-41A and then go to the next operating adjustment.

In the following table, note the new amounts on the financial statements for the various operating changes listed:

Original	1	2	3	4	5
Net income					
Total assets					
Total liabilities					
Total stockholders' equity					
Total liabilities & stockholders' equity					

Independent Operating Adjustments

1. Revenue and the related Accounts Receivable increased $10,000.
2. Revenue and the related Accounts Receivable decreased $10,000.
3. Operating Expenses and the related Accounts Payable decreased $400.
4. Operating Expenses and the related Accounts Payable increased $400.
5. Dividends paid decreased $500 and cash changed accordingly.

ATC 2-10 Spreadsheet Assignment *Mastering Excel*

Refer to Problem 2-41A. Complete the requirements using an Excel spreadsheet. Refer to Chapter 1 problem ATC 1-8 for ideas on how to structure the spreadsheet.

COMPREHENSIVE PROBLEM

The trial balance of Pacilio Security Services Inc. as of January 1, 2012, was as follows:

Cash	$8,500
Land	4,000
Notes Payable	5,000
Common Stock	6,000
Retained Earnings	1,500

During 2012, Pacilio Security Services experienced the following transactions:

1. Acquired an additional $2,000 from the issue of common stock.
2. Paid $3,000 on the debt owed to the Small Business Government Agency. The loan is interest free.
3. Performed $21,000 of security services for numerous local events during the year; $15,000 was on account and $6,000 was cash.
4. On May 1, rented a small office building. Paid $2,400 for 12 months' rent in advance.
5. Purchased supplies on account for $650.
6. Paid salaries expense for the year of $8,000.
7. Incurred other operating expenses on account, $6,200.
8. On September 1, 2012, a customer paid $600 for services to be provided over the next six months.
9. Collected $13,500 of accounts receivable during the year.
10. Paid $5,800 on accounts payable.
11. Paid $1,500 of advertising expenses for the year.
12. Paid a cash dividend to the shareholders of $1,000.
13. The market value of the land was determined to be $5,000 at December 31, 2012.

Information for Adjustments

14. There was $65 of supplies on hand at the end of the year.
15. Recognized the expired rent.
16. Recognized the revenue earned from Transaction 8.
17. Accrued salaries were $1,200 at December 31, 2012.

Required

a. Record the above transactions in an accounting equation. Provide the appropriate account titles for the amounts shown in the Retained Earnings column.

b. Prepare an income statement, statement of changes in stockholders' equity, balance sheet, and statement of cash flows for 2012.

CHAPTER 3

The Double-Entry Accounting System

LEARNING OBJECTIVES

After you have mastered the material in this chapter, you will be able to:

LO 3-1 Record business events in T-accounts using debit/credit terminology.

LO 3-2 Record transactions using the general journal format.

LO 3-3 Prepare a trial balance and explain how it is used to prepare financial statements.

LO 3-4 Prepare closing entries in general journal format.

LO 3-5 Use a return on assets ratio, a debt to assets ratio, and a return on equity ratio to analyze financial statements.

APPENDIX

LO 3-6 Record depreciation and interest using journal entries and T-accounts, and show how these entries affect financial statements.

Video lectures and accompanying self-assessment quizzes are available for all learning objectives through McGraw-Hill Connect® Plus Accounting.

CHAPTER OPENING

To prepare financial statements, a company must have a system for accurately capturing the vast numbers of business transactions in which it engages each year. The most widely used such system, double-entry accounting, is so effective it has been in use for hundreds of years! This chapter explains the rules for recording transactions using double-entry accounting.

Double-entry accounting rules are analogous to other rules people adopt to achieve various goals, such as rules governing traffic signals. A red signal means "stop," but it could just as easily mean "go." What matters is that all drivers agree on what red means. Similarly, double-entry accounting rules could have developed differently. In fact, the rules sometimes seem backwards at first. You likely use accounting terms like "debit" or "credit" from a consumer's point of view. To learn the accounting rules, however, you must view them from a business perspective. With practice, they will become second nature and you will know them as well as you know traffic signals.

The Curious Accountant

Most companies prepare financial statements at least once each year. The year about which financial statements report is called a **fiscal year.** Illustrations in this textbook usually assume the fiscal year coincides with the calendar year; that is, it ends on December 31. In practice, the fiscal years of many companies do not end on December 31. For example, **Levi Strauss**, a company that produces clothing, ends its fiscal year on the last Sunday in November. **Gap, Inc.**, a company that sells clothing, ends its fiscal year on the last Saturday or the first Saturday in February.

Why would these companies choose these dates to end their fiscal years? (Answers on pages 163 and 164.)

DEBIT/CREDIT TERMINOLOGY

LO 3-1

Record business events in T-accounts using debit/credit terminology.

An account form known as a **T-account** is a good starting point for learning double-entry recording procedures. A T-account looks like the letter "T" drawn on a piece of paper. The account title is written across the top of the horizontal bar of the T. The left side of the vertical bar is the **debit** side, and the right side is the **credit** side. An account has been *debited* when an amount is written on the left side and *credited* when an amount is written on the right side. Accountants often abbreviate the term *debit* as "dr." and *credit* as "cr." For any given account, the difference between the total debit and credit amounts is the **account balance.**

The rules for using debits and credits to record transactions in T-accounts are as follows:

Assets		=	Liabilities		+	Equity	
Debit +	Credit −		Debit −	Credit +		Debit −	Credit +

Notice that a debit can represent an increase or a decrease. Likewise, a credit can represent an increase or a decrease. Whether a debit or credit is an increase or a decrease depends on the type of account (asset, liability, or stockholders' equity) in question. The rules of debits and credits are summarized as follows:

1. Debits increase asset accounts; credits decrease asset accounts.
2. Debits decrease liability and stockholders' equity accounts; credits increase liability and stockholders' equity accounts.

RECORDING TRANSACTIONS IN T-ACCOUNTS

To illustrate the rules for debits and credits we record the 2016 accounting events for a small business, Collins Brokerage Services, Inc. Collins begins the accounting period with the following balances in its permanent accounts: Cash, \$5,000; Common Stock, \$4,000; and Retained Earnings, \$1,000. The beginning balances for the temporary accounts (Revenues, Expenses, and Dividends) are zero because these accounts were closed at the end of the previous period. The events are organized into four categories including: asset source, asset exchange, asset use, and claims exchange.

Asset Source Transactions

A business may obtain assets from three primary sources: (1) from stockholders, (2) from creditors, or (3) through operating activities (earning revenue). An asset source transaction increases an asset account and a corresponding liability or stockholders' equity account. The increase in the asset account is recorded with a debit entry. The increase in a liability or stockholders' equity account is recorded with a credit entry. The following section demonstrates recording procedures for common asset source transactions.

EVENT 1 **Acquired \$25,000 cash from the issue of common stock.**

This accounting event increases both assets and stockholders' equity. The increase in assets (Cash) is recorded with a debit, and the increase in stockholders' equity (Common Stock) is recorded with a credit, shown in T-account form as follows:

Assets		=	Liabilities		+	Equity	
Cash						Common Stock	
Debit	Credit					Debit	Credit
+							+
(1) 25,000							25,000 (1)

Notice the entry included both debiting an account and crediting an account. This system is called **double-entry accounting.** Recording any transaction requires at least one debit and at least one credit. The total of the debit amounts must equal the total of the credit amounts. These requirements provide accountants with a built-in error detection tool. For your convenience, the event number is shown parenthetically in the T-accounts beside the transaction amounts.

This entry has the following effects on the financial statements:

Assets	=	Liab.	+	Equity	Rev.	−	Exp.	=	Net Inc.	Cash Flow
Cash	=			Com. Stk.						
25,000	=	NA	+	25,000	NA	−	NA	=	NA	25,000 FA

EVENT 2 Purchased $850 of supplies on account.

Purchasing supplies on account increases both assets and liabilities. The increase in assets (Supplies) is recorded with a debit, and the increase in liabilities (Accounts Payable) is recorded with a credit, as shown in the following T-accounts:

Assets		=	Liabilities		+	Equity
Supplies			Accounts Payable			
Debit	Credit		Debit	Credit		
+				+		
(2) 850				850 (2)		

This entry has the following effects on the financial statements:

Assets	=	Liab.	+	Equity	Rev.	−	Exp.	=	Net Inc.	Cash Flow
Supplies	=	Accts. pay.								
850	=	850	+	NA	NA	−	NA	=	NA	NA

EVENT 3 Collected $1,800 cash as an advance to provide future services over a one-year period starting March 1.

Accepting the $1,800 in advance creates an obligation for Collins. The obligation is to provide future services to a customer. Collins will recognize a liability called *unearned revenue.* Recording the event increases both assets and liabilities. The increase in assets

(Cash) is recorded with a debit, and the increase in liabilities (Unearned Revenue) is recorded with a credit, as shown in the following T-accounts:

Assets		=	Liabilities		+	Equity
Cash			**Unearned Revenue**			
Debit +	Credit		Debit	Credit +		
(3) 1,800				1,800 (3)		

This entry has the following effects on the financial statements:

Assets	=	Liab.	+	Equity	Rev.	−	Exp.	=	Net Inc.	Cash Flow
Cash	=	Unearned Revenue								
1,800	=	1,800	+	NA	NA	−	NA	=	NA	1,800 OA

EVENT 4 **Provided $15,760 of services on account.**

Recognizing revenue earned on account increases both assets and stockholders' equity. The increase in assets (Accounts Receivable) is recorded with a debit, and the increase in stockholders' equity (Service Revenue) is recorded with a credit, as shown in the following T-accounts:

Assets		=	Liabilities	+	Equity	
Accounts Receivable					**Service Revenue**	
Debit +	Credit				Debit	Credit +
(4) 15,760						15,760 (4)

This entry has the following effects on the financial statements:

Assets	=	Liab.	+	Equity	Rev.	−	Exp.	=	Net Inc.	Cash Flow
Accts. Rec.	=			Ret. Earn.						
15,760	=	NA	+	15,760	15,760	−	NA	=	15,760	NA

Summary of the Previous Asset Source Transactions

Events 1 through 4 are asset source transactions. In each case, an asset account and a corresponding liability or equity account increased. The increase in the asset account was recorded with a debit and the increase in the liability or stockholders' equity account was recorded with a credit. Any transaction that provides assets to a business is recorded similarly.

CHECK YOURSELF 3.1

What are the three sources of assets? Which accounts are debited and credited when a business acquires an asset?

Answer The three sources of assets are creditors, investors, and earnings. When a company acquires an asset, the asset account is debited and the source account is credited. For example, if a company earns revenue on account, the Receivables account is debited and the Revenue account is credited.

Asset Exchange Transactions

Asset exchange transactions involve trading one asset for another asset. One asset account increases; the other decreases. The total amount of assets remains unchanged. Asset exchange transactions are recorded by debiting the asset account that is increasing and crediting the asset account that is decreasing. In T-account form, asset exchange transactions have the following effects on the accounting equation:

Assets				=	Claims
Asset 1		Asset 2			
Debit	Credit	Debit	Credit		
+			−		

EVENT 5 **Purchased land for $26,000 cash.**

The increase in assets (Land) is recorded with a debit, and the decrease in assets (Cash) is recorded with a credit, as shown in the following T-accounts:

Assets				=	Claims
Cash		Land			
Debit	Credit	Debit	Credit		
	−	+			
	26,000 (5)	(5) 26,000			

This entry has the following effects on the financial statements:

Assets			=	Liab.	+	Equity	Rev.	−	Exp.	=	Net Inc.	Cash Flow	
Cash	+	Land											
(26,000)	+	26,000	=	NA	+	NA	NA	−	NA	=	NA	(26,000)	IA

EVENT 6 **Paid $1,200 cash for a one-year insurance policy with coverage starting August 1.**

The increase in assets (Prepaid Insurance) is recorded with a debit, and the decrease in assets (Cash) is recorded with a credit, as shown in the following T-accounts:

Assets				=	Claims
Cash		Prepaid Insurance			
Debit	Credit	Debit	Credit		
	−	+			
	1,200 (6)	(6) 1,200			

This entry has the following effects on the financial statements:

Assets		=	Liab.	+	Equity	Rev.	−	Exp.	=	Net Inc.	Cash Flow
Cash	+ Prepaid Insurance										
(1,200) +	1,200	=	NA	+	NA	NA	−	NA	=	NA	(1,200) OA

EVENT 7 **Collected $13,400 cash from accounts receivable.**

The increase in assets (Cash) is recorded with a debit, and the decrease in assets (Accounts Receivable) is recorded with a credit, as shown in the following T-accounts:

Assets				=	Claims
Cash		Accounts Receivable			
Debit	Credit	Debit	Credit		
+			−		
(7) 13,400			13,400 (7)		

This entry has the following effects on the financial statements:

Assets		=	Liab.	+	Equity	Rev.	−	Exp.	=	Net Inc.	Cash Flow
Cash	+ Accts. Rec.										
13,400 +	(13,400)	=	NA	+	NA	NA	−	NA	=	NA	13,400 OA

Summary of the Previous Asset Exchange Transactions

Events 5 through 7 are asset exchange transactions. In each case, one asset account increased and another decreased. The asset account that increased was debited, and the asset account that decreased was credited. These asset exchange transactions did not affect the total amounts of assets, liabilities, or equity.

Asset Use Transactions

There are three primary asset use transactions: (1) expenses may use assets, (2) settling liabilities may use assets, or (3) paying dividends may use assets. An asset use transaction decreases an asset account and also decreases a liability or equity account. The decrease in the asset account is recorded with a credit and the decrease in the liability or equity account is recorded with a debit.

EVENT 8 Paid $9,500 cash for salaries expense.

The decrease in assets (Cash) is recorded with a credit, and the decrease in stockholders' equity (Salaries Expense) is recorded with a debit, as shown in the following T-accounts:

Assets		=	Liabilities	+	Equity	
Cash					**Salaries Expense**	
Debit	Credit				Debit	Credit
	−				+ Expense	
	9,500 (8)				− Equity	
					(8) 9,500	

The debit to Salaries Expense represents an *increase* in the salaries expense account, which is actually a *decrease* in stockholders' equity (Retained Earnings). Debit entries increase expense accounts. Expenses, however, decrease stockholders' equity (Retained Earnings). Debiting an expense account, therefore, reduces stockholders' equity.

This entry has the following effects on the financial statements:

Assets	=	Liab.	+	Equity	Rev.	−	Exp.	=	Net Inc.	Cash Flow
Cash	=			Ret. Earn.						
(9,500)	=	NA	+	(9,500)	NA	−	9,500	=	(9,500)	(9,500) OA

EVENT 9 Paid an $800 cash dividend.

The decrease in assets (Cash) is recorded with a credit, and the decrease in stockholders' equity (Dividends) is recorded with a debit, as shown in the following T-accounts:

Assets		=	Liabilities	+	Equity	
Cash					**Dividends**	
Debit	Credit				Debit	Credit
	−				+ Div.	
	800 (9)				− Equity	
					(9) 800	

The debit to Dividends represents both an increase in the dividends account and a decrease in stockholders' equity (Retained Earnings). Since dividends decrease stockholders' equity, an increase in the Dividends account reduces stockholders' equity. Recall that dividends are wealth transfers, not expenses.

This entry has the following effects on the financial statements:

Assets	=	Liab.	+	Equity	Rev.	−	Exp.	=	Net Inc.	Cash Flow
Cash	=			Ret. Earn.						
(800)	=	NA	+	(800)	NA	−	NA	=	NA	(800) FA

EVENT 10 **Paid $850 cash to settle accounts payable.**

The decrease in assets (Cash) is recorded with a credit, and the decrease in liabilities (Accounts Payable) is recorded with a debit, as shown in the following T-accounts:

Assets		=	Liabilities		+	Equity
Cash			Accounts Payable			
Debit	Credit		Debit	Credit		
	−		−			
	850 (10)		(10) 850			

This entry has the following effects on the financial statements:

Assets	=	Liab.	+	Equity	Rev.	−	Exp.	=	Net Inc.	Cash Flow
Cash	=	Accts. pay.								
(850)	=	(850)	+	NA	NA	−	NA	=	NA	(850) OA

Summary of Asset Use Transactions

Events 8 through 10 each reduced an asset account as well as either a liability or stockholders' equity account. Even though debit entries to expense and dividends accounts represent increases in those accounts, the balances in expense and dividends accounts reduce stockholders' equity. Any asset use transaction is recorded with a debit to a liability or a stockholders' equity account and a credit to an asset account.

Claims Exchange Transactions

Certain transactions involve exchanging one claims account for another claims account. The total amount of claims remains unchanged. Such transactions are recorded by debiting the claims account which is decreasing and crediting the claims account which is increasing.

EVENT 11 **Recognized $1,900 other operating expenses on account.**

This event increases liabilities and decreases stockholders' equity. The increase in liabilities (Accounts Payable) is recorded with a credit, and the decrease in stockholders' equity (Other Operating Expense) is recorded with a debit, as shown in the following T-accounts:

Assets	=	Liabilities		+	Equity	
		Accounts Payable			Other Operating Expense	
		Debit	Credit		Debit	Credit
			+		+ Expense	
			1,900 (11)		− Equity	
					(11) 1,900	

This entry has the following effects on the financial statements:

Assets	=	Liab.	+	Equity	Rev.	−	Exp.	=	Net Inc.	Cash Flow
		Accts. pay.	+	Ret. Earn.						
NA	=	1,900	+	(1,900)	NA	−	1,900	=	(1,900)	NA

Summary of Claims Exchange Transaction

Event 11 reflects an exchange on the claims side of the accounting equation. In this case, one claims account (Other Operating Expense) was debited, and another claims account (Accounts Payable) was credited. Claims exchange transactions do not affect the total amounts of either assets or claims.

Adjusting the Accounts

Assume Collins's fiscal year ends on December 31, 2016. Collins has several unrecorded accruals and deferrals that must be recognized before the financial statements can be prepared. The appropriate adjustments are discussed below.

ADJUSTMENT 1 **As of December 31, 2016, Collins had earned $750 of accrued interest revenue.**

Recognizing the revenue increases both assets and stockholders' equity. The increase in assets (Interest Receivable) is recorded with a debit, and the increase in stockholders' equity (Interest Revenue) is recorded with a credit, as shown in the following T-accounts:

Assets		=	Liabilities		+	Equity	
Interest Receivable						**Interest Revenue**	
Debit	Credit					Debit	Credit
+							+
(Adj. 1) 750							750 (Adj. 1)

This entry has the following effects on the financial statements:

Assets	=	Liab.	+	Equity	Rev.	−	Exp.	=	Net Inc.	Cash Flow
Int. Rec.	=			Ret. Earn.						
750	=	NA	+	750	750	−	NA	=	750	NA

ADJUSTMENT 2 **As of December 31, 2016, Collins had earned $1,500 of the $1,800 of the revenue it deferred in Event 3.**

Recall that Collins collected $1,800 in advance for a one-year contract starting March 1. By December 31, 2016, Collins would have provided professional services for 10 months, earning $1,500 ($1,800 ÷ 12 = $150; $150 × 10 = $1,500) of the revenue during 2016. This amount must be transferred from the liability account (Unearned Revenue) to an equity account (Service Revenue). Recognizing the revenue decreases liabilities and increases stockholders' equity. The decrease in liabilities (Unearned Revenue) is recorded with a debit, and the increase in stockholders' equity (Service Revenue) is recorded with a credit, as shown in the following T-accounts:

Assets	=	Liabilities		+	Equity	
		Unearned Revenue			**Service Revenue**	
		Debit	Credit		Debit	Credit
		−				+
		(Adj. 2) 1,500				1,500 (Adj. 2)

This adjustment has the following effects on the financial statements:

Assets	=	Liab.	+	Equity	Rev.	−	Exp.	=	Net Inc.	Cash Flow
		Unearned Revenue	+	Ret. Earn.						
NA	=	(1,500)	+	1,500	1,500	−	NA	=	1,500	NA

ADJUSTMENT 3 **As of December 31, 2016, Collins had $800 of accrued salary expenses that will be paid in 2017.**

Assume that Collins owes $800 to employees for work done in 2016. Collins will pay these salaries in 2017. The required adjusting entry increases liabilities and decreases stockholders' equity. The increase in liabilities (Salaries Payable) is recorded with a credit, and the decrease in stockholders' equity (Salaries Expense) is recorded with a debit, as shown in the following T-accounts:

Assets	=	Liabilities		+	Equity	
		Salaries Payable			Salaries Expense	
		Debit	Credit + 800 (Adj. 3)		Debit + Expense − Equity (Adj. 3) 800	Credit

This adjustment has the following effects on the financial statements:

Assets	=	Liab.	+	Equity	Rev.	−	Exp.	=	Net Inc.	Cash Flow
		Sal. Pay.	+	Ret. Earn.						
NA	=	800	+	(800)	NA	−	800	=	(800)	NA

ADJUSTMENT 4 **As of December 31, 2016, Collins had used $500 of the $1,200 of insurance coverage that was prepaid in Event 6.**

Recall that Collins paid $1,200 in advance for insurance coverage for one year. The monthly insurance cost is therefore $100 ($1,200 ÷ 12 months). By December 31, Collins had *used* the insurance coverage for five months in 2016. Insurance expense for those five months is therefore $500 ($100 × 5). Recognizing the insurance expense decreases both assets and stockholders' equity. The decrease in assets (Prepaid Insurance) is recorded with a credit, and the decrease in stockholders' equity (Insurance Expense) is recorded with a debit, as shown in the following T-accounts:

Assets		=	Liabilities	+	Equity	
Prepaid Insurance					Insurance Expense	
Debit	Credit − 500 (Adj. 4)				Debit + Expense − Equity (Adj. 4) 500	Credit

This adjustment has the following effects on the financial statements:

Assets	=	Liab.	+	Equity	Rev.	−	Exp.	=	Net Inc.	Cash Flow
Prep. Ins.	=			Ret. Earn.						
(500)	=	NA	+	(500)	NA	−	500	=	(500)	NA

ADJUSTMENT 5 **As of December 31, 2016, a physical count of the supplies on hand revealed that $125 of unused supplies were available for future use.**

Collins used $725 ($850 − $125) of supplies during the period. Recognizing the supplies expense decreases both assets and stockholders' equity. The decrease in assets (Supplies) is recorded with a credit and the decrease in stockholders' equity (Supplies Expense) is recorded with a debit, as shown in the following T-accounts:

Assets		=	Liabilities	+	Equity	
Supplies					Supplies Expense	
Debit	Credit − 725 (Adj. 5)				Debit + Expense − Equity (Adj. 5) 725	Credit

This adjustment has the following effects on the financial statements:

Assets	=	Liab.	+	Equity	Rev.	−	Exp.	=	Net Inc.	Cash Flow
Supplies	=			Ret. Earn.						
(725)	=	NA	+	(725)	NA	−	725	=	(725)	NA

CHECK YOURSELF 3.2

Can an asset exchange transaction be an adjusting entry?

Answer No. Adjusting entries always involve revenue or expense accounts. Since an asset exchange transaction involves only asset accounts, it cannot be an adjusting entry.

Overview of Debit/Credit Relationships

Panel A of Exhibit 3.1 summarizes the rules for debits and credits. Panel B illustrates these rules in T-account form.

The balance in each account, which is the difference between all the debit entries and all the credit entries, is written on the plus (increase) side of that account. Asset, expense, and dividend accounts normally have *debit balances;* liability, stockholders' equity, and revenue accounts normally have *credit balances.*

THE GENERAL JOURNAL

LO 3-2

Record transactions using the general journal format.

Businesses find it impractical to record every individual transaction directly into general ledger accounts. Imagine the number of cash transactions a grocery store has each day. To simplify recordkeeping, businesses rely on **source documents** such as cash register tapes as the basis for entering transaction data into the accounting system. Other source documents include invoices, time cards, check registers, and deposit tickets.

EXHIBIT 3.1

Debit/Credit Relationships

Panel A

Account	Debits	Credits
Assets	Increase	Decrease
Liabilities	Decrease	Increase
Stockholders' Equity	Decrease	Increase
Common Stock	Decrease	Increase
Retained Earnings	Decrease	Increase
Revenue	Decrease	Increase
Expenses	Increase	Decrease
Dividends	Increase	Decrease

Panel B

Assets		=	Liabilities		+	Stockholders' Equity	
Debit	Credit		Debit	Credit		Debit	Credit
+	−		−	+		−	+

Specific Equity Accounts

Common Stock	
Debit −	Credit +

Retained Earnings	
Debit −	Credit +

Dividends	
Debit − Equity + Div.	Credit + Equity − Div.

Revenue	
Debit −	Credit +

Expense	
Debit − Equity + Exp.	Credit + Equity − Exp.

Accountants further simplify recordkeeping by initially recording data from source documents into **journals.** Journals provide a chronological record of business transactions. *Transactions are recorded in journals before they are entered into ledger accounts.* Journals are therefore **books of original entry.** Companies may use different **special journals** to record specific types of recurring transactions. For example, a company may use one special journal to record sales on account, another to record purchases on account, a third to record cash receipts, and a fourth to record cash payments. Transactions that do not fall into any of these categories are recorded in the **general journal.** Although special journals are useful, companies can keep records without them by recording all transactions in the general journal. For simplicity, this text illustrates a general journal only.

REALITY BYTES

Do all accounting systems require using debits and credits? The answer is a definite no. Many small businesses use a single-entry system. A checkbook constitutes a sufficient accounting system for many business owners. Deposits represent revenues, and payments constitute expenses. Many excellent automated accounting systems do not require data entry through a debit/credit recording scheme. **QuickBooks** is a good example of this type of system. Data are entered into the QuickBooks software program through a user-friendly computer interface that does not require knowledge of debit/credit terminology. Even so, the QuickBooks program produces traditional financial reports such as an income statement, balance sheet, and statement of cash flows. How is this possible? Before you become too ingrained in the debit/credit system, recall that throughout the first two chapters of this text, we illustrated accounting records without using debits and credits. Financial reports can be produced in many ways without using a double-entry system. Having recognized this point, we also note that the vast majority of medium- to large-size companies use the double-entry system. Indeed, debit/credit terminology is a part of common culture. Most people have an understanding of what is happening when a business tells them that their account is being debited or credited. It is important for you to embrace the double-entry system as well as other financial reporting systems.

At a minimum, the general journal shows the dates, the account titles, and the amounts of each transaction. The date is recorded in the first column, followed by the title of the account to be debited. The title of the account to be credited is indented and written on the line directly below the account to be debited. The dollar amount of the transaction is recorded in the Debit and Credit columns. Dollar signs are not used when recording journal entries. For example, providing services for $1,000 cash on August 1 would be recorded in general journal format as follows:

Date	Account Title	Debit	Credit
Aug. 1	Cash	1,000	
	Service Revenue		1,000

Exhibit 3.2 shows a summary of Collins's 2016 transactions and demonstrates how the transactions are recorded in general journal format. For easy reference the journal column normally used for the transaction date contains the event numbers and the references for the adjusting entries. After transactions are initially recorded in a journal, the dollar amounts of each debit and credit are copied into the ledger accounts through a process called **posting.**

Most companies today use computer technology to record transactions and prepare financial statements. Computers can record and post data pertaining to vast numbers of transactions with incredible speed and unparalleled accuracy. Both manual and computerized accounting systems, however, use the same underlying design. Analyzing a manual accounting system is a useful way to gain insight into how computer-based systems work.

The collection of all the accounts used by a particular business is called the **general ledger.** The general ledger for Collins is displayed in Exhibit 3.3. In a manual system, the ledger could be a book with pages for each account where entries are recorded by hand. In more sophisticated systems, the general ledger is maintained in electronic form. Data are entered into electronic ledgers using computer keyboards or scanners. Companies typically assign each ledger account a name and a number. A list of all ledger accounts and their account numbers is called the **chart of accounts.**

EXHIBIT 3.2

Transaction Summary

Event 1 Acquired $25,000 cash from the issue of common stock.
Event 2 Purchased $850 of supplies on account.
Event 3 Collected $1,800 cash as an advance to provide future services over a one-year period starting March 1.
Event 4 Provided $15,760 of services on account.
Event 5 Purchased land for $26,000 cash.
Event 6 Paid $1,200 cash for a one-year insurance policy with coverage starting August 1.
Event 7 Collected $13,400 cash from accounts receivable.
Event 8 Paid $9,500 cash for salaries expense.
Event 9 Paid an $800 cash dividend.
Event 10 Paid $850 cash to settle accounts payable.
Event 11 Recognized $1,900 other operating expenses on account.

Adjustments

Adj. 1 Recognized $750 of accrued interest revenue.
Adj. 2 Recognized $1,500 of deferred service revenue.
Adj. 3 Recognized $800 of accrued salaries expense.
Adj. 4 Recognized $500 of deferred insurance expense.
Adj. 5 Recognized $725 of deferred supplies expense.

General Journal Entries

Event No.	Account Titles	Debit	Credit
1	Cash	25,000	
	Common Stock		25,000
2	Supplies	850	
	Accounts Payable		850
3	Cash	1,800	
	Unearned Service Revenue		1,800
4	Accounts Receivable	15,760	
	Service Revenue		15,760
5	Land	26,000	
	Cash		26,000
6	Prepaid Insurance	1,200	
	Cash		1,200
7	Cash	13,400	
	Accounts Receivable		13,400
8	Salaries Expense	9,500	
	Cash		9,500
9	Dividends	800	
	Cash		800
10	Accounts Payable	850	
	Cash		850
11	Other Operating Expenses	1,900	
	Accounts Payable		1,900
Adj. 1	Interest Receivable	750	
	Interest Revenue		750
Adj. 2	Unearned Service Revenue	1,500	
	Service Revenue		1,500
Adj. 3	Salaries Expense	800	
	Salaries Payable		800
Adj. 4	Insurance Expense	500	
	Prepaid Insurance		500
Adj. 5	Supplies Expense	725	
	Supplies		725

EXHIBIT 3.3

General Ledger

Assets = Liabilities + Stockholders' Equity

Assets

Cash			
Bal.	5,000	26,000	(5)
(1)	25,000	1,200	(6)
(3)	1,800	9,500	(8)
(7)	13,400	800	(9)
		850	(10)
Bal.	6,850		

Accounts Receivable			
(4)	15,760	13,400	(7)
Bal.	2,360		

Interest Receivable			
(Adj. 1)	750		

Prepaid Insurance			
(6)	1,200	500	(Adj. 4)
Bal.	700		

Supplies			
(2)	850	725	(Adj. 5)
Bal.	125		

Land			
(5)	26,000		

Liabilities

Accounts Payable			
(10)	850	850	(2)
		1,900	(11)
		1,900	Bal.

Salaries Payable			
		800	(Adj. 3)

Unearned Service Revenue			
(Adj. 2)	1,500	1,800	(3)
		300	Bal.

Stockholders' Equity

Common Stock			
		4,000	Bal.
		25,000	(1)
		29,000	Bal.

Retained Earnings			
		1,000	Bal.

Dividends			
(9)	800		

Service Revenue			
		15,760	(4)
		1,500	(Adj. 2)
		17,260	Bal.

Interest Revenue			
		750	(Adj. 1)

Salaries Expense			
(8)	9,500		
(Adj. 3)	800		
Bal.	10,300		

Other Operating Expenses			
(11)	1,900		

Insurance Expense			
(Adj. 4)	500		

Supplies Expense			
(Adj. 5)	725		

TRIAL BALANCE AND FINANCIAL STATEMENTS

LO 3-3

Prepare a trial balance and explain how it is used to prepare financial statements.

To test whether debits equal credits in the general ledger, accountants regularly prepare an internal accounting schedule called a **trial balance.** A trial balance lists every ledger account and its balance. Debit balances are listed in one column and credit balances are listed in an adjacent column. The columns are totaled and the totals are compared. Exhibit 3.4 displays the trial balance for Collins Brokerage Services, Inc., after the adjusting entries have been posted to the ledger.

If the debit total does not equal the credit total, the accountant knows to search for an error. Even if the totals are equal, however, there may be errors in the accounting records. For example, equal trial balance totals would not disclose errors like the following: failure to record transactions; misclassifications, such as debiting the wrong account; or incorrectly recording the amount of a transaction, such as recording a $200 transaction as $2,000. Equal debits and credits in a trial balance provide evidence rather than proof of accuracy.

Supplemented with details from the Cash and Common Stock ledger accounts, the adjusted trial balance (Exhibit 3.4) provides the information to prepare the financial statements for Collins Brokerage Services, Inc. The income statement, statement of changes in stockholders' equity, balance sheet, and statement of cash flows are shown in Exhibits 3.5, 3.6, 3.7, and 3.8.

EXHIBIT 3.4

COLLINS BROKERAGE SERVICES, INC.
Adjusted Trial Balance
December 31, 2016

Account Title	Debit	Credit
Cash	$ 6,850	
Accounts receivable	2,360	
Interest receivable	750	
Prepaid insurance	700	
Supplies	125	
Land	26,000	
Accounts payable		$ 1,900
Salaries payable		800
Unearned service revenue		300
Common stock		29,000
Retained earnings		1,000
Dividends	800	
Service revenue		17,260
Interest revenue		750
Salaries expense	10,300	
Insurance expense	500	
Supplies expense	725	
Other operating expense	1,900	
Totals	$51,010	$51,010

EXHIBIT 3.5

COLLINS BROKERAGE SERVICES, INC.
Income Statement
For the Year Ended December 31, 2016

Revenues		
Service revenue	$ 17,260	
Interest revenue	750	
Total revenue		$18,010
Expenses		
Salaries expense	(10,300)	
Other operating expenses	(1,900)	
Insurance expense	(500)	
Supplies expense	(725)	
Total expenses		(13,425)
Net income		$ 4,585

EXHIBIT 3.6

COLLINS BROKERAGE SERVICES, INC.
Statement of Changes in Stockholders' Equity
For the Year Ended December 31, 2016

Beginning common stock	$ 4,000	
Plus: Common stock issued	25,000	
Ending common stock		$29,000
Beginning retained earnings	1,000	
Plus: Net income	4,585	
Less: Dividends	(800)	
Ending retained earnings		4,785
Total stockholders' equity		$33,785

EXHIBIT 3.7

COLLINS BROKERAGE SERVICES, INC.
Balance Sheet
As of December 31, 2016

Assets		
Cash	$ 6,850	
Accounts receivable	2,360	
Interest receivable	750	
Prepaid insurance	700	
Supplies	125	
Land	26,000	
Total assets		$36,785
Liabilities		
Accounts payable	$ 1,900	
Salaries payable	800	
Unearned service revenue	300	
Total liabilities		$ 3,000
Stockholders' equity		
Common stock	29,000	
Retained earnings	4,785	
Total stockholders' equity		33,785
Total liabilities and stockholders' equity		$36,785

EXHIBIT 3.8

COLLINS BROKERAGE SERVICES, INC.
Statement of Cash Flows
For the Year Ended December 31, 2016

Cash flows from operating activities		
Cash receipts from customers	$15,200*	
Cash payments for salaries expense	(9,500)	
Cash payments for insurance expense	(1,200)	
Cash payments for supplies	(850)	
Net cash flow from operating activities		$ 3,650
Cash flows from investing activities		
Cash payment to purchase land		(26,000)
Cash flows from financing activities		
Cash receipts from issue of common stock	25,000	
Cash payment for dividends	(800)	
Net cash flow from financing activities		24,200
Net increase in cash		1,850
Plus: Beginning cash balance		5,000
Ending cash balance		$ 6,850

*$13,400 accounts receivable collections + $1,800 unearned service revenue collection.

Answers to The Curious Accountant

Part 1

The process of closing the books and going through a year-end audit is time-consuming for a business. Also, it is time spent that does not produce revenue. Thus, companies whose business is highly seasonal often choose "slow" periods to end their fiscal year. **Gap, Inc.**, does heavy business during the Christmas season, so it might find December 31 an inconvenient time to close its books. Toward the end of January, business activity is slow, and inventory levels are at their low points. This is a good time to count the inventory and to assess the financial condition of the company. For these reasons, Gap, Inc., has chosen to close its books to end its fiscal year around the end of January.

Now that you know why a business like Gap, Inc., might choose to end its fiscal year at the end of January, can you think of a reason why **Levi Strauss** closes its books at the end of November? (See page 164.)

Closing Entries

LO 3-4

Prepare closing entries in general journal format.

Exhibit 3.9 shows **closing entries** for Collins Brokerage Services, Inc. These entries move all 2016 data from the temporary accounts (revenues, expenses, and dividends) into the Retained Earnings account. For example, the first closing entry in Exhibit 3.9 moves the balance in the Service Revenue account to the Retained Earnings account. As shown in the adjusted trial balance (Exhibit 3.4), the Service Revenue account has a $17,260 credit balance before it is closed. Debiting the account for $17,260 brings its after-closing balance to zero. The corresponding $17,260 credit to Retained Earnings increases the balance in that account.

The third closing entry moves the balance in the Salaries Expense account to the Retained Earnings account. Before closing, the Salaries Expense account has a $10,300 debit balance; crediting the account for $10,300 leaves it with an after-closing balance of zero. The corresponding $10,300 debit to the Retained Earnings account reduces the

EXHIBIT 3.9

Closing Entries

Date	Account Titles	Debit	Credit
Dec. 31	Service Revenue	17,260	
	Retained Earnings		17,260
31	Interest Revenue	750	
	Retained Earnings		750
31	Retained Earnings	10,300	
	Salaries Expense		10,300
31	Retained Earnings	1,900	
	Other Operating Expenses		1,900
31	Retained Earnings	500	
	Insurance Expense		500
31	Retained Earnings	725	
	Supplies Expense		725
31	Retained Earnings	800	
	Dividends		800

Answers to The Curious Accountant

Part 2

Levi Strauss does not sell its clothes directly to consumers; rather, it sells most of its clothes through retailers. Levi Strauss must deliver its jeans to retailers before Thanksgiving if the stores are going to have goods available to sell during the Christmas season. So, Levi's "Christmas season" is probably over by early November, making the end of November a good time to end its fiscal year. Some clothing manufacturers, such as **Tommy Hilfiger** and Polo **Ralph Lauren**, close their books around the end of March. By then, goods for both the Christmas and spring seasons have been shipped to retailers.

balance in that account. The remaining entries close the other revenue, expense, and dividend accounts to the Retained Earnings account.

Closing entries can be recorded more efficiently than in Exhibit 3.9. For example, the two revenue accounts could be closed with one compound journal entry, like the one below.

Date	Account Title	Debit	Credit
Dec. 31	Service Revenue	17,260	
	Interest Revenue	750	
	Retained Earnings		18,010

Furthermore, revenue, expense, and dividend accounts could all be closed in a single compound journal entry. The form of the closing entries is not important. What matters is that all revenue, expense, and dividend amounts be moved to the Retained Earnings account. After the closing entries are posted to the ledger accounts, all revenue, expense, and dividend accounts have zero balances. The temporary accounts are then ready to capture revenue, expense, and dividend data for the next fiscal year.

If all companies closed their books on December 31 each year, accountants, printers, lawyers, government agencies, and others would be overburdened by the effort to produce the accounting reports of all companies at the same time. In an effort to balance the workload, many companies close their books at the end of the natural business year. A natural business year ends when operating activities are at their lowest point. For many companies the lowest point in the operating cycle occurs on a date other than December 31. A recent survey found that almost one-half of the companies sampled closed their books in months other than December (see Exhibit 3.10).

EXHIBIT 3.10

Distribution of Fiscal Closing Dates

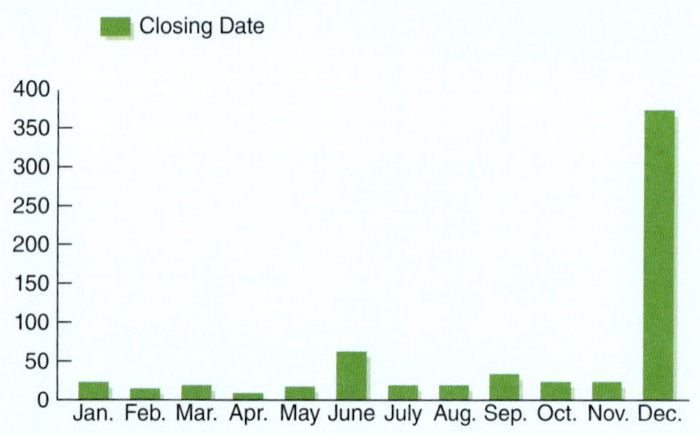

Data Source: AICPA Accounting Trends and Techniques.

Post-Closing Trial Balance

How often should companies prepare a trial balance? Some companies prepare a trial balance daily; others may prepare one monthly, quarterly, or annually, depending on the needs of management. The heading of a trial balance describes the status of the account balances in it. For example, the trial balance in Exhibit 3.11 is described as a *Post-Closing Trial Balance* because it reflects the account balances immediately after the closing entries were posted. In contrast, the trial balance in Exhibit 3.4 is described as an *Adjusted Trial Balance* because it shows the account balances immediately after the adjusting entries were posted. A trial balance prepared at the end of each day may be described as a *Daily Trial Balance*.

CHECK YOURSELF 3.3

Describe an error that would not cause a trial balance to be out of balance.

Answer Many potential errors would not cause a trial balance to be out of balance, such as debiting or crediting the wrong account. For example, if revenue earned on account were recorded with a debit to Cash instead of Accounts Receivable, total assets would be correct and the totals in the trial balance would equal each other even though the balances in the Cash and Accounts Receivable accounts would be incorrect. Recording the same incorrect amount in both the debit and credit part of an entry also would not cause a trial balance to be out of balance. For example, if $20 of revenue earned on account were recorded as a $200 debit to Accounts Receivable and a $200 credit to Consulting Revenue, the totals in the trial balance would equal each other although Accounts Receivable and Consulting Revenue amounts would be incorrect.

THE FINANCIAL ANALYST

Suppose a company earned net income of $1,000,000. Is the company's performance good or poor? If the company is Comcast, the performance is poor. If it is a small shoe store, the performance is outstanding. So, how do financial analysts compare the performance of differing size companies? Financial ratios are helpful in this regard.

LO 3-5

Use a return on assets ratio, a debt to assets ratio, and a return on equity ratio to analyze financial statements.

Assessing the Effective Use of Assets

Evaluating performance requires considering the size of the investment base used to produce the income. In other words, you expect someone who has a $10 million investment base to earn more than someone who has a $10 thousand base. The relationship between the level of income and the size of the investment can be expressed as the **return on assets ratio,** as follows:

$$\frac{\text{Net income}^{1}}{\text{Total assets}}$$

This ratio permits meaningful comparisons between different-size companies. Compare Dollar Tree, Inc., a retailer that prices all of its merchandise at $1.00, to Wal-Mart Stores, Inc. In their 2013 fiscal years, Dollar Tree reported net income of $596.7 million, while Walmart reported net income of $17.8 billion. Walmart's earnings were almost 30 times the earnings of Dollar Tree. However, the return on asset ratios for the two companies reveal that Dollar Tree produced higher earnings relative to the assets invested. Walmart's ratio was 8.7 percent, while Dollar Tree's was 21.6 percent. Even though Dollar Tree earned fewer dollars of net income, the company used its assets more efficiently than Walmart.

The preceding example demonstrates the usefulness of the relationship between income and assets. Two more ratios that enhance financial statement analysis are discussed in the following paragraphs.

EXHIBIT 3.11

COLLINS BROKERAGE SERVICES, INC.
Post-Closing Trial Balance
December 31, 2016

Account Title	Debit	Credit
Cash	$ 6,850	
Accounts receivable	2,360	
Interest receivable	750	
Prepaid insurance	700	
Supplies	125	
Land	26,000	
Accounts payable		$ 1,900
Salaries payable		800
Unearned service revenue		300
Common stock		29,000
Retained earnings		4,785
Totals	$36,785	$36,785

[1]The use of net income in this ratio ignores the effects of debt financing and income taxation. The effect of these variables on the return on assets ratio is explained in a later chapter.

Assessing Debt Risk

Borrowing money can be a risky business. To illustrate, assume two companies have the following financial structures:

	Assets	=	Liabilities	+	Stockholders' Equity
Eastern Company	100	=	20	+	80
Western Company	100	=	80	+	20

Which company has the greater financial risk? If each company incurred a $30 loss, the financial structures would change as follows:

	Assets	=	Liabilities	+	Stockholders' Equity
Eastern Company	70	=	20	+	50
Western Company	70	=	80	+	(10)

Clearly, Western Company is at greater risk. Eastern Company could survive a $30 loss that reduced assets and stockholders' equity. It would still have a $50 balance in stockholders' equity and more than enough assets ($70) to satisfy the $20 obligation to creditors. In contrast, a $30 loss would throw Western Company into bankruptcy. The company would have a $10 deficit (negative) balance in stockholders' equity and the remaining assets ($70) would be less than the $80 obligation to creditors.

The level of debt risk can be measured in part by using a **debt to assets ratio,** as follows:

$$\frac{\text{Total debt}}{\text{Total assets}}$$

For example, Eastern Company's debt to assets ratio is 20 percent ($20 ÷ $100) while Western Company's is 80 percent ($80 ÷ $100). Why would the owners of Western Company be willing to accept greater debt risk? Assume that both companies produce $12 of revenue and each must pay 10 percent interest on money owed to creditors. Income statements for the two companies appear as follows:[2]

	Eastern Company	Western Company
Revenue	$12	$12
Interest Expense	2	8
Net Income	$10	$ 4

At first glance, the owners of Eastern Company appear better off because Eastern produced higher net income. In fact, however, the owners of *Western* Company are better off. The owners of Eastern Company get $10 of income for investing $80 of their own money into the business, a return on their invested funds of 12.5 percent ($10 ÷ $80). In contrast, the owners of Western Company obtain $4 of net income for their $20 investment, a return on invested funds of 20 percent ($4 ÷ $20).

The relationship between net income and stockholders' equity used above is the **return on equity ratio,** computed as

$$\frac{\text{Net income}}{\text{Stockholders' equity}}$$

Using borrowed money to increase the return on stockholders' investment is called **financial leverage.** Financial leverage explains why companies are willing to accept the risk of debt. Companies borrow money to make money. If a company can borrow money at 10 percent and invest it at 12 percent, the owners will be better off by 2 percent

[2]This illustration ignores the effect of income taxes on debt financing. This subject is discussed in a later chapter.

FOCUS ON INTERNATIONAL ISSUES

HOW DOES IFRS DIFFER FROM U.S. GAAP?

Chapter 1 discussed the progression toward a single global GAAP in the form of International Financial Reporting Standards (IFRS). That discussion noted that the United States does not currently allow domestic companies to use IFRS; they must follow GAAP. Let's briefly consider just how U.S. GAAP differs from IFRS.

The differences can be summarized in a few broad categories. First, some differences are relatively minor. Consider the case of bank overdrafts. Under IFRS, some bank overdrafts are included as a cash inflow and reported on the statement of cash flows. U.S. GAAP does not permit this. Conversely, some differences relate to very significant issues. Both IFRS and GAAP use historical cost as their primary method for reporting information on financial statements, but both allow exceptions in some circumstances. However, IFRS permits more exceptions to historical cost than GAAP does. Some of these differences will be discussed in later chapters.

Some of the differences affect how financial statements are presented in annual reports. IFRS requires companies to report all financial statements for the current year and the prior year—two years of comparative data. Rules of the Securities and Exchange Commission require U.S. companies to report two years of balance sheets, the current and prior year, and three years of all other statements. See the financial statements of Target Corporation in Appendix B as an example. Of course, companies can show additional years if they wish.

As you would expect in the first course of accounting, some of the differences between IFRS and GAAP are simply too complex to be covered. Examples of such items relate to business combinations (when one company buys another) and foreign currency translations (when a company has subsidiaries that operate outside the United States).

Do not be overwhelmed by the differences between IFRS and GAAP. There are many more rules that are alike than are different. A person who has a reasonable understanding of U.S. GAAP should be able to read financial statements prepared under IFRS without too much difficulty. If you are interested in more detailed, up-to-date information about IFRS versus GAAP, the large international accounting firms have websites that can help. Two examples are: www.iasplus.com, which is presented by the firm of Deloitte Touche Tohmatsu, and www.kpmg.com/global/en/topics/global-ifrs-institute/, which is presented by the firm of KPMG.

of the amount borrowed. A business that does not borrow may be missing an opportunity to increase its return on equity.

Real-World Data

Exhibit 3.12 shows the debt to assets, return on assets, and return on equity ratios for six real-world companies in two different industries. The data are drawn from the companies' 2013 annual reports. Notice that **Aflac**'s return on assets ratio was 2.6 percent and **Aetna**'s was 3.8 percent. Neither ratio seems good; banks sometimes pay more than 2.6 percent interest on deposits in savings accounts. The *return on equity* ratios, however, show a different picture; Aflac's was 21.6 percent and Aetna's was 13.6 percent—much better than banks pay depositors.

Exhibit 3.12 shows that while **ExxonMobil**'s return on assets ratio was almost four times higher than Aflac's (9.4 percent versus 2.6 percent), its return on equity ratio was much closer (18.1 percent versus 21.6 percent). How did this happen? Compare their debt to assets ratios. Aflac financed 88 percent of its assets with debt compared to Exxon's 48 percent. Financial leverage is the biggest factor causing these results, but it is not the only factor that affects this ratio.

EXHIBIT 3.12

Three Ratios (in Percentages) for Six Real-World Companies

Industry	Company	Debt to Assets	Return on Assets	Return on Equity
Insurance	Aetna	72	3.8	13.6
	Aflac	88	2.6	21.6
	Progressive	76	4.8	18.8
Oil	Chevron	41	8.4	14.4
	ExxonMobil	48	9.4	18.1
	Marathon Oil	46	4.9	9.1

Since financial leverage offers the opportunity to increase return on equity, why doesn't every company leverage itself to the maximum? There is a downside. When the economy turns down, companies may not be able to produce investment returns that exceed interest rates. A company that has borrowed money at a fixed rate of 8 percent that can only earn 6 percent on its investments will suffer from financial leverage. In other words, financial leverage is a double-edged sword. It can have a negative as well as a positive impact on a company's return on equity ratio.

Finally, compare the ratios in Exhibit 3.12 for companies in the oil industry to the same ratios for companies in the insurance industry. There are significant differences *between* industries, but there are considerable similarities *within* each industry. The debt to assets ratio is much higher for the insurance industry than for the oil industry. However, within each industry, the ratios are clustered fairly close together. Distinct differences between industries and similarities within industries are common business features. When you compare accounting information for different companies, you must consider the industries in which those companies operate.

SCOPE OF COVERAGE

Throughout this text, we introduce ratios directly related to chapter topics. Only a few of the many ratios available to users of financial statements are introduced. Introductory finance courses typically include a more extensive study of ratios and other topics related to financial statement analysis. Many business programs offer an entire course on financial statement analysis. These courses help students learn to judge whether the ratio results signal good or poor performance. Developing such judgment requires understanding how accounting policies and procedures can affect financial ratios. The ratios introduced in this text will enhance your understanding of accounting as a basis for studying more advanced topics in subsequent courses.

<< A Look Back

This chapter introduced the *double-entry accounting system*. This system was first documented in the 1400s, and is used by most companies today. Key components of the double-entry system are summarized below.

1. Business events can be classified concisely using debit/credit terminology. *Debits* are used to record increases in asset accounts and decreases in liability and stockholders' equity accounts. *Credits* are used to record decreases in asset accounts and increases in liability and stockholders' equity accounts.

2. *T-accounts* are frequently used to analyze and communicate account activity. The account title is placed at the top of the horizontal bar of the T, and increases and decreases are placed on either side of the vertical bar. In a T-account, debits are recorded on the left side and credits are recorded on the right side.
3. Accountants initially record transaction data in journals. The *general journal* is used not only for data entry but also as a shorthand communication tool. Each journal entry includes at least one debit and one credit. An entry is recorded using at least two lines, with the debit recorded on the top line and the credit on the bottom line. The credit is indented to distinguish it from the debit. The general journal format is illustrated here:

Debit	XXX	
Credit		XXX

4. Information is posted (copied) from the journals to *ledger* accounts. The ledger accounts provide the information used to prepare the financial statements.
5. *Trial balances* are used to check the mathematical accuracy of the recording process. Ledger accounts with their associated debit and credit balances are listed in the trial balance. The debit and credit amounts are totaled and compared. An equal amount of debits and credits provides evidence but not proof that transactions have been recorded correctly. If the debits and credits are *not* equal, it is proof that errors exist.

The double-entry system is just a way to organize accounting data. No matter how we organize the data, the objective is to summarize and report it in a way that is useful for making decisions.

A Look Forward >>

Chapters 1 through 3 focused on businesses that generate revenue by providing services to their customers. Examples of these types of businesses include consulting, real estate sales, medical services, and legal services. The next chapter introduces accounting practices for businesses that generate revenue by selling goods. Examples of these companies include **Walmart**, **Best Buy**, **Office Depot**, and **Lowe's**.

APPENDIX

Journal Entries for Long-Term Assets and Depreciation

LO 3-6

Record depreciation and interest using journal entries and T-accounts, and show how these entries affect financial statements.

To illustrate the journal entries associated with the acquisition and depreciation of long-term assets, assume Evans Company paid $34,000 cash to purchase a computer. The computer has a $4,000 salvage value and a three-year useful life. The journal entry necessary to record the purchase of the computer is shown here.

Account Title	Debit	Credit
Computer	34,000	
Cash		34,000

Depreciation expense is determined as follows:

($34,000 cost − $4,000 salvage) / 3-year useful life = $10,000 per year

The journal entry to record the depreciation expense at the end of each year is shown here.

Account Title	Debit	Credit
Depreciation Expense	10,000	
Accumulated Depreciation		10,000

Journal Entries for Notes Payable and Interest Expense

To illustrate the journal entries associated with issuing a promissory note and associated interest, assume Evans Company acquired $20,000 cash by issuing a note to the State Bank. The note was dated October 1, 2016. It stipulated a one-year term and a 9 percent annual interest rate. The entry necessary to record the issue of the note on October 1 is shown here.

Account Title	Debit	Credit
Cash	20,000	
Note Payable		20,000

Accrued interest as of December 31, 2016, is computed as follows:

$20,000 principal × .09 annual interest × 3/12 = $450

The journal entry required to record the accrued interest as of December 31, 2016, is shown here:

Account Title	Debit	Credit
Interest Expense	450	
Interest Payable		450

The note matures on September 30, 2017. The accrued interest expense for the nine months the note was outstanding in 2017 is computed as follows:

$20,000 principal × .09 annual interest × 9/12 = $1,350

The journal entry required to record the accrued interest is shown here:

Account Title	Debit	Credit
Interest Expense	1,350	
Interest Payable		1,350

The journal entry required to pay the interest due and the principal balance of the note on September 30, 2017, is shown here:

Account Title	Debit	Credit
Interest Payable	1,800	
Notes Payable	20,000	
Cash		21,800

SELF-STUDY REVIEW PROBLEM

A step-by-step audio-narrated series of slides is available in the Connect library.

The following events apply to the first year of operations for Mestro Financial Services Company:

1. Acquired $28,000 cash by issuing common stock on January 1, 2016.
2. Purchased $1,100 of supplies on account.
3. Paid $12,000 cash in advance for a one-year lease on office space.
4. Earned $23,000 of consulting revenue on account.
5. Incurred $16,000 of general operating expenses on account.
6. Collected $20,000 cash from receivables.
7. Paid $13,000 cash on accounts payable.
8. Paid a $1,000 cash dividend to stockholders.

Information for Adjusting Entries

9. There was $200 of supplies on hand at the end of the accounting period.
10. The one-year lease on the office space was effective beginning on October 1, 2016.
11. There was $1,200 of accrued salaries at the end of 2016.

Required

a. Record the preceding events in general journal format.
b. Post the transaction data from the general journal into general ledger T-accounts.
c. Prepare an adjusted trial balance.
d. Prepare an income statement, statement of changes in stockholders' equity, balance sheet, and statement of cash flows.
e. Prepare the appropriate closing entries in general journal format.

Solution to Requirement a

Event No.	Account Title	Debit	Credit
1	Cash	28,000	
	Common Stock		28,000
2	Supplies	1,100	
	Accounts Payable		1,100
3	Prepaid Rent	12,000	
	Cash		12,000
4	Accounts Receivable	23,000	
	Consulting Revenue		23,000
5	General Operating Expenses	16,000	
	Accounts Payable		16,000
6	Cash	20,000	
	Accounts Receivable		20,000
7	Accounts Payable	13,000	
	Cash		13,000
8	Dividends	1,000	
	Cash		1,000
9	Supplies Expense	900	
	Supplies		900
10	Rent Expense	3,000	
	Prepaid Rent		3,000
11	Salaries Expense	1,200	
	Salaries Payable		1,200

Solution to Requirement b

MESTRO FINANCIAL SERVICES COMPANY
T-Accounts, 2016

Assets = Liabilities + Equity

Assets

Cash

1.	28,000	3.	12,000
6.	20,000	7.	13,000
		8.	1,000
Bal.	22,000		

Accounts Receivable

4.	23,000	6.	20,000
Bal.	3,000		

Supplies

2.	1,100	9.	900
Bal.	200		

Prepaid Rent

3.	12,000	10.	3,000
Bal.	9,000		

Liabilities

Accounts Payable

7.	13,000	2.	1,100
		5.	16,000
		Bal.	4,100

Salaries Payable

		11.	1,200
		Bal.	1,200

Equity

Common Stock

		1.	28,000
		Bal.	28,000

Dividends

8.	1,000		

Consulting Revenue

		4.	23,000

General Operating Expenses

5.	16,000		

Salaries Expense

11.	1,200		

Supplies Expense

9.	900		

Rent Expense

10.	3,000		

Solution to Requirement c

MESTRO FINANCIAL SERVICES COMPANY
Trial Balance
December 31, 2016

Account Titles	Debit	Credit
Cash	$22,000	
Accounts receivable	3,000	
Supplies	200	
Prepaid rent	9,000	
Accounts payable		$ 4,100
Salaries payable		1,200
Common stock		28,000
Dividends	1,000	
Consulting revenue		23,000
General operating expenses	16,000	
Salaries expense	1,200	
Supplies expense	900	
Rent expense	3,000	
Totals	$56,300	$56,300

Solution to Requirement d

MESTRO FINANCIAL SERVICES COMPANY
Financial Statements

Income Statement
For the Year Ended December 31, 2016

Consulting revenue		$23,000
Expenses		
General operating expenses	$16,000	
Salaries expense	1,200	
Supplies expense	900	
Rent expense	3,000	
Total expenses		(21,100)
Net income		$ 1,900

Statement of Changes in Stockholders' Equity
For the Year Ended December 31, 2016

Beginning common stock	$ 0	
Plus: Common stock issued	28,000	
Ending common stock		$28,000
Beginning retained earnings	0	
Plus: Net income	1,900	
Less: Dividends	(1,000)	
Ending retained earnings		900
Total stockholders' equity		$28,900

Balance Sheet
As of December 31, 2016

Assets		
Cash	$22,000	
Accounts receivable	3,000	
Supplies	200	
Prepaid rent	9,000	
Total assets		$34,200
Liabilities		
Accounts payable	$ 4,100	
Salaries payable	1,200	
Total liabilities		$ 5,300
Stockholders' equity		
Common stock	28,000	
Retained earnings	900	
Total stockholders' equity		28,900
Total liabilities and stockholders' equity		$34,200

continued

Statement of Cash Flows For the Year Ended December 31, 2016		
Cash flows from operating activities		
Inflow from customers	$20,000	
Outflow for expenses	(25,000)	
Net cash flow from operating activities		$ (5,000)
Cash flows from investing activities		0
Cash flows from financing activities		
Inflow from issue of common stock	28,000	
Outflow for dividends	(1,000)	
Net cash flow from financing activities		27,000
Net change in cash		22,000
Plus: Beginning cash balance		0
Ending cash balance		$22,000

Solution to Requirement e

Date	Account Title	Debit	Credit
Dec. 31	Consulting Revenue	23,000	
	Retained Earnings		23,000
Dec. 31	Retained Earnings	21,100	
	General Operating Expenses		16,000
	Salaries Expense		1,200
	Supplies Expense		900
	Rent Expense		3,000
Dec. 31	Retained Earnings	1,000	
	Dividends		1,000

KEY TERMS

Account balance 148
Books of original entry 158
Chart of accounts 159
Closing entries 163
Credit 148
Debit 148
Debt to assets ratio 166
Double-entry accounting 149
Financial leverage 166
Fiscal year 147
General journal 158
General ledger 159
Journals 158
Posting 159
Return on assets ratio 165
Return on equity ratio 166
Source documents 157
Special journals 158
T-account 148
Trial balance 161

QUESTIONS

1. What are the two fundamental equality requirements of the double-entry accounting system?
2. Define *debit* and *credit*. How are assets, liabilities, common stock, retained earnings, revenues, expenses, and dividends affected (increased or decreased) by debits and by credits?
3. How is the balance of an account determined?
4. What are the three primary sources of business assets?
5. What are the three primary ways a business may use assets?
6. Give an example of an asset exchange transaction.
7. How does a debit to an expense account ultimately affect retained earnings? Stockholders' equity?
8. What accounts normally have debit balances? What accounts normally have credit balances?
9. What is the primary source of information for preparing the financial statements?
10. What is the purpose of a journal?
11. What is the difference between the *general journal* and special journals?
12. What is a ledger? What is its function in the accounting system?
13. What is the purpose of closing entries?
14. Do all companies close their books on December 31? Why or why not?
15. At a minimum, what information is recorded in the general journal?
16. What is the purpose of a trial balance?
17. When should a trial balance be prepared?
18. What does the term *posting* mean?

19. What information does the return on assets ratio provide about a company?

20. What information does the debt to assets ratio provide about a company?

21. What is financial leverage?

22. Explain how financial leverage impacts the return on equity ratio.

MULTIPLE-CHOICE QUESTIONS

Multiple-choice questions are available in the Connect library.

EXERCISES—SERIES A

connect plus+ ACCOUNTING ***All applicable Exercises in Series A are available with McGraw-Hill's Connect Plus Accounting.***

Exercise 3-1A *Matching debit and credit terminology with accounting elements* LO 3-1

Required

Complete the following table by indicating whether a debit or credit is used to increase or decrease the balance of accounts belonging to each category of financial statement elements. The appropriate debit/credit terminology has been identified for the first category (assets) as an example.

Category of Elements	Used to Increase This Element	Used to Decrease This Element
Assets	Debit	Credit
Liabilities		
Common Stock		
Retained Earnings		
Revenue		
Expense		
Dividends		

Exercise 3-2A *Debit/credit terminology* LO 3-1

Two introductory accounting students were arguing about how to record a transaction involving an exchange of cash for land. Laura stated that the transaction should have a debit to Land and a credit to Cash; Clark argued that the reverse (debit to Cash and credit to Land) represented the appropriate treatment.

Required

Which student was correct? Defend your position.

Exercise 3-3A *Matching debit and credit terminology with account titles* LO 3-1

Required

Indicate whether each of the following accounts normally has a debit balance or a credit balance:

a. Salaries Expense
b. Consulting Revenue
c. Unearned Revenue
d. Accounts Payable
e. Dividends
f. Land
g. Salaries Payable
h. Cash
i. Prepaid Insurance
j. Common Stock
k. Interest Revenue
l. Rent Expense

LO 3-1

Exercise 3-4A *Applying debit/credit terminology to accounting events*

Required

a. In parallel columns, list the accounts that would be debited and credited for each of the following unrelated transactions:

(1) Acquired cash from the issue of common stock.
(2) Provided services for cash.
(3) Paid cash for salaries expense.
(4) Purchased supplies for cash.
(5) Paid in advance for two-year lease on office space.
(6) Provided services on account.
(7) Recognized expense for prepaid rent that had been used up by the end of the accounting period.
(8) Recognized accrued interest revenue.
(9) Recorded accrued salaries at the end of the accounting period.

b. Show how each transaction affects the financial statements by placing a + for increase, − for decrease, and NA for not affected under each component in a horizontal statements model like the one shown below. Also, in the Cash Flow column, use the letters OA to designate operating activity, IA for investing activity, and FA for financing activity. The first event is recorded as an example.

Assets	=	Liab.	+	Equity	Rev.	−	Exp.	=	Net Inc.	Cash Flow
+		NA		+	NA		NA		NA	+ FA

LO 3-1

Exercise 3-5A *Debit/credit terminology*

Required

For each of the following independent events, identify the account that would be debited and the account that would be credited. The accounts for the first event are identified as an example.

Event	Account Debited	Account Credited
a	Cash	Common Stock

a. Received cash by issuing common stock.
b. Received cash for services to be performed in the future.
c. Paid salaries payable.
d. Provided services on account.
e. Paid cash for operating expenses.
f. Purchased supplies on account.
g. Recognized revenue for services completed. Cash had been collected in Event *b*.
h. Recognized accrued salaries expense.
i. Recognized expense for supplies used during the period.
j. Performed services for cash.
k. Recognized accrued interest revenue.
l. Paid accounts payable.
m. Received cash in payment of accounts receivable.
n. Paid a cash dividend to the stockholders.

LO 3-1

Exercise 3-6A *Identifying transaction type, its effect on the accounting equation, and whether the effect is recorded with a debit or credit*

Required

Identify whether each of the following transactions is an asset source (AS), asset use (AU), asset exchange (AE), or claims exchange (CE). Also explain how each event affects the accounting equation by placing a + for increase, − for decrease, and NA for not affected under each of the components of the accounting equation. Finally, indicate whether the effect requires a debit or credit entry. The first event is recorded as an example.

						Stockholders' Equity		
Event	Type of Event	Assets	=	Liabilities	+	Common Stock	+	Retained Earnings
a	AS	+ Debit		+ Credit		NA		NA

a. Purchased supplies on account.
b. Acquired cash from the issue of common stock.
c. Paid cash in advance for one year of rent.
d. Paid salaries payable.
e. Received cash for services to be performed in the future.
f. Paid a cash dividend to the stockholders.
g. Received cash in payment of accounts receivable.
h. Paid accounts payable.
i. Provided services for cash.
j. Recognized expense for supplies used during the period.
k. Recognized revenue for services completed for which cash had been collected previously.
l. Recognized accrued interest revenue.
m. Incurred other operating expenses on account.
n. Purchased land with cash.

Exercise 3-7A *Identifying increases and decreases in T-accounts* LO 3-1

Required

For each of the following T-accounts, indicate the side of the account that should be used to record an increase or decrease in the account balance:

Cash

Debit	Credit

Accounts Payable

Debit	Credit

Common Stock

Debit	Credit

Accounts Receivable

Debit	Credit

Salaries Payable

Debit	Credit

Dividends

Debit	Credit

Supplies

Debit	Credit

Service Revenue

Debit	Credit

Other Operating Expense

Debit	Credit

Exercise 3-8A *T-accounts and the accounting equation* LO 3-1

Required

Record each of the following Fred Co. events in T-accounts, and then explain how the event affects the accounting equation:

a. Received $20,000 cash by issuing common stock.
b. Purchased supplies for $1,000 cash.
c. Purchased land for $10,000 cash.
d. Performed services for $3,200 cash.

LO 3-1

Exercise 3-9A *Recording receivables and identifying their effect on financial statements*

Davos Company performed services on account for $160,000 in 2016. Davos collected $120,000 cash from accounts receivable during 2016, and the remaining $40,000 was collected in cash during 2017.

Required

a. Record the 2016 transactions in T-accounts.

b. Record the 2016 transactions in a horizontal statements model like the following one:

Assets			=	Liab.	+	Equity	Rev.	−	Exp.	=	Net Inc.	Cash Flow
Cash	+	Accts. Rec.	=			Ret. Earn.						

c. Determine the amount of revenue Davos would report on the 2016 income statement.

d. Determine the amount of cash flow from operating activities Davos would report on the 2016 statement of cash flows.

e. Open a T-account for Retained Earnings, and close the 2016 Service Revenue account to the Retained Earnings account.

f. Record the 2017 cash collection in the appropriate T-accounts.

g. Record the 2017 transaction in a horizontal statements model like the one shown in Requirement *b*.

h. Assuming no other transactions occur in 2017, determine the amount of net income and the net cash flow from operating activities for 2017.

LO 3-1, 3-3, 3-4

Exercise 3-10A *Recording supplies and identifying their effect on financial statements*

Sye Chase started and operated a small family architectural firm in 2016. The firm was affected by two events: (1) Chase provided $25,000 of services on account, and (2) he purchased $2,800 of supplies on account. There were $250 of supplies on hand as of December 31, 2016.

Required

a. Open T-accounts and record the two transactions in the accounts.

b. Record the required year-end adjusting entry to reflect the use of supplies.

c. Record the preceding transactions in a horizontal statements model like the following one:

Assets			=	Liab.	+	Equity	Rev.	−	Exp.	=	Net Inc.	Cash Flow
Accts. Rec.	+	Supplies	=	Accts. Pay.	+	Ret. Earn.						

d. Explain why the amounts of net income and net cash flow from operating activities differ.

e. Record and post the required closing entries, and prepare a post-closing trial balance.

LO 3-1

Exercise 3-11A *Recording unearned revenue and identifying its effect on financial statements*

Raylan received a $60,000 cash advance payment on June 1, 2016, for consulting services to be performed in the future. Services were to be provided for a one-year term beginning June 1, 2016.

Required

a. Record the June 1 cash receipt in T-accounts.

b. Record in T-accounts the adjustment required as of December 31, 2016.

c. Record the preceding transaction and related adjustment in a horizontal statements model like the following one:

Assets	=	Liab.	+	Equity	Rev.	−	Exp.	=	Net Inc.	Cash Flow

d. Determine the amount of net income on the 2016 income statement. What is the amount of net cash flow from operating activities for 2016?

e. What amount of liabilities would Raylan report on the 2016 balance sheet?

Exercise 3-12A *Using a T-account to determine cash flow from operating activities* LO 3-1

River Co. began the accounting period with a $132,000 debit balance in its Accounts Receivable account. During the accounting period, River Co. earned revenue on account of $180,000. The ending Accounts Receivable balance was $116,000.

Required

Based on this information alone, determine the amount of cash inflow from operating activities during the accounting period. (*Hint:* Use a T-account for Accounts Receivable. Enter the debits and credits for the given events, and solve for the missing amount.)

Exercise 3-13A *Using a T-account to determine cash flow from operating activities* LO 3-1

The Garden Company began the accounting period with a $60,000 credit balance in its Accounts Payable account. During the accounting period, Garden Co. incurred expenses on account of $152,000. The ending Accounts Payable balance was $64,000.

Required

Based on this information, determine the amount of cash outflow for expenses during the accounting period. (*Hint:* Use a T-account for Accounts Payable. Enter the debits and credits for the given events, and solve for the missing amount.)

Exercise 3-14A *Recording events in the general journal and identifying their effect on financial statements* LO 3-2

Required

Record each of the following transactions in general journal form and then show the effect of the transaction in a horizontal statements model. The first transaction is shown as an example.

Account Title	Debit	Credit
Accounts Receivable	8,200	
Service Revenue		8,200

Assets	=	Liab.	+	Equity	Rev.	−	Exp.	=	Net Inc.	Cash Flow
8,200				8,200	8,200		NA		8,200	NA

a. Performed $8,200 of services on account.

b. Collected $5,600 cash on accounts receivable.

c. Paid $1,450 cash in advance for an insurance policy.

d. Paid $400 on accounts payable.

e. Recorded the adjusting entry to recognize $300 of insurance expense.

f. Recorded the adjusting entry to recognize $200 accrued interest revenue.

g. Received $1,600 cash for services to be performed at a later date.

h. Purchased land for $9,000 cash.

i. Purchased supplies for $350 cash.

Exercise 3-15A *Recording prepaid items and identifying their effect on financial statements* LO 3-2

Cherokee Company began operations when it issued common stock for $80,000 cash. It paid $60,000 cash in advance for a one-year contract to lease delivery equipment for the business. It signed the lease agreement on March 1, 2016, which was effective immediately. Cherokee received $98,000 of cash revenue in 2016.

Required

a. Record the March 1 cash payment in general journal format.
b. Record in general journal format the adjustment required as of December 31, 2016.
c. Record all events in a horizontal statements model like the following one:

Assets			=	Liab.	+	Equity			Rev.	−	Exp.	=	Net Inc.	Cash Flow
Cash	+	Prep. Rent	=			Common Stock	+	Ret. Earn.						

d. What amount of net income will Cherokee Company report on the 2016 income statement? What is the amount of net cash flow from operating activities for 2016?
e. Determine the amount of prepaid rent Cherokee Company would report on the December 31, 2016, balance sheet.

LO 3-2

Exercise 3-16A *Recording accrued salaries and identifying their effect on financial statements*

On December 31, 2016, BIG Company had accrued salaries of $6,400.

Required

a. Record in general journal format the adjustment required as of December 31, 2016.
b. Record the above adjustment in a horizontal statements model like the following one:

Assets	=	Liab.	+	Equity	Rev.	−	Exp.	=	Net Inc.	Cash Flow
		Sal. Pay.	+	Ret. Earn.						

c. Determine the amount of net income BIG would report on the 2016 income statement, assuming that BIG received $36,000 of cash revenue. What is the amount of net cash flow from operating activities for 2016?
d. What amount of salaries payable would BIG report on the December 31, 2016, balance sheet?

LO 3-4

Exercise 3-17A *Preparing closing entries*

The following financial information was taken from the books of Zone Health Club, a small spa and fitness club:

Account Balances as of December 31, 2016	
Accounts Receivable	$12,450
Accounts Payable	6,200
Salaries Payable	3,150
Cash	36,750
Dividends	2,000
Operating Expense	35,300
Prepaid Rent	1,200
Rent Expense	8,400
Retained Earnings 1/1/2016	41,250
Salaries Expense	14,500
Service Revenue	65,400
Supplies	650
Supplies Expense	3,150
Common Stock	7,000
Unearned Revenue	6,400
Land	15,000

Required

a. Prepare the journal entries necessary to close the temporary accounts at December 31, 2016, for Zone Health Club.

b. What is the balance in the Retained Earnings account after the closing entries are posted?

Exercise 3-18A *Recording transactions in the general journal and T-accounts*

LO 3-1, 3-2

The following events apply to Montgomery Company for 2016, its first year of operation:

1. Received cash of $36,000 from the issue of common stock.
2. Performed $48,000 of services on account.
3. Incurred $6,500 of other operating expenses on account.
4. Paid $21,000 cash for salaries expense.
5. Collected $34,500 of accounts receivable.
6. Paid a $3,000 dividend to the stockholders.
7. Performed $9,500 of services for cash.
8. Paid $5,500 of the accounts payable.

Required

a. Record the preceding transactions in general journal form.

b. Post the entries to T-accounts and determine the ending balance in each account.

c. Determine the amount of total assets at the end of 2016.

d. Determine the amount of net income for 2016.

Exercise 3-19A *Preparing a trial balance*

LO 3-3

Required

On December 31, 2016, Morgan Company had the following normal account balances in its general ledger. Use this information to prepare a trial balance.

Land	$30,000
Unearned Revenue	32,000
Dividends	8,000
Prepaid Rent	5,600
Cash	90,000
Salaries Expense	18,000
Accounts Payable	7,000
Common Stock	80,000
Operating Expense	41,000
Office Supplies	2,500
Advertising Expense	3,500
Retained Earnings, 1/1/2016	9,000
Service Revenue	86,000
Accounts Receivable	15,400

Exercise 3-20A *Determining the effect of errors on the trial balance*

LO 3-3

Required

Explain how each of the following posting errors affects a trial balance. State whether the trial balance will be out of balance because of the posting error, and indicate which side of the trial balance will have a higher amount after each independent entry is posted. If the posting error does not affect the equality of debits and credits in the trial balance, state that the error will not cause an inequality and explain why.

a. An $900 credit to Unearned Revenue was credited to Service Revenue.

b. A $3,400 credit to Accounts Payable was not posted.

c. An $900 debit to Rent Expense was posted twice.

d. A $1,250 debit to Office Supplies was debited to Office Supplies Expense.

e. A $560 debit to Cash was posted as a $650 debit.

LO 3-1, 3-2, 3-3

Exercise 3-21A *Recording events in the general journal, posting to T-accounts, and preparing a trial balance*

The following events apply to Equipment Services Inc. in its first year of operation:

1. Acquired $60,000 cash from the issue of common stock.
2. Received a $8,200 cash advance for services to be provided in the future.
3. Purchased $2,000 of supplies on account.
4. Earned $36,000 of service revenue on account.
5. Incurred $16,100 of operating expenses on account.
6. Collected $28,500 cash from accounts receivable.
7. Made a $15,100 payment on accounts payable.
8. Paid a $2,000 cash dividend to the stockholders.
9. Recognized $1,600 of supplies expense.
10. Recorded $3,100 of accrued salaries expense.
11. Recognized $3,100 of revenue for services provided to the customer in Event 2.
12. Recognized $500 of accrued interest revenue.

Required

a. Record the events in T-accounts and determine the ending account balances.

b. Test the equality of the debit and credit balances of the T-accounts by preparing a trial balance.

LO 3-1, 3-2, 3-3, 3-4

Exercise 3-22A *Recording events in the general journal, posting to T-accounts, and preparing closing entries*

At the beginning of 2016, Oak Consulting had the following normal balances in its accounts:

Account	Balance
Cash	$42,000
Accounts Receivable	25,000
Accounts Payable	8,400
Common Stock	24,000
Retained Earnings	34,600

The following events apply to Oak's Consulting for 2016:

1. Provided $185,000 of services on account.
2. Incurred $45,800 of operating expenses on account.
3. Collected $140,000 of accounts receivable.
4. Paid $120,000 cash for salaries expense.
5. Paid $31,400 cash as a partial payment on accounts payable.
6. Paid an $10,000 cash dividend to the stockholders.

Required

a. Record these transactions in a general journal.

b. Open T-accounts, and post the beginning balances and the preceding transactions to the appropriate accounts.

c. Record the beginning balances and the transactions in a horizontal statements model such as the following one:

Assets			=	Liab.	+	Equity			Rev. − Exp. = Net Inc.	Cash Flow
Cash	+	Accts. Rec.	=	Accts. Pay.	+	Common Stock	+	Ret. Earn.		

d. Record the closing entries in the general journal and post them to the T-accounts. What is the amount of net income for the year?

e. What is the amount of *change* in retained earnings for the year? Is the change in retained earnings different from the amount of net income? If so, why?

f. Prepare a post-closing trial balance.

Exercise 3-23A *Using ratio analysis to assess financial risk*

LO 3-5

The following information was drawn from the balance sheets of two companies:

Company	Assets	=	Liabilities	+	Equity
Ever-Well	320,000		96,000		224,000
Eat-Right	700,000		280,000		420,000

Required

a. Compute the debt to assets ratio to measure the level of financial risk of both companies.

b. Compare the two ratios computed in Requirement *a* to identify which company has the higher level of financial risk.

Exercise 3-24A *IFRS and U.S. GAAP*

IFRS

a. Describe some ways that U.S. GAAP and IFRS are different.

b. How are U.S. GAAP and IFRS alike for reporting purposes?

PROBLEMS—SERIES A

connect plus+ ACCOUNTING ***All applicable Problems in Series A are available with McGraw-Hill's Connect Plus Accounting.***

Problem 3-25A *Identifying debit and credit balances*

Required

Indicate whether each of the following accounts normally has a debit or credit balance:

a. Interest Receivable
b. Interest Revenue
c. Prepaid Insurance
d. Land
e. Salaries Payable
f. Salaries Expense
g. Supplies Expense
h. Consulting Revenue
i. Utilities Payable
j. Supplies
k. Service Revenue
l. Accounts Payable
m. Operating Expense
n. Unearned Revenue
o. Dividends
p. Cash
q. Insurance Expense
r. Accounts Receivable
s. Utilities Expense
t. Retained Earnings
u. Common Stock

CHECK FIGURES
a. Interest Receivable: Debit
j. Supplies: Debit

Problem 3-26A *Transaction type and debit/credit terminology*

LO 3-1

The following events apply to Kate Enterprises:

1. Collected $16,200 cash for services to be performed in the future.
2. Acquired $50,000 cash from the issue of common stock.
3. Paid salaries to employees, $3,500 cash.
4. Paid cash to rent office space for the next 12 months, $12,000.
5. Paid cash of $17,500 for other operating expenses.
6. Paid on account payable, $1,752.

7. Paid cash for utilities expense, $804.
8. Recognized $45,000 of service revenue on account.
9. Paid a $2,500 cash dividend to the stockholders.
10. Purchased $3,200 of supplies on account.
11. Received $12,500 cash for services rendered.
12. Recognized $5,200 of accrued salaries expense.
13. Recognized $1,300 of accrued interest revenue.
14. Recognized $3,000 of rent expense. Cash had been paid in a prior transaction (see Event 4).
15. Recognized $5,000 of revenue for services performed. Cash had been previously collected (see Event 1).

Required

Identify each event as an asset source (AS), asset use (AU), asset exchange (AE), or claims exchange (CE). Also identify the account that is to be debited and the account that is to be credited when the transaction is recorded. The first event is recorded as an example.

Event No.	Type of Event	Account Debited	Account Credited
1	AS	Cash	Unearned Revenue

LO 3-1, 3-3

CHECK FIGURE
b. Total debits: $207,500

Problem 3-27A *Recording events in a statements model and T-accounts and preparing a trial balance*

The following accounting events apply to Mary's Designs for the year 2016:

Asset Source Transactions

1. Began operations by acquiring $90,000 of cash from the issue of common stock.
2. Performed services and collected cash of $9,000.
3. Collected $36,000 of cash in advance for services to be provided over the next 12 months.
4. Provided $58,000 of services on account.
5. Purchased supplies of $5,200 on account.

Asset Exchange Transactions

6. Purchased $21,000 of land for cash.
7. Collected $49,000 of cash from accounts receivable.
8. Purchased $3,150 of supplies with cash.
9. Paid $12,000 for one year's rent in advance.

Asset Use Transactions

10. Paid $24,000 cash for salaries of employees.
11. Paid a cash dividend of $5,000 to the stockholders.
12. Paid off $3,600 of the accounts payable with cash.

Claims Exchange Transactions

13. Placed an advertisement in the local newspaper for $2,600 on account.
14. Incurred utility expense of $1,800 on account.

Adjusting Entries

15. Recognized $12,000 of revenue for performing services. The collection of cash for these services occurred in a prior transaction. (See Event 3.)
16. Recorded $8,000 of accrued salary expense at the end of 2016.
17. Recorded supplies expense. Had $1,900 of supplies on hand at the end of the accounting period.
18. Recognized four months of expense for prepaid rent that had been used up during the accounting period.
19. Recognized $500 of accrued interest revenue.

Required

a. Record each of the preceding events in T-accounts.

b. Prepare a before-closing trial balance.

c. Use a horizontal statements model to show how each event affects the balance sheet, income statement, and statement of cash flows. Indicate whether the event increases (+), decreases (−), or does not affect (NA) each element of the financial statements. Also, in the Cash Flow column, use the letters OA to designate operating activity, IA for investing activity, and FA for financing activity. The first event is recorded as an example.

Assets	=	Liab.	+	Equity	Rev.	−	Exp.	=	Net Inc.	Cash Flow
+		NA		+	NA		NA		NA	+ FA

Problem 3-28A *Effect of journal entries on financial statements*

LO 3-2

Event No.	Account Title	Debit	Credit
1	Cash Common Stock	XXX	 XXX
2	Prepaid Rent Cash	XXX	 XXX
3	Accounts Receivable Service Revenue	XXX	 XXX
4	Cash Unearned Revenue	XXX	 XXX
5	Cash Accounts Receivable	XXX	 XXX
6	Supplies Accounts Payable	XXX	 XXX
7	Salaries Expense Cash	XXX	 XXX
8	Utilities Expense Cash	XXX	 XXX
9	Supplies Expense Supplies	XXX	 XXX
10	Unearned Revenue Service Revenue	XXX	 XXX
11	Cash Service Revenue	XXX	 XXX
12	Dividends Cash	XXX	 XXX
13	Rent Expense Prepaid Rent	XXX	 XXX

Required

The preceding 13 different accounting events are presented in general journal format. Use a horizontal statements model to show how each event affects the balance sheet, income statement, and statement of cash flows. Indicate whether the event increases (+), decreases (−), or does not affect (NA) each element of the financial statements. Also, in the Cash Flow column, use the letters OA to designate operating activity, IA for investing activity, and FA for financing activity. The first event is recorded as an example.

Assets	=	Liab.	+	Equity	Rev.	−	Exp.	=	Net Inc.	Cash Flow
+		NA		+	NA		NA		NA	+ FA

LO 3-2

Problem 3-29A *Identifying accounting events from journal entries*

Required

The following information is from the records of attorney Glenn Price. Write a brief explanation of the accounting event represented in each of the general journal entries.

Date	Account Titles	Debit	Credit
Jan. 1	Cash	40,000	
	Common Stock		40,000
Feb. 1	Cash	24,000	
	Service Revenue		24,000
Mar. 1	Prepaid Rent	1,600	
	Cash		1,600
Apr. 1	Accounts Receivable	48,000	
	Service Revenue		48,000
May 1	Supplies	2,000	
	Cash		2,000
June 10	Cash	8,000	
	Unearned Revenue		8,000
July 10	Cash	8,800	
	Accounts Receivable		8,800
Aug. 1	Salaries Expense	4,000	
	Cash		4,000
Oct. 1	Dividends	2,000	
	Cash		2,000
Nov. 1	Property Tax Expense	3,000	
	Cash		3,000
Dec. 31	Rent Expense	4,400	
	Prepaid Rent		4,400
31	Unearned Revenue	2,240	
	Service Revenue		2,240
31	Supplies Expense	800	
	Supplies		800

LO 3-2

Problem 3-30A *Recording adjusting entries in general journal format*

Required

Each of the following independent events requires a year-end adjusting entry. Record each event and the related adjusting entry in general journal format. The first event is recorded as an example. Assume a December 31 closing date.

Event No.	Date	Account Titles	Debit	Credit
a	July 1	Prepaid Rent	48,000	
		Cash		48,000
a	Dec. 31	Rent Expense (48,000 × 6/12)	24,000	
		Prepaid Rent		24,000

a. Paid $48,000 cash in advance on July 1 for a one-year lease on office space.

b. Purchased $5,000 of supplies on account on April 15. At year-end, $500 of supplies remained on hand.

c. Received a $9,600 cash advance on July 1 for a contract to provide services for one year beginning immediately.

d. Paid $5,400 cash in advance on February 1 for a one-year insurance policy.

Problem 3-31A *Effect of errors on the trial balance*

LO 3-3

CHECK FIGURE
Corrected Cash Balance: $69,710

The following trial balance was prepared from the ledger accounts of Ricardo Company:

RICARDO COMPANY
Trial Balance
April 30, 2016

Account Title	Debit	Credit
Cash	$ 68,900	
Accounts Receivable	30,000	
Supplies	1,800	
Prepaid Insurance	3,600	
Land		$ 12,000
Accounts Payable		9,600
Common Stock		100,000
Retained Earnings		27,510
Dividends	8,000	
Service Revenue		60,000
Rent Expense	9,600	
Salaries Expense	31,500	
Operating Expense	32,400	
Totals	$185,800	$209,110

When the trial balance failed to balance, the accountant reviewed the records and discovered the following errors:

1. The company received $560 as payment for services rendered. The credit to Service Revenue was recorded correctly, but the debit to Cash was recorded as $650.
2. A $900 receipt of cash that was received from a customer on accounts receivable was not recorded.
3. A $600 purchase of supplies on account was properly recorded as a debit to the Supplies account. However, the credit to Accounts Payable was not recorded.
4. Land valued at $12,000 was contributed to the business in exchange for common stock. The entry to record the transaction was recorded as a $12,000 credit to both the Land account and the Common Stock account.
5. A $500 rent payment was properly recorded as a credit to Cash. However, the Salaries Expense account was incorrectly debited for $500.

Required

Based on this information, prepare a corrected trial balance for Ricardo Company.

Problem 3-32A *Comprehensive problem: single cycle*

LO 3-1, 3-2, 3-3, 3-4

CHECK FIGURE
d. Net Income: $50,880
Total Assets: $98,180

The following transactions pertain to Smith Training Company for 2016:

Jan.	30	Established the business when it acquired $45,000 cash from the issue of common stock.
Feb.	1	Paid rent for office space for two years, $24,000 cash.
Apr.	10	Purchased $3,200 of supplies on account.
July	1	Received $24,000 cash in advance for services to be provided over the next year.
	20	Paid $1,500 of the accounts payable from April 10.
Aug.	15	Billed a customer $18,000 for services provided during August.
Sept.	15	Completed a job and received $8,400 cash for services rendered.
Oct.	1	Paid employee salaries of $12,000 cash.
	15	Received $15,000 cash from accounts receivable.
Nov.	16	Billed customers $42,000 for services rendered on account.
Dec.	1	Paid a dividend of $15,000 cash to the stockholders.
	31	Adjusted records to recognize the services provided on the contract of July 1.
	31	Recorded $3,600 of accrued salaries as of December 31.
	31	Recorded the rent expense for the year. (See February 1.)
	31	Physically counted supplies; $280 was on hand at the end of the period.

Required

a. Record the preceding transactions in the general journal.
b. Post the transactions to T-accounts and calculate the account balances.
c. Prepare a trial balance.
d. Prepare the income statement, statement of changes in stockholders' equity, balance sheet, and statement of cash flows.
e. Prepare the closing entries at December 31.
f. Prepare a trial balance after the closing entries are posted.

LO 3-1, 3-2, 3-3, 3-4

CHECK FIGURES

Ending Cash
b. Balance, 2016: $29,500
g. Net Income, 2017: $20,750

Problem 3-33A *Two complete accounting cycles*

Colton Enterprises experienced the following events for 2016, the first year of operation:

1. Acquired $35,000 cash from the issue of common stock.
2. Paid $12,000 cash in advance for rent. The payment was for the period April 1, 2016, to March 31, 2017.
3. Performed services for customers on account for $72,000.
4. Incurred operating expenses on account of $35,000.
5. Collected $55,500 cash from accounts receivable.
6. Paid $21,000 cash for salary expense.
7. Paid $28,000 cash as a partial payment on accounts payable.

Adjusting Entries

8. Made the adjusting entry for the expired rent. (See Event 2.)
9. Recorded $2,400 of accrued salaries at the end of 2016.

Events for 2017

1. Paid $2,400 cash for the salaries accrued at the end of the prior accounting period.
2. Performed services for cash of $21,000.
3. Purchased $2,800 of supplies on account.
4. Paid $13,200 cash in advance for rent. The payment was for one year beginning April 1, 2017.
5. Performed services for customers on account for $88,000.
6. Incurred operating expenses on account of $44,500.
7. Collected $89,000 cash from accounts receivable.
8. Paid $39,000 cash as a partial payment on accounts payable.
9. Paid $31,500 cash for salary expense.
10. Paid a $10,000 cash dividend to stockholders.

Adjusting Entries

11. Made the adjusting entry for the expired rent. (*Hint:* Part of the rent was paid in 2016.)
12. Recorded supplies expense. A physical count showed that $450 of supplies were still on hand.

Required

a. Record the events and adjusting entries for 2016 in general journal form.
b. Post the 2016 events to T-accounts.
c. Prepare a trial balance for 2016.
d. Prepare an income statement, statement of changes in stockholders' equity, balance sheet, and statement of cash flows for 2016.
e. Record the entries to close the 2016 temporary accounts to Retained Earnings in the general journal and post to the T-accounts.
f. Prepare a post-closing trial balance for December 31, 2016.
g. Repeat requirements *a* through *f* for 2017.

Problem 3-34A *Using ratio analysis to make comparisons between companies* LO 3-5

At the end of 2016 the following information is available for the Alaska Company and the Colorado Company:

	Alaska Co.	Colorado Co.
Total assets	$245,000	$926,000
Total liabilities	152,000	501,000
Stockholders' equity	93,000	425,000
Net income	20,000	65,000

Required

a. For each company, compute the debt to assets ratio and the return on equity ratio.
b. Determine what percentage of each company's assets were financed by the owners.
c. Which company has the greatest level of financial risk?
d. Based on profitability alone, which company performed better?
e. Do the above ratios support the concept of financial leverage? Explain.

Problem 3-35A *Notes payable (Appendix)* LO 3-6

TARVON Inc. acquired $50,000 cash by issuing a promissory note to the National Bank on May 1, 2016. Duval issued a promissory note with a one-year term and a 6% annual interest rate.

Required

Prepare the general journal entries to record:

a. The issue of the note on May 1, 2016.
b. Accrued interest on December 31, 2016.
c. Accrued interest on April 30, 2017.
d. Cash paid to settle the amount of interest payable on April 30, 2017.
e. Cash paid to settle the principal balance of the obligation to the bank on April 30, 2017.

Problem 3-36A *Comprehensive problem including depreciation (Appendix)* LO 3-6

Bower Consulting Company started the period with cash of $25,000, common stock of $13,000, and retained earnings of $12,000. Bower engaged in the following transactions in 2016:

Transactions during 2016

1. On January 1, 2016, purchased office furniture for $12,000.
2. On March 1, paid $5,400 for an insurance policy that provides coverage for 12 months beginning immediately.
3. Purchased $1,800 of supplies for cash.
4. Provided $39,000 of services for cash.
5. Paid $9,000 for salaries expense.
6. On April 1, received $12,000 for services that will be performed over the next 12 months beginning immediately.

Information for Adjusting Entries

7. The furniture had an estimated life of four years and a $2,000 salvage value.
8. Recognized the expired insurance.
9. An inventory of supplies showed $250 of supplies on hand as of December 31.
10. Recognized the revenue associated with Event 6 as of December 31.

Required

a. Record the 10 events in general journal format.
b. Prepare an income statement, balance sheet, and statement of cash flows.

MULTIPLE-CHOICE QUESTIONS

Multiple-choice questions are available in the Connect library.

EXERCISES—SERIES B

LO 3-1

Exercise 3-1B *Matching debit and credit terminology with accounts*

Required

Complete the following table by indicating whether a debit or credit is used to increase or decrease the balance of the following accounts. The appropriate debit/credit terminology has been identified for the first account as an example.

Account Titles	Used to Increase This Account	Used to Decrease This Account
Insurance Expense	Debit	Credit
Rent Expense		
Prepaid Rent		
Interest Revenue		
Accounts Receivable		
Accounts Payable		
Common Stock		
Land		
Unearned Revenue		
Service Revenue		
Retained Earnings		

LO 3-1

Exercise 3-2B *Debit/credit rules*

Jake, Mollie, and Neil, three accounting students, are discussing the rules of debits and credits. Jake says that debits increase account balances and credits decrease account balances. Mollie says that Jake is wrong, that credits increase account balances and debits decrease account balances. Neil interrupts and declares that they are both correct.

Required

Explain what Neil means and give examples of transactions where debits increase account balances, credits decrease account balances, credits increase account balances, and debits decrease account balances.

LO 3-1

Exercise 3-3B *Matching debit and credit terminology with account titles*

Required

Indicate whether each of the following accounts normally has a debit balance or a credit balance.

a. Unearned Revenue
b. Service Revenue
c. Dividends
d. Land
e. Accounts Receivable
f. Cash
g. Common Stock
h. Prepaid Rent
i. Supplies
j. Accounts Payable
k. Interest Revenue
l. Rent Expense

LO 3-1

Exercise 3-4B *Applying debit/credit terminology to accounting events*

Required

a. In parallel columns, list the accounts that would be debited and credited for each of the following unrelated transactions:
(1) Provided services for cash.
(2) Recognized accrued salaries at the end of the period.

(3) Recognized accrued interest revenue.
(4) Provided services on account.
(5) Paid cash for operating expenses.
(6) Acquired cash from the issue of common stock.
(7) Purchased supplies on account.
(8) Purchased land for cash.
(9) Paid a cash dividend to the stockholders.

b. Show how each transaction affects the financial statements by placing a + for increase, − for decrease, and NA for not affected under each component in a horizontal statements model like the one shown below. Also, in the Cash Flow column, use the letters OA to designate operating activity, IA for investing activity, and FA for financing activity. The first event is recorded as an example.

Assets	=	Liab.	+	Equity	Rev.	−	Exp.	=	Net Inc.	Cash Flow
+		NA		+	+		NA		+	+ OA

Exercise 3-5B *Debit/credit terminology* LO 3-1

Required

For each of the following independent events, identify the account that would be debited and the account that would be credited. The accounts for the first event are identified as an example.

Event	Account Debited	Account Credited
a	Cash	Unearned Revenue

a. Received cash for services to be performed in the future.
b. Purchased supplies on account.
c. Paid cash in advance for one year's rent.
d. Received cash by issuing common stock.
e. Provided services on account.
f. Paid accounts payable.
g. Paid salaries payable.
h. Recognized revenue for services completed; previously collected the cash in Event *a*.
i. Paid cash for operating expenses.
j. Paid salaries expense.
k. Received cash in payment of accounts receivable.
l. Recognized expense for prepaid rent that had been used up by the end of the accounting period.
m. Recognized accrued interest revenue.
n. Paid cash dividends to the stockholders.

Exercise 3-6B *Identifying transaction type, its effect on the accounting equation, and whether the effect is recorded with a debit or credit* LO 3-1

Required

Identify whether each of the following transactions is an asset source (AS), asset use (AU), asset exchange (AE), or claims exchange (CE). Also explain how each event affects the accounting equation by placing a + for increase, − for decrease, and NA for not affected under each of the components of the accounting equation. Finally, indicate whether the effect requires a debit or credit entry. The first event is recorded as an example.

						Stockholders' Equity		
Event	Type of Event	Assets	=	Liabilities	+	Common Stock	+	Retained Earnings
a	AS	+ Debit		NA		NA		+ Credit

a. Provided services for cash.
b. Received cash in payment of accounts receivable.
c. Recognized revenue for services completed; cash collected previously.
d. Purchased land by paying cash.
e. Recognized accrued interest revenue.
f. Purchased supplies on account.
g. Paid salaries payable.
h. Recognized expense for prepaid rent that had been used up by the end of the accounting period.
i. Incurred other operating expenses on account.
j. Recognized expense for supplies used during the period.
k. Received cash for services to be performed in the future.
l. Paid a cash dividend to the stockholders.
m. Paid cash in advance for one year's rent.
n. Provided services on account.

LO 3-1

Exercise 3-7B *Identifying increases and decreases in T-accounts*

Required

For each of the following T-accounts, indicate the side of the account that should be used to record an increase or decrease in the financial statement element:

Assets		=	Liabilities		+	Stockholders' Equity	
Debit	Credit		Debit	Credit		Debit	Credit
						Revenue	
						Debit	Credit
						Expense	
						Debit	Credit

LO 3-1

Exercise 3-8B *T-accounts and the accounting equation*

Required

Record each of the following Wilson Co. events in T-accounts and then explain how the event affects the accounting equation:

a. Received $40,000 cash by issuing common stock.
b. Purchased supplies for $1,800 cash.
c. Performed services on account for $14,000.
d. Paid cash for $8,000 of salaries expense.

LO 3-1

Exercise 3-9B *Recording receivables and identifying their effect on financial statements*

Ross Company performed services on account for $30,000 in 2016, its first year of operations. Ross collected $24,000 cash from accounts receivable during 2016 and the remaining $6,000 in cash during 2017.

Required

a. Record the 2016 transactions in T-accounts.
b. Record the 2016 transactions in a horizontal statements model like the following one:

Assets			=	Liab.	+	Equity	Rev.	−	Exp.	=	Net Inc.	Cash Flow
Cash	+	Accts. Rec.	=			Ret. Earn.						

c. Determine the amount of revenue that would be reported on the 2016 income statement.

d. Determine the amount of cash flow from operating activities that would be reported on the 2016 statement of cash flows.

e. Open a T-account for Retained Earnings, and close the 2016 Service Revenue account to the Retained Earnings account.

f. Record the 2017 cash collection in the appropriate T-accounts.

g. Record the 2017 transaction in a horizontal statements model like the one shown in Requirement *b*.

h. Assuming no other transactions occur in 2017, determine the amount of net income and the net cash flow from operating activities for 2017.

Exercise 3-10B *Recording supplies and identifying their effect on financial statements*

LO 3-1, 3-3, 3-4

Laura Moss started and operated a small family consulting firm in 2016. The firm was affected by two events: (1) Moss provided $36,000 of services on account, and (2) she purchased $10,000 of supplies on account. There were $1,800 of supplies on hand as of December 31, 2016.

Required

a. Open T-accounts and record the two transactions in the accounts.

b. Record the required year-end adjusting entry to reflect the use of supplies.

c. Record the above transactions in a horizontal statements model like the following one:

Assets			=	Liab.	+	Equity	Rev.	−	Exp.	=	Net Inc.	Cash Flow
Accts. Rec.	+	Supplies	=	Accts. Pay.	+	Ret. Earn.						

d. Explain why the amounts of net income and net cash flow from operating activities differ.

e. Record and post the required closing entries, and prepare a post-closing trial balance.

Exercise 3-11B *Recording unearned revenue and identifying its effect on financial statements*

LO 3-1

James Jones received a $90,000 cash advance on March 1, 2016, for legal services to be performed in the future. Services were to be provided for a one-year term beginning March 1, 2016.

Required

a. Record the March 1 cash receipt in T-accounts.

b. Record in T-accounts the adjustment required as of December 31, 2016.

c. Record the preceding transaction and related adjustment in a horizontal statements model like the following one:

Assets	=	Liab.	+	Equity	Rev.	−	Exp.	=	Net Inc.	Cash Flow

d. Determine the amount of net income on the 2016 income statement. What is the amount of net cash flow from operating activities for 2016?

e. What amount of unearned revenue would Jones report on the December 31, 2016, balance sheet?

Exercise 3-12B *Using a T-account to determine cash flow from operating activities*

LO 3-1

Barnes Inc. began the accounting period with a $105,000 debit balance in its Accounts Receivable account. During the accounting period, Barnes earned revenue on account of $448,000. The ending Accounts Receivable balance was $86,000.

Required

Based on this information alone, determine the amount of cash inflow from operating activities during the accounting period. (*Hint:* Use a T-account for Accounts Receivable. Enter the debits and credits for the given events, and solve for the missing amount.)

LO 3-1

Exercise 3-13B *Using a T-account to determine cash flow from operating activities*

Hun Company began the accounting period with a $36,000 credit balance in its Accounts Payable account. During the accounting period, Hun incurred expenses on account of $108,000. The ending Accounts Payable balance was $48,000.

Required

Based on this information, determine the amount of cash outflow for expenses during the accounting period. (*Hint:* Use a T-account for Accounts Payable. Enter the debits and credits for the given events, and solve for the missing amount.)

LO 3-2

Exercise 3-14B *Recording events in the general journal and identifying their effect on financial statements*

Required

Record each of the following transactions in general journal form and then show the effect of the transaction in the horizontal statements model. The first transaction is shown as an example.

Account Title	Debit	Credit
Accounts Receivable	50,000	
Service Revenue		50,000

Assets	=	Liab.	+	Equity	Rev.	−	Exp.	=	Net Inc.	Cash Flow
50,000		NA		50,000	50,000		NA		50,000	NA

a. Performed $50,000 worth of services on account.
b. Charged $2,000 on account for operating expense.
c. Collected $27,000 cash on accounts receivable.
d. Paid $700 on accounts payable.
e. Paid $6,800 cash in advance for an insurance policy.
f. Recorded the adjusting entry to recognize $4,500 of insurance expense.
g. Recorded the adjusting entry to recognize $800 of accrued interest revenue.
h. Received $4,000 cash for services to be performed at a later date.
i. Purchased supplies for $2,400 cash.

LO 3-2

Exercise 3-15B *Recording accrued salaries and identifying their effect on financial statements*

On December 31, 2016, Zeal Company had accrued salaries of $12,000.

Required

a. Record in general journal format the adjustment required as of December 31, 2016.
b. Record the above adjustment in a horizontal statements model like the following one:

Assets	=	Liab.	+	Equity	Rev.	−	Exp.	=	Net Inc.	Cash Flow
		Sal. Pay.	+	Ret. Earn.						

c. Determine the amount of net income Zeal would report on the 2016 income statement, assuming that Zeal received $29,000 of cash revenue. What is the amount of net cash flow from operating activities for 2016?

d. What amount of salaries payable would Zeal report on the December 31, 2016, balance sheet?

Exercise 3-16B *Recording prepaid items and identifying their effect on financial statements*

LO 3-2

Virginia Mining began operations by issuing common stock for $150,000. The company paid $135,000 cash in advance for a one-year contract to lease machinery for the business. The lease agreement was signed on March 1, 2016, and was effective immediately. Virginia Mining received $172,500 of cash revenue in 2016.

Required

a. Record the March 1 cash payment in general journal format.

b. Record in general journal format the adjustment required as of December 31, 2016.

c. Record all 2016 events in a horizontal statements model like the following one:

Assets			=	Liab.	+	Equity			Rev. − Exp. = Net Inc.	Cash Flow
Cash	+	Prep. Rent	=			Common Stock	+	Ret. Earn.		

d. What amount of net income would be reported on the 2016 income statement? What is the amount of net cash flow from operating activities for 2016?

e. Determine the amount of prepaid rent that would be reported on the December 31, 2016, balance sheet.

Exercise 3-17B *Preparing closing entries*

LO 3-4

The following financial information was taken from the books of Serenity Spa:

Account Balances as of December 31, 2016	
Accounts Receivable	$ 54,000
Accounts Payable	15,000
Advertising Expense	7,000
Cash	80,600
Common Stock	40,000
Dividends	10,000
Land	27,000
Prepaid Rent	6,400
Rent Expense	15,600
Retained Earnings 1/1/2016	38,800
Salaries Expense	64,000
Salaries Payable	23,600
Service Revenue	153,000
Supplies	800
Supplies Expense	5,000

Required

a. Prepare the journal entries necessary to close the temporary accounts December 31, 2016, for Serenity Spa.

b. What is the balance in the Retained Earnings account after the closing entries are posted?

Exercise 3-18B *Recording transactions in general journal and T-accounts*

LO 3-1, 3-2

The following events apply to Colton Training Co. for 2016, its first year of operation:

1. Received cash of $60,000 from the issue of common stock.
2. Performed $100,000 worth of services on account.

3. Paid $74,000 cash for salaries expense.
4. Purchased supplies for $13,000 on account.
5. Collected $79,000 of accounts receivable.
6. Paid $9,500 of the accounts payable.
7. Paid a $6,000 dividend to the stockholders.
8. Had $2,500 of supplies on hand at the end of the period.

Required

a. Record these events in general journal form.
b. Post the entries to T-accounts and determine the ending balance in each account.
c. Determine the amount of total assets at the end of 2016.
d. Determine the amount of net income for 2016.

LO 3-3

Exercise 3-19B *Preparing a trial balance*

Required

On December 31, 2016, Wages Company had the following normal account balances in its general ledger. Use this information to prepare a trial balance.

Common Stock	$ 50,000
Salaries Expense	32,000
Office Supplies	3,600
Advertising Expense	5,000
Retained Earnings, 1/1/2016	28,400
Unearned Revenue	36,000
Accounts Receivable	13,000
Cash	120,000
Service Revenue	152,000
Dividends	10,000
Prepaid Insurance	12,800
Land	44,000
Rent Expense	30,000
Accounts Payable	4,000

LO 3-3

Exercise 3-20B *Determining the effect of errors on the trial balance*

Required

Explain how each of the following posting errors affects a trial balance. State whether the trial balance will be out of balance because of the posting error, and indicate which side of the trial balance will have a higher amount after each independent entry is posted. If the posting error does not affect the equality of debits and credits in the trial balance, state that the error will not cause an inequality and explain why.

a. A $2,000 credit to Salaries Payable was not posted.
b. A $5,400 debit to Cash was posted as a $4,500 debit.
c. A $3,000 debit to Prepaid Rent was debited to Rent Expense.
d. A $2,500 credit to Accounts Payable was posted as a credit to Cash.
e. The collection of $400 of accounts receivable was posted to Accounts Receivable twice.

LO 3-1, 3-2, 3-3

Exercise 3-21B *Recording events in the general journal, posting to T-accounts, and preparing a trial balance*

The following events apply to Perry Carpet Cleaners in 2016, its first year of operations:

1. Received $45,000 cash from the issue of common stock.
2. Earned $37,500 of service revenue on account.
3. Incurred $15,000 of operating expenses on account.

4. Received $30,000 cash for performing services.
5. Paid $12,000 cash to purchase land.
6. Collected $33,000 of cash from accounts receivable.
7. Received a $9,000 cash advance for services to be provided in the future.
8. Purchased $1,350 of supplies on account.
9. Made an $11,250 payment on accounts payable.
10. Paid a $7,500 cash dividend to the stockholders.
11. Recognized $750 of supplies expense.
12. Recognized $7,500 of revenue for services provided to the customer in Event 7.
13. Recognized $1,350 of accrued interest revenue.

Required

a. Record the events in the general journal.
b. Post the events to T-accounts and determine the ending account balances.
c. Test the equality of the debit and credit balances of the T-accounts by preparing a trial balance.

Exercise 3-22B *Recording events in the general journal, posting to T-accounts, and preparing closing entries*

LO 3-1, 3-2, 3-3, 3-4

At the beginning of 2016, Event Services Co. had the following normal balances in its accounts:

Account	Balance
Cash	$60,000
Accounts Receivable	38,000
Accounts Payable	24,800
Common Stock	48,000
Retained Earnings	25,200

The following events apply to Event Services Co. for 2016:

1. Provided $130,000 of services on account.
2. Incurred $6,200 of operating expenses on account.
3. Collected $112,000 of accounts receivable.
4. Paid $72,000 cash for salaries expense.
5. Paid $30,000 cash as a partial payment on accounts payable.
6. Paid a $16,000 cash dividend to the stockholders.

Required

a. Record these events in a general journal.
b. Open T-accounts and post the beginning balances and the preceding transactions to the appropriate accounts. Determine the balance of each account.
c. Record the beginning balances and the events in a horizontal statements model such as the following one:

Assets			=	Liab.	+	Equity			Rev.	−	Exp.	=	Net Inc.	Cash Flow
Cash	+	Accts. Rec.	=	Accts. Pay.	+	Common Stock	+	Ret. Earn.						

d. Record the closing entries in the general journal and post them to the T-accounts. What is the amount of net income for the year?
e. What is the amount of *change* in retained earnings for the year? Is the change in retained earnings different from the amount of net income? If so, why?
f. Prepare a post-closing trial balance.

LO 3-5

Exercise 3-23B *Using ratio analysis to assess financial risk*

The following information was drawn from the balance sheets of two companies:

Company	Assets	=	Liabilities	+	Equity
North	$100,000		$ 24,500		$ 75,500
South	500,000		220,000		280,000

Required

a. Compute the debt to assets ratio to measure the level of financial risk of both companies.

b. Compare the two ratios computed in Requirement *a* to identify which company has the higher level of financial risk.

IFRS

Exercise 3-24B *IFRS and U.S. GAAP*

Using one of the websites referenced in the Focus on International Issues feature on page 167, define the IASB and describe its function.

PROBLEMS—SERIES B

LO 3-1

Problem 3-25B *Identifying debit and credit balances*

Required

Indicate whether each of the following accounts normally has a debit or credit balance:

a. Retained Earnings
b. Prepaid Insurance
c. Insurance Expense
d. Accounts Receivable
e. Salaries Payable
f. Cash
g. Common Stock
h. Rent Expense
i. Salaries Expense
j. Land
k. Interest Receivable
l. Interest Revenue
m. Dividends
n. Operating Expense
o. Unearned Revenue
p. Accounts Payable
q. Supplies
r. Service Revenue
s. Prepaid Rent
t. Supplies Expense

LO 3-1

Problem 3-26B *Transaction type and debit/credit terminology*

The following events apply to Un Enterprises:

1. Acquired $30,000 cash from the issue of common stock.
2. Recognized $28,000 of service revenue on account.
3. Paid cash to rent office space for the next 12 months, $7,800.
4. Paid cash of $9,200 for operating expenses.
5. Collected $9,000 cash for services to be performed in the future.
6. Paid salaries to employees, $8,000 cash.
7. Paid cash for utilities expense, $1,200.
8. Paid on accounts payable, $1,200.
9. Paid a $5,000 cash dividend to the stockholders.
10. Purchased $2,000 of supplies on account.
11. Received $18,000 cash for services rendered.
12. Recognized $400 of accrued interest revenue.
13. Recognized $3,250 of rent expense related to cash paid in a prior transaction (see Event 3).

14. Recognized $6,000 of revenue for services performed for which cash had been previously collected (see Event 5).
15. Recognized $4,800 of accrued salaries expense.

Required

Identify each event as asset source (AS), asset use (AU), asset exchange (AE), or claims exchange (CE). Also identify the account to be debited and the account to be credited when the transaction is recorded. The first event is recorded as an example.

Event No.	Type of Event	Account Debited	Account Credited
1	AS	Cash	Common Stock

Problem 3-27B *Recording events in a statements model and T-accounts and preparing a trial balance*

LO 3-1, 3-3

The following accounting events apply to Little Co. for the year 2016:

Asset Source Transactions

1. Began operations when the business acquired $40,000 cash from the issue of common stock.
2. Performed services and collected cash of $2,000.
3. Collected $9,000 of cash in advance for services to be provided over the next 12 months.
4. Provided $24,000 of services on account.
5. Purchased supplies of $840 on account.

Asset Exchange Transactions

6. Purchased $8,000 of land for cash.
7. Collected $17,000 of cash from accounts receivable.
8. Purchased $1,000 of supplies with cash.
9. Paid $7,200 in advance for one year's rent.

Asset Use Transactions

10. Paid $6,000 cash for salaries of employees.
11. Paid a cash dividend of $4,000 to the stockholders.
12. Paid $840 for supplies that had been purchased on account.

Claims Exchange Transactions

13. Placed an advertisement in the local newspaper for $300 and agreed to pay for the ad later.
14. Incurred utilities expense of $250 on account.

Adjusting Entries

15. Recognized $6,000 of revenue for performing services. The collection of cash for these services occurred in a prior transaction. (See Event 3.)
16. Recorded $1,800 of accrued salary expense at the end of 2016.
17. Recorded supplies expense. Had $240 of supplies on hand at the end of the accounting period.
18. Recognized that three months of prepaid rent had been used up during the accounting period.
19. Recognized $900 of accrued interest revenue.

Required

a. Record each of the preceding transactions in T-accounts and determine the balance of each account.
b. Prepare a before-closing trial balance.

c. Use a horizontal statements model to show how each event affects the balance sheet, income statement, and statement of cash flows. Indicate whether the event increases (+), decreases (−), or does not affect (NA) each element of the financial statements. Also, in the Cash Flow column, use the letters OA to designate operating activity, IA for investing activity, and FA for financing activity. The first event is recorded as an example.

Assets	=	Liab.	+	Equity	Rev.	−	Exp.	=	Net Inc.	Cash Flow
+		NA		+	NA		NA		NA	+ FA

LO 3-2

Problem 3-28B *Effect of journal entries on financial statements*

Event No.	Account Title	Debit	Credit
1	Cash Common Stock	XXX	 XXX
2	Accounts Receivable Service Revenue	XXX	 XXX
3	Cash Accounts Receivable	XXX	 XXX
4	Supplies Accounts Payable	XXX	 XXX
5	Cash Unearned Revenue	XXX	 XXX
6	Cash Service Revenue	XXX	 XXX
7	Property Tax Expense Cash	XXX	 XXX
8	Prepaid Rent Cash	XXX	 XXX
9	Salaries Expense Cash	XXX	 XXX
10	Unearned Revenue Service Revenue	XXX	 XXX
11	Rent Expense Prepaid Rent	XXX	 XXX
12	Supplies Expense Supplies	XXX	 XXX
13	Dividends Cash	XXX	 XXX

Required

The preceding 13 different accounting events are presented in general journal format. Use a horizontal statements model to show how each event affects the balance sheet, income statement, and statement of cash flows. Indicate whether the event increases (+), decreases (−), or does not affect (NA) each element of the financial statements. Also, in the Cash Flow column, use the letters OA to designate operating activity, IA for investing activity, and FA for financing activity. The first event is recorded as an example.

Assets	=	Liab.	+	Equity	Rev.	−	Exp.	=	Net Inc.	Cash Flow
+		NA		+	NA		NA		NA	+ FA

Problem 3-29B *Identifying accounting events from journal entries*

LO 3-2

Required

The following information is from the records of Floral Design. Write a brief explanation of the accounting event represented in each of the general journal entries.

Date	Account Titles	Debit	Credit
Jan. 1	Cash	18,750	
	Common Stock		18,750
Feb. 1	Prepaid Rent	15,300	
	Cash		15,300
Mar. 1	Cash	19,500	
	Unearned Revenue		19,500
Apr. 1	Accounts Receivable	27,600	
	Service Revenue		27,600
May 1	Supplies	2,325	
	Accounts Payable		2,325
31	Salaries Expense	9,150	
	Cash		9,150
June 30	Property Tax Expense	4,500	
	Cash		4,500
Sept. 1	Cash	13,000	
	Service Revenue		13,000
Oct. 2	Cash	16,000	
	Accounts Receivable		16,000
Dec. 1	Dividends	4,000	
	Cash		4,000
Dec. 31	Supplies Expense	2,100	
	Supplies		2,100
31	Rent Expense	9,600	
	Prepaid Rent		9,600
31	Unearned Revenue	12,500	
	Service Revenue		12,500

Problem 3-30B *Recording adjusting entries in general journal format*

LO 3-2

Required

Each of the following independent events requires a year-end adjusting entry. Record each event and the related adjusting entry in general journal format. The first event is recorded as an example. Assume a December 31 closing date.

Date	Account Titles	Debit	Credit
Oct. 1	Prepaid Rent	8,400	
	Cash		8,400
Dec. 31	Rent Expense (8,400 × 3/12)	2,100	
	Prepaid Rent		2,100

a. Paid $8,400 cash in advance on October 1 for a one-year lease on office space.

b. Paid $4,800 cash in advance on May 1 for a one-year insurance policy.

c. Purchased $1,600 of supplies on account on June 15. At year end, $200 of supplies remained on hand.

d. Received a $4,800 cash advance on September 1 for a contract to provide services for one year beginning immediately..

LO 3-3

Problem 3-31B *Effect of errors on the trial balance*

The following trial balance was prepared from the ledger accounts of Klein Inc.:

KLEIN INC. Trial Balance May 31, 2016		
Account Titles	**Debit**	**Credit**
Cash	$ 7,200	
Accounts Receivable	1,770	
Supplies	420	
Prepaid Insurance	2,400	
Land	5,000	
Accounts Payable		$ 1,500
Common Stock		1,800
Retained Earnings		7,390
Dividends	400	
Service Revenue		19,600
Rent Expense	3,600	
Salaries Expense	9,000	
Operating Expenses	2,500	
Totals	$32,290	$30,290

The accountant for Klein, Inc., made the following errors during May 2016:

1. The cash purchase of land for $3,000 was recorded as a $5,000 debit to Land and a $3,000 credit to Cash.
2. A $1,600 purchase of supplies on account was properly recorded as a debit to the Supplies account but was incorrectly recorded as a credit to the Cash account.
3. The company provided services valued at $7,800 to a customer on account. The accountant recorded the transaction in the proper accounts but in the incorrect amount of $8,700.
4. A $1,200 cash receipt from a customer on an account receivable was not recorded.
5. An $800 cash payment of an account payable was not recorded.
6. The May utility bill, which amounted to $1,050 on account, was not recorded.

Required

a. Identify the errors that would cause a difference in the total amounts of debits and credits that would appear in a trial balance. Indicate whether the Debit or Credit column would be larger as a result of the error.

b. Indicate whether each of the preceding errors would overstate, understate, or have no effect on the amount of total assets, liabilities, and equity. Your answer should take the following form:

Event No.	Assets	=	Liabilities	+	Stockholders' Equity
1	Overstate		No effect		No effect

c. Prepare a corrected trial balance.

Problem 3-32B *Comprehensive problem: single cycle*

LO 3-1, 3-2, 3-3, 3-4

The following transactions pertain to Price Corporation for 2016:

Jan.	1	Began operations when the business acquired $25,000 cash from the issue of common stock.
Mar.	1	Paid rent for office space for two years, $8,400 cash.
Apr.	14	Purchased $400 of supplies on account.
June	30	Received $12,000 cash in advance for services to be provided over the next year.
July	5	Paid $300 of the accounts payable from April 14.
Aug.	1	Billed a customer $4,800 for services provided during July.
	8	Completed a job and received $1,600 cash for services rendered.
Sept.	1	Paid employee salaries of $18,000 cash.
	9	Received $4,250 cash from accounts receivable.
Oct.	5	Billed customers $17,000 for services rendered on account.
Nov.	2	Paid a $500 cash dividend to the stockholders.
Dec.	31	Adjusted records to recognize the services provided on the contract of June 30.
	31	Recorded $1,100 of accrued salaries as of December 31.
	31	Recorded the rent expense for the year. (See March 1.)
	31	Physically counted supplies; $50 was on hand at the end of the period.

Required

a. Record the preceding transactions in the general journal.

b. Post the transactions to T-accounts and calculate the account balances.

c. Prepare a trial balance.

d. Prepare the income statement, statement of changes in stockholders' equity, balance sheet, and statement of cash flows.

e. Prepare the closing entries at December 31.

f. Prepare a trial balance after the closing entries are posted.

Problem 3-33B *Two complete accounting cycles*

LO 3-1, 3-2, 3-3, 3-4

Anchor Machining experienced the following events during 2016:

1. Started operations by acquiring $100,000 of cash from the issue of common stock.
2. Paid $12,000 cash in advance for rent during the period from February 1, 2016, to February 1, 2017.
3. Received $9,600 cash in advance for services to be performed evenly over the period from September 1, 2016, to September 1, 2017.
4. Performed services for customers on account for $130,400.
5. Incurred operating expenses on account of $63,000.
6. Collected $113,800 cash from accounts receivable.
7. Paid $44,000 cash for salaries expense.
8. Paid $56,000 cash as a partial payment on accounts payable.

Adjusting Entries

9. Made the adjusting entry for the expired rent. (See Event 2.)
10. Recognized revenue for services performed in accordance with Event 3.
11. Recorded $4,200 of accrued salaries at the end of 2016.

Events for 2017

1. Paid $4,200 cash for the salaries accrued at the end of the previous year.
2. Performed services for cash, $81,000.
3. Paid $50,000 cash to purchase land.
4. Paid $10,800 cash in advance for rent during the period from February 1, 2017, to February 1, 2018.

5. Performed services for customers on account for $164,000.
6. Incurred operating expenses on account of $98,200.
7. Collected $152,600 cash from accounts receivable.
8. Paid $96,000 cash as a partial payment on accounts payable.
9. Paid $82,000 cash for salaries expense.
10. Paid a $10,000 cash dividend to the stockholders.

Adjusting Entries

11. Recognized revenue for services performed in accordance with Event 3 in 2016.
12. Made the adjusting entry for the expired rent. (*Hint:* Part of the rent was paid in 2016.)
13. Recorded $7,000 of accrued salaries at the end of 2017.

Required

a. Record the events and adjusting entries for 2016 in general journal form.
b. Post the events for 2016 to T-accounts.
c. Prepare a trial balance for 2016.
d. Prepare an income statement, statement of changes in stockholders' equity, balance sheet, and statement of cash flows for 2016.
e. Record the entries to close the 2016 temporary accounts to Retained Earnings in the general journal and post to the T-accounts.
f. Prepare a post-closing trial balance for December 31, 2016.
g. Repeat requirements *a* through *f* for 2017.

LO 3-5

Problem 3-34B *Using ratio analysis to make comparisons between companies*

At the end of 2016 the following information is available for Delaware Company and Florida Company:

	Delaware Co.	Florida Co.
Total assets	$127,000	$753,000
Total liabilities	93,000	452,000
Stockholders' equity	34,000	301,000
Net income	8,000	45,000

Required

a. For each company, compute the debt to assets ratio and the return on equity ratio.
b. Determine what percentage of each company's assets were financed by the owners.
c. Which company has the greatest level of financial risk?
d. Based on profitability alone, which company performed better?
e. Do the above ratios support the concept of financial leverage? Explain.

LO 3-6

Problem 3-35B *Notes payable (Appendix)*

Black Inc. acquired $10,000 cash by issuing a promissory note to the National Bank on November 1, 2016. The note stipulated a one-year term and a 9 percent annual interest rate.

Required

Prepare the general journal entries to record:

a. The issue of the note on November 1, 2016.
b. Accrued interest on December 31, 2016.
c. Accrued interest on October 31, 2017.
d. Cash paid to settle the amount of interest payable on October 31, 2017.
e. Cash paid to settle the principal balance of the obligation to the bank on October 31, 2017.

Problem 3-36B *Comprehensive problem including depreciation (Appendix)*

LO 3-6

Vox Company started the period with cash of $22,000, common stock of $12,000, and retained earnings of $10,000. Vox engaged in the following transactions in 2016:

Transactions During 2016

1. On January 1, 2016, purchased a computer for $7,500 cash.
2. On February 1, paid $6,600 cash for rent for a 12-month period beginning immediately.
3. Purchased $1,100 of supplies for cash.
4. Provided $56,000 of services for cash.
5. Paid $18,000 cash for salaries expense.
6. On May 1, received $9,000 for services that will be performed over the next 12 months.

Information for Adjusting Entries

7. The computer had an estimated life of three years and a $2,400 salvage value.
8. Recognized the expired rent.
9. An inventory of supplies showed $120 of supplies on hand as of December 31.
10. Recognized the revenue associated with Event 6 as of December 31.

Required

a. Record the 10 events in general journal format.
b. Prepare an income statement, balance sheet, and statement of cash flows.

ANALYZE, THINK, COMMUNICATE

ATC 3-1 Business Applications Case *Understanding real-world annual reports*

Required

Use the Target Corporation's annual report in Appendix B to answer the following questions:

a. What was Target's debt to assets ratio for its fiscal-year ended February 1, 2014 (2013) and 2012?
b. What was Target's return on assets ratio for 2013 and 2012?
c. What was Target's return on equity ratio for 2013 and 2012?
d. Why was Target's return on equity ratio higher than its return on assets ratio for 2013 and 2012?

ATC 3-2 Group Assignment *Financial statement analysis*

The beginning account balances for Miller Company were as follows for 2016, 2017, and 2018:

	January 1		
	2016	2017	2018
Cash	$12,000	$19,000	$42,600
Accounts Receivable	6,000	10,000	6,000
Land	9,000	9,000	9,000
Prepaid Rent	0	1,000	1,400
Accounts Payable	12,300	11,300	15,300
Salaries Payable	0	0	2,100
Common Stock	10,000	10,000	10,000
Retained Earnings	4,700	17,700	31,600

Miller Company experienced the following events for the accounting periods 2016, 2017, and 2018:

2016

1. Performed services for $36,000 on account.
2. Paid rent of $6,000 for the period March 1, 2016, to March 1, 2017.

3. Incurred operating expenses of $18,000 on account.
4. Collected $32,000 of accounts receivable.
5. Paid $19,000 of accounts payable.
6. Recorded expired rent.

2017

1. Performed services on account of $48,000.
2. Paid rent of $8,400 for the period March 1, 2017, to March 1, 2018, and recorded the expired rent for the period January 1, 2017, to March 1, 2017.
3. Incurred operating expenses of $24,000 on account.
4. Collected $52,000 of accounts receivable.
5. Paid $20,000 of accounts payable.
6. Recorded expired rent.
7. Recorded accrued salaries of $2,100.

2018

1. Paid accrued salaries.
2. Performed services on account of $56,000.
3. Paid rent of $9,000 for the period March 1, 2018, to March 1, 2019, and recorded the expired rent for the period January 1, 2018, to March 1, 2018.
4. Incurred operating expenses of $32,000 on account.
5. Collected $55,000 of accounts receivable.
6. Paid $33,000 of accounts payable.
7. Sold land for $5,000; the land had a cost of $5,000.
8. Recorded expired rent.

Required

Divide the class into groups of four or five students. Organize the groups into three sections. Assign each section of groups the financial data for one of the preceding accounting periods.

Group Task

a. Prepare an income statement, balance sheet, and statement of cash flows. It may be helpful to open T-accounts and post transactions to these accounts before attempting to prepare the statements.

Class Discussion

b. Review the cash flows associated with the collection of receivables and the payment of payables. Comment on the company's collection and payment strategy.
c. Did net income increase or decrease between 2016 and 2017? What were the primary causes?
d. Did net income increase or decrease between 2017 and 2018? What were the primary causes?

ATC 3-3 Real-World Case *Choice of fiscal year*

Consider the following brief descriptions of four companies from different industries. Michaels Stores claims to be the largest arts and crafts specialty retailer in North America. It operates over 1,100 retail stores. Pulte Group, Inc., builds houses throughout the United States. In 2013, it completed 17,766 new houses. Toro Company manufactures and sells professional and residential lawn care products, such as irrigation systems. Vail Resorts, Inc., operates ski resorts in Colorado, including Breckenridge Mountain and Vail Mountain Resort, the largest in the United States.

The chapter explained that companies often choose to close their books when business is slow. Each of these companies ends its fiscal year on a different date. The closing dates, listed chronologically, are as follows:

February 2
July 31
October 31
December 31

Required

a. Try to determine which fiscal year-end matches which company. Write a brief explanation of the reason for your decisions.

b. Because many companies deliberately choose to prepare their financial statements at a slow time of year, try to identify problems this may present for someone trying to analyze the balance sheet for Michaels Stores. Write a brief explanation of the issues you identify.

ATC 3-4 Business Applications Case *Performing ratio analysis using real-world data*

The following data were taken from Netflix, Inc.'s 2013 annual report. *All dollar amounts are in millions.*

	Fiscal Years Ending	
	December 31, 2013	**December 31, 2012**
Total assets	$5,412,563	$3,967,890
Total liabilities		
Stockholders' equity	1,333,561	744,673
Net income	112,403	17,152

Required

a. For each year, compute Netflix's debt to assets ratio, return on assets ratio, and return on equity ratio. You will need to compute total liabilities.

b. Did the company's level of financial risk increase or decrease from 2012 to 2013?

c. In which year did the company appear to manage its assets most efficiently?

d. Do the above ratios support the concept of financial leverage? Explain.

ATC 3-5 Business Applications Case *Performing ratio analysis using real-world data*

The following data were taken from the 2013 annual reports of Biogen Idec, Inc., and Amgen Inc. Both companies are leaders in biotechnology. *All dollar amounts are in millions.*

	Biogen Idec	Amgen
	December 31, 2013	**December 31, 2013**
Total assets	$11,863	$66,125
Total liabilities	3,242	44,029
Stockholders' equity	8,621	22,096
Net income	1,862	5,081

Required

a. For each company, compute the debt to assets ratio, return on assets ratio, and return on equity ratio.

b. Which company has the greatest level of financial risk? Explain.

c. Which company appears to have managed its assets most efficiently? Explain.

d. Which company performed better from the perspective of the owners? Explain.

ATC 3-6 Writing Assignment *Effect of land sale on return on assets*

Toyo Company is holding land that cost $900,000 for future use. However, plans have changed and the company may not need the land in the foreseeable future. The president is concerned about the return on assets. Current net income is $425,000 and total assets are $3,500,000.

Required

a. Write a memo to the company president explaining the effect of disposing of the land, assuming that it has a current value of $1,500,000.

b. Write a memo to the company president explaining the effect of disposing of the land, assuming that it has a current value of $600,000.

ATC 3-7 Ethical Dilemma *Choice of brothers: ethics, risk, and accounting numbers in a medieval setting*

In the late 1400s, a wealthy land owner named Caster was trying to decide which of his twin sons, Rogan or Argon, to designate as the first heir to the family fortune. He decided to set up each son with a small farm consisting of 300 sheep and 20 acres of land. Each twin would be allowed to manage his property as he deemed appropriate. After a designated period, Caster would call his sons before him to account for their actions. The heir to the family fortune would be chosen on the basis of which son had produced a larger increase in wealth during the test period.

On the appointed day of reckoning, Argon boasted that he had 714 sheep under his control while Rogan had only 330. Furthermore, Argon stated that he had increased his land holdings to 27 acres. The seven-acre increase resulted from two transactions: first, on the day the contest started, Argon used 20 sheep to buy 10 additional acres; and second, he sold three of these acres for a total of 9 sheep on the day of reckoning. Also, Argon's flock had produced 75 newborn sheep during the period of accounting. He had been able to give his friends 50 sheep in return for the help that they had given him in building a fence, thereby increasing not only his own wealth but the wealth of his neighbors as well. Argon boasted that the fence was strong and would keep his herd safe from predatory creatures for five years (assume the fence had been used for one year during the contest period). Rogan countered that Argon was holding 400 sheep that belonged to another herder. Argon had borrowed these sheep on the day that the contest had started. Furthermore, Argon had agreed to return 424 sheep to the herder. The 24 additional sheep represented consideration for the use of the herder's flock. Argon had agreed to return the sheep immediately after the day of reckoning.

During the test period, Rogan's flock had produced 37 newborn sheep, but 2 sheep had gotten sick and died during the accounting period. Rogan had also lost 5 sheep to predatory creatures. He had no fence, and some of his sheep strayed from the herd, thereby exposing themselves to danger. Knowing that he was falling behind, Rogan had taken a wife in order to boost his productivity. His wife owned 170 sheep on the day they were married; her sheep had produced 16 newborn sheep since the date of her marriage to Rogan. Argon had not included the wife's sheep in his count of Rogan's herd. If his wife's sheep had been counted, Rogan's herd would contain 516 instead of 330 sheep suggested by Argon's count.

Argon charged that seven of Rogan's sheep were sick with symptoms similar to those exhibited by the two sheep that were now dead. Rogan interjected that he should not be held accountable for acts of nature such as illness. Furthermore, he contended that by isolating the sick sheep from the remainder of the herd, he had demonstrated prudent management practices that supported his case to be designated first heir.

Required

a. Prepare an income statement, balance sheet, statement of sheep flow (cash flow) for each twin, using contemporary accounting standards for the current year. Note that you have to decide whether to include the sheep owned by Rogan's wife when making his financial statements (what is the accounting entity?). (*Hint:* Use the number of sheep rather than the number of dollars as the common unit of measure.)

b. Refer to the statements you prepared in Requirement *a* to answer the following questions:

(1) Which twin has more owner's equity at the end of the accounting period?

(2) Which twin produced the higher net income during the accounting period?

(3) Which son should be designated heir based on conventional accounting and reporting standards?

c. What is the difference in the value of the land of the twins if the land is valued at market value (that is, three sheep per acre) rather than historical cost (that is, two sheep per acre)?

d. Did Argon's decision to borrow sheep increase his profitability? Support your answer with appropriate financial data.

e. Was Argon's decision to build a fence financially prudent? Support your answer with appropriate financial data.

f. Assuming that the loan resulted in a financial benefit to Argon, identify some reasons that the shepherd who owned the sheep may have been willing to loan them to Argon.

g. Which twin is likely to take risks to improve profitability? What would be the financial condition of each twin if one-half of the sheep in both flocks died as a result of illness? How should such risk factors be reported in financial statements?

h. Should Rogan's decision to "marry for sheep" be considered from an ethical perspective, or should the decision be made solely on the basis of the bottom-line net income figure?

i. Prepare a report that recommends which twin should be designated heir to the family business. Include a set of financial statements that supports your recommendation. Since this is a managerial report that will not be distributed to the public, you are not bound by generally accepted accounting principles.

ATC 3-8 Research Assignment *Investigating Nike's 10-K report*

Many companies must file financial reports with the SEC. Many of these reports are available electronically through the EDGAR database. EDGAR is an acronym for Electronic Data Gathering, Analysis, and Retrieval system, and it is accessible through the World Wide Web on the Internet. Instructions for using EDGAR are in Appendix A.

Using the most current 10-K available on EDGAR or on the company's website at www.nikebiz.com, answer the following questions about Nike Company:

a. In what year did Nike begin operations?

b. Other than the Nike brand, what business does Nike operate?

c. How many employees does Nike have?

d. Describe, in dollar amounts, Nike's accounting equation at the end of the most recent year.

e. Has Nike's performance been improving or deteriorating over the past three years? Explain your answer.

ATC 3-9 Spreadsheet Assignment *Use of Excel*

Adams Company started operations on January 1, 2016. Six months later on June 30, 2016, the company decided to prepare financial statements. The company's accountant decided to problem solve for the adjusting journal entries and the final adjusted account balances by using an electronic spreadsheet. Once the spreadsheet is complete, she will record the adjusting entries in the general journal and post them to the ledger. The accountant has started the following spreadsheet but wants you to finish it for her.

Required

a. On a blank spreadsheet, enter the following trial balance in Columns A through C. Also enter the headings for Columns E through I.

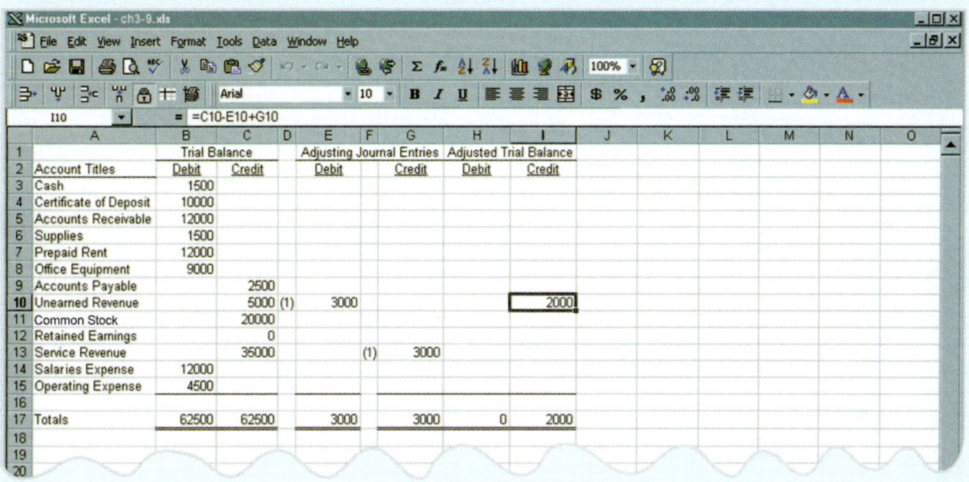

	A	B	C	D	E	F	G	H	I
1		Trial Balance			Adjusting Journal Entries			Adjusted Trial Balance	
2	Account Titles	Debit	Credit		Debit		Credit	Debit	Credit
3	Cash	1500							
4	Certificate of Deposit	10000							
5	Accounts Receivable	12000							
6	Supplies	1500							
7	Prepaid Rent	12000							
8	Office Equipment	9000							
9	Accounts Payable		2500						
10	Unearned Revenue		5000	(1)	3000				2000
11	Common Stock		20000						
12	Retained Earnings		0						
13	Service Revenue		35000			(1)	3000		
14	Salaries Expense	12000							
15	Operating Expense	4500							
16									
17	Totals	62500	62500		3000		3000	0	2000

b. Each of the following events requires an adjusting journal entry. Instead of recording entries in general journal format, record the adjusting entries in the Debit and Credit columns under the heading Adjusting Journal Entries. Entry (1) has already been recorded as an example. Be sure to number your adjusting entries on the spreadsheet. It will be necessary to insert new accounts for the adjustments. Recall that the accounting period is for six months.

(1) Received a $5,000 cash advance on April 1 for a contract to provide five months of service.

(2) Had accrued salaries on June 30 amounting to $1,500.

(3) On January 1 invested in a one-year, $10,000 certificate of deposit that had a 5 percent interest rate.

(4) On January 1 paid $12,000 in advance for a one-year lease on office space.

(5) Received in the mail a utility bill dated June 30 for $150.

(6) Purchased $1,500 of supplies on January 1. As of June 30, $700 of supplies remained on hand.

(7) Paid $9,000 for office equipment on January 1. The equipment was expected to have a four-year useful life and a $1,000 salvage value. Depreciation is computed on a straight-line basis.

c. Develop formulas to sum both the Debit and Credit columns under the Adjusting Journal Entries heading.

d. Develop formulas to derive the adjusted balances for the adjusted trial balance. For example, the formula for the ending balance of Unearned Revenue is =C10−E10+G10. In other words, a credit balance minus debit entries plus credit entries equals the ending balance. Once an ending balance is formulated for one credit account, that formula can be copied to all other credit accounts; the same is true for debit accounts. Once an ending balance is formulated for a debit account, that formula can be copied to all other debit accounts.

e. Develop formulas to sum both the Debit and Credit columns under the Adjusted Trial Balance heading.

Spreadsheet Tips

1. Rows and columns can be inserted by positioning the mouse on the immediate row or column after the desired position. Click on the *right* mouse button. With the *left* mouse button, choose Insert and then either Entire Column or Entire Row. Use the same method to delete columns or rows.
2. Enter the sequential numbering of the adjusting entries as labels rather than values by positioning an apostrophe in front of each entry. The first adjusting entry should be labeled '(1).

ATC 3-10 Spreadsheet Assignment *Mastery of Excel*

At the end of the accounting period, Adams Company's general ledger contained the following adjusted balances:

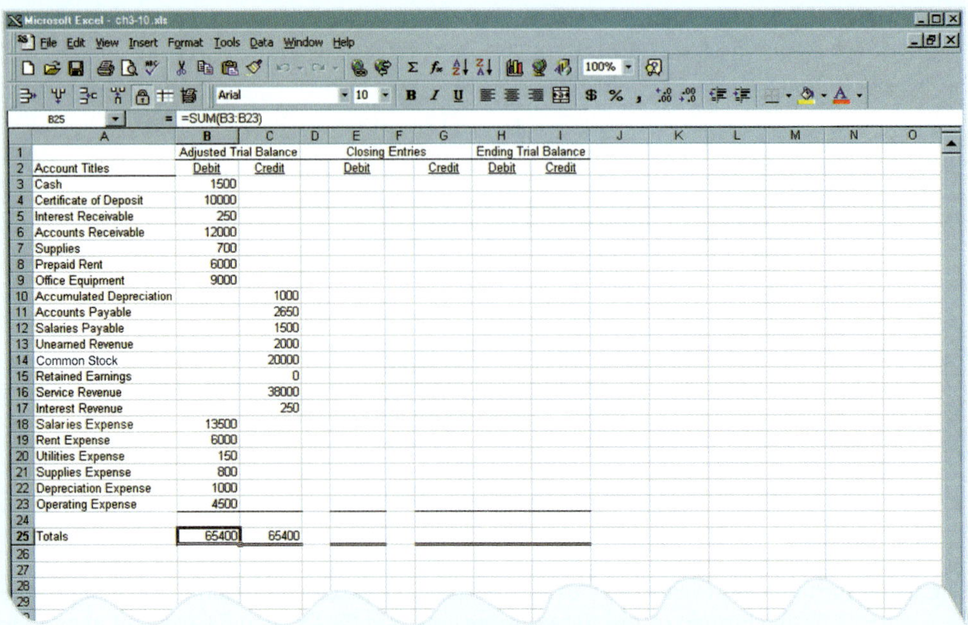

	Adjusted Trial Balance		Closing Entries		Ending Trial Balance	
Account Titles	Debit	Credit	Debit	Credit	Debit	Credit
Cash	1500					
Certificate of Deposit	10000					
Interest Receivable	250					
Accounts Receivable	12000					
Supplies	700					
Prepaid Rent	6000					
Office Equipment	9000					
Accumulated Depreciation		1000				
Accounts Payable		2650				
Salaries Payable		1500				
Unearned Revenue		2000				
Common Stock		20000				
Retained Earnings		0				
Service Revenue		38000				
Interest Revenue		250				
Salaries Expense	13500					
Rent Expense	6000					
Utilities Expense	150					
Supplies Expense	800					
Depreciation Expense	1000					
Operating Expense	4500					
Totals	65400	65400				

Required

1. Set up the preceding spreadsheet format. (The spreadsheet tips for ATC 3-9 also apply for this problem.)
2. Record the closing entries in the Closing Entries column of the spreadsheet.
3. Compute the Ending Trial Balance amounts.

COMPREHENSIVE PROBLEM

The trial balance of Pacilio Security Services Inc. as of January 1, 2013, had the following normal balances:

Cash	$8,900
Accounts Receivable	1,500
Supplies	65
Prepaid Rent	800
Land	4,000
Accounts Payable	1,050
Unearned Revenue	200
Salaries Payable	1,200
Notes Payable	2,000
Common Stock	8,000
Retained Earnings	2,815

During 2013, Pacilio Security Services experienced the following transactions:

1. Paid the salaries payable from 2012.
2. Paid the balance of $2,000 on the debt owed to the Small Business Government Agency. The loan is interest free.
3. Performed $32,000 of security services for numerous local events during the year; $21,000 was on account and $11,000 was for cash.
4. On May 1, paid $3,000 for 12 months' rent in advance.
5. Purchased supplies on account for $700.
6. Paid salaries expense for the year of $9,000.
7. Incurred other operating expenses on account, $4,200.
8. On October 1, 2013, a customer paid $1,200 for services to be provided over the next 12 months.
9. Collected $19,000 of accounts receivable during the year.
10. Paid $5,950 on accounts payable.
11. Paid $1,800 of advertising expenses for the year.
12. Paid a cash dividend to the shareholders of $4,650.
13. The market value of the land was determined to be $5,500 at December 31, 2013.

Adjustments

14. There was $120 of supplies on hand at the end of the year.
15. Recognized the expired rent.
16. Recognized the earned revenue from 2012 and transaction no. 8.
17. Accrued salaries were $1,000 at December 31, 2013.

Required

a. Record the above transactions in general journal form.
b. Post the transactions to T-accounts and determine the account balances.
c. Prepare a trial balance.
d. Prepare an income statement, statement of changes in stockholders' equity, balance sheet, and statement of cash flows for 2013.
e. Prepare the closing entries and post to the T-accounts.
f. Prepare a post-closing trial balance.

CHAPTER 4

Accounting for Merchandising Businesses

LEARNING OBJECTIVES

After you have mastered the material in this chapter, you will be able to:

LO 4-1 Record and report on inventory transactions using the perpetual system.

LO 4-2 Show how transportation costs, cash discounts, returns and allowances, and inventory shrinkage affect financial statements.

LO 4-3 Explain how gains, losses, and other items are shown on a multistep income statement.

LO 4-4 Determine the amount of net sales.

LO 4-5 Use common size financial statements and ratio analysis to evaluate managerial performance.

APPENDIX

LO 4-6 Identify the primary features of the periodic inventory system.

Video lectures and accompanying self-assessment quizzes are available for all learning objectives through McGraw-Hill Connect® Plus Accounting.

CHAPTER OPENING

Previous chapters have discussed accounting for service businesses. These businesses obtain revenue by providing some kind of service such as medical or legal advice to their customers. Other examples of service companies include dry cleaning companies, housekeeping companies, and car washes. This chapter introduces accounting for merchandising businesses. **Merchandising businesses** generate revenue by selling goods. They buy the merchandise they sell from companies called suppliers. The goods purchased for resale are called **merchandise inventory.** Merchandising businesses include **retail companies** (companies that sell goods to the final consumer) and **wholesale companies** (companies that sell to other businesses). **Sears**, **JCPenney**, **Target**, and **Sam's Club** are real-world merchandising businesses.

The Curious Accountant

Jason recently purchased a new Ford automobile from a dealer near his home. When he told his friend Ryan that he was able to purchase the car for $1,000 less than the sticker price, Ryan told Jason he had gotten a lousy deal. "Everybody knows there is a huge markup on cars," Ryan said. "You could have gotten a much lower price if you'd shopped around."

Jason responded, "If there is such a big profit margin on cars, why did so many of the car manufacturers get into financial trouble?" Ryan told him that he was confusing the maker of the car with the dealer. Ryan argued that although the manufacturers may not have high profit margins, the dealers do, and told him again that he had paid too much.

Exhibit 4.1 presents the income statements for **AutoNation, Inc.**, and **Ford Motor Company**. Based on these statements, do you think either of these guys is correct? For example, if you pay $20,000 for a vehicle from a dealership operated by AutoNation, the largest auto retailer in the United States, how much did the car cost the company? Also, how much did the car cost the Ford Motor Company to manufacture? (Answers on page 236.)

EXHIBIT 4.1 Comparative Income Statements

AUTONATION, INC.
Consolidated Statements of Income (Partial)
For the Years Ended December 31,
(In millions, except per share data)

	2013	2012	2011
Revenue:			
New vehicle	$ 9,949.6	$ 8,906.9	$ 7,498.9
Used vehicle	4,127.4	3,714.7	3,512.8
Parts and service	2,597.4	2,399.2	2,293.1
Finance and insurance, net	674.0	571.2	474.5
Other	169.2	76.8	53.0
Total revenue	17,517.6	15,668.8	13,832.3
Cost of Sales:			
New vehicle	9,333.2	8,327.4	6,951.2
Used vehicle	3,797.7	3,415.4	3,228.0
Parts and service	1,491.6	1,391.3	1,323.0
Other	135.2	48.3	26.1
Total cost of sales	14,757.7	13,182.4	11,528.3
Gross Profit:			
New vehicle	616.4	579.5	547.7
Used vehicle	329.7	299.3	284.8
Parts and service	1,105.8	1,007.9	970.1
Finance and insurance	674.0	571.2	474.5
Other	34.0	28.5	26.9
Total gross profit	2,759.9	2,486.4	2,304.0
Selling, general & administrative expenses	1,935.0	1,749.5	1,649.4
Depreciation and amortization	95.3	87.3	83.7
Franchise rights impairment	—	4.2	—
Other expenses (income), net	(10.7)	0.1	(1.1)
Operating income	740.3	645.3	572.0
Floorplan interest expense	(53.4)	(45.5)	(42.7)
Other interest expense	(88.3)	(86.9)	(66.0)
Loss on debt extinguishment	—	—	(2.2)
Interest income	0.2	0.3	0.7
Other income (losses), net	5.6	3.6	(0.5)
Income (loss) from continuing operations before income taxes	604.4	516.8	461.3
Income tax provision	228.6	199.5	177.1
Net income from continuing operations	375.8	317.3	284.2
Loss from discontinued operations, net of income taxes	(0.9)	(0.9)	(2.8)
Net income	$ 374.9	$ 316.4	$ 281.4

continued

EXHIBIT 4.1 *Concluded*

FORD MOTOR COMPANY AND SUBSIDIARIES
Consolidated Income Statements (Partial)
For the Years Ended December 31,
(In millions, except per share amounts)

	2013	2012	2011
Sales and revenues			
Automotive sales	$139,369	$126,567	$128,168
Financial Services revenues	7,548	6,992	7,437
Total sales and revenues	146,917	133,559	135,605
Costs and expenses			
Automotive cost of sales	125,234	112,992	113,611
Selling, administrative and other expenses	13,176	11,494	10,884
Interest expense	2,860	3,115	3,614
Financial Services provision for credit and insurance losses	208	77	(36)
Total costs and expenses	141,478	127,678	128,073
Automotive interest expense	829	713	817
Automotive interest income and other income/(loss), net	974	1,599	1,091
Financial Services other income/(loss), net	348	365	375
Equity in net income/(loss) of affiliated companies	1,069	588	500
Income before income taxes	7,001	7,720	8,681
Provision for/(Benefit from) income taxes	(147)	2,056	(11,541)
Net income	7,148	5,664	20,222
Less: Income/(Loss) attributable to noncontrolling interests	(7)	(1)	9
Net income attributable to Ford Motor Company	$ 7,155	$ 5,665	$ 20,213

ACCOUNTING FOR INVENTORY TRANSACTIONS

LO 4-1

Record and report on inventory transactions using the perpetual system.

Companies report inventory costs on the balance sheet in the asset account Merchandise Inventory. All costs incurred to acquire merchandise and ready it for sale are included in the inventory account. Examples of inventory costs include the price of goods purchased, shipping and handling costs, transit insurance, and storage costs. Since inventory items are referred to as products, inventory costs are frequently called **product costs.**

Costs that are not included in inventory are usually called **selling and administrative costs.** Examples of selling and administrative costs include advertising, administrative salaries, sales commissions, and insurance. Since selling and administrative costs are usually recognized as expenses *in the period* in which they are incurred, they are sometimes called **period costs.** In contrast, product costs are expensed when inventory is sold regardless of when it was purchased. In other words, product costs are matched directly with sales revenue, while selling and administrative costs are matched with the period in which they are incurred.

Allocating Inventory Cost between Asset and Expense Accounts

The cost of inventory that is available for sale during a specific accounting period is determined as follows:

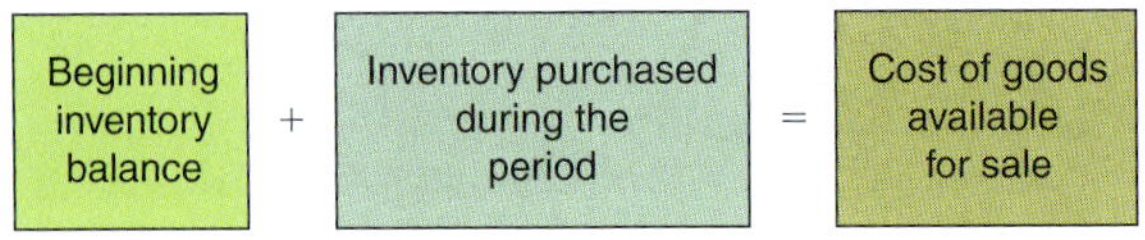

The **cost of goods available for sale** is allocated between the asset account Merchandise Inventory and an expense account called **Cost of Goods Sold.** The cost of inventory items that have not been sold (Merchandise Inventory) is reported as an asset on the balance sheet, and the cost of the items sold (Cost of Goods Sold) is expensed on the income statement. This allocation is depicted graphically as follows.

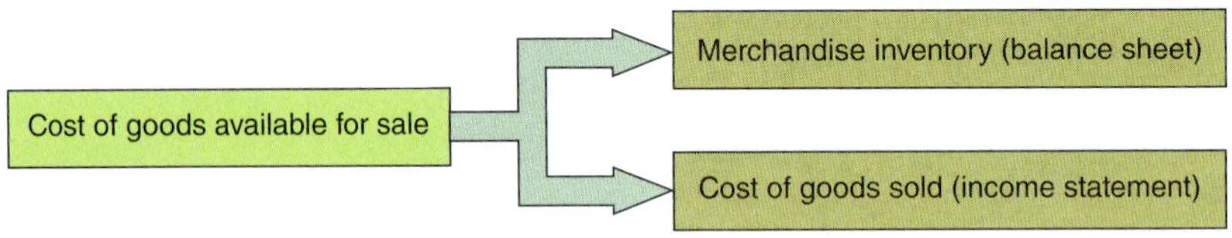

The difference between the sales revenue and the cost of goods sold is called **gross margin** or **gross profit.** The selling and administrative expenses (period costs) are subtracted from gross margin to obtain the net income.

Exhibit 4.1 displays income statements from the annual reports of AutoNation and Ford. For each company, review the most current income statement and determine the amount of gross margin on automobile sales. You should find a gross profit of $946.1 for AutoNation and a gross margin of $14,135 ($139,369 − $125,234) for Ford.

Perpetual Inventory System

Most modern companies maintain their inventory records using the **perpetual inventory system,** so-called because the inventory account is adjusted perpetually (continually) throughout the accounting period. Each time merchandise is purchased, the inventory account is increased; each time it is sold, the inventory account is decreased. The following illustration demonstrates the basic features of the perpetual inventory system.

June Gardener loved plants and grew them with such remarkable success that she decided to open a small retail plant store. She started June's Plant Shop (JPS) on January 1, 2016. The following discussion explains and illustrates the effects of the five events the company experienced during its first year of operation.

Effects of 2016 Events on Financial Statements

EVENT 1 JPS acquired $15,000 cash by issuing common stock.

This event is an asset source transaction. It increases both assets (cash) and stockholders' equity (common stock). The income statement is not affected. The statement of cash flows reflects an inflow from financing activities. The journal entry and its effects on the financial statements are shown here:

Account Title	Debit	Credit
Cash	15,000	
Common Stock		15,000

Assets			=	Liab.	+	Stockholders' Equity					
Cash +	Inventory +	Land	=	Accts. Pay.	+	Com. Stk. +	Ret. Earn.	Rev. −	Exp. =	Net Inc.	Cash Flow
15,000 +	NA +	NA	=	NA	+	15,000 +	NA	NA −	NA =	NA	15,000 FA

EVENT 2 JPS purchased merchandise inventory (plants) for $14,000 cash.

This event is an asset exchange transaction. One asset, cash, decreases and another asset, merchandise inventory, increases; total assets remain unchanged. Because product costs are expensed when inventory is sold, not when the goods are purchased, the event does not affect the income statement. The cash outflow, however, is reported in the operating activities section of the statement of cash flows. The journal entry and its effects on the financial statements are shown here:

Account Title	Debit	Credit
Merchandise Inventory	14,000	
Cash		14,000

Assets			=	Liab.	+	Stockholders' Equity					
Cash +	Inventory +	Land	=	Accts. Pay.	+	Com. Stk. +	Ret. Earn.	Rev. −	Exp. =	Net Inc.	Cash Flow
(14,000) +	14,000 +	NA	=	NA	+	NA +	NA	NA −	NA =	NA	(14,000) OA

EVENT 3a JPS recognized sales revenue from selling inventory for $12,000 cash.

The revenue recognition is the first part of a two-part transaction. The *sales part* represents a source of assets (cash increases from earning sales revenue). Both assets (cash) and stockholders' equity (retained earnings) increase. Sales revenue on the income statement increases. The $12,000 cash inflow is reported in the operating activities section of the statement of cash flows. The journal entry and its effects on the financial statements are shown here:

Account Title	Debit	Credit
Cash	12,000	
Sales Revenue		12,000

Assets			=	Liab.	+	Stockholders' Equity					
Cash +	Inventory +	Land	=	Accts. Pay.	+	Com. Stk. +	Ret. Earn.	Rev. −	Exp. =	Net Inc.	Cash Flow
12,000 +	NA +	NA	=	NA	+	NA +	12,000	12,000 −	NA =	12,000	12,000 OA

EVENT 3b JPS recognized $8,000 of cost of goods sold.

The expense recognition is the second part of the two-part transaction. The *expense part* represents a use of assets. Both assets (merchandise inventory) and stockholders' equity (retained earnings) decrease. An expense account, Cost of Goods Sold, is reported on the income statement. This part of the transaction does not affect the statement of cash flows. A cash outflow occurred when these goods were bought, not when they were sold. The journal entry and its effects on the financial statements are shown here:

Account Title	Debit	Credit
Cost of Goods Sold	8,000	
Merchandise Inventory		8,000

Assets			=	Liab.	+	Stockholders' Equity		Rev. − Exp. = Net Inc.			Cash Flow
Cash	+ Inventory	+ Land	=	Accts. Pay.	+	Com. Stk.	+ Ret. Earn.	Rev.	− Exp.	= Net Inc.	Cash Flow
NA	+ (8,000)	+ NA	=	NA	+	NA	+ (8,000)	NA	− 8,000	= (8,000)	NA

EVENT 4 JPS paid $1,000 cash for selling and administrative expenses.

This event is an asset use transaction. The payment decreases both assets (cash) and stockholders' equity (retained earnings). The increase in selling and administrative expenses decreases net income. The $1,000 cash payment is reported in the operating activities section of the statement of cash flows. The journal entry and its effects on the financial statements are shown here:

Account Title	Debit	Credit
Selling and Administrative Expenses	1,000	
Cash		1,000

Assets			=	Liab.	+	Stockholders' Equity		Rev. − Exp. = Net Inc.			Cash Flow
Cash	+ Inventory	+ Land	=	Accts. Pay.	+	Com. Stk.	+ Ret. Earn.	Rev.	− Exp.	= Net Inc.	Cash Flow
(1,000)	+ NA	+ NA	=	NA	+	NA	+ (1,000)	NA	− 1,000	= (1,000)	(1,000) OA

EVENT 5 JPS paid $5,500 cash to purchase land for a place to locate a future store.

Buying the land increases the Land account and decreases the Cash account on the balance sheet. This is an asset exchange transaction. The income statement is not affected. The statement of cash flows shows a cash outflow to purchase land in the investing activities section of the statement of cash flows. The journal entry and its effects on the financial statements are shown here:

Account Title	Debit	Credit
Land	5,500	
Cash		5,500

Assets			=	Liab.	+	Stockholders' Equity		Rev. − Exp. = Net Inc.			Cash Flow
Cash	+ Inventory	+ Land	=	Accts. Pay.	+	Com. Stk.	+ Ret. Earn.	Rev.	− Exp.	= Net Inc.	Cash Flow
(5,500)	+ NA	+ 5,500	=	NA	+	NA	+ NA	NA	− NA	= NA	(5,500) IA

Ledger Accounts and Financial Statements

Panel A of Exhibit 4.2 provides a summary of the 2016 accounting events. Panel B of Exhibit 4.2 shows the general ledger T-accounts after the journal entries have been posted to them. The ledger accounts provide the data for the financial statements in Exhibit 4.3.

Although Exhibit 4.2 does not include the 2016 year-end closing entries, recall that the closing entries will transfer the amounts from the Revenue and Expense accounts to the Retained Earnings account. The balance in the Retained Earnings account after closing will be $3,000. Before reading further, trace the transaction data from each journal entry in Panel A to the ledger accounts in Panel B and then from the ledger accounts to the financial statements in Exhibit 4.3.

EXHIBIT 4.2

Journal Entries and General Ledger Accounts for 2016

Panel A Accounting Events

The 2016 transactions JPS experienced are summarized below.

Event 1	JPS acquired $15,000 cash by issuing common stock.
Event 2	JPS purchased merchandise inventory (plants) for $14,000 cash.
Event 3a	JPS recognized sales revenue from selling inventory for $12,000 cash.
Event 3b	JPS recognized $8,000 of cost of goods sold.
Event 4	JPS paid $1,000 cash for selling and administrative expenses.
Event 5	JPS paid $5,500 cash to purchase land.

Panel B General Ledger Accounts

Assets = **Liabilities** + **Equity**

Assets

Cash

(1)	15,000	14,000	(2)
(3a)	12,000	1,000	(4)
		5,500	(5)
Bal.	6,500		

Merchandise Inventory

(2)	14,000	8,000	(3b)
Bal.	6,000		

Land

(5)	5,500		

Liabilities

Accounts Payable

		0	Bal.

Equity

Common Stock

		15,000	(1)
		15,000	Bal.

Retained Earnings

Sales Revenue

		12,000	(3a)

Cost of Goods Sold

(3b)	8,000		

Selling and Admin. Expenses

(4)	1,000		

EXHIBIT 4.3 Financial Statements

2016 Income Statement

Sales revenue	$12,000
Cost of goods sold	(8,000)
Gross margin	4,000
Less: Operating exp.	
Selling and admin. exp.	(1,000)
Net income	$ 3,000

12/31/16 Balance Sheet

Assets		
Cash	$ 6,500	
Merchandise inventory	6,000	
Land	5,500	
Total assets		$18,000
Liabilities		$ 0
Stockholders' equity		
Common stock	$15,000	
Retained earnings	3,000*	
Total stockholders' equity		18,000
Total liab. and stk. equity		$18,000

2016 Statement of Cash Flows

Operating activities		
Inflow from customers	$ 12,000	
Outflow for inventory	(14,000)	
Outflow for selling & admin. exp.	(1,000)	
Net cash outflow from operating activities		$ (3,000)**
Investing activities		
Outflow to purchase land		(5,500)
Financing activities		
Inflow from stock issue		15,000
Net change in cash		6,500
Plus: Beginning cash balance		0
Ending cash balance		$ 6,500

*The balance in the Retained Earnings account is the after-closing balance (Revenue $12,000 − Cost of Goods Sold $8,000 − Selling and Admin. Expenses $1,000).

**Cash $3,000 net cash outflow from operating activities is computed as $12,000 cash inflow from Revenue minus $14,000 cash outflow for the purchase of Inventory and $1,000 cash outflow paid for Selling and Admin. Exp.

JPS had no beginning inventory in its first year, so the cost of merchandise inventory available for sale was $14,000 (the amount of inventory purchased during the period). Recall that JPS must allocate the Cost of Goods (Inventory) Available for Sale between the Cost of Goods Sold ($8,000) and the ending balance ($6,000) in the Merchandise Inventory account. The cost of goods sold is reported as an expense on the income statement and the ending balance of merchandise inventory is reported as an asset on the balance sheet. The difference between the sales revenue ($12,000) and the cost of goods sold ($8,000) is labeled gross margin ($4,000) on the income statement.

CHECK YOURSELF 4.1

Phambroom Company began 2016 with $35,600 in its Inventory account. During the year, it purchased inventory costing $356,800 and sold inventory that had cost $360,000 for $520,000. Based on this information alone, determine (1) the inventory balance as of December 31, 2016, and (2) the amount of gross margin Phambroom would report on its 2016 income statement.

Answer

1. Beginning inventory + Purchases = Goods available − Ending inventory = Cost of goods sold

   $35,600 + $356,800 = $392,400 − Ending inventory = $360,000

   Ending inventory = $32,400
2. Sales revenue − Cost of goods sold = Gross margin

   $520,000 − $360,000 = $160,000

TRANSPORTATION COST, PURCHASE RETURNS AND ALLOWANCES, AND CASH DISCOUNTS RELATED TO INVENTORY PURCHASES

LO 4-2

Show how transportation costs, cash discounts, returns and allowances, and inventory shrinkage affect financial statements.

Purchasing inventory often involves: (1) incurring transportation costs, (2) returning inventory or receiving purchase allowances (cost reductions), and (3) taking cash discounts (also cost reductions). During its second accounting cycle, JPS encountered these kinds of events. The final account balances at the end of the 2016 fiscal year become the beginning balances for 2017: Cash, $6,500; Merchandise Inventory, $6,000; Land, $5,500; Common Stock, $15,000; and Retained Earnings, $3,000.

Effects of 2017 Events on Financial Statements

JPS experienced the following events during its 2017 accounting period. The effects of each of these events are explained and illustrated in the following discussion.

EVENT 1 **JPS borrowed $4,000 cash by issuing a note payable.**

JPS borrowed the money to enable it to purchase an additional plot of land for a future site for a store it planned to build in the near future. Borrowing the money increases the Cash account and the Notes Payable account on the balance sheet. The income statement is not affected. The statement of cash flows shows a cash flow from financing activities. The journal entry and its effects on the financial statements are shown here:

Account Title	Debit	Credit
Cash	4,000	
Notes Payable		4,000

Assets							=	Liabilities			+	Stockholders' Equity							
Cash	+	Accts. Rec.	+	Inventory	+	Land	=	Accts. Pay.	+	Notes Pay.	+	Com. Stk.	+	Ret. Earn.	Rev.	−	Exp.	=	Net Inc.	Cash Flow
4,000	+	NA	+	NA	+	NA	=	NA	+	4,000	+	NA	+	NA	NA	−	NA	=	NA	4,000 FA

EVENT 2 **JPS purchased on account merchandise inventory with a list price of $11,000.**

The inventory purchase increases both assets (merchandise inventory) and liabilities (accounts payable) on the balance sheet. The income statement is not affected until later, when inventory is sold. Since the inventory was purchased on account, there was no cash outflow. The journal entry and its effects on the financial statements are shown here:

Account Title	Debit	Credit
Merchandise Inventory	11,000	
Accounts Payable		11,000

Assets							=	Liab.			+	Stockholders' Equity								
Cash	+	Accts. Rec.	+	Inventory	+	Land	=	Accts. Pay.	+	Notes Pay.	+	Com. Stk.	+	Ret. Earn.	Rev.	−	Exp.	=	Net Inc.	Cash Flow
NA	+	NA	+	11,000	+	NA	=	11,000	+	NA	+	NA	+	NA	NA	−	NA	=	NA	NA

Accounting for Purchase Returns and Allowances

EVENT 3 **JPS returned some of the inventory purchased in Event 2. The list price of the returned merchandise was $1,000.**

To promote customer satisfaction, many businesses allow customers to return goods for reasons such as wrong size, wrong color, wrong design, or even simply because the purchaser changed his mind. The effect of a purchase return is the *opposite* of the original purchase. For JPS the *purchase return* decreases both assets (merchandise inventory) and liabilities (accounts payable). There is no effect on either the income statement or the statement of cash flows. The journal entry and its effects on the financial statements are shown here:

Account Title	Debit	Credit
Accounts Payable	1,000	
Merchandise Inventory		1,000

Assets							=	Liab.			+	Stockholders' Equity								
Cash	+	Accts. Rec.	+	Inventory	+	Land	=	Accts. Pay.	+	Notes Pay.	+	Com. Stk.	+	Ret. Earn.	Rev.	−	Exp.	=	Net Inc.	Cash Flow
NA	+	NA	+	(1,000)	+	NA	=	(1,000)	+	NA	+	NA	+	NA	NA	−	NA	=	NA	NA

Sometimes dissatisfied buyers will agree to keep goods instead of returning them if the seller offers to reduce the price. Such reductions are called allowances. *Purchase allowances* affect the financial statements the same way purchase returns do. On financial statements, returns and allowances are combined in one entry, called **purchase returns and allowances**.

Purchase Discounts

EVENT 4 JPS received a cash discount on goods purchased in Event 2. The credit terms were 2/10, n/30.

To encourage buyers to pay promptly, sellers sometimes offer **cash discounts.** To illustrate, assume JPS purchased the inventory in Event 2 under **credit terms** *2/10, n/30* (two-ten, net thirty). These terms mean the seller will allow a 2 percent cash discount if the purchaser pays cash within 10 days from the date of purchase. The amount not paid within the first 10 days is due at the end of 30 days from date of purchase. Recall that in Event 3 JPS returned $1,000 of the inventory purchased in Event 2, leaving a $10,000 balance ($11,000 list price − $1,000 purchase return). If JPS pays for the inventory within 10 days, the amount of the discount is $200 ($10,000 × .02).

When a cash discount is applied to a purchase it is called a **purchase discount.** When it is applied to a sale, it is called a sales discount. Sales discounts will be discussed later in the chapter. A purchase discount reduces the cost of the inventory and the associated account payable on the balance sheet. A purchase discount does not directly affect the income statement or the statement of cash flows. The journal entry and its effects on the financial statements are shown here:

Account Title	Debit	Credit
Accounts Payable	200	
Merchandise Inventory		200

Assets				=	Liab.		+	Stockholders' Equity				
Cash	+ Accts. Rec.	+ Inventory	+ Land	=	Accts. Pay.	+ Notes Pay.	+	Com. Stk.	+ Ret. Earn.	Rev. − Exp. = Net Inc.		Cash Flow
NA	+ NA	+ (200)	+ NA	=	(200)	+ NA	+	NA	+ NA	NA − NA = NA		NA

If JPS paid the account payable after 10 days, there would be no purchase discount. In this case the balances in the Inventory and Account Payable accounts would remain at $10,000.

EVENT 5 JPS paid the $9,800 balance due on the account payable.

The remaining balance in the accounts payable is $9,800 ($10,000 list price − $200 purchase discount). Paying cash to settle the liability reduces cash and accounts payable on the balance sheet. The income statement is not affected. The cash outflow is shown in the operating section of the statement of cash flows. The journal entry and its effects on the financial statements are shown here:

Account Title	Debit	Credit
Accounts Payable	9,800	
Cash		9,800

Assets				=	Liab.		+	Stockholders' Equity				
Cash	+ Accts. Rec.	+ Inventory	+ Land	=	Accts. Pay.	+ Notes Pay.	+	Com. Stk.	+ Ret. Earn.	Rev. − Exp. = Net Inc.		Cash Flow
(9,800)	+ NA	+ NA	+ NA	=	(9,800)	+ NA	+	NA	+ NA	NA − NA = NA		(9,800) OA

REALITY BYTES

Many real-world companies have found it more effective to impose a penalty for late payment than to use a cash discount to encourage early payment. The invoice from **Arley Water Works** is an example of the penalty strategy. Notice that the amount due, if paid by the due date, is \$18.14. A \$1.88 late charge is imposed if the bill is paid after the due date. The \$1.88 late charge is in fact interest. If Arley Water Works collects the payment after the due date, the utility will receive cash of \$20.02. The collection will increase cash (\$20.02), reduce accounts receivable (\$18.14), and increase interest revenue (\$1.88).

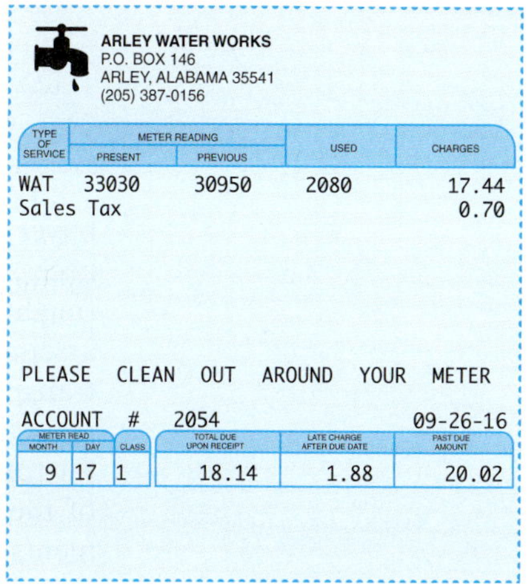

ARLEY WATER WORKS
P.O. BOX 146
ARLEY, ALABAMA 35541
(205) 387-0156

TYPE OF SERVICE	METER READING PRESENT	METER READING PREVIOUS	USED	CHARGES
WAT	33030	30950	2080	17.44
Sales Tax				0.70

PLEASE CLEAN OUT AROUND YOUR METER

ACCOUNT # 2054 09-26-16

METER READ MONTH	METER READ DAY	CLASS	TOTAL DUE UPON RECEIPT	LATE CHARGE AFTER DUE DATE	PAST DUE AMOUNT
9	17	1	18.14	1.88	20.02

The Cost of Financing Inventory

Suppose you buy inventory this month and sell it next month. Where do you get the money to pay for the inventory at the time you buy it? One way to finance the purchase is to buy it on account and withhold payment until the last day of the term for the account payable. For example, suppose you buy inventory under terms 2/10, net/30. Under these circumstances you could delay payment for 30 days after the day of purchase. This way you may be able to collect enough money from the inventory you sell to pay for the inventory you purchased. Refusing the discount allows you the time needed to generate the cash necessary to pay off the liability (account payable). Unfortunately, this is usually a very expensive way to finance the purchase of inventory.

While the amount of a cash discount may appear small, the discount period is short. Consider the terms 2/10, net/30. Since you can pay on the tenth day and still receive the discount, you obtain financing for only 20 days (30-day full credit term − 10-day discount term). In other words, you must forgo a 2 percent discount to obtain a loan with a 20-day term. What is the size of the discount in annual terms? The answer is determined by the following formula.

$$\text{Annual rate} = \text{Discount rate} \times (365 \text{ days} \div \text{Term of the loan})$$

$$\text{Annual rate} = 2\% \times (365 \div 20)$$

$$\text{Annual rate} = 36.5\%$$

This means that a 2 percent discount rate for 20 days is equivalent to a 36.5 percent annual rate of interest. So, if you do not have the money to pay the account payable, but can borrow money from a bank at less than 36.5 percent annual interest, you should borrow the money and pay off the account payable within the discount period.

Accounting for Transportation Costs

EVENT 6 **The shipping terms for the inventory purchased in Event 2 were FOB shipping point. JPS paid the freight company \$300 cash for delivering the merchandise.**

The terms **FOB shipping point** and **FOB destination** identify whether the buyer or the seller is responsible for transportation costs. If goods are delivered FOB shipping point, the buyer is responsible for the freight cost. If goods are delivered FOB destination, the seller is responsible. When the buyer is responsible, the freight cost is called

transportation-in. When the seller is responsible, the cost is called **transportation-out.** The following table summarizes freight cost terms:

Responsible Party	Buyer	Seller
Freight terms	FOB shipping point	FOB destination
Account title	Merchandise inventory	Transportation-out

Event 6 indicates the inventory was delivered FOB shipping point, so JPS (the buyer) is responsible for the $300 freight cost. Since incurring transportation-in costs is necessary to obtain inventory, these costs are added to the inventory account. The freight cost increases one asset account (Merchandise Inventory) and decreases another asset account (Cash). The income statement is not affected by this transaction because transportation-in costs are not expensed when they are incurred. Instead they are expensed as part of *cost of goods sold* when the inventory is sold. However, the cash paid for transportation-in costs is reported as an outflow in the operating activities section of the statement of cash flows. The journal entry and its effects on the financial statements are shown here:

Account Title	Debit	Credit
Merchandise Inventory	300	
Cash		300

Assets							=	Liab.			+	Stockholders' Equity								
Cash	+	Accts. Rec.	+	Inventory	+	Land	=	Accts. Pay.	+	Notes Pay.	+	Com. Stk.	+	Ret. Earn.	Rev.	−	Exp.	=	Net Inc.	Cash Flow
(300)	+	NA	+	300	+	NA	=	NA	+	NA	+	NA	+	NA	NA	−	NA	=	NA	(300) OA

EVENT 7a **JPS recognized $24,750 of revenue on the cash sale of merchandise that cost $11,500.**

The sale increases assets (cash) and stockholders' equity (retained earnings). The revenue recognition increases net income. The $24,750 cash inflow from the sale is reported in the operating activities section of the statement of cash flows. The journal entry and its effects on the financial statements are shown here:

Account Title	Debit	Credit
Cash	24,750	
Sales		24,750

Assets							=	Liab.			+	Stockholders' Equity								
Cash	+	Accts. Rec.	+	Inventory	+	Land	=	Accts. Pay.	+	Notes Pay.	+	Com. Stk.	+	Ret. Earn.	Rev.	−	Exp.	=	Net Inc.	Cash Flow
24,750	+	NA	+	NA	+	NA	=	NA	+	NA	+	NA	+	24,750	24,750	−	NA	=	24,750	24,750 OA

EVENT 7b **JPS recognized $11,500 of cost of goods sold.**

When goods are sold, the product cost—*including a proportionate share of transportation-in and adjustments for purchase returns and allowances*—is transferred from the Merchandise Inventory account to the expense account, Cost of Goods Sold.

Recognizing cost of goods sold decreases both assets (merchandise inventory) and stockholders' equity (retained earnings). The expense recognition for cost of goods sold decreases net income. Cash flow is not affected. The journal entry and its effects on the financial statements are shown here:

Account Title	Debit	Credit
Cost of Goods Sold	11,500	
Merchandise Inventory		11,500

Assets								=	Liab.			+	Stockholders' Equity										
Cash	+	Accts. Rec.	+	Inventory	+	Land		=	Accts. Pay.	+	Notes Pay.	+	Com. Stk.	+	Ret. Earn.		Rev.	−	Exp.	=	Net Inc.		Cash Flow
NA	+	NA	+	(11,500)	+	NA		=	NA	+	NA	+	NA	+	(11,500)		NA	−	11,500	=	(11,500)		NA

EVENT 8 JPS paid $450 cash for freight costs on inventory delivered to customers.

Assume the merchandise sold in Event 7a was shipped FOB destination. Also assume JPS paid the freight cost in cash. FOB destination means the seller is responsible for the freight cost, which is called transportation-out. Transportation-out is reported on the income statement as an operating expense in the section below gross margin. The cost of freight on goods shipped to customers is incurred *after* the goods are sold. It is not part of the costs to obtain goods or ready them for sale. Recognizing the expense of transportation-out reduces assets (cash) and stockholders' equity (retained earnings). Operating expenses increase and net income decreases. The cash outflow is reported in the operating activities section of the statement of cash flows. The journal entry and its effects on the financial statements are shown here:

Account Title	Debit	Credit
Transportation-Out	450	
Cash		450

Assets								=	Liab.			+	Stockholders' Equity										
Cash	+	Accts. Rec.	+	Inventory	+	Land		=	Accts. Pay.	+	Notes Pay.	+	Com. Stk.	+	Ret. Earn.		Rev.	−	Exp.	=	Net Inc.		Cash Flow
(450)	+	NA	+	NA	+	NA		=	NA	+	NA	+	NA	+	(450)		NA	−	450	=	(450)		(450) OA

If the terms had been FOB shipping point, the customer would have been responsible for the transportation cost and JPS would not have recorded an expense.

EVENT 9 JPS paid $5,000 cash for selling and administrative expenses.

The effect on the balance sheet is to decrease both assets (cash) and stockholders' equity (retained earnings). Recognizing the selling and administrative expenses decreases net income. The $5,000 cash outflow is reported in the operating activities section of the statement of cash flows. The journal entry and its effects on the financial statements are shown here:

Account Title	Debit	Credit
Selling and Administrative Expenses	5,000	
Cash		5,000

Assets				=	Liab.	+	Stockholders' Equity						
Cash	+ Accts. Rec.	+ Inventory	+ Land	=	Accts. Pay.	+ Notes Pay.	+ Com. Stk.	+ Ret. Earn.	Rev.	− Exp.	= Net Inc.	Cash Flow	
(5,000)	+ NA	+ NA	+ NA	=	NA	+ NA	+ NA	+ (5,000)	NA	− 5,000	= (5,000)	(5,000)	OA

EVENT 10 **JPS paid $360 cash for interest expense on the note payable described in Event 1.**

The effect on the balance sheet is to decrease both assets (cash) and stockholders' equity (retained earnings). Recognizing the interest expense decreases net income. The $360 cash outflow is reported in the operating activities section of the statement of cash flows. The journal entry and its effects on the financial statements are shown here:

Account Title	Debit	Credit
Interest Expense	360	
Cash		360

Assets				=	Liab.	+	Stockholders' Equity						
Cash	+ Accts. Rec.	+ Inventory	+ Land	=	Accts. Pay.	+ Notes Pay.	+ Com. Stk.	+ Ret. Earn.	Rev.	− Exp.	= Net Inc.	Cash Flow	
(360)	+ NA	+ NA	+ NA	=	NA	+ NA	+ NA	+ (360)	NA	− 360	= (360)	(360)	OA

Adjustment for Lost, Damaged, or Stolen Inventory

EVENT 11 **JPS took a physical count of its inventory and found $4,100 of inventory on hand.**

Most merchandising companies experience some level of inventory **shrinkage**, a term that reflects decreases in inventory for reasons other than sales to customers. Inventory may be stolen by shoplifters, damaged by customers or employees, or even simply lost or misplaced. Since the *perpetual* inventory system is designed to record purchases and sales of inventory as they occur, the balance in the merchandise inventory account represents the amount of inventory that *should* be on hand at any given time. For example, based on the previous transactions, the book balance of JPS's Inventory account can be computed as follows:

Beginning balance	$ 6,000
Purchases	11,000
Purchase returns	(1,000)
Purchase discounts	(200)
Transportation-in	300
Goods available for sale	16,100
Cost of goods sold	(11,500)
Ending balance	$ 4,600

Assume that JPS takes a physical count of its inventory on hand and finds that it has only $4,100 of inventory. By comparing the $4,600 book balance in the Merchandise Inventory account with the $4,100 of actual inventory counted, we determine that the company has experienced $500 of shrinkage. Under these circumstances JPS must make an adjusting entry to write off the inventory shrinkage so that the balance of the Inventory account reported on the financial statements agrees with the amount of inventory actually on hand at the end of the period. The write-off decreases both assets (inventory) and stockholders' equity (retained earnings). The write-off increases expenses and decreases net income. Cash flow is not affected. The journal entry and its effects on the financial statements are shown here:

Account Title	Debit	Credit
Inventory Loss (Cost of Goods Sold)	500	
Inventory		500

Assets								=	Liab.			+	Stockholders' Equity									
Cash	+	Accts. Rec.	+	Inventory	+	Land		=	Accts. Pay.	+	Notes Pay.	+	Com. Stk.	+	Ret. Earn.	Gain	−	Exp.	=	Net Inc.		Cash Flow
NA	+	NA	+	(500)	+	NA		=	NA	+	NA	+	NA	+	(500)	NA	−	500	=	(500)		NA

Theoretically, inventory losses are operating expenses. However, because such losses are normally immaterial in amount, they are usually added to cost of goods sold for external reporting purposes.

GAINS, LOSSES, AND A MULTISTEP INCOME STATEMENT

EVENT 12 **JPS sold the land that had cost $5,500 for $6,200 cash.**

LO 4-3

Explain how gains, losses, and other items are shown on a multistep income statement.

When JPS sells merchandise inventory for more than it cost, the difference between the sales revenue and the cost of the goods sold is called the *gross margin.* In contrast, when JPS sells land for more than it cost, the difference between the sales price and the cost of the land is called a **gain.** Why is one called *gross margin* and the other a *gain*? The terms are used to alert financial statement users to the fact that the nature of the underlying transactions is different.

JPS's primary business is selling inventory, not land. The term *gain* indicates profit resulting from transactions that are not likely to regularly recur. Similarly, had the land sold for less than cost the difference would have been labeled **loss** rather than expense. This term also indicates the underlying transaction is not from normal, recurring operating activities. Gains and losses are shown separately on the income statement to communicate the expectation that they are nonrecurring.

The presentation of gains and losses in the income statement is discussed in more detail in a later section of the chapter. At this point note that the sale increases cash, decreases land, and increases retained earnings on the balance sheet. The income statement shows a gain on the sale of land and net income increases. The $6,200 cash inflow is shown as an investing activity on the statement of cash flows. The journal entry and its effects on the financial statements are shown here:

Account Title	Debit	Credit
Cash	6,200	
Land		5,500
Gain on Sale of Land		700

Assets								=	Liab.			+	Stockholders' Equity				Gain	−	Exp.	=	Net Inc.	Cash Flow	
Cash	+	Accts. Rec.	+	Inventory	+	Land		=	Accts. Pay.	+	Notes Pay.	+	Com. Stk.	+	Ret. Earn.								
6,200	+	NA	+	NA	+	(5,500)		=	NA	+	NA	+	NA	+	700		700	−	NA	=	700	6,200	IA

CHECK YOURSELF 4.2

Tsang Company purchased $32,000 of inventory on account with payment terms of 2/10, n/30 and freight terms FOB shipping point. Freight costs were $1,100. Tsang obtained a $2,000 purchase allowance because the inventory was damaged upon arrival. Tsang paid for the inventory within the discount period. Based on this information alone, determine the balance in the Inventory account.

Answer

List price of inventory	$32,000
Plus: Transportation-in costs	1,100
Less: Purchase returns and allowances	(2,000)
Less: Purchase discount [($32,000 − $2,000) × .02]	(600)
Balance in inventory account	$30,500

Exhibit 4.4 summarizes the accounting events and ledger T-accounts for the 2017 accounting period. Before reading further, trace the effects of each event to the ledger accounts. Then trace the information in the ledger accounts to the 2017 financial statements displayed in Exhibits 4.5, 4.7, and 4.8.

EXHIBIT 4.4

Accounting Events and Ledger Accounts for 2017

Panel A Accounting Events

Event 1	JPS borrowed $4,000 cash by issuing a note payable.
Event 2	JPS purchased on account merchandise inventory with a list price of $11,000.
Event 3	JPS returned some of the inventory purchased in Event 2. The list price of the returned merchandise was $1,000.
Event 4	JPS received a cash discount on goods purchased in Event 2. The credit terms were 2/10, n/30.
Event 5	JPS paid the $9,800 balance due on the account payable.
Event 6	The inventory purchased in Event 2 was delivered FOB shipping point. JPS paid the freight company $300 cash for delivering the merchandise.
Event 7a	JPS recognized $24,750 of revenue on the cash sale of merchandise that cost $11,500.
Event 7b	JPS recognized $11,500 of cost of goods sold.
Event 8	JPS paid $450 cash for freight costs on inventory delivered to customers.
Event 9	JPS paid $5,000 cash for selling and administrative expenses.
Event 10	JPS paid $360 cash for interest expense on the note payable described in Event 1.
Event 11	JPS took a physical count of its inventory and found $4,100 of inventory on hand.
Event 12	JPS sold the land that had cost $5,500 for $6,200 cash.

continued

EXHIBIT 4.4 *Concluded*

Accounting Events and Ledger Accounts for 2017

Panel B Ledger Accounts

Assets = Liabilities + Equity

Assets

Cash

	Debit	Credit	
Bal.	6,500	9,800	(5)
(1)	4,000	300	(6)
(7a)	24,750	450	(8)
(12)	6,200	5,000	(9)
		360	(10)
Bal.	25,540		

Merchandise Inventory

	Debit	Credit	
Bal.	6,000	1,000	(3)
(2)	11,000	200	(4)
(6)	300	11,500	(7b)
		500	(11)
Bal.	4,100		

Land

	Debit	Credit	
Bal.	5,500	5,500	(12)
Bal.	-0-		

Liabilities

Accounts Payable

	Debit	Credit	
(3)	1,000	11,000	(2)
(4)	200		
(5)	9,800		
		-0-	Bal.

Notes Payable

	Debit	Credit	
		4,000	(1)
		4,000	Bal.

Equity

Common Stock

	Debit	Credit	
		15,000	Bal.

Retained Earnings

	Debit	Credit	
		3,000	Bal.
		7,640	(Cl)
		10,640	Bal.

Sales Revenue

	Debit	Credit	
(Cl)	24,750	24,750	(7a)
		-0-	Bal.

Gain on Sale of Land

	Debit	Credit	
(Cl)	700	700	(12)
		-0-	Bal.

Cost of Goods Sold

	Debit	Credit	
(7b)	11,500	12,000	(Cl)
(11)	500		
Bal.	-0-		

Transportation-Out

	Debit	Credit	
(8)	450	450	(Cl)
Bal.	-0-		

Selling and Admin. Expenses

	Debit	Credit	
(9)	5,000	5,000	(Cl)
Bal.	-0-		

Interest Expense

	Debit	Credit	
(10)	360	360	(Cl)
Bal.	-0-		

Total Assets	=	Total Liabilities	+	Total Equity
$29,640		$4,000		$25,640

JPS's 2017 income statement is shown in Exhibit 4.5. Observe the form of this statement carefully. It is more informative than one which simply subtracts expenses from revenues. First, it compares sales revenue with the cost of the goods that were sold to produce that revenue. The difference between the sales revenue and the cost of goods sold is called *gross margin.* Next, the operating expenses are subtracted from the gross margin to determine the *operating income*. **Operating income** is the amount of income that is generated from the normal recurring operations of a business. Items that are not expected to recur on a regular basis are subtracted from the operating income to determine the amount of *net income.*[1]

[1]Revenue and expense items with special characteristics may be classified as discontinued or extraordinary items. These items are shown separately just above net income regardless of whether a company uses a single-step or multistep format. Further discussion of these items is beyond the scope of this text.

EXHIBIT 4.5

JUNE'S PLANT SHOP Income Statement For the Period Ended December 31, 2017	
Sales revenue	$ 24,750
Cost of goods sold*	(12,000)
Gross margin	12,750
Less: Operating expenses	
Selling and administrative expense	(5,000)
Transportation-out	(450)
Operating income	7,300
Nonoperating items	
Interest expense	(360)
Gain on the sale of land	700
Net income	$ 7,640

*$11,500 inventory sold + $500 shrinkage.

EXHIBIT 4.6

Income Statement Format Used by U.S. Companies

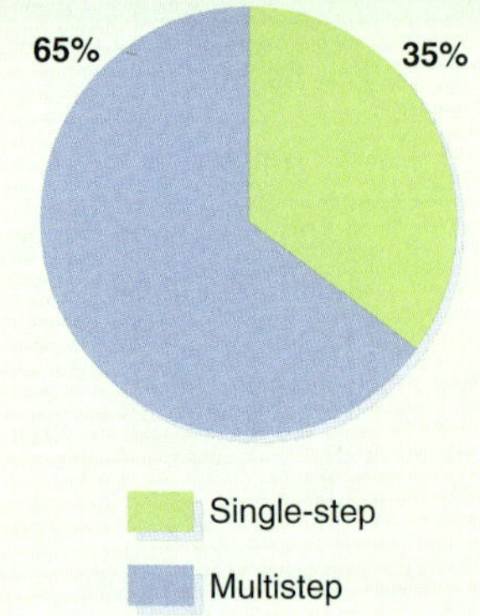

Data Source: AICPA, *Accounting Trends and Techniques.*

Income statements that show these additional relationships are called **multistep income statements.** Income statements that display a single comparison of all revenues minus all expenses are called **single-step income statements.** To this point in the text we have shown only single-step income statements to promote simplicity. However, the multistep form is used more frequently in practice. Exhibit 4.6 shows the percentage of companies that use the multistep versus the single-step format. Go to Exhibit 4.1 and identify the company that presents its income statement in the multistep format. You should have identified AutoNation as the company using the multistep format. Ford's statement is shown in the single-step format.

Note that interest is reported as a *nonoperating* item on the income statement in Exhibit 4.5. In contrast, it is shown in the *operating* activities section of the statement of cash flows in Exhibit 4.8. Generally accepted accounting principles (GAAP) requires interest to be reported in the operating activities section of the statement of cash flows. There is no corresponding requirement for the treatment of interest on the income statement. Prior to the requirement for reporting interest as an operating activity on the statement of cash flows, interest was considered to be a nonoperating item. Most companies continued to report interest as a nonoperating item on their income statements even though they were required to change how it was reported on the statement of cash flows. As a result, there is frequent inconsistency in the way interest is reported on the two financial statements.

REALITY BYTES

Good inventory management is essential for merchandising and manufacturing companies. Even if a company uses a perpetual inventory system, the amount of inventory believed to be on hand may be incorrect because of lost, damaged, or stolen goods, so a physical count is still required. Unfortunately, counting inventory is not a revenue-generating activity. If a company's employees are used to conduct the physical count, it takes time that may be better used for other activities. In fact, it may be so time-consuming that the business must close temporarily so employees will have the time to complete the inventory count.

To avoid this problem many businesses hire outside companies to count their inventory. These outside vendors can bring in a large crew of specially trained workers and complete a count very quickly. There are many companies that provide inventory counting services, but **RIGIS, LLC**, claims to be the world's largest. RIGIS reports that its 25,000 employees have counted over 400 billion items in the more than four million inventory counts it has conducted since beginning operations in 1958. On second thought, counting inventory *is* a revenue-producing activity if you are a company that counts inventory for others.

EXHIBIT 4.7

JUNE'S PLANT SHOP Balance Sheet As of December 31, 2017		
Assets		
Cash	$25,540	
Merchandise inventory	4,100	
Total assets		$29,640
Liabilities		
Notes payable		$ 4,000
Stockholders' equity		
Common stock	$15,000	
Retained earnings	10,640	
Total stockholders' equity		25,640
Total liabilities and stockholders' equity		$29,640

EXHIBIT 4.8

JUNE'S PLANT SHOP Statement of Cash Flows For the Year Ended December 31, 2017		
Operating activities		
Inflow from customers	$ 24,750	
Outflow for inventory*	(10,100)	
Outflow for transportation-out	(450)	
Outflow for selling and administrative expense	(5,000)	
Outflow for interest expense	(360)	
Net cash outflow for operating activities		$ 8,840
Investing activities		
Inflow from sale of land		6,200
Financing activities		
Inflow from issue of note payable		4,000
Net change in cash		19,040
Plus beginning cash balance		6,500
Ending cash balance		$25,540

*Net cost of inventory $9,800 + Transportation-in $300 = $10,100

Also note that while the gain on the sale of land is shown on the income statement, it is not included in the operating activities section of the statement of cash flows. Since the gain is a nonoperating item, it is included in the cash inflow from the sale of land shown in the investing activities section. In this case the full cash inflow from the sale of land ($6,200) is shown in the investing activities section of the statement of cash flows in Exhibit 4.8. Finally, note that the ending inventory balance is shown on the balance sheet in Exhibit 4.7.

EVENTS AFFECTING SALES

LO 4-4

Determine the amount of net sales.

To this point we have assumed JPS did not offer cash discounts to its customers. However, sales, as well as purchases of inventory, can be affected by returns, allowances, and discounts. **Sales discounts** are price reductions offered by sellers to encourage buyers to pay promptly. To illustrate, assume JPS engaged in the following selected events during 2018.

EVENT 1a **JPS sold on account merchandise with a list price of $8,500. Payment terms were 1/10, n/30. The merchandise had cost JPS $4,000.**

The sale increases both assets (accounts receivable) and shareholders' equity (retained earnings). Recognizing revenue increases net income. The statement of cash flows is not affected. The journal entry for this event and its effects on the financial statements follow:

Account Title	Debit	Credit
Accounts Receivable	8,500	
Sales Revenue		8,500

Assets					=	Liab.	+	Stockholders' Equity			Rev.	−	Exp.	=	Net Inc.	Cash Flow
Cash	+	Accts. Rec.	+	Inventory	=	Note Pay.	+	Com. Stk.	+	Retained Earnings						
NA	+	8,500	+	NA	=	NA	+	NA	+	8,500	8,500	−	NA	=	8,500	NA

EVENT 1b **JPS recognized $4,000 of cost of goods sold.**

Recognizing the expense decreases assets (merchandise inventory) and stockholders' equity (retained earnings). Cost of goods sold increases and net income decreases. Cash flow is not affected. The journal entry for this event and its effects on the financial statements follow:

Account Title	Debit	Credit
Cost of Goods Sold	4,000	
Merchandise Inventory		4,000

Assets					=	Liab.	+	Stockholders' Equity			Rev.	−	Exp.	=	Net Inc.	Cash Flow
Cash	+	Accts. Rec.	+	Inventory	=	Note Pay.	+	Com. Stk.	+	Retained Earnings						
NA	+	NA	+	(4,000)	=	NA	+	NA	+	(4,000)	NA	−	4,000	=	(4,000)	NA

Accounting for Sales Returns and Allowances

EVENT 2a **A customer from Event 1a returned inventory with a $1,000 list price. The merchandise had cost JPS $450.**

The sales return decreases both assets (accounts receivable) and stockholders' equity (retained earnings) on the balance sheet. Sales and net income decrease. Cash flow is not affected. The journal entry for this event and its effects on the financial statements follow:

Account Title	Debit	Credit
Sales Revenue	1,000	
Accounts Receivable		1,000

Assets					=	Liab.	+	Stockholders' Equity			Rev.	−	Exp.	=	Net Inc.	Cash Flow
Cash	+	Accts. Rec.	+	Inventory	=	Note Pay.	+	Com. Stk.	+	Retained Earnings						
NA	+	(1,000)	+	NA	=	NA	+	NA	+	(1,000)	(1,000)	−	NA	=	(1,000)	NA

EVENT 2b The cost of the goods ($450) is returned to the inventory account.

Since JPS got the inventory back, the sales return increases both assets (merchandise inventory) and stockholders' equity (retained earnings). The expense (cost of goods sold) decreases and net income increases. Cash flow is not affected. The journal entry for this event and its effects on the financial statements follow:

Account Title	Debit	Credit
Merchandise Inventory	450	
Cost of Goods Sold		450

Assets					=	Liab.	+	Stockholders' Equity			Rev.	−	Exp.	=	Net Inc.	Cash Flow
Cash	+	Accts. Rec.	+	Inventory	=	Note Pay.	+	Com. Stk.	+	Retained Earnings						
NA	+	NA	+	450	=	NA	+	NA	+	450	NA	−	(450)	=	450	NA

Accounting for Sales Discounts

EVENT 3 JPS collected the balance of the accounts receivable generated in Event 1a. Recall the goods were sold under terms 1/10, net/30.

ALTERNATIVE 1 The collection occurs before the discount period has expired (within 10 days from the date of the sale).

JPS would give the buyer a 1 percent discount. Given the original sales amount of $8,500 and a sales return of $1,000, the amount of the discount is $75 [($8,500 − $1,000) × .01]. The sales discount reduces the amount of accounts receivable and retained earnings on the balance sheet. It also reduces the amount of revenue and the net income shown on the balance sheet. It does not affect the statement of cash flows. These effects are shown below.

Account Title	Debit	Credit
Sales Revenue	75	
Accounts Receivable		75

Assets					=	Liab.	+	Stockholders' Equity			Rev.	−	Exp.	=	Net Inc.	Cash Flow
Cash	+	Accts. Rec.	+	Inventory	=	Note Pay.	+	Com. Stk.	+	Retained Earnings						
NA	+	(75)	+	NA	=	NA	+	NA	+	(75)	(75)	−	NA	=	(75)	NA

The balance due on the account receivable is $7,425 ($8,500 original sales − $1,000 sales return − $75 discount). The collection increases the Cash account and decreases the Accounts Receivable account. The income statement is not affected. The cash inflow is shown in the operating activities section of the statement of cash flows. The journal entry for this event and its effects on the financial statements follow:

Account Title	Debit	Credit
Cash	7,425	
Accounts Receivable		7,425

Assets					=	Liab.	+	Stockholders' Equity			Rev.	−	Exp.	=	Net Inc.	Cash Flow
Cash	+	Accts. Rec.	+	Inventory	=	Accts. Pay.	+	Com. Stk.	+	Retained Earnings						
7,425	+	(7,425)	+	NA	=	NA	+	NA	+	NA	NA	−	NA	=	NA	7,425 OA

Net Sales

The gross amount of sales minus **sales returns and allowances** and sales discounts is commonly called **net sales.** Companies are not required by GAAP to show sales returns and allowances and sales discounts on their income statement. Indeed, most companies show only the amount of *net sales* on the income statement. In this case the net sales amount to $7,425 ($8,500 original sales − $1,000 sales return − $75 discount).

ALTERNATIVE 2 The collection occurs after the discount period has expired (after 10 days from the date of the sale).

Under these circumstances there is no sales discount. The amount collected is $7,500 ($8,500 original sale − $1,000 sales return). Net sales shown on the income statement would also be $7,500.

THE FINANCIAL ANALYST

LO 4-5

Use common size financial statements and ratio analysis to evaluate managerial performance.

Merchandising is a highly competitive business. In order to succeed, merchandisers develop different strategies to distinguish themselves in the marketplace. For example, some companies like Walmart, Kmart, and Costco focus on price competition while others such as Neiman Marcus and Saks Fifth Avenue sell high-priced goods that offer high quality, style, and strong guarantees. Financial analysts have developed specific tools that are useful in scrutinizing the success or failure of a company's sales strategy. The first step in the analytical process is to develop common size statements so that comparisons can be made between companies.

Common Size Financial Statements

How good is a $1,000,000 increase in net income? The answer is not clear because there is no indication as to the size of the company. A million dollar increase may be excellent for a small company but would be virtually meaningless for a company the size of Exxon. To enable meaningful comparisons analysts prepare **common size financial statements.** Common size statements display information in percentages as well as absolute dollar amounts.

To illustrate, we expand the income statements for JPS to include percentages. The results are shown in Exhibit 4.9. The percentage data are computed by defining net sales as the base figure, or 100 percent. The other amounts on the statements are then shown as a percentage of net sales. For example, the *cost of goods sold percentage* is the dollar amount of *cost of goods sold* divided by the dollar amount of *net sales,* which produces a percentage of 66.7 percent ($8,000 ÷ $12,000) for 2016 and 48.5 percent ($12,000 ÷ $24,750) for 2017. Other income statement items are computed using the same approach.

Ratio Analysis

Two of the percentages shown in Exhibit 4.9 are used frequently in business to make comparisons within a specific company or between two or more different companies. These two commonly used percentages are the **gross margin percentage** and the **net income percentage.** The gross margin percentage provides insight about a company's pricing strategy. All other things being equal, a high gross margin percentage means that a company is charging high prices in relation to its cost of goods sold. These percentages are calculated as follows:

$$\text{Gross margin percentage} = \frac{\text{Gross margin}}{\text{Net sales}}$$

$$\text{Net income percentage} = \frac{\text{Net income}}{\text{Net sales}}$$

EXHIBIT 4.9 Common Size Financial Statements

JUNE'S PLANT SHOP
Income Statement
For the Years Ended December 31,

	2016		2017	
Net sales*	$12,000	100.0%	$ 24,750	100.0%
Cost of goods sold	(8,000)	66.7	(12,000)	48.5
Gross margin	4,000	33.3	12,750	51.5
Less: Operating expenses				
Selling and administrative expense	(1,000)	8.3	(5,000)	20.2
Transportation-out			(450)	1.8
Operating income	3,000	25.0	7,300	29.5
Nonoperating items				
Interest expense			(360)	(1.5)
Gain on the sale of land			700	2.8
Net income	$ 3,000	25.0	$ 7,640	30.9

*Since JPS did not offer sales discounts or have sales returns and allowances during 2016 or 2017, the amount of sales revenue is equal to the amount of net sales. We use the term *net sales* here because it is more commonly used in business practice. Percentages do not add exactly because they have been rounded.

In practice, the *net income percentage* is frequently called the **return on sales** ratio. The return on sales ratio provides insight as to how much of each sales dollar remains as net income after all expenses are paid. All other things being equal, companies with high ratios are doing a better job of controlling expenses.

Comparisons within a Particular Company

To illustrate comparisons within a particular company, assume that JPS relocated its store in an upscale mall in early 2017. Management realized that the company would have to pay more for operating expenses but believed those expenses could be offset by charging significantly higher prices. We use the gross margin percentage and the net income percentage to assess the success of JPS's strategy. Exhibit 4.9 shows an increase in the *gross margin percentage* from 33.3 to 51.5. This confirms that JPS was able to increase prices relative to its cost of goods sold. The increase in the *return on sales* ratio (25 percent to 30.9 percent) confirms that the increase in gross margin was larger than the increase in total expenses. We therefore conclude that JPS's strategy to relocate was successful. This may also explain why JPS sold its land in late 2017. Considering the success the company experienced at the new location, there was no longer a motive to build a store on the land.

Since net income is affected by nonoperating items, some financial analysts would prefer to use *operating income* instead of *net income* when computing the *return on sales* ratio. In this case the nonoperating items are immaterial. Indeed, to simplify the discussion in this chapter we always assume immateriality when computing this ratio. However, when nonoperating items are significant, it is more insightful to use *operating income* as the numerator of the *return on sales* ratio.

Comparisons between Companies

Does Walmart sell merchandise at a higher or lower price than Target? The *gross margin percentage* is useful in answering questions such as this. Since Walmart's 2013 fiscal year annual report shows a gross margin percentage of 24.3 while Target's report shows a gross margin percentage of 29.5, we conclude that there is validity to Walmart's claim of having low prices. The next section of the chapter provides insight as to how the *gross margin percentage* and the *return on sales* ratio can be used to gain insight about the operations of several real-world companies.

CHECK YOURSELF 4.3

The following sales data are from the records of two retail sales companies. All amounts are in thousands.

	Company A	Company B
Sales	$ 21,234	$ 43,465
Cost of goods sold	(14,864)	(34,772)
Gross margin	$ 6,370	$ 8,693

One company is an upscale department store, and the other is a discount store. Which company is the upscale department store?

Answer The gross margin percentage for Company A is approximately 30 percent ($6,370 ÷ $21,234). The gross margin percentage for Company B is 20 percent ($8,693 ÷ $43,465). These percentages suggest that Company A is selling goods with a higher markup than Company B, which implies that Company A is the upscale department store.

Answers to The Curious Accountant

As data from the income statement for **AutoNation** show, automobile dealers do not have big markups on the cars they sell. The new vehicles the company sold for $9,949.6 million in 2013 cost the company $9,333.2 to purchase, resulting in a gross margin of $616.4, or 6.2 percent. In other words, if you bought an "average" car from AutoNation for $20,000, the company's gross profit on it was only $1,240 ($20,000 × .062), meaning it paid **Ford** $18,760 ($20,000 − $1,240). Furthermore, the company still had other expenses to pay besides its cost of goods sold. In 2013, only 2.1 percent of each dollar of AutoNation's sales was net profit ($374.9 ÷ $17,517.6). Remember, the amount shown for sales on AutoNation's income statement is based on what customers actually paid for the cars the company sold, not the "sticker price."

Meanwhile, if Ford sold the car to AutoNation for $18,760, it earned a 10.1 percent gross margin on the sale, or $1,895 [$14,135 ÷ $139,369 = 10.1%; ($139,369 − $125,234 = $14,135)] [$18,760 × .101 = $1,895]. Like AutoNation, Ford still had other expenses to pay for besides the cost of goods sold. In 2013, Ford earned 4.9 percent of net profit on each dollar of sales ($7,155 ÷ $146,917).

Most consumers significantly overestimate the profit margins of the companies from which they buy goods. Retailers, especially, operate with small profit margins, so inventory management, discussed in Chapter 5, is very important to their success.

Real-World Data

Exhibit 4.10 shows the gross margin percentages and return on sales ratios for 10 companies. Three of the companies are manufacturers that produce pharmaceutical products, and the remaining seven companies sell various products at the retail level. These data are for the companies' 2013 fiscal years.

EXHIBIT 4.10

Industry/Company	Gross Margin %	Return on Sales %
Pharmaceutical manufacturers		
GlaxoSmithKline	67.6	21.2
Johnson & Johnson	68.7	19.4
Merck & Co.	61.5	10.5
Retail pharmacies		
CVS	18.7	3.6
Rite Aid	28.8	0.5
Walgreens	29.2	3.4
Department stores		
Macy's	40.3	4.8
Walmart	24.3	3.8
Office supplies		
Office Depot	23.4	−0.2
Staples	26.6	−0.9

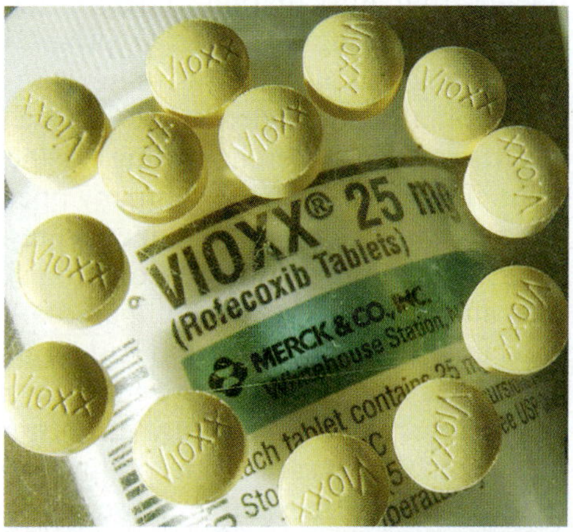

A review of the data confirms our earlier finding that ratios for companies in the same industry are often more similar than are ratios for companies from different industries. For example, note that the manufacturers have much higher margins, both for gross profit and for net earnings, than do the retailers. Manufacturers are often able to charge higher prices than are retailers because they obtain patents which give them a legal monopoly on the products they create. When a company such as Merck develops a new drug, no one else can produce that drug until the patent expires, giving it lots of control over its price at the wholesale level. Conversely, when Walgreens sells Merck's drug at the retail level, it faces price competition from CVS Caremark (CVS), a company that is trying to sell the same drug to the same consumers. One way CVS can try to get customers to shop at its store is to charge lower prices than its competitors, but this reduces its profit margins, since it must pay the same price to get Merck's drug as did Walgreens. As the data in Exhibit 4.10 show, in 2013 CVS had a lower gross margin percentage than Walgreens, indicating it is charging lower prices for similar goods. However, CVS still managed to generate a higher return on sales percentage.

In the examples presented in Exhibit 4.10, some companies with higher gross margin percentages have higher return on sales ratios than their competitors, but this is not always the case. Office Depot had a gross margin percentage that was 12 percent lower than Staples [(26.6 − 23.4) ÷ 26.6], but its return on sales ratio was higher, although neither company's ratio was very good.

A Look Back <<

Merchandising companies earn profits by selling inventory at prices that are higher than the cost paid for the goods. Merchandising companies include *retail companies* (companies that sell goods to the final consumer) and *wholesale companies* (companies that sell to other merchandising companies). The products sold by merchandising companies are called *inventory.* The costs to purchase inventory, to receive it, and to ready it for sale are *product costs,* which are first accumulated in an inventory account (balance sheet asset account) and then recognized as cost of goods sold (income statement expense account) in the period in which goods are sold. Purchases and sales of inventory can be recorded continually as goods are bought and sold (perpetual system) or at the end of the accounting period (periodic system, discussed in the chapter appendix).

Accounting for inventory includes the treatment of cash discounts, transportation costs, returns and allowances, and shrinkage. The cost of inventory is the list price less any purchase returns and allowances and purchase discounts, plus transportation-in costs. The cost of freight paid to acquire inventory (*transportation-in*) is considered a product cost. The cost of freight paid to deliver inventory to customers (*transportation-out*) is a selling expense. *Sales returns and allowances* and *sales discounts* are subtracted from sales revenue to determine the amount of *net sales* reported on the income statement. Purchase returns and allowances reduce product cost. Theoretically, the cost of lost, damaged, or stolen inventory (shrinkage) is an operating expense. However, because these costs are usually immaterial in amount they are typically included as part of cost of goods sold on the income statement.

Some companies use a *multistep income statement*, which reports product costs separately from selling and administrative costs. Cost of goods sold is subtracted from sales revenue to determine *gross margin.* Selling and administrative expenses are subtracted from gross margin to determine income from operations. Other companies report income using a *single-step format*, in which the cost of goods sold is listed along with selling and administrative items in a single expense category that is subtracted in total from revenue to determine income from operations.

Managers of merchandising businesses operate in a highly competitive environment. They must manage company operations carefully to remain profitable. *Common size financial statements* (statements presented on a percentage basis) and ratio analysis are useful monitoring tools. Common size financial statements permit ready comparisons among different-size companies. Although a $1 million increase in sales may be good for a small company and bad for a large company, a 10 percent increase can apply to any size company. The two most common ratios used by merchandising companies are the *gross margin percentage* (gross margin ÷ net sales) and the *net income percentage* (net income ÷ net sales). Interpreting these ratios requires an understanding of industry characteristics. For example, a discount store such as **Walmart** would be expected to have a much lower gross margin percentage than an upscale store such as **Neiman Marcus**.

Managers should be aware of the financing cost of carrying inventory. By investing funds in inventory, a firm loses the opportunity to invest them in interest-bearing assets. The cost of financing inventory is an *opportunity cost.* To minimize financing costs, a company should minimize the amount of inventory it carries, the length of time it holds the inventory, and the time it requires to collect accounts receivable after the inventory is sold.

>> A Look Forward

To this point, the text has explained the basic accounting cycle for service and merchandising businesses. Future chapters more closely address specific accounting issues. For example, in Chapter 5 you will learn how to deal with inventory items that are purchased at differing prices. Other chapters will discuss a variety of specific practices that are widely used by real-world companies.

APPENDIX

LO 4-6

Identify the primary features of the periodic inventory system.

Periodic Inventory System

Under certain conditions, it is impractical to record inventory sales transactions as they occur. Consider the operations of a fast-food restaurant. To maintain perpetual inventory records, the restaurant would have to transfer from the Inventory account to the

Cost of Goods Sold account the *cost* of each hamburger, order of fries, soft drink, or other food item as it was sold. Obviously, recording the cost of each item at the point of sale would be impractical without using highly sophisticated computer equipment. Recording the selling price the customer pays is captured by cash registers; the difficulty lies in capturing inventory cost.

The **periodic inventory system** offers a practical solution for recording inventory transactions in a low-technology, high-volume environment. As shown in Exhibit 4.11, inventory costs are recorded in a Purchases account at the time of purchase. Purchase

EXHIBIT 4.11

General Journal Entries for 2017 (Periodic Method)

Event No.	Account Title	Debit	Credit
1	Cash	4,000	
	Notes Payable		4,000
2	Purchases	11,000	
	Accounts Payable		11,000
3	Accounts Payable	1,000	
	Purchase Returns and Allowances		1,000
4	Accounts Payable	200	
	Purchase Discounts		200
5	Accounts Payable	9,800	
	Cash		9,800
6	Transportation-In	300	
	Cash		300
7a	Cash	24,750	
	Sales		24,750
7b	Under the periodic system the cost of goods sold is recorded at the end of the period in the adjusting entry shown below.		
8	Transportation-Out	450	
	Cash		450
9	Selling and Administrative Expenses	5,000	
	Cash		5,000
10	Interest Expense	360	
	Cash		360
11	The effects of this event are included as part of cost of goods sold in the adjusting entry shown below.		
12	Cash	6,200	
	Land		5,500
	Gain on Sale of Land		700
Adj	Cost of Goods Sold	12,000	
	Merchandise Inventory (Ending Balance)	4,100	
	Purchase Returns and Allowances	1,000	
	Purchase Discounts	200	
	Purchases		11,000
	Transportation-In		300
	Merchandise Inventory (Beginning Balance)		6,000
CL	Revenue	24,750	
	Gain on Sale of Land	700	
	Cost of Goods Sold		12,000
	Transportation-Out		450
	Selling and Administrative Expenses		5,000
	Interest Expense		360
	Retained Earnings		7,640

EXHIBIT 4.12

Schedule of Cost of Goods Sold for 2017

Beginning inventory	$ 6,000
Purchases	11,000
Purchase returns and allowances	(1,000)
Purchase discounts	(200)
Transportation-in	300
Cost of goods available for sale	16,100
Ending inventory	(4,100)
Cost of goods sold	$12,000

returns and allowances and transportation-in are recorded in separate accounts. No entries for the cost of merchandise purchases or sales are recorded in the Inventory account during the period. The cost of goods sold is determined at the end of the period as shown in Exhibit 4.12.

The perpetual and periodic inventory systems represent alternative procedures for recording the same information. The amounts of cost of goods sold and ending inventory reported in the financial statements will be the same regardless of the method used. Exhibit 4.11 presents the general journal entries JPS would make if it used the periodic inventory method for the 2017 transactions. Cost of goods sold is recorded in an adjusting entry at the end of the accounting period.

The **schedule of cost of goods sold** presented in Exhibit 4.12 is used for internal reporting purposes. It is normally not shown in published financial statements. The amount of cost of goods sold is reported as a single line item on the income statement. The income statement in Exhibit 4.5 will be the same whether JPS maintains perpetual or periodic inventory records.

Advantages and Disadvantages of the Periodic System versus the Perpetual System

The chief advantage of the periodic method is recording efficiency. Recording inventory transactions occasionally (periodically) requires less effort than recording them continually (perpetually). Historically, practical limitations offered businesses like fast-food restaurants or grocery stores no alternative to using the periodic system. The sheer volume of transactions made recording individual decreases to the Inventory account balance as each item was sold impossible. Imagine the number of transactions a grocery store would have to record every business day to maintain perpetual records.

Although the periodic system provides a recordkeeping advantage over the perpetual system, perpetual inventory records provide significant control advantages over periodic records. With perpetual records, the book balance in the Inventory account should agree with the amount of inventory in stock at any given time. By comparing that book balance with the results of a physical inventory count, management can determine the amount of lost, damaged, destroyed, or stolen inventory. Perpetual records also permit more timely and accurate reorder decisions and profitability assessments.

When a company uses the *periodic* inventory system, lost, damaged, or stolen merchandise is automatically included in the cost of goods sold. Because such goods are not included in the year-end physical count, they are treated as sold regardless of the reason for their absence. Since the periodic system does not separate the cost of lost, damaged, or stolen merchandise from the cost of goods sold, the amount of any inventory shrinkage is unknown. This feature is a major disadvantage of the periodic system. Without knowing the amount of inventory losses, management cannot weigh the costs of various security systems against the potential benefits.

Advances in such technology as electronic bar code scanning and increased computing power have eliminated most of the practical constraints that once prevented merchandisers with high-volume, low dollar-value inventories from recording inventory transactions on a continual basis. As a result, use of the perpetual inventory system has expanded rapidly in recent years and continued growth can be expected. This text, therefore, concentrates on the perpetual inventory system.

SELF-STUDY REVIEW PROBLEM

A step-by-step audio-narrated series of slides is available in the Connect library.

Academy Sales Company (ASC) started the 2016 accounting period with the balances given in the financial statements model shown below. During 2016 ASC experienced the following business events.

1. Purchased $16,000 of merchandise inventory on account, terms 2/10, n/30.
2. The goods that were purchased in Event 1 were delivered FOB shipping point. Freight costs of $600 were paid in cash by the responsible party.
3. Returned $500 of goods purchased in Event 1.

4a. Recorded the cash discount on the goods purchased in Event 1.

4b. Paid the balance due on the account payable within the discount period.

5a. Recognized $21,000 of cash revenue from the sale of merchandise.

5b. Recognized $15,000 of cost of goods sold.

6. The merchandise in Event 5a was sold to customers FOB destination. Freight costs of $950 were paid in cash by the responsible party.
7. Paid cash of $4,000 for selling and administrative expenses.
8. Sold the land for $5,600 cash.

Required

a. Record the above transactions in a financial statements model like the one shown below.

Event No.	Cash	+	Inventory	+	Land	=	Accts. Pay.	+	Com. Stk.	+	Ret. Earn.	Rev./ Gain	−	Exp.	=	Net Inc.	Cash Flow
Bal.	25,000	+	3,000	+	5,000	=	-0-	+	18,000	+	15,000	NA	−	NA	=	NA	NA

b. Prepare a schedule of cost of goods sold. (Appendix)

c. Prepare a multistep income statement. Include common size percentages on the income statement.

d. ASC's gross margin percentage in 2015 was 22 percent. Based on the common size data in the income statement, did ASC raise or lower its prices in 2016?

e. Assuming a 10 percent rate of growth, what is the amount of net income expected for 2017?

Answer

a.

Event No.	Cash	+	Inventory	+	Land	=	Accts. Pay.	+	Com. Stk.	+	Ret. Earn.	Rev./ Gain	−	Exp.	=	Net Inc.	Cash Flow
Bal.	25,000	+	3,000	+	5,000	=	-0-	+	18,000	+	15,000	NA	−	NA	=	NA	NA
1		+	16,000			=	16,000	+		+			−		=		
2	(600)	+	600			=		+		+			−		=		(600) OA
3		+	(500)			=	(500)	+		+			−		=		
4a		+	(310)			=	(310)	+		+			−		=		
4b	(15,190)	+				=	(15,190)	+		+			−		=		(15,190) OA
5a	21,000	+				=		+		+	21,000	21,000	−		=	21,000	21,000 OA
5b		+	(15,000)			=		+		+	(15,000)		−	15,000	=	(15,000)	
6	(950)	+				=		+		+	(950)		−	950	=	(950)	(950) OA
7	(4,000)	+				=		+		+	(4,000)		−	4,000	=	(4,000)	(4,000) OA
8	5,600	+			(5,000)	=		+		+	600	600	−		=	600	5,600 IA
Bal.	30,860	+	3,790		-0-	=	-0-	+	18,000	+	16,650	21,600	−	19,950	=	1,650	5,860 NC

b.

ACADEMY SALES COMPANY Schedule of Cost of Goods Sold For the Period Ended December 31, 2016	
Beginning inventory	$ 3,000
Plus purchases	16,000
Less: Purchase returns and allowances	(500)
Less: Purchases discounts	(310)
Plus: Transportation-in	600
Goods available for sale	18,790
Less: Ending inventory	(3,790)
Cost of goods sold	$15,000

c.

ACADEMY SALES COMPANY Income Statement* For the Period Ended December 31, 2016		
Net sales	$ 21,000	100.0%
Cost of goods sold	(15,000)	71.4
Gross margin	6,000	28.6
Less: Operating expenses		
Selling and administrative expense	(4,000)	19.0
Transportation-out	(950)	4.5
Operating income	1,050	5.0
Nonoperating items		
Gain on the sale of land	600	2.9
Net income	$ 1,650	7.9

*Percentages do not add exactly because they have been rounded.

d. All other things being equal, the higher the gross margin percentage, the higher the sales prices. Since the gross margin percentage increased from 22 percent to 28.6 percent, the data suggest that Academy raised its sales prices.

e. $1,155 [$1,050 + (.10 × $1,050)]. Note that the gain is not expected to recur.

KEY TERMS

Cash discount 222
Common size financial statements 234
Cost of goods available for sale 216
Cost of goods sold 216
Credit terms 222
FOB destination 223
FOB shipping point 223
Gain 227
Gross margin 216
Gross margin percentage 234
Gross profit 216
Loss 227
Merchandise inventory 213
Merchandising businesses 212
Multistep income statement 230
Net income percentage 234
Net sales 234
Operating income (or loss) 229
Period costs 215
Periodic inventory system 239
Perpetual inventory system 216
Product costs 215
Purchase discount 222
Purchase returns and allowances 221
Retail companies 213
Return on sales 235
Sales discounts 231
Sales returns and allowances 234
Schedule of cost of goods sold 240
Selling and administrative costs 215
Shrinkage 226
Single-step income statement 230
Transportation-in 224
Transportation-out 224
Wholesale companies 213

QUESTIONS

1. Define *merchandise inventory*. What types of costs are included in the Merchandise Inventory account?
2. What is the difference between a product cost and a selling and administrative cost?
3. How is the cost of goods available for sale determined?
4. What portion of cost of goods available for sale is shown on the balance sheet? What portion is shown on the income statement?

5. When are period costs expensed? When are product costs expensed?
6. If PetCo had net sales of $600,000, goods available for sale of $450,000, and cost of goods sold of $375,000, what is its gross margin? What amount of inventory will be shown on its balance sheet?
7. Describe how the perpetual inventory system works. What are some advantages of using the perpetual inventory system? Is it necessary to take a physical inventory when using the perpetual inventory system?
8. What are the effects of the following types of transactions on the accounting equation? Also identify the financial statements that are affected. (Assume that the perpetual inventory system is used.)
   - **a.** Acquisition of cash from the issue of common stock.
   - **b.** Contribution of inventory by an owner of a company.
   - **c.** Purchase of inventory with cash by a company.
   - **d.** Sale of inventory for cash.
9. Northern Merchandising Company sold inventory that cost $12,000 for $20,000 cash. How does this event affect the accounting equation? What financial statements and accounts are affected? (Assume that the perpetual inventory system is used.)
10. If goods are shipped FOB shipping point, which party (buyer or seller) is responsible for the shipping costs?
11. Define *transportation-in.* Is it a product or a period cost?
12. Quality Cellular Co. paid $80 for freight on merchandise that it had purchased for resale to customers (transportation-in) and paid $135 for freight on merchandise delivered to customers (transportation-out). What account is debited for the $80 payment? What account is debited for the $135 payment?
13. Why would a seller grant an allowance to a buyer of the seller's merchandise?
14. Dyer Department Store purchased goods with the terms 2/10, n/30. What do these terms mean?
15. Eastern Discount Stores incurred a $5,000 cash cost. How does the accounting for this cost differ if the cash were paid for inventory versus commissions to sales personnel?
16. What is the purpose of giving credit terms to customers?
17. Define *transportation-out.* Is it a product cost or a period cost for the seller?
18. Ball Co. purchased inventory with a list price of $4,000 with the terms 2/10, n/30. What amount will be debited to the Merchandise Inventory account?
19. Explain the difference be-tween gains and revenues.
20. Explain the difference between losses and expenses.
21. Suda Company sold land that cost $40,000 for $37,000 cash. Explain how this transaction would be shown on the statement of cash flows.
22. Explain the difference between purchase returns and sales returns. How do purchase returns affect the financial statements of both buyer and seller? How do sales returns affect the financial statements of both buyer and seller?
23. How is net sales determined?
24. What is the difference between a multistep income statement and a single-step income statement?
25. What is the advantage of using common size income statements to present financial information for several accounting periods?
26. What information is provided by the net income percentage (return on sales ratio)?
27. What is the purpose of preparing a schedule of cost of goods sold? (Appendix)
28. Explain how the periodic inventory system works. What are some advantages of using the periodic inventory system? What are some disadvantages of using the periodic inventory system? Is it necessary to take a physical inventory when using the periodic inventory system? (Appendix)
29. Why does the periodic inventory system impose a major disadvantage for management in accounting for lost, stolen, or damaged goods? (Appendix)

MULTIPLE-CHOICE QUESTIONS

Multiple-choice questions are available in the Connect library.

EXERCISES—SERIES A

All applicable Exercises in Series A are available with McGraw-Hill's Connect Plus Accounting.

When the instructions for *any* exercise or problem call for the preparation of an income statement, use the *multistep format* unless otherwise indicated.

LO 4-1

Exercise 4-1A *Comparing a merchandising company with a service company*

The following information is available for two different types of businesses for the 2016 accounting year. Hopkins CPAs is a service business that provides accounting services to small businesses. Sports Clothing is a merchandising business that sells sports clothing to college students.

Data for Hopkins CPAs

1. Borrowed $90,000 from the bank to start the business.
2. Provided $50,000 of services to clients and collected $50,000 cash.
3. Paid salary expense of $32,000.

Data for Sports Clothing

1. Borrowed $90,000 from the bank to start the business.
2. Purchased $50,000 inventory for cash.
3. Inventory costing $26,000 was sold for $50,000 cash.
4. Paid $8,000 cash for operating expenses.

Required

a. Prepare an income statement, balance sheet, and statement of cash flows for each of the companies.
b. Which of the two businesses would have product costs? Why?
c. Why does Hopkins CPAs not compute gross margin on its income statement?
d. Compare the assets of both companies. What assets do they have in common? What assets are different? Why?

LO 4-1, 4-3

Exercise 4-2A *Effect of inventory transactions on journals, ledgers, and financial statements: Perpetual system*

Dan Watson started a small merchandising business in 2016. The business experienced the following events during its first year of operation. Assume that Watson uses the perpetual inventory system.

1. Acquired $30,000 cash from the issue of common stock.
2. Purchased inventory for $18,000 cash.
3. Sold inventory costing $15,000 for $32,000 cash.

Required

a. Record the events in general journal format.
b. Post the entries to T-accounts.
c. Prepare an income statement for 2016 (use the multistep format).
d. What is the amount of net cash flow from operating activities for 2016?

LO 4-1

Exercise 4-3A *Effect of inventory transactions on the income statement and statement of cash flows: Perpetual system*

During 2016, Hardy Merchandising Company purchased $40,000 of inventory on account. Hardy sold inventory on account that cost $24,500 for $38,000. Cash payments on accounts payable were $22,000. There was $26,000 cash collected from accounts receivable. Hardy also paid $5,100 cash for operating expenses. Assume that Hardy started the accounting period with $20,000 in both cash and common stock.

Required

a. Identify the events described in the preceding paragraph and record them in a horizontal statements model like the following one:

Assets					=	Liab.	+	Equity			Rev.	−	Exp.	=	Net Inc.	Cash Flow
Cash	+	Accts. Rec.	+	Inv.	=	Accts. Pay.	+	Com. Stk.	+	Ret. Earn.						
20,000	+	NA	+	NA	=	NA	+	20,000	+	NA	NA	−	NA	=	NA	NA

b. What is the balance of accounts receivable at the end of 2016?

c. What is the balance of accounts payable at the end of 2016?

d. What are the amounts of gross margin and net income for 2016?

e. Determine the amount of net cash flow from operating activities.

f. Explain why net income and retained earnings are the same for Hardy. Normally would these amounts be the same? Why or why not?

Exercise 4-4A *Recording inventory transactions in the general journal and posting entries to T-accounts: Perpetual system* LO 4-1

Milo Clothing experienced the following events during 2016, its first year of operation:

1. Acquired $30,000 cash from the issue of common stock.
2. Purchased inventory for $15,000 cash.
3. Sold inventory costing $9,000 for $20,000 cash.
4. Paid $1,500 for advertising expense.

Required

a. Record the general journal entries for the preceding transactions.

b. Post each of the entries to T-accounts.

c. Prepare a trial balance to prove the equality of debits and credits.

Exercise 4-5A *Understanding the freight terms FOB shipping point and FOB destination* LO 4-2

Required

For each of the following events, indicate whether the freight terms are FOB destination or FOB shipping point.

a. Sold merchandise and the buyer paid the freight costs.

b. Purchased merchandise and the seller paid the freight costs.

c. Sold merchandise and paid the freight costs.

d. Purchased merchandise and paid the freight costs.

Exercise 4-6A *Determining the cost of inventory* LO 4-2

Required

For each of the following cases determine the ending balance in the inventory account. (*Hint:* First, determine the total cost of inventory available for sale. Next, subtract the cost of the inventory sold to arrive at the ending balance.)

a. Jill's Dress Shop had a beginning balance in its inventory account of $40,000. During the accounting period Jill's purchased $75,000 of inventory, returned $5,000 of inventory, and obtained $750 of purchases discounts. Jill's incurred $1,000 of transportation-in cost and $600 of transportation-out cost. Salaries of sales personnel amounted to $31,000. Administrative expenses amounted to $35,600. Cost of goods sold amounted to $82,300.

b. Ken's Bait Shop had a beginning balance in its inventory account of $8,000. During the accounting period Ken's purchased $36,900 of inventory, obtained $1,200 of purchases allowances, and received $360 of purchases discounts. Sales discounts amounted to $640. Ken's incurred $900 of transportation-in cost and $260 of transportation-out cost. Selling and administrative cost amounted to $12,300. Cost of goods sold amounted to $33,900.

LO 4-2, 4-3

Exercise 4-7A *Effect of purchase returns and allowances and freight costs on the journal, ledger, and financial statements: Perpetual system*

The trial balance for Terry's Auto Shop as of January 1, 2016, follows:

Account Titles	Debit	Credit
Cash	$16,000	
Inventory	8,000	
Common Stock		$20,000
Retained Earnings		4,000
Total	$24,000	$24,000

The following events affected the company during the 2016 accounting period:

1. Purchased merchandise on account that cost $15,000.
2. The goods in Event 1 were purchased FOB shipping point with freight cost of $800 cash.
3. Returned $2,600 of damaged merchandise for credit on account.
4. Agreed to keep other damaged merchandise for which the company received an $1,100 allowance.
5. Sold merchandise that cost $15,000 for $31,000 cash.
6. Delivered merchandise to customers in Event 5 under terms FOB destination with freight costs amounting to $500 cash.
7. Paid $8,000 on the merchandise purchased in Event 1.

Required

a. Record the events in general journal format.

b. Open general ledger T-accounts with the appropriate beginning balances, and post the journal entries to the T-accounts.

c. Prepare an income statement, balance sheet, and statement of cash flows. (Assume that closing entries have been made.)

d. Explain why a difference does or does not exist between net income and net cash flow from operating activities.

LO 4-2

Exercise 4-8A *Accounting for product costs: Perpetual inventory system*

Which of the following would be *debited* to the Inventory account for a merchandising business using the perpetual inventory system?

Required

a. Transportation-out.

b. Purchase discount.

c. Transportation-in.

d. Purchase of a new computer to be used by the business.

e. Purchase of inventory.

f. Allowance received for damaged inventory.

Exercise 4-9A *Effect of product cost and period cost: Horizontal statements model* LO 4-2

The Pet Store experienced the following events for the 2016 accounting period:

1. Acquired $60,000 cash from the issue of common stock.
2. Purchased $65,000 of inventory on account.
3. Received goods purchased in Event 2 FOB shipping point; freight cost of $900 paid in cash.
4. Sold inventory on account that cost $38,000 for $71,000.
5. Freight cost on the goods sold in Event 4 was $620. The goods were shipped FOB destination. Cash was paid for the freight cost.
6. Customer in Event 4 returned $4,200 worth of goods that had a cost of $2,150.
7. Collected $58,300 cash from accounts receivable.
8. Paid $59,200 cash on accounts payable.
9. Paid $2,600 for advertising expense.
10. Paid $3,100 cash for insurance expense.

Required

a. Which of these events affect period (selling and administrative) costs? Which result in product costs? If neither, label the transaction NA.

b. Record each event in a horizontal statements model like the following one. The first event is recorded as an example.

Assets					=	Liab.	+	Equity			Rev.	–	Exp.	=	Net Inc.	Cash Flow
Cash	+	Accts. Rec.	+	Inv.	=	Accts. Pay.	+	C. Stk.	+	Ret. Earn.						
60,000	+	NA	+	NA	=	NA	+	60,000	+	NA	NA	–	NA	=	NA	60,000 FA

Exercise 4-10A *Cash discounts and purchase returns* LO 4-2

On April 6, 2016, Home Furnishings purchased $25,200 of merchandise from Una Imports, terms 2/10 n/45. On April 8, Home returned $2,400 of the merchandise to Una Imports for credit. Home paid cash for the merchandise on April 15, 2016.

Required

a. What is the amount that Home must pay Una Imports on April 15?

b. Record the events in a horizontal statements model like the following one.

Assets			=	Liab.	+	Equity			Rev.	–	Exp.	=	Net Inc.	Cash Flow
Cash	+	Inv.	=	Accts. Pay.	+	C. Stock	+	Ret. Earn.						

c. How much must Home pay for the merchandise purchased if the payment is not made until April 20, 2016?

d. Record the payment in Requirement *c* in a horizontal statements model like the one above.

e. Why would Home want to pay for the merchandise by April 15?

Exercise 4-11A *Determining the effect of inventory transactions on the horizontal statements model: Perpetual system* LO 4-2

Bali Sales Company experienced the following events:

1. Purchased merchandise inventory for cash.
2. Purchased merchandise inventory on account.

3. Returned merchandise purchased on account.
4. Sold merchandise inventory for cash. Label the revenue recognition 4a and the expense recognition 4b.
5. Paid cash on accounts payable not within the discount period.
6. Sold merchandise inventory on account. Label the revenue recognition 6a and the expense recognition 6b.
7. Paid cash for selling and administrative expenses.
8. Paid cash for transportation-in.
9. Collected cash from accounts receivable.
10. Paid cash for transportation-out.

Required

Identify each event as asset source (AS), asset use (AU), asset exchange (AE), or claims exchange (CE). Also explain how each event affects the financial statements by placing a + for increase, − for decrease, or NA for not affected under each of the components in the following statements model. Assume the use of the perpetual inventory system. The first event is recorded as an example.

Event No.	Event Type	Assets	=	Liab.	+	Equity	Rev.	−	Exp.	=	Net Inc.	Cash Flow
1	AE	+ −	=	NA	+	NA	NA	−	NA	=	NA	− OA

LO 4-2

Exercise 4-12A *Effect of inventory losses: Perpetual system*

Ho Designs experienced the following events during 2016, its first year of operation:

1. Started the business when it acquired $70,000 cash from the issue of common stock.
2. Paid $41,000 cash to purchase inventory.
3. Sold inventory costing $37,500 for $56,200 cash.
4. Physically counted inventory; had inventory of $3,200 on hand at the end of the accounting period.

Required

a. Open appropriate ledger T-accounts, and record the events in the accounts.
b. Prepare an income statement and balance sheet.
c. If all purchases and sales of merchandise are reflected as increases or decreases to the Merchandise Inventory account, why is it necessary for management to even bother to take a physical count of goods on hand (ending inventory) at the end of the year?

LO 4-3

Exercise 4-13A *Multistep income statement*

In 2016, Kim Company sold land for $80,000 cash. The land had originally cost $60,000. Also, Kim sold inventory that had cost $110,000 for $198,000 cash. Operating expenses amounted to $36,000.

Required

a. Prepare a 2016 multistep income statement for Kim Company.
b. Assume that normal operating activities grow evenly by 10% during 2017. Prepare a 2017 multistep income statement for Kim Company.
c. Determine the percentage change in net income between 2016 and 2017.
d. Should the stockholders have expected the results determined in Requirement *c*? Explain your answer.

Exercise 4-14A ***Sales returns, discounts, gain, and a multistep income statement*** LO 4-2, 4-3

The following information was drawn from the 2016 accounting records of Ozark Merchandisers:

1. Inventory that had cost $21,200 was sold for $39,900 under terms 2/20, net/30.
2. Customers returned merchandise to Ozark five days after the purchase. The merchandise had been sold for a price of $1,520. The merchandise had cost Ozark $920.
3. All customers paid their accounts within the discount period.
4. Selling and administrative expenses amounted to $4,200.
5. Interest expense paid amounted to $360.
6. Land that had cost $8,000 was sold for $9,250 cash.

Required

a. Determine the amount of net sales.
b. Prepare a multistep income statement.
c. Where would the interest expense be shown on the statement of cash flows?
d. How would the sale of the land be shown on the statement of cash flows?
e. Explain the difference between a gain and revenue.

Exercise 4-15A ***Single-step and multistep income statements*** LO 4-3

The following information was taken from the accounts of Green Market, a small grocery store at December 31, 2016. The accounts are listed in alphabetical order, and all have normal balances. Dollar amounts are given in thousands.

Accounts payable	$ 800
Accounts receivable	2,250
Advertising expense	600
Cash	1,850
Common stock	2,000
Cost of goods sold	2,950
Interest expense	120
Merchandise inventory	1,250
Prepaid rent	720
Retained earnings, 1/1/2016	2,610
Sales revenue	5,600
Salaries expense	960
Rent expense	510
Gain on sale of land	200

Required

First, prepare an income statement for the year using the single-step approach. Then prepare another income statement using the multistep approach.

Exercise 4-16A ***Effect of sales returns and allowances and freight costs on the journal, ledger, and financial statements: Perpetual system*** LO 4-2, 4-4

Powell Company began the 2016 accounting period with $40,000 cash, $86,000 inventory, $60,000 common stock, and $66,000 retained earnings. During 2016, Powell experienced the following events:

1. Sold merchandise costing $58,000 for $99,500 on account to Prentise Furniture Store.
2. Delivered the goods to Prentise under terms FOB destination. Freight costs were $900 cash.
3. Received returned goods from Prentise. The goods cost Powell $4,000 and were sold to Prentise for $5,900.
4. Granted Prentise a $3,000 allowance for damaged goods that Prentise agreed to keep.
5. Collected partial payment of $81,000 cash from accounts receivable.

Required

a. Record the events in general journal format.

b. Open general ledger T-accounts with the appropriate beginning balances and post the journal entries to the T-accounts.

c. Prepare a multistep income statement, a balance sheet, and a statement of cash flows.

d. Why would Prentise agree to keep the damaged goods? Who benefits more?

LO 4-2, 4-3, 4-4, 4-5

Exercise 4-17A *Comprehensive exercise with sales discounts*

Junker's Stash started the 2016 accounting period with the balances given in the financial statements model shown below. During 2016 Junker's Stash experienced the following business events:

1. Paid cash to purchase $70,000 of merchandise inventory.
2. The goods that were purchased in Event 1 were delivered FOB destination. Freight costs of $1,400 were paid in cash by the responsible party.

3a. Sold merchandise for $72,000 under terms 1/10, n/30.

3b. Recognized $41,900 of cost of goods sold.

4a. Junker's Stash customers returned merchandise that was sold for $2,100.

4b. The merchandise returned in Event 4a had cost Junker's Stash $1,250.

5. The merchandise in Event 3a was sold to customers FOB destination. Freight costs of $1,650 were paid in cash by the responsible party.

6a. The customers paid for the merchandise sold in Event 3a within the discount period. Recognized the sales discount.

6b. Collected the balance in the accounts receivable account.

7. Paid cash of $6,850 for selling and administrative expenses.
8. Sold the land for $9,100 cash.

Required

a. Record the above transactions in a financial statements model like the one shown below:

Event No.	Cash	+	Accts. Rec.	+	Inventory	+	Land	=	Com. Stk.	+	Ret. Earn.	Rev./Gain	−	Exp.	=	Net Inc.	Cash Flow
Bal.	80,000	+	0	+	15,000	+	11,000	=	70,000	+	36,000	NA	−	NA	=	NA	NA

b. Determine the amount of net sales.

c. Prepare a multistep income statement. Include common size percentages on the income statement.

d. Junker's Stash return on sales ratio in 2015 was 12 percent. Based on the common size data in the income statement, did Junker's Stash expenses increase or decrease in 2016?

e. Explain why the term *loss* is used to describe the results due to the sale of land.

LO 4-5

Exercise 4-18A *Using ratios to make comparisons*

The following income statements were drawn from the annual reports of the Denver Company and the Reno Company:

	Denver*	Reno*
Net sales	$ 190,000	$ 180,000
Cost of goods sold	(114,000)	(126,000)
Gross margin	76,000	54,000
Less: Operating exp.		
Selling and admin. exp.	(62,700)	(39,600)
Net income	$ 13,300	$ 14,400

*All figures are reported in thousands of dollars.

Required

a. One of the companies is a high-end retailer that operates in exclusive shopping malls. The other operates discount stores that are located in low-cost, stand-alone buildings. Identify the high-end retailer and the discounter. Support your answer with appropriate ratios.

b. If Denver and Reno have equity of $130,000 and $160,000, respectively, which company is in the more profitable business?

Exercise 4-19A *Using common size statements and ratios to make comparisons* LO 4-5

At the end of 2016 the following information is available for Jackson and Fargo companies:

	Jackson	Fargo
Sales	$1,000,000	$1,000,000
Cost of goods sold	700,000	600,000
Operating expenses	250,000	300,000
Total assets	1,200,000	1,200,000
Stockholders' equity	360,000	360,000

Required

a. Prepare a common size income statement for each company.

b. Compute the return on assets and return on equity for each company.

c. Which company is more profitable from the stockholders' perspective?

d. One company is a high-end retailer, and the other operates a discount store. Which is the discounter? Support your selection by referring to the appropriate ratios.

Exercise 4-20A *Effect of inventory transactions on the income statement and balance sheet: Periodic system (Appendix)* LO 4-6

Bill Rose owns Rose Sporting Goods. At the beginning of the year, Rose Sporting Goods had $18,000 in inventory. During the year, Rose Sporting Goods purchased inventory that cost $66,000. At the end of the year, inventory on hand amounted to $28,500.

Required

Calculate the following:

a. Cost of goods available for sale during the year.

b. Cost of goods sold for the year.

c. Amount of inventory Rose Sporting Goods would report on the year-end balance sheet.

Exercise 4-21A *Determining cost of goods sold: Periodic system (Appendix)* LO 4-6

Tippah Antiques uses the periodic inventory system to account for its inventory transactions. The following account titles and balances were drawn from Tippah's records for the year 2016: beginning balance in inventory, $42,000; purchases, $128,000; purchase returns and allowances, $12,000; sales, $520,000; sales returns and allowances, $3,900; freight-in, $1,000; and operating expenses, $130,000. A physical count indicated that $26,000 of merchandise was on hand at the end of the accounting period.

Required

a. Prepare a schedule of cost of goods sold.

b. Prepare a multistep income statement.

Exercise 4-22A *Basic transactions: Periodic system, single cycle (Appendix)* LO 4-6

The following transactions apply to Bob's Bike Shop for 2016, its first year of operations:

1. Acquired $35,000 cash from the issue of common stock.
2. Acquired $9,600 of merchandise from Bob Hall, the owner, who had acquired the merchandise prior to opening the shop. Issued common stock to Bob in exchange for the merchandise inventory.

3. Purchased $85,000 of inventory on account.
4. Paid $2,800 for radio ads.
5. Sold inventory for $165,000 cash.
6. Paid $28,000 in salary to a part-time salesperson.
7. Paid $65,000 on accounts payable (see Event 3).
8. Physically counted inventory, which indicated that $28,500 of inventory was on hand at the end of the accounting period.

Required

a. Record each of these transactions in general journal form using the periodic method.
b. Post each of the transactions to ledger T-accounts.
c. Prepare an income statement, statement of changes in stockholders' equity, balance sheet, and statement of cash flows for 2016.
d. Prepare the necessary closing entries at the end of 2016, and post them to the appropriate T-accounts.
e. Prepare a post-closing trial balance.
f. Give an example of a business that may want to use the periodic system. Give an example of a business that may use the perpetual system.
g. Give some examples of assets other than cash that are commonly contributed to a business in exchange for stock.

PROBLEMS—SERIES A

All applicable Problems in Series A are available with McGraw-Hill's Connect Plus Accounting.

LO 4-1, 4-3

Problem 4-23A *Basic transactions for three accounting cycles: Perpetual system*

Blooming Flower Company was started in 2016 when it acquired $60,000 cash from the issue of common stock. The following data summarize the company's first three years' operating activities. Assume that all transactions were cash transactions.

	2016	2017	2018
Purchases of inventory	$50,000	$60,000	$ 85,000
Sales	68,000	85,000	130,000
Cost of goods sold	34,000	43,000	71,000
Selling and administrative expenses	29,000	35,000	42,000

Required

Prepare an income statement (use multistep format) and balance sheet for each fiscal year. (*Hint:* Record the transaction data for each accounting period in T-accounts before preparing the statements for that year.)

LO 4-2

Problem 4-24A *Identifying freight costs*

Required

For each of the following events, determine the amount of freight paid by The Box Company. Also indicate whether the freight cost would be classified as a product or period (selling and administrative) cost.

a. Purchased merchandise with freight costs of $650. The merchandise was shipped FOB shipping point.
b. Shipped merchandise to customers, freight terms FOB shipping point. The freight costs were $310.

c. Purchased inventory with freight costs of $1,500. The goods were shipped FOB destination.
d. Sold merchandise to a customer. Freight costs were $520. The goods were shipped FOB destination.

Problem 4-25A *Identifying product and period costs*

LO 4-2

Required

Indicate whether each of the following costs is a product cost or a period (selling and administrative) cost:

a. Goods purchased for resale.
b. Salaries of salespersons.
c. Advertising costs.
d. Transportation-out.
e. Interest on a note payable.
f. Salary of the company president.
g. Transportation-in.
h. Insurance on the office building.
i. Office supplies.
j. Costs incurred to improve the quality of goods available for sale.

Problem 4-26A *Comprehensive cycle problem: Perpetual system*

LO 4-2, 4-3, 4-4

At the beginning of 2016, the Redd Company had the following balances in its accounts:

Cash	$ 6,900
Inventory	15,000
Land	7,000
Common stock	15,000
Retained earnings	13,900

During 2016, the company experienced the following events:

1. Purchased inventory that cost $5,200 on account from Ross Company under terms 1/10, n/30. The merchandise was delivered FOB shipping point. Freight costs of $190 were paid in cash.
2. Returned $400 of the inventory that it had purchased because the inventory was damaged in transit. The seller agreed to pay the return freight cost.
3. Paid the amount due on its account payable to Ross Company within the cash discount period.
4. Sold inventory that had cost $6,800 for $12,100 on account, under terms 2/10, n/45.
5. Received merchandise returned from a customer. The merchandise originally cost $900 and was sold to the customer for $1,680 cash. The customer was paid $1,680 cash for the returned merchandise.
6. Delivered goods FOB destination in Event 4. Freight costs of $140 were paid in cash.
7. Collected the amount due on the account receivable within the discount period.
8. Sold the land for $8,500.
9. Recognized accrued interest income of $600.
10. Took a physical count indicating that $13,400 of inventory was on hand at the end of the accounting period.

Required

a. Identify each of these events as asset source (AS), asset use (AU), asset exchange (AE), or claims exchange (CE). Also explain how each event would affect the financial statements by placing a + for increase, − for decrease, or NA for not affected under each of the components in the following statements model. Assume that the perpetual inventory method is used. When an event has more than one part, use letters to distinguish the effects of each part. The first event is recorded as an example.

Event No.	Event Type	Assets	=	Liab.	+	Stk. Equity	Rev.	−	Exp.	=	Net Inc.	Cash Flow
1a	AS	+	=	+	+	NA	NA	−	NA	=	NA	NA
1b	AE	+ −	=	NA	+	NA	NA	−	NA	=	NA	− OA

b. Record the events in general journal format.

c. Open ledger T-accounts, and post the beginning balances and the events to the accounts.

d. Prepare a multistep income statement, a statement of changes in stockholders' equity, a balance sheet, and a statement of cash flows.

e. Record and post the closing entries, and prepare a post-closing trial balance.

LO 4-3, 4-5

Problem 4-27A *Multistep and common size income statements*

The following information was drawn from the records of Toner Sales Company:

	2016	2017
Net sales	$200,000	$200,000
Cost of goods sold	(90,000)	(80,000)
Operating expenses	(60,000)	(50,000)
Loss on the sale of land	–0–	(24,000)

Required

a. Prepare a multistep income statement for each year.

b. Prepare a common size income statement for each year.

c. At a recent meeting of the stockholders, Toner's president stated 2018 would be a very good year with net income rising significantly. Write a brief memo explaining whether you agree or disagree with the president. Assume that the operating trends between 2016 and 2017 continue through 2018.

LO 4-6

Problem 4-28A *Preparing schedule of cost of goods sold and multistep and single-step income statements: Periodic system (Appendix)*

The following account titles and balances were taken from the adjusted trial balance of King Co. for 2016. The company uses the periodic inventory system.

Account Title	Balance
Sales returns and allowances	$ 3,500
Miscellaneous expense	900
Transportation-out	2,200
Sales	15,300
Advertising expense	6,200
Salaries expense	21,000
Transportation-in	3,800
Purchases	88,000
Interest expense	250
Merchandise inventory, January 1	11,200
Rent expense	12,000
Merchandise inventory, December 31	10,700
Purchase returns and allowances	2,100
Loss on sale of land	3,100
Utilities expense	1,850

Required

a. Prepare a schedule to determine the amount of cost of goods sold.
b. Prepare a multistep income statement.
c. Prepare a single-step income statement.

Problem 4-29A *Comprehensive cycle problem: Periodic system (Appendix)* LO 4-6

The following trial balance pertains to Benji's Grocery as of January 1, 2016:

Account Title	Debit	Credit
Cash	$ 64,000	
Accounts receivable	12,000	
Merchandise inventory	90,000	
Accounts payable		$ 7,500
Common stock		89,000
Retained earnings		69,500
Totals	$166,000	$166,000

The following events occurred in 2016. Assume that Benji's uses the periodic inventory method.

1. Purchased land for $30,000 cash.
2. Purchased merchandise on account for $230,000, terms 1/10 n/45.
3. Paid freight of $2,100 cash on merchandise purchased FOB shipping point.
4. Returned $8,600 of defective merchandise purchased in Event 2.
5. Sold merchandise for $186,000 cash.
6. Sold merchandise on account for $236,000, terms 2/10 n/30.
7. Paid cash within the discount period on accounts payable due on merchandise purchased in Event 2.
8. Paid $28,500 cash for selling expenses.
9. Collected $156,000 of the accounts receivable from Event 6 within the discount period.
10. Collected $56,000 of the accounts receivable but not within the discount period.
11. Paid $17,100 of other operating expenses.
12. A physical count indicated that $48,300 of inventory was on hand at the end of the accounting period.

Required

a. Record these transactions in a general journal.
b. Post the transactions to ledger T-accounts.
c. Prepare a schedule of costs of goods sold, income statement, statement of changes in stockholders' equity, balance sheet, and statement of cash flows for 2016.

MULTIPLE-CHOICE QUESTIONS

Multiple-choice questions are available in the Connect library.

EXERCISES—SERIES B

When the instructions for *any* exercise or problem call for the preparation of an income statement, use the *multistep format* unless otherwise indicated.

Exercise 4-1B *Comparing a merchandising company with a service company* LO 4-1

The following information is available for two different types of businesses for the 2016 accounting year. Diamond Consulting is a service business that provides consulting services to small businesses. University Bookstore is a merchandising business that sells books to college students.

Data for Diamond Consulting

1. Borrowed $80,000 by issuing a note to the bank to start the business.
2. Performed services for clients and collected $60,000 cash.
3. Paid salary expense of $38,400.

Data for University Bookstore

1. Borrowed $80,000 by issuing a note to the bank to start the business.
2. Purchased $38,000 of inventory for cash.
3. Inventory costing $33,600 was sold for $60,000 cash.
4. Paid $4,800 cash for operating expenses.

Required

a. Prepare an income statement, balance sheet, and statement of cash flows for each of the companies.
b. What is different about the income statements of the two businesses?
c. What is different about the balance sheets of the two businesses?
d. How are the statements of cash flow different for the two businesses?

LO 4-1, 4-3

Exercise 4-2B *Effect of inventory transactions on journals, ledgers, and financial statements: Perpetual system*

Jason Kidd started a small merchandising business in 2016. The business experienced the following events during its first year of operation. Assume that Kidd uses the perpetual inventory system.

1. Acquired $30,000 cash from the issue of common stock.
2. Purchased inventory for $60,000 cash.
3. Sold inventory costing $48,000 for $82,000 cash.

Required

a. Record the events in general journal format.
b. Post the entries to T-accounts.
c. Prepare an income statement for 2016 (use the multistep format).
d. What is the amount of total assets at the end of the period?

LO 4-1

Exercise 4-3B *Effect of inventory transactions on the income statement and statement of cash flows: Perpetual system*

During 2016, Rondor Merchandising Company purchased $40,000 of inventory on account. The company sold inventory on account that cost $30,000 for $50,000. Cash payments on accounts payable were $24,500. There was $38,000 cash collected from accounts receivable. Rondor also paid $9,000 cash for operating expenses. Assume that Rondor started the accounting period with $20,000 in both cash and common stock.

Required

a. Identify the events described in the preceding paragraph and record them in a horizontal statements model like the following one:

Assets					=	Liab.	+	Equity			Rev.	−	Exp.	=	Net Inc.	Cash Flow
Cash	+	Accts. Rec.	+	Inv.	=	Accts. Pay.	+	Com. Stk.	+	Ret. Earn.						
20,000	+	NA	+	NA	=	NA	+	20,000	+	NA	NA	−	NA	=	NA	NA

b. What is the balance of accounts receivable at the end of 2016?
c. What is the balance of accounts payable at the end of 2016?
d. What are the amounts of gross margin and net income for 2016?

e. Determine the amount of net cash flow from operating activities.

f. Explain any differences between net income and net cash flow from operating activities.

Exercise 4-4B *Recording inventory transactions in the general journal and posting entries to T-accounts: Perpetual system*

LO 4-1

Jones Shoe shop experienced the following events during 2016, its first year of operation:

1. Acquired $25,000 cash from the issue of common stock.
2. Purchased inventory for $32,000 cash.
3. Sold inventory costing $19,000 for $36,000 cash.
4. Paid $3,100 for advertising expense.

Required

a. Record the general journal entries for the preceding transactions.

b. Post each of the entries to T-accounts.

c. Prepare a trial balance to prove the equality of debits and credits.

Exercise 4-5B *Determining which party is responsible for freight cost*

LO 4-2

Required

Determine which party, buyer or seller, is responsible for freight charges in each of the following situations:

a. Purchased merchandise, freight terms, FOB destination.

b. Purchased merchandise, freight terms, FOB shipping point.

c. Sold merchandise, freight terms, FOB destination.

d. Sold merchandise, freight terms, FOB shipping point.

Exercise 4-6B *Purchase discounts and transportation costs*

LO 4-2

Musgrove Basket Company had an $8,500 beginning balance in its Merchandise Inventory account. The following information regarding Musgrove's purchases and sales of inventory during its 2016 accounting period was drawn from the company's accounting records:

1. Purchased $45,000 of inventory under terms 1/10, net/60. Transportation costs amounted to $700. The goods were delivered FOB shipping point. Musgrove paid for the inventory within the discount period.
2. Purchased $40,000 of inventory under terms 2/10, net/30. Transportation costs amounted to $900. The goods were delivered to Musgrove FOB destination. Musgrove paid for the inventory after the discount period had expired.
3. Sold inventory that cost $56,000 for $94,000. Transportation costs for goods delivered to customers amounted to $3,200. The goods were delivered FOB destination.

Required

a. Determine the balance in the Inventory account at the end of the accounting period.

b. Is Musgrove or its customers responsible for the transportation costs described in Event 3?

c. Determine the gross margin.

Exercise 4-7B *Effect of purchase returns and allowances and freight costs on the journal, ledger, and financial statements: Perpetual system*

LO 4-2, 4-3

The trial balance for The Bolt Co. as of January 1, 2016, was as follows:

Account Titles	Debit	Credit
Cash	$12,000	
Inventory	6,000	
Common Stock		$15,000
Retained Earnings		3,000
Total	$18,000	$18,000

The following events affected the company during the 2016 accounting period:

1. Purchased merchandise on account that cost $8,200.
2. The goods in Event 1 were purchased FOB shipping point with freight cost of $600 cash.
3. Returned $800 of damaged merchandise for credit on account.
4. Agreed to keep other damaged merchandise for which the company received a $400 allowance.
5. Sold merchandise that cost $5,500 for $9,500 cash.
6. Delivered merchandise to customers under terms FOB destination with freight costs amounting to $300 cash.
7. Paid $5,000 on the merchandise purchased in Event 1.

Required

a. Record the transactions in general journal format.
b. Open general ledger T-accounts with the appropriate beginning balances, and post the journal entries to the T-accounts.
c. Prepare an income statement and statement of cash flows for 2016.
d. Explain why a difference does or does not exist between net income and net cash flow from operating activities.

LO 4-2

Exercise 4-8B *Accounting for product costs: Perpetual inventory system*

Which of the following would be *debited* to the Inventory account for a merchandising business using the perpetual inventory system?

Required

a. Transportation-in.
b. Allowance received for damaged inventory.
c. Purchase of inventory.
d. Purchase of office supplies.
e. Transportation-out.
f. Cash discount given on goods sold.

LO 4-2

Exercise 4-9B *Effect of product cost and period cost: Horizontal statements model*

Wild Rose Co. experienced the following events for the 2016 accounting period:

1. Acquired $20,000 cash from the issue of common stock.
2. Purchased $36,000 of inventory on account.
3. Received goods purchased in Event 2 FOB shipping point. Freight cost of $900 paid in cash.
4. Returned $4,000 of goods purchased in Event 2 because of poor quality.
5. Sold inventory on account that cost $28,000 for $82,000.
6. Freight cost on the goods sold in Event 5 was $200. The goods were shipped FOB destination. Cash was paid for the freight cost.
7. Collected $33,000 cash from accounts receivable.
8. Paid $27,000 cash on accounts payable.
9. Paid $4,500 for advertising expense.
10. Paid $7,200 cash for insurance expense.

Required

a. Which of these transactions affect period (selling and administrative) costs? Which result in product costs? If neither, label the transaction NA.

b. Record each event in a horizontal statements model like the following one. The first event is recorded as an example.

Assets					=	Liab.	+	Equity			Rev.	−	Exp.	=	Net Inc.	Cash Flow
Cash	+	Accts. Rec.	+	Inv.	=	Accts. Pay.	+	C. Stk.	+	Ret. Earn.						
20,000	+	NA	+	NA	=	NA	+	20,000	+	NA	NA	−	NA	=	NA	20,000 FA

Exercise 4-10B *Cash discounts and purchase returns*

LO 4-2

On March 6, 2016, Salon Express purchased merchandise from Hair Fashions with a list price of \$19,000, terms 2/10, n/45. On March 10, Salon returned merchandise to Hair Fashions for credit. The list price of the returned merchandise was \$8,500. Salon paid cash to settle the accounts payable on March 15, 2016.

Required

a. What is the amount of the check that Salon must write to Hair Fashions on March 15?

b. Record the events in a horizontal statements model like the following one.

Assets			=	Liab.	+	Equity			Rev.	−	Exp.	=	Net Inc.	Cash Flow
Cash	+	Inv.	=	Accts. Pay.	+	C. Stk	+	Ret. Earn.						

c. How much would Salon pay for the merchandise purchased if the payment is not made until March 20, 2016?

d. Record the payment of the merchandise in Requirement *c* in a horizontal statements model like the one shown above.

e. Why would Hair Fashions sell merchandise with the terms 2/10, n/45?

Exercise 4-11B *Determining the effect of inventory transactions on the financial statements model: Perpetual system*

LO 4-2

TRS Company experienced the following events:

1. Purchased merchandise inventory for cash.
2. Sold merchandise inventory on account. Label the revenue recognition 2a and the expense recognition 2b.
3. Returned merchandise purchased on account.
4. Purchased merchandise inventory on account.
5. Paid cash on accounts payable within the discount period.
6. Paid cash for selling and administrative expenses.
7. Sold merchandise inventory for cash. Label the revenue recognition 7a and the expense recognition 7b.
8. Paid cash for transportation-out.
9. Paid cash for transportation-in.
10. Collected cash from accounts receivable not within the discount period.

Required

Identify each event as asset source (AS), asset use (AU), asset exchange (AE), or claims exchange (CE). Also explain how each event affects the financial statements by placing a + for increase, − for decrease, or NA for not affected under each of the components in the following horizontal statements model. Assume the company uses the perpetual inventory system. The first event is recorded as an example.

Event No.	Event Type	Assets	=	Liab.	+	Equity	Rev.	−	Exp.	=	Net Inc.	Cash Flow
1	AE	+ −	=	NA	+	NA	NA	−	NA	=	NA	− OA

LO 4-2

Exercise 4-12B *Effect of inventory losses: Perpetual system*

Raabe Sales experienced the following events during 2016, its first year of operation:

1. Started the business when it acquired $80,000 cash from the issue of common stock.
2. Paid $35,000 cash to purchase inventory.
3. Sold inventory costing $21,000 for $40,500 cash.
4. Physically counted inventory showing $13,500 inventory was on hand at the end of the accounting period.

Required

a. Open appropriate ledger T-accounts, and record the events in the accounts.
b. Prepare an income statement and balance sheet for 2016.
c. Explain how differences between the book balance and the physical count of inventory could arise. Why is being able to determine whether differences exist useful to management?

LO 4-3

Exercise 4-13B *Multistep income statement*

In 2016, Image Incorporated sold land for $82,000 cash. The land had originally cost $50,000. Also, Image sold inventory that had cost $176,000 for $265,000 cash. Operating expenses amounted to $41,000.

Required

a. Prepare a 2016 multistep income statement for Image Incorporated.
b. Assume that normal operating activities grow evenly by 10% during 2017. Prepare a 2017 multistep income statement for Image Incorporated.
c. Determine the percentage change in net income between 2016 and 2017.
d. Should the stockholders have expected the results determined in Requirement *c*? Explain your answer.

LO 4-2, 4-3

Exercise 4-14B *Purchase returns, discounts, loss, and a multistep income statement*

The following information was drawn from the 2016 accounting records of Cozart Merchandisers.

1. Inventory with a list price of $40,000 was purchased under terms 2/10, net/30.
2. Cozart returned $4,200 of the inventory to the supplier five days after purchase.
3. The accounts payable was settled within the discount period.
4. The inventory was sold for $69,000.
5. Selling and administrative expenses amounted to $12,000.
6. Interest expense paid amounted to $800.
7. Land that cost $15,000 was sold for $20,000 cash.

Required

a. Determine the cost of the inventory sold.
b. Prepare a multistep income statement.
c. Where would the interest expense be shown on the statement of cash flows?
d. How would the sale of the land be shown on the statement of cash flows?
e. Explain the difference between a loss and an expense.

Exercise 4-15B *Single-step and multistep income statements*

LO 4-3

The following information was taken from the accounts of Adams's Eatery, a delicatessen, at December 31, 2016. The accounts are listed in alphabetical order, and each has a normal balance.

Accounts payable	$1,200
Accounts receivable	800
Advertising expense	400
Cash	820
Common stock	400
Cost of goods sold	1,200
Interest expense	140
Loss on sale of land	50
Merchandise inventory	900
Prepaid rent	80
Rent expense	220
Retained earnings	1,000
Salaries expense	260
Sales revenue	2,000

Required

First, prepare an income statement for the year using the single-step approach. Then prepare another income statement using the multistep approach.

Exercise 4-16B *Effect of sales returns and allowances and freight costs on the journal, ledger, and financial statements: Perpetual system*

LO 4-2, 4-4

Hollis Company began the 2016 accounting period with $36,000 cash, $80,000 inventory, $70,000 common stock, and $46,000 retained earnings. During the 2016 accounting period, Hollis experienced the following events:

1. Sold merchandise costing $51,500 for $92,900 on account to RJ's General Store.
2. Delivered the goods to RJ's under terms FOB destination. Freight costs were $500 cash.
3. Received returned goods from RJ's. The goods cost Hollis Company $3,200 and were sold to RJ's for $4,700.
4. Granted RJ's a $1,500 allowance for damaged goods that RJ's agreed to keep.
5. Collected partial payment of $71,000 cash from accounts receivable.

Required

a. Record the transactions in general journal format.
b. Open general ledger T-accounts with the appropriate beginning balances and post the journal entries to the T-accounts.
c. Prepare an income statement, balance sheet, and statement of cash flows.
d. Why would Hollis grant the $1,500 allowance to RJ's? Who benefits more?

Exercise 4-17B *Comprehensive exercise with purchases discounts*

LO 4-2, 4-3, 4-4, 4-5

Custom Auto Parts (CAP) started the 2016 accounting period with the balances given in the financial statements model shown below. During 2016, CAP experienced the following business events:

1. Purchased $60,000 of merchandise inventory on account, terms 2/10, n/30.
2. The goods that were purchased in Event 1 were delivered FOB shipping point. Freight costs of $1,500 were paid in cash by the responsible party.
3. Returned $3,000 of goods purchased in Event 1.

4a. Recorded the cash discount on the goods purchased in Event 1.
4b. Paid the balance due on the account payable within the discount period.
5a. Recognized $59,000 of cash revenue from the sale of merchandise.
5b. Recognized $45,000 of cost of goods sold.
6. The merchandise in Event 5a was sold to customers FOB destination. Freight costs of $1,400 were paid in cash by the responsible party.
7. Paid cash of $9,000 for selling and administrative expenses.
8. Sold the land for $14,500 cash.

Required

a. Record the above transactions in a financial statements model like the one shown below.

Event No.	Cash	+	Inventory	+	Land	=	Accts. Pay.	+	Com. Stk.	+	Ret. Earn.	Rev./ Gain	−	Exp.	=	Net Inc.	Cash Flow
Bal.	60,000	+	8,000	+	12,000	=	−0−	+	50,000	+	30,000	NA	−	NA	=	NA	NA

b. Prepare a multistep income statement. Include common size percentages on the income statement.
c. CAP's gross margin percentage in 2015 was 34%. Based on the common size data in the income statement, did CAP raise or lower its prices in 2016?
d. Assuming a 5% rate of growth, what is the amount of net income expected for 2017?

LO 4-5

Exercise 4-18B *Using ratios to make comparisons*

The following income statements were drawn from the annual reports of Athens Company and Boulder Company:

	Athens*	Boulder*
Net sales	$ 32,600	$ 86,200
Cost of goods sold	(24,450)	(47,410)
Gross margin	8,150	38,790
Less: Operating exp.		
Selling and admin. exp.	(6,200)	(34,480)
Net income	$ 1,950	$ 4,310

*All figures are reported in thousands of dollars.

Required

a. One of the companies is a high-end retailer that operates in exclusive shopping malls. The other operates discount stores that are located in low-cost, stand-alone buildings. Identify the high-end retailer and the discounter. Support your answer with appropriate ratios.
b. If Athens and Boulder have equity of $22,000 and $39,000, respectively, which company is in the more profitable business?

LO 4-5

Exercise 4-19B *Using common size statements and ratios to make comparisons*

At the end of 2016 the following information is available for Billings and Phoenix companies:

	Billings	Phoenix
Sales	$3,000,000	$3,000
Cost of goods sold	1,800,000	2,100
Operating expenses	960,000	780
Total assets	3,750,000	3,750
Stockholders' equity	1,000,000	1,200

Required

a. Prepare a common size income statement for each company.

b. Compute the return on assets and return on equity for each company.

c. Which company is more profitable from the stockholders' perspective?

d. One company is a high-end retailer, and the other operates a discount store. Which is the discounter? Support your selection by referring to the appropriate ratios.

Exercise 4-20B *Effect of inventory transactions on the income statement and balance sheet: Periodic system (Appendix)*

LO 4-6

Rick Dove is the owner of RD Cleaning. At the beginning of the year, Dove had $4,800 in inventory. During the year, Dove purchased inventory that cost $26,000. At the end of the year, inventory on hand amounted to $3,600.

Required

Calculate the following:

a. Cost of goods available for sale during the year.

b. Cost of goods sold for the year.

c. Inventory amount RD Cleaning would report on its year-end balance sheet.

Exercise 4-21B *Determining cost of goods sold: Periodic system (Appendix)*

LO 4-6

Far East Retailers uses the periodic inventory system to account for its inventory transactions. The following account titles and balances were drawn from Far East's records for the year 2016: beginning balance in inventory, $46,200; purchases, $352,400; purchase returns and allowances, $14,600; sales, $840,000; sales returns and allowances, $7,520; transportation-in, $2,150; and operating expenses, $65,100. A physical count indicated that $35,100 of merchandise was on hand at the end of the accounting period.

Required

a. Prepare a schedule of cost of goods sold.

b. Prepare a multistep income statement.

Exercise 4-22B *Basic transactions: Periodic system, single cycle (Appendix)*

LO 4-6

The following events apply to Sally's Gift Shop for 2016, its first year of operation:

1. Acquired $60,000 cash from the issue of common stock.
2. Issued common stock to Sally Quin, one of the owners, in exchange for merchandise inventory worth $3,200 Sally had acquired prior to opening the shop.
3. Purchased $56,200 of inventory on account.
4. Paid $4,500 for advertising expense.
5. Sold inventory for $98,300 cash.
6. Paid $12,000 in salary to a part-time salesperson.
7. Paid $47,000 on accounts payable (see Event 3).
8. Physically counted inventory, which indicated that $16,000 of inventory was on hand at the end of the accounting period.

Required

a. Record each of these events in general journal form. Sally's Gift Shop uses the periodic system.

b. Post each of the events to ledger T-accounts.

c. Prepare an income statement, statement of changes in stockholders' equity, balance sheet, and statement of cash flows for 2016.

d. Prepare the necessary closing entries at the end of 2016, and post them to the appropriate T-accounts.

e. Prepare a post-closing trial balance.
f. Discuss an advantage of using the periodic system instead of the perpetual system.
g. Why is the common stock issued on the statement of changes in stockholders' equity different from the common stock issued in the cash flow from financing activities section of the cash flow statement?

PROBLEMS—SERIES B

LO 4-1, 4-3

Problem 4-23B *Basic transactions for three accounting cycles: Perpetual system*

Mano Company was started in 2016 when it acquired $40,000 from the issue of common stock. The following data summarize the company's first three years' operating activities. Assume that all transactions were cash transactions.

	2016	2017	2018
Purchases of inventory	$30,000	$36,000	$57,000
Sales	42,000	56,000	72,000
Cost of goods sold	22,000	39,000	51,000
Selling and administrative expenses	6,500	9,100	11,200

Required

Prepare an income statement (use the multistep format) and balance sheet for each fiscal year. (*Hint:* Record the transaction data for each accounting period in T-accounts before preparing the statements for that year.)

LO 4-2

Problem 4-24B *Identifying freight cost*

Required

For each of the following events, determine the amount of freight paid by Cycle Parts House. Also indicate whether the freight is classified as a product or period cost.

a. Purchased merchandise with costs of $500, FOB shipping point.
b. Sold merchandise to a customer. Freight costs were $800, FOB shipping point.
c. Purchased inventory with freight costs of $1,400, FOB destination.
d. Shipped merchandise to customers with freight costs of $300, FOB destination.

LO 4-2

Problem 4-25B *Identifying product and period costs*

Required

Indicate whether each of the following costs is a product cost or a period cost:

a. Cleaning supplies for the office.
b. Freight on goods purchased for resale.
c. Salary of the marketing director.
d. Freight on goods sold to customer with terms FOB destination.
e. Utilities expense incurred for office building.
f. Advertising expense.
g. Insurance on vans used to deliver goods to customers.
h. Salaries of sales supervisors.
i. Monthly maintenance expense for a copier.
j. Goods purchased for resale.

Problem 4-26B *Comprehensive cycle problem: Perpetual system*

LO 4-2, 4-3, 4-4

At the beginning of 2016, EuRo Enterprises had the following balances in its accounts:

Cash	$16,800
Inventory	4,000
Land	2,000
Common stock	12,000
Retained earnings	10,800

During 2016, EuRo Enterprises experienced the following events:

1. Purchased inventory costing $11,200 on account from Ivey Company under terms 2/10, n/30. The merchandise was delivered FOB shipping point. Freight costs of $800 were paid in cash.
2. Returned $600 of the inventory that it had purchased because the inventory was damaged in transit. The seller agreed to pay the return freight cost.
3. Paid the amount due on its account payable to Ivey Company within the cash discount period.
4. Sold inventory that had cost $8,000 for $13,500. The sale was on account under terms 2/10, n/45.
5. Received merchandise returned from a customer. The merchandise had originally cost $1,200 and had been sold to the customer for $2,100 cash. The customer was paid $2,100 cash for the returned merchandise.
6. Delivered goods in Event 4 FOB destination. Freight costs of $800 were paid in cash.
7. Collected the amount due on accounts receivable within the discount period.
8. Sold the land for $3,500.
9. Recognized $500 of accrued interest revenue.
10. Took a physical count indicating that $6,500 of inventory was on hand at the end of the accounting period.

Required

a. Identify each of these events as asset source (AS), asset use (AU), asset exchange (AE), or claims exchange (CE). Also explain how each event affects the financial statements by placing a + for increase, − for decrease, or NA for not affected under each of the components in the following horizontal statements model. Assume that the perpetual inventory method is used. When an event has more than one part, use letters to distinguish the effects of each part. The first event is recorded as an example.

Event No.	Event Type	Assets	=	Liab.	+	Stk. Equity	Rev.	−	Exp.	=	Net Inc.	Cash Flow
1a	AS	+	=	+	+	NA	NA	−	NA	=	NA	NA
1b	AE	+ −	=	NA	+	NA	NA	−	NA	=	NA	− OA

b. Record the events in general journal format.

c. Open ledger T-accounts and post the beginning balances and the events to the accounts.

d. Prepare a multistep income statement, statement of changes in stockholders' equity, balance sheet, and statement of cash flows.

e. Record and post the closing entries, and prepare a post-closing trial balance.

Problem 4-27B *Multistep and common size income statements*

LO 4-3, 4-5

The following information was drawn from the records of Moore Sales Company:

	2016	2017
Net sales	$60,000	$70,000
Cost of goods sold	(25,000)	(26,500)
Operating expenses	(13,200)	(16,100)
Gain on the sale of land	0	5,000

Required

a. Prepare a multistep income statement for each year.
b. Prepare a common size income statement for each year.
c. Assume that the operating trends between 2016 and 2017 continue through 2018. Write a brief memo indicating whether you expect net income to increase or decrease in 2018.

LO 4-6

Problem 4-28B *Preparing a schedule of cost of goods sold and multistep and single-step income statements: Periodic system (Appendix)*

The following account titles and balances were taken from the adjusted trial balance of Hogan Sales Co. at December 31, 2016. The company uses the periodic inventory method.

Account Title	Balance
Advertising expense	$ 20,800
Interest expense	10,000
Merchandise inventory, January 1	36,000
Merchandise inventory, December 31	40,200
Miscellaneous expense	1,600
Purchases	300,000
Purchase returns and allowances	5,400
Rent expense	36,000
Salaries expense	106,000
Sales	640,000
Sales returns and allowances	16,000
Transportation-in	12,400
Transportation-out	21,600
Gain on sale of land	8,000
Utilities expense	22,400

Required

a. Prepare a schedule to determine the amount of cost of goods sold.
b. Prepare a multistep income statement.
c. Prepare a single-step income statement.

LO 4-6

Problem 4-29B *Comprehensive cycle problem: Periodic system (Appendix)*

The following trial balance pertains to Simmons Hardware as of January 1, 2016:

Account Title	Debit	Credit
Cash	$ 28,000	
Accounts receivable	18,000	
Merchandise inventory	120,000	
Accounts payable		$ 10,000
Common stock		140,000
Retained earnings		16,000
Total	$166,000	$166,000

The following events occurred in 2016. Assume that Simmons Hardware uses the periodic inventory system.

1. Purchased land for $16,000 cash.
2. Purchased merchandise on account for $46,000, terms 2/10 n/30.
3. The merchandise purchased by Simmons was shipped FOB shipping point for $460 cash.

4. Returned $4,000 of defective merchandise purchased in Event 2.
5. Sold merchandise for $54,000 cash.
6. Sold merchandise on account for $100,000, terms 1/20 n/30.
7. Paid cash within the discount period on accounts payable due on merchandise purchased in Event 2.
8. Paid $2,400 cash for selling expenses.
9. Collected $70,000 of accounts receivable within the discount period.
10. Collected $24,000 of accounts receivable but not within the discount period.
11. Paid $6,400 of other operating expenses.
12. Performed a physical count indicating that $60,000 of inventory was on hand at the end of the accounting period.

Required

a. Record these transactions in a general journal.
b. Post the transactions to ledger T-accounts.
c. Prepare a schedule of cost of goods sold, income statement, statement of changes in stockholders' equity, balance sheet, and statement of cash flows for 2016.

ANALYZE, THINK, COMMUNICATE

ATC 4-1 Business Applications Case *Understanding real-world annual reports*

Required

a. Use the Target Corporation's annual report in Appendix B to answer the following questions:
   (1) What was Target's gross margin percentage for the fiscal year ended February 1, 2014 (2013) and 2012?
   (2) What was Target's return on sales percentage for 2013 and 2012?
   (3) Target's return on sales percentage for 2013 was lower than it was in 2012. Ignoring taxes, how much higher would Target's 2013 net income have been if its return on sales percentage in 2013 had been the same as for 2012?

ATC 4-2 Group Exercise *Multistep income statement*

The following quarterly information is given for Rossie for the year ended 2016 (amounts shown are in millions):

	First Quarter	Second Quarter	Third Quarter	Fourth Quarter
Net Sales	$736.0	$717.4	$815.2	$620.1
Gross Margin	461.9	440.3	525.3	252.3
Net Income	37.1	24.6	38.6	31.4

Required

a. Divide the class into groups and organize the groups into four sections. Assign each section financial information for one of the quarters.
   (1) Each group should compute the cost of goods sold and operating expenses for the specific quarter assigned to its section and prepare a multistep income statement for the quarter.
   (2) Each group should compute the gross margin percentage and cost of goods sold percentage for its specific quarter.
   (3) Have a representative of each group put that quarter's sales, cost of goods sold percentage, and gross margin percentage on the board.

Class Discussion

b. Have the class discuss the change in each of these items from quarter to quarter and explain why the change might have occurred. Which was the best quarter and why?

ATC 4-3 Real World Case *Identifying companies based on financial statement information*

Presented here is selected information from the 2013 fiscal-year 10-K reports of four companies. The four companies, in alphabetical order, are: Caterpillar, Inc., a manufacturer of heavy machinery; Oracle Corporation, a company that develops software; Starbucks, a company that sells coffee products; and Tiffany & Company, a company that operates high-end jewelry and department stores. The data for the companies, presented in the order of the amount of their sales in millions of dollars, are:

	A	B	C	D
Sales	$3,794.2	$14,892.2	$37,180	$55,656
Cost of goods sold	1,631.0	6,382.3	7,113	40,727
Net earings	416.2	8.8	10,925	5,722
Inventory	173.0	1,111.2	240	12,625
Accounts receivable	2,234.3	561.4	6,049	17,234
Total assets	4,630.9	11,516.7	81,812	84,896

Required

Based on these financial data and your knowledge and assumptions about the nature of the businesses that the companies operate, determine which data relate to which companies. Write a memorandum explaining your decisions. Include a discussion of which ratios you used in your analysis, and show the computations of these ratios in your memorandum.

ATC 4-4 Real World Case *Performing ratio analysis using real-world data*

Bloomin' Brands, Inc., is the corporation behind five restaurant chains: Outback Steakhouse, Carrabba's Italian Grill, Bonefish Grill, Fleming's Prime Steakhouse and Wine Bar, and Roy's. The following data were taken from its 2013 annual report. All dollar amounts are in thousands.

	Fiscal Years Ending	
	December 31, 2013	December 31, 2012
Total restaurant sales	$4,089,128	$3,946,116
Cost of goods sold	1,333,842	1,281,002
Net income	214,568	61,304

Required

a. Compute Bloomin' Brands' gross margin percentage for 2013 and 2012.

b. Compute Bloomin' Brands' return on sales percentage for 2013 and 2012.

c. Based on the percentages computed in Requirements *a* and *b*, did Bloomin' Brands' performance get better or worse from 2012 to 2013?

d. Compare Bloomin' Brands' gross margin percentages and return on sales percentages to those of the other real-world companies discussed in this chapter and discuss whether or not it appears to have better than average financial performance.

ATC 4-5 Business Applications Case *Performing ratio analysis using real-world data*

The Kroger Co. was founded in 1883 and it is one of the largest retailers in the world based on annual sales. Whole Food Markets claims to be the world's largest retailer of natural and organic foods. Whole Foods offers specialty products to customers with sufficient disposable income to spend on such goods.

The following data were taken from these companies' 2013 annual reports. All dollar amounts are in millions.

	Kroger Co. February 2, 2013	Whole Foods September 29, 2013
Sales	$96,751	$12,917
Cost of goods sold	76,858	8,288
Net income	1,508	551

Required

a. Before performing any calculations, speculate as to which company will have the highest gross margin and return on sales percentage. Explain the rationale for your decision.

b. Calculate the gross margin percentages for Kroger and Whole Foods Market.

c. Calculate the return on sales percentages for Kroger and Whole Foods Market.

d. Do the calculations from Requirements *b* and *c* confirm your speculations in Requirement *a*?

ATC 4-6 Written Assignment, Critical Thinking *Effect of sales returns on financial statements*

Bell Farm and Garden Equipment Co. reported the following information for 2016:

Net sales of equipment	$ 2,450,567
Other income	6,786
Cost of goods sold	(1,425,990)
Selling, general, and administrative expense	(325,965)
Depreciation and amortization	(3,987)
Net operating income	$ 701,411

Selected information from the balance sheet as of December 31, 2016, follows:

Cash and marketable securities	$113,545
Inventory	248,600
Accounts receivable	82,462
Property, plant, and equipment—net	335,890
Other assets	5,410
Total assets	$785,907

Assume that a major customer returned a large order to Bell on December 31, 2016. The amount of the sale had been $146,800 with a cost of sales of $94,623. The return was recorded in the books on January 1, 2017. The company president does not want to correct the books. He argues that it makes no difference as to whether the return is recorded in 2016 or 2017. Either way, the return has been duly recognized.

Required

a. Assume that you are the CFO for Bell Farm and Garden Equipment Co. Write a memo to the president explaining how omitting the entry on December 31, 2016, could cause the financial statements to be misleading to investors and creditors. Explain how omitting the return from the customer would affect net income and the balance sheet.

b. Why might the president want to record the return on January 1, 2017, instead of December 31, 2016?

c. Would the failure to record the customer return violate the AICPA Code of Professional Conduct? (See Exhibit 2.9 in Chapter 2.)

d. If the president of the company refuses to correct the financial statements, what action should you take?

ATC 4-7 Ethical Dilemma *Wait until I get mine*

Ada Fontanez is the president of a large company that owns a chain of athletic shoe stores. The company was in dire financial condition when she was hired three years ago. In an effort to motivate Fontanez, the board of directors included a bonus plan as part of her compensation package. According to her employment contract, on January 15 of each year, Fontanez is paid a cash bonus equal to 5 percent of the amount of net income reported on the preceding December 31 income statement. Fontanez was sufficiently motivated. Through her leadership, the company prospered. Her efforts were recognized throughout the industry, and she received numerous lucrative offers to leave the company. One offer was so enticing that she decided to change jobs. Her decision was made in late December 2016. However, she decided to resign effective February 1, 2017, to ensure the receipt of her January bonus. On December 31, 2016, the chief accountant, Walter Smith, advised Fontanez that the company had a sizable quantity of damaged inventory. A warehouse fire had resulted in smoke and water damage to approximately $600,000 of inventory. The warehouse was not insured, and the accountant recommended that the loss be recognized immediately. After examining the inventory, Fontanez argued that it could be sold as *damaged goods* to customers at reduced prices. Accordingly, she refused to allow the write-off the accountant recommended. She stated that so long as she is president, the inventory stays on the books at cost. She told the accountant that he could take up the matter with the new president in February.

Required

a. How would an immediate write-off of the damaged inventory affect the December 31, 2016, income statement, balance sheet, and statement of cash flows?

b. How would the write-off affect Fontanez's bonus?

c. If the new president is given the same bonus plan, how will Fontanez's refusal to recognize the loss affect his or her bonus?

d. Assuming that the damaged inventory is truly worthless, comment on the ethical implications of Fontanez's refusal to recognize the loss in the 2016 accounting period.

e. Assume that the damaged inventory is truly worthless and that you are Smith. How would you react to Fontanez's refusal to recognize the loss?

ATC 4-8 Research Assignment *Analyzing Alcoa's profit margins*

Using either Alcoa's most current Form 10-K or the company's annual report, answer the questions below. To obtain the Form 10-K you can use the EDGAR system, following the instructions in Appendix A, or it can be found on the company's website. The company's annual report is available on its website.

Required

a. What was Alcoa's gross margin percentage for the most current year?

b. What was Alcoa's gross margin percentage for the previous year? Has it changed significantly?

c. What was Alcoa's return on sales percentage for the most current year?

d. What percentage of Alcoa's total sales for the most current year was from operations in the United States?

e. Comment on the appropriateness of comparing Alcoa's gross margin with that of Microsoft. If Microsoft has a higher/lower margin, does that mean that Microsoft is a better managed company?

ATC 4-9 Spreadsheet Analysis *Using Excel*

The following accounts, balances, and other financial information are drawn from the records of Vong Company for the year 2016:

Net sales revenue	$18,800	Beginning common stock	$ 9,000
Unearned revenue	2,600	Land	8,000
Accounts receivable	6,000	Certificate of deposit	10,000
Cost of goods sold	6,000	Interest revenue	100
Inventory	5,000	Interest receivable	100
Accounts payable	5,800	Dividends	1,500
Notes payable	6,000	Beginning retained earnings	8,500
Interest expense	550	Cash from stock issued	3,000
Interest payable	550	Cash	7,200
Supplies	50	Gain on sale of land	1,050
Supplies expense	750	Loss on sale of property	50
Office equipment	3,500	Salaries expense	1,400
Depreciation expense	500	Salaries payable	400
Accumulated depreciation	1,000	Rent expense	1,100
Transportation-out expense	500	Prepaid rent	100
Miscellaneous operating expense	4,500		

The Cash account revealed the following cash flows:

Received cash from advances from customers	$ 2,600
Purchased office equipment	(3,500)
Received cash from issuing stock	3,000
Collected cash from accounts receivable	3,800
Purchased land	(8,000)
Received cash from borrowing funds	6,000
Paid cash for rent	(1,200)
Sold land	10,000
Paid cash for dividends	(1,500)
Paid cash for operating expenses	(1,000)
Purchased certificate of deposit	(10,000)

Required

Build an Excel spreadsheet to construct a multistep income statement, statement of changes in stockholders' equity, balance sheet, and statement of cash flows for the year 2016.

ATC 4-10 Spreadsheet Analysis *Mastering Excel*

At the end of 2016, the following information is available for Short and Wise Companies:

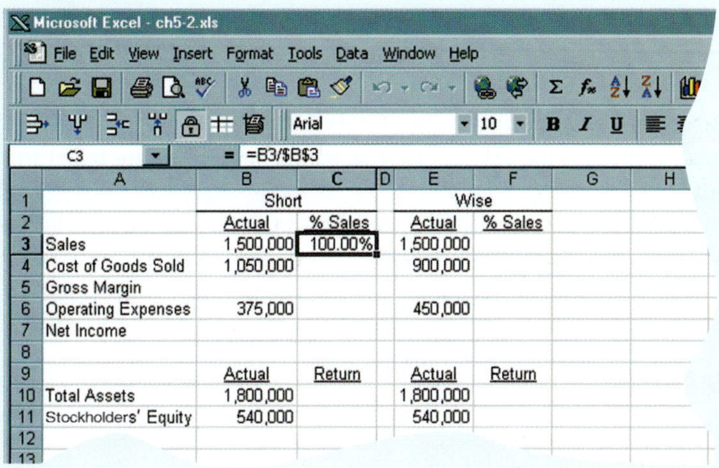

	A	B	C	D	E	F	G	H
1		Short			Wise			
2		Actual	% Sales		Actual	% Sales		
3	Sales	1,500,000	100.00%		1,500,000			
4	Cost of Goods Sold	1,050,000			900,000			
5	Gross Margin							
6	Operating Expenses	375,000			450,000			
7	Net Income							
8								
9		Actual	Return		Actual	Return		
10	Total Assets	1,800,000			1,800,000			
11	Stockholders' Equity	540,000			540,000			
12								
13								

Required

a. Set up the spreadsheet shown here. Complete the income statements by using Excel formulas.

b. Prepare a common size income statement for each company by completing the % Sales columns.

c. One company is a high-end retailer, and the other operates a discount store. Which is the discounter? Support your selection by referring to the common size statements.

d. Compute the return on assets and return on equity for each company.

e. Which company is more profitable from the stockholders' perspective?

f. Assume that a shortage of goods from suppliers is causing cost of goods sold to increase 10 percent for each company. Change the respective cost of goods sold balances in the Actual income statement column for each company. Note the new calculated amounts on the income statement and in the ratios. Which company's profits and returns are more sensitive to inventory price hikes?

COMPREHENSIVE PROBLEM

The trial balance of Pacilio Security Services Inc. as of January 1, 2014, had the following normal balances:

Cash	$12,500
Accounts Receivable	3,500
Supplies	120
Prepaid Rent	1,000
Land	4,000
Unearned Revenue	900
Salaries Payable	1,000
Common Stock	8,000
Retained Earnings	11,220

In 2014, Pacilio Security Services decided to expand its business to sell security systems and offer 24-hour alarm monitoring services. It plans to phase out its current service of providing security personnel at various events. The following summary transactions occurred during 2014.

1. Paid the salaries payable from 2013.
2. Acquired an additional $42,000 cash from the issue of common stock.
3. Rented a larger building on May 1; paid $6,000 for 12 months' rent in advance.
4. Paid $780 cash for supplies to be used over the next several months by the business.
5. Purchased 50 alarm systems for resale at a cost of $12,000. The alarm systems were purchased on account with the terms 2/10, n/30.
6. Returned one of the alarm systems that had a cost of $240.
7. Installed 40 alarm systems during the year for a total sales amount of $20,000. The cost of these systems amounted to $9,440. $15,000 of the sales were on account and $5,000 were cash sales.
8. Paid the installers and other employees a total of $9,500 in salaries.
9. Sold $36,000 of monitoring services for the year. The services are billed to the customers each month.
10. Paid cash on accounts payable. The payment was made before the discount period expired. At the time of purchase, the inventory had a cost of $7,920.
11. Paid cash to settle additional accounts payable. The payment was made after the discount period expired. At the time of purchase, the inventory had a cost of $2,880.
12. Collected $43,000 of accounts receivable during the year.
13. Performed $12,000 of security services for area events; $9,000 was on account and $3,000 was for cash.
14. Paid advertising cost of $1,620 for the year.

15. Paid $1,100 for utilities expense for the year.
16. Paid a dividend of $12,000 to the shareholders.

Adjustment Information

17. Supplies of $150 were on hand at the end of the year.
18. Recognized the expired rent for the year.
19. Recognized the balance of the unearned revenue; cash was received in 2013.
20. Accrued salaries at December 31, 2014, were $1,500.

Required

a. Record the above transactions in general journal form. (Round amounts to the nearest dollar.)
b. Post the transactions to T-accounts.
c. Prepare a trial balance.
d. Prepare an income statement, statement of changes in stockholders' equity, balance sheet, and statement of cash flows.
e. Close the temporary accounts to retained earnings.
f. Post the closing entries to the T-accounts and prepare a post-closing trial balance.

CHAPTER 5

Accounting for Inventories

LEARNING OBJECTIVES

After you have mastered the material in this chapter, you will be able to:

LO 5-1 Determine the amount of cost of goods sold and ending inventory using the specific identification, FIFO, LIFO, and weighted average cost flow methods.

LO 5-2 Apply the lower-of-cost-or-market rule to inventory valuation.

LO 5-3 Explain how fraud can be avoided through inventory control.

LO 5-4 Use the gross margin method to estimate ending inventory.

LO 5-5 Explain the importance of inventory turnover to a company's profitability.

Video lectures and accompanying self-assessment quizzes are available for all learning objectives through McGraw-Hill Connect® Plus Accounting.

CHAPTER OPENING

In the previous chapter we used the simplifying assumption that identical inventory items cost the same amount. In practice, businesses often pay different amounts for identical items. Suppose The Mountain Bike Company (TMBC) sells high-end Model 201 helmets. Since all Model 201 helmets are identical, does the helmet supplier charge TMBC the same amount for each helmet? Probably not. You have likely observed that prices change frequently.

Assume TMBC purchases one Model 201 helmet at a cost of $100. Two weeks later TMBC purchases a second Model 201 helmet. Because the supplier has raised prices, the second helmet costs $110. If TMBC sells one of its two helmets, should it record $100 or $110 as cost of goods sold? The following section of this chapter discusses several acceptable alternative methods for determining the amount of cost of goods sold from which companies may choose under generally accepted accounting principles.

The Curious Accountant

The Kroger Company is one of the world's largest retail chains, operating about 2,424 stores. As of February 2, 2013, the company reported approximately $5.1 billion of inventory on its balance sheet. In the notes to its financial statements, Kroger reported that it uses an inventory method that assumes its newest goods are sold first and its oldest goods are kept in inventory.

Can you think of any reason why a company selling perishable goods such as milk and vegetables would use an inventory method that assumes older goods are kept while newer goods are sold? (Answer on page 289.)

INVENTORY COST FLOW METHODS

LO 5-1

Determine the amount of cost of goods sold and ending inventory using the specific identification, FIFO, LIFO, and weighted average cost flow methods.

Recall that when goods are sold, product costs flow (are transferred) from the Inventory account to the Cost of Goods Sold account. Four acceptable methods for determining the amount of cost to transfer are (1) specific identification; (2) first-in, first-out (FIFO); (3) last-in, first-out (LIFO); and (4) weighted average.

Specific Identification

Suppose The Mountain Bike Company (TMBC) tags inventory items so that it can identify which one is sold at the time of sale. TMBC could then charge the actual cost of the specific item sold to cost of goods sold. Recall that the first inventory item TMBC purchased cost \$100 and the second item cost \$110. Using **specific identification,** cost of goods sold would be \$100 if the first item purchased was sold or \$110 if the second item purchased was sold.

When a company's inventory consists of many low-priced, high-turnover goods, the recordkeeping necessary to use specific identification isn't practical. Imagine the difficulty of recording the cost of each specific food item in a grocery store. Another disadvantage of the specific identification method is the opportunity for managers to manipulate the income statement. For example, TMBC can report a lower cost of goods sold by selling the first instead of the second item. Specific identification is, however, frequently used for high-priced, low-turnover inventory items such as automobiles. For big ticket items like cars, customer demands for specific products limit management's ability to select which merchandise is sold and volume is low enough to manage the recordkeeping.

First-In, First-Out (FIFO)

The **first-in, first-out (FIFO) cost flow method** requires that the cost of the items purchased *first* be assigned to cost of goods sold. Using FIFO, TMBC's cost of goods sold is \$100.

Last-In, First-Out (LIFO)

The **last-in, first-out (LIFO) cost flow method** requires that the cost of the items purchased *last* be charged to cost of goods sold. Using LIFO, TMBC's cost of goods sold is \$110.

Weighted Average

To use the **weighted-average cost flow method,** first calculate the average cost per unit by dividing the *total cost* of the inventory available by the *total number* of units available. In the case of TMBC, the average cost per unit of the inventory is \$105 [(\$100 + \$110) ÷ 2]. Cost of goods sold is then calculated by multiplying the average cost per unit by the number of units sold. Using weighted average, TMBC's cost of goods sold is \$105 (\$105 × 1).

Physical Flow

The preceding discussion pertains to the flow of *costs* through the accounting records, *not* the actual **physical flow of goods.** Goods usually move physically on a FIFO basis, which means that the first items of merchandise acquired by a company (first-in) are the first items sold to its customers (first-out). The inventory items on hand at the end of the accounting period are typically the last items in (the most recently acquired goods). If companies did not sell their oldest inventory items first, inventories would include dated, less marketable merchandise. *Cost flow,* however, can differ from *physical flow.* For example, a company may use LIFO or weighted average for financial reporting even if its goods flow physically on a FIFO basis.

Effect of Cost Flow on Financial Statements

Effect on Income Statement

The cost flow method a company uses can significantly affect the gross margin reported in the income statement. To demonstrate, assume that TMBC sold the inventory item discussed previously for $120. The amounts of gross margin using the FIFO, LIFO, and weighted-average cost flow assumptions are shown in the following table:

	FIFO	LIFO	Weighted Average
Sales	$120	$120	$120
Cost of goods sold	100	110	105
Gross margin	$ 20	$ 10	$ 15

Even though the physical flow is assumed to be identical for each method, the gross margin reported under FIFO is double the amount reported under LIFO. Companies experiencing identical economic events (same units of inventory purchased and sold) can report significantly different results in their financial statements. Meaningful financial analysis requires an understanding of financial reporting practices.

Effect on Balance Sheet

Since total product costs are allocated between costs of goods sold and ending inventory, the cost flow method a company uses affects its balance sheet as well as its income statement. Since FIFO transfers the first cost to the income statement, it leaves the last cost on the balance sheet. Similarly, by transferring the last cost to the income statement, LIFO leaves the first cost in ending inventory. The weighted-average method bases both cost of goods sold and ending inventory on the average cost per unit. To illustrate, the ending inventory TMBC would report on the balance sheet using each of the three cost flow methods is shown in the following table:

	FIFO	LIFO	Weighted Average
Ending inventory	$110	$100	$105

The FIFO, LIFO, and weighted-average methods are all used extensively in business practice. The same company may even use one cost flow method for some of its products and different cost flow methods for other products. Exhibit 5.1 illustrates the relative use of the different cost flow methods among U.S. companies.

EXHIBIT 5.1

Use of Inventory Cost Flow Methods

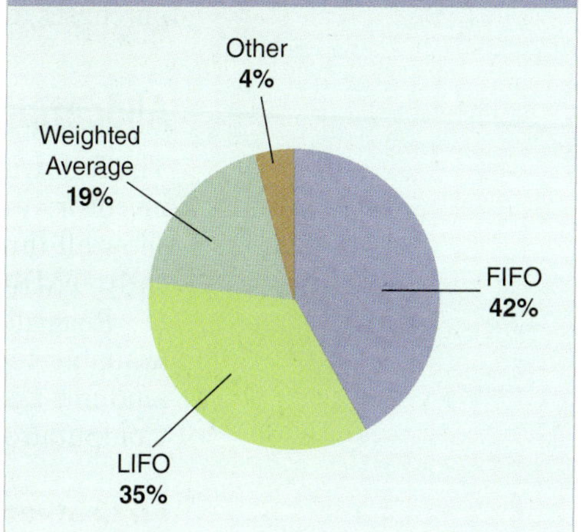

Data Source: AICPA, *Accounting Trends and Techniques.*

CHECK YOURSELF 5.1

Nash Office Supply (NOS) purchased two Model 303 copiers at different times. The first copier purchased cost $400 and the second copier purchased cost $450. NOS sold one of the copiers for $600. Determine the gross margin on the sale and the ending inventory balance assuming NOS accounts for inventory using (1) FIFO, (2) LIFO, and (3) weighted average.

Answer

	FIFO	LIFO	Weighted Average
Sales	$600	$600	$600
Cost of goods sold	(400)	(450)	(425)
Gross margin	$200	$150	$175
Ending inventory	$450	$400	$425

Multiple Layers with Multiple Quantities

The previous example illustrates different **inventory cost flow methods** using only two cost layers ($100 and $110) with only one unit of inventory in each layer. Actual business inventories are considerably more complex. Most real-world inventories are composed of multiple cost layers with different quantities of inventory in each layer. The underlying allocation concepts, however, remain unchanged.

For example, a different inventory item The Mountain Bike Company (TMBC) carries in its stores is a bike called the Eraser. TMBC's beginning inventory and two purchases of Eraser bikes are described below.

Jan. 1	Beginning inventory	10 units @ $200	=	$ 2,000
Mar. 18	First purchase	20 units @ $220	=	4,400
Aug. 21	Second purchase	25 units @ $250	=	6,250
Total cost of the 55 bikes available for sale				$12,650

The accounting records for the period show that TMBC paid cash for all Eraser bike purchases and sold 43 bikes at a cash price of $350 each.

Allocating Cost of Goods Available for Sale

The following discussion shows how to determine the cost of goods sold and ending inventory amounts using FIFO, LIFO, and weighted average cost flow methods. We show all three methods to demonstrate how they affect the financial statements differently; TMBC would actually use only one of the methods.

Regardless of the cost flow method chosen, TMBC must allocate the cost of goods available for sale ($12,650) between cost of goods sold and ending inventory. The amounts assigned to each category will differ depending on TMBC's cost flow method. Computations for each method are shown below.

FIFO Inventory Cost Flow

Recall that TMBC sold 43 Eraser bikes during the accounting period. The FIFO method transfers to the Cost of Goods Sold account the *cost of the first 43 bikes* TMBC had available to sell. The first 43 bikes acquired by TMBC were the 10 bikes in the beginning inventory (these were purchased in the prior period) plus the 20 bikes purchased in March and 13 of the bikes purchased in August. The expense recognized for the cost of these bikes ($9,650) is computed as follows:

Jan. 1	Beginning inventory	10 units @ $200	=	$2,000
Mar. 18	First purchase	20 units @ $220	=	4,400
Aug. 21	Second purchase	13 units @ $250	=	3,250
Total cost of the 43 bikes sold				$9,650

Since TMBC had 55 bikes available for sale it would have 12 bikes (55 available − 43 sold) in ending inventory. The cost assigned to these 12 bikes (the ending balance in the Inventory account) equals the cost of goods available for sale minus the cost of goods sold as shown below:

Cost of goods available for sale	$12,650
Cost of goods sold	9,650
Ending inventory balance	$ 3,000

We show the allocation of the cost of goods available for sale between cost of goods sold and ending inventory graphically below.

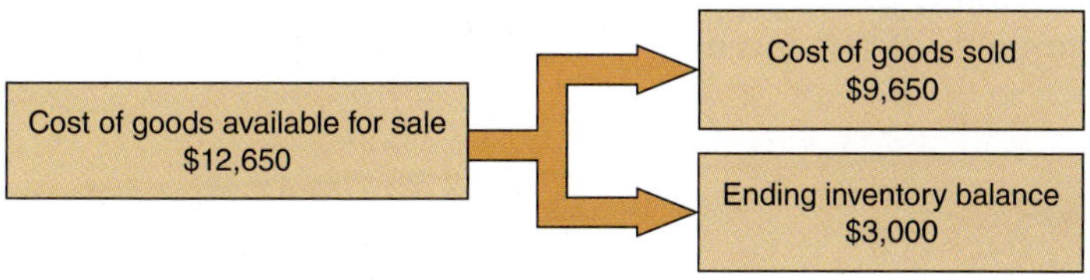

LIFO Inventory Cost Flow

Under LIFO, the cost of goods sold is the cost of the last 43 bikes acquired by TMBC, computed as follows:

Aug. 21	Second purchase	25 units @ $250	=	$ 6,250
Mar. 18	First purchase	18 units @ $220	=	3,960
Total cost of the 43 bikes sold				$10,210

The LIFO cost of the 12 bikes in ending inventory is computed as shown below:

Cost of goods available for sale	$12,650
Cost of goods sold	10,210
Ending inventory balance	$ 2,440

We show the allocation of the cost of goods available for sale between cost of goods sold and ending inventory graphically below.

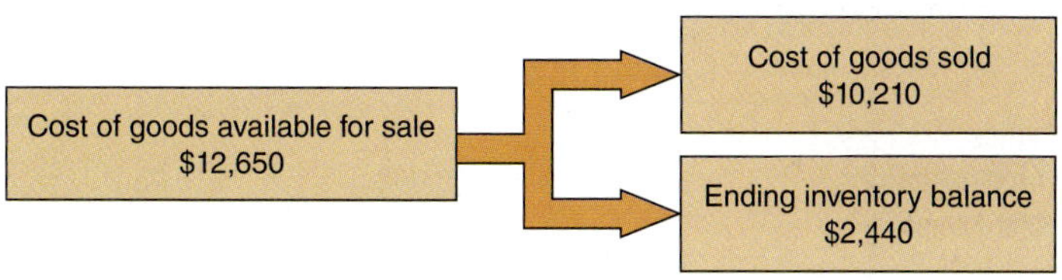

Weighted-Average Cost Flow

The weighted-average cost per unit is determined by dividing the *total cost of goods available for sale* by the *total number of units* available for sale. For TMBC, the weighted-average cost per unit is \$230 (\$12,650 ÷ 55). The weighted-average cost of goods sold is determined by multiplying the average cost per unit by the number of units sold (\$230 × 43 = \$9,890). The cost assigned to the 12 bikes in ending inventory is \$2,760 (12 × \$230).

We show the allocation of the cost of goods available for sale between cost of goods sold and ending inventory graphically below.

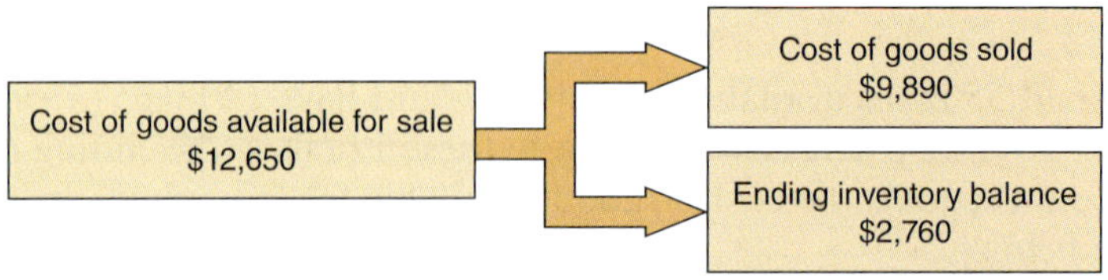

Effect of Cost Flow on Financial Statements

Exhibit 5.2 displays partial financial statements for The Mountain Bike Company (TMBC). This exhibit includes only information pertaining to the Eraser bikes inventory item described above. Other financial statement data are omitted.

Recall that assets are reported on the balance sheet in order of liquidity (how quickly they are expected to be converted to cash). Since companies frequently sell inventory on account, inventory is less liquid than accounts receivable. As a result, companies commonly report inventory below accounts receivable on the balance sheet.

EXHIBIT 5.2

TMBC COMPANY
Comparative Financial Statements

Partial Income Statements

	FIFO	LIFO	Weighted Average
Sales	\$15,050	\$ 15,050	\$15,050
Cost of goods sold	(9,650)	(10,210)	(9,890)
Gross margin	5,400	4,840	5,160

Partial Balance Sheets

	FIFO	LIFO	Weighted Average
Assets			
Cash	\$ XX	\$ XX	\$ XX
Accounts receivable	XX	XX	XX
Inventory	3,000	2,440	2,760

Partial Statements of Cash Flows

	FIFO	LIFO	Weighted Average
Operating Activities			
Cash inflow from customers	\$ 15,050	\$ 15,050	\$ 15,050
Cash outflow for inventory	(10,650)	(10,650)	(10,650)

Exhibit 5.2 demonstrates that the amounts reported for gross margin on the income statement and inventory on the balance sheet differ significantly. The cash flow from operating activities on the statement of cash flows, however, is identical under all three methods. Regardless of cost flow reporting method, TMBC paid $10,650 cash ($4,400 first purchase + $6,250 second purchase) to purchase inventory and received $15,050 cash for inventory sold.

The Impact of Income Tax

Based on the financial statement information in Exhibit 5.2, which cost flow method should TMBC use? Most people initially suggest FIFO because FIFO reports the highest gross margin and the largest balance in ending inventory. However, other factors are relevant. FIFO produces the highest gross margin; it also produces the highest net income and the highest income tax expense. In contrast, LIFO results in recognizing the lowest gross margin, lowest net income, and the lowest income tax expense.

Will investors favor a company with more assets and higher net income or one with lower tax expense? Recognize that specific identification, FIFO, LIFO, and weighted average are *different methods of reporting the same information.* TMBC experienced only one set of events pertaining to Eraser bikes. Exhibit 5.2 reports those same events three different ways. However, if the FIFO reporting method causes TMBC to pay more taxes than the LIFO method, using FIFO will cause a real reduction in the value of the company. Paying more money in taxes leaves less money in the company. Knowledgeable investors would be more attracted to TMBC if it uses LIFO because the lower tax payments allow the company to keep more value in the business.

Research suggests that, as a group, investors are knowledgeable. They make investment decisions based on economic substance regardless of how information is reported in financial statements.

The Income Statement versus the Tax Return

In some instances companies may use one accounting method for financial reporting and a different method to compute income taxes (the tax return must explain any differences). With respect to LIFO, however, the Internal Revenue Service requires that companies using LIFO for income tax purposes must also use LIFO for financial reporting. A company could not, therefore, get both the lower tax benefit provided by LIFO and the financial reporting advantage offered under FIFO.

Inflation versus Deflation

Our illustration assumes an inflationary environment (rising inventory prices). In a deflationary environment, the impact of using LIFO versus FIFO is reversed. LIFO produces tax advantages in an inflationary environment, while FIFO produces tax advantages in a deflationary environment. Companies operating in the computer industry—where prices are falling—would obtain a tax advantage by using FIFO. In contrast, companies that sell medical supplies in an inflationary environment would obtain a tax advantage by using LIFO.

Full Disclosure and Consistency

Generally accepted accounting principles allow each company to choose the inventory cost flow method best suited to its reporting needs. Because results can vary considerably among methods, however, the GAAP principle of **full disclosure** requires that financial statements disclose the method chosen. In addition, so that a company's financial statements are comparable from year to year, the GAAP principle of **consistency** generally requires that companies use the same cost flow method each period. The limited exceptions to the consistency principle are described in more advanced accounting courses.

CHECK YOURSELF 5.2

The following information was drawn from the inventory records of Fields, Inc.

Beginning inventory	200 units @ $20
First purchase	400 units @ $22
Second purchase	600 units @ $24

Assume that Fields sold 900 units of inventory.

1. Determine the amount of cost of goods sold using FIFO.
2. Would using LIFO produce a higher or lower amount of cost of goods sold? Why?

Answer

1. Cost of goods sold using FIFO

Beginning inventory	200 units @ $20	=	$ 4,000
First purchase	400 units @ $22	=	8,800
Second purchase	300 units @ $24	=	7,200
Total cost of goods sold			$20,000

2. The inventory records reflect an inflationary environment of steadily rising prices. Since LIFO charges the latest costs (in this case the highest costs) to the income statement, using LIFO (as opposed to FIFO) would produce a higher amount of cost of goods sold.

Inventory Cost Flow When Sales and Purchases Occur Intermittently

In the previous illustrations, all purchases were made before any goods were sold. This section addresses more realistic conditions, when sales transactions occur intermittently with purchases. Consider a third product The Mountain Bike Company (TMBC) carries in its inventory, an energy bar called NeverStop. NeverStop is sold at concession booths sponsored by TMBC at bike races. TMBC purchases and sells NeverStop in bulk boxes. It refers to each box as a unit of product. TMBC's beginning inventory, purchases, and sales of NeverStop for the period are described below.

Date	Transaction	Description
Jan. 1	Beginning inventory	100 units @ $20.00
Feb. 14	Purchased	200 units @ $21.50
Apr. 5	Sold	220 units @ $30.00
June 21	Purchased	160 units @ $22.50
Aug. 18	Sold	100 units @ $30.00
Sept. 2	Purchased	280 units @ $23.50
Nov. 10	Sold	330 units @ $30.00

FIFO Cost Flow

Exhibit 5.3 displays the computations for cost of goods sold and inventory if TMBC uses the FIFO cost flow method. The inventory records are maintained in layers. Each time a sales transaction occurs, the unit cost in the first layer of inventory is assigned to

EXHIBIT 5.3

Inventory Balance and Cost of Goods Sold using FIFO Cost Flow Method

		Inventory					Cost of Goods Sold
Date	**Description**	**Units**		**Cost**		**Total**	
Jan. 1	Beginning balance	100	@	$20.00	=	$2,000	
Feb. 14	Purchase	200	@	21.50	=	4,300	
Apr. 5	Sale of 220 units	(100)	@	20.00	=	(2,000)	
		(120)	@	21.50	=	(2,580)	$ 4,580
	Inventory balance after sale	80	@	21.50	=	1,720	
June 21	Purchase	160	@	22.50	=	3,600	
Aug. 18	Sale of 100 units	(80)	@	21.50	=	(1,720)	
		(20)	@	22.50	=	(450)	2,170
	Inventory balance after sale	140	@	22.50	=	3,150	
Sept. 2	Purchase	280	@	23.50	=	6,580	
Nov. 10	Sale of 330 units	(140)	@	22.50	=	(3,150)	
		(190)	@	23.50	=	(4,465)	7,615
	Ending inventory balance	90	@	23.50	=	$2,115	
	Total cost of goods sold						$14,365

the items sold. If the number of items sold exceeds the number of items in the first layer, the unit cost of the next layer is assigned to the remaining number of units sold, and so on. For example, the cost assigned to the 220 units of inventory sold on April 5 is determined as follows:

100 units of inventory in the first layer × $20.00 per unit	=	$2,000
+ 120 units of inventory in the second layer × $21.50 per unit	=	2,580
220 units for total cost of goods sold for the April 5 sale	=	$4,580

The cost of goods sold for subsequent sales transactions is similarly computed.

Using FIFO, and assuming a selling price of $30 per unit, gross margin for the period is computed as follows:

Sales (650 units @ $30 each)	$19,500
Cost of goods sold	14,365
Gross margin	$ 5,135

Weighted-Average and LIFO Cost Flows

When maintaining perpetual inventory records, using the weighted-average or LIFO cost flow methods leads to timing difficulties. For example, under LIFO, the cost of the *last* items purchased *during an accounting period* is the first amount transferred to cost of goods sold. When sales and purchases occur intermittently, the cost of the last items purchased isn't known at the time earlier sales occur. For example, when TMBC sold merchandise in April, it did not know what the replacement inventory purchased in September would cost.

Accountants can solve cost flow timing problems by keeping perpetual records of the quantities (number of units) of items purchased and sold separately from the related

FOCUS ON INTERNATIONAL ISSUES

LIFO IN OTHER COUNTRIES

This chapter introduced a rather strange inventory cost flow assumption called LIFO. As explained, the primary advantage of LIFO is to reduce a company's income taxes. Given the choice, companies that use LIFO to reduce their taxes would probably prefer to use another method when preparing their GAAP–based financial statements, but the IRS does not permit this. Thus, they are left with no choice but to use the seemingly counterintuitive LIFO assumption for financial reporting purposes in order to reap the benefits of LIFO in their income tax reporting.

What happens in countries other than the United States? International Financial Reporting Standards (IFRS) do not allow the use of LIFO. Most industrialized nations are now using IFRS. You can see the impact of this disparity if you review the annual report of a U.S. company that uses LIFO *and* has significant operations in other countries. Very often it will explain that LIFO is used to calculate inventory (and cost of goods sold) for domestic operations, but another method is used for activities outside the United States.

For example, here is an excerpt from General Electric's 2013 Form 10-K, Note 1.

> *All inventories are stated at the lower of cost or realizable values. Cost for a significant portion of GE U.S. inventories is determined on a last-in, first-out (LIFO) basis. Cost of other GE inventories is determined on a first-in, first-out (FIFO) basis. LIFO was used for 39% and 37% of GE inventories at December 31, 2013 and 2012, respectively.*

If the company has its headquarters in the United States, why not simply use LIFO in its foreign operations? In addition to having to prepare financial statements for the United States, the company probably has to prepare statements for its local operations using the reporting standards of the local country.

Prior to the establishment of IFRS, each country was responsible for issuing its own, local GAAP. Even then, most countries did not allow for the use of LIFO.

---

costs. Keeping records of quantities moving in and out of inventory, even though cost information is unavailable, provides many of the benefits of a perpetual inventory system. For example, management can determine the quantity of lost, damaged, or stolen goods and the point at which to reorder merchandise. At the end of the accounting period, when the cost of all inventory purchases is available, costs are assigned to the quantity data that have been maintained perpetually. Although further discussion of the weighted-average and LIFO cost flow methods is beyond the scope of this text, recognize that timing problems associated with intermittent sales are manageable.

LOWER-OF-COST-OR-MARKET RULE

LO 5-2

Apply the lower-of-cost-or-market rule to inventory valuation.

Regardless of whether a company uses FIFO, LIFO, weighted average, or specific identification, once the cost of ending inventory has been determined, generally accepted accounting principles require that the cost be compared with the end of period market value and that the inventory be reported at *lower of cost or market. Market* is defined as the amount the company would have to pay to *replace* the merchandise. If the replacement cost is less than the actual cost, regardless of whether the decline in market value is due to physical damage, deterioration, obsolescence, or a general price-level decline, the loss must be recognized in the current period.

The **lower-of-cost-or-market rule** can be applied to (1) each individual inventory item, (2) major classes or categories of inventory, or (3) the entire stock of inventory in the aggregate. The most common practice is the individualized application. To illustrate applying the rule to individual inventory items, assume that The Mountain Bike Company (TMBC) has in ending inventory 100 T-shirts it purchased at a cost of $14 each. If the year-end replacement cost of the shirts is above $14, TMBC will report the ending

REALITY BYTES

To avoid spoilage or obsolescence, most companies use a first-in, first-out (FIFO) approach for the flow of physical goods. The older goods (first units purchased) are sold before the newer goods are sold. For example, **Safeway** and other food stores stack older merchandise at the front of the shelf where customers are more likely to pick it up first. As a result, merchandise is sold before it becomes dated. However, when timing is not an issue, convenience may dictate the use of the last-in, first-out (LIFO) method. Examples of products that frequently move on a LIFO basis include rock, gravel, dirt, or other nonwasting assets. Indeed, rock, gravel, and dirt are normally stored in piles that are unprotected from weather. New inventory is simply piled on top of the old. Inventory that is sold is taken from the top of the pile because it is convenient to do so. Accordingly, the last inventory purchased is the first inventory sold. For example, **Vulcan Materials Co.**, which claims to be the nation's largest producer of construction aggregates (stone and gravel), uses LIFO. Regardless of whether the flow of physical goods occurs on a LIFO or FIFO basis, costs can flow differently. The flow of inventory through the physical facility is a separate issue from the flow of costs through the accounting system.

inventory at cost (100 × \$14 = \$1,400). However, if outsourcing permits the manufacturer to reduce the unit price of the shirts to \$11, then TMBC's replacement cost falls below the historical cost, and the inventory must be written down to \$1,100 (100 × \$11).

Exhibit 5.4 illustrates computing the ending inventory value on an item-by-item basis for a company that has four different inventory items. The company must write down the \$30,020 historical cost of its ending inventory to \$28,410. This \$1,610 write-down reduces the company's gross margin for the period. If the company keeps perpetual inventory records, the effect of the write-down and the journal entry to record it are as follows:

Assets	=	Liab.	+	Equity	Rev.	−	Exp.	=	Net Inc.	Cash Flow
(1,610)	=	NA	+	(1,610)	NA	−	1,610	=	(1,610)	NA

Account Title	Debit	Credit
Cost of Goods Sold (Inventory Loss)	1,610	
Inventory		1,610

EXHIBIT 5.4

Determination of Ending Inventory at Lower of Cost or Market

Item	Quantity (a)	Unit Cost (b)	Unit Market (c)	Total Cost (a × b)	Total Market (a × c)	Lower of Cost or Market
A	320	\$21.50	\$22.00	\$ 6,880	\$ 7,040	\$ 6,880
B	460	18.00	16.00	8,280	7,360	7,360
C	690	15.00	14.00	10,350	9,660	9,660
D	220	20.50	23.00	4,510	5,060	4,510
				\$30,020	\$29,120	\$28,410

FOCUS ON INTERNATIONAL ISSUES

THE LOWER-OF-COST-OR-MARKET RULE AND IFRS

Suppose a company has inventory with a historical cost of $1,000,000, the market value of which falls to $700,000. The company would have to write down the inventory and take a loss of $300,000. Now suppose that before the inventory was sold the market value recovered to $900,000. What would the company do? Nothing under U.S. GAAP; the inventory would remain on the books at $700,000 until it is sold or its market value declines further. However, under IFRS the inventory would be written up from $700,000 to $900,000 and a gain of $200,000 would be recognized.

Conceptually, the loss should be reported as an operating expense on the income statement. However, if the amount is immaterial, it can be included in cost of goods sold.

AVOIDING FRAUD IN MERCHANDISING BUSINESSES

LO 5-3

Explain how fraud can be avoided through inventory control.

For merchandising businesses, inventory is often the largest single asset reported on the balance sheet and cost of goods sold is normally the largest single expense reported on the income statement. For example, a recent income statement for Publix (a large grocery store chain) reported $28.9 billion of sales and approximately $20.9 billion of cost of goods sold, which means cost of goods sold for Publix was about 72 percent of revenue. In contrast, the next largest expense (operating and administrative expense) was approximately $5.9 billion, or 20 percent of revenue. While cost of goods sold represents only one expense account, the operating and administrative expense category actually combines many, perhaps hundreds, of individual expense accounts, such as depreciation, salaries, utilities, and so on. Because the inventory and cost of goods sold accounts are so significant, they are attractive targets for concealing fraud. For example, suppose a manager attempts to perpetrate a fraud by deliberately understating expenses. The understatement is less likely to be detected if it is hidden in the $20.9 billion Cost of Goods Sold account than if it is recorded in one of the smaller operating expense accounts.

Because the inventory and cost of goods sold accounts are susceptible to abuse, auditors and financial analysts carefully examine them for signs of fraud. Using tools to detect possible inventory misstatements requires understanding how overstatement or understatement of inventory affects the financial statements. To illustrate, assume that a company overstates its year-end inventory balance by $1,000. This inventory overstatement results in a $1,000 understatement of cost of goods sold, as shown in the following schedule:

	Ending Inventory Is Accurate	Ending Inventory Is Overstated	Effect
Beginning inventory	$ 4,000	$ 4,000	
Purchases	6,000	6,000	
Cost of goods available for sale	10,000	10,000	
Ending inventory	(3,000)	(4,000)	$1,000 Overstated
Cost of goods sold	$ 7,000	$ 6,000	$1,000 Understated

The understatement of cost of goods sold results in the overstatement of gross margin, which leads to an overstatement of net earnings, as indicated in the following income statement:

	Ending Inventory Is Accurate	Ending Inventory Is Overstated	Effect
Sales	$11,000	$11,000	
Cost of goods sold	(7,000)	(6,000)	$1,000 Understated
Gross margin	$ 4,000	$ 5,000	$1,000 Overstated

On the balance sheet, assets (inventory) and stockholders' equity (retained earnings) are overstated as follows:

	Ending Inventory Is Accurate	Ending Inventory Is Overstated	Effect
Assets			
Cash	$1,000	$ 1,000	
Inventory	3,000	4,000	$1,000 Overstated
Other assets	5,000	5,000	
Total assets	$9,000	$10,000	
Stockholders' equity			
Common stock	$5,000	$ 5,000	
Retained earnings	4,000	5,000	$1,000 Overstated
Total stockholders' equity	$9,000	$10,000	

Managers may be tempted to overstate the physical count of the ending inventory in order to report higher amounts of gross margin on the income statement and larger amounts of assets on the balance sheet. How can companies discourage managers from deliberately overstating the physical count of the ending inventory? The first line of defense is to assign the task of recording inventory transactions to different employees from those responsible for counting inventory.

Recall that under the perpetual system, increases and decreases in inventory are recorded at the time inventory is purchased and sold. If the records are maintained accurately, the balance in the inventory account should agree with the amount of physical inventory on hand. If a manager were to attempt to manipulate the financial statements by overstating the physical count of inventory, there would be a discrepancy between the accounting records and the physical count. In other words, a successful fraud requires controlling both the physical count and the recording process. If the counting and recording duties are performed by different individuals, fraud requires collusion, which reduces the likelihood of its occurrence. The separation of duties is an internal control procedure discussed further in the next chapter.

Because motives for fraud persist, even the most carefully managed companies cannot guarantee that no fraud will ever occur. As a result, auditors and financial analysts have developed tools to test for financial statement manipulation. The gross margin method of estimating the ending inventory balance is such a tool.

ESTIMATING THE ENDING INVENTORY BALANCE

LO 5-4

Use the gross margin method to estimate ending inventory.

The **gross margin method** assumes that the percentage of gross margin to sales remains relatively stable over time. To the extent that this assumption is accurate, the gross margin ratio from prior periods can be used to accurately estimate the current period's ending inventory. To illustrate, first review the information in Exhibit 5.5 which pertains to The T-Shirt Company.

The estimated cost of ending inventory can be computed as follows:

1. Calculate the expected gross margin ratio using financial statement data from prior periods. Accuracy may be improved by averaging gross margin and sales data over several accounting periods. For The T-Shirt Company, assume the average gross margin for the prior five years ÷ the average sales for the same five-year period = 25% expected gross margin ratio.
2. Multiply the expected gross margin ratio by the current period's sales ($22,000 × 0.25 = $5,500) to estimate the amount of gross margin.
3. Subtract the estimated gross margin from sales ($22,000 − $5,500 = $16,500) to estimate the amount of cost of goods sold.
4. Subtract the estimated cost of goods sold from the amount of goods available for sale ($23,600 − $16,500 = $7,100) to estimate the amount of ending inventory.

The estimated amount of ending inventory ($7,100) can be compared to the book balance and the physical count of inventory. If the book balance or the physical count is significantly higher than the estimated inventory balance, the analysis suggests the possibility of financial statement manipulation.

Other analytical comparisons are also useful. For example, the current year's gross margin ratio can be compared to last year's ratio. If cost of goods sold has been understated (ending inventory overstated), the gross margin ratio will be inflated. If this year's ratio is significantly higher than last year's, further analysis is required.

Although it may seem common because of the intense publicity generated when it occurs, fraud is the exception rather than the norm. In fact, growth in the inventory account balance usually results from natural business conditions. For example, a company that is adding new stores is expected to report growth in its inventory balance. Nevertheless, significant growth in inventory that is not explained by accompanying sales growth signals the need to analyze further for evidence of manipulation.

Since one year's ending inventory balance becomes the next year's beginning inventory balance, inaccuracies carry forward from one accounting period to the next. Persistent inventory overstatements result in an inventory account balance that spirals higher and higher. A fraudulently increasing inventory balance is likely to be discovered eventually.

EXHIBIT 5.5

THE T-SHIRT COMPANY
Schedule for Estimating the Ending Inventory Balance
For the Six Months Ending June 30, 2016

Beginning inventory	$ 5,100	
Purchases	18,500	
Cost of goods available for sale		$23,600
Sales through June 30, 2016	22,000	
Less: Estimated gross margin*	?	
Estimated cost of goods sold		?
Estimated ending inventory		$?

*Historically, gross margin has amounted to approximately 25 percent of sales.

Answers to The Curious Accountant

Even though **Kroger** uses the last-in, first-out *cost flow assumption* for financial reporting purposes, it, like most other companies, actually sells its oldest inventory first. As explained in the text material, GAAP allows a company to report its costs of goods sold in an order that is different from the actual physical flow of its goods. The primary reason some companies use the LIFO assumption is to reduce income taxes. Over the years, Kroger has saved approximately $379 million in taxes by using the LIFO versus the FIFO cost flow assumption when computing its taxable income.

To avoid detection, a manager who has previously overstated inventory will need to write the inventory back down in a subsequent accounting period. Therefore significant decreases, as well as increases, in the inventory balance or the gross margin ratio should be investigated. A manager may try to justify inventory write-downs by claiming that the inventory was lost, damaged, stolen, or had declined in value below historical cost. While there are valid reasons for writing down inventory, the possibility of fraud should be investigated.

CHECK YOURSELF 5.3

A physical count of Cantrell Inc.'s inventory revealed an ending balance of $6,020. The company's auditor decided to use the gross margin method to test the accuracy of the physical count. The accounting records indicate that the beginning inventory balance had been $20,000. During the period Cantrell had purchased $70,000 of inventory and had recognized $140,000 of sales revenue. Cantrell's gross margin percentage is normally 40 percent of sales. Develop an estimate of the amount of ending inventory and comment on the accuracy of the physical count.

Answer Goods available for sale is $90,000 ($20,000 beginning inventory + $70,000 purchases). Estimated cost of goods sold is $84,000 [$140,000 sales − ($140,000 × 0.40) gross margin]. Estimated ending inventory is $6,000 ($90,000 goods available for sale − $84,000 cost of goods sold). The difference between the physical count and the estimated balance ($6,020 − $6,000 = $20) is immaterial. Therefore the gross margin estimate is consistent with the physical count.

THE FINANCIAL ANALYST

LO 5-5

Explain the importance of inventory turnover to a company's profitability.

Assume a grocery store sells two brands of kitchen cleansers, Zjax and Cosmos. Zjax costs $1 and sells for $1.25, resulting in a gross margin of $0.25 ($1.25 − $1.00). Cosmos costs $1.20 and sells for $1.60, resulting in a gross margin of $0.40 ($1.60 − $1.20). Is it more profitable to stock Cosmos than Zjax? Not if the store can sell significantly more cans of Zjax.

Suppose the lower price results in higher customer demand for Zjax. If the store can sell 7,000 units of Zjax but only 3,000 units of Cosmos, Zjax will provide a total gross margin of $1,750 (7,000 units × $0.25 per unit), while Cosmos will provide only $1,200 (3,000 units × $0.40 per unit). How fast inventory sells is as important as the spread between cost and selling price. To determine how fast inventory is selling, financial analysts calculate a ratio that measures the *average number of days it takes to sell inventory.*

Average Number of Days to Sell Inventory

The first step in calculating the average number of days it takes to sell inventory is to compute the **inventory turnover,** as follows:

$$\frac{\text{Cost of goods sold}}{\text{Inventory}}$$

The result of this computation is the number of times the balance in the Inventory account is turned over (sold) each year. To more easily interpret the inventory turnover ratio, analysts often take a further step and determine the **average number of days to sell inventory** (also called the **average days in inventory**), computed as

$$\frac{365}{\text{Inventory turnover}}$$

Is It a Marketing or an Accounting Decision?

As suggested, overall profitability depends upon two elements: gross margin and inventory turnover. The most profitable combination would be to carry high margin inventory that turns over rapidly. To be competitive, however, companies must often concentrate on one or the other of the elements. For example, *discount merchandisers* such as Costco offer lower prices to stimulate greater sales. In contrast, fashionable stores such as Neiman Marcus charge higher prices to compensate for their slower inventory turnover. These upscale stores justify their higher prices by offering superior style, quality, convenience, service, etc. While decisions about pricing, advertising, service, and so on are often viewed as marketing decisions, effective choices require understanding the interaction between the gross margin percentage and inventory turnover.

Real-World Data

Exhibit 5.6 shows the *average number of days to sell inventory* for seven real-world companies in three different industries. The numbers pertain to the 2013 fiscal year. The data raise several questions.

First, why do D.R. Horton and Toll Brothers take so long to sell their inventories compared with the other companies? Both of these companies build and sell houses. It takes a lot longer to build a house than it does to make a hamburger. Furthermore, once a house is built it may take months to find a buyer. Finally, inventory of home builders includes the land on which the houses are constructed. A large subdivision may take several years to complete, but all of the land may have been purchased months, or even years, before the first house was started.

Why does Starbucks hold its inventory so much longer than the other two fast-food businesses? Starbucks's inventory is mostly coffee. It is more difficult for

EXHIBIT 5.6

Industry	Company	Average Number of Days to Sell Inventory
Fast Food	McDonald's	7
	Starbucks	32
	Yum! Brands	17
Department Stores	Macy's	117
	Walmart	45
Home Construction	D.R. Horton	433
	Toll Brothers	796

Starbucks to obtain coffee than it is for **McDonald's** to obtain beef or **Yum! Brands** to obtain flour, cheese, and fresh vegetables for its Pizza Hut pizza. Very little coffee is grown in the United States (Hawaii is the only state that produces coffee). Since purchasing coffee requires substantial delivery time, Starbucks cannot order its inventory at the last minute. This problem is further complicated by the fact that coffee harvests are seasonal. Cattle, on the other hand, can be processed into hamburgers year-round. As a result, Starbucks must hold inventory longer than McDonald's or Yum! Brands.

Why do department stores such as **Macy's** and **Walmart** take longer to sell inventory than McDonald's? Part of the answer is that food is perishable and clothing is not. But there is also the fact that department stores carry many more inventory items than do fast-food restaurants. It is much easier to anticipate customer demand if a company sells only 20 different items than if the company sells 20,000 different items. The problem of anticipating customer demand is solved by holding larger quantities of inventory.

Finally, notice that Walmart sells it merchandise in 45 days, while Macy's takes 117. This would seem to be an advantage for Walmart, but recall from Chapter 4 that in its 2013 fiscal year Walmart's gross margin percentage was 24.9 while Macy's was 40.3. Macy's higher gross margin percentage helps to make up for the additional time it takes to sell merchandise. Different companies use different business strategies to achieve their objectives. In the end, Macy's return on sales percentage, at 4.8 percent, was higher than Walmart's, which was 3.8 percent.

Effects of Cost Flow on Ratio Analysis

Since the amounts of ending inventory and cost of goods sold are affected by the cost flow method (FIFO, LIFO, etc.) a company uses, the gross margin and inventory turnover ratios are also affected by the cost flow method used. Further, since cost of goods sold affects the amount of net income and retained earnings, many other ratios are also affected by the inventory cost flow method that a company uses. Financial analysts must consider that the ratios they use can be significantly influenced by which accounting methods a company chooses.

A Look Back <<

This chapter discussed the specific identification, first-in, first-out (FIFO), last-in, first-out (LIFO), and weighted average inventory cost flow methods. Under *specific identification*, the actual cost of the goods is reported on the income statement and the balance sheet. Under *FIFO,* the cost of the items purchased first is reported on the income statement, and the cost of the items purchased last is reported on the balance sheet. Under *LIFO,* the cost of the items purchased last is reported on the income statement, and the cost of the items purchased first is reported on the balance sheet. Finally, under the *weighted-average method,* the average cost of inventory is reported on both the income statement and the balance sheet.

Generally accepted accounting principles often allow companies to account for the same types of events in different ways. The different cost flow methods presented in this chapter—FIFO, LIFO, weighted average, and specific identification—are examples of alternative accounting procedures allowed by GAAP. Financial analysts must be aware that financial statement amounts are affected by the accounting methods that a company uses as well as the economic activity it experiences.

This chapter also explained how to calculate the time it takes a company to sell its inventory. The measure of how fast inventory sells is called *inventory turnover;* it is computed by dividing cost of goods sold by inventory. The result of this computation is the number of times the balance in the inventory account is turned over each year. The *average number of days to sell inventory* can be determined by dividing the number of days in a year (365) by the inventory turnover ratio.

>> A Look Forward

Chapter 6 examines accounting for cash and the system of internal controls. Internal controls are the accounting practices and procedures that companies use to protect assets and ensure that transactions are recorded accurately. You will learn that companies account for small disbursements of cash, called *petty cash disbursements,* differently than they do for large disbursements. You will also learn how to prepare a formal bank reconciliation.

SELF-STUDY REVIEW PROBLEM

A step-by-step audio-narrated series of slides is available in the Connect library.

Erie Jewelers sells gold earrings. Its beginning inventory of Model 407 gold earrings consisted of 100 pairs of earrings at $50 per pair. Erie purchased two batches of Model 407 earrings during the year. The first batch purchased consisted of 150 pairs at $53 per pair; the second batch consisted of 200 pairs at $56 per pair. During the year, Erie sold 375 pairs of Model 407 earrings.

Required

Determine the amount of product cost Erie would allocate to cost of goods sold and ending inventory assuming that Erie uses (a) FIFO, (b) LIFO, and (c) weighted average.

Solution to Requirements a–c

Goods Available for Sale					
Beginning inventory	100	@	$50	=	$ 5,000
First purchase	150	@	53	=	7,950
Second purchase	200	@	56	=	11,200
Goods available for sale	450				$24,150

a. FIFO

Cost of Goods Sold	Pairs		Cost per Pair		Cost of Goods Sold
From beginning inventory	100	@	$50	=	$ 5,000
From first purchase	150	@	53	=	7,950
From second purchase	125	@	56	=	7,000
Total pairs sold	375				$19,950

Ending inventory = Goods available for sale − Cost of goods sold
Ending inventory = $24,150 − $19,950 = $4,200

b. LIFO

Cost of Goods Sold	Pairs		Cost per Pair		Cost of Goods Sold
From second purchase	200	@	$56	=	$11,200
From first purchase	150	@	53	=	7,950
From beginning inventory	25	@	50	=	1,250
Total pairs sold	375				$20,400

Ending inventory = Goods available for sale − Cost of goods sold
Ending inventory = $24,150 − $20,400 = $3,750

c. Weighted average

Goods available for sale ÷ Total pairs = Cost per pair
$24,150 ÷ 450 = $53.6667
Cost of goods sold 375 units @ $53.6667 = $20,125
Ending inventory 75 units @ $53.6667 = $4,025

KEY TERMS

Average number of days to sell inventory (or average days in inventory) 290
Consistency 281
First-in, first-out (FIFO) cost flow method 276
Full disclosure 281
Gross margin method 287
Inventory cost flow methods 278
Inventory turnover 290
Last-in, first-out (LIFO) cost flow method 276
Lower-of-cost-or-market rule 284
Physical flow of goods 276
Specific identification 276
Weighted-average cost flow method 276

QUESTIONS

1. Name and describe the four cost flow methods discussed in this chapter.
2. What are some advantages and disadvantages of the specific identification method of accounting for inventory?
3. What are some advantages and disadvantages of using the FIFO method of inventory valuation?
4. What are some advantages and disadvantages of using the LIFO method of inventory valuation?
5. In an inflationary period, which inventory cost flow method will produce the highest net income? Explain.
6. In an inflationary period, which inventory cost flow method will produce the largest amount of total assets on the balance sheet? Explain.
7. What is the difference between the flow of costs and the physical flow of goods?
8. Does the choice of cost flow method (FIFO, LIFO, or weighted average) affect the statement of cash flows? Explain.
9. Assume that Key Co. purchased 1,000 units of merchandise in its first year of operations for $25 per unit. The company sold 850 units for $40. What is the amount of cost of goods sold using FIFO? LIFO? Weighted average?
10. Assume that Key Co. purchased 1,500 units of merchandise in its second year of operation for $27 per unit. Its beginning inventory was determined in Question 9. Assuming that 1,500 units are sold, what is the amount of cost of goods sold using FIFO? LIFO? Weighted average?
11. Refer to Questions 9 and 10. Which method might be preferable for financial statements? For income tax reporting? Explain.
12. In an inflationary period, which cost flow method, FIFO or LIFO, produces the larger cash flow? Explain.
13. Which inventory cost flow method produces the highest net income in a deflationary period?
14. How does the phrase *lower-of-cost-or-market* apply to inventory valuation?
15. If some merchandise declines in value because of damage or obsolescence, what effect will the lower-of-cost-or-market rule have on the income statement? Explain.

16. What is a situation in which estimates of the amount of inventory may be useful or even necessary?
17. How can management manipulate net income using inventory fraud?
18. If the amount of goods available for sale is $123,000, the amount of sales is $130,000, and the gross margin is 25 percent of sales, what is the amount of ending inventory?
19. Assume that inventory is overstated by $1,500 at the end of 2016 but is corrected in 2017. What effect will this have on the 2016 income statement? The 2016 balance sheet? The 2017 income statement? The 2017 balance sheet?
20. What information does inventory turnover provide?
21. What is an example of a business that would have a high inventory turnover? A low inventory turnover?

MULTIPLE-CHOICE QUESTIONS

Multiple-choice questions are available in the Connect library.

EXERCISES—SERIES A

connect plus+ ACCOUNTING ***All applicable Exercises in Series A are available with McGraw-Hill's Connect Plus Accounting.***

LO 5-1

Exercise 5-1A *Effect of inventory cost flow assumption on financial statements*

Required

For each of the following situations, indicate whether FIFO, LIFO, or weighted average applies:

a. In a period of falling prices, net income would be highest.
b. In a period of falling prices, the unit cost of goods would be the same for ending inventory and cost of goods sold.
c. In a period of rising prices, net income would be highest.
d. In a period of rising prices, cost of goods sold would be highest.
e. In a period of rising prices, ending inventory would be highest.

LO 5-1

Exercise 5-2A *Allocating product cost between cost of goods sold and ending inventory*

Jones Co. started the year with no inventory. During the year, it purchased two identical inventory items at different times. The first purchase cost $1,060 and the other, $1,380. Jones sold one of the items during the year.

Required

Based on this information, how much product cost would be allocated to cost of goods sold and ending inventory on the year-end financial statements, assuming use of

a. FIFO?
b. LIFO?
c. Weighted average?

LO 5-1

Exercise 5-3A *Allocating product cost between cost of goods sold and ending inventory: multiple purchases*

Cortez Company sells chairs that are used at computer stations. Its beginning inventory of chairs was 100 units at $60 per unit. During the year, Cortez made two batch purchases of this chair. The first was a 150-unit purchase at $68 per unit; the second was a 200-unit purchase at $72 per unit. During the period, it sold 270 chairs.

Required

Determine the amount of product costs that would be allocated to cost of goods sold and ending inventory, assuming that Cortez uses

a. FIFO.
b. LIFO.
c. Weighted average.

Exercise 5-4A *Effect of inventory cost flow (FIFO, LIFO, and weighted average) on gross margin*

LO 5-1

The following information pertains to Mason Company for 2016:

Beginning inventory	90 units @ $40
Units purchased	310 units @ $45

Ending inventory consisted of 30 units. Mason sold 370 units at $90 each. All purchases and sales were made with cash. Operating expenses amounted to $4,100.

Required

a. Compute the gross margin for Mason Company using the following cost flow assumptions: (1) FIFO, (2) LIFO, and (3) weighted average.

b. What is the amount of net income using FIFO, LIFO, and weighted average? (Ignore income tax considerations.)

c. Compute the amount of ending inventory using (1) FIFO, (2) LIFO, and (3) weighted average.

Exercise 5-5A *Effect of inventory cost flow on ending inventory balance and gross margin*

LO 5-1

The Shirt Shop had the following transactions for T-shirts for 2016, its first year of operations:

Jan. 20	Purchased 400 units @ $ 8	=	$3,200
Apr. 21	Purchased 200 units @ $10	=	2,000
July 25	Purchased 280 units @ $13	=	3,640
Sept. 19	Purchased 90 units @ $15	=	1,350

During the year, The Shirt Shop sold 810 T-shirts for $30 each.

Required

a. Compute the amount of ending inventory The Shirt Shop would report on the balance sheet, assuming the following cost flow assumptions: (1) FIFO, (2) LIFO, and (3) weighted average.

b. Record the above transactions in general journal form and post to T-accounts assuming (1) FIFO, (2) LIFO, and (3) weighted average methods. Use a separate set of journal entries and T-accounts for each method. Assume all transactions are cash transactions.

c. Compute the difference in gross margin between the FIFO and LIFO cost flow assumptions.

Exercise 5-6A *Income tax effect of shifting from FIFO to LIFO*

LO 5-1

The following information pertains to the inventory of Parvin Company:

Jan. 1	Beginning inventory	400 units @ $30
Apr. 1	Purchased	2,000 units @ $35
Oct. 1	Purchased	600 units @ $38

During 2016, Parvin sold 2,700 units of inventory at $90 per unit and incurred $41,500 of operating expenses. Parvin currently uses the FIFO method but is considering a change to LIFO. All transactions are cash transactions. Assume a 30 percent income tax rate. Parvin started the period with cash of $75,000, inventory of $12,000, common stock of $50,000, and retained earnings of $37,000.

Required

a. Record the above transactions in general journal form and post to T-accounts using (1) FIFO and (2) LIFO. Use a separate set of journal entries and T-accounts for each method.

b. Prepare income statements using FIFO and LIFO.

c. Determine the amount of income tax that Parvin would pay using each cost flow method.

d. Determine the cash flow from operating activities under FIFO and LIFO.

e. Why is the cash flow from operating activities different under FIFO and LIFO?

LO 5-1

Exercise 5-7A *Effect of FIFO versus LIFO on income tax expense*

The Brick Company had cash sales of $280,000 for 2016, its first year of operation. On April 2, the company purchased 210 units of inventory at $390 per unit. On September 1, an additional 160 units were purchased for $425 per unit. The company had 110 units on hand at the end of the year. The company's income tax rate is 40 percent. All transactions are cash transactions.

Required

a. The preceding paragraph describes five accounting events: (1) a sales transaction, (2) the first purchase of inventory, (3) a second purchase of inventory, (4) the recognition of cost of goods sold expense, and (5) the payment of income tax expense. Record the amounts of each event in horizontal statements models like the following ones, assuming first a FIFO and then a LIFO cost flow.

Effect of Events on Financial Statements

Panel 1: FIFO Cost Flow

Event No.	Balance Sheet					Income Statement					Statement of Cash Flows
	Cash	+	Inventory	=	Ret. Earn.	Rev.	−	Exp.	=	Net Inc.	

Panel 2: LIFO Cost Flow

Event No.	Balance Sheet					Income Statement					Statement of Cash Flows
	Cash	+	Inventory	=	Ret. Earn.	Rev.	−	Exp.	=	Net Inc.	

b. Compute net income using FIFO.

c. Compute net income using LIFO.

d. Explain the difference, if any, in the amount of income tax expense incurred using the two cost flow assumptions.

e. Which method, FIFO or LIFO, produced the larger amount of assets on the balance sheet?

LO 5-1

Exercise 5-8A *Recording inventory transactions using the perpetual method: intermittent sales and purchases*

The following inventory transactions apply to Green Company for 2016:

Jan. 1	Purchased	260 units @ $50
Apr. 1	Sold	130 units @ $85
Aug. 1	Purchased	390 units @ $56
Dec. 1	Sold	490 units @ $96

The beginning inventory consisted of 180 units at $48 per unit. All transactions are cash transactions.

Required

a. Record these transactions in general journal format assuming Green uses the FIFO cost flow assumption and keeps perpetual records.

b. Compute cost of goods sold for 2016.

Exercise 5-9A *Effect of cost flow on ending inventory: intermittent sales and purchases*

LO 5-1

The Hat Store had the following series of transactions for 2016:

Date	Transaction	Description
Jan. 1	Beginning inventory	50 units @ $40
Mar. 15	Purchased	200 units @ $42
May 30	Sold	170 units @ $95
Aug. 10	Purchased	275 units @ $46
Nov. 20	Sold	340 units @ $96

Required

a. Determine the quantity and dollar amount of inventory at the end of the year, assuming The Hat Store uses the FIFO cost flow assumption and keeps perpetual records.

b. Write a memo explaining why The Hat Store would have difficulty applying the weighted-average method on a perpetual basis.

Exercise 5-10A *Lower-of-cost-or-market rule: perpetual system*

LO 5-2

The following information pertains to Hagen Metal Work's ending inventory for the current year:

Item	Quantity	Unit Cost	Unit Market Value
C	90	$24	$16
D	75	22	20
K	40	25	28
M	22	15	17

Required

a. Determine the value of the ending inventory using the lower-of-cost-or-market rule applied to (1) each individual inventory item and (2) the inventory in aggregate.

b. Prepare any necessary journal entries, assuming the decline in value is immaterial. Hagen Metal Works uses the perpetual inventory system. (Make entries for both methods.)

Exercise 5-11A *Lower-of-cost-or-market rule*

LO 5-2

Brooks Company carries three inventory items. The following information pertains to the ending inventory:

Item	Quantity	Unit Cost	Unit Market Value
A	120	$60	$55
F	170	80	75
K	110	30	40

Required

a. Determine the ending inventory that Brooks will report on the balance sheet, assuming that it applies the lower-of-cost-or-market rule to individual inventory items.

b. Prepare the necessary journal entry, assuming the decline in value was immaterial.

Exercise 5-12A *Estimating ending inventory*

LO 5-3, 5-4

A substantial portion of inventory owned by Prentiss Sporting Goods was recently destroyed when the roof collapsed during a rainstorm. Prentiss also lost some of its accounting records. Prentiss must estimate the loss from the storm for insurance reporting and financial statement purposes. Prentiss uses the periodic inventory system. The following accounting information was recovered from the damaged records:

Beginning inventory	$ 60,000
Purchases to date of storm	190,000
Sales to date of storm	250,000

The value of undamaged inventory counted was $3,600. Historically Prentiss's gross margin percentage has been approximately 25 percent of sales.

Required

Estimate the following:

a. Gross margin in dollars.
b. Cost of goods sold.
c. Ending inventory.
d. Amount of lost inventory.

LO 5-3, 5-4

Exercise 5-13A *Estimating ending inventory: perpetual system*

Brad Essary owned a small company that sold garden equipment. The equipment was expensive, and a perpetual system was maintained for control purposes. Even so, lost, damaged, and stolen merchandise normally amounted to 5 percent of the inventory balance. On June 14, Essary's warehouse was destroyed by fire. Just prior to the fire, the accounting records contained a $280,000 balance in the Inventory account. However, inventory costing $42,000 had been sold and delivered to customers but had not been recorded in the books at the time of the fire. The fire did not affect the showroom, which contained inventory that cost $58,000.

Required

Estimate the amount of inventory destroyed by fire.

LO 5-3

Exercise 5-14A *Effect of inventory error on financial statements: perpetual system*

Stubbs Company failed to count $55,000 of inventory in its 2016 year-end physical count.

Required

Write a memo explaining how Stubbs Company's balance sheet will be affected in 2016. Assume Stubbs uses the perpetual inventory system.

LO 5-3

Exercise 5-15A *Effect of inventory error on elements of financial statements*

The ending inventory for Carver Co. was incorrectly adjusted, which caused it to be understated by $15,300 for 2016.

Required

Was each of the following amounts overstated, understated, or not affected by the error?

Item No.	Year	Amount
1	2016	Beginning inventory
2	2016	Purchases
3	2016	Goods available for sale
4	2016	Cost of goods sold
5	2016	Gross margin
6	2016	Net income
7	2017	Beginning inventory
8	2017	Purchases
9	2017	Goods available for sale
10	2017	Cost of goods sold
11	2017	Gross margin
12	2017	Net income

Exercise 5-16A *Explaining multiple inventory methods at one real-world company*

LO 5-1, IFRS

The following note related to accounting for inventory was taken from the 2013 annual report of Alcoa, Inc.:

> **Inventory Valuation** Inventories are carried at the lower of cost or market, with cost for a substantial portion of U.S. and Canadian inventories determined under the last-in, first-out (LIFO) method. The cost of other inventories is principally determined under the average-cost method.

Required

Write a brief report explaining the reason or reasons that best explain why Alcoa uses the LIFO cost flow method for its inventories kept in the United States and Canada, but the average cost method for its other inventories.

Exercise 5-17A *GAAP versus IFRS*

IFRS

Generally accepted accounting principles (GAAP) and International Financial Reporting Standards (IFRS) treat the LIFO inventory cost flow method differently.

Required

a. Briefly describe the position GAAP takes with respect to LIFO.

b. Briefly describe the position IFRS takes with respect to LIFO.

c. Explain the primary force that motivates the different positions.

PROBLEMS—SERIES A

Problem 5-18A *Effect of different inventory cost flow methods on financial statements*

LO 5-1

CHECK FIGURES

a. Cost of Goods Sold FIFO: $62,650

b. Net Income LIFO: $22,012

The accounting records of Wall's China Shop reflected the following balances as of January 1, 2016:

Cash	$80,100
Beginning inventory	33,000 (220 units @ $150)
Common stock	50,000
Retained earnings	63,100

The following five transactions occurred in 2016:

1. First purchase (cash) 150 units @ $155
2. Second purchase (cash) 160 units @ $160
3. Sales (all cash) 410 units @ $320
4. Paid $38,000 cash for salaries expense.
5. Paid cash for income tax at the rate of 25 percent of income before taxes.

Required

a. Compute the cost of goods sold and ending inventory, assuming (1) FIFO cost flow, (2) LIFO cost flow, and (3) weighted-average cost flow. Compute the income tax expense for each method.

b. Record the five transactions in general journal form and post to T-accounts assuming (1) FIFO cost flow, (2) LIFO cost flow, and (3) weighted-average cost flow.

c. Use a vertical model to show the 2016 income statement, balance sheet, and statement of cash flows under FIFO, LIFO, and weighted average. (*Hint:* Record the events under an accounting equation before preparing the statements.)

LO 5-1

CHECK FIGURES
b. Cost of Goods Sold: $49,250
c. Ending Inventory: $17,550

Problem 5-19A *Allocating product costs between cost of goods sold and ending inventory: intermittent purchases and sales of merchandise*

Pam's Creations had the following sales and purchase transactions during 2016. Beginning inventory consisted of 60 items at $350 each. The company uses the FIFO cost flow assumption and keeps perpetual inventory records.

Date	Transaction	Description
Mar. 5	Purchased	50 items @ $370
Apr. 10	Sold	30 items @ $450
June 19	Sold	60 items @ $450
Sept. 16	Purchased	70 items @ $390
Nov. 28	Sold	45 items @ $480

Required

a. Record the inventory transactions in general journal format.

b. Calculate the gross margin Pam's Creations would report on the 2016 income statement.

c. Determine the ending inventory balance Pam's Creations would report on the December 31, 2016, balance sheet.

LO 5-2

CHECK FIGURES
a. $26,250
b. $26,980

Problem 5-20A *Inventory valuation based on the lower-of-cost-or-market rule*

At the end of the year, Randy's Parts Co. had the following items in inventory:

Item	Quantity	Unit Cost	Unit Market Value
P1	60	$ 85	$ 90
P2	40	70	72
P3	80	130	120
P4	70	125	130

Required

a. Determine the amount of ending inventory using the lower-of-cost-or-market rule applied to each individual inventory item.

b. Provide the general journal entry necessary to write down the inventory based on Requirement *a.* Assume that Randy's Parts Co. uses the perpetual inventory system.

c. Determine the amount of ending inventory, assuming that the lower-of-cost-or-market rule is applied to the total inventory in aggregate.

d. Provide the general journal entry necessary to write down the inventory based on Requirement *c.* Assume that Randy's Parts Co. uses the perpetual inventory system.

e. Explain how the inventory loss would be reported when the periodic inventory system is used.

LO 5-4

CHECK FIGURES
a. Gross Margin: $330,000
b. Total Inventory Loss: $25,000

Problem 5-21A *Estimating ending inventory: gross margin method*

The inventory of Don's Grocery was destroyed by a tornado on October 6 of the current year. Fortunately, some of the accounting records were at the home of one of the owners and were not damaged. The following information was available for the period of January 1 through October 6:

Beginning inventory, January 1	$ 140,000
Purchases through October 6	670,000
Sales through October 6	1,100,000

Gross margin for Don's has traditionally been 30 percent of sales.

Required

a. For the period ending October 6, compute the following:
   (1) Estimated gross margin.
   (2) Estimated cost of goods sold.
   (3) Estimated inventory at October 6.

b. Assume that $15,000 of the inventory was not damaged. What is the amount of the loss from the tornado?

c. If Don's had used the perpetual inventory system, how would it have determined the amount of the inventory loss?

Problem 5-22A *Estimating ending inventory: gross margin method*

LO 5-4

Toyland wishes to produce quarterly financial statements, but it takes a physical count of inventory only at year-end. The following historical data were taken from the 2016 and 2017 accounting records:

CHECK FIGURE
b. Estimated ending inventory: $19,200

	2016	2017
Net sales	$150,000	$190,000
Cost of goods sold	76,000	89,200

At the end of the first quarter of 2018, Toyland's ledger had the following account balances:

Sales	$210,000
Purchases	90,000
Beginning inventory 1/1/2018	32,100
Ending inventory 3/31/2018	16,000

Based on purchases and sales, the Toyland accountant thinks inventory is low.

Required

Using the information provided, estimate the following for the first quarter of 2018:

a. Cost of goods sold. (Use the average cost of goods sold percentage.)

b. Ending inventory at March 31.

c. What could explain the difference between actual and estimated inventory?

Problem 5-23A *Effect of inventory errors on financial statements*

LO 5-3

The following income statement was prepared for Frame Supplies for the year 2016:

FRAME SUPPLIES Income Statement For the Year Ended December 31, 2016	
Sales	$ 250,000
Cost of goods sold	(140,000)
Gross margin	110,000
Operating expenses	(69,500)
Net income	$ 40,500

During the year-end audit, the following errors were discovered:

1. A $2,500 payment for repairs was erroneously charged to the Cost of Goods Sold account. (Assume that the perpetual inventory system is used.)
2. Sales to customers for $1,800 at December 31, 2016, were not recorded in the books for 2016. Also, the $980 cost of goods sold was not recorded.
3. A mathematical error was made in determining ending inventory. Ending inventory was understated by $2,150. (The Inventory account was mistakenly written down to the Cost of Goods Sold account.)

Required

Determine the effect, if any, of each of the errors on the following items. Give the dollar amount of the effect and whether it would overstate (O), understate (U), or not affect (NA) the account. The first item for each error is recorded as an example.

Error No. 1	Amount of Error	Effect
Sales, 2016	NA	NA
Ending inventory, December 31, 2016		
Gross margin, 2016		
Beginning inventory, January 1, 2017		
Cost of goods sold, 2016		
Net income, 2016		
Retained earnings, December 31, 2016		
Total assets, December 31, 2016		
Error No. 2	**Amount of Error**	**Effect**
Sales, 2016	$1,800	U
Ending inventory, December 31, 2016		
Gross margin, 2016		
Beginning inventory, January 1, 2017		
Cost of goods sold, 2016		
Net income, 2016		
Retained earnings, December 31, 2016		
Total assets, December 31, 2016		
Error No. 3	**Amount of Error**	**Effect**
Sales, 2016	NA	NA
Ending inventory, December 31, 2016		
Gross margin, 2016		
Beginning inventory, January 1, 2017		
Cost of goods sold, 2016		
Net income, 2016		
Retained earnings, December 31, 2016		
Total assets, December 31, 2016		

LO 5-5

Problem 5-24A *Using ratios to make comparisons*

The following accounting information pertains to Phoenix Co. and Roswell Co. companies at the end of 2017. The only difference between the two companies is that Phoenix Co. uses FIFO while Roswell Co. uses LIFO.

	Phoenix Co.	Roswell Co.
Cash	$ 96,000	$ 96,000
Accounts receivable	385,000	385,000
Merchandise Inventory	290,000	220,000
Accounts payable	260,000	260,000
Cost of goods sold	1,440,000	1,510,000
Building	480,000	480,000
Sales	2,400,000	2,400,000

Required

a. Compute the gross margin percentage for each company and identify the company that *appears* to be charging the higher prices in relation to its cost.

b. For each company, compute the inventory turnover ratio and the average days to sell inventory. Identify the company that *appears* to be incurring the higher inventory financing cost.

c. Explain why a company with the lower gross margin percentage has the higher inventory turnover ratio.

EXERCISES—SERIES B

Exercise 5-1B *Effect of inventory cost flow assumption on financial statements* LO 5-1

Required

For each of the following situations, fill in the blank with *FIFO, LIFO,* or *weighted average:*

a. ______ would produce the highest amount of net income in an inflationary environment.

b. ______ would produce the highest amount of assets in an inflationary environment.

c. ______ would produce the lowest amount of net income in a deflationary environment.

d. ______ would produce the same unit cost for assets and cost of goods sold in an inflationary environment.

e. ______ would produce the lowest amount of net income in an inflationary environment.

f. ______ would produce an asset value that was the same regardless of whether the environment was inflationary or deflationary.

g. ______ would produce the lowest amount of assets in an inflationary environment.

h. ______ would produce the highest amount of assets in a deflationary environment.

Exercise 5-2B *Allocating product cost between cost of goods sold and ending inventory* LO 5-1

Harris Co. started the year with no inventory. During the year, it purchased two identical inventory items. The inventory was purchased at different times. The first purchase cost $3,600 and the other, $4,200. One of the items was sold during the year.

Required

Based on this information, how much product cost would be allocated to cost of goods sold and ending inventory on the year-end financial statements, assuming use of

a. FIFO?

b. LIFO?

c. Weighted average?

Exercise 5-3B *Allocating product cost between cost of goods sold and ending inventory: multiple purchases* LO 5-1

Marley Company sells coffee makers used in business offices. Its beginning inventory of coffee makers was 400 units at $50 per unit. During the year, Marley made two batch purchases of coffee makers. The first was a 500-unit purchase at $55 per unit; the second was a 600-unit purchase at $58 per unit. During the period, Marley sold 1,200 coffee makers.

Required

Determine the amount of product costs that would be allocated to cost of goods sold and ending inventory, assuming that Marley uses

a. FIFO.

b. LIFO.

c. Weighted average.

Exercise 5-4B *Effect of inventory cost flow (FIFO, LIFO, and weighted average) on gross margin* LO 5-1

The following information pertains to Stanley Company for 2016:

Beginning inventory	90 units @ $15
Units purchased	320 units @ $19

Ending inventory consisted of 40 units. Stanley sold 370 units at $30 each. All purchases and sales were made with cash.

Required

a. Compute the gross margin for Stanley Company using the following cost flow assumptions: (1) FIFO, (2) LIFO, and (3) weighted average.

b. What is the dollar amount of difference in net income between using FIFO versus LIFO? (Ignore income tax considerations.)

c. Determine the cash flow from operating activities, using each of the three cost flow assumptions listed in Requirement *a.* Ignore the effect of income taxes. Explain why these cash flows have no differences.

LO 5-1

Exercise 5-5B *Effect of inventory cost flow on ending inventory balance and gross margin*

Scott Sales had the following transactions for jackets in 2016, its first year of operations:

Jan. 20	Purchased 80 units @ $15	=	$1,200
Apr. 21	Purchased 420 units @ $16	=	6,720
July 25	Purchased 250 units @ $20	=	5,000
Sept. 19	Purchased 150 units @ $22	=	3,300

During the year, Scott Sales sold 830 jackets for $40 each.

Required

a. Compute the amount of ending inventory Scott would report on the balance sheet, assuming the following cost flow assumptions: (1) FIFO, (2) LIFO, and (3) weighted average.

b. Record the above transactions in general journal form and post to T-accounts using (1) FIFO, (2) LIFO, and (3) weighted average. Use a separate set of journal entries and T-accounts for each method. Assume all transactions are cash transactions.

c. Compute the difference in gross margin between the FIFO and LIFO cost flow assumptions.

LO 5-1

Exercise 5-6B *Income tax effect of shifting from FIFO to LIFO*

The following information pertains to the inventory of the Bryant Company:

Jan. 1	Beginning Inventory	300 units @ $25
Apr. 1	Purchased	2,800 units @ $30
Oct. 1	Purchased	1,000 units @ $32

During the year, Bryant sold 3,500 units of inventory at $50 per unit and incurred $21,000 of operating expenses. Bryant currently uses the FIFO method but is considering a change to LIFO. All transactions are cash transactions. Assume a 30 percent income tax rate. Bryant started the period with cash of $36,000, inventory of $7,500, common stock of $20,000, and retained earnings of $23,500.

Required

a. Record the above transactions in general journal form and post to T-accounts using (1) FIFO and (2) LIFO. Use a separate set of journal entries and T-accounts for each method.

b. Prepare income statements using FIFO and LIFO.

c. Determine the amount of income tax Bryant would save if it changed cost flow methods.

d. Determine the cash flow from operating activities under FIFO and LIFO.

e. Explain why cash flow from operating activities is lower under FIFO when that cost flow method produced the higher gross margin.

Exercise 5-7B *Effect of FIFO versus LIFO on income tax expense* LO 5-1

Home Gifts Inc. had cash sales of $112,500 for 2016, its first year of operation. On April 2, the company purchased 150 units of inventory at $180 per unit. On September 1, an additional 200 units were purchased for $200 per unit. The company had 50 units on hand at the end of the year. The company's income tax rate is 40 percent. All transactions are cash transactions.

Required

a. The preceding paragraph describes five accounting events: (1) a sales transaction, (2) the first purchase of inventory, (3) a second purchase of inventory, (4) the recognition of cost of goods sold expense, and (5) the payment of income tax expense. Record the amounts of each event in horizontal statements models like the following ones, assuming first a FIFO and then a LIFO cost flow.

Effect of Events on Financial Statements

Panel 1: FIFO Cost Flow

Event No.	Balance Sheet								Income Statement					Statement of Cash Flows
	Cash	+	Inventory	=	Com. Stk.	+	Ret. Earn.		Rev.	−	Exp.	=	Net Inc.	

Panel 2: LIFO Cost Flow

Event No.	Balance Sheet								Income Statement					Statement of Cash Flows
	Cash	+	Inventory	=	Com. Stk.	+	Ret. Earn.		Rev.	−	Exp.	=	Net Inc.	

b. Compute net income using FIFO.

c. Compute net income using LIFO.

d. Explain the difference, if any, in the amount of income tax expense incurred using the two cost flow assumptions.

e. How does the use of the FIFO versus the LIFO cost flow assumptions affect the statement of cash flows?

Exercise 5-8B *Recording inventory transactions using the perpetual system: intermittent sales and purchases* LO 5-1

The following inventory transactions apply to Duncan Steel Company for 2016:

Jan. 1	Purchased	200 units @ $12
Apr. 1	Sold	150 units @ $20
Aug. 1	Purchased	300 units @ $15
Dec. 1	Sold	450 units @ $25

The beginning inventory consisted of 180 units at $10 per unit. All transactions are cash transactions.

Required

a. Record these transactions in general journal format assuming Duncan Steel Company uses the FIFO cost flow assumption and keeps perpetual records.

b. Compute the ending balance in the Inventory account.

LO 5-1

Exercise 5-9B *Effect of cost flow on ending inventory: intermittent sales and purchases*

Nash Auto Parts, Inc., had the following transactions for 2016:

Date	Transaction	Description
Jan. 1	Beginning inventory	40 units @ $22
Mar. 15	Purchased	150 units @ $24
May 30	Sold	175 units @ $48
Aug. 10	Purchased	320 units @ $26
Nov. 20	Sold	300 units @ $50

Required

a. Determine the quantity and dollar amount of inventory at the end of the year, assuming Nash Auto Parts, Inc., uses the FIFO cost flow assumption and keeps perpetual records.

b. Write a memo explaining why Nash Auto Parts, Inc., would have difficulty applying the LIFO method on a perpetual basis. Include a discussion of how to overcome these difficulties.

LO 5-2

Exercise 5-10B *Lower-of-cost-or-market rule: perpetual system*

The following information pertains to James Hardware's ending inventory for the current year:

Item	Quantity	Unit Cost	Unit Market Value
M	200	$10	$ 8
N	100	12	10
0	40	8	9
P	30	5	10

Required

a. Determine the value of the ending inventory using the lower-of-cost-or-market rule applied to (1) each individual inventory item and (2) the inventory in aggregate.

b. Prepare any necessary journal entries, assuming the decline in value is immaterial, using the (1) individual method and (2) aggregate method. James Hardware uses the perpetual inventory system.

LO 5-2

Exercise 5-11B *Lower-of-cost-or-market rule*

Harvey Company carries three inventory items. The following information pertains to the ending inventory:

Item	Quantity	Unit Cost	Unit Market Value
A	400	$20	$18
B	500	25	24
C	300	10	12

Required

a. Determine the ending inventory that will be reported on the balance sheet, assuming that Harvey applies the lower-of-cost-or-market rule to individual inventory items.

b. Prepare the necessary journal entry, assuming the decline in value is immaterial.

Exercise 5-12B ***Estimating ending inventory using the gross margin method*** **LO 5-3, 5-4**

Frank Jones, the owner of Frank's Hunting Supplies, is surprised at the amount of actual inventory at the end of the year. He thought there should be more inventory on hand based on the amount of sales for the year. The following information is taken from the books of Frank's Hunting Supplies:

Beginning inventory	$250,000
Purchases for the year	500,000
Sales for the year	850,000
Inventory at the end of the year (based on actual count)	40,000

Historically, Frank has made a 20 percent gross margin on his sales. Frank thinks there may be some problem with the inventory. Evaluate the situation based on the historical gross profit percentage.

Required

Estimate the following:

a. Gross margin in dollars.

b. Cost of goods sold in dollars.

c. Estimated ending inventory.

d. Inventory shortage.

e. Provide an explanation for the shortage.

Exercise 5-13B ***Estimating ending inventory: perpetual system*** **LO 5-4**

Beth Malone owned a small company that sold boating equipment. The equipment was expensive, and a perpetual system was maintained for control purposes. Even so, lost, damaged, and stolen merchandise normally amounted to 5 percent of the inventory balance. On June 14, Beth's warehouse was destroyed by fire. Just prior to the fire, the accounting records contained a $130,000 balance in the Inventory account. However, inventory costing $20,000 had been sold and delivered to customers the day of the fire but had not been recorded in the books at the time of the fire. The fire did not affect the showroom, which contained inventory that cost $50,000.

Required

Estimate the amount of inventory destroyed by fire.

Exercise 5-14B ***Effect of inventory error on financial statements: perpetual system*** **LO 5-4**

Bosh Company failed to count $22,000 of inventory in its 2016 year-end physical count.

Required

Explain how this error will affect Bosh's 2016 financial statements, assuming that Bosh uses the perpetual inventory system.

Exercise 5-15B ***Effect of inventory misstatement on elements of financial statements*** **LO 5-4**

The ending inventory for Oak Co. was erroneously written down, causing an understatement of $6,500 at the end of 2016.

Required

Was each of the following amounts overstated, understated, or not affected by the error?

Item No.	Year	Amount
1	2016	Beginning inventory
2	2016	Purchases
3	2016	Goods available for sale
4	2016	Cost of goods sold
5	2016	Gross margin
6	2016	Net income
7	2017	Beginning inventory
8	2017	Purchases
9	2017	Goods available for sale
10	2017	Cost of goods sold
11	2017	Gross margin
12	2017	Net income

LO 5-1, IFRS

Exercise 5-16B *Explaining multiple inventory methods at one real-world company*

The following note related to accounting for inventory was taken from the 2013 annual report of Walmart Stores, Inc.:

> ***Inventories*** The Company values inventories at the lower of cost or market as determined primarily by the retail method of accounting, using the last-in, first-out ("LIFO") method for substantially all of the Walmart U.S. segment's inventories. The retail method of accounting results in inventory being valued at the lower of cost or market since permanent markdowns are currently taken as a reduction of the retail value of inventory. The Walmart International segment's inventories are primarily valued by the retail method of accounting, using the first-in, first-out ("FIFO") method. The Sam's Club segment's inventories are valued based on weighted-average cost using the LIFO method. At January 31, 2013 and 2012, the Company's inventories valued at LIFO approximate those inventories as if they were valued at FIFO.

Required

Write a brief report explaining the reason or reasons that best explain why Walmart uses the LIFO cost flow method for its operations in the United States, but the FIFO method for its non–U.S. operations.

IFRS

Exercise 5-17B *GAAP versus IFRS*

Po River Winery Inc. has inventory that cost $500,000. The aging process for the inventory requires several years. At the company's closing date (December 31, 2016) the inventory had a market value of $400,000. During 2017 the market value recovered to an estimated $480,000.

Required

a. Assuming Po River uses GAAP, determine the book value and the amount of any gain or loss recognized on the 2016 and 2017 financial statements.

b. Assuming Po River uses IFRS, determine the book value and the amount of any gain or loss recognized on the 2016 and 2017 financial statements.

PROBLEMS—SERIES B

LO 5-1

Problem 5-18B *Effect of different inventory cost flow methods on financial statements*

The accounting records of Allen Insulation, Inc., reflected the following balances as of January 1, 2016:

Cash	$36,000
Beginning inventory	24,000 (200 units @ $120)
Common stock	25,000
Retained earnings	35,000

The following five transactions occurred in 2016:

1. First purchase (cash) 130 units @ $124
2. Second purchase (cash) 220 units @ $128
3. Sales (all cash) 350 units @ $320
4. Paid $24,000 cash for operating expenses.
5. Paid cash for income tax at the rate of 40 percent of income before taxes.

Required

a. Compute the cost of goods sold and ending inventory, assuming (1) FIFO cost flow, (2) LIFO cost flow, and (3) weighted-average cost flow. Compute income tax expense for each method.

b. Record the above transactions in general journal form and post to T-accounts assuming (1) FIFO cost flow, (2) LIFO cost flow, and (3) weighted-average cost flow.

c. Use a vertical model to show the 2016 income statement, balance sheet, and statement of cash flows under FIFO, LIFO, and weighted average.

Problem 5-19B *Allocating product costs between cost of goods sold and ending inventory: intermittent purchases and sales of merchandise* LO 5-1

Donovan, Inc., had the following sales and purchase transactions during 2016. Beginning inventory consisted of 120 items at $80 each. Donovan uses the FIFO cost flow assumption and keeps perpetual inventory records.

Date	Transaction	Description
Mar. 5	Purchased	100 items @ $90
Apr. 10	Sold	70 items @ $175
June 19	Sold	80 items @ $175
Sept. 16	Purchased	50 items @ $95
Nov. 28	Sold	60 items @ $180

Required

a. Record the inventory transactions in general journal format.

b. Calculate the gross margin Donovan would report on the 2016 income statement.

c. Determine the ending inventory balance Donovan would report on the December 31, 2016, balance sheet.

Problem 5-20B *Inventory valuation based on the lower-of-cost-or-market rule* LO 5-2

At the end of the year, Ronaldo Jewelers had the following items in inventory:

Item	Quantity	Unit Cost	Unit Market Value
D1	30	$80	$90
D2	10	60	55
D3	41	30	32
D4	20	90	75

Required

a. Determine the amount of ending inventory using the lower-of-cost-or-market rule applied to each individual inventory item.

b. Provide the general journal entry necessary to write down the inventory based on Requirement *a.* Assume that Ronaldo Jewelers uses the perpetual inventory system.

c. Determine the amount of ending inventory, assuming that the lower-of-cost-or-market rule is applied to the inventory in aggregate.

d. Provide the general journal entry necessary to write down the inventory based on Requirement *c.* Assume that Ronaldo Jewelers uses the perpetual inventory system.

LO 5-4

Problem 5-21B *Estimating ending inventory: gross margin method*

A hurricane destroyed the inventory of Coleman Feed Store on September 21 of the current year. Although some of the accounting information was destroyed, the following information was discovered for the period of January 1 through September 21:

Beginning inventory, January 1	$120,000
Purchases through September 21	450,000
Sales through September 21	800,000

The gross margin for Coleman Feed Store has traditionally been 35 percent of sales.

Required

a. For the period ending September 21, compute the following:

(1) Estimated gross margin.

(2) Estimated cost of goods sold.

(3) Estimated inventory at September 21.

b. Assume that $8,000 of the inventory was not damaged. What is the amount of the loss from the hurricane?

c. Coleman Feed Store uses the perpetual inventory system. If some of the accounting records had not been destroyed, how would Coleman determine the amount of the inventory loss?

LO 5-4

Problem 5-22B *Estimating ending inventory: gross margin method*

Sam Todd, owner of Todd Company, is reviewing the quarterly financial statements and thinks the cost of goods sold is out of line with past years. The following historical data are available for 2016 and 2017:

	2016	2017
Net sales	$220,000	$250,000
Cost of goods sold	99,000	117,200

At the end of the first quarter of 2018, Todd Company's ledger had the following account balances:

Sales	$280,000
Purchases	210,000
Beginning inventory, January 1, 2018	70,000

Required

Using the information provided, estimate the following for the first quarter of 2018:

a. Cost of goods sold. (Use average cost of goods sold percentage.)

b. Ending inventory at March 31 based on the historical cost of goods sold percentage.

c. Inventory shortage if the inventory balance as of March 31 is $125,000.

LO 5-3

Problem 5-23B *Effect of inventory errors on financial statements*

The following income statement was prepared for Rice Company for the year 2016:

RICE COMPANY Income Statement For the Year Ended December 31, 2016	
Sales	$ 75,000
Cost of goods sold	(41,250)
Gross margin	33,750
Operating expenses	(10,120)
Net income	$ 23,630

During the year-end audit, the following errors were discovered:

1. An $1,800 payment for repairs was erroneously charged to the Cost of Goods Sold account. (Assume that the perpetual inventory system is used.)
2. Sales to customers for $3,400 at December 31, 2016, were not recorded in the books for 2016. Also, the $1,870 cost of goods sold was not recorded.
3. A mathematical error was made in determining ending inventory. Ending inventory was understated by $1,700. (The Inventory account was written down in error to the Cost of Goods Sold account.)

Required

Determine the effect, if any, of each of the errors on the following items. Give the dollar amount of the effect and whether it would overstate (O), understate (U), or not affect (NA) the account. The effect on sales is recorded as an example.

Error No. 1	Amount of Error	Effect
Sales, 2016	NA	NA
Ending inventory, December 31, 2016		
Gross margin, 2016		
Beginning inventory, January 1, 2017		
Cost of goods sold, 2016		
Net income, 2016		
Retained earnings, December 31, 2016		
Total assets, December 31, 2016		
Error No. 2	**Amount of Error**	**Effect**
Sales, 2016	$2,400	U
Ending inventory, December 31, 2016		
Gross margin, 2016		
Beginning inventory, January 1, 2017		
Cost of goods sold, 2016		
Net income, 2016		
Retained earnings, December 31, 2016		
Total assets, December 31, 2016		
Error No. 3	**Amount of Error**	**Effect**
Sales, 2016	NA	NA
Ending inventory, December 31, 2016		
Gross margin, 2016		
Beginning inventory, January 1, 2017		
Cost of goods sold, 2016		
Net income, 2016		
Retained earnings, December 31, 2016		
Total assets, December 31, 2016		

Problem 5-24B *Using ratios to make comparisons* LO 5-5

The following accounting information pertains to Mobile and Casper companies at the end of 2016. The only difference between the two companies is that Mobile uses FIFO while Casper uses LIFO.

	Mobile Co.	Casper Co.
Cash	$ 70,000	$ 70,000
Accounts receivable	230,000	230,000
Merchandise inventory	220,000	190,000
Accounts payable	210,000	210,000
Cost of goods sold	1,350,000	1,380,000
Building	300,000	300,000
Sales	1,800,000	1,800,000

Required

a. Compute the gross margin percentage for each company and identify the company that *appears* to be charging the higher prices in relation to its cost.

b. For each company, compute the inventory turnover ratio and the average days to sell inventory. Identify the company that *appears* to be incurring the higher inventory financing cost.

c. Explain why a company with the lower gross margin percentage has the higher inventory turnover ratio.

ANALYZE, THINK, COMMUNICATE

ATC 5-1 Business Applications Case *Understanding real-world annual reports*

Required

Use the Target Corporation's annual report in Appendix B to answer the following questions.

a. What was Target's inventory turnover ratio and average days to sell inventory for the fiscal year ended February 1, 2014 (2013) and 2012?

b. Is the company's management of inventory getting better or worse?

c. What cost flow method(s) did Target use to account for inventory?

ATC 5-2 Group Assignment *Inventory cost flow*

The accounting records of Blue Bird Co. showed the following balances at January 1, 2016:

Cash	$30,000
Beginning inventory (100 units @ $50, 70 units @ $55)	8,850
Common stock	20,000
Retained earnings	18,850

Transactions for 2016 were as follows:

Purchased 100 units @ $54 per unit.
Sold 220 units @ $80 per unit.
Purchased 250 units @ $58 per unit.
Sold 200 units @ $90 per unit.
Paid operating expenses of $3,200.
Paid income tax expense. The income tax rate is 30%.

Required

a. Organize the class into three sections, and divide each section into groups of three to five students. Assign each section one of the cost flow methods, FIFO, LIFO, or weighted average. The company uses the perpetual inventory system.

Group Tasks

Determine the amount of ending inventory, cost of goods sold, gross margin, and net income after income tax for the cost flow method assigned to your section. Also prepare an income statement using that cost flow assumption.

Class Discussion

b. Have a representative of each section put its income statement on the board. Discuss the effect that each cost flow method has on assets (ending inventory), net income, and cash flows. Which method is preferred for tax reporting? For financial reporting? What restrictions are placed on the use of LIFO for tax reporting?

ATC 5-3 Real-World Case *Inventory management issues at the Penske Automotive Group*

The following data were extracted from the 2013 financial statements of Penske Automotive Group, Inc. This company operates automobile dealerships, mostly in the United States and the United Kingdom. The company had 327 dealerships as of the end of 2013. Dollar amounts are in millions.

	December 31, 2013	December 31, 2012
Revenue from car sales	$11,858.7	$10,453.8
Cost of sales—cars	10,962.8	9,625.5
Gross profit—car sales	895.9	828.3
Operating income before taxes	375.4	290.1
Net income (loss)	245.7	187.2
Ending inventory—cars	2,538.3	1,975.7

Required

a. Compute Penske's gross margin percentage for 2013 and 2012.

b. Compute Penske's average days to sell inventory for 2013 and 2012.

c. How much higher or lower would Penske's *earnings before taxes* have been in 2013 if its gross margin percentage had been the same as it was in 2012? Show all supporting computations.

ATC 5-4 Business Applications Case *Performing ratio analysis using real-world data*

Safeway, Inc., operated 1,335 stores as of December 28, 2013. The following data were taken from the company's annual report. All dollar amounts are in millions.

	Fiscal Years Ending	
	December 28, 2013	December 29, 2012
Revenue	$36,139.1	$44,206.5
Cost of goods sold	26,645.1	32,486.5
Net income	3,522.2	598.1
Merchandise inventory	2,089.6	2,562.0

Required

a. Compute Safeway's inventory turnover ratio for 2013 and 2012.

b. Compute Safeway's average days to sell inventory for 2013 and 2012.

c. Based on your computations in Requirements *a* and *b*, did Safeway's inventory management get better or worse from 2012 to 2013?

ATC 5-5 Business Applications Case *Performing ratio analysis using real-world data*

Ruby Tuesday's, Inc., operated 706 casual dining restaurants across the United States as of June 4, 2013. Zale Corporation claims to be a leading retailer of fine jewelry. The following data were taken from these companies' 2013 annual reports. All dollar amounts are in thousands.

	Ruby Tuesday's June 4, 2013	Zale Corporation July 31, 2013
Revenue	$1,245,226	$1,888,016
Cost of goods sold	341,512	903,602
Net income	(39,413)	10,012
Merchandise inventory	21,779	767,540

Required

a. Before performing any calculations, speculate as to which company will take the longest to sell its inventory. Explain the rationale for your decision.

b. Calculate the inventory turnover ratios for Ruby Tuesday's and Zale Corporation.

c. Calculate the average days to sell inventory for Ruby Tuesday's and Zale Corporation.

d. Do the calculations from Requirements *b* and *c* confirm your speculations in Requirement *a*?

ATC 5-6 Writing Assignment *Use of LIFO*

The following information is available for Leno Company:

Sales	$695,000
Goods available for sale	535,000
Ending inventory (using FIFO)	246,000

Leno Company currently uses the FIFO cost flow method for financial statement reporting and tax reporting. It is considering changing to the LIFO cost flow method for tax reporting purposes. If Leno uses LIFO, its ending inventory would be $175,000.

Required

a. Why would Leno want to change to LIFO for tax reporting?

b. Discuss any changes that Leno would have to make for GAAP reporting if it does change to LIFO for tax reporting.

ATC 5-7 Ethical Dilemma *Show them only what you want them to see*

Clair Coolage is the chief accountant for a sales company called Far Eastern Imports. The company has been highly successful and is trying to increase its capital base by attracting new investors. The company operates in an inflationary environment and has been using the LIFO inventory cost flow method to minimize its net earnings and thereby reduce its income taxes. Katie Bailey, the vice president of finance, asked Coolage to estimate the change in net earnings that would occur if the company switched to FIFO. After reviewing the company's books, Coolage estimated that pretax income would increase by $1,200,000 if the company adopted the FIFO cost flow method. However, the switch would result in approximately $400,000 of additional taxes. The overall effect would result in an increase of $800,000 in net earnings. Bailey told Coolage to avoid the additional taxes by preparing the tax return on a LIFO basis but to prepare a set of statements on a FIFO basis to be distributed to potential investors.

Required

a. Comment on the legal and ethical implications of Bailey's decision.

b. How will the switch to FIFO affect Far Eastern's balance sheet?

c. If Bailey reconsiders and makes a decision to switch to FIFO for tax purposes as well as financial reporting purposes, net income will increase by $800,000. Comment on the wisdom of paying $400,000 in income taxes to obtain an additional $800,000 of net income.

ATC 5-8 Research Assignment *Analyzing inventory at Gap Company*

Using either Gap's most current Form 10-K or the company's annual report, answer the questions below. To obtain the Form 10-K use either the EDGAR system, following the instructions in Appendix A, or the company's website. The company's annual report is available on its website.

Required

a. How many stores did Gap operate at year-end? (Do not include "Franchise store locations.")

b. What was the average amount of inventory per store? Use *all* stores operated by The Gap, Inc., not just those called *The Gap.* (*Hint:* The answer to this question must be computed. The number of stores in operation at the end of the most recent year can be found in the MD&A of the 10-K.)

c. Using the quarterly financial information in the 10-K, complete the following chart.

Quarter	Sales During Each Quarter
1	$
2	
3	
4	

d. Referring to the chart in Requirement *c*, explain why Gap's sales vary so widely throughout its fiscal year. Do you believe that Gap's inventory level varies throughout the year in relation to sales?

ATC 5-9 Spreadsheet Analysis *Using Excel*

At January 1, 2016, the accounting records of Ginger's Boutique had the following balances:

Cash	$1,000
Inventory	2,250 (150 units @ $15)
Common stock	2,000
Retained earnings	1,250

During January, Ginger's Boutique entered into five cash transactions:

1. Purchased 120 units of inventory @ $16 each.
2. Purchased 160 units of inventory @ $17 each.
3. Sold 330 units of inventory @ $30 each.
4. Incurred $1,700 of operating expenses.
5. Paid income tax at the rate of 30 percent of income before taxes.

Required

a. Set up rows 1 through 10 of the following spreadsheet to compute cost of goods sold and ending inventory, assuming (1) FIFO, (2) LIFO, and (3) weighted-average cost flows. Notice that the FIFO cost flow has already been completed for you. Use columns O through W to complete the LIFO and weighted-average cost flow computations. Be sure to use formulas for all calculations.

Microsoft Excel - ch8-1.xls

File Edit View Insert Format Tools Data Window Help

B16 = =K7

	A	B	C	D	E	F	G	H	I	J	K	L	M	N
1	Cost of Goods Available For Sale					FIFO Ending Inventory			FIFO Cost of Goods Sold			LIFO Ending Inventory		
2			Unit	Total			Unit	Total		Unit	Total		Unit	Total
3		Units	Price	Cost		Units	Price	Cost	Units	Price	Cost	Units	Price	Cost
4	Beginning Inventory	150	$15	$2,250					150	$15	$2,250			
5	First Purchase (cash)	120	$16	$1,920					120	$16	$1,920			
6	Second Purchase (cash)	160	$17	$2,720		100	$17	$1,700	60	$17	$1,020			
7	Total Cost of Goods Available for Sale	430		$6,890		100		$1,700	330		$5,190			
8														
9	Average Cost		$16.02				Check:	EI + CGS	430	Units				
10								EI + CGS	$6,890	Total Cost				

	A	B	C	D
11				
12				
13				WEIGHTED
14	**Income Statements**	FIFO	LIFO	AVERAGE
15	Sales (330 units @ $30 each) (cash)	$9,900		
16	Cost of Goods Sold	5,190		
17	Gross Margin	4,710		
18	Operating Expenses (cash)	1,700		
19	Income Before Taxes	3,010		
20	Income Tax Expense (30%) (cash)	903		
21	Net Income	$2,107		
22				
23	**Statement of Cash Flows**	FIFO		
24	Cash from Operating Activities:			
25	Cash received from Customers	$9,900		
26	Cash paid for Inventory Purchased	(4,640)		
27	Cash paid for Operating Expenses	(1,700)		
28	Cash paid for Income Taxes	(903)		
29	Net Cash Flow from Operating Activities	2,657		
30	Beginning Cash	1,000		
31	Ending Cash	$3,657		
32				

b. In rows 13 through 31, compute the amount of net income and net cash flow from operations under FIFO, LIFO, and weighted average. The FIFO column has been provided as an example.

ATC 5-10 Spreadsheet Assignment *Mastering Excel*

Required

Complete ATC 5-5 using an Excel spreadsheet. Use Excel problem ATC 5-9 as a resource for structuring the spreadsheet.

COMPREHENSIVE PROBLEM

The trial balance of Pacilio Security Services Inc. as of January 1, 2015, had the following normal balances:

Cash	$62,860
Accounts receivable	20,500
Supplies	150
Prepaid rent	2,000
Merchandise inventory (9 @ $240)	2,160
Land	4,000
Accounts payable	980
Salaries payable	1,500
Common stock	50,000
Retained earnings	39,190

During 2015, Pacilio Security Services experienced the following transactions:

1. Paid the salaries payable from 2014.
2. On January 15, purchased 20 standard alarm systems for cash at a cost of $250 each.
3. On February 1, paid the accounts payable of $980, but not within the discount period. (The company uses the gross method.)
4. On March 1, leased a business van. Paid $4,800 for one year's lease in advance.
5. Paid $7,200 on May 1 for one year's rent on the office in advance.
6. Purchased with cash $500 of supplies to be used over the next several months by the business.
7. Purchased with cash another 25 alarm systems on August 1 for resale at a cost of $260 each.
8. On September 5, purchased on account 30 standard alarm systems at a cost of $265.
9. Installed 60 standard alarm systems for $33,000. $22,000 of the sales were on account and $11,000 were cash sales. (*Note:* Be sure to record cost of goods sold using the perpetual FIFO method.)
10. Made a full refund to a dissatisfied customer who returned her alarm system. The sale had been a cash sale for $550 with a cost of $260.
11. Paid installers and other employees a total of $21,000 cash for salaries.
12. Sold $45,000 of monitoring services during the year. The services are billed to the customers each month.
13. Sold an additional monitoring service for $1,200 for one year's service. The customer paid the full amount of $1,200 on October 1.
14. Collected $74,000 of accounts receivable during the year.
15. Paid an additional $6,000 to settle some of the accounts payable.
16. Paid $3,500 of advertising expense during the year.
17. Paid $2,320 of utilities expense for the year.
18. Paid a dividend of $15,000 to the shareholders.

Adjustments

19. There was $200 of supplies on hand at the end of the year.

20. Recognized the expired rent for both the van and the office building for the year.

21. Recognized the revenue earned from transaction 13.

22. Accrued salaries at December 31, 2015, were $1,000.

Required

a. Record the above transactions in general journal form.

b. Post the transactions to T-accounts.

c. Prepare a trial balance.

d. Prepare an income statement, statement of changes in stockholders' equity, balance sheet, and statement of cash flows.

e. Close the temporary accounts to retained earnings.

f. Post the closing entries to the T-accounts and prepare an after-closing trial balance.

CHAPTER 6

Internal Control and Accounting for Cash

LEARNING OBJECTIVES

After you have mastered the material in this chapter, you will be able to:

LO 6-1 Identify the key elements of a strong system of internal control.

LO 6-2 Identify special internal controls for cash.

LO 6-3 Prepare a bank reconciliation.

LO 6-4 Explain the use of a petty cash fund.

LO 6-5 Describe the auditor's role in financial reporting.

Video lectures and accompanying self-assessment quizzes are available for all learning objectives through McGraw-Hill Connect® Plus Accounting.

CHAPTER OPENING

To operate successfully, businesses must establish systems of control. How can Walmart's upper-level managers ensure that every store will open on time? How can the president of General Motors be confident that the company's financial reports fairly reflect the company's operations? How can the owner of a restaurant prevent a waiter from serving food to his friends and relatives without charging them for it? The answer: by exercising effective control over company activities. The policies and procedures used to provide reasonable assurance that the objectives of an enterprise will be accomplished are called **internal controls.**

Internal controls can be divided into two categories: (1) **accounting controls** are designed to safeguard company assets and ensure reliable accounting records; and (2) **administrative controls** are concerned with evaluating performance and assessing the degree of compliance with company policies and public laws.

The Curious Accountant

On December 29, 2013, **Target Corporation** announced that unauthorized access had been made to its system for processing customers' credit and debit cards. It reported that 40 million accounts had been impacted between November 27, 2013, and December 15, 2013.

On January 10, 2014, Target announced that, in addition to the debit and credit card data, customers' account information had been inappropriately accessed by unauthorized parties. The information stolen included names, mailing addresses, phone numbers, and/or e-mail addresses for up to 70 million individuals.

On January 22, 2014, **Neiman Marcus Group** announced that between July 16, 2013, and October 30, 2013, the credit card information of approximately 1.1 million customers had been viewed by unauthorized parties. To date, it had heard of 2,400 customers' cards that had been used fraudulently.

On February 14, 2014, *The Wall Street Journal* reported that members of Target's "computer security staff raised concerns about vulnerabilities in the retailer's payment card system at least two months before hackers stole 40 million credit and debit card numbers from its servers." The article also noted that the company "has an extensive cyber-security intelligence team, which sees numerous threats each week and could prioritize only so many issues."

Companies' responsibilities under the Sarbanes-Oxley Act (SOX) were introduced in Chapter 2, and SOX is discussed further in this chapter. Do you think SOX was intended to require companies to protect their customers from the type of cyber-security frauds reported here? If not, are there other aspects of financial accounting systems that should protect a company's customers? (Answers on page 324.)

KEY FEATURES OF INTERNAL CONTROL SYSTEMS

LO 6-1

Identify the key elements of a strong system of internal control.

During the early 2000s a number of accounting-related scandals cost investors billions. In 2001, Enron's share price went from $85 to $0.30 after it was revealed that the company had billions of dollars in losses that were not reported on the financial statements. Several months later, WorldCom reported an $11 billion accounting fraud, which included hundreds of millions in personal loans to then CEO, Bernie Ebbers.

The Enron and WorldCom accounting scandals had such devastating effects that they led Congress to pass the Sarbanes-Oxley Act of 2002 (SOX). SOX requires public companies to evaluate their internal control and to publish those findings with their SEC filings. *Internal control* is the process designed to ensure reliable financial reporting, effective and efficient operations, and compliance with applicable laws and regulations. Safeguarding assets against theft and unauthorized use, acquisition, or disposal is also part of internal control.

Section 404 of Sarbanes-Oxley requires a statement of management's responsibility for establishing and maintaining adequate internal control over financial reporting by public companies. This section includes an assessment of the controls and the identification of the framework used for the assessment. The framework established by The Committee of Sponsoring Organizations of the Treadway Commission (COSO) in 1992 is the de facto standard by which SOX compliance is judged.[1] COSO's framework, titled *Internal Control—An Integrated Framework,* recognizes five interrelated components, including:

1. *Control Environment.* The integrity and ethical values of the company, including its code of conduct, involvement of the board of directors, and other actions that set the tone of the organization.
2. *Risk Assessment.* Management's process of identifying potential risks that could result in misstated financial statements and developing actions to address those risks.
3. *Control Activities.* These are the activities usually thought of as "the internal controls." They include such things as segregation of duties, account reconciliations, and information processing controls that are designed to safeguard assets and enable an organization to prepare reliable financial statements in a timely manner.
4. *Information and Communication.* The internal and external reporting process, including an assessment of the technology environment.
5. *Monitoring.* Assessing the quality of a company's internal control over time and taking actions as necessary to ensure it continues to address the risks of the organization.

In 2004, COSO updated the framework to help entities design and implement effective enterprisewide approaches to risk management. The updated document is titled *Enterprise Risk Management (ERM)—An Integrated Framework.* The ERM framework introduces an enterprisewide approach to risk management as well as concepts such as risk appetite, risk tolerance, and portfolio view. While SOX applies only to U.S. public companies, the ERM framework has been adopted by both public and private organizations around the world.

[1]As of the publication of this text, COSO is engaged in a multiyear project to update its *Internal Control–Integrated Framework*. The COSO Board has emphasized that the key concepts and principles embedded in the 1992 Framework remain fundamentally sound for designing, implementing, and maintaining systems of internal control. The original framework will be superseded in December 2014.

The ERM framework does not replace the internal control framework. Instead, it incorporates the internal control framework within it. Accordingly, companies may decide to look to the ERM framework both to satisfy their internal control needs and to move toward a fuller risk management process.

While a detailed discussion of the COSO documents is beyond the scope of this text, the following overview of the more common *control activities* of the internal control framework is insightful.

Segregation of Duties

The likelihood of fraud or theft is reduced if employees must work together to accomplish it. Clear **segregation of duties** is frequently used as a deterrent to corruption. When duties are segregated, the work of one employee can act as a check on the work of another employee. For example, a person selling seats to a movie may be tempted to steal money received from customers who enter the theater. This temptation is reduced if the person staffing the box office is required to issue tickets that a second employee collects as people enter the theater. If ticket stubs collected by the second employee are compared with the cash receipts from ticket sales, any cash shortages will become apparent. Furthermore, friends and relatives of the ticket agent cannot easily enter the theater without paying. Theft or unauthorized entry would require collusion between the ticket agent and the usher who collects the tickets. Both individuals would have to be dishonest enough to steal, yet trustworthy enough to convince each other they would keep the embezzlement secret. Whenever possible, the functions of *authorization, recording,* and *custody of assets* should be performed by separate individuals.

Quality of Employees

A business is only as good as the people it employs. Cheap labor is not a bargain if the employees are incompetent. Employees should be properly trained. In fact, they should be trained to perform a variety of tasks. The ability of employees to substitute for one another prevents disruptions when co-workers are absent because of illnesses, vacations, or other commitments. The capacity to rotate jobs also relieves boredom and increases respect for the contributions of other employees. Every business should strive to maximize the productivity of every employee. Ongoing training programs are essential to a strong system of internal control.

Bonded Employees

The best way to ensure employee honesty is to hire individuals with *high levels of personal integrity.* Employers should screen job applicants using interviews, background checks, and recommendations from prior employers or educators. Even so, screening programs may fail to identify character weaknesses. Further, unusual circumstances may cause honest employees to go astray. Therefore, employees in positions of trust should be bonded. A **fidelity bond** provides insurance that protects a company from losses caused by employee dishonesty.

Required Absences

Employees should be required to take regular vacations and their duties should be rotated periodically. Employees may be able to cover up fraudulent activities if they are always present at work. Consider the case of a parking meter collection agent who covered the same route for several years with no vacation. When the agent became sick, a substitute collected more money each day than the regular reader usually reported. Management checked past records and found that the ill meter reader had been understating the cash receipts and pocketing the difference. If management had required vacations or rotated the routes, the embezzlement would have been discovered much earlier.

Procedures Manual

Appropriate accounting procedures should be documented in a **procedures manual.** The manual should be routinely updated. Periodic reviews should be conducted to ensure that employees are following the procedures outlined in the manual.

Authority and Responsibility

Employees are motivated by clear lines of authority and responsibility. They work harder when they have the authority to use their own judgment and they exercise reasonable caution when they are held responsible for their actions. Businesses should prepare an **authority manual** that establishes a definitive *chain of command*. The authority manual should guide both specific and general authorizations. **Specific authorizations** apply to specific positions within the organization. For example, investment decisions are authorized at the division level while hiring decisions are authorized at the departmental level. In contrast, **general authority** applies across different levels of management. For example, employees at all levels may be required to fly economy class or to make purchases from specific vendors.

Prenumbered Documents

How would you know if a check were stolen from your checkbook? If you keep a record of your check numbers, the missing number would tip you off immediately. Businesses also use prenumbered checks to avoid the unauthorized use of their bank accounts. In fact, prenumbered forms are used for all important documents such as purchase orders, receiving reports, invoices, and checks. To reduce errors, prenumbered forms should be as simple and easy to use as possible. Also, the documents should allow for authorized signatures. For example, credit sales slips should be signed by the customer to clearly establish who made the purchase, reducing the likelihood of unauthorized transactions.

Physical Control

Employees walk away with billions of dollars of business assets each year. To limit losses, companies should establish adequate physical control over valuable assets. For example, inventory should be kept in a storeroom and not released without proper authorization. Serial numbers on equipment should be recorded along with the name of the individual who is responsible for the equipment. Unannounced physical counts should be conducted randomly to verify the presence of company-owned equipment. Certificates of deposit and marketable securities should be kept in fireproof vaults. Access to these vaults should be limited to authorized personnel. These procedures protect the documents from fire and limit access to only those individuals who have the appropriate security clearance to handle the documents.

In addition to safeguarding assets, there should be physical control over the accounting records. The accounting journals, ledgers, and supporting documents should be kept in a fireproof safe. Only personnel responsible for recording transactions in the journals should have access to them. With limited access, there is less chance that someone will change the records to conceal fraud or embezzlement.

Performance Evaluations

Because few people can evaluate their own performance objectively, internal controls should include independent verification of employee performance. For example, someone other than the person who has control over inventory should take a physical count of inventory. Internal and external audits serve as independent verification of performance. Auditors should evaluate the effectiveness of the internal control system as well as verify the accuracy of the accounting records. In addition, the external auditors attest to the company's use of generally accepted accounting principles in the financial statements.

Limitations

A system of internal controls is designed to prevent or detect errors and fraud. However, no control system is foolproof. Internal controls can be circumvented by collusion among employees. Two or more employees working together can hide embezzlement by covering for each other. For example, if an embezzler goes on vacation, fraud will not be reported by a replacement who is in collusion with the embezzler. No system can prevent all fraud. However, a good system of internal controls minimizes illegal or unethical activities by reducing temptation and increasing the likelihood of early detection.

CHECK YOURSELF 6.1

What are nine features of an internal control system?

Answer The nine features follow:

1. Separating duties so that fraud or theft requires collusion.
2. Hiring and training competent employees.
3. Bonding employees to recover losses through insurance.
4. Requiring employees to be absent from their jobs so that their replacements can discover errors or fraudulent activity that might have occurred.
5. Establishing proper procedures for processing transactions.
6. Establishing clear lines of authority and responsibility.
7. Using prenumbered documents.
8. Implementing physical controls such as locking cash in a safe.
9. Conducting performance evaluations through independent internal and external audits.

ACCOUNTING FOR CASH

LO 6-2

Identify special internal controls for cash.

For financial reporting purposes, **cash** generally includes currency and other items that are payable *on demand,* such as checks, money orders, bank drafts, and certain savings accounts. Savings accounts that impose substantial penalties for early withdrawal should be classified as *investments* rather than cash. Postdated checks or IOUs represent *receivables* and should not be included in cash. As illustrated in Exhibit 6.1, most companies combine currency and other payable-on-demand items in a single balance sheet account with varying titles.

Companies must maintain a sufficient amount of cash to pay employees, suppliers, and other creditors. When a company fails to pay its legal obligations, its creditors can force the company into bankruptcy. Even so, management should avoid accumulating more cash than is needed. The failure to invest excess cash in earning assets reduces profitability. Cash inflows and outflows must be managed to prevent a shortage or surplus of cash.

EXHIBIT 6.1

Balance Sheet Classifications that Include the Word Cash

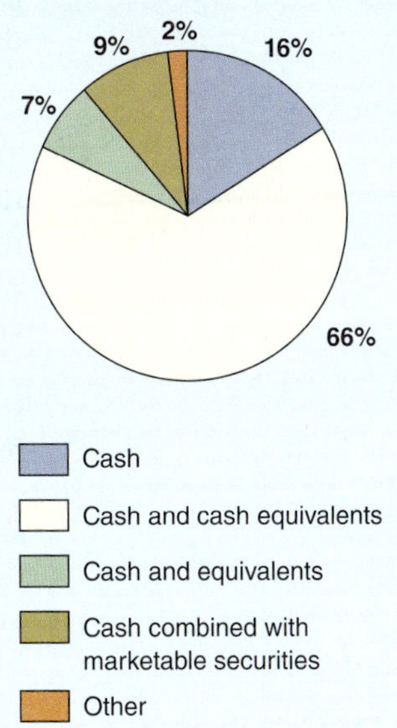

Data Source: AICPA, *Accounting Trends and Techniques.*

Controlling Cash

Controlling cash, more than any other asset, requires strict adherence to internal control procedures. Cash has universal appeal. A relatively small suitcase filled with high-denomination currency can represent significant value. Furthermore, the rightful owner of currency is difficult to prove. In most cases, possession constitutes ownership. As a result, cash is highly susceptible to theft and must be carefully protected. Cash is most susceptible to embezzlement when it is received or disbursed. The following controls should be employed to reduce the likelihood of theft.

Cash Receipts

A record of all cash collections should be prepared immediately upon receipt. The amount of cash on hand should be counted regularly. Missing amounts of money can be detected by comparing the actual cash on hand with the book balance. Employees who receive cash should give customers a copy of a written receipt. Customers usually review their receipts to ensure they have gotten credit for the amount paid and call any errors to the receipts clerk's attention. This not only reduces errors but also provides a control on the clerk's honesty. Cash receipts should be deposited in a bank on a timely basis. Cash collected late in the day should be deposited in a night depository. Every effort should be made to minimize the amount of cash on hand. Keeping large amounts of

Answers to The Curious Accountant

The Sarbanes-Oxley Act (SOX) placed a lot of emphasis on companies having a good system of internal controls, primarily to ensure proper financial reporting. But SOX was intended mostly to protect a company's investors, not its customers. Fraud involving stealing customers' credit card information is not a financial reporting issue. However, as this chapter has explained, good internal controls are about more than accurate financial reporting; they should also protect the company's resources, and customers are a major company resource.

The fraud that occurred at **Target** and **Neiman Marcus** certainly inconvenienced their customers, but the fraud was also very expensive for the companies. First, each company issued assurances that customers would not be responsible for fraudulent charges made to their cards due to the security breaches. Who pays for the fraudulent charges? Target and Neiman Marcus. According to a *Wall Street Journal* report on February 18, 2014, one analyst estimated that Target could pay as much as $1.1 billion for fraudulent credit card charges. Additionally, both companies offered to pay for one-year of free credit monitoring and identity theft protection for every customer whose information was compromised. Credit monitoring for 70 million customers will be expensive. Then, there is the potential for lost sales if customers stop or reduce their purchases at the affected companies. After the breach was announced, Target's sales began to drop, resulting in fourth quarter sales for 2013 that were 3.8 percent lower than for the same quarter of 2012. For Target, a 3.8 percent decline in fourth quarter sales amounted to $854 million! Furthermore, it is likely this event will continue to negatively impact future sales. It is much easier to lose customers' trust that it is to gain it.

cash on hand not only increases the risk of loss from theft but also places employees in danger of being harmed by criminals who may be tempted to rob the company.

Cash Payments

To effectively control cash, a company should make all disbursements using checks, thereby providing a record of cash payments. All checks should be prenumbered, and unused checks should be locked up. Using prenumbered checks allows companies to easily identify lost or stolen checks by comparing the numbers on unused and canceled checks with the numbers used for legitimate disbursements.

The duties of approving disbursements, signing checks, and recording transactions should be segregated. If one person is authorized to approve, sign, and record checks, he or she could falsify supporting documents, write an unauthorized check, and record a cover-up transaction in the accounting records. By separating these duties, the check signer reviews the documentation provided by the approving individual before signing the check. Likewise, the recording clerk reviews the work of both the approving person and the check signer when the disbursement is recorded in the accounting records. Thus writing unauthorized checks requires trilevel collusion.

Supporting documents with authorized approval signatures should be required when checks are presented to the check signer. For example, a warehouse receiving order should be matched with a purchase order before a check is approved to pay a bill

REALITY BYTES

THE COST OF PROTECTING CASH

Could you afford to buy a safe like the one shown here? The vault is only one of many expensive security devices used by banks to safeguard cash. By using checking accounts, companies are able to avoid many of the costs associated with keeping cash safe. In addition to providing physical control, checking accounts enable companies to maintain a written audit trail of cash receipts and payments. Checking accounts represent the most widely used internal control device in modern society. It is difficult to imagine a business operating without the use of checking accounts.

from a supplier. Before payments are approved, invoice amounts should be checked and payees verified as valid vendors. Matching supporting documents with proper authorization discourages employees from creating phony documents for a disbursement to a friend or fictitious business. Also, the approval process serves as a check on the accuracy of the work of all employees involved.

Supporting documents should be marked *Paid* when the check is signed. If the documents are not indelibly marked, they could be retrieved from the files and resubmitted for a duplicate, unauthorized payment. A payables clerk could collude with the payee to split extra cash paid out by submitting the same supporting documents for a second payment.

All spoiled and voided checks should be defaced and retained. If defaced checks are not retained, an employee could steal a check and then claim that it was written incorrectly and thrown away. The clerk could then use the stolen check to make an unauthorized payment.

Checking Account Documents

The previous section explained the need for businesses to use checking accounts. Next we will describe the four main types of forms associated with a bank checking account.

Signature Card

A bank **signature card** shows the bank account number and the signatures of the people authorized to sign checks. The card is retained in the bank's files. If a bank employee is unfamiliar with the signature on a check, he or she can refer to the signature card to verify the signature before cashing the check.

Deposit Ticket

Each deposit of cash or checks is accompanied by a **deposit ticket,** which normally identifies the account number and the name of the account. The depositor lists the individual amounts of currency, coins, and checks, as well as the total deposited, on the deposit ticket.

Bank Check

A written check affects three parties: (1) the person or business writing the check (the *payer*); (2) the bank on which the check is drawn; and (3) the person or business to whom the check is payable (the *payee*). Companies often write **checks** using multicopy, prenumbered forms, with the name of the issuing business preprinted on the face of each check. A remittance notice is usually attached to the check forms. This portion of the form provides the issuer space to record what the check is for (e.g., what invoices are being paid), the amount being disbursed, and the date of payment. When signed by the person whose signature is on the signature card, the check authorizes the bank to transfer the face amount of the check from the payer's account to the payee.

Bank Statement

Periodically, the bank sends the depositor a **bank statement.** The bank statement is presented from the bank's point of view. Checking accounts are liabilities to a bank because the bank is obligated to pay back the money that customers have deposited in their accounts. Therefore, in the bank's accounting records a customer's checking account has a *credit* balance. As a result, **bank statement debit memos** describe transactions that reduce the customer's account balance (the bank's liability). **Bank statement credit memos** describe activities that increase the customer's account balance (the bank's liability). Since a checking account is an asset (cash) to the depositor, a *bank statement debit memo* requires a *credit entry* to the Cash account on the depositor's books. Likewise, when a bank tells you that it has credited your account, you will debit your Cash account in response.

Bank statements normally report (a) the balance of the account at the beginning of the period; (b) additions for customer deposits made during the period; (c) other additions described in credit memos (e.g., for interest earned); (d) subtractions for the payment of checks drawn on the account during the period; (e) other subtractions described in debit memos (e.g., for service charges); (f) a running balance of the account; and (g) the balance of the account at the end of the period. The sample bank statement in Exhibit 6.2 illustrates these items with references to the preceding letters in parentheses.

EXHIBIT 6.2

FIRST STATE BANK
of Frisco County
2121 Westbury Drive • Harrison, Nevada • 54269 - 0001

Green Shades Resorts, Inc.
1439 Lazy Lane
Harrison, Nevada 54275 - 0023

Account Number
53-9872-3

Checking Account Summary	On This Date	Your Balance Was	Deposits Added	No. Deposits	Checks Paid	No. Checks
	8/31/2016	4,779.86	3,571.72	5	4,537.22	22
	Other Debits	Resulting in a Balance of		On This Date		Enclosures
	297.91	3,516.45		9/30/2016		29

Checks and Debits		Deposits and Credits	Date	Balance
15.82	24.85	600.25	9/3	5,339.44
249.08	497.00		9/5	4,593.36
42.53	124.61		9/7	4,426.22
79.87	859.38		9/8	3,486.97
685.00	742.59	711.43	9/9	2,770.81
25.75	38.98		9/12	2,706.08
36.45	59.91		9/14	2,609.72
	8.40 DM	940.00 CM	9/15	3,541.32
61.40		689.47	9/18	4,169.39
289.51 NS			9/19	3,879.88
71.59	82.00		9/21	3,726.29
312.87			9/24	3,413.42
25.00		630.57	9/27	4,018.99
227.00			9/28	3,791.99
95.06	180.48		9/30	3,516.45

LEGEND – NS Nonsufficient Funds • DM Debit Memo • CM Credit Memo

FIRST STATE BANK OF FRISCO COUNTY

RECONCILING THE BANK ACCOUNT

LO 6-3

Prepare a bank reconciliation.

Usually the ending balance reported on the bank statement differs from the balance in the depositor's Cash account as of the same date. The discrepancy is normally attributable to timing differences. For example, a depositor deducts the amount of a check from its Cash account when it writes the check. However, the bank does not deduct the amount of the check from the depositor's account until the payee presents it for payment, which may be days, weeks, or even months after the check is written. As a result, the balance on the depositor's books is lower than the balance on the bank's books. Companies prepare a **bank reconciliation** to explain the differences between the cash balance reported on the bank statement and the cash balance recorded in the depositor's accounting records.

Determining True Cash Balance

A bank reconciliation normally begins with the cash balance reported by the bank, which is called the **unadjusted bank balance.** The adjustments necessary to determine the amount of cash that the depositor actually owns as of the date of the bank statement are then added to and subtracted from the unadjusted bank balance. The final total is the **true cash balance.** The true cash balance is independently reached a second time by making adjustments to the **unadjusted book balance.** The bank account is reconciled when the true cash balance determined from the perspective of the unadjusted *bank* balance agrees with the true cash balance determined from the perspective of the unadjusted *book* balance. The procedures a company uses to determine the *true cash balance* from the two different perspectives are outlined here.

Adjustments to the Bank Balance

A typical format for determining the true cash balance beginning with the unadjusted bank balance is

Unadjusted bank balance
+ Deposits in transit
− Outstanding checks
= True cash balance

Deposits in Transit

Companies frequently leave deposits in the bank's night depository or make them on the day following the receipt of cash. Such deposits are called **deposits in transit.** Since these deposits have been recorded in the depositor's accounting records but have not yet been added to the depositor's account by the bank, they must be added to the unadjusted bank balance.

Outstanding Checks

These are disbursements that have been properly recorded as cash deductions on the depositor's books. However, the bank has not deducted the amounts from the depositor's bank account because the checks have not yet been presented by the payee to the bank for payment; that is, the checks have not cleared the bank. **Outstanding checks** must be subtracted from the unadjusted bank balance to determine the true cash balance.

Adjustments to the Book Balance

A typical format for determining the true cash balance beginning with the unadjusted book balance is as follows:

Unadjusted book balance
+ Accounts receivable collections
+ Interest earned
− Bank service charges
− Non-sufficient-funds (NSF) checks
= True cash balance

Accounts Receivable Collections

To collect cash as quickly as possible, many companies have their customers send payments directly to the bank. The bank adds the collection directly to the depositor's account and notifies the depositor about the collection through a credit memo that is included on the bank statement. The depositor adds the amount of the cash collections to the unadjusted book balance in the process of determining the true cash balance.

Interest Earned

Banks pay interest on certain checking accounts. The amount of the interest is added directly to the depositor's bank account. The bank notifies the depositor about the interest through a credit memo that is included on the bank statement. The depositor adds the amount of the interest revenue to the unadjusted book balance in the process of determining the true cash balance.

Service Charges

Banks frequently charge depositors fees for services performed. They may also charge a penalty if the depositor fails to maintain a specified minimum cash balance throughout the period. Banks deduct such fees and penalties directly from the depositor's account and advise the depositor of the deduction through a debit memo that is included on the bank statement. The depositor deducts such **service charges** from the unadjusted book balance to determine the true cash balance.

Non-Sufficient-Funds (NSF) Checks

Non-sufficient-funds (NSF) checks are checks that a company obtains from its customers and deposits in its checking account. However, when the checks are submitted to the customers' banks for payment, the banks refuse payment because there is insufficient money in the customers' accounts. When such checks are returned, the amounts of the checks are deducted from the company's bank account balance. The company is advised of NSF checks through debit memos that appear on the bank statement. The depositor deducts the amounts of the NSF checks from the unadjusted book balance in the process of determining the true cash balance.

Correction of Errors

In the course of reconciling the bank statement with the Cash account, the depositor may discover errors in the bank's records, the depositor's records, or both. If an error is found on the bank statement, an adjustment for it is made to the unadjusted bank balance to determine the true cash balance, and the bank should be notified immediately to correct its records. Errors made by the depositor require adjustments to the book balance to arrive at the true cash balance.

Certified Checks

A **certified check** is guaranteed for payment by a bank. Whereas a regular check is deducted from the customer's account when it is presented for payment, a certified check is deducted from the customer's account when the bank certifies that the check is good. Certified checks, therefore, *have* been deducted by the bank in determining the unadjusted bank balance, whether they have cleared the bank or remain outstanding as of the date of the bank statement. Since certified checks are deducted both from bank and depositor records immediately, they do not cause differences between the depositor and bank balances. As a result, certified checks are not included in a bank reconciliation.

Illustrating a Bank Reconciliation

The following example illustrates a bank reconciliation for Green Shades Resorts, Inc. (GSRI). The bank statement for GSRI is displayed in Exhibit 6.2. Exhibit 6.3 illustrates the completed bank reconciliation. The items on the reconciliation are described in the discussion that follows.

Adjustments to the Bank Balance

As of September 30, 2016, the bank statement showed an unadjusted balance of \$3,516.45. A review of the bank statement disclosed three adjustments that had to be made to the unadjusted bank balance to determine GSRI's true cash balance.

1. Comparing the deposits on the bank statement with deposits recorded in GSRI's accounting records indicated there was \$724.11 of deposits in transit.
2. An examination of the returned checks disclosed that the bank had erroneously deducted a \$25 check written by Green Valley Resorts from GSRI's bank account. This amount must be added back to the unadjusted bank balance to determine the true cash balance.
3. The checks returned with the bank statement were sorted and compared to the cash records. Three checks with amounts totaling \$235.25 were outstanding.

After these adjustment are made, GSRI's true cash balance is determined to be \$4,030.31.

Adjustments to the Book Balance

As indicated in Exhibit 6.3, GSRI's unadjusted book balance as of September 30, 2016, was \$3,361.22. This balance differs from GSRI's true cash balance because of four unrecorded accounting events:

1. The bank collected a \$940 account receivable for GSRI.
2. GSRI's accountant made a \$27 recording error.

EXHIBIT 6.3

GREEN SHADES RESORTS, INC.
Bank Reconciliation
September 30, 2016

Unadjusted bank balance, September 30, 2016	\$3,516.45
Add: Deposits in transit	724.11
Bank error: Check drawn on Green Valley Resorts charged to GSRI	25.00
Less: Outstanding checks	

Check No.	Date	Amount
639	Sept. 18	\$ 13.75
646	Sept. 20	29.00
672	Sept. 27	192.50

Total	(235.25)
True cash balance, September 30, 2016	\$4,030.31
Unadjusted book balance, September 30, 2016	\$3,361.22
Add: Receivable collected by bank	940.00
Error made by accountant (Check no. 633 recorded as \$63.45 instead of \$36.45)	27.00
Less: Bank service charges	(8.40)
NSF check	(289.51)
True cash balance, September 30, 2016	\$4,030.31

3. The bank charged GSRI an $8.40 service fee.
4. GSRI had deposited a $289.51 check from a customer who did not have sufficient funds to cover the check.

Two of these four adjustments increase the unadjusted cash balance. The other two decrease the unadjusted cash balance. After the adjustments have been recorded, the Cash account reflects the true cash balance of $4,030.31 ($3,361.22 unadjusted cash balance + $940.00 receivable collection + $27.00 recording error − $8.40 service charge − $289.51 NSF check). Since the true balance determined from the perspective of the bank statement agrees with the true balance determined from the perspective of GSRI's books, the bank statement has been successfully reconciled with the accounting records.

Updating GSRI's Accounting Records

Each of the adjustments to the book balance must be recorded in GSRI's financial records. The effects of each adjustment on the financial statements are as follows.

ADJUSTMENT 1 **Recording the $940 receivable collection increases Cash and reduces Accounts Receivable.**

The event is an asset exchange transaction. The journal entry and its effects on the financial statements are shown here:

Account Title	Debit	Credit
Cash	940.00	
Accounts Receivable		940.00

Assets			=	Liab.	+	Equity	Rev.	−	Exp.	=	Net Inc.	Cash Flow
Cash	+	Accts. Rec.										
940.00	+	(940.00)	=	NA	+	NA	NA	−	NA	=	NA	940.00 OA

ADJUSTMENT 2 **Assume the $27 recording error occurred because GSRI's accountant accidentally transposed two numbers when recording check no. 633 for utilities expense.**

The check was written to pay utilities expense of $36.45 but was recorded as a $63.45 disbursement. Since cash payments are overstated by $27.00 ($63.45 − $36.45), this amount must be added back to GSRI's Cash balance and deducted from the Utilities Expense account, which increases net income. The journal entry and its effects on the financial statements are shown here:

Account Title	Debit	Credit
Cash	27.00	
Utilities Expense		27.00

Assets	=	Liab.	+	Equity	Rev.	−	Exp.	=	Net Inc.	Cash Flow
Cash	=			Ret. Earn.						
27.00	=	NA	+	27.00	NA	−	(27.00)	=	27.00	27.00 OA

ADJUSTMENT 3 **The $8.40 service charge is an expense that reduces assets, stockholders' equity, net income, and cash.**

The journal entry and its effects on the financial statements are shown here:

Account Title	Debit	Credit
Bank Service Charge Expense	8.40	
Cash		8.40

Assets	=	Liab.	+	Equity	Rev.	−	Exp.	=	Net Inc.	Cash Flow
Cash	=			Ret. Earn.						
(8.40)	=	NA	+	(8.40)	NA	−	8.40	=	(8.40)	(8.40) OA

ADJUSTMENT 4 **The $289.51 NSF check reduces GSRI's cash balance.**

When it originally accepted the customer's check, GSRI increased its Cash account. Since there is not enough money in the customer's bank account to pay the check, GSRI didn't actually receive cash so GSRI must reduce its Cash account. GSRI will still try to collect the money from the customer. In the meantime, it will show the amount of the NSF check as an account receivable. The adjusting entry to record the NSF check is an asset exchange transaction. Cash decreases and Accounts Receivable increases. The journal entry and its effects on the financial statements are shown here:

Account Title	Debit	Credit
Accounts Receivable	289.51	
Cash		289.51

Assets			=	Liab.	+	Equity	Rev.	−	Exp.	=	Net Inc.	Cash Flow
Cash	+	Accts. Rec.										
(289.51)	+	289.51	=	NA	+	NA	NA	−	NA	=	NA	(289.51) OA

Cash Short and Over

Sometimes employees make mistakes when collecting cash from or making change for customers. When such errors occur, the amount of money in the cash register will not agree with the amount of cash receipts recorded on the cash register tape. For example, suppose that when a customer paid for $17.95 of merchandise with a $20 bill, the sales clerk returned $3.05 in change instead of $2.05. If, at the end of the day, the cash register tape shows total receipts of $487.50, the cash drawer would contain only $486.50. The actual cash balance is less than the expected cash balance by $1. Any shortage of cash or excess of cash is recorded in a special account called **Cash Short and Over.** In this example, the shortage is recorded with the following journal entry:

Account Title	Debit	Credit
Cash	486.50	
Cash Short and Over	1.00	
Sales		487.50

A cash shortage is an expense. It is recorded by debiting the Cash Short and Over account. An overage of cash represents revenue and is recorded by crediting the Cash Short and Over account. As with other expense and revenue items, the balance of the Cash Short and Over account is closed to the Retained Earnings account at the end of the accounting period.

CHECK YOURSELF 6.2

The following information was drawn from Reliance Company's October bank statement. The unadjusted bank balance on October 31 was $2,300. The statement showed that the bank had collected a $200 account receivable for Reliance. The statement also included $20 of bank service charges for October and a $100 check payable to Reliance that was returned NSF. A comparison of the bank statement with company accounting records indicates that there was a $500 deposit in transit and $1,800 of checks outstanding at the end of the month. Based on this information, determine the true cash balance on October 31.

Answer Since the unadjusted book balance is not given, start with the unadjusted bank balance to determine the true cash balance. The collection of the receivable, the bank service charges, and the NSF check are already recognized in the unadjusted bank balance, so these items are not used to determine the true cash balance. To determine the true cash balance, add the deposit in transit to the unadjusted bank balance and then subtract the outstanding checks. The true cash balance is $1,000 ($2,300 unadjusted bank balance + $500 deposit in transit − $1,800 outstanding checks).

USING PETTY CASH FUNDS

LO 6-4

Explain the use of a petty cash fund.

Although businesses use checks for most disbursements, they often pay for small items such as postage, delivery charges, taxi fares, employees' supper money, and so on with currency. They frequently establish a **petty cash fund** to maintain effective control over these small cash disbursements. The fund is established for a specified dollar amount, such as $300, and is controlled by one employee, called the *petty cash custodian.*

Petty cash funds are usually maintained on an **imprest basis,** which means that the money disbursed is periodically replenished. The fund is created by drawing a check on the regular checking account, cashing it, and giving the currency to the petty cash custodian. The custodian normally keeps the currency under lock and key. The amount of the petty cash fund depends on what it is used for, how often it is used, and how often it is replenished. It should be large enough to handle disbursements for a reasonable time period, such as several weeks or a month.

Establishing a petty cash fund merely transfers money from a bank to a safety box inside the company offices. The establishment is an asset exchange event. The Cash account decreases, and an account called Petty Cash increases. The journal entry and its effects on the financial statements are shown here:

Account Title	Debit	Credit
Petty Cash	300.00	
Cash		300.00

Assets			=	Liab.	+	Equity	Rev.	−	Exp.	=	Net Inc.	Cash Flow
Cash	+	Petty Cash										
(300.00)	+	300.00	=	NA	+	NA	NA	−	NA	=	NA	NA

EXHIBIT 6.4

Petty cash voucher no. ________

To: ____________________________ Date ________, 20____

Explanation: Account No. ____________ Amount ________

Approved by ____________ Received by ____________

When money is disbursed from the petty cash fund, the custodian should complete a **petty cash voucher,** such as the one in Exhibit 6.4. Any supporting documents, such as an invoice, restaurant bill, or parking fee receipt, should be attached to the petty cash voucher. The person who receives the currency should sign the voucher as evidence of receiving the money. The total of the amounts recorded on the petty cash vouchers plus the remaining coins and currency should equal the balance of the petty cash ledger account. *No journal entry is made in the accounting records when petty cash funds are disbursed.* The effects on the financial statements are recorded only when the petty cash fund is replenished or increased (when additional currency is put into the petty cash safety box).

When the amount of currency in the petty cash fund is relatively low, the fund is replenished. The petty cash vouchers are totaled, the amount of any cash short or over is determined, and a check is issued to the bank to obtain the currency needed to return the fund to its imprest balance. For example, suppose the $300 petty cash fund is replenished when the total of the petty cash vouchers is $216. The vouchers can be classified according to different types of expenses or listed in total as miscellaneous expense. Assuming the company classifies petty cash expenditures as miscellaneous expense, the journal entries to record replenishing the fund are as follows:

Account Title	Debit	Credit
Miscellaneous Expense	216.00	
Petty Cash		216.00
To record expenses paid from the petty cash fund		
Petty Cash	216.00	
Cash		216.00
To replenish the petty cash fund		

If desired, the effect of the entries could be recorded more efficiently. Since the credit to the Petty Cash account is offset by a debit to the same account, a single entry debiting miscellaneous expense and crediting cash would have the same effect on the accounts. The entry more frequently used in practice to record replenishing petty cash is

Account Title	Debit	Credit
Miscellaneous Expense	216.00	
Cash		216.00

The replenishment affects the financial statements in the same manner as any other cash expense. It reduces assets, stockholders' equity, net income, and cash flow, as follows:

Assets	=	Liab.	+	Equity	Rev.	−	Exp.	=	Net Inc.	Cash Flow
Cash	=			Ret. Earn.						
(216.00)	=	NA	+	(216.00)	NA	−	216.00	=	(216.00)	(216.00) OA

If management desires more detailed information about petty cash expenditures, the vouchers can be sorted into postage, $66; delivery charges, $78.40; taxi fares, $28; and supper money, $43.60, in which case the journal entry to replenish the fund would be recorded as follows:

Account Title	Debit	Credit
Postage Expense	66.00	
Delivery Expense	78.40	
Taxi Fares Expense	28.00	
Employee Meal Expense	43.60	
Cash		216.00

Once the vouchers are checked, the fund replenished, and the journal entry recorded, the vouchers should be indelibly marked *Paid* so they cannot be reused.

Sometimes, cash shortages and overages are discovered when the money in the petty cash fund is physically counted. Suppose that a physical count discloses $212.30 in petty cash vouchers and only $87 in currency and coins. Assuming an imprest petty cash balance of $300, the journal entry necessary to replenish the fund is as follows:

Account Title	Debit	Credit
Miscellaneous Expense	212.30	
Cash Short and Over	.70	
Cash		213.00
To replenish the petty cash fund		

If cash shortages or overages do not occur frequently and are of insignificant amounts, companies are likely to include them in miscellaneous expense or miscellaneous revenue.

CHECK YOURSELF 6.3

Cornerstone Corporation established a $400 petty cash fund that was replenished when it contained $30 of currency and coins and $378 of receipts for miscellaneous expenses. Based on this information, determine the amount of cash short or over to be recognized. Explain how the shortage or overage would be reported in the financial statements. Also determine the amount of petty cash expenses that were recognized when the fund was replenished.

Answer The fund contained $408 of currency and receipts ($30 currency + $378 of receipts), resulting in a cash overage of $8 ($408 − $400). The overage would be reported as miscellaneous revenue on the income statement. The amount of petty cash expenses recognized would equal the amount of the expense receipts, which is $378.

THE FINANCIAL ANALYST

Companies communicate information to analysts and other users through a document called the *annual report.* These reports are usually printed in color on high-quality paper and contain lots of photographs. However, in an effort to reduce cost, some companies issue their annual reports in black and white on low-grade paper or in electronic form. A company's annual report contains much more than the financial statements. Annual reports often have 40 or more pages. The financial statements require only four to six pages. What is printed on all those other pages? In general, the annual report of a large company has four major sections: (1) financial statements, (2) notes to the financial statements, (3) management's discussion and analysis, and (4) auditors' report. The notes and management's discussion and analysis make up the bulk of the report.

Notes to the Financial Statements

Accountants frequently have to make estimates when preparing financial statements. Also, GAAP may offer alternative ways of reporting certain transactions. **Notes to the financial statements** explain some of the estimates that were made as well as which reporting options were used. Reading the notes is critical to understanding the financial statements. The financial statements include a caveat such as "the accompanying notes are an integral part of these financial statements."

Management's Discussion and Analysis

Management's discussion and analysis (MD&A) is located at the beginning of the annual report. MD&A is the section of the annual report in which management explains the company's past performance and future plans. For example, MD&A typically compares current year earnings with those of past periods and explains the reasons for significant changes. If the company is planning significant acquisitions of assets or other businesses, this information is usually included in MD&A. Likewise, any plans to discontinue part of the existing business are outlined in MD&A.

Role of the Independent Auditor

LO 6-5

Describe the auditor's role in financial reporting.

As previously explained, financial statements are prepared in accordance with certain rules called *generally accepted accounting principles (GAAP)*. Thus, when **General Electric** publishes its financial statements, it is saying, "here are our financial statements prepared according to GAAP." How can a financial analyst know that a company really did follow GAAP? Analysts and other statement users rely on **audits** conducted by **certified public accountants (CPAs).**

The primary roles of an independent auditor (CPA) are summarized below:

1. Conducts a financial audit (a detailed examination of a company's financial statements and underlying accounting records).
2. Assumes both legal and professional responsibilities to the public as well as to the company paying the auditor.
3. Determines if financial statements are *materially* correct rather than *absolutely* correct.
4. Presents conclusions in an audit report that includes an opinion as to whether the statements are prepared in conformity with GAAP. In rare cases, the auditor issues a disclaimer.
5. Maintains professional confidentiality of client records. The auditor is not, however, exempt from legal obligations such as testifying in court.

The Financial Statements Audit

What is an audit? There are several different types of audits. The type most relevant to this course is a **financial statements audit.** The financial audit is a detailed examination of a company's financial statements and the documents that support those statements. It also tests the reliability of the accounting system used to produce the financial reports. A financial audit is conducted by an **independent auditor** who must be a CPA.

The term *independent auditor* typically refers to a *firm* of certified public accountants. CPAs are licensed by state governments to provide services to the public. They are to be independent of the companies they audit. To help assure independence, CPAs may not be employees of the companies they audit. Further, they cannot have investments in the companies they audit. Although CPAs are paid by the companies they audit, the audit fee may not be based on the outcome of the audit.

Although the independent auditors are chosen by, paid by, and can be fired by their client companies, the auditors are primarily responsible to *the public.* In fact, auditors have a legal responsibility to those members of the public who have a financial interest in the company being audited. If investors in a company lose money, they sometimes sue the independent auditors in an attempt to recover their losses, especially if the losses were related to financial failure. A lawsuit against auditors will succeed only if the auditors failed in their professional responsibilities when conducting the audit. Auditors are not responsible for the success or failure of a company. Instead, they are responsible for the appropriate auditing of the reporting of that success or failure. While recent debacles such as Bernard Madoff Investments produce spectacular headlines, auditors are actually not sued very often, considering the number of audits they perform.

Materiality and Financial Statements Audits

Auditors do not guarantee that financial statements are absolutely correct—only that they are *materially* correct. This is where things get a little fuzzy. What is a *material error?* The concept of materiality is very subjective. If ExxonMobil inadvertently overstated its sales by $1 million, would this be material? In its 2013 fiscal-year, Exxon Mobil had approximately $438 billion of sales! A $1 million error in computing sales at Exxon Mobil is like a $1 error in computing the pay of a person who makes $438,000 per year—not material at all! An error, or other reporting problem, is **material** if knowing about it would influence the decisions of an *average prudent investor.*

Financial audits are not directed toward the discovery of fraud. Auditors are, however, responsible for providing *reasonable assurance* that statements are free from material misstatements, whether caused by errors or fraud. Also, auditors are responsible for evaluating whether internal control procedures are in place to help prevent fraud. If fraud is widespread in a company, normal audit procedures should detect it.

Accounting majors take at least one and often two or more courses in auditing to understand how to conduct an audit. An explanation of auditing techniques is beyond the scope of this course, but at least be aware that auditors do not review how the company accounted for every transaction. Along with other methods, auditors use statistics to choose representative samples of transactions to examine.

Types of Audit Opinions

Once an audit is complete, the auditors present their conclusions in a report that includes an *audit opinion.* There are three basic types of audit opinions.

An **unqualified opinion,** despite its negative-sounding name, is the most favorable opinion auditors can express. It means the auditor believes the financial statements are in compliance with GAAP without material qualification, reservation, or exception. Most audits result in unqualified opinions because companies correct any material reporting deficiencies the auditors find before the financial statements are released.

The most negative report an auditor can issue is an **adverse opinion.** An adverse opinion means that one or more departures from GAAP are so material the financial statements do not present a fair picture of the company's status. The auditor's report explains the unacceptable accounting practice(s) that resulted in the adverse opinion being issued. Adverse opinions are very rare because public companies are required by law to follow GAAP.

A **qualified opinion** falls between an unqualified and an adverse opinion. A qualified opinion means that for the most part, the company's financial statements are in compliance with GAAP, but the auditors have reservations about something in the statements. The auditors' report explains why the opinion is qualified. A qualified opinion usually does not imply a serious accounting problem, but users should read the auditors' report and draw their own conclusions.

If an auditor is unable to perform the audit procedures necessary to determine whether the statements are prepared in accordance with GAAP, the auditor cannot issue an opinion on the financial statements. Instead, the auditor issues a **disclaimer of opinion.** A disclaimer is neither negative nor positive. It simply means that the auditor is unable to obtain enough information to confirm compliance with GAAP.

Regardless of the type of report they issue, auditors are only expressing their judgment about whether the financial statements present a fair picture of a company. They do not provide opinions regarding the investment quality of a company.

The ultimate responsibility for financial statements rests with the executives of the reporting company. Just like auditors, management can be sued by investors who believe they lost money due to improper financial reporting. This is one reason all business persons should understand accounting fundamentals.

Confidentiality

The **confidentiality** rules in the code of ethics for CPAs prohibit auditors from *voluntarily disclosing* information they have acquired as a result of their accountant-client relationships. However, accountants may be required to testify in a court of law. In general, federal law does not recognize an accountant-client privilege as it does with attorneys and clergy. Some federal courts have taken exception to this position, especially as it applies to tax cases. State law varies with respect to accountant-client privilege. Furthermore, if auditors terminate a client relationship because of ethical or legal disagreements and they are subsequently contacted by a successor auditor, they may be required to inform the successor of the reasons for the termination. In addition, auditors must consider the particular circumstances of a case when assessing the appropriateness of disclosing confidential information. Given the diverse legal positions governing accountant-client confidentiality, auditors should seek legal counsel prior to disclosing any information obtained in an accountant-client relationship.

To illustrate, assume that Joe Smith, CPA, discovers that his client Jane Doe is misrepresenting information reported in her financial statements. Smith tries to convince Doe to correct the misrepresentations, but she refuses to do so. Smith is required by the code of ethics to terminate his relationship with Doe. However, Smith is not permitted to disclose Doe's dishonest reporting practices unless he is called on to testify in a legal hearing or to respond to an inquiry by Doe's successor accountant.

With respect to the discovery of significant fraud, the auditor is required to inform management at least one level above the position of the employee who is engaged in the fraud and to notify the board of directors of the company. Suppose that Joe Smith, CPA, discovers that Mary Adams, employee of Western Company, is embezzling money from Western. Smith is required to inform Adams's supervisor and to notify Western's board of directors. However, Smith is prohibited from publicly disclosing the fraud.

The Securities and Exchange Commission

The annual reports of public companies often differ from those of private companies because public companies are registered with the **Securities and Exchange Commission (SEC).** Public companies, sometimes called SEC companies, have to follow the reporting rules of the SEC as well as GAAP. SEC rules require some additional disclosures not required by GAAP. For example, an MD&A section is required by the SEC, but not by GAAP. As a result, annual reports of non-SEC companies usually do not include MD&A.

The SEC is a government agency authorized to establish and enforce the accounting rules for public companies. Although the SEC can overrule GAAP, it has very seldom done so. Recall that GAAP is established by the Financial Accounting Standards Board, a private professional accounting organization. While SEC rules seldom conflict with GAAP, they frequently require additional disclosures. All companies whose stock trades on public stock exchanges, and some whose stock does not, are required to register with the SEC. The SEC has no jurisdiction over non-SEC companies.

SEC companies must file specific information directly with the SEC annually, quarterly, and in-between if required. The most common reports are filed on Form 10-K (annually) and Form 10-Q (quarterly). The 10-Qs are less detailed than the 10-Ks. While there is significant overlap between the 10-Ks (SEC report) and the annual reports that companies issue directly to the public, the 10-Ks usually contain more information but fewer photographs. Most of the reports filed with the SEC are available electronically through the SEC's EDGAR database. EDGAR is an acronym for Electronic Data Gathering, Analysis, and Retrieval, and it is accessible through the World Wide Web on the Internet. Appendix A provides instructions for using EDGAR.

REALITY BYTES

In 2008, Bernard Madoff was arrested on suspicion of having defrauded the clients of his investment company, Bernard L. Madoff Investments (BMI), of $60 billion. Although his clients believed the money they sent to BMI was being invested in the stock market, it was just being deposited into bank accounts. Clients were sent monthly statements falsely showing that their investments were earning income and growing at a steady rate, even when the overall stock market was falling. This occurred even though BMI's books received an "unqualified" auditor's opinion.

Federal prosecutors announced that BMI's auditor, David Friehling, did very little in the way of auditing the company's books. On March 18, 2009, he also was arrested and charged with falsely certifying BMI's financial statements. It is worth noting that the auditor was not charged with participating in the fraud, but of providing faulty audits. The specific complaints against the auditor were that (1) he did not verify that the investments Mr. Madoff claimed to have made actually existed; (2) he did not review the activity in the firm's primary checking account; and (3) the auditor and his family had investments with Mr. Madoff, which is a violation of the conflict of interest rules.

In November 2009, the auditor pled guilty to nine criminal charges and began cooperating with federal prosecutors investigating the Madoff fraud, partly in the hope of reducing his prison sentence of potentially 105 years. As of 2014 he was still assisting prosecutors and still awaiting sentencing, but he had already paid a high price for his failures. He claims his family lost $4.5 million from investments in BMI; he was working low-paying, part-time jobs; and in November of 2012, his 23-year-old son committed suicide.

This incompetent audit, coupled with a dishonest investment manager, cost thousands of clients billions of dollars. Many of Mr. Madoff's clients lost their entire life's savings and virtually all of their retirement income, although some of their money has been recovered. Auditors usually practice their profession unseen by the public but, as this unfortunate event demonstrates, the results of their efforts—and the consequences of their mistakes—can be almost unimaginably important to investors.

The SEC regulates audit standards as well as financial reporting. Prior to passage of the Sarbanes-Oxley Act in July 2002, the SEC left much of the regulation and oversight of independent auditors to the American Institute of Certified Public Accountants, a private professional organization. However, a key provision of Sarbanes-Oxley establishes the Public Company Accounting Oversight Board (PCAOB). This board assumes the primary responsibility for establishing and enforcing auditing standards for CPA firms that audit SEC companies. The board has five financially astute members, three of whom cannot be CPAs.

<< A Look Back

The policies and procedures used to provide reasonable assurance that the objectives of an enterprise will be accomplished are called *internal controls,* and they can be subdivided into two categories: accounting controls and administrative controls. *Accounting controls* are composed of procedures designed to safeguard the assets and ensure that the accounting records contain reliable information. *Administrative controls* are designed to evaluate performance and the degree of compliance with company policies and public laws. While the mechanics of internal control systems vary from company to company, the more prevalent features include the following: segregation of duties, quality of employees, bonded employees, required absence, a procedures manual, authority and responsibility, prenumbered documents, physical control, and performance evaluations.

Because cash is such an important business asset and because it is tempting to steal, much of the discussion of internal controls in this chapter focused on cash controls. Special procedures should be employed to control the receipts and payments of cash. One of the most common control policies is to use *checking accounts* for all except petty cash disbursements.

A *bank reconciliation* should be prepared each month to explain differences between the bank statement and a company's internal accounting records. A common reconciliation format determines the true cash balance based on both bank and book records. Items that typically appear on a bank reconciliation include the following:

Unadjusted bank balance	xxx	Unadjusted book balance	xxx
Add		Add	
Deposits in transit	xxx	Interest revenue	xxx
		Collection of receivables	xxx
Subtract		Subtract	
Outstanding checks	xxx	Bank service charges	xxx
		NSF checks	xxx
True cash balance	xxx	True cash balance	xxx

Agreement of the two true cash balances provides evidence that accounting for cash transactions has been accurate.

Another common internal control policy for protecting cash is using a *petty cash fund.* Normally, an employee who is designated as the petty cash custodian is entrusted with a small amount of cash. The custodian reimburses employees for small expenditures made on behalf of the company in exchange for authorized receipts from the employees at the time they are reimbursed. The total of these receipts plus the remaining currency in the fund should always equal the amount of funds entrusted to the custodian. Journal entries to recognize the expenses incurred are made at the time the fund is replenished.

Finally, the chapter discussed the auditor's role in financial reporting, including the materiality concept and the types of audit opinions that may be issued.

A Look Forward >>

Accounting for receivables and payables was introduced in Chapter 2 using relatively simple illustrations. For example, we assumed that customers who purchased services on account always paid their bills. In real business practice, some customers do not pay their bills. Among other topics, Chapter 7 examines how companies account for uncollectible accounts receivable.

SELF-STUDY REVIEW PROBLEM

A step-by-step audio-narrated series of slides is available in the Connect library.

The following information pertains to Terry's Pest Control Company (TPCC) for July:

1. The unadjusted bank balance at July 31 was $870.
2. The bank statement included the following items:
   (a) A $60 credit memo for interest earned by TPCC.
   (b) A $200 NSF check made payable to TPCC.
   (c) A $110 debit memo for bank service charges.
3. The unadjusted book balance at July 31 was $1,400.
4. A comparison of the bank statement with company accounting records disclosed the following:
   (a) A $400 deposit in transit at July 31.
   (b) Outstanding checks totaling $120 at the end of the month.

Required

a. Prepare a bank reconciliation.

b. Prepare in general journal format the entries necessary to adjust TPCC's cash account to its true balance.

Solution to Requirement a

TERRY'S PEST CONTROL COMPANY Bank Reconciliation July 31	
Unadjusted bank balance	$ 870
Add: Deposits in transit	400
Less: Outstanding checks	(120)
True cash balance	$1,150
Unadjusted book balance	$1,400
Add: Interest revenue	60
Less: NSF check	(200)
Less: Bank service charges	(110)
True cash balance	$1,150

Solution to Requirement b

Ref.	Account Title	Debit	Credit
1.	Cash	60	
	Interest Revenue		60
2.	Accounts Receivable	200	
	Cash		200
3.	Service Charge Expense	110	
	Cash		110

KEY TERMS

Accounting controls 318
Administrative controls 318
Adverse opinion 336
Audits 335
Authority manual 322
Bank reconciliation 327
Bank statement 326
Bank statement credit memo 326
Bank statement debit memo 326
Cash 323
Cash short and over 331
Certified check 328
Certified public accountants (CPAs) 335
Checks 325
Confidentiality 337
Deposit ticket 325
Deposits in transit 327
Disclaimer of opinion 336
Fidelity bond 321
Financial statements audit 335
General authority 322
Imprest basis 332
Independent auditor 335
Internal controls 318
Management's discussion and analysis (MD&A) 335
Material 336
Non-sufficient-funds (NSF) checks 328
Notes to the financial statements 335
Outstanding checks 327
Petty cash fund 332
Petty cash voucher 333
Procedures manual 321
Qualified opinion 336
Securities and Exchange Commission (SEC) 337
Segregation of duties 321
Service charges 328
Signature card 325
Specific authorizations 322
True cash balance 327
Unadjusted bank balance 327
Unadjusted book balance 327
Unqualified opinion 336

QUESTIONS

1. What motivated Congress to pass the Sarbanes-Oxley Act (SOX) of 2002?
2. Define the term *internal control*.
3. Explain the relationship between SOX and COSO.
4. Name and briefly define the five components of COSO's internal control framework.
5. Explain how COSO's *Enterprise Risk Management—An Integrated Framework* project relates to COSO's *Internal Control—An Integrated Framework* project.
6. What is the difference between accounting controls and administrative controls?
7. What are several features of an effective internal control system?
8. What is meant by *segregation of duties*? Give an illustration.
9. What are the attributes of a high-quality employee?
10. What is a fidelity bond? Explain its purpose.
11. Why is it important that every employee periodically take a leave of absence or vacation?
12. What are the purpose and importance of a procedures manual?
13. What is the difference between specific and general authorizations?

14. Why should documents (checks, invoices, receipts) be prenumbered?
15. What procedures are important in the physical control of assets and accounting records?
16. What is the purpose of independent verification of performance?
17. What items are considered cash?
18. Why is cash more susceptible to theft or embezzlement than other assets?
19. Giving written copies of receipts to customers can help prevent what type of illegal acts?
20. What procedures can help to protect cash receipts?
21. What procedures can help protect cash disbursements?
22. What effect does a debit memo in a bank statement have on the Cash account? What effect does a credit memo in a bank statement have on the Cash account?
23. What information is normally included in a bank statement?
24. Why might a bank statement reflect a balance that is larger than the balance recorded in the depositor's books? What could cause the bank balance to be smaller than the book balance?
25. What is the purpose of a bank reconciliation?
26. What is an outstanding check?
27. What is a deposit in transit?
28. What is a certified check?
29. How is an NSF check accounted for in the accounting records?
30. What is the purpose of the Cash Short and Over account?
31. What is the purpose of a petty cash fund?
32. What types of expenditures are usually made from a petty cash fund?
33. What is a financial statement audit? Who is qualified to perform it?
34. What is an independent auditor? Why must auditors be independent?
35. What makes an error in the financial statements material?
36. What three basic types of auditors' opinions can be issued on audited financial statements? Describe each.
37. What are the implications of an unqualified audit opinion?
38. When might an auditor issue a disclaimer on financial statements?
39. In what circumstances can an auditor disclose confidential information about a client without the client's permission?
40. What is the purpose of internal controls in an organization?

MULTIPLE-CHOICE QUESTIONS

Multiple-choice questions are available in the Connect library.

EXERCISES—SERIES A

connect plus+ ACCOUNTING ***All applicable Exercises in Series A are available with McGraw-Hill's Connect Plus Accounting.***

Exercise 6-1A *SOX and COSO's internal control frameworks* LO 6-1

Required

a. Discuss the requirements of Section 404 of the Sarbanes-Oxley Act and how it relates to COSO.

b. What type of companies do these rules apply to?

Exercise 6-2A *Features of a strong internal control system* LO 6-1

Required

List and describe nine features of a strong internal control system discussed in this chapter.

Exercise 6-3A *Internal control procedures to prevent embezzlement* LO 6-1

Anna Chun was in charge of the returns department at The Luggage Company. She was responsible for evaluating returned merchandise. She sent merchandise that was reusable back to the warehouse, where it was restocked in inventory. Chun was also responsible for taking the merchandise that she determined to be defective to the city dump for disposal. She had agreed to buy a friend a tax planning program at a discount through her contacts at work. That is when the idea came to her. She could simply classify one of the reusable returns as defective and bring it home instead of taking it to the dump. She did so and made a quick $150. She was happy, and her friend was ecstatic; he was able to buy a $400 software package for only $150. He told his friends about the deal, and soon Chun had a regular set of customers. She was caught when a retail store owner complained to the marketing manager that his pricing strategy was being undercut by The Luggage Company's direct sales to the public. The marketing manager was suspicious because The Luggage Company had no direct marketing program. When the outside sales were ultimately traced back to Chun, the company discovered that it had lost over $10,000 in sales revenue because of her criminal activity.

Required

Identify an internal control procedure that could have prevented the company's losses. Explain how the procedure would have stopped the embezzlement.

LO 6-1

Exercise 6-4A *Internal control procedures to prevent deception*

Regional Medical Centers (RMC) hired a new physician, Fred Clark, who was an immediate success. Everyone loved his bedside manner; he could charm the most cantankerous patient. Indeed, he was a master salesman as well as an expert physician. Unfortunately, Clark misdiagnosed a case that resulted in serious consequences to the patient. The patient filed suit against RMC. In preparation for the defense, RMC's attorneys discovered that Clark was indeed an exceptional salesman. He had worked for several years as district marketing manager for a pharmaceutical company. In fact, he was not a physician at all! He had changed professions without going to medical school. He had lied on his application form. His knowledge of medical terminology had enabled him to fool everyone. RMC was found negligent and lost a $3 million lawsuit.

Required

Identify the relevant internal control procedures that could have prevented the company's losses. Explain how these procedures would have prevented Clark's deception.

LO 6-2

Exercise 6-5A *Internal control for cash*

Required

a. Why are special controls needed for cash?

b. What is included in the definition of *cash*?

LO 6-1, 6-2

Exercise 6-6A *Internal controls for small businesses*

Required

Assume you are the owner of a small business that has only two employees.

a. Which of the internal control procedures are most important to you?

b. How can you overcome the limited opportunity to use the segregation-of-duties control procedure?

LO 6-4

Exercise 6-7A *Treatment of NSF check*

Han's Supplies' bank statement contained a $270 NSF check that one of its customers had written to pay for supplies purchased.

Required

a. Show the effects of recognizing the NSF check on the financial statements by recording the appropriate amounts in a horizontal statements model like the following one:

Assets			=	Liab.	+	Equity	Rev.	−	Exp.	=	Net Inc.	Cash Flow
Cash	+	Accts. Rec.										

b. Is the recognition of the NSF check on Han's books an asset source, use, or exchange transaction?

c. Suppose the customer redeems the check by giving Han $290 cash in exchange for the bad check. The additional $20 paid a service fee charged by Han. Show the effects on the financial statements in the horizontal statements model in Requirement *a.*

d. Is the receipt of cash referenced in Requirement *c* an asset source, use, or exchange transaction?

e. Record in general journal form the adjusting entry for the NSF check and the entry for redemption of the check by the customer.

Exercise 6-8A *Adjustments to the balance per books* LO 6-3

Required

Identify which of the following items are added to or subtracted from the unadjusted *book balance* to arrive at the true cash balance. Distinguish the additions from the subtractions by placing a + beside the items that are added to the unadjusted book balance and a − beside those that are subtracted from it. The first item is recorded as an example.

Reconciling Items	Book Balance Adjusted?	Added or Subtracted?
Credit memo	Yes	+
Interest revenue		
Deposits in transit		
Debit memo		
Service charge		
Charge for printing checks		
NSF check from customer		
Note receivable collected by the bank		
Outstanding checks		

Exercise 6-9A *Adjustments to the balance per bank* LO 6-3

Required

Identify which of the following items are added to or subtracted from the unadjusted *bank balance* to arrive at the true cash balance. Distinguish the additions from the subtractions by placing a + beside the items that are added to the unadjusted bank balance and a − beside those that are subtracted from it. The first item is recorded as an example.

Reconciling Items	Bank Balance Adjusted?	Added or Subtracted?
Bank service charge	No	NA
Outstanding checks		
Deposits in transit		
Debit memo		
Credit memo		
Certified checks		
Petty cash voucher		
NSF check from customer		
Interest revenue		

Exercise 6-10A *Adjusting the cash account* LO 6-3

As of June 30, 2016, the bank statement showed an ending balance of $19,500. The unadjusted Cash account balance was $15,200. The following information is available:

1. Deposit in transit, $2,400.
2. Credit memo in bank statement for interest earned in June, $30.
3. Outstanding check, $6,690.
4. Debit memo for service charge, $20.

Required

a. Determine the true cash balance by preparing a bank reconciliation as of June 30, 2016, using the preceding information.

b. Record in general journal format the adjusting entries necessary to correct the unadjusted book balance.

LO 6-3

Exercise 6-11A *Determining the true cash balance, starting with the unadjusted bank balance*

The following information is available for Trinkle Company for the month of June:

1. The unadjusted balance per the bank statement on June 30 was $81,500.
2. Deposits in transit on June 30 were $3,150.
3. A debit memo was included with the bank statement for a service charge of $40.
4. A $5,611 check written in June had not been paid by the bank.
5. The bank statement included a $950 credit memo for the collection of a note. The principal of the note was $900, and the interest collected amounted to $50.

Required

Determine the true cash balance as of June 30. (*Hint:* It is not necessary to use all of the preceding items to determine the true balance.)

LO 6-3

Exercise 6-12A *Determining the true cash balance, starting with the unadjusted book balance*

Nickleson Company had an unadjusted cash balance of $7,750 as of May 31. The company's bank statement, also dated May 31, included a $72 NSF check written by one of Nickleson's customers. There were $800 in outstanding checks and $950 in deposits in transit as of May 31. According to the bank statement, service charges were $50, and the bank collected a $800 note receivable for Nickleson. The bank statement also showed $13 of interest revenue earned by Nickleson.

Required

Determine the true cash balance as of May 31. (*Hint:* It is not necessary to use all of the preceding items to determine the true balance.)

LO 6-4

Exercise 6-13A *Effect of establishing a petty cash fund*

Chen Company established a $200 petty cash fund on January 1, 2016.

Required

a. Is the establishment of the petty cash fund an asset source, use, or exchange transaction?
b. Record the establishment of the petty cash fund in a horizontal statements model like the following one:

Assets			=	Liab.	+	Equity	Rev.	−	Exp.	=	Net Inc.	Cash Flow
Cash	+	Petty Cash										

c. Record the establishment of the fund in general journal format.

LO 6-4

Exercise 6-14A *Effect of petty cash events on the financial statements*

Fresh Foods established a petty cash fund of $100 on January 2. On January 31, the fund contained cash of $9.20 and vouchers for the following cash payments:

Maintenance expense	$61.50
Office supplies	12.50
Transportation expense	15.00

The three distinct accounting events affecting the petty cash fund for the period were (1) establishment of the fund, (2) reimbursements made to employees, and (3) recognition of expenses and replenishment of the fund.

Required

a. Record each of the three events in a horizontal statements model like the following one. In the Cash Flow column, indicate whether the item is an operating activity (OA), investing activity (IA), or a financing activity (FA). Use NA to indicate that an account was not affected by the event.

Assets			=	Liab.	+	Equity	Rev.	−	Exp.	=	Net Inc.	Cash Flow
Cash	+	Petty Cash										

b. Record the events in general journal format.

Exercise 6-15A *Determining the amount of petty cash expense* — LO 6-4

Consider the following events:

1. A petty cash fund of $200 was established on April 1, 2016.
2. Employees were reimbursed when they presented petty cash vouchers to the petty cash custodian.
3. On April 30, 2016, the petty cash fund contained vouchers totaling $196.50 plus $2.20 of currency.

Required

Answer the following questions:

a. How did the establishment of the petty cash fund affect (increase, decrease, or have no effect on) total assets?
b. What is the amount of total petty cash expenses to be recognized during April?
c. When are petty cash expenses recognized (at the time of establishment, reimbursement, or replenishment)?

Exercise 6-16A *Confidentiality and the auditor* — LO 6-5

Cal Lopez discovered significant fraud in the accounting records of a high profile client. The story has been broadcast on national airways. Lopez was unable to resolve his remaining concerns with the company's management team and ultimately resigned from the audit engagement. Lopez knows that he will be asked by several interested parties, including his friends and relatives, the successor auditor, and prosecuting attorneys in a court of law, to tell what he knows. He has asked you for advice.

Required

Write a memo that explains Lopez's disclosure responsibilities to each of the interested parties.

PROBLEMS—SERIES A

All applicable Problems in Series A are available with McGraw-Hill's Connect Plus Accounting.

Problem 6-17A *Using internal control to restrict illegal or unethical behavior* — LO 6-1, 6-2

Required

For each of the following fraudulent acts, describe one or more internal control procedures that could have prevented (or helped prevent) the problems.

a. Everyone in the office has noticed what a dedicated employee Carley Trap is. She never misses work, not even for a vacation. Trap is in charge of the petty cash fund. She transfers funds from the company's bank account to the petty cash account on an as-needed basis. During a surprise audit, the petty cash fund was found to contain fictitious receipts. Over a three-year period, Trap had used more than $4,000 of petty cash to pay for personal expenses.

b. Doug Clampet was hired as the vice president of the manufacturing division of a corporation. His impressive resume listed a master's degree in business administration from a large state university and numerous collegiate awards and activities, when in fact Clampet had only a high school diploma. In a short time, the company was in poor financial condition because of his inadequate knowledge and bad decisions.

c. Stone Manufacturing has good internal control over its manufacturing materials inventory. However, office supplies are kept on open shelves in the employee break room. The office supervisor has noticed that he is having to order paper, tape, staplers, and pens with increasing frequency.

LO 6-3

Problem 6-18A *Preparing a bank reconciliation*

Rick Hall owns a card shop, Hall's Cards. The following cash information is available for the month of August 2016.

As of August 31, the bank statement shows a balance of $16,140. The August 31 unadjusted balance in the Cash account of Hall's Cards is $14,100. A review of the bank statement revealed the following information:

1. A deposit of $4,150 on August 31, 2016, does not appear on the August bank statement.
2. It was discovered that a check to pay for baseball cards was correctly written and paid by the bank for $4,500 but was recorded on the books as $5,400.
3. When checks written during the month were compared with those paid by the bank, three checks amounting to $5,370 were found to be outstanding.
4. A debit memo for $80 was included in the bank statement for the purchase of a new supply of checks.

Required

a. Prepare a bank reconciliation at the end of August showing the true cash balance.
b. Prepare any necessary journal entries to adjust the books to the true cash balance.

LO 6-3

Problem 6-19A *Missing information in a bank reconciliation*

The following data apply to Pro Beauty Supply Inc. for May 2016:

1. Balance per the bank on May 31, $9,150.
2. Deposits in transit not recorded by the bank, $1,510.
3. Bank error; check written by Best Beauty Supply was charged to Pro Beauty Supply's account, $560.
4. The following checks written and recorded by Pro Beauty Supply were not included in the bank statement:

3013	$ 510
3054	640
3056	1,520

5. Note collected by the bank, $500.
6. Service charge for collection of note, $20.
7. The bookkeeper recorded a check written for $320 to pay for the May utilities expense as $230 in the cash disbursements journal.
8. Bank service charge in addition to the note collection fee, $40.
9. Customer checks returned by the bank as NSF, $310.

Required

Determine the amount of the unadjusted cash balance per Pro Beauty Supply's books.

LO 6-3

Problem 6-20A *Adjustments to the cash account based on the bank reconciliation*

Required

Determine whether the following items included in Wong Company's January 2016 bank reconciliation will require adjusting or correcting entries on Wong's books. When an entry is required, record it in general journal format.

a. Service charges of $50 for the month of January were listed on the bank statement.

b. The bank charged a $250 check drawn on Wing Restaurant to Wong's account. The check was included in Wong's bank statement.

c. A check of $62 was returned to the bank because of insufficient funds and was noted on the bank statement. Wong received the check from a customer and thought that it was good when it was deposited into the account.

d. A $990 deposit was recorded by the bank as $980.

e. Four checks totaling $810 written during the month of January were not included with the January bank statement.

f. A $75 check written to Office Max for office supplies was recorded in the general journal as $57.

g. The bank statement indicated that the bank had collected a $450 note for Wong.

h. Wong recorded $900 of receipts on January 31, 2016, which were deposited in the night depository of the bank. These deposits were not included in the bank statement.

Problem 6-21A *Bank reconciliation and adjustments to the cash account*

LO 6-3

CHECK FIGURE

a. True Cash Balance, July 31, 2016: $16,234

The following information is available for Park Valley Spa for July 2016:

Bank Statement

STATE BANK

Bolta Vista, NV 10001

Park Valley Spa 10 Main Street Bolta Vista, NV 10001	Account number 12-4567 July 31, 2016

Beginning balance 6/30/2016	$ 9,031
Total deposits and other credits	29,800
Total checks and other debits	23,902
Ending balance 7/31/2016	14,929

Checks and Debits		Deposits and Credits	
Check No.	Amount	Date	Amount
2350	$3,761	July 1	$1,102
2351	1,643	July 10	6,498
2352	8,000	July 15	4,929
2354	2,894	July 21	6,174
2355	1,401	July 26	5,963
2357	6,187	July 30	2,084
DM	16	CM	3,050

The following is a list of checks and deposits recorded on the books of the Park Valley Spa for July 2016:

Date	Check No.	Amount of Check	Date	Amount of Deposit
July 2	2351	$1,643	July 8	$6,498
July 4	2352	8,000	July 14	4,929
July 10	2353	1,500	July 21	6,174
July 10	2354	2,894	July 26	5,963
July 15	2355	1,401	July 29	2,084
July 20	2356	745	July 30	3,550
July 22	2357	6,187		

Other Information

1. Check no. 2350 was outstanding from June.
2. The credit memo was for collection of notes receivable.
3. All checks were paid at the correct amount.

4. The debit memo was for printed checks.
5. The June 30 bank reconciliation showed a deposit in transit of $1,102.
6. The unadjusted Cash account balance at July 31 was $13,200.

Required

a. Prepare the bank reconciliation for Park Valley Spa at the end of July.
b. Record in general journal form any necessary entries to the Cash account to adjust it to the true cash balance.

LO 6-3

Problem 6-22A *Effect of adjustments to cash on the accounting equation*

After reconciling its bank account, Watson Company made the following adjusting entries:

Entry No.	Account Titles	Debit	Credit
1	Cash Supplies Expense *To correct overstatement of expense*	20	 20
2	Cash Accounts Receivable *To record bank collection*	845	 845
3	Cash Interest Revenue *To record interest revenue*	44	 44
4	Service Charge Expense Cash *To record bank service charge*	35	 35
5	Accounts Receivable Cash *To record NSF check from Beat*	174	 174

Required

Identify the event depicted in each journal entry as asset source (AS), asset use (AU), asset exchange (AE), or claims exchange (CE). Also explain how each entry affects the accounting equation by placing a + for increase, − for decrease, or NA for not affected under the following components of the accounting equation. The first event is recorded as an example.

						Stockholders' Equity		
Event No.	Type of Event	Assets	=	Liabilities	+	Common Stock	+	Retained Earnings
1	AS	+		NA		NA		+

LO 6-1, 6-2, 6-3

Problem 6-23A *Bank reconciliation and internal control*

Following is a bank reconciliation for Zocar Enterprises for June 30, 2016:

	Cash Account	Bank Statement
Balance as of 6/30/2016	$ 1,918	$ 3,000
Deposit in transit		600
Outstanding checks		(1,507)
Note collected by bank	2,000	
Bank service charge	(25)	
NSF check	(1,800)	
Adjusted cash balance as of 6/30/2016	$ 2,093	$ 2,093

When reviewing the bank reconciliation, Zocar's auditor was unable to locate any reference to the NSF check on the bank statement. Furthermore, the clerk who reconciles the bank account and records the adjusting entries could not find the actual NSF check that should have been included in the bank statement. Finally, there was no specific reference in the accounts receivable supporting records identifying a party who had written a bad check.

Required

a. Prepare the adjusting entry that the clerk would have made to record the NSF check.

b. Assume that the clerk who prepares the bank reconciliation and records the adjusting entries also makes bank deposits. Explain how the clerk could use a fictitious NSF check to hide the theft of cash.

c. How could Zocar avoid the theft of cash that is concealed by the use of fictitious NSF checks?

Problem 6-24A *Petty cash fund* LO 6-4

Austin Co. established a petty cash fund by issuing a check for $300 and appointing Steve Mack as petty cash custodian. Mack had vouchers for the following petty cash payments during the month:

Stamps	$62
Miscellaneous items	20
Employee supper money	70
Taxi fare	50
Window-washing service	75

There was $21 of currency in the petty cash box at the time it was replenished.

Required

a. Prepare all general journal entries necessary to (1) establish the fund, (2) reimburse employees, (3) recognize expenses, and (4) replenish the fund. (*Hint:* Journal entries may not be required for all the events.)

b. Explain how the Cash Short and Over account required in this case will affect the income statement.

c. Identify the event depicted in each journal entry recorded in Requirement *a* as asset source (AS), asset use (AU), asset exchange (AE), or claims exchange (CE).

d. Record the effects of the events in Requirement *a* on the financial statements using a horizontal statements model like the following one. In the Cash Flow column, indicate whether the item is an operating activity (OA), investing activity (IA), or financing activity (FA). Use NA to indicate that an account was not affected by the event.

Assets	= Liab. + Equity	Rev. − Exp. = Net Inc.	Cash Flow
Cash + Petty Cash			

Problem 6-25A *Auditor responsibilities* LO 6-5

You have probably heard it is unwise to bite the hand that feeds you. Independent auditors are chosen by, paid by, and can be fired by the companies they audit. What keeps the auditor independent? In other words, what stops an auditor from blindly following the orders of a client?

Required

Write a memo that explains the reporting responsibilities of an independent auditor.

EXERCISES—SERIES B

Exercise 6-1B *SOX and COSO's internal control frameworks* LO 6-1

Required

a. Explain what the acronym SOX refers to.

b. Define the acronym COSO and explain how it relates to SOX.

c. Name and briefly define the five components of COSO's internal control framework.

d. Define the acronym ERM and explain how it relates to COSO's internal control framework.

LO 6-1

Exercise 6-2B *Internal control procedures*

Required

a. Name and describe the two categories of internal controls.

b. What is the purpose of internal controls?

LO 6-1

Exercise 6-3B *Internal control procedures*

Stan Oden is opening a new business that will sell sporting goods. It will initially be a small operation, and he is concerned about the security of his assets. He will not be able to be at the business all of the time and will have to rely on his employees and internal control procedures to ensure that transactions are properly accounted for and assets are safeguarded. He will have a store manager and two other employees who will be sales personnel and stock personnel and who will also perform any other duties necessary. Stan will be in the business on a regular basis. He has come to you for advice.

Required

Write a memo to Stan outlining the procedures that he should implement to ensure that his store assets are protected and that the financial transactions are properly recorded.

LO 6-1

Exercise 6-4B *Internal controls to prevent theft*

Sally Knox worked as the parts manager for East River Automobiles, a local automobile dealership. Sally was very dedicated and never missed a day of work. Since East River was a small operation, she was the only employee in the parts department. Her duties consisted of ordering parts for stock and as needed for repairs, receiving the parts and checking them in, distributing them as needed to the shop or to customers for purchase, and keeping track of and taking the year-end inventory of parts. East River decided to expand and needed to secure additional financing. The local bank agreed to a loan contingent on an audit of the dealership. One requirement of the audit was to oversee the inventory count of both automobiles and parts on hand. Sally was clearly nervous, explaining that she had just inventoried all parts in the parts department. She supplied the auditors with a detailed list. The inventory showed parts on hand worth $225,000. The auditors decided they needed to verify a substantial part of the inventory. When the auditors began their counts, a pattern began to develop. Each type of part seemed to be one or two items short when the actual count was taken. This raised more concern. Although Sally assured the auditors the parts were just misplaced, the auditors continued the count. After completing the count of parts on hand, the auditors could document only $155,000 of actual parts. Suddenly, Sally quit her job and moved to another state.

Required

a. What do you suppose caused the discrepancy between the actual count and the count that Sally had supplied?

b. What procedures could be put into place to prevent this type of problem?

LO 6-2

Exercise 6-5B *Features of internal control procedures for cash*

Required

List and discuss effective internal control procedures that apply to cash.

LO 6-1

Exercise 6-6B *Internal controls for equipment*

Required

List the internal control procedures that pertain to the protection of business equipment.

LO 6-3

Exercise 6-7B *Treatment of NSF check*

The bank statement of Hibbert Supplies included a $300 NSF check that one of Hibbert's customers had written to pay for services that were provided by Hibbert.

Required

a. Show the effects of recognizing the NSF check on the financial statements by recording the appropriate amounts in a horizontal statements model like the following one:

Assets			=	Liab.	+	Equity	Rev.	−	Exp.	=	Net Inc.	Cash Flow
Cash	+	Accts. Rec.										

b. Is the recognition of the NSF check on Hibbert's books an asset source, use, or exchange transaction?

c. Suppose the customer redeems the check by giving Hibbert $325 cash in exchange for the bad check. The additional $25 paid a service fee charged by Hibbert. Show the effects on the financial statements in the horizontal statements model in Requirement *a.*

d. Is the receipt of cash referred to in Requirement *c* an asset source, use, or exchange transaction?

e. Record in general journal form the adjusting entry for the NSF check and the subsequent entry for redemption of the check by the customer.

Exercise 6-8B *Adjustments to the balance per books* LO 6-3

Required

Identify which of the following items are added to or subtracted from the unadjusted *book balance* to arrive at the true cash balance. Distinguish the additions from the subtractions by placing a + beside the items that are added to the unadjusted book balance and a − beside those that are subtracted from it. The first item is recorded as an example.

Reconciling Items	Book Balance Adjusted?	Added or Subtracted?
Automatic debit for utility bill	Yes	−
Charge for printing new checks		
NSF check from customer		
ATM fee		
Outstanding checks		
Interest revenue earned on the account		
Deposits in transit		
Service charge		

Exercise 6-9B *Adjustments to the balance per bank* LO 6-3

Required

Identify which of the following items are added to or subtracted from the unadjusted *bank balance* to arrive at the true cash balance. Distinguish the additions from the subtractions by placing a + beside the items that are added to the unadjusted bank balance and a − beside those that are subtracted from it. The first item is recorded as an example.

Reconciling Items	Bank Balance Adjusted?	Added or Subtracted?
Credit memo	No	N/A
ATM fee		
Petty cash voucher		
NSF check from customer		
Interest revenue		
Bank service charge		
Outstanding checks		
Deposits in transit		
Debit memo		

LO 6-3

Exercise 6-10B *Adjusting the cash account*

As of May 31, 2016, the bank statement showed an ending balance of $26,100. The unadjusted Cash account balance was $27,350. The following information is available:

1. Deposit in transit, $6,981.
2. Credit memo in bank statement for interest earned in May, $36.
3. Outstanding check, $5,720.
4. Debit memo for service charge, $25.

Required

a. Determine the true cash balance by preparing a bank reconciliation as of May 31, 2016, using the preceding information.

b. Record in general journal format the adjusting entries necessary to correct the unadjusted book balance.

LO 6-3

Exercise 6-11B *Determining the true cash balance, starting with the unadjusted bank balance*

The following information is available for Jenkins Company for the month of August:

1. The unadjusted balance per the bank statement on August 31 was $35,200.
2. Deposits in transit on August 31 were $3,750.
3. A debit memo was included with the bank statement for a service charge of $35.
4. A $2,120 check written in August had not been paid by the bank.
5. The bank statement included a $1,550 credit memo for the collection of a note. The principal of the note was $1,500, and the interest collected was $50.

Required

Determine the true cash balance as of August 31. (*Hint:* It is not necessary to use all of the preceding items to determine the true balance.)

LO 6-3

Exercise 6-12B *Determining the true cash balance, starting with the unadjusted book balance*

Burson Company had an unadjusted cash balance of $8,120 as of April 30. The company's bank statement, also dated April 30, included a $200 NSF check written by one of Burson's customers. There were $1,525 in outstanding checks and $900 in deposits in transit as of April 30. According to the bank statement, service charges were $50, and the bank collected a $500 note receivable for Burson. The bank statement also showed $31 of interest revenue earned by Burson.

Required

Determine the true cash balance as of April 30. (*Hint:* It is not necessary to use all of the preceding items to determine the true balance.)

LO 6-4

Exercise 6-13B *Effect of establishing a petty cash fund*

Mountain Timber Company established a $180 petty cash fund on January 1, 2016.

Required

a. Is the establishment of the petty cash fund an asset source, use, or exchange transaction?

b. Record the establishment of the petty cash fund in a horizontal statements model like the following one:

Assets			=	Liab.	+	Equity	Rev.	−	Exp.	=	Net Inc.	Cash Flow
Cash	+	Petty Cash										

c. Record the establishment of the fund in general journal format.

Exercise 6-14B *Effect of petty cash events on the financial statements* LO 6-4

Payton Inc. established a petty cash fund of $150 on January 2. On January 31, the fund contained cash of $8.20 and vouchers for the following cash payments:

Postage and office supplies	$76.30
Entertainment expense	36.50
Maintenance expense	25.00

The three distinct accounting events affecting the petty cash fund for the period were (1) establishment of the fund, (2) reimbursements made to employees, and (3) recognition of expenses and replenishment of the fund.

Required

a. Record each of the three events in a horizontal statements model like the following one. In the Cash Flow column, indicate whether the item is an operating activity (OA), investing activity (IA), or a financing activity (FA). Use NA to indicate that an account was not affected by the event.

Assets			=	Liab.	+	Equity	Rev.	−	Exp.	=	Net Inc.	Cash Flow
Cash	+	Petty Cash										

b. Record the events in general journal format.

Exercise 6-15B *Determining the amount of petty cash expense* LO 6-4

Consider the following events:

1. A petty cash fund of $200 was established on April 1, 2016.
2. Employees were reimbursed when they presented petty cash vouchers to the petty cash custodian.
3. On April 30, 2016, the petty cash fund contained vouchers totaling $171.40 plus $26.10 of currency.

Required

Answer the following questions:

a. How did the establishment of the petty cash fund affect (increase, decrease, or have no effect on) total assets?

b. What is the amount of total petty cash expenses to be recognized during April?

c. When are petty cash expenses recognized (at the time of establishment, reimbursement, or replenishment)?

Exercise 6-16B *Materiality and the auditor* LO 6-5

Sarah Bale is an auditor. Her work at two companies disclosed inappropriate recognition of revenue. Both cases involved dollar amounts in the $100,000 range. In one case, Bale considered the item material and required her client to restate earnings. In the other case, Bale dismissed the misstatement as being immaterial.

Required

Write a memo that explains how a $100,000 misstatement of revenue is acceptable for one company but unacceptable for a different company.

PROBLEMS—SERIES B

Problem 6-17B *Using internal control to restrict illegal or unethical behavior* LO 6-1, 6-2

Required

For each of the following fraudulent acts, describe one or more internal control procedures that could have prevented (or helped prevent) the problems.

a. Linda Hinson, the administrative assistant in charge of payroll, created a fictitious employee, wrote weekly checks to the fictitious employee, and then personally cashed the checks for her own benefit.

b. Jim Stewart, the receiving manager of Western Lumber, created a fictitious supplier named B&A Building Supply. B&A regularly billed Western Lumber for supplies purchased. Stewart had printed shipping slips and billing invoices with the name of the fictitious company and opened a post office box as the mailing address. Stewart simply prepared a receiving report and submitted it for payment to the accounts payable department. The accounts payable clerk then paid the invoice when it was received because Stewart acknowledged receipt of the supplies.

c. Jalie Thomas works at a local hobby shop and usually operates the cash register. She has developed a way to give discounts to her friends. When they come by, she rings a lower price or does not charge the friend for some of the material purchased. At first, Thomas thought she would get caught, but no one seemed to notice. Indeed, she has become so sure that there is no way for the owner to find out that she has started taking home some supplies for her own personal use.

LO 6-3

Problem 6-18B *Preparing a bank reconciliation*

Bill Lewis owns a construction business, Lewis Supply Co. The following cash information is available for the month of October 2016.

As of October 31, the bank statement shows a balance of $21,400. The October 31 unadjusted balance in the Cash account of Lewis Supply Co. is $18,400. A review of the bank statement revealed the following information:

1. A deposit of $2,600 on October 31, 2016, does not appear on the October 31 bank statement.
2. A debit memo for $75 was included in the bank statement for the purchase of a new supply of checks.
3. When checks written during the month were compared with those paid by the bank, three checks amounting to $2,075 were found to be outstanding.
4. It was discovered that a check to pay for repairs was correctly written and paid by the bank for $1,500 but was recorded on the books as $5,100.

Required

a. Prepare a bank reconciliation at the end of October showing the true cash balance.

b. Prepare any necessary journal entries to adjust the books to the true cash balance.

LO 6-3

Problem 6-19B *Missing information in a bank reconciliation*

The following data apply to Woods Sports Inc. for April 2016:

1. Balance per the bank on April 30, $13,750.
2. Deposits in transit not recorded by the bank, $3,600.
3. Bank error; check written by Glen Woods on his personal checking account was drawn on Woods Sports Inc.'s account, $800.
4. The following checks written and recorded by Woods Sports Inc. were not included in the bank statement:

1901	$ 265
1920	650
1921	1,200

5. Credit memo for note collected by the bank, $1,100.
6. Service charge for collection of note, $50.
7. The bookkeeper recorded a check written for $760 to pay for April's office supplies as $670 in the cash disbursements journal.
8. Bank service charge in addition to the note collection fee, $45.
9. NSF checks returned by the bank, $175.

Required

Determine the amount of the unadjusted cash balance per Woods Sports Inc.'s books.

Problem 6-20B *Adjustments to the cash account based on the bank reconciliation*

LO 6-3

Determine whether the following items in China Imports' bank reconciliation require adjusting or correcting entries on China Imports' books. When an entry is required, record it in general journal format.

a. The bank statement indicated that China Imports earned $60 of interest revenue.
b. China Imports' accountant mistakenly recorded a $430 check that was written to purchase supplies as $350.
c. Bank service charges for the month were $45.
d. The bank reconciliation disclosed that $800 had been stolen from China Imports' business.
e. Outstanding checks amounted to $2,600.
f. The bank collected $4,000 of China Imports' accounts receivable. China Imports had instructed its customers to send their payments directly to the bank.
g. The bank mistakenly gave Imports Inc. credit for a $800 deposit made by China Imports.
h. Deposits in transit were $6,200.
i. China Imports' bank statement contained a $525 NSF check. China Imports had received the check from a customer and had included it in one of its bank deposits.

Problem 6-21B *Bank reconciliation and adjustments to the cash account*

LO 6-3

The following information is available for Pyle Garage for March 2016:

BANK STATEMENT
HAZARD STATE BANK
215 MAIN STREET
HAZARD, GA 30321

Pyle Garage 629 Main Street Hazard, GA 30321	Account number 62-00062 March 31, 2016
Beginning balance 3/1/2016	$15,000.00
Total deposits and other credits	7,000.00
Total checks and other debits	6,000.00
Ending balance 3/31/2016	16,000.00

Checks and Debits		Deposits and Credits	
Check No.	Amount	Date	Amount
1462	$1,163.00	March 1	$1,000.00
1463	62.00	March 2	1,340.00
1464	1,235.00	March 6	210.00
1465	750.00	March 12	1,940.00
1466	1,111.00	March 17	855.00
1467	964.00	March 22	1,480.00
DM	15.00	CM	175.00
1468	700.00		

The following is a list of checks and deposits recorded on the books of Pyle Garage for March 2016:

Date	Check No.	Amount of Check	Date	Amount of Deposit
March 1	1463	$ 62.00	March 1	$1,340.00
March 5	1464	1,235.00	March 5	210.00
March 6	1465	750.00		
March 9	1466	1,111.00	March 10	1,940.00
March 10	1467	964.00		
March 14	1468	70.00	March 16	855.00
March 19	1469	1,500.00	March 19	1,480.00
March 28	1470	102.00	March 29	2,000.00

Other Information

1. Check no. 1462 was outstanding from February.
2. A credit memo for collection of accounts receivable was included in the bank statement.
3. All checks were paid at the correct amount.
4. The bank statement included a debit memo for service charges.
5. The February 28 bank reconciliation showed a deposit in transit of $1,000.
6. Check no. 1468 was for the purchase of equipment.
7. The unadjusted Cash account balance at March 31 was $16,868.

Required

a. Prepare the bank reconciliation for Pyle Garage at the end of March.

b. Record in general journal form any necessary entries to the Cash account to adjust it to the true cash balance.

LO 6-3

Problem 6-22B *Effect of adjustments to cash on the accounting equation*

After reconciling its bank account, Addy Equipment Company made the following adjusting entries:

Entry No.	Account Titles	Debit	Credit
1	Accounts Receivable Cash *To record NSF check from Wilson*	250	250
2	Rent Expense Cash *To correct understatement of expense*	35	35
3	Service Charge Expense Cash *To record bank service charge*	15	15
4	Cash Accounts Receivable *To record bank collection*	175	175
5	Cash Interest Revenue *To record interest revenue*	40	40

Required

Identify the event depicted in each journal entry as an asset source (AS), asset use (AU), asset exchange (AE), or claims exchange (CE). Also explain how each entry affects the accounting equation by placing a + for increase, − for decrease, or NA for not affected under the following components of the accounting equation. The first event is recorded as an example.

						Stockholders' Equity		
Event No.	Type of Event	Assets	=	Liabilities	+	Common Stock	+	Retained Earnings
1	AE	+/−		NA		NA		NA

Problem 6-23B *Bank reconciliation and internal control*

LO 6-1, 6-2, 6-3

Following is a bank reconciliation for BBQ Express for May 31, 2016:

	Cash Account	Bank Statement
Balance as of 5/31/2016	$25,000	$22,000
Deposit in transit		4,250
Outstanding checks		(465)
Note collected by bank	1,815	
Bank service charge	(30)	
Automatic payment on loan	(1,000)	
Adjusted cash balance as of 5/31/2016	$25,785	$25,785

Because of limited funds, BBQ Express employed only one accountant who was responsible for receiving cash, recording receipts and disbursements, preparing deposits, and preparing the bank reconciliation. The accountant left the company on June 8, 2016, after preparing the May 31 bank reconciliation. His replacement compared the checks returned with the bank statement to the cash disbursements journal and found the total of outstanding checks to be $4,600.

Required

a. Prepare a corrected bank reconciliation.

b. What is the total amount of cash missing, and how was the difference between the "true cash" per the bank and the "true cash" per the books hidden on the reconciliation prepared by the former employee?

c. What could BBQ Express do to avoid cash theft in the future?

Problem 6-24B *Petty cash fund*

LO 6-4

The following data pertain to the petty cash fund of Marsh Company:

CHECK FIGURE
a. Cash Short: $3

1. The petty cash fund was established on an imprest basis at $250 on March 1.
2. On March 31, a physical count of the fund disclosed $13 in currency and coins, vouchers authorizing meal allowances totaling $120, vouchers authorizing purchase of postage stamps of $21, and vouchers for payment of delivery charges of $93.

Required

a. Prepare all general journal entries necessary to (1) establish the fund, (2) reimburse employees, and (3) recognize the expenses and replenish the fund as of March 31. (*Hint:* Journal entries may not be required for all three events.)

b. Explain how the Cash Short and Over account required in this case affects the income statement.

c. Identify the event depicted in each journal entry recorded in Requirement *a* as asset source (AS), asset use (AU), asset exchange (AE), or claims exchange (CE).

d. Record the effects on the financial statements of the events in Requirement *a* using a horizontal statements model like the following one. In the Cash Flow column, indicate whether the item is an operating activity (OA), investing activity (IA), or financing activity (FA). Use NA to indicate that an account was not affected by the event.

Assets			=	Liab.	+	Equity	Rev.	−	Exp.	=	Net Inc.	Cash Flow
Cash	+	Petty Cash										

LO 6-5

Problem 6-25B *Types of audit reports*

Connie Stevens is a partner in a regional accounting firm. Ms. Stevens was hired by a client to audit the company's books. After extensive work, Ms. Stevens determined that she was unable to perform the appropriate audit procedures.

Required

a. Name the type of audit report that Ms. Stevens should issue with respect to the work that she did accomplish.

b. If Ms. Stevens had been able to perform the necessary audit procedures, there are three types of audit reports that she could have issued depending on the outcome of the audit. Name and describe these three types of audit reports.

ANALYZE, THINK, COMMUNICATE

ATC 6-1 Business Applications Case *Understanding real-world annual reports*

Required

Use the Target Corporation's annual report in Appendix B to answer the following questions.

a. Who are the independent auditors for Target?

b. What type of opinion did the independent auditors issue on Target's financial statements?

c. On what date does it appear the independent auditors completed their work related to Target's financial statements for the fiscal-year ended February 1, 2014 (2013)?

d. Does the auditors' report give any information about how the audit was conducted? If so, what does it suggest was done?

e. Does the auditors' report tell the reader that the audit was concerned with materiality rather than absolute accuracy in the financial statements?

ATC 6-2 Group Assignment *Bank reconciliations*

The following cash and bank information is available for three companies at June 30, 2016:

Cash and Adjustment Information	Peach Co.	Apple Co.	Pear Co.
Unadjusted cash balance per books, 6/30	$45,620	$32,450	$23,467
Outstanding checks	1,345	2,478	2,540
Service charge	50	75	35
Balance per bank statement, 6/30	48,632	37,176	24,894
Credit memo for collection of notes receivable	4,500	5,600	3,800
NSF check	325	145	90
Deposits in transit	2,500	3,200	4,800
Credit memo for interest earned	42	68	12

Required

a. Organize the class into three sections and divide each section into groups of three to five students. Assign Peach Co. to section 1, Apple Co. to section 2, and Pear Co. to section 3.

Group Tasks

(1) Prepare a bank reconciliation for the company assigned to your group.

(2) Prepare any necessary journal entries for the company assigned to your group.

(3) Select a representative from a group in each section to put the bank reconciliation and required journal entries on the board.

Class Discussion:

b. Discuss the cause of the difference between the unadjusted cash balance and the ending balance for the bank statement. Also, discuss types of adjustments that are commonly made to the bank balance and types of adjustments that are commonly made to the unadjusted book balance.

ATC 6-3 Real-World Case *Evaluating management's responsibilities*

The following excerpt was taken from Google, Inc.'s 10-K report for its 2013 fiscal year:

CONTROLS AND PROCEDURES

Evaluation of Disclosure Controls and Procedures

Our management, with the participation of our chief executive officer and chief financial officer, evaluated the effectiveness of our disclosure controls and procedures. . . .

Based on this evaluation, our chief executive officer and chief financial officer concluded that, as of December 31, 2013, our disclosure controls and procedures are designed at a reasonable assurance level and are effective to provide reasonable assurance that information we are required to disclose in reports that we file or submit under the Exchange Act is recorded, processed, summarized, and reported within the time periods specified in the SEC's rules and forms, and that such information is accumulated and communicated to our management, including our chief executive officer and chief financial officer, as appropriate, to allow timely decisions regarding required disclosure. . . .

Management's Report on Internal Control over Financial Reporting

Our management is responsible for establishing and maintaining adequate internal control over financial reporting, as defined in Rule 13a-15(f) of the Exchange Act. Our management conducted an evaluation of the effectiveness of our internal control over financial reporting based on the framework in Internal Control—Integrated Framework *issued by the Committee of Sponsoring Organizations of the Treadway Commission. Based on this evaluation, management concluded that our internal control over financial reporting was effective as of December 31, 2013. Management reviewed the results of its assessment with our Audit Committee. The effectiveness of our internal control over financial reporting as of December 31, 2013, has been audited by Ernst & Young LLP, an independent registered public accounting firm, as stated in its report which is included in Item 8 of this Annual Report on Form 10-K.*

Limitations on Effectiveness of Controls and Procedures

In designing and evaluating the disclosure controls and procedures, management recognizes that any controls and procedures, no matter how well designed and operated, can provide only reasonable assurance of achieving the desired control objectives. In addition, the design of disclosure controls and procedures must reflect the fact that there are resource constraints and that management is required to apply its judgment in evaluating the benefits of possible controls and procedures relative to their costs.

Required

Based on information in the text, list some of the elements of internal control you would expect the company's management to have established. You do not need to read the report of the Treadway Commission.

ATC 6-4 Business Applications Case *Decisions about materiality*

The accounting firm of Brooke & Doggett, CPAs, recently completed the audits of three separate companies. During these audits, the following events were discovered, and Brooke & Doggett is trying to decide if each event is material. If an item is material, the CPA firm will insist that the company modify the financial statements.

1. In 2016, Major Company reported service revenues of $1,000,000 and earnings before tax of $80,000. Because of an accounting error, the company recorded $6,000 as revenue in 2016 for services that will not be performed until early 2017.
2. Willis Company plans to report a cash balance of $70,000. Because of an accounting error, this amount is $5,000 too high. Willis also plans to report total assets of $4,000,000 and net earnings of $415,000.
3. Adams Company's 2016 balance sheet shows a cash balance of $200,000 and total assets of $9,000,000. For 2016, the company had a net income of $750,000. These balances are all correct, but they would have been $5,000 higher if the president of the company had not claimed business travel expenses that were, in fact, the cost of personal vacations for him and his family. He charged the costs of these trips on the company's credit card. The president of Adams Company owns 25 percent of the business.

Required

Write a memorandum to the partners of Brooke & Doggett, explaining whether each of these events is material.

ATC 6-5 Business Applications Case *Limitations of audit opinion*

The statement of financial position (balance sheet) of Trident Company reports assets of \$5,500,000. Lisa Kimpton advises you that a major accounting firm has audited the statements and attested that they were prepared in accordance with generally accepted accounting principles. She tells you that she can buy the total owner's interest in the business for only \$3,800,000 and is seriously considering the opportunity. She says that the auditor's unqualified opinion validates the \$5,500,000 value of the assets. Lisa believes she would be foolish to pass up the opportunity to purchase the assets at a price of only \$3,800,000.

Required

a. What part of the accounting equation is Lisa failing to consider?

b. Comment on Lisa's misconceptions regarding the auditor's role in providing information that is useful in making investment decisions.

ATC 6-6 Writing Assignment *Internal control procedures*

Sarah Johnson was a trusted employee of Evergreen Trust Bank. She was involved in everything. She worked as a teller, she accounted for the cash at the other teller windows, and she recorded many of the transactions in the accounting records. She was so loyal that she never would take a day off, even when she was really too sick to work. She routinely worked late to see that all the day's work was posted into the accounting records. She would never take even a day's vacation because they might need her at the bank. Adam and Jammie, CPAs, were hired to perform an audit, the first complete audit that had been done in several years. Johnson seemed somewhat upset by the upcoming audit. She said that everything had been properly accounted for and that the audit was a needless expense. When Adam and Jammie examined some of the bank's internal control procedures, the firm discovered problems. In fact, as the audit progressed, it became apparent that a large amount of cash was missing. Numerous adjustments had been made to customer accounts with credit memorandums, and many of the transactions had been posted several days late. In addition, there were numerous cash payments for "office expenses." When the audit was complete, it was determined that more than \$100,000 of funds was missing or improperly accounted for. All fingers pointed to Johnson. The bank's president, who was a close friend of Johnson, was bewildered. How could this type of thing happen at this bank?

Required

Prepare a written memo to the bank president, outlining the procedures that should be followed to prevent this type of problem in the future.

ATC 6-7 Ethical Dilemma *I need just a little extra money*

John Riley, a certified public accountant, has worked for the past eight years as a payroll clerk for Southeast Industries, a small furniture manufacturing firm in the northeast. John recently experienced unfortunate circumstances. His teenage son required minor surgery and the medical bills not covered by John's insurance have financially strained John's family.

John works hard and is a model employee. Although he received regular performance raises during his first few years with Southeast, John's wages have not increased in three years. John asked his supervisor, Bill Jameson, for a raise. Bill agreed that John deserved a raise, but told him he could not currently approve one because of sluggish sales.

A disappointed John returned to his duties while the financial pressures in his life continued. Two weeks later, Larry Tyler, an assembly worker at Southeast, quit over a dispute with management. John conceived an idea. John's duties included not only processing employee terminations but also approving time cards before paychecks were issued and then distributing the paychecks to firm personnel. John decided to delay processing Mr. Tyler's termination, to forge timecards for Larry Tyler for the next few weeks, and to cash the checks himself. Since he distributed paychecks, no one would find out, and John reasoned that he was really entitled to the extra money anyway. In fact, no one did discover his maneuver and John stopped the practice after three weeks.

Required

a. Does John's scheme affect Southeast's balance sheet? Explain your answer.

b. Review the AICPA's Articles of Professional Conduct (see Chapter 2) and comment on any of the standards that have been violated.

c. Identify the three elements of unethical and criminal conduct recognized in the fraud triangle.

ATC 6-8 Research Assignment *Investigating cash and management issues at Smucker's*

Using the most current annual report available on the company's website, answer the following questions about the J. M. Smucker Company.

Required

a. Instead of "Cash," the company's balance sheet uses the account name "Cash and cash equivalents." How does the company define cash equivalents?

b. The annual report has two reports in which management clearly acknowledges its responsibility for the company's financial reporting and internal controls. What are the names of these reports and on what pages are they located?

ATC 6-9 Spreadsheet Assignment *Using Excel*

At the end of 2016, the following accounting information is available for Bainbridge and Crist Companies:

Microsoft Excel - ch6-3.xls

B8 = =SUM(B5:B7)

	A	B	C	D	E	F	G
1	**Classified Balance Sheet**	**Bainbridge**	**Crist**		**Multistep Income Statement**	**Bainbridge**	**Crist**
2	**Assets**						
3					Sales	500,000	575,000
4	**Current Assets**				Cost of Goods Sold	170,000	200,000
5	Cash	18,000	22,500		Gross Margin	330,000	375,000
6	Accounts Receivable	19,000	19,500		Operating Expenses	285,000	345,000
7	Inventory	14,000	18,000		Net Income	45,000	30,000
8	Total Current Assets	51,000	60,000				
9							
10	**Property, Plant and Equipment**				**RATIOS**		
11	Land	52,500	50,000		Current Ratio	1.46	0.85
12	Building	135,000	120,000		Debt to Total Assets	46.12%	82.83%
13	Total Property, Plant and Equipment	187,500	170,000		Equity to Total Assets	53.88%	17.17%
14					Gross Margin Percentage	66.00%	65.22%
15	Total Assets	238,500	230,000		Return on Sales	9.00%	5.22%
16					Return on Assets	18.87%	13.04%
17	**Liabilities**				Return on Equity	35.02%	75.95%
18	**Current Liabilities**						
19	Accounts Payable	20,000	52,500				
20	Wages Payable	15,000	18,000				
21	Total Current Liabilities	35,000	70,500				
22							
23	**Long-Term Liabilities**						
24	Notes Payable	75,000	120,000				
25							
26	Total Liabilities	110,000	190,500				
27							
28	**Equity**						
29	Common Stock	30,000	9,500				
30	Retained Earnings	98,500	30,000				
31							
32	Total Equity	128,500	39,500				
33							
34	Total Liabilities and Equity	238,500	230,000				
35							

problem | Problem(2) | Problem 6-3 solution | Problem 6-3 Solı

Required

a. Set up the preceding spreadsheet. Complete the balance sheet and income statement. Use Excel formulas for rows that "total" on the balance sheet and for gross margin and net income on the income statement.

b. Calculate the designated ratios using Excel formulas.

c. Which company is more likely to be able to pay its current liabilities?
d. Which company carries a greater financial risk?
e. Which company is more profitable from the stockholders' perspective?
f. Based on profitability alone, which company performed better?
g. Assume that sales increased 10 percent and that the additional sales were made on account. Adjust the balance sheet and income statement for the effects. Notice that Retained Earnings will also need to be adjusted to keep the balance sheet in balance. What is the resultant effect on the ratios?

COMPREHENSIVE PROBLEM

The trial balance of Pacilio Security Services Inc. as of January 1, 2016, had the following normal balances:

Cash	$74,210
Accounts Receivable	13,500
Supplies	200
Prepaid Rent	3,200
Merchandise Inventory (24 @ $265; 1 @ $260)	6,620
Land	4,000
Accounts Payable	1,950
Unearned Revenue	900
Salaries Payable	1,000
Common Stock	50,000
Retained Earnings	47,880

During 2016 Pacilio Security Services experienced the following transactions:

1. Paid the salaries payable from 2015.
2. On March 1, 2016, Pacilio established a $100 petty cash fund to handle small expenditures.
3. Paid $4,800 on March 1, 2016, for one year's lease on the company van in advance.
4. Paid $7,200 on May 2, 2016, for one year's office rent in advance.
5. Purchased $400 of supplies on account.
6. Purchased 100 alarm systems for $28,000 cash during the year.
7. Sold 102 alarm systems for $57,120. All sales were on account. (Compute cost of goods sold using the FIFO cost flow method.)
8. Paid $2,100 on accounts payable during the year.
9. Replenished the petty cash fund on August 1. At this time, the petty cash fund had only $7 of currency left. It contained the following receipts: office supplies expense, $23; cutting grass, $55; and miscellaneous expense, $14.
10. Billed $52,000 of monitoring services for the year.
11. Paid installers and other employees a total of $25,000 cash for salaries.
12. Collected $89,300 of accounts receivable during the year.
13. Paid $3,600 of advertising expense during the year.
14. Paid $2,500 of utilities expense for the year.
15. Paid a dividend of $10,000 to the shareholders.

Adjustments

16. There was $160 of supplies on hand at the end of the year.
17. Recognized the expired rent for both the van and the office building for the year. (The rent for both the van and the office remained the same for 2015 and 2016.)
18. Recognized the balance of the revenue earned in 2016 where cash had been collected in 2015.
19. Accrued salaries at December 31, 2016, were $1,400.

Required

a. Record the above transactions in general journal form.

b. Post the transactions to the T-accounts.

c. Prepare a bank reconciliation at the end of the year. The following information is available for the bank reconciliation:

(1) Checks written but not paid by the bank, $8,350.

(2) A deposit of $6,500 made on December 31, 2016, had been recorded but was not shown on the bank statement.

(3) A debit memo for $55 for a new supply of checks. (*Hint:* Use Office Supplies Expense account.)

(4) A credit memo for $30 for interest earned on the checking account.

(5) An NSF check for $120.

(6) The balance shown on the bank statement was $80,822.

d. Record and post any adjustments necessary from the bank reconciliation.

e. Prepare a trial balance.

f. Prepare an income statement, statement of changes in stockholders' equity, balance sheet, and statement of cash flows.

g. Close the temporary accounts to retained earnings.

h. Post the closing entries to the T-accounts and prepare a post-closing trial balance.

CHAPTER 7

Accounting for Receivables

LEARNING OBJECTIVES

After you have mastered the material in this chapter, you will be able to:

LO 7-1 Use the percent of revenue method to account for uncollectible accounts expense.

LO 7-2 Use the percent of receivables method to account for uncollectible accounts expense.

LO 7-3 Use aging of accounts receivable to estimate uncollectible accounts expense.

LO 7-4 Show how the direct write-off method of accounting for uncollectible accounts affects financial statements.

LO 7-5 Explain how accounting for notes receivable and accrued interest affects financial statements.

LO 7-6 Explain how accounting for credit card sales affects financial statements.

LO 7-7 Explain the effects of the cost of financing credit sales.

Video lectures and accompanying self-assessment quizzes are available for all learning objectives through McGraw-Hill Connect® Plus Accounting.

CHAPTER OPENING

Many people buy on impulse. If they must wait, the desire to buy wanes. To take advantage of impulse buyers, most merchandising companies offer customers credit because it increases their sales. A disadvantage of this strategy occurs when some customers are unable or unwilling to pay their bills. Nevertheless, the widespread availability of credit suggests that the advantages of increased sales outweigh the disadvantages of some uncollectible accounts.

When a company allows a customer to "buy now and pay later," the company's right to collect cash in the future is called an **account receivable.** Typically, amounts due from individual accounts receivable are relatively small and the collection period is short. Most accounts receivable are collected within 30 days. When a longer credit term is needed or when a receivable is large, the seller usually requires the buyer to issue a note reflecting a credit agreement between the parties. The note specifies the maturity date, interest rate, and other credit terms. Receivables evidenced by such notes are called **notes receivable.** Accounts and notes receivable are reported as assets on the balance sheet.

The Curious Accountant

General Dynamics Corporation is an aerospace and defense company that provides both products and services in business aviation; combat vehicles, weapons systems, and munitions; shipbuilding; and communications and information technology. Its products include Gulfstream business jet airplanes. In 2013, 62 percent of its revenues were earned from the U.S. government, 18 percent from commercial customers in the United States, 13 percent from international commercial customers, and the remaining 7 percent from international government defense customers.

Suppose the U.S. government contracted with General Dynamics to purchase four Gulfstream airplanes at a total cost of $200 million. Assume the government offers to pay for the airplanes the day they are delivered (a cash purchase) or 30 days later (a purchase on account). Assume that General Dynamics is absolutely sure the government will pay its account when due.

Do you think the company should care whether the government pays for the services upon delivery or 30 days later? Why? (Answer on page 367.)

ESTIMATING UNCOLLECTIBLE ACCOUNTS EXPENSE USING THE PERCENT OF REVENUE METHOD

LO 7-1

Use the percent of revenue method to account for uncollectible accounts expense.

Most companies do not expect to collect the full amount (face value) of their accounts receivable. Even carefully screened credit customers sometimes don't pay their bills. The **net realizable value** of accounts receivable represents the amount of receivables a company estimates it will actually collect. The net realizable value is the *face value* less an *allowance for doubtful accounts.*

The **allowance for doubtful accounts** represents a company's estimate of the amount of uncollectible receivables. To illustrate, assume a company with total accounts receivable of $50,000 estimates that $2,000 of its receivables will not be collected. The net realizable value of receivables is computed as follows:

Accounts receivable	$50,000
Less: Allowance for doubtful accounts	(2,000)
Net realizable value of receivables	$48,000

A company cannot know today, of course, the exact amount of the receivables it will not be able to collect in the future. The *allowance for doubtful accounts* and the *net realizable value* are necessarily *estimated amounts.* The net realizable value, however, more closely measures the cash that will ultimately be collected than does the face value. To avoid overstating assets, companies report receivables on their balance sheets at the net realizable value.

Reporting accounts receivable in the financial statements at net realizable value is commonly called the **allowance method of accounting for uncollectible accounts.** As indicated above, the allowance method requires accountants to estimate the amount of uncollectible accounts. How do accountants make these estimates? One approach is to base the estimates on a percentage of revenue. The following section of this chapter illustrates accounting for uncollectible accounts when the percentage of revenue approach is employed.

Accounting Events Affecting the 2016 Period

Allen's Tutoring Services (ATS) is a small company that provides tutoring services to college students. ATS started operations on January 1, 2016. During 2016, ATS experienced three types of accounting events. These events are discussed below.

EVENT 1 Revenue Recognition

Allen's Tutoring Services (ATS) recognized $3,750 of service revenue earned on account during 2016.

This is an asset source transaction. ATS obtained assets (accounts receivable) by providing services to customers. Both assets and stockholders' equity (retained earnings) increase. The event increases revenue and net income. Cash flow is not affected. The journal entry and its effects on the financial statements are shown here:

Account Title	Debit	Credit
Accounts Receivable	3,750	
Service Revenue		3,750

Assets	=	Liab.	+	Equity	Rev.	−	Exp.	=	Net Inc.	Cash Flow
Accts. Rec.	=			Ret. Earn.						
3,750	=	NA	+	3,750	3,750	−	NA	=	3,750	NA

Answers to The Curious Accountant

General Dynamics would definitely prefer to make the sale to the government in cash rather than on account. Even though it may be certain to collect its accounts receivable, the sooner the company gets its cash, the sooner the cash can be reinvested.

The interest cost related to a small account receivable of $50 that takes 30 days to collect may seem immaterial; at 4 percent the lost interest amounts to $.20. However, when one considers that General Dynamics had approximately $4.4 billion of accounts receivable on December 31, 2013, and took an average of 51 days to collect them, the cost of financing receivables for a real-world company becomes apparent. At 4 percent the cost of waiting 51 days to collect $4.4 billion of cash is $24.6 million ($4.4 billion × .04 × 51/365). For a full year, the cost to General Dynamics would be $176 million ($4.4 billion × .04). In 2013 the weighted-average interest rate on General Dynamics's debt was approximately 4 percent.

EVENT 2 Collection of Receivables

ATS collected $2,750 cash from accounts receivable in 2016.

This event is an asset exchange transaction. The asset cash increases; the asset accounts receivable decreases. Total assets remains unchanged. Net income is not affected because the revenue was recognized in the previous transaction. The cash inflow is reported in the operating activities section of the statement of cash flows. The journal entry and its effects on the financial statements are shown here:

Account Title	Debit	Credit
Cash	2,750	
Accounts Receivable		2,750

Assets			=	Liab.	+	Equity	Rev.	−	Exp.	=	Net Inc.	Cash Flow
Cash	+	Accts. Rec.										
2,750	+	(2,750)	=	NA	+	NA	NA	−	NA	=	NA	2,750 OA

EVENT 3 Recognizing Uncollectible Accounts Expense

ATS recognized uncollectible accounts expense for accounts expected to be uncollectible in the future.

While ATS has collected cash for some of the revenue earned in 2016, some of the remaining receivables may never be collected. ATS will not know the *actual amount* of uncollectible accounts until 2017 when the customers fail to pay. However, the company can estimate the amount of revenue that it expects will be uncollectible. The *estimated amount* of uncollectible accounts can then be recognized as an expense on the 2016 income statement. Recognizing the estimated expense improves the matching of revenues and expenses and therefore increases the accuracy of the financial statements.

Many accountants determine the estimated uncollectible accounts expense by taking a percentage of revenue. This approach is commonly called the **percent of revenue method.** The percentage used to make the estimate is usually based on the company's past collection experiences. However, the percentage may be adjusted for anticipated future circumstances. For example, the percentage may be reduced if the company plans to adopt more rigorous credit approval standards. Alternatively, the percentage may be increased if economic forecasts signal an economic downturn that would make customer defaults more likely.

Since this is ATS's first year of operation, there is no prior experience for determining the estimated percentage of uncollectible accounts. Instead ATS will have to base its estimate on industry averages. To illustrate the accounting procedures for recognizing uncollectible accounts expense, assume that ATS estimates that 2 percent of revenue will be uncollectible. Under these circumstances, ATS would recognize \$75 (\$3,750 of revenue × 2%) of uncollectible accounts expense on the 2016 income statement.

The estimated amount of **uncollectible accounts expense** is recognized in a year-end adjusting entry. The adjusting entry reduces the net realizable value of receivables, stockholders' equity, and the amount of reported net income. The statement of cash flows is not affected. The journal entry and its effects on the financial statements are shown here:

Account Title	Debit	Credit
Uncollectible Accounts Expense	75	
Allowance for Doubtful Accounts		75

Assets	=	Liab.	+	Equity	Rev.	−	Exp.	=	Net Inc.	Cash Flow
Net Realizable Value of Receivables	=			Ret. Earn.						
(75)	=	NA	+	(75)	NA	−	75	=	(75)	NA

The Accounts Receivable account is not reduced directly because none of the receivables have *actually* been determined to be uncollectible. The decrease in the net realizable value of receivables represents an *estimate* of what will be uncollectible some time in the future. To distinguish the actual balance in accounts receivable from the net realizable value, accountants use a **contra asset account** called Allowance for Doubtful Accounts. The allowance account is called a *contra account* because it has a credit balance instead of the debit balance normally seen in asset accounts. Indeed, the credit balance in the Allowance for Doubtful Accounts is subtracted from the debit balance in the Accounts Receivable account to determine the net realizable value of receivables that is shown on the balance sheet. The net realizable value of receivables for ATS is determined as follows:

Accounts receivable	\$1,000*
Less: Allowance for doubtful accounts	(75)
Net realizable value of receivables	\$ 925

*(\$3,750 revenue on account − \$2,750 of collections)

Generally accepted accounting principles require disclosure of both the net realizable value and the amount of the allowance account. Many companies disclose these amounts directly in the balance sheet in a manner similar to that shown in the text box above. Other companies disclose allowance information in the notes to the financial statements.

Recording and Reporting Uncollectible Accounts Events in the Double-Entry System

Exhibit 7.1, Panel A, shows a summary of the 2016 transactions for ATC. Panel B shows the general ledger T-accounts after the journal entries have been posted to them. Panel C contains the financial statements. Although Exhibit 7.1 does not illustrate the 2016 year-end closing entries, recall that the closing entries will transfer the amounts from the revenue and expense accounts to the Retained Earnings account. The balance in the Retained Earnings account after closing will be $3,675, as reported on the year-end balance sheet.

Financial Statements

As previously indicated, estimating uncollectible accounts improves the usefulness of the 2016 financial statements in two ways. First, the balance sheet reports the amount of cash ($1,000 − $75 = $925) the company actually expects to collect (net realizable value of accounts receivable). Second, the income statement provides a clearer picture

EXHIBIT 7.1

The Big Picture

Panel A Transactions Summary

Event 1	ATS earned $3,750 of revenue on account.
Event 2	ATS collected $2,750 cash from accounts receivable.
Event 3	ATS adjusted its accounts to reflect management's estimate that uncollectible accounts expense would be $75.

Panel B General Ledger Accounts

Assets = Liabilities + Equity

Cash

	Debit	Credit	
(2)	2,750		
Bal.	2,750		

Accounts Receivable

	Debit	Credit	
(1)	3,750	2,750	(2)
Bal.	1,000		

Allowance for Doubtful Accounts

	Debit	Credit	
		75	(3)
		75	Bal.

Retained Earnings

	Debit	Credit	

Service Revenue

	Debit	Credit	
		3,750	(1)

Uncollectible Accts. Expense

	Debit	Credit	
(3)	75		

Panel C Financial Statements for 2016

Income Statement

Service revenue	$3,750
Uncollectible accts. exp.	(75)
Net income	$3,675

Balance Sheet

Assets		
Cash		$2,750
Accounts receivable	$1,000	
Less: Allowance	(75)	
Net realizable value		925
Total assets		$3,675
Stockholders' equity		
Retained earnings		$3,675

Statement of Cash Flows

Operating Activities	
Inflow from customers	$2,750
Investing Activities	0
Financing Activities	0
Net change in cash	2,750
Plus: Beginning cash balance	0
Ending cash balance	$2,750

of managerial performance because it better *matches* the uncollectible accounts expense with the revenue it helped produce. The statements in Exhibit 7.1 show that the cash flow from operating activities ($2,750) differs from net income ($3,675). The statement of cash flows reports only cash collections, whereas the income statement reports revenues earned on account less the estimated amount of uncollectible accounts expense.

CHECK YOURSELF 7.1

Pamlico Inc. began operations on January 1, 2016. During 2016, it earned $400,000 of revenue on account. The company collected $370,000 of accounts receivable. At the end of the year, Pamlico estimates uncollectible accounts expense will be 1 percent of revenue. Based on this information alone, what is the net realizable value of accounts receivable as of December 31, 2016?

Answer Accounts receivable at year-end are $30,000 ($400,000 sales on account − $370,000 collection of receivables). The recognition of uncollectible accounts expense would result in a $4,000 ($400,000 × 0.01) balance in the allowance account. The net realizable value of accounts receivable is therefore $26,000 ($30,000 − $4,000).

Accounting Events Affecting the 2017 Period

To further illustrate accounting for uncollectible accounts, we discuss six accounting events affecting Allen's Tutoring Services (ATS) during 2017.

EVENT 1 **Write-Off of Uncollectible Accounts Receivable**
ATS wrote off $70 of uncollectible accounts receivable.

This is an asset exchange transaction. The amount of the uncollectible accounts is removed from the Accounts Receivable account and from the Allowance for Doubtful Accounts account. Since the balances in both the Accounts Receivable and the Allowance accounts decrease, the net realizable value of receivables—and therefore total assets—remains unchanged. The write-off does not affect the income statement. Since the uncollectible accounts expense was recognized in the previous year, the expense would be double counted if it were recognized again at the time an uncollectible account is written off. Finally, the statement of cash flows is not affected by the write-off. The journal entry and its effects on the financial statements are shown here:

Account Title	Debit	Credit
Allowance for Doubtful Accounts	70	
Accounts Receivable		70

Assets	=	Liab.	+	Equity	Rev.	−	Exp.	=	Net Inc.	Cash Flow
Net Realizable Value of Receivables										
NA	=	NA	+	NA	NA	−	NA	=	NA	NA

The computation of the *net realizable value,* before and after the write-off, is shown below:

	Before Write-Off	After Write-Off
Accounts receivable	$1,000	$930
Less: Allowance for doubtful accounts	(75)	(5)
Net realizable value	$ 925	$925

EVENT 2 **Revenue Recognition**
ATS provided $10,000 of tutoring services on account during 2017.

Assets (accounts receivable) and stockholders' equity (retained earnings) increase. Recognizing revenue increases net income. Cash flow is not affected. The journal entry and its effects on the financial statements are shown here:

Account Title	Debit	Credit
Accounts Receivable	10,000	
Service Revenue		10,000

Assets	=	Liab.	+	Equity	Rev.	−	Exp.	=	Net Inc.	Cash Flow
Accts. Rec.	=			Ret. Earn.						
10,000	=	NA	+	10,000	10,000	−	NA	=	10,000	NA

EVENT 3 **Collection of Accounts Receivable**
ATS collected $8,430 cash from accounts receivable.

The balance in the Cash account increases, and the balance in the Accounts Receivable account decreases. Total assets are unaffected. Net income is not affected because revenue was recognized previously. The cash inflow is reported in the operating activities section of the statement of cash flows. The journal entry and its effects on the financial statements are shown here:

Account Title	Debit	Credit
Cash	8,430	
Accounts Receivable		8,430

Assets			=	Liab.	+	Equity	Rev.	−	Exp.	=	Net Inc.	Cash Flow
Cash	+	Accts. Rec.										
8,430	+	(8,430)	=	NA	+	NA	NA	−	NA	=	NA	8,430 OA

EVENT 4 **Recovery of an Uncollectible Account: Reinstate Receivable**
ATS recovered a receivable that it had previously written off.

Occasionally, a company receives payment from a customer whose account was previously written off. In such cases, the customer's account should be reinstated and the cash received should be recorded the same way as any other collection on account. The account receivable is reinstated because a complete record of the customer's payment history may be useful if the customer requests credit again at some future date. To illustrate, assume that ATS received a $10 cash payment from a customer whose account had previously been written off. The first step is to **reinstate** the account receivable by reversing the previous write-off. The balances in the Accounts Receivable and the Allowance accounts increase. Since the Allowance is a contra asset account, the increase in it offsets the increase in the Accounts Receivable account, and total assets are unchanged. Net income and cash flow are unaffected. The journal entry and its effects on the financial statements are shown here:

Account Title	Debit	Credit
Accounts Receivable	10	
Allowance for Doubtful Accounts		10

Assets	=	Liab.	+	Equity	Rev.	−	Exp.	=	Net Inc.	Cash Flow
Net Realizable Value of Receivables										
NA	=	NA	+	NA	NA	−	NA	=	NA	NA

EVENT 5 **Recovery of an Uncollectible Account: Collection of Receivable**
ATS recorded collection of the reinstated receivable.

The collection of $10 is recorded like any other collection of a receivable account. Cash increases, and Accounts Receivable decreases. The journal entry and its effects on the financial statements are shown here:

Account Title	Debit	Credit
Cash	10	
Accounts Receivable		10

Cash	+	Accts. Rec.	=	Liab.	+	Equity	Rev.	−	Exp.	=	Net Inc.	Cash Flow
10	+	(10)	=	NA	+	NA	NA	−	NA	=	NA	10 OA

EVENT 6 **Adjustment for Recognition of Uncollectible Accounts Expense**
Using the percent of revenue method, ATS recognized uncollectible accounts expense for 2017.

Assuming management continues to estimate uncollectible accounts expense at 2 percent of revenue, ATS will recognize $200 ($10,000 revenue × .02) of uncollectible accounts expense in a year-end adjusting entry. The adjusting entry and its effects on the financial statements are shown here:

Account Title	Debit	Credit
Uncollectible Accounts Expense	200	
Allowance for Doubtful Accounts		200

Assets	=	Liab.	+	Equity	Rev.	−	Exp.	=	Net Inc.	Cash Flow
Net Realizable Value of Receivables	=			Ret. Earn.						
(200)	=	NA	+	(200)	NA	−	200	=	(200)	NA

Recording and Reporting Uncollectible Accounts Events in the Double-Entry System

Panel A of Exhibit 7.2 shows a summary of the 2017 accounting events for ATS. Panel B of the exhibit shows the general ledger T-accounts after the journal entries have been posted to them. Panel C contains the financial statements. Exhibit 7.2 does not include the closing entries. Closing the accounts will transfer the amounts from the revenue and expense accounts to the Retained Earnings account, resulting in a $13,475 ending balance in this account as shown on the 2017 balance sheet.

EXHIBIT 7.2

The Big Picture

Panel A Transactions Summary

Event 1	ATS wrote off $70 of uncollectible accounts receivable.
Event 2	ATS earned $10,000 of revenue on account.
Event 3	ATS collected $8,430 cash from accounts receivable.
Event 4	ATS reinstated a $10 account receivable it had previously written off.
Event 5	ATS recorded the collection of $10 from the reinstated receivable referenced in Event 4.
Event 6	ATS adjusted its accounts to recognize $200 of uncollectible accounts expense.

Panel B General Ledger Accounts

Assets = Liabilities + Equity

Cash

	Debit	Credit	
Bal.	2,750		
(3)	8,430		
(5)	10		
Bal.	11,190		

Accounts Receivable

	Debit	Credit	
Bal.	1,000	70	(1)
(2)	10,000	8,430	(3)
(4)	10	10	(5)
Bal.	2,500		

Allowance for Doubtful Accounts

	Debit	Credit	
(1)	70	75	Bal.
		10	(4)
		200	(6)
		215	Bal.

Retained Earnings

	Debit	Credit	
		3,675	Bal.

Service Revenue

	Debit	Credit	
		10,000	(2)

Uncollectible Accts. Expense

	Debit	Credit	
(6)	200		

Panel C Financial Statements for 2017

Income Statement

Service revenue	$10,000
Uncollectible accts. exp.	(200)
Net income	$ 9,800

Balance Sheet

Assets		
Cash		$11,190
Accounts receivable	$2,500	
Less: Allowance	(215)	
Net realizable value		2,285
Total assets		$13,475
Stockholders' equity		
Retained earnings		$13,475

Statement of Cash Flows

Operating Activities	
Inflow from customers	$ 8,440
Investing Activities	0
Financing Activities	0
Net change in cash	8,440
Plus: Beginning cash balance	2,750
Ending cash balance	$11,190

Analysis of Financial Statements

Exhibit 7.2 Panel C displays the 2017 financial statements. The amount of uncollectible accounts expense ($200) differs from the ending balance of the Allowance account ($215). The balance in the Allowance account was $15 before the 2017 adjusting entry for uncollectible accounts expense was recorded. At the end of 2016, Allen's Tutoring Services estimated there would be $75 of uncollectible accounts as a result of 2016 credit sales. Actual write-offs, however, amounted to $70 and $10 of that amount was recovered, indicating the actual uncollectible accounts expense for 2016 was only $60. Hindsight shows the expense for 2016 was overstated by $15. However, if no estimate had been made, the amount of uncollectible accounts expense would have been understated by $60. In some accounting periods estimated uncollectible accounts expense will likely be overstated; in others it may be understated. The allowance method cannot produce perfect results, but it does improve the accuracy of the financial statements.

Since no dividends were paid, retained earnings at the end of 2017 equals the December 31, 2016, retained earnings plus 2017 net income (that is, $3,675 + $9,800 = $13,475). Again, the cash flow from operating activities ($8,440) differs from net income ($9,800) because the statement of cash flows does not include the effects of revenues earned on account or the recognition of uncollectible accounts expense.

CHECK YOURSELF 7.2

Maher Company had beginning balances in Accounts Receivable and Allowance for Doubtful Accounts of $24,200 and $2,000, respectively. During the accounting period Maher earned $230,000 of revenue on account and collected $232,500 of cash from receivables. The company also wrote off $1,950 of uncollectible accounts during the period. Maher estimates uncollectible accounts expense will be 1 percent of credit sales. Based on this information, what is the net realizable value of receivables at the end of the period?

Answer The balance in the Accounts Receivable account is $19,750 ($24,200 + $230,000 − $232,500 − $1,950). The amount of uncollectible accounts expense for the period is $2,300 ($230,000 × 0.01). The balance in the Allowance for Doubtful Accounts is $2,350 ($2,000 − $1,950 + $2,300). The net realizable value of receivables is therefore $17,400 ($19,750 − $2,350).

ESTIMATING UNCOLLECTIBLE ACCOUNTS EXPENSE USING THE PERCENT OF RECEIVABLES METHOD

LO 7-2

Use the percent of receivables method to account for uncollectible accounts expense.

Some accountants believe they can better estimate the amount of uncollectible expense by basing their estimates on a percentage of accounts receivable rather than a percentage of revenue. This approach is commonly called the **percent of receivables method** of estimating uncollectible accounts expense. The approach focuses on estimating the most accurate balance for the Allowance for Doubtful Accounts account that appears on the year-end balance sheet.

To illustrate, assume that before adjusting its accounts on December 31, 2016, Pyramid Corporation had a $56,000 balance in its Accounts Receivable account and a $500 credit balance in its Allowance for Doubtful Accounts account. Further assume that Pyramid estimates it will be unable to collect 6 percent of its accounts receivable. In other words, Pyramid estimates that $3,360 ($56,000 × .06) of the accounts receivable will be uncollectible. Accordingly, the *ending credit balance* in the Allowance for Doubtful Accounts account that appears on the December 31, 2016, balance sheet must be $3,360.

Since the Allowance account currently has a $500 credit balance, Pyramid must record an adjusting entry that adds a $2,860 ($3,360 − $500) credit to the Allowance account before preparing the financial statements. The offsetting debit in the adjusting entry is to Uncollectible Accounts Expense. In other words, *the amount of the uncollectible accounts expense is determined by calculating the amount necessary to achieve the required ending balance in the Allowance account.*

The adjusting entry necessary to recognize the uncollectible accounts expense and its effects on the financial statements is as follows:

Account Title	Debit	Credit
Uncollectible Accounts Expense	2,860	
Allowance for Doubtful Accounts		2,860

Assets	=	Liab.	+	Equity	Rev.	−	Exp.	=	Net Inc.	Cash Flow
Net Realizable Value of Receivables	=			Ret. Earn.						
(2,860)	=	NA	+	(2,860)	NA	−	2,860	=	(2,860)	NA

CHECK YOURSELF 7.3

During 2016, Oron Company earned $100,000 of revenue. Before adjusting its accounts on December 31, 2016, Oron had a $20,000 balance in its Accounts Receivable Account and a $50 credit balance in its Allowance for Doubtful Accounts account. Determine the amount of uncollectible accounts expense Oron will recognize on its 2016 income statement assuming the company estimates uncollectible accounts expense to be 4 percent of receivables.

Answer The ending balance in the Allowance for Doubtful Accounts account after the adjusting entries are posted to the ledger accounts is an $800 ($20,000 accounts receivable × .04) credit balance. Since there is an unadjusted credit balance of $50 in the Allowance account, the adjusting entry must include a $750 credit to the Allowance account. A corresponding $750 debit to the Uncollectible Accounts Expense account would be required. Accordingly, the amount of uncollectible expense recognized on the 2016 income statement is $750.

Aging Accounts Receivable

LO 7-3

Use aging of accounts receivable to estimate uncollectible accounts expense.

History suggests that an account receivable that is past its due date is less likely to be collected than one that is not yet currently due. The longer an account receivable remains past due, the less likely it is to be collected. Accordingly, the accuracy of the amount of estimated uncollectible expense can be improved by **aging of accounts receivable**, which involves applying higher uncollectible percentage estimates to older receivables. To illustrate, assume that Pyramid Corporation prepared the aging of accounts receivable schedule shown in Exhibit 7.3.

The amount of accounts receivable that is estimated to be uncollectible (the ending balance in the Allowance for Doubtful Accounts account) is determined by applying different percentages to each category in the aging schedule. The percentage for each category is based on a company's previous collection experience for each of the categories. The percentages become progressively higher as the accounts become older. Exhibit 7.4 illustrates computing the ending balance required for Pyramid Corporation's December 31, 2016, balance sheet.

EXHIBIT 7.3

PYRAMID CORPORATION
Accounts Receivable Aging Schedule
December 31, 2016

Customer Name	Total Balance	Current	Number of Days Past Due 0–30	31–60	61–90	Over 90
J. Davis	$ 6,700	$ 6,700				
B. Diamond	4,800	2,100	$ 2,700			
K. Eppy	9,400	9,400				
B. Gilman	2,200				$1,000	$1,200
A. Kelly	7,300	7,300				
L. Niel	8,600	1,000	6,000	$ 1,600		
L. Platt	4,600			4,600		
J. Turner	5,500			3,000	2,000	500
H. Zachry	6,900		3,000	3,900		
Total	$56,000	$26,500	$11,700	$13,100	$3,000	$1,700

EXHIBIT 7.4

Balance Required in the Allowance for Doubtful Accounts at December 31, 2016

Number of Days Past Due	Receivables Amount	Percentage Likely to Be Uncollectible	Required Allowance Account Balance
Current	$26,500	.01	$ 265
0–30	11,700	.05	585
31–60	13,100	.10	1,310
61–90	3,000	.25	750
Over 90	1,700	.50	850
Total	$56,000		$3,760

The computations in Exhibit 7.4 show that the *ending balance* in the Allowance for Doubtful Accounts account shown must be $3,760. Since Pyramid has an unadjusted $500 credit balance in its Allowance account, the amount of uncollectible expense to be recognized in the adjusting entry is $3,260 ($3,760 required ending balance − $500 current unadjusted balance). Except for the amount of the estimated expense, the journal entry and the effects on the financial statement would be the same as previously shown. Remember that aging is designed to improve the estimated amount of uncollectible accounts expense. It does not affect how the recognition of the expense affects the financial statements.

Matching Revenues and Expenses versus Asset Measurement

The *percent of revenue* method, with its focus on determining the uncollectible accounts expense, is often called the income statement approach. The *percent of receivables* method, focused on determining the best estimate of the allowance balance, is frequently called the balance sheet approach. Which estimating method is better? In any given year, the results will vary slightly between approaches. In the long run, however, the percentages used in either approach are based on a company's actual history of uncollectible accounts. Accountants routinely revise their estimates as more data become available, using hindsight to determine if the percentages should be increased or decreased. Either approach provides acceptable results.

RECOGNIZING UNCOLLECTIBLE ACCOUNTS EXPENSE USING THE DIRECT WRITE-OFF METHOD

LO 7-4

Show how the direct write-off method of accounting for uncollectible accounts affects financial statements.

If uncollectible accounts are not material, generally accepted accounting principles allow companies to account for them using the **direct write-off method.** Under the direct write-off method, a company simply recognizes uncollectible accounts expense *in the period in which it identifies and writes off uncollectible accounts.* No estimates, allowance account, or adjusting entries are needed.

The direct write-off method fails to match revenues with expenses. Revenues are recognized in one period and any related uncollectible accounts expense is recognized in a later period. Also, the direct write-off method overstates assets because receivables are reported at *face value* rather than *net realizable value.* If the amount of uncollectible accounts is immaterial, however, companies accept the minor reporting inaccuracies as a reasonable trade-off for recording convenience.

To illustrate the direct write-off method, return to the first year (2016) that Allen's Tutoring Services (ATS) operated. Assume ATS decided the direct write-off method was appropriate to account for its receivables. Recall that during 2016 ATS recognized $3,750 of revenue on account. The journal entry and its effects on the financial statements are shown below:

Account Title	Debit	Credit
Accounts Receivable	3,750	
Service Revenue		3,750

Assets	=	Liab.	+	Equity	Rev.	−	Exp.	=	Net Inc.	Cash Flow
Accts. Rec.	=			Ret. Earn.						
3,750	=	NA	+	3,750	3,750	−	NA	=	3,750	NA

ATS believed only an immaterial amount of the $3,750 of accounts receivable would prove uncollectible. It therefore made no year-end adjusting entry for estimated uncollectible accounts. Instead, ATS recognizes uncollectible accounts expense when it determines an account is uncollectible.

In its second accounting period (2017), ATS determined that $70 of accounts receivable were uncollectible. ATS recognized the uncollectible accounts expense in the entry to write off the uncollectible receivables. With the direct write-off method, the write-off reduces the asset account Accounts Receivable and decreases the stockholders' equity account Retained Earnings. On the income statement, expenses increase and net income decreases. The statement of cash flows is not affected by the write-off. The journal entry and its effects on the financial statements are shown below:

Account Title	Debit	Credit
Uncollectible Accounts Expense	70	
Accounts Receivable		70

Assets	=	Liab.	+	Equity	Rev.	−	Exp.	=	Net Inc.	Cash Flow
Accts. Rec.	=			Ret. Earn.						
(70)	=	NA	+	(70)	NA	−	70	=	(70)	NA

Also in 2017 ATS recovered a $10 account receivable it had previously written off. Recording the recovery of a previously written-off account requires two entries. First, ATS must *reinstate* the receivable (merely reverse the write-off entry above) because it has proven to be collectible after all. Second, ATS must record collecting the reinstated account. With the direct write-off method, reinstating the receivable increases the asset account Accounts Receivable and increases the stockholders' equity account Retained Earnings. On the income statement, expenses decrease and net income increases. The statement of cash flows is not affected. The journal entry and its effects on the financial statements are shown below:

Account Title	Debit	Credit
Accounts Receivable	10	
Uncollectible Accounts Expense		10

Assets	=	Liab.	+	Equity	Rev.	−	Exp.	=	Net Inc.	Cash Flow
Accts. Rec.	=			Ret. Earn.						
10	=	NA	+	10	NA	−	(10)	=	10	NA

Like the collection of any other receivable, collection of the reinstated account receivable increases the asset account Cash and decreases the asset account Accounts Receivable. The income statement is not affected. The cash inflow is reported in the operating activities section of the statement of cash flows. The journal entry and its effects on the financial statements are shown below:

Account Title	Debit	Credit
Cash	10	
Accounts Receivable		10

Assets			=	Liab.	+	Equity	Rev.	−	Exp.	=	Net Inc.	Cash Flow
Cash	−	Accts. Rec.										
10		(10)	=	NA	+	NA	NA	−	NA	=	NA	10 OA

ACCOUNTING FOR NOTES RECEIVABLE

LO 7-5

Explain how accounting for notes receivable and accrued interest affects financial statements.

Companies typically do not charge their customers interest on accounts receivable that are not past due. When a company extends credit for a long time or when the amount of credit it extends is large, however, the cost of granting free credit and the potential for disputes about payment terms both increase. To address these concerns, the parties frequently enter into a credit agreement, the terms of which are legally documented in a **promissory note.**

To illustrate, assume in 2018 Allen's Tutoring Services (ATS) generates excess cash that it loans to an individual, Stanford Cummings, so Cummings can buy a car. ATS and Cummings agree that Cummings will repay the money borrowed plus interest at the end of one year. They also agree that ATS will hold the title to the car to secure the debt. Exhibit 7.5 illustrates a promissory note that outlines this credit agreement. For ATS, the credit arrangement represents a *note receivable.*

EXHIBIT 7.5

Promissory Note

Promissory Note

$15,000 (3)	*November 1, 2018*
Amount	**Date**

For consideration received, Stanford Cummings (1) **hereby promises to pay to the order of:**

Allen's Tutoring Services (2)

Fifteen thousand and no/100 (3) **Dollars**

payable on October 31, 2019 (5)

plus interest thereon at the rate of 6 **percent per year.** (4)

Collateral Description Automobile title (6)

Signature *Stanford Cummings* (1)

Features of this note are discussed below. Each feature is cross-referenced with a number that corresponds to an item on the promissory note in Exhibit 7.5. Locate each feature in Exhibit 7.5 and read the corresponding description of the feature below:

1. Maker—The person responsible for making payment on the due date is the **maker** of the note. The maker may also be called the *borrower* or *debtor.*
2. Payee—The person to whom the note is made payable is the **payee.** The payee may also be called the *creditor* or *lender.* The payee loans money to the maker and expects the return of the principal and the interest due.
3. Principal—The amount of money loaned by the payee to the maker of the note is the **principal.**
4. Interest—The economic benefit earned by the payee for loaning the principal to the maker is **interest,** which is normally expressed as an annual percentage of the principal amount. For example, a note with a 6 percent interest rate requires interest payments equal to 6 percent of the principal amount every year the loan is outstanding.
5. Maturity Date—The date on which the maker must repay the principal and make the final interest payment to the payee is the **maturity date.**
6. Collateral—Assets belonging to the maker that are assigned as security to ensure that the principal and interest will be paid when due are called **collateral.** In this example, if Cummings fails to pay ATS the amount due, ownership of the car Cummings purchased will be transferred to ATS.

Recording and Reporting Transactions Related to Notes Receivable

We illustrate accounting for notes receivable using the credit agreement evidenced by the promissory note in Exhibit 7.5. Allen's Tutoring Services engaged in many transactions during 2018; we discuss here only transactions directly related to the note receivable.

EVENT 1 Loan of Money

The note shows that ATS loaned $15,000 to Stanford Cummings on November 1, 2018. This event is an asset exchange. The asset account Cash decreases and the asset account Notes Receivable increases. The income statement is not affected. The statement of cash flows shows a cash outflow for investing activities. The journal entry and its effects on the financial statements are shown below:

Account Title	Debit	Credit
Notes Receivable	15,000	
Cash		15,000

	Assets					=	Liab.	+	Equity	Rev.	−	Exp.	=	Net Inc.	Cash Flow
Date	Cash	+	Notes Rec.	+	Int. Rec.	=			Ret. Earn.						
11/01/18	(15,000)	+	15,000	+	NA	=	NA	+	NA	NA	−	NA	=	NA	(15,000) IA

EVENT 2 Accrual of Interest

For ATS, loaning money represents an investment in the note receivable. ATS will collect the principal ($15,000) plus interest of 6 percent of the principal amount (0.06 × $15,000 = $900), or a total of $15,900, on October 31, 2019, one year from the date the loan was made.

Conceptually, lenders *earn* interest continually even though they do not *collect* cash continually. Each day, the amount of interest due, called **accrued interest**, is greater than the day before. Companies would find it highly impractical to attempt to record (recognize) accrued interest continually as the amount due increased.

Businesses typically solve the recordkeeping problem by only recording accrued interest when it is time to prepare financial statements or when the interest is due. At such times, the accounts are *adjusted* to reflect the amount of interest currently due. For example, ATS recorded the asset exchange immediately upon investing in the Note Receivable on November 1, 2018. ATS did not, however, recognize any interest earned on the note until the balance sheet date, December 31, 2018. At year-end, ATS made an entry to recognize the interest it had earned during the previous two months (November 1 through December 31). This entry is an **adjusting entry** because it adjusts (updates) the account balances prior to preparing financial statements.

ATS computed the amount of accrued interest by multiplying the principal amount of the note by the annual interest rate and by the length of time for which the note has been outstanding.

$$\text{Principal} \times \text{Annual interest rate} \times \text{Time outstanding} = \text{Interest revenue}$$
$$\$15{,}000 \times 0.06 \times (2/12) = \$150$$

ATS recognized the $150 of interest revenue in 2018 although ATS will not collect the cash until 2019. This practice illustrates the **matching concept.** Interest revenue is recognized in (matched with) the period in which it is earned regardless of when the related cash is collected. The adjusting entry is an asset source transaction. The asset account Interest Receivable increases, and the stockholders' equity account Retained Earnings increases. The income statement reflects an increase in revenue and net income. The statement of cash flows is not affected because ATS will not collect cash until the maturity date (October 31, 2019). The adjusting entry and its effects on the financial statements are shown below:

Account Title	Debit	Credit
Interest Receivable	150	
Interest Revenue		150

	Assets					=	Liab.	+	Equity	Rev.	−	Exp.	=	Net Inc.	Cash Flow
Date	Cash	+	Notes Rec.	+	Int. Rec.	=			Ret. Earn.						
12/31/18	NA	+	NA	+	150	=	NA	+	150	150	−	NA	=	150	NA

EVENT 3 Collection of Principal and Interest on the Maturity Date

ATS collected \$15,900 cash on the maturity date. The collection included \$15,000 for the principal plus \$900 for the interest. Recall that ATS previously accrued interest in the December 31, 2018, adjusting entry for the two months in 2018 that the note was outstanding. Since year-end, ATS has earned an additional 10 months of interest revenue. ATS must recognize this interest revenue before recording the cash collection. The amount of interest earned in 2019 is computed as follows:

$$\text{Principal} \times \text{Annual interest rate} \times \text{Time outstanding} = \text{Interest revenue}$$
$$\$15{,}000 \times 0.06 \times (10/12) = \$750$$

The journal entry and effects on the financial statements are shown below:

Account Title	Debit	Credit
Interest Receivable	750	
Interest Revenue		750

	Assets					=	Liab.	+	Equity	Rev.	−	Exp.	=	Net Inc.	Cash Flow
Date	Cash	+	Notes Rec.	+	Int. Rec.	=			Ret. Earn.						
10/31/19	NA	+	NA	+	750	=	NA	+	750	750	−	NA	=	750	NA

The total amount of accrued interest is now \$900 (\$150 accrued in 2018 plus \$750 accrued in 2019). The \$15,900 cash collection is an asset exchange transaction. The asset account Cash increases and two asset accounts, Notes Receivable and Interest Receivable, decrease. The income statement is not affected. The statement of cash flows shows a \$15,000 inflow from investing activities (recovery of principal) and a \$900 inflow from operating activities (interest collection). The journal entry and effects on the financial statements are shown below:

Account Title	Debit	Credit
Cash	15,900	
Notes Receivable		15,000
Interest Receivable		900

	Assets					=	Liab.	+	Equity	Rev.	−	Exp.	=	Net Inc.	Cash Flow
Date	Cash	+	Notes Rec.	+	Int. Rec.	=			Ret. Earn.						
10/31/19	15,900	+	(15,900)	+	(900)	=	NA	+	NA	NA	−	NA	=	NA	15,000 IA 900 OA

To clarify the illustration, we showed the interest accrual and the cash collection as two separate entries. Experienced accountants often record the two events in a single journal entry as follows:

Account Title	Debit	Credit
Cash	15,900	
Notes Receivable		15,000
Interest Receivable		150
Interest Revenue		750

Financial Statements

The financial statements reveal key differences between the timing of revenue recognition and the exchange of cash. These differences are highlighted below:

	2018	2019	Total
Interest revenue recognized	$150	$750	$900
Cash inflow from operating activities	0	900	900

Accrual accounting calls for recognizing revenue in the period in which it is earned regardless of when cash is collected.

Income Statement

Although generally accepted accounting principles require reporting receipts of or payments for interest on the statement of cash flows as operating activities, they do not specify how to classify interest on the income statement. In fact, companies traditionally report interest on the income statement as a nonoperating item. Interest is therefore frequently reported in two different categories within the same set of financial statements.

Balance Sheet

As with other assets, companies report interest receivable and notes receivable on the balance sheet in order of their liquidity. **Liquidity** refers to how quickly assets are expected to be converted to cash during normal operations. In the preceding example, Allen's Tutoring Services expects to convert its accounts receivable to cash before it collects the interest receivable and note receivable. Companies commonly report interest and notes receivable after accounts receivable. Exhibit 7.6 shows a partial balance sheet for ATS to illustrate the presentation of receivables.

CHECK YOURSELF 7.4

On October 1, 2016, Mei Company accepted a promissory note for a loan it made to the Asia Pacific Company. The note had a $24,000 principal amount, a four-month term, and an annual interest rate of 4 percent. Determine the amount of interest revenue and the cash inflow from operating activities Mei will report in its 2016 and 2017 financial statements. Also provide in general journal form the year-end adjusting entry needed to recognize 2016 interest revenue.

Answer The computation of accrued interest revenue is shown below. The interest rate is stated in annual terms even though the term of the note is only four months. Interest rates are commonly expressed as an annual percentage regardless of the term of the note. The *time outstanding* in the following formulas is therefore expressed as a fraction of a year. Mei charged annual interest of 4 percent, but the note was outstanding for only 3/12 of a year in 2016 and 1/12 of a year in 2017.

2016

Principal	×	Annual interest rate	×	Time outstanding	=	Interest revenue
$24,000	×	0.04	×	(3/12)	=	$240

2017

Principal	×	Annual interest rate	×	Time outstanding	=	Interest revenue
$24,000	×	0.04	×	(1/12)	=	$80

In 2016, Mei's cash inflow from interest will be zero.

In 2017, Mei will report a $320 ($240 + $80) cash inflow from operating activities for interest. The adjusting entry to recognize 2016 accrued interest is as follows:

Interest Receivable	240	
Interest Revenue		240

EXHIBIT 7.6

Typical Balance Sheet Presentation of Receivables

ALLEN'S TUTORING SERVICES Partial Balance Sheet As of December 31, 2018		
Cash		XXXX
Accounts receivable	XXXX	
Less: Allowance for doubtful accounts	(XXXX)	
Net realizable value of accounts receivable		XXXX
Interest receivable		XXXX
Notes receivable		XXXX

ACCOUNTING FOR CREDIT CARD SALES

LO 7-6

Explain how accounting for credit card sales affects financial statements.

Maintaining accounts and notes receivable is expensive. In addition to uncollectible accounts expense, companies extending credit to their customers incur considerable costs for such clerical tasks as running background checks and maintaining customer records. Many businesses find it more efficient to accept third-party credit cards instead of offering credit directly to their customers. Credit card companies service the merchant's credit sales for a fee that typically ranges between 1 and 5 percent of gross sales.

The credit card company usually provides customers with plastic cards that permit cardholders to charge purchases at various retail outlets. When a sale takes place, the seller records the transaction on a receipt the customer usually signs. The receipt is forwarded to the credit card company, which immediately pays the merchant.

The credit card company deducts its service fee from the gross amount of the sale and pays the merchant the net balance (gross amount of sale less credit card fee) in cash. The credit card company collects the gross sale amount directly from the customer. The merchant avoids the risk of uncollectible accounts as well as the cost of maintaining customer credit records. To illustrate, assume that Allen's Tutoring Services experiences the following events.

EVENT 1 Recognition of Revenue and Expense on Credit Card Sales

ATS accepts a credit card payment for $1,000 of services rendered.

Assume the credit card company charges a 5 percent fee for handling the transaction ($1,000 × 0.05 = $50). ATS's income increases by the amount of revenue ($1,000) and decreases by the amount of the credit card expense ($50). Net income increases by $950. The event increases an asset, accounts receivable, due from the credit card company, and stockholders' equity (retained earnings) by $950 ($1,000 revenue − $50 credit card expense). Cash flow is not affected. The journal entry and its effects on the financial statements are shown here:

Account Title	Debit	Credit
Accounts Receivable—Credit Card Company	950	
Credit Card Expense	50	
Service Revenue		1,000

Assets	=	Liab.	+	Equity	Rev.	−	Exp.	=	Net Inc.	Cash Flow
Accts. Rec.	=			Ret. Earn.						
950	=	NA	+	950	1,000	−	50	=	950	NA

EVENT 2 **Collection of Credit Card Receivable**

The collection of the receivable due from the credit card company is recorded like any other receivable collection.

When ATS collects the net amount of $950 ($1,000 − $50) from the credit card company, one asset account (Cash) increases and another asset account (Accounts Receivable) decreases. Total assets are not affected. The income statement is not affected. A $950 cash inflow is reported in the operating activities section of the statement of cash flows. The journal entry and its effects on the financial statements are shown here:

Account Title	Debit	Credit
Cash	950	
Accounts Receivable—Credit Card Company		950

Assets			=	Liab.	+	Equity	Rev.	−	Exp.	=	Net Inc.	Cash Flow
Cash	+	Accts. Rec.										
950	+	(950)	=	NA	+	NA	NA	−	NA	=	NA	950 OA

THE FINANCIAL ANALYST

Costs of Credit Sales

LO 7-7

Explain the effects of the cost of financing credit sales.

As mentioned earlier, two costs of extending credit to customers are uncollectible accounts expense and recordkeeping costs. These costs can be significant. Large companies spend literally millions of dollars to buy the equipment and pay the staff necessary to operate entire departments devoted to managing accounts receivable. Further, there is an implicit interest cost associated with extending credit. When a customer is permitted to delay payment, the creditor forgoes the opportunity to invest the amount the customer owes.

Exhibit 7.7 presents part of a note from the 2013 annual report of Rent-A-Center. This excerpt provides insight into the credit costs real companies incur. First, observe that Rent-A-Center was owed $62.4 million of receivables. These receivables represent

EXHIBIT 7.7

RENT-A-CENTER, INC. December 31, 2013
Partial Note C Regarding Accountants Receivable and Allowance for Doubtful Accounts (amounts shown in thousands)

Receivables consist of the following:

	2013	2012
Installment sales receivable	$ 51,335	$ 46,753
Trade and notes receivables	11,051	8,986
Total	62,386	55,739
Less allowance for doubtful accounts	(3,700)	(2,920)
Net receivables	$ 58,686	$ 52,819

Changes in the Company's allowance for doubtful accounts are as follows:

	2013	2012
Beginning balance	$ 2,920	$ 3,919
Bad debt expense	14,589	12,953
Accounts written off	(18,348)	(17,432)
Recoveries	4,539	3,480
Ending balance	$ 3,700	$ 2,920

money that could be in the bank earning interest if all sales had been made in cash. If Rent-A-Center could have earned interest at 5 percent on that money, the opportunity cost of this lost interest is approximately \$3.1 million (\$62.4 million × .05) a year. Next, observe that Rent-A-Center expects to have uncollectible accounts amounting to \$3.7 million (balance in the allowance account). These are significant costs to a company whose net income was \$128.2 million in 2013.

Average Number of Days to Collect Accounts Receivable

The longer it takes to collect accounts receivable, the greater the opportunity cost of lost income. Also, business experience indicates that the older an account receivable becomes, the less likely it is to be collected. Finally, taking longer to collect an account typically costs more for salaries, equipment, and supplies used in the process of trying to collect it. Businesses are therefore concerned about how long it takes to collect their receivables.

Two ratios help management, or other users, measure a company's collection period. One is the **accounts receivable turnover ratio,** computed as:[1]

$$\frac{\text{Sales}}{\text{Accounts receivable}}$$

Dividing a company's sales by its accounts receivable tells how many times the accounts receivable balance is "turned over" (converted into cash) each year. The higher the turnover, the shorter the collection period. To simplify its interpretation, the accounts receivable turnover ratio is often taken one step further to determine the **average number of days to collect accounts receivable,** sometimes called the *average collection period.* This is computed as:

$$\frac{365}{\text{Accounts receivable turnover ratio}}$$

This ratio measures how many days, on average, it takes a company to collect its accounts receivable. Since longer collection periods increase costs, shorter periods are obviously more desirable. To illustrate computing the *average number of days to collect accounts receivable* for Allen's Tutoring Services, refer to the 2017 financial statements in Exhibit 7.2. On average, the company takes 83 days to collect its receivables, computed in two steps:

1. The accounts receivable turnover is 4.376 (\$10,000 ÷ \$2,285) times.
2. The average number of days to collect receivables is 83 (365 ÷ 4.376) days.

In the preceding computations, the net realizable value of accounts receivable was used because that is the amount typically reported in published financial statements. The results would not have been materially different had total accounts receivable been used.

Real-World Data

What is the collection period for real companies? The time required to collect receivables varies among industries and among companies within industries. The fourth column in Exhibit 7.8 displays the average number of days to collect receivables for seven companies in three different industries. These numbers are for 2013.

Since customers in fast-food restaurants typically pay cash when they purchase hamburgers or coffee, why do these companies have accounts receivable? The accounts receivable for **McDonald's** and **Yum! Brands** arise because these companies sell goods to restaurants that are independent franchisees. So, for example, McDonald's accounts

[1]To be more precise, the ratio could be computed using only credit sales and average accounts receivable. Usually, however, companies do not report credit sales separately from cash sales in published financial statements. Average accounts receivable, if desired, is computed as [(Beginning receivables + Ending receivables) ÷ 2]. For this course, use the simpler computation shown here (Sales ÷ Accounts receivable).

EXHIBIT 7.8

Industry	Company	Average Days to Sell Inventory	Average Days to Collect Receivables	Length of Operating Cycle
Fast Food	McDonald's	7	17	24
	Starbucks	32	47*	79
	Yum! Brands	17	9	26
Department Stores	Macy's	117	5	122
	Walmart	42	4	46
Home Construction	D.R. Horton	433	0	433
	Toll Brothers	796	30	826

*Estimate based on sales to franchised shops and retailers only.

receivable represents future collections from restaurant owners, not customers who purchase hamburgers.

Although there are many franchised Starbucks coffee shops, most of the company's revenues come from shops that are owned and operated by the company itself. Starbucks does not have accounts receivable from its own shops; its receivables come from sales to outside customers and from credit card sales in its own shops. In addition to accounts receivable related to franchised coffee shops, Starbucks sells coffee products such as coffee beans to retailers such as grocery stores. Most of these companies do not pay Starbucks "cash on delivery," but purchase their goods on account. One way companies manage their cash flow is to take time to pay their bills, and large companies such as Kroger can essentially force their suppliers to sell them goods on credit. At 47 days, Starbucks's business customers are taking their time to pay.

Some companies allow their customers extended time to pay their bills because the customers would otherwise have difficulty coming up with the money. Many small companies do not have cash available to pay up front. Buying on credit is the only way they can obtain the inventory they need. If a manufacturer or wholesaler wants to sell to such companies, credit sales represent the only option available.

The length of the **operating cycle** is the average time it takes a business to convert inventory to accounts receivable plus the time it takes to convert accounts receivable into cash. The average number of days to collect receivables is one component of the operating cycle for a particular company. The other component is the average number of days to sell inventory that was explained in Chapter 5. The length of the operating cycles for the real-world companies in Exhibit 7.8 is shown in the last column.

What is the significance of the different operating cycle lengths in Exhibit 7.8? As previously explained, the longer the operating cycle takes, the more it costs the company. Exhibit 7.8 shows it takes Macy's an average of 76 days longer than Walmart to complete an operating cycle. All other things being equal, approximately how much did this longer time reduce Macy's earnings? Assume Macy's could invest excess cash at 8 percent (or alternatively, assume it pays 8 percent to finance its inventory and accounts receivable). Using the accounting information reported in Macy's 2013 financial statements, we can answer the question as follows:

Macy's investment in inventory	×	Interest rate	×	Time	=	Cost
\$5,308,000,000	×	8%	×	76/365	=	\$88,418,192

With 3 operating cycles per year (365 ÷ 122), the extended operating cycle costs Macy's \$265 million annually. Based on the assumptions used here, Macy's would have increased its after-tax earnings by approximately 8 percent, if it could have reduced its operating cycle by 76 days. Although this illustration is a rough estimate, it demonstrates that it is important for businesses to minimize the length of their operating cycles.

REALITY BYTES

This chapter explains that, in general, companies want to collect their receivables as quickly as possible. There is a notable exception to this generalization. If a company charges its customers interest on unpaid receivables, the company makes money on the unpaid balance. Many sellers of "big-ticket" goods like furniture, large appliances, and automobiles offer to finance their customers' purchases, allowing customers extended time to pay off their receivables in exchange for the customers' paying additional charges for interest.

For example, most people probably think of **Harley-Davidson** as a company that makes its profits selling motorcycles, and that is largely true. However, Harley-Davidson also made a substantial amount of profit from financing the motorcycles that it sells. During 2011, 2012, and 2013, the company earned 72 percent of its operating income from motorcycle sales and 28 percent from financing those sales. This amounted to $506 million of income before taxes. Therefore, the fact that it took Harley-Davidson 140 days to collect its receivables in 2013 was probably not a reason for concern.

CHECK YOURSELF 7.5

Randolph Corporation had sales for the year of $535,333 and an accounts receivable balance at year-end of $22,000. Determine Randolph's average number of days to collect accounts receivable.

Answer The accounts receivable turnover is 24.33 ($535,333 ÷ $22,000) times per year. The average number of days to collect accounts receivable is 15 (365 ÷ 24.33).

FOCUS ON INTERNATIONAL ISSUES

A ROSE BY ANY OTHER NAME . . .

If a person who studied U.S. GAAP wanted to look at the financial statements of a non-U.S. company, choosing statements of a company from another English-speaking country might seem logical. Presumably, this would eliminate language differences, and only the differences in GAAP would remain. However, this is not true.

When an accountant in the United States uses the term *turnover,* she or he is usually thinking of a financial ratio, such as the accounts receivable turnover ratio. However, in the United Kingdom, the term *turnover* refers to what U.S. accountants call *sales.* U.K. balance sheets do not usually show an account named *Inventory;* rather, they use the term *Stocks.* In the United States, accountants typically use the term *stocks* to refer to certificates representing ownership in a corporation. Finally, if an accountant or banker from the United Kingdom should ever ask you about your *gearing ratio,* he or she probably is not interested in your bicycle but in your debt to assets ratio.

Although IFRS has significantly increased the uniformity of financial reporting throughout the world, it does not seek to impose absolute uniformity. IFRS often allows alternate ways of accounting for the same business event, as will be discussed in Chapter 8. Even when different companies choose the same IFRS option for accounting for a given event, they are allowed some flexibility in the application of the IFRS rule, as are companies in the United States who follow GAAP. And, obviously, companies in different countries are allowed to prepare financial reports in their own language. As we will see in Chapter 9, companies in different countries may even use significantly different formats for their balance sheets.

<< A Look Back

We first introduced accounting for receivables in Chapter 2. This chapter presented additional complexities related to accounts receivable, such as the *allowance method of accounting for uncollectible accounts.* The allowance method improves matching of expenses with revenues. It also provides a more accurate measure of the value of accounts receivable on the balance sheet.

Under the allowance method, estimated uncollectible accounts expense is recorded in an adjusting entry at the end of the period in which a company has made credit sales. There are two methods commonly used to estimate the amount of uncollectible accounts expense: the percent of revenue method and the percent of receivables method. With the percent of revenue method, uncollectible accounts expense is measured as a percent of the period's sales. With the percent of receivables method, a company analyzes its accounts receivable at the end of the period, usually classifying them by age, to estimate the amount of the accounts receivable balance that is likely to be uncollectible. The balance in the Allowance for Doubtful Accounts account is then adjusted to equal the estimated amount of uncollectible accounts. Uncollectible accounts expense decreases the net realizable value of receivables (accounts receivable − allowance for doubtful accounts), stockholders' equity, and net income.

The allowance method of accounting for uncollectible accounts is conceptually superior to the *direct write-off method,* in which uncollectible accounts expense is recognized when an account is determined to be uncollectible. The direct write-off method fails to match revenues with expenses and overstates accounts receivable on the balance sheet. It is easier to use, however, and is permitted by generally accepted accounting principles if the amount of uncollectible accounts expense is immaterial.

The chapter also introduced notes receivable and accounting for *accrued interest.* When the term of a promissory note extends over more than one accounting period, companies must record adjusting entries to recognize interest in the appropriate accounting period, even if the cash exchange of interest occurs in a different accounting period.

We also discussed accounting for credit card sales, a vehicle that shifts uncollectible accounts expense to the credit card issuer. Many companies find the benefits of accepting major credit cards to be worth the credit card expense consequently incurred.

Finally, we addressed the costs of making credit sales. In addition to uncollectible accounts expense, interest is a major cost of financing receivables. The length of the collection period provides a measure of the quality of receivables. Short collection periods usually indicate lower amounts of uncollectible accounts and interest cost. Long collection periods imply higher costs. The collection period can be measured in two steps. First, divide sales by the accounts receivable balance to determine the accounts receivable turnover ratio. Then divide the number of days in the year (365) by the accounts receivable turnover ratio.

>> A Look Forward

Chapter 8 discusses accounting for long-term assets such as buildings and equipment. As with inventory cost flow, discussed in Chapter 5, GAAP allows companies to use different accounting methods to report on similar types of business events. Life would be easier for accounting students if all companies used the same accounting methods. However, the business world is complex. For the foreseeable future, people are likely to continue to have diverse views as to the best way to account for a variety of business transactions. To function effectively in today's business environment, it is important for you to be able to recognize differences in reporting practices.

SELF-STUDY REVIEW PROBLEM

A step-by-step audio-narrated series of slides is available in the Connect library.

During 2016 Calico Company experienced the following accounting events:

1. Provided $120,000 of services on account.
2. Collected $85,000 cash from accounts receivable.
3. Wrote off $1,800 of accounts receivable that were uncollectible.
4. Loaned $3,000 to an individual, Emma Gardner, in exchange for a note receivable.
5. Paid $90,500 cash for operating expenses.
6. Estimated that uncollectible accounts expense would be 2 percent of credit sales. Recorded the year-end adjusting entry.
7. Recorded the year-end adjusting entry for accrued interest on the note receivable (see Event 4). Calico made the loan on August 1. It had a six-month term and a 6 percent rate of interest.

Calico's ledger balances on January 1, 2016 were as follows:

Event No.	Assets							=	Liab.	+	Equity		
	Cash	+	Net Realizable Value of Receivables	+	Notes Rec.	+	Int. Rec.	=			Com. Stk.	+	Ret. Earn.
Bal.	12,000		15,800	+	NA	+	NA	=	NA	+	20,000	+	7,800

Required

a. Record the 2016 events in ledger accounts using the horizontal format shown above.
b. Determine net income for 2016.
c. Determine net cash flow from operating activities for 2016.
d. Determine the net realizable value of accounts receivable at December 31, 2016.
e. What amount of interest revenue will Calico recognize on its note receivable in 2017?

Solution to Requirement a

Event No.	Assets							=	Liab.	+	Equity		
	Cash	+	Net Realizable Value of Receivables	+	Notes Rec.	+	Int. Rec.	=			Com. Stk.	+	Ret. Earn.
Bal.	12,000	+	15,800	+	NA	+	NA	=	NA	+	20,000	+	7,800
1	NA	+	120,000	+	NA	+	NA	=	NA	+	NA	+	120,000
2	85,000	+	(85,000)	+	NA	+	NA	=	NA	+	NA	+	NA
3	NA	+	NA	+	NA	+	NA	=	NA	+	NA	+	NA
4	(3,000)	+	NA	+	3,000	+	NA	=	NA	+	NA	+	NA
5	(90,500)	+	NA	+	NA	+	NA	=	NA	+	NA	+	(90,500)
6	NA	+	(2,400)	+	NA	+	NA	=	NA	+	NA	+	(2,400)
7	NA	+	NA	+	NA	+	75*	=	NA	+	NA	+	75
Totals	3,500	+	48,400	+	3,000	+	75	=	NA	+	20,000	+	34,975

*$3,000 × .06 × 5/12 = $75.

Solution to Requirements b–e

b. Net income is $27,175 ($120,000 − $90,500 − $2,400 + $75).
c. Net cash flow from operating activities is an outflow of $5,500 ($85,000 − $90,500).
d. The net realizable value of accounts receivable is $48,400 ($51,200 − $2,800).
e. In 2017, Calico will recognize interest revenue for one month: $3,000 × .06 × 1/12 = $15.

KEY TERMS

Account receivable 364
Accounts receivable turnover ratio 385
Accrued interest 380
Adjusting entry 380
Aging of accounts receivable 375
Allowance for doubtful accounts 366
Allowance method of accounting for uncollectible accounts 366
Average number of days to collect accounts receivable 385
Collateral 379
Contra asset account 368
Direct write-off method 377
Interest 379
Liquidity 382
Maker 379
Matching concept 380
Maturity date 379
Net realizable value 366
Notes receivable 365
Operating cycle 386
Payee 379
Percent of receivables method 374
Percent of revenue method 368
Principal 379
Promissory note 378
Reinstate 371
Uncollectible accounts expense 368

QUESTIONS

1. What is the difference between accounts receivable and notes receivable?
2. What is the *net realizable value* of receivables?
3. What type of account is the Allowance for Doubtful Accounts?
4. What are two ways in which estimating uncollectible accounts improves the accuracy of the financial statements?
5. When using the allowance method, why is uncollectible accounts expense an estimated amount?
6. What is the most common format for reporting accounts receivable on the balance sheet? What information does this method provide beyond showing only the net amount?
7. Why is it necessary to make an entry to reinstate a previously written off account receivable before the collection is recorded?
8. What are some factors considered in estimating the amount of uncollectible accounts receivable?
9. What is the effect on the accounting equation of recognizing uncollectible accounts expense?
10. What is the effect on the accounting equation of writing off an uncollectible account receivable when the allowance method is used? When the direct write-off method is used?
11. How does the recovery of a previously written-off account affect the income statement when the allowance method is used? How does the recovery of a previously written-off account affect the statement of cash flows when the allowance method is used?
12. What is the advantage of using the allowance method of accounting for uncollectible accounts? What is the advantage of using the direct write-off method?
13. How do companies determine the percentage estimate of uncollectible accounts when using the percent of revenue method?
14. What is an advantage of using the percent of receivables method of estimating uncollectible accounts expense?
15. What is "aging of accounts receivable"?
16. What is the difference between the allowance method and the direct write-off method of accounting for uncollectible accounts?
17. When is it acceptable to use the direct write-off method of accounting for uncollectible accounts?
18. What is a promissory note?
19. Define the following terms:
    a. Maker
    b. Payee
    c. Principal
    d. Interest
    e. Maturity date
    f. Collateral
20. What is the formula for computing interest revenue?
21. What is accrued interest?
22. When is an adjusting entry for accrued interest generally recorded?
23. Assume that on July 1, 2016, Big Corp. loaned Little Corp. $12,000 for a period of one year at 6 percent interest. What amount of interest revenue will Big report for 2016? What amount of cash will Big receive upon maturity of the note?
24. In which section of the statement of cash flows will Big report the cash collected in Question 23?
25. Why is it generally beneficial for a business to accept major credit cards as payment for goods and services even when the fee charged by the credit card company is substantial?
26. What types of costs do businesses avoid when they accept major credit cards as compared with handling credit sales themselves?
27. How is the accounts receivable turnover ratio computed? What information does the ratio provide?
28. How is the average number of days to collect accounts receivable computed? What information does the ratio provide?
29. Is accounting terminology standard in all countries? What term is used in the United Kingdom to refer to *sales?* What term is used to refer to *inventory?* What is a *gearing ratio?* Is it important to know about these differences?
30. What is the operating cycle of a business?

MULTIPLE-CHOICE QUESTIONS

Multiple-choice questions are available in the Connect library.

EXERCISES—SERIES A

connect plus+ ACCOUNTING ***All applicable Exercises in Series A are available with McGraw-Hill's Connect Plus Accounting.***

Exercise 7-1A *Analysis of financial statement effects of accounting for uncollectible accounts under the allowance method* LO 7-1

Businesses using the allowance method for the recognition of uncollectible accounts expense commonly experience four accounting events:

1. Recognition of uncollectible accounts expense through a year-end adjusting entry.
2. Write-off of uncollectible accounts.
3. Recognition of revenue on account.
4. Collection of cash from accounts receivable.

Required

Show the effect of each event on the elements of the financial statements, using a horizontal statements model like the one shown here. Use the following coding scheme to record your answers: increase is +, decrease is −, not affected is NA. In the cash flow column, indicate whether the item is an operating activity (OA), investing activity (IA), or financing activity (FA). The first transaction is entered as an example.

Event No.	Assets	=	Liab.	+	Equity	Rev.	−	Exp.	=	Net Inc.	Cash Flow
1	−		NA		−	NA		+		−	NA

Exercise 7-2A *Accounting for uncollectible accounts: allowance method* LO 7-1

Holmes Cleaning Service began operation on January 1, 2016. The company experienced the following events for its first year of operations:

Events Affecting 2016:

1. Provided $84,000 of cleaning services on account.
2. Collected $76,000 cash from accounts receivable.
3. Paid salaries of $28,500 for the year.
4. Adjusted the accounts to reflect management's expectations that uncollectible accounts expense would be $1,650. The expense was determined using the percent of revenue method.

Required

a. Prepare general journal entries for the above events.
b. Post the general journal entries to T-accounts.
c. Prepare an income statement, balance sheet, and statement of cash flows for 2016.

Exercise 7-3A *Analyzing account balances for a company using the allowance method of accounting for uncollectible accounts* LO 7-1

The following account balances come from the records of Ourso Company:

	Beginning Balance	Ending Balance
Accounts Receivable	$2,800	$3,600
Allowance for Doubtful Accounts	280	350

During the accounting period, Ourso recorded $14,000 of sales revenue on account. The company also wrote off a $150 account receivable.

Required

a. Determine the amount of cash collected from receivables.

b. Determine the amount of uncollectible accounts expense recognized during the period.

LO 7-1

Exercise 7-4A *Effect of recognizing uncollectible accounts expense on financial statements: percent of revenue allowance method*

Rosie Dry Cleaning was started on January 1, 2016. It experienced the following events during its first two years of operation:

Events Affecting 2016

1. Provided $45,000 of cleaning services on account.
2. Collected $39,000 cash from accounts receivable.
3. Adjusted the accounting records to reflect the estimate that uncollectible accounts expense would be 1 percent of the cleaning revenue on account.

Events Affecting 2017

1. Wrote off a $300 account receivable that was determined to be uncollectible.
2. Provided $62,000 of cleaning services on account.
3. Collected $61,000 cash from accounts receivable.
4. Adjusted the accounting records to reflect the estimate that uncollectible accounts expense would be 1 percent of the cleaning revenue on account.

Required

a. Record the events for 2016 in T-accounts.

b. Determine the following amounts:

(1) Net income for 2016.

(2) Net cash flow from operating activities for 2016.

(3) Balance of accounts receivable at the end of 2016.

(4) Net realizable value of accounts receivable at the end of 2016.

c. Repeat Requirements *a* and *b* for the 2017 accounting period.

LO 7-1

Exercise 7-5A *Analyzing financial statement effects of accounting for uncollectible accounts using the percent of revenue allowance method*

Grover Inc. uses the allowance method to account for uncollectible accounts expense. Grover, Inc. experienced the following four accounting events in 2016:

1. Recognized $92,000 of revenue on account.
2. Collected $78,000 cash from accounts receivable.
3. Wrote off uncollectible accounts of $720.
4. Recognized uncollectible accounts expense. Grover estimated that uncollectible accounts expense will be 1 percent of sales on account.

Required

a. Show the effect of each event on the elements of the financial statements, using a horizontal statements model like the one shown here. Use + for increase, − for decrease, and NA for not affected. In the cash flow column, indicate whether the item is an operating activity (OA), investing activity (IA), or financing activity (FA). The first transaction is entered as an example.

Event No.	Assets	=	Liab.	+	Equity	Rev.	−	Exp.	=	Net Inc.	Cash Flow
1	+		NA		+	+		NA		+	NA

b. Record the above transactions in general journal form.

Exercise 7-6A *Effect of recovering a receivable previously written off*

LO 7-1

The accounts receivable balance for Renue Spa at December 31, 2015, was $61,000. Also on that date, the balance in the Allowance for Doubtful Accounts was $3,750. During 2016, $2,100 of accounts receivable were written off as uncollectible. In addition, Renue unexpectedly collected $500 of receivables that had been written off in a previous accounting period. Services provided on account during 2016 were $215,000, and cash collections from receivables were $218,000. Uncollectible accounts expense was estimated to be 2 percent of the sales on account for the period.

Required

a. Record the transactions in general journal form and post to T-accounts.
b. Based on the preceding information, compute (after year-end adjustment):
   (1) Balance of Allowance for Doubtful Accounts at December 31, 2016.
   (2) Balance of Accounts Receivable at December 31, 2016.
   (3) Net realizable value of Accounts Receivable at December 31, 2016.
c. What amount of uncollectible accounts expense will Renue report for 2016?
d. Explain how the $500 recovery of receivables affects the income statement.

Exercise 7-7A *Accounting for uncollectible accounts: percent of receivables allowance method*

LO 7-2, 7-3

Vulcan Service Co. experienced the following transactions for 2016, its first year of operations:

1. Provided $91,000 of services on account.
2. Collected $72,000 cash from accounts receivable.
3. Paid $36,000 of salaries expense for the year.
4. Adjusted the accounts using the following information from an accounts receivable aging schedule:

Number of Days Past Due	Amount	Percent Likely to Be Uncollectible	Allowance Balance
Current	$7,800	.01	
0–30	4,500	.05	
31–60	2,000	.10	
61–90	2,200	.20	
Over 90 days	2,500	.50	

Required

a. Record the above transactions in general journal form and post to T-accounts.
b. Prepare the income statement for Vulcan Service Co. for 2016.
c. What is the net realizable value of the accounts receivable at December 31, 2016?

Exercise 7-8A *Effect of recognizing uncollectible accounts on the financial statements: percent of receivables allowance method*

LO 7-2

Leach Inc. experienced the following events for the first two years of its operations:

2016:

1. Issued $10,000 of common stock for cash.
2. Provided $78,000 of services on account.
3. Provided $36,000 of services and received cash.
4. Collected $69,000 cash from accounts receivable.
5. Paid $38,000 of salaries expense for the year.
6. Adjusted the accounting records to reflect uncollectible accounts expense for the year. Leach estimates that 5 percent of the ending accounts receivable balance will be uncollectible.

2017:

1. Wrote off an uncollectible account for $650.
2. Provided $88,000 of services on account.
3. Provided $32,000 of services and collected cash.
4. Collected $81,000 cash from accounts receivable.
5. Paid $65,000 of salaries expense for the year.
6. Adjusted the accounts to reflect uncollectible accounts expense for the year. Leach estimates that 5 percent of the ending accounts receivable balance will be uncollectible.

Required

a. Record the 2016 events in general journal form and post them to T-accounts.
b. Prepare the income statement, statement of changes in stockholders' equity, balance sheet, and statement of cash flows for 2016.
c. What is the net realizable value of the accounts receivable at December 31, 2016?
d. Repeat Requirements *a*, *b*, and *c* for 2017.

LO 7-4

Exercise 7-9A *Accounting for uncollectible accounts: direct write-off method*

Patel Service Co. does make a few sales on account but is mostly a cash business. Consequently, it uses the direct write-off method to account for uncollectible accounts. During 2016 Patel Service Co. earned $35,000 of cash revenue and $4,500 of revenue on account. Cash operating expenses were $19,000. After numerous attempts to collect a $120 account receivable from Sam Stephens, the account was determined to be uncollectible in 2016.

Required

a. Record the effects of (1) cash revenue, (2) revenue on account, (3) cash expenses, and (4) write off of the uncollectible account on the financial statements using a horizontal statements model like the one shown here. In the Cash Flow column, indicate whether the item is an operating activity (OA), investing activity (IA), or financing activity (FA). Use NA to indicate that an element is not affected by the event.

Assets			=	Liab.	+	Equity	Rev.	−	Exp.	=	Net Inc.	Cash Flow
Cash	+	Accts. Rec.										

b. What amount of net income did Patel Service Co. report on the 2016 income statement?
c. Prepare the general journal entries for the four accounting events listed in Requirement *a*.

LO 7-1, 7-4

Exercise 7-10A *Accounting for uncollectible accounts: percent of revenue allowance versus direct write-off method*

Joey's Bike Shop sells new and used bicycle parts. Although a majority of its sales are cash sales, it makes a significant amount of credit sales. During 2016, its first year of operations, Joey's Bike Shop experienced the following:

Sales on account	$260,000
Cash sales	580,000
Collections of accounts receivable	235,000
Uncollectible accounts charged off during the year	1,250

Required

a. Assume that Joey's Bike Shop uses the allowance method of accounting for uncollectible accounts and estimates that 1 percent of its sales on account will not be collected. Answer the following questions:

(1) What is the Accounts Receivable balance at December 31, 2016?

(2) What is the ending balance of the Allowance for Doubtful Accounts at December 31, 2016, after all entries and adjusting entries are posted?

(3) What is the amount of uncollectible accounts expense for 2016?

(4) What is the net realizable value of accounts receivable at December 31, 2016?

b. Assume that Joey's Bike Shop uses the direct write-off method of accounting for uncollectible accounts. Answer the following questions:

(1) What is the Accounts Receivable balance at December 31, 2016?

(2) What is the amount of uncollectible accounts expense for 2016?

(3) What is the net realizable value of accounts receivable at December 31, 2016?

Exercise 7-11A *Accounting for notes receivable* LO 7-5

Rainey Enterprises loaned $20,000 to Small Co. on June 1, 2016, for one year at 6 percent interest.

Required

a. Record these general journal entries for Rainey Enterprises:

(1) The loan to Small Co.

(2) The adjusting entry at December 31, 2016.

(3) The adjusting entry and collection of the note on June 1, 2017.

b. Show the effects of the three above transactions in a horizontal statements model like the one shown below:

	Assets					=	Liab.	+	Equity	Rev.	−	Exp.	=	Net Inc.	Cash Flows
Date	Cash	+	Notes Rec.	+	Int. Rec.	=		+	Ret. Earn.						

Exercise 7-12A *Notes receivable—accrued interest* LO 7-5

On May 1, 2016, Benz's Sandwich Shop loaned $10,000 to Mark Henry for one year at 6 percent interest.

Required

Answer the following questions:

a. What is Benz's interest income for 2016?

b. What is Benz's total amount of receivables at December 31, 2016?

c. How will the loan and interest be reported on Benz's 2016 statement of cash flows?

d. What is Benz's interest income for 2017?

e. What is the total amount of cash that Benz's will collect in 2017 from Mark Henry?

f. How will the loan and interest be reported on Benz's 2017 statement of cash flows?

g. What is the total amount of interest that Benz's earned on the loan to Mark Henry?

Exercise 7-13A *Effect of credit card sales on financial statements* LO 7-6

Ultra Day Spa provided $120,000 of services during 2016. All customers paid for the services with credit cards. Ultra submitted the credit card receipts to the credit card company immediately. The credit card company paid Ultra cash in the amount of face value less a 5 percent service charge.

Required

a. Record the credit card sales and the subsequent collection of accounts receivable in a horizontal statements model like the one shown here. In the Cash Flow column, indicate whether the item is an operating activity (OA), investing activity (IA), or financing activity (FA). Use NA to indicate that an element is not affected by the event.

Assets			=	Liab.	+	Equity	Rev.	−	Exp.	=	Net Inc.	Cash Flow
Cash	+	Accts. Rec.										

b. Based on this information alone, answer the following questions:
   (1) What is the amount of total assets at the end of the accounting period?
   (2) What is the amount of revenue reported on the income statement?
   (3) What is the amount of cash flow from operating activities reported on the statement of cash flows?
   (4) What costs would a business incur if it maintained its own accounts receivable? What cost does a business incur by accepting credit cards?

LO 7-6

Exercise 7-14A *Recording credit card sales*

Luna Company accepted credit cards in payment for $6,000 of services performed during July 2016. The credit card company charged Luna a 4 percent service fee; it paid Luna as soon as it received the invoices.

Required

a. Prepare the general journal entry to record the service revenue.
b. Prepare the general journal entry for the collection of the receivable from the credit card company.
c. Based on this information alone, what is the amount of net income earned during the month of July?

LO 7-1, 7-5, 7-6

Exercise 7-15A *Comprehensive single-cycle problem*

The following post-closing trial balance was drawn from the accounts of Little Grocery Supplier (LGS) as of December 31, 2015:

	Debit	Credit
Cash	$ 9,000	
Accounts Receivable	41,000	
Allowance for Doubtful Accounts		$ 2,500
Inventory	78,000	
Accounts Payable		21,000
Common Stock		50,000
Retained Earnings		54,500
Totals	$128,000	$128,000

Transactions for 2016

1. LGS acquired an additional $20,000 cash from the issue of common stock.
2. LGS purchased $85,000 of inventory on account.
3. LGS sold inventory that cost $91,000 for $160,000. Sales were made on account.
4. The company wrote off $900 of uncollectible accounts.
5. On September 1, LGS loaned $18,000 to Eden Co. The note had an 8 percent interest rate and a one-year term.
6. LGS paid $19,000 cash for operating expenses.
7. The company collected $161,000 cash from accounts receivable.
8. A cash payment of $92,000 was paid on accounts payable.
9. The company paid a $5,000 cash dividend to the stockholders.
10. Accepted credit cards for sales amounting to $7,000. The cost of goods sold was $4,000. The credit card company charges a 4% service charge. The cash has not been received.
11. Uncollectible accounts are estimated to be 1 percent of sales on account.
12. Recorded the accrued interest at December 31, 2016 (see item 5).

Required

a. Record the above transactions in general journal form.
b. Open T-accounts and record the beginning balances and the 2016 transactions.
c. Prepare an income statement, statement of changes in stockholders' equity, balance sheet, and statement of cash flows for 2016.

Exercise 7-16A *Accounts receivable turnover and average days to collect accounts receivable*

LO 7-7

The following information is available for Bergstrom Inc. and Sineann Inc. at December 31, 2016:

Accounts	Bergstrom	Sineann
Accounts Receivable	$ 790,000	$ 540,100
Allowance for Doubtful Accounts	15,800	9,700
Sales Revenue	8,360,200	3,780,600

Required

a. What is the accounts receivable turnover for each of the companies for 2016?
b. What is the average days to collect the receivables for 2016?
c. Assuming both companies use the percent of receivables allowance method, what is the estimated percentage of uncollectible accounts for each company?

PROBLEMS—SERIES A

connect plus+ ACCOUNTING ***All applicable Problems in Series A are available with McGraw-Hill's Connect Plus Accounting.***

Problem 7-17A *Accounting for uncollectible accounts: two cycles using the percent of revenue allowance method*

LO 7-1

CHECK FIGURES
c. Ending Accounts Receivable, 2016: $48,000
d. Net Income, 2017: $113,400

The following transactions apply to Jova Company for 2016, the first year of operation:

1. Issued $10,000 of common stock for cash.
2. Recognized $210,000 of service revenue earned on account.
3. Collected $162,000 from accounts receivable.
4. Paid $125,000 cash for operating expenses.
5. Adjusted the accounts to recognize uncollectible accounts expense. Jova uses the allowance method of accounting for uncollectible accounts and estimates that uncollectible accounts expense will be 1 percent of sales on account.

The following transactions apply to Jova for 2017:

1. Recognized $320,000 of service revenue on account.
2. Collected $335,000 from accounts receivable.
3. Determined that $2,150 of the accounts receivable were uncollectible and wrote them off.
4. Collected $800 of an account that had previously been written off.
5. Paid $205,000 cash for operating expenses.
6. Adjusted the accounts to recognize uncollectible accounts expense for 2017. Jova estimates uncollectible accounts expense will be 0.5 percent of sales on account.

Required

Complete the following requirements for 2016 and 2017. Complete all requirements for 2016 prior to beginning the requirements for 2017.

a. Identify the type of each transaction (asset source, asset use, asset exchange, or claims exchange).
b. Show the effect of each transaction on the elements of the financial statements, using a horizontal statements model like the one shown here. Use + for increase, − for decrease, and NA

for not affected. Also, in the Cash Flow column, indicate whether the item is an operating activity (OA), investing activity (IA), or financing activity (FA). The first transaction is entered as an example. (*Hint:* Closing entries do not affect the statements model.)

Event No.	Assets	=	Liab.	+	Equity	Rev.	−	Exp.	=	Net Inc.	Cash Flow
1	+		NA		+	+		NA		+	NA

c. Record the transactions in general journal form and post them to T-accounts (begin 2017 with the ending T-account balances from 2016).

d. Prepare the income statement, statement of changes in stockholders' equity, balance sheet, and statement of cash flows.

e. Prepare closing entries and post these closing entries to the T-accounts. Prepare the post-closing trial balance.

LO 7-1

Problem 7-18A *Determining account balances and preparing journal entries: percent of revenue allowance method of accounting for uncollectible accounts*

CHECK FIGURE
d. Net Realizable Value: $43,100

During the first year of operation, 2016, Direct Service Co. recognized $290,000 of service revenue on account. At the end of 2016, the accounts receivable balance was $46,000. For this first year in business, the owner believes uncollectible accounts expense will be about 1 percent of sales on account.

Required

a. What amount of cash did Direct Service collect from accounts receivable during 2016?

b. Assuming Direct Service uses the allowance method to account for uncollectible accounts, what amount should Direct Service record as uncollectible accounts expense for 2016?

c. Prepare the general journal entries to:

(1) Record service revenue on account.

(2) Record collections from accounts receivable.

(3) Record the entry to recognize uncollectible accounts expense.

d. What is the net realizable value of receivables at the end of 2016?

e. Show the effects of the transactions in Requirement *c* on the financial statements by recording the appropriate amounts in a horizontal statements model like the one shown here. In the Cash Flow column, indicate whether the item is an operating activity (OA), investing activity (IA), or financing activity (FA). Use NA for not affected.

Assets			=	Liab.	+	Equity	Rev.	−	Exp.	=	Net Inc.	Cash Flow
Cash	+	Net Realizable Value of Receivables										

LO 7-2

Problem 7-19A *Determination of account balances and preparation of journal entries—percent of receivables allowance method of accounting for uncollectible accounts*

CHECK FIGURE
b. Net Realizable Value: $66,864

The following information is available for Quality Book Sales' sales on account and accounts receivable:

Accounts receivable balance, January 1, 2016	$ 78,500
Allowance for doubtful accounts, January 1, 2016	4,710
Sales on account, 2016	550,000
Collection on accounts receivable, 2016	556,000

After several collection attempts, Quality Book Sales wrote off $2,850 of accounts that could not be collected. Quality Book Sales estimates that 4 percent of the ending accounts receivable balance will be uncollectible.

Required

a. Compute the following amounts:

  (1) Using the allowance method, the amount of uncollectible accounts expense for 2016.

  (2) Net realizable value of receivables at the end of 2016.

b. Record the general journal entries to:

  (1) Record sales on account for 2016.

  (2) Record cash collections from accounts receivable for 2016.

  (3) Write off the accounts that are not collectible.

  (4) Record the estimated uncollectible accounts expense for 2016.

c. Explain why the uncollectible accounts expense amount is different from the amount that was written off as uncollectible.

Problem 7-20A *Accounting for uncollectible accounts: percent of receivables allowance method*

LO 7-2, 7-3

CHECK FIGURES
b. Net Income: $61,430
Total Assets: $133,430

Roth Inc. experienced the following transactions for 2016, its first year of operations:

1. Issued common stock for $50,000 cash.
2. Purchased $140,000 of merchandise on account.
3. Sold merchandise that cost $110,000 for $250,000 on account.
4. Collected $236,000 cash from accounts receivable.
5. Paid $118,000 on accounts payable.
6. Paid $50,000 of salaries expense for the year.
7. Paid other operating expenses of $28,000.
8. Roth adjusted the accounts using the following information from an accounts receivable aging schedule:

Number of Days Past Due	Amount	Percent Likely to Be Uncollectible	Allowance Balance
Current	$10,000	.01	
0–30	2,000	.05	
31–60	1,200	.10	
61–90	500	.20	
Over 90 days	300	.50	

Required

a. Record the above transactions in general journal form and post to T-accounts.

b. Prepare the income statement, statement of changes in stockholders' equity, balance sheet, and statement of cash flows for Roth Inc. for 2016.

c. What is the net realizable value of the accounts receivable at December 31, 2016?

Problem 7-21A *Accounting for credit card sales and uncollectible accounts: percent of receivables allowance method*

LO 7-2, 7-6

CHECK FIGURES
c. Net Income: $280,300
Total Assets: $480,300

Northwest Sales had the following transactions in 2016:

1. The business was started when it acquired $200,000 cash from the issue of common stock.
2. Northwest purchased $900,000 of merchandise for cash in 2016.
3. During the year, the company sold merchandise for $1,200,000. The merchandise cost $710,000. Sales were made under the following terms:

a. $520,000	Cash sales
b. 380,000	Credit card sales (The credit card company charges a 4 percent service fee.)
c. 300,000	Sales on account

4. The company collected all the amount receivable from the credit card company.
5. The company collected $210,000 of accounts receivable.
6. The company paid $190,000 cash for selling and administrative expenses.
7. Determined that 5 percent of the ending accounts receivable balance would be uncollectible.

Required

a. Show the effects of each of the transactions on the elements of the financial statements, using a horizontal statements model like the one shown here. Use + for increase, − for decrease, and NA for not affected. The first transaction is entered as an example. (*Hint:* Closing entries do not affect the statements model.)

Event No.	Assets	=	Liab.	+	Equity	Rev.	−	Exp.	=	Net Inc.	Cash Flow
1	+		NA		+	NA		NA		NA	+ FA

b. Prepare general journal entries for each of the transactions and post them to T-accounts.
c. Prepare an income statement, statement of changes in stockholders' equity, balance sheet, and statement of cash flows for 2016.

LO 7-4, 7-5

Problem 7-22A *Accounting for notes receivable and uncollectible accounts using the direct write-off method*

The following transactions apply to Hooper Co. for 2016, its first year of operations:

1. Issued $60,000 of common stock for cash.
2. Provided $90,000 of services on account.
3. Collected $78,000 cash from accounts receivable.
4. Loaned $20,000 to Mosby Co. on November 30, 2016. The note had a one-year term to maturity and a 6 percent interest rate.
5. Paid $26,000 of salaries expense for the year.
6. Paid a $2,000 dividend to the stockholders.
7. Recorded the accrued interest on December 31, 2016 (see item 4).
8. Determined that $920 of accounts receivable were uncollectible.

Required

a. Record the above transactions in general journal form.
b. Post the entries to T-accounts.
c. Prepare the income statement, balance sheet, and statement of cash flows for 2016.
d. Show the effects of the above transactions in a horizontal statements model like the one shown below:

	Assets							= Liab. +	Equity			Rev. − Exp. = Net Inc.	Cash Flows
Event	Cash	+	Accts. Rec.	+	Notes Rec.	+	Int. Rec.	=	Com. Stk.	+	Ret. Earn.		

LO 7-4, 7-5, 7-6

Problem 7-23A *Effect of transactions on the elements of financial statements*

Required

Identify each of the following independent transactions as asset source (AS), asset use (AU), asset exchange (AE), or claims exchange (CE). Also explain how each event affects assets, liabilities, stockholders' equity, net income, and cash flow by placing a + for increase, − for decrease, or NA for not affected under each of the categories. The first event is recorded as an example.

Event	Type of Event	Assets	Liabilities	Common Stock	Retained Earnings	Net Income	Cash Flow
a	AS	+	NA	NA	+	+	NA

a. Provided services on account.

b. Wrote off an uncollectible account (use the direct write-off method).

c. Loaned cash to H. Phillips for one year at 6 percent interest.

d. Collected cash from customers paying their accounts.

e. Paid cash for land.

f. Sold merchandise at a price above cost. Accepted payment by credit card. The credit card company charges a service fee. The receipts have not yet been forwarded to the credit card company.

g. Provided services for cash.

h. Paid cash for operating expenses.

i. Paid cash for salaries expense.

j. Recovered an uncollectible account that had been previously written off (assume the direct write-off method is used to account for uncollectible accounts).

k. Paid cash to creditors on accounts payable.

l. Recorded three months of accrued interest on the note receivable (see item *c*).

m. Submitted receipts to the credit card company (see *f* above) and collected cash.

n. Sold land at its cost.

Problem 7-24A *Multistep income statement and balance sheet* LO 7-1, 7-5

Required

Use the following information to prepare a multistep income statement and a balance sheet for Sherman Equipment Co. for 2016. (*Hint:* Some of the items will *not* appear on either statement, and ending retained earnings must be calculated.)

CHECK FIGURES
Total Assets: $273,800
Total Liabilities: $58,000

Salaries Expense	$ 69,000	Operating Expenses	$ 62,000
Common Stock	100,000	Cash Flow from Investing Activities	78,400
Notes Receivable (short term)	24,000	Prepaid Rent	12,500
Allowance for Doubtful Accounts	7,800	Land	40,000
Uncollectible Accounts Expense	8,100	Cash	48,100
Supplies	1,200	Inventory	98,300
Interest Revenue	5,400	Accounts Payable	46,000
Sales Revenue	320,000	Salaries Payable	12,000
Dividends	5,000	Cost of Goods Sold	148,000
Interest Receivable (short term)	1,500	Accounts Receivable	56,000
Beginning Retained Earnings	81,000		

Problem 7-25A *Missing information* LO 7-1, 7-5

The following information comes from the accounts of James Company:

Account Title	Beginning Balance	Ending Balance
Accounts Receivable	$36,000	$34,000
Allowance for Doubtful Accounts	1,800	1,600
Note Receivable	40,000	40,000
Interest Receivable	1,400	2,800

Required

a. There were $190,000 of sales on account during the accounting period. Write-offs of uncollectible accounts were $1,450. What was the amount of cash collected from accounts receivable? What amount of uncollectible accounts expense was reported on the income statement? What was the net realizable value of receivables at the end of the accounting period?

b. The note receivable has a two-year term with a 7 percent interest rate. What amount of interest revenue was recognized during the period? How much cash was collected from interest?

LO 7-1, 7-3, 7-5, 7-6

Problem 7-26A ***Comprehensive accounting cycle problem (uses percent of revenue allowance method)***

The following trial balance was prepared for Tile, Etc., Inc., on December 31, 2016, after the closing entries were posted:

Account Title	Debit	Credit
Cash	$110,000	
Accounts Receivable	125,000	
Allowance for Doubtful Accounts		$ 18,000
Inventory	425,000	
Accounts Payable		95,000
Common Stock		450,000
Retained Earnings		97,000
Totals	$660,000	$660,000

Tile, Etc. had the following transactions in 2017:

1. Purchased merchandise on account for $580,000.
2. Sold merchandise that cost $420,000 for $890,000 on account.
3. Sold for $245,000 cash merchandise that had cost $160,000.
4. Sold merchandise for $190,000 to credit card customers. The merchandise had cost $96,000. The credit card company charges a 4 percent fee.
5. Collected $620,000 cash from accounts receivable.
6. Paid $610,000 cash on accounts payable.
7. Paid $145,000 cash for selling and administrative expenses.
8. Collected cash for the full amount due from the credit card company (see item 4).
9. Loaned $60,000 to J. Parks. The note had an 8 percent interest rate and a one-year term to maturity.
10. Wrote off $7,500 of accounts as uncollectible.
11. Made the following adjusting entries:
    (a) Recorded uncollectible accounts expense estimated at 1 percent of sales on account.
    (b) Recorded seven months of accrued interest on the note at December 31, 2017 (see item 9).

Required

a. Prepare general journal entries for these transactions; post the entries to T-accounts; and prepare an income statement, a statement of changes in stockholders' equity, a balance sheet, and a statement of cash flows for 2017.

b. Compute the net realizable value of accounts receivable at December 31, 2017.

c. If Tile, Etc. used the direct write-off method, what amount of uncollectible accounts expense would it report on the income statement?

EXERCISES—SERIES B

Exercise 7-1B *Analysis of financial statement effects of accounting for uncollectible accounts under the allowance method* LO 7-1

Hardin Services Co. experienced the following events in 2016:

1. Provided services on account.
2. Collected cash for accounts receivable.
3. Attempted to collect an account and, when unsuccessful, wrote the amount off to uncollectible accounts expense.

Required

Show the effect of each event on the elements of the financial statements, using a horizontal statements model like the one shown here. Use + for increase, − for decrease, and NA for not affected. In the cash flow column, indicate whether the item is an operating activity (OA), investing activity (IA), or financing activity (FA).

Event No.	Assets	=	Liab.	+	Equity	Rev.	−	Exp.	=	Net Inc.	Cash Flow

Exercise 7-2B *Accounting for bad debts: allowance method* LO 7-1

Sandy's Accounting Service began operation on January 1, 2016. The company experienced the following events for its first year of operations:

Events Affecting 2016:

1. Provided $96,000 of accounting services on account.
2. Collected $80,000 cash from accounts receivable.
3. Paid salaries of $32,000 for the year.
4. Adjusted the accounts to reflect management's expectations that uncollectible accounts expense would be $1,600.

Required

a. Prepare general journal entries for the above events.
b. Post the general journal entries to T-accounts.
c. Prepare an income statement, balance sheet, and statement of cash flows for 2016.

Exercise 7-3B *Analyzing account balances for a company using the allowance method of accounting for uncollectible accounts* LO 7-1

The following account balances come from the records of Stone Company:

	Beginning Balance	Ending Balance
Accounts Receivable	$4,000	$4,500
Allowance for Doubtful Accounts	150	250

During the accounting period, Stone recorded $21,000 of service revenue on account. The company also wrote off a $180 account receivable.

Required

a. Determine the amount of cash collected from receivables.
b. Determine the amount of uncollectible accounts expense recognized during the period.

LO 7-1

Exercise 7-4B *Effect of recognizing uncollectible accounts expense on financial statements: percent of revenue allowance method*

Reliable Auto Service was started on January 1, 2016. The company experienced the following events during its first two years of operation:

Events Affecting 2016

1. Provided $45,000 of repair services on account.
2. Collected $32,000 cash from accounts receivable.
3. Adjusted the accounting records to reflect the estimate that uncollectible accounts expense would be 1 percent of the service revenue on account.

Events Affecting 2017

1. Wrote off a $320 account receivable that was determined to be uncollectible.
2. Provided $65,000 of repair services on account.
3. Collected $66,000 cash from accounts receivable.
4. Adjusted the accounting records to reflect the estimate that uncollectible accounts expense would be 1 percent of the service revenue on account.

Required

a. Record the events for 2016 in general journal form and post them to T-accounts.

b. Determine the following amounts:

   (1) Net income for 2016.

   (2) Net cash flow from operating activities for 2016.

   (3) Balance of accounts receivable at the end of 2016.

   (4) Net realizable value of accounts receivable at the end of 2016.

c. Repeat Requirements *a* and *b* for the 2017 accounting period.

LO 7-1

Exercise 7-5B *Analyzing financial statement effects of accounting for uncollectible accounts using the percent of revenue allowance method*

Tull Bros. uses the allowance method to account for uncollectible accounts expense. Tull experienced the following four events in 2016:

1. Recognized $68,000 of revenue on account.
2. Collected $62,000 cash from accounts receivable.
3. Determined that $500 of accounts receivable were not collectible and wrote them off.
4. Recognized uncollectible accounts expense for the year. Tull estimates that uncollectible accounts expense will be 2 percent of its sales.

Required

a. Show the effect of each of these events on the elements of the financial statements, using a horizontal statements model like the following one. Use + for increase, − for decrease, and NA for not affected. In the cash flow column, indicate whether the item is an operating activity (OA), investing activity (IA), or financing activity (FA).

Event No.	Assets			=	Liab.	+	Equity	Rev.	−	Exp.	=	Net Inc.	Cash Flow
	Cash	+	Net Realizable Value of Rec.	=			Ret. Earn.						

b. Record the above transactions in general journal form.

LO 7-1

Exercise 7-6B *Effect of recovering a receivable previously written off*

The accounts receivable balance for Edd's Shoe Repair at December 31, 2016, was $76,000. Also on that date, the balance in the Allowance for Doubtful Accounts was $3,200. During 2017, $2,900 of accounts receivable were written off as uncollectible. In addition, Edd's Shoe Repair unexpectedly collected $200 of receivables that had been written off in a previous accounting period. Sales on account during 2017 were $210,000, and cash collections from receivables were $215,000. Uncollectible accounts expense was estimated to be 1 percent of the sales on account for the period.

Required

a. Record the transactions in general journal form and post them to T-accounts.

b. Based on the preceding information, compute (after year-end adjustment):

(1) Balance of Allowance for Doubtful Accounts at December 31, 2017.

(2) Balance of Accounts Receivable at December 31, 2017.

(3) Net realizable value of Accounts Receivable at December 31, 2017.

c. What amount of uncollectible accounts expense will Edd's Shoe Repair report for 2017?

d. Explain how the $200 recovery of receivables affected the accounting equation.

Exercise 7-7B *Accounting for uncollectible accounts: percent of receivables allowance method*

LO 7-2, 7-3

Pollard Service Co. experienced the following transactions for 2016, its first year of operations:

1. Provided $86,000 of services on account.
2. Collected $72,000 cash from accounts receivable.
3. Paid $39,000 of salaries expense for the year.
4. Pollard adjusted the accounts using the following information from an accounts receivable aging schedule:

Number of Days Past Due	Amount	Percent Likely to Be Uncollectible	Allowance Balance
Current	$7,500	.01	
0–30	2,000	.05	
31–60	1,500	.10	
61–90	1,000	.30	
Over 90 days	2,000	.50	

Required

a. Record the above transactions in general journal form and post them to T-accounts.

b. Prepare the income statement for Pollard Service Co. for 2016.

c. What is the net realizable value of the accounts receivable at December 31, 2016?

Exercise 7-8B *Effect of recognizing uncollectible accounts on the financial statements: percent of receivables allowance method*

LO 7-2

Juno Inc. experienced the following events for the first two years of its operations:

2016:

1. Issued $5,000 of common stock for cash.
2. Provided $80,000 of services on account.
3. Provided $22,000 of services and received cash.
4. Collected $65,000 cash from accounts receivable.
5. Paid $24,000 of salaries expense for the year.
6. Adjusted the accounting records to reflect uncollectible accounts expense for the year. Juno estimates that 5 percent of the ending accounts receivable balance will be uncollectible.

2017:

1. Wrote off an uncollectible account of $620.
2. Provided $95,000 of services on account.
3. Provided $15,000 of services and collected cash.
4. Collected $90,000 cash from accounts receivable.
5. Paid $35,000 of salaries expense for the year.

6. Adjusted the accounts to reflect uncollectible accounts expense for the year. Juno estimates that 5 percent of the ending accounts receivable balance will be uncollectible.

Required

a. Record the 2016 events in general journal form and post them to T-accounts.
b. Prepare the income statement, statement of changes in stockholders' equity, balance sheet, and statement of cash flows for 2016.
c. What is the net realizable value of the accounts receivable at December 31, 2016?
d. Repeat Requirements *a*, *b*, and *c* for 2017.

LO 7-4

Exercise 7-9B *Accounting for uncollectible accounts: direct write-off method*

Applied Business Systems has a small number of sales on account but is mostly a cash business. Consequently, it uses the direct write-off method to account for uncollectible accounts. During 2016, Applied Business Systems earned $46,000 of cash revenue and $9,000 of revenue on account. Cash operating expenses were $32,100. After numerous attempts to collect a $325 account receivable from J.C. Mims, the account was determined to be uncollectible in 2017.

Required

a. Record the effects of (1) cash revenue, (2) revenue on account, (3) cash expenses, and (4) write-off of the uncollectible account on the financial statements using a horizontal statements model like the one shown here. In the Cash Flow column, indicate whether the item is an operating activity (OA), investing activity (IA), or financing activity (FA). Use NA to indicate that an element is not affected by the event.

Assets			=	Liab.	+	Equity	Rev.	−	Exp.	=	Net Inc.	Cash Flow
Cash	+	Accts. Rec.										

b. What amount of net income did Applied Business Systems report on the 2016 income statement?
c. Prepare the general journal entries for the four accounting events listed in Requirement *a*.

LO 7-1, 7-4

Exercise 7-10B *Accounting for uncollectible accounts: percent of revenue allowance versus direct write-off method*

Classic Auto Parts sells new and used auto parts. Although a majority of its sales are cash sales, it makes a significant amount of credit sales. During 2016, its first year of operations, Classic Auto Parts experienced the following:

Sales on account	$320,000
Cash sales	680,000
Collections of accounts receivable	295,000
Uncollectible accounts charged off during the year	1,400

Required

a. Assume that Classic Auto Parts uses the allowance method of accounting for uncollectible accounts and estimates that 1 percent of its sales on account will not be collected. Answer the following questions:
   (1) What is the Accounts Receivable balance at December 31, 2016?
   (2) What is the ending balance of the Allowance for Doubtful Accounts at December 31, 2016, after all entries and adjusting entries are posted?
   (3) What is the amount of uncollectible accounts expense for 2016?
   (4) What is the net realizable value of accounts receivable at December 31, 2016?

b. Assume that Classic Auto Parts uses the direct write-off method of accounting for uncollectible accounts. Answer the following questions:

(1) What is the Accounts Receivable balance at December 31, 2016?

(2) What is the amount of uncollectible accounts expense for 2016?

(3) What is the net realizable value of accounts receivable at December 31, 2016?

Exercise 7-11B *Accounting for notes receivable* — LO 7-5

Cachet Enterprises loaned $30,000 to Craft Co. on September 1, 2016, for one year at 6 percent interest.

Required

a. Record these general journal entries for Cachet Enterprises:

(1) The loan to Craft Co.

(2) The adjusting entry at December 31, 2016.

(3) The adjusting entry and collection of the note on September 1, 2017.

b. Show the effects of the three above transactions in a horizontal statements model like the one shown below.

	Assets					=	Liab.	+	Equity	Rev.	−	Exp.	=	Net Inc.	Cash Flows
Date	Cash	+	Notes Rec.	+	Int. Rec.	=			Ret. Earn.						

Exercise 7-12B *Notes receivable—accrued interest* — LO 7-5

On March 1, 2016, Taylor's Deli loaned $18,000 to Style Studio for one year at 5 percent interest.

Required

Answer the following questions:

a. What is Taylor's interest income for 2016?

b. What is Taylor's total amount of receivables at December 31, 2016?

c. How will the loan and interest be reported on Taylor's 2016 statement of cash flows?

d. What is Taylor's interest income for 2017?

e. What is the total amount of cash that Taylor's will collect in 2017 from Style Studio?

f. How will the loan and interest be reported on Taylor's 2017 statement of cash flows?

g. What is the total amount of interest Taylor's Deli earned from the loan to Style Studio?

Exercise 7-13B *Effect of credit card sales on financial statements* — LO 7-6

Advanced Carpet Cleaning provided $76,000 of services during 2016, its first year of operations. All customers paid for the services with major credit cards. Advanced Carpet submitted the credit card receipts to the credit card company immediately. The credit card company paid Advanced Carpet cash in the amount of face value less a 3 percent service charge.

Required

a. Record the credit card sales and the subsequent collection of accounts receivable in a horizontal statements model like the one shown here. In the Cash Flow column, indicate whether the item is an operating activity (OA), investing activity (IA), or financing activity (FA). Use NA to indicate that an element is not affected by the event.

Assets			=	Liab.	+	Equity	Rev.	−	Exp.	=	Net Inc.	Cash Flow
Cash	+	Accts. Rec.										

b. Answer the following questions:

(1) What is the amount of total assets at the end of the accounting period?

(2) What is the amount of revenue reported on the income statement?

(3) What is the amount of cash flow from operating activities reported on the statement of cash flows?

(4) Why would Advanced Carpet Cleaning accept credit cards instead of providing credit directly to its customers? In other words, why would Advanced Carpet be willing to pay 3 percent of sales to have the credit card company handle its sales on account?

LO 7-6

Exercise 7-14B *Recording credit card sales*

Jung Company accepted credit cards in payment for $8,650 of services performed during March 2016. The credit card company charged Jung a 4 percent service fee. The credit card company paid Jung as soon as it received the invoices.

Required

a. Prepare the general journal entry to record the service revenue.

b. Prepare the general journal entry for the collection of the receivable from the credit card company.

c. Based on this information alone, what is the amount of net income earned during the month of March?

LO 7-1, 7-5, 7-6

Exercise 7-15B *Comprehensive single-cycle problem*

The following post-closing trial balance was drawn from the accounts of Southern Timber Co. as of December 31, 2015:

	Debit	Credit
Cash	$16,000	
Accounts receivable	18,000	
Allowance for doubtful accounts		$ 2,000
Inventory	25,000	
Accounts payable		9,200
Common stock		30,000
Retained earnings		17,800
Totals	$59,000	$59,000

Transactions for 2016

1. Acquired an additional $20,000 cash from the issue of common stock.
2. Purchased $80,000 of inventory on account.
3. Sold inventory that cost $61,000 for $98,000. Sales were made on account.
4. Wrote off $1,500 of uncollectible accounts.
5. On September 1, Southern loaned $10,000 to Pine Co. The note had a 6 percent interest rate and a one-year term.
6. Paid $24,500 cash for salaries expense.
7. Collected $99,000 cash from accounts receivable.
8. Paid $78,000 cash on accounts payable.
9. Paid a $5,000 cash dividend to the stockholders.
10. Accepted credit cards for sales amounting to $5,000. The cost of goods sold was $3,500. The credit card company charges a 4% service charge. The cash has not been received.
11. Estimated uncollectible accounts expense to be 1 percent of sales on account.
12. Recorded the accrued interest at December 31, 2016.

Required

a. Record the above transactions in general journal form.

b. Open T-accounts and record the beginning balances and the 2016 transactions.

c. Prepare an income statement, statement of changes in stockholders' equity, balance sheet, and statement of cash flows for 2016.

Exercise 7-16B *Accounts receivable turnover and average days to collect accounts receivable*

LO 7-7

The following information is available for Bradford Inc. and Windsor Inc. at December 31, 2017:

Accounts	Bradford	Windsor
Accounts Receivable	$ 92,500	$ 220,200
Allowance for Doubtful Accounts	3,250	8,100
Sales Revenue	716,500	1,978,200

Required

a. What is the accounts receivable turnover for each of the companies for 2017?

b. What is the average days to collect the receivables for 2017?

c. Assuming both companies use the percent of receivables allowance method, what is the estimated percentage of uncollectible accounts for each company?

PROBLEMS—SERIES B

Problem 7-17B *Accounting for uncollectible accounts—two cycles using the percent of revenue allowance method*

LO 7-1

The following transactions apply to Sports Consulting for 2016, the first year of operation:

1. Issued $5,000 of common stock for cash.
2. Recognized $70,000 of service revenue earned on account.
3. Collected $62,000 from accounts receivable.
4. Adjusted accounts to recognize uncollectible accounts expense. Sports uses the allowance method of accounting for uncollectible accounts and estimates that uncollectible accounts expense will be 2 percent of sales on account.

The following transactions apply to Sports Consulting for 2017:

1. Recognized $84,000 of service revenue on account.
2. Collected $70,000 from accounts receivable.
3. Determined that $1,100 of the accounts receivable were uncollectible and wrote them off.
4. Collected $200 of an account that had been previously written off.
5. Paid $51,200 cash for operating expenses.
6. Adjusted accounts to recognize uncollectible accounts expense for 2017. Sports estimates that uncollectible accounts expense will be 1 percent of sales on account.

Required

Complete all the following requirements for 2016 and 2017. Complete all requirements for 2016 prior to beginning the requirements for 2017.

a. Identify the type of each transaction (asset source, asset use, asset exchange, or claims exchange).

b. Show the effect of each transaction on the elements of the financial statements, using a horizontal statements model like the one shown here. Use + for increase, − for decrease, and NA for not affected. Also, in the Cash Flow column, indicate whether the item is an operating activity (OA), investing activity (IA), or financing activity (FA). The first transaction is entered as an example. (*Hint:* Closing entries do not affect the statements model.)

Event No.	Assets	=	Liab.	+	Equity	Rev.	−	Exp.	=	Net Inc.	Cash Flow
1	+		NA		+	+		NA		+	NA

c. Record the transactions in general journal form and post them to T-accounts (begin 2017 with the ending T-account balances from 2016).

d. Prepare the income statement, statement of changes in stockholders' equity, balance sheet, and statement of cash flows.

e. Prepare closing entries and post these closing entries to the T-accounts. Prepare a post-closing trial balance.

LO 7-1

Problem 7-18B *Determining account balances and preparing journal entries: percent of revenue allowance method of accounting for uncollectible accounts*

The following information pertains to Kee Cabinet Company's sales on account and accounts receivable:

Accounts Receivable Balance, January 1, 2016	$ 96,200
Allowance for Doubtful Accounts, January 1, 2016	6,250
Sales on Account, 2016	726,000
Cost of Goods Sold, 2016	473,000
Collections of Accounts Receivable, 2016	715,000

After several collection attempts, Kee Cabinet Company wrote off $3,100 of accounts that could not be collected. Kee estimates that uncollectible accounts expense will be 0.5 percent of sales on account.

Required

a. Prepare the general journal entries to:

(1) Record sales on account for 2016.

(2) Record cash collections from accounts receivable for 2016.

(3) Write off the accounts that are not collectible.

(4) Record the estimated uncollectible accounts expense for 2016.

b. Compute the following amounts:

(1) Using the allowance method, the amount of uncollectible accounts expense for 2016.

(2) Net realizable value of receivables at the end of 2016.

c. Explain why the uncollectible accounts expense amount is different from the amount that was written off as uncollectible.

LO 7-2

Problem 7-19B *Determination of account balances and preparation of journal entries—percent of receivables allowance method of accounting for uncollectible accounts*

During the first year of operation, 2016, Home Renovation recognized $261,000 of service revenue on account. At the end of 2016, the accounts receivable balance was $46,300. Even though this is his first year in business, the owner believes he will collect all but about 4 percent of the ending balance.

Required

a. What amount of cash was collected by Home Renovation during 2016?

b. Assuming the use of an allowance system to account for uncollectible accounts, what amount should Home Renovation record as uncollectible accounts expense in 2016?

c. Prepare the journal entries to

(1) Record service revenue on account.

(2) Record collection of accounts receivable.

(3) Record the entry to recognize uncollectible accounts expense.

d. What is the net realizable value of receivables at the end of 2016?

e. Show the effect of the transactions listed in Requirement *c* on the financial statements by recording the appropriate amounts in a horizontal statements model like the one shown here. When you record amounts in the Cash Flow column, indicate whether the item is an operating activity (OA), investing activity (IA), or financing activity (FA). The letters NA indicate that an element is not affected by the event.

Assets			=	Liab.	+	Equity	Rev.	−	Exp.	=	Net Inc.	Cash Flow
Cash	+	Net Realizable Value of Receivables										

Problem 7-20B ***Accounting for uncollectible accounts: percent of receivables allowance method*** **LO 7-2, 7-3**

Thorne Inc. experienced the following transactions for 2016, its first year of operations:

1. Issued common stock for $60,000 cash.
2. Purchased $210,000 of merchandise on account.
3. Sold merchandise that cost $165,000 for $310,000 on account.
4. Collected $288,000 cash from accounts receivable.
5. Paid $190,000 on accounts payable.
6. Paid $46,000 of salaries expense for the year.
7. Paid other operating expenses of $62,000.
8. Thorne adjusted the accounts using the following information from an accounts receivable aging schedule.

Number of Days Past Due	Amount	Percent Likely to Be Uncollectible	Allowance Balance
Current	$15,700	.01	
0–30	8,500	.05	
31–60	4,000	.10	
61–90	2,600	.20	
Over 90 days	1,200	.50	

Required

a. Record the above transactions in general journal form and post them to T-accounts.
b. Prepare the income statement, statement of changes in stockholders' equity, balance sheet, and statement of cash flows for Thorne Inc. for 2016.
c. What is the net realizable value of the accounts receivable at December 31, 2016?

Problem 7-21B ***Accounting for credit card sales and uncollectible accounts: percent of receivables allowance method*** **LO 7-2, 7-6**

Diamond Supply Company had the following transactions in 2016:

1. Acquired $50,000 cash from the issue of common stock.
2. Purchased $120,000 of merchandise for cash in 2016.
3. Sold merchandise that cost $95,000 for $180,000 during the year under the following terms:

$ 50,000	Cash sales
115,000	Credit card sales (The credit card company charges a 3 percent service fee.)
15,000	Sales on account

4. Collected all the amount receivable from the credit card company.
5. Collected $11,300 of accounts receivable.
6. Paid selling and administrative expenses of $51,500.
7. Determined that 5 percent of the ending accounts receivable balance would be uncollectible.

Required

a. Show the effects of each of the transactions on the elements of the financial statements, using a horizontal statements model like the one shown here. Use + for increase, − for decrease, and NA for not affected. The first transaction is entered as an example. (*Hint:* Closing entries do not affect the statements model.)

Event No.	Assets	=	Liab.	+	Equity	Rev.	−	Exp.	=	Net Inc.	Cash Flow
1	+		NA		+	NA		NA		NA	+ FA

b. Prepare general journal entries for each of the transactions and post them to T-accounts.

c. Prepare an income statement, statement of changes in stockholders' equity, balance sheet, and statement of cash flows for 2016.

LO 7-4, 7-5

Problem 7-22B *Accounting for notes receivable and uncollectible accounts using the direct write-off method*

The following transactions apply to Cheng Co. for 2016, its first year of operations:

1. Issued $60,000 of common stock for cash.
2. Provided $94,000 of services on account.
3. Collected $84,500 cash from accounts receivable.
4. Loaned $10,000 to Swan Co. on October 1, 2016. The note had a one-year term to maturity and a 6 percent interest rate.
5. Paid $41,000 of salaries expense for the year.
6. Paid a $3,000 dividend to the stockholders.
7. Recorded the accrued interest on December 31, 2016 (see item 4).
8. Determined that $990 of accounts receivable were uncollectible. The company uses the direct write-off method.

Required

a. Record the above transactions in general journal form.

b. Post the entries to T-accounts.

c. Prepare the income statement, balance sheet, and statement of cash flows for 2016.

d. Show the effects of the above transactions in a horizontal statements model like the one shown below.

	Assets							= Liab. +	Equity			Rev. − Exp. = Net Inc.	Cash Flows
Event	Cash	+	Accts. Rec.	+	Notes Rec.	+	Int. Rec.	=	Com. Stk.	+	Ret. Earn.		

LO 7-4, 7-5, 7-6

Problem 7-23B *Effect of transactions on the elements of financial statements*

Required

Identify each of the following independent transactions as an asset source (AS), asset use (AU), asset exchange (AE), or claims exchange (CE). Also explain how each event affects assets, liabilities, stockholders' equity, net income, and cash flow by placing a + for increase, − for decrease, or NA for not affected under each of the categories. The first event is recorded as an example.

Event	Type of Event	Assets	Liabilities	Common Stock	Retained Earnings	Net Income	Cash Flow
a	AS/AU	+/−	NA	NA	+	+	NA

a. Sold merchandise at a price above cost. Accepted payment by credit card. The credit card company charges a service fee. The receipts have not yet been forwarded to the credit card company.
b. Sold land for cash at its cost.
c. Paid cash to satisfy salaries payable.
d. Submitted receipts to the credit card company (see *a* above) and collected cash.
e. Loaned Carl Maddox cash. The loan had a 5 percent interest rate and a one-year term to maturity.
f. Paid cash to creditors on accounts payable.
g. Accrued three months' interest on the note receivable (see *e* above).
h. Provided services for cash.
i. Paid cash for salaries expense.
j. Provided services on account.
k. Wrote off an uncollectible account (use direct write-off method).
l. Collected cash from customers paying their accounts.
m. Recovered an uncollectible account that was previously written off (assume direct write-off method was used).
n. Paid cash for land.
o. Paid cash for other operating expenses.

Problem 7-24B *Multistep income statement and balance sheet* LO 7-1, 7-5

Required

Use the following information to prepare a multistep income statement and a balance sheet for Trias Company for 2016. (*Hint:* Some of the items will *not* appear on either statement, and ending retained earnings must be calculated.)

Operating Expenses	$ 45,000	Allowance for Doubtful Accounts	$ 6,500
Accounts Payable	48,000	Sales Revenue	350,000
Land	45,000	Uncollectible Accounts Expense	9,600
Dividends	10,000	Accounts Receivable	92,000
Beginning Retained Earnings	120,100	Salaries Payable	10,500
Interest Revenue	12,000	Supplies	4,500
Inventory	105,000	Prepaid Rent	16,000
Notes Receivable (short term)	15,000	Common Stock	60,000
Cash	16,700	Cost of Goods Sold	225,000
Interest Receivable (short term)	2,100	Salaries Expense	61,200
Cash Flow from Investing Activities	(91,600)	Unearned Revenue	40,000

Problem 7-25B *Missing information* LO 7-1, 7-5

The following information comes from the accounts of Legoria Company:

Account Title	Beginning Balance	Ending Balance
Accounts Receivable	$36,000	$32,000
Allowance for Doubtful Accounts	2,000	2,200
Notes Receivable	50,000	50,000
Interest Receivable	2,000	5,000

Required

a. There were \$160,000 in sales on account during the accounting period. Write offs of uncollectible accounts were \$1,200. What was the amount of cash collected from accounts receivable? What amount of uncollectible accounts expense was reported on the income statement? What was the net realizable value of receivables at the end of the accounting period?

b. The note has a 6 percent interest rate and 24 months to maturity. What amount of interest revenue was recognized for the year? How much cash was collected for interest?

LO 7-1, 7-5, 7-6

Problem 7-26B ***Comprehensive accounting cycle problem (uses percent of revenue allowance method)***

The following trial balance was prepared for Village Cycle Sales and Service on December 31, 2016, after the closing entries were posted:

Account Title	Debit	Credit
Cash	\$ 46,200	
Accounts Receivable	21,300	
Allowance for Doubtful Accounts		\$ 1,350
Inventory	85,600	
Accounts Payable		28,000
Common Stock		80,000
Retained Earnings		43,750
Totals	\$153,100	\$153,100

Village Cycle had the following transactions in 2017:

1. Purchased merchandise on account for \$260,000.
2. Sold merchandise that cost \$243,000 on account for \$340,000.
3. Performed \$80,000 of services for cash.
4. Sold merchandise for \$60,000 to credit card customers. The merchandise cost \$41,250. The credit card company charges a 5 percent fee.
5. Collected \$348,000 cash from accounts receivable.
6. Paid \$265,000 cash on accounts payable.
7. Paid \$115,000 cash for selling and administrative expenses.
8. Collected cash for the full amount due from the credit card company (see item 4).
9. Loaned \$50,000 to Lee Supply. The note had a 9 percent interest rate and a one-year term to maturity.
10. Wrote off \$830 of accounts as uncollectible.
11. Made the following adjusting entries:
    (a) Recorded three months' interest on the note at December 31, 2017 (see item 9).
    (b) Estimated uncollectible accounts expense to be .5 percent of sales on account.

Required

Prepare general journal entries for these transactions; post the entries to T-accounts; and prepare an income statement, a statement of changes in stockholders' equity, a balance sheet, and a statement of cash flows for 2017.

ANALYZE, THINK, COMMUNICATE

ATC 7-1 **Business Applications Case** ***Understanding real-world annual reports***

Required

To answer this question, you will need to refer to Target Corporation's annual report in Appendix B.

Target did not report any accounts receivables or credit card receivables on its February 1, 2014 (2013), balance sheet. Explain why. You will need to read the MD&A to the financial statements.

ATC 7-2 Group Assignment *Missing information*

The following selected financial information is available for three companies:

	Expo	White	Zina
Total sales	$125,000	$210,000	?
Cash sales	?	26,000	$120,000
Sales on account	40,000	?	75,000
Accounts receivable, January 1, 2016	6,200	42,000	?
Accounts receivable, December 31, 2016	5,600	48,000	7,500
Allowance for doubtful accounts, January 1, 2016	?	?	405
Allowance for doubtful accounts, December 31, 2016	224	1,680	?
Uncollectible accounts expense, 2016	242	1,200	395
Uncollectible accounts written off	204	1,360	365
Collections of accounts receivable, 2016	?	?	75,235

Required

a. Divide the class into three sections and divide each section into groups of three to five students. Assign one of the companies to each of the sections.

Group Tasks

(1) Determine the missing amounts for your company.

(2) Determine the percentage of accounts receivable estimated to be uncollectible at the end of 2015 and 2016 for your company.

(3) Determine the percentage of total sales that are sales on account for your company.

(4) Determine the accounts receivable turnover for your company.

Class Discussion

b. Have a representative of each section put the missing information on the board and explain how it was determined.

c. Which company has the highest percentage of sales that are on account?

d. Which company is doing the best job of collecting its accounts receivable? What procedures and policies can a company use to better collect its accounts receivable?

ATC 7-3 Real-World Case *Time needed to collect accounts receivable*

Presented here are the average days to collect accounts receivable for four companies in different industries. The data are for 2013.

Company	Average Days to Collect Accounts Receivable
Boeing (aircraft manufacturer)	27
Colgate-Palmolive Company (consumer products manufacturer)	34
Ethan Allen (furniture retailer)	6
General Motors (auto sales only)	22

Required

Write a brief memorandum that provides possible answers to each of the following questions:

a. Why would a company that manufactures and sells airplanes (Boeing) and a company that manufacturers and sells automobiles (General Motors) collect their accounts receivables in such relatively short times?

b. Why would a company that sells furniture (Ethan Allen) collect its receivables so much quicker than a company that sells toothpaste and soap (Colgate-Palmolive)?

ATC 7-4 Business Applications Case *Performing ratio analysis using real-world data*

The following data were taken from Hershey Foods Corporation's 2013 annual report. All dollar amounts are in thousands.

	Fiscal Years Ending	
	December 31, 2013	December 31, 2012
Sales	$7,146,079	$6,644,252
Accounts receivable	444,912	461,383

Required

a. Compute Hershey's accounts receivable turnover ratios for 2013 and 2012.

b. Compute Hershey's average days to collect accounts receivables for 2013 and 2012.

c. Based on the ratios computed in Requirements *a* and *b*, did Hershey's performance get better or worse from 2012 to 2013?

d. In 2013 Hershey issued long-term notes payable with an interest rate of 4.2 percent. Assume it took Hershey 30 days to collect its receivables. Using an interest rate of 4.2 percent, calculate how much it cost Hershey's to finance its receivables for 30 days in 2013.

ATC 7-5 Business Applications Case *Performing ratio analysis using real-world data*

AutoZone, Inc., claims to be "the nation's leading auto parts retailer." It sells replacement auto parts directly to the consumer. BorgWarner, Inc., has over 17,000 employees and produces automobile parts, such as transmissions and cooling systems, for the world's vehicle manufacturers. The following data were taken from these companies' 2013 annual reports. All dollar amounts are in thousands.

	Fiscal Years Ending	
	AutoZone August 31, 2013	BorgWarner December 31, 2013
Sales	$9,147,530	$7,436,600
Accounts receivable	171,638	1,248,500

Required

a. Before performing any calculations, speculate as to which company will take the longest to collect its accounts receivable. Explain the rationale for your decision.

b. Calculate the accounts receivable turnover ratios for AutoZone and BorgWarner.

c. Calculate the average days to collect accounts receivable for AutoZone and BorgWarner.

d. Do the calculations from Requirements *b* and *c* confirm your speculations in Requirement *a*?

ATC 7-6 Writing Assignment *Cost of charge sales*

Paul Smith is opening a plumbing supply store in University City. He plans to sell plumbing parts and materials to both wholesale and retail customers. Since contractors (wholesale customers) prefer to charge parts and materials and pay at the end of the month, Paul expects he will have to offer charge accounts. He plans to offer charge sales to the wholesale customers only and to require retail customers to pay with either cash or credit cards. Paul wondered what expenses his business would incur relative to the charge sales and the credit cards.

Required

a. What issues will Paul need to consider if he allows wholesale customers to buy plumbing supplies on account?

b. Write a memo to Paul Smith outlining the potential cost of accepting charge customers. Discuss the difference between the allowance method for uncollectible accounts and the direct write-off method. Also discuss the cost of accepting credit cards.

ATC 7-7 Ethical Dilemma *How bad can it be?*

Alonzo Saunders owns a small training services company that is experiencing growing pains. The company has grown rapidly by offering liberal credit terms to its customers. Although his competitors require payment for services within 30 days, Saunders permits his customers to delay payment for up to 90 days. Saunders's customers thereby have time to fully evaluate the training that employees receive before they must pay for that training. Saunders guarantees satisfaction. If a customer is unhappy, the customer does not have to pay. Saunders works with reputable companies, provides top-quality training, and rarely encounters dissatisfied customers.

The long collection period, however, has created a cash flow problem. Saunders has a \$100,000 accounts receivable balance but needs cash to pay current bills. He has recently negotiated a loan agreement with National Bank of Brighton County that should solve his cash flow problems. The loan agreement requires that Saunders pledge the accounts receivable as collateral for the loan. The bank agreed to loan Saunders 70 percent of the receivables balance, thereby giving him access to \$70,000 cash. Saunders is satisfied with this arrangement because he estimates he needs approximately \$60,000.

On the day Saunders was to execute the loan agreement, he heard a rumor that his biggest customer was experiencing financial problems and might declare bankruptcy. The customer owed Saunders \$45,000. Saunders promptly called the customer's chief accountant and learned "off the record" that the rumor was true. The accountant told Saunders that the company's net worth was negative and most of its assets were pledged as collateral for bank loans. In his opinion, Saunders was unlikely to collect the balance due. Saunders's immediate concern was the impact the circumstances would have on his loan agreement with the bank.

Saunders uses the direct write-off method to recognize uncollectible accounts expense. Removing the \$45,000 receivable from the collateral pool would leave only \$55,000 of receivables, reducing the available credit to \$38,500 (\$55,000 × 0.70). Even worse, recognizing the uncollectible accounts expense would so adversely affect his income statement that the bank might further reduce the available credit by reducing the percentage of receivables allowed under the loan agreement. Saunders will have to attest to the quality of the receivables at the date of the loan but reasons that since the information he obtained about the possible bankruptcy was "off the record" he is under no obligation to recognize the uncollectible accounts expense until the receivable is officially uncollectible.

Required

a. How are income and assets affected by the decision not to act on the bankruptcy information?

b. Review the AICPA's Articles of Professional Conduct (see Chapter 2) and comment on any of the standards that would be violated by the actions Saunders is contemplating.

c. Identify the elements of unethical and criminal conduct recognized in the fraud triangle (see Chapter 2), and explain how they apply to this case.

ATC 7-8 Research Assignment *Comparing Whirlpool Corporation's and Papa John's time to collect accounts receivable*

Using the most current annual reports or Forms 10-K for **Whirlpool Corporation** and **Papa John's International, Inc.**, complete the requirements below. To obtain the Forms 10-K, use either the EDGAR system, following the instructions in Appendix A, or the companies' websites. The annual reports can be found on the companies' websites.

Required

a. What was Whirlpool's average days to collect accounts receivable? Show your computations.

b. What percentage of accounts receivable did Whirlpool estimate would not be collected?

c. What was Papa John's average days to collect accounts receivable? Show your computations.

d. What percentage of accounts receivable did Papa John's estimate would not be collected?

e. Briefly explain why Whirlpool would take longer than Papa John's to collect its accounts receivable.

ATC 7-9 Spreadsheet Analysis *Using Excel*

Set up the following spreadsheet comparing Vong and Crist Companies:

Microsoft Excel - ch7-9.xls

	A	B	C	D	E	F
1						
2		**Vong**		**Crist**		
3	Sales	$800,000		$1,100,000		
4	Cost of Goods Sold	600,000		660,000		
5	Gross Profit					
6						
7	Gross Profit Percentage					
8						
9	Accounts Receivable	130,000		270,000		
10	Allowance for Doubtful Accounts	10,000		27,000		
11	Net Realizable Value					
12						
13	Accounts Receivable Turnover					
14						
15	Average Days to Collect					

Required

a. For each company, compute gross profit, gross profit percentage, net realizable value, accounts receivable turnover, and average days to collect.

b. In relation to cost, which company is charging more for its merchandise?

c. Which company is likely to incur higher financial costs associated with granting credit to customers? Explain the reasons for your answer.

d. Which company appears to have more restrictive credit standards when authorizing credit to customers? How do you know?

COMPREHENSIVE PROBLEM

The trial balance of Pacilio Security Services Inc. as of January 1, 2017, had the following normal balances:

Cash	$78,972
Petty Cash	100
Accounts Receivable	33,440
Supplies	160
Prepaid Rent	3,200
Merchandise Inventory (23 @ $280)	6,440
Land	4,000
Accounts Payable	250
Salaries Payable	1,400
Common Stock	50,000
Retained Earnings	74,662

During 2017 Pacilio Security Services experienced the following transactions:

1. Paid the salaries payable from 2016.
2. Paid $4,800 on March 1, 2017, for one year's lease in advance on the company van.

3. Paid $8,400 on May 2, 2017, for one year's office rent in advance.
4. Purchased $550 of supplies on account.
5. Paid cash to purchase 105 alarm systems at a cost of $285 each.
6. Pacilio has noticed its accounts receivable balance is growing more than desired and some collection problems exist. It appears that uncollectible accounts expense is approximately 3 percent of total credit sales. Pacilio has decided it will, starting this year, adopt the allowance method of accounting for uncollectible accounts. It will record an adjusting entry to recognize the estimate at the end of the year.
7. In trying to collect several of its delinquent accounts, Pacilio has learned that these customers have either declared bankruptcy or moved and left no forwarding address. These uncollectible accounts amount to $1,900.
8. Sold 110 alarm systems for $63,800. All sales were on account. (Compute cost of goods sold using the FIFO cost flow method.)
9. Paid the balance of the accounts payable.
10. Pacilio began accepting credit cards for some of its monitoring service sales. The credit card company charges a fee of 4 percent. Total monitoring services for the year were $68,000. Pacilio accepted credit cards for $24,000 of this amount. The other $44,000 was sales on account.
11. On July 1, 2017, Pacilio replenished the petty cash fund. The fund contained $21 of currency and receipts of $50 for yard mowing, $22 for office supplies expense, and $9 for miscellaneous expenses.
12. Collected the amount due from the credit card company.
13. Paid installers and other employees a total of $45,000 cash for salaries.
14. Collected $116,800 of accounts receivable during the year.
15. Paid $9,500 of advertising expense during the year.
16. Paid $5,200 of utilities expense for the year.
17. Paid a dividend of $20,000 to the shareholders.

Adjustments

18. There was $250 of supplies on hand at the end of the year.
19. Recognized the expired rent for both the van and the office for the year.
20. Recognized the uncollectible accounts expense for the year using the allowance method.
21. Accrued salaries at December 31, 2017, were $2,100.

Required

a. Record the above transactions in general journal form.
b. Post the transactions to the T-accounts.
c. Prepare a trial balance.
d. Prepare an income statement, statement of changes in stockholders' equity, balance sheet, and statement of cash flows.
e. Close the temporary accounts to retained earnings.
f. Post the closing entries to the T-accounts and prepare a post-closing trial balance.

CHAPTER 8

Accounting for Long-Term Operational Assets

LEARNING OBJECTIVES

After you have mastered the material in this chapter, you will be able to:

LO 8-1 Identify and determine the cost of long-term operational assets.

LO 8-2 Explain how straight-line depreciation affects financial statements.

LO 8-3 Explain how double-declining-balance depreciation affects financial statements.

LO 8-4 Explain how units-of-production depreciation affects financial statements.

LO 8-5 Show how asset disposals affect financial statements.

LO 8-6 Identify some of the tax issues that affect long-term operational assets.

LO 8-7 Show how revising estimates affects financial statements.

LO 8-8 Explain how continuing expenditures for operational assets affect financial statements.

LO 8-9 Explain how the depletion of natural resources affects financial statements.

LO 8-10 Identify and determine the cost of intangible assets.

LO 8-11 Explain how the amortization of intangible assets affects financial statements.

LO 8-12 Show how expense recognition choices and industry characteristics affect financial performance measures.

Video lectures and accompanying self-assessment quizzes are available for all learning objectives through McGraw-Hill Connect® Plus Accounting.

CHAPTER OPENING

Companies use assets to produce revenue. Some assets, like inventory or office supplies, are called **current assets** because they are used relatively quickly (within a single accounting period). Other assets, like equipment or buildings, are used for extended periods of time (two or more accounting periods). These assets are called **long-term operational assets.**[1] Accounting

[1]Classifying assets as current versus long term is explained in more detail in Chapter 9.

for long-term assets raises several questions. For example, what is the cost of the asset? Is it the list price only or should the cost of transportation, transit insurance, setup, and so on be added to the list price? Should the cost of a long-term asset be recognized as expense in the period the asset is purchased or should the cost be expensed over the useful life of the asset? What happens in the accounting records when a long-term asset is retired from use? This chapter answers these questions. It explains accounting for long-term operational assets from the date of purchase through the date of disposal.

The Curious Accountant

Most companies have various types of long-term assets that they use to operate their business. Common types of long-term assets include buildings, machinery, and equipment. But there are other types as well. A major category of long-term assets for a mining company is the mineral reserves from which they extract ore.

Freeport-McMoRan Copper & Gold, Inc. (referred to as FCX) is one of the largest mining operations in the world. It produces copper, gold, and molybdenum from 12 major mines located on four continents. As of December 31, 2013, it owned proven mineral reserves that cost \$4.7 billion and buildings, machinery, and equipment that cost \$18.6 billion.

As you learned in Chapters 2 and 4, except for land, over time most assets are consumed in a company's efforts to produce revenues, and as they are consumed, the asset account is decreased and an expense account is increased. How do you think the way a mining company uses its buildings and equipment differs from the way it uses its mineral reserves, and how do you think these differences affect the way these assets are accounted for? (Answers on page 439.)

TANGIBLE VERSUS INTANGIBLE ASSETS

LO 8-1

Identify and determine the cost of long-term operational assets.

Long-term assets may be tangible or intangible. **Tangible assets** have a physical presence; they can be seen and touched. Tangible assets include equipment, machinery, natural resources, and land. In contrast, intangible assets have no physical form. Although they may be represented by physical documents, **intangible assets** are, in fact, rights or privileges. They cannot be seen or touched. For example, a patent represents an exclusive legal *privilege* to produce and sell a particular product. It protects inventors by making it illegal for others to profit by copying their inventions. Although a patent may be represented by legal documents, the privilege is the actual asset. Since the privilege cannot be seen or touched, the patent is an intangible asset.

Tangible Long-Term Assets

Tangible long-term assets are classified as (1) property, plant, and equipment; (2) natural resources; or (3) land.

Property, Plant, and Equipment

Property, plant, and equipment is sometimes called *plant assets* or *fixed assets.* Examples of property, plant, and equipment include furniture, cash registers, machinery, delivery trucks, computers, mechanical robots, and buildings. The level of detail used to account for these assets varies. One company may include all office equipment in one account, whereas another company might divide office equipment into computers, desks, chairs, and so on. The term used to recognize expense for property, plant, and equipment is **depreciation.**

Natural Resources

Mineral deposits, oil and gas reserves, timber stands, coal mines, and stone quarries are examples of **natural resources.** Conceptually, natural resources are inventories. When sold, the cost of these assets is frequently expensed as *cost of goods sold.* Although inventories are usually classified as short-term assets, natural resources are normally classified as long term because the resource deposits generally have long lives. For example, it may take decades to extract all of the diamonds from a diamond mine. The term used to recognize expense for natural resources is **depletion.**

Land

Land is classified separately from other property because land is not subject to depreciation or depletion. Land has an infinite life. It is not worn out or consumed as it is used. When buildings or natural resources are purchased simultaneously with land, the amount paid must be divided between the land and the other assets because of the nondepreciable nature of the land.

Intangible Assets

Intangible assets fall into two categories, those with *identifiable useful lives* and those with *indefinite useful lives.*

Intangible Assets with Identifiable Useful Lives

Intangible assets with identifiable useful lives include patents and copyrights. These assets may become obsolete (a patent may become worthless if new technology provides a superior product) or may reach the end of their legal lives. The term used when recognizing expense for intangible assets with identifiable useful lives is called **amortization.**

Intangible Assets with Indefinite Useful Lives

The benefits of some intangible assets may extend so far into the future that their useful lives cannot be estimated. For how many years will the Coca-Cola trademark attract customers? When will the value of a McDonald's franchise end? There are no answers to these questions. Intangible assets such as renewable franchises, trademarks, and goodwill have indefinite useful lives. The costs of such assets are not expensed unless the value of the assets becomes impaired.

DETERMINING THE COST OF LONG-TERM ASSETS

The **historical cost concept** requires that an asset be recorded at the amount paid for it. This amount includes the purchase price plus any costs necessary to get the asset in the location and condition for its intended use. Common cost components are:

- ***Buildings:*** (1) purchase price, (2) sales taxes, (3) title search and transfer document costs, (4) realtor's and attorney's fees, and (5) remodeling costs.
- ***Land:*** (1) purchase price, (2) sales taxes, (3) title search and transfer document costs, (4) realtor's and attorney's fees, (5) costs for removal of old buildings, and (6) grading costs.
- ***Equipment:*** (1) purchase price (less discounts), (2) sales taxes, (3) delivery costs, (4) installation costs, and (5) costs to adapt for intended use.

The cost of an asset does not include payments for fines, damages, and so on that could have been avoided.

CHECK YOURSELF 8.1

Sheridan Construction Company purchased a new bulldozer that had a $260,000 list price. The seller agreed to allow a 4 percent cash discount in exchange for immediate payment. The bulldozer was delivered FOB shipping point at a cost of $1,200. Sheridan hired a new employee to operate the dozer for an annual salary of $36,000. The employee was trained to operate the dozer for a one-time training fee of $800. The cost of the company's theft insurance policy increased by $300 per year as a result of adding the dozer to the policy. The dozer had a five-year useful life and an expected salvage value of $26,000. Determine the asset's cost.

Answer

List price	$260,000
Less: Cash discount ($260,000 × 0.04)	(10,400)
Shipping cost	1,200
Training cost	800
Total asset cost (amount capitalized)	$251,600

Basket Purchase Allocation

Acquiring a group of assets in a single transaction is known as a **basket purchase.** The total price of a basket purchase must be allocated among the assets acquired. Accountants commonly allocate the purchase price using the **relative market value method.** To illustrate, assume that Beatty Company purchased land and a building for $240,000 cash. A real estate appraiser determined the market value of each asset to be

Building	$270,000
Land	90,000
Total	$360,000

The appraisal indicates that the land is worth 25 percent ($90,000 ÷ $360,000) of the total value and the building is worth 75 percent ($270,000 ÷ $360,000). Using these percentages, the actual purchase price is allocated as follows:

Building	0.75 × $240,000 =	$180,000
Land	0.25 × $240,000 =	60,000
Total		$240,000

METHODS OF RECOGNIZING DEPRECIATION EXPENSE

The life cycle of an operational asset involves (1) acquiring the funds to buy the asset, (2) purchasing the asset, (3) using the asset, and (4) retiring (disposing of) the asset. These stages are illustrated in Exhibit 8.1. The stages involving (1) acquiring funds and (2) purchasing assets have been discussed previously. This section of the chapter describes how accountants recognize the *use* of assets (Stage 3). As they are used, assets suffer from wear and tear called *depreciation*. Ultimately, assets depreciate to the point that they are no longer useful in the process of earning revenue. This process usually takes several years. The amount of an asset's cost that is allocated to expense during an accounting period is called **depreciation expense.**

EXHIBIT 8.1

Life Cycle of an Operational Asset

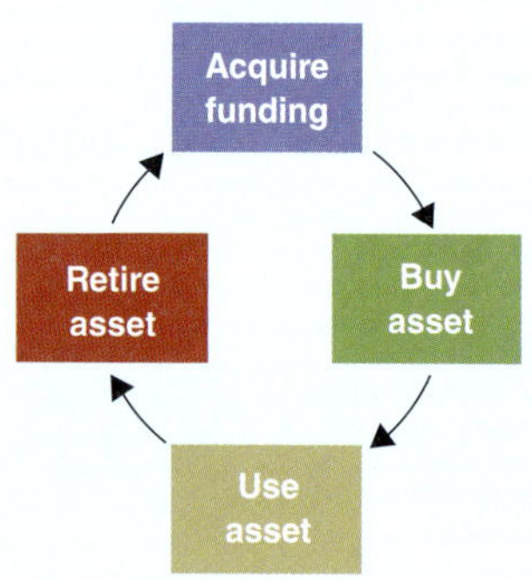

An asset that is fully depreciated by one company may still be useful to another company. For example, a rental car that is no longer useful to Hertz may still be useful to a local delivery company. As a result, companies are frequently able to sell their fully depreciated assets to other companies or individuals. The expected market value of a fully depreciated asset is called its **salvage value.** The total amount of depreciation a company recognizes for an asset, its **depreciable cost,** is the difference between its original cost and its salvage value.

For example, assume a company purchases an asset for $5,000. The company expects to use the asset for 5 years (the **estimated useful life**) and then to sell it for $1,000 (salvage value). The depreciable cost of the asset is $4,000 ($5,000 − $1,000). The portion of the depreciable cost ($4,000) that represents its annual usage is recognized as depreciation expense.

Accountants must exercise judgment to estimate the amount of depreciation expense to recognize each period. For example, suppose you own a personal computer. You know how much the computer cost, and you know you will eventually need to replace it. How would you determine the amount the computer depreciates each year you use it? Businesses may use any of several acceptable methods to estimate the amount of depreciation expense to recognize each year.

EXHIBIT 8.2

Depreciation Methods Used by U.S. Companies

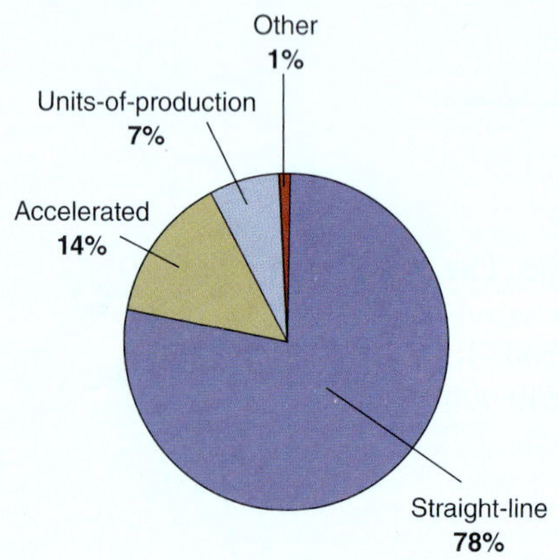

Data Source: AICPA Accounting Trends and Techniques.

The method used to recognize depreciation expense should match the asset's usage pattern. More expense should be recognized in periods when the asset is used more and less in periods when the asset is used less. Since assets are used to produce revenue, matching expense recognition with asset usage also matches expense recognition with revenue recognition. Three alternative methods for recognizing depreciation expense are (1) straight-line, (2) double-declining-balance, and (3) units-of-production.

The *straight-line* method produces the same amount of depreciation expense each accounting period. *Double-declining-balance,* an accelerated method, produces more depreciation expense in the early years of an asset's life, with a declining amount of expense in later years. *Units-of-production* produces varying amounts of depreciation expense in different accounting periods (more in some accounting periods and less in others). Exhibit 8.2 contrasts the different depreciation methods that U.S. companies use.

Dryden Enterprises Illustration

To illustrate the different depreciation methods, consider a van purchased by Dryden Enterprises. Dryden plans to use the van as rental property. The van had a list price of \$23,500. Dryden obtained a 10 percent cash discount from the dealer. The van was delivered FOB shipping point, and Dryden paid an additional \$250 for transportation costs. Dryden also paid \$2,600 for a custom accessory package to increase the van's appeal as a rental vehicle. The cost of the van is computed as follows:

List price	\$23,500	
Less: Cash discount	(2,350)	\$23,500 × 0.10
Plus: Transportation costs	250	
Plus: Cost of customization	2,600	
Total	\$24,000	

The van has an estimated *salvage value* of \$4,000 and an *estimated useful life* of four years. The following section examines three different patterns of expense recognition for this van.

Straight-Line Depreciation

LO 8-2

Explain how straight-line depreciation affects financial statements.

The first scenario assumes the van is used evenly over its four-year life. The revenue from renting the van is assumed to be \$8,000 per year. The matching concept calls for the expense recognition pattern to match the revenue stream. Since the same amount of revenue is recognized in each accounting period, Dryden should use **straight-line depreciation** because it produces equal amounts of depreciation expense each year.

The first phase of the asset life cycle is to acquire funds to purchase the asset. Assume Dryden acquired \$25,000 cash on January 1, 2016, by issuing common stock. The journal entry and its effects on the financial statements are shown here:

Account Title	Debit	Credit
Cash	25,000	
Common Stock		25,000

Assets			=	Equity			Rev.	−	Exp.	=	Net Inc.	Cash Flow
Cash	+	Book Value of Van	=	Com. Stk.	+	Ret. Earn.						
25,000	+	NA	=	25,000	+	NA	NA	−	NA	=	NA	25,000 FA

The second phase of the life cycle is to purchase the van. Assume Dryden bought the van on January 1, 2016, using funds from the stock issue. The cost of the van, previously computed, was \$24,000 cash. The journal entry and its effects on the financial statements are shown here:

Account Title	Debit	Credit
Van	24,000	
Cash		24,000

Assets			=	Equity			Rev.	−	Exp.	=	Net Inc.	Cash Flow
Cash	+	Book Value of Van	=	Com. Stk.	+	Ret. Earn.						
(24,000)	+	24,000	=	NA	+	NA	NA	−	NA	=	NA	(24,000) IA

Dryden used the van by renting it to customers. The rent revenue each year is $8,000 cash. The annual journal entry and its effects on the financial statements are shown here:

Account Title	Debit	Credit
Cash	8,000	
Rent Revenue		8,000

Assets			=	Equity			Rev.	−	Exp.	=	Net Inc.	Cash Flow
Cash	+	Book Value of Van	=	Com. Stk.	+	Ret. Earn.						
8,000	+	NA	=	NA	+	8,000	8,000	−	NA	=	8,000	8,000 OA

Although illustrated only once, these effects occur four times—once for each year Dryden earns revenue by renting the van.

At the end of each year, Dryden adjusts its accounts to recognize depreciation expense. The amount of depreciation recognized using the straight-line method is calculated as follows:

$$(\text{Asset cost} - \text{Salvage value}) \div \text{Useful life} = \text{Depreciation expense}$$
$$(\$24{,}000 - \$4{,}000) \div 4 \text{ years} = \$5{,}000 \text{ per year}$$

Recognizing depreciation expense is an asset use transaction that reduces assets and equity. The asset reduction is reported using a **contra asset account** called **Accumulated Depreciation.** Like other contra asset accounts, the Accumulated Depreciation account has a credit balance. The **book value** of a long-term tangible asset is determined by subtracting the credit balance in the Accumulated Depreciation account from the debit balance in the associated asset account. The book value may also be called the **carrying value.**

While recognizing depreciation expense decreases net income, it *does not affect cash flow.* The $24,000 cash outflow occurred in January 2016 when Dryden purchased the van. In contrast, the $5,000 depreciation expense is recognized each year as the van is used. The December 31, 2016, journal entry recognizing depreciation expense and its effects on the financial statements are shown here:

Account Title	Debit	Credit
Depreciation Expense	5,000	
Accumulated Depreciation		5,000

Assets			=	Equity			Rev.	−	Exp.	=	Net Inc.	Cash Flow
Cash	+	Book Value of Van	=	Com. Stk.	+	Ret. Earn.						
NA	+	(5,000)	=	NA	+	(5,000)	NA	−	5,000	=	(5,000)	NA

The book value of the van as of December 31, 2016, is $19,000, computed as shown here:

Van	$24,000
Accumulated depreciation	(5,000)
Book value	$19,000

Depreciation expense is recognized each year the van is used. Like other expense accounts, the Depreciation Expense account is a temporary account that is closed to retained earnings at the end of each accounting cycle. In other words, each year $5,000 is recognized in the Depreciation Expense account and then closed to the Retained Earnings account. As a result, the Depreciation Expense account will never have a balance that is larger than $5,000.

In contrast, the Accumulated Depreciation account is a permanent account. As its name implies, the total amount in the Accumulated Depreciation account increases (accumulates) each time depreciation expense is recognized. For example, at the end of 2017 Dryden will recognize $5,000 of depreciation expense and the balance in the Accumulated Depreciation account will increase to $10,000. At the end of 2018 Dryden will recognize $5,000 of depreciation expense and increase the balance in the Accumulated Depreciation account to $15,000, and so on.

Financial Statements

Exhibit 8.3 displays a vertical statements model that shows the financial results for the Dryden illustration from 2016 through 2019. Study the exhibit until you understand how all the figures were derived. The amount of depreciation expense ($5,000) reported on the income statement is constant each year from 2016 through 2019. The amount of accumulated depreciation reported on the balance sheet grows from $5,000 to $10,000, to $15,000, and finally to $20,000. The Accumulated Depreciation account is a *contra asset account* that is subtracted from the Van account in determining total assets.

EXHIBIT 8.3 Financial Statements under Straight-Line Depreciation

DRYDEN ENTERPRISES
Financial Statements

	2016	2017	2018	2019
Income Statements				
Rent revenue	$ 8,000	$ 8,000	$ 8,000	$ 8,000
Depreciation expense	(5,000)	(5,000)	(5,000)	(5,000)
Net income	$ 3,000	$ 3,000	$ 3,000	$ 3,000
Balance Sheets				
Assets				
Cash	$ 9,000	$17,000	$25,000	$33,000
Van	24,000	24,000	24,000	24,000
Accumulated depreciation	(5,000)	(10,000)	(15,000)	(20,000)
Total assets	$28,000	$31,000	$34,000	$37,000
Stockholders' equity				
Common stock	$25,000	$25,000	$25,000	$25,000
Retained earnings	3,000	6,000	9,000	12,000
Total stockholders' equity	$28,000	$31,000	$34,000	$37,000
Statements of Cash Flows				
Operating Activities				
Inflow from customers	$ 8,000	$ 8,000	$ 8,000	$ 8,000
Investing Activities				
Outflow to purchase van	(24,000)			
Financing Activities				
Inflow from stock issue	25,000			
Net Change in Cash	9,000	8,000	8,000	8,000
Beginning cash balance	0	9,000	17,000	25,000
Ending cash balance	$ 9,000	$17,000	$25,000	$33,000

Notice the differences between cash flow from operating activities and the income statement. For example, in 2016 Dryden paid \$24,000 cash to purchase the van. However, only \$5,000 of this cost is shown as an operating expense on the income statement. Further, there is no effect on cash flow from operating activities. Instead the entire \$24,000 cash outflow is shown as an investing activity. These differences highlight the fact that cash flow from operating activities and the income statement are purposefully designed to inform users about different aspects of the business' operations.

Double-Declining-Balance Depreciation

LO 8-3

Explain how double-declining-balance depreciation affects financial statements.

For the second scenario, assume demand for the van is strong when it is new, but fewer people rent the van as it ages. As a result, the van produces smaller amounts of revenue as time goes by. To match expenses with revenues, it is reasonable to recognize more depreciation expense in the van's early years and less as it ages.

Double-declining-balance depreciation produces a large amount of depreciation in the first year of an asset's life and progressively smaller levels of expense in each succeeding year. Since the double-declining-balance method recognizes depreciation expense more rapidly than the straight-line method does, it is called an **accelerated depreciation method.** Depreciation expense recognized using double-declining-balance is computed in three steps.

1. *Determine the straight-line rate.* Divide one by the asset's useful life. Since the estimated useful life of Dryden's van is four years, the straight-line rate is 25 percent (1 ÷ 4) per year.
2. *Determine the double-declining-balance rate.* Multiply the straight-line rate by 2 (*double* the rate). The double-declining-balance rate for the van is 50 percent (25 percent × 2).
3. *Determine the depreciation expense.* Multiply the double-declining-balance rate by the book value of the asset *at the beginning of the period* (recall that book value is historical cost minus *accumulated depreciation*). The following table shows the amount of depreciation expense Dryden will recognize over the van's useful life (2016–2019).

Year	Book Value at Beginning of Period	×	Double the Straight-Line Rate	=	Annual Depreciation Expense	
2016	(\$24,000 − \$ 0)	×	0.50	=	\$12,000	
2017	(24,000 − 12,000)	×	0.50	=	6,000	
2018	(24,000 − 18,000)	×	0.50	=	~~3,000~~	2,000
2019	(24,000 − 20,000)	×	0.50	=	~~2,000~~	0

Regardless of the depreciation method used, *an asset cannot be depreciated below its salvage value.* This restriction affects depreciation computations for the third and fourth years. Because the van had a cost of \$24,000 and a salvage value of \$4,000, the total amount of depreciable cost (historical cost − salvage value) is \$20,000 (\$24,000 − \$4,000). Since \$18,000 (\$12,000 + \$6,000) of the depreciable cost is recognized in the first two years, only \$2,000 (\$20,000 − \$18,000) remains to be recognized after the second year. Depreciation expense recognized in the third year is therefore \$2,000 even though double-declining-balance computations suggest that \$3,000 should be recognized. Similarly, zero depreciation expense is recognized in the fourth year even though the computations indicate a \$2,000 charge.

Effects on the Financial Statements

Exhibit 8.4 displays financial statements for the life of the asset assuming Dryden uses double-declining-balance depreciation. The illustration assumes a cash revenue stream of $15,000, $9,000, $5,000, and $3,000 for the years 2016, 2017, 2018, and 2019, respectively. Trace the depreciation expense from the table above to the income statements. Reported depreciation expense is greater in the earlier years and smaller in the later years of the asset's life.

The double-declining-balance method smoothes the amount of net income reported over the asset's useful life. In the early years, when heavy asset use produces higher revenue, depreciation expense is also higher. Similarly, in the later years, lower levels of revenue are matched with lower levels of depreciation expense. Net income is constant at $3,000 per year.

The depreciation method a company uses *does not* affect how it acquires the financing, invests the funds, and retires the asset. For Dryden's van, the accounting effects of these life cycle phases are the same as under the straight-line approach. Similarly, the *recording procedures* are not affected by the depreciation method. Different depreciation methods affect only the amounts of depreciation expense recorded each year, not which accounts are used. The general journal entries are therefore not illustrated for the double-declining-balance or the units-of-production depreciation methods.

EXHIBIT 8.4 Financial Statements under Double-Declining-Balance Depreciation

DRYDEN ENTERPRISES Financial Statements				
	2016	**2017**	**2018**	**2019**
Income Statements				
Rent revenue	$15,000	$ 9,000	$ 5,000	$ 3,000
Depreciation expense	(12,000)	(6,000)	(2,000)	0
Net income	$ 3,000	$ 3,000	$ 3,000	$ 3,000
Balance Sheets				
Assets				
Cash	$16,000	$25,000	$30,000	$33,000
Van	24,000	24,000	24,000	24,000
Accumulated depreciation	(12,000)	(18,000)	(20,000)	(20,000)
Total assets	$28,000	$31,000	$34,000	$37,000
Stockholders' equity				
Common stock	$25,000	$25,000	$25,000	$25,000
Retained earnings	3,000	6,000	9,000	12,000
Total stockholders' equity	$28,000	$31,000	$34,000	$37,000
Statements of Cash Flows				
Operating Activities				
Inflow from customers	$15,000	$ 9,000	$ 5,000	$ 3,000
Investing Activities				
Outflow to purchase van	(24,000)			
Financing Activities				
Inflow from stock issue	25,000			
Net Change in Cash	16,000	9,000	5,000	3,000
Beginning cash balance	0	16,000	25,000	30,000
Ending cash balance	$16,000	$25,000	$30,000	$33,000

CHECK YOURSELF 8.2

Olds Company purchased an asset that cost $36,000 on January 1, 2016. The asset had an expected useful life of five years and an estimated salvage value of $5,000. Assuming Olds uses the double-declining-balance method, determine the amount of depreciation expense and the amount of accumulated depreciation Olds would report on the 2018 financial statements.

Answer

Year	Book Value at Beginning of Period	×	Double the Straight-Line Rate*	=	Annual Depreciation Expense
2016	($36,000 − $ 0)	×	0.40	=	$14,400
2017	(36,000 − 14,400)	×	0.40	=	8,640
2018	(36,000 − 23,040)	×	0.40	=	5,184
Total accumulated depreciation at December 31, 2018					$28,224

*Double-declining-balance rate = 2 × Straight-line rate = 2 × (1 ÷ 5 years) = 0.40

Units-of-Production Depreciation

LO 8-4

Explain how units-of-production depreciation affects financial statements.

Suppose rental demand for Dryden's van depends on general economic conditions. In a robust economy, travel increases, and demand for renting vans is high. In a stagnant economy, demand for van rentals declines. In such circumstances, revenues fluctuate from year to year. To accomplish the matching objective, depreciation should also fluctuate from year to year. A method of depreciation known as **units-of-production depreciation** accomplishes this goal by basing depreciation expense on actual asset usage.

Computing depreciation expense using units-of-production begins with identifying a measure of the asset's productive capacity. For example, the number of miles Dryden expects its van to be driven may be a reasonable measure of its productive capacity. If the depreciable asset were a saw, an appropriate measure of productive capacity could be the number of board feet the saw was expected to cut during its useful life. In other words, the basis for measuring production depends on the nature of the depreciable asset.

To illustrate computing depreciation using the units-of-production depreciation method, assume that Dryden measures productive capacity based on the total number of miles the van will be driven over its useful life. Assume Dryden estimates this productive capacity to be 100,000 miles. The first step in determining depreciation expense is to compute the cost per unit of production. For Dryden's van, this amount is total depreciable cost (historical cost − salvage value) divided by total units of expected productive capacity (100,000 miles). The depreciation cost per mile is therefore $0.20 [($24,000 cost − $4,000 salvage) ÷ 100,000 miles]. Annual depreciation expense is computed by multiplying the cost per mile by the number of miles driven. Odometer readings indicate the van was driven 40,000 miles, 20,000 miles, 30,000 miles, and 15,000 miles in 2016, 2017, 2018, and 2019, respectively. Based on these data, Dryden developed the following schedule of depreciation charges:

Year	Cost per Mile (a)	Miles Driven (b)	Depreciation Expense (a × b)
2016	$.20	40,000	$8,000
2017	.20	20,000	4,000
2018	.20	30,000	6,000
2019	.20	15,000	~~3,000~~ 2,000

As pointed out in the discussion of the double-declining-balance method, an asset cannot be depreciated below its salvage value. Since $18,000 of the $20,000 ($24,000 cost − $4,000 salvage) depreciable cost is recognized in the first three years of using the van, only $2,000 ($20,000 − $18,000) remains to be charged to depreciation in the fourth year, even though the depreciation computations suggest the charge should be $3,000. As the preceding table indicates, the general formula for computing units-of-production depreciation is

$$\frac{\text{Cost} - \text{Salvage value}}{\text{Total estimated units of production}} \times \begin{array}{c}\text{Units of production}\\ \text{in current}\\ \text{year}\end{array} = \begin{array}{c}\text{Annual}\\ \text{depreciation}\\ \text{expense}\end{array}$$

Exhibit 8.5 displays financial statements that assume Dryden uses units-of-production depreciation. The exhibit assumes a cash revenue stream of $11,000, $7,000, $9,000, and $5,000 for 2016, 2017, 2018, and 2019, respectively. Trace the depreciation expense from the schedule above to the income statements. Depreciation expense is greater in years the van is driven more and smaller in years the van is driven less, providing a reasonable matching of depreciation expense with revenue produced. Net income is again constant at $3,000 per year.

EXHIBIT 8.5 Financial Statements under Units-of-Production Depreciation

DRYDEN ENTERPRISES
Financial Statements

	2016	2017	2018	2019
Income Statements				
Rent revenue	$11,000	$ 7,000	$ 9,000	$ 5,000
Depreciation expense	(8,000)	(4,000)	(6,000)	(2,000)
Net income	$ 3,000	$ 3,000	$ 3,000	$ 3,000
Balance Sheets				
Assets				
Cash	$12,000	$19,000	$28,000	$33,000
Van	24,000	24,000	24,000	24,000
Accumulated depreciation	(8,000)	(12,000)	(18,000)	(20,000)
Total assets	$28,000	$31,000	$34,000	$37,000
Stockholders' equity				
Common stock	$25,000	$25,000	$25,000	$25,000
Retained earnings	3,000	6,000	9,000	12,000
Total stockholders' equity	$28,000	$31,000	$34,000	$37,000
Statements of Cash Flows				
Operating Activities				
Inflow from customers	$11,000	$ 7,000	$ 9,000	$ 5,000
Investing Activities				
Outflow to purchase van	(24,000)			
Financing Activities				
Inflow from stock issue	25,000			
Net Change in Cash	12,000	7,000	9,000	5,000
Beginning cash balance	0	12,000	19,000	28,000
Ending cash balance	$12,000	$19,000	$28,000	$33,000

Accounting for the Disposal of Long-Term Operational Assets

LO 8-5

Show how asset disposals affect financial statements.

Regardless of which method of depreciation a company chooses to use, the van will ultimately cease to be useful for the purpose of generating revenue. At this point, the company will have to dispose of the asset. To illustrate accounting for the disposal of the asset, assume Dryden retires the van from service and sells it on January 1, 2020, for $4,500 cash. On this date the van's book value is $4,000 ($24,000 cost − $20,000 accumulated depreciation). Under these circumstances, Dryden would recognize a $500 gain ($4,500 book value − $4,000 sales price) on the sale. Recording the disposal of the asset requires the following journal entry:

Account Title	Debit	Credit
Cash	4,500	
Accumulated Depreciation	20,000	
Van		24,000
Gain on Sale of Van		500

The debit to the Cash account records the amount of the cash received from the sale of the asset. The debit to the Accumulated Depreciation account removes the amount of accumulated depreciation associated with the van from the accounting records. The credit to the Van account removes the original cost of the van from the accounting records. The credit to the Gain account recognizes the gain that was generated from the sale of the van. The effects of the compound journal entry on the financial statements is shown here:

Assets			=	Equity			Rev. or Gain.	−	Exp. Or Loss.	=	Net Inc.	Cash Flow
Cash	+	Book Value of Van	=	Com. Stk.	+	Ret. Earn.						
4,500	+	(4,000)	=	NA	+	500	500	−	NA	=	500	4,500 IA

Total assets increase by $500 because the amount of cash collected is more than the book value of the van. The gain causes the amount of net income and ultimately stockholders' equity to increase. The amount of the gain is not reported on the statement of cash flows. Instead, the entire $4,500 is shown in the statement of cash flows as an inflow from investing activities. Since selling vans is not part of Dryden's normal operations, the gain will be reported separately, after operating income, on the income statement.

Comparing the Depreciation Methods

The total amount of depreciation expense Dryden recognized using each of the three methods was $20,000 ($24,000 cost − $4,000 salvage value). The different methods affect the *timing,* but not the *total amount,* of expense recognized. The different methods simply assign the $20,000 to different accounting periods. Exhibit 8.6 presents graphically the differences among the three depreciation methods discussed above. A company should use the method that most closely matches expenses with revenues.

EXHIBIT 8.6

Depreciation Expense under Different Depreciation Methods

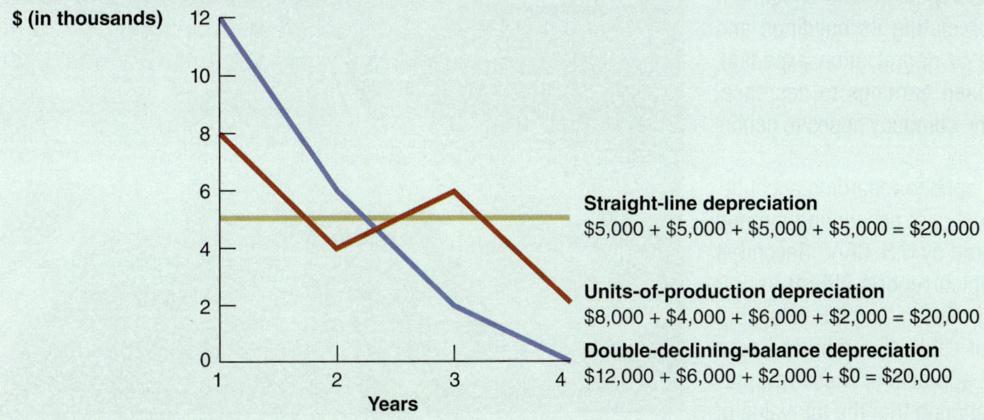

INCOME TAX CONSIDERATIONS

LO 8-6

Identify some of the tax issues that affect long-term operational assets.

The matching principle is not relevant to income tax reporting. The objective of tax reporting is to minimize tax expense. For tax purposes the most desirable depreciation method is the one that produces the highest amount of depreciation expense. Higher expenses mean lower taxes.

The maximum depreciation currently allowed by tax law is computed using an accelerated depreciation method known as the **modified accelerated cost recovery system (MACRS).** MACRS specifies the useful life for designated categories of assets. For example, under the law, companies must base depreciation computations for automobiles, light trucks, technological equipment, and other similar asset types on a 5-year useful life. In contrast, a 7-year life must be used for office furniture, fixtures, and many types of conventional machinery. The law classifies depreciable property, excluding real estate, into one of six categories: 3-year property, 5-year property, 7-year property, 10-year property, 15-year property, and 20-year property. Tables have been established for each category that specify the percentage of cost that can be expensed (deducted) in determining the amount of taxable income. A tax table for 5- and 7-year property is shown here as an example.

Year	5-Year Property, %	7-Year Property, %
1	20.00	14.29
2	32.00	24.49
3	19.20	17.49
4	11.52	12.49
5	11.52	8.93
6	5.76	8.92
7		8.93
8		4.46

The amount of depreciation a company can deduct each year for tax purposes is determined by multiplying the cost of a depreciable asset by the percentage shown in the table. For example, the depreciation expense for year 1 of a 7-year property asset is the cost of the asset multiplied by 14.29 percent. Depreciation for year 2 is the cost multiplied by 24.49 percent.

FOCUS ON INTERNATIONAL ISSUES

As you have learned, U.S. GAAP requires companies to use historical cost when accounting for property, plant, and equipment (PPE). Once a company begins depreciating its buildings and equipment, expenses increase (due to depreciation expense), which causes net income and retained earnings to decrease. This, of course, ignores the revenue the company hopes to generate by using the asset.

Under IFRS a company has two options regarding accounting of PPE. First, it can use a historical cost accounting method that is virtually identical to that required by U.S. GAAP. Second, it can use the "revaluation model," which reports PPE at its fair value. There can be different ways of determining fair value, but the preferred approach is to base fair value on a market-based appraisal, performed by professional appraisers. These revaluations must be conducted frequently enough that the fair value of an asset is not materially different from its recorded book value.

Basically, the revaluation model works as follows. The company periodically compares the current book value of its PPE to the fair value at that same date. This fair value relates to the value of the used asset, not the amount required to replace it with a new asset. If the fair value of an asset is higher than its currently recorded book value, the recorded amount for the asset is increased, which increases total assets. However, the increase in the asset's fair value is *not* reported on the company's income statement, as would a gain from selling the asset. Rather, the increase is reported in a special section of stockholders' equity, which balances the increase that was recorded for assets. However, if the new fair value is *lower* than the asset's current book value, the decrease is charged to net income, as well as to assets. This is another example of the conservatism principle at work. Not surprisingly, there are exceptions to these rules. Once a new fair value is established, future depreciation expense is based on these values.

One concern might be that companies, hoping to manipulate earnings, would pick and choose some assets to account for under historical costs and others to account for under the revaluation model. This is not permitted. Although a company does not have to use a single method for all its assets, it must use a single method for all the assets in a given class of assets. For example, historical costs could be used for all factory equipment, and the revaluation model used for all its buildings.

As significant as the difference between the historical cost method and the fair value approach might be, the majority of companies continue to use historical costs. Professors H. B. Christensen and V. Nikolaev conducted a study of the use of revaluation accounting for nonfinancial assets by companies in Germany and the United Kingdom. Their research found that only 3.2 percent of the 1,539 companies surveyed used the revaluation model for property, plant, and equipment.*

*Source: Christensen, H. B. and Nikolaev, V., "Who Uses Fair Value Accounting for Nonfinancial Assets after IFRS Adoption?" The University of Chicago Booth School of Business Working Paper No. 09-12, February 2009.

The tables present some apparent inconsistencies. For example, if MACRS is an accelerated depreciation method, why is less depreciation permitted in year 1 than in years 2 and 3? Also, why is depreciation computed in year 6 for property with a 5-year life and in year 8 for property with a 7-year life? These conditions are the consequence of using the **half-year convention.**

The half-year convention is designed to simplify computing taxable income. Instead of requiring taxpayers to calculate depreciation from the exact date of purchase to the exact date of disposal, the tax code requires one-half year's depreciation to be charged in the year in which an asset is acquired and one-half year's depreciation in the final year of depreciation. As a result, the percentages shown in the table for the first and last years represent depreciation for one-half year instead of the actual time of usage.

To illustrate computing depreciation using MACRS, assume that Wilson Company purchased furniture (7-year property) for $10,000 cash on July 21. Tax depreciation charges over the useful life of the asset are computed as shown:

Year	Table Factor, %	×	Cost	=	Depreciation Amount
1	14.29		$10,000		$1,429
2	24.49		10,000		2,449
3	17.49		10,000		1,749
4	12.49		10,000		1,249
5	8.93		10,000		893
6	8.92		10,000		892
7	8.93		10,000		893
8	4.46		10,000		446
Total over useful life					$10,000

As an alternative to MACRS, the tax code permits using straight-line depreciation. For certain types of assets such as real property (buildings), the tax code requires using straight-line depreciation.

There is no requirement that depreciation methods used for financial reporting be consistent with those used in preparing the income tax return. For example, a company may use straight-line depreciation in its financial statements and MACRS for the tax return. A company making this choice would reduce taxes in the early years of an asset's life because it would report higher depreciation charges on the tax return than in the financial statements. In later years, however, taxes will be higher because under MACRS, the amount of depreciation declines as the asset becomes older. Taxes are delayed but not avoided. The amount of taxes delayed for future payment represent a **deferred tax liability.** Delaying tax payments is advantageous. During the delay period, the money that would have been used to pay taxes can be used instead to make revenue-generating investments.

REVISION OF ESTIMATES

LO 8-7

Show how revising estimates affects financial statements.

In order to report useful financial information on a timely basis, accountants must make many estimates of future results, such as the salvage value and useful life of depreciable assets. Estimates are frequently revised when new information surfaces. Because revisions of estimates are common, generally accepted accounting principles call for incorporating the revised information into present and future calculations. Prior reports are not corrected.

To illustrate, assume that McGraw Company purchased a machine on January 1, 2016, for $50,000. McGraw estimated the machine would have a useful life of eight years and a salvage value of $3,000. Using the straight-line method, McGraw determined the annual depreciation charge as follows:

($50,000 − $3,000) ÷ 8 years = $5,875 per year

At the beginning of the fifth year, accumulated depreciation on the machine is $23,500 ($5,875 × 4). The machine's book value is $26,500 ($50,000 − $23,500). At this point, what happens if McGraw changes its estimates of useful life or the salvage value? Consider the following revision examples independently of each other.

Revision of Life

Assume McGraw revises the expected life to 14, rather than 8, years. The machine's *remaining* life would then be 10 more years instead of 4 more years. Assume salvage value remains $3,000. Depreciation for each remaining year is

($26,500 book value − $3,000 salvage) ÷ 10-year remaining life = $2,350

Revision of Salvage

Alternatively, assume the original expected life remained eight years, but McGraw revised its estimate of salvage value to $6,000. Depreciation for each of the remaining four years would be

($26,500 book value − $6,000 salvage) ÷ 4-year remaining life = $5,125

The revised amounts are determined for the full year, regardless of when McGraw revised its estimates. For example, if McGraw decides to change the estimated useful life on October 1, 2018, the change would be effective as of January 1, 2018. The year-end adjusting entry for depreciation would include a full year's depreciation calculated on the basis of the revised estimated useful life.

CONTINUING EXPENDITURES FOR PLANT ASSETS

LO 8-8

Explain how continuing expenditures for operational assets affect financial statements.

Most plant assets require additional expenditures for maintenance or improvement during their useful lives. Accountants must determine if these expenditures should be expensed or capitalized (recorded as assets).

Costs That Are Expensed

The costs of routine maintenance and minor repairs that are incurred to *keep* an asset in good working order are expensed in the period in which they are incurred. Because they reduce net income when incurred, accountants often call repair and maintenance costs **revenue expenditures** (companies subtract them from revenue).

With respect to the previous example, assume McGraw spent $500 for routine lubrication and to replace minor parts. The journal entry and its effects on the financial statements are shown here:

Account Title	Debit	Credit
Repairs Expense	500	
Cash		500

Assets	=	Equity			Rev.	−	Exp.	=	Net Inc.	Cash Flow
Cash	=	Com. Stk.	+	Ret. Earn.						
(500)	=	NA	+	(500)	NA	−	500	=	(500)	500 OA

Costs That Are Capitalized

Substantial amounts spent to improve the quality or extend the life of an asset are described as **capital expenditures.** Capital expenditures are accounted for in one of two ways, depending on whether the cost incurred *improves the quality* or *extends the life* of the asset.

Improving Quality

Expenditures such as adding air conditioning to an existing building or installing a trailer hitch on a vehicle improve the quality of service these assets provide. If a capital expenditure improves an asset's quality, the amount is added to the historical cost of the asset. The additional cost is expensed through higher depreciation charges over the asset's remaining useful life.

To demonstrate, return to the McGraw Company example. Recall that the machine originally cost $50,000, had an estimated salvage value of $3,000, and had a predicted life of eight years. Recall further that accumulated depreciation at the beginning of the fifth year is $23,500 ($5,875 × 4) so the book value is $26,500 ($50,000 − $23,500). Assume McGraw makes a major expenditure of $4,000 in the machine's fifth year to improve its productive capacity. The journal entry and its effects on the financial statements are shown here:

Account Title	Debit	Credit
Machine	4,000	
Cash		4,000

Assets			=	Equity			Rev.	−	Exp.	=	Net Inc.	Cash Flow
Cash	+	Book Value of Mach.	=	Com. Stk.	+	Ret. Earn.						
(4,000)	+	4,000	=	NA	+	NA	NA	−	NA	=	NA	(4,000) IA

After recording the expenditure, the machine account balance is $54,000 and the asset's book value is $30,500 ($54,000 − $23,500). The depreciation charges for each of the remaining four years are

($30,500 book value − $3,000 salvage) ÷ 4-year remaining life = $6,875

Extending Life

Expenditures such as replacing the roof of an existing building or putting a new engine in an older vehicle extend the useful life of these assets. If a capital expenditure extends the life of an asset rather than improving the asset's quality of service, accountants view the expenditure as canceling some of the depreciation previously charged to expense. The event is still an asset exchange; cash decreases, and the book value of the machine increases. However, the increase in the book value of the machine results from reducing the balance in the contra asset account, Accumulated Depreciation.

To illustrate, assume that instead of increasing productive capacity, McGraw's $4,000 expenditure had extended the useful life of the machine by two years. The journal entry and its effects on the financial statements are shown here:

Account Title	Debit	Credit
Accumulated Depreciation–Machine	4,000	
Cash		4,000

Assets			=	Equity			Rev.	−	Exp.	=	Net Inc.	Cash Flow
Cash	+	Book Value of Mach.	=	Com. Stk.	+	Ret. Earn.						
(4,000)	+	4,000	=	NA	+	NA	NA	−	NA	=	NA	(4,000) IA

After the expenditure is recorded, the book value is the same as if the $4,000 had been added to the Machine account ($50,000 cost − $19,500 adjusted balance in Accumulated Depreciation = $30,500). Depreciation expense for each of the remaining six years follows:

($30,500 book value − $3,000 salvage) ÷ 6-year remaining life = $4,583

CHECK YOURSELF 8.3

On January 1, 2016, Dager Inc. purchased an asset that cost $18,000. It had a five-year useful life and a $3,000 salvage value. Dager uses straight-line depreciation. On January 1, 2018, it incurred a $1,200 cost related to the asset. With respect to this asset, determine the amount of expense and accumulated depreciation Dager would report in the 2018 financial statements under each of the following assumptions.

1. The $1,200 cost was incurred to repair damage resulting from an accident.
2. The $1,200 cost improved the operating capacity of the asset. The total useful life and salvage value remained unchanged.
3. The $1,200 cost extended the useful life of the asset by one year. The salvage value remained unchanged.

Answer

1. Dager would report the $1,200 repair cost as an expense. Dager would also report depreciation expense of $3,000 [($18,000 − $3,000) ÷ 5]. Total expenses related to this asset in 2018 would be $4,200 ($1,200 repair expense + $3,000 depreciation expense). Accumulated depreciation at the end of 2018 would be $9,000 ($3,000 depreciation expense × 3 years).
2. The $1,200 cost would be capitalized in the asset account, increasing both the book value of the asset and the annual depreciation expense.

	After-Effects of Capital Improvement
Amount in asset account ($18,000 + $1,200)	$19,200
Less: Salvage value	(3,000)
Accumulated depreciation on January 1, 2018	(6,000)
Remaining depreciable cost before recording 2018 depreciation	$10,200
Depreciation for 2018 ($10,200 ÷ 3 years)	$ 3,400
Accumulated depreciation at December 31, 2018 ($6,000 + $3,400)	$ 9,400

3. The $1,200 cost would be subtracted from the Accumulated Depreciation account, increasing the book value of the asset. The remaining useful life would increase to four years, which would decrease the depreciation expense.

	After-Effects of Capital Improvement
Amount in asset account	$18,000
Less: Salvage value	(3,000)
Accumulated depreciation on January 1, 2018 ($6,000 + $1,200)	(4,800)
Remaining depreciable cost before recording 2018 depreciation	$10,200
Depreciation for 2018 ($10,200 ÷ 4 years)	$ 2,550
Accumulated depreciation at December 31, 2018 ($4,800 + $2,550)	$ 7,350

NATURAL RESOURCES

LO 8-9

Explain how the depletion of natural resources affects financial statements.

The cost of natural resources includes not only the purchase price but also related items such as the cost of exploration, geographic surveys, and estimates. The process of expensing natural resources is commonly called depletion.[2] The most common method used to calculate depletion is units-of-production.

[2]In practice, the depletion charge is considered a product cost and allocated between inventory and cost of goods sold. This text uses the simplifying assumption that all resources are sold in the same accounting period in which they are extracted. The full depletion charge is therefore expensed in the period in which the resources are extracted.

Answers to The Curious Accountant

As assets lose their productive capacity, either from being used or due to obsolescence, the asset account is reduced and an expense account is increased. Assets such as buildings and equipment may decline faster if they are used, but, due to obsolescence, they usually continue to decline even if they are not used. For this reason, a time-based depreciation method, such as straight-line or double-declining-balance, is almost always used for buildings and more often than not for equipment. In contrast, a mineral reserve does not lose its capacity unless ore is extracted. After all, the gold the FCX is mining today has been in the earth for millions of years. For this reason, companies typically use the units-of-production method to calculate depletion on mineral reserves. In both cases, the objective should be to achieve the best matching of expenses incurred with the revenues they generate.

To illustrate, assume Apex Coal Mining paid $4,000,000 cash to purchase a mine with an estimated 16,000,000 tons of coal. The unit depletion charge is

$4,000,000 ÷ 16,000,000 tons = $0.25 per ton

If Apex mines 360,000 tons of coal in the first year, the depletion charge is

360,000 tons ÷ $0.25 per ton = $90,000

The depletion of a natural resource has the same effect on the accounting equation as other expense recognition events. Assets (in this case, a *coal mine*) and stockholders' equity decrease. The depletion expense reduces net income. The journal entries necessary to record the acquisition and depletion of the coal mine and their effects on the financial statements are shown here:

Account Title	Debit	Credit
Coal Mine	4,000,000	
Cash		4,000,000
Depletion Expense	90,000	
Coal Mine		90,000

Assets			=	Equity			Rev.	−	Exp.	=	Net Inc.	Cash Flow
Cash	+	Coal Mine	=	Com. Stk.	+	Ret. Earn.						
(4,000,000)	+	4,000,000	=	NA	+	NA	NA	−	NA	=	NA	(4,000,000) IA
NA	+	(90,000)	=	NA	+	(90,000)	NA	−	90,000	=	(90,000)	NA

INTANGIBLE ASSETS

LO 8-10

Identify and determine the cost of intangible assets.

Intangible assets provide rights, privileges, and special opportunities to businesses. Common intangible assets include trademarks, patents, copyrights, franchises, and goodwill. Some of the unique characteristics of these intangible assets are described in the following sections.

FOCUS ON INTERNATIONAL ISSUES

RESEARCH *AND* DEVELOPMENT VS. RESEARCH *OR* DEVELOPMENT

For many years some thought the companies that followed U.S. GAAP were at a disadvantage when it came to research and development (R&D) costs, because these companies had to immediately expense such cost, while the accounting rules of some other countries allowed R&D cost to be capitalized. Remember, recording costs as an asset—capitalizing it—means that net income is not immediately reduced. The global movement toward using IFRS is reducing, but not eliminating, the different accounting treatments for R&D.

Like U.S. GAAP, IFRS requires *research* costs to be expensed, but it allows *development* costs to be capitalized. This IFRS rule itself can present challenges, because sometimes it is not clear where research ends and development begins. Basically, once research has produced a product, patent, and so forth that the company believes will result in a revenue-generating outcome, any additional costs to get it ready for market are development costs.

Trademarks

A **trademark** is a name or symbol that identifies a company or a product. Familiar trademarks include the Polo emblem, the name *Coca-Cola*, and the Nike slogan, "Just do it." Trademarks are registered with the federal government and have an indefinite legal lifetime.

The costs incurred to design, purchase, or defend a trademark are capitalized in an asset account called Trademarks. Companies want their trademarks to become familiar but also face the risk of a trademark being used as the generic name for a product. To protect a trademark, companies in this predicament spend large sums on legal fees and extensive advertising programs to educate consumers. Well-known trademarks that have been subject to this problem include Coke, Xerox, Kleenex, and Vaseline.

Patents

A **patent** grants its owner an exclusive legal right to produce and sell a product that has one or more unique features. Patents issued by the U.S. Patent Office have a legal life of 20 years. Companies may obtain patents through purchase, lease, or internal development. The costs capitalized in the Patent account are usually limited to the purchase price and legal fees to obtain and successfully defend the patent. The research and development costs that are incurred to develop patentable products are usually expensed in the period in which they are incurred.

Copyrights

A **copyright** protects writings, musical compositions, works of art, and other intellectual property for the exclusive benefit of the creator or persons assigned the right by the creator. The cost of a copyright includes the purchase price and any legal costs associated with obtaining and defending the copyright. Copyrights granted by the federal government extend for the life of the creator plus 70 years. A radio commercial could legally use a Bach composition as background music; it could not, however, use the theme song from the most recent academy award winning movie without obtaining permission from the copyright owner. The cost of a copyright is often expensed early because future royalties may be uncertain.

REALITY BYTES

In 2013, **Hewlett-Packard Company** (HP) reported that it had paid $174 million to acquire **Digital Risk LLC**, even though the company's land, buildings, equipment, patents, and so on had a fair value of only $62 million. Why would HP pay the owners of Digital Risk almost three times the value of the assets shown on the company's balance sheet?

HP believed that Digital Risk had *goodwill* that would enable the company to use its assets in a manner that would generate above-average earnings in the future. In other words, HP was paying for an asset not shown on Digital Risk's balance sheet. Keep in mind that such decisions are based on assumptions, estimates, and predictions about future events. These predictions are not always proven correct.

Consider another example involving HP. In 2011 HP purchased a software company named **Autonomy** for $11 billion; $6.6 billion of this amount was for goodwill. Within a year HP had determined that it had grossly overpaid for Autonomy. In Note 6 of its 2013 Form 10-K, HP reported:

> *HP initiated its annual goodwill impairment analysis in the fourth quarter of fiscal 2012 and concluded that fair value was below carrying amount for the Autonomy reporting unit. . . . Based on the analysis, HP recorded an impairment charge of $3.1 billion on intangible assets [and] . . . a goodwill impairment charge of $5.7 billion.*

What had been seen as an asset worth $11 billion was now valued at only $2.2 billion. As noted above, predictions about the future are not always proven correct.

Franchises

Franchises grant exclusive rights to sell products or perform services in certain geographic areas. Franchises may be granted by governments or private businesses. Franchises granted by governments include federal broadcasting licenses. Private business franchises include fast-food restaurant chains and brand labels such as **Healthy Choice**. The legal and useful lives of a franchise are frequently difficult to determine. Judgment is often crucial to establishing the estimated useful life for franchises.

Goodwill

Goodwill is the value attributable to favorable factors such as reputation, location, and superior products. Consider the most popular restaurant in your town. If the owner sold the restaurant, do you think the acquisition price would be simply the total value of the chairs, tables, kitchen equipment, and building? Certainly not, because much of the restaurant's value lies in its popularity; in other words, its ability to generate a high return is based on the goodwill (reputation) of the business.

Calculating goodwill can be complex; here we present a simple example to illustrate how it is determined. Suppose the accounting records of a restaurant named Bendigo's show

Assets	=	Liabilities	+	Stockholders' equity
$200,000	=	$50,000	+	$150,000

Assume a buyer agrees to acquire the restaurant by paying the owner $300,000 cash and assuming the existing liabilities. In other words, the restaurant is acquired at a price of $350,000 ($300,000 cash + $50,000 assumed liabilities). Now assume that the assets of the business (tables, chairs, kitchen equipment, etc.) have a fair value of only $280,000. Why would the buyer pay $350,000 to purchase assets with a fair value of $280,000? Obviously, the buyer is purchasing more than just the assets. The buyer is acquiring the business's goodwill. The amount of the goodwill is the difference between the purchase price and the fair value of the assets. In this case, the goodwill is $70,000 ($350,000 − $280,000). The journal entry to record the acquisition and its effects on the financial statements are shown here:

Account Title	Debit	Credit
Restaurant Assets	280,000	
Goodwill	70,000	
Cash		300,000
Liabilities		50,000

Assets					=	Liab.	+	Equity	Rev.	−	Exp.	=	Net Inc.	Cash Flow
Cash	+	Rest. Assets	+	Goodwill										
(300,000)	+	280,000	+	70,000	=	50,000	+	NA	NA	−	NA	=	NA	(300,000) IA

The fair value of the restaurant assets represents the historical cost to the new owner. It becomes the basis for future depreciation charges.

Expense Recognition for Intangible Assets

LO 8-11

Explain how the amortization of intangible assets affects financial statements.

As mentioned earlier, intangible assets fall into two categories, those with *identifiable useful lives* and those with *indefinite useful lives.* Expense recognition for intangible assets depends on which classification applies.

Expensing Intangible Assets with Identifiable Useful Lives

The costs of intangible assets with identifiable useful lives are normally expensed on a straight-line basis using a process called *amortization.* An intangible asset should be amortized over the shorter of two possible time periods: (1) its legal life or (2) its useful life.

To illustrate, assume that Flowers Industries purchased a newly granted patent for $44,000 cash. Although the patent has a legal life of 20 years, Flowers estimates that it will be useful for only 11 years. The annual amortization charge is therefore $4,000 ($44,000 ÷ 11 years). The journal entries to record the patent purchase and first year amortization and their effects on the financial statements are shown here:

Account Title	Debit	Credit
Patent	44,000	
Cash		44,000
Amortization Expense, Patent	4,000	
Patent		4,000

Assets			=	Equity			Rev.	−	Exp.	=	Net Inc.	Cash Flow
Cash	+	Patent	=	Com. Stk.	+	Ret. Earn.						
(44,000)	+	44,000	=	NA	+	NA	NA	−	NA	=	NA	(44,000) IA
NA	+	(4,000)	=	NA	+	(4,000)	NA	−	4,000	=	(4,000)	NA

Impairment Losses for Intangible Assets with Indefinite Useful Lives

Intangible assets with indefinite useful lives must be tested for impairment annually. The impairment test consists of comparing the fair value of the intangible asset to its carrying value (book value). If the fair value is less than the book value, an impairment loss must be recognized.

To illustrate, return to the example of the Bendigo's restaurant acquisition. Recall that the buyer of Bendigo's paid $70,000 for goodwill. Assume the restaurant experiences a significant decline in revenue because many of its former regular customers are dissatisfied with the food prepared by the new chef. Suppose the decline in revenue is so substantial that the new owner believes the Bendigo's name is permanently impaired. The owner decides to hire a different chef and change the name of the restaurant. In this case, the business has suffered a permanent decline in value of goodwill. The company must recognize an impairment loss.

The restaurant's name has lost its value, but the owner believes the location continues to provide the opportunity to produce above-average earnings. Some, but not all, of the goodwill has been lost. Assume the fair value of the remaining goodwill is determined to be $40,000. The impairment loss to recognize is $30,000 ($70,000 − $40,000). The loss reduces the intangible asset (goodwill), stockholder's equity (retained earnings), and net income. The statement of cash flows is not affected. The journal entry and its effects on the financial statements follow:

Account Title	Debit	Credit
Impairment Loss	30,000	
Goodwill		30,000

Assets	=	Liab.	+	Equity	Rev.	−	Exp./Loss	=	Net Inc.	Cash Flow
Goodwill	=			Ret. Earn.						
(30,000)	=	NA	+	(30,000)	NA	−	(30,000)	=	(30,000)	NA

Balance Sheet Presentation

This chapter explained accounting for the acquisition, expense recognition, and disposal of a wide range of long-term assets. Exhibit 8.7 illustrates the typical balance sheet presentation of many of the assets discussed.

EXHIBIT 8.7

Balance Sheet Presentation of Operational Assets

Partial Balance Sheet			
Long-Term Assets			
Plant and equipment			
Buildings	$4,000,000		
Less: Accumulated depreciation	(2,500,000)	$1,500,000	
Equipment	1,750,000		
Less: Accumulated depreciation	(1,200,000)	550,000	
Total plant and equipment			$2,050,000
Land			850,000
Natural resources			
Mineral deposits (Less: Depletion)		2,100,000	
Oil reserves (Less: Depletion)		890,000	
Total natural resources			2,990,000
Intangibles			
Patents (Net of amortization)		38,000	
Goodwill		175,000	
Total intangible assets			213,000
Total long-term assets			$6,103,000

THE FINANCIAL ANALYST

LO 8-12

Show how expense recognition choices and industry characteristics affect financial performance measures.

Managers may have differing opinions about which allocation method (straight-line, accelerated, or units-of-production) best matches expenses with revenues. As a result, one company may use straight-line depreciation while another company in similar circumstances uses double-declining-balance. Since the allocation method a company uses affects the amount of expense it recognizes, analysts reviewing financial statements must consider the accounting procedures companies use in preparing the statements.

Effect of Judgment and Estimation

Assume that two companies, Alpha and Zeta, experience identical economic events in 2016 and 2017. Both generate revenue of \$50,000 and incur cost of goods sold of \$30,000 during each year. In 2016, each company pays \$20,000 for an asset with an expected useful life of five years and no salvage value. How will the companies' financial statements differ if one uses straight-line depreciation and the other uses the double-declining-balance method? To answer this question, first compute the depreciation expense for both companies for 2016 and 2017.

If Alpha Company uses the straight-line method, depreciation for 2016 and 2017 is

(Cost − Salvage)	÷ Useful life	=	Depreciation expense per year
(\$20,000 − \$0)	÷ 5 years	=	\$4,000

In contrast, if Zeta Company uses the double-declining-balance method, Zeta recognizes the following amounts of depreciation expense for 2016 and 2017

	(Cost − Accumulated Depreciation)	×	2 × (Straight-Line Rate)	=	Depreciation Expense
2016	(\$20,000 − \$ 0)	×	[2 × (1 ÷ 5)]	=	\$8,000
2017	(\$20,000 − \$8,000)	×	[2 × (1 ÷ 5)]	=	\$4,800

Based on these computations, the income statements for the two companies are

Income Statements

	2016		2017	
	Alpha Co.	Zeta Co.	Alpha Co.	Zeta Co.
Sales	\$ 50,000	\$ 50,000	\$ 50,000	\$ 50,000
Cost of goods sold	(30,000)	(30,000)	(30,000)	(30,000)
Gross margin	20,000	20,000	20,000	20,000
Depreciation expense	(4,000)	(8,000)	(4,000)	(4,800)
Net income	\$ 16,000	\$ 12,000	\$ 16,000	\$ 15,200

The relevant sections of the balance sheets are

Plant Assets

	2016		2017	
	Alpha Co.	Zeta Co.	Alpha Co.	Zeta Co.
Asset	\$20,000	\$20,000	\$20,000	\$ 20,000
Accumulated depreciation	(4,000)	(8,000)	(8,000)	(12,800)
Book value	\$16,000	\$12,000	\$12,000	\$ 7,200

The depreciation method is not the only aspect of expense recognition that can vary between companies. Companies may also make different assumptions about the useful lives and salvage values of long-term operational assets. Thus, even if the same depreciation method is used, depreciation expense may still differ.

Since the depreciation method and the underlying assumptions regarding useful life and salvage value affect the determination of depreciation expense, they also affect the amounts of net income, retained earnings, and total assets. Financial statement analysis is affected if it is based on ratios that include these items. Previously defined ratios that are affected include the (1) debt to assets ratio, (2) return on assets ratio, (3) return on equity ratio, and (4) return on sales ratio.

To promote meaningful analysis, GAAP requires companies to disclose all significant accounting policies used to prepare their financial statements. This disclosure is provided in the notes that accompany the financial statements.

Effect of Industry Characteristics

As indicated in previous chapters, industry characteristics affect financial performance measures. For example, companies in manufacturing industries invest heavily in machinery while insurance companies rely more on human capital. Manufacturing companies therefore have relatively higher depreciation charges than insurance companies. To illustrate how the type of industry affects financial reporting, examine Exhibit 8.8. This exhibit compares the ratio of sales to property, plant, and equipment for two companies in each of three different industries. These data are for 2013.

The table indicates that for every $1.00 invested in property, plant, and equipment, Manpower produced $122.00 of sales. In contrast, Verizon and Southwest Airlines produced only $1.37 and $1.36, respectively, for each $1.00 they invested in operational assets. Does this mean the management of Manpower is doing a better job than the management of Verizon or Southwest Airlines? Not necessarily. It means that these companies operate in different economic environments. In other words, it takes significantly more equipment to operate a cable company or an airline than it takes to operate an employment agency.

Effective financial analysis requires careful consideration of industry characteristics, accounting policies, and the reasonableness of assumptions such as useful life and salvage value.

EXHIBIT 8.8

Industry Data Reflecting the Use of Long-Term Tangible Assets

Industry	Company	Sales ÷ Property, Plant, and Equipment
Broadband Communications	Comcast Corp.	2.17
	Verizon Communications	1.37
Airlines	Alaska Air Group	1.32
	Southwest Airlines	1.36
Employment Agencies	Kelly Services	58.80
	Manpower, Inc.	122.00

<< A Look Back

This chapter explains that the primary objective of recognizing depreciation is to match the cost of a long-term tangible asset with the revenues the asset is expected to generate. The matching concept also applies to natural resources (depletion) and intangible assets (amortization). The chapter explains how alternative methods can be used to account for the same event (e.g., straight-line versus double-declining-balance depreciation). Companies experiencing exactly the same business events could produce different financial statements. The alternative accounting methods for depreciating, depleting, or amortizing assets include the (1) straight-line, (2) double-declining-balance, and (3) units-of-production methods.

The *straight-line method* produces equal amounts of expense in each accounting period. The amount of the expense recognized is determined using the formula [(cost − salvage) ÷ number of years of useful life]. The *double-declining-balance method* produces proportionately larger amounts of expense in the early years of an asset's useful life and increasingly smaller amounts of expense in the later years of the asset's useful life. The formula for calculating double-declining-balance depreciation is [book value at beginning of period × (2 × the straight-line rate)]. The *units-of-production method* produces expense in direct proportion to the number of units produced during an accounting period. The formula for the amount of expense recognized each period is [(cost − salvage) ÷ total estimated units of production = allocation rate × units of production in current accounting period].

The chapter also discussed *MACRS depreciation,* an accelerated tax reporting method. MACRS is not acceptable under GAAP for public reporting. A company may use MACRS depreciation for tax purposes and straight-line or one of the other methods for public reporting. As a result, differences may exist between the amount of tax expense and the amount of tax liability. Such differences are reported as *deferred income taxes.*

This chapter showed how to account for *changes in estimates* such as the useful life or the salvage value of a depreciable asset. Changes in estimates do not affect the amount of depreciation recognized previously. Instead, the remaining book value of the asset is expensed over its remaining useful life.

After an asset has been placed into service, companies typically incur further costs for maintenance, quality improvement, and extensions of useful life. *Maintenance costs* are expensed in the period in which they are incurred. *Costs that improve the quality* of an asset are added to the cost of the asset, increasing the book value and the amount of future depreciation charges. *Costs that extend the useful life* of an asset are subtracted from the asset's Accumulated Depreciation account, increasing the book value and the amount of future depreciation charges.

>> A Look Forward

In Chapter 9 we move from the assets section of the balance sheet to issues in accounting for short-term liabilities. You will also study the basic components of a payroll accounting system.

SELF-STUDY REVIEW PROBLEM

A step-by-step audio-narrated series of slides is available in the Connect library.

The following information pertains to a machine purchased by Bakersfield Company on January 1, 2016:

Purchase price	$ 63,000
Delivery cost	$ 2,000
Installation charge	$ 3,000
Estimated useful life	8 years
Estimated units the machine will produce	130,000
Estimated salvage value	$ 3,000

The machine produced 14,400 units during 2016 and 17,000 units during 2017.

Required

Determine the depreciation expense Bakersfield would report for 2016 and 2017 using each of the following methods:

a. Straight-line.

b. Double-declining-balance.

c. Units-of-production.

d. MACRS, assuming that the machine is classified as seven-year property.

Solution to Requirements a–d

a. Straight-line

Purchase price	$63,000	
Delivery cost	2,000	
Installation charge	3,000	
Total cost of machine	68,000	
Less: Salvage value	(3,000)	
	$65,000	÷ 8 = $8,125 Depreciation per year
2016	$ 8,125	
2017	$ 8,125	

b. Double-declining-balance

Year	Cost	−	Accumulated Depreciation at Beginning of Year	×	2 × S-L Rate	=	Annual Depreciation
2016	$68,000	−	$ 0	×	(2 × 0.125)	=	$17,000
2017	68,000	−	17,000	×	(2 × 0.125)	=	12,750

c. Units-of-production

(1) (Cost − Salvage value) ÷ Estimated units of production = Depreciation cost per unit produced

$$\frac{\$68{,}000 - \$3{,}000}{130{,}000} = \$0.50 \text{ per unit}$$

(2) Cost per unit × Annual units produced = Annual depreciation expense

2016 $0.50 × 14,400 = $7,200

2017 0.50 × 17,000 = 8,500

d. MACRS

Cost × MACRS percentage = Annual depreciation

2016	**$68,000 × 0.1429**	**=**	**$ 9,717**
2017	**68,000 × 0.2449**	**=**	**16,653**

KEY TERMS

Accelerated depreciation method 428
Accumulated Depreciation 426
Amortization 422
Basket purchase 423
Book value 426
Capital expenditures 436
Carrying value 426
Contra asset account 426
Copyright 440
Current assets 420
Deferred tax liability 435
Depletion 422
Depreciable cost 424
Depreciation 422
Depreciation expense 424
Double-declining-balance depreciation 428
Estimated useful life 424
Franchise 441
Goodwill 441
Half-year convention 434
Historical cost concept 423
Intangible assets 422
Long-term operational assets 420
Modified accelerated cost recovery system (MACRS) 433
Natural resources 422
Patent 440
Property, plant, and equipment 422
Relative market value method 423
Revenue expenditures 436
Salvage value 424
Straight-line depreciation 425
Tangible assets 422
Trademark 440
Units-of-production depreciation 430

QUESTIONS

1. What is the difference between the functions of long-term operational assets and investments?
2. What is the difference between tangible and intangible assets? Give an example of each.
3. What is the difference between goodwill and specifically identifiable intangible assets?
4. Define *depreciation*. What kind of asset depreciates?
5. Why do you think natural resources are called *wasting assets?*
6. Is land a depreciable asset? Why or why not?
7. Define *amortization*. What kind of assets are amortized?
8. Explain the historical cost concept as it applies to long-term operational assets. Why is the book value of an asset likely to be different from the current fair market value of the asset?
9. What different kinds of expenditures might be included in the recorded cost of a building?
10. What is a basket purchase of assets? When a basket purchase is made, how is cost assigned to individual assets?
11. What are the stages in the life cycle of a long-term operational asset?
12. Explain straight-line, units-of-production, and double-declining-balance depreciation. When is it appropriate to use each of these depreciation methods?
13. What effect does the recognition of depreciation expense have on total assets? On total equity?
14. Does the recognition of depreciation expense affect cash flows? Why or why not?
15. MalMax purchased a depreciable asset. What would be the difference in total assets at the end of the first year if MalMax chooses straight-line depreciation versus double-declining-balance depreciation?
16. John Smith mistakenly expensed the cost of a long-term tangible fixed asset. Specifically, he charged the cost of a truck to a delivery expense account. How will this error affect the income statement and the balance sheet in the year in which the mistake is made?
17. What is *salvage value?*
18. What type of account (classification) is Accumulated Depreciation?
19. How is the book value of an asset determined?
20. Why is depreciation that has been recognized over the life of an asset shown in a contra account? Why not just reduce the asset account?
21. Assume that a piece of equipment cost \$5,000 and had accumulated depreciation recorded of \$3,000. What is the book value of the equipment? Is the book value equal to the fair market value of the equipment? Explain.
22. Why would a company choose to depreciate one piece of equipment using the double-declining-balance method and another piece of equipment using straight-line depreciation?
23. Explain MACRS depreciation. When is its use appropriate?
24. Does the method of depreciation required to be used for tax purposes reflect the use of a piece of equipment? Can you use double-declining-balance depreciation for tax purposes?
25. Define *deferred taxes.* Where does the account *Deferred Taxes* appear in the financial statements?
26. Why may it be necessary to revise the estimated life of a plant asset? When the estimated life is revised, does it affect the amount of depreciation per year? Why or why not?
27. How are capital expenditures made to improve the quality of a capital asset accounted for? Would the answer change if the expenditure extended the life of the asset but did not improve quality? Explain.
28. When a long-term operational asset is sold at a gain, how is the balance sheet affected? Is the statement of cash flows affected? If so, how?
29. Define *depletion.* What is the most commonly used method of computing depletion?
30. List several common intangible assets. How is the life determined that is to be used to compute amortization?
31. List some differences between U.S. GAAP and IFRS for long-term operational assets.
32. How do differences in expense recognition and industry characteristics affect financial performance measures?

MULTIPLE-CHOICE QUESTIONS

Multiple-choice questions are available in the Connect library.

EXERCISES—SERIES A

connect plus+ ACCOUNTING ***All applicable Exercises in Series A are available with McGraw-Hill's Connect Plus Accounting.***

Unless specifically included, ignore income tax considerations in all exercises and problems.

Exercise 8-1A *Long-term operational assets used in a business* LO 8-1

Required

Give some examples of long-term operational assets that each of the following companies is likely to own: *(a)* **Caterpillar**, *(b)* **Amtrak**, *(c)* **Facebook**, and *(d)* **Bank of America Corp.**

Exercise 8-2A *Identifying long-term operational assets* LO 8-1

Required

Which of the following items should be classified as long-term operational assets?

a. Prepaid insurance
b. Coal mine
c. Office equipment
d. Accounts receivable
e. Supplies
f. Copyright
g. Delivery van
h. Land used in the business
i. Goodwill
j. Cash
k. Filing cabinet
l. Tax library of accounting firm

Exercise 8-3A *Classifying tangible and intangible assets* LO 8-1

Required

Identify each of the following long-term operational assets as either tangible (T) or intangible (I):

a. Pizza oven
b. Land
c. Franchise
d. Filing cabinet
e. Copyright
f. Silver mine
g. Office building
h. Drill press
i. Patent
j. Oil well
k. Desk
l. Goodwill

Exercise 8-4A *Determining the cost of an asset* LO 8-1

Southwest Milling Co. purchased a front-end loader to move stacks of lumber. The loader had a list price of $140,000. The seller agreed to allow a 4 percent discount because Southwest Milling paid cash. Delivery terms were FOB shipping point. Freight cost amounted to $1,200. Southwest Milling had to hire a specialist to calibrate the loader. The specialist's fee was $1,800. The loader operator is paid an annual salary of $60,000. The cost of the company's theft insurance policy increased by $800 per year as a result of acquiring the loader. The loader had a four-year useful life and an expected salvage value of $6,000.

Required

a. Determine the amount to be capitalized in an asset account for the purchase of the loader.
b. Record the purchase in general journal format.

Exercise 8-5A *Allocating costs on the basis of relative market values* LO 8-1

Carver Inc. purchased a building and the land on which the building is situated for a total cost of $700,000 cash. The land was appraised at $320,000 and the building at $480,000.

Required

a. Determine the amount of the purchase cost to allocate to the land and the amount to allocate to the building.

b. Would the company recognize a gain on the purchase? Why or why not?

c. Record the purchase in a statements model like the following one:

Assets					=	Liab.	+	Equity	Rev.	−	Exp.	=	Net Inc.	Cash Flow
Cash	+	Land	+	Building										

d. Record the purchase in general journal format.

LO 8-1

Exercise 8-6A *Allocating costs for a basket purchase*

Pitney Co. purchased an office building, land, and furniture for $500,000 cash. The appraised value of the assets was as follows:

Land	$180,000
Building	300,000
Furniture	120,000
Total	$600,000

Required

a. Compute the amount to be recorded on the books for each asset.

b. Record the purchase in a horizontal statements model like the following one:

Assets							=	Liab.	+	Equity	Rev.	−	Exp.	=	Net Inc.	Cash Flow
Cash	+	Land	+	Building	+	Furn.										

c. Prepare the general journal entry to record the purchase.

LO 8-2

Exercise 8-7A *Effect of depreciation on the accounting equation and financial statements*

The following events apply to Gulf Seafood for the 2016 fiscal year:

1. The company started when it acquired $60,000 cash by issuing common stock.
2. Purchased a new cooktop that cost $40,000 cash.
3. Earned $72,000 in cash revenue.
4. Paid $25,000 cash for salaries expense.
5. Adjusted the records to reflect the use of the cooktop. Purchased on January 1, 2016, the cooktop has an expected useful life of four years and an estimated salvage value of $4,000. Use straight-line depreciation. The adjusting entry was made as of December 31, 2016.

Required

a. Record the events in general journal format and post to T-accounts.

b. Prepare a balance sheet and a statement of cash flows for the 2016 accounting period.

c. What is the net income for 2016?

d. What amount of depreciation expense would Gulf Seafood report on the 2017 income statement?

e. What amount of accumulated depreciation would Gulf Seafood report on the December 31, 2017, balance sheet?

f. Would the cash flow from operating activities be affected by depreciation in 2017?

Exercise 8-8A ***Effect of double-declining-balance depreciation on financial statements*** **LO 8-3**

Golden Manufacturing Company started operations by acquiring $150,000 cash from the issue of common stock. On January 1, 2016, the company purchased equipment that cost $120,000 cash, had an expected useful life of six years, and had an estimated salvage value of $4,000. Golden Manufacturing earned $72,000 and $83,000 of cash revenue during 2016 and 2017, respectively. Golden Manufacturing uses double-declining-balance depreciation.

Required

Prepare income statements, balance sheets, and statements of cash flows for 2016 and 2017. Use a vertical statements format. (*Hint:* Record the events in T-accounts prior to preparing the statements.)

Exercise 8-9A ***Events related to the acquisition, use, and disposal of a tangible plant asset: straight-line depreciation*** **LO 8-2, 8-5**

City Taxi Service purchased a new auto to use as a taxi on January 1, 2016, for $36,000. In addition, City paid sales tax and title fees of $1,200 for the vehicle. The taxi is expected to have a five-year life and a salvage value of $4,000.

Required

a. Using the straight-line method, compute the depreciation expense for 2016 and 2017.

b. Prepare the general journal entry to record the 2016 depreciation.

c. Assume that the taxi was sold on January 1, 2018, for $22,000. Prepare the journal entry for the sale of the taxi in 2018.

Exercise 8-10A ***Computing and recording straight-line versus double-declining-balance depreciation*** **LO 8-2, 8-3**

At the beginning of 2016, Copland Drugstore purchased a new computer system for $52,000. It is expected to have a five-year life and a $7,000 salvage value.

Required

a. Compute the depreciation for each of the five years, assuming that the company uses

(1) Straight-line depreciation.

(2) Double-declining-balance depreciation.

b. Record the purchase of the computer system and the depreciation expense for the first year under straight-line and double-declining-balance methods in a financial statements model like the following one:

		Assets	=	Equity	Rev.	−	Exp.	=	Net Inc.	Cash Flow
Cash	+	Book Value of Comp. Sys.	=	Ret. Earn.						

c. Prepare the journal entries to recognize depreciation for each of the five years, assuming that the company uses

(1) Straight-line depreciation.

(2) Double-declining-balance depreciation.

Exercise 8-11A ***Effect of the disposal of plant assets on the financial statements*** **LO 8-5**

Un Company sold office equipment with a cost of $23,000 and accumulated depreciation of $12,000 for $14,000.

Required

a. What is the book value of the asset at the time of sale?

b. What is the amount of gain or loss on the disposal?

c. How would the sale affect net income (increase, decrease, no effect) and by how much?

d. How would the sale affect the amount of total assets shown on the balance sheet (increase, decrease, no effect) and by how much?

e. How would the event affect the statement of cash flows (inflow, outflow, no effect) and in what section?

LO 8-5

Exercise 8-12A *Effect of gains and losses on the accounting equation and financial statements*

On January 1, 2016, Prairie Enterprises purchased a parcel of land for $28,000 cash. At the time of purchase, the company planned to use the land for a warehouse site. In 2018, Prairie Enterprises changed its plans and sold the land.

Required

a. Assume that the land was sold for $29,500 in 2018.
   (1) Show the effect of the sale on the accounting equation.
   (2) What amount would Prairie report on the 2018 income statement related to the sale of the land?
   (3) What amount would Prairie report on the 2018 statement of cash flows related to the sale of the land?

b. Assume that the land was sold for $24,000 in 2018.
   (1) Show the effect of the sale on the accounting equation.
   (2) What amount would Prairie report on the 2018 income statement related to the sale of the land?
   (3) What amount would Prairie report on the 2018 statement of cash flows related to the sale of the land?

LO 8-3, 8-4

Exercise 8-13A *Double-declining-balance and units-of-production depreciation: gain or loss on disposal*

Exact Photo Service purchased a new color printer at the beginning of 2016 for $38,000. The printer is expected to have a four-year useful life and a $3,500 salvage value. The expected print production is estimated at 1,500,000 pages. Actual print production for the four years was as follows:

2016	390,000
2017	410,000
2018	420,000
2019	300,000
Total	1,520,000

The printer was sold at the end of 2019 for $1,650.

Required

a. Compute the depreciation expense for each of the four years, using double-declining-balance depreciation.

b. Compute the depreciation expense for each of the four years, using units-of-production depreciation.

c. Calculate the amount of gain or loss from the sale of the asset under each of the depreciation methods.

LO 8-6

Exercise 8-14A *Computing depreciation for tax purposes*

Crossroads Eye Care Company purchased $60,000 of equipment on March 1, 2016.

Required

a. Compute the amount of depreciation expense that is deductible under MACRS for 2016 and 2017, assuming that the equipment is classified as seven-year property.

b. Compute the amount of depreciation expense that is deductible under MACRS for 2016 and 2017, assuming that the equipment is classified as five-year property.

Exercise 8-15A *Revision of estimated useful life* LO 8-7

On January 1, 2016, Poultry Processing Company purchased a freezer and related installation equipment for $42,000. The equipment had a three-year estimated life with a $3,000 salvage value. Straight-line depreciation was used. At the beginning of 2018, Poultry Processing revised the expected life of the asset to four years rather than three years. The salvage value was revised to $2,000.

Required

Compute the depreciation expense for each of the four years, 2016–2019.

Exercise 8-16A *Distinguishing between revenue expenditures and capital expenditures* LO 8-8

Bill's Wrecker Service has just completed a minor repair on a tow truck. The repair cost was $1,550, and the book value prior to the repair was $6,500. In addition, the company spent $12,000 to replace the roof on a building. The new roof extended the life of the building by five years. Prior to the roof replacement, the general ledger reflected the Building account at $85,000 and related Accumulated Depreciation account at $32,000.

Required

After the work was completed, what book value should appear on the balance sheet for the tow truck and the building?

Exercise 8-17A *Effect of revenue expenditures versus capital expenditures on financial statements* LO 8-8

Sellers Construction Company purchased a compressor for $28,000 cash. It had an estimated useful life of four years and a $4,000 salvage value. At the beginning of the third year of use, the company spent an additional $6,000 related to the equipment. The company's financial condition just prior to this expenditure is shown in the following statements model:

Assets			=	Equity			Rev.	–	Exp.	=	Net Inc.	Cash Flow
Cash	+	Book Value of Compressor	=	Com. Stk.	+	Ret. Earn.						
45,000	+	16,000	=	40,000	+	21,000	NA	–	NA	=	NA	NA

Required

Record the $6,000 expenditure in the statements model under each of the following *independent* assumptions:

a. The expenditure was for routine maintenance.

b. The expenditure extended the compressor's life.

c. The expenditure improved the compressor's operating capacity.

Exercise 8-18A *Effect of revenue expenditures versus capital expenditures on financial statements* LO 8-8

On January 1, 2016, Webb Construction Company overhauled four cranes resulting in a slight increase in the life of the cranes. Such overhauls occur regularly at two-year intervals and have been treated as maintenance expense in the past. Management is considering whether to capitalize this year's $22,000 cash cost in the Cranes asset account or to expense it as a maintenance expense. Assume that the cranes have a remaining useful life of two years and no expected salvage value. Assume straight-line depreciation.

Required

a. Determine the amount of additional depreciation expense Webb would recognize in 2016 and 2017 if the cost were capitalized in the Cranes account.

b. Determine the amount of expense Webb would recognize in 2016 and 2017 if the cost were recognized as maintenance expense.

c. Determine the effect of the overhaul on cash flow from operating activities for 2016 and 2017 if the cost were capitalized and expensed through depreciation charges.

d. Determine the effect of the overhaul on cash flow from operating activities for 2016 and 2017 if the cost were recognized as maintenance expense.

LO 8-9

Exercise 8-19A *Computing and recording depletion expense*

Colorado Mining paid $600,000 to acquire a mine with 40,000 tons of coal reserves. The following statements model reflects Colorado Mining's financial condition just prior to purchasing the coal reserves. The company extracted 15,000 tons of coal in year 1 and 18,000 tons in year 2.

Assets			=	Equity			Rev.	−	Exp.	=	Net Inc.	Cash Flow
Cash	+	Coal Res.	=	Com. Stk.	+	Ret. Earn.						
800,000	+	NA	=	800,000	+	NA	NA	−	NA	=	NA	NA

Required

a. Compute the depletion charge per unit.

b. Record the acquisition of the coal reserves and the depletion expense for years 1 and 2 in a financial statements model like the preceding one.

c. Prepare the general journal entries to record the depletion expense for years 1 and 2.

LO 8-10, 8-11

Exercise 8-20A *Computing and recording the amortization of intangibles*

Dynamo Manufacturing paid cash to acquire the assets of an existing company. Among the assets acquired were the following items:

Patent with 4 remaining years of legal life	$40,000
Goodwill	35,000

Dynamo's financial condition just prior to the acquisition of these assets is shown in the following statements model:

Assets					=	Liab.	+	Equity	Rev.	−	Exp.	=	Net Inc.	Cash Flow
Cash	+	Patent	+	Goodwill										
90,000	+	NA	+	NA	=	NA	+	90,000	NA	−	NA	=	NA	NA

Required

a. Compute the annual amortization expense for these items.

b. Record the acquisition of the intangible assets and the related amortization expense for year 1 in a horizontal statements model like the one shown above.

c. Prepare the journal entries to record the acquisition of the intangible assets and the related amortization for year 1.

LO 8-10

Exercise 8-21A *Computing and recording goodwill*

Arizona Corp. acquired the business Data Systems for $320,000 cash and assumed all liabilities at the date of purchase. Data's books showed tangible assets of $260,000, liabilities of $40,000, and stockholders' equity of $220,000. An appraiser assessed the fair market value of the tangible assets at $250,000 at the date of acquisition. Arizona Corp.'s financial condition just prior to the acquisition is shown in the following statements model:

Assets					=	Liab.	+	Equity	Rev.	−	Exp.	=	Net Inc.	Cash Flow
Cash	+	Tang. Assets	+	Goodwill										
450,000	+	NA	+	NA	=	NA	+	450,000	NA	−	NA	=	NA	NA

Required

a. Compute the amount of goodwill acquired.

b. Record the acquisition in a financial statements model like the preceding one.

c. When will the goodwill be written off under the impairment rules?

d. Record the acquisition in general journal format.

Exercise 8-22A *R&D costs GAAP vs IFRS*

IFRS

The Naples Corp. incurred $2,500,000 of research cost and $1,700,000 of development cost during 2016.

Required

a. Determine the amount of expense recognized on the 2016 income statement assuming Naples uses U.S. GAAP.

b. Determine the amount of expense recognized on the 2016 income statement assuming Naples uses IFRS.

Exercise 8-23A *Accounting for land and buildings under IFRS*

IFRS

Assume the following. Pescara Company purchased a parcel of land on January 1, 2012, for $600,000. It constructed a building on the land at a cost of $3,000,000. The building was occupied on January 1, 2015, and is expected to have a useful life of 40 years and an estimated salvage value of $1,000,000.

As of December 31, 2016, and 2017, the fair value of the land had not been formally revalued because the real estate market had not changed significantly. Due to a jump in real estate prices, during 2018 the value of the land had increased to $650,000, and the fair value of the building was $3,000,000. The salvage value of the building is still estimated at $1,000,000. The land and the building were reevaluated by the company in 2018.

Required

a. Under U.S. accounting rules, what amount would be reported on the company's 2017 and 2018 balance sheets for the land and for the building? Show any necessary computations.

b. Under U.S. accounting rules, what amount of depreciation expense would be reported in 2018 for the building? Show any necessary computations.

c. Under the IFRS revaluation model, what amount would be reported on the company's 2017 and 2018 balance sheets for the land and for the building? Show any necessary computations.

d. Under the IFRS revaluation model, what amount of depreciation expense would be reported in 2018 for the building? Show any necessary computations.

PROBLEMS—SERIES A

connect plus+ ACCOUNTING ***All applicable Problems in Series A are available with McGraw-Hill's Connect Plus Accounting.***

Problem 8-24A *Accounting for acquisition of assets including a basket purchase*

LO 8-1

CHECK FIGURES

Total cost of equipment: $62,800

Cost allocated to copier: $16,500

Trinkle Co., Inc., made several purchases of long-term assets in 2016. The details of each purchase are presented here.

New Office Equipment

1. List price: $60,000; terms: 2/10 n/30; paid within discount period.
2. Transportation-in: $1,500.

3. Installation: $2,500.
4. Cost to repair damage during unloading: $650.
5. Routine maintenance cost after six months: $350.

Basket Purchase of Copier, Computer, and Scanner for $30,000 with Fair Market Values

1. Copier, $22,000.
2. Computer, $10,000.
3. Scanner, $8,000.

Land for New Warehouse with an Old Building Torn Down

1. Purchase price, $250,000.
2. Demolition of building, $18,000.
3. Lumber sold from old building, $6,000.
4. Grading in preparation for new building, $22,000.
5. Construction of new building, $510,000.

Required

In each of these cases, determine the amount of cost to be capitalized in the asset accounts.

LO 8-2, 8-5

Problem 8-25A *Accounting for depreciation over multiple accounting cycles: straight-line depreciation*

CHECK FIGURES
Net Income, 2016: $16,100
Total Assets, 2019: $137,900

Bensen Company started business by acquiring $60,000 cash from the issue of common stock on January 1, 2016. The cash acquired was immediately used to purchase equipment for $50,000 that had a $10,000 salvage value and an expected useful life of four years. The equipment was used to produce the following revenue stream (assume that all revenue transactions are for cash). At the beginning of the fifth year, the equipment was sold for $8,800 cash. Bensen uses straight-line depreciation.

	2016	2017	2018	2019	2020
Revenue	$26,100	$28,500	$32,000	$31,300	$0

Required

Prepare income statements, statements of changes in stockholders' equity, balance sheets, and statements of cash flows for each of the five years. Present the statements in the form of a vertical statements model.

LO 8-2, 8-3, 8-7, 8-8

Problem 8-26A *Purchase and use of tangible asset: three accounting cycles, straight-line depreciation*

CHECK FIGURES
Net Income, 2016: $34,100
Total Assets, 2018: $174,450

The following transactions relate to Academy Towing Service. Assume the transactions for the purchase of the wrecker and any capital improvements occur on January 1 of each year.

2016

1. Acquired $70,000 cash from the issue of common stock.
2. Purchased a used wrecker for $32,000. It has an estimated useful life of three years and a $5,000 salvage value.
3. Paid sales tax on the wrecker of $3,000.
4. Collected $56,100 in towing fees.
5. Paid $12,000 for gasoline and oil.
6. Recorded straight-line depreciation on the wrecker for 2016.
7. Closed the revenue and expense accounts to Retained Earnings at the end of 2016.

2017

1. Paid for a tune-up for the wrecker's engine, $900.
2. Bought four new tires, $1,250.

3. Collected $62,000 in towing fees.
4. Paid $18,000 for gasoline and oil.
5. Recorded straight-line depreciation for 2017.
6. Closed the revenue and expense accounts to Retained Earnings at the end of 2017.

2018

1. Paid to overhaul the wrecker's engine, $4,800, which extended the life of the wrecker to a total of four years. The salvage value did not change.
2. Paid for gasoline and oil, $19,100.
3. Collected $65,000 in towing fees.
4. Recorded straight-line depreciation for 2018.
5. Closed the revenue and expense accounts at the end of 2018.

Required

a. Use a horizontal statements model like the following one to show the effect of these transactions on the elements of financial statements. Use + for increase, − for decrease, and NA for not affected. The first event is recorded as an example.

2016 Event No.	Assets	=	Liabilities	+	Equity	Net Inc.	Cash Flow
1	+		NA		+	NA	+ FA

b. For each year, record the transactions in general journal form and post them to T-accounts.

c. Use a vertical model to present financial statements for 2016, 2017, and 2018.

Problem 8-27A *Calculating depreciation expense using four different methods*

LO 8-2, 8-3, 8-4, 8-6

CHECK FIGURES
a. Depreciation Expense, 2016: $14,000
d. Depreciation Expense, 2017: $18,123

Banko Inc. manufactures sporting goods. The following information applies to a machine purchased on January 1, 2016:

Purchase price	$ 70,000
Delivery cost	$ 3,000
Installation charge	$ 1,000
Estimated life	5 years
Estimated units	140,000
Salvage estimate	$ 4,000

During 2016, the machine produced 36,000 units and during 2017, it produced 38,000 units.

Required

Determine the amount of depreciation expense for 2016 and 2017 using each of the following methods:

a. Straight-line.
b. Double-declining-balance.
c. Units of production.
d. MACRS, assuming that the machine is classified as seven-year property.

Problem 8-28A *Effect of straight-line versus double-declining-balance depreciation on the recognition of expense and gains or losses*

LO 8-2, 8-3, 8-5

Becker Office Service purchased a new computer system in 2016 for $40,000. It is expected to have a five-year useful life and a $5,000 salvage value. The company expects to use the system more extensively in the early years of its life.

CHECK FIGURES
a. Depreciation Expense, Year 2: $7,000
b. Depreciation Expense, Year 2: $9,600

Required

a. Calculate the depreciation expense for each of the five years, assuming the use of straight-line depreciation.
b. Calculate the depreciation expense for each of the five years, assuming the use of double-declining-balance depreciation.
c. Would the choice of one depreciation method over another produce a different amount of cash flow for any year? Why or why not?
d. Assume that Becker Office Service sold the computer system at the end of the fourth year for $15,000. Compute the amount of gain or loss using each depreciation method.
e. Explain any differences in gain or loss due to using the different methods.

LO 8-4, 8-5

Problem 8-29A *Computing and recording units-of-production depreciation*

Sabel Co. purchased assembly equipment for $500,000 on January 1, 2016. Sabel's financial condition immediately prior to the purchase is shown in the following horizontal statements model:

Assets			=	Equity			Rev.	−	Exp.	=	Net Inc.	Cash Flow
Cash	+	Book Value of Equip.	=	Com. Stk.	+	Ret. Earn.						
800,000	+	NA	=	800,000	+	NA	NA	−	NA	=	NA	NA

CHECK FIGURES
a. Depreciation Expense, 2016: $134,400
c. Gain on Sale: $600

The equipment is expected to have a useful life of 200,000 machine hours and a salvage value of $20,000. Actual machine-hour use was as follows:

2016	56,000
2017	61,000
2018	42,000
2019	36,000
2020	10,000

Required

a. Compute the depreciation for each of the five years, assuming the use of units-of-production depreciation.
b. Assume that Sabel earns $230,000 of cash revenue during 2016. Record the purchase of the equipment and the recognition of the revenue and the depreciation expense for the first year in a financial statements model like the preceding one.
c. Assume that Sabel sold the equipment at the end of the fifth year for $20,600. Record the general journal entry for the sale.

LO 8-2, 8-3, 8-4

Problem 8-30A *Determining the effect of depreciation expense on financial statements*

CHECK FIGURES
a. Company A, Net Income: $28,750
c. Company C, Book Value: $16,700

Three different companies each purchased trucks on January 1, 2016, for $50,000. Each truck was expected to last four years or 200,000 miles. Salvage value was estimated to be $5,000. All three trucks were driven 66,000 miles in 2016, 42,000 miles in 2017, 40,000 miles in 2018, and 60,000 miles in 2019. Each of the three companies earned $40,000 of cash revenue during each of the four years. Company A uses straight-line depreciation, company B uses double-declining-balance depreciation, and company C uses units-of-production depreciation.

Required

Answer each of the following questions. Ignore the effects of income taxes.

a. Which company will report the highest amount of net income for 2016?
b. Which company will report the lowest amount of net income for 2019?
c. Which company will report the highest book value on the December 31, 2018, balance sheet?

d. Which company will report the highest amount of retained earnings on the December 31, 2019, balance sheet?

e. Which company will report the lowest amount of cash flow from operating activities on the 2018 statement of cash flows?

Problem 8-31A *Accounting for depletion*

LO 8-7, 8-9

Flannery Company engages in the exploration and development of many types of natural resources. In the last two years, the company has engaged in the following activities:

Jan. 1, 2016	Purchased for $1,500,000 a silver mine estimated to contain 100,000 tons of silver ore.
July 1, 2016	Purchased for $1,700,000 a tract of timber estimated to yield 1,000,000 board feet of lumber and the residual value of the land was estimated at $100,000.
Feb. 1, 2017	Purchased for $2,700,000 a gold mine estimated to yield 50,000 tons of gold-veined ore.
Sept. 1, 2017	Purchased oil reserves for $1,300,000. The reserves were estimated to contain 270,000 barrels of oil, of which 10,000 would be unprofitable to pump.

CHECK FIGURES
a. Silver Mine Depletion, 2016: $210,000
b. Total Natural Resources: $4,844,000

Required

a. Prepare the journal entries to account for the following:

(1) The 2016 purchases.

(2) Depletion on the 2016 purchases, assuming that 14,000 tons of silver were mined and 500,000 board feet of lumber were cut.

(3) The 2017 purchases.

(4) Depletion on the four natural resource assets, assuming that 20,000 tons of silver ore, 300,000 board feet of lumber, 4,000 tons of gold ore, and 50,000 barrels of oil were extracted.

b. Prepare the portion of the December 31, 2017, balance sheet that reports natural resources.

c. Assume that in 2018 the estimates changed to reflect only 20,000 tons of gold ore remaining. Prepare the depletion journal entry in 2018 to account for the extraction of 10,000 tons of gold ore.

Problem 8-32A *Recording continuing expenditures for plant assets*

LO 8-2, 8-8

Morris Inc. recorded the following transactions over the life of a piece of equipment purchased in 2016:

Jan. 1, 2016	Purchased equipment for $90,000 cash. The equipment was estimated to have a five-year life and $5,000 salvage value and was to be depreciated using the straight-line method.
Dec. 31, 2016	Recorded depreciation expense for 2016.
Sept. 30, 2017	Undertook routine repairs costing $900.
Dec. 31, 2017	Recorded depreciation expense for 2017.
Jan. 1, 2018	Made an adjustment costing $2,500 to the equipment. It improved the quality of the output but did not affect the life and salvage value estimates.
Dec. 31, 2018	Recorded depreciation expense for 2018.
June 1, 2019	Incurred $850 cost to oil and clean the equipment.
Dec. 31, 2019	Recorded depreciation expense for 2019.
Jan. 1, 2020	Had the equipment completely overhauled at a cost of $9,000. The overhaul was estimated to extend the total life to seven years. The salvage value did not change.
Dec. 31, 2020	Recorded depreciation expense for 2020.
Oct. 1, 2021	Received and accepted an offer of $19,000 for the equipment.

CHECK FIGURES
b. 2018 Depreciation Expense: $17,833
d. Gain on sale: $2,820

Required

a. Use a horizontal statements model like the following one to show the effects of these transactions on the elements of the financial statements. Use + for increase, − for decrease, and NA for not affected. The first event is recorded as an example.

Date	Assets	=	Liabilities	+	Equity	Net Inc.	Cash Flow
Jan. 1, 2016	+ −		NA		NA	NA	− IA

b. Determine the amount of depreciation expense to be reported on the income statements for the years 2016 through 2020.

c. Determine the book value (cost − accumulated depreciation) Morris will report on the balance sheets at the end of the years 2016 through 2021.

d. Determine the amount of the gain or loss Morris will report on the disposal of the equipment on October 1, 2021.

e. Prepare the journal entry for the disposal of the equipment on October 1, 2021.

LO 8-2, 8-8

CHECK FIGURE
b. Depreciation Expense: $8,000

Problem 8-33A *Continuing expenditures with statements model*

Tower Company owned a service truck that was purchased at the beginning of 2016 for $31,000. It had an estimated life of three years and an estimated salvage value of $4,000. Tower Company uses straight-line depreciation. Its financial condition as of January 1, 2018, is shown in the following financial statements model:

Assets			=	Equity			Rev.	−	Exp.	=	Net Inc.	Cash Flow
Cash	+	Book Value of Truck	=	Com. Stk.	+	Ret. Earn.						
20,000	+	13,000	=	9,000	+	24,000	NA	−	NA	=	NA	NA

In 2018, Tower Company spent the following amounts on the truck:

Jan. 4	Overhauled the engine for $6,000. The estimated life was extended one additional year, and the salvage value was revised to $3,000.
July 6	Obtained oil change and transmission service, $250.
Aug. 7	Replaced the fan belt and battery, $350.
Dec. 31	Purchased gasoline for the year, $7,500.
31	Recognized 2018 depreciation expense.

Required

a. Record the 2018 transactions in a statements model like the preceding one.

b. Prepare journal entries for the 2018 transactions.

LO 8-10

CHECK FIGURE
b. Depletion Expense: $4,000

Problem 8-34A *Accounting for intangible assets*

Mitre Company acquired Midwest Transportation Co. for $1,400,000. The fair market values of the assets acquired were as follows. No liabilities were assumed.

Equipment	$510,000
Land	150,000
Building	520,000
Franchise (10-year life)	40,000

Required

a. Calculate the amount of goodwill acquired.

b. Prepare the journal entry to record the amortization of the franchise fee at the end of year 1.

LO 8-11

Problem 8-35A *Accounting for goodwill*

Rossie Equipment Manufacturing Co. acquired the assets of Alba Inc., a competitor, in 2016. It recorded goodwill of $70,000 at acquisition. Because of defective machinery Alba had produced prior to the acquisition, it has been determined that all of the acquired goodwill has been permanently impaired.

Required

Prepare the journal entry to record the permanent impairment of the goodwill.

EXERCISES—SERIES B

Unless specifically included, ignore income tax considerations in all exercises and problems.

Exercise 8-1B *Long-term operational assets used in a business* LO 8-1

Required

Give some examples of long-term operational assets that each of the following companies is likely to own: *(a)* Sears, *(b)* Princess Cruise Lines, *(c)* Southwest Airlines, and *(d)* Harley-Davidson Co.

Exercise 8-2B *Identifying long-term operational assets* LO 8-1

Required

Which of the following items should be classified as long-term operational assets?

a. Cash
b. Buildings
c. Production machinery
d. Accounts receivable
e. Prepaid rent
f. Franchise
g. Inventory
h. Patent
i. Tract of timber
j. Land
k. Computer
l. Goodwill

Exercise 8-3B *Classifying tangible and intangible assets* LO 8-1

Required

Identify each of the following long-term operational assets as either tangible (T) or intangible (I).

a. Retail store building
b. Shelving for inventory
c. Trademark
d. Gas well
e. Drilling rig
f. FCC license for TV station
g. 18-wheel truck
h. Timber
i. Log loader
j. Dental chair
k. Goodwill
l. Computer software

Exercise 8-4B *Determining the cost of an asset* LO 8-1

Oregon Logging Co. purchased an electronic saw to cut various types and sizes of logs. The saw had a list price of $160,000. The seller agreed to allow a 5 percent discount because Oregon paid cash. Delivery terms were FOB shipping point. Freight cost amounted to $3,200. Oregon had to hire an individual to operate the saw. Oregon had to build a special platform to mount the saw. The cost of the platform was $2,500. The saw operator was paid an annual salary of $50,000. The cost of the company's theft insurance policy increased by $1,800 per year as a result of acquiring of the saw. The saw had a five-year useful life and an expected salvage value of $25,000.

Required

a. Determine the amount to be capitalized in an asset account for the purchase of the saw.
b. Record the purchase in general journal format.

Exercise 8-5B *Allocating costs on the basis of relative market values* LO 8-1

Florida Company purchased a building and the land on which the building is situated for a total cost of $800,000 cash. The land was appraised at $300,000 and the building at $700,000.

Required

a. What is the accounting term for this type of acquisition?
b. Determine the amount of the purchase cost to allocate to the land and the amount to allocate to the building.

c. Would the company recognize a gain on the purchase? Why or why not?

d. Record the purchase in a statements model like the following one:

Assets					=	Liab.	+	Equity	Rev.	−	Exp.	=	Net Inc.	Cash Flow
Cash	+	Land	+	Building										

e. Record the purchases in general journal format.

LO 8-1

Exercise 8-6B *Allocating costs for a basket purchase*

Usrey Company purchased a restaurant building, land, and equipment for $600,000 cash. The appraised value of the assets was as follows:

Land	$200,000
Building	480,000
Equipment	120,000
Total	$800,000

Required

a. Compute the amount to be recorded on the books for each of the assets.

b. Record the purchase in a horizontal statements model like the following one:

Assets							=	Liab.	+	Equity	Rev.	−	Exp.	=	Net Inc.	Cash Flow
Cash	+	Land	+	Building	+	Equip.										

c. Prepare the general journal entry to record the purchase.

LO 8-2

Exercise 8-7B *Effect of depreciation on the accounting equation and financial statements*

The following events apply to The Soda Shop for the 2016 fiscal year:

1. The company started when it acquired $20,000 cash from the issue of common stock.
2. Purchased a new ice cream machine that cost $20,000 cash.
3. Earned $36,000 in cash revenue.
4. Paid $21,000 cash for salaries expense.
5. Paid $6,000 cash for operating expenses.
6. Adjusted the records to reflect the use of the machine to make ice cream sodas. The machine, purchased on January 1, 2016, has an expected useful life of five years and an estimated salvage value of $5,000. Use straight-line depreciation. The adjusting entry was made as of December 31, 2016.

Required

a. Record the events in general journal format and post to T-accounts.

b. What amount of depreciation expense would The Soda Shop report on the 2017 income statement?

c. What amount of accumulated depreciation would The Soda Shop report on the December 31, 2017, balance sheet?

d. Would the cash flow from operating activities be affected by depreciation in 2017?

LO 8-3

Exercise 8-8B *Effect of double-declining-balance depreciation on financial statements*

Hinds Company started operations by acquiring $120,000 cash from the issue of common stock. On January 1, 2016, the company purchased equipment that cost $110,000 cash. The equipment had an expected useful life of five years and an estimated salvage value of $10,000. Hinds Company earned $85,000 and $72,000 of cash revenue during 2016 and 2017, respectively. Hinds Company uses double-declining-balance depreciation.

Required

Prepare income statements, balance sheets, and statements of cash flows for 2016 and 2017. Use a vertical statements format. (*Hint:* Record the events in T-accounts prior to preparing the statements.)

Exercise 8-9B *Events related to the acquisition, use, and disposal of a tangible plant asset: straight-line depreciation* LO 8-2, 8-5

Pete's Pizza purchased a delivery van on January 1, 2016, for $35,000. In addition, Pete's paid sales tax and title fees of $1,500 for the van. The van is expected to have a four-year life and a salvage value of $6,500.

Required

a. Using the straight-line method, compute the depreciation expense for 2016 and 2017.

b. Prepare the general journal entry to record the 2016 depreciation.

c. Assume the van was sold on January 1, 2019, for $21,000. Prepare the journal entry for the sale of the van in 2019.

Exercise 8-10B *Computing and recording straight-line versus double-declining-balance depreciation* LO 8-2, 8-3

At the beginning of 2016, Hill Manufacturing purchased a new computerized drill press for $75,000. It is expected to have a five-year life and a $15,000 salvage value.

Required

a. Compute the depreciation for each of the five years, assuming that the company uses

(1) Straight-line depreciation.

(2) Double-declining-balance depreciation.

b. Record the purchase of the drill press and the depreciation expense for the first year under the straight-line and double-declining-balance methods in a financial statements model like the following one:

		Assets	=	Equity	Rev.	−	Exp.	=	Net Inc.	Cash Flow
Cash	+	Book Value of Drill Press	=	Ret. Earn.						

c. Prepare the journal entries to recognize depreciation for each of the five years, assuming that the company uses

(1) Straight-line depreciation.

(2) Double-declining-balance depreciation.

Exercise 8-11B *Effect of the disposal of plant assets on the financial statements* LO 8-5

A plant asset with a cost of $50,000 and accumulated depreciation of $41,000 is sold for $10,000.

Required

a. What is the book value of the asset at the time of sale?

b. What is the amount of gain or loss on the disposal?

c. How would the sale affect net income (increase, decrease, no effect) and by how much?

d. How would the sale affect the amount of total assets shown on the balance sheet (increase, decrease, no effect) and by how much?

e. How would the event affect the statement of cash flows (inflow, outflow, no effect) and in what section?

LO 8-5

Exercise 8-12B *Effect of gains and losses on the accounting equation and financial statements*

On January 1, 2016, Heflin Enterprises purchased a parcel of land for $20,000 cash. At the time of purchase, the company planned to use the land for future expansion. In 2017, Heflin Enterprises changed its plans and sold the land.

Required

a. Assume that the land was sold for $22,500 in 2017.
   (1) Show the effect of the sale on the accounting equation.
   (2) What amount would Heflin report on the income statement related to the sale of the land?
   (3) What amount would Heflin report on the statement of cash flows related to the sale of the land?

b. Assume that the land was sold for $18,500 in 2017.
   (1) Show the effect of the sale on the accounting equation.
   (2) What amount would Heflin report on the income statement related to the sale of the land?
   (3) What amount would Heflin report on the statement of cash flows related to the sale of the land?

LO 8-3, 8-4

Exercise 8-13B *Double-declining-balance and units-of-production depreciation: gain or loss on disposal*

Design Service Co. purchased a new color copier at the beginning of 2016 for $47,000. The copier is expected to have a five-year useful life and a $7,000 salvage value. The expected copy production was estimated at 2,000,000 copies. Actual copy production for the five years was as follows:

2016	560,000
2017	490,000
2018	430,000
2019	350,000
2020	210,000
Total	2,040,000

The copier was sold at the end of 2020 for $7,600.

Required

a. Compute the depreciation expense for each of the five years, using double-declining-balance depreciation.

b. Compute the depreciation expense for each of the five years, using units-of-production depreciation. (Round cost per unit to three decimal places.)

c. Calculate the amount of gain or loss from the sale of the asset under each of the depreciation methods.

LO 8-6

Exercise 8-14B *Computing depreciation for tax purposes*

Ripley Lumber Company purchased $240,000 of equipment on September 1, 2016.

Required

a. Compute the amount of depreciation expense that is deductible under MACRS for 2016 and 2017, assuming that the equipment is classified as seven-year property.

b. Compute the amount of depreciation expense that is deductible under MACRS for 2016 and 2017, assuming that the equipment is classified as five-year property.

LO 8-7

Exercise 8-15B *Revision of estimated useful life*

On January 1, 2016, Mead Machining Co. purchased a compressor and related installation equipment for $72,500. The equipment had a three-year estimated life with a $12,500 salvage value. Straight-line depreciation was used. At the beginning of 2018, Mead revised the expected life of the asset to four years rather than three years. The salvage value was revised to $2,500.

Required

Compute the depreciation expense for each of the four years.

MCS

Exercise 8-16B *Distinguishing between revenue expenditures and capital expenditures*

LO 8-8

Efficient Shredding Service has just completed a minor repair on a shredding machine. The repair cost was $1,900, and the book value prior to the repair was $6,000. In addition, the company spent $12,000 to replace the roof on a building. The new roof extended the life of the building by five years. Prior to the roof replacement, the general ledger reflected the Building account at $110,000 and related Accumulated Depreciation account at $30,000.

Required

After the work was completed, what book value should Efficient have reported on the balance sheet for the shredding machine and the building?

Exercise 8-17B *Effect of revenue expenditures versus capital expenditures on financial statements*

LO 8-8

Ford Construction Company purchased a forklift for $150,000 cash. It had an estimated useful life of four years and a $10,000 salvage value. At the beginning of the third year of use, the company spent an additional $9,000 that was related to the forklift. The company's financial condition just prior to this expenditure is shown in the following statements model:

		Assets	=			Equity	Rev.	−	Exp.	=	Net Inc.	Cash Flow
Cash	+	Book Value of Forklift	=	Com. Stk.	+	Ret. Earn.						
15,000	+	80,000	=	45,000	+	50,000	NA	−	NA	=	NA	NA

Required

Record the $9,000 expenditure in the statements model under each of the following *independent* assumptions:

a. The expenditure was for routine maintenance.

b. The expenditure extended the forklift's life.

c. The expenditure improved the forklift's operating capacity.

Exercise 8-18B *Effect of revenue expenditures versus capital expenditures on financial statements*

LO 8-8

On January 1, 2016, Midstate Power Company overhauled four turbine engines that generate power for customers. The overhaul resulted in a slight increase in the capacity of the engines to produce power. Such overhauls occur regularly at two-year intervals and have been treated as maintenance expense in the past. Management is considering whether to capitalize this year's $22,000 cash cost in the engine asset account or to expense it as a maintenance expense. Assume that the engines have a remaining useful life of two years and no expected salvage value. Assume straight-line depreciation.

Required

a. Determine the amount of additional depreciation expense Midstate would recognize in 2016 and 2017 if the cost were capitalized in the Engine account.

b. Determine the amount of expense Midstate would recognize in 2016 and 2017 if the cost were recognized as maintenance expense.

c. Determine the effect of the overhaul on cash flow from operating activities for 2016 and 2017 if the cost were capitalized and expensed through depreciation charges.

d. Determine the effect of the overhaul on cash flow from operating activities for 2016 and 2017 if the cost were recognized as maintenance expense.

LO 8-9

Exercise 8-19B *Computing and recording depletion expense*

Fulton Sand and Gravel paid $800,000 to acquire 1,200,000 cubic yards of sand reserves. The following statements model reflects Fulton's financial condition just prior to purchasing the sand reserves. The company extracted 650,000 cubic yards of sand in year 1 and 450,000 cubic yards in year 2.

Assets			=	Equity			Rev.	−	Exp.	=	Net Inc.	Cash Flow
Cash	+	Sand Res.	=	Com. Stk.	+	Ret. Earn.						
900,000	+	NA	=	900,000	+	NA	NA	−	NA	=	NA	NA

Required

a. Compute the depletion charge per cubic yard.

b. Record the acquisition of the sand reserves and the depletion expense for years 1 and 2 in a financial statements model like the preceding one.

c. Prepare the general journal entries to record the depletion expense for years 1 and 2.

LO 8-10, 8-11

Exercise 8-20B *Computing and recording the amortization of intangibles*

Garth Manufacturing paid cash to acquire the assets of an existing company. Among the assets acquired were the following items:

Patent with 5 remaining years of legal life	$48,000
Goodwill	35,000

Garth's financial condition just prior to the purchase of these assets is shown in the following statements model:

Assets					=	Liab.	+	Equity	Rev.	−	Exp.	=	Net Inc.	Cash Flow
Cash	+	Patent	+	Goodwill										
94,000	+	NA	+	NA	=	NA	+	94,000	NA	−	NA	=	NA	NA

Required

a. Compute the annual amortization expense for these items if applicable.

b. Record the acquisition of the intangible assets and the related amortization expense for year 1 in a horizontal statements model like the preceding one.

c. Prepare the journal entries to record the acquisition of the intangible assets and the related amortization for year 1.

LO 8-10

Exercise 8-21B *Computing and recording goodwill*

Horn Co. acquired the business Medical Supply Co. for $275,000 cash and assumed all liabilities at the date of acquisition. Medical's books showed tangible assets of $250,000, liabilities of $10,000, and equity of $240,000. An appraiser assessed the fair market value of the tangible assets at $265,000 at the date of acquisition. Horn's financial condition just prior to the acquisition is shown in the following statements model:

Assets					=	Liab.	+	Equity	Rev.	−	Exp.	=	Net Inc.	Cash Flow
Cash	+	Tang. Assets	+	Goodwill										
450,000	+	NA	+	NA	=	NA	+	450,000	NA	−	NA	=	NA	NA

Required

a. Compute the amount of goodwill acquired.

b. Record the acquisition in a financial statements model like the preceding one.

c. Record the acquisition in general journal format.

Exercise 8-22B *Depreciable assets under IFRS*

IFRS

The Transnational Business Inc. (TBI) purchased an asset that cost $60,000 on January 1, 2016. The asset had a four-year useful life and a $10,000 salvage value.

Required

a. Determine the amount of expense recognized on the 2016 income statement assuming TBI uses U.S. GAAP.

b. Determine the amount of expense or gain recognized on the income statement assuming TBI uses the IFRS revaluation model and the asset is determined to have a fair value of $55,000 as of December 31, 2016.

c. Determine the amount of expense or gain recognized on the income statement assuming TBI uses the IFRS revaluation model and the asset is determined to have a fair value of $65,000 as of December 31, 2016.

Exercise 8-23B *Accounting for land and buildings under IFRS*

IFRS

Assume the following. Madrid Company purchased a parcel of land on January 1, 2012, for $400,000. It constructed a building on the land at a cost of $2,000,000. The building was occupied on January 1, 2015, and is expected to have a useful life of 40 years and an estimated salvage value of $600,000.

As of December 31, 2016 and 2017, the fair value of the land had not been formally revalued because the real estate market had not changed significantly. Due to a jump in real estate prices, during 2018 the value of the land had increased to $450,000, and the fair value of the building was $2,000,000. The salvage value of the building is still estimated at $600,000. The land and the building were reevaluated by the company in 2018.

Required

a. Under U.S. accounting rules, what amount would be reported on the company's 2017 and 2018 balance sheets for the land and for the building? Show any necessary computations.

b. Under U.S. accounting rules, what amount of depreciation expense would be reported in 2018 for the building? Show any necessary computations.

c. Under the IFRS revaluation model, what amount would be reported on the company's 2017 and 2018 balance sheets for the land and for the building? Show any necessary computations.

d. Under the IFRS revaluation model, what amount of depreciation expense would be reported in 2018 for the building? Show any necessary computations.

PROBLEMS—SERIES B

Problem 8-24B *Accounting for acquisition of assets including a basket purchase*

LO 8-1

Floyd Company made several purchases of long-term assets in 2016. The details of each purchase are presented here.

New Office Equipment

1. List price: $50,000; terms: 1/10 n/30; paid within the discount period.
2. Transportation-in: $1,200.
3. Installation: $1,000.
4. Cost to repair damage during unloading: $700.
5. Routine maintenance cost after eight months: $240.

Basket Purchase of Office Furniture, Copier, Computers, and Laser Printers for $70,000 with Fair Market Values

1. Office furniture, $48,000.
2. Copier, $12,000.
3. Computers and printers, $20,000.

Land for New Headquarters with Old Barn Torn Down

1. Purchase price, $100,000.
2. Demolition of barn, $7,000.
3. Lumber sold from old barn, $2,000.
4. Grading in preparation for new building, $11,000.
5. Construction of new building, $310,000.

Required

In each of these cases, determine the amount of cost to be capitalized in the asset accounts.

LO 8-2, 8-5

Problem 8-25B *Accounting for depreciation over multiple accounting cycles: straight-line depreciation*

Scott Company began operations when it acquired $40,000 cash from the issue of common stock on January 1, 2016. The cash acquired was immediately used to purchase equipment for $40,000 that had a $4,000 salvage value and an expected useful life of four years. The equipment was used to produce the following revenue stream (assume all revenue transactions are for cash). At the beginning of the fifth year, the equipment was sold for $4,500 cash. Scott uses straight-line depreciation.

	2016	2017	2018	2019	2020
Revenue	$9,500	$10,000	$10,500	$8,500	$0

Required

Prepare income statements, statements of changes in stockholders' equity, balance sheets, and statements of cash flows for each of the five years.

LO 8-2, 8-3, 8-7, 8-8

Problem 8-26B *Purchase and use of tangible asset: three accounting cycles, double-declining-balance depreciation*

The following transactions pertain to Accounting Solutions Inc. Assume the transactions for the purchase of the computer and any capital improvements occur on January 1 each year.

2016

1. Acquired $80,000 cash from the issue of common stock.
2. Purchased a computer system for $35,000. It has an estimated useful life of five years and a $5,000 salvage value.
3. Paid $2,450 sales tax on the computer system.
4. Collected $65,000 in fees from clients.
5. Paid $1,500 in fees to service the computers.
6. Recorded double-declining-balance depreciation on the computer system for 2016.
7. Closed the revenue and expense accounts to Retained Earnings at the end of 2016.

2017

1. Paid $1,000 for repairs to the computer system.
2. Bought off-site backup services to maintain the computer system, $1,500.
3. Collected $68,000 in fees from clients.
4. Paid $1,500 in fees to service the computers.
5. Recorded double-declining-balance depreciation for 2017.
6. Closed the revenue and expense accounts to Retained Earnings at the end of 2017.

2018

1. Paid $6,000 to upgrade the computer system, which extended the total life of the system to six years. The salvage value did not change.
2. Paid $1,200 in fees to service the computers.
3. Collected $70,000 in fees from clients.
4. Recorded double-declining-balance depreciation for 2018.
5. Closed the revenue and expense accounts at the end of 2018.

Required

a. Use a horizontal statements model like the following one to show the effect of these transactions on the elements of the financial statements. Use + for increase, − for decrease, and NA for not affected. The first event is recorded as an example.

2016 Event No.	Assets	=	Liabilities	+	Equity	Net Inc.	Cash Flow
1	+		NA		+	NA	+ FA

b. For each year, record the transactions in general journal form and post them to T-accounts.

c. Use a vertical model to present financial statements for 2016, 2017, and 2018.

Problem 8-27B *Calculating depreciation expense using four different methods*

LO 8-2, 8-3, 8-4, 8-6

Todd Service Company purchased a copier on January 1, 2016, for $25,000 and paid an additional $500 for delivery charges. The copier was estimated to have a life of four years or 1,000,000 copies. Salvage value was estimated at $1,500. The copier produced 250,000 copies in 2016 and 270,000 copies in 2017.

Required

Compute the amount of depreciation expense for the copier for calendar years 2016 and 2017, using these methods:

a. Straight-line.

b. Units-of-production.

c. Double-declining-balance.

d. MACRS, assuming that the copier is classified as five-year property.

Problem 8-28B *Effect of straight-line versus double-declining-balance depreciation on the recognition of expense and gains or losses*

LO 8-2, 8-3, 8-5

National Laundry Services purchased a new steam press on January 1, for $42,000. It is expected to have a five-year useful life and a $4,000 salvage value. National expects to use the steam press more extensively in the early years of its life.

Required

a. Calculate the depreciation expense for each of the five years, assuming the use of straight-line depreciation.

b. Calculate the depreciation expense for each of the five years, assuming the use of double-declining-balance depreciation.

c. Would the choice of one depreciation method over another produce a different amount of cash flow for any year? Why or why not?

d. Assume that National Laundry Services sold the steam press at the end of the third year for $22,000. Compute the amount of gain or loss using each depreciation method.

Problem 8-29B *Computing and recording units-of-production depreciation*

LO 8-4, 8-5

Friendly Corporation purchased a delivery van for $28,500 in 2016. The firm's financial condition immediately prior to the purchase is shown in the following horizontal statements model:

Assets			=	Equity			Rev.	−	Exp.	=	Net Inc.	Cash Flow
Cash	+	Book Value of Van	=	Com. Stk.	+	Ret. Earn.						
50,000	+	NA	=	50,000	+	NA	NA	−	NA	=	NA	NA

The van was expected to have a useful life of 200,000 miles and a salvage value of $2,500. Actual mileage was as follows:

2016	60,000
2017	50,000
2018	55,000

Required

a. Compute the depreciation for each of the three years, assuming the use of units-of-production depreciation.

b. Assume that Friendly earns $26,000 of cash revenue during 2016. Record the purchase of the van and the recognition of the revenue and the depreciation expense for the first year in a financial statements model like the one shown above.

c. Assume that Friendly sold the van at the end of the third year for $8,000. Record the general journal entry for the sale.

LO 8-2, 8-3, 8-4

Problem 8-30B *Determining the effect of depreciation expense on financial statements*

Three different companies each purchased a machine on January 1, 2016, for $64,000. Each machine was expected to last five years or 200,000 hours. Salvage value was estimated to be $6,000. All three machines were operated for 50,000 hours in 2016, 55,000 hours in 2017, 40,000 hours in 2018, 44,000 hours in 2019, and 31,000 hours in 2020. Each of the three companies earned $30,000 of cash revenue during each of the five years. Company A uses straight-line depreciation, company B uses double-declining-balance depreciation, and company C uses units-of-production depreciation.

Required

Answer each of the following questions. Ignore the effects of income taxes.

a. Which company will report the highest amount of net income for 2016?

b. Which company will report the lowest amount of net income for 2018?

c. Which company will report the highest book value on the December 31, 2018, balance sheet?

d. Which company will report the highest amount of retained earnings on the December 31, 2019, balance sheet?

e. Which company will report the lowest amount of cash flow from operating activities on the 2018 statement of cash flows?

LO 8-7, 8-9

Problem 8-31B *Accounting for depletion*

Metals Exploration Corporation engages in the exploration and development of many types of natural resources. In the last two years, the company has engaged in the following activities:

Jan. 1, 2016	Purchased a coal mine estimated to contain 300,000 tons of coal for $900,000.
July 1, 2016	Purchased for $2,000,000 a tract of timber estimated to yield 3,000,000 board feet of lumber and to have a residual land value of $200,000.
Feb. 1, 2017	Purchased a silver mine estimated to contain 30,000 tons of silver for $850,000.
Aug. 1, 2017	Purchased for $875,000 oil reserves estimated to contain 270,000 barrels of oil, of which 20,000 would be unprofitable to pump.

Required

a. Prepare the journal entries to account for the following:

(1) The 2016 purchases.

(2) Depletion on the 2016 purchases, assuming that 80,000 tons of coal were mined and 1,000,000 board feet of lumber were cut.

(3) The 2017 purchases.

(4) Depletion on the four reserves, assuming that 68,000 tons of coal, 1,200,000 board feet of lumber, 9,000 tons of silver, and 80,000 barrels of oil were extracted.

b. Prepare the portion of the December 31, 2017, balance sheet that reports natural resources.

c. Assume that in 2018 the estimates changed to reflect only 50,000 tons of coal remaining. Prepare the depletion journal entry for 2018 to account for the extraction of 40,000 tons of coal.

Problem 8-32B *Recording continuing expenditures for plant assets* LO 8-2, 8-8

Tringle Inc. recorded the following transactions over the life of a piece of equipment purchased in 2016:

Jan. 1, 2016	Purchased the equipment for $38,000 cash. The equipment is estimated to have a five-year life and $3,000 salvage value and was to be depreciated using the straight-line method.
Dec. 31, 2016	Recorded depreciation expense for 2016.
May 5, 2017	Undertook routine repairs costing $900.
Dec. 31, 2017	Recorded depreciation expense for 2017.
Jan. 1, 2018	Made an adjustment costing $4,000 to the equipment. It improved the quality of the output but did not affect the life and salvage value estimates.
Dec. 31, 2018	Recorded depreciation expense for 2018.
Mar. 1, 2019	Incurred $410 cost to oil and clean the equipment.
Dec. 31, 2019	Recorded depreciation expense for 2019.
Jan. 1, 2020	Had the equipment completely overhauled at a cost of $9,000. The overhaul was estimated to extend the total life to seven years and revised the salvage value to $2,500.
Dec. 31, 2020	Recorded depreciation expense for 2020.
July 1, 2021	Sold the equipment for $8,500 cash.

Required

a. Use a horizontal statements model like the following one to show the effects of these transactions on the elements of the financial statements. Use + for increase, − for decrease, and NA for not affected. The first event is recorded as an example.

Date	Assets	=	Liabilities	+	Equity	Net Inc.	Cash Flow
Jan. 1, 2016	+ −		NA		NA	NA	− IA

b. Determine the amount of depreciation expense Tringle will report on the income statements for the years 2016 through 2020.

c. Determine the book value (cost − accumulated depreciation) Tringle will report on the balance sheets at the end of the years 2016 through 2020.

d. Determine the amount of the gain or loss Tringle will report on the disposal of the equipment on July 1, 2021.

e. Prepare the journal entry for the disposal of the equipment on July 1, 2021.

Problem 8-33B *Accounting for continuing expenditures* LO 8-2, 8-8

Delta Manufacturing paid $62,000 to purchase a computerized assembly machine on January 1, 2016. The machine had an estimated life of eight years and a $2,000 salvage value. Delta's financial condition as of January 1, 2019, is shown in the following financial statements model. Delta uses the straight-line method for depreciation.

Assets			=	Equity			Rev.	−	Exp.	=	Net Inc.	Cash Flow
Cash	+	Book Value of Mach.	=	Com. Stk.	+	Ret. Earn.						
15,000	+	39,500	=	10,500	+	44,000	NA	−	NA	=	NA	NA

Delta Manufacturing made the following expenditures on the computerized assembly machine in 2019:

Jan. 2	Added an overdrive mechanism for $8,000 that would improve the overall quality of the performance of the machine but would not extend its life. The salvage value was revised to $2,500.
Aug. 1	Performed routine maintenance, $1,250.
Oct. 2	Replaced some computer chips (considered routine), $800.
Dec. 31	Recognized 2019 depreciation expense.

Required

a. Record the 2019 transactions in a statements model like the preceding one.

b. Prepare journal entries for the 2019 transactions.

LO 8-10

Problem 8-34B *Accounting for intangible assets*

Doug's Diner acquired a fast-food restaurant for $1,500,000. The fair market values of the assets acquired were as follows. No liabilities were assumed.

Equipment	$380,000
Land	200,000
Building	680,000
Franchise (5-year life)	120,000

Required

a. Calculate the amount of goodwill acquired.

b. Prepare the journal entry to record the amortization of the franchise fee at the end of year 1.

LO 8-11

Problem 8-35B *Accounting for goodwill*

Bostick Co. acquired the assets of Belk Co. for $1,200,000 in 2016. The estimated fair market value of the assets at the acquisition date was $1,000,000. Goodwill of $200,000 was recorded at acquisition. In 2017, because of negative publicity, one-half of the goodwill acquired from Belk Co. was judged to be permanently impaired.

Required

a. How will Bostick account for the impairment of the goodwill?

b. Prepare the journal entry to record the permanent impairment of goodwill.

ANALYZE, THINK, COMMUNICATE

ATC 8-1 Business Applications Case *Understanding real-world annual reports*

Required

Use the Target Corporation's annual report in Appendix B to answer the following questions.

a. What method of depreciation does Target use?

b. What types of intangible assets does Target have?

c. What are the estimated lives that Target uses for the various types of long-term assets?

d. As of February 1, 2014 (2013 fiscal-year), what is the original cost of Target's: Land; Buildings and improvements; and Fixtures and equipment?

e. What was Target's depreciation expense and amortization expense for 2013?

ATC 8-2 Group Assignment *Different depreciation methods*

Sweet's Bakery makes cakes, pies, and other pastries that it sells to local grocery stores. The company experienced the following transactions during 2016.

1. Started business by acquiring $60,000 cash from the issue of common stock.
2. Purchased bakery equipment for $46,000.
3. Had sales in 2016 amounting to $42,000.

4. Paid $8,200 of cash for supplies which were all used during the year to make baked goods.
5. Incurred other operating expenses of $12,000 for 2016.
6. Recorded depreciation assuming the equipment had a four-year life and a $6,000 salvage value. The MACRS recovery period is five years.
7. Paid income tax. The rate is 30 percent.

Required

a. Organize the class into three sections and divide each section into groups of three to five students. Assign each section a depreciation method: straight-line, double-declining-balance, or MACRS.

Group Task

Prepare an income statement and balance sheet using the preceding information and the depreciation method assigned to your group.

Class Discussion

b. Have a representative of each section put its income statement on the board. Are there differences in net income? In the amount of income tax paid? How will these differences in the amount of depreciation expense change over the life of the equipment?

ATC 8-3 Real-World Case *Identifying companies based on financial statement information*

The following ratios are for four companies in different industries. Some of these ratios have been discussed in the textbook, others have not, but their names explain how the ratio was computed. These data are for the companies' 2013 fiscal years. The four sets of ratios, presented randomly are:

Ratio	Company 1	Company 2	Company 3	Company 4
Current assets ÷ Total assets	11%	10%	22%	81%
Average days to sell inventory	50 days	29 days	43 days	70 days
Average days to collect receivables	4 days	35 days	8 days	40 days
Return-on-assets	38%	4%	15%	6%
Gross margin	69%	58%	58%	27%
Sales ÷ Property, plant and equipment	1.9 times	3.0 times	19.8 times	6.4 times
Sales ÷ Number of full-time employees	$41,514	$339,921	$68,965	$522,014

The four companies to which these ratios relate, listed in alphabetical order, are:

Molson Coors Brewing Company is a company that produces beer and related products.

Darden Restaurants, Inc., operates approximately 2,150 restaurants under 10 different names, including Olive Garden, Red Lobster, and LongHorn Steakhouse.

Deere & Company is a company that manufactures heavy construction equipment.

Weight Watchers International, Inc., is a company that provides weight loss services and products. Its fiscal year-end was December 31, 2013, during which 49 percent of its revenues came from meeting fees, 20 percent from product sales, and 31 percent from online services.

Required

Determine which company should be matched with each set of ratios. Write a memorandum explaining the rationale for your decisions.

ATC 8-4 Business Applications Case *Performing ratio analysis using real-world data*

American Greetings Corporation manufactures and sells greeting cards and related items such as gift wrapping paper. CSX Corporation is one of the largest railway networks in the nation. The following data were taken from one of the companies' December 27, 2013, annual report and from the other's February 28, 2013, annual report. Revealing which data relate to which company was intentionally omitted. For one company, the dollar amounts are in thousands, while for the other they are in millions.

	Company 1	Company 2
Sales	$1,868,739	$12,026
Depreciation costs	44,326	1,104
Net earnings	49,918	1,864
Current assets	661,906	2,602
Property, plant, and equipment	372,452	27,291
Total assets	1,583,463	31,782

Required

a. Calculate depreciation costs as a percentage of sales for each company.

b. Calculate property, plant, and equipment as a percentage of total assets for each company.

c. Based on the information now available to you, decide which data relate to which company. Explain the rationale for your decision.

d. Which company appears to be using its assets most efficiently? Explain your answer.

ATC 8-5 Business Applications Case *Performing ratio analysis using real-world data*

Companies in the gas and oil business use a lot of property, plant, and equipment. Not only is there the significant investment they must make in equipment used to find, extract, and process the oil and natural gas, but they must also purchase the rights to the energy reserves themselves.

Chesapeake Energy Corporation claims to be "the second-largest producer of natural gas, a top 11 producer of liquids and the most active driller of wells in the U.S. We own interests in approximately 45,400 producing natural gas and oil wells . . ."

Anadarko Petroleum Corporation is a large independent exploration and production company in the gas and oil industry. In addition to its wells in seven U.S. states and the Gulf of Mexico, it has operations in 11 other countries around the world.

The following information was taken from the companies' December 31, 2013, annual reports. All dollar amounts are in millions.

	Chesapeake Energy Corporation	Anadarko Petroleum Corporation
Sales	$17,506	$14,581
Depreciation and depletion costs	2,903	3,927
Property, plant, and equipment (net of accumulated depreciation)	37,134	40,929
Total assets	41,782	55,781
Depreciation method	Straight-line	Straight-line
Depletion method	Units of production	Units of production
Estimated life of assets		
Buildings	10 to 39 years	up to 40 years
Machinery and equipment	3 to 20 years	3 to 15 years
Net income	$ 744*	$ 801

*Includes income attributable to noncontrolling interests.

Required

a. Calculate depreciation costs as a percentage of sales for each company.

b. Calculate property, plant, and equipment as a percentage of total assets for each company.

c. Based only on the percentages calculated in Requirements *a* and *b*, which company appears to be using its assets most efficiently? Explain your answer.

d. Calculate the return on assets ratio for each company. Based on this ratio, which company appears to be using its assets most efficiently? Explain your answer.

e. Identify some of the problems a financial analyst would encounter in comparing the use of long-term assets at Chesapeake versus Anadarko.

ATC 8-6 Writing Assignment *Impact of historical cost on asset presentation on the balance sheet*

Assume that you are examining the balance sheets of two companies and note the following information:

	Company A	Company B
Equipment	$1,130,000	$900,000
Accumulated Depreciation	(730,000)	(500,000)
Book Value	$ 400,000	$400,000

Maxie Smith, a student who has had no accounting courses, remarks that Company A and Company B have the same amount of equipment.

Required

In a short paragraph, explain to Maxie that the two companies do not have equal amounts of equipment. You may want to include in your discussion comments regarding the possible age of each company's equipment, the impact of the historical cost concept on balance sheet information, and the impact of different depreciation methods on book value.

ATC 8-7 Ethical Dilemma *What's an expense?*

Several years ago, Wilson Blowhard founded a communications company. The company became successful and grew by expanding its customer base and acquiring some of its competitors. In fact, most of its growth resulted from acquiring other companies. Mr. Blowhard is adamant about continuing the company's growth and increasing its net worth. To achieve these goals, the business's net income must continue to increase at a rapid pace.

If the company's net worth continues to rise, Mr. Blowhard plans to sell the company and retire. He is, therefore, focused on improving the company's profit any way he can.

In the communications business, companies often use the lines of other communications companies. This line usage is a significant operating expense for Mr. Blowhard's company. Generally accepted accounting principles require operating costs like line use to be expensed as they are incurred each year. Each dollar of line cost reduces net income by a dollar.

After reviewing the company's operations, Mr. Blowhard concluded that the company did not currently need all of the line use it was paying for. It was really paying the owner of the lines now so that the line use would be available in the future for all of Mr. Blowhard's expected new customers. Mr. Blowhard instructed his accountant to capitalize all of the line cost charges and depreciate them over 10 years. The accountant reluctantly followed Mr. Blowhard's instructions and the company's net income for the current year showed a significant increase over the prior year's net income. Mr. Blowhard had found a way to report continued growth in the company's net income and increase the value of the company.

Required

a. How does Mr. Blowhard's scheme affect the amount of income that the company would otherwise report in its financial statements and how does the scheme affect the company's balance sheet? Explain your answer.

b. Review the AICPA's Articles of Professional Conduct (see Chapter 2) and comment on any of the principles that were violated.

c. Review the elements of the fraud triangle (see Chapter 2) and comment on which of these features are evident in this case.

ATC 8-8 Research Assignment *Comparing Microsoft's and Intel's operational assets*

This chapter discussed how companies in different industries often use different proportions of current versus long-term assets to accomplish their business objective. The technology revolution resulting from the silicon microchip has often been led by two well-known companies: Microsoft and Intel. Although often thought of together, these companies are really very different. Using either the most current Forms 10-K or annual reports for Microsoft Corporation and Intel Corporation, complete the requirements below. Obtain the Forms 10-K using either the EDGAR system, following the instructions in Appendix A, or the company's website. Microsoft's annual report is available on its website; Intel's annual report is its Form 10-K.

Required

a. Fill in the missing data in the following table. The percentages must be computed; they are not included in the companies' 10-Ks. (*Note:* The percentages for current assets and property, plant, and equipment will not sum to 100.)

	Current Assets	Property, Plant, and Equipment	Total Assets
Microsoft			
Dollar Amount	$	$	$
% of Total Assets	%	%	100%
Intel			
Dollar Amount	$	$	$
% of Total Assets	%	%	100%

b. Briefly explain why these two companies have different percentages of their assets in current assets versus property, plant, and equipment.

ATC 8-9 Spreadsheet Assignment *Reporting to the IRS versus financial statement reporting*

Crist Company operates a lawn mowing service. Crist has chosen to depreciate its equipment for financial statement purposes using the straight-line method. However, to save cash in the short run, Crist has elected to use the MACRS method for income tax reporting purposes.

Required

a. Set up the following spreadsheet to reflect the two different methods of reporting. Notice that the first two years of revenues and operating expenses are provided.

b. Enter the effects of the following items for 2016.

(1) At the beginning of 2016, Crist purchased for $10,000 cash a lawn mower it expects to use for five years. Salvage value is estimated to be $2,000. As stated, Crist uses the straight-line method of depreciation for financial statement purposes and the MACRS method for income tax purposes. Use formulas to calculate depreciation expense for each method.

(2) No equipment was sold during 2016; therefore, no gain or loss would be reported this year.

(3) The income tax rate is 30 percent. For simplicity, assume that the income tax payable was paid in 2016.

(4) Complete the schedules for income reporting, reporting of equipment, and reporting of cash flows for 2016. Use formulas for all calculations.

c. Enter the effects of the following items for 2017.

(1) Crist used the mower for the entire 2017 year. Enter 2017 depreciation expense amounts for the income reporting section of your spreadsheet.

(2) At December 31, Crist sold the lawn mower for $7,000. Calculate the gain or loss on the sale for the income reporting section. Use formulas to make the calculations.

(3) The income tax rate is 30 percent. For simplicity, assume that the income tax payable was paid in 2017.

(4) Complete the schedules for income reporting and reporting of cash flows for 2017.

d. Calculate the Total columns for the income reporting and reporting of cash flows sections.

e. Respond to the following.

(1) In 2016, by adopting the MACRS method of depreciation for tax purposes instead of the straight-line method, what is the difference in the amount of cash paid for income taxes?

(2) In the long term, after equipment has been disposed of, is there any difference in total income under the two methods?

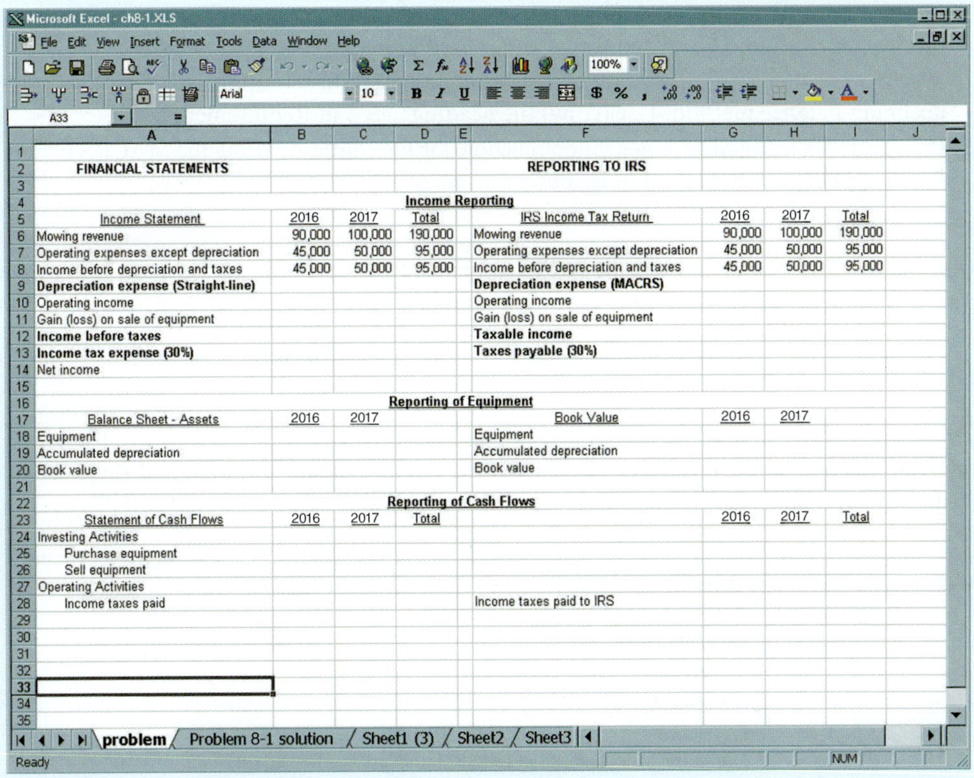

	A	B	C	D	F	G	H	I
1								
2	FINANCIAL STATEMENTS				REPORTING TO IRS			
3								
4				Income Reporting				
5	Income Statement	2016	2017	Total	IRS Income Tax Return	2016	2017	Total
6	Mowing revenue	90,000	100,000	190,000	Mowing revenue	90,000	100,000	190,000
7	Operating expenses except depreciation	45,000	50,000	95,000	Operating expenses except depreciation	45,000	50,000	95,000
8	Income before depreciation and taxes	45,000	50,000	95,000	Income before depreciation and taxes	45,000	50,000	95,000
9	**Depreciation expense (Straight-line)**				**Depreciation expense (MACRS)**			
10	Operating income				Operating income			
11	Gain (loss) on sale of equipment				Gain (loss) on sale of equipment			
12	**Income before taxes**				**Taxable income**			
13	**Income tax expense (30%)**				**Taxes payable (30%)**			
14	Net income							
15								
16				Reporting of Equipment				
17	Balance Sheet - Assets	2016	2017		Book Value	2016	2017	
18	Equipment				Equipment			
19	Accumulated depreciation				Accumulated depreciation			
20	Book value				Book value			
21								
22				Reporting of Cash Flows				
23	Statement of Cash Flows	2016	2017	Total		2016	2017	Total
24	Investing Activities							
25	Purchase equipment							
26	Sell equipment							
27	Operating Activities							
28	Income taxes paid				Income taxes paid to IRS			
29–35								

(3) In the long term, after equipment has been disposed of, is there any difference between total income tax expense and total income tax paid?

(4) Explain why Crist Company would use two different depreciation methods, particularly the straight-line method for the financial statements and an accelerated method (MACRS) for reporting to the IRS.

ATC 8-10 Spreadsheet Assignment *Alternative methods of depreciation*

Short Company purchased a computer on January 1, 2016, for $5,000. An additional $100 was paid for delivery charges. The computer was estimated to have a life of five years or 10,000 hours. Salvage value was estimated at $300. During the five years, the computer was used as follows:

2016	2,500 hours
2017	2,400 hours
2018	2,000 hours
2019	1,700 hours
2020	1,400 hours

Required

a. Prepare a five-year depreciation schedule for the computer using the straight-line depreciation method. Be sure to use formulas for all computations including depreciation expense. Set up the following headings for your schedule:

	Beginning				Ending		
Year	Cost	Accumulated Depreciation	Book Value	Depreciation Expense	Cost	Accumulated Depreciation	Book Value

b. Prepare another five-year depreciation schedule for the computer using the units-of-production method. Use (copy) the headings used in Requirement *a.*

c. Prepare another five-year depreciation schedule for the computer using the double-declining-balance method. Use (copy) the headings used in Requirement *a.*

d. Prepare another five-year depreciation schedule for the computer using the MACRS method. Use (copy) the headings used in Requirement *a.*

Spreadsheet Tip

After the year 2016, enter subsequent dates automatically. Position the mouse in the lower right-hand corner of the highlighted cell "2016" until a thin cross appears. Click and drag down four additional rows.

COMPREHENSIVE PROBLEM

The trial balance of Pacilio Security Services Inc. as of January 1, 2018, had the following normal balances:

Cash	$93,708
Petty cash	100
Accounts receivable	22,540
Allowance for doubtful accounts	1,334
Supplies	250
Prepaid rent	3,600
Merchandise inventory (18 @ $285)	5,130
Land	4,000
Salaries payable	2,100
Common stock	50,000
Retained earnings	75,894

During 2018 Pacillo Security Services experienced the following transactions:

1. Paid the salaries payable from 2017.
2. Purchased equipment and a van for a lump sum of $36,000 cash on January 2, 2018. The equipment was appraised for $10,000 and the van was appraised for $30,000.
3. Paid $9,000 on May 1, 2018, for one year's office rent in advance.
4. Purchased $300 of supplies on account.
5. Purchased 120 alarm systems at a cost of $280 each. Paid cash for the purchase.
6. After numerous attempts to collect from customers, wrote off $2,350 of uncollectible accounts receivable.
7. Sold 115 alarm systems for $580 each. All sales were on account. (Be sure to compute cost of goods sold using the FIFO cost flow method.)
8. Billed $86,000 of monitoring services for the year. Credit card sales amounted to $36,000, and the credit card company charged a 4 percent fee. The remaining $50,000 were sales on account.
9. Replenished the petty cash fund on June 30. The fund had $12 cash and receipts of $45 for yard mowing, $28 for office supplies expense, and $11 for miscellaneous expenses.
10. Collected the amount due from the credit card company.
11. Paid installers and other employees a total of $52,000 cash for salaries.
12. Collected $115,500 of accounts receivable during the year.
13. Paid $12,500 of advertising expense during the year.
14. Paid $6,800 of utilities expense for the year.
15. Sold the land, which was purchased in 2011, for $12,000.
16. Paid the accounts payable.
17. Paid a dividend of $10,000 to the shareholders.

Adjustments

18. Determined that $180 of supplies were on hand at the end of the year.

19. Recognized the expired rent for both the old van and the office building for the year. The lease on the van was not renewed. Rent paid on March 1, 2017, for the van was $4,800.

20. Recognized uncollectible accounts expense for the year using the allowance method. Pacilio estimates that 3 percent of sales on account will not be collected.

21. Recognized depreciation expense on the equipment and the van. The equipment has a five-year life and a $2,000 salvage value. The van has a four-year life and a $6,000 salvage value. The company uses double-declining-balance for the van and straight-line for the equipment.

22. Accrued salaries at December 31, 2018, were $1,500.

Required

a. Record the above transactions in general journal form.

b. Post the transactions to T-accounts.

c. Prepare a trial balance.

d. Prepare an income statement, statement of changes in stockholders' equity, balance sheet, and statement of cash flows.

e. Close the temporary accounts to retained earnings.

f. Post the closing entries to the T-accounts and prepare a post-closing trial balance.

CHAPTER 9

Accounting for Current Liabilities and Payroll

LEARNING OBJECTIVES

After you have mastered the material in this chapter, you will be able to:

LO 9-1 Show how notes payable and related interest expense affect financial statements.

LO 9-2 Show how sales tax liabilities affect financial statements.

LO 9-3 Define contingent liabilities and explain how they are reported in financial statements.

LO 9-4 Explain how warranty obligations affect financial statements.

LO 9-5 Determine payroll taxes and explain how they affect financial statements.

LO 9-6 Prepare a classified balance sheet.

LO 9-7 Use the current ratio to assess the level of liquidity.

APPENDIX

LO 9-8 Show how discount notes and related interest charges affect financial statements.

Video lectures and accompanying self-assessment quizzes are available for all learning objectives through McGraw-Hill Connect® Plus Accounting.

CHAPTER OPENING

Chapter 7 explained the need to estimate the net realizable value of receivables (the amount of receivables a company expects to actually collect). Do companies also estimate the net realizable value of payables (the amount they expect to actually pay)? The answer is no. Unless there is evidence to the contrary, companies are assumed to be going concerns that will continue to operate. Under this **going concern assumption**, companies expect to pay their obligations in full. Accounts and notes payable are therefore reported at face value. In addition to reporting liabilities for which the amounts due are known, companies report liabilities for which the amounts due are uncertain. Liabilities that are uncertain as to amount are contingent liabilities.

Chapter 2 discussed several types of liabilities with known amounts due, including accounts payable, salaries payable, and unearned revenue. This chapter introduces other liabilities with known amounts due: notes payable, sales tax payable, and payroll liabilities; and contingent liabilities including warranties payable and vacation pay. We limit the discussion in this chapter to *current liabilities,* those that are payable within one year or the operating cycle, whichever is longer.

The Curious Accountant

Rusty Rohr had worked as a plumber or plumber's assistant since high school. When he turned 30, he started his own plumbing business. In addition to working himself, he hired two friends, each of whom he planned to pay $25 per hour plus reasonable benefits. One reason Rusty wanted his own business was because he felt small companies often did not provide employees reasonable benefits. Rusty planned to charge customers $50 per hour for plumbing services. He believed charging double the rate he paid his employees would cover his operating expenses and still provide a profit on the employees' work.

Rusty hired a local accounting firm for his accounting needs, including handling his company's payroll records. After getting the business established, he and his employees kept busy, but the business was not as profitable as Rusty had expected. His accountant explained that the total compensation cost of his employees was averaging around $35 per hour. Rusty's knew the employees would cost more than their $25 per hour wage rate because of their fringe benefits, but he had not expected the benefits cost to be 40 percent of their base pay.

What could cause Rusty's compensation expenses to be so unexpectedly high? (Answers on page 497.)

ACCOUNTING FOR NOTES PAYABLE

LO 9-1

Show how notes payable and related interest expense affect financial statements.

Our discussion of promissory notes in Chapter 7 focused on the payee, the company with a note receivable on its books. In this chapter we focus on the maker of the note, the company with a note payable on its books. Since the maker of the note issues (gives) the note to the payee, the maker is sometimes called the **issuer.**

To illustrate, assume that on September 1, 2016, Herrera Supply Company (HSC) borrowed $90,000 (the principal amount) from National Bank. As evidence of the debt, Herrera issued a **note payable** that had a one-year term and an annual interest rate of 9 percent.

Issuing the note is an asset source transaction. The asset account Cash increases and the liability account Notes Payable increases. The income statement is not affected. The statement of cash flows shows a $90,000 cash inflow from financing activities. The journal entry and its effects on the financial statements are shown here:

Account Title	Debit	Credit
Cash	90,000	
Notes Payable		90,000

Date	Assets	=	Liabilities			+	Stockholders' Equity			Rev.	−	Exp.	=	Net Inc.	Cash Flow
	Cash	=	Notes Pay.	+	Int. Pay.	+	Com. Stk.	+	Ret. Earn.						
09/01/16	90,000	=	90,000	+	NA	+	NA	+	NA	NA	−	NA	=	NA	90,000 FA

On December 31, 2016, HSC would record an adjusting entry to recognize four months (September 1 through December 31) of accrued interest expense. The accrued interest is $2,700 [$90,000 × 0.09 × (4 ÷ 12)]. The adjusting entry is a claims exchange. The liability account Interest Payable increases, and the equity account Retained Earnings decreases. The income statement would report interest expense although HSC had not paid any cash for interest in 2016. The journal entry and its effects on the financial statements are shown here:

Account Title	Debit	Credit
Interest Expense	2,700	
Interest Payable		2,700

Date	Assets	=	Liabilities			+	Stockholders' Equity			Rev.	−	Exp.	=	Net Inc.	Cash Flow
	Cash	=	Notes Pay.	+	Int. Pay.	+	Com. Stk.	+	Ret. Earn.						
12/31/16	NA	=	NA	+	2,700	+	NA	+	(2,700)	NA	−	2,700	=	(2,700)	NA

HSC would record three journal entries on August 31, 2017 (the maturity date). The first entry recognizes $5,400 of interest expense that accrued in 2017 from January 1 through August 31 [$90,000 × 0.09 × (8 ÷ 12)]. The entry and its effects on the financial statements are shown here:

Account Title	Debit	Credit
Interest Expense	5,400	
Interest Payable		5,400

	Assets	=	Liabilities			+	Stockholders' Equity			Rev.	–	Exp.	=	Net Inc.	Cash Flow
Date	Cash	=	Notes Pay.	+	Int. Pay.	+	Com. Stk.	+	Ret. Earn.						
08/31/17	NA	=	NA	+	5,400	+	NA	+	(5,400)	NA	–	5,400	=	(5,400)	NA

The second entry records HSC's cash payment for interest on August 31, 2017. This entry is an asset use transaction that reduces both the Cash and Interest Payable accounts for the total amount of interest due, \$8,100 [\$90,000 × 0.09 × (12 ÷ 12)]. The interest payment includes the four months' interest accrued in 2016 and the eight months accrued in 2017 (\$2,700 + \$5,400 = \$8,100). There is no effect on the income statement because HSC recognized the interest expense in two previous journal entries. The statement of cash flows would report an \$8,100 cash outflow from operating activities. The journal entry and its effects on the financial statements are shown here:

Account Title	Debit	Credit
Interest Payable	8,100	
Cash		8,100

	Assets	=	Liabilities			+	Stockholders' Equity			Rev.	–	Exp.	=	Net Inc.	Cash Flow
Date	Cash	=	Notes Pay.	+	Int. Pay.	+	Com. Stk.	+	Ret. Earn.						
08/31/17	(8,100)	=	NA	+	(8,100)	+	NA	+	NA	NA	–	NA	=	NA	(8,100) OA

The third entry on August 31, 2017, reflects repaying the principal. This entry is an asset use transaction. The Cash account and the Notes Payable account each decrease by \$90,000. There is no effect on the income statement. The statement of cash flows would show a \$90,000 cash outflow from financing activities. Recall that paying interest is classified as an operating activity even though repaying the principal is a financing activity. The journal entry and its effects on the financial statements are shown here:

Account Title	Debit	Credit
Notes Payable	90,000	
Cash		90,000

	Assets	=	Liabilities			+	Stockholders' Equity			Rev.	–	Exp.	=	Net Inc.	Cash Flow
Date	Cash	=	Notes Pay.	+	Int. Pay.	+	Com. Stk.	+	Ret. Earn.						
08/31/17	(90,000)	=	(90,000)	+	NA	+	NA	+	NA	NA	–	NA	=	NA	(90,000) FA

Alternatively, HSC could combine the three separate journal entries recorded on the maturity date (August 31, 2017) into a single compound journal entry as shown below:

Account Title	Debit	Credit
Interest Expense	5,400	
Interest Payable	2,700	
Notes Payable	90,000	
Cash		98,100

CHECK YOURSELF 9.1

On October 1, 2016, Mellon Company issued an interest-bearing note payable to Better Banks Inc. The note had a $24,000 principal amount, a four-month term, and an annual interest rate of 4 percent. Determine the amount of interest expense and the cash outflow from operating activities Mellon will report in its 2016 and 2017 financial statements. Also provide in general journal form the adjusting entry necessary to recognize interest expense in 2016.

Answer The computation of accrued interest expense is shown below. Unless otherwise specified, the interest rate is stated in annual terms even though the term of the note is only four months. Interest rates are commonly expressed as an annual percentage regardless of the term of the note. The *time outstanding* in the following formulas is therefore expressed as a fraction of a year. Mellon paid interest at an annual rate of 4 percent, but the note was outstanding for only 3/12 of a year in 2016 and 1/12 of a year in 2017.

2016

Principal	×	Annual interest rate	×	Time outstanding	=	Interest expense
$24,000	×	0.04	×	(3/12)	=	$240

2017

Principal	×	Annual interest rate	×	Time outstanding	=	Interest expense
$24,000	×	0.04	×	(1/12)	=	$80

Mellon will report a $320 ($240 + $80) cash outflow from operating activities for interest in 2017. The adjusting entry required to recognize accrued interest at the end of 2016 is as follows:

Account	Debit	Credit
Interest Expense	240	
Interest Payable		240

ACCOUNTING FOR SALES TAX

LO 9-2

Show how sales tax liabilities affect financial statements.

Most states require retail companies to collect a sales tax on items sold to their customers. The retailer collects the tax from its customers and remits the tax to the state at regular intervals. The retailer has a current liability for the amount of sales tax collected but not yet paid to the state.

To illustrate, assume Herrera Supply Company (HSC) sells merchandise to a customer for $2,000 cash in a state where the sales tax rate is 6 percent. The journal entry to record the sale and its effects on the financial statements are shown here:

Account Title	Debit	Credit
Cash	2,120	
Sales Tax Payable		120
Sales Revenue[1]		2,000

Assets	=	Liab.	+	Equity			Rev.	−	Exp.	=	Net Inc.	Cash Flow
Cash	=	Sales Tax Pay.	+	Com. Stk.	+	Ret. Earn.						
2,120	=	120	+	NA	+	2,000	2,000	−	NA	=	2,000	2,120 OA

[1]The entry to record cost of goods sold for this sale is intentionally omitted.

Remitting the tax (paying cash to the tax authority) is an asset use transaction. Both the Cash account and the Sales Tax Payable account decrease. The journal entry and its effects on the financial statements are shown here:

Account Title	Debit	Credit
Sales Tax Payable	120	
Cash		120

Assets	=	Liab.	+	Equity			Rev.	−	Exp.	=	Net Inc.	Cash Flow
Cash	=	Sales Tax Pay.	+	Com. Stk.	+	Ret. Earn.						
(120)	=	(120)	+	NA	+	NA	NA	−	NA	=	NA	(120) OA

CONTINGENT LIABILITIES

LO 9-3

Define contingent liabilities and explain how they are reported in financial statements.

A **contingent liability** is a potential obligation arising from a past event. The amount or existence of the obligation depends on some future event. A pending lawsuit, for example, is a contingent liability. Depending on the outcome, a defendant company could be required to pay a monetary settlement or could be relieved of any obligation. Generally accepted accounting principles require that companies classify contingent liabilities into three different categories depending on the likelihood of their becoming actual liabilities. The categories and the accounting for each are described below:

1. If the likelihood of a future obligation arising is *probable* (likely) and its amount can be *reasonably estimated,* a liability is recognized in the financial statements. Contingent liabilities in this category include warranties, vacation pay, and sick leave.
2. If the likelihood of a future obligation arising is *reasonably possible* but not likely, or if it is probable but *cannot be reasonably estimated,* no liability is reported on the balance sheet. The potential liability is, however, disclosed in the notes to the financial statements. Contingent liabilities in this category include legal challenges, environmental damages, and government investigations.
3. If the likelihood of a future obligation arising is *remote,* no liability need be recognized in the financial statements or disclosed in the notes to the statements.[2]

Determining whether a contingent liability is probable, reasonably possible, or remote requires professional judgment. Even seasoned accountants seek the advice of attorneys, engineers, insurance agents, and government regulators before classifying significant contingent liabilities. Professional judgment is also required to distinguish between contingent liabilities and **general uncertainties.** All businesses face uncertainties such as competition and damage from floods or storms. Such uncertainties are not contingent liabilities, however, because they do not arise from past events.

Exhibit 9.1 summarizes the three categories of contingent liabilities and the accounting for each category.

[2]Companies may, if desired, voluntarily disclose contingent liabilities classified as remote.

EXHIBIT 9.1

Reporting Contingent Liabilities

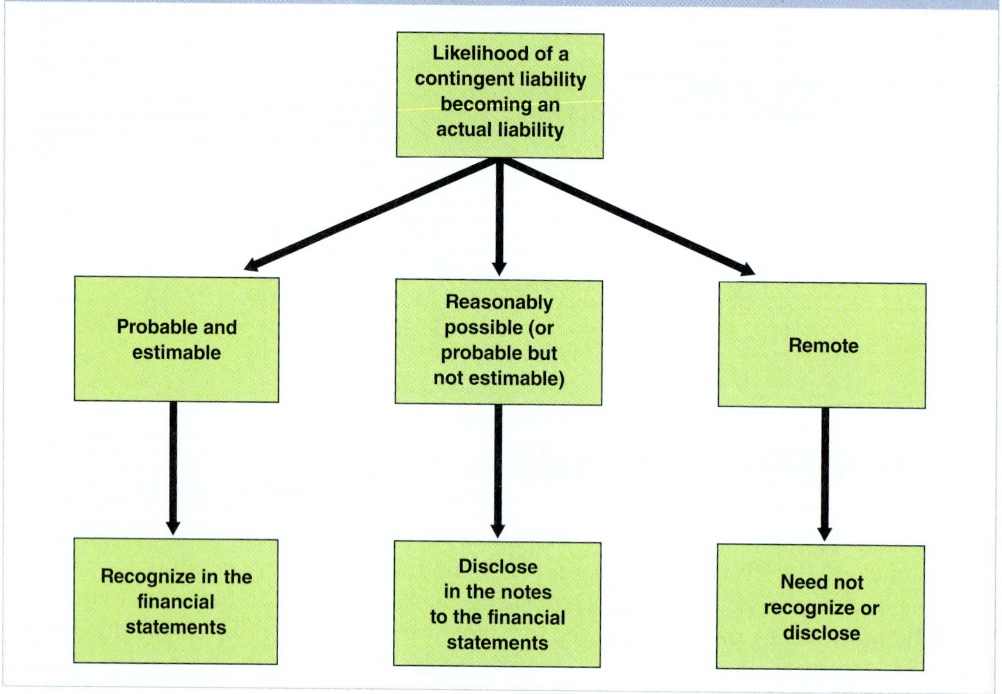

WARRANTY OBLIGATIONS

LO 9-4

Explain how warranty obligations affect financial statements.

To attract customers, many companies guarantee their products or services. Such guarantees are called **warranties.** Warranties take many forms. Usually, they extend for a specified period of time. Within this period, the seller promises to replace or repair defective products without charge. Although the amount and timing of warranty obligations are uncertain, warranties usually represent liabilities that must be reported in the financial statements.

To illustrate accounting for warranty obligations, assume Herrera Supply Company (HSC) had cash of $2,000, inventory of $6,000, common stock of $5,000, and retained earnings of $3,000 on January 1, 2016. The 2016 accounting period is affected by three accounting events: (1) sale of merchandise under warranty; (2) recognition of warranty obligations to customers who purchased the merchandise; and (3) settlement of a customer's warranty claim.

EVENT 1 **HSC sold for $7,000 cash merchandise that had cost $4,000.**

In the following statements model, revenue from the sale is labeled 1a and the cost of the sale is labeled 1b. The journal entries for the sales transaction and their effects on the financial statements are shown here:

Account Title	Debit	Credit
Cash	7,000	
Sales Revenue		7,000
Cost of Goods Sold	4,000	
Inventory		4,000

Event No.	Assets			=	Liab.	+	Equity	Rev.	−	Exp.	=	Net Inc.	Cash Flow
	Cash	+	Inventory	=			Ret. Earn.						
1a	7,000	+	NA	=	NA	+	7,000	7,000	−	NA	=	7,000	7,000 OA
1b	NA	+	(4,000)	=	NA	+	(4,000)	NA	−	4,000	=	(4,000)	NA

EVENT 2 HSC guaranteed the merchandise sold in Event 1 to be free from defects for one year following the date of sale.

Although the exact amount of future warranty claims is unknown, HSC must inform financial statement users of the company's obligation. HSC must estimate the amount of the warranty liability and report the estimate in the 2016 financial statements. Assume the warranty obligation is estimated to be $100. Recognizing this obligation increases liabilities (warranties payable) and reduces stockholders' equity (retained earnings). Recognizing the warranty expense reduces net income. The statement of cash flows is not affected when the obligation and the corresponding expense are recognized. The journal entry and its effects on the financial statements are shown here:

Account Title	Debit	Credit
Warranty Expense	100	
Warranties Payable		100

Event No.	Assets	=	Liab.	+	Equity	Rev.	−	Exp.	=	Net Inc.	Cash Flow
			Warr. Pay.	+	Ret. Earn.						
2	NA	=	100	+	(100)	NA	−	100	=	(100)	NA

EVENT 3 HSC paid $40 cash to repair defective merchandise returned by a customer.

The cash payment for the repair is not an expense. Warranty expense was recognized in the period in which the sale was made (when the Warranties Payable account was credited). The payment reduces an asset (cash) and a liability (warranties payable). The income statement is not affected by the repairs payment. However, there is a $40 cash outflow reported in the operating activities section of the statement of cash flows. The journal entry and its effects on the financial statements are shown here:

Account Title	Debit	Credit
Warranties Payable	40	
Cash		40

Event No.	Assets	=	Liab.	+	Equity	Rev.	−	Exp.	=	Net Inc.	Cash Flow
	Cash	=	Warr. Pay.	+	Ret. Earn.						
3	(40)	=	(40)	+	NA	NA	−	NA	=	NA	(40) OA

General Ledger T-Accounts and Financial Statements

Panel A of Exhibit 9.2 summarizes the 2016 accounting events. Panel B presents the ledger accounts in T-account form. The event numbers are shown parenthetically in the T-accounts to facilitate your review. The closing entries (Event 4 in Panel A) are included and referenced with the abbreviation "cl." The financial statements are shown in Panel C of the exhibit. You should study Exhibit 9.2 to strengthen your understanding of how the warranty events affect the financial statements.

EXHIBIT 9.2

The Big Picture

Panel A: Transaction Summary

1. Sold merchandise that cost $4,000 for $7,000 cash.
2. Recognized a $100 warranty obligation and the corresponding expense.
3. Paid $40 to satisfy a warranty claim.
4. Closed the revenue and expense accounts (referenced *cl.*).

Panel B: General Ledger

Assets = **Liabilities** + **Equity**

Assets

Cash

	Debit	Credit	
Bal.	2,000	40	(3)
(1a)	7,000		
Bal.	8,960		

Inventory

	Debit	Credit	
Bal.	6,000	4,000	(1b)
Bal.	2,000		

Liabilities

Warranties Payable

	Debit	Credit	
(3)	40	100	(2)
		60	Bal.

Equity

Common Stock

	Debit	Credit	
		5,000	Bal.

Retained Earnings

	Debit	Credit	
		3,000	Bal.
		2,900	(cl.)
		5,900	Bal.

Sales Revenue

	Debit	Credit	
(cl.)	7,000	7,000	(1a)
		0	Bal.

Cost of Goods Sold

	Debit	Credit	
(1b)	4,000	4,000	(cl.)
Bal.	0		

Warranty Expense

	Debit	Credit	
(2)	100	100	(cl.)
Bal.	0		

Panel C: Financial Statements for 2016

Income Statement

Sales revenue	$ 7,000
Cost of goods sold	(4,000)
Gross margin	3,000
Warranty expense	(100)
Net income	$ 2,900

Balance Sheet

Assets	
Cash	$ 8,960
Inventory	2,000
Total assets	$10,960
Liabilities	
Warranties payable	$ 60
Stockholders' equity	
Common stock	5,000
Retained earnings	5,900
Total liab. and stockholders' equity	$10,960

Statement of Cash Flows

Operating Activities		
Inflow from customers	$7,000	
Outflow for warranty	(40)	
Net Inflow from Operating activities		6,960
Investing Activities		0
Financing Activities		0
Net change in cash		6,960
Plus: Beginning cash balance		2,000
Ending cash balance		$8,960

CHECK YOURSELF 9.2

Flotation Systems Inc. (FSI) began operations in 2016. Its sales were $360,000 in 2016 and $410,000 in 2017. FSI estimates the cost of its one-year product warranty will be 2 percent of sales. Actual cash payments for warranty claims amounted to $5,400 during 2016 and $8,500 during 2017. Prepare the journal entries required to record warranty expense and cash paid to settle warranty claims for 2016 and 2017. Determine the amount of warranties payable FSI would report on its 2016 and 2017 year-end balance sheets.

Answer Journal Entries for 2016

Account Title	Debit	Credit
Warranty Expense ($360,000 × .02)	7,200	
Warranties Payable		7,200
Warranties Payable	5,400	
Cash		5,400

Journal Entries for 2017

Account Title	Debit	Credit
Warranty Expense ($410,000 × .02)	8,200	
Warranties Payable		8,200
Warranties Payable	8,500	
Cash*		8,500

*The 2017 cash payment exceeds the 2017 accrued expense because some of the warranty expense accrued in 2016 was actually paid in 2017.

FSI would report Warranties Payable on the December 31, 2016, balance sheet of $1,800 ($7,200 − $5,400). Warranties Payable on the December 31, 2017, balance sheet is $1,500 ($1,800 + $8,200 − $8,500).

ACCOUNTING FOR PAYROLL

LO 9-5

Determine payroll taxes and explain how they affect financial statements.

If you've had a job, you know the amount of your paycheck is less than the amount of your salary. Employers are required to withhold part of each employee's earnings. The money withheld is used to pay such items as income taxes, union dues, and medical insurance premiums for which the *employee* is responsible. The *employer* is also required to make matching payments for certain items such as social security and to pay additional amounts for unemployment taxes. This section of the chapter explains how employers account for *employee withholdings* as well as *employer payroll expenses.*

Identifying Employees

Businesses use the services of independent contractors as well as employees. They must distinguish between the two because payroll taxes apply only to employees. When a business supervises, directs, and controls an individual's work, the individual is an **employee** of the business. When a business pays an individual for specific services, but the individual supervises and controls the work, then that individual is an **independent contractor.**

REALITY BYTES

Many of the items we purchase come with a manufacturer's warranty, but companies that sell electronics and electrical appliances often offer to sell you an extended warranty that provides protection after the manufacturer's warranty has expired. Why do they offer this option to customers, and how do these warranties differ from the standard manufacturers' warranties?

Companies such as Best Buy offer to sell customers extended warranties because they make a significant profit on them. If you buy an extended warranty from Best Buy, the retailer is not actually the one who is promising to repair your product; that will be done by a third party. Best Buy simply receives a commission for selling the warranty. In its 2013 fiscal-year such commissions accounted for 2.8 percent of the company's total revenues, and since it had to incur very little expense to earn these revenues, they are mostly profit.

The typical manufacturer's warranty, as you have learned in this chapter, is an expense recognized at the time of the sale. However, companies that provide extended warranties must recognize the warranty revenue over the life of the warranty, not immediately upon sale. Remember, this is referring to the third-party warranty provider, not Best Buy. Since Best Buy is simply earning a commission from selling the warranty, it gets to recognize all of the revenue at the time of the sale.

The distinction between independent contractor and employee depends upon control and supervision rather than the type of work performed. A company's chief financial officer (CFO) is a company *employee;* the company's outside auditor is an *independent contractor.* Although both individuals provide accounting services, the company controls the CFO's work while the auditor is independent. If a business hired Rusty Rohr's company (see The Curious Accountant at the start of the chapter) for plumbing services, Rusty would be an independent contractor with respect to his customer. Rusty's workers, however, are employees of Rusty's plumbing company.

Employees' Gross Earnings

The compensation earned by employees who are paid based on the number of hours they work is normally called **wages.** The compensation earned by employees who are paid a set amount per week, month, or other earnings period regardless of the number of hours worked is normally called **salaries.** The total amount of wages or salaries earned, before any deductions for withholding, represents employees' **gross earnings.** Gross earnings is the sum of regular pay plus any bonuses, overtime, or other additions.

Deductions from Employees' Gross Earnings

Employers withhold money from employees' gross earnings. Employers are obligated (have liabilities) to pay the funds withheld on behalf of the employees. Employers determine each employee's net pay (cash paid to the employee) by *deducting* the withholdings from the gross earnings. This section of the chapter introduces common withholdings.

Federal Income Taxes

To help the federal government collect income taxes due on a timely basis, the tax laws adopted by Congress require employers to withhold income taxes from employee earnings. The employers then pay the withheld taxes directly to the government.

For example, assume an employee earns $2,000. Assume further the employee owes $300 of income tax on these earnings. On payday, the employer withholds $300 of the earnings and pays the employee $1,700 cash. The employer then has a $300 liability (obligation) to the federal government for the income tax withheld. The employer will use the money withheld to pay the employee's federal income tax liability. The journal entry to record paying the employee and its effects on the financial statements are shown here:

Account Title	Debit	Credit
Salary Expense	2,000	
Employee Income Tax Payable		300
Cash		1,700

Assets	=	Liab.	+	Equity			Rev.	−	Exp.	=	Net Inc.	Cash Flow
Cash	=	EIT Pay.	+	Com. Stk.	+	Ret. Earn.						
(1,700)	=	300	+	NA	+	(2,000)	NA	−	2,000	=	(2,000)	(1,700) OA

When the employer pays the liability, both cash and liabilities will decrease. The income statement will not be affected. The statement of cash flows will show a cash outflow from operating activities. The journal entry and its effects on the financial statements are shown here:

Account Title	Debit	Credit
Employee Income Tax Payable	300	
Cash		300

Assets	=	Liab.	+	Equity			Rev.	−	Exp.	=	Net Inc.	Cash Flow
Cash	=	EIT Pay.	+	Com. Stk.	+	Ret. Earn.						
(300)	=	(300)	+	NA	+	NA	NA	−	NA	=	NA	(300) OA

The federal tax laws require employers to withhold funds for employee Social Security and Medicare (FICA) taxes as well as income taxes. Employers may also be required to withhold amounts to pay state, county, and municipal government taxes from employees' paychecks. These withholdings have the same effects on the financial statements as those described above for federal income taxes.

Federal Income Tax Documents

The amount withheld from an employee's salary depends on the employee's *gross pay* and the number of *withholding allowances* the employee claims. Each allowance reduces the amount the employer must withhold. Employees are generally allowed to claim one allowance for themselves and one for each legal dependent. For example, a married person with two dependent children could claim four allowances (the employee, the dependent spouse, and the two dependent children). Exhibit 9.3 shows an **Employee's Withholding Allowance Certificate, Form W-4,** the form used to document the number of allowances claimed by an employee.

The federal government provides tax withholding tables that indicate the amount to withhold for any amount of earnings and any number of allowances. At the end of the calendar year, the employer must notify each employee of the amount of his or her gross earnings for the year and of the amounts the employer withheld. Employers provide this information to employees on a **Wage and Tax Statement, Form W-2,** illustrated

EXHIBIT 9.3

Employee's Withholding Allowance Certificate Form W-4

Separate here and give Form W-4 to your employer. Keep the top part for your records.

Form **W-4**
Department of the Treasury
Internal Revenue Service

Employee's Withholding Allowance Certificate

▶ **Whether you are entitled to claim a certain number of allowances or exemption from withholding is subject to review by the IRS. Your employer may be required to send a copy of this form to the IRS.**

OMB No. 1545-0074
2014

1 Your first name and middle initial	Last name	2 **Your social security number**

Home address (number and street or rural route)

3 ☐ Single ☐ Married ☐ Married, but withhold at higher Single rate.
Note. If married, but legally separated, or spouse is a nonresident alien, check the "Single" box.

City or town, state, and ZIP code

4 **If your last name differs from that shown on your social security card, check here. You must call 1-800-772-1213 for a replacement card.** ▶ ☐

5 Total number of allowances you are claiming (from line **H** above **or** from the applicable worksheet on page 2) 5

6 Additional amount, if any, you want withheld from each paycheck . . . . 6 $

7 I claim exemption from withholding for 2014, and I certify that I meet **both** of the following conditions for exemption.
- Last year I had a right to a refund of **all** federal income tax withheld because I had **no** tax liability, **and**
- This year I expect a refund of **all** federal income tax withheld because I expect to have **no** tax liability.

If you meet both conditions, write "Exempt" here . . . . ▶ 7

Under penalties of perjury, I declare that I have examined this certificate and, to the best of my knowledge and belief, it is true, correct, and complete.

Employee's signature
(This form is not valid unless you sign it.) ▶ **Date** ▶

8 Employer's name and address (Employer: Complete lines 8 and 10 only if sending to the IRS.)	9 Office code (optional)	10 Employer identification number (EIN)

For Privacy Act and Paperwork Reduction Act Notice, see page 2. Cat. No. 10220Q Form **W-4** (2014)

in Exhibit 9.4. The employer sends one copy of Form W-2 to the Social Security Administration and other copies to the employee.

Employers are required to file the **Employer's Quarterly Federal Tax Return, Form 941** no later than one month after each quarter ends. This form reports the amounts due and paid to the government for federal withholdings. Failure to pay withheld taxes in a timely manner is serious. The government has the right to impose significant penalties and can even close a business, seize its assets, and take legal action against those who fail to pay taxes due.

Social Security and Medicare Taxes (FICA)

Congress adopted the Federal Insurance Contributions Act (FICA) to provide funding for the Social Security and Medicare programs. **Social Security** provides qualified individuals with old age, survivor's, and disability insurance (OASDI); **Medicare** provides health insurance. During their working years, employees pay a percentage of their earnings (up to a specified limit) to the federal government for Social Security. At retirement, a qualified person is entitled to receive monthly Social Security payments. Workers who become disabled before retirement are eligible to receive disability benefits. If a worker or retired person dies, any legal dependents are eligible to receive survivor benefits.

In order to meet the required benefit payments, Congress has frequently increased the amount of earnings to which the rates apply. Future changes in FICA tax rates and earnings maximums are likely. These changes will affect only the amount of FICA taxes, however, not how to account for them. *To simplify computations this text assumes a Social*

EXHIBIT 9.4

Wage and Tax Statement Form W-2

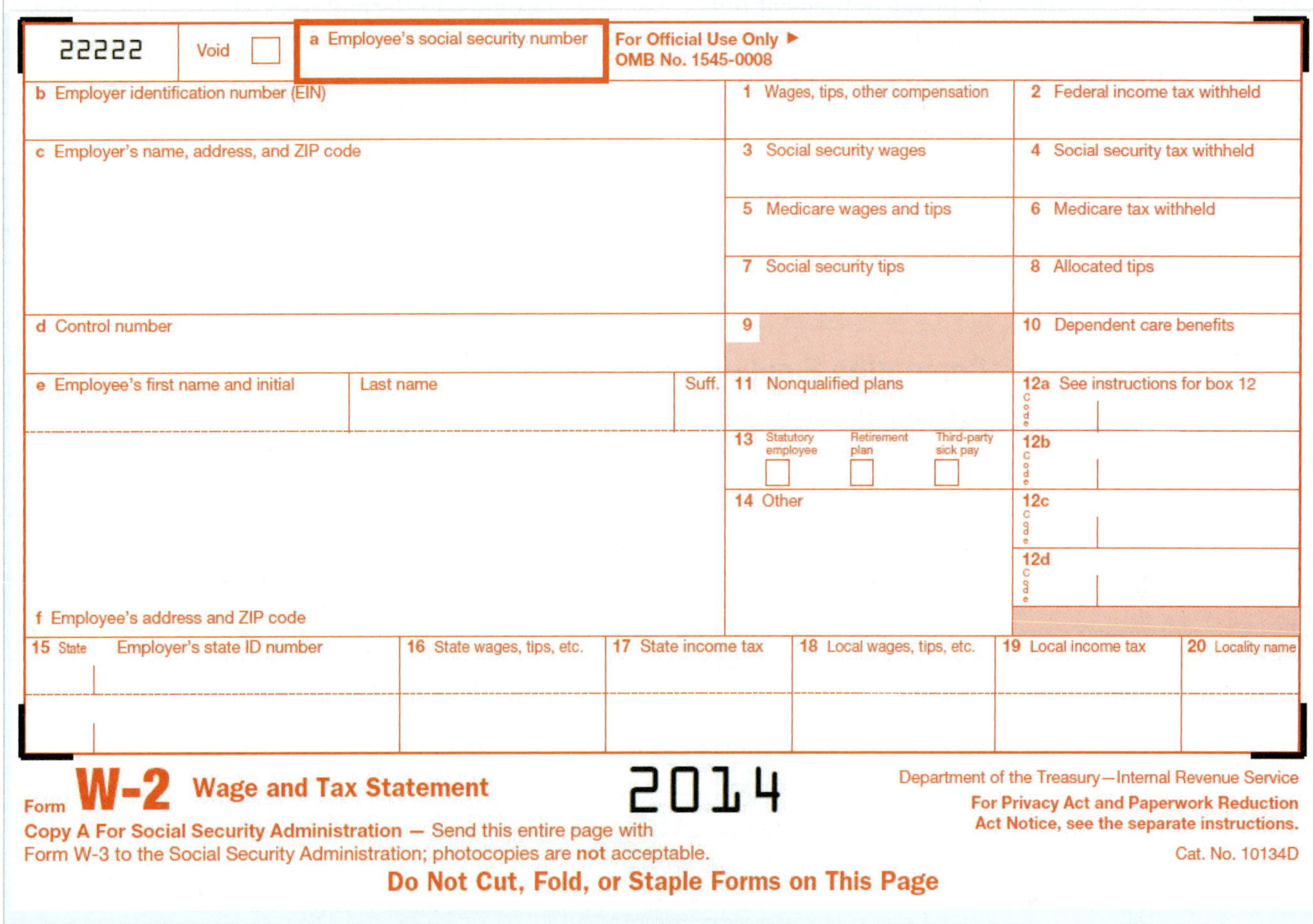
22222 Void a Employee's social security number For Official Use Only ► OMB No. 1545-0008

b Employer identification number (EIN)

1 Wages, tips, other compensation

2 Federal income tax withheld

c Employer's name, address, and ZIP code

3 Social security wages

4 Social security tax withheld

5 Medicare wages and tips

6 Medicare tax withheld

7 Social security tips

8 Allocated tips

d Control number

9

10 Dependent care benefits

e Employee's first name and initial Last name Suff.

11 Nonqualified plans

12a See instructions for box 12 Code

13 Statutory employee Retirement plan Third-party sick pay

12b Code

14 Other

12c Code

12d Code

f Employee's address and ZIP code

15 State Employer's state ID number 16 State wages, tips, etc. 17 State income tax 18 Local wages, tips, etc. 19 Local income tax 20 Locality name

Form W-2 Wage and Tax Statement 2014

Department of the Treasury—Internal Revenue Service

For Privacy Act and Paperwork Reduction Act Notice, see the separate instructions.

Copy A For Social Security Administration — Send this entire page with Form W-3 to the Social Security Administration; photocopies are not acceptable.

Cat. No. 10134D

Do Not Cut, Fold, or Staple Forms on This Page

Security rate of 6 percent on the first \$110,000 of income and a Medicare rate of 1.5 percent on all earnings.[3] For example, an employee earning \$100,000 per year will have the following FICA taxes withheld from his or her salary:

Social Security	\$100,000	×	6.0%	=	\$6,000
Medicare	100,000	×	1.5%	=	1,500
Total withheld					\$7,500

Not only employees are required to pay FICA taxes; the FICA legislation requires employers to pay a matching amount. The total FICA tax paid to the federal government for an employee earning \$100,000 per year is \$15,000 (\$7,500 × 2), half paid by the employee and half paid by the employer. We discuss accounting for employer taxes later in the chapter.

Voluntary Withholdings (Deductions)

One reason governments require employers to withhold taxes from employee earnings is that many people have difficulty managing their spending. If employees received their gross earnings amount, they might not be able to pay their taxes because they would spend the money on other things first. Many people have this tendency with regard to

[3]The actual rates are 6.2% and 1.45%.

other spending responsibilities as well. To ensure they make important payments, they voluntarily allow their employer to withhold money from their salaries. The employer then uses the money withheld to make payment in the employees' names for such items as medical insurance premiums, union dues, charitable contributions, and contributions to private retirement funds or savings accounts. Even employees who manage their personal finances without difficulty find it convenient to allow their employers to withhold funds and make payments on their behalf.

Withholding voluntary deductions from an employee's gross earnings represents a service on the employer's part. The employer must deduct the amounts authorized by each employee and remit the withheld money to the proper recipients. The employer must maintain additional records and undertake additional transactions to ensure the proper amounts are withheld and paid as specified on a timely basis. Employers normally itemize all deductions from gross pay on the pay stub to explain how an employee's net pay was determined.

Computing Employee Net Pay

Net pay is the employee's gross earnings less all deductions (withholdings). Net pay, often called take-home pay, is the amount of cash the employee receives from the employer.

To illustrate assume that Herrera Supply Company (HSC) has an employee named Sarah Jennings. Ms. Jennings earns a monthly salary of \$6,000. Based on Ms. Jennings's Form W-4, the tax tables require withholding \$450 per month for income taxes. Since Ms. Jennings earns less than \$110,000 per year, her full monthly salary is subject to FICA withholdings. Ms. Jennings has authorized HSC to deduct \$320 per month for medical insurance and \$25 per month for a charitable contribution to the American Cancer Society. Ms. Jennings's net pay is computed as follows:

Gross monthly salary		\$6,000
Deductions		
Federal income taxes	\$450	
FICA Tax—Social Security (\$6,000 × 6%)	360	
FICA Tax—Medicare (\$6,000 × 1.5%)	90	
Medical insurance premiums	320	
American Cancer Society	25	
Total deductions		1,245
Net pay		\$4,755

The journal entry to recognize salary expense for Ms. Jennings and its effects on HSC's financial statements are shown here:

Account Title	Debit	Credit
Salary Expense	6,000	
Employee Income Tax Payable		450
FICA Tax—Social Security Payable		360
FICA Tax—Medicare Payable		90
Medical Insurance Premiums Payable		320
American Cancer Society Payable		25
Cash		4,755

Assets =	Liab. +	Equity	Rev. − Exp. = Net Inc.	Cash Flow
Cash =	Various Payables +	Com. Stk. + Ret. Earn.		
(4,755) =	1,245 +	NA + (6,000)	NA − 6,000 = (6,000)	(4,755) OA

Employer Payroll Taxes

As mentioned above, employers are required to match employees' FICA taxes, and FICA tax rates are subject to change. This text uses the same assumed tax rates for employers as it uses for employees. *Assume a Social Security rate of 6 percent on the first $110,000 of each employee's earnings and a Medicare rate of 1.5 percent on all earnings.* The employer's portion of FICA taxes is a payroll tax expense to the employer.

Employers also incur a payroll tax expense for *unemployment* taxes. Congress adopted the **Federal Unemployment Tax Act (FUTA)** to finance temporary relief to qualified *unemployed* persons. The tax is determined by multiplying the wages of employees (up to a specified maximum limit) by a specified rate. The FUTA tax provides money to both state and federal government workforce agencies. States may enact supplemental unemployment tax laws based on higher maximum earnings or tax rates and could assess employees, rather than employers, for all or part of the supplemental coverage.

As of January 2014, the unemployment tax rate was 6.0 percent of the first $7,000 of wages earned by each employee during a calendar year. FUTA allows employers a credit of up to 5.4 percent for amounts paid to a state unemployment program, leaving a rate of 0.6 percent to be paid to the federal government. For example, on a tax of $420 (6.0% × $7,000), an employer would pay $42 (0.6% × $7,000) to the federal government and $378 (5.4% × $7,000) to the state government. State governments receive a larger percentage because they are responsible for administering the unemployment programs. The rates may be reduced to reward employers with few or no unemployment claims.

Recording and Reporting Payroll Taxes

To illustrate computing employer payroll tax expense, return to HSC's employee, Ms. Jennings, who earns $6,000 per month. HSC's February payroll tax expense for Ms. Jennings is computed as follows:

FICA tax expense—Social Security ($6,000 × 6%)	$360
FICA tax expense—Medicare ($6,000 × 1.5%)	90
Federal unemployment tax expense ($1,000 × 0.6%)	6
State unemployment tax expense ($1,000 × 5.4%)	54
Total payroll tax expense	$510

The unemployment taxes apply only to the first $7,000 of income earned each year by each employee. Since Ms. Jennings earned $6,000 in January, unemployment tax only applies to $1,000 of her February salary. The journal entry to record the payroll tax expense and its effects on the financial statements are shown here:

Account Title	Debit	Credit
Payroll Tax Expense	510	
FICA Tax—Social Security Payable		360
FICA Tax—Medicare Payable		90
Federal Unemployment Tax Payable		6
State Unemployment Tax Payable		54

Assets	=	Liab.	+	Equity			Rev. − Exp. = Net Inc.	Cash Flow
Cash	=	Various Payables	+	Com. Stk.	+	Ret. Earn.		
NA	=	510	+	NA	+	(510)	NA − 510 = (510)	NA

CHECK YOURSELF 9.3

Bill Chavez, an employee of Bombay Company, earns a salary of $110,000 per year. Based on the tax rates assumed in this chapter, determine the annual payroll tax expense Bombay Company would incur with respect to Mr. Chavez. How much payroll tax would Mr. Chavez be required to pay?

Answer

Payroll tax expense for Bombay Company	
FICA tax expense—Social Security ($110,000 × 6%)	$6,600
FICA tax expense—Medicare ($110,000 × 1.5%)	1,650
Federal unemployment tax expense ($7,000 × 0.6%)	42
State unemployment tax expense ($7,000 × 5.4%)	378
Total payroll tax expense	$8,670

Mr. Chavez would not pay any payroll taxes. Payroll taxes apply to employers, not employees.

Employee Fringe Benefits

In addition to salaries and wages, many employers provide their employees with a variety of fringe benefits such as paid vacations, sick leave, maternity leave, and medical, dental, life, and disability insurance. These benefits plus payroll taxes frequently amount to as much as 25 percent of the employees' gross salaries and wages. Fringe benefits are reported as expenses on the income statement.

To illustrate, assume HSC provides the following fringe benefits to an employee, Alice Worthington. Ms. Worthington accrues $200 per month in vacation pay. HSC pays $250 per month for Ms. Worthington's medical insurance and contributes $150 per month to a pension (retirement) program for Ms. Worthington. The monthly entry to record the accrued fringe benefits expenses and its effects on the financial statements are shown here:

Account Title	Debit	Credit
Vacation Pay Expense	200	
Employee Medical Insurance Expense	250	
Employee Pension Expense	150	
Vacation Pay Payable		200
Employee Medical Insurance Payable		250
Employee Pension Liability		150

Assets	=	Liab.	+	Equity			Rev. − Exp. = Net Inc.	Cash Flow
Cash	=	Various Payables	+	Com. Stk.	+	Ret. Earn.		
NA	=	600	+	NA	+	(600)	NA − 600 = (600)	NA

THE FINANCIAL ANALYST

Current versus Noncurrent

LO 9-6

Prepare a classified balance sheet.

Because meeting obligations on time is critical to business survival, financial analysts and creditors are interested in whether companies will have enough money available to pay bills when they are due. Most businesses provide information about their bill-paying ability by classifying their assets and liabilities according to liquidity. The more quickly an asset is converted to cash or consumed, the more *liquid* it is. Assets are usually divided

Answers to The Curious Accountant

As the chapter explains, not only do employees have 7.65 percent of their wages withheld for Social Security taxes, but their employers also must pay 7.65 percent, which is $1.91 per hour for someone being paid $25 per hour. Additionally, federal and state unemployment insurance taxes must be paid. Workers' compensation insurance must be provided to assist workers who are injured on the job. And then, there are the benefits that Rusty voluntarily provides his workers, such as health care, vacation pay, and contributions to their retirement plans. According to the **U.S. Bureau of Labor Statistics** (BLS), in 2013 the average pay for plumbers was around $24 per hour. The BLS further reported that benefits for workers in private industry averaged 42.2 percent of their base pay.

Based on the information provided by the BLS survey, fringe benefits and payroll taxes would increase Rusty's payroll costs per hour by around $10.55 ($25 × 0.422), bringing the total cost to $35.55. An additional problem is that Rusty can only charge his customers for "billable hours," but he must pay his employees for 40 hours per week. Obviously plumbers cannot work 40 billable hours per week since they must travel from job to job. The $25 markup Rusty is charging his customers ($50 − $25) has to pay for these nonbillable hours as well as his employees' fringe benefits and, he hopes, a profit.

into two major classifications: *current* and *noncurrent*. Current items are also referred to as *short term* and noncurrent items as *long term*.

A **current (short-term) asset** is expected to be converted to cash or consumed within one year or an operating cycle, whichever is longer. An **operating cycle** is defined as the average time it takes a business to convert cash to inventory, inventory to accounts receivable, and accounts receivable back to cash. The financial tools used to measure the length of an operating cycle for particular businesses are discussed in Chapter 7. For most businesses, the operating cycle is less than one year. As a result, the one-year rule normally prevails with respect to classifying assets as current. The current assets section of a balance sheet typically includes the following items:

Current Assets
Cash
Marketable securities
Accounts receivable
Short-term notes receivable
Interest receivable
Inventory
Supplies
Prepaid items

Given the definition of current assets, it seems reasonable to assume that **current (short-term) liabilities** would be those due within one year or an operating cycle, whichever is longer. This assumption is usually correct. However, an exception is made for long-term renewable debt. For example, consider a liability that was issued with a 20-year term to maturity. After 19 years, the liability becomes due within one year and is, therefore, a current liability. Even so, the liability will be classified as long term if the company plans to issue new long-term debt and to use the proceeds from that debt to repay the maturing liability. This situation is described as *refinancing short-term debt on* *a long-term basis.* In general, if a business does not plan to use any of its current assets to repay a debt, that debt is listed as long term even if it is due within one year. The current liabilities section of a balance sheet typically includes the following items:

Current Liabilities
Accounts payable
Short-term notes payable
Wages payable
Taxes payable
Interest payable

Balance sheets that distinguish between current and noncurrent items are called **classified balance sheets.** To enhance the usefulness of accounting information, most real-world balance sheets are classified. Exhibit 9.5 displays an example of a classified balance sheet.

EXHIBIT 9.5

LIMBAUGH COMPANY
Classified Balance Sheet
As of December 31, 2016

Assets			
Current Assets			
Cash		$ 20,000	
Accounts receivable		35,000	
Inventory		230,000	
Prepaid rent		3,600	
Total current assets			$288,600
Property, Plant, and Equipment			
Office equipment	$ 80,000		
Less: Accumulated depreciation	(25,000)	55,000	
Building	340,000		
Less: Accumulated depreciation	(40,000)	300,000	
Land		120,000	
Total property, plant, and equipment			475,000
Total assets			$763,600
Liabilities and Stockholders' Equity			
Current Liabilities			
Accounts payable		$ 32,000	
Notes payable		120,000	
Salaries payable		32,000	
Unearned revenue		9,800	
Total current liabilities			$193,800
Long-Term Liabilities			
Note payable			100,000
Total liabilities			293,800
Stockholders' Equity			
Common stock		200,000	
Retained earnings		269,800	469,800
Total liabilities and stockholders' equity			$763,600

Liquidity versus Solvency

LO 9-7

Use the current ratio to assess the level of liquidity.

Liquidity describes the ability to generate sufficient short-term cash flows to pay obligations as they come due. **Solvency** is the ability to repay liabilities in the long run. Liquidity and solvency are both important to the survival of a business. Financial analysts rely on several ratios to help them evaluate a company's liquidity and solvency. The *debt to assets* ratio introduced in Chapter 3 is one tool used to measure solvency. The primary ratio used to evaluate liquidity is the current ratio.

The **current ratio** is defined as:

$$\frac{\text{Current assets}}{\text{Current liabilities}}$$

Since current assets normally exceed current liabilities, this ratio is usually greater than 100 percent. For example, if a company has \$250 in current assets and \$100 in current liabilities, current assets are 250 percent of current liabilities. The current ratio is traditionally expressed as a decimal rather than as a percentage, however; most analysts would describe this example as a current ratio of 2.5 to 1 (\$250 ÷ \$100 = \$2.50 in current assets for every \$1 in current liabilities). This book uses the traditional format when referring to the current ratio.

The current ratio is among the most widely used ratios in analyzing financial statements. Current ratios can be too high as well as too low. A low ratio suggests that the company may have difficulty paying its short-term obligations. A high ratio suggests

FOCUS ON INTERNATIONAL ISSUES

WHY ARE THESE BALANCE SHEETS BACKWARD?

As discussed in earlier chapters, most industrialized countries require companies to use international financial accounting standards (IFRS), which are similar to the GAAP used in the United States. The globalization of accounting standards should, therefore, make it easier to read a company's annual report regardless of its country or origin. However, there are still language differences between companies; German companies prepare their financial reports using IFRS, but in German, while U.K. companies use English.

Suppose language is not an issue. For example, companies in the United States, the United Kingdom (U.K.), and even India, prepare their annual reports in English. Thus, one would expect to find few differences between financial reports prepared by companies in these countries. However, if a person who learned accounting in the United States looks at the balance sheet of a U.K. company he or she might think the statement is a bit "backward," and likewise, the balance sheet of an Indian company might seem upside down.

Like U.S. companies, U.K. companies report assets at the top, or left, of the balance sheet, and liabilities and stockholders' equity on the bottom or right. However, unlike the United States, U.K. companies typically show long-term assets before current assets. Even more different are balance sheets of Indian companies, which begin with stockholders' equity and then liabilities at the top or left, and then show assets on the bottom or right. Like the U.K. statements, those in India show long-term assets before current assets. Realize that most of the accounting rules established by IFRS or U.S. GAAP deal with measurement issues. Assets can be measured using the same rules but they must be disclosed in different manners. IFRS requires companies to classify assets and liabilities as current versus noncurrent, but the order in which these categories are listed on the balance sheet is not specified.

For an example of a financial statement for a U.K. company, go to **www.itvplc.com**. Click on "Investors" and then "Reports and Results." For an example of an Indian company's annual report, go to **www.colgate.co.in**. Click on "For Investors," then "Financials Reports," and then on "Annual Reports."

that a company is not maximizing its earnings potential because investments in liquid assets usually do not earn as much money as investments in other assets. Companies must try to maintain an effective balance between liquid assets (so they can pay bills on time) and nonliquid assets (so they can earn a good return).

Real-World Data

Exhibit 9.6 presents the current ratios and debt to assets ratios for six companies in three different industries. These data are for the 2013 fiscal years.

EXHIBIT 9.6

Industry	Company	Current Ratio	Debt to Assets Ratio
Electric utilities	American Electric Power	0.71	0.71
	Dominion Resources	0.85	0.76
Clothing stores	American Eagle Outfitters	2.62	0.38
	The Gap	1.76	0.61
Building supplies	Home Depot	1.34	0.57
	Lowe's	1.27	0.58

Which of these companies has the highest level of financial risk? Perhaps Dominion Resources because it has the highest debt to assets ratio. The electric utilities have higher debt to assets ratios and lower current ratios than those of the companies in the building supplies business. Does this mean that electric utilities are riskier investments? Not necessarily; since the companies are in different industries, the ratios may not be comparable. Utility companies have a more stable revenue base than building supplies companies. If the economy turns downward, people are likely to continue to use electricity. However, they are less likely to buy a new home or add on to their existing home. Because utility companies have a stable source of revenue, creditors are likely to feel comfortable with higher levels of debt for them than they would for building supplies companies. As previously stated, the industry must be considered when interpreting ratios. American Eagle Outfitters appears to have the lowest financial risk based on its debt to assets ratio being lowest and its current ratio being the highest. Finally, note that the debt to assets ratios tend to be grouped by industry.

<< A Look Back

Chapter 9 discussed accounting for current liabilities and payroll. Current liabilities are obligations due within one year or the company's operating cycle, whichever is longer. The chapter expanded the discussion of promissory notes begun in Chapter 7. Chapter 7 introduced accounting for the note payee, the lender; Chapter 9 discussed accounting for the note maker (issuer), the borrower. Notes payable and related interest payable are reported as liabilities on the balance sheet. Chapter 9 also discussed accounting for sales tax liabilities, warranty obligations, and contingent liabilities.

Payroll costs and payroll taxes constitute a major expense for most businesses. An employer is responsible for withholding money from an employee's salary. The most common withholdings are for federal income taxes, FICA taxes, insurance premiums, savings or retirement contributions, union dues, and charitable donations. The employer uses the withholdings to pay the employees' obligations. The difference between the *gross pay* and the money withheld is called net pay. The *net pay* is the amount of cash the employer pays to the employee.

In addition to making payments for its employees, the employer is responsible for certain taxes on its employees' salaries and wages. These taxes are called payroll taxes. They include matching FICA Social Security and Medicare taxes, and federal and state unemployment taxes. Governments periodically change the rates of these taxes. The accounting for them, however, is not affected by rate changes. The rates used in this text are as follows: FICA Social Security—6 percent of the first $110,000 of each employee's wages with a matching payment for the employer; FICA Medicare—1.5 percent of the total wages of each employee with a matching payment for the employer; federal unemployment taxes—0.6 percent (6.0 percent less a 5.4 percent credit for state unemployment taxes) of the first $7,000 of each employee's wages; and state unemployment—5.4 percent of the first $7,000 of each employee's wages.

Finally, Chapter 9 discussed assessing companies' liquidity. The current ratio is current assets divided by current liabilities. The higher the current ratio, the more liquid the business.

A Look Forward >>

Chapter 10 investigates issues related to accounting for long-term liabilities. As you will learn, income tax consequences enter into decisions to borrow money.

APPENDIX

Accounting for Discount Notes

LO 9-8

Show how discount notes and related interest charges affect financial statements.

All notes payable discussed previously have been "add-on" **interest-bearing notes.** The amount due at maturity for add-on notes is the *face value* of the note *plus accrued interest.* In contrast, the interest on a **discount note** is included in the face value of the note. A $5,000 face value discount note is repaid with $5,000 cash at maturity. This payment includes both principal and accrued interest.

Accounting Events Affecting 2016

To illustrate, assume Beacon Management Services experienced the following four events in 2016: (1) borrowed money by issuing a discount note; (2) recognized operating expenses; (3) recognized revenue; and (4) recognized accrued interest.

EVENT 1 Beacon Management Services was started when it issued a $10,000 face value discount note to State Bank on March 1, 2016.

The note had a 9 percent *discount rate* and a one-year term to maturity. As with interest-bearing notes, the *issuer* of a discount note exchanges the promissory note for cash. Accounting for the discount note requires dividing the face amount between the **discount** and the **principal,** or **proceeds** (amount of cash borrowed). The discount is computed by multiplying the face value of the note by the interest rate by the time period. Subtracting the discount from the face value of the note determines the principal (proceeds). The computations follow:

Face value of note	$10,000
Less discount ($10,000 × 0.09 × 1) =	900
Proceeds (amount borrowed)	$ 9,100

On the issue date, both assets and liabilities increase by the amount borrowed (the $9,100 principal). The borrowing transaction on the issue date has no effect on the income statement. The $9,100 cash inflow is reported in the financing activities section of the statement of cash flows. The journal entry to record issuing the discount note and its effects on the financial statements are shown here:

Account Title	Debit	Credit
Cash	9,100	
Discount on Notes Payable	900	
Notes Payable		10,000

Event No.	Assets	=	Liabilities			+	Equity			Rev.	−	Exp.	=	Net Inc.	Cash Flow
	Cash	=	Notes Pay.	−	Disc. on N/P	+	Com. Stk.	+	Ret. Earn.						
1	9,100	=	10,000	−	900	+	NA	+	NA	NA	−	NA	=	NA	9,100 FA

The discount is recorded in a **contra liability account** called **Discount on Notes Payable.** The *carrying value* of the liability is the difference between the Notes Payable and Discount accounts. Carrying value, also called *book value,* is the amount at which the liability is carried on the books. In this case, the Notes Payable account in Beacon's ledger has a $10,000 credit balance and the Discount on Notes Payable account has a $900 debit balance. The carrying value on the issue date is as follows:

Notes payable	$10,000
Discount on notes payable	(900)
Carrying value of liability	$ 9,100

EVENT 2 **Beacon incurred $8,000 of cash operating expenses.**

Paying these expenses reduces both assets and stockholders' equity. The effect on the income statement is to increase expenses and decrease net income. The cash outflow is reported in the operating activities section of the statement of cash flows. The journal entry and its effects on the financial statements are shown here:

Account Title	Debit	Credit
Operating Expenses	8,000	
Cash		8,000

Event No.	Assets	=	Liabilities			+	Equity			Rev.	−	Exp.	=	Net Inc.	Cash Flow
	Cash	=	Notes Pay.	−	Disc. on N/P	+	Com. Stk.	+	Ret. Earn.						
2	(8,000)	=	NA	−	NA	+	NA	+	(8,000)	NA	−	(8,000)	=	(8,000)	(8,000) OA

EVENT 3 **Beacon recognized $12,000 of cash service revenue.**

Recognizing revenue increases both assets and stockholders' equity. Net income increases. The cash inflow is reported in the operating activities section of the statement of cash flows. The journal entry and its effects on the financial statements are shown here:

Account Title	Debit	Credit
Cash	12,000	
Service Revenue		12,000

Event No.	Assets	=	Liabilities			+	Equity			Rev.	−	Exp.	=	Net Inc.	Cash Flow
	Cash	=	Notes Pay.	−	Disc. on N/P	+	Com. Stk.	+	Ret. Earn.						
3	12,000	=	NA	−	NA	+	NA	+	12,000	12,000	−	NA	=	12,000	12,000 OA

EVENT 4 **Beacon recorded an adjusting entry to recognize interest accrued since March 1.**

On December 31, 2016, Beacon must adjust its accounting records to recognize the 10 months of interest expense it incurred in 2016. For this note, interest expense accrues at \$75 per month (\$900 discount ÷ 12). As of December 31, \$750 (\$75 × 10) of interest expense has accrued. Since no cash payment is due until the note matures in 2017, the reduction in equity from recognizing the interest expense is accompanied by an increase in liabilities.

The increase in liabilities is recorded by *reducing the contra liability account,* Discount on Notes Payable. Recall that the carrying value of the liability was \$9,100 on the day the note was issued. The adjusting entry to record the accrued interest expense removes \$750 from the Discount account, leaving a discount balance of \$150 (\$900 − \$750) after the adjusting entry is posted.

The bookkeeping technique of converting the discount to interest expense over the term of the loan is described as **amortizing** the discount. After amortizing 10 months' interest expense, the carrying value of the liability reported on the December 31, 2016, balance sheet (see Exhibit 9.7) is \$9,850 (\$10,000 face value − \$150 discount). The effect of the interest recognition on the income statement is to increase expenses and decrease net income by \$750. The statement of cash flows is not affected by the accrual. Beacon recognizes the cash effects of the interest on the maturity date when it pays the maturity (face) value of the note to State Bank.

The journal entry to amortize the discount and its effects on the financial statements are shown here:

Account Title	Debit	Credit
Interest Expense	750	
Discount on Notes Payable		750

Event No.	Assets	=	Liabilities			+	Equity			Rev.	−	Exp.	=	Net Inc.	Cash Flow
	Cash	=	Notes Pay.	−	Disc. on N/P	+	Com. Stk.	+	Ret. Earn.						
4	NA	=	NA	−	(750)	+	NA	+	(750)	NA	−	750	=	(750)	NA

General Ledger T-Accounts and Financial Statements

Panel A of Exhibit 9.7 summarizes the 2016 accounting events. Panel B presents the ledger accounts in T-account form. The event numbers are shown in the T-accounts to facilitate your review. The closing entries are included and referenced with the abbreviation "cl." The financial statements are shown parenthetically in Panel C of the exhibit. You should study Exhibit 9.7 to strengthen your understanding of how the accounting for discount notes affects the financial statements.

EXHIBIT 9.7

The Big Picture

Panel A: Transaction Summary

1. Beacon issued a $10,000 face value, one-year, discount note with a 9 percent discount rate.
2. Beacon paid $8,000 cash for operating expenses.
3. Beacon earned cash service revenue of $12,000.
4. Beacon recognized $750 of accrued interest expense.
5. Beacon closed the revenue and expense accounts. The letters *cl* are the posting reference for the closing entry.

Panel B: General Ledger

Assets = Liabilities + Equity

Assets — Cash

	Debit	Credit	
(1)	9,100	8,000	(2)
(3)	12,000		
Bal.	13,100		

Liabilities — Notes Payable

	Debit	Credit	
		10,000	(1)
		10,000	Bal.

Liabilities — Discount on Notes Payable

	Debit	Credit	
(1)	900	750	(4)
Bal.	150		

Equity — Retained Earnings

	Debit	Credit	
		3,250	(cl.)
		3,250	Bal.

Equity — Service Revenue

	Debit	Credit	
(cl.)	12,000	12,000	(3)
		0	Bal.

Equity — Operating Expenses

	Debit	Credit	
(2)	8,000	8,000	(cl.)
Bal.	0		

Equity — Interest Expense

	Debit	Credit	
(4)	750	750	(cl.)
Bal.	0		

Panel C: Financial Statements for 2016

Income Statement

Service revenue	$12,000
Operating expenses	(8,000)
Operating income	4,000
Interest expense	(750)
Net income	$ 3,250

Balance Sheet

Assets		
Cash		$13,110
Liabilities		
Notes payable	$10,000	
Less: Disc. on notes pay.	(150)	
Total liabilities		$ 9,850
Stockholders' equity		
Retained earnings		3,250
Total liab. and stockholders' equity		$13,100

Statement of Cash Flows

Operating Activities	
Inflow from customers	$12,000
Outflow for expenses	(8,000)
Net inflow from operating activities	4,000
Investing Activities	0
Financing Activities	
Inflow from creditors	9,100
Net change in cash	13,100
Plus: Beginning cash balance	0
Ending cash balance	$13,100

Accounting Events Affecting 2017

In 2017, Beacon Management Services experienced the following four accounting events: (1) recognized accrued interest for 2017; (2) paid the face value of the note; (3) recognized revenue; and (4) recognized operating expenses.

EVENT 1 **Beacon recorded an adjusting entry to recognize interest accrued since December 31.**

Since the note had a one-year term, interest for two months remains to be accrued at the maturity date on February 28, 2017. Interest on this note accrues at $75 per month

($900 discount ÷ 12), so there is $150 ($75 × 2) of interest expense to recognize in 2017. Recognizing the interest increases liabilities (the Discount account is reduced to zero) and decreases stockholders' equity. The effect on the income statement of recognizing interest is to increase expenses and decrease net income by $150. The statement of cash flows is not affected by the interest recognition. The journal entry and its effects on the financial statements are shown here:

Account Title	Debit	Credit
Interest Expense	150	
Discount on Notes Payable		150

Event No.	Assets	=	Liabilities			+	Equity			Rev.	−	Exp.	=	Net Inc.	Cash Flow
	Cash	=	Notes Pay.	−	Disc. on N/P	+	Com. Stk.	+	Ret. Earn.						
1	NA	=	NA	−	(150)	+	NA	+	(150)	NA	−	150	=	(150)	NA

EVENT 2 Beacon paid the face value of the note.

The face value ($10,000) of the note is due on the maturity date. Paying the maturity value is an asset use transaction that decreases both assets and liabilities. The income statement is not affected by the payment. The $10,000 cash payment includes $900 for interest and $9,100 for principal. On the statement of cash flows a $900 outflow for interest is reported in the operating activities section and a $9,100 outflow for repaying the loan is reported in the financing activities section. The journal entry and its effects on the financial statements are shown here:

Account Title	Debit	Credit
Notes Payable	10,000	
Cash		10,000

Event No.	Assets	=	Liabilities			+	Equity			Rev.	−	Exp.	=	Net Inc.	Cash Flow
	Cash	=	Notes Pay.	−	Disc. on N/P	+	Com. Stk.	+	Ret. Earn.						
2	(10,000)	=	(10,000)	−	NA	+	NA	+	NA	NA	−	NA	=	NA	(900) OA (9,100) FA

EVENT 3 Beacon recognized $13,000 of cash service revenue.

Recognizing the revenue increases both assets and stockholders' equity. Net income also increases. The cash inflow is reported in the operating activities section of the statement of cash flows. The journal entry and its effects on the financial statements are shown here:

Account Title	Debit	Credit
Cash	13,000	
Service Revenue		13,000

Event No.	Assets	=	Liabilities			+	Equity			Rev.	−	Exp.	=	Net Inc.	Cash Flow
	Cash	=	Notes Pay.	−	Disc. on N/P	+	Com. Stk.	+	Ret. Earn.						
3	13,000	=	NA	−	NA	+	NA	+	13,000	13,000	−	NA	=	13,000	13,000 OA

EVENT 4 Beacon incurred $8,500 of cash operating expenses.

This event decreases both assets and stockholders' equity. Net income also decreases. The cash outflow is reported in the operating activities section of the statement of cash flows. The journal entry and its effects on the financial statements are shown here:

Account Title	Debit	Credit
Operating Expenses	8,500	
Cash		8,500

Event No.	Assets	=	Liabilities			+	Equity			Rev.	−	Exp.	=	Net Inc.	Cash Flow
	Cash	=	Notes Pay.	−	Disc. on N/P	+	Com. Stk.	+	Ret. Earn.						
4	(8,500)	=	NA	−	NA	+	NA	+	(8,500)	NA	−	8,500	=	(8,500)	(8,500) OA

General Ledger T-Accounts and Financial Statements

Panel A of Exhibit 9.8 summarizes the 2017 accounting events. Panel B presents the ledger accounts in T-account form. The event numbers are shown in the T-accounts

EXHIBIT 9.8

The Big Picture

Panel A: Transaction Summary

Event 1	Recognized accrued interest for 2017.
Event 2	Paid face value of note.
Event 3	Recognized revenue.
Event 4	Recognized operating expenses.

Panel B: General Ledger

Assets = Liabilities + Equity

Assets — Cash

	Debit	Credit	
Bal.	13,100	10,000	(2)
(3)	13,000	8,500	(4)
Bal.	7,600		

Liabilities — Notes Payable

	Debit	Credit	
(2)	10,000	10,000	Bal.
		0	Bal.

Discount on Notes Payable

	Debit	Credit	
Bal.	150	150	(1)
Bal.	0		

Equity — Retained Earnings

	Debit	Credit	
		3,250	Bal.
		4,350	(cl.)
		7,600	Bal.

Service Revenue

	Debit	Credit	
(cl.)	13,000	13,000	(3)
		0	Bal.

Operating Expenses

	Debit	Credit	
(4)	8,500	8,500	(cl.)
Bal.	0		

Interest Expense

	Debit	Credit	
(1)	150	150	(cl.)
Bal.	0		

continued

EXHIBIT 9.8 *Concluded*

Panel C: Financial Statements for 2017

Income Statement	
Service revenue	$13,000
Operating expenses	(8,500)
Operating income	4,500
Interest expense	(150)
Net income	$ 4,350

Balance Sheet	
Assets	
Cash	$7,600
Liabilities	$ 0
Stockholders' equity	
Retained earnings	7,600
Total liab. and stockholders' equity	$7,600

Statement of Cash Flows	
Operating Activities	
Inflow from customers	$13,000
Outflow for expenses	(8,500)
Outflow for interest	(900)
Net inflow from operating activities	3,600
Investing Activities	0
Financing Activities	
Outflow to creditors	(9,100)
Net change in cash	(5,500)
Plus: Beginning cash balance	13,100
Ending cash balance	$ 7,600

to facilitate your review. The closing entries are included and referenced with the abbreviation "cl." The financial statements are shown parenthetically in Panel C of the exhibit.

You should study Exhibit 9.8 to strengthen your understanding of how accounting for discount notes affects the financial statements. Observe that no liabilities are reported in the balance sheet because Beacon has paid off the note and interest before the closing date. Since Beacon has not paid dividends since its inception, retained earning represents the sum of net income recognized for 2016 and 2017.

SELF-STUDY REVIEW PROBLEM

A step-by-step audio-narrated series of slides is available in the Connect library.

Perfect Picture Inc. (PPI) experienced the following transactions during 2016. The transactions are summarized (transaction data pertain to the full year) and limited to those that affect the company's current liabilities.

1. PPI had cash sales of $820,000. The state requires that PPI charge customers an 8 percent sales tax (ignore cost of goods sold).
2. PPI paid the state sales tax authority $63,000.
3. On March 1, PPI issued a note payable to County Bank. PPI received $50,000 cash (principal balance). The note had a one-year term and a 6 percent annual interest rate.
4. On December 31, PPI recognized accrued interest on the note issued in Event 3.
5. On December 31, PPI recognized warranty expense at the rate of 3 percent of sales.
6. PPI paid $22,000 cash to settle warranty claims.
7. PPI has five employees. Four of the employees each earn $40,000 per year. The fifth employee, the store manager, earns $120,000 per year. The annual amount withheld for income tax for all employees is $54,000. Each of the five employees has volunteered to have $50 per month withheld as a charitable contribution to the United Way. Record the net pay as a liability.
8. Based on the salary data described in Event 7, PPI recognized payroll tax expense for FICA and unemployment taxes.
9. During the year PPI remitted the following amounts of cash in partial settlement of the indicated liabilities.

Employee income tax payable	$ 52,000
FICA tax—Social Security payable	27,000
FICA tax—Medicare payable	7,000
United Way payable	2,500
Salaries payable	190,250
Federal unemployment tax payable	200
State unemployment tax payable	1,500

10. PPI pays $320 per month for medical insurance premiums for each employee. The company also contributes an amount equal to 4 percent of salaries to a pension fund for each employee. Each employee accrues vacation pay at a rate of $300 per month.
11. During the year PPI remitted the following amount of cash in partial settlement of the indicated liabilities.

Medical insurance payable	$18,000
Employee pension fund payable	8,200
Vacation pay payable	16,400

Required

a. Prepare in general journal form the entries to record the transactions described above.

b. Prepare the current liabilities section of the December 31, 2016, balance sheet.

Solution to Requirement a

Event No.	Account Title	Debit	Credit
1	Cash	885,600	
	Sales Revenue		820,000
	Sales Tax Payable		65,600
2	Sales Tax Payable	63,000	
	Cash		63,000
3	Cash	50,000	
	Notes Payable		50,000
4	Interest Expense ($50,000 × 0.06 × 10/12)	2,500	
	Interest Payable		2,500
5	Warranty Expense ($820,000 × 0.03)	24,600	
	Warranties Payable		24,600
6	Warranties Payable	22,000	
	Cash		22,000
7	Salary Expense [(4 × $40,000) + $120,000)]	280,000	
	Employee Income Tax Payable		54,000
	FICA Tax—Social Security Payable*		16,200
	FICA Tax—Medicare Payable ($280,000 × 0.015)		4,200
	United Way Payable ($50 × 5 × 12)		3,000
	Salaries Payable		202,600
8	Payroll Tax Expense	22,500	
	FICA Tax—Social Security Payable*		16,200
	FICA Tax—Medicare Payable ($280,000 × 0.015)		4,200
	Federal Unemployment Tax Payable ($7,000 × 5 × 0.006)		210
	State Unemployment Tax Payable ($7,000 × 5 × 0.054)		1,890
			continued

*Recall that the chapter assumes Social Security tax is applied to a maximum limit of $110,000.
[($40,000 × 0.06 = $2,400 × 4 = $9,600) + ($110,000 × 0.06 = $6,600)] = $16,200

Event No.	Account Title	Debit	Credit
9	Employee Income Tax Payable	52,000	
	FICA Tax—Social Security Payable	27,000	
	FICA Tax—Medicare Payable	7,000	
	United Way Payable	2,500	
	Salaries Payable	190,250	
	Federal Unemployment Tax Payable	200	
	State Unemployment Tax Payable	1,500	
	Cash		280,450
10	Fringe Benefits Expense	48,400	
	Medical Insurance Payable ($320 × 12 × 5)		19,200
	Employee Pension Fund Payable ($280,000 × 0.04)		11,200
	Vacation Pay Payable ($300 × 12 × 5)		18,000
11	Medical Insurance Payable	18,000	
	Employee Pension Fund Payable	8,200	
	Vacation Pay Payable	16,400	
	Cash		42,600

Solution to Requirement b

PERFECT PICTURE INC.
Partial Balance Sheet
December 31, 2016

Current Liabilities	
Sales tax payable ($65,600 − $63,000)	$ 2,600
Notes payable	50,000
Interest payable	2,500
Warranties payable ($24,600 − $22,000)	2,600
Employee income tax payable ($54,000 − $52,000)	2,000
FICA—Social Security payable ($16,200 + $16,200 − $27,000)	5,400
FICA—Medicare payable ($4,200 + $4,200 − $7,000)	1,400
United Way payable ($3,000 − $2,500)	500
Salaries payable ($202,600 − $190,250)	12,350
Federal unemployment tax payable ($210 − $200)	10
State unemployment tax payable ($1,890 − $1,500)	390
Medical insurance payable ($19,200 − $18,000)	1,200
Employee pension fund payable ($11,200 − $8,200)	3,000
Vacation pay payable ($18,000 − $16,400)	1,600
Total current liabilities	$85,550

KEY TERMS

Amortizing 503
Classified balance sheets 498
Contingent liability 485
Contra liability account 502
Current (short-term) asset 497
Current (short-term) liabilities 497
Current ratio 499
Discount 501
Discount note 501
Discount on Notes Payable 502
Employee 489
Employee's Withholding Allowance Certificate, Form W-4 491
Employer's Quarterly Federal Tax Return, Form 941 492
Federal Unemployment Tax Act (FUTA) 495
General uncertainties 485
Going concern assumption 480
Gross earnings 490
Independent contractor 489
Interest-bearing notes 501
Issuer 482
Liquidity 499
Medicare 492
Net pay 494
Note payable 482
Operating cycle 497
Principal 501
Proceeds 501
Salaries 490
Social Security 492
Solvency 499
Wage and Tax Statement, Form W-2 491
Wages 490
Warranties 486

QUESTIONS

1. What type of transaction is a cash payment to creditors? How does this type of transaction affect the accounting equation?
2. What is a current liability? Distinguish between a current liability and a long-term debt.
3. What is included in the entry to record accrued interest expense? How does it affect the accounting equation?
4. Who is the maker of a note payable?
5. What is the going concern assumption? Does it affect the way liabilities are reported in the financial statements?
6. Why is it necessary to make an adjusting entry at the end of the accounting period for unpaid interest on a note payable?
7. Assume that on October 1, 2016, Big Company borrowed $10,000 from the local bank at 6 percent interest. The note is due on October 1, 2017. How much interest does Big pay in 2016? How much interest does Big pay in 2017? What amount of cash does Big pay back in 2017?
8. When a business collects sales tax from customers, is it revenue? Why or why not?
9. What is a contingent liability?
10. List the three categories of contingent liabilities.
11. Are contingent liabilities recorded on a company's books? Explain.
12. What is the difference in accounting procedures for a liability that is probable and estimable and one that is reasonably possible but not estimable?
13. What type of liabilities are not recorded on a company's books?
14. What does the term *warranty* mean?
15. What effect does recognizing future warranty obligations have on the balance sheet? On the income statement?
16. When is warranty cost reported on the statement of cash flows?
17. What is the difference between an employee and an independent contractor?
18. What is the difference between wages and salaries?
19. What is the purpose of the W-2 form? What is the purpose of the W-4 form?
20. What two taxes are components of the FICA tax? What programs do they fund?
21. Who pays the FICA tax? Is there a ceiling on the amount of tax that is paid?
22. What is the difference between gross pay and net pay for an employee?
23. Why are amounts withheld from employees' pay considered liabilities of the employer?
24. What is the purpose of the Federal Unemployment Tax? What is the maximum amount of wages subject to the tax?
25. What items are included in compensation cost for a company in addition to the gross salaries of the employees?
26. Give two examples of fringe benefits.
27. What is a classified balance sheet?
28. What is the difference between the liquidity and the solvency of a business?
29. The higher the company's current ratio, the better the company's financial condition. Do you agree with this statement? Explain.
30. What is the difference between an interest-bearing note and a discount note?
31. How is the carrying value of a discount note computed?
32. Will the effective rate of interest be the same on a $10,000 face value, 6 percent interest-bearing note and a $10,000 face value, 6 percent discount note? Is the amount of cash received upon making these two loans the same? Why or why not?
33. How does the *amortization* of a discount affect the income statement, balance sheet, and statement of cash flows?
34. How does issuing an $8,000 discount note with an 8 percent discount rate and a one-year term to maturity affect the accounting equation?
35. What type of account is Discount on Notes Payable?

MULTIPLE-CHOICE QUESTIONS

Multiple-choice questions are available in the Connect library.

EXERCISES—SERIES A

connect plus+ ACCOUNTING — ***All applicable Exercises in Series A are available with McGraw-Hill's Connect Plus Accounting.***

LO 9-1

Exercise 9-1A *Recognizing accrued interest expense*

Abardeen Corporation borrowed $90,000 from the bank on October 1, 2016. The note had an 8 percent annual rate of interest and matured on March 31, 2017. Interest and principal were paid in cash on the maturity date.

Required

a. What amount of cash did Abardeen pay for interest in 2016?

b. What amount of interest expense was recognized on the 2016 income statement?

c. What amount of total liabilities was reported on the December 31, 2016, balance sheet?

d. What total amount of cash was paid to the bank on March 31, 2017, for principal and interest?

e. What amount of interest expense was reported on the 2017 income statement?

Exercise 9-2A *Effects of recognizing accrued interest on financial statements* LO 9-1

Bill Darby started Darby Company on January 1, 2016. The company experienced the following events during its first year of operation:

1. Earned $16,200 of cash revenue.
2. Borrowed $12,000 cash from the bank.
3. Adjusted the accounting records to recognize accrued interest expense on the bank note. The note, issued on September 1, 2016, had a one-year term and an 8 percent annual interest rate.

Required

a. What is the amount of interest payable at December 31, 2016?

b. What is the amount of interest expense in 2016?

c. What is the amount of interest paid in 2016?

d. Use a horizontal statements model to show how each event affects the balance sheet, income statement, and statement of cash flows. Indicate whether the event increases (I), decreases (D), or does not affect (NA) each element of the financial statements. In the Cash Flows column, designate the cash flows as operating activities (OA), investing activities (IA), or financing activities (FA). The first transaction has been recorded as an example.

Event No.	Balance Sheet									Income Statement					Statement of Cash Flows
	Cash	=	Notes Pay.	+	Int. Pay.	+	Com. Stk.	+	Ret. Earn.	Rev.	–	Exp.	=	Net Inc.	
1	I	=	NA	+	NA	+	NA	+	I	I	–	NA	=	I	I OA

Exercise 9-3A *Recording sales tax* LO 9-2

Vail Book Mart sells books and other supplies to students in a state where the sales tax rate is 8 percent. Vail Book Mart engaged in the following transactions for 2016. Sales tax of 8 percent is collected on all sales.

1. Book sales, not including sales tax, for 2016 amounted to $250,000 cash.
2. Cash sales of miscellaneous items in 2016 were $85,000, not including tax.
3. Cost of goods sold was $190,000 for the year.
4. Paid $117,000 in operating expenses for the year.
5. Paid the sales tax collected to the state agency.

Required

a. What is the total amount of sales tax Vail Book Mart collected and paid for the year?

b. Prepare the journal entries for the above transactions.

c. What is Vail Book Mart's net income for the year?

Exercise 9-4A *Recognizing sales tax payable* LO 9-2

The following selected transactions apply to Topeca Supply for November and December 2016. November was the first month of operations. Sales tax is collected at the time of sale but is not paid to the state sales tax agency until the following month.

1. Cash sales for November 2016 were $165,000 plus sales tax of 7 percent.
2. Topeca Supply paid the November sales tax to the state agency on December 10, 2016.
3. Cash sales for December 2016 were $180,000 plus sales tax of 7 percent.

Required

a. Record the above transactions in general journal form.

b. Show the effect of the above transactions on a horizontal statements model like the one shown below.

Assets:	=	Liabilities	+	Equity			Income Statement					Cash Flow
Cash	=	Sales Tax Pay.	+	Com. Stk.	+	Ret. Earn.	Rev.	−	Exp.	=	Net Inc.	

c. What was the total amount of sales tax paid in 2016?

d. What was the total amount of sales tax collected in 2016?

e. What amount of sales tax expense will be reported on the 2016 income statement?

LO 9-3

Exercise 9-5A *Contingent liabilities*

The following three independent sets of facts relate to contingent liabilities:

1. In November of the current year an automobile manufacturing company recalled all pickup trucks manufactured during the past two years. A flaw in the battery cable was discovered and the recall provides for replacement of the defective cables. The estimated cost of this recall is \$2 million.
2. The EPA has notified a company of violations of environmental laws relating to hazardous waste. These actions seek cleanup costs, penalties, and damages to property. The company is reasonably certain there will be cost associated with the cleanup, but cannot estimate the amount. The cleanup cost could be as high as \$4,000,000 or as little as \$500,000 and insurance could reimburse all or part of the cost. There is no way to more accurately estimate the cost to the company at this time.
3. Holland Company does not carry property damage insurance because of the cost. The company has suffered substantial losses each of the past three years. However, it has had no losses for the current year. Management thinks this is too good to be true and is sure there will be significant losses in the coming year. However, the exact amount cannot be determined.

Required

a. Discuss the various categories of contingent liabilities.

b. For each item above, determine the correct accounting treatment. Prepare any required journal entries.

LO 9-4

Exercise 9-6A *Effect of warranties on income and cash flow*

To support herself while attending school, Daun Deloch sold stereo systems to other students. During the first year of operations, Daun purchased the stereo systems for \$140,000 and sold them for \$250,000 cash. She provided her customers with a one-year warranty against defects in parts and labor. Based on industry standards, she estimated that warranty claims would amount to 2 percent of sales. During the year she paid \$2,820 cash to replace a defective tuner.

Required

Prepare an income statement and statement of cash flows for Daun's first year of operation. Based on the information given, what is Daun's total warranties liability at the end of the accounting period?

LO 9-4

Exercise 9-7A *Effect of warranty obligations and payments on financial statements*

The Chair Company provides a 120-day parts-and-labor warranty on all merchandise it sells. The Chair Company estimates the warranty expense for the current period to be \$2,650. During the period a customer returned a product that cost \$1,830 to repair.

Required

a. Show the effects of these transactions on the financial statements using a horizontal statements model like the example shown here. Use + for increase, − for decrease, and NA for not affected. In the Cash Flow column, indicate whether the item is an operating activity (OA), investing activity (IA), or financing activity (FA).

Assets	=	Liab.	+	Equity	Rev.	−	Exp.	=	Net Inc.	Cash Flow

b. Prepare the journal entry to record the warranty expense for the period.

c. Prepare the journal entry to record payment for the actual repair costs.

d. Why do companies estimate warranty expense and record the expense before the repairs are actually made?

Exercise 9-8A *Current liabilities*

LO 9-1, 9-2, 9-4

The following transactions apply to Ozark Sales for 2016:

1. The business was started when the company received $50,000 from the issue of common stock.
2. Purchased equipment inventory of $380,000 on account.
3. Sold equipment for $510,000 cash (not including sales tax). Sales tax of 8 percent is collected when the merchandise is sold. The merchandise had a cost of $330,000.
4. Provided a six-month warranty on the equipment sold. Based on industry estimates, the warranty claims would amount to 2 percent of sales.
5. Paid the sales tax to the state agency on $400,000 of the sales.
6. On September 1, 2016, borrowed $50,000 from the local bank. The note had a 4 percent interest rate and matured on March 1, 2017.
7. Paid $6,200 for warranty repairs during the year.
8. Paid operating expenses of $78,000 for the year.
9. Paid $250,000 of accounts payable.
10. Recorded accrued interest on the note issued in transaction no. 6.

Required

a. Show the effect of these transactions on the financial statements using a horizontal statements model like the one shown here. Use + for increase, − for decrease, and NA for not affected. In the Cash Flow column, indicate whether the item is an operating activity (OA), investing activity (IA), or financing activity (FA). The first transaction is recorded as an example.

Assets	=	Liabilities	+	Equity	Rev.	−	Exp.	=	Net Inc.	Cash Flow
+		NA		+	NA		NA		NA	+ FA

b. Prepare the journal entries for the above transactions and post them to the appropriate T-accounts.

c. Prepare the income statement, balance sheet, and statement of cash flows for 2016.

d. What is the total amount of current liabilities at December 31, 2016?

Exercise 9-9A *Calculating payroll*

LO 9-5

Zolnick Enterprises has two hourly employees, Kelly and Jon. Both employees earn overtime at the rate of 1½ times the hourly rate for hours worked in excess of 40 per week. Assume the Social Security tax rate is 6 percent on the first $110,000 of wages and the Medicare tax rate is 1.5 percent on all earnings. Federal income tax withheld for Kelly and Jon was $260 and $220, respectively, for the first week of January. The following information is for the first week in January 2016:

Employee	Hours Worked	Wage Rate per Hour
Kelly	54	$32
Jon	44	$26

Required

a. Calculate the gross pay for each employee for the week.

b. Calculate the net pay for each employee for the week.

c. Prepare the general journal entry to record payment of the wages.

LO 9-5

Exercise 9-10A *Calculating payroll*

Old Town Entertainment has two employees in 2016. Clay earns \$3,600 per month and Philip, the manager, earns \$10,800 per month. Neither is paid extra for working overtime. Assume the Social Security tax rate is 6 percent on the first \$110,000 of earnings and the Medicare tax rate is 1.5 percent on all earnings. The federal income tax withholding is 15 percent of gross earnings for Clay and 20 percent for Philip. Both Clay and Philip have been employed all year.

Required

a. Calculate the net pay for both Clay and Philip for March.

b. Calculate the net pay for both Clay and Philip for December.

c. Is the net pay the same in March and December for both employees? Why or why not?

d. What amounts will Old Town report on the 2016 W-2s for each employee?

LO 9-5

Exercise 9-11A *Calculating employee and employer payroll taxes*

Sky Co. employed Tom Mills in 2016. Tom earned \$5,100 per month and worked the entire year. Assume the Social Security tax rate is 6 percent for the first \$110,000 of earnings and the Medicare tax rate is 1.5 percent. Tom's federal income tax withholding amount is \$900 per month. Use 5.4 percent for the state unemployment tax rate and .06 percent for the federal unemployment tax rate on the first \$7,000 of earnings per employee.

Required

a. Answer the following questions.

(1) What is Tom's net pay per month?

(2) What amount does Tom pay monthly in FICA payroll taxes?

(3) What is the total payroll tax expense for Sky Co. for January 2016? February 2016? March 2016? December 2016?

b. Assume that instead of \$5,100 per month Tom earned \$9,600 per month. Answer the questions in Requirement *a*.

LO 9-5

Exercise 9-12A *Fringe benefits and payroll expense*

Silver Co. provides various fringe benefits for its two employees. It provides vacation and personal leave at the rate of one day for each month worked. Its employees earn a combined total of approximately \$420 per day. In addition, Silver Co. pays \$650 per month in medical insurance premiums for its employees. Silver also contributes \$400 per month into a retirement plan for the employees. The federal unemployment tax rate is .06 percent and the state unemployment tax rate is 4.0 percent on the first \$7,000 of earnings per employee.

Required

a. Prepare the monthly journal entry for the accrued fringe benefits.

b. Show the effect of the above transaction on a horizontal statements model like the one shown below.

Assets =	Liabilities	+	Equity			Income Statement	Cash Flow
Cash =	Various Payables	+	Com. Stk.	+	Ret. Earn.	Rev. − Exp. = Net Inc.	

c. If the three employees each worked 250 days, what is Silver Co.'s total payroll cost (salary, payroll taxes, and fringe benefits) for the year? (Assume that each employee earns \$315 per day.)

Exercise 9-13A *Comprehensive single cycle problem*

LO 9-1, 9-2, 9-4, 9-5

The following transactions apply to Park Co. for 2016:

1. Received $50,000 cash from the issue of common stock.
2. Purchased inventory on account for $180,000.
3. Sold inventory for $250,000 cash that had cost $140,000. Sales tax was collected at the rate of 5 percent on the inventory sold.
4. Borrowed $50,000 from First State Bank on March 1, 2016. The note had a 7 percent interest rate and a one-year term to maturity.
5. Paid the accounts payable (see transaction 2).
6. Paid the sales tax due on $190,000 of sales. Sales tax on the other $60,000 is not due until after the end of the year.
7. Salaries for the year for the one employee amounted to $46,000. Assume the Social Security tax rate is 6 percent and the Medicare tax rate is 1.5 percent. Federal income tax withheld was $5,300.
8. Paid $5,800 for warranty repairs during the year.
9. Paid $36,000 of other operating expenses during the year.
10. Paid a dividend of $2,000 to the shareholders.

Adjustments:

11. The products sold in transaction 3 were warranted. Park estimated that the warranty cost would be 3 percent of sales.
12. Record the accrued interest at December 31, 2016.
13. Record the accrued payroll tax at December 31, 2016. Assume no payroll taxes have been paid for the year and that the unemployment tax rate is 6 percent (federal unemployment tax rate is .06 percent and the state unemployment tax rate is 5.4 percent on the first $7,000 of earnings per employee).

Required

a. Record the above transactions in general journal form.

b. Post the transactions to T-accounts.

c. Prepare an income statement, statement of changes in stockholders' equity, balance sheet, and statement of cash flows for 2016.

Exercise 9-14A *Preparing a classified balance sheet*

LO 9-6

Required

Use the following information to prepare a classified balance sheet for Alpha Co. at the end of 2016.

Accounts receivable	$26,500
Accounts payable	12,200
Cash	20,500
Common stock	30,000
Land	10,000
Long-term notes payable	17,500
Merchandise inventory	26,300
Retained earnings	23,600

Exercise 9-15A *Using the current ratio to make comparisons*

LO 9-7

The following information was drawn from the 2017 balance sheets of the Cedar and Maple companies:

	Cedar	Maple
Current assets	$40,000	$70,000
Current liabilities	25,000	55,000

Required

a. Compute the current ratio for each company.

b. Which company has the greater likelihood of being able to pay its bills?

c. Assume that both companies have the same amount of total assets. Speculate as to which company would produce the higher return on assets ratio.

LO 9-8

Exercise 9-16A *Effect of a discount note on financial statements (Appendix)*

Helen Parish started a design company on January 1, 2016. On April 1, 2016, Parish borrowed cash from a local bank by issuing a one-year $120,000 face value note with annual interest based on an 8 percent discount. During 2016, Parish provided services for $72,000 cash.

Required

Answer the following questions. (*Hint:* Record the events in T-accounts prior to answering the questions.)

a. What is the amount of total liabilities on the December 31, 2016, balance sheet?

b. What is the amount of net income on the 2016 income statement?

c. What is the amount of cash flow from operating activities on the 2016 statement of cash flows?

d. Provide the general journal entries necessary to record issuing the note on April 1, 2016; recognizing accrued interest on December 31, 2016; and repaying the loan on March 31, 2017.

LO 9-1, 9-8

Exercise 9-17A *Comparing effective interest rates on discount versus interest-bearing notes (Appendix)*

Sheldon Jones borrowed money by issuing two notes on March 1, 2016. The financing transactions are described here.

1. Borrowed funds by issuing a $52,000 face value discount note to Farmers Bank. The note had an 8 percent discount rate, a one-year term to maturity, and was paid off on March 1, 2017.
2. Borrowed funds by issuing a $52,000 face value, interest-bearing note to Valley Bank. The note had an 8 percent stated rate of interest, a one-year term to maturity, and was paid off on March 1, 2017.

Required

a. Show the effects of issuing the two notes on the financial statements using separate horizontal financial statement models like the ones here. Record the transaction amounts under the appropriate categories. In the Cash Flow column, indicate whether the item is an operating activity (OA), investing activity (IA), or financing activity (FA). Record only the events occurring on the date of issue. Do not record accrued interest or the repayment at maturity.

Discount Note

Assets =	Liabilities	+ Equity	Rev. − Exp. = Net Inc.	Cash Flow
Cash =	Notes Pay. − Disc. on Notes Pay.	+ Ret. Earn.		

Interest-Bearing Note

Assets	=	Liabilities	+	Equity	Rev.	−	Exp.	=	Net Inc.	Cash Flow
Cash	=	Notes Pay.	+	Ret. Earn.						

b. What is the total amount of interest to be paid on each note?

c. What amount of cash was received from each note when it was issued?

d. Which note has the higher effective interest rate? Support your answer with appropriate computations.

Exercise 9-18A *Recording accounting events for a discount note (Appendix)*

LO 9-8

Harden Co. issued a $60,000 face value discount note to National Bank on July 1, 2016. The note had a 6 percent discount rate and a one-year term to maturity.

Required

Prepare general journal entries for the following:

a. The issuance of the note on July 1, 2016.
b. The adjustment for accrued interest at the end of the year, December 31, 2016.
c. Recording interest expense for 2017 and repaying the principal on June 30, 2017.

PROBLEMS—SERIES A

connect plus+ ACCOUNTING ***All applicable Problems in Series A are available with McGraw-Hill's Connect Plus Accounting.***

Problem 9-19A *Effect of accrued interest on financial statements*

LO 9-1

Malco Enterprises issued $10,000 of common stock when the company was started. In addition, Malco borrowed $36,000 from a local bank on July 1, 2016. The note had a 6 percent annual interest rate and a one-year term to maturity. Malco Enterprises recognized $72,500 of revenue on account in 2016 and $85,200 of revenue on account in 2017. Cash collections of accounts receivable were $61,300 in 2016 and $71,500 in 2017. Malco paid $39,000 of other operating expenses in 2016 and $45,000 of other operating expenses in 2017. Malco repaid the loan and interest at the maturity date.

CHECK FIGURES
a. $1,080
b. $22,300

Required

Based on this information, answer the following questions. (*Hint:* Record the events in the accounting equation before answering the questions.)

a. What amount of interest expense would Malco report on the 2016 income statement?
b. What amount of net cash flow from operating activities would Malco report on the 2016 statement of cash flows?
c. What amount of total liabilities would Malco report on the December 31, 2016, balance sheet?
d. What amount of retained earnings would Malco report on the December 31, 2016, balance sheet?
e. What amount of net cash flow from financing activities would Malco report on the 2016 statement of cash flows?
f. What amount of interest expense would Malco report on the 2017 income statement?
g. What amount of net cash flow from operating activities would Malco report on the 2017 statement of cash flows?
h. What amount of total assets would Malco report on the December 31, 2017, balance sheet?
i. What amount of net cash flow from investing activities would Malco report on the 2017 statement of cash flows?
j. If Malco Enterprises paid a $2,000 dividend during 2017, what retained earnings balance would it report on the December 31, 2017, balance sheet?

Problem 9-20A *Account for short-term debt and sales tax—two accounting cycles*

LO 9-1, 9-2

The following transactions apply to Walnut Enterprises for 2016, its first year of operations:

CHECK FIGURES
c. Net Income, 2013: $65,750
f. Total Assets, 2014: $164,460

1. Received $50,000 cash from the issue of a short-term note with a 6 percent interest rate and a one-year maturity. The note was made on April 1, 2016.
2. Received $130,000 cash plus applicable sales tax from performing services. The services are subject to a sales tax rate of 6 percent.
3. Paid $62,000 cash for other operating expenses during the year.
4. Paid the sales tax due on $110,000 of the service revenue for the year. Sales tax on the balance of the revenue is not due until 2017.
5. Recognized the accrued interest at December 31, 2016.

The following transactions apply to Walnut Enterprises for 2017:

1. Paid the balance of the sales tax due for 2016.
2. Received $201,000 cash plus applicable sales tax from performing services. The services are subject to a sales tax rate of 6 percent.
3. Repaid the principal of the note and applicable interest on April 1, 2017.
4. Paid $102,500 of other operating expenses during the year.
5. Paid the sales tax due on $185,000 of the service revenue. The sales tax on the balance of the revenue is not due until 2018.

Required

a. Record the 2016 transactions in general journal form.
b. Post the transactions to T-accounts.
c. Prepare a balance sheet, statement of changes in stockholders' equity, income statement, and statement of cash flows for 2016.
d. Prepare the closing entries and post them to the T-accounts.
e. Prepare a post-closing trial balance.
f. Repeat Requirements *a* through *e* for 2017.

LO 9-3

Problem 9-21A *Contingent liabilities*

Required

a. Give an example of a contingent liability that is probable and reasonably estimable. How would this type of liability be shown in the accounting records?
b. Give an example of a contingent liability that is reasonably possible or probable but not reasonably estimable. How would this type of liability be shown in the accounting records?
c. Give an example of a contingent liability that is remote. How is this type of liability shown in the accounting records?

LO 9-1, 9-2, 9-3, 9-4

CHECK FIGURE

b. Total Current Liabilities: $22,600

Problem 9-22A *Current liabilities*

The following selected transactions were taken from the books of Ripley Company for 2016:

1. On February 1, 2016, borrowed $70,000 cash from the local bank. The note had a 6 percent interest rate and was due on June 1, 2016.
2. Cash sales for the year amounted to $240,000 plus sales tax at the rate of 7 percent.
3. Ripley provides a 90-day warranty on the merchandise sold. The warranty expense is estimated to be 1 percent of sales.
4. Paid the sales tax to the state sales tax agency on $210,000 of the sales.
5. Paid the note due on June 1 and the related interest.
6. On November 1, 2016, borrowed $20,000 cash from the local bank. The note had a 6 percent interest rate and a one-year term to maturity.
7. Paid $2,100 in warranty repairs.
8. A customer has filed a lawsuit against Ripley for $1 million for breach of contract. The company attorney does not believe the suit has merit.

Required

a. Answer the following questions:
   (1) What amount of cash did Ripley pay for interest during 2016?
   (2) What amount of interest expense is reported on Ripley's income statement for 2016?
   (3) What is the amount of warranty expense for 2016?
b. Prepare the current liabilities section of the balance sheet at December 31, 2016. (*Hint:* First post the liabilities transactions to T-accounts.)
c. Show the effect of these transactions on the financial statements using a horizontal statements model like the one on the next page. Use + for increase, − for decrease, and NA for not affected. In the Cash Flow column, indicate whether the item is an operating

activity (OA), investing activity (IA), or financing activity (FA). The first transaction has been recorded as an example.

Assets	=	Liabilities	+	Equity	Rev.	−	Exp.	=	Net Inc.	Cash Flow
+		+		NA	NA		NA		NA	+ FA

Problem 9-23A *Accounting for payroll and payroll taxes*

LO 9-5

Electronics Service Co. pays salaries monthly on the last day of the month. The following information is available from Electronics for the month ended December 31, 2016:

Administrative salaries	$96,000
Sales salaries	57,000
Office salaries	38,000

Assume the Social Security tax rate is 6 percent on the first $110,000 of salaries. Duke reached the $110,000 amount in September. His salary in December amounted to $11,500 and is included in the $96,000. No one else will reach the $110,000 amount for the year. None of the employee salaries are subject to unemployment tax in December.

Other amounts withheld from salaries in December were as follows:

Federal income tax	$21,500
State income tax	11,200
Employee savings plan	4,000

Required

a. Prepare the journal entry to record the payment of payroll on December 31, 2016.

b. Prepare the journal entry to record the payroll tax expense for Electronics Service Co. for December 2016.

Problem 9-24A *Computation of net pay and payroll expense*

LO 9-5

CHECK FIGURE
e. $4,055.24

The following information is available for the employees of Webber Packing Company for the first week of January 2016:

1. Kayla earns $28 per hour and 1½ times her regular rate for hours over 40 per week. Kayla worked 52 hours the first week in January. Kayla's federal income tax withholding is equal to 15 percent of her gross pay. Webber pays medical insurance of $50 per week for Kayla and contributes $50 per week to a retirement plan for her.
2. Paula earns a weekly salary of $1,600. Paula's federal income tax withholding is 18 percent of her gross pay. Webber pays medical insurance of $80 per week for Paula and contributes $100 per week to a retirement plan for her.
3. Vacation pay is accrued at the rate of 2 hours per week (based on the regular pay rate) for Kayla and $60 per week for Paula.

Assume the Social Security tax rate is 6 percent on the first $110,000 of salaries and the Medicare tax rate is 1.5 percent of total salaries. The state unemployment tax rate is 5.4 percent and the federal unemployment tax rate is 0.6 percent of the first $7,000 of salary for each employee.

Required

a. Compute the gross pay for Kayla for the first week in January.

b. Compute the net pay for both Kayla and Paula for the first week in January.

c. Prepare the journal entry to record the payment of the payroll for the week.

d. Prepare the journal entry to record the payroll tax expense and fringe benefit expense for Webber Packing Company for the week.

e. What is the total cost of compensation expense for the first week of January 2016 for Webber Packing Company?

LO 9-6

Problem 9-25A *Multistep income statement and classified balance sheet*

CHECK FIGURES
Total Current Assets: $212,700
Total Current Liabilities: $67,500

Required

Use the following information to prepare a multistep income statement and a classified balance sheet for Eller Equipment Co. for 2016. (*Hint:* Some of the items will *not* appear on either statement, and ending retained earnings must be calculated.)

Salaries expense	$ 72,000	Beginning retained earnings	$134,150
Common stock	50,000	Warranties payable (short term)	2,500
Notes receivable (short term)	10,000	Gain on sale of equipment	8,500
Allowance for doubtful accounts	6,500	Operating expenses	96,000
Accumulated depreciation	42,300	Cash flow from investing activities	125,000
Notes payable (long term)	80,000	Prepaid rent	14,000
Salvage value of building	6,000	Land	70,000
Interest payable (short term)	1,500	Cash	26,300
Uncollectible accounts expense	7,150	Inventory	110,500
Supplies	1,800	Accounts payable	32,000
Equipment	97,500	Interest expense	8,600
Interest revenue	3,600	Salaries payable	5,200
Sales revenue	510,000	Unearned revenue	26,300
Dividends	$ 11,500	Cost of goods sold	310,000
Warranty expense	9,600	Accounts receivable	56,000
Interest receivable (short term)	600	Depreciation expense	1,000

LO 9-7

Problem 9-26A *Using ratios to make comparisons*

CHECK FIGURE
a. Charles Current Ratio: 1.33 to 1.0

The following accounting information exists for Charles and James companies at the end of 2016:

	Charles	James
Cash	$ 15,000	$ 25,000
Wages payable	20,000	25,000
Merchandise inventory	30,000	55,000
Building	80,000	80,000
Accounts receivable	35,000	30,000
Long-term notes payable	90,000	120,000
Land	45,000	50,000
Accounts payable	40,000	45,000
Sales revenue	220,000	270,000
Expenses	190,000	245,000

Required

a. Identify the current assets and current liabilities and compute the current ratio for each company.

b. Assuming that all assets and liabilities are listed here, compute the debt to assets ratios for each company.

c. Determine which company has the greater financial risk in both the short term and the long term.

LO 9-8

Problem 9-27A *Accounting for a discount note across two accounting cycles (Appendix)*

CHECK FIGURES
e. Net Income, 2016: $160,200
Total Assets, 2017: $323,400

Don Terry opened Terry Company, an accounting practice, in 2016. The following summarizes transactions that occurred during 2016:

1. Issued a $120,000 face value discount note to First National Bank on July 1, 2016. The note had an 8 percent discount rate and a one-year term to maturity.
2. Recognized cash revenue of $310,000.
3. Incurred and paid $145,000 of operating expenses.
4. Adjusted the books to recognize interest expense at December 31, 2016.
5. Prepared the necessary closing entries at December 31, 2016.

The following summarizes transactions that occurred in 2017:

1. Recognized $346,000 of cash revenue.
2. Incurred and paid $178,000 of operating expenses.
3. Recognized the interest expense for 2017 and paid the face value of the note.
4. Prepared the necessary closing entries at December 31, 2017.

Required

a. Show the effects of each of the transactions on the elements of the financial statements, using a horizontal statements model like the one shown here. Use + for increase, − for decrease, and NA for not affected. The first transaction is entered as an example. (*Hint:* Closing entries do not affect the statements model.)

Event No.	Assets	=	Liab.	+	Equity	Rev.	−	Exp.	=	Net Inc.	Cash Flow
1	+		+		NA	NA		NA		NA	+ FA

b. Prepare entries in general journal form for the transactions for 2016 and 2017, and post them to T-accounts.

c. Prepare an income statement, statement of changes in stockholders' equity, balance sheet, and statement of cash flows for 2016 and 2017.

EXERCISES—SERIES B

Exercise 9-1B *Recognizing accrued interest expense*

LO 9-1

Union Corporation borrowed $60,000 from the bank on November 1, 2016. The note had a 6 percent annual rate of interest and matured on April 30, 2017. Interest and principal were paid in cash on the maturity date.

Required

a. What amount of cash did Union pay for interest in 2016?
b. What amount of interest expense was reported on the 2016 income statement?
c. What amount of total liabilities was reported on the December 31, 2016, balance sheet?
d. What total amount of cash was paid to the bank on April 30, 2017, for principal and interest?
e. What amount of interest expense was reported on the 2017 income statement?

Exercise 9-2B *Effects of recognizing accrued interest on financial statements*

LO 9-1

Danny Bell started Bell Company on January 1, 2016. The company experienced the following events during its first year of operation:

1. Earned $3,000 of cash revenue for performing services.
2. Borrowed $4,800 cash from the bank.
3. Adjusted the accounting records to recognize accrued interest expense on the bank note. The note, issued on August 1, 2016, had a one-year term and a 6 percent annual interest rate.

Required

a. What is the amount of interest expense in 2016?
b. What amount of cash was paid for interest in 2016?
c. Use a horizontal statements model to show how each event affects the balance sheet, income statement, and statement of cash flows. Indicate whether the event increases (I), decreases (D), or does not affect (NA) each element of the financial statements. In the Cash Flows column, designate the cash flows as operating activities (OA), investing activities (IA), or financing activities (FA). The first transaction has been recorded as an example.

Event No.	Balance Sheet									Income Statement					Statement of Cash Flows
	Cash	=	Notes Pay.	+	Int. Pay.	+	Com. Stk.	+	Ret. Earn.	Rev.	−	Exp.	=	Net Inc.	
1	I	=	NA	+	NA	+	NA	+	I	I	−	NA	=	I	I OA

LO 9-2

Exercise 9-3B *Recording sales tax*

The Tiger Book Store sells books and other supplies to students in a state where the sales tax rate is 7 percent. The Tiger Book Store engaged in the following transactions for 2016. Sales tax of 7 percent is collected on all sales.

1. Book sales, not including sales tax, for 2016 amounted to $215,000 cash.
2. Cash sales of miscellaneous items in 2016 were $160,000, not including tax.
3. Cost of goods sold amounted to $195,000 for the year.
4. Paid $95,000 in operating expenses for the year.
5. Paid the sales tax collected to the state agency.

Required

a. What is the total amount of sales tax the Tiger Book Store collected and paid for the year?
b. Prepare the journal entries for the above transactions.
c. What is the Tiger Book Store's net income for the year?

LO 9-2

Exercise 9-4B *Recognizing sales tax payable*

The following selected transactions apply to Fast Stop for November and December 2016. November was the first month of operations. Sales tax is collected at the time of sale but is not paid to the state sales tax agency until the following month.

1. Cash sales for November 2016 were $85,000 plus sales tax of 8 percent.
2. Fast Stop paid the November sales tax to the state agency on December 10, 2016.
3. Cash sales for December 2016 were $98,000 plus sales tax of 8 percent.

Required

a. Record the above transactions in general journal form.
b. Show the effect of the above transactions on a horizontal statements model like the one shown below.

Assets	=	Liabilities	+	Equity			Income Statement					Cash Flow
Cash	=	Sales Tax Pay.	+	Com. Stk.	+	Ret. Earn.	Rev.	−	Exp.	=	Net Inc.	

c. What was the total amount of sales tax paid in 2016?
d. What was the total amount of sales tax collected in 2016?
e. What is the amount of the sales tax liability as of December 31, 2016?
f. On what financial statement will the sales tax liability appear?

LO 9-3

Exercise 9-5B *Contingent liabilities*

The following legal situations apply to Zier Corp. for 2016:

1. A customer slipped and fell on a slick floor while shopping in the retail store. The customer has filed a $5 million lawsuit against the company. Zier's attorney knows that the company will have to pay some damages but is reasonably certain that the suit can be settled for $750,000.
2. The EPA has assessed a fine against Zier of $320,000 for hazardous emissions from one of its manufacturing plants. The EPA had previously issued a warning to Zier and required Zier to

make repairs within six months. Zier began to make the repairs, but was not able to complete them within the six-month period. Since Zier has started the repairs, Zier's attorney thinks the fine will be reduced to $120,000. He is approximately 80 percent certain that he can negotiate the fine reduction because of the repair work that has been completed.

3. One of Zier's largest manufacturing facilities is located in "tornado alley." Property is routinely damaged by storms. Zier estimates it may have property damage of as much as $450,000 this coming year.

Required

For each item above, determine the correct accounting treatment. Prepare any required journal entries.

Exercise 9-6B *Effect of warranties on income and cash flow* — LO 9-4

To support himself while attending school, Steve Owens sold computers to other students. During the year Steve purchased computers for $150,000 and sold them for $280,000 cash. He provided his customers with a one-year warranty against defects in parts and labor. Based on industry standards, he estimated that warranty claims would amount to 5 percent of sales. During the year he paid $1,545 cash to replace a defective hard drive.

Required

a. Prepare the journal entries to record the
  (1) Purchase of inventory.
  (2) Sale of computers.
  (3) Warranty expense.
  (4) Payment for repairs.

b. Post the above transactions to T-accounts.

c. Prepare an income statement and statement of cash flows for Steve's first year of operation.

d. Explain the difference between net income and the amount of cash flow from operating activities.

Exercise 9-7B *Effect of warranty obligations and payments on financial statements* — LO 9-4

The Malon Appliance Co. provides a 120-day parts-and-labor warranty on all merchandise it sells. Malon estimates the warranty expense for the current period to be $2,450. During the period a customer returned a product that cost $1,950 to repair.

Required

a. Show the effects of these transactions on the financial statements using a horizontal statements model like the example shown here. Use + for increase, − for decrease, and NA for not affected. In the Cash Flow column, indicate whether the item is an operating activity (OA), investing activity (IA), or financing activity (FA).

Assets	=	Liab.	+	Equity	Rev.	−	Exp.	=	Net Inc.	Cash Flow

b. Prepare the journal entry to record the warranty expense for the period.

c. Prepare the journal entry to record payment for the actual repair costs.

d. Discuss the advantage of estimating the amount of warranty expense.

Exercise 9-8B *Current liabilities* — LO 9-1, 9-2, 9-4

The following transactions apply to Farmer's Equipment Sales Corp. for 2016:

1. The business was started when Farmer's received $60,000 from the issue of common stock.
2. Purchased $160,000 of merchandise on account.
3. Sold merchandise for $220,000 cash (not including sales tax). Sales tax of 8 percent is collected when the merchandise is sold. The merchandise had a cost of $140,000.

4. Provided a six-month warranty on the merchandise sold. Based on industry estimates, the warranty claims would amount to 4 percent of merchandise sales.
5. Paid the sales tax to the state agency on $180,000 of the sales.
6. On September 1, 2016, borrowed $40,000 from the local bank. The note had a 6 percent interest rate and matures on March 1, 2017.
7. Paid $6,600 for warranty repairs during the year.
8. Paid operating expenses of $61,000 for the year.
9. Paid $145,000 of accounts payable.
10. Recorded accrued interest at the end of the year.

Required

a. Show the effect of these transactions on the financial statements using a horizontal statements model like the one shown here. Use + for increase, − for decrease, and NA for not affected. In the Cash Flow column, indicate whether the item is an operating activity (OA), investing activity (IA), or financing activity (FA). The first transaction is recorded as an example.

Assets	=	Liabilities	+	Equity	Rev.	−	Exp.	=	Net Inc.	Cash Flow
+		NA		+	NA		NA		NA	+ FA

b. Prepare the journal entries for the above transactions and post them to the appropriate T-accounts.
c. Prepare the income statement, balance sheet, and statement of cash flows for 2016.
d. What is the total amount of current liabilities at December 31, 2016?

LO 9-5

Exercise 9-9B *Calculating payroll*

Wilkins Enterprises has two hourly employees, Marcia and Clark. Both employees earn overtime at the rate of 1½ times the hourly rate for hours worked in excess of 40 per week. Assume the Social Security tax rate is 6 percent on the first $110,000 of wages and the Medicare tax rate is 1.5 percent on all earnings. Federal income tax withheld for Marcia and Clark was $280 and $250, respectively. The following information is for the first week in January 2016:

Employee	Hours Worked	Wage Rate per Hour
Marcia	54	$25
Clark	48	$35

Required

a. Calculate the gross pay for each employee for the week.
b. Calculate the net pay for each employee for the week.
c. Prepare the general journal entry to record payment of the wages.

LO 9-5

Exercise 9-10B *Calculating payroll*

Easy Stop has two employees in 2016. Catherine earns $4,500 per month and Jordan, the manager, earns $11,000 per month. Neither is paid extra if they work overtime. Assume the Social Security tax rate is 6 percent on the first $110,000 of earnings and the Medicare tax rate is 1.5 percent on all earnings. The federal income tax withholding is 15 percent of gross earnings for Catherine and 20 percent for Jordan. Both Catherine and Jordan have been employed all year.

Required

a. Calculate the net pay for both Catherine and Jordan for March.
b. Calculate the net pay for both Catherine and Jordan for December.
c. Is the net pay the same in March and December for both employees? Why or why not?
d. What amounts will Easy Stop report on the 2016 W-2s for each employee?

Exercise 9-11B *Calculating employee and employer payroll taxes* LO 9-5

Culver Co. employed Jen Sing in 2016. Jen earned $5,200 per month and worked the entire year. Assume the Social Security tax rate is 6 percent on the first $110,000 of earnings and the Medicare tax rate is 1.5 percent. Jen's federal income tax withholding amount is $800 per month. Use 6.0 percent for the unemployment tax rate for the first $7,000 of earnings per employee.

Required

a. Answer the following questions:
   (1) What is Jen's net pay per month?
   (2) What amount does Jen pay monthly in FICA payroll taxes?
   (3) What is the total payroll tax expense for Culver Co. for January 2016? February 2016? March 2016? December 2016?

b. Assume that instead of $5,200 per month, Jen earned $10,000 per month. Answer the questions in Requirement *a*.

Exercise 9-12B *Fringe benefits and payroll expense* LO 9-5

Oswald Co. provides various fringe benefits for its two employees. It provides vacation and personal leave at the rate of one day for each month worked. Its employees earn a combined total of approximately $500 per day. In addition, Oswald Co. pays $780 per month in medical insurance premiums for its employees. Oswald also contributes $400 per month into a retirement plan for the employees. Assume the Social Security tax rate is 6 percent of the first $110,000 of salaries and the Medicare tax rate is 1.5 percent. The unemployment tax rate is 6.0 percent on the first $7,000 of earnings per employee.

Required

a. Prepare the monthly journal entry for the accrued fringe benefits.

b. Show the effect of the above transaction on a statements model like the one shown below:

Assets =	Liabilities +	Equity	Income Statement	Cash Flow
Cash =	Various Payables +	Com. Stk. + Ret. Earn.	Rev. − Exp. = Net Inc.	

c. If the two employees each worked 250 days for the year, what is Oswald Co.'s total payroll cost (salary, payroll taxes, and fringe benefits) for the year? (Assume that each employee earns $250 per day.)

Exercise 9-13B *Comprehensive single cycle problem* LO 9-1, 9-2, 9-4, 9-5

The following transactions apply to Ritter Co. for 2016:

1. Received $40,000 cash from the issue of common stock.
2. Purchased inventory on account for $128,000.
3. Sold inventory for $200,000 cash that had cost $110,000. Sales tax was collected at the rate of 5 percent on the inventory sold.
4. Borrowed $40,000 from First State Bank on October 1, 2016. The note had a 6 percent interest rate and a one-year term to maturity.
5. Paid the accounts payable (see transaction 2).
6. Paid the sales tax due on $160,000 of sales. Sales tax on the other $40,000 is not due until after the end of the year.
7. Salaries for the year for the one employee amounted $45,000. Assume the Social Security tax rate is 6 percent and the Medicare tax rate is 1.5 percent. Federal income tax withheld was $5,600.
8. Paid $3,200 for warranty repairs during the year.
9. Paid $24,000 of other operating expenses during the year.
10. Paid a dividend of $5,000 to the shareholders.

Adjustments:

11. The products sold in transaction 3 were warranted. Ritter estimated that the warranty cost would be 3 percent of sales.
12. Record the accrued interest at December 31, 2016.
13. Record the accrued payroll tax at December 31, 2016. Assume no payroll taxes have been paid for the year and that the unemployment tax rate is 6.0 percent (the federal unemployment tax rate is 0.6 percent and the state unemployment tax rate is 5.4 percent on the first $7,000 of earnings per employee).

Required

a. Record the above transactions in general journal form.

b. Post the transactions to T-accounts.

c. Prepare an income statement, statement of changes in stockholders' equity, balance sheet, and statement of cash flows for 2016.

LO 9-6

Exercise 9-14B *Preparing a classified balance sheet*

Required

Use the following information to prepare a classified balance sheet for Latimer Co. at the end of 2016:

Accounts receivable	$36,200
Accounts payable	12,400
Cash	29,650
Common stock	50,000
Long-term notes payable	45,500
Merchandise inventory	38,300
Office equipment	36,400
Retained earnings	36,250
Prepaid insurance	3,600

LO 9-7

Exercise 9-15B *Using the current ratio to make comparisons*

The following information was drawn from the 2016 balance sheets of the Augusta and Reno Companies:

	Augusta Company	Reno Company
Current assets	$45,000	$72,000
Current liabilities	28,000	54,000

Required

a. Compute the current ratio for each company.

b. Which company has the greater likelihood of being able to pay its bills?

c. Assume that both companies have the same amount of total assets. Speculate as to which company would produce the higher return on assets ratio.

LO 9-8

Exercise 9-16B *Effect of a discount note on financial statements (Appendix)*

Mark Miller started a moving company on January 1, 2016. On March 1, 2016, Miller borrowed cash from a local bank by issuing a one-year $80,000 face value note with annual interest based on a 12 percent discount. During 2016, Miller provided services for $65,400 cash.

Required

Answer the following questions. Record the events in T-accounts prior to answering the questions.

a. What is the amount of total liabilities on the December 31, 2016, balance sheet?

b. What is the amount of net income on the 2016 income statement?

c. What is the amount of cash flow from operating activities on the 2016 statement of cash flows?

d. Provide the general journal entries necessary to record issuing the note on March 1, 2016; recognizing accrued interest on December 31, 2016; and repaying the loan on February 28, 2017.

Exercise 9-17B *Comparing effective interest rates on discount versus interest-bearing notes (Appendix)*

LO 9-1, 9-8

Jim Hanks borrowed money by issuing two notes on January 1, 2016. The financing transactions are described here.

1. Borrowed funds by issuing a $60,000 face value discount note to State Bank. The note had an 8 percent discount rate, a one-year term to maturity, and was paid off on December 31, 2016.
2. Borrowed funds by issuing a $60,000 face value, interest-bearing note to Community Bank. The note had an 8 percent stated rate of interest, a one-year term to maturity, and was paid off on December 31, 2016.

Required

a. Show the effects of issuing the two notes on the financial statements using separate horizontal financial statement models like the ones here. Record the transaction amounts under the appropriate categories. In the Cash Flow column, indicate whether the item is an operating activity (OA), investing activity (IA), or financing activity (FA). Record only the events occurring on the date of issue. Do not record accrued interest or the repayment at maturity.

Discount Note

Assets =	Liabilities	+ Equity	Rev. − Exp. = Net Inc.	Cash Flow
Cash =	Notes Pay. − Disc. on Notes Pay.	+ Ret. Earn.		

Interest-Bearing Note

Assets	=	Liabilities	+	Equity	Rev.	−	Exp.	=	Net Inc.	Cash Flow
Cash	=	Notes Pay.	+	Ret. Earn.						

b. What is the total amount of interest to be paid on each note?

c. What amount of cash was received from each note when it was issued?

d. Which note has the higher effective interest rate? Support your answer with appropriate computations.

Exercise 9-18B *Recording accounting events for a discount note (Appendix)*

LO 9-8

Bricca Co. issued a $60,000 face value discount note to First Bank on June 1, 2016. The note had a 6 percent discount rate and a one-year term to maturity.

Required

Prepare general journal entries for the following transactions:

a. The issuance of the note on June 1, 2016.

b. The adjustment for accrued interest at the end of the year, December 31, 2016.

c. Recording interest expense for 2017 and repaying the principal on May 31, 2017.

PROBLEMS—SERIES B

LO 9-1

Problem 9-19B *Effect of accrued interest on financial statements*

Ingals Co. issued $10,000 of common stock when the company was started. In addition, Ingals borrowed $20,000 from the local bank on April 1, 2016. The note had an 8 percent annual interest rate and a one-year term to maturity. Ingals Co. recognized $54,000 of revenue on account in 2016 and $65,000 of revenue on account in 2017. Cash collections from accounts receivable were $46,000 in 2016 and $63,000 in 2017. Ingals Co. paid $27,000 of salaries expense in 2016 and $36,000 of salaries expense in 2017. Ingals Co. paid the loan and interest at the maturity date.

Required

Based on the preceding information, answer the following questions. (*Hint:* Record the events in the accounting equation before answering the questions.)

a. What amount of net cash flow from operating activities would Ingals report on the 2016 cash flow statement?

b. What amount of interest expense would Ingals report on the 2016 income statement?

c. What amount of total liabilities would Ingals report on the December 31, 2016, balance sheet?

d. What amount of retained earnings would Ingals report on the December 31, 2016, balance sheet?

e. What amount of cash flow from financing activities would Ingals report on the 2016 statement of cash flows?

f. What amount of interest expense would Ingals report on the 2017 income statement?

g. What amount of cash flows from operating activities would Ingals report on the 2017 cash flows statement?

h. What amount of total assets would Ingals report on the December 31, 2017, balance sheet?

LO 9-1, 9-2

Problem 9-20B *Accounting for short-term debt and sales tax—two accounting cycles*

The following transactions apply to Barclay Co. for 2016, its first year of operations:

1. Received $50,000 cash from the issue of a short-term note with a 5 percent interest rate and a one-year maturity. The note was made on April 1, 2016.
2. Received $140,000 cash plus applicable sales tax from performing services. The services are subject to a sales tax rate of 6 percent.
3. Paid $84,000 cash for other operating expenses during the year.
4. Paid the sales tax due on $110,000 of the service revenue for the year. Sales tax on the balance of the revenue is not due until 2017.
5. Recognized the accrued interest at December 31, 2016.

The following transactions apply to Barclay Co. for 2017:

1. Paid the balance of the sales tax due for 2016.
2. Received $155,000 cash plus applicable sales tax from performing services. The services are subject to a sales tax rate of 6 percent.
3. Repaid the principal of the note and applicable interest on April 1, 2017.
4. Paid $96,000 of other operating expenses during the year.
5. Paid the sales tax due on $135,000 of the service revenue. The sales tax on the balance of the revenue is not due until 2018.

Required

a. Record the 2016 transactions in general journal form.

b. Post the transactions to T-accounts.

c. Prepare a balance sheet, statement of changes in stockholders' equity, income statement, and statement of cash flows for 2016.

d. Prepare the closing entries and post them to the T-accounts.

e. Prepare a post-closing trial balance.
f. Repeat Requirements *a* through *e* for 2017.

Problem 9-21B *Contingent liabilities* LO 9-3

Required

How should each of the following situations be reported in the financial statements?

a. It has been determined that one of the company's products has caused a safety hazard. It is considered probable that liabilities have been incurred and a reasonable estimate of the amount can be made.
b. A company warehouse is located in a section of the city that has routinely flooded in the past. Consequently the company can no longer find a source of insurance for the warehouse. No flood has yet occurred this year.
c. Because of newly passed legislation, a company will have to upgrade its facilities over the next two years. Significant expenditures will occur, but at this time the amount has not been determined.

Problem 9-22B *Current liabilities* LO 9-1, 9-2, 9-3, 9-4

The following selected transactions were taken from the books of Dodson Company for 2016:

1. On March 1, 2016, borrowed $60,000 cash from the local bank. The note had a 6 percent interest rate and was due on September 1, 2016.
2. Cash sales for the year amounted to $240,000 plus sales tax at the rate of 7 percent.
3. Dodson provides a 90-day warranty on the merchandise sold. The warranty expense is estimated to be 2 percent of sales.
4. Paid the sales tax to the state sales tax agency on $200,000 of the sales.
5. Paid the note due on September 1 and the related interest.
6. On October 1, 2016, borrowed $50,000 cash from the local bank. The note had a 7 percent interest rate and a one-year term to maturity.
7. Paid $3,800 in warranty repairs.
8. A customer has filed a lawsuit against Dodson for $150,000 for breach of contract. The company attorney does not believe the suit has merit.

Required

a. Answer the following questions:
   (1) What amount of cash did Dodson pay for interest during the year?
   (2) What amount of interest expense is reported on Dodson's income statement for the year?
   (3) What is the amount of warranty expense for the year?
b. Prepare the current liabilities section of the balance sheet at December 31, 2016. (*Hint:* first post the liabilities transactions to T-accounts.)
c. Show the effect of these transactions on the financial statements using a horizontal statements model like the one shown here. Use + for increase, − for decrease, and NA for not affected. In the Cash Flow column, indicate whether the item is an operating activity (OA), investing activity (IA), or financing activity (FA). The first transaction is recorded as an example.

Assets	=	Liabilities	+	Equity	Rev.	−	Exp.	=	Net Inc.	Cash Flow
+		+		NA	NA		NA		NA	+ FA

Problem 9-23B *Accounting for payroll and payroll taxes* LO 9-5

Maddox Co. pays salaries monthly on the last day of the month. The following information is available from Maddox Co. for the month ended December 31, 2016.

Administrative salaries	$85,000
Sales salaries	66,000
Office salaries	48,000

Assume the Social Security tax rate is 6 percent on the first $110,000 of salaries and the Medicare tax rate is 1.5 percent on all salaries. James reached the $110,000 amount in October. His salary in December amounted to $11,000 and is included in the $85,000. No one else will reach the $110,000 amount for the year. None of the employee salaries are subject to unemployment tax in December.

Other amounts withheld from salaries in December were as follows:

Federal income tax	$24,500
State income tax	7,200
Employee savings plan	3,000

Required

a. Prepare the journal entry to record the payment of payroll on December 31, 2016.

b. Prepare the journal entry to record the payroll tax expense for Maddox Co. for December 2016.

LO 9-5

Problem 9-24B *Computation of net pay and payroll expense*

The following information is available for the employees of Yui Company for the first week of January 2016:

1. Sam earns $32 per hour and 1½ times his regular rate for hours over 40 per week. Sam worked 46 hours the first week in January. Sam's federal income tax withholding is equal to 10 percent of his gross pay. Yui pays medical insurance of $75 per week for Sam and contributes $50 per week to a retirement plan for him.
2. Adam earns a weekly salary of $1,200. Adam's federal income tax withholding is 15 percent of his gross pay. Yui pays medical insurance of $110 per week for Adam and contributes $100 per week to a retirement plan for him.
3. Vacation pay is accrued at the rate of 1/4 of the regular pay rate per hour for Sam and $60 per week for Adam.

Assume the Social Security tax rate is 6 percent on the first $110,000 of salaries and the Medicare tax rate is 1.5 percent of total salaries. The state unemployment tax rate is 5.4 percent and the federal unemployment tax rate is 0.6 percent of the first $7,000 of salary for each employee.

Required

a. Compute the gross pay for Sam for the first week in January.

b. Compute the net pay for both Sam and Adam for the first week in January.

c. Prepare the journal entry to record the payment of the payroll for the week.

d. Prepare the journal entry to record the payroll tax expense and fringe benefit expense for Yui for the week.

e. What is the total cost of compensation expense for the first week of January 2016 for Yui Company?

LO 9-6

Problem 9-25B *Multistep income statement and classified balance sheet*

Required

Use the following information to prepare a multistep income statement and a classified balance sheet for Brown Company for 2016. (*Hint:* Some of the items will *not* appear on either statement, and ending retained earnings must be calculated.)

Operating expenses	$ 45,000	Cash	$ 46,000
Land	75,000	Interest receivable (short term)	1,600
Accumulated depreciation	46,000	Cash flow from investing activities	(96,000)
Accounts payable	35,000	Allowance for doubtful accounts	14,000
Unearned revenue	27,000	Interest payable (short term)	6,000
Warranties payable (short term)	4,500	Sales revenue	900,000
Equipment	96,000	Uncollectible accounts expense	25,000
Notes payable (long term)	140,000	Interest expense	16,000
Salvage value of equipment	10,000	Accounts receivable	88,000
Dividends	15,000	Salaries payable	48,000
Warranty expense	7,200	Supplies	4,500
Beginning retained earnings	41,100	Prepaid rent	18,000
Interest revenue	4,200	Common stock	90,000
Gain on sale of equipment	7,000	Cost of goods sold	575,000
Inventory	126,000	Salaries expense	102,000
Notes receivable (short term)	12,500	Building	110,000

Problem 9-26B *Using ratios to make comparisons* LO 9-7

The following accounting information exists for Collie and Spaniel companies at the end of 2016:

	Collie	Spaniel
Cash	$ 12,000	$ 15,000
Wages payable	10,000	12,000
Merchandise inventory	20,000	55,000
Building	90,000	80,000
Accounts receivable	22,000	25,000
Long-term notes payable	80,000	100,000
Land	35,000	40,000
Accounts payable	25,000	35,000
Sales revenue	220,000	250,000
Expenses	190,000	230,000

Required

a. Identify the current assets and current liabilities and compute the current ratio for each company.

b. Assuming that all assets and liabilities are listed here, compute the debt to assets ratios for each company.

c. Determine which company has the greater financial risk in both the short term and the long term.

Problem 9-27B *Accounting for a discount note—two accounting cycles (Appendix)* LO 9-8

Ball Company was started in 2016. The following summarizes transactions that occurred during 2016:

1. Issued a $40,000 face value discount note to Golden Savings Bank on April 1, 2016. The note had a 6 percent discount rate and a one-year term to maturity.
2. Recognized revenue from services performed for cash, $130,000.
3. Incurred and paid $98,000 cash for selling and administrative expenses.
4. Amortized the discount on the note at the end of the year, December 31, 2016.
5. Prepared the necessary closing entries at December 31, 2016.

The following summarizes transactions that occurred in 2017:

1. Recognized $215,000 of service revenue in cash.
2. Incurred and paid $151,000 for selling and administrative expenses.
3. Amortized the remainder of the discount for 2017 and paid the face value of the note.
4. Prepared the necessary closing entries at December 31, 2017.

Required

a. Show the effects of each of the transactions on the elements of the financial statements, using a horizontal statements model like the one shown here. Use + for increase, − for decrease, and NA for not affected. The first transaction is entered as an example. (*Hint:* Closing entries do not affect the statements model.)

Event No.	Assets	=	Liab.	+	Equity	Rev.	−	Exp.	=	Net Inc.	Cash Flow
1	+		+		NA	NA		NA		NA	+ FA

b. Prepare entries in general journal form for the transactions for 2016 and 2017, and post them to T-accounts.

c. Prepare an income statement, statement of changes in stockholders' equity, balance sheet, and statement of cash flows for 2016 and 2017.

ANALYZE, THINK, COMMUNICATE

ATC 9-1 Business Applications Case *Understanding real-world annual reports*

Required

Use the Target Corporation's annual report in Appendix B to answer the following questions.

a. What was Target's current ratio for its fiscal-year ended February 1, 2014 (2013) and 2012?

b. Did the current ratio get stronger or weaker from 2012 to 2013? Explain briefly why this happened.

c. Target's balance sheet reports "Accrued and other current liabilities." What is included in this category? (See the notes to the financial statements.)

ATC 9-2 Group Assignment *Accounting for payroll*

The following payroll information is available for three companies for 2016. Each company has two employees. Assume that the Social Security tax rate is 6 percent on the first $110,000 of earnings and the Medicare tax rate is 1.5 percent on all earnings.

Brooks Company				
Brooks Company	**Hourly Rate**	**Regular Hours**	**Overtime Rate**	**Overtime Hours**
Employee No. 1	$40	2,000	$60	300
Employee No. 2	20	2,000	30	100

Other benefits provided for the employees:	
Medical insurance	$250 per month for each employee
Pension benefits	$100 per month for one employee

Federal income tax withheld is 15 percent of gross earnings for each employee. The state unemployment tax rate is 5.4 percent and the federal unemployment tax rate is 0.6 percent on the first $7,000 of earnings per employee.

Hill Company				
Hill Company	Weekly Rate/Hourly Rate	Weeks/Hours Worked	Overtime Rate	Overtime Hours
Employee No. 1	$2,000	52	NA	NA
Employee No. 2	18/hr.	2,000	$27/hr.	60

Other benefits provided for the employees:	
Medical and dental insurance	$325 per month for each employee
Pension benefits	$150 per month for one employee and $100 per month for the other employee

Federal income tax withheld is 15 percent of gross earnings for each employee. The state unemployment tax rate is 5.4 percent and the federal unemployment tax rate is 0.6 percent on the first $7,000 of earnings per employee.

Valley Company				
Valley Company	Monthly Rate/Hourly Rate	Monthly/Hours Worked	Overtime Rate	Overtime Hours
Employee No. 1	$10,500	12	NA	NA
Employee No. 2 (part time)	20/hr.	860	NA	NA

Other benefits provided for the employees:	
Medical and dental insurance	$375 per month for only one employee
Pension benefits	10% of gross salary for the full time employee

Federal income tax withheld is 15 percent of gross earnings for each employee. The state unemployment tax rate is 5.4 percent and the federal unemployment tax rate is 0.6 percent on the first $7,000 of earnings per employee.

Required

a. Divide the class into groups of four or five students. Organize the groups into three sections. Assign each section of groups the payroll data for one of the above companies.

Group Tasks

(1) Determine the gross and net payroll for your company for the year.

(2) Determine the total compensation cost for your company for the year.

(3) Have a representative from each section put the compensation on the board broken down by salaries cost, payroll tax, and fringe benefit cost.

Class Discussion

b. Have the class discuss how the categories of compensation cost are similar and why some are more or less than those of the other companies.

ATC 9-3 Real-World Case *Unusual types of liabilities*

In the liabilities section of its 2013 balance sheet, Bank of America reported "noninterest-bearing deposits" in U.S. offices of over $373 billion. Bank of America is a very large banking company. In the liabilities section of its 2013 balance sheet, Newmont Mining Corporation reported "reclamation and remediation liabilities" of more than $1.5 billion. Newmont Mining is involved in gold mining and refining activities. In its 2013 balance sheet, Delta Air Lines's largest current liability reported was $4.1 billion for "air traffic liability."

Required

a. For each of the preceding liabilities, write a brief explanation of what you believe the nature of the liability to be and how the company will pay it off. To develop your answers, think about the nature of the industry in which each of the companies operates.

b. Of the three liabilities described, which do you think poses the most risk for the company? In other words, for which liability are actual costs most likely to exceed the liability reported on the balance sheet? Uncertainty creates risk.

ATC 9-4 Business Applications Case *Performing ratio analysis using real-world data*

Not surprisingly, Newell Rubbermaid, Inc., is the marketer of the well known Rubbermaid plastic containers, but it also markets many other consumer brands, including Sharpie, Calphalon, Parker and Waterman writing instruments, and Lenox hand and power tools. The following data were taken from the company's 2013 annual report. Dollar amounts are in millions.

	Fiscal Years Ending	
	December 31, 2013	December 31, 2012
Current assets	$2,295.6	$2,271.1
Current liabilities	1,599.5	1,570.8
Total assets	6,079.7	6,222.0
Total liabilities	4,004.7	4,221.8

Required

a. Compute Rubbermaid's current ratios for 2013 and 2012.

b. Compute Rubbermaid's debt to assets ratios for 2013 and 2012.

c. Based on the ratios computed in Requirements *a* and *b*, did Rubbermaid's liquidity get better or worse from 2012 to 2013?

d. Based on the ratios computed in Requirements *a* and *b*, did Rubbermaid's solvency get better or worse from 2012 to 2013?

ATC 9-5 Business Applications Case *Performing ratio analysis using real-world data*

Advanced Micro Devices, Inc. (AMD) is "a global semiconductor company with facilities around the world." AMD began operations in 1969. Texas Instruments, Inc., is the company that invented the integrated circuit over 45 years ago. It has over 100,000 customers in 35 countries. The following data were taken from the companies' 2013 annual reports. Dollar amounts are in millions.

	Advanced Micro Devices	Texas Instruments
Current assets	$2,884	$ 8,019
Current liabilities	1,618	2,747
Total assets	4,337	18,938
Total liabilities	3,793	8,131

Required

a. Compute the current ratio for each company.

b. Compute the debt to assets ratio for each company.

c. Based on the ratios computed in Requirements *a* and *b*, which company had the better liquidity in 2013?

d. Based on the ratios computed in Requirements *a* and *b*, which company had the better solvency in 2013?

ATC 9-6 Writing Assignment *Payroll tax costs*

Nancy, who graduated from State University in June 2016, has just landed her first real job. She is excited because her salary is $4,000 per month. Nancy is single and has been planning all month about how she will spend her $4,000. When she received her first paycheck on June 30, 2016, she was very disappointed. The amount of her check was only $3,100. Explain to Nancy why (generally) her check was not for $4,000.

ATC 9-7 Ethical Dilemma *Who pays FICA taxes?*

Scott Putman owns and operates a lawn care company. Like most companies in the lawn care business, his company experiences a high level of employee turnover. However, he finds it relatively easy to replace employees because he pays above-market wages. He attributes his ability to pay high wages to a little accounting trick he discovered several years ago. Instead of paying his half of each employee's FICA taxes to the government, he decided to pay that money to the employees in the form of higher wages. He then doubles their FICA tax payroll deduction and uses half of the deduction to pay his share of the Social Security tax. For example, suppose he plans to pay an employee $2,000 per month. Technically, the employee would have to pay 7.5 percent FICA and Medicare tax ($2,000 × .075 = $150) and Mr. Putman's company would have to make a $150 matching payment. Instead of doing it this way, he devised the following plan. He pays the employee $2,150 and then deducts $300 for FICA and Medicare tax from the employee's salary. The end result is the same. Either way the employee ends up with net pay of $1,850 ($2,000 − $150 = $1,850 or $2,150 − $300 = $1,850). Also, the government gets $300 FICA tax, regardless of how it gets divided between the employee and the employer. Mr. Putman is convinced that he is right in what he is doing. Certainly, it benefits his company by allowing him to offer higher starting salaries. Further, he believes it is a more honest way of showing the real cost of Social Security and Medicare.

Required

a. Is Mr. Putnam right in his assumption that the total tax paid is the same under his approach as it would be if proper accounting procedures were applied? Explain.

b. Assuming that Mr. Putman is a CPA, do his actions violate any of the articles of the AICPA Code of Professional Conduct shown in Chapter 2 (Exhibit 2.9)? If so, discuss some of the articles that are violated.

c. Discuss Mr. Putman's actions within the context of the fraud triangle's elements of ethical misconduct that were outlined in Chapter 2.

ATC 9-8 Research Assignment *Analyzing Pep Boys's liquidity*

Using either the most current Form 10-K for The Pep Boys—Manny, Moe & Jack or the company's annual report, answer the questions below. To obtain the Form 10-K, either use the EDGAR system (following the instructions in Appendix A), or the company's website. The company's annual report is available on its website.

Required

a. What is Pep Boys's current ratio?

b. Which of Pep Boys's current assets had the largest balance?

c. What percentage of Pep Boys's total assets consisted of current assets?

d. Did Pep Boys have any "currently maturing" long-term debt included in current liabilities on its balance sheet?

e. If Pep Boys were a company that manufactured auto parts rather than a retailer of auto parts, how do you think its balance sheet would be different?

ATC 9-9 Excel Assignment

The following information is available for Lumberton Co. for the week ending June 28, 2016. All employees are paid time and one-half for all hours over 40. Each employee has cumulative salary of over $7,000, but less than $110,000. Assume the Social Security tax rate is 6 percent on the first $110,000 of wages and the Medicare tax rate is 1.5 percent of total wages. The company contributes the retirement cost to a retirement plan for the employee.

Employee	Rate of Pay	Hours	Fed WH %	Contributions to Retirement Plans
Jillian	$15 per hour	32	12%	$20 per week
Carl	18	46	10	10% of gross pay
Yolanda	16	45	10	10% of gross pay

Required

a. Set up a spreadsheet to compute the net pay for each of the above employees. You will need to insert the appropriate Excel formulas.

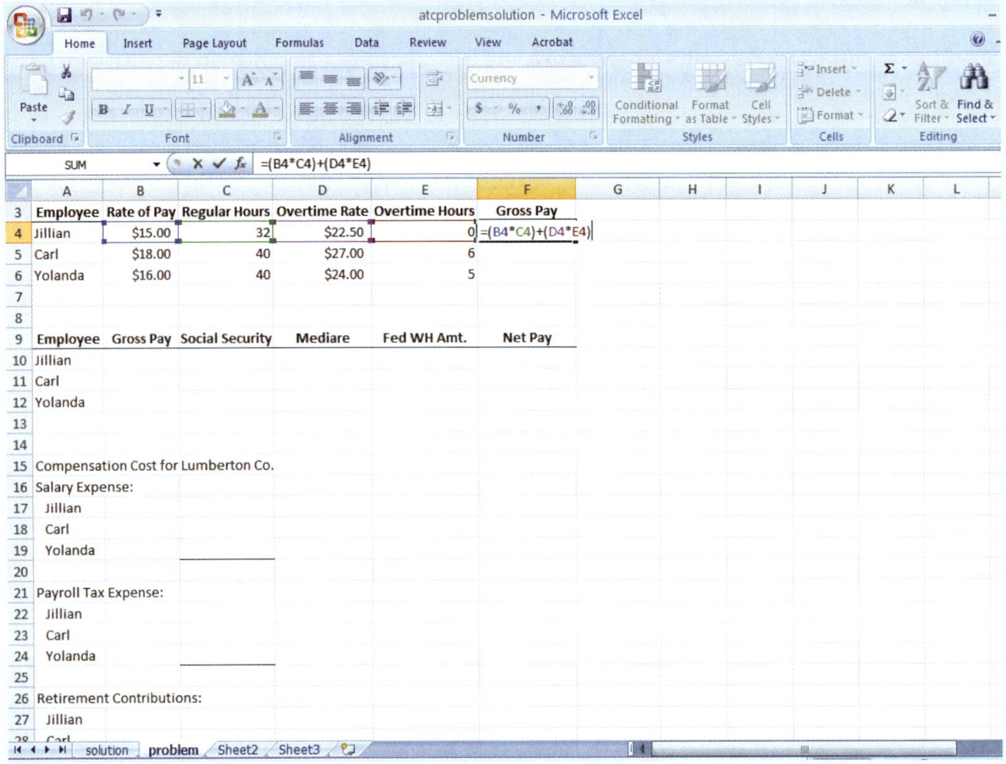

b. What is the total amount of compensation cost (salary cost plus payroll tax cost) for Lumberton Co. for the week ending June 28, 2016?

c. Lumberton is considering adding group health insurance coverage for its employees to its benefits package. If the average cost of health insurance per employee is $3,900 per year, how much additional cost would be added to weekly compensation cost for Lumberton? Assume the addition of health insurance and recompute the total compensation cost for Lumberton for the week ending June 28, 2016.

ATC 9-10

Refer to Problem 9-17A. Complete requirement *a*, *b*, *c*, and *d*, using an Excel spreadsheet. Refer to Chapter 1, Problem ATC 1-8 for ideas on how to structure the spreadsheet.

COMPREHENSIVE PROBLEM

The trial balance of Pacilio Security Services Inc. as of January 1, 2019, had the following normal balances:

Cash	$93,380
Petty cash	100
Accounts receivable	21,390
Allowance for doubtful accounts	2,485
Supplies	180
Prepaid rent	3,000
Merchandise inventory (23 @ $280)	6,440
Equipment	9,000
Van	27,000
Accumulated depreciation	14,900
Salaries payable	1,500
Common stock	50,000
Retained earnings	91,605

During 2019 Pacilio Security Services experienced the following transactions:

1. Paid the salaries payable from 2018.
2. Paid $9,000 on May 2, 2019, for one year's office rent in advance.
3. Purchased $425 of supplies on account.

4. Purchased 145 alarm systems at a cost of $290 each. Paid cash for the purchase.
5. After numerous attempts to collect from customers, wrote off $2,060 of uncollectible accounts receivable.
6. Sold 130 alarm systems for $580 each plus sales tax of 5 percent. All sales were on account. (Be sure to compute cost of goods sold using the FIFO cost flow method.)
7. Billed $107,000 of monitoring services for the year. Credit card sales amounted to $42,000, and the credit card company charged a 4 percent fee. The remaining $65,000 were sales on account. Sales tax is not charged on this service.
8. Replenished the petty cash fund on June 30. The fund had $5 cash and has receipts of $60 for yard mowing, $15 for office supplies expense, and $17 for miscellaneous expenses.
9. Collected the amount due from the credit card company.
10. Paid the sales tax collected on $69,600 of the alarm sales.
11. Paid installers and other employees a total of $65,000 for salaries for the year. Assume the Social Security tax rate is 6 percent and the Medicare tax rate is 1.5 percent. Federal income taxes withheld amounted to $7,500. Cash was paid for the net amount of salaries due.
12. Pacilio now offers a one-year warranty on its alarm systems. Paid $1,950 in warranty repairs during the year.
13. On September 1, borrowed $12,000 from State Bank. The note had an 8 percent interest rate and a one-year term to maturity.
14. Collected $136,100 of accounts receivable during the year.
15. Paid $15,000 of advertising expense during the year.
16. Paid $7,200 of utilities expense for the year.
17. Paid the payroll taxes, both the amounts withheld from the salaries plus the employer share of Social Security tax and Medicare tax, on $60,000 of the salaries plus $7,000 of the federal income tax that was withheld. (Unemployment taxes were not paid at this time.)
18. Paid the accounts payable.
19. Paid a dividend of $10,000 to the shareholders.

Adjustments

20. There was $165 of supplies on hand at the end of the year.
21. Recognized the expired rent for the office building for the year.
22. Recognized uncollectible accounts expense for the year using the allowance method. The company revised its estimate of uncollectible accounts based on prior years' experience. This year Pacilio estimates that 2.75 percent of sales on account will not be collected.
23. Recognized depreciation expense on the equipment and the van. The equipment has a 5-year life and a $2,000 salvage value. The van has a 4-year life and a $6,000 salvage value. The company uses double-declining-balance for the van and straight-line for the equipment. (A full year's depreciation was taken in 2018, the year of acquisition.)
24. The alarm systems sold in transaction 6 were covered with a one-year warranty. Pacilio estimated that the warranty cost would be 3 percent of alarm sales.
25. Recognized the accrued interest on the note payable at December 31, 2019.
26. The unemployment tax on salaries has not been paid. Recorded the accrued unemployment tax on the salaries for the year. The unemployment tax rate is 4.5 percent. ($14,000 of salaries is subject to this tax.)
27. Recognized the employer Social Security and Medicare payroll tax that has not been paid on $5,000 of salaries expense.

Required

a. Record the above transactions in general journal form. Round all amounts to the nearest whole dollar.

b. Post the transactions to the T-accounts.

c. Prepare a trial balance.

d. Prepare an income statement, statement of changes in stockholders' equity, a classified balance sheet, and statement of cash flows.

e. Close the temporary accounts to retained earnings.

f. Post the closing entries to the T-accounts and prepare a post-closing trial balance.

CHAPTER 10

Accounting for Long-Term Debt

LEARNING OBJECTIVES

After you have mastered the material in this chapter, you will be able to:

LO 10-1 Show how an installment note affects financial statements.

LO 10-2 Show how a line of credit affects financial statements.

LO 10-3 Describe bond features and show how bonds issued at face value affect financial statements.

LO 10-4 Use the straight-line method to amortize bond discounts.

LO 10-5 Use the straight-line method to amortize bond premiums.

LO 10-6 Use the effective interest rate method to amortize bond discounts.

LO 10-7 Use the effective interest rate method to amortize bond premiums.

LO 10-8 Explain the advantages and disadvantages of debt financing.

Video lectures and accompanying self-assessment quizzes are available for all learning objectives through McGraw-Hill Connect® Plus Accounting.

CHAPTER OPENING

Most businesses finance their investing activities with long-term debt. Recall that current liabilities mature within one year or a company's operating cycle, whichever is longer. Other liabilities are **long-term liabilities.** Long-term debt agreements vary with respect to requirements for paying interest charges and repaying principal (the amount borrowed). Interest payments may be due monthly, annually, at some other interval, or at the maturity date. Interest charges may be based on a **fixed interest rate** that remains constant during the term of the loan or a **variable interest rate** that fluctuates up or down during the loan period.

Principal repayment is generally required either in one lump sum at the maturity date or in installments that are spread over the life of the loan. For example, each monthly payment on your car loan probably includes both paying interest and repaying some of the principal. Repaying a portion of the principal with regular payments that also include interest is often called loan **amortization.**[1] This chapter explains accounting for interest and principal with respect to the major forms of long-term debt financing.

[1]In Chapter 8 the term *amortization* described the expense recognized when the *cost of an intangible asset* is systematically allocated to expense over the useful life of the asset. This chapter shows that the term amortization refers more broadly to a variety of allocation processes. Here it means the systematic process of allocating interest to the periods in which the loan is outstanding.

The Curious Accountant

In its 2013 fiscal year **Panasonic Corporation** reported a loss of ¥775 billion, which is approximately 7.6 billion U.S. dollars. ¥ is the symbol for the Japanese yen.

With such a huge loss on its income statement, do you think Panasonic was able to make the interest payments on its debt? If so, how? (Answer on page 541.)

INSTALLMENT NOTES PAYABLE

LO 10-1

Show how an installment note affects financial statements.

Loans that require payments of principal and interest at regular intervals (amortizing loans) are typically represented by **installment notes.** The terms of installment notes usually range from two to five years. To illustrate accounting for installment notes, assume Blair Company was started on January 1, 2016, when it borrowed $100,000 cash from National Bank. In exchange for the money, Blair issued the bank a five-year installment note with a 9 percent fixed interest rate. The journal entry to record issuing the note and its effects on the financial statements are as follows:

Date	Account Title	Debit	Credit
2016 Jan. 1	Cash Installment Note Payable	100,000	 100,000

	Assets	=	Liab.	+	Equity			Rev.	−	Exp.	=	Net Inc.	Cash Flow
Date	Cash	=	Note Pay.	+	Com. Stk.	+	Ret. Earn.						
2016 Jan. 1	100,000	=	100,000	+	NA	+	NA	NA	−	NA	=	NA	100,000 FA

The loan agreement required Blair to pay five equal installments of $25,709[2] on December 31 of each year from 2016 through 2020. Exhibit 10.1 shows the allocation of each payment between principal and interest. When Blair pays the final installment, both the principal and interest will be paid in full. The amounts shown in Exhibit 10.1 are computed as follows:

1. The Interest Expense (Column D) is computed by multiplying the Principal Balance on Jan. 1 (Column B) by the interest rate. For example, interest expense for 2016 is $100,000 × 0.09 = $9,000; for 2017 it is $83,291 × 0.09 = $7,496; and so on.
2. The Principal Repayment (Column E) is computed by subtracting the Interest Expense (Column D) from the Cash Payment on Dec. 31 (Column C). For example, the Principal Repayment for 2016 is $25,709 − $9,000 = $16,709; for 2017 it is $25,709 − $7,496 = $18,213; and so on.

EXHIBIT 10.1

Amortization Schedule for Installment Note Payable

Accounting Period Column A	Principal Balance on Jan. 1 Column B	Cash Payment on Dec. 31 Column C	Interest Expense Column D	Principal Repayment Column E	Principal Balance on Dec. 31 Column F
2016	$100,000	$25,709	$9,000	$16,709	$83,291
2017	83,291	25,709	7,496	18,213	65,078
2018	65,078	25,709	5,857	19,852	45,226
2019	45,226	25,709	4,070	21,639	23,587
2020	23,587	25,710*	2,123	23,587	0

*All computations are rounded to the nearest dollar. To fully liquidate the liability, the final payment is one dollar more than the others because of rounding differences.

[2]The amount of the annual payment is determined using the present value concepts presented in Appendix F at the end of this textbook. Usually the lender (bank or other financial institution) calculates the amount of the payment for the customer.

Answers to The Curious Accountant

Even though **Panasonic** reported a $7.6 billion loss in 2013, it was able to make the interest payments on its debt with no difficulty for two reasons. First, interest is paid with cash, not accrual earnings. Many of the expenses on the company's income statement did not require the use of cash. For example, Panasonic reported depreciation and amortization expense of $3.3 billion, which did not require cash in 2013. Also, it reported $3.9 billion of charges for impairments of long-term assets and goodwill, but only $0.1 billion of these required cash payments.

Second, the net loss the company incurred was *after* interest expense of $252 million had been deducted. The company's statement of cash flows shows that net cash flow from operating activities in 2013, *after making interest payments,* was a positive $3.3 billion. The capacity of operations to support interest payments is measured by the amount of earnings before interest deductions. For example, look at the 2016 income statement for Blair Company in Exhibit 10.2. This statement shows only $3,000 of net income, but $12,000 of cash revenue was available for the payment of interest. Similarly, Panasonic's 2013 net loss is not an indication of the company's ability to pay interest in the short run.

3. The Principal Balance on Dec. 31 (Column F) is computed by subtracting the Principal Repayment (Column E) from the Principal Balance on Jan. 1 (Column B). For example, the Principal Balance on Dec. 31 for 2016 is $100,000 − $16,709 = $83,291; on December 31, 2017, the principal balance is $83,291 − $18,213 = $65,078; and so on. The Principal Balance on Dec. 31 (ending balance) for 2016 ($83,291) is also the Principal Balance on Jan. 1 (beginning balance) for 2017; the principal balance on December 31, 2017, is the principal balance on January 1, 2018, and so on.

Although the amounts for interest expense and principal repayment differ each year, the effects of the annual payment on the financial statements are the same. On the balance sheet, assets (cash) decrease by the total amount of the payment; liabilities (note payable) decrease by the amount of the principal repayment; and stockholders' equity (retained earnings) decreases by the amount of interest expense. Net income decreases from recognizing interest expense. On the statement of cash flows, the portion of the cash payment applied to interest is reported in the operating activities section and the portion applied to principal is reported in the financing activities section. The journal entry to record the December 31, 2016, cash payment and its effects on the financial statements are as follows:

Date	Account Title	Debit	Credit
2016 Dec. 31	Interest Expense Installment Note Payable Cash	9,000 16,709	 25,709

	Assets	=	Liab.	+	Equity			Rev.	−	Exp.	=	Net Inc.	Cash Flow
Date	Cash	=	Note Pay.	+	Com. Stk.	+	Ret. Earn.						
2016 Dec. 31	(25,709)	=	(16,709)	+	NA	+	(9,000)	NA	−	9,000	=	(9,000)	(9,000) OA (16,709) FA

EXHIBIT 10.2

BLAIR COMPANY
Financial Statements

	2016	2017	2018	2019	2020
Income Statements					
Rent revenue	$ 12,000	$12,000	$12,000	$ 12,000	$12,000
Interest expense	(9,000)	(7,496)	(5,857)	(4,070)	(2,123)
Net income	$ 3,000	$ 4,504	$ 6,143	$ 7,930	$ 9,877
Balance Sheets					
Assets					
Cash	$ 86,291	$72,582	$58,873	$ 45,164	$31,454
Liabilities					
Note payable	$ 83,291	$65,078	$45,226	$ 23,587	$ 0
Stockholders' equity					
Retained earnings	3,000	7,504	13,647	21,577	31,454
Total liabilities and stk. equity	$ 86,291	$72,582	$58,873	$ 45,164	$31,454
Statements of Cash Flows					
Operating Activities					
Inflow from customers	$ 12,000	$12,000	$12,000	$ 12,000	$12,000
Outflow for interest	(9,000)	(7,496)	(5,857)	(4,070)	(2,123)
Investing Activities	0	0	0	0	0
Financing Activities					
Inflow from note issue	100,000	0	0	0	0
Outflow to repay note	(16,709)	(18,213)	(19,852)	(21,639)	(23,587)
Net Change in Cash	86,291	(13,709)	(13,709)	(13,709)	(13,710)
Plus: Beginning cash balance	0	86,291	72,582	58,873	45,164
Ending cash balance	$ 86,291	$72,582	$58,873	$ 45,164	$31,454

Exhibit 10.2 displays income statements, balance sheets, and statements of cash flows for Blair Company for the accounting periods 2016 through 2020. The illustration assumes that Blair earned $12,000 of rent revenue each year. Since some of the principal is repaid each year, the note payable amount reported on the balance sheet and the amount of the interest expense on the income statement both decline each year.

CHECK YOURSELF 10.1

On January 1, 2016, Krueger Company issued a $50,000 installment note to State Bank. The note had a 10-year term and an 8 percent interest rate. Krueger agreed to repay the principal and interest in 10 annual payments of $7,451.47 at the end of each year. Determine the amount of principal and interest Krueger paid during the first and second year that the note was outstanding.

Answer

Accounting Period	Principal Balance January 1 A	Cash Payment December 31 B	Applied to Interest C = A × 0.08	Applied to Principal B − C
2016	$50,000.00	$7,451.47	$4,000.00	$3,451.47
2017	46,548.53	7,451.47	3,723.88	3,727.59

LINE OF CREDIT

LO 10-2

Show how a line of credit affects financial statements.

A **line of credit** enables a company to borrow or repay funds as needed. For example, a business may borrow $50,000 one month and make a partial repayment of $10,000 the next month. Credit agreements usually specify a limit on the amount that can be borrowed. Exhibit 10.3 shows that credit agreements are widely used.

Interest rates on lines of credit normally vary with fluctuations in some designated interest rate benchmark such as the rate paid on U.S. Treasury bills. For example, a company may pay 4 percent interest one month and 4.5 percent the next month, even if the principal balance remains constant.

Lines of credit typically have one-year terms. Although they are classified on the balance sheet as short-term liabilities, lines of credit are frequently extended indefinitely by simply renewing the credit agreement.

To illustrate accounting for a line of credit, assume Lagoon Company owns a wholesale jet-ski distributorship. In the spring, Lagoon borrows money using a line of credit to finance building up its inventory. Lagoon repays the loan over the summer months using cash generated from jet-ski sales. Borrowing or repaying events occur on the first of the month. Interest payments occur at the end of each month. Exhibit 10.4 presents all 2016 line of credit events.

Each borrowing event (March 1, April 1, and May 1) is an asset source transaction. Both cash and the line of credit liability increase. Each repayment (June 1, July 1, and August 1) is an asset use transaction. Both cash and the line of credit liability decrease. Each month's interest expense recognition and payment is an asset use transaction. Assets (cash) and stockholders' equity (retained earnings) decrease, as does net income. The journal entries to record the events are shown in Panel A of Exhibit 10.5. The effects of the events on the financial statements are shown in Panel B.

EXHIBIT 10.3

Percentage of U.S. Companies Disclosing Credit Agreements

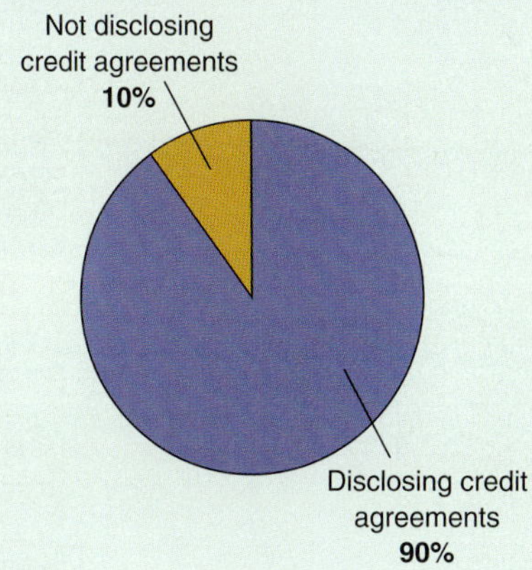

Data Source: AICPA, *Accounting Trends and Techniques.*

EXHIBIT 10.4

Summary of Line of Credit Events

Date	Amount Borrowed (Repaid)	Loan Balance at End of Month	Effective Interest Rate per Month (%)	Interest Expense (rounded to nearest $1)
Mar. 1	$ 20,000	$ 20,000	0.09 ÷ 12	$150
Apr. 1	30,000	50,000	0.09 ÷ 12	375
May 1	50,000	100,000	0.105 ÷ 12	875
June 1	(10,000)	90,000	0.10 ÷ 12	750
July 1	(40,000)	50,000	0.09 ÷ 12	375
Aug. 1	(50,000)	0	0.09 ÷ 12	0

EXHIBIT 10.5

Panel A: Journal Entries

Date	Account Titles	Debit	Credit
Mar. 1	Cash	20,000	
	Note Payable		20,000
Mar. 31	Interest Expense	150	
	Cash		150
Apr. 1	Cash	30,000	
	Note Payable		30,000

continued

EXHIBIT 10.5 *Concluded*

Apr. 30	Interest Expense Cash	375	 375
May 1	Cash Note Payable	50,000	 50,000
May 31	Interest Expense Cash	875	 875
June 1	Note Payable Cash	10,000	 10,000
June 30	Interest Expense Cash	750	 750
July 1	Note Payable Cash	40,000	 40,000
July 31	Interest Expense Cash	375	 375
Aug. 1	Note Payable Cash	50,000	 50,000

Panel B: Effects on Financial Statements

Date	Assets	=	Liabilities	+	Equity	Rev.	−	Exp.	=	Net Inc.	Cash Flow	
Mar. 1	20,000	=	20,000	+	NA	NA	−	NA	=	NA	20,000	FA
31	(150)	=	NA	+	(150)	NA	−	150	=	(150)	(150)	OA
Apr. 1	30,000	=	30,000	+	NA	NA	−	NA	=	NA	30,000	FA
30	(375)	=	NA	+	(375)	NA	−	375	=	(375)	(375)	OA
May 1	50,000	=	50,000	+	NA	NA	−	NA	=	NA	50,000	FA
31	(875)	=	NA	+	(875)	NA	−	875	=	(875)	(875)	OA
June 1	(10,000)	=	(10,000)	+	NA	NA	−	NA	=	NA	(10,000)	FA
30	(750)	=	NA	+	(750)	NA	−	750	=	(750)	(750)	OA
July 1	(40,000)	=	(40,000)	+	NA	NA	−	NA	=	NA	(40,000)	FA
31	(375)	=	NA	+	(375)	NA	−	375	=	(375)	(375)	OA
Aug. 1	(50,000)	=	(50,000)	+	NA	NA	−	NA	=	NA	(50,000)	FA
31	NA	=	NA	+	NA	NA	−	NA	=	NA	NA	

BOND LIABILITIES

LO 10-3

Describe bond features and show how bonds issued at face value affect financial statements.

Many companies borrow money directly from the public by selling **bond certificates,** otherwise called *issuing* bonds. Bond certificates describe a company's obligation to pay interest and to repay the principal. The seller, or **issuer,** of a bond is the borrower; the buyer of a bond, or **bondholder,** is the lender.

From the issuer's point of view, a bond represents an obligation to pay a sum of money to the bondholder on the bond's maturity date. The amount due at maturity is the **face value** of the bond. Most bonds also require the issuer to make cash interest payments based on a **stated interest rate** at regular intervals over the life of the bond. Exhibit 10.6 shows a typical bond certificate.

Advantages of Issuing Bonds

Bond financing offers companies the following advantages:

1. Bonds usually have longer terms than notes issued to banks. While typical bank loan terms range from 2 to 5 years, bonds normally have 20-year terms to maturity.

EXHIBIT 10.6

Bond Certificate

Longer terms to maturity allow companies to implement long-term strategic plans without having to worry about frequent refinancing arrangements.

2. Bond interest rates may be lower than bank interest rates. Banks earn profits by borrowing money from the public (depositors) at low interest rates, then loaning that money to companies at higher rates. By issuing bonds directly to the public, companies can pay lower interest costs by eliminating the middleman (banks).

Security of Bonds

Bonds may be either secured or unsecured.

1. **Secured bonds** grant their holders a priority legal claim on specified identifiable assets should the issuer default. A common type of secured bond is a **mortgage bond,** which conditionally transfers the title of designated property to the bondholder until the bond is paid.
2. **Unsecured bonds,** also called **debentures,** are issued based on the general strength of the borrower's credit. Bond certificates often specify the priority of debenture holders' claims relative to other creditors. Holders of **subordinated debentures** have lower priority claims than other creditors, whereas holders of **unsubordinated debentures** have equal claims.

Timing of Maturity

The maturity dates of bonds can be specified in various ways. Even bonds sold as separate components of a single issue may have different maturity dates.

1. **Term bonds** mature on a specified date in the future.
2. **Serial bonds** mature at specified intervals throughout the life of the total issue. For example, bonds with a total face value of $1,000,000 may mature in increments of $100,000 every year for 10 years.

REALITY BYTES

Throughout this textbook various financial ratios have been discussed, along with explanations of how they are used by financial analysts. Ratios are also often included as covenants in loan agreements when a company borrows money. If the company violates a ratio covenant in the loan agreement, the lender can force the company to renegotiate the loan or pay back the borrowed funds much earlier than originally agreed. This can have dire consequences for the company. Consider the excerpts below taken from the "Management's Discussion and Analysis... - *Capital Financing Overview*" of the **Las Vegas Sands Corporation**'s 2013 Form 10-K.

> *Through December 31, 2013, we have funded our development projects primarily through borrowings from our credit facilities ... The U.S. credit facility, which was amended in December 2013, requires our Las Vegas operations to comply with a financial covenant at the end of each quarter to the extent that any revolving loans or certain letters of credit are outstanding. This financial covenant requires our Las Vegas operations to maintain a maximum leverage ratio of net debt, as defined, to trailing twelve-month adjusted earnings before interest, income taxes, depreciation and amortization, as defined ("Adjusted EBITDA"). The maximum leverage ratio is 5.5x for all quarterly periods through maturity ... If we are unable to maintain compliance with the financial covenants under these credit facilities, we would be in default under the respective credit facilities ... Any defaults or cross-defaults under these agreements would allow the lenders, in each case, to exercise their rights and remedies as defined under their respective agreements. If the lenders were to exercise their rights to accelerate the due dates of the indebtedness outstanding, there can be no assurance that we would be able to repay or refinance any amounts that may become due and payable under such agreements . . .*

Simply put, the company is warning investors that if it violates the ratio covenants, which it seems likely to do, the company could go into bankruptcy. Ratios matter!

To ensure there is enough cash available at maturity to pay off the debt, a bond agreement may require the issuer to make regular payments into a **sinking fund.** Money deposited in the sinking fund is usually managed by an independent trustee who invests the funds until the bonds mature. At maturity, the funds and the proceeds from the investments are used to repay the bond debt.

Special Features

Some bonds feature one or both of the following characteristics.

1. **Convertible bonds** are liabilities that can be exchanged at the option of the bondholder for common stock or some other specified ownership interest. The issuing company benefits because bondholders (investors) are willing to accept a lower interest rate in exchange for the conversion feature. Bondholders benefit because they obtain the option to share in potential rewards of ownership. If the market value of the company's stock increases, bondholders can convert their bonds to stock. If the stock price does not increase, bondholders are still guaranteed interest payments and priority claims in bankruptcy settlements.
2. **Callable bonds** allow the issuing company to redeem (pay off) the bond debt before the maturity date. If interest rates decline, this feature benefits the issuing company because it could borrow additional money at a lower rate and use the proceeds to pay off its higher rate bonds. Since an early redemption would eliminate their higher interest bond investments, bondholders consider call features undesirable. To encourage investors to buy callable bonds, the **call price** normally exceeds the *face value* of the bonds. For example, the issuing company may agree to pay the holder of a $1,000 face value bond a call price of $1,050 if the bond is redeemed before its maturity date. The difference between the call price and the face value ($50 [$1,050 − $1,000] in this case) is commonly called a **call premium.**

Bond Ratings

Three financial services analyze the risk of default for corporate bond issues and publish ratings of the risk as guides to bond investors. These agencies are Fitch, Moody's, and Standard & Poor's. The highest rating (lowest risk) a company can achieve is AAA, the next highest is AA, and so forth. Bond issuers try to maintain high credit ratings because lower ratings require them to pay higher interest rates.

Restrictive Covenants

In general, large loans with long terms to maturity pose more risk to lenders (creditors) than small loans with short terms. To reduce the risk that they won't get paid, lenders frequently require borrowers (debtors) to pledge designated assets as **collateral** for loans. For example, when a bank makes a car loan, it usually retains legal title to the car until the loan is fully repaid. If the borrower fails to make the monthly payments, the bank repossesses the car, sells it to someone else, and uses the proceeds to pay the original owner's debt. Similarly, assets like accounts receivable, inventory, equipment, buildings, and land may be pledged as collateral for business loans.

In addition to requiring collateral, creditors often obtain additional protection by including **restrictive covenants** in loan agreements. Such covenants may restrict additional borrowing, limit dividend payments, or restrict salary increases. If the loan restrictions are violated, the borrower is in default and the loan balance is due immediately.

Finally, creditors often ask owners and executives of nonpublic companies to provide copies of their personal tax returns and financial statements. The financial condition of the owners and executives is important because they may be asked to pledge personal property as collateral for business loans.

Bonds Issued at Face Value

Assume Marsha Mason needs cash in order to seize a business opportunity. Mason knows of a company seeking a plot of land on which to store its inventory of crushed stone. Mason also knows of a suitable tract of land she could purchase for $100,000. The company has agreed to lease the land it needs from Mason for $12,000 per year. Mason lacks the funds to buy the land.

Some of Mason's friends recently complained about the low interest rates banks were paying on certificates of deposit. Mason suggested that her friends invest in bonds instead of CDs. She offered to sell them bonds with a 9 percent stated interest rate. The terms specified in the bond agreement Mason drafted included making interest payments in cash on December 31 of each year, a five-year term to maturity, and pledging the land as collateral for the bonds.[3] Her friends were favorably impressed, and Mason issued the bonds to them in exchange for cash on January 1, 2016.

Mason used the bond proceeds to purchase the land and immediately contracted to lease it for five years. On December 31, 2020, the maturity date of the bonds, Mason sold the land for its $100,000 book value and used the proceeds from the sale to repay the bond liability.

Journal Entries and Financial Statement Effects

Mason's business venture involved six distinct accounting events, described below.

EVENT 1 Issued Bonds for $100,000 Cash.

Assets (cash) and liabilities (bonds payable) increase. Net income is not affected. The $100,000 cash inflow is reported in the financing activities section of the

[3]In practice, bonds are usually issued for much larger sums of money, often hundreds of millions of dollars. Also, terms to maturity are normally long, with 20 years being common. Using such large amounts for such long terms is unnecessarily cumbersome for instructional purposes. The effects of bond issues can be illustrated efficiently by using smaller amounts of debt with shorter maturities, as assumed in the case of Marsha Mason.

statement of cash flows. The journal entry and its effects on the financial statements are shown here:

Account Title	Debit	Credit
Cash	100,000	
Bonds Payable		100,000

Assets	=	Liab.	+	Equity	Rev.	−	Exp.	=	Net Inc.	Cash Flow
Cash	=	Bonds Pay.								
100,000	=	100,000	+	NA	NA	−	NA	=	NA	100,000 FA

EVENT 2 Paid $100,000 cash to purchase land.

The asset cash decreases and the asset land increases. The income statement is not affected. The cash outflow is reported in the investing activities section of the statement of cash flows. The journal entry and its effects on the financial statements are shown here:

Account Title	Debit	Credit
Land	100,000	
Cash		100,000

Assets			=	Liab.	+	Equity	Rev.	−	Exp.	=	Net Inc.	Cash Flow
Cash	+	Land										
(100,000)	+	100,000	=	NA	+	NA	NA	−	NA	=	NA	(100,000) IA

EVENT 3 Recognized $12,000 cash revenue from renting the land.

This event is repeated each year from 2016 through 2020. The event increases assets and stockholders' equity. Recognizing revenue increases net income. The cash inflow is reported in the operating activities section of the statement of cash flows. The journal entry and its effects on the financial statements are shown here:

Account Title	Debit	Credit
Cash	12,000	
Rent Revenue		12,000

Assets	=	Liab.	+	Equity	Rev.	−	Exp.	=	Net Inc.	Cash Flow
Cash	=			Ret. Earn.						
12,000	=	NA	+	12,000	12,000	−	NA	=	12,000	12,000 OA

EVENT 4 Paid $9,000 cash for interest.

This event is also repeated each year from 2016 through 2020. The interest payment is an asset use transaction. Cash and stockholders' equity (retained earnings) decrease. The expense recognition decreases net income. The cash outflow is reported in the operating activities section of the statement of cash flows. The journal entry and its effects on the financial statements are shown here:

Account Title	Debit	Credit
Interest Expense	9,000	
Cash		9,000

Assets	=	Liab.	+	Equity	Rev.	−	Exp.	=	Net Inc.	Cash Flow
Cash	=			Ret. Earn.						
(9,000)	=	NA	+	(9,000)	NA	−	9,000	=	(9,000)	(9,000) OA

EVENT 5 Sold the land for cash equal to its $100,000 book value.

Cash increases and land decreases. Since there was no gain or loss on the sale, the income statement is not affected. The cash inflow is reported in the investing activities section of the statement of cash flows. The journal entry and its effects on the financial statements are shown here:

Account Title	Debit	Credit
Cash	100,000	
Land		100,000

Assets			=	Liab.	+	Equity	Rev.	−	Exp.	=	Net Inc.	Cash Flow
Cash	+	Land										
100,000	+	(100,000)	=	NA	+	NA	NA	−	NA	=	NA	100,000 IA

EVENT 6 Repaid the face value of the bond liability.

Cash and bonds payable decrease. The income statement is not affected. The cash outflow is reported in the financing activities section of the statement of cash flows. The journal entry and its effects on the financial statements are shown here:

Account Title	Debit	Credit
Bonds Payable	100,000	
Cash		100,000

Assets	=	Liab.	+	Equity	Rev.	−	Exp.	=	Net Inc.	Cash Flow
Cash	=	Bonds Pay.								
(100,000)	=	(100,000)	+	NA	NA	−	NA	=	NA	(10,000) FA

Financial Statements

Exhibit 10.7 displays Mason Company's financial statements. For simplicity, the income statement does not distinguish between operating and other items. Rent revenue and interest expense are constant across all accounting periods, so Mason recognizes $3,000 of net income in each accounting period. On the balance sheet, cash increases by $3,000 each year because cash revenue exceeds cash paid for interest. Land remains constant each year at its $100,000 historical cost until it is sold in 2020. Similarly, the bonds payable liability is reported at $100,000 from the date the bonds were issued in 2016 until they are paid off on December 31, 2020.

EXHIBIT 10.7

Mason Company Financial Statements

Bonds Issued at Face Value	2016	2017	2018	2019	2020
Income Statements					
Rent revenue	$ 12,000	$ 12,000	$ 12,000	$ 12,000	$ 12,000
Interest expense	(9,000)	(9,000)	(9,000)	(9,000)	(9,000)
Net income	$ 3,000	$ 3,000	$ 3,000	$ 3,000	$ 3,000
Balance Sheets					
Assets					
Cash	$ 3,000	$ 6,000	$ 9,000	$ 12,000	$ 15,000
Land	100,000	100,000	100,000	100,000	0
Total assets	$103,000	$106,000	$109,000	$112,000	$ 15,000
Liabilities					
Bonds payable	$100,000	$100,000	$100,000	$100,000	$ 0
Stockholders' equity					
Retained earnings	3,000	6,000	9,000	12,000	15,000
Total liabilities and stockholders' equity	$103,000	$106,000	$109,000	$112,000	$ 15,000
Statements of Cash Flows					
Operating Activities					
Inflow from customers	$ 12,000	$ 12,000	$ 12,000	$ 12,000	$ 12,000
Outflow for interest	(9,000)	(9,000)	(9,000)	(9,000)	(9,000)
Investing Activities					
Outflow to purchase land	(100,000)				
Inflow from sale of land					100,000
Financing Activities					
Inflow from bond issue	100,000				
Outflow to repay bond liab.					(100,000)
Net change in cash	3,000	3,000	3,000	3,000	3,000
Plus: Beginning cash balance	0	3,000	6,000	9,000	12,000
Ending cash balance	$ 3,000	$ 6,000	$ 9,000	$ 12,000	$ 15,000

Compare Blair Company's income statements in Exhibit 10.2 with Mason Company's income statements in Exhibit 10.7. Both Blair and Mason borrowed $100,000 cash at a 9 percent stated interest rate for five-year terms. Blair, however, repaid its liability under the terms of an installment note while Mason did not repay any principal until the end of the five-year bond term. Because Blair repaid part of the principal balance on the installment loan each year, Blair's interest expense declined each year. The interest expense on Mason's bond liability, however, remained constant because the full principal amount was outstanding for the entire five-year bond term.

AMORTIZATION USING THE STRAIGHT-LINE METHOD

LO 10-4

Use the straight-line method to amortize bond discounts.

Bonds Issued at a Discount

Return to the Mason Company illustration with one change. Assume Mason's bond certificates have a 9 percent stated rate of interest printed on them. Suppose Mason's friends find they can buy bonds from another entrepreneur willing to pay a higher rate of interest. They explain to Mason that business decisions cannot be made on the basis of friendship. Mason provides a counteroffer. There is no time to change the bond certificates, so Mason offers to accept $95,000 for the bonds today and still repay the full face value of $100,000 at the maturity date. The $5,000 difference is called a **bond discount.** Mason's friends agree to buy the bonds for $95,000.

Effective Interest Rate

The bond discount increases the interest Mason must pay. First, Mason must still make the annual cash payments described in the bond agreement. In other words, Mason must pay cash of $9,000 (0.09 × $100,000) annually even though she actually borrowed only $95,000. Second, Mason will have to pay back $5,000 more than she received ($100,000 − $95,000). The extra $5,000 (bond discount) is additional interest. Although the $5,000 of additional interest is not paid until maturity, when spread over the life of the bond, it amounts to $1,000 of additional interest expense per year.

The actual rate of interest that Mason must pay is called the **effective interest rate.** A rough estimate of the effective interest rate for the discounted Mason bonds is 10.5 percent ([$9,000 annual stated interest + $1,000 annual amortization of the discount] ÷ $95,000 amount borrowed). Selling the bonds at a $5,000 discount permits Mason to raise the 9 percent stated rate of interest to an effective rate of roughly 10.5 percent. Deeper discounts would raise the effective rate even higher. More shallow discounts would reduce the effective rate of interest. Mason can set the effective rate of interest to any level desired by adjusting the amount of the discount.

Bond Prices

It is common business practice to use discounts to raise the effective rate of interest above the stated rate. Bonds frequently sell for less than face value. Bond prices are normally expressed *as a percentage of the face value.* For example, Mason's discounted bonds sold for 95, meaning the bonds sold at 95 percent of face value ($100,000 × 0.95 = $95,000). Amounts of less than 1 percentage point are usually expressed as a fraction. Therefore, a bond priced at 98 3/4 sells for 98.75 percent of face value.

Journal Entries and Financial Statement Effects

To illustrate accounting for bonds issued at a discount, return to the Mason Company example using the assumption the bonds are issued for 95 instead of face value. We examine the same six events using this revised assumption. This revision changes some amounts reported on the financial statements. For example, Event 1 in year 2016 reflects receiving only $95,000 cash from the bond issue. Since Mason had only $95,000 available to invest in land, the illustration assumes that Mason acquired a less desirable piece of property which generated only $11,400 of rent revenue per year.

EVENT 1 Bonds with a face value of $100,000 are issued at 95.

Because Mason must pay the face value at maturity, the $100,000 face value of the bonds is recorded in the Bonds Payable account. The $5,000 discount is recorded in a separate contra liability account called **Discount on Bonds Payable.** As shown below, the contra account is subtracted from the face value to determine the **carrying value** (book value) of the bond liability on January 1, 2016.

Bonds payable	$100,000
Less: Discount on bonds payable	(5,000)
Carrying value	$ 95,000

The bond issue is an asset source transaction. Both assets and total liabilities increase by $95,000. Net income is not affected. The cash inflow is reported in the financing activities section of the statement of cash flows. The journal entry and its effects on the financial statements are shown here:

Account Title	Debit	Credit
Cash	95,000	
Discount on Bonds Payable	5,000	
Bonds Payable		100,000

Assets	=	Liabilities	+	Equity	Rev.	−	Exp.	=	Net Inc.	Cash Flow
Cash	=	Carrying Value of Bond Liability	+	Equity						
95,000	=	95,000	+	NA	NA	−	NA	=	NA	95,000 FA

EVENT 2 Paid $95,000 cash to purchase land.

The asset cash decreases and the asset land increases. The income statement is not affected. The cash outflow is reported in the investing activities section of the statement of cash flows. The journal entry and its effects on the financial statements are shown here:

Account Title	Debit	Credit
Land	95,000	
Cash		95,000

Assets			=	Liab.	+	Equity	Rev.	−	Exp.	=	Net Inc.	Cash Flow
Cash	+	Land										
(95,000)	+	95,000	=	NA	+	NA	NA	−	NA	=	NA	(95,000) IA

EVENT 3 Recognized $11,400 cash revenue from renting the land.

This event is repeated each year from 2016 through 2020. The event is an asset source transaction that increases assets and stockholders' equity. Recognizing revenue increases net income. The cash inflow is reported in the operating activities section of the statement of cash flows. The journal entry and its effects on the financial statements are shown here:

Account Title	Debit	Credit
Cash	11,400	
Rent Revenue		11,400

Assets	=	Liab.	+	Equity	Rev.	−	Exp.	=	Net Inc.	Cash Flow
Cash	=			Ret. Earn.						
11,400	=	NA	+	11,400	11,400	−	NA	=	11,400	11,400 OA

EVENT 4 Recognized interest expense. The interest cost of borrowing has two components: the $9,000 paid in cash each year and the $5,000 discount paid at maturity.

Using **straight-line amortization,** the amount of the discount recognized as expense in each accounting period is $1,000 ($5,000 discount ÷ 5 years). Mason will therefore recognize $10,000 of interest expense each year ($9,000 at the stated interest rate plus

$1,000 amortization of the bond discount). On the balance sheet, the asset cash decreases by $9,000, the carrying value of the bond liability increases by $1,000 (through a decrease in the bond discount), and retained earnings (interest expense) decreases by $10,000. The journal entry and its effects on the financial statements are shown here:

Account Title	Debit	Credit
Interest Expense	10,000	
Cash		9,000
Discount on Bonds Payable		1,000

Assets	=	Liabilities	+	Equity	Rev.	−	Exp.	=	Net Inc.	Cash Flow
Cash	=	Carrying Value of Bond Liability	+	Ret. Earn.						
(9,000)	=	1,000	+	(10,000)	NA	−	10,000	=	(10,000)	(9,000) OA

EVENT 5 Sold the land for cash equal to its $95,000 book value.

Cash increases and land decreases. Since there was no gain or loss on the sale, the income statement is not affected. The cash inflow is reported in the investing activities section of the statement of cash flows. The journal entry and its effects on the financial statements are shown here:

Account Title	Debit	Credit
Cash	95,000	
Land		95,000

Assets			=	Liab.	+	Equity	Rev.	−	Exp.	=	Net Inc.	Cash Flow
Cash	+	Land										
95,000	+	(95,000)	=	NA	+	NA	NA	−	NA	=	NA	95,000 IA

EVENT 6 Paid the bond liability.

Cash and bonds payable decrease. The income statement is not affected. For reporting purposes, the cash outflow is separated into two parts on the statement of cash flows: $95,000 of the cash outflow is reported in the financing activities section because it represents repaying the principal amount borrowed; the remaining $5,000 cash outflow is reported in the operating activities section because it represents the interest arising from issuing the bonds at a discount. In practice, the amount of the discount is frequently immaterial and is combined in the financing activities section with the principal repayment. The journal entry and its effects on the financial statements are shown here:

Account Title	Debit	Credit
Bond Payable	100,000	
Cash		100,000

Assets	=	Liab.	+	Equity	Rev.	−	Exp.	=	Net Inc.	Cash Flow
Cash	=	Bonds Pay.								
(100,000)	=	(100,000)	+	NA	NA	−	NA	=	NA	(95,000) FA (5,000) OA

Financial Statements

Exhibit 10.8 displays Mason Company's financial statements assuming the bonds were issued at a discount. Contrast the net income reported in Exhibit 10.8 (bonds issued at a discount) with the net income reported in Exhibit 10.7 (bonds sold at face value). Two factors cause the net income in Exhibit 10.8 to be lower. First, since the bonds were sold at a discount, Mason Company had less money to spend on its land investment. It bought less desirable land which generated less revenue. Second, the effective interest rate was higher than the stated rate, resulting in higher interest expense. Lower revenues coupled with higher expenses result in less profitability.

On the balance sheet, the carrying value of the bond liability increases each year until the maturity date, December 31, 2020, when it is equal to the $100,000 face value of the bonds (the amount Mason is obligated to pay). Because Mason did not pay any dividends, retained earnings ($7,000) on December 31, 2020, is equal to the total amount of net income reported over the five-year period ($1,400 × 5). All earnings were retained in the business.

EXHIBIT 10.8

Mason Company Financial Statements

Bonds Issued at a Discount	2016	2017	2018	2019	2020
Income Statements					
Rent revenue	$ 11,400	$ 11,400	$ 11,400	$ 11,400	$ 11,400
Interest expense	(10,000)	(10,000)	(10,000)	(10,000)	(10,000)
Net income	$ 1,400	$ 1,400	$ 1,400	$ 1,400	$ 1,400
Balance Sheets					
Assets					
Cash	$ 2,400	$ 4,800	$ 7,200	$ 9,600	$ 7,000
Land	95,000	95,000	95,000	95,000	0
Total assets	$ 97,400	$ 99,800	$102,200	$104,600	$ 7,000
Liabilities					
Bonds payable	$100,000	$100,000	$100,000	$100,000	$ 0
Discount on bonds payable	(4,000)	(3,000)	(2,000)	(1,000)	0
Carrying value of bond liab.	96,000	97,000	98,000	99,000	0
Stockholders' equity					
Retained earnings	1,400	2,800	4,200	5,600	7,000
Total liabilities and stockholders' equity	$ 97,400	$ 99,800	$102,200	$104,600	$ 7,000
Statements of Cash Flows					
Operating Activities					
Inflow from customers	$ 11,400	$ 11,400	$ 11,400	$ 11,400	$ 11,400
Outflow for interest	(9,000)	(9,000)	(9,000)	(9,000)	(14,000)
Investing Activities					
Outflow to purchase land	(95,000)				
Inflow from sale of land					95,000
Financing Activities					
Inflow from bond issue	95,000				
Outflow to repay bond liab.					(95,000)
Net change in cash	2,400	2,400	2,400	2,400	(2,600)
Plus: Beginning cash balance	0	2,400	4,800	7,200	9,600
Ending cash balance	$ 2,400	$ 4,800	$ 7,200	$ 9,600	$ 7,000

Several factors account for the differences between net income and cash flow. First, although $10,000 of interest expense is reported on each income statement, only $9,000 of cash was paid for interest each year until 2020, when $14,000 was paid for interest ($9,000 based on the stated rate + $5,000 for discount). The $1,000 difference between interest expense and cash paid for interest in 2016, 2017, 2018, and 2019 results from amortizing the bond discount. The cash outflow for the interest related to the discount is included in the $100,000 payment made at maturity on December 31, 2020. Even though $14,000 of cash is paid for interest in 2020, only $10,000 is recognized as interest expense on the income statement that year. Although the total increase in cash over the five-year life of the business ($7,000) is equal to the total net income reported for the same period, there are significant timing differences between when the interest expense is recognized and when the cash outflows occur to pay for it.

CHECK YOURSELF 10.2

On January 1, 2016, Moffett Company issued bonds with a $600,000 face value at 98. The bonds had a 9 percent annual interest rate and a 10-year term. Interest is payable in cash on December 31 of each year. What amount of interest expense will Moffett report on the 2018 income statement? What carrying value for bonds payable will Moffett report on the December 31, 2018, balance sheet?

Answer The bonds were issued at a $12,000 ($600,000 × 0.02) discount. The discount will be amortized over the 10-year life at the rate of $1,200 ($12,000 ÷ 10 years) per year. The amount of interest expense for 2018 is $55,200 ($600,000 × 0.09 = $54,000 annual cash interest + $1,200 discount amortization).

The carrying value of the bond liability is equal to the face value less the unamortized discount. By the end of 2018, $3,600 of the discount will have been amortized ($1,200 × 3 years = $3,600). The unamortized discount as of December 31, 2018, will be $8,400 ($12,000 − $3,600). The carrying value of the bond liability as of December 31, 2018, will be $591,600 ($600,000 − $8,400).

Effect of Semiannual Interest Payments

The previous examples assumed that interest payments were made annually. In practice, most bond agreements call for interest to be paid semiannually, which means that interest is paid in cash twice each year. If Marsha Mason's bond certificate had stipulated semiannual interest payments, her company would have paid $4,500 ($100,000 × 0.09 = $9,000 ÷ 2 = $4,500) cash to bondholders for interest on June 30 and December 31 of each year. The journal entries to record semiannual interest payments each year (for the bonds issued at a discount) are as follows:

Date	Account Title	Debit	Credit
June 30	Interest Expense	5,000	
	Discount on Bonds Payable		500
	Cash		4,500
Dec. 31	Interest Expense	5,000	
	Discount on Bonds Payable		500
	Cash		4,500

Bonds Issued at a Premium

LO 10-5

Use the straight-line method to amortize bond premiums.

When bonds are sold for more than their face value, the difference between the amount received and the face value is called a **bond premium.** Bond premiums reduce the effective interest rate. For example, assume Mason Company issued its 9 percent bonds at 105, receiving $105,000 cash on the issue date. The company is still only required to repay the $100,000 face value of the bonds at the maturity date. The $5,000 difference between the amount received and the amount repaid at maturity reduces the total amount of interest expense. The premium is recorded in a separate liability account called **Premium on Bonds Payable.** This account is reported on the balance sheet as an addition to Bonds Payable, increasing the carrying value of the bond liability. On the issue date, the bond liability would be reported on the balance sheet as follows:

Bonds payable	$100,000
Plus: Premium on bonds payable	5,000
Carrying value	$105,000

The entire $105,000 cash inflow is reported in the financing activities section of the statement of cash flows even though the $5,000 premium is conceptually an operating activities cash flow because it pertains to interest. In practice, premiums are usually so small they are immaterial and the entire cash inflow is normally classified as a financing activity.

The journal entries to record issuing the bonds at a premium and the first interest payment are as follows (assume annual interest payments):

Date	Account Title	Debit	Credit
Jan. 1	Cash	105,000	
	Bonds Payable		100,000
	Premium on Bonds Payable		5,000
Dec. 31	Interest Expense	8,000	
	Premium on Bonds Payable	1,000	
	Cash		9,000

The effects on the financial statements are shown here:

	Assets	=	Liabilities	+	Equity	Rev.	−	Exp.	=	Net Inc.	Cash Flow
Date	Cash	=	Carrying Value of Bond Liability								
Jan. 1	105,000	=	105,000	+	NA	NA	−	NA	=	NA	105,000 FA
Dec. 31	(9,000)		(1,000)		(8,000)			8,000		(8,000)	9,000 OA

The Market Rate of Interest

When a bond is issued, the effective interest rate is determined by current market conditions. Market conditions are influenced by many factors, such as the state of the economy, government policy, and the law of supply and demand. These conditions are collectively reflected in the **market interest rate.** The *effective rate of interest* investors are willing to accept *for a particular bond* equals the *market rate of interest* for other investments with similar levels of risk at the time the bond is issued. When the market rate of interest is higher than the stated rate of interest, bonds will sell at a discount so as to increase the effective rate of interest to the market rate. When the market rate is lower than the stated rate, bonds will sell at a premium so as to reduce the effective rate to the market rate.

Bond Redemptions

In the previous illustration, Mason Company's five-year, 9 percent bonds were redeemed (paid off) on the maturity date. After Mason Company paid the bondholders the face value of the bonds, the balance in the bonds payable account was zero. The balance in the fully amortized discount account was also zero.

Companies may redeem bonds with a *call provision* prior to the maturity date. If a company calls bonds prior to maturity, it must pay the bondholders the call price. As explained previously, the call price is normally above face value. For example, suppose Mason Company's bond certificate allows it to call the bonds at 103. Assume Marsha Mason's client breaks the land rental contract two years early, at the end of 2018. Mason is forced to sell the land and pay off the bonds. Assuming the bonds were originally issued at a $5,000 discount, Exhibit 10.8 shows there is a $2,000 balance in the Discount on Bonds Payable account at the end of 2018.

To redeem the bonds on January 1, 2019, Mason must pay the bondholders $103,000 ($100,000 face value × 1.03 call price). Since the book value of the bond liability is $98,000 ($100,000 face value − $2,000 remaining discount), Mason recognizes a $5,000 loss ($103,000 redemption price − $98,000 book value) when the bonds are called. The early redemption decreases cash, the carrying value of the bond liability, and stockholders' equity.

The entire $103,000 cash outflow is reported in the financing activities section of the statement of cash flows. Conceptually, some of this outflow is attributable to activities other than financing. In practice, the amounts paid in an early redemption which are not attributable to financing activities are usually immaterial and the entire cash outflow is therefore classified as a financing activity.

The general journal entry to record the bond redemption and its effects on the financial statements are shown here:

Account Title	Debit	Credit
Loss on Bond Redemption	5,000	
Bonds Payable	100,000	
Discount on Bonds Payable		2,000
Cash		103,000

Assets	=	Liabilities	+	Equity	Rev.	−	Exp.	=	Net Inc.	Cash Flow
Cash	=	Carrying Value of Bond Liability	+	Ret. Earn.						
(103,000)	=	(98,000)	+	(5,000)	NA	−	5,000	=	(5,000)	(103,000) FA

AMORTIZATION USING THE EFFECTIVE INTEREST RATE METHOD

To this point we have demonstrated the straight-line method for amortizing bond discounts and premiums. While this method is easy to understand, it is inaccurate because it does not show the correct amount of interest expense incurred during each accounting period. To illustrate, return to the case of Mason Company demonstrated in Exhibit 10.8 (page 554). Recall that the exhibit shows the effects of accounting for a $100,000 face value bond with a 9 percent stated rate of interest that was issued at a price of 95. The carrying value of the bond liability on the January 1, 2016, issue date was $95,000. The bond discount was amortized using the straight-line method.

Recall that the straight-line method amortizes the discount equally over the life of the bond. Specifically, there is a $5,000 discount which is amortized over a 5-year life resulting in a $1,000 amortization per year. As the discount is amortized the bond liability (carrying value of the bond) increases. Specifically, the carrying value of the bond liability shown in Exhibit 10.8 increases as follows:

Accounting Period	2016	2017	2018	2019
Carrying value as of December 31	$96,000	$97,000	$98,000	$99,000

While the carrying value of the bond liability increases steadily, the straight-line method recognizes the same amount of interest expense ($9,000 stated rate of interest + $1,000 discount amortization = $10,000 interest expense) per year. This straight-line recognition pattern is irrational because the amount of interest expense recognized should increase as the carrying value of the bond liability increases. A more accurate recognition pattern can be accomplished by using an approach called the **effective interest rate method.**

Amortizing Bond Discounts

LO 10-6

Use the effective interest rate method to amortize bond discounts.

The effective interest rate is determined by the price that the buyer of a bond is willing to pay on the issue date. In the case of Mason Company the issue price of $95,000 for bonds with a $100,000 face value, a 9 percent stated rate of interest, and a 5-year term produces an effective interest rate of approximately 10.33 percent.[4] Since the effective interest rate is based on the market price of the bonds on the day of issue, it is sometimes called *the market rate of interest.*

Interest recognition under the effective interest rate method is accomplished as follows:

1. Determine the cash payment for interest by multiplying the stated rate of interest times the face value of the bonds.
2. Determine the amount of interest expense by multiplying the effective rate of interest times the carrying value of the bond liability.
3. Determine the amount of the amortization of the bond discount by subtracting the cash payment from the interest expense.
4. Update the carrying value of the liability by adding the amount of the discount amortization to the amount of the carrying value at the beginning of the accounting period.

Applying these procedures to the Mason Company illustration produces the amortization schedule shown in Exhibit 10.9.

The recognition of interest expense at the end of each accounting period has the following effects on the financial statements. On the balance sheet, assets decrease, liabilities increase, and retained earnings decrease. On the income statement, expenses

EXHIBIT 10.9

Amortization Schedule for Bond Discount

	(A) Cash Payment	(B) Interest Expense	(C) Discount Amortization	(D) Carrying Value
January 1, 2016				$ 95,000
December 31, 2016	$ 9,000	$ 9,814	$ 814	95,814
December 31, 2017	9,000	9,898	898	96,712
December 31, 2018	9,000	9,990	990	97,702
December 31, 2019	9,000	10,093	1,093	98,795
December 31, 2020	9,000	10,205	1,205	100,000
Totals	$45,000	$50,000	$5,000	

(A) Stated rate of interest times the face value of the bonds ($100,000 × 0.09).
(B) Effective interest rate times the carrying value at the beginning of the period. For the 2016 accounting period the amount is $9,814 ($95,000 × 0.1033).
(C) Interest Expense − Cash Payment. For 2016 the discount amortization is $814 ($9,814 − $9,000 = $814).
(D) Carrying value at beginning of period plus portion of discount amortized. For the accounting period ending December 31, 2016, the amount is $95,814 ($95,000 + $814).

[4]In practice the effective rate of interest is calculated using software programs, interest formulas, or interest tables. For further discussion see Appendix F, which is located at the end of this textbook.

increase and net income decreases. There is a cash outflow in the operating activities section of the statement of cash flows. The journal entry and its effects on the financial statements are shown here:

Account Title	Debit	Credit
Interest Expense	9,814	
Cash		9,000
Discount on Bonds Payable		814

Assets	=	Liabilities	+	Equity	Rev.	−	Exp.	=	Net Inc.	Cash Flow
Cash	=	Carrying Value of Bond Liab.	+	Ret. Earn.						
(9,000)	=	814	+	(9,814)	NA	−	9,814	=	(9,814)	(9,000) OA

Exhibit 10.10 shows the financial statements for Mason Company for 2016 through 2020. The statements assume the same events as those used to construct Exhibit 10.8 (page 554). These events are summarized below:

1. Mason issues a $100,000 face value bond with a 9 percent stated rate of interest. The bond has a 5-year term and is issued at a price of 95. Annual interest is paid with cash on December 31 of each year.
2. Mason uses the proceeds from the bond issue to purchase land.
3. Leasing the land produces rent revenue of $11,400 cash per year.
4. On the maturity date of the bond, the land is sold and the proceeds from the sale are used to repay the bond liability.

The only difference between the two exhibits is that Exhibit 10.8 was constructed assuming that the bond discount was amortized using the straight-line method while Exhibit 10.10 assumes that the discount was amortized using the effective interest rate method.

Notice that interest expense under the effective interest rate method (Exhibit 10.10) increases each year while interest expense under the straight-line method (Exhibit 10.8) remains constant for all years. This result occurs because the effective interest rate method amortizes increasingly larger amounts of the discount (see Column C of Exhibit 10.9) as the carrying value of the bond liability increases. In contrast, the straight-line method amortized the bond discount at a constant rate of $1,000 per year over the life of the bond. Even so, the total amount of interest expense recognized over the life of the bond is the same ($50,000) under both methods. Since the effective interest rate method matches the interest expense with the carrying value of the bond liability, it is the theoretically preferred approach. Indeed, accounting standards require the use of the effective interest rate method when the differences between it and the straight-line method are material.

The amortization of the discount affects the carrying value of the bond as well as the amount of interest expense. Under the effective interest rate method the rate of growth of the carrying value of the bond increases as the maturity date approaches. In contrast, under the straight-line method the rate of growth of the carrying value of the bond remains constant at $1,000 per year throughout the life of the bond.

Finally, notice that cash flow is not affected by the method of amortization. The exact same cash flow consequences occur under both the straight-line (Exhibit 10.8) and the effective interest rate method (Exhibit 10.10).

Amortizing Bond Premiums

LO 10-7

Use the effective interest rate method to amortize bond premiums.

Bond premiums can also be amortized using the effective interest rate method. To illustrate, assume United Company issued a $100,000 face value bond with a 10 percent stated rate of interest. The bond had a 5-year term. The bond was issued at a price of

EXHIBIT 10.10

Financial Statements

Under the Assumption that Bonds Are Issued at a Discount

	2016	2017	2018	2019	2020
Income Statements					
Rent revenue	$ 11,400	$ 11,400	$ 11,400	$ 11,400	$ 11,400
Interest expense	(9,814)	(9,898)	(9,990)	(10,093)	(10,205)
Net income	$ 1,586	$ 1,502	$ 1,410	$ 1,307	$ 1,195
Balance Sheets					
Assets:					
Cash	$ 2,400	$ 4,800	$ 7,200	$ 9,600	$ 7,000
Land	95,000	95,000	95,000	95,000	0
Total assets	$ 97,400	$ 99,800	$102,200	$104,600	$ 7,000
Liabilities					
Bond payable	$100,000	$100,000	$100,000	$100,000	$ 0
Discount on bonds payable	(4,186)	(3,288)	(2,298)	(1,205)	0
Carrying value of bond liab.	95,814	96,712	97,702	98,795	0
Equity					
Retained earnings	1,586	3,088	4,498	5,805	7,000
Total liabilities and equity	$ 97,400	$ 99,800	$102,200	$104,600	$ 7,000
Statements of Cash Flows					
Operating Activities					
Inflow from customers	$ 11,400	$ 11,400	$ 11,400	$ 11,400	$ 11,400
Outflow for interest	(9,000)	(9,000)	(9,000)	(9,000)	(14,000)
Investing Activities					
Outflow to purchase land	(95,000)				
Inflow from sale of land					95,000
Financing Activities					
Inflow from bond issue	95,000				
Outflow to repay bond liab.					(95,000)
Net change in cash	2,400	2,400	4,800	7,200	(2,600)
Beginning cash balance	0	2,400	2,400	2,400	9,600
Ending cash balance	$ 2,400	$ 4,800	$ 7,200	$ 9,600	$ 7,000

$107,985. The effective rate of interest is 8 percent. United's accountant prepared the amortization schedule shown in Exhibit 10.11.

The recognition of interest expense at the end of each accounting period has the following effects on the financial statements. On the balance sheet assets decrease, liabilities decrease, and retained earnings decrease. On the income statement expenses increase and net income decreases. There is a cash outflow in the operating activities section of the statement of cash flows. The journal entry and its effects on the financial statements are shown here.

Account Title	Debit	Credit
Interest Expense	8,639	
Premium on Bonds Payable	1,361	
Cash		10,000

EXHIBIT 10.11

Amortization Schedule for Bond Premium

	(A) Cash Payment	(B) Interest Expense	(C) Discount Amortization	(D) Carrying Value
January 1, 2016				$107,985
December 31, 2016	$10,000	$ 8,639	$1,361	106,624
December 31, 2017	10,000	8,530	1,470	105,154
December 31, 2018	10,000	8,413	1,587	103,567
December 31, 2019	10,000	8,285	1,715	101,852
December 31, 2020	10,000	8,148	1,852	100,000
Totals	$50,000	$42,015	$7,985	

(A) Stated rate of interest times the face value of the bonds ($100,000 × 0.10).
(B) Effective interest times the carrying value at the beginning of the period. For the 2016 accounting period the amount is $8,639 ($107,985 × 0.08).
(C) Cash Payment − Interest Expense. For 2016 the premium amortization is $1,361 ($10,000 − $8,639 = $1,361).
(D) Carrying value at beginning of period minus the portion of premium amortized. For the accounting period ending December 31, 2016, the amount is $106,624 ($107,985 − $1,361).

Assets	=	Liabilities	+	Equity	Rev.	−	Exp.	=	Net Inc.	Cash Flow
Cash	=	Carrying Value of Bond Liab.	+	Ret. Earn.						
(10,000)	=	(1,361)	+	(8,639)	NA	−	8,639	=	(8,639)	(10,000) OA

THE FINANCIAL ANALYST

Bond financing has advantages and disadvantages for the stockholders of a business. Assessing a company's investment potential requires understanding both the potential rewards and the potential risks of debt financing.

LO 10-8

Explain the advantages and disadvantages of debt financing.

Financial Leverage and Tax Advantage of Debt Financing

As with other forms of credit, bonds may provide companies increased earnings through **financial leverage.** If a company can borrow money at 7 percent through a bond issue and invest the proceeds at 12 percent, the company's earnings benefit from the 5 percent (12 percent − 7 percent) **spread.**

Also, bond interest expense, like other forms of interest expense, is tax deductible, making the effective cost of borrowing less than the interest expense because the interest expense reduces the tax expense. Because dividend payments are not tax deductible, equity financing (e.g., issuing common stock) does not offer this advantage.

To illustrate, assume its organizers obtain $100,000 to start Maduro Company. During its first year of operation, Maduro earns $60,000 of revenue and incurs $40,000 of expenses other than interest expense. Consider two different forms of financing. First, assume the initial $100,000 is obtained by issuing common stock (equity financing) and Maduro pays an 8 percent dividend ($100,000 × 0.08 = $8,000 dividend). Second, assume Maduro issues $100,000 of bonds that pay 8 percent annual interest

($100,000 × 0.08 = $8,000). Assuming a 30 percent tax rate, which form of financing produces the larger increase in retained earnings? Refer to the following computations:

Computation of Addition to Retained Earnings

	Equity Financing	Debt Financing
Revenue	$ 60,000	$ 60,000
Expense (excluding interest)	(40,000)	(40,000)
Earnings before interest and taxes	20,000	20,000
Interest ($100,000 × 8%)	0	(8,000)
Pretax income	20,000	12,000
Income tax (30%)	(6,000)	(3,600)
Net income	14,000	8,400
Dividend	(8,000)	0
Addition to retained earnings	$ 6,000	$ 8,400

Debt financing produces $2,400 more retained earnings than equity financing. If equity financing is obtained, the company pays $6,000 in income taxes; debt financing requires only $3,600 of income taxes. Maduro's cost of financing, whether paid in dividends to investors or interest to creditors, is $8,000. With debt financing, however, the Internal Revenue Service receives $2,400 less.

The after-tax interest cost of debt can be computed as

Total interest expense × (1.0 − Tax rate)
$8,000 × (1.0 − 0.30) = $5,600

The after-tax interest rate that Maduro is paying can be computed using the same logic:

Debt interest rate × (1.0 − Tax rate)
8% × (1.0 − 0.30) = 5.6%

Unlike interest expense, there is no difference in the before-tax and after-tax effects of a dividend. For Maduro, $1 of dividends costs the company a full $1 of retained earnings, while $1 of interest has an after-tax cost of only $0.70 (assuming a 30 percent tax rate). This tax benefit only applies to profitable businesses. There are no tax savings if a company has no income because businesses that produce losses pay no taxes.

EBIT and Ratio Analysis

The tax consequences of debt financing can influence ratio analysis. For example, consider the *return on assets* (ROA) ratio discussed in Chapter 3. In that chapter ROA was defined as:

Net income ÷ Total assets

Recall that the ROA ratio is used to measure the effectiveness of asset management. In general, higher ROAs suggest better performance. However, the Maduro example demonstrates that a higher ROA can be obtained by using equity financing rather than debt financing without regard to how assets are managed. Recall that Maduro obtained $100,000 of assets whether through equity or debt financing. The assets were used exactly the same way regardless of the financing method used. With equity financing, Maduro's ROA is 14 percent ($14,000 ÷ $100,000) and with debt financing it is 8.4 percent ($8,400 ÷ $100,000). The difference in the ROA results from the financing approach rather than asset management.

The effects of the financing strategy can be avoided in ROA calculations by using *earnings before interest and taxes* (EBIT) rather than net income when computing the ratio. For example, if Maduro uses EBIT to compute ROA, the result is 20 percent ($20,000 ÷ $100,000) regardless of whether debt or equity financing is used. Using EBIT to compute ROA provides a less biased measure of asset utilization. For simplicity, however, this text uses net income to determine ROA unless otherwise indicated.

Times Interest Earned Ratio

Financing with bonds also has disadvantages. The issuer is legally obligated to make interest payments on time and to repay the principal at maturity. If a company fails to make scheduled payments, the creditors (bondholders) can force the company into bankruptcy. The claims on a company's assets held by bondholders and other creditors have priority over the claims of the owners. If a company in bankruptcy is forced to liquidate its assets, creditor claims must be fully paid before any owner claims can be paid. Bond issues therefore increase the owners' risk.

Financial analysts use several ratios to help assess the risk of bankruptcy. One is the *debt to assets ratio,* explained in Chapter 3. Another is the **times interest earned** ratio, defined as

EBIT ÷ Interest expense

This ratio measures *how many times* a company would be able to pay its interest using its earnings. The *times interest earned ratio* is based on EBIT rather than net income because it is the amount of earnings before interest and taxes that is available to pay interest. The higher the ratio, the less likely a company will be unable to make its interest payments. Higher times interest earned ratios suggest lower levels of risk. Examples of times interest earned ratios and debt to assets ratios for six real-world companies follow. These numbers are based on financial data for the year 2013.

Industry	Company	Times Interest Earned	Debt to Assets
Breakfast cereal	Kellogg's	12.1	0.77
	General Mills	9.0	0.64
Cosmetics	Avon	2.4	0.83
	Esteé Lauder	20.6	0.54
Hotels	Starwood Hotels	9.3	0.62
	Wyndham Worldwide	6.2	0.83

Since bills are paid with cash, not income, a company may be able to make interest payments even if it has a negative times interest earned ratio. A company with no EBIT may yet have cash. Meaningful financial statement analysis cannot rely on any single ratio or any set of ratios. Making sound business decisions requires considering other information in addition to the insights provided from analyzing ratios. A company with inferior ratios and a patent on a newly discovered drug that cures cancer may be a far better investment than a company with great ratios and a patent on a chemotherapy product that will soon be out of date. Ratio computations are based on historical data. They are useful only to the extent that history is likely to repeat itself.

CHECK YOURSELF 10.3

Selected financial data pertaining to Shaver Company and Goode Company follow (amounts are in thousands):

	Shaver Company	Goode Company
Earnings before interest and taxes	$750,720	$2,970,680
Interest expense	234,600	645,800

Based on this information, which company is more likely to be able to make its interest payments?

Answer The times interest earned ratio for Shaver Company is 3.2 ($750,720 ÷ $234,600) times. The times interest earned ratio for Goode Company is 4.6 ($2,970,680 ÷ $645,800) times. Based on these data, Goode Company is more likely to be able to make its interest payments.

<< A Look Back

This chapter explained basic accounting for long-term debt. *Long-term notes payable* usually mature in two to five years and require payments that include a return of principal plus interest. *Lines of credit* enable companies to borrow limited amounts on an as-needed basis. Although lines of credit normally have one-year terms, companies frequently renew them, extending the effective maturity date to the intermediate range of five or more years. Interest on a line of credit is normally paid monthly.

Long-term debt financing for more than 10 years usually requires issuing *bonds.* Bond agreements normally commit a company to pay *semiannual interest* at a fixed percentage of the bond face value. The amount of interest required by the bond agreement is based on the *stated interest rate.* If bonds are issued when the *market interest rate* is different from the stated interest rate, companies will receive more or less than the face value in order for the effective rate of interest to be consistent with market conditions. Selling bonds at a *discount* (below face value) increases the effective interest rate above the stated rate. Selling bonds at a *premium* decreases the effective rate of interest.

This chapter explained the tax advantages of using debt versus equity financing. Interest is a *tax-deductible expense* subtracted prior to determining taxable income. In contrast, dividends paid to owners are not deductible in determining taxable income.

>> A Look Forward

A company seeking long-term financing might choose to use debt, such as the types of bonds or term loans that were discussed in this chapter. Owners' equity is another source of long-term financing. Several equity alternatives are available, depending on the type of business organization the owners choose to establish. For example, a company could be organized as a sole proprietorship, partnership, or corporation. Chapter 11 presents accounting issues related to equity transactions for each of these types of business structures.

SELF-STUDY REVIEW PROBLEM

A step-by-step audio-narrated series of slides is available in the Connect library.

During 2016 and 2017, Herring Corp. completed the following selected transactions relating to its bond issue. The corporation's fiscal year ends on December 31.

2016

Jan. 1 Sold $400,000 of 10-year, 9 percent bonds at 97. Interest is payable in cash on December 31 each year.

Dec. 31 Paid the bond interest and recorded the amortization of the discount using the straight-line method.

2017

Dec. 31 Paid the bond interest and recorded the amortization of the discount using the straight-line method.

Required

a. Show how these events would affect Herring's financial statements by recording them in a financial statements model like the following one.

	Assets	=	Liab.	+	Equity	Rev.	−	Exp.	=	Net Inc.	Cash Flow
Date	Cash	=	Carrying Value of Bond Liability	+	Ret. Earn.						
1/1/16											
12/31/16											
12/31/17											

b. Determine the carrying value of the bond liability as of December 31, 2017.

c. Assuming Herring had earnings before interest and taxes of $198,360 in 2017, calculate the times interest earned ratio.

Solution

a.

	Assets	=	Liab.	+	Equity	Rev.	−	Exp.	=	Net Inc.	Cash Flow
Date	Cash	=	Carrying Value of Bond Liability	+	Ret. Earn.						
1/1/16	388,000	=	388,000	+	NA	NA	−	NA	=	NA	388,000 FA
12/31/16	(36,000)	=	1,200	+	(37,200)	NA	−	37,200	=	(37,200)	(36,000) OA
12/31/17	(36,000)	=	1,200	+	(37,200)	NA	−	37,200	=	(37,200)	(36,000) OA

b. The unamortized discount as of December 31, 2017, is $9,600 ($12,000 − $1,200 − $1,200). The carrying value of the bond liability is $390,400 ($400,000 − $9,600).

c. The times interest earned ratio is 5.3 times ($198,360 ÷ $37,200).

KEY TERMS

Amortization 539
Bond certificates 544
Bond discount 551
Bondholder 544
Bond premium 555
Call premium 546
Call price 546
Callable bonds 546
Carrying value 551
Collateral 547
Convertible bonds 546
Debentures 545
Discount on Bonds Payable 551
Effective interest rate 551
Effective interest rate method 558
Face value 544
Financial leverage 561
Fixed interest rate 538
Installment notes 540
Issuer 544
Line of credit 543
Long-term liabilities 538
Market interest rate 556
Mortgage bond 545
Premium on Bonds Payable 556
Restrictive covenants 547
Secured bonds 545
Serial bonds 545
Sinking fund 546
Spread 561
Stated interest rate 544
Straight-line amortization 552
Subordinated debentures 545
Term bonds 545
Times interest earned 563
Unsecured bonds 545
Unsubordinated debentures 545
Variable interest rate 538

QUESTIONS

1. What is the difference between classification of a note as short term or long term?
2. At the beginning of year 1, B Co. has a note payable of $72,000 that calls for an annual payment of $16,246, which includes both principal and interest. If the interest rate is 8 percent, what is the amount of interest expense in year 1 and in year 2? What is the balance of the note at the end of year 2?
3. What is the purpose of a line of credit for a business? Why would a company choose to obtain a line of credit instead of issuing bonds?
4. What are the primary sources of debt financing for most large companies?
5. What are some advantages of issuing bonds versus borrowing from a bank?
6. What are some disadvantages of issuing bonds?

7. Why can a company usually issue bonds at a lower interest rate than the company would pay if the funds were borrowed from a bank?
8. What effect does income tax have on the cost of borrowing funds for a business?
9. What is the concept of financial leverage?
10. Which type of bond, secured or unsecured, is likely to have a lower interest rate? Explain.
11. What is the function of restrictive covenants attached to bond issues?
12. What is the difference between term bonds and serial bonds?
13. What is the purpose of establishing a sinking fund?
14. What is the call price of a bond? Is it usually higher or lower than the face amount of the bond? Explain.
15. If Roc Co. issued $100,000 of 5 percent, 10-year bonds at the face amount, what is the effect of the issuance of the bonds on the financial statements? What amount of interest expense will Roc Co. recognize each year?
16. What mechanism is used to adjust the stated interest rate to the market rate of interest?
17. When the effective interest rate is higher than the stated interest rate on a bond issue, will the bond sell at a discount or premium? Why?
18. What type of transaction is the issuance of bonds by a company?
19. What factors may cause the effective interest rate and the stated interest rate to be different?
20. If a bond is selling at 97 ½, how much cash will the company receive from the sale of a $1,000 bond?
21. How is the carrying value of a bond computed?
22. Gay Co. has a balance in the Bonds Payable account of $25,000 and a balance in the Discount on Bonds Payable account of $5,200. What is the carrying value of the bonds? What is the total amount of the liability?
23. When the effective interest rate is higher than the stated interest rate, will interest expense be higher or lower than the amount of interest paid?
24. Assuming that the selling price of the bond and the face value are the same, would the issuer of a bond prefer to make annual or semiannual interest payments? Why?
25. Rato Co. called some bonds and had a loss on the redemption of the bonds of $2,850. How is this amount reported on the income statement?
26. Which method of financing, debt or equity, is generally more advantageous from a tax standpoint? Why?
27. If a company has a tax rate of 30 percent and interest expense was $10,000, what is the after-tax cost of the debt?
28. Which type of financing, debt or equity, increases the risk factor of a business? Why?
29. What information does the times interest earned ratio provide?

MULTIPLE-CHOICE QUESTIONS

Multiple-choice questions are available in the Connect library.

EXERCISES—SERIES A

connect plus+ ACCOUNTING

All applicable Exercises in Series A are available with McGraw-Hill's Connect Plus Accounting.

LO 10-1

Exercise 10-1A *Interest only versus an installment note*

Sanders Co. is planning to finance an expansion of its operations by borrowing $150,000. City Bank has agreed to loan Sanders the funds. Sanders has two repayment options: (1) to issue a note with the principal due in 10 years and with interest payable annually or (2) to issue a note to repay $15,000 of the principal each year along with the annual interest based on the unpaid principal balance. Assume the interest rate is 8 percent for each option.

Required

a. What amount of interest will Sanders pay in year 1

 (1) Under option 1?

 (2) Under option 2?

b. What amount of interest will Sanders pay in year 2

 (1) Under option 1?

 (2) Under option 2?

c. Explain the advantage of each option.

Exercise 10-2A *Amortization schedule for an installment note* LO 10-1

On January 1, 2016, Beatie Co. borrowed $200,000 cash from Central Bank by issuing a five-year, 6 percent note. The principal and interest are to be paid by making annual payments in the amount of $47,479. Payments are to be made December 31 of each year, beginning December 31, 2016.

Required

Prepare an amortization schedule for the interest and principal payments for the five-year period.

Exercise 10-3A *Financial statement effects of an installment note* LO 10-1

Dan Dayle started a business by issuing an $80,000 face value note to First State Bank on January 1, 2016. The note had an 8 percent annual rate of interest and a five-year term. Payments of $20,037 are to be made each December 31 for five years.

Required

a. What portion of the December 31, 2016, payment is applied to
 (1) Interest expense?
 (2) Principal?
b. What is the principal balance on January 1, 2017?
c. What portion of the December 31, 2017, payment is applied to
 (1) Interest expense?
 (2) Principal?

Exercise 10-4A *Financial statement effects of an installment note* LO 10-1

A partial amortization schedule for a 10-year note payable issued on January 1, 2016, is shown below:

Accounting Period	Principal Balance January 1	Cash Payment	Applied to Interest	Applied to Principal
2016	$200,000	$27,174	$12,000	$15,174
2017	184,826	27,174	11,090	16,084
2018	168,742	27,174	10,125	17,049

Required

a. Using a financial statements model like the one shown here, record the appropriate amounts for the following two events:
 (1) January 1, 2016, issue of the note payable.
 (2) December 31, 2016, payment on the note payable.

Event No.	Assets	=	Liab.	+	Equity	Rev.	−	Exp.	=	Net Inc.	Cash Flow
1											

b. If the company earned $62,000 cash revenue and paid $45,000 in cash expenses in addition to the interest in 2016, what is the amount of each of the following?
 (1) Net income for 2016.
 (2) Cash flow from operating activities for 2016.
 (3) Cash flow from financing activities for 2016.
c. What is the amount of interest expense on this loan for 2019?

Exercise 10-5A *Journal entries for a line of credit* LO 10-2

Singer Company has a line of credit with United Bank. Singer can borrow up to $400,000 at any time over the course of the 2016 calendar year. The following table shows the prime rate expressed as an annual percentage along with the amounts borrowed and repaid during the first three months of 2016. Singer agreed to pay interest at an annual rate equal to 2 percent above the bank's prime rate. Funds are borrowed or repaid on the first day of each month. Interest is payable in cash on the last day of the month. The interest rate is applied to the outstanding monthly balance. For example, Singer pays 6.5 percent (4.5 percent + 2 percent) annual interest on $140,000 for the month of February.

Month	Amount Borrowed or (Repaid)	Prime Rate for the Month
January	$80,000	4.0%
February	60,000	4.5
March	(20,000)	4.0

Required

Provide all journal entries pertaining to Singer's line of credit for the first three months of 2016.

LO 10-3

Exercise 10-6A *Two accounting cycles for bonds issued at face value*

Doyle Company issued $500,000 of 10-year, 7 percent bonds on January 1, 2016. The bonds were issued at face value. Interest is payable in cash on December 31 of each year. Doyle immediately invested the proceeds from the bond issue in land. The land was leased for an annual $125,000 of cash revenue, which was collected on December 31 of each year, beginning December 31, 2016.

Required

a. Prepare the journal entries for these events, and post them to T-accounts for 2016 and 2017.

b. Prepare the income statement, balance sheet, and statement of cash flows for 2016 and 2017.

LO 10-3

Exercise 10-7A *Two accounting cycles for bonds issued at face value*

On January 1, 2016, Bell Corp. issued $180,000 of 10-year, 6 percent bonds at their face amount. Interest is payable on December 31 of each year with the first payment due December 31, 2016.

Required

Prepare all the general journal entries related to these bonds for 2016 and 2017.

LO 10-3

Exercise 10-8A *Journal entries for callable bonds*

Nivan Co. issued $500,000 of 5 percent, 10-year, callable bonds on January 1, 2016, at their face value. The call premium was 3 percent (bonds are callable at 103). Interest was payable annually on December 31. The bonds were called on December 31, 2020.

Required

Prepare the journal entries to record the bond issue on January 1, 2016, and the bond redemption on December 31, 2020. Entries for accrual and payment of interest are not required.

LO 10-3

Exercise 10-9A *Annual versus semiannual interest for bonds issued at face value*

Milan Company issued bonds with a face value of $200,000 on January 1, 2016. The bonds had a 7 percent stated rate of interest and a six-year term. The bonds were issued at face value. Interest is payable on an annual basis.

Required

Write a memo explaining whether the total cash outflow for interest would be more, less, or the same if the bonds pay semiannual versus annual interest.

Exercise 10-10A *Determining cash receipts from bond issues*

LO 10-4, 10-5

Required

Compute the cash proceeds from bond issues under the following terms. For each case, indicate whether the bonds sold at a premium or discount:

a. Pear, Inc., issued $400,000 of 10-year, 8 percent bonds at 103.

b. Apple, Inc., issued $200,000 of five-year, 12 percent bonds at 97 ½.

c. Cherry Co. issued $100,000 of five-year, 6 percent bonds at 102 ¼.

d. Grape, Inc., issued $120,000 of four-year, 8 percent bonds at 96.

Exercise 10-11A *Stated rate of interest versus the market rate of interest*

LO 10-3, 10-4, 10-5

Required

Indicate whether a bond will sell at a premium (P), discount (D), or face value (F) for each of the following conditions:

a. ____ The stated rate of interest is higher than the market rate.

b. ____ The market rate of interest is equal to the stated rate.

c. ____ The market rate of interest is less than the stated rate.

d. ____ The stated rate of interest is less than the market rate.

e. ____ The market rate of interest is higher than the stated rate.

Exercise 10-12A *Identifying bond premiums and discounts*

LO 10-4, 10-5

Required

In each of the following situations, state whether the bonds will sell at a premium or discount:

a. Valley issued $300,000 of bonds with a stated interest rate of 7 percent. At the time of issue, the market rate of interest for similar investments was 6 percent.

b. Spring issued $220,000 of bonds with a stated interest rate of 5 percent. At the time of issue, the market rate of interest for similar investments was 6 percent.

c. River Inc. issued $150,000 of callable bonds with a stated interest rate of 5 percent. The bonds were callable at 102. At the date of issue, the market rate of interest was 6 percent for similar investments.

Exercise 10-13A *Determining the amount of bond premiums and discounts*

LO 10-4, 10-5

Required

For each of the following situations, calculate the amount of bond discount or premium, if any.

a. Gray Co. issued $80,000 of 6 percent bonds at 101 ¼.

b. Bush, Inc., issued $200,000 of 10-year, 6 percent bonds at 97 ½.

c. Oak, Inc., issued $100,000 of 20-year, 6 percent bonds at 103.

d. Willow Co. issued $180,000 of 15-year, 7 percent bonds at 99.

Exercise 10-14A *Straight-line amortization of a bond discount*

LO 10-4

Diaz Company issued $180,000 face value of bonds on January 1, 2016. The bonds had a 7 percent stated rate of interest and a five-year term. Interest is paid in cash annually, beginning December 31, 2016. The bonds were issued at 98. The straight-line method is used for amortization.

Required

a. Use a financial statements model like the one shown below to demonstrate how (1) the January 1, 2016, bond issue and (2) the December 31, 2016, recognition of interest expense, including the amortization of the discount and the cash payment, affect the company's financial statements. Use + for increase, − for decrease, and NA for not affected.

Event No.	Assets	=	Liab.	+	Equity	Rev.	−	Exp.	=	Net Inc.	Cash Flow
1											

b. Determine the carrying value (face value less discount or plus premium) of the bond liability as of December 31, 2016.
c. Determine the amount of interest expense reported on the 2016 income statement.
d. Determine the carrying value (face value less discount or plus premium) of the bond liability as of December 31, 2017.
e. Determine the amount of interest expense reported on the 2017 income statement.

LO 10-5

Exercise 10-15A *Straight-line amortization of a bond premium*

The Square Foot Grill, Inc., issued $200,000 of 10-year, 6 percent bonds on July 1, 2016, at 102. Interest is payable in cash semiannually on June 30 and December 31. The straight-line method is used for amortization.

Required

a. Prepare the journal entries to record issuing the bonds and any necessary journal entries for 2016 and 2017. Post the journal entries to T-accounts. Prepare any necessary closing entries for 2016.
b. Prepare the liabilities section of the balance sheet at the end of 2016 and 2017.
c. What amount of interest expense will Square Foot report on the financial statements for 2016 and 2017?
d. What amount of cash will Square Foot pay for interest in 2016 and 2017?

LO 10-4

Exercise 10-16A *Straight-line amortization for bonds issued at a discount*

On January 1, 2016, Price Co. issued $190,000 of five-year, 6 percent bonds at 96 ½. Interest is payable annually on December 31. The discount is amortized using the straight-line method.

Required

Prepare the journal entries to record the bond transactions for 2016 and 2017.

LO 10-5

Exercise 10-17A *Straight-line amortization of a bond premium*

Stuart Company issued $150,000 face value of bonds on January 1, 2016. The bonds had a 6 percent stated rate of interest and a five-year term. Interest is paid in cash annually, beginning December 31, 2016. The bonds were issued at 103. The straight-line method is used for amortization.

Required

a. Use a financial statements model like the one shown below to demonstrate how (1) the January 1, 2016, bond issue and (2) the December 31, 2016, recognition of interest expense, including the amortization of the premium and the cash payment, affect the company's financial statements. Use + for increase, − for decrease, and NA for not affected.

Event No.	Assets	=	Liab.	+	Equity	Rev.	−	Exp.	=	Net Inc.	Cash Flow
1											

b. Determine the carrying value (face value less discount or plus premium) of the bond liability as of December 31, 2016.
c. Determine the amount of interest expense reported on the 2016 income statement.
d. Determine the carrying value of the bond liability as of December 31, 2017.
e. Determine the amount of interest expense reported on the 2017 income statement.

LO 10-5

Exercise 10-18A *Straight-line amortization for bonds issued at a premium*

On January 1, 2016, Sayers Company issued $280,000 of five-year, 6 percent bonds at 102. Interest is payable semiannually on June 30 and December 31. The premium is amortized using the straight-line method.

Required

Prepare the journal entries to record the bond transactions for 2016 and 2017.

Exercise 10-19A *Effective interest amortization of a bond discount* LO 10-6

On January 1, 2016, the Diamond Association issued bonds with a face value of $300,000, a stated rate of interest of 6 percent, and a 10-year term to maturity. Interest is payable in cash on December 31 of each year. The effective rate of interest was 7 percent at the time the bonds were issued. The bonds sold for $278,932. Diamond used the effective interest rate method to amortize the bond discount.

Required

a. Determine the amount of the discount on the day of issue.
b. Determine the amount of interest expense recognized on December 31, 2016.
c. Determine the carrying value of the bond liability on December 31, 2016.
d. Provide the general journal entry necessary to record the December 31, 2016, interest expense.

Exercise 10-20A *Effective interest amortization of a bond discount* LO 10-6

On January 1, 2016, Parker Company issued bonds with a face value of $80,000, a stated rate of interest of 8 percent, and a five-year term to maturity. Interest is payable in cash on December 31 of each year. The effective rate of interest was 9 percent at the time the bonds were issued. The bonds sold for $76,888. Parker used the effective interest rate method to amortize the bond discount.

Required

a. Prepare an amortization table as shown below:

	Cash Payment	Interest Expense	Discount Amortization	Carrying Value
January 1, 2016				76,888
December 31, 2016	6,400	6,920	520	77,408
December 31, 2017	?	?	?	?
December 31, 2018	?	?	?	?
December 31, 2019	?	?	?	?
December 31, 2020	?	?	?	?
Totals	32,000	35,112	3,112	

b. What item(s) in the table would appear on the 2019 balance sheet?
c. What item(s) in the table would appear on the 2019 income statement?
d. What item(s) in the table would appear on the 2019 statement of cash flows?

Exercise 10-21A *Effective interest amortization of a bond premium* LO 10-7

On January 1, 2016, Young Company issued bonds with a face value of $300,000, a stated rate of interest of 7 percent, and a 10-year term to maturity. Interest is payable in cash on December 31 of each year. The effective rate of interest was 6 percent at the time the bonds were issued. The bonds sold for $323,165. Young used the effective interest rate method to amortize the bond premium.

Required

a. Determine the amount of the premium on the day of issue.
b. Determine the amount of interest expense recognized on December 31, 2016.
c. Determine the carrying value of the bond liability on December 31, 2016.
d. Provide the general journal entry necessary to record the December 31, 2016, interest expense.

Exercise 10-22A *Effective interest amortization for a bond premium* LO 10-7

On January 1, 2016, Hart Company issued bonds with a face value of $150,000, a stated rate of interest of 8 percent, and a five-year term to maturity. Interest is payable in cash on December 31 of each year. The effective rate of interest was 7 percent at the time the bonds were issued. The bonds sold for $156,150. Hart used the effective interest rate method to amortize the bond premium.

Required

a. Prepare an amortization table as shown below:

	Cash Payment	Interest Expense	Premium Amortization	Carrying Value
January 1, 2016				156,150
December 31, 2016	12,000	10,931	1,069	155,081
December 31, 2017	?	?	?	?
December 31, 2018	?	?	?	?
December 31, 2019	?	?	?	?
December 31, 2020	?	?	?	?
Totals	60,000	53,850	6,150	

b. What item(s) in the table would appear on the 2019 balance sheet?

c. What item(s) in the table would appear on the 2019 income statement?

d. What item(s) in the table would appear on the 2019 statement of cash flows?

LO 10-5, 10-7

Exercise 10-23A *Effective interest versus straight-line amortization*

On January 1, 2016, the Christie Companies issued bonds with a face value of $500,000, a stated rate of interest of 10 percent, and a 20-year term to maturity. Interest is payable in cash on December 31 of each year. The effective rate of interest was 8 percent at the time the bonds were issued.

Required

Write a brief memo explaining whether the effective interest rate method or the straight-line method will produce the highest amount of interest expense recognized on the 2016 income statement.

LO 10-8

Exercise 10-24A *Determining the after-tax cost of debt*

The following 2016 information is available for three companies:

	Crow Co.	Robin Co.	Sparrow Co.
Face value of bonds payable	$300,000	$600,000	$500,000
Interest rate	8%	7%	6%
Income tax rate	35%	20%	25%

Required

a. Determine the annual before-tax interest cost for each company *in dollars.*

b. Determine the annual after-tax interest cost for each company *in dollars.*

c. Determine the annual after-tax interest cost for each company as *a percentage* of the face value of the bonds.

LO 10-8

Exercise 10-25A *Determining the effects of financing alternatives on ratios*

Composite Solutions Company (CSC) has the following account balances:

Current assets	$150,000	Current liabilities	$100,000
Noncurrent assets	350,000	Noncurrent liabilities	250,000
		Stockholders' equity	150,000

The company wishes to raise $80,000 in cash and is considering two financing options: CSC can sell $80,000 of bonds payable, or it can issue additional common stock for $80,000. To help in the decision process, CSC's management wants to determine the effects of each alternative on its current ratio and debt to assets ratio.

Required

a. Help CSC's management by completing the following chart:

Ratio	Currently	If Bonds Are Issued	If Stock Is Issued
Current ratio			
Debt to asset ratio			

b. Assume that after the funds are invested, EBIT amounts to $60,000. Also assume the company pays $6,000 in dividends or $6,000 in interest depending on which source of financing is used. Based on a 40 percent tax rate, determine the amount of the increase in retained earnings that would result under each financing option.

PROBLEMS—SERIES A

connect plus+ ACCOUNTING ***All applicable Problems in Series A are available with McGraw-Hill's Connect Plus Accounting.***

Problem 10-26A *Effect of an installment note on financial statements*

LO 10-1

On January 1, 2016, Brown Co. borrowed cash from First Bank by issuing a $100,000 face value, four-year term note that had an 8 percent annual interest rate. The note is to be repaid by making annual cash payments of $30,192 that include both interest and principal on December 31 of each year. Brown used the proceeds from the loan to purchase land that generated rental revenues of $52,000 cash per year.

CHECK FIGURES

a. 2016 Ending Principal Balance: $77,808

b. 2016 Net Income: $44,000

Required

a. Prepare an amortization schedule for the four-year period.
b. Prepare an income statement, balance sheet, and statement of cash flows for each of the four years. (*Hint:* Record the transactions for each year in T-accounts before preparing the financial statements.)
c. Given that revenue is the same for each period, explain why net income increases each year.

Problem 10-27A *Effect of a line of credit on financial statements*

LO 10-2

Boyd Company has a line of credit with State Bank. Boyd can borrow up to $400,000 at any time over the course of the 2016 calendar year. The following table shows the prime rate expressed as an annual percentage along with the amounts borrowed and repaid during 2016. Boyd agreed to pay interest at an annual rate equal to 2 percent above the bank's prime rate. Funds are borrowed or repaid on the first day of each month. Interest is payable in cash on the last day of the month. The interest rate is applied to the outstanding monthly balance. For example, Boyd pays 7 percent (5 percent + 2 percent) annual interest on $100,000 for the month of January.

CHECK FIGURES

a. Interest Expense: $11,088

Total Assets: $83,912

Month	Amount Borrowed or (Repaid)	Prime Rate for the Month
January	$100,000	5%
February	70,000	6
March	(30,000)	7
April through October	No change	No change
November	(50,000)	6
December	(40,000)	5

Boyd earned $45,000 of cash revenue during 2016.

Required

a. Prepare an income statement, balance sheet, and statement of cash flows for 2016. (*Note:* Round computations to the nearest dollar.)

b. Write a memo to explain how the business was able to generate retained earnings when the owner contributed no assets to the business.

LO 10-3

CHECK FIGURES
b. Interest Expense: $48,000
Loss on Bond Redemptions: $24,000

Problem 10-28A *Recording transactions for callable bonds*

Arnold Corp. issued $600,000 of 20-year, 8 percent, callable bonds on January 1, 2016, with interest payable annually on December 31. The bonds were issued at their face amount. The bonds are callable at 104. The fiscal year of the corporation ends December 31.

Required

a. Show the effect of the following events on the financial statements by recording the appropriate amounts in a horizontal statements model like the following one. In the Cash Flow column, indicate whether the item is an operating activity (OA), investing activity (IA), or financing activity (FA). Use NA if an element was not affected by the event.
   (1) Issued the bonds on January 1, 2016.
   (2) Paid interest due to bondholders on December 31, 2016.
   (3) On January 1, 2021, Arnold Corp. called the bonds. Assume that all interim entries were correctly recorded.

Event No.	Assets	=	Liab.	+	Equity	Rev.	−	Exp.	=	Net Inc.	Cash Flow
1											

b. Prepare journal entries for the three events listed in Requirement *a.*

LO 10-5

Problem 10-29A *Straight-line amortization of a bond premium*

Pine Land Co. was formed when it acquired cash from the issue of common stock. The company then issued bonds at a premium on January 1, 2016. Interest is payable annually on December 31 of each year, beginning December 31, 2016. On January 2, 2016, Pine Land Co. purchased a piece of land and leased it for an annual rental fee. The rent is received annually on December 31, beginning December 31, 2016. At the end of the eight-year period (December 31, 2023), the land was sold at a gain, and the bonds were paid off. A summary of the transactions for each year follows:

2016

1. Acquired cash from the issue of common stock.
2. Issued eight-year bonds.
3. Purchased land.
4. Received land rental income.
5. Recognized interest expense including the straight-line amortization of the premium and made the cash payment for interest on December 31.
6. Prepared the December 31 entry to close Rent Revenue.
7. Prepared the December 31 entry to close Interest Expense.

2017–2022

8. Received land rental income.
9. Recognized interest expense including the straight-line amortization of the premium and made the cash payment for interest on December 31.
10. Prepared the December 31 entry to close Rent Revenue.
11. Prepared the December 31 entry to close Interest Expense.

2023

12. Sold land at a gain.
13. Retired bonds at face value.

Required

Identify each of these 13 events and transactions as an asset source (AS), asset use (AU), asset exchange (AE), or claims exchange (CE). Explain how each event affects assets, liabilities, equity, net income, and cash flow by placing a + for increase, − for decrease, or NA for not affected under each category. In the Cash Flow column, indicate whether the item is an operating activity (OA), investing activity (IA), or financing activity (FA). The first event is recorded as an example.

Event No.	Types of Event	Assets	=	Liabilities	+	Common Stock	+	Retained Earnings	Net Income	Cash Flow
1	AS	+		NA		+		NA	NA	+ FA

Problem 10-30A *Straight-line amortization of a bond discount*

LO 10-4

CHECK FIGURES

d. 2016 Interest Expense: $18,600

e. 2016 Interest Paid: $18,000

During 2016 and 2017, Agatha Corp. completed the following transactions relating to its bond issue. The corporation's fiscal year is the calendar year.

2016

Jan. 1 Issued $300,000 of 10-year, 6 percent bonds for $294,000. The annual cash payment for interest is due on December 31.

Dec. 31 Recognized interest expense, including the straight-line amortization of the discount, and made the cash payment for interest.

Dec. 31 Closed the interest expense account.

2017

Dec. 31 Recognized interest expense, including the straight-line amortization of the discount, and made the cash payment for interest.

Dec. 31 Closed the interest expense account.

Required

a. When the bonds were issued, was the market rate of interest more or less than the stated rate of interest? If Agatha had sold the bonds at their face amount, what amount of cash would Agatha have received?

b. Prepare the general journal entries for these transactions.

c. Prepare the liabilities section of the balance sheet at December 31, 2016 and 2017.

d. Determine the amount of interest expense that will be reported on the income statements for 2016 and 2017.

e. Determine the amount of interest that will be paid in cash to the bondholders in 2016 and 2017.

Problem 10-31A *Straight-line amortization of a bond discount*

LO 10-4

Oz Company was started when it issued bonds with a $500,000 face value on January 1, 2016. The bonds were issued for cash at 96. Oz uses the straight-line method of amortization. They had a 20-year term to maturity and an 8 percent annual interest rate. Interest was payable on December 31 of each year. Oz Company immediately purchased land with the proceeds (cash received) from the bond issue. Oz leased the land for $60,000 cash per year. On January 1, 2019, the company sold the land for $500,000 cash. Immediately after the sale of the land, Oz redeemed the bonds at 98. Assume that no other accounting events occurred during 2019.

Required

Prepare an income statement, statement of changes in equity, balance sheet, and statement of cash flows for the 2016, 2017, 2018, and 2019 accounting periods. Assume that the company closes its books on December 31 of each year. Prepare the statements using a vertical statements format. (*Hint:* Record each year's transactions in T-accounts prior to preparing the financial statements.)

LO 10-5

Problem 10-32A *Effect of bond transactions on financial statements*

The three typical accounting events associated with borrowing money through a bond issue are:

1. Exchanging the bonds for cash on the day of issue.
2. Making cash payments for interest expense and recording amortization when applicable.
3. Repaying the principal at maturity.

Required

a. Assuming the bonds are issued at face value, show the effect of each of the three events on the financial statements using a horizontal statements model like the following one. Use + for increase, − for decrease, and NA for not affected.

Event No.	Assets	=	Liab.	+	Equity	Rev.	−	Exp.	=	Net Inc.	Cash Flow
1											

b. Repeat the requirements in Requirement *a,* but assume instead that the bonds are issued at a discount.

c. Repeat the requirements in Requirement *a,* but assume instead that the bonds are issued at a premium.

LO 10-4, 10-6

Problem 10-33A *Effective interest versus straight-line amortization*

On January 1, 2016, Twain Corp. sold $500,000 of its own 7 percent, 10-year bonds. Interest is payable annually on December 31. The bonds were sold to yield an effective interest rate of 8 percent. Twain uses the effective interest rate method. The bonds sold for $477,422.

Required

a. Prepare the journal entry for the issuance of the bonds.

b. Prepare the journal entry for the amortization of the bond discount and the payment of the interest at December 31, 2016. (Assume effective interest amortization.)

c. Prepare the journal entry for the amortization of the bond discount and the payment of interest on December 31, 2016. (Assume straight-line amortization.)

d. Calculate the amount of interest expense for 2017. (Assume effective interest amortization.)

e. Calculate the amount of interest expense for 2017. (Assume straight-line amortization.)

LO 10-8

Problem 10-34A *Using ratios to make comparisons*

The following information pertains to Bob's Pest Services and Sarah's Critter Control at the end of 2016:

Account Title	Bob's Pest Services	Sarah's Critter Control
Current assets	$ 45,000	$ 45,000
Total assets	800,000	800,000
Current liabilities	78,000	57,000
Total liabilities	675,000	500,000
Stockholders' equity	125,000	300,000
Interest expense	62,000	45,000
Income tax expense	69,000	75,500
Net income	105,000	115,000

Required

a. Compute each company's debt to assets ratio, current ratio, and times interest earned (EBIT must be computed). Identify the company with the greater financial risk.

b. Compute each company's return on equity ratio and return on assets ratio. Use EBIT instead of net income when computing the return on assets ratio. Identify the company that is managing its assets more effectively. Identify the company that is producing the higher return from the stockholders' perspective. Explain how one company was able to produce a higher return on equity than the other.

EXERCISES—SERIES B

Exercise 10-1B *Interest only versus an installment note* LO 10-1

Pare Co. borrowed $80,000 from National Bank by issuing a note with a five-year term. Pare has two options with respect to the payment of interest and principal. Option 1 requires the payment of interest only on an annual basis with the full amount of the principal due at maturity. Option 2 calls for an annual payment that includes interest due plus a partial repayment of the principal balance. The effective annual interest rate on both notes is identical.

Required

Write a memo explaining how the two alternatives will affect *(a)* the carrying value of liabilities, *(b)* the amount of annual interest expense, *(c)* the total amount of interest that will be paid over the life of the note, and *(d)* the cash flow consequences.

Exercise 10-2B *Amortization schedule for an installment note* LO 10-1

On January 1, 2016, Monroe Co. borrowed $80,000 cash from First Bank by issuing a four-year, 6 percent note. The principal and interest are to be paid by making annual payments in the amount of $23,087. Payments are to be made December 31 of each year, beginning December 31, 2016.

Required

Prepare an amortization schedule for the interest and principal payments for the four-year period.

Exercise 10-3B *Financial statement effects of an installment note* LO 10-1

Lek Hood started a business by issuing a $70,000 face value note to State National Bank on January 1, 2016. The note had a 6 percent annual rate of interest and a 10-year term. Payments of $9,581 are to be made each December 31 for 10 years.

Required

a. What portion of the December 31, 2016, payment is applied to
  (1) Interest expense?
  (2) Principal?
b. What is the principal balance on January 1, 2017?
c. What portion of the December 31, 2017, payment is applied to
  (1) Interest expense?
  (2) Principal?

Exercise 10-4B *Financial statement effects of an installment note* LO 10-1

A partial amortization schedule for a five-year note payable that Mercury Co. issued on January 1, 2016, is shown here:

Accounting Period	Principal Balance January 1	Cash Payment	Applied to Interest	Applied to Principal
2016	$60,000	$13,858	$3,000	$10,858
2017	49,142	13,858	2,457	11,401

Required

a. What rate of interest is Mercury Co. paying on the note?

b. Using a financial statements model like the one shown below, record the appropriate amounts for the following two events:

(1) January 1, 2016, issue of the note payable.

(2) December 31, 2017, payment on the note payable.

Event No.	Assets	=	Liab.	+	Equity	Rev.	−	Exp.	=	Net Inc.	Cash Flow
1											

c. If the company earned $75,000 cash revenue and paid $32,000 in cash expenses in addition to the interest in 2016, what is the amount of each of the following?

(1) Net income for 2016.

(2) Cash flow from operating activities for 2016.

(3) Cash flow from financing activities for 2016.

d. What is the amount of interest expense on this loan for 2018?

LO 10-2

Exercise 10-5B *Journal entries for a line of credit*

Colson Company has a line of credit with Federal Bank. Colson can borrow up to $800,000 at any time over the course of the 2016 calendar year. The following table shows the prime rate expressed as an annual percentage along with the amounts borrowed and repaid during the first four months of 2016. Colson agreed to pay interest at an annual rate equal to 2 percent above the bank's prime rate. Funds are borrowed or repaid on the first day of each month. Interest is payable in cash on the last day of the month. The interest rate is applied to the outstanding monthly balance. For example, Colson pays 6 percent (4 percent + 2 percent) annual interest on $80,000 for the month of January.

Month	Amount Borrowed or (Repaid)	Prime Rate for the Month
January	$80,000	4.0%
February	50,000	4.25%
March	(30,000)	4.5%
April	20,000	4.25%

Required

Provide all journal entries pertaining to Colson's line of credit for the first four months of 2016.

LO 10-3

Exercise 10-6B *Two accounting cycles for bonds issued at face value*

Pluto Company issued $300,000 of 20-year, 6 percent bonds on January 1, 2016. The bonds were issued at face value. Interest is payable in cash on December 31 of each year. Pluto immediately invested the proceeds from the bond issue in land. The land was leased for an annual $50,000 of cash revenue, which was collected on December 31 of each year, beginning December 31, 2016.

Required

a. Prepare the journal entries and appropriate closing entries for these events and post them to T-accounts for 2016 and 2017.

b. Prepare the income statement, balance sheet, and statement of cash flows for 2016 and 2017.

LO 10-3

Exercise 10-7B *Two accounting cycles for bonds issued at face value*

On January 1, 2016, Hazman Corp. issued $200,000 of 10-year, 6 percent bonds at their face value. Interest is payable on December 31 of each year with the first payment due December 31, 2016.

Required

Prepare all the general journal entries related to these bonds for 2016 and 2017.

Exercise 10-8B *Journal entries for callable bonds*

LO 10-3

Tyler Co. issued $250,000 of 6 percent, 10-year, callable bonds on January 1, 2016, at their face value. The call premium was 2 percent (bonds are callable at 102). Interest was payable annually on December 31. The bonds were called on December 31, 2019.

Required

Prepare the journal entries to record the bond issue on January 1, 2016, and the bond redemption on December 31, 2019. Entries to accrue and pay interest are not required.

Exercise 10-9B *Annual versus semiannual interest for bonds issued at face value*

LO 10-3

Jupiter Co. issued bonds with a face value of $150,000 on January 1, 2016. The bonds had a 6 percent stated rate of interest and a five-year term. The bonds were issued at face value.

Required

a. What total amount of interest will Jupiter pay in 2016 if bond interest is paid annually each December 31?

b. What total amount of interest will Jupiter pay in 2016 if bond interest is paid semiannually each June 30 and December 31?

c. Write a memo explaining which option Jupiter would prefer.

Exercise 10-10B *Determining cash receipts from bond issues*

LO 10-4, 10-5

Required

Compute the cash proceeds from bond issues under the following terms. For each case, indicate whether the bonds sold at a premium or discount:

a. Hett, Inc., issued $400,000 of 8-year, 8 percent bonds at 101.

b. Holt Co. issued $250,000 of 4-year, 6 percent bonds at 98.

c. Holmes Co. issued $300,000 of 10-year, 7 percent bonds at 102 ¼.

d. Hart, Inc., issued $200,000 of 5-year, 6 percent bonds at 97 ½.

Exercise 10-11B *Stated rate of interest versus the market rate of interest*

LO 10-3, 10-4, 10-5

Required

Indicate whether a bond will sell at a premium (P), discount (D), or face value (F) for each of the following conditions:

a. ____ The stated rate of interest is less than the market rate.

b. ____ The market rate of interest is equal to the stated rate.

c. ____ The market rate of interest is less than the stated rate.

d. ____ The market rate of interest is higher than the stated rate.

e. ____ The stated rate of interest is higher than the market rate.

Exercise 10-12B *Identifying bond premiums and discounts*

LO 10-4, 10-5

Required

In each of the following situations, state whether the bonds will sell at a premium or discount:

a. Carver issued $400,000 of bonds with a stated interest rate of 7 percent. At the time of issue, the market rate of interest for similar investments was 6 percent.

b. Herring issued $200,000 of bonds with a stated interest rate of 6 percent. At the time of issue, the market rate of interest for similar investments was 8 percent.

c. Watson, Inc., issued callable bonds with a stated interest rate of 6 percent. The bonds were callable at 102. At the date of issue, the market rate of interest was 7 percent for similar investments.

LO 10-4, 10-5

Exercise 10-13B *Determining the amount of bond premiums and discounts*

Required

For each of the following situations, calculate the amount of bond discount or premium, if any:

a. Jones Co. issued $120,000 of 6 percent bonds at 101.

b. Jude, Inc., issued $80,000 of 10-year, 8 percent bonds at 98.

c. James, Inc., issued $200,000 of 15-year, 9 percent bonds at 102 ¼.

d. Jolly Co. issued $400,000 of 20-year, 8 percent bonds at 99 ¾.

LO 10-4

Exercise 10-14B *Straight-line amortization of a bond discount*

Frey Company issued $300,000 face value of bonds on January 1, 2016. The bonds had a 6 percent stated rate of interest and a 10-year term. Interest is paid in cash annually, beginning December 31, 2016. The bonds were issued at 98. Frey uses the straight-line method of amortization.

Required

a. Use a financial statements model like the one shown below to demonstrate how (1) the January 1, 2016, bond issue and (2) the December 31, 2016, recognition of interest expense, including the amortization of the discount and the cash payment, affect the company's financial statements. Use + for increase, − for decrease, and NA for not affected.

Event No.	Assets	=	Liab.	+	Equity	Rev.	−	Exp.	=	Net Inc.	Cash Flow
1											

b. Determine the amount of interest expense reported on the 2016 income statement.

c. Determine the carrying value (face value less discount or plus premium) of the bond liability as of December 31, 2016.

d. Determine the amount of interest expense reported on the 2017 income statement.

e. Determine the carrying value (face value less discount or plus premium) of the bond liability as of December 31, 2017.

LO 10-4

Exercise 10-15B *Straight-line amortization of a bond discount*

Dixon Construction, Inc., issued $300,000 of 10-year, 6 percent bonds on July 1, 2016, at 96. Interest is payable in cash semiannually on June 30 and December 31. Dixon uses the straight-line method of amortization.

Required

a. Prepare the journal entries to record issuing the bonds and any necessary journal entries for 2016 and 2017. Prepare any necessary closing entries for 2016. Post the entries to T-accounts.

b. Prepare the liabilities section of the balance sheet at the end of 2016 and 2017.

c. What amount of interest expense will Dixon Construction report on the financial statements for 2016 and 2017?

d. What amount of cash will Dixon Construction pay for interest in 2016 and 2017?

LO 10-4

Exercise 10-16B *Straight-line amortization for bonds issued at a discount*

On January 1, 2016, Files Co. issued $400,000 of five-year, 6 percent bonds at 97. Interest is payable annually on December 31. The discount is amortized using the straight-line method.

Required

Prepare the journal entries to record the bond transactions for 2016 and 2017.

LO 10-5

Exercise 10-17B *Straight-line amortization of a bond premium*

Ramsey Company issued $300,000 face value of bonds on January 1, 2016. The bonds had a 6 percent stated rate of interest and a 10-year term. Interest is paid in cash annually, beginning December 31, 2016. The bonds were issued at 101 ½. The straight-line method is used for amortization.

Required

a. Use a financial statements model like the one shown below to demonstrate how (1) the January 1, 2016 bond issue and (2) the December 31, 2016 recognition of interest expense, including the amortization of the premium and the cash payment, affect the company's financial statements. Use + for increase, − for decrease, and NA for not affected.

Event No.	Assets	=	Liab.	+	Equity	Rev.	−	Exp.	=	Net Inc.	Cash Flow
1											

b. Determine the carrying value (face value plus premium) of the bond liability as of December 31, 2016.
c. Determine the amount of interest expense reported on the 2016 income statement.
d. Determine the carrying value of the bond liability as of December 31, 2017.
e. Determine the amount of interest expense reported on the 2017 income statement.

Exercise 10-18B *Straight-line amortization for bonds issued at a premium* LO 10-5

On January 1, 2016, Chen Company issued $300,000 of five-year, 6 percent bonds at 101. Interest is payable annually on December 31. The premium is amortized using the straight-line method.

Required

Prepare the journal entries to record the bond transactions for 2016 and 2017.

Exercise 10-19B *Effective interest amortization of a bond discount* LO 10-6

On January 1, 2016, Seaside Condo Association issued bonds with a face value of $250,000, a stated rate of interest of 8 percent, and a 10-year term to maturity. Interest is payable in cash on December 31 of each year. The effective rate of interest was 10 percent at the time the bonds were issued. The bonds sold for $219,277. Seaside used the effective interest rate method to amortize the bond discount.

Required

a. Determine the amount of the discount on the day of issue.
b. Determine the amount of interest expense recognized on December 31, 2016.
c. Determine the carrying value of the bond liability on December 31, 2016.
d. Provide the general journal entry necessary to record the December 31, 2016, interest expense.

Exercise 10-20B *Effective interest amortization of a bond discount* LO 10-6

On January 1, 2016, Valley Enterprises issued bonds with a face value of $60,000, a stated rate of interest of 8 percent, and a five-year term to maturity. Interest is payable in cash on December 31 of each year. The effective rate of interest was 9 percent at the time the bonds were issued. The bonds sold for $57,666. Valley used the effective interest rate method to amortize the bond discount.

Required

a. Prepare an amortization table as shown below:

	Cash Payment	Interest Expense	Discount Amortization	Carrying Value
January 1, 2016				57,666
December 31, 2016	4,800	5,190	390	58,056
December 31, 2017	?	?	?	?
December 31, 2018	?	?	?	?
December 31, 2019	?	?	?	?
December 31, 2020	?	?	?	?
Totals	24,000	26,334	2,334	

b. What item(s) in the table would appear on the 2017 balance sheet?

c. What item(s) in the table would appear on the 2017 income statement?
d. What item(s) in the table would appear on the 2017 statement of cash flows?

LO 10-7

Exercise 10-21B *Effective interest amortization of a bond premium*

On January 1, 2016, Omega Company issued bonds with a face value of $200,000, a stated rate of interest of 6 percent, and a 10-year term to maturity. Interest is payable in cash on December 31 of each year. The effective rate of interest was 5 percent at the time the bonds were issued. The bonds sold for $215,443. Omega used the effective interest rate method to amortize the bond discount.

Required

a. Determine the amount of the premium on the day of issue.
b. Determine the amount of interest expense recognized on December 31, 2016.
c. Determine the carrying value of the bond liability on December 31, 2016.
d. Provide the general journal entry necessary to record the December 31, 2016, interest expense.

LO 10-7

Exercise 10-22B *Effective interest amortization for a bond premium*

On January 1, 2016, Reese Incorporated issued bonds with a face value of $120,000, a stated rate of interest of 8 percent, and a five-year term to maturity. Interest is payable in cash on December 31 of each year. The effective rate of interest was 7 percent at the time the bonds were issued. The bonds sold for $124,920. Pitre used the effective interest rate method to amortize the bond discount.

Required

a. Prepare an amortization table as shown below:

	Cash Payment	Interest Expense	Premium Amortization	Carrying Value
January 1, 2016				124,920
December 31, 2016	9,600	8,744	856	124,064
December 31, 2017	?	?	?	?
December 31, 2018	?	?	?	?
December 31, 2019	?	?	?	?
December 31, 2020	?	?	?	?
Totals	48,000	43,080	4,920	

b. What item(s) in the table would appear on the 2018 balance sheet?
c. What item(s) in the table would appear on the 2018 income statement?
d. What item(s) in the table would appear on the 2018 statement of cash flows?

LO 10-4, 10-6

Exercise 10-23B *Effective interest versus straight-line amortization*

On January 1, 2016, Wright and Associates issued bonds with a face value of $800,000, a stated rate of interest of 8 percent, and a 20-year term to maturity. Interest is payable in cash on December 31 of each year. The effective rate of interest was 9 percent at the time the bonds were issued.

Required

Write a brief memo explaining whether the effective interest rate method or the straight-line method will produce the highest amount of interest expense recognized on the 2016 income statement.

LO 10-8

Exercise 10-24B *Determining the after-tax cost of debt*

The following 2016 information is available for three companies:

	Bass Co.	Carp Co.	Perch Co.
Face value of bonds payable	$300,000	$600,000	$500,000
Interest rate	10%	9%	8%
Income tax rate	40%	30%	35%

Required

a. Determine the annual before-tax interest cost for each company *in dollars.*

b. Determine the annual after-tax interest cost for each company *in dollars.*

c. Determine the annual after-tax interest cost for each company as *a percentage* of the face value of the bonds.

Exercise 10-25B *Determining the effects of financing alternatives on ratios*

LO 10-8

Cascade Industries has the following account balances:

Current assets	$ 30,000	Current liabilities	$15,000
Noncurrent assets	120,000	Noncurrent liabilities	75,000
		Stockholders' equity	60,000

The company wishes to raise $50,000 in cash and is considering two financing options: Cascade can sell $50,000 of bonds payable, or it can issue additional common stock for $50,000. To help in the decision process, Cascade's management wants to determine the effects of each alternative on its current ratio and debt to assets ratio.

Required

a. Help Cascade's management by completing the following chart:

Ratio	Currently	If Bonds Are Issued	If Stock Is Issued
Current ratio			
Debt to asset ratio			

b. Assume that after the funds are invested, EBIT amounts to $18,000. Also assume the company pays $5,000 in dividends or $5,000 in interest, depending on which source of financing is used. Based on a 30 percent tax rate, determine the amount of the increase in retained earnings that would result under each financing option.

PROBLEMS—SERIES B

Problem 10-26B *Effect of an installment note on financial statements*

LO 10-1

On January 1, 2016, Kramer Co. borrowed cash from First City Bank by issuing a $90,000 face value, three-year term note that had a 7 percent annual interest rate. The note is to be repaid by making annual payments of $34,295 that include both interest and principal on December 31. Kramer invested the proceeds from the loan in land that generated lease revenues of $45,000 cash per year.

Required

a. Prepare an amortization schedule for the three-year period.

b. Prepare an income statement, balance sheet, and statement of cash flows for each of the three years. (*Hint:* Record the transactions for each year in T-accounts before preparing the financial statements.)

c. Does cash outflow from operating activities remain constant or change each year? Explain.

Problem 10-27B *Effect of a line of credit on financial statements*

LO 10-2

Mott Company has a line of credit with Bay Bank. Mott can borrow up to $400,000 at any time over the course of the 2016 calendar year. The following table shows the prime rate expressed as an annual percentage along with the amounts borrowed and repaid during 2016. Mott agreed to pay interest at an annual rate equal to 1 percent above the bank's prime rate. Funds are borrowed or repaid on the first day of each month. Interest is payable in cash on the last day of the month. The interest rate is applied to the outstanding monthly balance. For example, Mott pays 6 percent (5 percent + 1 percent) annual interest on $60,000 for the month of January.

Month	Amount Borrowed or (Repaid)	Prime Rate for the Month
January	$60,000	5%
February	40,000	5
March	(30,000)	6
April through October	No change	No change
November	(20,000)	6
December	(10,000)	5

Mott earned $25,000 of cash revenue during 2016.

Required

a. Prepare an income statement, balance sheet, and statement of cash flows for 2016.

b. Write a memo discussing the advantages to a business of arranging a line of credit.

LO 10-3

Problem 10-28B *Recording transactions for callable bonds*

Dame Co. issued $250,000 of 10-year, 6 percent, callable bonds on January 1, 2016, with interest payable annually on December 31. The bonds were issued at their face amount. The bonds are callable at 101 ½. The fiscal year of the corporation is the calendar year.

Required

a. Show the effect of the following events on the financial statements by recording the appropriate amounts in a horizontal statements model like the following one. In the Cash Flow column, indicate whether the item is an operating activity (OA), investing activity (IA), or financing activity (FA). Use NA if an element was not affected by the event.

(1) Issued the bonds on January 1, 2016.

(2) Paid interest due to bondholders on December 31, 2016.

(3) On January 1, 2020, Dame Co. called the bonds. Assume that all interim entries were correctly recorded.

Event No.	Assets	=	Liab.	+	Equity	Rev.	−	Exp.	=	Net Inc.	Cash Flow
1											

b. Prepare journal entries for the three events listed in Requirement *a.*

LO 10-4

Problem 10-29B *Straight-line amortization of a bond discount*

White Co. was formed when it acquired cash from the issue of common stock. The company then issued bonds at a discount on January 1, 2016. Interest is payable on December 31 with the first payment made December 31, 2016. On January 2, 2016, White Co. purchased a piece of land that produced rent revenue annually. The rent is collected on December 31 of each year, beginning December 31, 2016. At the end of the six-year period (January 1, 2022), the land was sold at a gain and the bonds were paid off at face value. A summary of the transactions for each year follows:

2016

1. Acquired cash from the issue of common stock.
2. Issued six-year bonds.
3. Purchased land.
4. Received land rental income.
5. Recognized interest expense, including the straight-line amortization of the discount, and made the cash payment for interest on December 31.
6. Prepared December 31 entry to close Rent Revenue.
7. Prepared December 31 entry to close Interest Expense.

2017–2021

8. Received land rental income.

9. Recognized interest expense, including the straight-line amortization of the discount, and made the cash payment for interest December 31.

10. Prepared December 31 entry to close Rent Revenue.

11. Prepared December 31 entry to close Interest Expense.

2022

12. Sold the land at a gain.

13. Retired the bonds at face value.

Required

Identify each of these 13 events and transactions as an asset source (AS), asset use (AU), asset exchange (AE), or claims exchange (CE). Explain how each event affects assets, liabilities, equity, net income, and cash flow by placing a + for increase, − for decrease, or NA for not affected under each of the categories. In the Cash Flow column, indicate whether the item is an operating activity (OA), investing activity (IA), or financing activity (FA). The first event is recorded as an example.

Event No.	Type of Event	Assets	= Liabilities +	Common Stock	+ Retained Earnings	Net Income	Cash Flow
1	AS	+	NA	+	NA	NA	+ FA

Problem 10-30B *Straight-line amortization of a bond discount*

LO 10-4

During 2016 and 2017, Kale Co. completed the following transactions relating to its bond issue. The company's fiscal year ends on December 31.

2016

Mar. 1 Issued $200,000 of eight-year, 6 percent bonds for $194,000. The semiannual cash payment for interest is due on March 1 and September 1, beginning September 2016.

Sept. 1 Recognized interest expense, including the straight-line amortization of the discount, and made the semiannual cash payment for interest.

Dec. 31 Recognized accrued interest expense, including the straight-line amortization of the discount.

Dec. 31 Closed the interest expense account.

2017

Mar. 1 Recognized interest expense, including the straight-line amortization of the discount, and made the semiannual cash payment for interest.

Sept. 1 Recognized interest expense, including the straight-line amortization of the discount, and made the semiannual cash payment for interest.

Dec. 31 Recognized accrued interest expense, including the amortization of the discount.

Dec. 31 Closed the interest expense account.

Required

a. When the bonds were issued, was the market rate of interest more or less than the stated rate of interest? If the bonds had sold at face value, what amount of cash would Kale Co. have received?

b. Prepare the general journal entries for these transactions.

c. Prepare the liabilities section of the balance sheet at December 31, 2016 and 2017.

d. Determine the amount of interest expense Kale would report on the income statements for 2016 and 2017.

e. Determine the amount of interest Kale would pay to the bondholders in 2016 and 2017.

Problem 10-31B *Straight-line amortization of a bond premium*

LO 10-5

Whitten Company was started when it issued bonds with $300,000 face value on January 1, 2016. The bonds were issued for cash at 103. Whitten uses the straight-line method of amortization.

They had a 15-year term to maturity and a 6 percent annual interest rate. Interest was payable annually. Whitten immediately purchased land with the proceeds (cash received) from the bond issue. Whitten leased the land for \$36,000 cash per year. On January 1, 2019, the company sold the land for \$310,000 cash. Immediately after the sale, Whitten repurchased its bonds (repaid the bond liability) at 104. Assume that no other accounting events occurred in 2019.

Required

Prepare an income statement, statement of changes in equity, balance sheet, and statement of cash flows for each of the 2016, 2017, 2018, and 2019 accounting periods. Assume that the company closes its books on December 31 of each year. Prepare the statements using a vertical statements format. (*Hint:* Record each year's transactions in T-accounts prior to preparing the financial statements.)

LO 10-1, 10-2, 10-4, 10-5

Problem 10-32B *Effect of financing transactions on financial statements*

Required

Show the effect of each of the following independent accounting events on the financial statements using a horizontal statements model like the following one. Use + for increase, − for decrease, and NA for not affected. The first event is recorded as an example.

Event No.	Assets	=	Liab.	+	Equity	Rev.	−	Exp.	=	Net Inc.	Cash Flow
1	+		+		NA	NA		NA		NA	FA +

a. Issued a bond at a premium.
b. Made an interest payment on a bond that had been issued at a premium and amortized the premium.
c. Borrowed funds using a line of credit.
d. Made an interest payment for funds that had been borrowed against a line of credit.
e. Made a cash payment on a note payable for both interest and principal.
f. Issued a bond at face value.
g. Made an interest payment on a bond that had been issued at face value.
h. Issued a bond at a discount.
i. Made an interest payment on a bond that had been issued at a discount and amortized the discount.

LO 10-5, 10-7

Problem 10-33B *Effective interest versus straight-line amortization*

On January 1, 2016, Mason Corp. sold \$100,000 of its own 6 percent, 10-year bonds. Interest is payable annually on December 31. The bonds were sold to yield an effective interest rate of 5 percent. Mason Corp. uses the effective interest rate method. The bonds sold for \$104,330.

Required

a. Prepare the journal entry for the issuance of the bonds.
b. Prepare the journal entry for the amortization of the bond premium and the payment of the interest on December 31, 2018. (Assume effective interest amortization.)
c. Prepare the journal entry for the amortization of the bond premium and the payment of interest on December 31, 2018. (Assume straight-line amortization.)
d. Calculate the amount of interest expense for 2019. (Assume effective interest amortization.)
e. Calculate the amount of interest expense for 2019. (Assume straight-line amortization.)

Problem 10-34B *Using ratios to make comparisons*

LO 10-8

The following information pertains to Tacoma and Olympia companies at the end of 2016:

Account Title	Tacoma Co.	Olympia Co.
Current assets	$ 60,000	$ 60,000
Total assets	1,000,000	1,000,000
Current liabilities	55,000	50,000
Total liabilities	800,000	600,000
Stockholders' equity	200,000	400,000
Interest expense	60,000	45,000
Income tax expense	95,000	100,000
Net income	145,000	155,000

Required

a. Compute each company's debt to assets ratio, current ratio, and times interest earned (EBIT must be computed). Identify the company with the greater financial risk.

b. Compute each company's return on equity ratio and return on assets ratio. Use EBIT instead of net income when computing the return on assets ratio. Identify the company that is managing its assets more effectively. Identify the company that is producing the higher return from the stockholders' perspective. Explain how one company was able to produce a higher return on equity than the other.

ANALYZE, THINK, COMMUNICATE

ATC 10-1 Business Application Case *Understanding real-world annual reports*

Use the Target Corporation's annual report in Appendix B to answer the following questions:

Required

a. What was the average interest rate on Target's long-term debt in the fiscal-year ended February 1, 2014 (2013)?

b. Target has an "unsecured revolving credit facility" (i.e., a line of credit). What is the total amount of credit available under this facility? How much of this total amount available had Target used as of February 1, 2014?

c. Target's balance sheet shows a line titled "Other noncurrent liabilities." What are the types of debt included in this category?

ATC 10-2 Group Assignment *Missing information*

The following three companies issued the following bonds:

1. Carr, Inc., issued $100,000 of 8 percent, five-year bonds at 102 ¼ on January 1, 2016. Interest is payable annually on December 31.
2. Kim, Inc., issued $100,000 of 8 percent, five-year bonds at 98 on January 1, 2016. Interest is payable annually on December 31.
3. Jay, Inc., issued $100,000 of 8 percent, five-year bonds at 104 on January 1, 2016. Interest is payable annually on December 31.

Required

a. Organize the class into three sections and divide each section into groups of three to five students. Assign each of the sections one of the companies.

Group Tasks

(1) Compute the following amounts for your company (use straight-line amortization):
  (a) Cash proceeds from the bond issue.
  (b) Interest paid in 2016.
  (c) Interest expense for 2016.

(2) Prepare the liabilities section of the balance sheet as of December 31, 2016.

Class Discussion

b. Have a representative of each section put the liabilities section for its company on the board.
c. Is the amount of interest expense different for the three companies? Why or why not?
d. Is the amount of interest paid different for each of the companies? Why or why not?
e. Is the amount of total liabilities different for each of the companies? Why or why not?

ATC 10-3 Real-World Case *Using accounting numbers to assess creditworthiness*

Automatic Data Processing, Inc. (ADP) is "one of the world's leading providers of human capital management solutions to employers, as well as integrated computing solutions to vehicle dealers around the world ... We offer solutions to businesses of all sizes, whether they have simple or complex needs, and serve approximately 620,000 clients in more than 125 countries."

The Boeing Company is one of the world's major aerospace firms and operates "in five principal segments: Commercial Airplanes; Military Aircraft; Network & Space Systems; Global Services & Support; and Boeing Capital Corporation."

HCA, Inc., is a holding company, which, through its subsidiary companies, owns and operates approximately 165 hospitals and 115 surgery centers in the United States and England.

J.C. Penney, Inc., operates approximately 1,100 stores, making it one of the largest apparel and home furnishing retailers in the United States.

Each company received a different rating from Standards & Poor's (S&P). In descending order, the ratings for these companies were AAA, A, BB, and CCC+. These rating are as of March 7, 2014. All dollar amounts are in millions.

	Net Income	Cash Flow from Operations	Current Ratio	Debt to Assets Ratio	Times Interest Earned	Return on Assets Ratio
Automatic Data Processing, Inc.						
2012	$1,389	$1,910	1.08	0.80	276.60	0.045
2013	1,406	1,577	1.06	0.81	234.63	0.043
Boeing						
2012	4,585	7,508	1.27	0.84	17.14	0.044
2013	3,900	8,179	1.26	0.93	13.76	0.046
HCA						
2012	2,006	4,175	1.26	1.30	2.61	0.071
2013	1,996	3,680	1.41	1.24	2.59	0.69
J.C. Penney						
2012	(152)	820	1.84	0.65	0.33	−0.013
2013	(985)	(10)	1.43	0.68	−3.43	−0.091

Required

Determine which credit rating was assigned to which company. Write a memorandum explaining the rationale for your decisions.

ATC 10-4 Business Applications Case *Performing ratio analysis using real-world data*

Sonic Corporation began business in 1953. In 2013 it was operating 3,522 drive-in hamburger restaurants throughout the United States and Mexico. The following data were taken from the company's 2013 annual report. All dollar amounts are in thousands.

	Fiscal Years Ending	
Account Title	**August 31, 2013**	**August 31, 2012**
Current assets	$140,722	$107,151
Total assets	660,794	680,760
Current liabilities	72,930	80,516
Total liabilities	583,330	621,513
Stockholders' equity	77,464	59,247
Interest expense	29,098	31,608
Income tax expense	19,598	21,877
Net income	36,701	36,085

Required

a. Calculate the EBIT for each year.

b. Calculate the times interest earned ratio for each year.

c. Calculate the current ratio and debt to assets ratio for each year.

d. Did the company's level of financial risk increase or decrease from 2012 to 2013? Explain.

ATC 10-5 Business Applications Case *Performing ratio analysis using real-world data*

Jos. A. Bank Clothiers, Inc., operates 602 retail clothing stores in 44 states and the District of Columbia. The Men's Wearhouse, Inc., operates 1,075 men's clothing stores in the United States, and 1,143 in Canada. These stores do business under the names Men's Wearhouse, K&G Fashion Superstores, and Moores Clothing for Men. The following information was taken from these companies' February 2, 2013, annual reports. All dollar amounts are in thousands.

Account Title	Jos. A. Banks	Men's Wearhouse
Current assets	$742,189	$ 855,153
Total assets	894,847	1,496,347
Current liabilities	170,349	294,183
Total liabilities	227,284	387,112
Stockholders' equity	667,563	1,109,235
Interest expense	26	1,544
Income tax expense	49,147	65,609
Net income	79,696	132,063

Required

a. Calculate the EBIT for each company.

b. Calculate each company's debt to assets ratio, current ratio, and the times interest earned ratio.

c. Calculate each company's return on assets ratio using EBIT instead of net earnings. Calculate each company's return on equity ratio using net earnings.

d. Men's Wearhouse reported interest expense of $1,544, before taxes. What was its after-tax interest expense in dollars? (*Hint:* You will need to compute its tax rate by dividing income tax expense by *earnings before taxes,* which must be computed.)

ATC 10-6 Writing Assignment *Debt versus equity financing*

Mack Company plans to invest $50,000 in land that will produce annual rent revenue equal to 15 percent of the investment starting on January 1, 2016. The revenue will be collected in cash at the end of each year, starting December 31, 2016. Mack can obtain the cash necessary to purchase the land from two sources. Funds can be obtained by issuing $50,000 of 10 percent, five-year bonds at their face amount. Interest due on the bonds is payable on December 31 of each year with the first payment due on December 31, 2016. Alternatively, the $50,000 needed to invest in land can be obtained from equity financing. In this case, the stockholders (holders of the equity) will be paid a $5,000 annual cash dividend. Mack Company is in a 30 percent income tax bracket.

Required

a. Prepare an income statement and statement of cash flows for 2016 under the two alternative financing proposals.

b. Write a short memorandum explaining why one financing alternative provides more net income but less cash flow than the other.

ATC 10-7 Ethical Dilemma *I don't want to pay taxes*

Dana Harbert recently started a very successful small business. Indeed, the business had grown so rapidly that she was no longer able to finance its operations by investing her own resources in the business. She needed additional capital but had no more of her own money to put into the business. A friend, Gene Watson, was willing to invest $100,000 in the business. Harbert estimated that with Watson's investment, the company would be able to increase revenue by $40,000. Furthermore, she believed that operating expenses would increase by only 10 percent. Harbert and Watson agree that Watson's investment should entitle him to receive a cash dividend equal to 20 percent of net income. A set of forecasted statements with and without Watson's investment is presented here. (Assume that all transactions involving revenue, expense, and dividends are cash transactions.)

Financial Statements

	Forecast 1 without Watson's Investment	Forecast 2 with Watson's Investment
Income Statements		
Revenue	$120,000	$160,000
Operating expenses	(70,000)	(77,000)
Income before interest and taxes	50,000	83,000
Income tax expense (effective tax rate is 30%)	(15,000)	(24,900)
Net income	$ 35,000	$ 58,100
Statements of Changes in Stockholders' Equity		
Beginning retained earnings	$ 15,000	$ 15,000
Plus: Net income	35,000	58,100
Less: Dividend to Watson (20% of $58,100)	0	(11,620)
Ending retained earnings	$ 50,000	$ 61,480
Balance Sheets		
Assets (computations explained in following paragraph)	$400,000	$511,480
Liabilities	$ 0	$ 0
Equity		
Common stock	350,000	450,000
Retained earnings	50,000	61,480
Total liabilities and equity	$400,000	$511,480

The balance for assets in Forecast 1 is computed as the beginning balance of $365,000 plus net income of $35,000. The balance for assets in Forecast 2 is computed as the beginning balance of $365,000, plus the $100,000 cash investment, plus net income of $58,100, less the $11,620 dividend. Alternatively, total assets can be computed by determining the amount of total claims (total assets = total claims).

Harbert tells Watson that there would be a $3,486 tax advantage associated with debt financing. She says that if Watson is willing to become a creditor instead of an owner, she could pay him an additional $697.20 (that is, 20 percent of the tax advantage). Watson tells Harbert that he has no interest in participating in the management of the business, but Watson wants an ownership interest to guarantee that he will always receive 20 percent of the profits of the business. Harbert suggests that they execute a formal agreement in which Watson is paid 11.62 percent interest on his $100,000 loan to the business. This agreement will be used for income tax reporting. In addition, Harbert says that she is willing to establish a private agreement to write Watson a personal check for any additional amount necessary to make Watson's total return equal to 20 percent of all profits plus a $697.20 bonus for his part of the tax advantage. She tells Watson, "It's just like ownership. The only difference is that we call it debt for the Internal Revenue Service. If they want to have some silly rule that says if you call it debt, you get a tax break, then we are foolish if we don't call it debt. I will call it anything they want, just as long as I don't have to pay taxes on it."

Required

a. Construct a third set of forecasted financial statements (Forecast 3) at 11.62 percent annual interest, assuming that Watson is treated as creditor (he loans the business $100,000).

b. Verify the tax advantage of debt financing by comparing the balances of the Retained Earnings account in Forecast 2 and Forecast 3.

c. If you were Watson, would you permit Harbert to classify the equity transaction as debt to provide a higher return to the business and to you?

d. Comment on the ethical implications of misnaming a financing activity for the sole purpose of reducing income taxes.

ATC 10-8 Research Assignment *Analyzing long-term debt at Union Pacific Railroad*

Many companies have a form of debt called *capital leases.* A capital lease is created when a company agrees to rent an asset, such as equipment or a building, for such a long time that GAAP treats this lease as if the asset was purchased using borrowed funds. A capital lease creates a liability for the company that acquired the leased asset because it has promised to make payments to another company for several years in the future. If a company has any capital leases, it must disclose them in the notes to the financial statements and will sometimes disclose them in a separate account in the liabilities section of the balance sheet.

Using the most current Forms 10-K for **Union Pacific Corporation**, complete the requirements below. To obtain the 10-K you can either use the EDGAR system, following the instructions in Appendix A, or they can be found on the company's website.

Required

a. What was Union Pacific's debt to asset ratio?

b. How much interest expense did Union Pacific incur?

c. What amount of liabilities did Union Pacific have as a result of capital leases? Footnotes 14 and 16 present information about Union Pacific's leases.

d. What percentage of Union Pacific's long-term liabilities was the result of capital leases?

e. Many companies try to structure (design) leasing agreements so that their leases will *not* be classified as capital leases. Explain why a company such as Union Pacific might want to avoid having capital leases.

ATC 10-9 Spreadsheet Assignment *Using Excel*

On January 1, 2016, Bainbridge Company borrowed $100,000 cash from a bank by issuing a 10-year, 9 percent note. The principal and interest are to be paid by making annual payments in the amount of $15,582. Payments are to be made December 31 of each year beginning December 31, 2016.

Required

a. Set up the spreadsheet as shown below. Notice that Excel can be set up to calculate the loan payment. If you're unfamiliar with this, see the following Spreadsheet Tips section. The Beginning Principal Balance (B12) and Cash Payment (C12) can be referenced from the Loan Information section. The interest rate used to calculate Interest Expense (D12) can also be referenced from the Loan Information section.

b. Complete the spreadsheet for the 10 periods.

c. In Row 23, calculate totals for cash payments, interest expense, and applied to principal.

d. Consider how the amounts would differ if Bainbridge were to borrow the $100,000 at different interest rates and time periods. The results of the original data (option 1) have been entered in the following schedule. In the spreadsheet, delete 9 percent and 10 from cells B4 and B5, respectively. Enter the data for the second option (8 percent and 10 years) in cells B4 and B5. Enter the recomputed payment and total interest in the schedule for the second option. Continue the same process for options 3 through 9 by deleting the prior rate and number of periods in the spreadsheet and entering in the next option's data. The number of years scheduled (rows 12 through 21) will have to be shortened for the 7-year options and lengthened for the 13-year options.

	Option								
	1	2	3	4	5	6	7	8	9
Rate	9%	8%	10%	9%	8%	10%	9%	8%	10%
Years	10	10%	10	7	7	7	13	13	13
Payment	15,582								
Total interest	55,820								

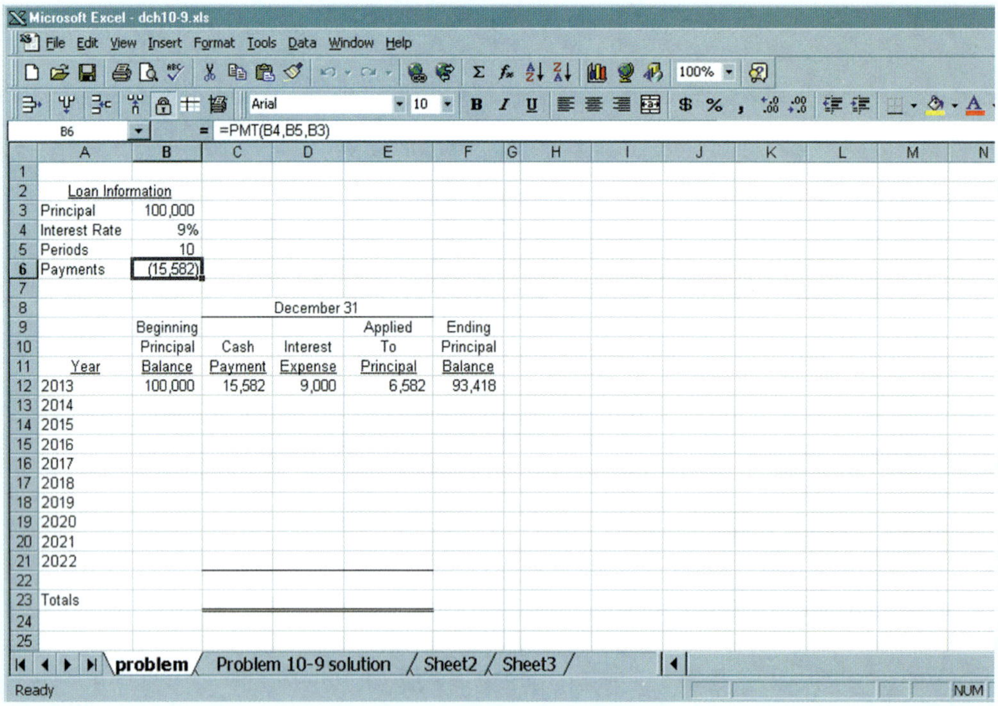

Microsoft Excel - dch10-9.xls

B6 = =PMT(B4,B5,B3)

	A	B	C	D	E	F
1						
2	Loan Information					
3	Principal	100,000				
4	Interest Rate	9%				
5	Periods	10				
6	Payments	(15,582)				
7						
8				December 31		
9		Beginning			Applied	Ending
10		Principal	Cash	Interest	To	Principal
11	Year	Balance	Payment	Expense	Principal	Balance
12	2013	100,000	15,582	9,000	6,582	93,418
13	2014					
14	2015					
15	2016					
16	2017					
17	2018					
18	2019					
19	2020					
20	2021					
21	2022					
22						
23	Totals					
24						
25						

problem / Problem 10-9 solution / Sheet2 / Sheet3

Spreadsheet Tips

1. Excel will calculate an installment loan payment. The interest rate (%), number of periods (nper), and amount borrowed or otherwise known as present value (PV) must be entered in the payment formula. The formula for the payment is =PMT(rate,nper,pv). The rate, number of periods, and amount borrowed (present value) may be entered as actual amounts or referenced to other cells. In the preceding spreadsheet, the payment formula can be either =PMT(9%,10,100000) or =PMT(B4,B5,B3). In our case, the latter is preferred so that variables can be altered in the spreadsheet without also having to rewrite the payment formula. Notice that the payment is a negative number.

2. Using positive numbers is preferred in the amortization schedule. The loan payment (cell B6) in the loan information section shows up as a negative number. Any reference to it in the amortization schedule should be preceded by a minus sign to convert it to a positive number. For example, the formula in cell C12 for the cash payment is =−B6.
3. Recall that to copy a fixed number, a $ sign must be positioned before the column letter and row number. The complete formula then for cell C12 is =−B6.

ATC 10-10 Spreadsheet Analysis *Mastering Excel*

Wise Company was started on January 1, 2016, when it issued 20-year, 10 percent, $200,000 face value bonds at a price of 90. Interest is payable annually at December 31 of each year. Wise immediately purchased land with the proceeds (cash received) from the bond issue. Wise leased the land for $27,000 cash per year. The lease revenue payments are due every December 31.

Required

Set up the following horizontal statements model on a blank spreadsheet. The SCF Activity column is for the classifications operating, financing, or investing.

a. Enter the effects of the 2016 transactions. Assume that both the interest and lease payments occurred on December 31. Notice that the entry for the lease has already been entered as an example. Calculate the ending balances.

b. Enter the effects of the 2017 transactions. Assume that both the interest and lease payments occurred on December 31. Calculate the ending balances.

c. Enter the effects of the 2018 transactions. Assume that both the interest and lease payments occurred on December 31. Calculate the ending balances.

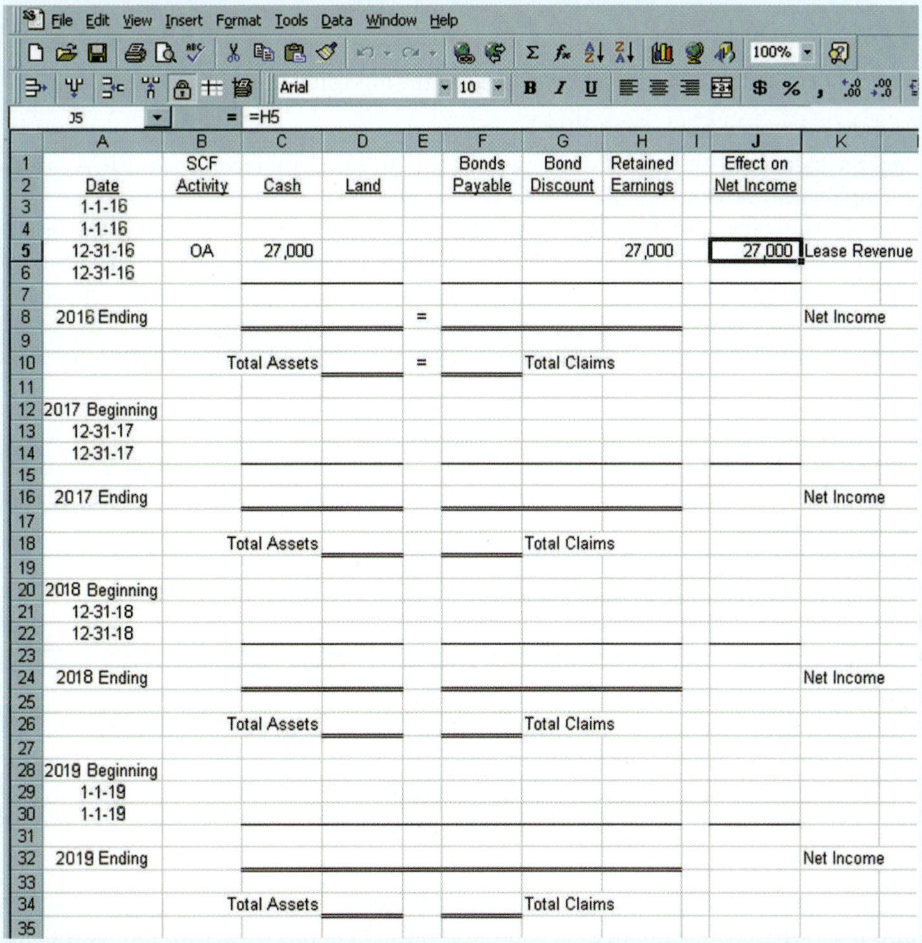

	A	B	C	D	E	F	G	H	I	J	K
1		SCF				Bonds	Bond	Retained		Effect on	
2	Date	Activity	Cash	Land		Payable	Discount	Earnings		Net Income	
3	1-1-16										
4	1-1-16										
5	12-31-16	OA	27,000					27,000		27,000	Lease Revenue
6	12-31-16										
7											
8	2016 Ending				=						Net Income
9											
10			Total Assets		=		Total Claims				
11											
12	2017 Beginning										
13	12-31-17										
14	12-31-17										
15											
16	2017 Ending										Net Income
17											
18			Total Assets				Total Claims				
19											
20	2018 Beginning										
21	12-31-18										
22	12-31-18										
23											
24	2018 Ending										Net Income
25											
26			Total Assets				Total Claims				
27											
28	2019 Beginning										
29	1-1-19										
30	1-1-19										
31											
32	2019 Ending										Net Income
33											
34			Total Assets				Total Claims				
35											

d. On January 1, 2019, Wise Company sold the land for $190,000 cash. Immediately after the sale of the land, Wise repurchased its bond at a price of 93. Assume that no other accounting events occurred during 2019. Enter the effects of the 2019 transactions. Calculate the ending balances.

COMPREHENSIVE PROBLEM

The trial balance of Pacilio Security Services Inc. as of January 1, 2020, had the following normal balances:

Cash	$122,475
Petty cash	100
Accounts receivable	27,400
Allowance for doubtful accounts	4,390
Supplies	165
Prepaid rent	3,000
Merchandise inventory (38 @ $290)	11,020
Equipment	9,000
Van	27,000
Accumulated depreciation	23,050
Sales tax payable	290
Employee income tax payable	500
FICA—Social Security tax payable	600
FICA—Medicare tax payable	150
Warranty payable	312
Unemployment tax payable	630
Interest payable	320
Notes payable	12,000
Common stock	50,000
Retained earnings	107,918

During 2020 Pacilio Security Services experienced the following transactions:

1. Paid the sales tax payable from 2019.
2. Paid the balance of the payroll liabilities due for 2019 (federal income tax, FICA taxes, and unemployment taxes).
3. On January 1, 2020, purchased land and a building for $150,000. The building was appraised at $125,000 and the land at $25,000. Pacilio paid $50,000 cash and financed the balance. The balance was financed with a 10-year installment note. The note had an interest rate of 7 percent and annual payments of $14,238 due on the last day of the year.
4. On January 1, 2020, issued $50,000 of 6 percent, five year bonds. The bonds were issued at 98.
5. Purchase $660 of supplies on account.
6. Purchased 170 alarm systems at a cost of $300. Cash was paid for the purchase.
7. After numerous attempts to collect from customers, wrote off $2,450 of uncollectible accounts receivable.
8. Sold 160 alarm systems for $580 each plus sales tax of 5 percent. All sales were on account. (Be sure to compute cost of goods sold using the FIFO cost flow method.)
9. Billed $120,000 of monitoring services for the year. Credit card sales amounted to $36,000, and the credit card company charged a 4 percent fee. The remaining $84,000 were sales on account. Sales tax is not charged on this service.
10. Replenished the petty cash fund on June 30. The fund had $11 cash and receipts of $65 for yard mowing and $24 for office supplies expense.
11. Collected the amount due from the credit card company.
12. Paid the sales tax collected on $85,000 of the alarm sales.
13. Collected $167,000 of accounts receivable during the year.
14. Paid installers and other employees a total of $82,000 for salaries for the year. Assume the Social Security tax rate is 6 percent and the Medicare tax rate is 1.5 percent. Federal income taxes withheld amounted to $9,600. The net amount of salaries was paid in cash.
15. Paid $1,250 in warranty repairs during the year.
16. On September 1, paid the note and interest owed to State Bank.

17. Paid $18,000 of advertising expense during the year.
18. Paid $5,600 of utilities expense for the year.
19. Paid the payroll liabilities, both the amounts withheld from the salaries plus the employer share of Social Security tax and Medicare tax, on $75,000 of the salaries plus $8,600 of the federal income tax that was withheld. (Disregard unemployment taxes in this entry.)
20. Paid the accounts payable.
21. Paid bond interest and amortized the discount.
22. Paid the annual installment on the amortized note.
23. Paid a dividend of $10,000 to the shareholders.

Adjustments

24. There was $210 of supplies on hand at the end of the year.
25. Recognized the expired rent for the office building for the year.
26. Recognized the uncollectible accounts expense for the year using the allowance method. Pacilio now estimates that 1.5 percent of sales on account will not be collected.
27. Recognized depreciation expense on the equipment, van, and building. The equipment has a five-year life and a $2,000 salvage value. The van has a four-year life and a $6,000 salvage value. The building has a 40-year life and a $10,000 salvage value. The company uses double-declining-balance for the van and straight-line for the equipment and the building. The equipment and van were purchased in 2018 and a full year of depreciation was taken for both in 2018.
28. The alarms systems sold in transaction 8 were covered with a one-year warranty. Pacilio estimated that the warranty cost would be 2 percent of alarm sales.
29. The unemployment tax on the three employees has not been paid. Record the accrued unemployment tax on the salaries for the year. The unemployment tax rate is 4.5 percent and gross wages for all employees exceeded $7,000.
30. Recognized the employer Social Security and Medicare payroll tax that has not been paid on $7,000 of salaries expense.

Required

a. Record the above transactions in general journal form. Round all amounts to the nearest whole dollar.
b. Post the transactions to the T-accounts.
c. Prepare a trial balance.
d. Prepare an income statement, statement of changes in stockholders' equity, classified balance sheet, and statement of cash flows.
e. Close the temporary accounts to retained earnings.
f. Post the closing entries to the T-accounts and prepare an after-closing trial balance.

CHAPTER 11

Proprietorships, Partnerships, and Corporations

LEARNING OBJECTIVES

After you have mastered the material in this chapter, you will be able to:

LO 11-1 Identify the primary characteristics of sole proprietorships, partnerships, and corporations.

LO 11-2 Explain how different types of capital stock affect financial statements.

LO 11-3 Show how treasury stock transactions affect financial statements.

LO 11-4 Explain how dividends, stock splits, and appropriations affect financial statements.

LO 11-5 Explain some uses of accounting information in making stock investment decisions.

Video lectures and accompanying self-assessment quizzes are available for all learning objectives through McGraw-Hill Connect® Plus Accounting.

CHAPTER OPENING

You want to start a business. How should you structure it? Should it be a sole proprietorship, partnership, or corporation? Each form of business structure presents advantages and disadvantages. For example, a sole proprietorship allows maximum independence and control while partnerships and corporations allow individuals to pool resources and talents with other people. This chapter discusses these and other features of the three primary forms of business structure.

The Curious Accountant

Imagine your rich uncle rewarded you for doing well in your first accounting course by giving you $10,000 to invest in the stock of one company. After reviewing many recent annual reports, you narrowed your choice to two companies with the following characteristics:

Mystery Company A: This company began operations in 2006, was incorporated in 2007, and began selling its stock to the public on November 7, 2013. It has lost money every year it has been in existence. In 2013 alone its losses were $645 million, and by December 31, 2013, it had total lifetime losses of approximately $995 million. Even so, the company provides one of the most influential services on the planet. At its current price of $54 you could buy 185 shares. A friend tells you that a person whose attention span is as short as yours would be crazy not to buy this company's stock.

Mystery Company B: This company has been in existence since 1870 and has made a profit most years. In 2013 alone its net earnings were $2.1 billion, and it paid dividends of $1.2 billion. Unlike Company A, Company B sells items that everyone uses but few people talk about. Its stock is selling for about $109 per share, so you can buy 92 shares. Your friend says that buying this company's stock would be the most boring investment you would ever make.

The names of the real-world companies described above are disclosed later. Based on the information provided, which company's stock would you buy? (Answer on page 599.)

FORMS OF BUSINESS ORGANIZATIONS

LO 11-1

Identify the primary characteristics of sole proprietorships, partnerships, and corporations.

Sole proprietorships are owned by a single individual who is responsible for making business and profit distribution decisions. If you want to be the absolute master of your destiny, you should organize your business as a proprietorship. Establishing a sole proprietorship is usually as simple as obtaining a business license from local government authorities. Usually no legal ownership agreement is required.

Partnerships allow persons to share their talents, capital, and the risks and rewards of business ownership. Since two or more individuals share ownership, partnerships require clear agreements about how authority, risks, and profits will be shared. Prudent partners minimize misunderstandings by hiring attorneys to prepare a **partnership agreement** which defines the responsibilities of each partner and describes how income or losses will be divided. Since the measurement of income affects the distribution of profits, partnerships frequently hire accountants to ensure that records are maintained in accordance with generally accepted accounting principles (GAAP). Partnerships (and sole proprietorships) also may need professional advice to deal with tax issues.

A **corporation** is a separate legal entity created by the authority of a state government. The paperwork to start a corporation is complex. For most laypersons, engaging professional attorneys and accountants to assist with the paperwork is well worth the fees charged.

Each state has separate laws governing establishing corporations. Many states follow the standard provisions of the Model Business Corporation Act. All states require the initial application to provide **articles of incorporation**, which normally include the following information: (1) the corporation's name and proposed date of incorporation; (2) the purpose of the corporation; (3) the location of the business and its expected life (which can be *perpetuity,* meaning *endless*); (4) provisions for capital stock; and (5) the names and addresses of the members of the first board of directors, the individuals with the ultimate authority for operating the business. If the articles are in order, the state establishes the legal existence of the corporation by issuing a charter of incorporation. The charter and the articles are public documents.

Each form of business organization presents a different combination of advantages and disadvantages. Persons wanting to start a business or invest in one should consider the characteristics of each type of business structure.

Regulation

Few laws specifically affect the operations of proprietorships and partnerships. Corporations, however, are usually heavily regulated. The extent of government regulation depends on the size and distribution of a company's ownership interests. Ownership interests in corporations are normally evidenced by **stock certificates.**

Ownership of corporations can be transferred from one individual to another through exchanging stock certificates. As long as the exchanges (buying and selling of shares of stock, often called *trading*) are limited to transactions between individuals, a company is defined as a **closely held corporation.** However, once a corporation reaches a certain size, it may list its stock on a stock exchange such as the New York Stock Exchange. Trading on a stock exchange is limited to the stockbrokers who are members of the exchange. These brokers represent buyers and sellers who are willing to pay the brokers commissions for exchanging stock certificates on their behalf. Although closely held corporations are relatively free from government regulation, companies whose stock is publicly traded on the exchanges by brokers are subject to extensive regulation.

The extensive regulation of trading on stock exchanges began in the 1930s. The stock market crash of 1929 and the subsequent Great Depression led Congress to pass the **Securities Act of 1933** and the **Securities Exchange Act of 1934** to regulate issuing stock and to govern the exchanges. The 1934 act also created the Securities and Exchange Commission (SEC) to enforce the securities laws. Congress gave the SEC legal authority to establish accounting principles for corporations that are registered on

Answers to The Curious Accountant

Mystery Company A is **Twitter, Inc.**, as of March 7, 2014. In its initial public offering on November 7, 2013, its stock price was $26 per share, and by the end of the day it was selling for $44.90. Four months later the stock was trading at $53.53.

Mystery Company B is **Kimberly-Clark Corporation**, as of March 7, 2014. Its well-known products include Kleenex, Scott toilet tissue, Huggies, Depend, and Cottonelle. During the first four months of trading, Twitter's stock price rose from $26 to $53.53. During the same four months, K-C's stock went from $107.88 to $108.95. Of course, only the future will reveal which company is the better investment in the long run.

the exchanges. However, the SEC has generally deferred its rule-making authority to the independent, private sector Financial Accounting Standards Board (FASB).

A number of high-profile business failures around the turn of this century raised questions about the effectiveness of financial statement audits to protect the public. The **Sarbanes-Oxley Act of 2002** was adopted to address these concerns. The act creates a five-member Public Company Accounting Oversight Board (PCAOB) with the authority to set and enforce auditing, attestation, quality control, and ethics standards for auditors of public companies. The PCAOB is empowered to impose disciplinary and remedial sanctions for violations of its rules, securities laws, and professional auditing and accounting standards. Public corporations operate in a complex regulatory environment that requires the services of attorneys and professional accountants.

Double Taxation

Corporations pay income taxes on their earnings and then owners pay income taxes on distributions (dividends) received from corporations. As a result, distributed corporate profits are taxed twice—first when income is reported on the corporation's income tax return and a second time when distributions are reported on individual owners' tax returns. This phenomenon is commonly called **double taxation** and is a significant disadvantage of the corporate form of business organization.

To illustrate, assume Glide Corporation earns pretax income of $100,000. Glide is in a 30 percent tax bracket. The corporation itself will pay income tax of $30,000 ($100,000 × 0.30). If the corporation distributes the after-tax income of $70,000 ($100,000 − $30,000) to individual stockholders who are taxed at 15 percent, the $70,000 dividend will be reported on the individual tax returns, requiring tax payments of $10,500 ($70,000 × 0.15). Total income tax of $40,500 ($30,000 + $10,500) is due on $100,000 of earned income. In contrast, consider a proprietorship that is owned by an individual in a 30 percent tax bracket. If the proprietorship earns and distributes $100,000 profit, the total tax would be only $30,000 ($100,000 × 0.30).

Double taxation can be a burden for small companies. To reduce that burden, tax laws permit small closely held corporations to elect "S Corporation" status. S Corporation income is not taxed at the corporate level but instead flows through to the owners who pay individual income taxes. Also, many states have enacted laws permitting the formation of **limited liability companies (LLCs),** which offer many of the benefits of corporate ownership yet are in general taxed as sole proprietorships or partnerships. Since proprietorships and partnerships are not separate taxable entities, company earnings are taxable to the owners rather than the company itself.

Limited Liability

Given the disadvantages of increased regulation and double taxation, why would anyone choose the corporate form of business structure over a partnership or proprietorship? A major reason is that the corporate form limits an investor's potential liability as an owner of a business venture. Because a corporation is legally separate from its owners, creditors cannot claim owners' personal assets as payment for the company's debts. Also, plaintiffs must sue the corporation, not its owners. The most that owners of a corporation can lose is the amount they have invested in the company (the value of the company's stock).

Unlike corporate stockholders, the owners of proprietorships and partnerships are *personally liable* for actions they take in the name of their companies. In fact, partners are responsible not only for their own actions but also for those taken by any other partner on behalf of the partnership. The benefit of **limited liability** is one of the most significant reasons limited liability companies and corporations are so popular.

Continuity

Unlike partnerships or proprietorships, which terminate with the departure of their owners, a corporation's life continues when a shareholder dies or sells his or her stock. Because of **continuity** of existence, many corporations formed in the 1800s still thrive today.

Transferability of Ownership

The **transferability** of corporate ownership is easy. An investor simply buys or sells stock to acquire or give up an ownership interest in a corporation. Hundreds of millions of shares of stock are bought and sold on the major stock exchanges each day.

Transferring the ownership of proprietorships is much more difficult. To sell an ownership interest in a proprietorship, the proprietor must find someone willing to purchase the entire business. Since most proprietors also run their businesses, transferring ownership also requires transferring management responsibilities. Consider the difference in selling $1 million of ExxonMobil stock versus selling a locally owned gas station. The stock could be sold on the New York Stock Exchange within minutes. In contrast, it could take years to find a buyer who is financially capable of and interested in owning and operating a gas station.

Transferring ownership in partnerships can also be difficult. As with proprietorships, ownership transfers may require a new partner to make a significant investment and accept management responsibilities in the business. Further, a new partner must accept and be accepted by the other partners. Personality conflicts and differences in management style can cause problems in transferring ownership interests in partnerships.

Management Structure

Partnerships and proprietorships are usually managed by their owners. Corporations, in contrast, have three tiers of management authority. The *owners* (**stockholders**) represent the highest level of organizational authority. The stockholders *elect* a **board of directors** to oversee company operations. The directors then *hire* professional executives to manage the company on a daily basis. Since large corporations can offer high salaries and challenging career opportunities, they can often attract superior managerial talent.

Ability to Raise Capital

Because corporations can have millions of owners (shareholders), they have the opportunity to raise huge amounts of capital. Few individuals have the financial means to build and operate a telecommunications network such as AT&T or a marketing distribution system such as Walmart. However, by pooling the resources of millions of owners through public stock and bond offerings, corporations generate the billions of dollars of capital needed for such massive investments. In contrast, the capital resources of proprietorships

and partnerships are limited to a relatively small number of private owners. Although proprietorships and partnerships can also obtain resources by borrowing, the amount creditors are willing to lend them is usually limited by the size of the owners' net worth.

Appearance of Capital Structure in Financial Statements

The ownership interest (equity) in a business is composed of two elements: (1) owner/investor contributions and (2) retained earnings. The way these two elements are reported in the financial statements differs for each type of business structure (proprietorship, partnership, or corporation).

Presentation of Equity in Proprietorships

Owner contributions and retained earnings are combined in a single Capital account on the balance sheets of proprietorships. To illustrate, assume that Worthington Sole Proprietorship was started on January 1, 2016, when it acquired a $5,000 capital contribution from its owner, Phil Worthington. During the first year of operation, the company generated $4,000 of cash revenues, incurred $2,500 of cash expenses, and distributed $1,000 cash to the owner. Exhibit 11.1 displays 2016 financial statements for Worthington's company. Note on the *capital statement* that distributions are called **withdrawals.** Verify that the $5,500 balance in the Capital account on the balance sheet includes the $5,000 owner contribution and the retained earnings of $500 ($1,500 net income − $1,000 withdrawal).

EXHIBIT 11.1

WORTHINGTON SOLE PROPRIETORSHIP
Financial Statements
As of December 31, 2016

Income Statement	
Revenue	$4,000
Expenses	2,500
Net income	$1,500

Capital Statement	
Beginning capital balance	$ 0
Plus: Investment by owner	5,000
Plus: Net income	1,500
Less: Withdrawal by owner	(1,000)
Ending capital balance	$5,500

Balance Sheet	
Assets	
Cash	$5,500
Equity	
Worthington, capital	$5,500

CHECK YOURSELF 11.1

Weiss Company was started on January 1, 2016, when it acquired $50,000 cash from its owner(s). During 2016 the company earned $72,000 of net income. Explain how the equity section of Weiss's December 31, 2016, balance sheet would differ if the company were a proprietorship versus a corporation.

Answer *Proprietorship* records combine capital acquisitions from the owner and earnings from operating the business in a single capital account. In contrast, *corporation* records separate capital acquisitions from the owners and earnings from operating the business. If Weiss were a proprietorship, the equity section of the year-end balance sheet would report a single capital component of $122,000. If Weiss were a corporation, the equity section would report two separate equity components, most likely common stock of $50,000 and retained earnings of $72,000.

EXHIBIT 11.2

SLATER AND JOHNSON PARTNERSHIP
Financial Statements
As of December 31, 2017

Income Statement	
Revenue	$5,000
Expenses	3,000
Net income	$2,000

Capital Statement	
Beginning capital balance	$ 0
Plus: Investment by owner	6,000
Plus: Net income	2,000
Less: Withdrawal by owner	(600)
Ending capital balance	$7,400

Balance Sheet	
Assets	
Cash	$7,400
Equity	
Slater, capital	$2,700
Johnson, capital	4,700
Total capital	$7,400

Presentation of Equity in Partnerships

The financial statement format for reporting partnership equity is similar to that used for proprietorships. Contributed capital and retained earnings are combined. However, a separate capital account is maintained for each partner in the business to reflect each partner's ownership interest.

To illustrate, assume that Sara Slater and Jill Johnson formed a partnership on January 1, 2017. The partnership acquired $2,000 of capital from Slater and $4,000 from Johnson. The partnership agreement called for each partner to receive an annual distribution equal to 10 percent of her capital contribution. Any further earnings were to be retained in the business and divided equally between the partners. During 2017, the company earned $5,000 of cash revenue and incurred $3,000 of cash expenses, for net income of $2,000 ($5,000 − $3,000). As specified by the partnership agreement, Slater received a $200 ($2,000 × 0.10) cash withdrawal and Johnson received $400 ($4,000 × 0.10). The remaining $1,400 ($2,000 − $200 − $400) of income was retained in the business and divided equally, adding $700 to each partner's capital account.

Exhibit 11.2 displays financial statements for the Slater and Johnson partnership. Again, note that distributions are called *withdrawals.* Also find on the balance sheet a *separate capital account* for each partner. Each capital account includes the amount of the partner's contributed capital plus her proportionate share of the earnings.

Presentation of Equity in Corporations

Corporations have more complex capital structures than proprietorships and partnerships. Explanations of some of the more common features of corporate capital structures and transactions follow.

ACCOUNTING FOR CAPITAL STOCK

LO 11-2

Explain how different types of capital stock affect financial statements.

Stock issued by corporations may have a variety of different characteristics. For example, a company may issue different classes of stock that grant owners different rights and privileges. Also, the number of shares a corporation can legally issue may differ from the number it actually has issued. Further, a corporation can even buy back its own stock. Finally, a corporation may assign different values to the stock it issues. Accounting for corporate equity transactions is discussed in the next section of the text.

Par Value

Many states require assigning a **par value** to stock. Historically, par value represented the maximum liability of the investors. Par value multiplied by the number of shares of stock issued represents the minimum amount of assets that must be retained in the company as protection for creditors. This amount is known as **legal capital**. To ensure that the amount of legal capital is maintained in a corporation, many states require that purchasers pay at least the par value for a share of stock initially purchased from a corporation. To minimize the amount of assets that owners must maintain in the business, many corporations issue stock with very low par values, often $1 or less. Therefore, *legal capital* as defined by par value has come to have very little relevance to investors or creditors. As a result, many states allow corporations to issue no-par stock.

Stated Value

No-par stock may have a stated value. Like par value, **stated value** is an arbitrary amount assigned by the board of directors to the stock. It also has little relevance to investors and creditors. Stock with a par value and stock with a stated value are accounted for exactly the same way. When stock has no par or stated value, accounting for it is slightly different. These accounting differences are illustrated later in this chapter.

Other Valuation Terminology

The price an investor must pay to purchase a share of stock is the **market value.** The sales price of a share of stock may be more or less than the par value. Another term analysts frequently associate with stock is *book value.* **Book value per share** is calculated by dividing total stockholders' equity (assets − liabilities) by the number of shares of stock owned by investors. Book value per share differs from market value per share because equity is measured in historical dollars and market value reflects investors' estimates of a company's current value.

Stock: Authorized, Issued, and Outstanding

As part of the regulatory function, states approve the maximum number of shares of stock corporations are legally permitted to issue. This maximum number is called **authorized stock.** Authorized stock that has been sold to the public is called **issued stock.** When a corporation buys back some of its issued stock from the public, the repurchased stock is called **treasury stock.** Treasury stock is still considered to be issued stock, but it is no longer outstanding. **Outstanding stock** (total issued stock minus treasury stock) is stock owned by investors outside the corporation. For example, assume a company that is authorized to issue 150 shares of stock issues 100 shares to investors, and then buys back 20 shares of treasury stock. There are 150 shares authorized, 100 shares issued, and 80 shares outstanding.

Classes of Stock

The corporate charter defines the number of shares of stock authorized, the par value or stated value (if any), and the classes of stock that a corporation can issue. Most stock issued is classified as either *common* or *preferred.*

Common Stock

All corporations issue **common stock.** Common stockholders bear the highest risk of losing their investment if a company is forced to liquidate. On the other hand, they reap the greatest rewards when a corporation prospers. Common stockholders generally enjoy several rights, including: (1) the right to buy and sell stock, (2) the right to share in the distribution of profits, (3) the right to share in the distribution of corporate assets in the case of liquidation, (4) the right to vote on significant matters that affect the corporate charter, and (5) the right to participate in the election of directors.

Preferred Stock

Many corporations issue **preferred stock** in addition to common stock. Holders of preferred stock receive certain privileges relative to holders of common stock. In exchange for special privileges in some areas, preferred stockholders give up rights in other areas. Preferred stockholders usually have no voting rights and the amount of their dividends is usually limited. Preferences granted to preferred stockholders include the following:

1. *Preference as to assets.* Preferred stock often has a liquidation value. In case of bankruptcy, preferred stockholders must be paid the liquidation value before any assets are distributed to common stockholders. However, preferred stockholder claims still fall behind creditor claims.
2. *Preference as to dividends.* Preferred shareholders are frequently guaranteed the right to receive dividends before common stockholders. The amount of the preferred dividend is normally stated on the stock certificate. It may be stated as a dollar value (say, $5) per share or as a percentage of the par value. Most preferred stock has **cumulative dividends,** meaning that if a corporation is unable to pay the preferred dividend in any year, the dividend is not lost but begins to accumulate. Cumulative dividends that have not been paid are called **dividends in arrears.** When a company pays dividends, any preferred stock arrearages must be paid before any other dividends are paid. Noncumulative preferred stock is not often issued because preferred stock is much less attractive if missed dividends do not accumulate.

To illustrate the effects of preferred dividends, consider Dillion, Incorporated, which has the following shares of stock outstanding:

Preferred stock, 4%, $10 par, 10,000 shares
Common stock, $10 par, 20,000 shares

Assume the preferred stock dividend has not been paid for two years. If Dillion pays $22,000 in dividends, how much will each class of stock receive? It depends on whether the preferred stock is cumulative.

Allocation of Distribution for Cumulative Preferred Stock

	To Preferred	To Common
Dividends in arrears	$ 8,000	$ 0
Current year's dividends	4,000	10,000
Total distribution	$12,000	$10,000

Allocation of Distribution for Noncumulative Preferred Stock

	To Preferred	To Common
Dividends in arrears	$ 0	$ 0
Current year's dividends	4,000	18,000
Total distribution	$ 4,000	$18,000

The total annual dividend on the preferred stock is $4,000 (0.04 × $10 par × 10,000 shares). If the preferred stock is cumulative, the $8,000 in arrears must be paid first. Then $4,000 for the current year's dividend is paid next. The remaining $10,000 goes to common stockholders. If the preferred stock is noncumulative, the $8,000 of dividends from past periods is ignored. This year's $4,000 preferred dividend is paid first, with the remaining $18,000 going to common.

Other features of preferred stock may include the right to participate in distributions beyond the established amount of the preferred dividend, the right to convert preferred stock to common stock or to bonds, and the potential for having the preferred stock called (repurchased) by the corporation. Detailed discussion of these topics is left to more advanced courses. Exhibit 11.3 indicates that roughly 25 percent of U.S. companies have preferred shares outstanding.

EXHIBIT 11.3

Presence of Preferred Stock in the Capital Structure of U.S. Companies

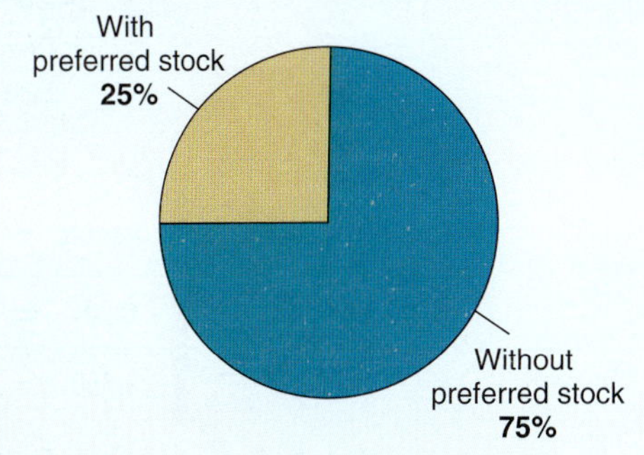

Data Source: AICPA, *Accounting Trends and Techniques.*

Accounting for Stock Transactions

Issuing stock with a par or stated value is accounted for differently from issuing no-par stock. For stock with either a par or stated value, the total amount acquired from the owners is divided between two separate equity accounts. The amount of the par or stated value is recorded in the stock account. Any amount received above the par or stated value is recorded in an account called **Paid-in Capital in Excess of Par** (or **Stated) Value.**

Issuing Par Value Stock

To illustrate the issue of common stock with a par value, assume that Nelson Incorporated is authorized to issue 250 shares of common stock. During 2016, Nelson issued 100 shares of $10 par common stock for $22 per share. The event increases assets and stockholders' equity by $2,200 ($22 × 100 shares). The increase in stockholders' equity is divided into two parts, $1,000 of par value ($10 per share × 100 shares) and $1,200 ($2,200 − $1,000) received in excess of par value. The income statement is not affected. The $2,200 cash inflow is reported in the financing activities section of the statement of cash flows. The journal entry and its effects on the financial statements are shown here.

Account Title	Debit	Credit
Cash	2,200	
Common Stock, $10 Par Value		1,000
Paid-in Capital in Excess of Par Value—Common		1,200

Assets	=	Liab.	+	Equity			Rev.	−	Exp.	=	Net Inc.	Cash Flow
Cash	=			Com. Stk.	+	PIC in Excess						
2,200	=	NA	+	1,000	+	1,200	NA	−	NA	=	NA	2,200 FA

The *legal capital* of the corporation is $1,000, the total par value of the issued common stock. The number of shares issued can be easily verified by dividing the total amount in the common stock account by the par value ($1,000 ÷ $10 = 100 shares).

Stock Classification

Assume Nelson Incorporated obtains authorization to issue 400 shares of Class B, $20 par value common stock. The company issues 150 shares of this stock at $25 per share. The event increases assets and stockholders' equity by $3,750 ($25 × 150 shares). The increase in stockholders' equity is divided into two parts, $3,000 of par value ($20 per share × 150 shares) and $750 ($3,750 − $3,000) received in excess of par value. The income statement is not affected. The $3,750 cash inflow is reported in the financing activities section of the statement of cash flows. The journal entry and its effects on the financial statements are shown here:

Account Title	Debit	Credit
Cash	3,750	
Common Stock, Class B, $20 Par Value		3,000
Paid-in Capital in Excess of Par Value—Class B Common		750

Assets	=	Liab.	+	Equity			Rev.	−	Exp.	=	Net Inc.	Cash Flow
Cash	=			Com. Stk.	+	PIC in Excess						
3,750	=	NA	+	3,000	+	750	NA	−	NA	=	NA	3,750 FA

As the preceding event suggests, companies can issue numerous classes of common stock. The specific rights and privileges for each class are described in the individual stock certificates.

Stock Issued at Stated Value

Assume Nelson Incorporated is authorized to issue 300 shares of a third class of stock, 7 percent cumulative preferred stock with a stated value of $10 per share. Nelson issued 100 shares of the preferred stock at a price of $22 per share. The effect on the financial statements is identical to that described for the issue of the $10 par value common stock. The journal entry differs only to reflect the name of the different class of stock.

Account Title	Debit	Credit
Cash	2,200	
Preferred Stock, $10 Stated Value, 7% cumulative		1,000
Paid-in Capital in Excess of Stated Value—Preferred		1,200

Assets	=	Liab.	+	Equity			Rev.	−	Exp.	=	Net Inc.	Cash Flow
Cash	=			Pfd. Stk.	+	PIC in Excess						
2,200	=	NA	+	1,000	+	1,200	NA	−	NA	=	NA	2,200 FA

Stock Issued with No Par Value

Assume that Nelson Incorporated is authorized to issue 150 shares of a fourth class of stock. This stock is no-par common stock. Nelson issues 100 shares of this no-par stock at $22 per share. The entire amount received ($22 × 100 = $2,200) is recorded in the stock account. The journal entry and its effects on the financial statements are shown here:

Account Title	Debit	Credit
Cash	2,200	
Common Stock, No Par		2,200

Assets	=	Liab.	+	Equity			Rev.	−	Exp.	=	Net Inc.	Cash Flow
Cash	=			Com. Stk.	+	PIC in Excess						
2,200	=	NA	+	2,200	+	NA	NA	−	NA	=	NA	2,200 FA

Financial Statement Presentation

Exhibit 11.4 displays Nelson Incorporated's balance sheet after the four stock issuances described above. The exhibit assumes that Nelson earned and retained $5,000 of income during 2016. The stock accounts are presented first, followed by the paid-in capital in excess of par (or stated) value accounts. A wide variety of reporting formats is used in practice. For example, another popular format is to group accounts by stock class, with the paid-in capital in excess accounts listed with their associated stock accounts. Alternatively, many companies combine the different classes of stock into a single amount and provide the detailed information in notes to the financial statements.

EXHIBIT 11.4

NELSON INCORPORATED
Balance Sheet
As of December 31, 2016

Assets	
Cash	$15,350
Stockholders' equity	
Preferred stock, $10 stated value, 7% cumulative, 300 shares authorized, 100 issued and outstanding	$ 1,000
Common stock, $10 par value, 250 shares authorized, 100 issued and outstanding	1,000
Common stock, class B, $20 par value, 400 shares authorized, 150 issued and outstanding	3,000
Common stock, no par, 150 shares authorized, 100 issued and outstanding	2,200
Paid-in capital in excess of stated value—Preferred	1,200
Paid-in capital in excess of par value—Common	1,200
Paid-in capital in excess of par value—Class B common	750
Total paid-in capital	10,350
Retained earnings	5,000
Total stockholders' equity	$15,350

TREASURY STOCK

LO 11-3

Show how treasury stock transactions affect financial statements.

When a company buys its own stock, the stock purchased is called *treasury stock.* Why would a company buy its own stock? Common reasons include (1) to have stock available to give employees pursuant to stock option plans, (2) to accumulate stock in preparation for a merger or business combination, (3) to reduce the number of shares outstanding in order to increase earnings per share, (4) to keep the price of the stock high when it appears to be falling, and (5) to avoid a hostile takeover (removing shares from the open market reduces the opportunity for outsiders to obtain enough voting shares to gain control of the company).

Conceptually, purchasing treasury stock is the reverse of issuing stock. When a business issues stock, the assets and equity of the business increase. When a business buys treasury stock, the assets and equity of the business decrease. To illustrate, return to the Nelson Incorporated example. Assume that in 2017 Nelson paid $20 per share to buy back 50 shares of the $10 par value common stock that it originally issued at $22 per share. The purchase of treasury stock is an asset use transaction. Assets and stockholders' equity decrease by the cost of the purchase ($20 × 50 shares = $1,000). The income statement is not affected. The cash outflow is reported in the financing activities section of the statement of cash flows. The journal entry and its effects on the financial statements are shown here:

Account Title	Debit	Credit
Treasury Stock	1,000	
Cash		1,000

Assets	=	Liab.	+	Equity			Rev.	−	Exp.	=	Net Inc.	Cash Flow
Cash	=			Other Equity Accts.	−	Treasury Stk.						
(1,000)	=	NA	+	NA	−	1,000	NA	−	NA	=	NA	(1,000) FA

REALITY BYTES

HOW MUCH TREASURY STOCK CAN A COMPANY PURCHASE?

A common practice in recent years has been for companies to purchase treasury stock frequently. Whereas in past years companies wishing to distribute more of their equity back to shareholders might have increased dividends, today they are more likely to use stock buybacks. Some companies seem to take the practice to extremes. Consider the excerpt below, taken from the shareholders' equity section of **Marriott International**'s recent balance sheets.

First, notice that the company has a balance in its Treasury Stock account that is larger than the balance in its Common Stock account. How can this be? Remember, when stock is issued to shareholders it is recorded in Common Stock at its issuance price, but it is recorded in Treasury Stock at the price the company paid to buy it back. The stock prices of successful companies rise over time.

Second, notice that Marriott has purchased so much treasury stock that its total shareholders' equity is negative. This is unusual. When a company has negative shareholders' equity it is usually because of a negative balance in Retained Earnings, but Marriott had almost $4 billion of retained earnings in 2013. The fact that the company had negative shareholders' equity means that, at least on paper, its liabilities were more than its assets. While this can present a problem for a company that is struggling, Marriott reported approximately $1 billion of earnings before interest and taxes (EBIT) and $1 billion of cash flow from operating activities in 2013 and 2012, so it was able to meet its debt obligations with no difficulty.

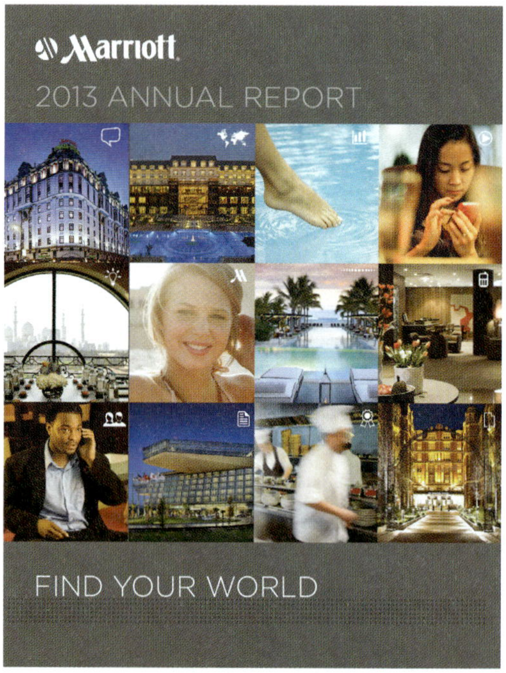

MARRIOTT INTERNATIONAL, INC.
Partial Balance Sheets
For the years ended
(in millions)

	December 31, 2013	December 28, 2012
Shareholders' deficit		
Class A common stock	$ 5	$ 5
Additional paid-in capital	2,716	2,585
Retained earnings	3,837	3,509
Treasury stock, at cost	(7,929)	(7,340)
Accumulated other comprehensive loss	(44)	(44)
Total shareholders' equity	(1,415)	(1,285)
Total liabilities and stockholders' equity	$ 6,794	$ 6,342

The Treasury Stock account is a contra equity account. It is deducted from the other equity accounts in determining total stockholders' equity. In this example, the Treasury Stock account is debited for the full amount paid ($1,000). The original issue price and the par value of the stock have no effect on the entry. Recording the full amount paid in the Treasury Stock account is called the **cost method of accounting for treasury stock** transactions. Although other methods could be used, the cost method is the most common.

Assume Nelson reissues 30 shares of treasury stock at a price of $25 per share. As with any other stock issue, the sale of treasury stock is an asset source transaction. In this case, assets and stockholders' equity increase by $750 ($25 × 30 shares). The income statement is not affected. The cash inflow is reported in the financing activities section of the statement of cash flows. The journal entry and its effects on the financial statements are shown here:

Account Title	Debit	Credit
Cash	750	
Treasury Stock		600
Paid-in Capital in Excess of Cost of Treasury Stock		150

Assets	=	Liab.	+	Equity					Rev.	−	Exp.	=	Net Inc.	Cash Flow
Cash	=			Other Equity Accounts	−	Treasury Stock	+	PIC from Treasury Stk.						
750	=	NA	+	NA	−	(600)	+	150	NA	−	NA	=	NA	750 FA

The decrease in the Treasury Stock account increases stockholders' equity. The $150 difference between the cost of the treasury stock ($20 per share × 30 shares = $600) and the sales price ($750) is *not* reported as a gain. The sale of treasury stock is a capital acquisition, not a revenue transaction. The $150 is additional paid-in capital. *Corporations do not recognize gains or losses on the sale of treasury stock.*

After selling 30 shares of treasury stock, 20 shares remain in Nelson's possession. These shares cost $20 each, so the balance in the Treasury Stock account is now $400 ($20 × 20 shares). Treasury stock is reported on the balance sheet directly below retained earnings. Although this placement suggests that treasury stock reduces retained earnings, the reduction actually applies to the entire stockholders' equity section. In the following section, we continue our discussion of Nelson Incorporated and show the presentation of treasury stock in the balance sheet. (See Exhibit 11.5 on page 613).

CHECK YOURSELF 11.2

On January 1, 2016, Janell Company's Common Stock account balance was $20,000. On April 1, 2016, Janell paid $12,000 cash to purchase some of its own stock. Janell resold this stock on October 1, 2016, for $14,500. What is the effect on the company's cash and stockholders' equity from both the April 1 purchase and the October 1 resale of the stock?

Answer The April 1 purchase would reduce both cash and stockholders' equity by $12,000. The treasury stock transaction represents a return of invested capital to those owners who sold stock back to the company.

The sale of the treasury stock on October 1 would increase both cash and stockholders' equity by $14,500. The difference between the sales price of the treasury stock and its cost ($14,500 − $12,000) represents additional paid-in capital from treasury stock transactions. The stockholders' equity section of the balance sheet would include Common Stock, $20,000, and Additional Paid-in Capital from Treasury Stock Transactions, $2,500.

DIVIDENDS, STOCK SPLITS, AND APPROPRIATIONS OF RETAINED EARNINGS

Cash Dividend

LO 11-4

Explain how dividends, stock splits, and appropriations affect financial statements.

Cash dividends are affected by three significant dates: *the declaration date, the date of record,* and *the payment date.* Assume that on October 15, 2017, the board of Nelson Incorporated declared the cash dividend on the 100 outstanding shares of its $10 stated value preferred stock. The dividend will be paid to stockholders of record as of November 15, 2017. The cash payment will be made on December 15, 2017.

Declaration Date

Although corporations are not required to declare dividends, they are legally obligated to pay dividends once they have been declared. They must recognize a liability on the **declaration date** (in this case, October 15, 2017). The increase in liabilities is accompanied by a decrease in retained earnings. The income statement and statement of cash flows are not affected. The journal entry and the effects on the financial statements of *declaring* the $70 (0.07 × $10 × 100 shares) dividend are shown here:

Account Title	Debit	Credit
Dividends	70	
Dividends Payable		70

Assets	=	Liab.	+	Equity			Rev.	−	Exp.	=	Net Inc.	Cash Flow
Cash	=	Div. Pay.	+	Com. Stk.	+	Ret. Earn.						
NA	=	70	+	NA	+	(70)	NA	−	NA	=	NA	NA

Date of Record

Cash dividends are paid to investors who owned the preferred stock on the **date of record** (in this case November 15, 2017). Any stock sold after the date of record but before the payment date (in this case December 15, 2017) is traded **ex-dividend,** meaning the buyer will not receive the upcoming dividend. The date of record is merely a cutoff date. It does not affect the financial statements.

Payment Date

Nelson Incorporated actually paid the cash dividend on the **payment date.** This event has the same effect as paying any other liability. Assets (cash) and liabilities (dividends payable) both decrease. The income statement is not affected. The cash outflow is reported in the financing activities section of the statement of cash flows. The journal entry and its effects on the financial statements are shown here:

Account Title	Debit	Credit
Dividends Payable	70	
Cash		70

Assets	=	Liab.	+	Equity			Rev.	−	Exp.	=	Net Inc.	Cash Flow
Cash	=	Div. Pay.	+	Com. Stk.	+	Ret. Earn.						
(70)	=	(70)	+	NA	+	NA	NA	−	NA	=	NA	(70) FA

REALITY BYTES

As you have learned, dividends, unlike interest on bonds, do not have to be paid. In fact, a company's board of directors must vote to pay dividends before they can be paid. Even so, once a company establishes a practice of paying a dividend of a given amount each period, usually quarterly, the company is reluctant to not pay the dividend. The amount of dividends that companies pay, relative to their earnings, varies widely.

Large, well-established companies usually do pay dividends, while young, growing companies often do not. Consider the 30 companies that make up the Dow Jones Industrials Average group. In 2013, 29 of these companies paid dividends. The only one that did not was **General Motors**. Of the remaining 29 companies, **UnitedHealth Group** paid out the lowest percentage of its earnings in dividends (12.1 percent). At the other extreme, in 2013 **Merck & Co.**, the large pharmaceutical company, paid $1.14 of dividends for every $1.00 it had in earnings. The average percentage of earnings paid out as dividends for all 30 companies in the Dow was 36.4 percent.

For comparison, consider two large, relatively young, technology companies: **Google** and **Facebook**. Although both of these companies have had positive earnings in recent years, (Google alone had $12.9 billion of earnings in 2013), neither has ever paid a dividend to its common shareholders. They are using their cash to grow their businesses, often by purchasing other companies.

Stock Dividend

Dividends are not always paid in cash. Companies sometimes choose to issue **stock dividends,** wherein they distribute additional shares of stock to the stockholders. To illustrate, assume that Nelson Incorporated decided to issue a 10 percent stock dividend on its class B, $20 par value common stock. Since dividends apply to outstanding shares only, Nelson will issue 15 (150 outstanding shares × 0.10) additional shares of class B stock.

Assume the new shares are distributed when the market value of the stock is $30 per share. As a result of the stock dividend, Nelson will transfer $450 ($30 × 15 new shares) from retained earnings to paid-in capital.[1] The stock dividend is an equity exchange transaction. The income statement and statement of cash flows are not affected. The journal entry and its effects on the financial statements are shown below.

Account Title	Debit	Credit
Retained Earnings	450	
Common Stock, Class B, $20 Par Value		300
Paid-in Capital in Excess of Par Value—Class B Common		150

Assets	=	Liab.	+	Equity					Rev.	−	Exp.	=	Net Inc.	Cash Flow
				Com. Stk.	+	PIC in Excess	+	Ret. Earn.						
NA	=	NA	+	300	+	150	+	(450)	NA	−	NA	=	NA	NA

Stock dividends have no effect on assets. They merely increase the number of shares of stock outstanding. Since a greater number of shares represents the same ownership interest in the same amount of assets, the market value per share of a company's stock normally declines when a stock dividend is distributed. A lower market price makes the

[1]The accounting here applies to small stock dividends. Accounting for large stock dividends is explained in a more advanced course.

FOCUS ON INTERNATIONAL ISSUES

PICKY, PICKY, PICKY . . .

Considering the almost countless number of differences that could exist between U.S. GAAP and IFRS, it is not surprising that some of those that do exist relate to very specific issues. Consider the case of the timing of stock splits.

Assume a company that ends its fiscal year on December 31, 2016, declares a 2-for-1 stock split on January 15, 2017, before it has issued its 2016 annual report. Should the company apply the effects of the stock split retroactively to its 2016 financial statements, or begin showing the effects of the split on its 2017 statements? Under U.S. GAAP the split must be applied retroactively to the 2016 statements since they had not been issued at the time of the split. Under IFRS the 2016 statements would not show the effects of the split, but the 2017 statements would. By the way, an event that occurs between a company's fiscal year-end and the date its annual report is released is called a *subsequent event* by accountants.

Obviously no one can know every rule under GAAP, much less all of the differences between GAAP and IFRS. This is why it is important to learn how to find answers to specific accounting questions as well as to develop an understanding of the basic accounting rules. Most important, if you are not sure you know the answer, do not assume you do.

stock more affordable and may increase demand for the stock, which benefits both the company and its stockholders.

Stock Split

A corporation may also reduce the market price of its stock through a **stock split.** A stock split replaces existing shares with a greater number of new shares. Any par or stated value of the stock is proportionately reduced to reflect the new number of shares outstanding. For example, assume Nelson Incorporated declared a 2-for-1 stock split on the 165 outstanding shares (150 originally issued + 15 shares distributed in a stock dividend) of its $20 par value, class B common stock. Nelson notes in the accounting records that the 165 old $20 par shares are replaced with 330 new $10 par shares. Investors who owned the 165 shares of old common stock would now own 330 shares of the new common stock.

Stock splits have no effect on the dollar amounts of assets, liabilities, and stockholders' equity. They only affect the number of shares of stock outstanding and the par value per share. In Nelson's case, the ownership interest that was previously represented by 165 shares of stock is now represented by 330 shares. Since twice as many shares now represent the same ownership interest, the market value per share should be one-half as much as it was prior to the split. However, as with a stock dividend, the lower market price will probably stimulate demand for the stock. As a result, doubling the number of shares will likely reduce the market price to slightly more than one-half of the pre-split value. For example, if the stock were selling for $30 per share before the 2-for-1 split, it might sell for $15.50 after the split.

Appropriation of Retained Earnings

The board of directors may restrict the amount of retained earnings available to distribute as dividends. The restriction may be required by credit agreements, or it may be discretionary. A retained earnings restriction, often called an *appropriation,* is an equity exchange event. It transfers a portion of existing retained earnings to **Appropriated Retained Earnings.** Total retained earnings remains unchanged. To illustrate, assume that Nelson Incorporated appropriates $1,000 of retained earnings for future expansion. The income statement and the statement of cash flows are not affected. The journal entry and its effects on the financial statements are shown here:

Account Title	Debit	Credit
Retained Earnings	1,000	
Appropriated Retained Earnings		1,000

Assets	=	Liab.	+	Equity					Rev.	−	Exp.	=	Net Inc.	Cash Flow
				Com. Stk.	+	Ret. Earn.	+	App. Ret. Earn.						
NA	=	NA	+	NA	+	(1,000)	+	1,000	NA	−	NA	=	NA	FA

Financial Statement Presentation

The 2016 and 2017 events for Nelson Incorporated are summarized below. Events 1 through 8 are cash transactions. The results of the 2016 transactions (nos. 1–5) are reflected in Exhibit 11.4 (see page 607). The results of the 2017 transactions (nos. 6–11) are shown in Exhibit 11.5.

1. Issued 100 shares of $10 par value common stock at a market price of $22 per share.
2. Issued 150 shares of class B, $20 par value common stock at a market price of $25 per share.
3. Issued 100 shares of $10 stated value, 7 percent cumulative preferred stock at a market price of $22 per share.
4. Issued 100 shares of no-par common stock at a market price of $22 per share.
5. Earned and retained $5,000 cash from operations.

EXHIBIT 11.5

NELSON INCORPORATED
Balance Sheet
As of December 31, 2017

Assets		
Cash		$21,030
Stockholders' equity		
Preferred stock, $10 stated value, 7% cumulative, 300 shares authorized, 100 issued and outstanding	$1,000	
Common stock, $10 par value, 250 shares authorized, 100 issued, and 80 outstanding	1,000	
Common stock, class B, $10 par, 800 shares authorized, 330 issued and outstanding	3,300	
Common stock, no par, 150 shares authorized, 100 issued and outstanding	2,200	
Paid-in capital in excess of stated value—Preferred	1,200	
Paid-in capital in excess of par value—Common	1,200	
Paid-in capital in excess of par value—Class B common	900	
Paid-in capital in excess of cost of treasury stock	150	
Total paid-in capital		$10,950
Retained Earnings		
Appropriated	1,000	
Unappropriated	9,480	
Total retained earnings		10,480
Less: Treasury stock, 20 shares @ $20 per share		(400)
Total stockholders' equity		$21,030

6. Purchased 50 shares of $10 par value common stock as treasury stock at a market price of $20 per share.
7. Sold 30 shares of treasury stock at a market price of $25 per share.
8. Declared and paid a $70 cash dividend on the preferred stock.
9. Issued a 10 percent stock dividend on the 150 shares of outstanding class B, $20 par value common stock (15 additional shares). The additional shares were issued when the market price of the stock was $30 per share. There are 165 (150 + 15) class B common shares outstanding after the stock dividend.
10. Issued a 2-for-1 stock split on the 165 shares of class B, $20 par value common stock. After this transaction, there are 330 shares outstanding of the class B common stock with a $10 par value.
11. Appropriated $1,000 of retained earnings.

The illustration assumes that Nelson earned net income of $6,000 in 2017. The ending retained earnings balance is determined as follows: Beginning balance $5,000 − $70 Cash dividend − $450 Stock dividend + $6,000 Net income = $10,480.

THE FINANCIAL ANALYST

LO 11-5

Explain some uses of accounting information in making stock investment decisions.

Stockholders may benefit in two ways when a company generates earnings. The company may distribute the earnings directly to the stockholders in the form of dividends. Alternatively, the company may retain some or all of the earnings to finance growth and increase its potential for future earnings. If the company retains earnings, the market value of its stock should increase to reflect its greater earnings prospects. How can analysts use financial reporting to help assess the potential for dividend payments or growth in market value?

Receiving Dividends

Is a company likely to pay dividends in the future? The financial statements can help answer this question. They show if dividends were paid in the past. Companies with a history of paying dividends usually continue to pay dividends. Also, to pay dividends in the future, a company must have sufficient cash and retained earnings. These amounts are reported on the balance sheet and the statement of cash flows.

Increasing the Price of Stock

Is the market value (price) of a company's stock likely to increase? Increases in a company's stock price occur when investors believe the company's earnings will grow. Financial statements provide information that is useful in predicting the prospects for earnings growth. Here also, a company's earnings history is an indicator of its growth potential. However, because published financial statements report historical information, investors must recognize their limitations. Investors want to know about the future. Stock prices are therefore influenced more by forecasts than by history.

For example:

- On January 30, 2014, Amazon.com, Inc., announced that revenues for the fourth quarter of the fiscal year ended December 31, 2013, were 20 percent higher than for the same quarter of the previous year and earnings were up 243 percent! In reaction to this news, the price of its stock *fell* by 8.2 percent on a day when the market as a whole was up 1 percent. Why did the stock market respond in this way? Amazon's stock price fell because the company's revenues and earnings for the quarter were less than had been expected by analysts who follow the company.

- On January 30, 2014, Pitney Bowes, Inc., announced that revenues for the fourth quarter of 2013 were only 1 percent higher than revenues for the fourth quarter of the fiscal year ended December 31, 2012, and that earnings were 20 percent lower. The stock market's reaction to the news was to *increase* the price of the company's stock by 16 percent. The market reacted this way because even though earnings and total revenues were down, revenues in its digital commerce operations were up by 17 percent, and the company expects this part of its business to become increasingly important in the future. Analysts seemed to agree.

In each case, investors reacted to the potential for earnings growth rather than the historical earnings reports. Because investors find forecasted statements more relevant to decision making than historical financial statements, most companies provide forecasts in addition to historical financial statements.

The value of a company's stock is also influenced by nonfinancial information that financial statements cannot provide. For example, suppose ExxonMobil announced in the middle of its fiscal year that it had just discovered substantial oil reserves on property to which it held drilling rights. Consider the following questions:

- What would happen to the price of ExxonMobil's stock on the day of the announcement?
- What would happen to ExxonMobil's financial statements on that day?

The price of ExxonMobil's stock would almost certainly increase as soon as the discovery was made public. However, nothing would happen to its financial statements on that day. There would probably be very little effect on its financial statements for that year. Only after the company began to develop the oil field and sell the oil would its financial statements reflect the discovery. Changes in financial statements tend to lag behind the announcements companies make regarding their earnings potential.

Stock prices are also affected by general economic conditions and consumer confidence as well as the performance measures reported in financial statements. For example, when political uncertainty in Ukraine caused Russia to escalate its military presence in Crimea on February 27, 2014, with talk of annexation, stock markets around the world reacted quickly and erratically. On March 3, the Russian stock market dropped 11 percent, which might be expected, but the U.S. stock market fell 0.7 percent even though the United States has little, if any, business presence in Crimea. The next day, when tensions seemed to be easing, the U.S. markets rose by 1.5 percent. These fluctuations were based mostly on rumors of what might happen, not actual warfare. Historically based financial statements are of little benefit in predicting general economic conditions or changes in political conditions that might affect future business activity.

Price-Earnings Ratio

The **price-earnings ratio,** frequently called the *P/E ratio,* is the most commonly reported measure of a company's value. The P/E ratio is a company's market price per share of stock divided by the company's annual earnings per share (EPS).[2]

Assume Western Company recently reported annual earnings per share of \$3. Western's stock is currently selling for \$54 per share. Western's stock is therefore selling at a P/E ratio of 18 (\$54 market price ÷ \$3 EPS). What does a P/E ratio of 18 mean? If Western continued earning \$3 per share of stock each year and paid out all its earnings to stockholders in the form of cash dividends, it would take 18 years for an investor to recover the price paid for the stock.

In contrast, assume the stock of Eastern Company, which reported EPS of \$4, is currently selling for \$48 per share. Eastern's P/E ratio is 12 (\$48 market price ÷ \$4 EPS).

[2]The amount of earnings per share is provided on the face of the income statement. In its simplest form, it is computed by dividing the company's net income (net earnings) by the number of shares of common stock outstanding.

Investors who buy Eastern Company stock would get their money back six years faster (18 − 12) than investors who buy Western Company stock.

Why would investors buy a stock with a P/E ratio of 18 when they could buy one with a P/E ratio of 12? If investors expect Western Company's earnings to grow faster than Eastern Company's earnings, the higher P/E ratio makes sense. For example, suppose Western Company's earnings were to double to \$6 per share while Eastern's remained at \$4 per share. Western's P/E ratio would drop to 9 (\$54 market price ÷ \$6 EPS) while Eastern's remains at 12. This explains why high-growth companies sell for higher P/E multiples than do low-growth companies.

Caution must be used when interpreting P/E ratios. A company can have a high P/E ratio due to very low earnings, rather than high optimism by investors. For example, if a company's EPS is \$0.02, and its stock is selling for \$0.50, it will have a P/E ratio of 25, which is high. In this case the high P/E ratio is the result of very low earnings, not optimism. If a company has a net loss, the P/E ratio is not computed.

Also, be aware that P/E ratios reported in the financial press are often based on *projected* EPS, rather than historical earnings. Sometimes P/E ratios based on historical earnings are referred to as being based on trailing earnings. In this course, compute the P/E ratio using the company's most recent, actual earnings amount rather than its forecasted earnings.

Exercising Control through Stock Ownership

The more influence an investor has over the operations of a company, the more the investor can benefit from owning stock in the company. For example, consider a power company that needs coal to produce electricity. The power company may purchase some common stock in a coal mining company to ensure a stable supply of coal. What percentage of the mining company's stock must the power company acquire to exercise significant influence over the mining company? The answer depends on how many investors own stock in the mining company and how the number of shares is distributed among the stockholders.

The greater its number of stockholders, the more *widely held* a company is. If stock ownership is concentrated in the hands of a few persons, a company is *closely held.* Widely held companies can generally be controlled with smaller percentages of ownership than closely held companies. Consider a company in which no existing investor owns more than 1 percent of the voting stock. A new investor who acquires a 5 percent interest would immediately become, by far, the largest shareholder and would likely be able to significantly influence board decisions. In contrast, consider a closely held company in which one current shareholder owns 51 percent of the company's stock. Even if another investor acquired the remaining 49 percent of the company, that investor could not control the company.

Financial statements contain some, but not all, of the information needed to help an investor determine ownership levels necessary to permit control. For example, the financial statements disclose the total number of shares of stock outstanding, but they normally contain little information about the number of shareholders and even less information about any relationships between shareholders. Relationships between shareholders are critically important because related shareholders, whether bound by family or business interests, might exercise control by voting as a bloc. For publicly traded companies, information about the number of shareholders and the identity of some large shareholders is disclosed in reports filed with the Securities and Exchange Commission.

<< A Look Back

Starting a business requires obtaining financing; it takes money to make money. Although some money may be borrowed, lenders are unlikely to make loans to businesses that lack some degree of owner financing. Equity financing is therefore critical to virtually all profit-oriented businesses. This chapter has examined some of the issues related to accounting for equity transactions.

The idea that a business must obtain financing from its owners was one of the first events presented in this textbook. This chapter discussed the advantages and disadvantages of organizing a business as a sole proprietorship versus a partnership versus a corporation. These advantages and disadvantages include the following:

1. *Double taxation*—Income of corporations is subject to double taxation, but that of proprietorships and partnerships is not.
2. *Regulation*—Corporations are subject to more regulation than are proprietorships and partnerships.
3. *Limited liability*—An investor's personal assets are not at risk as a result of owning corporate securities. The investor's liability is limited to the amount of the investment. In general proprietorships and partnerships do not offer limited liability. However, laws in some states permit the formation of limited liability companies which operate like proprietorships and partnerships yet place some limits on the personal liability of their owners.
4. *Continuity*—Proprietorships and partnerships dissolve when one of the owners leaves the business. Corporations are separate legal entities that continue to exist regardless of changes in ownership.
5. *Transferability*—Ownership interests in corporations are easier to transfer than those of proprietorships or partnerships.
6. *Management structure*—Corporations are more likely to have independent professional managers than are proprietorships or partnerships.
7. *Ability to raise capital*—Because they can be owned by millions of investors, corporations have the opportunity to raise more capital than proprietorships or partnerships.

Corporations issue different classes of common stock and preferred stock as evidence of ownership interests. In general, *common stock* provides the widest range of privileges, including the right to vote and participate in earnings. *Preferred stockholders* usually give up the right to vote in exchange for preferences such as the right to receive dividends or assets upon liquidation before common stockholders. Stock may have a *par value* or *stated value,* which relates to legal requirements governing the amount of capital that must be maintained in the corporation. Corporations may also issue *no-par stock,* avoiding some of the legal requirements that pertain to par or stated value stock.

Stock that a company issues and then repurchases is called *treasury stock.* Purchasing treasury stock reduces total assets and stockholders' equity. Reselling treasury stock represents a capital acquisition. The difference between the reissue price and the cost of the treasury stock is recorded directly in the equity accounts. Treasury stock transactions do not result in gains or losses on the income statement.

Companies may issue *stock splits* or *stock dividends.* These transactions increase the number of shares of stock without changing the net assets of a company. The per share market value usually drops when a company issues stock splits or dividends.

A Look Forward >>

Chapter 12 examines the statement of cash flows in more detail than past chapters have. It introduces a more practical way to prepare the statement than analyzing every single entry in the Cash account, and it presents the more formal format for the statement of cash flows used by most real-world companies.

SELF-STUDY REVIEW PROBLEM

A step-by-step audio-narrated series of slides is available in the Connect library.

Edwards Inc. experienced the following events:

1. Issued common stock for cash.
2. Declared a cash dividend.
3. Issued noncumulative preferred stock for cash.
4. Appropriated retained earnings.
5. Distributed a stock dividend.
6. Paid cash to purchase treasury stock.
7. Distributed a 2-for-1 stock split.
8. Issued cumulative preferred stock for cash.
9. Paid a cash dividend that had previously been declared.
10. Sold treasury stock for cash at a higher amount than the cost of the treasury stock.

Required

Show the effect of each event on the elements of the financial statements using a horizontal statements model like the one shown here. Use + for increase, − for decrease, and NA for not affected. In the Cash Flow column, indicate whether the item is an operating activity (OA), investing activity (IA), or financing activity (FA). The first transaction is entered as an example.

Event	Assets	=	Liab.	+	Equity	Rev.	−	Exp.	=	Net Inc.	Cash Flow
1	+		NA		+	NA		NA		NA	+ FA

Solution to Self-Study Review Problem

Event	Assets	=	Liab.	+	Equity	Rev.	−	Exp.	=	Net Inc.	Cash Flow
1	+		NA		+	NA		NA		NA	+ FA
2	NA		+		−	NA		NA		NA	NA
3	+		NA		+	NA		NA		NA	+ FA
4	NA		NA		−+	NA		NA		NA	NA
5	NA		NA		−+	NA		NA		NA	NA
6	−		NA		−	NA		NA		NA	− FA
7	NA		NA		NA	NA		NA		NA	NA
8	+		NA		+	NA		NA		NA	+ FA
9	−		−		NA	NA		NA		NA	− FA
10	+		NA		+	NA		NA		NA	+ FA

KEY TERMS

Appropriated retained earnings 612
Articles of incorporation 598
Authorized stock 603
Board of directors 600
Book value per share 603
Closely held corporation 598
Common stock 603
Continuity 600
Corporation 598
Cost method of accounting for treasury stock 609

Cumulative dividends 604
Date of record 610
Declaration date 610
Dividends in arrears 604
Double taxation 599
Ex-dividend 610
Issued stock 603
Legal capital 603
Limited liability 600
Limited liability companies (LLCs) 599
Market value 603
Outstanding stock 603
Paid-in Capital in Excess of Par Value 605
Par value 602
Partnership agreement 598
Partnerships 598
Payment date 610
Preferred stock 603
Price-earnings ratio 615
Sarbanes-Oxley Act of 2002 599
Securities Act of 1933 and Securities Exchange Act of 1934 598
Sole proprietorships 598
Stated value 603
Stock certificates 598
Stock dividends 611
Stockholders 600
Stock split 612
Transferability 600
Treasury stock 603
Withdrawals 601

QUESTIONS

1. What are the three major forms of business organizations? Describe each.
2. How are sole proprietorships formed?
3. Discuss the purpose of a partnership agreement. Is such an agreement necessary for partnership formation?
4. What is meant by the phrase *separate legal entity?* To which type of business organization does it apply?
5. What is the purpose of the articles of incorporation? What information do they provide?
6. What is the function of the stock certificate?
7. What prompted Congress to pass the Securities Act of 1933 and the Securities Exchange Act of 1934? What is the purpose of these laws?
8. What are the advantages and disadvantages of the corporate form of business organization?
9. What is a limited liability company? Discuss its advantages and disadvantages.
10. How does the term *double taxation* apply to corporations? Give an example of double taxation.
11. What is the difference between contributed capital and retained earnings for a corporation?
12. What are the similarities and differences in the equity structure of a sole proprietorship, a partnership, and a corporation?
13. Why is it easier for a corporation to raise large amounts of capital than it is for a partnership?
14. What is the meaning of each of the following terms with respect to the corporate form of organization?
    (a) Legal capital
    (b) Par value of stock
    (c) Stated value of stock
    (d) Market value of stock
    (e) Book value of stock
    (f) Authorized shares of stock
    (g) Issued stock
    (h) Outstanding stock
    (i) Treasury stock
    (j) Common stock
    (k) Preferred stock
    (l) Dividends
15. What is the difference between cumulative preferred stock and noncumulative preferred stock?
16. What is no-par stock? How is it recorded in the accounting records?
17. Assume that Best Co. has issued and outstanding 1,000 shares of $100 par value, 10 percent, cumulative preferred stock. What is the dividend per share? If the preferred dividend is two years in arrears, what total amount of dividends must be paid before the common shareholders can receive any dividends?
18. If Best Co. issued 10,000 shares of $20 par value common stock for $30 per share, what amount is credited to the Common Stock account? What amount of cash is received?
19. What is the difference between par value stock and stated value stock?
20. Why might a company repurchase its own stock?
21. What effect does the purchase of treasury stock have on the equity of a company?
22. Assume that Day Company repurchased 1,000 of its own shares for $30 per share and sold the shares two weeks later for $35 per share. What is the amount of gain on the sale? How is it reported on the balance sheet? What type of account is treasury stock?
23. What is the importance of the declaration date, record date, and payment date in conjunction with corporate dividends?
24. What is the difference between a stock dividend and a stock split?
25. Why would a company choose to distribute a stock dividend instead of a cash dividend?
26. What is the primary reason that a company would declare a stock split?
27. If Best Co. had 10,000 shares of $20 par value common stock outstanding and declared a 5-for-1 stock split, how many shares would then be outstanding and what would be their par value after the split?
28. When a company appropriates retained earnings, does the company set aside cash for a specific use? Explain.
29. What is the largest source of financing for most U.S. businesses?
30. What is meant by *equity financing?* What is meant by *debt financing?*
31. What is a widely held corporation? What is a closely held corporation?
32. What are some reasons that a corporation might not pay dividends?

MULTIPLE-CHOICE QUESTIONS

Multiple-choice questions are available in the Connect library.

EXERCISES—SERIES A

All applicable Exercises in Series A are available with McGraw-Hill's Connect Plus Accounting.

LO 11-1

Exercise 11-1A *Effect of accounting events on the financial statements of a sole proprietorship*

A sole proprietorship was started on January 1, 2016, when it received \$60,000 cash from Marlin Jones, the owner. During 2016, the company earned \$35,300 in cash revenues and paid \$16,200 in cash expenses. Jones withdrew \$1,000 cash from the business during 2016.

Required

Prepare an income statement, capital statement (statement of changes in equity), balance sheet, and statement of cash flows for Jone's 2016 fiscal year.

LO 11-1

Exercise 11-2A *Effect of accounting events on the financial statements of a partnership*

Faith Busby and Jeremy Beatty started the B&B partnership on January 1, 2016. The business acquired \$44,000 cash from Busby and \$66,000 from Beatty. During 2016, the partnership earned \$42,000 in cash revenues and paid \$18,400 for cash expenses. Busby withdrew \$2,000 cash from the business, and Beatty withdrew \$2,500 cash. The net income was allocated to the capital accounts of the two partners in proportion to the amounts of their original investments in the business.

Required

Prepare an income statement, capital statement, balance sheet, and statement of cash flows for B&B's 2016 fiscal year.

LO 11-2

Exercise 11-3A *Effect of accounting events on the financial statements of a corporation*

Astro Corporation was started with the issue of 2,000 shares of \$5 par stock for cash on January 1, 2016. The stock was issued at a market price of \$12 per share. During 2016, the company earned \$31,000 in cash revenues and paid \$17,000 for cash expenses. Also, a \$2,000 cash dividend was paid to the stockholders.

Required

Prepare an income statement, statement of changes in stockholders' equity, balance sheet, and statement of cash flows for Astro Corporation's 2016 fiscal year.

LO 11-2

Exercise 11-4A *Effect of issuing common stock on the balance sheet*

Newly formed S&J Iron Corporation has 50,000 shares of \$10 par common stock authorized. On March 1, 2016, S&J Iron issued 6,000 shares of the stock for \$16 per share. On May 2 the company issued an additional 10,000 shares for \$18 per share. S&J Iron was not affected by other events during 2016.

Required

a. Record the transactions in a horizontal statements model like the following one. In the Cash Flow column, indicate whether the item is an operating activity (OA), investing activity (IA), or financing activity (FA). Use NA to indicate that an element was not affected by the event.

Assets	=	Liab.	+	Equity			Rev. − Exp. = Net Inc.	Cash Flow
Cash	=			Com. Stk.	+	PIC in Excess		

b. Determine the amount S&J Iron would report for common stock on the December 31, 2016, balance sheet.
c. Determine the amount S&J Iron would report for paid-in capital in excess of par.
d. What is the total amount of capital contributed by the owners?
e. What amount of total assets would S&J Iron report on the December 31, 2016, balance sheet?
f. Prepare journal entries to record the March 1 and May 2 transactions.

Exercise 11-5A *Recording and reporting common and preferred stock transactions* LO 11-2

Eastport Inc. was organized on June 5, 2016. It was authorized to issue 300,000 shares of $10 par common stock and 50,000 shares of 5 percent cumulative class A preferred stock. The class A stock had a stated value of $50 per share. The following stock transactions pertain to Eastport Inc.:

1. Issued 15,000 shares of common stock for $12 per share.
2. Issued 5,000 shares of the class A preferred stock for $51 per share.
3. Issued 60,000 shares of common stock for $15 per share.

Required

a. Prepare general journal entries for these transactions.
b. Prepare the stockholders' equity section of the balance sheet immediately after these transactions.

Exercise 11-6A *Effect of no-par common and par preferred stock on the horizontal statements model* LO 11-2

Mercury Corporation issued 6,000 shares of no-par common stock for $45 per share. Mercury also issued 3,000 shares of $50 par, 5 percent noncumulative preferred stock at $52 per share.

Required

a. Record these events in a horizontal statements model like the following one. In the Cash Flow column, indicate whether the item is an operating activity (OA), investing activity (IA), or financing activity (FA). Use NA to indicate that an element was not affected by the event.

Assets =	Equity					Rev. − Exp. = Net Inc.	Cash Flow
Cash	=	Pfd. Stk.	+	Com. Stk.	+ PIC in Excess		

b. Prepare journal entries to record these transactions.

Exercise 11-7A *Issuing stock for assets other than cash* LO 11-2

Tom Yuppy, a wealthy investor, exchanged a plot of land that originally cost him $25,000 for 1,000 shares of $10 par common stock issued to him by Leuig Corp. On the same date, Leuig Corp. issued an additional 2,000 shares of stock to Yuppy for $25 per share.

Required

a. What was the value of the land at the date of the stock issue?
b. Show the effect of the two stock issues on Leuig's books in a horizontal statements model like the following one. In the Cash Flow column, indicate whether the item is an operating activity (OA), investing activity (IA), or financing activity (FA). Use NA to indicate that an element was not affected by the event.

Assets			=	Equity	Rev. − Exp. = Net Inc.	Cash Flow
Cash	+	Land	=	Com. Stk. + PIC in Excess		

c. Prepare the journal entries to record these transactions.

LO 11-3

Exercise 11-8A *Treasury stock transactions*

Elroy Corporation repurchased 4,000 shares of its own stock for $30 per share. The stock has a par of $10 per share. A month later Elroy resold 900 shares of the treasury stock for $32 per share.

Required

a. Record the two events in general journal format.

b. What is the balance of the treasury stock account after these transactions?

LO 11-3

Exercise 11-9A *Recording and reporting treasury stock transactions*

The following information pertains to JAE Corp. at January 1, 2016:

Common stock, $10 par, 20,000 shares authorized, 2,000 shares issued and outstanding	$20,000
Paid-in capital in excess of par, common stock	15,000
Retained earnings	82,000

JAE Corp. completed the following transactions during 2016:

1. Issued 3,000 shares of $10 par common stock for $25 per share.
2. Repurchased 500 shares of its own common stock for $26 per share.
3. Resold 200 shares of treasury stock for $30 per share.

Required

a. How many shares of common stock were outstanding at the end of the period?

b. How many shares of common stock had been issued at the end of the period?

c. Prepare journal entries for these transactions and post them to T-accounts.

d. Prepare the stockholders' equity section of the balance sheet reflecting these transactions. Include the number of shares authorized, issued, and outstanding in the description of the common stock.

LO 11-4

Exercise 11-10A *Effect of cash dividends on financial statements*

On May 1, 2016, Love Corporation declared a $50,000 cash dividend to be paid on May 31 to shareholders of record on May 15.

Required

a. Record the events occurring on May 1, May 15, and May 31 in a horizontal statements model like the following one. In the Cash Flow column, indicate whether the item is an operating activity (OA), investing activity (IA), or financing activity (FA).

Date	Assets = Liab. + Com. Stock + Ret. Earn.	Rev. − Exp. = Net Inc.	Cash Flow

b. Prepare journal entries for all events associated with the dividend.

LO 11-4

Exercise 11-11A *Accounting for cumulative preferred dividends*

When Crossett Corporation was organized in January 2016, it immediately issued 4,000 shares of $50 par, 6 percent, cumulative preferred stock and 50,000 shares of $20 par common stock. Its earnings history is as follows: 2016, net loss of $35,000; 2017, net income of $125,000; 2018, net income of $215,000. The corporation did not pay a dividend in 2016.

Required

a. How much is the dividend arrearage as of January 1, 2017?

b. Assume that the board of directors declares a $25,000 cash dividend at the end of 2017 (remember that the 2016 and 2017 preferred dividends are due). How will the dividend be divided between the preferred and common stockholders?

Exercise 11-12A *Cash dividends for preferred and common shareholders* LO 11-4

Weaver Corporation had the following stock issued and outstanding at January 1, 2016:

1. 150,000 shares of $1 par common stock.
2. 15,000 shares of $100 par, 6 percent, noncumulative preferred stock.

On June 10, Weaver Corporation declared the annual cash dividend on its 15,000 shares of preferred stock and a $0.50 per share dividend for the common shareholders. The dividends will be paid on July 1 to the shareholders of record on June 20.

Required

a. Determine the total amount of dividends to be paid to the preferred shareholders and common shareholders.

b. Prepare general journal entries to record the declaration and payment of the cash dividends (be sure to date your entries).

Exercise 11-13A *Cash dividends: common and preferred stock* LO 11-4

Nowell Inc. had the following stock issued and outstanding at January 1, 2016:

1. 150,000 shares of no-par common stock.
2. 30,000 shares of $50 par, 4 percent, cumulative preferred stock. (Dividends are in arrears for one year, 2015.)

On March 8, 2016, Nowell declared a $175,000 cash dividend to be paid March 31 to shareholders of record on March 20.

Required

a. What amount of dividends will be paid to the preferred shareholders versus the common shareholders?

b. Prepare the journal entries required for these transactions. (Be sure to include the dates of the entries.)

Exercise 11-14A *Accounting for stock dividends* LO 11-4

Beacon Corporation issued a 5 percent stock dividend on 30,000 shares of its $10 par common stock. At the time of the dividend, the market value of the stock was $15 per share.

Required

a. Compute the amount of the stock dividend.

b. Show the effects of the stock dividend on the financial statements using a horizontal statements model like the following one:

Assets	=	Liab.	+	Com. Stock	+	PIC in Excess	+	Ret. Earn.	Rev.	−	Exp.	=	Net Inc.	Cash Flow

c. Prepare the journal entry to record the stock dividend.

Exercise 11-15A *Determining the effects of stock splits on the accounting records* LO 11-4

The market value of Yeates Corporation's common stock had become excessively high. The stock was currently selling for $240 per share. To reduce the market price of the common stock, Yeates declared a 3-for-1 stock split for the 100,000 outstanding shares of its $10 par value common stock.

Required

a. What entry will be made on the books of Yeates Corporation for the stock split?

b. Determine the number of common shares outstanding and the par value after the split.

c. Explain how the market value of the stock will be affected by the stock split.

LO 11-5

Exercise 11-16A *Corporate announcements*

Discount Drugs (one of the three largest drug makers) just reported that its 2016 third quarter profits are essentially the same as the 2015 third quarter profits. In addition to this announcement, the same day, Discount Drugs also announced that the Food and Drug Administration has just approved a new drug used to treat high blood pressure that Discount Drugs developed. This new drug has been shown to be extremely effective and has few or no side effects. It will also be less expensive than the other drugs currently on the market.

Required

Using the above information, answer the following questions:

a. What do you think will happen to the stock price of Discount Drugs on the day these two announcements are made? Explain your answer.

b. How will the balance sheet be affected on that day by the above announcements?

c. How will the income statement be affected on that day by the above announcements?

d. How will the statement of cash flows be affected on that day by the above announcements?

LO 11-5

Exercise 11-17A *Using the P/E ratio*

During 2016 the Lake Corporation and the River Corporation reported net incomes of $700,000 and $960,000, respectively. Both companies had 200,000 shares of common stock issued and outstanding. The market price per share of Lake's stock was $50, while River's sold for $85 per share.

Required

a. Determine the P/E ratio for each company.

b. Based on the P/E ratios computed in Requirement *a*, which company do investors believe has the greater potential for growth in income?

LO 11-5

Exercise 11-18A *The P/E ratio*

Required

Write a memo explaining why one company's P/E ratio may be higher than another company's P/E ratio.

PROBLEMS—SERIES A

All applicable Problems in Series A are available with McGraw-Hill's Connect Plus Accounting.

LO 11-1

CHECK FIGURES
a. Net Income: $16,900
b. Cascade Capital: $29,160

Problem 11-19A *Effect of business structure on financial statements*

Cascade Company was started on January 1, 2016, when it acquired $60,000 cash from the owners. During 2016, the company earned cash revenues of $35,000 and incurred cash expenses of $18,100. The company also paid cash distributions of $4,000.

Required

Prepare a 2016 income statement, capital statement (statement of changes in equity), balance sheet, and statement of cash flows under each of the following assumptions. (Consider each assumption separately.)

a. Cascade is a sole proprietorship owned by Carl Cascade.

b. Cascade is a partnership with two partners, Carl Cascade and Beth Cascade. Carl Cascade invested $24,000 and Beth Cascade invested $36,000 of the $60,000 cash that was used to start the business. Beth was expected to assume the vast majority of the responsibility for operating the business. The partnership agreement called for Beth to receive 60 percent of the profits and Carl to get the remaining 40 percent. With regard to the $4,000 distribution, Beth withdrew $2,400 from the business and Carl withdrew $1,600.

c. Cascade is a corporation. It issued 5,000 shares of $5 par common stock for $60,000 cash to start the business.

Problem 11-20A *Different forms of business organization*

LO 11-1

Cal Cagle was working to establish a business enterprise with four of his wealthy friends. Each of the five individuals would receive a 20 percent ownership interest in the company. A primary goal of establishing the enterprise was to minimize the amount of income taxes paid. Assume that the five investors are in a 35 percent personal tax bracket and that the corporate tax rate is 25 percent. Also assume that the new company is expected to earn $220,000 of cash income before taxes during its first year of operation. All earnings are expected to be immediately distributed to the owners.

Required

Calculate the amount of after-tax cash flow available to each investor if the business is established as a partnership versus a corporation. Write a memo explaining the advantages and disadvantages of these two forms of business organization. Explain why a limited liability company may be a better choice than either a partnership or a corporation.

Problem 11-21A *Analyzing journal entries for treasury stock transactions*

LO 11-2, 11-3

CHECK FIGURE
b. 4,800

The following correctly prepared entries without explanations pertain to Corners Corporation:

	Account Title	Debit	Credit
1.	Cash	1,000,000	
	Common Stock		600,000
	Paid-in Capital in Excess of Par Value		400,000
2.	Treasury Stock	24,000	
	Cash		24,000
3.	Cash	21,000	
	Treasury Stock		18,000
	Paid-in Capital in Excess of Cost of Treasury Stock		3,000

The original sale (Entry 1) was for 400,000 shares, and the treasury stock was acquired for $5 per share (Entry 2).

Required

a. What was the sales price per share of the original stock issue?

b. How many shares of stock did the corporation acquire in Entry 2?

c. How many shares were reissued in Entry 3?

d. How many shares are outstanding immediately following Entries 2 and 3, respectively?

Problem 11-22A *Recording and reporting stock dividends*

LO 11-2, 11-4

CHECK FIGURE
c. Total Paid-In Capital: $608,000

Brice Co. completed the following transactions in 2016, the first year of operation:

1. Issued 40,000 shares of no-par common stock for $10 per share.
2. Issued 8,000 shares of $20 par, 6 percent, preferred stock for $20 per share.
3. Paid a cash dividend of $9,600 to preferred shareholders.
4. Issued a 10 percent stock dividend on no-par common stock. The market value at the dividend declaration date was $12 per share.
5. Later that year, issued a 2-for-1 split on the shares of outstanding common stock. The market price of the stock at that time was $50 per share.
6. Produced $140,000 of cash revenues and incurred $72,000 of cash operating expenses.
7. Closed the revenue, expense, and dividend accounts to retained earnings.

Required

a. Record each of these events in a horizontal statements model like the following one. In the Cash Flow column, indicate whether the item is an operating activity (OA), investing activity (IA), or financing activity (FA). Use NA to indicate that an element is not affected by the event.

Assets	=	Equity					Rev.	−	Exp.	=	Net Inc.	Cash Flow
		P. Stk.	+	C. Stk.	+	Ret. Earn.						

b. Record the 2016 transactions in general journal form and post them to T-accounts.

c. Prepare the stockholders' equity section of the balance sheet at the end of 2016. (Include all necessary information.)

d. Theoretically, what is the market value of the common stock after the stock split?

LO 11-2, 11-3, 11-4

CHECK FIGURES

b. Preferred Stock, 2016: $50,000

c. Common Shares Outstanding, 2017: 35,100

Problem 11-23A *Recording and reporting stock transactions and cash dividends across two accounting cycles*

Sun Corporation received a charter that authorized the issuance of 100,000 shares of $10 par common stock and 50,000 shares of $50 par, 5 percent cumulative preferred stock. Sun Corporation completed the following transactions during its first two years of operation:

2016

Jan. 5 Sold 6,000 shares of the $10 par common stock for $15 per share.
12 Sold 1,000 shares of the 5 percent preferred stock for $55 per share.
Apr. 5 Sold 30,000 shares of the $10 par common stock for $21 per share.
Dec. 31 During the year, earned $150,000 in cash revenue and paid $88,000 for cash operating expenses.
31 Declared the cash dividend on the outstanding shares of preferred stock for 2016. The dividend will be paid on February 15 to stockholders of record on January 10, 2017.
31 Closed the revenue, expense, and dividend accounts to the retained earnings account.

2017

Feb. 15 Paid the cash dividend declared on December 31, 2016.
Mar. 3 Sold 15,000 shares of the $50 par preferred stock for $53 per share.
May 5 Purchased 900 shares of the common stock as treasury stock at $24 per share.
Dec. 31 During the year, earned $210,000 in cash revenues and paid $98,000 for cash operating expenses.
31 Declared the annual dividend on the preferred stock and a $0.50 per share dividend on the common stock.
31 Closed revenue, expense, and dividend accounts to the retained earnings account.

Required

a. Prepare journal entries for these transactions for 2016 and 2017 and post them to T-accounts.

b. Prepare the balance sheets at December 31, 2016 and 2017.

c. What is the number of common shares *outstanding* at the end of 2016? At the end of 2017? How many common shares had been *issued* at the end of 2016? At the end of 2017? Explain any differences between issued and outstanding common shares for 2016 and for 2017.

LO 11-2, 11-3, 11-4

CHECK FIGURE

b. Total Paid-In Capital: $261,000

Problem 11-24A *Recording and reporting treasury stock transactions*

Choctaw Co. completed the following transactions in 2016, the first year of operation:

1. Issued 20,000 shares of $10 par common stock for $10 per share.
2. Issued 3,000 shares of $20 stated value preferred stock for $20 per share.
3. Purchased 1,000 shares of common stock as treasury stock for $12 per share.
4. Declared a $2,000 cash dividend on preferred stock.

5. Sold 500 shares of treasury stock for $14 per share.
6. Paid $2,000 cash for the preferred dividend declared in Event 4.
7. Earned cash revenues of $78,000 and incurred cash expenses of $41,000.
8. Closed revenue, expense, and dividend accounts to the retained earnings account.
9. Appropriated $8,000 of retained earnings.

Required

a. Prepare journal entries to record these transactions and post them to T-accounts.
b. Prepare a balance sheet as of December 31, 2016.

Problem 11-25A *Analyzing the stockholders' equity section of the balance sheet*

LO 11-2, 11-3, 11-4

The stockholders' equity section of the balance sheet for Mann Equipment Co. at December 31, 2016, is as follows:

CHECK FIGURES

a. Par Value per Share: $20
b. Dividend per Share: $1.20

Stockholders' Equity

Paid-in capital		
Preferred stock, ? par value, 6% cumulative, 100,000 shares authorized, 10,000 shares issued and outstanding	$ 200,000	
Common stock, $10 stated value, 200,000 shares authorized, 100,000 shares issued and outstanding	1,000,000	
Paid-in capital in excess of par—Preferred	25,000	
Paid-in capital in excess of stated value—Common	500,000	
Total paid-in capital		$1,725,000
Retained earnings		420,000
Total stockholders' equity		$2,145,000

Note: The market value per share of the common stock is $42, and the market value per share of the preferred stock is $26.

Required

a. What is the par value per share of the preferred stock?
b. What is the dividend per share on the preferred stock?
c. What was the average issue price per share (price for which the stock was issued) of the common stock?
d. Explain the difference between the par value and the market price of the preferred stock.
e. If Mann declares a 2-for-1 stock split on the common stock, how many shares will be outstanding after the split? What amount will be transferred from the retained earnings account because of the stock split? Theoretically, what will be the market price of the common stock immediately after the stock split?

Problem 11-26A *Effects of equity transactions on financial statements*

LO 11-2, 11-3, 11-4

The following events were experienced by Sequoia, Inc.:

1. Issued cumulative preferred stock for cash.
2. Issued common stock for cash.
3. Issued noncumulative preferred stock for cash.
4. Paid cash to purchase treasury stock.
5. Sold treasury stock for an amount of cash that was more than the cost of the treasury stock.
6. Declared a cash dividend.
7. Declared a 2-for-1 stock split on the common stock.
8. Distributed a stock dividend.
9. Appropriated retained earnings.
10. Paid a cash dividend that was previously declared.

Required

Show the effect of each event on the elements of the financial statements using a horizontal statements model like the following one. Use + for increase, − for decrease, and NA for not affected. In the Cash Flow column indicate whether the item is an operating activity (OA), investing activity (IA), or financing activity (FA). The first transaction is entered as an example.

Event No.	Assets	=	Liab.	+	Equity	Rev.	−	Exp.	=	Net Inc.	Cash Flow
1	+		NA		+	NA		NA		NA	+ FA

EXERCISES—SERIES B

LO 11-1

Exercise 11-1B *Effect of accounting events on the financial statements of a sole proprietorship*

A sole proprietorship was started on January 1, 2016, when it received $30,000 cash from Maria Lopez, the owner. During 2016, the company earned $50,000 in cash revenues and paid $22,300 in cash expenses. Lopez withdrew $10,000 cash from the business during 2016.

Required

Prepare an income statement, capital statement (statement of changes in equity), balance sheet, and statement of cash flows for Lopez's 2016 fiscal year.

LO 11-1

Exercise 11-2B *Effect of accounting events on the financial statements of a partnership*

D. Reed and J. Files started the RF partnership on January 1, 2016. The business acquired $70,000 cash from Reed and $140,000 from Files. During 2016, the partnership earned $75,000 in cash revenues and paid $39,000 for cash expenses. Reed withdrew $2,000 cash from the business, and Files withdrew $4,000 cash. The net income was allocated to the capital accounts of the two partners in proportion to the amounts of their original investments in the business.

Required

Prepare an income statement, capital statement, balance sheet, and statement of cash flows for the RF partnership for the 2016 fiscal year.

LO 11-2

Exercise 11-3B *Effect of accounting events on the financial statements of a corporation*

Bozeman Corporation was started with the issue of 10,000 shares of $10 par common stock for cash on January 1, 2016. The stock was issued at a market price of $16 per share. During 2016, the company earned $71,000 in cash revenues and paid $46,500 for cash expenses. Also a $5,000 cash dividend was paid to the stockholders.

Required

Prepare an income statement, statement of changes in stockholders' equity, balance sheet, and statement of cash flows for Bozeman Corporation's 2016 fiscal year.

LO 11-2

Exercise 11-4B *Effect of issuing common stock on the balance sheet*

Newly formed Irwin Services Corporation has 100,000 shares of $10 par common stock authorized. On March 1, 2016, Irwin Services issued 20,000 shares of the stock for $12 per share. On May 2 the company issued an additional 30,000 shares for $15 per share. Irwin Services was not affected by other events during 2016.

Required

a. Record the transactions in a horizontal statements model like the following one. In the Cash Flow column, indicate whether the item is an operating activity (OA), investing activity (IA), or financing activity (FA). Use NA to indicate that an element was not affected by the event.

Assets	=	Liab.	+	Equity			Rev.	−	Exp.	=	Net Inc.	Cash Flow
Cash	=			Com. Stk.	+	PIC in Excess						

b. Determine the amount Irwin Services would report for common stock on the December 31, 2016, balance sheet.

c. Determine the amount Irwin Services would report for paid-in capital in excess of par.

d. What is the total amount of capital contributed by the owners?

e. What amount of total assets would Irwin Services report on the December 31, 2016, balance sheet?

f. Prepare journal entries to record the March 1 and May 2 transactions.

Exercise 11-5B *Recording and reporting common and preferred stock transactions* LO 11-2

Reiss Inc. was organized on June 1, 2016. It was authorized to issue 500,000 shares of $10 par common stock and 100,000 shares of 4 percent cumulative class A preferred stock. The class A stock had a stated value of $50 per share. The following stock transactions pertain to Reiss Inc.:

1. Issued 40,000 shares of common stock for $16 per share.
2. Issued 20,000 shares of the class A preferred stock for $52 per share.
3. Issued 60,000 shares of common stock for $20 per share.

Required

a. Prepare general journal entries for these transactions.

b. Prepare the stockholders' equity section of the balance sheet immediately after these transactions.

Exercise 11-6B *Effect of no-par common and par preferred stock on the horizontal statements model* LO 11-2

Rice Corporation issued 10,000 shares of no-par common stock for $25 per share. Rice also issued 3,000 shares of $40 par, 6 percent noncumulative preferred stock at $42 per share.

Required

a. Record these events in a horizontal statements model like the following one. In the cash flow column, indicate whether the item is an operating activity (OA), investing activity (IA), or financing activity (FA). Use NA to indicate that an element was not affected by the event.

Assets	=	Equity					Rev.	−	Exp.	=	Net Inc.	Cash Flow
Cash	=	Pfd. Stk.	+	Com. Stk.	+	PIC in Excess						

b. Prepare journal entries to record these transactions.

Exercise 11-7B *Issuing stock for assets other than cash* LO 11-2

Carroll Corporation was formed when it issued shares of common stock to two of its shareholders. Carroll issued 10,000 shares of $5 par common stock to R. Flowler in exchange for $80,000 cash (the issue price was $8 per share). Carroll also issued 3,500 shares of stock to P. Jones in exchange for a one-year-old delivery van on the same day. Jones had originally paid $39,000 for the van.

Required

a. What was the market value of the delivery van on the date of the stock issue?

b. Show the effect of the two stock issues on Carroll's books in a horizontal statements model like the following one. In the Cash Flow column, indicate whether the item is an operating activity (OA), investing activity (IA), or financing activity (FA). Use NA to indicate that an element was not affected by the event.

Assets			=	Equity		
Cash	+	Van	=	Com. Stk.	+	PIC in Excess

Rev.	−	Exp.	=	Net Inc.	Cash Flow

c. Prepare the journal entries to record these transactions.

LO 11-3

Exercise 11-8B *Treasury stock transactions*

Earles Corporation repurchased 4,000 shares of its own stock for $30 per share. The stock has a par value of $10 per share. A month later Earles resold 2,500 shares of the treasury stock for $35 per share.

Required

a. Record the two events in general journal format.

b. What is the balance of the treasury stock account after these transactions?

LO 11-3

Exercise 11-9B *Recording and reporting treasury stock transactions*

The following information pertains to Ming Corp. at January 1, 2016:

Common stock, $10 par, 50,000 shares authorized, 3,000 shares issued and outstanding	$30,000
Paid-in capital in excess of par, common stock	12,000
Retained earnings	46,000

Ming Corp. completed the following transactions during 2016:

1. Issued 2,000 shares of $10 par common stock for $16 per share.
2. Repurchased 500 shares of its own common stock for $18 per share.
3. Resold 120 shares of treasury stock for $20 per share.

Required

a. How many shares of common stock were outstanding at the end of the period?

b. How many shares of common stock had been issued at the end of the period?

c. Prepare journal entries for these transactions and post them to T-accounts.

d. Prepare the stockholders' equity section of the balance sheet reflecting these transactions. Include the number of shares authorized, issued, and outstanding in the description of the common stock.

LO 11-4

Exercise 11-10B *Effect of cash dividends on financial statements*

On October 1, 2016, Nicholes Corporation declared a $50,000 cash dividend to be paid on December 15 to shareholders of record on November 1.

Required

a. Record the events occurring on October 1, November 1, and December 15 in a horizontal statements model like the following one. In the Cash Flow column, indicate whether the item is an operating activity (OA), investing activity (IA), or financing activity (FA).

Date	Assets	=	Liab.	+	Com. Stock	+	Ret. Earn.	Rev.	−	Exp.	=	Net Inc.	Cash Flow

b. Prepare journal entries for all events associated with the dividend.

LO 11-4

Exercise 11-11B *Accounting for cumulative preferred dividends*

When Ching Corporation was organized in January 2016, it immediately issued 10,000 shares of $50 par, 5 percent, cumulative preferred stock and 15,000 shares of $10 par common stock.

The company's earnings history is as follows: 2016, net loss of $18,000; 2017, net income of $95,000; 2018, net income of $90,000. The corporation did not pay a dividend in 2016.

Required

a. How much is the dividend arrearage as of January 1, 2017?

b. Assume that the board of directors declares a $65,000 cash dividend at the end of 2017 (remember that the 2016 and 2017 preferred dividends are due). How will the dividend be divided between the preferred and common stockholders?

Exercise 11-12B *Cash dividends for preferred and common shareholders* LO 11-4

ALR Corporation had the following stock issued and outstanding at January 1, 2016:

1. 200,000 shares of $10 par common stock.
2. 8,000 shares of $100 par, 4 percent, noncumulative preferred stock.

On May 10, ALR Corporation declared the annual cash dividend on its 8,000 shares of preferred stock and a $0.50 per share dividend for the common shareholders. The dividends will be paid on June 15 to the shareholders of record on May 30.

Required

a. Determine the total amount of dividends to be paid to the preferred shareholders and common shareholders.

b. Prepare general journal entries to record the declaration and payment of the cash dividends (be sure to date your entries).

Exercise 11-13B *Cash dividends: common and preferred stock* LO 11-4

Tyler Corp. had the following stock issued and outstanding at January 1, 2016:

1. 60,000 shares of no-par common stock.
2. 15,000 shares of $100 par, 4 percent, cumulative preferred stock. (Dividends are in arrears for one year, 2015.)

On February 1, 2016, Tyler declared a $150,000 cash dividend to be paid March 31 to shareholders of record on March 10.

Required

a. What amount of dividends will be paid to the preferred shareholders versus the common shareholders?

b. Prepare the journal entries required for these transactions. (Be sure to include the dates of the entries.)

Exercise 11-14B *Accounting for stock dividends* LO 11-4

Egrett Corporation issued a 4 percent stock dividend on 20,000 shares of its $10 par common stock. At the time of the dividend, the market value of the stock was $30 per share.

Required

a. Compute the amount of the stock dividend.

b. Show the effects of the stock dividend on the financial statements using a horizontal statements model like the following one.

Assets	=	Liab.	+	Com. Stock	+	PIC in Excess	+	Ret. Earn.	Rev.	−	Exp.	=	Net Inc.	Cash Flow

c. Prepare the journal entry to record the stock dividend.

Exercise 11-15B *Determining the effects of stock splits on the accounting records* LO 11-4

The market value of Granger Corporation's common stock had become excessively high. The stock was currently selling for $240 per share. To reduce the market price of the common stock, Granger declared a 3-for-1 stock split for the 200,000 outstanding shares of its $15 par common stock.

Required

a. How will Granger Corporation's books be affected by the stock split?

b. Determine the number of common shares outstanding and the par value after the split.

c. Explain how the market value of the stock will be affected by the stock split.

LO 11-5

Exercise 11-16B *Accounting information*

The Cutting Edge (TCE) is one of the world's largest lawn mower distributors. TCE is concerned about maintaining an adequate supply of the economy-line mowers that it sells in its stores. TCE currently obtains its economy-line mowers from two suppliers. To ensure a steady supply of mowers, the management of TCE is considering the purchase of an ownership interest in one of the companies that supplies its mowers. More specifically, TCE wants to own enough stock of one of the suppliers to enable it to exercise significant influence over the management of the company. The following is a description of the two suppliers.

The first supplier, Dobbs Incorporated, is a closely held company. Large blocks of the Dobbs stock are held by individual members of the Dobbs family. TCE's investment advisor has discovered that one of the members of the Dobbs family is interested in selling her 5 percent share of the company's stock.

The second supplier, National Mowers Inc., has widely disbursed ownership with no one single stockholder owning more than 1 percent of the stock. TCE's investment advisor believes that 5 percent of this company's stock could be acquired gradually over an extended period of time without having a significant effect on the company's stock price.

Required

Provide a recommendation to TCE's management as to whether it should pursue the purchase of 5 percent of Dobbs Incorporated, or 5 percent of National Mowers Inc. Your answer should be supported by an explanation of your recommendation.

LO 11-5

Exercise 11-17B *Using the P/E ratio*

During 2016, Davis, Inc., and Royal, Inc., reported net incomes of $81,000 and $93,000, respectively. Both companies had 10,000 shares of common stock issued and outstanding. The market price per share of Davis's stock was $130, while Royal's sold for $120 per share.

Required

a. Determine the P/E ratio for each company. (Round to the nearest whole number.)

b. Based on the P/E ratios computed in Requirement *a*, which company do investors believe has the greater potential for growth in income?

LO 11-5

Exercise 11-18B *The P/E ratio*

Pepper Company's earnings were approximately the same in 2016 and 2017. Even so, the company's P/E ratio dropped significantly.

Required

Speculate about why Pepper's P/E ratio dropped significantly while its earnings remained constant.

PROBLEMS—SERIES B

LO 11-1, 11-2

Problem 11-19B *Effect of business structure on financial statements*

Best Auto Parts Company was started on January 1, 2016, when the owners invested $120,000 cash in the business. During 2016, the company earned cash revenues of $80,000 and incurred cash expenses of $56,000. The company also paid cash distributions of $5,000.

Required

Prepare a 2016 income statement, capital statement (statement of changes in equity), balance sheet, and statement of cash flows using each of the following assumptions. (Consider each assumption separately.)

a. Best Auto Parts is a sole proprietorship owned by J. Smart.

b. Best Auto Parts is a partnership with two partners, Beth Song and J. Smart. Song invested $72,000 and Smart invested $48,000 of the $120,000 cash that was used to start the business.

Smart was expected to assume the vast majority of the responsibility for operating the business. The partnership agreement called for Smart to receive 60 percent of the profits and Song the remaining 40 percent. With regard to the $5,000 distribution, Smart withdrew $1,500 from the business and Song withdrew $3,500.

c. Best Auto Parts is a corporation. The owners were issued 10,000 shares of $10 par common stock when they invested the $120,000 cash in the business.

Problem 11-20B *Different forms of business organization*

LO 11-1

Bill Wheeler established a partnership with June Cramer. The new company, W&C Fuels, purchased coal directly from mining companies and contracted to ship the coal via waterways to a seaport where it was delivered to ships that were owned and operated by international utilities companies. Wheeler was primarily responsible for running the day-to-day operations of the business. Cramer negotiated the buy-and-sell agreements. She recently signed a deal to purchase and deliver $2,000,000 of coal to Solar Utilities. W&C Fuels purchased the coal on account from Miller Mining Company. After accepting title to the coal, W&C Fuels agreed to deliver the coal under terms FOB destination, Port of Long Beach. Unfortunately, Cramer failed to inform Wheeler of the deal in time for Wheeler to insure the shipment. While in transit, the vessel carrying the coal suffered storm damage that rendered the coal virtually worthless by the time it reached its destination. W&C Fuels immediately declared bankruptcy. The company not only was responsible for the $2,000,000 due to Miller Mining Company but also was sued by Solar for breach of contract. Cramer had a personal net worth of virtually zero, but Wheeler was a wealthy individual with a net worth approaching $2,500,000. Accordingly, Miller Mining and Solar filed suit against Wheeler's personal assets. Wheeler claimed that he was not responsible for the problem because Cramer had failed to inform him of the contracts in time to obtain insurance coverage. Cramer admitted that she was personally responsible for the disaster.

Required

Write a memo describing Wheeler's risk associated with his participation in the partnership. Comment on how other forms of ownership would have affected his level of risk.

Problem 11-21B *Recording and reporting treasury stock transactions*

LO 11-3

Edwards Corporation reports the following information in its January 1, 2016, balance sheet:

Stockholders' equity	
Common stock, $10 par value, 100,000 shares authorized, 50,000 shares issued and outstanding	$500,000
Paid-in capital in excess of par value	150,000
Retained earnings	120,000
Total stockholders' equity	$770,000

During 2016, Edwards was affected by the following accounting events:

1. Purchased 2,000 shares of treasury stock at $15 per share.
2. Reissued 1,200 shares of treasury stock at $18 per share.
3. Earned $72,000 of cash revenues.
4. Paid $41,000 of cash operating expenses.

Required

a. Provide journal entries to record these transactions.

b. Prepare the stockholders' equity section of the year-end balance sheet.

Problem 11-22B *Recording and reporting stock dividends*

LO 11-2, 11-4

Burk Corp. completed the following transactions in 2016, the first year of operation:

1. Issued 30,000 shares of $10 par common stock for $15 per share.
2. Issued 6,000 shares of $100 par, 5 percent, preferred stock at $101 per share.
3. Paid the annual cash dividend to preferred shareholders.
4. Issued a 5 percent stock dividend on the common stock. The market value at the dividend declaration date was $19 per share.

5. Later that year, issued a 2-for-1 split on the 31,500 shares of outstanding common stock.
6. Earned $165,000 of cash revenues and paid $98,000 of cash operating expenses.
7. Closed the revenue, expense, and dividend accounts to retained earnings.

Required

a. Record each of these events in a horizontal statements model like the following one. In the Cash Flow column, indicate whether the item is an operating activity (OA), investing activity (IA), or financing activity (FA). Use NA to indicate that an element is not affected by the event.

Assets = Liab. +	Equity	Rev. − Exp. = Net Inc.	Cash Flow
	Pfd. Stk. + Com. Stk. + PIC in Excess PS + PIC in Excess CS + Ret. Earn.		

b. Record the 2016 transactions in general journal form and post them to T-accounts.
c. Prepare the stockholders' equity section of the balance sheet at the end of 2016.

LO 11-2, 11-3, 11-4

Problem 11-23B *Recording and reporting stock transactions and cash dividends across two accounting cycles*

Edgar Corporation was authorized to issue 100,000 shares of $8 par common stock and 50,000 shares of $80 par, 4 percent, cumulative preferred stock. Edgar Corporation completed the following transactions during its first two years of operation:

2016

Jan. 2	Issued 25,000 shares of $8 par common stock for $10 per share.
15	Issued 2,000 shares of $80 par preferred stock for $90 per share.
Feb. 14	Issued 20,000 shares of $8 par common stock for $12 per share.
Dec. 31	During the year, earned $280,000 of cash revenues and paid $165,000 of cash operating expenses.
31	Declared the cash dividend on outstanding shares of preferred stock for 2016. The dividend will be paid on January 31 to stockholders of record on January 15, 2017.
31	Closed revenue, expense, and dividend accounts to the retained earnings account.

2017

Jan. 31	Paid the cash dividend declared on December 31, 2016.
Mar. 1	Issued 4,000 shares of $80 par preferred stock for $92 per share.
June 1	Purchased 1,000 shares of common stock as treasury stock at $14 per share.
Dec. 31	During the year, earned $185,000 of cash revenues and paid $110,000 of cash operating expenses.
31	Declared the dividend on the preferred stock and a $1.00 per share dividend on the common stock.
31	Closed revenue, expense, and dividend accounts to the retained earnings account.

Required

a. Prepare journal entries for these transactions for 2016 and 2017 and post them to T-accounts.
b. Prepare the stockholders' equity section of the balance sheet at December 31, 2016.
c. Prepare the balance sheet at December 31, 2017.

LO 11-2, 11-3, 11-4

Problem 11-24B *Recording and reporting treasury stock transactions*

Rabern Corp. completed the following transactions in 2016, the first year of operation:

1. Issued 15,000 shares of $10 par common stock at par.
2. Issued 5,000 shares of $50 stated value preferred stock at $52 per share.
3. Purchased 800 shares of common stock as treasury stock for $12 per share.
4. Declared a 5 percent cash dividend on preferred stock.
5. Sold 300 shares of treasury stock for $16 per share.
6. Paid the cash dividend on preferred stock that was declared in Event 4.

7. Earned revenue of $80,000 and incurred operating expenses of $48,000.
8. Closed revenue, expense, and dividend accounts to the retained earnings account.
9. Appropriated $6,000 of retained earnings.

Required

a. Prepare journal entries to record these transactions and post them to T-accounts.
b. Prepare the stockholders' equity section of the balance sheet as of December 31, 2016.

Problem 11-25B *Analyzing the stockholders' equity section of the balance sheet*

LO 11-2, 11-3, 11-4

The stockholders' equity section of the balance sheet for Stinson Company at December 31, 2016, is as follows:

Stockholders' Equity		
Paid-in capital		
Preferred stock, ? par value, 5% cumulative, 100,000 shares authorized, 40,000 shares issued and outstanding	$400,000	
Common stock, $20 stated value, 150,000 shares authorized, 40,000 shares issued and ? outstanding	800,000	
Paid-in capital in excess of par—Preferred	30,000	
Paid-in capital in excess of stated value—Common	100,000	
Total paid-in capital		$1,330,000
Retained earnings		250,000
Treasury stock, 2,000 shares		(25,000)
Total stockholders' equity		$1,555,000

Note: The market value per share of the common stock is $40, and the market value per share of the preferred stock is $12.

Required

a. What is the par value per share of the preferred stock?
b. What is the dividend per share on the preferred stock?
c. What is the number of common stock shares outstanding?
d. What was the average issue price per share (price for which the stock was issued) of the common stock?
e. Explain the difference between the average issue price and the market price of the common stock.
f. If Stinson declared a 2-for-1 stock split on the common stock, how many shares would be outstanding after the split? What amount would be transferred from the retained earnings account because of the stock split? Theoretically, what would be the market price of the common stock immediately after the stock split?

Problem 11-26B *Effects of equity transactions on financial statements*

LO 11-2, 11-3, 11-4

The following events were experienced by Halbart Inc.:

1. Issued common stock for cash.
2. Distributed a 2-for-1 stock split on the common stock.
3. Appropriated retained earnings.
4. Issued cumulative preferred stock for cash.
5. Sold treasury stock for an amount of cash that was more than the cost of the treasury stock.
6. Issued noncumulative preferred stock for cash.
7. Paid cash to purchase treasury stock.
8. Declared a cash dividend.
9. Distributed a stock dividend.
10. Paid the cash dividend declared in Event 8.

Required

Show the effect of each event on the elements of the financial statements using a horizontal statements model like the following one. Use + for increase, − for decrease, and NA for not affected. In the Cash Flow column, indicate whether the item is an operating activity (OA), investing activity (IA), or financing activity (FA). The first transaction is entered as an example.

Event No.	Assets	=	Liab.	+	Equity	Rev.	−	Exp.	=	Net Inc.	Cash Flow
1	+		NA		+	NA		NA		NA	+ FA

ANALYZE, THINK, COMMUNICATE

ATC 11-1 Business Applications Case *Understanding real-world annual reports*

Use the Target Corporation's annual report in Appendix B to answer the following questions:

Required

a. What is the par value per share of Target's stock? How was the par value established?

b. How many shares of Target's common stock were *outstanding* as of February 1, 2014?

c. Target's annual report provides some details about the company's executive officers. How many are identified? What is their minimum, maximum, and average age? How many are females?

d. Target's balance sheet does not show a balance for treasury stock. Does this mean the company has not repurchased any of its own stock? Explain.

ATC 11-2 Group Assignment *Missing information*

Listed here are the stockholders' equity sections of three public companies for years ending in 2013 and 2012:

	2013	2012
The Wendy's Company (in thousands)		
Stockholders' equity		
Common stock, ?? par value per share, authorized: 1,500,000; 470,424 shares issued	$ 47,042	$ 47,042
Additional paid-in capital	2,794,445	2,782,765
Retained earnings	(492,215)	(467,007)
Acc. other comp. income (loss)	(10,337)	5,981
Treasury stock, at cost: 77,637 in 2013 and 78,051 in 2012	(409,449)	(382,926)
Coca-Cola (in millions)		
Stockholders' equity		
Common stock, ?? par value per share, authorized: 11,200; issued: 7,040 shares in 2013 and 2012	1,760	1,760
Capital surplus	12,276	11,379
Reinvested earnings	61,660	58,045
Acc. other comp. inc. (loss)	(3,432)	(3,385)
Treasury stock, at cost: (2,638 shares in 2013 and 2,571 shares in 2012)	(39,091)	(35,009)
Harley-Davidson (in thousands)		
Stockholders' equity		
Common stock, 343,157 and 341,266 shares issued in 2013 and 2012, respectively	3,432	3,413
Additional paid-in capital	1,175,052	1,066,069
Retained earnings	7,852,729	7,306,424
Acc. other comp. inc. (loss)	(332,676)	(607,678)
Treasury stock, at cost: 123,198 and 115,166 shares in 2013 and 2012, respectively, at cost	(5,689,051)	(5,210,604)

Required

a. Divide the class in three sections and divide each section into groups of three to five students. Assign each section one of the companies.

Group Tasks

Based on the company assigned to your group, answer the following questions:

b. What is the per share par or stated value of the common stock in 2013?

c. What was the average issue price of the common stock for each year?

d. How many shares of stock are outstanding at the end of each year?

e. What is the average cost per share of the treasury stock for 2013?

f. Do the data suggest that your company was profitable in 2013?

g. Can you determine the amount of net income from the information given? What is missing?

h. What is the total stockholders' equity of your company for each year?

Class Discussion

i. Have each group select a representative to present the information about its company. Compare the share issue price and the par or stated value of the companies.

j. Compare the average issue price to the current market price for each of the companies. Speculate about what might cause the difference.

ATC 11-3 Real-World Case *Which stock is most valuable?*

Listed here are data for five companies. These data are for the companies' 2013 fiscal years. The market price per share is the closing price of the companies' stock as of March 7, 2014. Except for market price per share, all amounts are in thousands. The shares outstanding number is the weighted-average number of shares the company used to compute basic earnings per share.

Company	Net Earnings	Stockholders' Equity	Shares Outstanding	Market Price per Share
Berkshire Hathaway	$19,476,000	$224,485,000	1,644	$183,772.00
Carmax	434,284	3,019,167	228,095	48.60
Chevron	21,423,000	150,427,000	1,916,000	115.08
eBay	2,856,000	23,647,000	1,295,000	59.06
Pfizer	22,003,000	76,620,000	6,813,000	32.43

Required

a. Compute the earnings per share (EPS) for each company.

b. Compute the P/E ratio for each company.

c. Using the P/E ratios, rank the companies' stock in the order that the stock market appears to value the companies, from most valuable to least valuable. Identify reasons the ranking based on P/E ratios may not represent the market's optimism about one or two companies.

d. Compute the book value per share for each company.

e. Compare each company's book value per share to its market price per share. Based on the data, rank the companies from most valuable to least valuable. (The higher the ratio of market value to book value, the greater the value the stock market appears to be assigning to a company's stock.)

ATC 11-4 Business Applications Case *Performing ratio analysis using real-world data*

Ford Motor Company is one of the world's largest automobile manufacturing companies. The following data were taken from the company's 2013 annual report:

	Fiscal Years Ending	
	December 31, 2013	December 31, 2012
Net earnings (in millions)	$7,155	$5,665
Earnings per share	$ 1.82	$ 1.48
The following data were taken from public stock-price quotes:		
Stock price per share on March 3, 2014 (Two months after the end of Ford's 2013 fiscal year.)		$15.20
Stock price per share on March 1, 2013 (Two months after the end of Ford's 2012 fiscal year.)		$12.61

Required

a. Compute Ford's price-earnings ratio for March 3, 2014, and March 1, 2013.

b. Did the financial markets appear to be more optimistic about Ford's future performance on March 3, 2014, or March 3, 2013?

c. Based on the information provided, estimate approximately how many shares of stock Ford had outstanding as of December 31, 2013.

ATC 11-5 Business Applications Case *Performing ratio analysis using real-world data*

Google, Inc., operates the world's largest Internet search engine. International Business Machines Corporation (IBM) is one of the world's largest computer hardware and software companies. The following data were taken from the companies' December 31, 2013, annual reports:

	Google, Inc.	IBM
Net earnings (in millions)	$ 12,920	$16,483
Earnings per share	$ 38.82	$ 15.06
The following data were taken from public stock-price quotes:		
Stock price per share on March 3, 2014 (Two months after the end of their 2013 fiscal years.)	$1,202.69	$184.26

Required

a. Compute the price-earnings ratios for each company as of March 3, 2014.

b. Which company's future performance did the financial markets appear to be more optimistic about as of March 3, 2014?

c. Provide some reasons why the market may view one company's future more optimistically than the other.

ATC 11-6 Writing Assignment *Comparison of organizational forms*

Jim Baku and Scott Hanson are thinking about opening a new restaurant. Baku has extensive marketing experience but does not know that much about food preparation. However, Hanson is an excellent chef. Both will work in the business, but Baku will provide most of the funds necessary to start the business. At this time, they cannot decide whether to operate the business as a partnership or a corporation.

Required

Prepare a written memo to Baku and Hanson describing the advantages and disadvantages of each organizational form. Also, from the limited information provided, recommend the organizational form you think they should use.

ATC 11-7 Ethical Dilemma *Bad news versus very bad news*

Louise Stinson, the chief financial officer of Bostonian Corporation, was on her way to the president's office. She was carrying the latest round of bad news. There would be no executive bonuses this year. Corporate profits were down. Indeed, if the latest projections held true, the company would report a small loss on the year-end income statement. Executive bonuses were tied to corporate profits. The executive compensation plan provided for 10 percent of net earnings to be set aside for bonuses. No profits meant no bonuses. While things looked bleak, Stinson had a plan that might help soften the blow.

After informing the company president of the earnings forecast, Stinson made the following suggestion: Since the company was going to report a loss anyway, why not report a big loss? She reasoned that the directors and stockholders would not be much more angry if the company reported a large loss than if it reported a small one. There were several questionable assets that could be written down in the current year. This would increase the current year's loss but would reduce expenses in subsequent accounting periods. For example, the company was carrying damaged inventory that was estimated to have a value of $2,500,000. If this estimate were revised to $500,000, the company would have to recognize a $2,000,000 loss in the current year. However, next year when the goods were sold, the expense for cost of goods sold would be $2,000,000 less and profits would be higher by that amount. Although the directors would be angry this year, they would certainly be happy next year. The strategy would also have the benefit of adding $200,000 to next year's executive bonus pool ($2,000,000 × 0.10). Furthermore, it could not hurt this year's bonus pool because there would be no pool this year since the company is going to report a loss.

Some of the other items that Stinson is considering include (1) converting from straight-line to accelerated depreciation, (2) increasing the percentage of receivables estimated to be uncollectible in the current year and lowering the percentage in the following year, and (3) raising the percentage of estimated warranty claims in the current period and lowering it in the following period. Finally, Stinson notes that two of the company's department stores have been experiencing losses. The company could sell these stores this year and thereby improve earnings next year. Stinson admits that the sale would result in significant losses this year, but she smiles as she thinks of next year's bonus check.

Required

- **a.** Explain how each of the three numbered strategies for increasing the amount of the current year's loss would affect the stockholders' equity section of the balance sheet in the current year. How would the other elements of the balance sheet be affected?
- **b.** If Stinson's strategy were effectively implemented, how would it affect the stockholders' equity in subsequent accounting periods?
- **c.** Comment on the ethical implications of running the company for the sake of management (maximization of bonuses) versus the maximization of return to stockholders.
- **d.** Formulate a bonus plan that will motivate managers to maximize the value of the firm instead of motivating them to manipulate the reporting process.
- **e.** How would Stinson's strategy of overstating the amount of the reported loss in the current year affect the company's current P/E ratio?

ATC 11-8 Research Assignment *Analyzing Starbucks' equity structure*

Using either Starbucks Corporation's most current Form 10-K or the company's annual report, answer the questions below. To obtain the Form 10-K use either the EDGAR system, following the instructions in Appendix A, or the company's website. The company's annual report is available on its website.

Required

a. What is the *book value* of Starbucks' stockholders' equity that is shown on the company's balance sheet? What is its book value per share?

b. What is the par value of Starbucks' common stock?

c. Does Starbucks have any treasury stock? If so, how many shares of treasury stock does the company hold?

d. Why does the stock of a company such as Starbucks have a market value that is higher than its book value?

ATC 11-9 Spreadsheet Analysis *Using Excel*

Annette's Accessories had the following stock issued and outstanding at January 1, 2016:

150,000 shares of $1 par common stock
10,000 shares of $50 par, 8%, cumulative preferred stock

On March 5, 2016, Annette's declared a $100,000 cash dividend to be paid March 31 to shareholders of record on March 21.

Required

Set up a spreadsheet to calculate the total amount of dividends to be paid to preferred and common shareholders under the following alternative situations:

a. No dividends are in arrears for preferred shareholders.

b. One year's worth of dividends is in arrears for preferred shareholders.

c. Two years' worth of dividends is in arrears for preferred shareholders.

d. Instead of a $100,000 dividend, Annette's paid a $70,000 dividend and one year of dividends was in arrears.

Spreadsheet Tips

The following spreadsheet provides one method of setting up formulas for all possible alternatives. The spreadsheet also reflects the results of Requirement *a.*

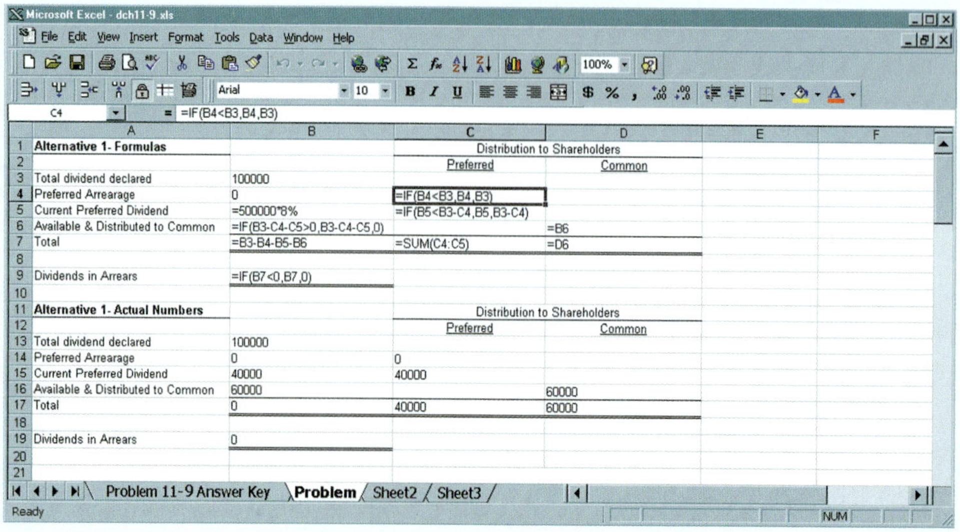
Microsoft Excel - dch11-9.xls

C4 = =IF(B4<B3,B4,B3)

	A	B	C	D
1	**Alternative 1- Formulas**		Distribution to Shareholders	
2			Preferred	Common
3	Total dividend declared	100000		
4	Preferred Arrearage	0	=IF(B4<B3,B4,B3)	
5	Current Preferred Dividend	=500000*8%	=IF(B5<B3-C4,B5,B3-C4)	
6	Available & Distributed to Common	=IF(B3-C4-C5>0,B3-C4-C5,0)		=B6
7	Total	=B3-B4-B5-B6	=SUM(C4:C5)	=D6
8				
9	Dividends in Arrears	=IF(B7<0,B7,0)		
10				
11	**Alternative 1- Actual Numbers**		Distribution to Shareholders	
12			Preferred	Common
13	Total dividend declared	100000		
14	Preferred Arrearage	0	0	
15	Current Preferred Dividend	40000	40000	
16	Available & Distributed to Common	60000		60000
17	Total	0	40000	60000
18				
19	Dividends in Arrears	0		
20				
21				

Problem 11-9 Answer Key | **Problem** | Sheet2 | Sheet3

Ready

Notice the use of the IF function. The IF function looks like =IF(condition, true, false). To use the IF function, first describe a certain condition to Excel. Next indicate the desired result if that condition is found to be true. Finally, indicate the desired result if that condition is found to be false. Notice in cell C4 of the spreadsheet (dividends in arrears distributed to preferred shareholders) that the condition provided is B4<B3, which is asking whether the dividends in arrears are less than the total dividend. If this condition is true, the formula indicates to display B4, which is the amount of the dividends in arrears. If the condition is false, the formula indicates that B3 should be displayed, which is the total amount of the dividend.

The IF function can also be used to determine the amount of the current dividend distributed to preferred shareholders, the amount available for common shareholders, and the dividends in arrears after the dividend.

ATC 11-10 Spreadsheet Assignment *Mastering Excel*

Required

Complete Requirement *a* of Problem 11-22A using an Excel spreadsheet.

COMPREHENSIVE PROBLEM

The trial balance of Pacilio Security Services Inc. as of January 1, 2021, had the following normal balances:

Cash	$113,718
Petty cash	100
Accounts receivable	39,390
Allowance for doubtful accounts	4,662
Supplies	210
Merchandise inventory (48 @ $300)	14,400
Equipment	9,000
Van	27,000
Building	125,000
Accumulated depreciation	28,075
Land	25,000
Sales tax payable	390
Employee income tax payable	1,000
FICA—Social Security tax payable	840
FICA—Medicare tax payable	210
Warranty payable	918
Unemployment tax payable	945
Notes payable—Building	92,762
Bonds payable	50,000
Discount on bonds payable	800
Common stock	50,000
Retained earnings	124,816

During 2021, Pacilio Security Services experienced the following transactions:

1. Paid the sales tax payable from 2020.
2. Paid the balance of the payroll liabilities due for 2020 (federal income tax, FICA taxes, and unemployment taxes).
3. Issued 5,000 additional shares of the $5 par value common stock for $8 per share and 1,000 shares of $50 stated value, 5 percent cumulative preferred stock for $52 per share.

4. Purchased $500 of supplies on account.
5. Purchased 190 alarm systems at a cost of $310. Cash was paid for the purchase.
6. After numerous attempts to collect from customers, wrote off $3,670 of uncollectible accounts receivable.
7. Sold 210 alarm systems for $600 each plus sales tax of 5 percent. All sales were on account. (Be sure to compute cost of goods sold using the FIFO cost flow method.)
8. Billed $125,000 of monitoring services for the year. Credit card sales amounted to $58,000, and the credit card company charged a 4 percent fee. The remaining $67,000 were sales on account. Sales tax is not charged on this service.
9. Replenished the petty cash fund on June 30. The fund had $10 cash and receipts of $75 for yard mowing and $15 for office supplies expense.
10. Collected the amount due from the credit card company.
11. Paid the sales tax collected on $105,000 of the alarm sales.
12. Collected $198,000 of accounts receivable during the year.
13. Paid installers and other employees a total of $96,000 for salaries for the year. Assume the Social Security tax rate is 6 percent and the Medicare tax rate is 1.5 percent. Federal income taxes withheld amounted to $10,600. No employee exceeded $110,000 in total wages. The net salaries were paid in cash.
14. On October 1, declared a dividend on the preferred stock and a $1 per share dividend on the common stock to be paid to shareholders of record on October 15, payable on November 1, 2021.
15. Paid $1,625 in warranty repairs during the year.
16. On November 1, 2021, paid the dividends that had been previously declared.
17. Paid $18,500 of advertising expense during the year.
18. Paid $6,100 of utilities expense for the year.
19. Paid the payroll liabilities, both the amounts withheld from the salaries plus the employer share of Social Security tax and Medicare tax, on $88,000 of the salaries plus $9,200 of the federal income tax that was withheld.
20. Paid the accounts payable.
21. Paid bond interest and amortized the discount. The bond was issued in 2020 and pays interest at 6 percent.
22. Paid the annual installment of $14,238 on the amortized note. The interest rate for the note is 7 percent.

Adjustments

23. There was $190 of supplies on hand at the end of the year.
24. Recognized the uncollectible accounts expense for the year using the allowance method. Pacilio now estimates that 1 percent of sales on account will not be collected.
25. Recognized depreciation expense on the equipment, van, and building. The equipment, purchased in 2018, has a five-year life and a $2,000 salvage value. The van has a four-year life and a $6,000 salvage value. The building has a 40-year life and a $10,000 salvage value. The company uses straight-line for the equipment and the building. The van is fully depreciated.
26. The alarm systems sold in transaction 7 were covered with a one-year warranty. Pacilio estimated that the warranty cost would be 2 percent of alarm sales.
27. The unemployment tax on the three employees has not been paid. Record the accrued unemployment tax on the salaries for the year. The unemployment tax rate is 4.5 percent and gross wages for all three employees exceeded $7,000.
28. Recognized the employer Social Security and Medicare payroll tax that has not been paid on $8,000 of salaries expense.

Required

a. Record the above transactions in general journal form. Round all amounts to the nearest whole dollar.

b. Post the transactions to the T-accounts.

c. Prepare a trial balance.

d. Prepare an income statement, a balance sheet, and a statement of cash flows.

e. Close the temporary accounts to retained earnings.

f. Post the closing entries to the T-accounts and prepare a post-closing trial balance.

CHAPTER 12

Statement of Cash Flows

LEARNING OBJECTIVES

After you have mastered the material in this chapter, you will be able to:

LO 12-1 Prepare the operating activities section of a statement of cash flows using the indirect method.

LO 12-2 Prepare the operating activities section of a statement of cash flows using the direct method.

LO 12-3 Prepare the investing activities section of a statement of cash flows.

LO 12-4 Prepare the financing activities section of a statement of cash flows.

Video lectures and accompanying self-assessment quizzes are available for all learning objectives through McGraw-Hill Connect® Plus Accounting.

CHAPTER OPENING

To make informed investment and credit decisions, financial statement users need information to help them assess the amounts, timing, and uncertainty of a company's prospective cash flows. This chapter explains more about the items reported on the statement of cash flows and describes a more practical way to prepare the statement than analyzing every entry in the cash account. As previously shown, the statement of cash flows reports how a company obtained and spent cash during an accounting period. Sources of cash are **cash inflows**, and uses are **cash outflows**. Cash receipts (inflows) and payments (outflows) are reported as either operating activities, investing activities, or financing activities.

The Curious Accountant

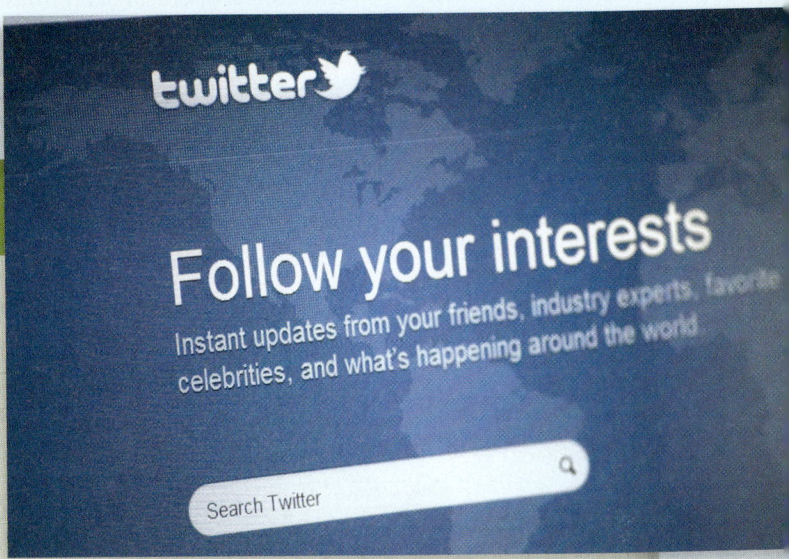

As described in *The Curious Accountant* for Chapter 11, **Twitter, Inc.**, began operations in 2006 and began selling its stock to the public on November 7, 2013. It has lost money every year it has been in existence. In 2013 alone its losses were $645 million, and by December 31, 2013, it had total lifetime losses of approximately $995 million.

How could Twitter lose so much money and still be able to pay its bills? (Answer on page 651.)

AN OVERVIEW OF THE STATEMENT OF CASH FLOWS

The statement of cash flows provides information about cash coming into and going out of a business during an accounting period. Cash flows are classified into one of three categories: operating activities, investing activities, or financing activities. A separate section also displays any significant noncash investing and financing activities. Descriptions of these categories and how they are presented in the statement of cash flows follow.

Operating Activities

Routine cash inflows and outflows resulting from running (operating) a business are reported in the **operating activities** section of the statement of cash flows. Cash flows reported as operating activities include:

1. Cash receipts from revenues, including interest and dividend revenue.
2. Cash payments for expenses, including interest expense. Recall that dividend payments are not expenses. Dividend payments are reported in the financing activities section.

Under generally accepted accounting principles, the operating activities section of the statement of cash flows can be presented using either the *direct* or the *indirect* method. The **direct method** explicitly (*directly*) identifies the major *sources* and *uses* of cash. To illustrate, assume that during 2016 New South Company earns revenue on account of $500 and collects $400 cash from customers. Further assume the company incurs $390 of expenses on account and pays $350 cash to settle accounts payable. Exhibit 12.1 shows the operating activities section of the statement of cash flows using the *direct method.*

EXHIBIT 12.1

Operating Activities—Direct Method

Cash Flows from Operating Activities	
Cash receipts from customers	$400
Cash payments for expenses	(350)
Net cash flow from operating activities	$ 50

In contrast, the **indirect method** starts with net income as reported on the income statement, followed by the adjustments necessary to convert the accrual-based net income figure to a cash-basis equivalent. To illustrate, begin with New South Company's income statement based on the above assumptions:

Revenues	$500
Expenses	(390)
Net income	$110

Converting the net income of $110 to the net cash flow from operating activities of $50 requires the following adjustments.

1. New South earned $500 of revenue but collected only $400 in cash. The remaining $100 will be collected in the next accounting period. This $100 *increase in accounts receivable* must be *subtracted* from net income to determine cash flow because it increased net income but did not increase cash.
2. New South incurred $390 of expense but paid only $350 in cash. The remaining $40 will be paid in the next accounting period. This $40 *increase in accounts payable* must be *added* back to net income to determine cash flow because it decreased net income but did not use cash.

EXHIBIT 12.2

Operating Activities—Indirect Method

Cash Flows from Operating Activities	
Net income	$110
Subtract: Increase in accounts receivable	(100)
Add: Increase in accounts payable	40
Net cash flow from operating activities	$ 50

Exhibit 12.2 shows the operating activities section of the statement of cash flows using the *indirect method.*

Compare the direct method presented in Exhibit 12.1 with the indirect method presented in Exhibit 12.2. Both methods report $50 of net cash flow from operating activities. They represent two different approaches to computing the same amount.

Because people typically find the direct method easier to understand, the Financial Accounting Standards Board (FASB) recommends it. Most companies, however, use the indirect method. Why? Back when the FASB adopted a requirement for companies to include a statement of cash flows in their published financial statements, most companies used accounting systems that were compatible with the indirect method. It was therefore easier to prepare the new statement under the indirect method using existing systems than to create new recordkeeping systems compatible with the direct method.

The FASB continues to advocate the direct method and a growing number of companies use it. Since the majority of companies continue to use the indirect method, however, financial statement users should understand both methods.

CHECK YOURSELF 12.1

Hammer, Inc., had a beginning balance of $22,400 in its Accounts Receivable account. During the accounting period, Hammer earned $234,700 of net income. The ending balance in the Accounts Receivable account was $18,200. Based on this information alone, determine the amount of cash flow from operating activities.

Answer

Account Title	Ending	Beginning	Change
Accounts receivable	$18,200	$22,400	$(4,200)

Applicable Rule	Cash Flow from Operating Activities	Amount
	Net Income	$234,700
Rule 1	Add: Decrease in accounts receivable	4,200
	Cash flow from operating activities	$238,900

Investing Activities

For a business, long-term assets are investments. Cash flows related to acquiring or disposing of long-term assets are therefore reported in the **investing activities** section of the statement of cash flows. Cash flows reported as investing activities include:

1. Cash receipts (inflows) from selling property, plant, equipment, or marketable securities as well as collections from credit instruments such as notes or mortgages receivable.
2. Cash payments (outflows) for purchasing property, plant, equipment, or marketable securities as well as for making loans to borrowers.

Financing Activities

Cash flows related to borrowing (short- or long-term) and stockholders' equity are reported in the **financing activities** section of the statement of cash flows. Cash flows reported as financing activities include:

1. Cash receipts (inflows) from borrowing money and issuing stock.
2. Cash payments (outflows) to repay debt, purchase treasury stock, and pay dividends.

The classification of cash flows is based on the type of activity, not the type of account. For example, buying another company's common stock is an investing activity, but issuing a company's own common stock is a financing activity. Receiving dividends from a common stock investment is an operating activity, and paying dividends to a company's own stockholders is a financing activity. Similarly, loaning money is an investing activity, although borrowing it is a financing activity. Focus on the type of activity rather than the type of account when classifying cash flows as operating, investing, or financing activities.

Noncash Investing and Financing Activities

Companies sometimes undertake significant **noncash investing and financing activities** such as acquiring a long-term asset in exchange for common stock. Since these types of transactions do not involve exchanging cash they are not reported in the main body of the statement of cash flows. However, because the FASB requires that all material investing and financing activities be disclosed, whether or not they involve exchanging cash, companies must include with the statement of cash flows a separate schedule of any noncash investing and financing activities.

Reporting Format for the Statement of Cash Flows

Cash flow categories are reported in the following order: (1) operating activities; (2) investing activities; and (3) financing activities. In each category, the difference between the inflows and outflows is presented as a net cash inflow or outflow for the category. These net amounts are combined to determine the net change (increase or decrease) in the company's cash for the period. The net change in cash is combined with the beginning cash balance to determine the ending cash balance. The ending cash balance on the statement of cash flows is the same as the cash balance reported on the balance sheet. The schedule of noncash investing and financing activities is typically presented at the bottom of the statement of cash flows. Exhibit 12.3 outlines this format.

EXHIBIT 12.3 Format for Statement of Cash Flows

WESTERN COMPANY Statement of Cash Flows For the Year Ended December 31, 2016	
Cash flows from operating activities	
Net increase (decrease) from operating activities	XXX
Cash flows from investing activities	
Net increase (decrease) from investing activities	XXX
Cash flows from financing activities	
Net increase (decrease) from financing activities	XXX
Net increase (decrease) in cash	XXX
Plus: Beginning cash balance	XXX
Ending cash balance	XXX
Schedule of Noncash Investing and Financing Activities	
List of significant noncash transactions	XXX

As indicated in Exhibit 12.4, most companies present the statement of cash flows as the last of the four primary financial statements. However, a sizable number of companies present it after the income statement and balance sheet but before the statement of changes in stockholders' equity. Some companies place the statement of cash flows first, before the other three statements.

EXHIBIT 12.4

Placement of Statement of Cash Flows Relative to Other Financial Statements

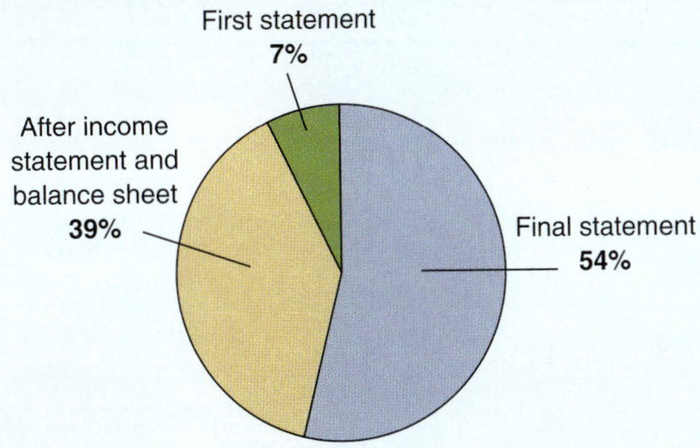

Data Source: AICPA, *Accounting Trends and Techniques.*

PREPARING A STATEMENT OF CASH FLOWS

Most of the data needed to construct a statement of cash flows can be obtained from two successive balance sheets and the intervening income statement. Certain information from the long-term asset records is also usually required. To illustrate, refer to the financial statements for New South Company presented in Exhibit 12.5. Notice that cash decreased from $400 at the end of 2016 to $300 at the end of 2017. The statement of cash flows explains what caused this $100 decrease.

EXHIBIT 12.5 Financial Statements for New South Company

NEW SOUTH COMPANY
Balance Sheets
As of December 31

	2017	2016
Current assets:		
Cash	$ 300	$ 400
Accounts receivable	1,000	1,200
Interest receivable	400	300
Inventory	8,900	8,200
Prepaid insurance	1,100	1,400
Total current assets	11,700	11,500
Long-term assets		
Investment securities	5,100	3,500
Store fixtures	5,400	4,800
Accumulated depreciation	(900)	(1,200)
Land	8,200	6,000
Total long-term assets	17,800	13,100
Total assets	$29,500	$24,600
Current liabilities:		
Accounts payable—inventory purchases	$ 800	$ 1,100
Salaries payable	1,000	900
Other operating expenses payable	1,500	1,300
Interest payable	300	500
Unearned rent revenue	600	1,600
Total current liabilities	4,200	5,400

continued

EXHIBIT 12.5 *Concluded*

NEW SOUTH COMPANY Balance Sheets As of December 31	2017	2016
Long-term liabilities		
Mortgage payable	2,200	0
Bonds payable	1,000	4,000
Total long-term liabilities	3,200	4,000
Stockholders' equity		
Common stock	10,000	8,000
Retained earnings	12,700	7,200
Treasury stock	(600)	0
Total stockholders' equity	22,100	15,200
Total liabilities and stockholders' equity	$29,500	$24,600

NEW SOUTH COMPANY Income Statement For the Year Ended December 31, 2017		
Sales revenue		$ 20,600
Cost of goods sold		(10,500)
Gross margin		10,100
Operating expenses		
Depreciation expense	$(1,000)	
Salaries expense	(2,700)	
Insurance expense	(1,300)	
Other operating expenses	(1,400)	
Total operating expenses		(6,400)
Income from sales business		3,700
Other income—rent revenue		2,400
Operating income		6,100
Nonoperating revenue and expense		
Interest revenue	700	
Interest expense	(400)	
Gain on sale of store fixtures	600	
Total nonoperating items		900
Net income		$ 7,000

Note 1: No investment securities were sold during 2017.

Note 2: During 2017, New South sold store fixtures that had originally cost $1,700. At the time of sale, accumulated depreciation on the fixtures was $1,300.

Note 3: Land was acquired during 2017 by issuing a mortgage note payable. No land sales occurred during 2017.

PREPARING THE OPERATING ACTIVITIES SECTION OF A STATEMENT OF CASH FLOWS USING THE INDIRECT METHOD

LO 12-1

Prepare the operating activities section of a statement of cash flows using the indirect method.

Recall that the indirect approach begins with the amount of net income. Many aspects of accrual accounting, such as recognizing revenues and expenses on account, can cause differences between the amount of net income reported on a company's income statement and the amount of net cash flow it reports from operating activities. Most of the

Answers to The Curious Accountant

First, it should be remembered that GAAP requires earnings and losses be computed on an accrual basis. A company can have negative earnings and still have positive cash flows from operating activities. This was not the case at Twitter. From 2011 through 2013, the company's cash flows from operating activities totaled a negative $97 million. Although this is less than the $853 million of cumulative net losses the company incurred during the same period, negative cash flows do not pay the bills.

In its early years of operations, Twitter, like many new companies, was able to stay in business because of the cash it raised through financing activities. Obviously, a company cannot operate indefinitely without generating cash from operating activities. Individuals and institutions who are willing to buy a company's stock or loan it cash in its early years will disappear if they do not believe the company will eventually begin earning profits and generating positive cash flows from operations. Exhibit 12.6 presents Twitter's statements of cash flows from 2011 through 2013.

EXHIBIT 12.6

TWITTER, INC.
Consolidated Statements of Cash Flows
(in thousands)

	Year Ended December 31		
	2013	**2012**	**2011**
Cash flows from operating activities			
Net loss	$ (645,323)	$ (79,399)	$(128,302)
Adjustments to reconcile net loss to net cash provided by (used in) operating activities:			
Depreciation and amortization	110,894	72,506	24,192
Stock-based compensation expense	600,367	25,741	60,384
Provision for bad debt	1,557	1,844	1,828
Deferred income tax benefit	(8,902)	(1,098)	(2,252)
Non-cash acquisition-related costs	704	1,715	—
Amortization of investment premium and other	3,457	4,102	2,739
Changes in assets and liabilities, net of assets acquired and liabilities assumed from acquisitions:			
Accounts receivable	(112,060)	(73,898)	(33,023)
Prepaid expenses and other assets	(12,045)	(6,691)	(2,597)
Accounts payable	7,957	2,931	(918)
Accrued and other liabilities	54,792	24,312	7,352
Net cash provided by (used in) operating activities	1,398	(27,935)	(70,597)
Cash flows from investing activities			
Purchases of property and equipment, net of proceeds from sales	(75,744)	(50,599)	(11,546)
Purchases of marketable securities	(1,573,489)	(542,638)	(487,595)
Proceeds from maturities of marketable securities	355,270	621,049	178,540
Proceeds from sales of marketable securities	42,816	26,300	19,277
Restricted cash	(10,847)	(3,143)	(4,645)
Business combinations, net of cash acquired and purchases of intangible assets	(44,072)	(1,526)	(18,906)
Net cash provided by (used in) investing activities	(1,306,066)	49,443	(324,875)

continued

EXHIBIT 12.6 *Concluded*

TWITTER, INC.
Consolidated Statements of Cash Flows
(in thousands)

	Year Ended December 31		
	2013	2012	2011
Cash flows from financing activities			
Net proceeds from issuance of common stock upon initial public offering	2,018,579	—	—
Taxes paid related to net share settlement of equity awards	(14,637)	—	—
Repayments of capital lease obligations	(70,445)	(39,436)	(15,103)
Proceeds from issuances of convertible preferred stock, net of issuance costs	—	—	485,006
Proceeds from exercise of stock options and sales of restricted stock to employees at fair value, net of repurchase	8,679	2,312	10,307
Net cash provided by (used in) financing activities	1,942,176	(37,124)	480,210
Net increase (decrease) in cash and cash equivalents	637,508	(15,616)	84,738
Foreign exchange effect on cash and cash equivalents	174	(52)	5
Cash and cash equivalents at beginning of period	203,328	218,996	134,253
Cash and cash equivalents at end of period	$ 841,010	$203,328	$218,996

differences between revenue and expense recognition and cash flows are related to changes in the balances of the noncash current assets and current liabilities.

Indirect Method—Reconciliation Approach

The following section of this chapter examines the relationships between items reported on the income statement and the related assets and liabilities. Begin by reconciling the *noncash* current asset and current liability amounts shown on the balance sheets in Exhibit 12.5. *Do not include Cash in this analysis.* The amount of the change in the cash balance is the result of not only operating activities but also investing and financing activities.

Reconciliation of Accounts Receivable

Use the information in Exhibit 12.5 to prepare the following reconciliation of Accounts Receivable. The beginning and ending balances appear on the balance sheets. The *increase due to revenue recognized on account* is the sales revenue reported on the income statement.

Table 1 Reconciliation of Accounts Receivable

$200 Decrease (Beginning → Ending)	Beginning balance	$ 1,200
	Increase due to revenue recognized on account	20,600
	Decrease due to cash collections from customers	? = (20,800)
	Ending balance	$ 1,000

To balance Accounts Receivable, the *decrease due to cash collections from customers* must be $20,800.[1]

The reconciliation shows that the $200 decrease in the accounts receivable balance occurred because *cash collections from customers* were $200 more than the amount of *revenue recognized on account* ($20,800 versus $20,600). Since the amount of cash collected is more than the amount of revenue recognized, we add $200 to the amount of

[1]This text uses the simplifying assumption that all sales occur on account.

net income to determine net cash flow from operating activities (Reference No. 1 in Exhibit 12.7, p. 656).

Reconciliation of Interest Receivable

The beginning and ending balances appear on the balance sheets in Exhibit 12.5. The *increase due to interest revenue recognized on account* is the interest revenue reported on the income statement.

Table 2 Reconciliation of Interest Receivable

$100 Increase	Beginning balance	$300
	Increase due to interest revenue recognized on account	700
	Decrease due to cash collections of interest receivable	? = (600)
	Ending balance	$400

To balance Interest Receivable, the *decrease due to cash collections of interest receivable* must be $600.

The reconciliation shows that the $100 increase in the interest receivable balance occurred because *cash collections of interest* were $100 less than the *interest revenue recognized on account* ($600 versus $700). Since the amount of cash collected is less than the amount of revenue recognized, we subtract the $100 from the amount of net income to determine net cash flow from operating activities (Reference No. 2 in Exhibit 12.7).

Reconciliation of Inventory and Accounts Payable

To simplify computing the amount of cash paid for inventory purchases, assume that all inventory purchases are made on account. The computation requires two steps. First, Inventory must be analyzed to determine the amount of inventory purchased. Second, Accounts Payable must be analyzed to determine the amount of cash paid to purchase inventory.

Use the financial statement information in Exhibit 12.5 to prepare the following Inventory reconciliation. The beginning and ending balances appear on the balance sheets. The *decrease due to recognizing cost of goods sold* is the cost of goods sold reported on the income statement.

Table 3 Reconciliation of Inventory

$700 Increase	Beginning balance	$ 8,200
	Increase due to inventory purchases	? = 11,200
	Decrease due to recognizing cost of goods sold	(10,500)
	Ending balance	$ 8,900

To balance Inventory, the *increase due to inventory purchases* must be $11,200.

Assuming the inventory was purchased on account, the $11,200 of inventory purchases determined above equals the *increase due to inventory purchases* used in the reconciliation of Accounts Payable below. The beginning and ending balances appear on the balance sheets in Exhibit 12.5.

Table 4 Reconciliation of Accounts Payable*

$300 Decrease	Beginning balance	$ 1,100
	Increase due to inventory purchases	11,200
	Decrease due to cash settlements of accounts payable—inv.	? = (11,500)
	Ending balance	$ 800

*Assume that Accounts Payable is used for purchases of inventory only.

To balance Accounts Payable, the *decrease due to cash settlements of accounts payable—inventory* (cash paid to purchase inventory) must be $11,500.

Since the amount of *cash paid to purchase inventory* is $1,000 more than the amount of *cost of goods sold* recognized on the income statement ($11,500 versus $10,500), we subtract the $1,000 difference from the amount of net income to determine net cash flow from operating activities. In Exhibit 12.7 the $1,000 subtraction is divided between a $700 increase in inventory (Reference No. 3 in Exhibit 12.7) and a $300 decrease in accounts payable (Reference No. 4 in Exhibit 12.7).

Reconciliation of Prepaid Insurance

Use the financial statement information in Exhibit 12.5 to reconcile Prepaid Insurance. The beginning and ending balances appear on the balance sheets. The *decrease due to recognizing insurance expense* is the insurance expense reported on the income statement.

Table 5 Reconciliation of Prepaid Insurance

$300 Decrease	Beginning balance	$ 1,400	
	Increase due to the cash purchase of insurance	?	= 1,000
	Decrease due to recognizing insurance expense	(1,300)	
	Ending balance	$ 1,100	

To balance Prepaid Insurance, the amount of the *increase due to the cash purchase of insurance* must be $1,000.

The reconciliation shows that the $300 decrease in the prepaid insurance balance occurred because *cash paid to purchase insurance* was $300 less than the amount of *insurance expense recognized* ($1,000 versus $1,300). Since the amount of cash paid is less than the amount of expense recognized, we add $300 to the amount of net income to determine the net cash flow from operating activities (Reference No. 5 in Exhibit 12.7).

Reconciliation of Salaries Payable

Use the financial statement information in Exhibit 12.5 to reconcile Salaries Payable. The beginning and ending balances appear on the balance sheets. The *increase due to recognizing salary expense on account* is the salaries expense reported on the income statement.

Table 6 Reconciliation of Salaries Payable

$100 Increase	Beginning balance	$ 900	
	Increase due to recognizing salary expense on account	2,700	
	Decrease due to cash settlements of salaries payable	?	= (2,600)
	Ending balance	$1,000	

To balance Salaries Payable, the amount of the *decrease due to cash settlements of salaries payable* (cash paid for salaries expense) must be $2,600. The reconciliation shows that the $100 increase in the salaries payable balance occurred because the *cash paid for salary expense* is $100 less than the amount of *salary expense recognized on account* ($2,600 versus $2,700). Since the amount of cash paid is less than the amount of expense recognized, we add $100 to the amount of net income to determine the cash flow from operating activities (Reference No. 6 in Exhibit 12.7).

Reconciliation of Other Operating Expenses Payable

Use the financial statement information in Exhibit 12.5 to reconcile Other Operating Expenses Payable. The beginning and ending balances appear on the balance sheets. The *increase due to recognizing other operating expenses on account* is the other operating expenses amount reported on the income statement.

$200 Increase

Table 7 Reconciliation of Other Operating Expenses Payable		
Beginning balance	$1,300	
Increase due to recognizing other operating expenses on account	1,400	
Decrease due to cash settlements of other operating expenses pay.	?	= (1,200)
Ending balance	$1,500	

To balance Other Operating Expenses Payable, the amount of the *decrease due to cash settlements of other operating expenses payable* must be $1,200.

The reconciliation shows that the $200 increase in the other operating expenses payable balance occurred because the *cash paid for other operating expenses* was $200 less than the amount of *other operating expenses recognized on account* ($1,200 versus $1,400). Since the amount of cash paid is less than the amount of expense recognized, we add $200 to the amount of net income to determine the net cash flow from operating activities (Reference No. 7 in Exhibit 12.7).

Reconciliation of Interest Payable

Use the financial statement information in Exhibit 12.5 to reconcile Interest Payable. The beginning and ending balances appear on the balance sheets. The *increase due to recognizing interest expense on account* is the interest expense reported on the income statement.

$200 Decrease

Table 8 Reconciliation of Interest Payable		
Beginning balance	$500	
Increase due to recognizing interest expense on account	400	
Decrease due to cash settlements of interest payable	?	= (600)
Ending balance	$300	

To balance Interest Payable, the amount of the *decrease due to cash settlements of interest payable* (cash paid for interest expense) must be $600.

The reconciliation shows that the $200 decrease in the interest payable balance occurred because the amount of *cash paid for interest expense* is $200 more than the amount of *interest expense recognized on account* ($600 versus $400). Since the amount of cash paid is more than the amount of interest expense recognized, we subtract $200 from the amount of net income to determine the net cash flow from operating activities (Reference No. 8 in Exhibit 12.7).

Reconciliation of Unearned Rent Revenue

Use the financial statement information in Exhibit 12.5 to reconcile Unearned Rent Revenue. The beginning and ending balances appear on the balance sheets. The *decrease due to recognizing other income—rent revenue* is the other income—rent revenue reported on the income statement.

$1,000 Decrease

Table 9 Reconciliation of Unearned Rent Revenue		
Beginning balance	$ 1,600	
Increase due to collecting cash in advance of providing rental services	?	= 1,400
Decrease due to recognizing other income—rent revenue	(2,400)	
Ending balance	$ 600	

To balance Unearned Rent Revenue, the amount of the *increase due to collecting cash in advance of providing rental services* must be $1,400.

The reconciliation shows that the $1,000 decrease in the unearned rent revenue balance occurred because the amount of *cash collected in advance of providing rental services* is $1,000 less than the amount of *rent revenue recognized* ($1,400 versus $2,400). Since the amount of cash collected is less than the amount of revenue recognized, we subtract $1,000 from the amount of net income to determine the net cash flow from operating activities (Reference No. 9 in Exhibit 12.7).

Noncash Expenses

The calculation of accrual-based net income frequently includes noncash expenses such as depreciation expense. Since noncash expenses are deducted in determining net income, they must be added back to the amount of net income when computing net cash flow from operating activities (Reference No. 10 in Exhibit 12.7).

Gains and Losses

When a company retires a long-term asset, the company may receive cash from the sale of the asset being retired. If the asset is sold for more than book value (cost − accumulated depreciation), the gain increases net income; if the asset is sold for less than book value, the loss decreases net income. In either case, the cash inflow is the total amount of cash collected from selling the asset, not the amount of the gain or loss, and this cash inflow is reported in the investing activities section of the statement of cash flows. Since gains increase net income and losses decrease net income, but neither represents the amount of cash received from an asset sale, gains must be subtracted from and losses added back to net income to determine net cash flow from operating activities (Reference No. 11 in Exhibit 12.7).

Indirect Method—Rule-Based Approach

The reconciliation process described in the previous section of this chapter leads to a set of rules that can be used to convert accrual-based revenues and expenses to their cash flow equivalents. These rules are summarized in Exhibit 12.8.

Although the rule-based approach offers less insight, it is easy to apply. To illustrate, return to the financial statement data in Exhibit 12.5. The *noncash* current assets and current liabilities reported on the balance sheets are summarized in Exhibit 12.9 for your convenience. The amount of the change in each balance is shown in the *Change* column.

Refer to the income statement to identify the amounts of net income, noncash expenses, gains, and losses. The income statement for New South Company in Exhibit 12.5 includes three relevant figures: net income of $7,000; depreciation expense of $1,000; and a $600 gain on the sale of store fixtures. Applying the rules in Exhibit 12.8 produces

EXHIBIT 12.7

Cash Flows from Operating Activities—Indirect Method

Reference No.	Cash Flows from Operating Activities	
	Net income	$7,000
	Adjustments to reconcile net income to net cash flow from operating activities:	
1	Decrease in accounts receivable	200
2	Increase in interest receivable	(100)
3	Increase in inventory	(700)
4	Decrease in accounts payable for inventory purchases	(300)
5	Decrease in prepaid insurance	300
6	Increase in salaries payable	100
7	Increase in other operating expenses payable	200
8	Decrease in interest payable	(200)
9	Decrease in unearned rent revenue	(1,000)
10	Depreciation expense	1,000
11	Gain on sale of store fixtures	(600)
	Net cash flow from operating activities	$5,900

the operating activities section of the statement of cash flows shown in Exhibit 12.10. The applicable rule for each item is referenced in the first column of the exhibit.

The operating activities section of the statements of cash flows shown in Exhibits 12.10 and 12.7 are identical. The rule-based approach is an alternative way to prepare this section when using the indirect method.

EXHIBIT 12.8

Cash Flows from Operating Activities—Indirect Method

	Net income	XXX
Rule 1	Add decreases and subtract increases in noncash current assets.	XXX
Rule 2	Add increases and subtract decreases in noncash current liabilities.	XXX
Rule 3	Add noncash expenses (e.g., depreciation).	XXX
Rule 4	Add losses and subtract gains.	XXX
	Net cash flow from operating activities	XXX

EXHIBIT 12.9

Noncash Current Assets and Current Liabilities

Account Title	2017	2016	Change
Accounts receivable	$1,000	$1,200	$ (200)
Interest receivable	400	300	100
Inventory	8,900	8,200	700
Prepaid insurance	1,100	1,400	(300)
Accounts payable—inventory purchases	800	1,100	(300)
Salaries payable	1,000	900	100
Other operating expenses payable	1,500	1,300	200
Interest payable	300	500	(200)
Unearned rent revenue	600	1,600	(1,000)

EXHIBIT 12.10 Cash Flows from Operating Activities—Indirect Method, Operating Activities

NEW SOUTH COMPANY
Statement of Cash Flows
For the Year Ended December 31, 2017

Applicable Rule	Cash Flows from Operating Activities	
	Net income	$ 7,000
	Adjustments to reconcile net income to net cash flow from operating activities:	
Rule 1	Decrease in accounts receivable	200
Rule 1	Increase in interest receivable	(100)
Rule 1	Increase in inventory	(700)
Rule 2	Decrease in accounts payable for inventory purchases	(300)
Rule 1	Decrease in prepaid insurance	300
Rule 2	Increase in salaries payable	100
Rule 2	Increase in other operating expenses payable	200
Rule 2	Decrease in interest payable	(200)
Rule 2	Decrease in unearned rent revenue	(1,000)
Rule 3	Depreciation expense	1,000
Rule 4	Gain on sale of store fixtures	(600)
	Net cash flow from operating activities	$ 5,900

CHECK YOURSELF 12.2

Q Magazine, Inc., reported $369,000 of net income for the month. At the beginning of the month, its Unearned Revenue account had a balance of $78,000. At the end of the month, the account had a balance of $67,000. Based on this information alone, determine the amount of net cash flow from operating activities.

Answer

Account Title	Ending	Beginning	Change
Unearned revenue	$67,000	$78,000	$(11,000)

Applicable Rule	Cash Flows from Operating Activities	Amount
	Net income	$369,000
Rule 2	Deduct: Decrease in unearned revenue	(11,000)
	Net cash flow from operating activities	$358,000

CHECK YOURSELF 12.3

The following account balances were drawn from the accounting records of Loeb, Inc.

Account Title	Ending Balance	Beginning Balance
Prepaid rent	$3,000	$4,200
Interest payable	2,650	2,900

Loeb reported $7,400 of net income during the accounting period. Based on this information alone, determine the amount of net cash flow from operating activities.

Answer Based on Rule 1, the $1,200 decrease ($4,200 − $3,000) in Prepaid Rent (current asset) must be added to net income to determine the amount of net cash flow from operating activities. Rule 2 requires that the $250 decrease ($2,900 − $2,650) in interest Payable (current liability) must be deducted from net income. Accordingly, the cash flow from operating activities is $8,350 ($7,400 + $1,200 − $250). Note that paying interest is defined as an operating activity and should not be confused with dividend payments, which are classified as financing activities.

CHECK YOURSELF 12.4

Arley Company's income statement reported net income (all amounts are in millions) of $326 for the year. The income statement included depreciation expense of $45 and a net loss on the sale of long-term assets of $22. Based on this information alone, determine the net cash flow from operating activities.

Answer Based on Rule 3 and Rule 4, both the depreciation expense and the loss would have to be added to net income to determine net cash flow from operating activities. Net cash flow from operating activities would be $393 million ($326 + $45 + $22).

PREPARING THE OPERATING ACTIVITIES SECTION OF A STATEMENT OF CASH FLOWS USING THE DIRECT METHOD

LO 12-2

Prepare the operating activities section of a statement of cash flows using the direct method.

The reconciliation tables developed earlier to determine net cash flow from operating activities under the *indirect method* also disclose the information needed to present the amount of net cash flow from operating activities under the *direct method.* Remember that the amount of net cash flow from operating activities is the same whether it is presented using the indirect or the direct method.

The direct method shows the specific sources and uses of cash that are associated with operating activities. It does not show adjustments to net income. To illustrate, examine Exhibit 12.11. The information in the reference column identifies the reconciliation table from which the cash flow amounts were drawn. The page number indicates where the reconciliation table is located in this chapter.

Table 3 is not included in Exhibit 12.11 because it does not directly involve a cash flow. Also, noncash expenses, gains, and losses are not used in the determination of net cash flow from operating activities when using the direct method.

EXHIBIT 12.11

Cash Flows from Operating Activities—Direct Method

Reference	Cash Flows from Operating Activities	
Table 1, page 652	Inflow from customers	$ 20,800
Table 2, page 653	Inflow from interest revenue	600
Table 4, page 653	Outflow for inventory purchases	(11,500)
Table 5, page 654	Outflow to purchase insurance	(1,000)
Table 6, page 654	Outflow to pay salary expense	(2,600)
Table 7, page 655	Outflow for other operating expenses	(1,200)
Table 8, page 655	Outflow to pay interest expense	(600)
Table 9, page 655	Inflow from rent revenue	1,400
	Net cash flow from operating activities	$ 5,900

PREPARING THE INVESTING ACTIVITIES SECTION OF A STATEMENT OF CASH FLOWS

LO 12-3

Prepare the investing activities section of a statement of cash flows.

The direct and indirect methods discussed above pertain only to the presentation of operating activities. The *investing activities* section of the statement of cash flows is the same regardless of whether the direct or indirect method is used for operating activities. The information necessary to identify cash inflows and outflows from investing activities is obtained by reconciling changes in a company's long-term assets. In general:

- Increases in long-term asset balances suggest cash outflows to purchase assets.
- Decreases in long-term asset balances suggest cash inflows from selling assets.

It is usually necessary to analyze data from the long-term asset records to determine details about long-term asset purchases and sales. In the New South Company example, these details are presented as notes at the bottom of the balance sheets.

To illustrate, return to the financial statements in Exhibit 12.5. New South Company reports the following three long-term assets on its balance sheets. *It is not necessary to reconcile accumulated depreciation since it does not affect cash flow.*

Long-Term Asset	2017	2016
Investment securities	$5,100	$3,500
Store fixtures	5,400	4,800
Land	8,200	6,000

For each long-term asset, reconcile the beginning and ending balances by identifying purchases and sales affecting it. Review the notes for additional relevant information. Begin with investment securities.

Reconciliation of Investment Securities

Reconciliation of Investment Securities	
Beginning balance in investment securities	$3,500
Increase due to purchase of investment securities	? = 1,600
Decrease due to sale of investment securities	0
Ending balance in investment securities	$5,100

Because Note 1 below the balance sheets indicates no investment securities were sold during 2017, the *decrease due to sale of investment securities* is zero. To balance Investment Securities, the *increase due to purchase of investment securities* must be $1,600. In the absence of contrary information, assume New South used cash to purchase the investment securities. This cash outflow is reported in the investing activities section of the statement of cash flows in Exhibit 12.12.

Reconciliation of Store Fixtures

Reconciliation of Store Fixtures	
Beginning balance in store fixtures	$ 4,800
Increase due to purchase of store fixtures	? = 2,300
Decrease due to sale of store fixtures	(1,700)
Ending balance in store fixtures	$ 5,400

Note 2 below the balance sheets indicates that the *decrease due to sale of store fixtures* is $1,700. What is the cash flow from this sale? The book value of these fixtures was $400 ($1,700 cost − $1,300 accumulated depreciation). Since the income statement reports a $600 gain on the sale of store fixtures, the cash collected from the sale was more than the book value of the store fixtures. Compute the amount of cash collected from the sale of store fixtures as follows:

Cash inflow = Book value + Gain = $400 + $600 = $1,000

The $1,000 cash inflow from the sale of store fixtures is reported in the investing activities section of the statement of cash flows in Exhibit 12.12.

To balance Store Fixtures, the *increase due to purchase of store fixtures* must be $2,300. In the absence of contrary information, assume New South used cash to purchase store fixtures. The cash outflow is reported in the investing activities section of the statement of cash flows in Exhibit 12.12.

Reconciliation of Land

Reconciliation of Land	
Beginning balance in land	$6,000
Increase due to purchase of land	? = 2,200
Decrease due to sale of land	0
Ending balance in land	$8,200

Because Note 3 below the balance sheets indicates no land was sold during 2017, the *decrease due to sale of land* is zero. To balance Land, the *increase due to purchase of land* must be $2,200. Since the land was acquired by issuing a mortgage note payable, New South did not use cash for the purchase. This type of transaction is reported in the *noncash investing and financing activities* section of the statement of cash flows, discussed in more detail later in the chapter. The cash inflows and outflows from investing activities are summarized in Exhibit 12.12.

EXHIBIT 12.12

Cash Flows from Investing Activities

Cash Flows from Investing Activities	
Cash outflow to purchase investment securities	$(1,600)
Cash inflow from the sale of store fixtures	1,000
Cash outflow to purchase store fixtures	(2,300)
Net cash outflow from investing activities	$(2,900)

CHECK YOURSELF 12.5

On January 1, 2016, Wyatt Company had an Equipment balance of $124,000. During 2016, Wyatt purchased equipment that cost $50,000. The balance in Equipment on December 31, 2016, was $90,000. The 2016 income statement included a $7,000 loss from the sale of equipment. On the date of sale, accumulated depreciation on the equipment sold was $49,000.

Required

a. Determine the cost of the equipment sold during 2016.

b. Determine the amount of cash flow from the sale of equipment that should be reported in the investing activities section of the 2016 statement of cash flows.

Solution

a.

Reconciliation of Equipment		
Beginning balance	$124,000	
Increase due to the purchase of equipment	50,000	
Decrease due to sale of equipment	?	= (84,000)
Ending balance	$ 90,000	

To balance Equipment, the *decrease due to sale of equipment* must be $84,000.

b. The book value of the equipment sold was $35,000 ($84,000 − $49,000 accumulated depreciation). Since Wyatt recognized a loss on the equipment sale, the amount of cash collected from the sale was less than the book value of the equipment. The cash collected from the sale of the equipment was $28,000 ($35,000 book value − $7,000 loss on sale).

PREPARING THE FINANCING ACTIVITIES SECTION OF A STATEMENT OF CASH FLOWS

LO 12-4

Prepare the financing activities section of a statement of cash flows.

Because the differences between the direct and the indirect methods of presenting the statement of cash flows pertain only to operating activities, the *financing activities* section is the same under either approach. The information necessary to identify cash inflows and outflows from financing activities is obtained by reconciling changes in short-term notes payable, long-term liabilities, and stockholders' equity. In general,

- Increases in short-term notes payable or long-term debt balances suggest cash inflows occurred from issuing debt instruments (notes or bonds).
- Decreases in short-term notes payable or long-term debt balances suggest cash outflows occurred for payment of debt (notes or bonds).
- Increases in contributed capital (common stock, preferred stock, or paid-in capital) suggest cash inflows occurred from issuing equity instruments.
- Increases or decreases in treasury stock suggest cash outflows or inflows occurred to purchase or sell a company's own stock.
- Decreases in retained earnings from cash dividends suggest cash outflows occurred to pay dividends.

To illustrate, return to the financial statements of the New South Company in Exhibit 12.5. The following long-term liability and stockholders' equity balances are reported on the New South balance sheets:

Account Title	2017	2016
Mortgage payable	$ 2,200	$ 0
Bonds payable	1,000	4,000
Common stock	10,000	8,000
Retained earnings	12,700	7,200
Treasury stock	600	0

For each account, reconcile the beginning and ending balances by identifying the increases and decreases affecting it. Review the notes for additional relevant information. Begin with the mortgage payable liability.

Reconciliation of Mortgage Payable

Reconciliation of Mortgage Payable		
Beginning balance in mortgage payable	$ 0	
Increase due to issuing mortgage payable	?	= 2,200
Decrease due to payment of mortgage payable	0	
Ending balance in mortgage payable	$2,200	

As previously discussed, Note 3 indicates a mortgage note payable was issued to acquire land. The *increase due to issuing mortgage payable* is $2,200. Since New South received land, not cash, by issuing the mortgage, the transaction is reported in the noncash investing and financing activities section of the statement of cash flows.

Reconciliation of Bonds Payable

Bonds Payable		
Beginning balance in bonds payable	$4,000	
Increase due to issuing bonds payable	0	
Decrease due to payment of bonds payable	?	= (3,000)
Ending balance in bonds payable	$1,000	

Since there is no indication that New South issued bonds during 2017, assume the *increase due to issuing bonds payable* is zero. To balance Bonds Payable, the *decrease due to payment of bonds payable* must be $3,000. The cash outflow is reported in the financing activities section in Exhibit 12.13.

Reconciliation of Common Stock

Reconciliation of Common Stock		
Beginning balance in common stock	$ 8,000	
Increase due to issuing common stock	?	= 2,000
Ending balance in common stock	$10,000	

To balance Common Stock, the *increase due to issuing common stock* has to be $2,000. The cash inflow is reported in the financing activities section in Exhibit 12.13.

Reconciliation of Retained Earnings

Reconciliation of Retained Earnings		
Beginning balance in retained earnings	$ 7,200	
Increase due to net income	7,000	
Decrease due to payment of dividends	?	= (1,500)
Ending balance in retained earnings	$12,700	

The *increase due to net income* comes from the income statement. To balance Retained Earnings, the decrease due to payment of dividends must be $1,500. In the absence of information to the contrary, assume the decrease is due to the cash payment of dividends. The cash outflow for payment of dividends is reported in the financing activities section of the statement of cash flows in Exhibit 12.13.

Reconciliation of Treasury Stock

Reconciliation of Treasury Stock		
Beginning balance in treasury stock	$ 0	
Increase due to purchasing treasury stock	?	= 600
Decrease due to reissuing treasury stock	0	
Ending balance in treasury stock	$600	

Since there is no indication that New South reissued treasury stock during 2017, the *decrease due to reissuing treasury stock* is zero. To balance Treasury Stock, the increase due to purchasing treasury stock must be $600. The cash outflow is reported in the financing activities section in Exhibit 12.13.

Exhibits 12.14 and 12.15 illustrate the complete statement of cash flows for New South Company under the two alternative methods. Exhibit 12.14 presents operating activities using the indirect method. Exhibit 12.15 presents operating activities using the direct method. The investing and financing activities do not differ between methods. Under either method the combined effects of operating, investing, and financing activities result in a net decrease in cash of $100 for 2017. This $100 decrease is necessarily consistent with the difference between the December 31, 2017, and the December 31, 2016, cash balances shown in the balance sheets in Exhibit 12.5.

EXHIBIT 12.13

Cash Flows from Financing Activities

Cash Flows from Financing Activities	
Cash outflow to reduce bonds payable	$(3,000)
Cash inflow from issuing common stock	2,000
Cash outflow to pay dividends	(1,500)
Cash outflow to purchase treasury stock	(600)
Net cash outflow from financing activities	$(3,100)

EXHIBIT 12.14 Statement of Cash Flows—Indirect Method

NEW SOUTH COMPANY
Statement of Cash Flows
For the Year Ended December 31, 2017

Cash Flows from Operating Activities		
Net income	$ 7,000	
Adjustments to reconcile net income to net cash flow from operating activities:		
Decrease in accounts receivable	200	
Increase in interest receivable	(100)	
Increase in inventory	(700)	
Decrease in accounts payable for inventory purchases	(300)	
Decrease in prepaid insurance	300	
Increase in salaries payable	100	
Increase in other operating expenses payable	200	
Decrease in interest payable	(200)	
Decrease in unearned rent revenue	(1,000)	
Depreciation expense	1,000	
Gain on sale of store fixtures	(600)	
Net cash flow from operating activities		$5,900
Cash Flows from Investing Activities		
Cash outflow to purchase investment securities	(1,600)	
Cash inflow from the sale of store fixtures	1,000	
Cash outflow to purchase store fixtures	(2,300)	
Net cash outflow from investing activities		(2,900)
Cash Flows from Financing Activities		
Cash outflow to reduce bonds payable	(3,000)	
Cash inflow from issuing common stock	2,000	
Cash outflow to pay dividends	(1,500)	
Cash outflow to purchase treasury stock	(600)	
Net cash outflow from financing activities		(3,100)
Net decrease in cash		(100)
Plus: Beginning cash balance		400
Ending cash balance		$ 300
Schedule of Noncash Investing and Financing Activities		
Issue mortgage for land		$2,200

EXHIBIT 12.15 Statement of Cash Flows—Direct Method

NEW SOUTH COMPANY
Statement of Cash Flows
For the Year Ended December 31, 2017

Cash Flows from Operating Activities		
Inflow from customers	$ 20,800	
Inflow from interest revenue	600	
Outflow for inventory purchases	(11,500)	
Outflow to purchase insurance	(1,000)	
Outflow to pay salary expense	(2,600)	
Outflow for other operating expenses	(1,200)	
Outflow to pay interest expense	(600)	
Inflow from rent revenue	1,400	
Net cash flow from operating activities		$5,900

continued

EXHIBIT 12.15 *Concluded*

NEW SOUTH COMPANY
Statement of Cash Flows
For the Year Ended December 31, 2017

Cash Flows from Investing Activities		
Cash outflow to purchase investment securities	(1,600)	
Cash inflow from the sale of store fixtures	1,000	
Cash outflow to purchase store fixtures	(2,300)	
Net cash outflow from investing activities		(2,900)
Cash Flows from Financing Activities		
Cash outflow to reduce bonds payable	(3,000)	
Cash inflow from issuing common stock	2,000	
Cash outflow to pay dividends	(1,500)	
Cash outflow to purchase treasury stock	(600)	
Net cash outflow from financing activities		(3,100)
Net decrease in cash		(100)
Plus: Beginning cash balance		400
Ending cash balance		$ 300
Schedule of Noncash Investing and Financing Activities		
Issue mortgage for land		$2,200

CHECK YOURSELF 12.6

On January 1, 2016, Sterling Company had a balance of $250,000 in Bonds Payable. During 2016, Sterling issued bonds with a $75,000 face value. The bonds were issued at face value. The balance in Bonds Payable on December 31, 2016, was $150,000.

Required

a. Determine the cash outflow for repayment of bond liabilities assuming the bonds were retired at face value.

b. Prepare the financing activities section of the 2016 statement of cash flows.

Solution

a.

Reconciliation of Bonds Payable

Beginning balance	$250,000
Increase due to issuing bonds payable	75,000
Decrease due to payment of bonds payable	?= (175,000)
Ending balance	$150,000

In order to balance Bonds Payable, the *decrease due to payment of bonds payable* must be $175,000. In the absence of information to the contrary, assume cash was used to pay the bond liabilities.

b.

Cash Flows from Financing Activities

Inflow from issuing bond liabilities	$ 75,000
Outflow for reduction of bond liabilities	(175,000)
Net cash outflow from financing activities	$(100,000)

PREPARING THE SCHEDULE OF NONCASH INVESTING AND FINANCING ACTIVITIES

As mentioned earlier, companies may engage in significant noncash investing and financing activities. For example, New South Company acquired land by issuing a \$2,200 mortgage note. Since these types of transactions do not involve exchanging cash, they are not reported in the main body of the statement of cash flows. However, the Financial Accounting Standards Board (FASB) requires disclosure of all material investing and financing activities whether or not they involve exchanging cash. Companies must therefore include with the statement of cash flows a separate schedule that reports noncash investing and financing activities. See the *Schedule of Noncash Investing and Financing Activities* at the bottom of Exhibits 12.14 and 12.15 for an example.

REALITY BYTES

How did Johnson & Johnson, Inc. **(J&J)**, acquire \$13.3 billion of assets in 2012 *without* spending cash? Oddly enough, the answer can be found on its statement of cash flows.

The supplemental "noncash transactions" information included at the bottom of J&J's statement of cash flows reveals that it acquired the assets by exchanging common stock directly for assets. A direct exchange of common stock for assets was responsible for \$13.3 billion of the \$17.8 billion purchase price of a company called Synthes, Inc. The remaining \$4.5 billion was paid with cash.

Had J&J issued \$13.3 billion of common stock and then used this cash to purchase \$13.3 billion of assets, it would have reported two separate cash events in the body of its statement of cash flows. A cash inflow would have been reported in the financing activities section for the issuance of the stock, and a cash outflow would have been reported in the investing activities section for the purchase of the assets. Acquiring large amounts of assets is considered important, even if there is no immediate exchange of cash, so generally accepted accounting principles require such events to be reported with the statement of cash flows or disclosed in the notes.

THE FINANCIAL ANALYST

Why are financial analysts interested in the statement of cash flows? Understanding the cash flows of a business is essential because cash is used to pay the bills. A company, especially one experiencing rapid growth, can be short of cash in spite of earning substantial net income. To illustrate, assume you start a computer sales business. You borrow \$2,000 and spend the money to purchase two computers for \$1,000 each. You sell one of the computers on account for \$1,500. If your loan required a payment at this time, you could not make it. Even though you have net income of \$500 (\$1,500 sales − \$1,000 cost of goods sold), you have no cash until you collect the \$1,500 account receivable. A business cannot survive without managing cash flow carefully. It is little wonder that financial analysts are keenly interested in cash flow.

Real-World Data

The statement of cash flows frequently provides a picture of business activity that otherwise would be lost in the complexities of accrual accounting. For example, as *The Curious Accountant* in Chapter 10 explained, even though Panasonic Corporation reported a loss of approximately $7.6 billion in 2013 on its income statement, its net cash flow from operating activities was a positive $3.3 billion.

Investors consider cash flow information so important they are willing to pay for it. Even though the FASB *prohibits* companies from disclosing *cash flow per share* in audited financial statements, one prominent stock analysis service, ***Value Line Investment Survey***, sells this information to a significant customer base. Clearly, Value Line's customers value information about cash flows.

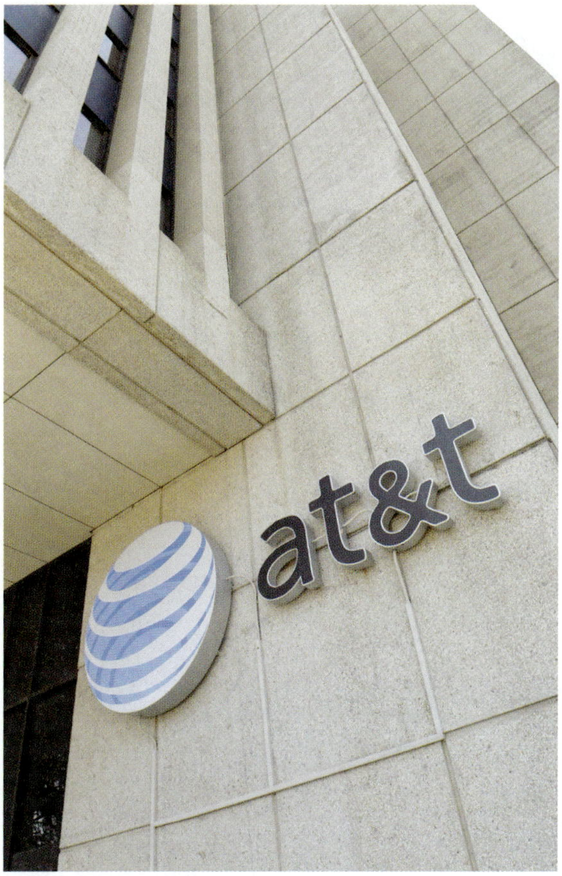

Exhibit 12.16 compares income from operations to cash flows from operating activities for six real-world companies for 2010 through 2013. Several things are apparent from this exhibit. The cash flow from operating activities exceeds income from operations for all but three of the 24 comparisons, and all of these relate to one company, **D. R. Horton**, a large home-building company. Cash flows often exceed income because depreciation, a noncash expense, is usually significant. The most dramatic example of the differences between cash flow and income is **AT&T**. For the four years shown in Exhibit 12.16, AT&T had cumulative net earnings of $50.5 billion, but its cash flows from operations were $146.6 billion, almost three times larger. During this period, AT&T's earnings ranged from a low of $4.2 billion to a high of $20.2 billion, a change of 480 percent, but its cash flow from operating activities ranged from $34.6 billion to $39.2 billion, a change of only 13 percent. The difference between cash flow from operating activities and net income helps explain how some companies can have significant losses over a few years and continue to stay in business and pay their bills.

EXHIBIT 12.16

Net Income versus Cash Flow from Operations (Amounts in millions)

	2013	2012	2011	2010
AT&T				
Net income	$18,553	$ 7,539	$ 4,184	$20,179
Cash flow—operations	34,796	39,176	34,648	34,993
Avon Products				
Net income	(52)	(38)	518	609
Cash flow—operations	540	556	656	689
Blackberry				
Operating income	(628)	1,164	3,411	2,457
Cash flow—operations	2,303	2,912	4,009	3,035
Chevron				
Net income	21,597	26,336	27,008	19,136
Cash flow—operations	35,002	38,812	41,098	31,359
D. R. Horton				
Net income	463	956	72	245
Cash flow—operations	(1,231)	(298)	15	709
McDonald's				
Net income	5,586	5,465	5,503	4,946
Cash flow—operations	7,121	6,966	7,150	6,342

The exhibit also shows that cash flow from operating activities can be more stable than operating income. Results for Avon Products demonstrate this clearly. Avon reported a loss in two of the four years presented. However, operating cash flows were not only positive in every year, but they were never lower than $539 million.

What could explain why D. R. Horton had *less* cash flow from operating activities than operating income in 2012 and 2013? The company was experiencing the kind of growth described earlier for your computer business. Its cash outflows were supporting growth in inventory. After the depressed real estate market that began in 2008, home buying began to increase. As a result, home builders had to add inventory, which in their business includes land, to meet the demand. In 2013 alone, D. R. Horton's inventory increased by 50 percent, or $2 billion.

The D. R. Horton situation highlights a potential weakness in the format of the statement of cash flows. Some accountants consider it misleading to classify all increases in long-term assets as *investing activities* and all changes in inventory as affecting cash flow from operating activities. In the case of D. R. Horton, they would argue that the increase in inventory that relates to expanding its business should be classified as an investing activity, just as the cost of a new warehouse is. Although inventory is classified as a current asset and buildings are classified as long-term assets, in reality there is a certain level of inventory a company must permanently maintain to stay in business. The GAAP format of the statement of cash flows penalizes cash flow from operating activities for increases in inventory that are really a permanent investment in assets.

Conversely, the same critics might argue that some purchases of long-term assets are not actually *investments* but merely replacements of old, existing property, plant, and equipment. In other words, the *investing activities* section of the statement of cash flows makes no distinction between expenditures that expand the business and those that simply replace old equipment (sometimes called *capital maintenance* expenditures).

Users of the statement of cash flows must exercise the same care interpreting it as when they use the balance sheet or the income statement. Numbers alone are insufficient. Users must evaluate numbers based on knowledge of the particular business and industry they are analyzing.

Accounting information alone cannot guide a businessperson to a sound decision. Making good business decisions requires an understanding of the business in question, the environmental and economic factors affecting the operation of that business, and the accounting concepts on which the financial statements of that business are based.

<< A Look Back

This chapter examined in detail only one financial statement, the statement of cash flows. The chapter provided a more comprehensive discussion of how accrual accounting relates to cash-based accounting. Effective use of financial statements requires understanding not only accrual and cash-based accounting systems but also how they relate to each other. That relationship is why a statement of cash flows can begin with a reconciliation of net income, an accrual measurement, to net cash flow from operating activities, a cash measurement. Finally, this chapter explained how the conventions for classifying cash flows as operating, investing, or financing activities require analysis and understanding to make informed decisions with the financial information.

A Look Forward >>

Chapter 13, which is available only online, provides expanded coverage of financial statement analysis. Your instructor will provide guidance as to how to access this chapter if he or she decides to cover it. If your journey ends here, we sincerely hope this text provided a meaningful learning experience that will serve you well as you progress through your academic training and, ultimately, your career. Good luck and best wishes.

SELF-STUDY REVIEW PROBLEM

A step-by-step audio-narrated series of slides is available in the Connect library.

The following financial statements pertain to Schlemmer Company.

Balance Sheets As of December 31	2017	2016
Cash	$ 48,400	$ 2,800
Accounts receivable	2,200	1,200
Inventory	5,600	6,000
Equipment	18,000	22,000
Accumulated depreciation—equip.	(13,650)	(17,400)
Land	17,200	10,400
Total assets	$ 77,750	$25,000
Accounts payable (inventory)	$ 5,200	$ 4,200
Long-term debt	5,600	6,400
Common stock	19,400	10,000
Retained earnings	47,550	4,400
Total liabilities and equity	$ 77,750	$25,000

Income Statement For the Year Ended December 31, 2017	
Sales revenue	$67,300
Cost of goods sold	(24,100)
Gross margin	43,200
Depreciation expense	(1,250)
Operating income	41,950
Gain on sale of equipment	2,900
Loss on disposal of land	(100)
Net income	$44,750

Additional Data

1. During 2017 equipment that had originally cost $11,000 was sold. Accumulated depreciation on this equipment was $5,000 at the time of sale.
2. Common stock was issued in exchange for land valued at $9,400 at the time of the exchange.

Required

Using the indirect method, prepare in good form a statement of cash flows for the year ended December 31, 2017.

Solution

SCHLEMMER COMPANY Statement of Cash Flows For the Year Ended December 31, 2017		
Cash Flows from Operating Activities		
Net income	$44,750	
Add:		
Decrease in inventory (1)	400	
Increase in accounts payable (2)	1,000	
Depreciation expense (3)	1,250	
Loss on disposal of land (4)	100	
Subtract:		
Increase in accounts receivable (1)	(1,000)	
Gain on sale of equipment (4)	(2,900)	
Net cash inflow from operating activities		$43,600
Cash Flows from Investing Activities		
Cash inflow from the sale of equipment (5)	8,900	
Cash outflow for the purchase of equipment (5)	(7,000)	
Cash inflow from sale of land (6)	2,500	
Net cash outflow from investing activities		4,400
Cash Flows from Financing Activities		
Cash outflow to repay long-term debt (7)	(800)	
Cash outflow to pay dividends (8)	(1,600)	
Net cash outflow from financing activities		(2,400)
Net Increase in Cash		45,600
Plus: Beginning cash balance		2,800
Ending cash balance		$48,400
Schedule of Noncash Investing and Financing Activities		
Issue of common stock for land (9)		$ 9,400

(1) Add decreases and subtract increases in current asset account balances to net income.

(2) Add increases and subtract decreases in current liability account balances to net income.

(3) Add noncash expenses (depreciation) to net income.

(4) Add losses on the sale of noncurrent assets to net income and subtract gains on the sale of long-term assets from net income.

(5) Information regarding the Equipment account is summarized in the following table.

Equipment Account Information	
Beginning balance in equipment	$ 22,000
Purchases of equipment (cash outflows)	? = 7,000
Sales of equipment (cash inflows)	(11,000)
Ending balance in equipment	$ 18,000

To balance the account, equipment costing $7,000 must have been purchased. In the absence of information to the contrary, we assume cash was used to make the purchase.

Note 1 to the financial statement shows that equipment sold had a book value of $6,000 ($11,000 cost − $5,000 accumulated depreciation). The amount of the cash inflow from this sale is computed as follows:

Cash inflow = Book value + Gain = $6,000 + $2,900 = $8,900

(6) The information regarding the Land account is as follows:

Land Account Information	
Beginning balance in land	$10,400
Purchases of land (issue of common stock)	9,400
Sales of land (cash inflows)	? = (2,600)
Ending balance in land	$17,200

Note 2 indicates that land valued at $9,400 was acquired by issuing common stock. Since there was no cash flow associated with this purchase, the event is shown in the *noncash investing and financing activities* section of the statement of cash flows.

To balance the account, the cost (book value) of land sold had to be $2,600. Since the income statement shows a $100 loss on the sale of land, the cash collected from the sale is computed as follows:

Cash inflow = Book value − Loss = $2,600 − $100 = $2,500

(7) The information regarding the Long-Term Debt account is as follows:

Long-Term Debt Information	
Beginning balance in long-term debt	$6,400
Issue of long-term debt instruments (cash inflow)	0
Payment of long-term debt (cash outflow)	? = (800)
Ending balance in long-term debt	$5,600

There is no information in the financial statements that suggests long-term debt was issued. Therefore, to balance the account, $800 of long-term debt had to be paid off, thereby resulting in a cash outflow.

(8) The information regarding the Retained Earnings account is as follows:

Retained Earnings Information	
Beginning balance in retained earnings	$ 4,400
Net income	44,750
Dividends (cash outflow)	? = (1,600)
Ending balance in retained earnings	$47,550

To balance the account, $1,600 of dividends had to be paid, thereby resulting in a cash outflow.

(9) Note 2 states that common stock was issued to acquire land valued at $9,400. This is a noncash investing and financing activity.

KEY TERMS

Cash inflows 644
Cash outflows 644
Direct method 646
Financing activities 647
Indirect method 646
Investing activities 647
Noncash investing and financing activities 648
Operating activities 646

QUESTIONS

1. What is the purpose of the statement of cash flows?
2. What are the three categories of cash flows reported on the cash flow statement? Discuss each and give an example of an inflow and an outflow for each category.
3. What are noncash investing and financing activities? Provide an example. How are such transactions shown on the statement of cash flows?
4. Albring Company had a beginning balance in accounts receivable of

$12,000 and an ending balance of $14,000. Net income amounted to $110,000. Based on this information alone, determine the amount of net cash flow from operating activities.

5. Forsyth Company had a beginning balance in utilities payable of $3,300 and an ending balance of $5,200. Net income amounted to $87,000. Based on this information alone, determine the amount of net cash flow from operating activities.
6. Clover Company had a beginning balance in unearned revenue of $4,300 and an ending balance of $3,200. Net income amounted to $54,000. Based on this information alone, determine the amount of net cash flow from operating activities.
7. Which of the following activities are financing activities?
   - **(a)** Payment of accounts payable.
   - **(b)** Payment of interest on bonds payable.
   - **(c)** Sale of common stock.
   - **(d)** Sale of preferred stock at a premium.
   - **(e)** Payment of a cash dividend.
8. Does depreciation expense affect net cash flow? Explain.
9. If Best Company sold land that cost $4,200 at a $500 gain, how much cash did it collect from the sale of land?
10. If Best Company sold office equipment that originally cost $7,500 and had $7,200 of accumulated depreciation at a $100 loss, what was the selling price for the office equipment?
11. In which section of the statement of cash flows would the following transactions be reported?
    - **(a)** The amount of the change in the balance of accounts receivable.
    - **(b)** Cash purchase of investment securities.
    - **(c)** Cash purchase of equipment.
    - **(d)** Cash sale of merchandise.
    - **(e)** Cash sale of common stock.
    - **(f)** The amount of net income.
    - **(g)** Cash proceeds from loan.
    - **(h)** Cash payment on bonds payable.
    - **(i)** Cash receipt from sale of old equipment.
    - **(j)** The amount of the change in the balance of accounts payable.
12. What is the difference between preparing the statement of cash flows using the direct method and using the indirect method?
13. Which method (direct or indirect) of presenting the statement of cash flows is more intuitively logical? Why?
14. What is the major advantage of using the indirect method to present the statement of cash flows?
15. What is the advantage of using the direct method to present the statement of cash flows?
16. How would Best Company report the following transactions on the statement of cash flows?
    - **(a)** Purchased new equipment for $46,000 cash.
    - **(b)** Sold old equipment for $8,700 cash. The equipment had a book value of $4,900.
17. Can a company report negative net cash flows from operating activities for the year on the statement of cash flows but still have positive net income on the income statement? Explain.

MULTIPLE-CHOICE QUESTIONS

Multiple-choice questions are available in the Connect library.

EXERCISES—SERIES A

All applicable Exercises in Series A are available with McGraw-Hill's Connect Plus Accounting.

LO 12-1

Exercise 12-1A *Use the indirect method to determine cash flows from operating activities*

An accountant for Southern Manufacturing Companies (SMC) computed the following information by making comparisons between SMC's 2016 and 2017 balance sheets. Further information was determined by examining the company's 2017 income statement.

1. The amount of cash dividends paid to the stockholders.
2. The amount of a decrease in the balance of an Unearned Revenue account.
3. The amount of an increase in the balance of an Inventory account.
4. The amount of an increase in the balance of a Land account.
5. The amount of a decrease in the balance of a Prepaid Rent account.
6. The amount of an increase in the balance of a Treasury Stock account.
7. The amount of an increase in the balance of the Accounts Receivable account.
8. The amount of a loss arising from the sale of land.
9. The amount of an increase in the balance of the Other Operating Expenses Payable account.

10. The amount of a decrease in the balance of the Bonds Payable account.

11. The amount of depreciation expense shown on the income statement.

Required

For each item described above indicate whether the amount should be added to or subtracted from the amount of net income when determining the amount of net cash flow from operating activities using the indirect method. Also identify any items that do not affect net cash flow from operating activities because they are reported as investing or financing activities.

Exercise 12-2A *Use the indirect method to determine cash flows from operating activities*

LO 12-1

Alfonza Incorporated presents its statement of cash flows using the indirect method. The following accounts and corresponding balances were drawn from the company's 2017 and 2016 year-end balance sheets:

Account Title	2017	2016
Accounts receivable	$16,200	$17,800
Accounts payable	7,600	9,100

The 2017 income statement showed net income of $31,600.

Required

a. Prepare the operating activities section of the statement of cash flows.

b. Explain why the change in the balance in accounts receivable was added to or subtracted from the amount of net income when you completed Requirement *a*.

c. Explain why the change in the balance in accounts payable was added to or subtracted from the amount of net income when you completed Requirement *a*.

Exercise 12-3A *Use the indirect method to determine cash flows from operating activities*

LO 12-1

Shim Company presents its statement of cash flows using the indirect method. The following accounts and corresponding balances were drawn from Shim's 2017 and 2016 year-end balance sheets:

Account Title	2017	2016
Accounts receivable	$36,000	$37,200
Prepaid rent	2,400	1,800
Interest receivable	600	400
Accounts payable	9,300	10,400
Salaries payable	4,500	5,200
Unearned revenue	3,600	5,400

The income statement reported a $1,500 gain on the sale of equipment, an $800 loss on the sale of land, and $3,600 of depreciation expense. Net income for the period was $47,300.

Required

Prepare the operating activities section of the statement of cash flows.

Exercise 12-4A *Use the direct method to determine cash flows from operating activities*

LO 12-2

The following accounts and corresponding balances were drawn from Avia Company's 2017 and 2016 year-end balance sheets:

Account Title	2017	2016
Unearned revenue	$7,600	$6,200
Prepaid rent	2,400	3,600

During the year, $46,000 of unearned revenue was recognized as having been earned. Rent expense for 2017 was $18,000.

Required

Based on this information alone, prepare the operating activities section of the statement of cash flows assuming the direct approach is used.

LO 12-2

Exercise 12-5A *Use the direct method to determine cash flows from operating activities*

The following accounts and corresponding balances were drawn from Marinelli Company's 2017 and 2016 year-end balance sheets:

Account Title	2017	2016
Accounts receivable	$35,200	$31,600
Interest receivable	4,200	4,800
Other operating expenses payable	21,000	18,500
Salaries payable	6,500	7,200

The 2017 income statement is shown below:

Income Statement	
Sales	$ 530,000
Salary expense	(214,000)
Other operating expenses	(175,000)
Operating income	141,000
Nonoperating items: Interest revenue	16,500
Net income	$ 157,500

Required

a. Use the direct method to compute the amount of cash inflows from operating activities.

b. Use the direct method to compute the amount of cash outflows from operating activities.

LO 12-1, 12-2

Exercise 12-6A *Direct versus indirect method of determining cash flows from operating activities*

Expert Electronics, Inc. (EEI), recognized $3,800 of sales revenue on account and collected $2,100 of cash from accounts receivable. Further, EEI recognized $900 of operating expenses on account and paid $700 cash as partial settlement of accounts payable.

Required

Based on this information alone:

a. Prepare the operating activities section of the statement of cash flows under the direct method.

b. Prepare the operating activities section of the statement of cash flows under the indirect method.

LO 12-1, 12-2

Exercise 12-7A *The direct versus the indirect method of determining cash flows from operating activities*

The following accounts and corresponding balances were drawn from Jogger Company's 2017 and 2016 year-end balance sheets:

Account Title	2017	2016
Accounts receivable	$57,000	$62,000
Prepaid rent	1,100	1,300
Utilities payable	900	750
Other operating expenses payable	21,300	22,400

The 2017 income statement is shown below:

Income Statement	
Sales	$268,000
Rent expense	(36,000)
Utilities expense	(18,300)
Other operating expenses	(79,100)
Net Income	$134,600

Required

a. Prepare the operating activities section of the statement of cash flows using the direct method.

b. Prepare the operating activities section of the statement of cash flows using the indirect method.

Exercise 12-8A *Determining cash flow from investing activities*

LO 12-3

On January 1, 2016, Shelton Company had a balance of $325,000 in its Land account. During 2016, Shelton sold land that had cost $106,500 for $132,000 cash. The balance in the Land account on December 31, 2016, was $285,000.

Required

a. Determine the cash outflow for the purchase of land during 2016.

b. Prepare the investing activities section of the 2016 statement of cash flows.

Exercise 12-9A *Determining cash flows from investing activities*

LO 12-3

On January 1, 2016, Bacco Company had a balance of $72,350 in its Delivery Equipment account. During 2016, Bacco purchased delivery equipment that cost $22,100. The balance in the Delivery Equipment account on December 31, 2016, was $69,400. The 2016 income statement reported a gain from the sale of equipment for $5,000. On the date of sale, accumulated depreciation on the equipment sold amounted to $22,000.

Required

a. Determine the original cost of the equipment that was sold during 2016.

b. Determine the amount of cash flow from the sale of delivery equipment that should be shown in the investing activities section of the 2016 statement of cash flows.

Exercise 12-10A *Determining cash flows from investing activities*

LO 12-3

The following accounts and corresponding balances were drawn from Delsey Company's 2017 and 2016 year-end balance sheets:

Account Title	2017	2016
Investment securities	$110,000	$116,500
Machinery	486,000	437,000
Land	160,000	100,000

Other information drawn from the accounting records:

1. Delsey incurred a $6,000 loss on the sale of investment securities during 2017.
2. Old machinery with a book value of $8,000 (cost of $36,000 minus accumulated depreciation of $28,000) was sold. The income statement showed a gain on the sale of machinery of $4,500.
3. Delsey did not sell land during the year.

Required

a. Compute the amount of cash flow associated with the sale of investment securities.
b. Compute the amount of cash flow associated with the purchase of machinery.
c. Compute the amount of cash flow associated with the sale of machinery.
d. Compute the amount of cash flow associated with the purchase of land.
e. Prepare the investing activities section of the statement of cash flows.

LO 12-4

Exercise 12-11A *Determining cash flows from financing activities*

On January 1, 2016, DIBA Company had a balance of $450,000 in its Bonds Payable account. During 2016, DIBA issued bonds with a $200,000 face value. There was no premium or discount associated with the bond issue. The balance in the Bonds Payable account on December 31, 2016, was $400,000.

Required

a. Determine the cash outflow for the repayment of bond liabilities assuming that the bonds were retired at face value.
b. Prepare the financing activities section of the 2016 statement of cash flows.

LO 12-4

Exercise 12-12A *Determining cash flows from financing activities*

On January 1, 2016, Hardy Company had a balance of $150,000 in its Common Stock account. During 2016, Hardy paid $20,000 to purchase treasury stock. Treasury stock is accounted for using the cost method. The balance in the Common Stock account on December 31, 2016, was $175,000. Assume that the common stock is no par stock.

Required

a. Determine the cash inflow from the issue of common stock.
b. Prepare the financing activities section of the 2016 statement of cash flows.

LO 12-4

Exercise 12-13A *Determining cash flows from financing activities*

The following accounts and corresponding balances were drawn from Dexter Company's 2017 and 2016 year-end balance sheets:

Account Title	2017	2016
Bonds payable	$350,000	$400,000
Common stock	450,000	420,000

Other information drawn from the accounting records:

1. Dividends paid during the period amounted to $50,000.
2. There were no bond liabilities issued during the period.

Required

a. Compute the amount of cash flow associated with the repayment of bond liabilities.
b. Compute the amount of cash flow associated with the issue of common stock.
c. Prepare the financing activities section of the statement of cash flows.

PROBLEMS—SERIES A

All applicable Problems in Series A are available with McGraw-Hill's Connect Plus Accounting.

Problem 12-14A *The direct versus the indirect method of determining cash flow from operating activities*

LO 12-1, 12-2

CHECK FIGURE
Net Cash Flow from Operating Activities: $105,200

Green Brands, Inc. (GBI), presents its statement of cash flows using the indirect method. The following accounts and corresponding balances were drawn from GBI's 2017 and 2016 year-end balance sheets:

Account Title	2017	2016
Accounts receivable	$48,000	$52,000
Merchandise inventory	78,000	72,000
Prepaid insurance	24,000	32,000
Accounts payable	31,000	28,000
Salaries payable	8,200	7,800
Unearned service revenue	2,400	3,600

The 2017 income statement is shown below:

Income Statement	
Sales	$ 720,000
Cost of goods sold	(398,000)
Gross margin	322,000
Service revenue	6,000
Insurance expense	(36,000)
Salaries expense	(195,000)
Depreciation expense	(12,000)
Operating income	85,000
Gain on sale of equipment	4,500
Net income	$ 89,500

Required

a. Prepare the operating activities section of the statement of cash flows using the direct method.

b. Prepare the operating activities section of the statement of cash flows using the indirect method.

Problem 12-15A *Determining cash flows from investing activities*

LO 12-3

CHECK FIGURES
b. $4,700
c. $10,000

The following information was drawn from the year-end balance sheets of Mass Trading Company:

Account Title	2017	2016
Investment securities	$ 47,200	$ 42,400
Equipment	246,000	218,000
Buildings	646,000	720,000
Land	95,000	72,000

Additional information regarding transactions occurring during 2017:

1. Investment securities that had cost $6,100 were sold. The 2017 income statement contained a loss on the sale of investment securities of $1,400.
2. Equipment with a cost of $38,000 was purchased.

3. The income statement showed a gain on the sale of equipment of $8,000. On the date of sale, accumulated depreciation on the equipment sold amounted to $8,000.
4. A building that had originally cost $210,000 was demolished.
5. Land that had cost $30,000 was sold for $27,000.

Required

a. Determine the amount of cash flow for the purchase of investment securities during 2017.
b. Determine the amount of cash flow from the sale of investment securities during 2017.
c. Determine the cost of the equipment that was sold during 2017.
d. Determine the amount of cash flow from the sale of equipment during 2017.
e. Determine the amount of cash flow for the purchase of buildings during 2017.
f. Determine the amount of cash flow for the purchase of land during 2017.
g. Prepare the investing activities section of the 2017 statement of cash flows.

LO 12-4

CHECK FIGURES

c. $15,000

e. Net Cash Flow from Financing Activities: ($206,000) outflow

Problem 12-16A *Determining cash flows from financing activities*

The following information was drawn from the year-end balance sheets of Fox River, Inc.:

Account Title	2017	2016
Bonds payable	$600,000	$800,000
Common stock	210,000	180,000
Treasury stock	20,000	5,000
Retained earnings	86,000	75,000

Additional information regarding transactions occurring during 2017:

1. Fox River, Inc., issued $100,000 of bonds during 2017. The bonds were issued at face value. All bonds retired were retired at face value.
2. Common stock did not have a par value.
3. Fox River, Inc., uses the cost method to account for treasury stock.
4. The amount of net income shown on the 2017 income statement was $32,000.

Required

a. Determine the amount of cash flow for the retirement of bonds that should appear on the 2017 statement of cash flows.
b. Determine the amount of cash flow from the issue of common stock that should appear on the 2017 statement of cash flows.
c. Determine the amount of cash flow for the purchase of treasury stock that should appear on the 2017 statement of cash flows.
d. Determine the amount of cash flow for the payment of dividends that should appear on the 2017 statement of cash flows.
e. Prepare the financing activities section of the 2017 statement of cash flows.

LO 12-1, 12-3, 12-4

Problem 12-17A *Preparing a statement of cash flows*

The following information can be obtained by examining a company's balance sheet and income statement information:

a. Increases in current asset account balances, other than cash.
b. Decreases in current asset account balances, other than cash.
c. Cash outflows to purchase long-term assets.
d. Decreases in current liability account balances.
e. Cash outflows to repay long-term debt.
f. Gains recognized on the sale of long-term assets.
g. Noncash expenses (e.g., depreciation).
h. Cash outflows to purchase treasury stock.

i. Increases in current liability account balances.
j. Cash inflows from the sale of long-term assets.
k. Cash inflows from the issue of common stock.
l. Cash outflows to pay dividends.
m. Losses incurred from the sale of long-term assets.
n. Cash inflows from the issue of long-term debt.

Required

Construct a table like the one shown below. For each item, indicate whether it would be used in the computation of net cash flows from operating, investing, or financing activities. Also, indicate whether the item would be added or subtracted when determining the net cash flow from operating, investing, or financing activities. Assume the indirect method is used to prepare the operating activities section of the statement of cash flows. The first item has been completed as an example.

Item	Type of Activity	Add or Subtract
a.	Operating	Subtract
b.		

Problem 12-18A *Using financial statements to prepare a statement of cash flows—Indirect method*

LO 12-1, 12-3, 12-4

CHECK FIGURES
Net Cash Flow from Operating Activities: $32,200
Net Increase in Cash: $16,200

The comparative balance sheets and income statements for Gypsy Company follow:

Balance Sheets
As of December 31

	2017	2016
Assets		
Cash	$ 32,500	$16,300
Accounts receivable	4,750	2,800
Inventory	11,200	9,800
Equipment	45,000	52,000
Accumulated depreciation—equipment	(17,800)	(21,800)
Land	28,000	12,000
Total assets	$103,650	$71,100
Liabilities and equity		
Accounts payable (inventory)	$ 3,750	$ 4,900
Long-term debt	5,800	7,800
Common stock	47,000	25,000
Retained earnings	47,100	33,400
Total liabilities and equity	$103,650	$71,100

Income Statement
For the Year Ended December 31, 2017

Sales revenue	$ 61,200
Cost of goods sold	(24,500)
Gross margin	36,700
Depreciation expense	(12,000)
Operating income	24,700
Gain on sale of equipment	1,500
Loss on disposal of land	(100)
Net income	$ 26,100

Additional Data

1. During 2017, the company sold equipment for $21,500; it had originally cost $36,000. Accumulated depreciation on this equipment was $16,000 at the time of the sale. Also, the company purchased equipment for $29,000 cash.
2. The company sold land that had cost $6,000. This land was sold for $5,900, resulting in the recognition of a $100 loss. Also, common stock was issued in exchange for title to land that was valued at $22,000 at the time of exchange.
3. Paid dividends of $12,400.

Required

Prepare a statement of cash flows using the indirect method.

LO 12-1, 12-3, 12-4

eXcel

CHECK FIGURES

Net Cash Flow from Operating Activities: $45,900

Net Decrease in Cash: $42,100

Problem 12-19A *Using financial statements to prepare a statement of cash flows—Indirect method*

The comparative balance sheets and an income statement for Raceway Corporation follow:

Balance Sheets
As of December 31

	2017	2016
Assets		
Cash	$ 6,300	$ 48,400
Accounts receivable	10,200	7,260
Merchandise inventory	45,200	56,000
Prepaid rent	700	2,140
Equipment	140,000	144,000
Accumulated depreciation	(73,400)	(118,000)
Land	116,000	50,000
Total assets	$245,000	$189,800
Liabilities		
Accounts payable (inventory)	$ 37,200	$ 40,000
Salaries payable	12,200	10,600
Stockholders' equity		
Common stock, $50 par value	150,000	120,000
Retained earnings	45,600	19,200
Total liabilities and equity	$245,000	$189,800

Income Statement
For the Year Ended December 31, 2017

Sales	$ 480,000
Cost of goods sold	(264,000)
Gross profit	216,000
Operating expenses	
Depreciation expense	(11,400)
Rent expense	(7,000)
Salaries expense	(95,200)
Other operating expenses	(76,000)
Net income	$ 26,400

Other Information

1. Purchased land for $66,000.
2. Purchased new equipment for $62,000.

3. Sold old equipment that cost $66,000 with accumulated depreciation of $56,000 for $10,000 cash.
4. Issued common stock for $30,000.

Required

Prepare the statement of cash flows for 2017 using the indirect method.

Problem 12-20A *Using transaction data to prepare a statement of cash flows—Direct method*

LO 12-2, 12-3, 12-4

CHECK FIGURE

Net Cash Flow from Operating Activities: $(900)

York Company engaged in the following transactions for the year 2016. The beginning cash balance was $86,000 and the ending cash balance was $59,100.

1. Sales on account were $548,000. The beginning receivables balance was $128,000 and the ending balance was $90,000.
2. Salaries expense for the period was $232,000. The beginning salaries payable balance was $16,000 and the ending balance was $8,000.
3. Other operating expenses for the period were $236,000. The beginning other operating expenses payable balance was $16,000 and the ending balance was $10,000.
4. Recorded $30,000 of depreciation expense. The beginning and ending balances in the Accumulated Depreciation account were $42,000 and $12,000, respectively.
5. The Equipment account had beginning and ending balances of $44,000 and $56,000 respectively. There were no sales of equipment during the period.
6. The beginning and ending balances in the Notes Payable account were $36,000 and $44,000, respectively. There were no payoffs of notes during the period.
7. There was $4,600 of interest expense reported on the income statement. The beginning and ending balances in the Interest Payable account were $8,400 and $7,500, respectively.
8. The beginning and ending Merchandise Inventory account balances were $22,000 and $29,400, respectively. The company sold merchandise with a cost of $83,600 (cost of goods sold for the period was $83,600). The beginning and ending balances in the Accounts Payable account were $8,000 and $6,400, respectively.
9. The beginning and ending balances in the Notes Receivable account were $60,000 and $100,000, respectively. Notes receivable result from long-term loans made to employees. There were no collections from employees during the period.
10. The beginning and ending balances in the Common Stock account were $120,000 and $160,000, respectively. The increase was caused by the issue of common stock for cash.
11. Land had beginning and ending balances of $24,000 and $14,000, respectively. Land that cost $10,000 was sold for $6,000, resulting in a loss of $4,000.
12. The tax expense for the period was $6,600. The Taxes Payable account had a $2,400 beginning balance and an $2,200 ending balance.
13. The Investments account had beginning and ending balances of $20,000 and $60,000, respectively. The company purchased investments for $50,000 cash during the period, and investments that cost $10,000 were sold for $22,000, resulting in a $12,000 gain.

Required

a. Determine the amount of cash flow for each item and indicate whether the item should appear in the operating, investing, or financing activities section of a statement of cash flows. Also identify any items that do not affect the cash flow statement. Assume York Company uses the direct method for showing net cash flow from operating activities.
b. Prepare a statement of cash flows based on the information you developed in Requirement *a*.

Problem 12-21A *Using financial statements to prepare a statement of cash flows—Direct method*

LO 12-2, 12-3, 12-4

The following financial statements were drawn from the records of Matrix Shoes:

CHECK FIGURES

Net Cash Flow from Operating Activities: $56,200

Net Increase in Cash: $80,200

Balance Sheets
As of December 31

	2017	2016
Assets		
Cash	$ 94,300	$ 14,100
Accounts receivable	36,000	40,000
Merchandise inventory	72,000	64,000
Notes receivable	0	16,000
Equipment	98,000	170,000
Accumulated depreciation—equipment	(47,800)	(94,000)
Land	46,000	30,000
Total assets	$298,500	$240,100
Liabilities		
Accounts payable	$ 24,000	$ 26,400
Salaries payable	15,000	10,000
Utilities payable	800	1,400
Interest payable	0	1,000
Notes payable (long-term)	0	24,000
Common stock	150,000	110,000
Retained earnings	108,700	67,300
Total liabilities and equity	$298,500	$240,100

Income Statement
For the Year Ended December 31, 2017

Sales revenue	$ 300,000
Cost of goods sold	(144,000)
Gross margin	156,000
Operating expenses	
Salary expense	(88,000)
Depreciation expense	(9,800)
Utilities expense	(6,400)
Operating income	51,800
Nonoperating items	
Interest expense	(2,400)
Loss on the sale of equipment	(800)
Net income	$ 48,600

Additional Information

1. Sold equipment costing $72,000 with accumulated depreciation of $56,000 for $15,200 cash.
2. Paid a $7,200 cash dividend to owners.

Required

Analyze the data and prepare a statement of cash flows using the direct method.

EXERCISES—SERIES B

LO 12-1

Exercise 12-1B *Use the indirect method to determine cash flows from operating activities*

An accountant for Farve Enterprise Companies (FEC) computed the following information by making comparisons between FEC's 2017 and 2016 balance sheets. Further information was determined by examining the company's 2017 income statement.

1. The amount of an increase in the balance of a Prepaid Rent account.
2. The amount of an increase in the balance of a Treasury Stock account.

3. The amount of a decrease in the balance of the Accounts Receivable account.
4. The amount of a gain arising from the sale of land.
5. The amount of an increase in the balance of the Salaries Payable account.
6. The amount of an increase in the balance of the Bonds Payable account.
7. The amount of depreciation expense shown on the income statement.
8. The amount of cash dividends paid to the stockholders.
9. The amount of an increase in the balance of an Unearned Revenue account.
10. The amount of a decrease in the balance of an Inventory account.
11. The amount of a decrease in the balance of a Land account.

Required

For each item described above, indicate whether the amount should be added to or subtracted from the amount of net income when determining the amount of net cash flow from operating activities using the indirect method. Also identify any items that do not affect net cash flow from operating activities because they are reported as investing or financing activities.

Exercise 12-2B *Use the indirect method to determine cash flows from operating activities*

LO 12-1

Napoleon Incorporated presents its statement of cash flows using the indirect method. The following accounts and corresponding balances were drawn from the company's 2017 and 2016 year-end balance sheets:

Account Title	2017	2016
Accounts receivable	$31,400	$28,600
Accounts payable	10,300	9,800

The 2017 income statement showed net income of $41,500.

Required

a. Prepare the operating activities section of the statement of cash flows.
b. Explain why the change in the balance in accounts receivable was added to or subtracted from the amount of net income when you completed Requirement *a.*
c. Explain why the change in the balance in accounts payable was added to or subtracted from the amount of net income when you completed Requirement *a.*

Exercise 12-3B *Use the indirect method to determine cash flows from operating activities*

LO 12-1

Pella Company presents its statement of cash flows using the indirect method. The following accounts and corresponding balances were drawn from Pella's 2017 and 2016 year-end balance sheets:

Account Title	2017	2016
Accounts receivable	$24,000	$21,000
Prepaid rent	1,650	1,900
Interest receivable	900	1,200
Accounts payable	10,200	8,500
Salaries payable	2,700	2,900
Unearned revenue	2,000	1,800

The income statement reported a $700 loss on the sale of equipment, a $900 gain on the sale of land, and $2,500 of depreciation expense. Net income for the period was $36,500.

Required

Prepare the operating activities section of the statement of cash flows.

LO 12-2

Exercise 12-4B *Use the direct method to determine cash flows from operating activities*

The following accounts and corresponding balances were drawn from Osprey Company's 2017 and 2016 year-end balance sheets:

Account Title	2017	2016
Unearned revenue	$4,500	$6,000
Prepaid rent	5,200	3,600

During the year, $84,000 of unearned revenue was recognized as having been earned. Rent expense for 2017 was $24,000.

Required

Based on this information alone, prepare the operating activities section of the statement of cash flows assuming the direct approach is used.

LO 12-2

Exercise 12-5B *Use the direct method to determine cash flows from operating activities*

The following accounts and corresponding balances were drawn from Pixi Company's 2017 and 2016 year-end balance sheets:

Account Title	2017	2016
Accounts receivable	$62,000	$56,000
Interest receivable	8,000	6,000
Other operating expenses payable	26,000	29,000
Salaries payable	12,000	9,000

The 2017 income statement is shown below:

Income Statement	
Sales	$ 650,000
Salary expense	(420,000)
Other operating expenses	(110,000)
Operating income	120,000
Nonoperating items: Interest revenue	15,000
Net income	$ 135,000

Required

a. Use the direct method to compute the amount of cash inflows from operating activities.

b. Use the direct method to compute the amount of cash outflows from operating activities.

LO 12-1, 12-2

Exercise 12-6B *Direct versus indirect method of determining cash flows from operating activities*

Ragg Shop, Inc. (RSI), recognized $3,800 of sales revenue on account and collected $2,950 of cash from accounts receivable. Further, RSI recognized $1,200 of operating expenses on account and paid $900 cash as partial settlement of accounts payable.

Required

Based on this information alone:

a. Prepare the operating activities section of the statement of cash flows under the direct method.

b. Prepare the operating activities section of the statement of cash flows under the indirect method.

Exercise 12-7B *The direct versus the indirect method of determining cash flows from operating activities*

LO 12-1, 12-2

The following accounts and corresponding balances were drawn from Geneses Company's 2017 and 2016 year-end balance sheets:

Account Title	2017	2016
Accounts receivable	$65,000	$72,000
Prepaid rent	1,400	1,950
Utilities payable	3,200	3,800
Other operating expenses payable	27,000	31,500

The 2017 income statement is shown below:

Income Statement	
Sales	$ 420,000
Rent expense	(52,000)
Utilities expense	(45,300)
Other operating expenses	(195,000)
Net income	$ 127,700

Required

a. Prepare the operating activities section of the statement of cash flows using the direct method.

b. Prepare the operating activities section of the statement of cash flows using the indirect method.

Exercise 12-8B *Determining cash flow from investing activities*

LO 12-3

On January 1, 2016, Poole Company had a balance of $178,000 in its Land account. During 2016, Poole sold land that had cost $71,000 for $95,000 cash. The balance in the Land account on December 31, 2016, was $210,000.

Required

a. Determine the cash outflow for the purchase of land during 2016.

b. Prepare the investing activities section of the 2016 statement of cash flows.

Exercise 12-9B *Determining cash flow from investing activities*

LO 12-3

On January 1, 2016, Sanita Company had a balance of $76,300 in its Office Equipment account. During 2016, Sanita purchased office equipment that cost $30,300. The balance in the Office Equipment account on December 31, 2016, was $75,400. The 2016 income statement contained a gain from the sale of equipment of $6,000. On the date of sale, accumulated depreciation on the equipment sold amounted to $14,400.

Required

a. Determine the cost of the equipment that was sold during 2016.

b. Determine the amount of cash flow from the sale of office equipment that should be shown in the investing activities section of the 2016 statement of cash flows.

LO 12-3

Exercise 12-10B *Determining cash flows from investing activities*

The following accounts and corresponding balances were drawn from Teva Company's 2017 and 2016 year-end balance sheets:

Account Title	2017	2016
Investment securities	$102,000	$110,000
Machinery	480,000	465,000
Land	75,000	95,000

Other information drawn from the accounting records:

1. Teva incurred a $3,000 loss on the sale of investment securities during 2017.
2. Old machinery with a book value of $8,000 (cost of $34,000 minus accumulated depreciation of $26,000) was sold. The income statement showed a gain on the sale of machinery of $7,500.
3. Teva incurred a loss of $4,000 on the sale of land in 2017.

Required

a. Compute the amount of cash flow associated with the sale of investment securities.
b. Compute the amount of cash flow associated with the purchase of machinery.
c. Compute the amount of cash flow associated with the sale of machinery.
d. Compute the amount of cash flow associated with the sale of land.
e. Prepare the investing activities section of the statement of cash flows.

LO 12-4

Exercise 12-11B *Determining cash flows from financing activities*

On January 1, 2016, Van Company had a balance of $800,000 in its Bonds Payable account. During 2016, Van issued bonds with a $300,000 face value. There was no premium or discount associated with the bond issue. The balance in the Bonds Payable account on December 31, 2016, was $600,000.

Required

a. Determine the cash outflow for the repayment of bond liabilities assuming that the bonds were retired at face value.
b. Prepare the financing activities section of the 2016 statement of cash flows.

LO 12-4

Exercise 12-12B *Determining cash flows from financing activities*

On January 1, 2016, Milam Company had a balance of $300,000 in its Common Stock account. During 2016, Milam paid $18,000 to purchase treasury stock. Treasury stock is accounted for using the cost method. The balance in the Common Stock account on December 31, 2016, was $350,000. Assume that the common stock is no par stock.

Required

a. Determine the cash inflow from the issue of common stock.
b. Prepare the financing activities section of the 2016 statement of cash flows.

LO 12-4

Exercise 12-13B *Determining cash flows from financing activities*

The following accounts and corresponding balances were drawn from Cushing Company's 2017 and 2016 year-end balance sheets:

Account Title	2017	2016
Bonds payable	$200,000	$150,000
Common stock	650,000	400,000

Other information drawn from the accounting records:

1. Dividends paid during the period amounted to $50,000.
2. There were no bond liabilities repaid during the period.

Required

a. Compute the amount of cash flow associated with the issue of bond liabilities.
b. Compute the amount of cash flow associated with the issue of common stock.
c. Prepare the financing activities section of the statement of cash flows.

PROBLEMS—SERIES B

Problem 12-14B *The direct versus the indirect method of determining cash flows from operating activities*

LO 12-1, 12-2

The following accounts and corresponding balances were drawn from Crimson Sports, Inc.'s 2017 and 2016 year-end balance sheets:

Account Title	2017	2016
Accounts receivable	$31,000	$36,000
Merchandise inventory	70,000	65,000
Prepaid insurance	25,000	24,000
Accounts payable	18,000	20,000
Salaries payable	5,100	4,500
Unearned service revenue	10,200	9,500

The 2017 income statement is shown below:

Income Statement	
Sales	$ 495,000
Cost of goods sold	(215,000)
Gross margin	280,000
Service revenue	20,000
Insurance expense	(42,000)
Salaries expense	(122,000)
Depreciation expense	(12,000)
Operating income	124,000
Gain on sale of equipment	1,500
Net income	$ 125,500

Required

a. Prepare the operating activities section of the statement of cash flows using the direct method.
b. Prepare the operating activities section of the statement of cash flows using the indirect method.

Problem 12-15B *Determining cash flows from investing activities*

LO 12-3

The following information was drawn from the year-end balance sheets of Vigotti Company:

Account Title	2017	2016
Investment securities	$ 51,000	$ 60,000
Equipment	310,000	275,000
Buildings	980,000	950,000
Land	135,000	110,000

Additional information regarding transactions occurring during 2017:

1. Investment securities that had cost $11,300 were sold. The 2017 income statement contained a loss on the sale of investment securities of $800.
2. Equipment with a cost of $80,000 was purchased.
3. The income statement showed a gain on the sale of equipment of $9,500. On the date of sale, accumulated depreciation on the equipment sold amounted to $38,000.
4. A building that had originally cost $90,000 was demolished.
5. Land that had cost $20,000 was sold for $15,000.

Required

a. Determine the amount of cash flow for the purchase of investment securities during 2017.
b. Determine the amount of cash flow from the sale of investment securities during 2017.
c. Determine the cost of the equipment that was sold during 2017.
d. Determine the amount of cash flow from the sale of equipment during 2017.
e. Determine the amount of cash flow for the purchase of buildings during 2017.
f. Determine the amount of cash flow for the purchase of land during 2017.
g. Prepare the investing activities section of the 2017 statement of cash flows.

LO 12-4

Problem 12-16B *Determining cash flows from financing activities*

The following information was drawn from the year-end balance sheets of Long's Wholesale, Inc.:

Account Title	2017	2016
Bonds payable	$400,000	$600,000
Common stock	190,000	150,000
Treasury stock	20,000	15,000
Retained earnings	96,000	80,000

Additional information regarding transactions occurring during 2017:

1. Long's Wholesale, Inc., issued $90,000 of bonds during 2017. The bonds were issued at face value. All bonds retired were retired at face value.
2. Common stock did not have a par value.
3. Long's Wholesale, Inc., uses the cost method to account for treasury stock. Long's Wholesale, Inc., did not resell any treasury stock in 2017.
4. The amount of net income shown on the 2017 income statement was $49,000.

Required

a. Determine the amount of cash flow for the retirement of bonds that should appear on the 2017 statement of cash flows.
b. Determine the amount of cash flow from the issue of common stock that should appear on the 2017 statement of cash flows.
c. Determine the amount of cash flow for the purchase of treasury stock that should appear on the 2017 statement of cash flows.
d. Determine the amount of cash flow for the payment of dividends that should appear on the 2017 statement of cash flows.
e. Prepare the financing activities section of the 2017 statement of cash flows.

LO 12-1, 12-3, 12-4

Problem 12-17B *Preparing a statement of cash flows*

The following information can be obtained by examining a company's balance sheet and income statement information:

a. Increases in current asset account balances, other than cash.
b. Cash outflows to purchase noncurrent assets.
c. Decreases in current liability account balances.
d. Noncash expenses (e.g., depreciation).
e. Cash outflows to purchase treasury stock.

f. Gains recognized on the sale of noncurrent assets.
g. Cash outflows to pay dividends.
h. Cash inflows from the issue of common stock.
i. Cash inflows from the sale of noncurrent assets.
j. Increases in current liability account balances.
k. Cash inflows from the issue of noncurrent debt.
l. Losses incurred from the sale of noncurrent assets.
m. Decreases in current asset account balances, other than cash.
n. Cash outflows to repay noncurrent debt.

Required

Construct a table like the one shown below. For each item, indicate whether it would be used in the computation of net cash flows from operating, investing, or financing activities. Also, indicate whether the item would be added or subtracted when determining the net cash flow from operating, investing, or financing activities. Assume the indirect method is used to prepare the operating activities section of the statement of cash flows. The first item has been completed as an example.

Item	Type of Activity	Add or Subtract
a.	Operating	Subtract
b.		

Problem 12-18B *Using financial statements to prepare a statement of cash flows—Indirect method*

LO 12-1, 12-3, 12-4

The following financial statements were drawn from the records of Culinary Products Co.:

Balance Sheets As of December 31		
	2017	2016
Assets		
Cash	$24,200	$ 2,800
Accounts receivable	2,000	1,200
Inventory	6,400	6,000
Equipment	19,000	42,000
Accumulated depreciation—equipment	(9,000)	(17,400)
Land	18,400	10,400
Total assets	$61,000	$ 45,000
Liabilities and stockholders' equity		
Accounts payable (inventory)	$ 2,600	$ 4,200
Long-term debt	2,800	6,400
Common stock	22,000	10,000
Retained earnings	33,600	24,400
Total liabilities and stockholders' equity	$61,000	$ 45,000

Income Statement For the Year Ended December 31, 2017	
Sales revenue	$ 35,700
Cost of goods sold	(14,150)
Gross margin	21,550
Depreciation expense	(3,600)
Operating income	17,950
Gain on sale of equipment	500
Loss on disposal of land	(50)
Net income	$ 18,400

Additional Data

1. During 2017, the company sold equipment for $18,500; it had originally cost $30,000. Accumulated depreciation on this equipment was $12,000 at the time of the sale. Also, the company purchased equipment for $7,000 cash.
2. The company sold land that had cost $4,000. This land was sold for $3,950, resulting in the recognition of a $50 loss. Also, common stock was issued in exchange for title to land that was valued at $12,000 at the time of exchange.
3. Paid dividends of $9,200.

Required

Prepare a statement of cash flows using the indirect method.

LO 12-1, 12-3, 12-4

Problem 12-19B *Using financial statements to prepare a statement of cash flows—Indirect method*

The comparative balance sheets and an income statement for Wang Beauty Products, Inc., are shown below.

Balance Sheets As of December 31		
	2017	2016
Assets		
Cash	$ 68,800	$ 40,600
Accounts receivable	30,000	22,000
Merchandise inventory	160,000	176,000
Prepaid rent	2,400	4,800
Equipment	256,000	288,000
Accumulated depreciation	(146,800)	(236,000)
Land	192,000	80,000
Total assets	$ 562,400	$ 375,400
Liabilities and equity		
Accounts payable (inventory)	$ 67,000	$ 76,000
Salaries payable	28,000	24,000
Stockholders' equity		
Common stock, $50 par value	250,000	200,000
Retained earnings	217,400	75,400
Total liabilities and equity	$ 562,400	$ 375,400

Income Statement For the Year Ended December 31, 2017	
Sales	$1,500,000
Cost of goods sold	(797,200)
Gross profit	702,800
Operating expenses	
Depreciation expense	(22,800)
Rent expense	(24,000)
Salaries expense	(256,000)
Other operating expenses	(258,000)
Net income	$ 142,000

Other Information

1. Purchased land for $112,000.
2. Purchased new equipment for $100,000.

3. Sold old equipment that cost $132,000 with accumulated depreciation of $112,000 for $20,000 cash.
4. Issued common stock for $50,000.

Required

Prepare the statement of cash flows for 2017 using the indirect method.

Problem 12-20B *Using transaction data to prepare a statement of cash flows—Direct method*

LO 12-2, 12-3, 12-4

The Electric Company engaged in the following transactions during 2017. The beginning cash balance was $43,000 and the ending cash balance was $48,600.

1. Sales on account were $274,000. The beginning receivables balance was $86,000 and the ending balance was $74,000.
2. Salaries expense was $115,000. The beginning salaries payable balance was $9,600 and the ending balance was $7,500.
3. Other operating expenses were $118,000. The beginning Other Operating Expenses Payable balance was $8,500 and the ending balance was $6,000.
4. Recorded $25,000 of depreciation expense. The beginning and ending balances in the Accumulated Depreciation account were $18,000 and $43,000, respectively.
5. The Equipment account had beginning and ending balances of $28,000 and $42,000, respectively. There were no sales of equipment during the period.
6. The beginning and ending balances in the Notes Payable account were $38,000 and $32,000, respectively. There were no notes payable issued during the period.
7. There was $4,600 of interest expense reported on the income statement. The beginning and ending balances in the Interest Payable account were $6,400 and $6,200, respectively.
8. The beginning and ending Merchandise Inventory account balances were $26,000 and $32,500, respectively. The company sold merchandise with a cost of $119,000. The beginning and ending balances in the Accounts Payable account were $10,000 and $12,500, respectively.
9. The beginning and ending balances in the Notes Receivable account were $80,000 and $20,000, respectively. Notes receivable result from long-term loans made to creditors. There were no loans made to creditors during the period.
10. The beginning and ending balances in the Common Stock account were $140,000 and $190,000, respectively. The increase was caused by the issue of common stock for cash.
11. Land had beginning and ending balances of $48,000 and $28,000, respectively. Land that cost $20,000 was sold for $16,000, resulting in a loss of $4,000.
12. The tax expense for the period was $6,600. The Tax Payable account had a $3,200 beginning balance and a $2,800 ending balance.
13. The Investments account had beginning and ending balances of $10,000 and $30,000, respectively. The company purchased investments for $40,000 cash during the period, and investments that cost $20,000 were sold for $26,000, resulting in a $6,000 gain.

Required

a. Determine the amount of cash flow for each item and indicate whether the item should appear in the operating, investing, or financing activities section of a statement of cash flows. Also identify any items that do not affect the cash flow statement. Assume The Electric Company uses the direct method for showing net cash flow from operating activities.

b. Prepare a statement of cash flows based on the information you developed in Requirement *a.*

Problem 12-21B *Using financial statements to prepare a statement of cash flows—Direct method*

LO 12-2, 12-3, 12-4

The following financial statements were drawn from the records of Boston Materials, Inc.:

Balance Sheets As of December 31		
	2017	**2016**
Assets		
Cash	$ 99,700	$ 25,400
Accounts receivable	72,000	60,000
Inventory	86,000	75,000
Notes receivable (long-term)	0	24,000
Equipment	104,000	152,000
Accumulated depreciation—equipment	(67,500)	(75,000)
Land	60,000	45,000
Total assets	$354,200	$306,400
Liabilities and equity		
Accounts payable	$ 35,300	$ 36,200
Salaries payable	18,200	15,500
Utilities payable	1,400	2,800
Interest payable	600	1,200
Notes payable (long-term)	0	36,000
Common stock	120,000	100,000
Retained earnings	178,700	114,700
Total liabilities and equity	$354,200	$306,400

Income Statement For the Year Ended December 31, 2017	
Sales revenue	$ 450,000
Cost of goods sold	(212,000)
Gross margin	238,000
Operating expenses	
Salary expense	(96,000)
Depreciation expense	(18,500)
Utilities expense	(7,500)
Operating income	116,000
Nonoperating items	
Interest expense	(3,500)
Gain on sale of equipment	1,500
Net income	$ 114,000

Additional Information

1. Sold equipment costing $48,000 with accumulated depreciation of $26,000 for $23,500 cash.
2. Paid a $50,000 cash dividend to owners.

Required

Analyze the data and prepare a statement of cash flows using the direct method.

ANALYZE, THINK, COMMUNICATE

ATC 12-1 Business Applications Case *Understanding real-world annual reports*

Required

Use the Target Corporation's annual report in Appendix B to answer the following questions.

a. For the year ended February 1, 2014 (2013), which was larger, Target's *net income* or its *cash flow from operating activities*? By what amount did they differ?

b. What two items are most responsible for the difference between Target's *net income* and its *cash flow from operating activities* in 2013?

c. In 2013 Target generated approximately $6.5 billion of cash from operating activities, and its cash balance decreased by $89 million. How did the company use this $6.6 billion of cash?

ATC 12-2 Real-World Case *Following the cash*

Tesla Motors Company, Inc., began operations in 2003 but did not begin selling its stock to the public until June 28, 2010. It has lost money every year it has been in existence, and by December 31, 2013, it had total lifetime losses of approximately $1.1 billion. The company makes the Tesla Model S, and it supplies electric car components to Daimler and Toyota. Tesla's statements of cash flows for 2011, 2012, and 2013 follow.

TESLA MOTORS, INC.
Consolidated Statements of Cash Flows
(in thousands)

	For the Years Ending December 31		
	2013	**2012**	**2011**
Cash flows from operating activities:			
Net income (loss)	$(396,213)	$(254,411)	$(154,328)
Adjustments to reconcile net loss to net cash used in operating activities:			
Depreciation and amortization	28,825	16,919	10,623
Change in fair value of warrant liabilities	1,854	2,750	5,022
Discounts and premiums on short-term marketable securities	56	(112)	—
Stock-based compensation	50,145	29,419	21,156
Excess tax benefits from stock-based compensation	—	—	(74)
Loss on abandonment of fixed assets	1,504	345	8
Inventory write-downs	4,929	1,828	951
Account receivables	(17,303)	(2,829)	(3,222)
Inventory	—	—	(20,115)
Inventories and operating lease vehicles	(194,726)	(13,638)	—
Prepaid expenses and other current assets	1,121	(248)	(4,977)
Other assets	(482)	(288)	(463)
Operating lease assets	—	—	(8,398)
Accounts payable	187,821	31,859	(212)
Accrued liabilities	9,603	12,321	13,345
Deferred development compensation	—	—	(156)
Deferred revenue	(526)	(1,927)	4,801
Reservation payments	47,056	61,006	4,707
Other long-term liabilities	10,255	2,641	3,515
Net cash flows from operating activities	(266,081)	(114,364)	(127,817)
Cash flows from investing activities:			
Purchase of marketable securities	(14,992)	(64,952)	—
Maturities of short-term marketable securities	40,000	40,000	—
Payments related to acquisition of Fremont manufacturing facility and related assets	—	—	(65,210)
Purchases of property and equipment excluding capital leases	(239,228)	(197,896)	(40,203)
Transfer of restricted cash into its dedicated Department of Energy account	—	—	(100,000)
Withdrawals out of (transfers into) our dedicated Department of Energy account, net	8,620	50,121	26,403
Decrease (increase) in restricted cash	(1,330)	(3,201)	(1,287)
Net cash flows from investing activities	(206,930)	(175,928)	(180,297)
Cash flows from financing activities:			
Proceeds from issuance of common stock in initial public offering	221,496	172,410	188,842
Proceeds from issuance of common stock in private placements	—	59,058	—
Proceeds from issuance of common stock in Toyota private placement	—	—	50,000
Proceeds from issuance of common stock in Panasonic private placement	—	—	30,000
Principal payments on capital leases and other debt	(2,832)	(416)	(315)
Proceeds from long-term debt and other long-term liabilities	188,796	204,423	71,828
Principal payments on long-term debt	(12,710)	—	—
Proceeds from exercise of stock options	—	—	1,350
Proceeds from exercise of stock options and other stock issuances	24,885	10,525	—
Excess tax benefits from stock-based compensation	—	—	74
Deferred common stock and loan facility issuance costs	—	—	(3,734)
Net cash flows from financing activities	419,635	446,000	338,045
Net increase (decrease) in cash and cash equivalents	(53,376)	155,708	29,931
Cash and cash equivalents at beginning of period	255,266	99,558	69,627
Cash and cash equivalents at end of period	$ 201,890	$ 255,266	$ 99,558

Required

a. As this chapter explained, many companies that report net losses on their earnings statements report positive cash flows from operating activities. How do Tesla's net incomes compare to its cash flows from operating activities?

b. Based only on the information in the statements of cash flows, does Tesla appear to be growing the capacity of its business? Explain.

c. In 2013 Tesla paid off $12.7 million of long-term borrowings and $2.8 million of capital leases and other debt. Where did it get the funds to repay this debt?

d. All things considered, based on the information in its statements of cash flows, does Tesla's cash position appear to be improving or deteriorating?

ATC 12-3 Group Assignment *Preparing a statement of cash flows*

The following financial statements and information are available for Blythe Industries Inc.

Balance Sheets As of December 31	2017	2016
Assets		
Cash	$ 160,200	$120,600
Accounts receivable	103,200	85,000
Inventory	186,400	171,800
Marketable securities (available for sale)	284,000	220,000
Equipment	650,000	490,000
Accumulated depreciation	(310,000)	(240,000)
Land	80,000	120,000
Total assets	$1,153,800	$967,400
Liabilities and equity		
Liabilities		
Accounts payable (inventory)	$ 36,400	$ 66,200
Notes payable—Long-term	230,000	250,000
Bonds payable	200,000	100,000
Total liabilities	466,400	416,200
Stockholders' equity		
Common stock, no par	240,000	200,000
Preferred stock, $50 par	110,000	100,000
Paid-in capital in excess of par—Preferred stock	34,400	26,800
Total paid-In capital	384,400	326,800
Retained earnings	333,000	264,400
Less: Treasury stock	(30,000)	(40,000)
Total stockholders' equity	687,400	551,200
Total liabilities and stockholders' equity	$1,153,800	$967,400

Income Statement For the Year Ended December 31, 2017		
Sales revenue		$1,050,000
Cost of goods sold		(766,500)
Gross profit		283,500
Operating expenses		
Supplies expense	$20,400	
Salaries expense	92,000	
Depreciation expense	90,000	
Total operating expenses		(202,400)
Operating income		81,100
Nonoperating items		
Interest expense		(16,000)
Gain from the sale of marketable securities		30,000
Gain from the sale of land and equipment		12,000
Net income		$ 107,100

Additional Information

1. Sold land that cost $40,000 for $44,000.
2. Sold equipment that cost $30,000 and had accumulated depreciation of $20,000 for $18,000.
3. Purchased new equipment for $190,000.
4. Sold marketable securities that were classified as available-for-sale and that cost $40,000 for $70,000.
5. Purchased new marketable securities, classified as available-for-sale, for $104,000.
6. Paid $20,000 on the principal of the long-term note.
7. Paid off a $100,000 bond issue and issued new bonds for $200,000.
8. Sold 100 shares of treasury stock at its cost.
9. Issued some new common stock.
10. Issued some new $50 par preferred stock.
11. Paid dividends. (*Note:* The only transactions to affect retained earnings were net income and dividends.)

Required

Organize the class into three sections and divide each section into groups of three to five students. Assign each section of groups an activity section of the statement of cash flows (operating activities, investing activities, or financing activities).

Group Task

Prepare your assigned portion of the statement of cash flows. Have a representative of your section put your activity section of the statement of cash flows on the board. As each section adds its information on the board, the full statement of cash flows will be presented.

Class Discussion

Have the class finish the statement of cash flows by computing the net change in cash. Also have the class answer the following questions:

a. What is the cost per share of the treasury stock?
b. What was the issue price per share of the preferred stock?
c. What was the book value of the equipment sold?

ATC 12-4 Business Applications Case *Identifying different presentation formats*

In *Statement of Financial Accounting Standards No. 95,* the Financial Accounting Standards Board (FASB) recommended but did not require that companies use the direct method. In Appendix B, Paragraphs 106–121, the FASB discussed its reasons for this recommendation.

Required

Obtain a copy of *Standard No. 95* and read Appendix B Paragraphs 106–121. Write a brief response summarizing the issues that the FASB considered and its specific reaction to those issues. Your response should draw heavily on paragraphs 119–121.

ATC 12-5 Writing Assignment *Explaining discrepancies between cash flow and operating income*

The following selected information was drawn from the records of Fleming Company:

Assets	2016	2017
Accounts receivable	$ 400,000	$ 840,200
Merchandise inventory	720,000	1,480,000
Equipment	1,484,000	1,861,200
Accumulated depreciation	(312,000)	(402,400)

Fleming is experiencing cash flow problems. Despite the fact that it reported significant increases in operating income, operating activities produced a net cash outflow. Recent financial forecasts predict that Fleming will have insufficient cash to pay its current liabilities within three months.

Required

Write an explanation of Fleming's cash shortage. Include a recommendation to remedy the problem.

ATC 12-6 Ethical Dilemma *Would I lie to you, baby?*

Andy and Jean Crocket are involved in divorce proceedings. When discussing a property settlement, Andy told Jean that he should take over their investment in an apartment complex because she would be unable to absorb the loss that the apartments are generating. Jean was somewhat distrustful and asked Andy to support his contention. He produced the following income statement, which was supported by a CPA's unqualified opinion that the statement was prepared in accordance with generally accepted accounting principles.

CROCKET APARTMENTS
Income Statement
For the Year Ended December 31, 2016

Rent revenue		$ 580,000
Less: Expenses		
Depreciation expense	$280,000	
Interest expense	184,000	
Operating expense	88,000	
Management fees	56,000	
Total expenses		(608,000)
Net loss		$ (28,000)

All revenue is earned on account. Interest and operating expenses are incurred on account. Management fees are paid in cash. The following accounts and balances were drawn from the 2015 and 2016 year-end balance sheets.

Account Title	2015	2016
Rent receivable	$40,000	$44,000
Interest payable	12,000	18,000
Accounts payable (oper. exp.)	6,000	4,000

Jean is reluctant to give up the apartments but feels that she must do so because her present salary is only $40,000 per year. She says that if she takes the apartments, the $28,000 loss would absorb a significant portion of her salary, leaving her only $12,000 with which to support herself. She tells you that while the figures seem to support her husband's arguments, she believes that she is failing to see something. She knows that she and her husband collected a $20,000 distribution from the business on December 1, 2016. Also, $150,000 cash was paid in 2016 to reduce the principal balance on a mortgage that was taken out to finance the purchase of the apartments two years ago. Finally, $24,000 cash was paid during 2016 to purchase a computer system used in the business. She wonders, "If the apartments are losing money, where is my husband getting all the cash to make these payments?"

Required

a. Prepare a statement of cash flows for the 2016 accounting period.

b. Compare the cash flow statement prepared in Requirement *a* with the income statement and provide Jean Crocket with recommendations.

c. Comment on the value of an unqualified audit opinion when using financial statements for decision-making purposes.

ATC 12-7 Research Assignment *Analyzing cash flow information*

In 2013 and 2012 Sears Holding Corporation reported net losses and negative cash flows from operating activities. Using the company's Form 10-K for the fiscal year ended February 1, 2014 (2013), complete the requirements below. The Form 10-K can be found on the company's website, where it is called the Annual Report. It can also be obtained using the EDGAR system following the instructions in Appendix A.

Required

a. Determine Sears' net incomes and cash flow from operating activities for 2012 and 2013.

b. How was Sears able to pay its bills given that it has such large, negative net cash flows from operating activities in 2012 and 2013? Provide a separate answer for each year.

APPENDIX A

ACCESSING THE EDGAR DATABASE THROUGH THE INTERNET

Successful business managers need many different skills, including communication, interpersonal, computer, and analytical. Most business students become very aware of the data analysis skills used in accounting, but they may not be as aware of the importance of "data-finding" skills. There are many sources of accounting and financial data. The more sources you are able to use, the better.

One very important source of accounting information is the EDGAR database. Others are probably available at your school through the library or business school network. Your accounting instructor will be able to identify these for you and make suggestions regarding their use. By making the effort to learn to use electronic databases, you will enhance your abilities as a future manager and your marketability as a business graduate.

These instructions assume that you know how to access and use an Internet browser. Follow the instructions to retrieve data from the Securities and Exchange Commission's EDGAR database. Be aware that the SEC may have changed its interface since this appendix was written. Accordingly, be prepared for slight differences between the following instructions and what appears on your computer screen. Take comfort in the fact that changes are normally designed to simplify user access. If you encounter a conflict between the following instructions and the instructions provided in the SEC interface, remember that the SEC interface is more current and should take precedence over the following instructions.

Most companies provide links to their SEC filings from their corporate website. These links are often simpler to use and provide more choices regarding file formats than the SEC's EDGAR site. On company websites, links to SEC filings are usually found under one of the following links: "Investor Relations," "Company Info," or "About Us."

1. Connect to the EDGAR database through the following address: **http://www.sec.gov/.**
2. After the SEC homepage appears, click on **Company Filings.**
3. On the screen that appears, enter the name of the company whose file you wish to retrieve.
4. The next screen will present a list of companies that have the same name as the one you entered, along with companies that have similar names. Identify the company you want and click on the CIK number beside it.
5. Enter the SEC form number that you want to retrieve in the window titled **Filing Type** that appears in the upper left portion of the screen. For example, if you want Form 10-K, which will usually be the case, enter **10-K** and click on the **Search** button.
6. A list of the forms you requested will be presented, along with the date they were filed. Click on the **Document** button next to the file you wish to retrieve.
7. Once the 10-K has been retrieved, you can search it online or save it on your computer.
8. Often the 10-K will have a table of contents that can help locate the part of the report you need. The financial statements are seldom located at the beginning of the Form 10-K. They are usually in either Section 8 or Section 15.

APPENDIX B

PORTION OF THE FORM 10-K FOR TARGET CORPORATION

This appendix contains a portion of the Form 10-K for the Target Corporation that was filed with the Securities and Exchange Commission on March 14, 2014. The document included in this appendix is Target's annual report, which was included *as a part* of its complete Form 10-K for the company's fiscal year ended February 1, 2014. Throughout this text this is referred to as the company's 2013 fiscal year.

This document is included for illustrative purposes, and it is intended to be used for educational purposes only. It should not be used for making investment decisions. Target Corporation's complete Form 10-K may be obtained from the SEC's EDGAR website, using the procedures explained in Appendix A. The Form 10-K may also be found on Target's website under "Investor Relations." From this page, click on the "SEC Filings" tab and scroll to locate the appropriate 10-K report.

UNITED STATES
SECURITIES AND EXCHANGE COMMISSION
Washington, D.C. 20549

FORM 10-K

(Mark One)

☒ **ANNUAL REPORT PURSUANT TO SECTION 13 OR 15(d) OF THE SECURITIES EXCHANGE ACT OF 1934**

For the fiscal year ended February 1, 2014

OR

☐ **TRANSITION REPORT PURSUANT TO SECTION 13 OR 15(d) OF THE SECURITIES EXCHANGE ACT OF 1934**

For the transition period from to

Commission file number **1-6049**

TARGET.

TARGET CORPORATION
(Exact name of registrant as specified in its charter)

Minnesota (State or other jurisdiction of incorporation or organization)	**41-0215170** (I.R.S. Employer Identification No.)
1000 Nicollet Mall, Minneapolis, Minnesota (Address of principal executive offices)	**55403** (Zip Code)

Registrant's telephone number, including area code: 612/304-6073

Securities Registered Pursuant To Section 12(B) Of The Act:

Title of Each Class	Name of Each Exchange on Which Registered
Common Stock, par value $0.0833 per share	**New York Stock Exchange**

Securities registered pursuant to Section 12(g) of the Act: **None**

Indicate by check mark if the registrant is a well-known seasoned issuer, as defined in Rule 405 of the Securities Act. Yes ☒ No ☐

Indicate by check mark if the registrant is not required to file reports pursuant to Section 13 or Section 15(d) of the Act. Yes ☐ No ☒

Note – Checking the box above will not relieve any registrant required to file reports pursuant to Section 13 or 15(d) of the Exchange Act from their obligations under those Sections.

Indicate by check mark whether the registrant (1) has filed all reports required to be filed by Section 13 or 15(d) of the Securities Exchange Act of 1934 during the preceding 12 months (or for such shorter period that the registrant was required to file such reports), and (2) has been subject to such filing requirements for the past 90 days. Yes ☒ No ☐

Indicate by checkmark whether the registrant has submitted electronically and posted on its corporate website, if any, every Interactive Data File required to be submitted and posted pursuant to Rule 405 of Regulation S-T (§232.405 of this chapter) during the preceding 12 months (or for such shorter period that the registrant was required to submit and post such files. Yes ☒ No ☐

Indicate by check mark if disclosure of delinquent filers pursuant to Item 405 of Regulation S-K (§229.405 of this chapter) is not contained herein, and will not be contained, to the best of registrant's knowledge, in definitive proxy or information statements incorporated by reference in Part III of this Form 10-K or any amendment to this Form 10-K. ☒

Indicate by check mark whether the registrant is a large accelerated filer, an accelerated filer, a non-accelerated filer or a smaller reporting company (as defined in Rule 12b-2 of the Act).

Large accelerated filer ☒ Accelerated filer ☐ Non-accelerated filer ☐ (Do not check if a smaller reporting company) Smaller reporting company ☐

Indicate by check mark whether the registrant is a shell company (as defined in Rule 12b-2 of the Act). Yes ☐ No ☒

Aggregate market value of the voting stock held by non-affiliates of the registrant on August 3, 2013 was $45,036,171,526, based on the closing price of $71.50 per share of Common Stock as reported on the New York Stock Exchange Composite Index.

Indicate the number of shares outstanding of each of registrant's classes of Common Stock, as of the latest practicable date. Total shares of Common Stock, par value $0.0833, outstanding at March 10, 2014 were 633,174,692.

DOCUMENTS INCORPORATED BY REFERENCE

1. Portions of Target's Proxy Statement to be filed on or about April 28, 2014 are incorporated into Part III.

TABLE OF CONTENTS

PART I

Item 1. Business

General

Target Corporation (Target, the Corporation or the Company) was incorporated in Minnesota in 1902. We offer our customers, referred to as "guests," both everyday essentials and fashionable, differentiated merchandise at discounted prices. Our ability to deliver a preferred shopping experience to our guests is supported by our strong supply chain and technology infrastructure, a devotion to innovation that is ingrained in our organization and culture, and our disciplined approach to managing our business and investing in future growth.

We operate as two reportable segments: U.S. and Canadian. Our U.S. Segment includes all of our U.S. retail operations, which are designed to enable guests to purchase products seamlessly in stores, online or through mobile devices. The U.S. Segment also includes our credit card servicing activities and certain centralized operating and corporate activities not allocated to our Canadian Segment. Our Canadian Segment includes all of our Canadian retail operations, including 124 stores opened during 2013. We currently do not have a digital sales channel within our Canadian Segment.

Prior to the first quarter of 2013, we operated a U.S. Credit Card Segment that offered credit to qualified guests through our branded credit cards: the Target Credit Card and the Target Visa Credit Card. In the first quarter of 2013, we sold our U.S. consumer credit card portfolio, and TD Bank Group (TD) now underwrites, funds and owns Target Credit Card and Target Visa consumer receivables in the U.S. We perform account servicing and primary marketing functions and earn a substantial portion of the profits generated by the portfolio. Following the sale of our U.S. consumer credit card portfolio to TD, we combined our historical U.S. Retail Segment and U.S. Credit Card Segment into one U.S. Segment. Refer to Item 7, Management's Discussion and Analysis of Financial Condition and Results of Operations, and Note 6 of the Consolidated Financial Statements included in Item 8, Financial Statements and Supplementary Data, for more information on the credit card receivables transaction and segment change.

Data Breach

During the fourth quarter of 2013, we experienced a data breach in which an intruder stole certain payment card and other guest information from our network (the Data Breach). For further information about the Data Breach, see Item 7, Management's Discussion and Analysis of Financial Condition and Results of Operations.

Financial Highlights

For information about our fiscal years, see Item 8, Financial Statements and Supplemental Data - Note 1, Summary of Accounting Policies, of this Annual Report on Form 10-K.

For information on key financial highlights and segment financial information, see the items referenced in Item 6, Selected Financial Data, Item 7, Management's Discussion and Analysis of Financial Condition and Results of Operations and Item 8, Financial Statements and Supplemental Data — Note 28, Segment Reporting, of this Annual Report on Form 10-K.

Seasonality

A larger share of annual revenues and earnings traditionally occurs in the fourth quarter because it includes the peak sales period from Thanksgiving to the end of December.

Merchandise

We sell a wide assortment of general merchandise and food. Our general merchandise and CityTarget stores offer an edited food assortment, including perishables, dry grocery, dairy and frozen items, while our SuperTarget stores offer a full line of food items comparable to traditional supermarkets. Our digital channels include a wide assortment of general merchandise, including many items found in our stores and a complementary assortment, such as extended sizes and colors, that are only sold online.

A significant portion of our sales is from national brand merchandise. Approximately one-third of 2013 sales related to our owned and exclusive brands, including but not limited to the following:

Owned Brands		
Archer Farms®	Gilligan & O'Malley®	Sutton & Dodge®
Simply Balanced™	Market Pantry®	Threshold™
Boots & Barkley®	Merona®	up & up®
CHEFS®	Room Essentials®	Wine Cube®
Circo®	Smith & Hawken®	Xhilaration®
Embark®	Spritz™	

Exclusive Brands		
Assets® by Sarah Blakely	Genuine Kids from OshKosh®	Nate Berkus for Target®
C9 by Champion®	Giada De Laurentiis™ for Target®	Nick & Nora®
Carlton®	Harajuku Mini for Target®	Shaun White
Chefmate®	Just One You made by Carter's	Simply Shabby Chic®
Cherokee®	Kid Made Modern®	Sonia Kashuk®
Converse® One Star®	Kitchen Essentials® from Calphalon®	Thomas O'Brien®
dENiZEN™ from Levi's®	Liz Lange® for Target	
Fieldcrest®	Mossimo Supply Company®	

We also sell merchandise through periodic exclusive design and creative partnerships, and also generate revenue from in-store amenities such as Target Café, Target Clinic, Target Pharmacy and Target Photo, and leased or licensed departments such as Target Optical, Pizza Hut, Portrait Studio and Starbucks.

Distribution

The vast majority of merchandise is distributed to our stores through our network of 40 distribution centers, 37 in the United States and 3 in Canada. General merchandise is shipped to and from our distribution centers by common carriers. Certain food items and other merchandise is shipped directly to our stores in the U.S. and Canada by vendors or third party distributors.

Employees

At February 1, 2014, we employed approximately 366,000 full-time, part-time and seasonal employees, referred to as "team members." During our peak sales period from Thanksgiving to the end of December, our employment levels peaked at approximately 416,000 team members. We offer a broad range of company-paid benefits to our team members. Eligibility for, and the level of, these benefits varies, depending on team members' full-time or part-time status, compensation level, date of hire and/or length of service. These company-paid benefits include a pension plan, 401(k) plan, medical and dental plans, a retiree medical plan, disability insurance, paid vacation, tuition reimbursement, various team member assistance programs, life insurance and merchandise discounts. We believe our team member relations are good.

Working Capital

Our working capital needs are greater in the months leading up to our peak sales period from Thanksgiving to the end of December, which we typically finance with cash flow provided by operations and short-term borrowings. Additional details are provided in the Liquidity and Capital Resources section in Item 7, Management's Discussion and Analysis of Financial Condition and Results of Operations.

Effective inventory management is key to our ongoing success. We use various techniques including demand forecasting and planning and various forms of replenishment management. We achieve effective inventory management by being in-stock in core product offerings, maintaining positive vendor relationships, and carefully planning inventory levels for seasonal and apparel items to minimize markdowns.

Competition

We compete with traditional and off-price general merchandise retailers, apparel retailers, internet retailers, wholesale clubs, category specific retailers, drug stores, supermarkets and other forms of retail commerce. Our ability to positively differentiate ourselves from other retailers and provide a compelling value proposition largely determine our competitive position within the retail industry.

Intellectual Property

Our brand image is a critical element of our business strategy. Our principal trademarks, including Target, SuperTarget and our "Bullseye Design," have been registered with the U.S. Patent and Trademark Office. We also seek to obtain and preserve intellectual property protection for our owned brands.

Geographic Information

The vast majority of our revenues are generated within the United States. During 2013, a modest percentage of our revenues were generated in Canada. The vast majority of our long-lived assets are located within the United States and Canada.

Available Information

Our Annual Report on Form 10-K, quarterly reports on Form 10-Q, current reports on Form 8-K and amendments to those reports filed or furnished pursuant to Section 13(a) or 15(d) of the Exchange Act are available free of charge at www.Target.com/Investors as soon as reasonably practicable after we file such material with, or furnish it to, the U.S. Securities and Exchange Commission (SEC). Our Corporate Governance Guidelines, Business Conduct Guide, Corporate Responsibility Report and the position descriptions for our Board of Directors and Board committees are also available free of charge in print upon request or at www.Target.com/Investors.

Item 1A. Risk Factors

Our business is subject to many risks. Set forth below are the most significant risks that we face.

If we are unable to positively differentiate ourselves from other retailers, our results of operations could be adversely affected.

The retail business is highly competitive. In the past we have been able to compete successfully by differentiating our guests' shopping experience by creating an attractive value proposition through a careful combination of price, merchandise assortment, convenience, guest service, loyalty programs and marketing efforts. Our ability to create a personalized guest experience through the collection and use of guest data is increasingly important to our ability to differentiate from other retailers. Guest perceptions regarding the cleanliness and safety of our stores, the functionality and reliability of our digital channels, our in-stock levels and other factors also affect our ability to compete. No single competitive factor is dominant, and actions by our competitors on any of these factors could have an adverse effect on our sales, gross margins and expenses.

We sell many products under our owned and exclusive brands. These brands are an important part of our business because they differentiate us from other retailers, generally carry higher margins than equivalent national brand products and represent a significant portion of our overall sales. If one or more of these brands experiences a loss of consumer acceptance or confidence, our sales and gross margins could be adversely affected.

The continuing migration and evolution of retailing to online and mobile channels has increased our challenges in differentiating ourselves from other retailers. In particular, consumers are able to quickly and conveniently comparison shop with digital tools, which can lead to decisions based solely on price. We work with our vendors to offer unique and distinctive merchandise, and encourage our guests to shop with confidence with our price match policy. Failure to effectively execute in these efforts, actions by our competitors in response to these efforts or failures of our vendors to manage their own channels and content could hurt our ability to differentiate ourselves from other retailers and, as a result, have an adverse effect on sales, gross margins and expenses.

Our continued success is substantially dependent on positive perceptions of Target which, if eroded, could adversely affect our business and our relationships with our guests and team members.

We believe that one of the reasons our guests prefer to shop at Target and our team members choose Target as a place of employment is the reputation we have built over many years for serving our four primary constituencies: guests, team members, the communities in which we operate, and shareholders. To be successful in the future, we must continue to preserve, grow and leverage the value of Target's reputation. Reputational value is based in large part on perceptions. While reputations may take decades to build, any negative incidents can quickly erode trust and confidence, particularly if they result in adverse mainstream and social media publicity, governmental investigations or litigation. Those types of incidents could have an adverse impact on perceptions and lead to tangible adverse effects on our business, including consumer boycotts, lost sales, loss of new store development opportunities, or team member retention and recruiting difficulties. For example, we experienced weaker than expected U.S. Segment sales following the announcement of the Data Breach and are unable to determine whether there will be a long-term impact to our relationship with our guests and whether we will need to engage in significant promotional or other activities to regain their trust.

If we are unable to successfully develop and maintain a relevant and reliable multichannel experience for our guests, our sales, results of operations and reputation could be adversely affected.

Our business has evolved from an in-store experience to interaction with guests across multiple channels (in-store, online, mobile and social media, among others). Our guests are using computers, tablets, mobile phones and other devices to shop in our stores and online and provide feedback and public commentary about all aspects of our business. We currently provide full and mobile versions of our website (Target.com), applications for mobile phones and tablets and interact with our guests through social media. Multichannel retailing is rapidly evolving and we must keep pace with changing guest expectations and new developments and technology investments by our competitors. If we are unable to attract and retain team members or contract with third parties having the specialized skills needed to support our multichannel efforts, implement improvements to our guest-facing technology in a timely manner, or provide a convenient and consistent experience for our guests regardless of the ultimate sales channel, our ability to compete and our results of operations could be adversely affected. In addition, if Target.com and our other guest-facing technology systems do not appeal to our guests or reliably function as designed, we may experience a loss of guest confidence, lost sales or be exposed to fraudulent purchases, which, if significant, could adversely affect our reputation and results of operations.

If we fail to anticipate and respond quickly to changing consumer preferences, our sales, gross margins and profitability could suffer.

A substantial part of our business is dependent on our ability to make trend-right decisions and effectively manage our inventory in a broad range of merchandise categories, including apparel, home décor, seasonal offerings, food and other merchandise. Failure to accurately predict constantly changing consumer tastes, preferences, spending patterns and other lifestyle decisions, and personalize our offerings to our guests may result in lost sales, spoilage and increased inventory markdowns, which would lead to a deterioration in our results of operations by hurting our sales, gross margins and profitability.

Our earnings are highly susceptible to the state of macroeconomic conditions and consumer confidence in the United States.

Most of our stores and all of our digital sales are in the United States, making our results highly dependent on U.S. consumer confidence and the health of the U.S. economy. In addition, a significant portion of our total sales is derived from stores located in five states: California, Texas, Florida, Minnesota and Illinois, resulting in further dependence on local economic conditions in these states. Deterioration in macroeconomic conditions or consumer confidence could negatively affect our business in many ways, including slowing sales growth or reduction in overall sales, and reducing gross margins. These same considerations impact the success of our credit card program. Even though we no longer own a consumer credit card receivables portfolio, we share in the economic performance of the credit card program with TD. Deterioration in macroeconomic conditions could adversely affect the volume of new credit accounts, the amount of credit card program balances and the ability of credit card holders to pay their balances. These conditions could result in us receiving lower profit-sharing payments.

We rely on a large, global and changing workforce of Target team members, contractors and temporary staffing. If we do not effectively manage our workforce and the concentration of work in certain global locations, our labor costs and results of operations could be adversely affected.

With approximately 366,000 team members, our workforce costs represent our largest operating expense, and our business is dependent on our ability to attract, train and retain the appropriate mix of qualified team members, contractors and temporary staffing. Many team members are in entry-level or part-time positions with historically high turnover rates. Our ability to meet our labor needs while controlling our costs is subject to external factors such as unemployment levels, prevailing wage rates, collective bargaining efforts, health care and other benefit costs and changing demographics. If we are unable to attract and retain adequate numbers and an appropriate mix of qualified team members, contractors and temporary staffing, our operations, guest service levels and support functions could suffer. Those factors, together with increasing wage and benefit costs, could adversely affect our results of operations. As of March 14, 2014, none of our team members were working under collective bargaining agreements. We are periodically subject to labor organizing efforts. If we become subject to one or more collective bargaining agreements in the future, it could adversely affect our labor costs and how we operate our business.

We have a concentration of support functions located in India where there has been greater political, financial, environmental and health instability than the United States. An extended disruption of our operations in India could adversely affect certain operations supporting stability and maintenance of our digital channels and information technology development.

If our capital investments in technology, new stores and remodeling existing stores do not achieve appropriate returns, our competitive position, financial condition and results of operations may be adversely affected.

Our business is becoming increasingly reliant on technology investments and the returns on these investments are less predictable than building new stores and remodeling existing stores. We are currently making, and will continue to make, significant technology investments to support our multichannel efforts, implement improvements to our guest-facing technology and transform our information processes and computer systems to more efficiently run our business and remain competitive and relevant to our guests. These technology initiatives might not provide the anticipated benefits or may provide them on a delayed schedule or at a higher cost. We must monitor and choose the right investments and implement them at the right pace. Targeting the wrong opportunities, failing to make the best investments, or making an investment commitment significantly above or below our needs could result in the loss of our competitive position and adversely impact our financial condition or results of operations.

In addition, our growth also depends, in part, on our ability to build new stores and remodel existing stores in a manner that achieves appropriate returns on our capital investment. We compete with other retailers and businesses for suitable locations for our stores. Many of our expected new store sites are located in fully developed markets, which are generally more time-consuming and expensive undertakings than expansion into undeveloped suburban and ex-urban markets.

Interruptions in our supply chain or increased commodity prices and supply chain costs could adversely affect our gross margins, expenses and results of operations.

We are dependent on our vendors to supply merchandise in a timely and efficient manner. If a vendor fails to deliver on its commitments, whether due to financial difficulties or other reasons, we could experience merchandise out-of-stocks that could lead to lost sales. In addition, a large portion of our merchandise is sourced, directly or indirectly, from outside the United States, with China as our single largest source. Political or financial instability, trade restrictions, the outbreak of pandemics, labor unrest, transport capacity and costs, port security, weather conditions, natural disasters or other events that could slow port activities and affect foreign trade are beyond our control and could disrupt our supply of merchandise and/or adversely affect our results of operations. In addition, changes in the costs of procuring commodities used in our merchandise or the costs related to our supply chain, including vendor costs, labor, fuel, tariffs, currency exchange rates and supply chain transparency initiatives, could have an adverse effect on gross margins, expenses and results of operations.

Failure to address product safety concerns could adversely affect our sales and results of operations.

If our merchandise offerings, including food, drug and children's products, do not meet applicable safety standards or our guests' expectations regarding safety, we could experience lost sales and increased costs and be exposed to legal and reputational risk. All of our vendors must comply with applicable product safety laws, and we are dependent on them to ensure that the products we buy comply with all safety standards. Events that give rise to actual, potential or perceived product safety concerns, including food or drug contamination, could expose us to government enforcement action or private litigation and result in costly product recalls and other liabilities. In addition, negative guest perceptions regarding the safety of the products we sell could cause our guests to seek alternative sources for their needs, resulting in lost sales. In those circumstances, it may be difficult and costly for us to regain the confidence of our guests.

The data breach we experienced in 2013 has resulted in government inquiries and private litigation, and if our efforts to protect the security of information about our guests and team members are unsuccessful, future issues may result in additional costly government enforcement actions and private litigation and our sales and reputation could suffer.

The nature of our business involves the receipt and storage of information about our guests and team members. We have a program in place to detect and respond to data security incidents. However, because the techniques used to obtain unauthorized access, disable or degrade service, or sabotage systems change frequently and may be difficult to detect for long periods of time, we may be unable to anticipate these techniques or implement adequate preventive measures. In addition, hardware, software or applications we develop or procure from third parties may contain defects in design or manufacture or other problems that could unexpectedly compromise information security. Unauthorized parties may also attempt to gain access to our systems or facilities through fraud, trickery or other forms of deceiving our team members, contractors and temporary staff. Until the fourth quarter of 2013, all incidents we experienced were insignificant. The Data Breach we experienced was significant and went undetected for several weeks. We experienced weaker than expected U.S. Segment sales immediately following the announcement of the Data Breach, and we are currently facing more than 80 civil lawsuits filed on behalf of guests, payment card issuing banks and shareholders. In addition, state and federal agencies, including State Attorneys General, the Federal Trade Commission and the SEC, are investigating events related to the Data Breach, including how it occurred, its consequences and our responses. Those claims and investigations may have an adverse effect on how we operate our business and our results of operations.

If we experience additional significant data security breaches or fail to detect and appropriately respond to significant data security breaches, we could be exposed to additional government enforcement actions and private litigation. In addition, our guests could further lose confidence in our ability to protect their information, which could cause them to discontinue using our REDcards or pharmacy services, or stop shopping with us altogether.

Our failure to comply with federal, state, local and international laws, or changes in these laws could increase our costs, reduce our margins and lower our sales.

Our business is subject to a wide array of laws and regulations in the United States, Canada and other countries in which we operate. Significant workforce-related legislative changes could increase our expenses and adversely affect our operations. Examples of possible workforce-related legislative changes include changes to an employer's obligation to recognize collective bargaining units, the process by which collective bargaining agreements are negotiated or imposed, minimum wage requirements, and health care mandates. In addition, changes in the regulatory environment affecting Medicare reimbursements, privacy and information security, product safety, supply chain transparency, or environmental protection, among others, could cause our expenses to increase without an ability to pass through any increased expenses through higher prices. For example, we are currently facing government inquiries related to the Data Breach that may result in the imposition of fines or other penalties. In addition, any legislative or regulatory changes adopted in reaction to the recent retail-industry data breaches could increase or accelerate our compliance costs. Also, our pharmacy and clinic operations are governed by various regulations, and a significant change in, or our noncompliance with, these regulations could have a material adverse effect on our compliance costs and results of operations. In addition, if we fail to comply with other applicable laws and regulations, including wage and hour laws, the Foreign Corrupt Practices Act and local anti-bribery laws, we could be subject to legal risk, including government enforcement action and class action civil litigation, which could adversely affect our results of operations by increasing our costs, reducing our margins and lowering our sales.

Weather conditions where our stores are located may impact consumer shopping patterns, which alone or together with natural disasters, particularly in areas where our sales are concentrated, could adversely affect our results of operations.

Uncharacteristic or significant weather conditions can affect consumer shopping patterns, particularly in apparel and seasonal items, which could lead to lost sales or greater than expected markdowns and adversely affect our short-term results of operations. In addition, our three largest states by total sales are California, Texas and Florida, areas where natural disasters are more prevalent. Natural disasters in those states or in other areas where our sales are concentrated could result in significant physical damage to or closure of one or more of our stores or distribution centers, and cause delays in the distribution of merchandise from our vendors to our distribution centers and stores, which could adversely affect our results of operations by increasing our costs and lowering our sales.

Changes in our effective income tax rate could adversely affect our net income.

A number of factors influence our effective income tax rate, including changes in tax law, tax treaties, interpretation of existing laws, and our ability to sustain our reporting positions on examination. Changes in any of those factors could change our effective tax rate, which could adversely affect our net income. In addition, our operations outside of the United States may cause greater volatility in our effective tax rate.

If we are unable to access the capital markets or obtain bank credit, our financial position, liquidity and results of operations could suffer.

We are dependent on a stable, liquid and well-functioning financial system to fund our operations and capital investments. In particular, we have historically relied on the public debt markets to fund portions of our capital investments and the commercial paper market and bank credit facilities to fund seasonal needs for working capital. Our continued access to these markets depends on multiple factors including the condition of debt capital markets, our operating performance and maintaining strong debt ratings. If rating agencies lower our credit ratings, it could adversely impact our ability to access the debt markets, our cost of funds and other terms for new debt issuances. Each of the credit rating agencies reviews its rating periodically, and there is no guarantee our current credit rating will remain the same. In addition, we use a variety of derivative products to manage our exposure to market risk, principally interest rate and equity price fluctuations. Disruptions or turmoil in the financial markets could reduce our ability to meet our capital requirements or fund our working capital needs, and lead to losses on derivative positions resulting from counterparty failures, which could adversely affect our financial position and results of operations.

A significant disruption in our computer systems and our inability to adequately maintain and update those systems could adversely affect our operations and our ability to maintain guest confidence.

We rely extensively on our computer systems to manage inventory, process guest transactions, manage guest data, communicate with our vendors and other third parties, service REDcard accounts and summarize and analyze results, and on continued and unimpeded access to the internet to use our computer systems. Our systems are subject to damage or interruption from power outages, telecommunications failures, computer viruses and malicious attacks, security breaches and catastrophic events. If our systems are damaged or fail to function properly, we may incur substantial repair or replacement costs, experience data loss and impediments to our ability to manage inventories or process guest transactions, and encounter lost guest confidence, which could adversely affect our results of operations. The Data Breach we experienced negatively impacted our ability to timely handle customer inquiries, and we experienced weaker than expected U.S. Segment sales following the announcement of the Data Breach.

We continually make significant technology investments that will help maintain and update our existing computer systems. Implementing significant system changes increases the risk of computer system disruption. Additionally, the potential problems and interruptions associated with implementing technology initiatives could disrupt or reduce our operational efficiency, and could impact the guest experience and guest confidence.

If we do not positively differentiate the Target experience and appeal to our new Canadian guests, our financial results could be adversely affected.

In fiscal 2013 we opened 124 Target stores in Canada, which was our first retail store expansion outside of the United States. Our initial sales and operating results in Canada have not met our initial expectations. Improving our sales in Canada is contingent on our ability to deploy new marketing programs that positively differentiate us from other retailers in Canada, and achieve market acceptance by Canadian guests. In addition, our sales and operating results in Canada are dependent on our ability to manage our inventory to offer the expected assortment of merchandise to our Canadian guests while avoiding overstock situations, and general macroeconomic conditions in Canada. If we do not effectively execute our marketing program and manage our inventory in Canada, our financial results could be adversely affected.

A disruption in relationships with third parties who provide us services in connection with certain aspects of our business could adversely affect our operations.

We rely on third parties to support a variety of business functions, including our Canadian supply chain, portions of our technology development and systems, our multichannel platforms and distribution network operations, credit and debit card transaction processing, and extensions of credit for our 5% REDcard Rewards loyalty program. If we are unable to contract with third parties having the specialized skills needed to support those strategies or integrate their products and services with our business, or if those third parties fail to meet our performance standards and expectations, including with respect to data security, our reputation, sales and results of operations could be adversely affected. In addition, we could face increased costs associated with finding replacement providers or hiring new team members to provide these services in-house.

We experienced a significant data security breach in the fourth quarter of fiscal 2013 and are not yet able to determine the full extent of its impact and the impact of government investigations and private litigation on our results of operations, which could be material.

The Data Breach we experienced involved the theft of certain payment card and guest information through unauthorized access to our network. Our investigation of the matter is ongoing, and it is possible that we will identify additional information that was accessed or stolen, which could materially worsen the losses and reputational damage we have experienced. For example, when the intrusion was initially identified, we thought the information stolen was limited to payment card information, but later discovered that other guest information was also stolen.

We are currently subject to a number of governmental investigations and private litigation and other claims relating to the Data Breach, and in the future we may be subject to additional investigations and claims of this sort. These investigations and claims could have a material adverse impact on our results of operations or profitability. Our financial liability arising from such investigations and claims will depend on many factors, one of which is whether, at the time of the Data Breach, the portion of our network that handles payment card data was in compliance with applicable payment card industry standards. While that portion of our network was determined to be compliant by an independent third-party assessor in the fall of 2013, we expect the forensic investigator working on behalf of the payment card networks to claim that we were not in compliance. Another factor is whether, and if so to what extent, any fraud losses or other expenses experienced by cardholders, card issuers and/or the payment card networks on or with respect to the payment card accounts affected by the Data Breach can be properly attributed to the Data Breach and whether, and if so to what extent, it would in any event be our legal responsibility. In addition, the governmental agencies investigating the Data Breach may seek to impose on us fines and/or other monetary relief and/or injunctive relief that could materially increase our data security costs, adversely impact how we operate our network and collect and use guest information, and put us at a competitive disadvantage with other retailers.

Finally, we believe that the greatest risk to our business arising out of the Data Breach is the negative impact on our reputation and loss of confidence of our guests, as well as the possibility of decreased participation in our REDcards Rewards loyalty program which our internal analysis has indicated drives meaningful incremental sales. We experienced weaker than expected U.S. Segment sales after the announcement of the Data Breach, but are unable to determine whether there will be a long-term impact to our relationship with our guests or whether we will need to engage in significant promotional or other activities to regain their trust, which could have a material adverse impact on our results of operations or profitability.

Item 1B. Unresolved Staff Comments

Not applicable.

Item 2. Properties

U.S. Stores at February 1, 2014	Stores	Retail Sq. Ft. (in thousands)		Stores	Retail Sq. Ft. (in thousands)
Alabama	22	3,150	Montana	7	780
Alaska	3	504	Nebraska	14	2,006
Arizona	47	6,264	Nevada	19	2,461
Arkansas	9	1,165	New Hampshire	9	1,148
California	262	34,718	New Jersey	43	5,701
Colorado	41	6,215	New Mexico	10	1,185
Connecticut	20	2,672	New York	69	9,437
Delaware	3	440	North Carolina	48	6,360
District of Columbia	1	179	North Dakota	4	554
Florida	123	17,345	Ohio	64	8,002
Georgia	54	7,398	Oklahoma	16	2,285
Hawaii	4	695	Oregon	19	2,280
Idaho	6	664	Pennsylvania	64	8,384
Illinois	91	12,514	Rhode Island	4	517
Indiana	33	4,377	South Carolina	19	2,359
Iowa	22	3,015	South Dakota	5	580
Kansas	19	2,577	Tennessee	32	4,114
Kentucky	14	1,660	Texas	149	20,976
Louisiana	16	2,246	Utah	13	1,953
Maine	5	630	Vermont	—	—
Maryland	38	4,938	Virginia	57	7,650
Massachusetts	36	4,734	Washington	36	4,194
Michigan	59	7,057	West Virginia	6	755
Minnesota	75	10,777	Wisconsin	39	4,773
Mississippi	6	743	Wyoming	2	187
Missouri	36	4,736			
			Total	**1,793**	**240,054**

Canadian Stores at February 1, 2014	Stores	Retail Sq. Ft. (in thousands)		Stores	Retail Sq. Ft. (in thousands)
Alberta	14	1,633	Nunavut	—	—
British Columbia	18	2,047	Ontario	50	5,772
Manitoba	4	457	Prince Edward Island	1	106
New Brunswick	3	320	Quebec	25	2,876
Newfoundland and Labrador	2	216	Saskatchewan	3	319
Northwest Territories	—	—	Yukon	—	—
Nova Scotia	4	443			
			Total	**124**	**14,189**

U.S. Stores and Distribution Centers at February 1, 2014	Stores	Distribution Centers [a]
Owned	1,535	31
Leased	91	6
Owned buildings on leased land	167	—
Total	**1,793**	**37**

[a] The 37 distribution centers have a total of 50,111 thousand square feet.

Canadian Stores and Distribution Centers at February 1, 2014	Stores	Distribution Centers [a]
Owned	—	3
Leased	124	—
Total	**124**	**3**

[a] The 3 distribution centers have a total of 3,963 thousand square feet.

We own our corporate headquarters buildings located in and around Minneapolis, Minnesota, and we lease and own additional office space in Minneapolis and elsewhere in the United States. We lease our Canadian headquarters in Mississauga, Ontario. Our international sourcing operations include 22 office locations in 14 countries, all of which are leased. We also lease office space in Bangalore, India, where we operate various support functions. Our properties are in good condition, well maintained, and suitable to carry on our business.

For additional information on our properties, see the Capital Expenditures section in Item 7, Management's Discussion and Analysis of Financial Condition and Results of Operations and Notes 12 and 20 of the Notes to Consolidated Financial Statements included in Item 8, Financial Statements and Supplementary Data.

Item 3. Legal Proceedings

No response is required under Item 103 of Regulation S-K, which requires disclosure of legal proceedings that are material, based on an analysis of the probability and magnitude of the outcome. For a description of other legal proceedings, including a discussion of litigation and government inquiries related to the Data Breach we experienced in the fourth quarter of fiscal 2013 in which certain payment card and guest information was stolen through unauthorized access to our network, see Item 7, Management's Discussion and Analysis of Financial Condition and Results of Operations and Note 17 of the Notes to Consolidated Financial Statements included in Item 8, Financial Statements and Supplementary Data.

Item 4. Mine Safety Disclosures

Not applicable.

Item 4A. Executive Officers

Executive officers are elected by, and serve at the pleasure of, the Board of Directors. There is neither a family relationship between any of the officers named and any other executive officer or member of the Board of Directors, nor any arrangement or understanding pursuant to which any person was selected as an officer.

Name	Title and Business Experience	Age
Timothy R. Baer	Executive Vice President, General Counsel and Corporate Secretary since March 2007.	53
Anthony S. Fisher	President, Target Canada since January 2011. Vice President, Merchandise Operations from February 2010 to January 2011. Divisional Merchandise Manager, Toys and Sporting Goods, from June 2008 to January 2010.	39
John D. Griffith	Executive Vice President, Property Development since February 2005.	52
Jeffrey J. Jones II	Executive Vice President and Chief Marketing Officer since April 2012. Partner and President of McKinney Ventures LLC from March 2006 to March 2012.	46
Jodeen A. Kozlak	Executive Vice President, Human Resources since March 2007.	50
John J. Mulligan	Executive Vice President and Chief Financial Officer since April 2012. Senior Vice President, Treasury, Accounting and Operations from February 2010 to April 2012. Vice President, Pay and Benefits from February 2007 to February 2010.	48
Tina M. Schiel	Executive Vice President, Stores since January 2011. Senior Vice President, New Business Development from February 2010 to January 2011. Senior Vice President, Stores from February 2001 to February 2010.	48
Gregg W. Steinhafel	Chairman of the Board, President and Chief Executive Officer since February 2009. President and Chief Executive Officer since May 2008. Director since January 2007. President since August 1999.	59
Kathryn A. Tesija	Executive Vice President, Merchandising and Supply Chain since October 2012. Executive Vice President, Merchandising from May 2008 to September 2012.	51
Laysha L. Ward	President, Community Relations and Target Foundation since July 2008.	46

PART II

Item 5. Market for the Registrant's Common Equity, Related Stockholder Matters and Issuer Purchases of Equity Securities

Our common stock is listed on the New York Stock Exchange under the symbol "TGT." We are authorized to issue up to 6,000,000,000 shares of common stock, par value \$0.0833, and up to 5,000,000 shares of preferred stock, par value \$0.01. At March 10, 2014, there were 15,875 shareholders of record. Dividends declared per share and the high and low closing common stock price for each fiscal quarter during 2013 and 2012 are disclosed in Note 29 of the Notes to Consolidated Financial Statements included in Item 8, Financial Statements and Supplementary Data.

In January 2012, our Board of Directors authorized the repurchase of \$5 billion of our common stock, with no stated expiration for the share repurchase program. We have repurchased 49.1 million shares of our common stock under this program for a total cash investment of \$3.1 billion (\$62.99 average price per share).

The table below presents Target common stock purchases made during the three months ended February 1, 2014 by Target, as defined in Rule 10b-18(a)(3) under the Exchange Act.

Period	Total Number of Shares Purchased [(a)(b)]	Average Price Paid per Share [(a)(b)]	Total Number of Shares Purchased as Part of the Current Program [(a)]	Dollar Value of Shares that May Yet Be Purchased Under the Program
November 3, 2013 through November 30, 2013	2,406	\$ —	49,148,329	\$ 1,904,324,394
December 1, 2013 through January 4, 2014	18,310	—	49,148,329	1,904,324,394
January 5, 2014 through February 1, 2014	147,537	—	49,148,329	1,904,324,394
	168,253	**\$ —**	**49,148,329**	**\$ 1,904,324,394**

(a) The table above includes shares reacquired upon settlement of prepaid forward contracts. At February 1, 2014, we held asset positions in prepaid forward contracts for 1 million shares of our common stock, for a total cash investment of \$63 million, or an average per share price of \$48.83. No shares were reacquired under such contracts during the fourth quarter. Refer to Notes 23 and 25 of the Notes to Consolidated Financial Statements included in Item 8, Financial Statements and Supplementary Data for further details of these contracts.

(b) The number of shares above includes shares of common stock reacquired from team members who tendered owned shares to satisfy the tax withholding on equity awards as part of our long-term incentive plans or to satisfy the exercise price on stock option exercises. For the three months ended February 1, 2014,168,253 shares were reacquired at an weighted average per share price of \$61.91 pursuant to our long-term incentive plan.

Comparison of Cumulative Five Year Total Return

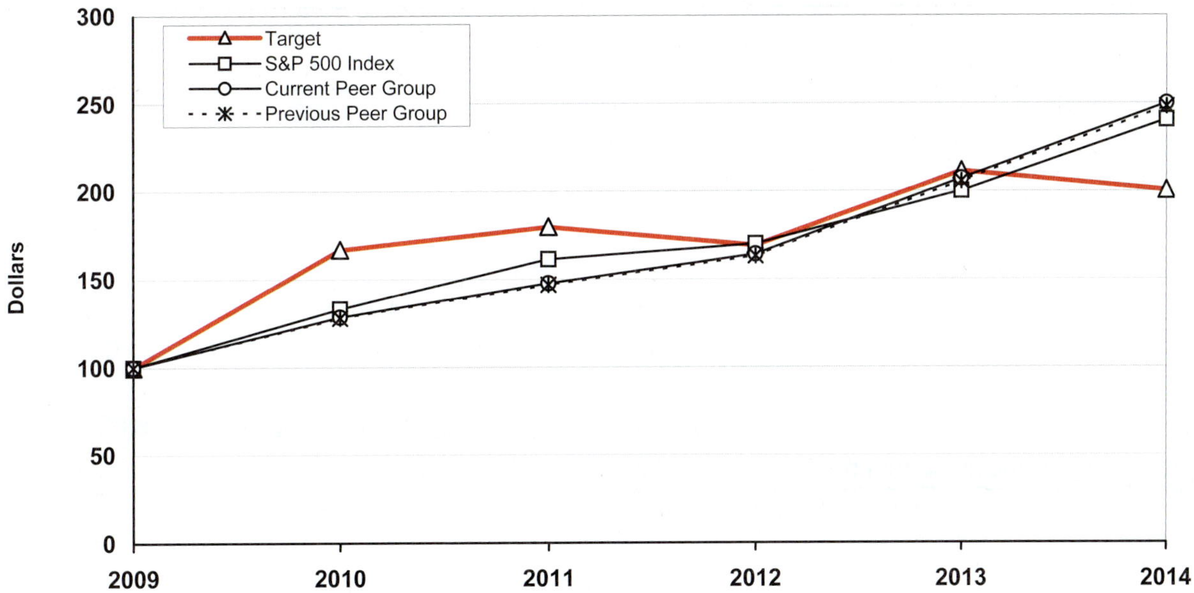

	Fiscal Years Ended					
	January 31, 2009	January 30, 2010	January 29, 2011	January 28, 2012	February 2, 2013	February 1, 2014
Target	$ 100.00	$ 167.08	$ 179.93	$ 169.27	$ 211.54	$ 200.64
S&P 500 Index	100.00	133.14	161.44	170.04	199.98	240.58
Previous Peer Group	100.00	128.10	146.82	163.21	205.64	247.92
Current Peer Group	100.00	128.46	147.71	164.25	207.23	249.77

The graph above compares the cumulative total shareholder return on our common stock for the last five fiscal years with (i) the cumulative total return on the S&P 500 Index, (ii) the peer group used in previous filings consisting of 15 online, general merchandise, department store, food and specialty retailers, which are large and meaningful competitors (Amazon.com, Best Buy, Costco, CVS Caremark, Home Depot, J. C. Penney, Kohl's, Kroger, Lowe's, Macy's, Safeway, Sears, Supervalu, Walgreens and Walmart) (Previous Peer Group), and (iii) a new peer group consisting of the companies in the Previous Peer Group excluding Supervalu. The change in peer groups was made to be consistent with the retail peer group used for our definitive Proxy Statement to be filed on or about April 28, 2014.

Both peer groups are weighted by the market capitalization of each component company. The graph assumes the investment of $100 in Target common stock, the S&P 500 Index, the Previous Peer Group and the Current Peer Group on January 31, 2009, and reinvestment of all dividends.

Item 6. Selected Financial Data

	As of or for the Year Ended					
(millions, except per share data)	**2013**	2012 [(a)]	2011	2010	2009	2008
Financial Results:						
Total revenues [(b)]	**$ 72,596**	$ 73,301	$ 69,865	$ 67,390	$ 65,357	$ 64,948
Net earnings	**1,971**	2,999	2,929	2,920	2,488	2,214
Per Share:						
Basic earnings per share	**3.10**	4.57	4.31	4.03	3.31	2.87
Diluted earnings per share	**3.07**	4.52	4.28	4.00	3.30	2.86
Cash dividends declared per share	**1.65**	1.38	1.15	0.92	0.67	0.62
Financial Position:						
Total assets	**44,553**	48,163	46,630	43,705	44,533	44,106
Long-term debt, including current portion	**13,782**	17,648	17,483	15,726	16,814	18,752

Note: This information should be read in conjunction with Management's Discussion and Analysis of Financial Condition and Results of Operations, included in Item 7 of this Report, and our consolidated financial statements and notes thereto, included in Item 8 of this Report.

(a) Consisted of 53 weeks.

(b) For 2013, total revenues include sales generated by our U.S. and Canadian retail operations. For 2012 and prior, total revenues include sales generated by our U.S. retail operations and credit card revenues.

Item 7. Management's Discussion and Analysis of Financial Condition and Results of Operations

Executive Summary

Fiscal 2013 included the following notable items:

- GAAP earnings per share were $3.07, including dilution of $1.13 related to the Canadian Segment.
- Adjusted earnings per share were $4.38 on a comparable sales decrease of 0.4 percent.
- We paid dividends of $1,006 million and repurchased 21.9 million of our shares for $1,474 million.
- We opened 124 stores in Canada, marking the biggest single-year store opening cycle in the Company's history and first year of international retail operations.
- We completed the sale of our U.S. consumer credit card portfolio to TD in March 2013 and recognized a gain of $391 million.
- We used $1.4 billion of the net proceeds received from the sale of our U.S. consumer credit card portfolio to repurchase, at market value, $970 million of debt.

Sales were $72,596 million for 2013, an increase of $636 million or 0.9 percent from the prior year. Consolidated earnings before interest expense and income taxes for 2013 decreased by $1,142 million or 21.3 percent from 2012 to $4,229 million. Cash flow provided by operations was $6,520 million, $5,325 million and $5,434 million for 2013, 2012 and 2011, respectively. In connection with the sale of our U.S. credit card receivables, we received cash of $5.7 billion. Of this amount, $2.7 billion is included in cash flow provided by operations and $3.0 billion is included in cash flow provided by investing activities.

Earnings Per Share				Percent Change	
	2013	2012 [(a)]	2011	**2013/2012**	2012/2011
GAAP diluted earnings per share	**$ 3.07**	$ 4.52	$ 4.28	**(32.1)%**	5.6%
Adjustments	**1.31**	0.24	0.13		
Adjusted diluted earnings per share	**$ 4.38**	$ 4.76	$ 4.41	**(8.0)%**	7.9%

Note: We have disclosed adjusted diluted earnings per share ("Adjusted EPS"), a non-GAAP metric, which excludes the impact of certain matters not related to our routine retail operations, including the impact of our Canadian market entry. Management believes that Adjusted EPS is meaningful in order to provide period-to-period comparisons of our operating results. A reconciliation of non-GAAP financial measures to GAAP measures is provided on page 25.

(a) Consisted of 53 weeks.

Data Breach

Description of Event

As previously disclosed, we experienced a data breach in which an intruder stole certain payment card and other guest information from our network (the Data Breach). Based on our investigation to date, we believe that the intruder accessed and stole payment card data from approximately 40 million credit and debit card accounts of guests who shopped at our U.S. stores between November 27 and December 15, 2013, through malware installed on our point-of-sale system in our U.S. stores. On December 15, we removed the malware from virtually all registers in our U.S. stores. Payment card data used in transactions made by 56 additional guests in the period between December 16 and December 17 was stolen prior to our disabling malware on one additional register that was disconnected from our system when we completed the initial malware removal on December 15. In addition, the intruder stole certain guest information, including names, mailing addresses, phone numbers or email addresses, for up to 70 million individuals. Our investigation of the matter is ongoing, and we are supporting law enforcement efforts to identify the responsible parties.

Expenses Incurred and Amounts Accrued

In the fourth quarter of 2013, we recorded $61 million of pretax Data Breach-related expenses, and expected insurance proceeds of $44 million, for net expenses of $17 million ($11 million after tax), or $0.02 per diluted share. These expenses were included in our Consolidated Statements of Operations as Selling, General and Administrative Expenses (SG&A), but were not part of our segment results. Expenses include costs to investigate the Data Breach, provide credit-monitoring services to our guests, increase staffing in our call centers, and procure legal and other professional services.

The $61 million of fourth quarter expenses also includes an accrual related to the expected payment card networks' claims by reason of the Data Breach. The ultimate amount of these claims will likely include amounts for incremental counterfeit fraud losses and non-ordinary course operating expenses (such as card reissuance costs) that the payment card networks believe they or their issuing banks have incurred. In order for us to have liability for such claims, we believe that a court would have to find among other things that (1) at the time of the Data Breach the portion of our network that handles payment card data was noncompliant with applicable data security standards in a manner that contributed to the Data Breach, and (2) the network operating rules around reimbursement of operating costs and counterfeit fraud losses are enforceable. While an independent third-party assessor found the portion of our network that handles payment card data to be compliant with applicable data security standards in the fall of 2013, we expect the forensic investigator working on behalf of the payment card networks nonetheless to claim that we were not in compliance with those standards at the time of the Data Breach. We base that expectation on our understanding that, in cases like ours where prior to a data breach the entity suffering the breach had been found by an independent third-party assessor to be fully compliant with those standards, the network-approved forensic investigator nonetheless regularly claims that the breached entity was not in fact compliant with those standards. As a result, we believe it is probable that the payment card networks will make claims against us. We expect to dispute the payment card networks' anticipated claims, and we think it is likely that our disputes would lead to settlement negotiations consistent with the experience of other entities that have suffered similar payment card breaches. We believe such negotiations would effect a combined settlement of both the payment card networks' counterfeit fraud loss allegations and their non-ordinary course operating expense allegations. We based our year-end accrual on the expectation of reaching negotiated settlements of the payment card networks' anticipated claims and not on any determination that it is probable we would be found liable on these claims were they to be litigated. Currently, we can only reasonably estimate a loss associated with settlements of the networks' expected claims for non-ordinary course operating expenses. The year-end accrual does not include any amounts associated with the networks' expected claims for alleged incremental counterfeit fraud losses because the loss associated with settling such claims, while probable in our judgment, is not reasonably estimable, in part because we have not yet received third-party fraud reporting from the payment card networks. We are not able to reasonably estimate a range of possible losses in excess of the year-end accrual related to the expected settlement of the payment card networks' claims because the investigation into the matter is ongoing and there are significant factual and legal issues to be resolved. We believe that the ultimate amount paid on payment card network claims could be material to our results of operations in future periods.

Litigation and Governmental Investigations

In addition, more than 80 actions have been filed in courts in many states and other claims have been or may be asserted against us on behalf of guests, payment card issuing banks, shareholders or others seeking damages or other related relief, allegedly arising out of the Data Breach. State and federal agencies, including the State Attorneys General, the Federal Trade Commission and the SEC are investigating events related to the Data Breach, including how it occurred, its consequences and our responses. Although we are cooperating in these investigations, we may be subject to fines or other obligations, which may have an adverse effect on how we operate our business and our results of operations. While a loss from these matters is reasonably possible, we cannot reasonably estimate a range of possible losses because our investigation into the matter is ongoing, the proceedings remain in the early stages, alleged damages have not been specified, there is uncertainty as to the likelihood of a class or classes being certified or the ultimate size of any class if certified, and there are significant factual and legal issues to be resolved. Further, we do not believe that a loss from these matters is probable; therefore, we have not recorded a loss contingency liability for litigation, claims and governmental investigations in the fourth quarter. See Note 17 of the Notes to Consolidated Financial Statements included in Item 8, Financial Statements and Supplementary Data.

Future Costs

We expect to incur significant investigation, legal and professional services expenses associated with the Data Breach in future periods. We will recognize these expenses as services are received. We also expect to incur additional expenses associated with incremental fraud and reissuance costs on Target REDcards.

Insurance Coverage

To limit our exposure to Data Breach losses, we maintain $100 million of network-security insurance coverage, above a $10 million deductible. This coverage and certain other insurance coverage may reduce our exposure. We will pursue recoveries to the maximum extent available under the policies. As of February 1, 2014, we have recorded a $44 million receivable for costs we believe are reimbursable and probable of recovery under our insurance coverage, which partially offsets the $61 million of expense relating to the Data Breach.

Future Capital Investments

We plan to accelerate a previously planned investment of approximately $100 million to equip our proprietary REDcards and all of our U.S. store card readers with chip-enabled smart-card technology by the first quarter of 2015.

In addition, we may accelerate or make additional investments in our information technology systems, but we are unable to estimate such investments because the nature and scope has not yet been determined. We do not expect such amounts to be material to any fiscal period.

Effect on Sales and Guest Loyalty

We believe the Data Breach adversely affected our fourth quarter U.S. Segment sales. Prior to our December 19, 2013 announcement of the Data Breach, our U.S. Segment fourth quarter comparable sales were positive, followed by meaningfully negative comparable sales results following the announcement. Comparable sales began to recover in January 2014. The collective interaction of year-over-year changes in the retail calendar (*e.g.*, the number of days between Thanksgiving and Christmas), combined with the broad array of competitive, consumer behavioral and weather factors makes any quantification of the precise impact of the Data Breach on sales infeasible.

Fourth quarter sales penetration on our REDcards was 20.9 percent, up 5.4 percentage points from 2012. While the rate of increase slowed following the Data Breach, year-over-year penetration continued to grow.

We know our guests' confidence in Target and the broader U.S. payment system has been shaken. We are committed to, and actively engaged in, activities to restore their confidence. We cannot predict the length or extent of any ongoing impact to sales.

Credit Card Receivables Transaction

In March 2013, we sold our entire U.S. consumer credit card portfolio to TD and recognized a gain of $391 million. This transaction was accounted for as a sale, and the receivables are no longer reported in our Consolidated Statements of Financial Position. Consideration received included cash of $5.7 billion, equal to the gross (par) value of the outstanding receivables at the time of closing, and a $225 million beneficial interest asset. The beneficial interest asset effectively represents a receivable for the present value of future profit-sharing we expect to receive on the receivables sold. Based on historical payment patterns, we estimate that the beneficial interest asset will be reduced over a four-year period following the sale, with larger reductions in the early years. As of February 1, 2014, a $127 million beneficial interest asset remained. Concurrent with the sale of the portfolio, we repaid the nonrecourse debt collateralized by credit card receivables (2006/2007 Series Variable Funding Certificate) at par of $1.5 billion, resulting in net cash proceeds of $4.2 billion.

TD now underwrites, funds and owns Target Credit Card and Target Visa consumer receivables in the U.S. TD controls risk management policies and oversees regulatory compliance, and we perform account servicing and primary marketing functions. We earn a substantial portion of the profits generated by the Target Credit Card and Target Visa portfolios. Income from the TD profit-sharing arrangement and our related account servicing expenses are classified within SG&A expenses in the U.S. Segment.

Beginning with the first quarter of 2013, we no longer report a U.S. Credit Card Segment.

Analysis of Results of Operations

U.S. Segment

U.S. Segment Results (dollars in millions)	2013	2012 [(a)]	2011	Percent Change 2013/2012	Percent Change 2012/2011
Sales	**$ 71,279**	$ 71,960	$ 68,466	**(0.9)%**	5.1%
Cost of sales	**50,039**	50,568	47,860	**(1.0)**	5.7
Gross margin	**21,240**	21,392	20,606	**(0.7)**	3.8
SG&A expenses [(b)]	**14,285**	13,759	13,079	**3.8**	5.2
EBITDA	**6,955**	7,633	7,527	**(8.9)**	1.4
Depreciation and amortization	**1,996**	2,044	2,084	**(2.4)**	(1.9)
EBIT	**$ 4,959**	$ 5,589	$ 5,443	**(11.3)%**	2.7%

Note: Prior period segment results have been revised to reflect the combination of our historical U.S. Retail Segment and U.S. Credit Card Segment into one U.S. Segment. Quarterly and full-year historical information for the three most recently completed years reflecting the results for the U.S. Segment and Canadian Segment are attached as Exhibit (99) to our current report on Form 8-K filed April 16, 2013.

Note: See Note 28 to our Consolidated Financial Statements for a reconciliation of our segment results to earnings before income taxes.

(a) Consisted of 53 weeks.

(b) SG&A includes credit card revenues and expenses for all periods presented prior to the March 2013 sale of our U.S. consumer credit card portfolio to TD. For 2013, SG&A also includes $653 million of profit-sharing income from the arrangement with TD.

U.S. Segment Rate Analysis	**Twelve Months Ended February 1, 2014**	Twelve Months Ended February 2, 2013: U.S. Segment, as revised	Twelve Months Ended February 2, 2013: Impact of Historical U.S. Credit Card Segment[(a)]	Twelve Months Ended February 2, 2013: Historical U.S. Retail Segment	2013 U.S. Segment Change vs. 2012: U.S. Segment, as revised	2013 U.S. Segment Change vs. 2012: Historical U.S. Retail Segment
Gross margin rate	**29.8%**	29.7%	— pp	29.7%	0.1pp	0.1pp
SG&A expense rate	**20.0**	19.1	(0.8)	19.9	0.9	0.1
EBITDA margin rate	**9.8**	10.6	0.8	9.8	(0.8)	—
Depreciation and amortization expense rate	**2.8**	2.8	—	2.8	—	—
EBIT margin rate	**7.0**	7.8	0.8	7.0	(0.8)	—

U.S. Segment Rate Analysis		Twelve Months Ended January 28, 2012			2012 U.S. Segment Change vs. 2011	
	Twelve Months Ended February 2, 2013	U.S. Segment, as revised	Impact of Historical U.S. Credit Card Segment[a]	Historical U.S. Retail Segment	U.S. Segment, as revised	Historical U.S. Retail Segment
Gross margin rate	**29.7%**	30.1%	— pp	30.1%	(0.4)pp	(0.4)pp
SG&A expense rate	**19.1**	19.1	(1.0)	20.1	—	(1.0)
EBITDA margin rate	**10.6**	11.0	1.0	10.0	(0.4)	0.6
Depreciation and amortization expense rate	**2.8**	3.0	—	3.0	(0.2)	(0.2)
EBIT margin rate	**7.8**	8.0	1.0	7.0	(0.2)	0.8

Rate analysis metrics are computed by dividing the applicable amount by sales.

(a) Represents the impact of combining the historical U.S. Credit Card Segment and the U.S. Retail Segment into one U.S. Segment. Compared with the historical U.S. Retail Segment results for the same period, segment results, as revised, reflect lower SG&A rates and increased EBIT and EBITDA margin rates resulting from the inclusion of credit card profits, net of expenses, within SG&A compared with historical U.S. Segment results for the same period.

Sales

Sales include merchandise sales, net of expected returns, and gift card breakage. Refer to Note 2 of the Notes to Consolidated Financial Statements for a definition of gift card breakage. The decrease in sales in 2013 reflects the impact of an additional week in 2012 and a decline in comparable sales, partially offset by the contribution from new stores. Sales growth in 2012 resulted from higher comparable sales, the contribution from new stores and a 1.7 percentage point benefit from an additional week in the fiscal year. Inflation did not materially affect sales in any period presented.

Comparable sales is a measure that highlights the performance of our existing stores and digital sales by measuring the change in sales for a period over the comparable, prior-year period of equivalent length. The method of calculating comparable sales varies across the retail industry. As a result, our comparable sales calculation is not necessarily comparable to similarly titled measures reported by other companies. Comparable sales include all sales, except sales from stores open less than thirteen months.

Comparable Sales	2013	2012	2011
Comparable sales change	**(0.4)%**	2.7%	3.0%
Drivers of change in comparable sales:			
Number of transactions	**(2.7)%**	0.5%	0.4%
Average transaction amount	**2.3 %**	2.3%	2.6%
Selling price per unit	**1.6 %**	1.3%	0.3%
Units per transaction	**0.7 %**	1.0%	2.3%

U.S. Sales by Product Category	Percentage of Sales		
	2013	2012	2011
Household essentials [(a)]	**25%**	25%	25%
Hardlines [(b)]	**18**	18	19
Apparel and accessories [(c)]	**19**	19	19
Food and pet supplies [(d)]	**21**	20	19
Home furnishings and décor [(e)]	**17**	18	18
Total	**100%**	100%	100%

(a) Includes pharmacy, beauty, personal care, baby care, cleaning and paper products.

(b) Includes electronics (including video game hardware and software), music, movies, books, computer software, sporting goods and toys.

(c) Includes apparel for women, men, boys, girls, toddlers, infants and newborns, as well as intimate apparel, jewelry, accessories and shoes.

(d) Includes dry grocery, dairy, frozen food, beverages, candy, snacks, deli, bakery, meat, produce and pet supplies.

(e) Includes furniture, lighting, kitchenware, small appliances, home décor, bed and bath, home improvement, automotive and seasonal merchandise such as patio furniture and holiday décor.

The collective interaction of a broad array of macroeconomic, competitive and consumer behavioral factors, as well as sales mix, and transfer of sales to new stores makes further analysis of sales metrics infeasible.

Credit is offered by TD to qualified guests through Target-branded credit cards: the Target Credit Card and the Target Visa Credit Card (Target Credit Cards). Additionally, we offer a branded proprietary Target Debit Card. Collectively, we refer to these products as REDcards®. Guests receive a 5 percent discount on virtually all purchases when they use a REDcard at Target. We monitor the percentage of sales that are paid for using REDcards (REDcard Penetration) because our internal analysis has indicated that a meaningful portion of incremental purchases on our REDcards are also incremental sales for Target.

REDcard Penetration	**2013**	2012	2011
Target Credit Cards	**9.3%**	7.9%	6.8%
Target Debit Card	**9.9**	5.7	2.5
Total store REDcard Penetration	**19.3%**	13.6%	9.3%

Note: The sum of Target Credit Cards and Target Debit Card penetration may not equal Total store REDcard Penetration due to rounding.

Gross Margin Rate

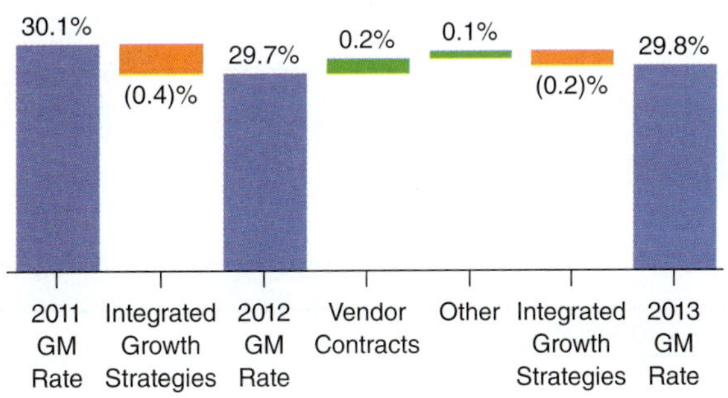

Our gross margin rate was 29.8 percent in 2013, 29.7 percent in 2012 and 30.1 percent in 2011. The 2013 increase is primarily the result of a change in vendor contracts regarding payments received in support of marketing programs. Increases to the rate were offset by our integrated growth strategies of our 5 percent REDcard Rewards loyalty program and our store remodel program.

The 2013 change to certain merchandise vendor contracts resulted in more vendor consideration being recognized as a reduction of our cost of sales rather than a reduction of SG&A. This change increased our gross margin rate for 2013, with an equal and offsetting increase in our SG&A rate, and has no impact on EBITDA or EBIT margin rates.

Selling, General and Administrative Expense Rate

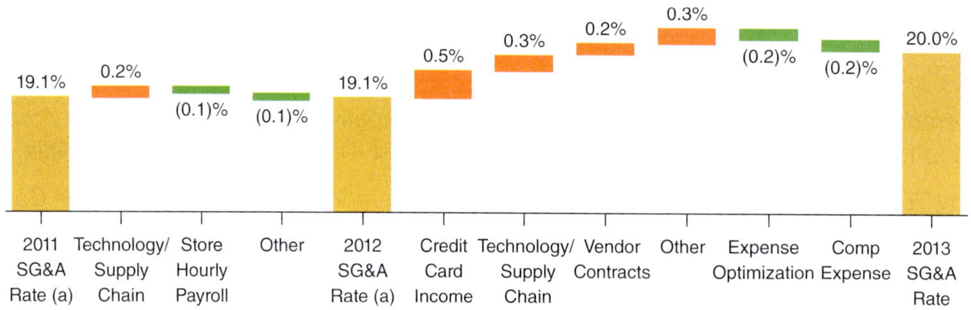

[(a)] Represents revised U.S. Segment results.

Our SG&A expense rate was 20.0 percent in 2013, and 19.1 percent in both 2012 and 2011. The increase in 2013 resulted from a smaller contribution from our credit card portfolio, investments in technology and supply chain in support of multichannel initiatives, changes in merchandise vendor contracts described on the previous page, and other increases. Increases were partially offset by the benefit from our company-wide expense optimization efforts and favorable incentive compensation and store hourly payroll. During 2012, investments in technology and supply chain were offset by improvements in store hourly payroll and disciplined expense management across the Company.

Store Data

Change in Number of Stores	2013	2012
Beginning store count	**1,778**	1,763
Opened	**19**	23
Closed	**(4)**	(5)
Relocated	—	(3)
Ending store count	**1,793**	1,778
Number of stores remodeled during the year	**100**	252

Number of Stores and Retail Square Feet	Number of Stores		Retail Square Feet [(a)]	
	February 1, 2014	February 2, 2013	**February 1, 2014**	February 2, 2013
Target general merchandise stores	**289**	391	**33,843**	46,584
Expanded food assortment stores	**1,245**	1,131	**160,891**	146,249
SuperTarget stores	**251**	251	**44,500**	44,500
CityTarget stores	**8**	5	**820**	514
Total	**1,793**	1,778	**240,054**	237,847

[(a)] In thousands, reflects total square feet less office, distribution center and vacant space.

Canadian Segment

Canadian Segment Results				Percent Change	
(dollars in millions)	**2013**	2012	2011	**2013/2012**	2012/2011
Sales	**$ 1,317**	$ —	$ —	**n/a**	n/a
Cost of sales	**1,121**	—	—	**n/a**	n/a
Gross margin	**196**	—	—	**n/a**	n/a
SG&A expenses	**910**	272	74	**234.9**	268.7
EBITDA	**(714)**	(272)	(74)	**162.6**	268.7
Depreciation and amortization	**227**	97	48	**133.6**	103.2
EBIT	**$ (941)**	$ (369)	$ (122)	**155.0%**	203.5%

Canadian Segment Rate Analysis	2013
Gross margin rate	**14.9%**
SG&A expense rate	**69.1**
EBITDA margin rate	**(54.2)**
Depreciation and amortization expense rate	**17.3**
EBIT margin rate	**(71.5)**

Note: Rate analysis metrics are computed by dividing the applicable amount by sales.
Due to the start-up nature of our Canadian Segment, the rates above may not be indicative of future results.

Sales

Sales include merchandise sales, net of expected returns, and gift card breakage. Refer to Note 2 of the Notes to Consolidated Financial Statements for a definition of gift card breakage.

We opened 124 Canadian Target general merchandise stores during 2013 with 14.2 million total retail square feet. Canadian sales of $1,317 million represent a partial year of operation, with approximately 55 percent of the stores opened during the first half of the year, 20 percent during the third quarter and the remaining 25 percent during the fourth quarter.

Credit is offered to guests by Royal Bank of Canada (RBC) through our co-branded credit card: the Target RBC MasterCard. Additionally, we offer a proprietary Target Debit Card. Consistent with our branded payment products in the U.S., these payment products are referred to as REDcards. Guests receive a 5 percent discount on virtually all purchases when they use a REDcard at Target.

REDcard Penetration	2013
Target Credit Cards	**1.4%**
Target Debit Card	**1.5**
Total store REDcard Penetration	**2.9%**

Gross Margin Rate

The gross margin rate of 14.9 percent reflects efforts to clear excess inventory following lower than anticipated sales and supply chain start-up challenges.

Selling, General and Administrative Expense Rate

In addition to operating expenses during 2013, our Canadian Segment SG&A expense for 2013, 2012 and 2011 included start-up costs including compensation, benefits and third-party service expenses.

Other Performance Factors

Consolidated Selling, General and Administrative Expenses

In addition to our selling, general and administrative expenses recorded within our segments, we recorded certain other expenses during 2013. These expenses included a $23 million workforce-reduction charge primarily related to severance and benefits costs, a $22 million charge related to part-time team member health benefit changes, $19 million in impairment charges related to certain parcels of undeveloped land, and $17 million of Data Breach-related costs, net of expected insurance proceeds. Additional information about these items is provided within the Reconciliation of Non-GAAP Financial Measures to GAAP Measures on page 25.

Net Interest Expense

Net interest expense was $1,126 million in 2013. This increase of 47.7 percent, or $364 million, from 2012 was due to a $445 million loss on early retirement of debt in 2013, partially offset by the benefit from 2013 debt reductions.

Net interest expense was $762 million for 2012. This decrease of 12.0 percent, or $104 million, from 2011 was primarily due to an $87 million loss on early retirement of debt in 2011.

Provision for Income Taxes

Our effective income tax rate increased to 36.5 percent in 2013, from 34.9 percent in 2012, which was driven by the net effect of increased losses related to Canadian operations combined with a lower year-over-year benefit from the favorable resolution of various income tax matters. The resolution of various income tax matters reduced tax expense by $16 million and $58 million in 2013 and 2012, respectively. A tax rate reconciliation is provided in Note 21 to our Consolidated Financial Statements.

Our effective income tax rate increased to 34.9 percent in 2012, from 34.3 percent in 2011, primarily due to a lower benefit associated with the favorable resolution of various income tax matters, combined with the effect of increased losses related to Canadian operations. Various income tax matters were resolved in 2012 and 2011 which reduced tax expense by $58 million and $85 million, respectively.

Reconciliation of Non-GAAP Financial Measures to GAAP Measures

To provide additional transparency, we have disclosed non-GAAP adjusted diluted earnings per share, which excludes the impact of our 2013 Canadian market entry, the gain on receivables transaction, favorable resolution of various income tax matters, the loss on early retirement of debt and other matters presented below. We believe this information is useful in providing period-to-period comparisons of the results of our U.S. operations. This measure is not in accordance with, or an alternative for, generally accepted accounting principles in the United States. The most comparable GAAP measure is diluted earnings per share. Non-GAAP adjusted EPS should not be considered in isolation or as a substitution for analysis of our results as reported under GAAP. Other companies may calculate non-GAAP adjusted EPS differently than we do, limiting the usefulness of the measure for comparisons with other companies.

	2013			2012			2011		
(millions, except per share data)	Pretax	Net of Tax	Per Share Amounts	Pretax	Net of Tax	Per Share Amounts	Pretax	Net of Tax	Per Share Amounts
GAAP diluted earnings per share			$ 3.07			$ 4.52			$ 4.28
Adjustments									
Total Canadian losses [(a)]	$ 1,018	$ 723	$ 1.13	$ 447	$ 315	$ 0.48	$ 166	$ 119	$ 0.17
Loss on early retirement of debt	445	270	0.42	—	—	—	87	55	0.08
Gain on receivables transaction [(b)]	(391)	(247)	(0.38)	(152)	(97)	(0.15)	—	—	—
Reduction of beneficial interest asset	98	61	0.09	—	—	—	—	—	—
Other [(c)]	64	40	0.06	—	—	—	—	—	—
Data Breach related costs, net of insurance receivable [(d)]	17	11	0.02	—	—	—	—	—	—
Resolution of income tax matters	—	(16)	(0.03)	—	(58)	(0.09)	—	(85)	(0.12)
Adjusted diluted earnings per share			$ 4.38			$ 4.76			$ 4.41

Note: A non-GAAP financial measures summary is provided on page 16. The sum of the non-GAAP adjustments may not equal the total adjustment amounts due to rounding.

[(a)] Total Canadian losses include interest expense of $77 million, $78 million and $44 million for 2013, 2012 and 2011, respectively.

[(b)] 2013 adjustment represents consideration received in the first quarter from the sale of our U.S. credit card receivables in excess of the recorded amount of the receivables. Consideration included a beneficial interest asset of $225 million. The 2012 adjustment represents the gain on receivables held for sale.

[(c)] Other includes a $23 million workforce-reduction charge primarily related to severance and benefits costs, a $22 million charge related to part-time team member health benefit changes and $19 million in impairment charges related to certain parcels of undeveloped land.

[(d)] For 2013, we recorded $61 million of pretax Data Breach-related expenses, and expected insurance proceeds of $44 million, for net pretax expenses of $17 million.

Analysis of Financial Condition

Liquidity and Capital Resources

Our period-end cash and cash equivalents balance was $695 million compared with $784 million in 2012. Short-term investments (highly liquid investments with an original maturity of three months or less from the time of purchase) of $3 million and $130 million were included in cash and cash equivalents at the end of 2013 and 2012, respectively. Our investment policy is designed to preserve principal and liquidity of our short-term investments. This policy allows investments in large money market funds or in highly rated direct short-term instruments that mature in 60 days or less. We also place dollar limits on our investments in individual funds or instruments.

Cash Flows

Our 2013 operations were funded by both internally generated funds and proceeds from the sale of our consumer credit card receivables portfolio. Cash flow provided by operations was $6,520 million in 2013 compared with $5,325 million in 2012. Our cash flows, combined with our prior year-end cash position, allowed us to pay current debt maturities, invest in the business, pay dividends and repurchase shares under our share repurchase program.

Concurrent with the sale of our U.S. credit card portfolio described in Note 6 of the Notes to Consolidated Financial Statements included in Item 8, Financial Statements and Supplementary Data, we repaid the nonrecourse debt collateralized by credit card receivables (2006/2007 Series Variable Funding Certificate) at par of $1.5 billion. Also during the first quarter of 2013, we used $1.4 billion of the net proceeds received from the sale to repurchase, at market value, $970 million of debt. We have applied additional proceeds from the sale to reduce our debt and repurchase shares.

Year-end inventory levels increased from $7,903 million in 2012 to $8,766 million in 2013, about half of which was for our 2013 Canadian market entry. Accounts payable increased by $627 million, or 8.9 percent over the same period.

Share Repurchases

During the first quarter of 2012, we completed a $10 billion share repurchase program authorized by our Board of Directors in November 2007, and began repurchasing shares under a new $5 billion program authorized by our Board of Directors in January 2012. During 2013, we repurchased 21.9 million shares of our common stock for a total investment of $1,474 million ($67.41 per share). We did not repurchase any shares during the second half of 2013 due to our performance and desire to maintain our strong investment grade credit ratings. During 2012, we repurchased 32.2 million shares of our common stock for a total investment of $1,900 million ($58.96 per share).

Dividends

We paid dividends totaling $1,006 million in 2013 and $869 million in 2012, for an increase of 15.8 percent. We declared dividends totaling $1,051 million ($1.65 per share) in 2013, for an increase of 16.4 percent over 2012. We declared dividends totaling $903 million ($1.38 per share) in 2012, an increase of 16.2 percent over 2011. We have paid dividends every quarter since our 1967 initial public offering, and it is our intent to continue to do so in the future.

Short-term and Long-term Financing

Our financing strategy is to ensure liquidity and access to capital markets, to manage our net exposure to floating interest rate volatility and to maintain a balanced spectrum of debt maturities. Within these parameters, we seek to minimize our borrowing costs. Our ability to access the long-term debt and commercial paper markets has provided us with ample sources of liquidity. Our continued access to these markets depends on multiple factors, including the condition of debt capital markets, our operating performance and maintaining strong debt ratings. As of February 1, 2014, our credit ratings were as follows:

Credit Ratings	Moody's	Standard and Poor's	Fitch
Long-term debt	A2	A+	A-
Commercial paper	P-1	A-1	F2

If our credit ratings were lowered, our ability to access the debt markets, our cost of funds and other terms for new debt issuances could be adversely impacted. Each credit rating agency reviews its rating periodically and there is no guarantee our current credit ratings will remain the same as described above. Our Standard and Poor's rating currently carries a negative outlook, and we believe that our recent operating performance may cause Standard and Poor's to lower their long-term debt rating by one level.

As a measure of our financial condition, we monitor our interest coverage ratio, representing the ratio of pretax earnings before fixed charges to fixed charges. Fixed charges include interest expense and the interest portion of rent expense. Our interest coverage ratio was 4.7x in 2013, 6.1x in 2012 and 5.9x in 2011. Refer to Exhibit (12) for a description of how the gain on sale of our U.S. credit card receivable portfolio and loss on early retirement of debt affected the 2013 calculation.

In 2013, we funded our peak sales season working capital needs through internally generated funds and the issuance of commercial paper. In 2012, we funded our peak sales season working capital needs through internally generated funds.

Commercial Paper (dollars in millions)	**2013**	2012	2011
Maximum daily amount outstanding during the year	**$ 1,465**	$ 970	$ 1,211
Average amount outstanding during the year	**408**	120	244
Amount outstanding at year-end	**80**	970	—
Weighted average interest rate	**0.13%**	0.16%	0.11%

We have additional liquidity through a committed $2.25 billion revolving credit facility obtained in October 2011, which was amended during 2013 to extend the expiration date to October 2018. No balances were outstanding at any time during 2013 or 2012 under this facility.

Most of our long-term debt obligations contain covenants related to secured debt levels. In addition to a secured debt level covenant, our credit facility also contains a debt leverage covenant. We are, and expect to remain, in compliance with these covenants. Additionally, at February 1, 2014, no notes or debentures contained provisions requiring acceleration of payment upon a debt rating downgrade, except that certain outstanding notes allow the note holders to put the notes to us if within a matter of months of each other we experience both (i) a change in control; and (ii) our long-term debt ratings are either reduced and the resulting rating is non-investment grade, or our long-term debt ratings are placed on watch for possible reduction and those ratings are subsequently reduced and the resulting rating is non-investment grade.

We believe our sources of liquidity will continue to be adequate to maintain operations, finance anticipated expansion and strategic initiatives, fund obligations incurred as a result of the Data Breach and any related future technology enhancements, pay dividends and continue purchases under our share repurchase program for the foreseeable future. We continue to anticipate ample access to commercial paper and long-term financing.

Capital Expenditures

Capital Expenditures	**2013**			2012			2011
(millions)	**U.S.**	**Canada**	**Total**	U.S.	Canada	Total	Total
New stores	**$ 536**	**$ 1,451**	**$ 1,987**	$ 673	$ 417	$ 1,090	$ 2,058
Store remodels and expansions	**281**	**—**	**281**	690	—	690	1,289
Information technology, distribution and other	**1,069**	**116**	**1,185**	982	515	1,497	1,021
Total	**$ 1,886**	**$ 1,567**	**$ 3,453**	$ 2,345	$ 932	$ 3,277	$ 4,368

Capital expenditures increased in 2013 from the prior year due to Canadian expenditures in advance of 2013 store openings, partially offset by fewer remodels and new stores in the U.S . The decrease in capital expenditures in 2012 from the prior year was primarily driven by the 2011 purchase of Zellers leases in Canada and fewer 2012 U.S. store remodels, partially offset by continued investment in new stores in the U.S. and Canada and technology and multichannel investments. We expect approximately $2.4 to $2.7 billion of capital expenditures in 2014, reflecting an estimated $2.1 to $2.3 billion in our U.S. Segment, including the previously discussed acceleration of our investment in chip-enabled smart card technology, and approximately $0.3 to $0.4 billion in our Canadian Segment.

Commitments and Contingencies

Contractual Obligations as of February 1, 2014 (millions)	Payments Due by Period				
	Total	Less than 1 Year	1-3 Years	3-5 Years	After 5 Years
Recorded contractual obligations:					
Long-term debt [(a)]	$ 11,708	$ 1,001	$ 778	$ 2,453	$ 7,476
Capital lease obligations [(b)]	5,313	204	390	307	4,412
Real estate liabilities [(c)]	144	144	—	—	—
Deferred compensation [(d)]	522	46	99	111	266
Tax contingencies [(e)]	—	—	—	—	—
Loss contingencies [(f)]	—	—	—	—	—
Unrecorded contractual obligations:					
Interest payments – long-term debt	8,618	590	1,145	917	5,966
Operating leases [(b)]	4,103	187	359	330	3,227
Real estate obligations [(g)]	305	289	16	—	—
Purchase obligations [(h)]	1,317	828	301	61	127
Future contributions to retirement plans [(i)]	—	—	—	—	—
Contractual obligations	$ 32,030	$ 3,289	$ 3,088	$ 4,179	$ 21,474

(a) Represents principal payments only, and excludes any fair market value adjustments recorded in long-term debt under derivative and hedge accounting rules. See Note 18 of the Notes to Consolidated Financial Statements for further information.

(b) Total contractual lease payments include $3,740 million and $2,105 million of capital and operating lease payments, respectively, related to options to extend the lease term that are reasonably assured of being exercised. These payments also include $80 million and $135 million of legally binding minimum lease payments for stores that are expected to open in 2014 or later for capital and operating leases, respectively. Capital lease obligations include interest. See Note 20 of the Notes to Consolidated Financial Statements for further information.

(c) Real estate liabilities include costs incurred but not paid related to the construction or remodeling of real estate and facilities.

(d) Deferred compensation obligations include commitments related to our nonqualified deferred compensation plans. The timing of deferred compensation payouts is estimated based on payments currently made to former employees and retirees, forecasted investment returns, and the projected timing of future retirements.

(e) Estimated tax contingencies of $241 million, including interest and penalties, are not included in the table above because we are not able to make reasonably reliable estimates of the period of cash settlement. See Note 21 of the Notes to Consolidated Financial Statements for further information.

(f) Estimated loss contingencies, including those related to the Data Breach, are not included in the table above because we are not able to make reasonably reliable estimates of the period of cash settlement. See Note 17 of the Notes to Consolidated Financial Statements for further information.

(g) Real estate obligations include commitments for the purchase, construction or remodeling of real estate and facilities.

(h) Purchase obligations include all legally binding contracts such as firm minimum commitments for inventory purchases, merchandise royalties, equipment purchases, marketing-related contracts, software acquisition/license commitments and service contracts. (Note: we expect to extend certain merchandise contracts during the first quarter of 2014, which could increase our minimum purchase commitment by approximately $1,500 million.) We issue inventory purchase orders in the normal course of business, which represent authorizations to purchase that are cancelable by their terms. We do not consider purchase orders to be firm inventory commitments; therefore, they are excluded from the table above. If we choose to cancel a purchase order, we may be obligated to reimburse the vendor for unrecoverable outlays incurred prior to cancellation. We also issue trade letters of credit in the ordinary course of business, which are excluded from this table as these obligations are conditioned on terms of the letter of credit being met.

(i) We have not included obligations under our pension and postretirement health care benefit plans in the contractual obligations table above because no additional amounts are required to be funded as of February 1, 2014. Our historical practice regarding these plans has been to contribute amounts necessary to satisfy minimum pension funding requirements, plus periodic discretionary amounts determined to be appropriate.

Off Balance Sheet Arrangements: Other than the unrecorded contractual obligations above, we do not have any arrangements or relationships with entities that are not consolidated into the financial statements.

Critical Accounting Estimates

Our analysis of operations and financial condition is based on our consolidated financial statements prepared in accordance with GAAP. Preparation of these consolidated financial statements requires us to make estimates and assumptions affecting the reported amounts of assets and liabilities at the date of the consolidated financial statements, reported amounts of revenues and expenses during the reporting period and related disclosures of contingent assets and liabilities. In the Notes to Consolidated Financial Statements, we describe the significant accounting policies used in preparing the consolidated financial statements. Our estimates are evaluated on an ongoing basis and are drawn from historical experience and other assumptions that we believe to be reasonable under the circumstances. Actual results could differ under other assumptions or conditions. However, we do not believe there is a reasonable likelihood that there will be a material change in future estimates or assumptions. Our senior management has discussed the development and selection of our critical accounting estimates with the Audit Committee of our Board of Directors. The following items in our consolidated financial statements require significant estimation or judgment:

Inventory and cost of sales: We use the retail inventory method to account for the majority of our inventory and the related cost of sales. Under this method, inventory is stated at cost using the last-in, first-out (LIFO) method as determined by applying a cost-to-retail ratio to each merchandise grouping's ending retail value. The cost of our inventory includes the amount we pay to our suppliers to acquire inventory, freight costs incurred in connection with the delivery of product to our distribution centers and stores, and import costs, reduced by vendor income and cash discounts. The majority of our distribution center operating costs, including compensation and benefits, are expensed to cost of sales in the period incurred. Since inventory value is adjusted regularly to reflect market conditions, our inventory methodology reflects the lower of cost or market. We reduce inventory for estimated losses related to shrink and markdowns. Our shrink estimate is based on historical losses verified by physical inventory counts. Historically, our actual physical inventory count results have shown our estimates to be reliable. Markdowns designated for clearance activity are recorded when the salability of the merchandise has diminished. Inventory is at risk of obsolescence if economic conditions change, including changing consumer demand, guest preferences, changing consumer credit markets or increasing competition. We believe these risks are largely mitigated because our inventory typically turns in less than three months. Inventory was $8,766 million and $7,903 million at February 1, 2014 and February 2, 2013, respectively, and is further described in Note 10 of the Notes to Consolidated Financial Statements.

Vendor income receivable: Cost of sales and SG&A expenses are partially offset by various forms of consideration received from our vendors. This "vendor income" is earned for a variety of vendor-sponsored programs, such as volume rebates, markdown allowances, promotions and advertising allowances, as well as for our compliance programs. We establish a receivable for the vendor income that is earned but not yet received. Based on the agreements in place, this receivable is computed by estimating when we have completed our performance and when the amount is earned. The majority of all year-end vendor income receivables are collected within the following fiscal quarter, and we do not believe there is a reasonable likelihood that the assumptions used in our estimate will change significantly. Historically, adjustments to our vendor income receivable have not been material. Vendor income receivable was $555 million and $621 million at February 1, 2014 and February 2, 2013, respectively, and is described further in Note 4 of the Notes to Consolidated Financial Statements.

Long-lived assets: Long-lived assets are reviewed for impairment whenever events or changes in circumstances indicate that the carrying amounts may not be recoverable. The evaluation is performed at the lowest level of identifiable cash flows independent of other assets. An impairment loss would be recognized when estimated undiscounted future cash flows from the operation and/or disposition of the assets are less than their carrying amount. Measurement of an impairment loss would be based on the excess of the carrying amount of the asset group over its fair value. Fair value is measured using discounted cash flows or independent opinions of value, as appropriate. We recorded impairments of $77 million, $37 million and $43 million in 2013, 2012 and 2011, respectively, and are described further in Note 12. As of February 1, 2014, a 10 percent decrease in the fair value of assets we intend to sell or close would result in additional impairment of $7 million in 2013. Historically, we have not realized material losses upon sale of long-lived assets.

Insurance/self-insurance: We retain a substantial portion of the risk related to certain general liability, workers' compensation, property loss and team member medical and dental claims. However, we maintain stop-loss coverage to limit the exposure related to certain risks. Liabilities associated with these losses include estimates of both claims filed and losses incurred but not yet reported. We use actuarial methods which consider a number of factors to estimate our ultimate cost of losses. General liability and workers' compensation liabilities are recorded at our estimate of their net present value; other liabilities referred to above are not discounted. Our workers' compensation and general liability accrual was $576 million and $627 million at February 1, 2014 and February 2, 2013, respectively. We believe that the amounts accrued are appropriate; however, our liabilities could be significantly affected if future occurrences or loss developments differ from our assumptions. For example, a 5 percent increase or decrease in average claim costs would impact our self-insurance expense by $28 million in 2013. Historically, adjustments to our estimates have not been material. Refer to Item 7A, Quantitative and Qualitative Disclosures About Market Risk, for further disclosure of the market risks associated with these exposures. We maintain insurance coverage to limit our exposure to certain events, including network security matters. As of February 1, 2014, we have recognized a $44 million insurance-recovery receivable relating to the Data Breach because we believe recovery is probable. However, it is possible that the insurance carriers could dispute our claims and that we may be unable to collect the recorded receivable.

Income taxes: We pay income taxes based on the tax statutes, regulations and case law of the various jurisdictions in which we operate. Significant judgment is required in determining the timing and amounts of deductible and taxable items, and in evaluating the ultimate resolution of tax matters in dispute with tax authorities. The benefits of uncertain tax positions are recorded in our financial statements only after determining it is likely the uncertain tax positions would withstand challenge by taxing authorities. We periodically reassess these probabilities, and record any changes in the financial statements as appropriate. Liabilities for uncertain tax positions, including interest and penalties, were $241 million and $280 million at February 1, 2014 and February 2, 2013, respectively. We believe the resolution of these matters will not have a material adverse impact on our consolidated financial statements. As of February 1, 2014 we had foreign net operating loss carryforwards of $1,466 million which are available to offset future income. These carryforwards are primarily related to the start-up operations of the Canadian Segment and expire between 2031 and 2033. We establish a valuation allowance for any portion of our deferred tax assets that we believe will not be realized. We have evaluated the positive and negative evidence and consider it more likely than not that these carryforwards will be fully utilized prior to expiration. Therefore, we have not established a valuation allowance. Income taxes are described further in Note 21 of the Notes to Consolidated Financial Statements.

Pension and postretirement health care accounting: We maintain a funded qualified, defined benefit pension plan, as well as several smaller and unfunded nonqualified plans and a postretirement health care plan for certain current and retired team members. The costs for these plans are determined based on actuarial calculations using the assumptions described in the following paragraphs. Eligibility and the level of benefits varies depending on team members' full-time or part-time status, date of hire and/or length of service. The benefit obligation and related expense for these plans are determined based on actuarial calculations using assumptions about the expected long-term rate of return, the discount rate and compensation growth rates. The assumptions used to determine the period-end benefit obligation also establish the expense for the next year, with adjustments made for any significant plan or participant changes.

Our expected long-term rate of return on plan assets of 8.0 percent is determined by the portfolio composition, historical long-term investment performance and current market conditions. Our compound annual rate of return on qualified plans' assets was 10.4 percent, 8.3 percent, 7.2 percent and 9.2 percent for the 5-year, 10-year, 15-year and 20-year periods, respectively. A one percentage point decrease in our expected long-term rate of return would increase annual expense by $29 million.

The discount rate used to determine benefit obligations is adjusted annually based on the interest rate for long-term high-quality corporate bonds, using yields for maturities that are in line with the duration of our pension liabilities. Our benefit obligation and related expense will fluctuate with changes in interest rates. A 0.5 percentage point decrease to the weighted average discount rate would increase annual expense by $30 million.

Based on our experience, we use a graduated compensation growth schedule that assumes higher compensation growth for younger, shorter-service pension-eligible team members than it does for older, longer-service pension-eligible team members.

Pension and postretirement health care benefits are further described in Note 26 of the Notes to Consolidated Financial Statements.

Legal and other contingencies: We are exposed to other claims and litigation arising in the ordinary course of business and use various methods to resolve these matters in a manner that we believe serves the best interest of our shareholders and other constituents. When a loss is probable, we record an accrual based on the reasonably estimable loss or range of loss. When no point of loss is more likely than another, we record the lowest amount in the estimated range of loss and disclose the estimated range. We do not record liabilities for reasonably possible loss contingencies, but do disclose a range of reasonably possible losses if they are material and we are able to estimate such a range. If we cannot provide a range of reasonably possible losses, we explain the factors that prevent us from determining such a range. Historically, adjustments to our estimates have not been material.

We believe the accruals recorded in our consolidated financial statements properly reflect loss exposures that are both probable and reasonably estimable. With the exception of Data Breach-related loss exposures, we do not believe any of the currently identified claims or litigation will materially affect our results of operations, cash flows or financial condition. However, litigation is subject to inherent uncertainties, and unfavorable rulings could occur. If an unfavorable ruling were to occur, it may cause a material adverse impact on the results of operations, cash flows or financial condition for the period in which the ruling occurs, or future periods.

For Data Breach-related exposures, we are unable to reasonably estimate a range of probable loss in excess of the recorded payment card network contingent losses. We believe that losses from the payment card networks in excess of the amounts recorded in fiscal 2013 are reasonably possible, and that these losses could be material to our results of operations in future periods, but we are unable to estimate a range of such reasonably possible losses. We are also unable to estimate a range of reasonably possible losses arising from Data Breach-related litigation and governmental investigations. See Item 7, Management's Discussion and Analysis of Financial Condition and Results of Operations and Note 17 of the Notes to the Consolidated Financial Statements included in Item 8, Financial Statements and Supplementary Data for further information on the Data Breach-related contingencies.

New Accounting Pronouncements

We do not expect that any recently issued accounting pronouncements will have a material effect on our financial statements.

Forward-Looking Statements

This report contains forward-looking statements, which are based on our current assumptions and expectations. These statements are typically accompanied by the words "expect," "may," "could," "believe," "would," "might," "anticipates," or words of similar import. The principal forward-looking statements in this report include: our financial performance, statements regarding the adequacy of and costs associated with our sources of liquidity, the fair value and amount of the beneficial interest asset, the continued execution of our share repurchase program, our expected capital expenditures, the impact of changes in the expected effective income tax rate on net income, the expected compliance with debt covenants, the expected impact of new accounting pronouncements, our intentions regarding future dividends, contributions and payments related to our pension and postretirement health care plans, the expected returns on pension plan assets, the effects of macroeconomic conditions, the adequacy of our reserves for general liability, workers' compensation and property loss, the expected outcome of, and adequacy of our reserves for, investigations, inquiries, claims and litigation, including those related to the Data Breach, expected insurance recoveries, expected changes to our contractual obligations, the expected ability to recognize deferred tax assets and liabilities, including foreign net operating loss carryforwards, and the resolution of tax matters.

All such forward-looking statements are intended to enjoy the protection of the safe harbor for forward-looking statements contained in the Private Securities Litigation Reform Act of 1995, as amended. Although we believe there is a reasonable basis for the forward-looking statements, our actual results could be materially different. The most important factors which could cause our actual results to differ from our forward-looking statements are set forth on our description of risk factors in Item 1A to this Form 10-K, which should be read in conjunction with the forward-looking statements in this report. Forward-looking statements speak only as of the date they are made, and we do not undertake any obligation to update any forward-looking statement.

Item 7A. Quantitative and Qualitative Disclosures About Market Risk

At February 1, 2014, our exposure to market risk was primarily from interest rate changes on our debt obligations, some of which are at a LIBOR-plus floating-rate. Our interest rate exposure is primarily due to the extent by which our floating rate debt obligations differ from our floating rate short term investments. At February 1, 2014, our floating rate debt exceeded our floating rate short term investments by approximately $1 billion. As a result, based on our balance sheet position at February 1, 2014, the annualized effect of a 0.1 percentage point increase in floating interest rates on our floating rate debt obligations, net of our short-term investments, would be to decrease earnings before income taxes by approximately $1 million. In general, we expect our floating rate debt to exceed our floating rate short-term investments over time, but that may vary in different interest rate environments. See further description of our debt and derivative instruments in Notes 18 and 19 of the Notes to Consolidated Financial Statements.

We record our general liability and workers' compensation liabilities at net present value; therefore, these liabilities fluctuate with changes in interest rates. Periodically, in certain interest rate environments, we economically hedge a portion of our exposure to these interest rate changes by entering into interest rate forward contracts that partially mitigate the effects of interest rate changes. Based on our balance sheet position at February 1, 2014, the annualized effect of a 0.5 percentage point decrease in interest rates would be to decrease earnings before income taxes by $8 million.

In addition, we are exposed to market return fluctuations on our qualified defined benefit pension plans. A 0.5 percentage point decrease to the weighted average discount rate would increase annual expense by $30 million. The value of our pension liabilities is inversely related to changes in interest rates. To protect against declines in interest rates, we hold high-quality, long-duration bonds and interest rate swaps in our pension plan trust. At year-end, we had hedged 50 percent of the interest rate exposure of our funded status.

As more fully described in Note 13 and Note 25 of the Notes to Consolidated Financial Statements, we are exposed to market returns on accumulated team member balances in our nonqualified, unfunded deferred compensation plans. We control the risk of offering the nonqualified plans by making investments in life insurance contracts and prepaid forward contracts on our own common stock that offset a substantial portion of our economic exposure to the returns on these plans. The annualized effect of a one percentage point change in market returns on our nonqualified defined contribution plans (inclusive of the effect of the investment vehicles used to manage our economic exposure) would not be significant.

There have been no other material changes in our primary risk exposures or management of market risks since the prior year.

Item 8. Financial Statements and Supplementary Data

Report of Management on the Consolidated Financial Statements

Management is responsible for the consistency, integrity and presentation of the information in the Annual Report. The consolidated financial statements and other information presented in this Annual Report have been prepared in accordance with accounting principles generally accepted in the United States and include necessary judgments and estimates by management.

To fulfill our responsibility, we maintain comprehensive systems of internal control designed to provide reasonable assurance that assets are safeguarded and transactions are executed in accordance with established procedures. The concept of reasonable assurance is based upon recognition that the cost of the controls should not exceed the benefit derived. We believe our systems of internal control provide this reasonable assurance.

The Board of Directors exercised its oversight role with respect to the Corporation's systems of internal control primarily through its Audit Committee, which is comprised of independent directors. The Committee oversees the Corporation's systems of internal control, accounting practices, financial reporting and audits to assess whether their quality, integrity and objectivity are sufficient to protect shareholders' investments.

In addition, our consolidated financial statements have been audited by Ernst & Young LLP, independent registered public accounting firm, whose report also appears on this page.

Gregg W. Steinhafel
Chairman, President and Chief Executive Officer
March 14, 2014

John J. Mulligan
Executive Vice President and
Chief Financial Officer

Report of Independent Registered Public Accounting Firm on Consolidated Financial Statements
The Board of Directors and Shareholders
Target Corporation

We have audited the accompanying consolidated statements of financial position of Target Corporation and subsidiaries (the Corporation) as of February 1, 2014 and February 2, 2013, and the related consolidated statements of operations, comprehensive income, cash flows, and shareholders' investment for each of the three years in the period ended February 1, 2014. These financial statements are the responsibility of the Corporation's management. Our responsibility is to express an opinion on these financial statements based on our audits.

We conducted our audits in accordance with the standards of the Public Company Accounting Oversight Board (United States). Those standards require that we plan and perform the audit to obtain reasonable assurance about whether the financial statements are free of material misstatement. An audit includes examining, on a test basis, evidence supporting the amounts and disclosures in the financial statements. An audit also includes assessing the accounting principles used and significant estimates made by management, as well as evaluating the overall financial statement presentation. We believe that our audits provide a reasonable basis for our opinion.

In our opinion, the financial statements referred to above present fairly, in all material respects, the consolidated financial position of Target Corporation and subsidiaries at February 1, 2014 and February 2, 2013, and the consolidated results of their operations and their cash flows for each of the three years in the period ended February 1, 2014, in conformity with U.S. generally accepted accounting principles.

We also have audited, in accordance with the standards of the Public Company Accounting Oversight Board (United States), the Corporation's internal control over financial reporting as of February 1, 2014, based on criteria established in *Internal Control—Integrated Framework* issued by the Committee of Sponsoring Organizations of the Treadway Commission (1992 Framework) and our report dated March 14, 2014, expressed an unqualified opinion thereon.

Ernst & Young LLP

Minneapolis, Minnesota
March 14, 2014

Report of Management on Internal Control over Financial Reporting

Our management is responsible for establishing and maintaining adequate internal control over financial reporting, as such term is defined in Exchange Act Rules 13a-15(f). Under the supervision and with the participation of our management, including our chief executive officer and chief financial officer, we assessed the effectiveness of our internal control over financial reporting as of February 1, 2014, based on the framework in *Internal Control—Integrated Framework (1992)*, issued by the Committee of Sponsoring Organizations of the Treadway Commission (1992 framework). Based on our assessment, we conclude that the Corporation's internal control over financial reporting is effective based on those criteria.

Our internal control over financial reporting as of February 1, 2014, has been audited by Ernst & Young LLP, the independent registered public accounting firm who has also audited our consolidated financial statements, as stated in their report which appears on this page.

Gregg W. Steinhafel
Chairman, President and Chief Executive Officer
March 14, 2014

John J. Mulligan
Executive Vice President and
Chief Financial Officer

Report of Independent Registered Public Accounting Firm on Internal Control over Financial Reporting
The Board of Directors and Shareholders
Target Corporation

We have audited Target Corporation and subsidiaries' (the Corporation) internal control over financial reporting as of February 1, 2014, based on criteria established in *Internal Control—Integrated Framework* issued by the Committee of Sponsoring Organizations of the Treadway Commission (1992 Framework) (the COSO criteria). The Corporation's management is responsible for maintaining effective internal control over financial reporting, and for its assessment of the effectiveness of internal control over financial reporting included in the accompanying Report of Management on Internal Control over Financial Reporting. Our responsibility is to express an opinion on the Corporation's internal control over financial reporting based on our audit.

We conducted our audit in accordance with the standards of the Public Company Accounting Oversight Board (United States). Those standards require that we plan and perform the audit to obtain reasonable assurance about whether effective internal control over financial reporting was maintained in all material respects. Our audit included obtaining an understanding of internal control over financial reporting, assessing the risk that a material weakness exists, testing and evaluating the design and operating effectiveness of internal control based on the assessed risk, and performing such other procedures as we considered necessary in the circumstances. We believe that our audit provides a reasonable basis for our opinion.

A company's internal control over financial reporting is a process designed to provide reasonable assurance regarding the reliability of financial reporting and the preparation of financial statements for external purposes in accordance with generally accepted accounting principles. A company's internal control over financial reporting includes those policies and procedures that (1) pertain to the maintenance of records that, in reasonable detail, accurately and fairly reflect the transactions and dispositions of the assets of the company, (2) provide reasonable assurance that transactions are recorded as necessary to permit preparation of financial statements in accordance with generally accepted accounting principles, and that receipts and expenditures of the company are being made only in accordance with authorizations of management and directors of the company, and (3) provide reasonable assurance regarding prevention or timely detection of unauthorized acquisition, use or disposition of the company's assets that could have a material effect on the financial statements.

Because of its inherent limitations, internal control over financial reporting may not prevent or detect misstatements. Also, projections of any evaluation of effectiveness to future periods are subject to the risk that controls may become inadequate because of changes in conditions or that the degree of compliance with the policies or procedures may deteriorate.

In our opinion, the Corporation maintained, in all material respects, effective internal control over financial reporting as of February 1, 2014, based on the COSO criteria.

We also have audited, in accordance with the standards of the Public Company Accounting Oversight Board (United States), the consolidated statements of financial position of Target Corporation and subsidiaries as of February 1, 2014 and February 2, 2013, and the related consolidated statements of operations, comprehensive income, cash flows and shareholders' investment for each of the three years in the period ended February 1, 2014, and our report dated March 14, 2014, expressed an unqualified opinion thereon.

Ernst & Young LLP

Minneapolis, Minnesota
March 14, 2014

Consolidated Statements of Operations

(millions, except per share data)	2013	2012	2011
Sales	$ 72,596	$ 71,960	$ 68,466
Credit card revenues	—	1,341	1,399
Total revenues	72,596	73,301	69,865
Cost of sales	51,160	50,568	47,860
Selling, general and administrative expenses	15,375	14,914	14,106
Credit card expenses	—	467	446
Depreciation and amortization	2,223	2,142	2,131
Gain on receivables transaction	(391)	(161)	—
Earnings before interest expense and income taxes	4,229	5,371	5,322
Net interest expense	1,126	762	866
Earnings before income taxes	3,103	4,609	4,456
Provision for income taxes	1,132	1,610	1,527
Net earnings	$ 1,971	$ 2,999	$ 2,929
Basic earnings per share	$ 3.10	$ 4.57	$ 4.31
Diluted earnings per share	$ 3.07	$ 4.52	$ 4.28
Weighted average common shares outstanding			
Basic	635.1	656.7	679.1
Dilutive effect of share-based awards[a]	6.7	6.6	4.8
Diluted	641.8	663.3	683.9

[a] Excludes 2.3 million, 5.0 million and 15.5 million share-based awards for 2013, 2012 and 2011, respectively, because their effects were antidilutive.

See accompanying Notes to Consolidated Financial Statements.

Consolidated Statements of Comprehensive Income

(millions)		**2013**		2012		2011
Net earnings	**$**	**1,971**	$	2,999	$	2,929
Other comprehensive income/(loss), net of tax						
Pension and other benefit liabilities, net of provision/(benefit) for taxes of **$71**, $58 and $(56)		**110**		92		(83)
Currency translation adjustment and cash flow hedges, net of provision/(benefit) for taxes of **$11**, $8 and $(11)		**(425)**		13		(17)
Other comprehensive income/(loss)		**(315)**		105		(100)
Comprehensive income	**$**	**1,656**	$	3,104	$	2,829

See accompanying Notes to Consolidated Financial Statements.

Consolidated Statements of Financial Position

(millions, except footnotes)		February 1, 2014		February 2, 2013
Assets				
Cash and cash equivalents, including short-term investments of **$3** and $130	$	**695**	$	784
Credit card receivables, held for sale		**—**		5,841
Inventory		**8,766**		7,903
Other current assets		**2,112**		1,860
Total current assets		**11,573**		16,388
Property and equipment				
Land		**6,234**		6,206
Buildings and improvements		**30,356**		28,653
Fixtures and equipment		**5,583**		5,362
Computer hardware and software		**2,764**		2,567
Construction-in-progress		**843**		1,176
Accumulated depreciation		**(14,402)**		(13,311)
Property and equipment, net		**31,378**		30,653
Other noncurrent assets		**1,602**		1,122
Total assets	$	**44,553**	$	48,163
Liabilities and shareholders' investment				
Accounts payable	$	**7,683**	$	7,056
Accrued and other current liabilities		**3,934**		3,981
Current portion of long-term debt and other borrowings		**1,160**		2,994
Total current liabilities		**12,777**		14,031
Long-term debt and other borrowings		**12,622**		14,654
Deferred income taxes		**1,433**		1,311
Other noncurrent liabilities		**1,490**		1,609
Total noncurrent liabilities		**15,545**		17,574
Shareholders' investment				
Common stock		**53**		54
Additional paid-in capital		**4,470**		3,925
Retained earnings		**12,599**		13,155
Accumulated other comprehensive loss				
Pension and other benefit liabilities		**(422)**		(532)
Currency translation adjustment and cash flow hedges		**(469)**		(44)
Total shareholders' investment		**16,231**		16,558
Total liabilities and shareholders' investment	$	**44,553**	$	48,163

Common Stock Authorized 6,000,000,000 shares, $0.0833 par value; **632,930,740** shares issued and outstanding at February 1, 2014; 645,294,423 shares issued and outstanding at February 2, 2013.

Preferred Stock Authorized 5,000,000 shares, $0.01 par value; no shares were issued or outstanding at February 1, 2014 or February 2, 2013.

See accompanying Notes to Consolidated Financial Statements.

Consolidated Statements of Cash Flows

(millions)	2013	2012	2011
Operating activities			
Net earnings	$ **1,971**	$ 2,999	$ 2,929
Adjustments to reconcile net earnings to cash provided by operations:			
Depreciation and amortization	**2,223**	2,142	2,131
Share-based compensation expense	**110**	105	90
Deferred income taxes	**(254)**	(14)	371
Bad debt expense [(a)]	**41**	206	154
Gain on receivables transaction	**(391)**	(161)	—
Loss on debt extinguishment	**445**	—	—
Noncash (gains)/losses and other, net	**82**	14	22
Changes in operating accounts:			
Accounts receivable originated at Target	**157**	(217)	(187)
Proceeds on sale of accounts receivable originated at Target	**2,703**	—	—
Inventory	**(885)**	15	(322)
Other current assets	**(267)**	(123)	(150)
Other noncurrent assets	**19**	(98)	43
Accounts payable	**625**	199	232
Accrued and other current liabilities	**(9)**	138	218
Other noncurrent liabilities	**(50)**	120	(97)
Cash provided by operations	**6,520**	5,325	5,434
Investing activities			
Expenditures for property and equipment	**(3,453)**	(3,277)	(4,368)
Proceeds from disposal of property and equipment	**86**	66	37
Change in accounts receivable originated at third parties	**121**	254	259
Proceeds from sale of accounts receivable originated at third parties	**3,002**	—	—
Cash paid for acquisitions, net of cash assumed	**(157)**	—	—
Other investments	**130**	102	(108)
Cash required for investing activities	**(271)**	(2,855)	(4,180)
Financing activities			
Change in commercial paper, net	**(890)**	970	—
Additions to short-term debt	—	—	1,500
Reductions of short-term debt	—	(1,500)	—
Additions to long-term debt	—	1,971	1,994
Reductions of long-term debt	**(3,463)**	(1,529)	(3,125)
Dividends paid	**(1,006)**	(869)	(750)
Repurchase of stock	**(1,461)**	(1,875)	(1,842)
Stock option exercises and related tax benefit	**456**	360	89
Other	—	(16)	(6)
Cash required for financing activities	**(6,364)**	(2,488)	(2,140)
Effect of exchange rate changes on cash and cash equivalents	**26**	8	(32)
Net decrease in cash and cash equivalents	**(89)**	(10)	(918)
Cash and cash equivalents at beginning of period	**784**	794	1,712
Cash and cash equivalents at end of period	$ **695**	$ 784	$ 794
Supplemental information			
Interest paid, net of capitalized interest	$ **1,120**	$ 775	$ 816
Income taxes paid	**1,386**	1,603	1,109
Noncash financing activities			
Property and equipment acquired through capital lease obligations	**211**	282	1,388

(a) Includes net write-offs of credit card receivables prior to the sale of our U.S. consumer credit card receivables on March 13, 2013, and bad debt expense on credit card receivables during the twelve months ended February 2, 2013.

See accompanying Notes to Consolidated Financial Statements.

Consolidated Statements of Shareholders' Investment

(millions, except footnotes)	Common Stock Shares	Stock Par Value	Additional Paid-in Capital	Retained Earnings	Accumulated Other Comprehensive Income/(Loss)	Total
January 29, 2011	704.0	$ 59	$ 3,311	$ 12,698	$ (581)	$ 15,487
Net earnings	—	—	—	2,929	—	2,929
Other comprehensive income	—	—	—	—	(100)	(100)
Dividends declared	—	—	—	(777)	—	(777)
Repurchase of stock	(37.2)	(3)	—	(1,891)	—	(1,894)
Stock options and awards	2.5	—	176	—	—	176
January 28, 2012	669.3	$ 56	$ 3,487	$ 12,959	$ (681)	$ 15,821
Net earnings	—	—	—	2,999	—	2,999
Other comprehensive income	—	—	—	—	105	105
Dividends declared	—	—	—	(903)	—	(903)
Repurchase of stock	(32.2)	(3)	—	(1,900)	—	(1,903)
Stock options and awards	8.2	1	438	—	—	439
February 2, 2013	645.3	$ 54	$ 3,925	$ 13,155	$ (576)	$ 16,558
Net earnings	**—**	**—**	**—**	**1,971**	**—**	**1,971**
Other comprehensive income	**—**	**—**	**—**	**—**	**(315)**	**(315)**
Dividends declared	**—**	**—**	**—**	**(1,051)**	**—**	**(1,051)**
Repurchase of stock	**(21.9)**	**(2)**	**—**	**(1,476)**	**—**	**(1,478)**
Stock options and awards	**9.5**	**1**	**545**	**—**	**—**	**546**
February 1, 2014	**632.9**	**$ 53**	**$ 4,470**	**$ 12,599**	**$ (891)**	**$ 16,231**

Dividends declared per share were $1.65, $1.38 and $1.15 in 2013, 2012 and 2011, respectively.

See accompanying Notes to Consolidated Financial Statements.

Notes to Consolidated Financial Statements

1. Summary of Accounting Policies

Organization Target Corporation (Target, the Corporation, or the Company) operates two reportable segments: U.S. and Canadian. Our U.S. Segment includes all of our U.S. retail operations, including digital sales. The U.S. Segment also includes our U.S. credit card servicing activities and certain centralized operating and corporate activities not allocated to our Canadian Segment. In 2013, following the sale of our U.S. consumer credit card portfolio to TD Bank Group (TD), we combined our historical U.S. Retail Segment and U.S. Credit Card Segment into one U.S. Segment. Our Canadian Segment includes all of our Canadian retail operations, including 124 stores opened in 2013. We currently do not have a digital sales channel in Canada.

Consolidation The consolidated financial statements include the balances of the Corporation and its subsidiaries after elimination of intercompany balances and transactions. All material subsidiaries are wholly owned. We consolidate variable interest entities where it has been determined that the Corporation is the primary beneficiary of those entities' operations.

Use of estimates The preparation of our consolidated financial statements in conformity with U.S. generally accepted accounting principles (GAAP) requires management to make estimates and assumptions affecting reported amounts in the consolidated financial statements and accompanying notes. Actual results may differ significantly from those estimates.

Fiscal year Our fiscal year ends on the Saturday nearest January 31. Unless otherwise stated, references to years in this report relate to fiscal years, rather than to calendar years. Fiscal 2013 ended February 1, 2014 and consisted of 52 weeks. Fiscal 2012 ended February 2, 2013, and consisted of 53 weeks. Fiscal 2011 ended January 28, 2012, and consisted of 52 weeks. Fiscal 2014 will end January 31, 2015, and will consist of 52 weeks.

Accounting policies Our accounting policies are disclosed in the applicable Notes to the Consolidated Financial Statements.

2. Revenues

Our retail stores generally record revenue at the point of sale. Sales from our online and mobile applications include shipping revenue and are recorded upon delivery to the guest. Total revenues do not include sales tax because we are a pass-through conduit for collecting and remitting sales taxes. Generally, guests may return merchandise within 90 days of purchase. Revenues are recognized net of expected returns, which we estimate using historical return patterns as a percentage of sales. Commissions earned on sales generated by leased departments are included within sales and were $29 million, $25 million and $22 million in 2013, 2012 and 2011, respectively.

Revenue from gift card sales is recognized upon gift card redemption. Our gift cards do not expire. Based on historical redemption rates, a small and relatively stable percentage of gift cards will never be redeemed, referred to as "breakage." Estimated breakage revenue is recognized over time in proportion to actual gift card redemptions and was not material in any period presented.

Guests receive a 5 percent discount on virtually all purchases and receive free shipping at Target.com when they use their REDcard. The discounts associated with loyalty programs are included as reductions in sales in our Consolidated Statements of Operations and were $833 million, $583 million and $340 million in 2013, 2012 and 2011, respectively.

3. Cost of Sales and Selling, General and Administrative Expenses

The following table illustrates the primary items classified in each major expense category:

Cost of Sales	Selling, General and Administrative Expenses
Total cost of products sold including • Freight expenses associated with moving merchandise from our vendors to our distribution centers and our retail stores, and among our distribution and retail facilities • Vendor income that is not reimbursement of specific, incremental and identifiable costs Inventory shrink Markdowns Outbound shipping and handling expenses associated with sales to our guests Payment term cash discounts Distribution center costs, including compensation and benefits costs Import costs	Compensation and benefit costs including • Stores • Headquarters Occupancy and operating costs of retail and headquarters facilities Advertising, offset by vendor income that is a reimbursement of specific, incremental and identifiable costs Pre-opening costs of stores and other facilities U.S. credit cards servicing expenses and profit sharing Litigation and defense costs and related insurance recovery Other administrative costs

Note: The classification of these expenses varies across the retail industry.

4. Consideration Received from Vendors

We receive consideration for a variety of vendor-sponsored programs, such as volume rebates, markdown allowances, promotions and advertising allowances and for our compliance programs, referred to as "vendor income." Vendor income reduces either our inventory costs or SG&A expenses based on the provisions of the arrangement. Under our compliance programs, vendors are charged for merchandise shipments that do not meet our requirements (violations), such as late or incomplete shipments. These allowances are recorded when violations occur. Substantially all consideration received is recorded as a reduction of cost of sales.

We establish a receivable for vendor income that is earned but not yet received. Based on provisions of the agreements in place, this receivable is computed by estimating the amount earned when we have completed our performance. We perform detailed analyses to determine the appropriate level of the receivable in the aggregate. The majority of year-end receivables associated with these activities are collected within the following fiscal quarter. We have not historically had significant write-offs for these receivables.

5. Advertising Costs

Advertising costs, which primarily consist of newspaper circulars, internet advertisements and media broadcast, are expensed at first showing or distribution of the advertisement, and are recorded net of related vendor income.

Advertising Costs (millions)	2013	2012	2011
Gross advertising costs	$ **1,744**	$ 1,653	$ 1,589
Vendor income [(a)]	**76**	231	229
Net advertising costs	$ **1,668**	$ 1,422	$ 1,360

(a) A 2013 change to certain merchandise vendor contracts resulted in more vendor funding being recognized as a reduction of our cost of sales rather than offsetting certain advertising expenses.

6. Credit Card Receivables Transaction

In March 2013, we sold our entire U.S. consumer credit card portfolio to TD and recognized a gain of $391 million. This transaction was accounted for as a sale, and the receivables are no longer reported in our Consolidated Statements of Financial Position. Consideration received included cash of $5.7 billion, equal to the gross (par) value of the outstanding receivables at the time of closing, and a $225 million beneficial interest asset. Concurrent with the sale of the portfolio, we repaid the nonrecourse debt collateralized by credit card receivables (2006/2007 Series Variable Funding Certificate) at par of $1.5 billion, resulting in net cash proceeds of $4.2 billion.

TD now underwrites, funds and owns Target Credit Card and Target Visa receivables in the U.S. TD controls risk management policies and oversees regulatory compliance, and we perform account servicing and primary marketing functions. We earn a substantial portion of the profits generated by the Target Credit Card and Target Visa portfolios. Income from the TD profit-sharing arrangement and our related account servicing expenses are classified within SG&A expenses in the U.S. Segment.

The U.S. Segment earned credit card revenues prior to the close of the transaction, and earned $653 million of profit-sharing from TD during 2013. On a consolidated basis, this profit-sharing income is offset by a $98 million reduction in the beneficial interest asset, for a net $555 million impact.

The $225 million beneficial interest asset recognized at the close of the transaction effectively represents a receivable for the present value of future profit-sharing we expect to receive on the receivables sold. It was reduced during 2013 by $96 million of profit-sharing payments related to sold receivables and a $2 million revaluation adjustment. As of February 1, 2014, a $127 million beneficial interest asset remains and is recorded within other current assets and other noncurrent assets in our Consolidated Statements of Financial Position. Based on historical payment patterns, we estimate that the remaining beneficial interest asset will be reduced over the next three years.

Prior to the sale, credit card revenues were recognized according to the contractual provisions of each credit card agreement. When accounts were written off, uncollected finance charges and late fees were recorded as a reduction of credit card revenues. Target retail sales charged on our credit cards totaled $5,807 million and $4,686 million in 2012 and 2011, respectively.

Historically, our credit card receivables were recorded at par value less an allowance for doubtful accounts. As of February 2, 2013, our consumer credit card receivables were recorded at the lower of cost (par) or fair value because they were classified as held for sale. Lower of cost (par) or fair value was determined on a segmented basis using the delinquency and credit-quality segmentation we have historically used to determine the allowance for doubtful accounts. Many nondelinquent balances were recorded at cost (par) because fair value exceeded cost. Delinquent balances were generally recorded at fair value, which reflected our expectation of losses on these receivables.

7. Canadian Leasehold Acquisition

During 2011, we purchased the leasehold interests in 189 sites operated by Zellers in Canada, in exchange for $1,861 million. In addition, we sold our right to acquire the leasehold interests in 54 of these sites to third-parties for a total of $225 million. These transactions resulted in a final net purchase price of $1,636 million, which was included in expenditures for property and equipment in the Consolidated Statements of Cash Flows.

As a result of the acquisition, the following net assets were recorded in our Canadian Segment: buildings and improvements of $2,887 million; finite-lived intangible assets of $23 million; unsecured debt and other borrowings of $1,274 million.

8. Fair Value Measurements

Fair value measurements are categorized into one of three levels based on the lowest level of significant input used: Level 1 (unadjusted quoted prices in active markets); Level 2 (observable market inputs available at the measurement date, other than quoted prices included in Level 1); and Level 3 (unobservable inputs that cannot be corroborated by observable market data).

Fair Value Measurements – Recurring Basis	Fair Value at February 1, 2014			Fair Value at February 2, 2013		
(millions)	Level 1	Level 2	Level 3	Level 1	Level 2	Level 3
Assets						
Cash and cash equivalents						
Short-term investments	$ 3	$ —	$ —	$ 130	$ —	$ —
Other current assets						
Interest rate swaps [(a)]	—	1	—	—	4	—
Prepaid forward contracts	73	—	—	73	—	—
Beneficial interest asset [(b)]	—	—	71	—	—	—
Other noncurrent assets						
Interest rate swaps [(a)]	—	62	—	—	85	—
Company-owned life insurance investments [(c)]	—	305	—	—	269	—
Beneficial interest asset [(b)]	—	—	56	—	—	—
Total	$ 76	$ 368	$ 127	$ 203	$ 358	$ —
Liabilities						
Other current liabilities						
Interest rate swaps [(a)]	$ —	$ —	$ —	$ —	$ 2	$ —
Other noncurrent liabilities						
Interest rate swaps [(a)]	$ —	$ 39	$ —	$ —	$ 54	$ —
Total	$ —	$ 39	$ —	$ —	$ 56	$ —

(a) There was one interest rate swap designated as an accounting hedge at February 1, 2014 and February 2, 2013. See Note 19 for additional information on interest rate swaps.

(b) A rollforward of the Level 3 beneficial interest asset is included in Note 6.

(c) Company-owned life insurance investments consist of equity index funds and fixed income assets. Amounts are presented net of nonrecourse loans that are secured by some of these policies. These loan amounts were $790 million at February 1, 2014 and $817 million at February 2, 2013.

Valuation Technique
Short-term investments - Carrying value approximates fair value because maturities are less than three months.
Prepaid forward contracts - Initially valued at transaction price. Subsequently valued by reference to the market price of Target common stock.
Interest rate swaps - Valuation models are calibrated to initial trade price. Subsequent valuations are based on observable inputs to the valuation model (*e.g.*, interest rates and credit spreads).
Company-owned life insurance investments - Includes investments in separate accounts that are valued based on market rates credited by the insurer.
Beneficial interest asset - Valued using a cash-flow based economic-profit model, which includes inputs of the forecasted performance of the receivables portfolio and a market-based discount rate. Internal data is used to forecast expected payment patterns and write-offs, revenue, and operating expenses (credit EBIT yield) related to the credit card portfolio. Changes in macroeconomic conditions in the United States could affect the estimated fair value. A one percentage point change in the forecasted EBIT yield would impact our fair value estimate by approximately $20 million. A one percentage point change in the forecasted discount rate would impact our fair value estimate by approximately $4 million. As described in Note 6, this beneficial interest asset effectively represents a receivable for the present value of future profit-sharing we expect to receive on the receivables sold. As a result, a portion of the profit-sharing payments we receive from TD will reduce the beneficial interest asset. As the asset is reduced over time, changes in the forecasted credit EBIT yield and the forecasted discount rate will have a similar impact on the estimated fair value.

The carrying amount and estimated fair value of debt, a significant financial instrument not measured at fair value in the Consolidated Statements of Financial Position, was $11,758 million and $13,184 million, respectively, at February 1, 2014, and $15,618 million and $18,143 million, respectively, at February 2, 2013. The fair value of debt is generally measured using a discounted cash flow analysis based on current market interest rates for similar types of financial instruments and would be classified as Level 2. These amounts exclude unamortized swap valuation adjustments and capital lease obligations.

As of February 2, 2013, our consumer credit card receivables were recorded at the lower of cost (par) or fair value because they were classified as held for sale. We estimated the fair value of our consumer credit card portfolio to be approximately $6.3 billion using a cash flow-based, economic-profit model using Level 3 inputs, including the forecasted performance of the portfolio and a market-based discount rate. We used internal data to forecast expected payment patterns and write-offs, revenue, and operating expenses (credit EBIT yield) related to the credit card portfolio. Refer to Note 6 for more information on our credit card receivables transaction.

The carrying amounts of accounts payable and certain accrued and other current liabilities approximate fair value due to their short terms.

9. Cash Equivalents

Cash equivalents include highly liquid investments with an original maturity of three months or less from the time of purchase. These investments were $3 million and $130 million at February 1, 2014 and February 2, 2013, respectively. Cash equivalents also include amounts due from third-party financial institutions for credit and debit card transactions. These receivables typically settle in less than five days and were $347 million and $371 million at February 1, 2014 and February 2, 2013, respectively.

10. Inventory

The majority of our inventory is accounted for under the retail inventory accounting method (RIM) using the last-in, first-out (LIFO) method. Inventory is stated at the lower of LIFO cost or market. The cost of our inventory includes the amount we pay to our suppliers to acquire inventory, freight costs incurred in connection with the delivery of product to our distribution centers and stores, and import costs, reduced by vendor income and cash discounts. The majority of our distribution center operating costs, including compensation and benefits, are expensed in the period incurred. Inventory is also reduced for estimated losses related to shrink and markdowns. The LIFO provision is calculated based on inventory levels, markup rates and internally measured retail price indices.

Under RIM, inventory cost and the resulting gross margins are calculated by applying a cost-to-retail ratio to the inventory retail value. RIM is an averaging method that has been widely used in the retail industry due to its practicality. The use of RIM will result in inventory being valued at the lower of cost or market because permanent markdowns are taken as a reduction of the retail value of inventory.

Certain other inventory is recorded at the lower of cost or market using the cost method. The valuation allowance for inventory valued under a cost method was not material to our Consolidated Financial Statements as of the end of fiscal 2013 or 2012.

We routinely enter into arrangements with vendors whereby we do not purchase or pay for merchandise until the merchandise is ultimately sold to a guest. Activity under this program is included in sales and cost of sales in the Consolidated Statements of Operations, but the merchandise received under the program is not included in inventory in our Consolidated Statements of Financial Position because of the virtually simultaneous purchase and sale of this inventory. Sales made under these arrangements totaled $1,833 million, $1,800 million and $1,736 million in 2013, 2012 and 2011, respectively.

11. Other Current Assets

Other Current Assets (millions)		**February 1, 2014**		February 2, 2013
Pharmacy, income tax and other receivables	**$**	**792**	$	478
Vendor income receivable		**555**		621
Prepaid expenses		**272**		310
Deferred taxes		**177**		193
Other		**316**		258
Total	**$**	**2,112**	$	1,860

12. Property and Equipment

Property and equipment is depreciated using the straight-line method over estimated useful lives or lease terms if shorter. We amortize leasehold improvements purchased after the beginning of the initial lease term over the shorter of the assets' useful lives or a term that includes the original lease term, plus any renewals that are reasonably assured at the date the leasehold improvements are acquired. Depreciation and capital lease amortization expense for 2013, 2012 and 2011 was $2,198 million, $2,120 million and $2,107 million, respectively. For income tax purposes, accelerated depreciation methods are generally used. Repair and maintenance costs are expensed as incurred. Facility pre-opening costs, including supplies and payroll, are expensed as incurred.

Estimated Useful Lives	Life (Years)
Buildings and improvements	8-39
Fixtures and equipment	2-15
Computer hardware and software	2-7

Long-lived assets are reviewed for impairment when events or changes in circumstances, such as a decision to relocate or close a store or make significant software changes, indicate that the asset's carrying value may not be recoverable. For asset groups classified as held for sale, the carrying value is compared to the fair value less cost to sell. We estimate fair value by obtaining market appraisals, valuations from third party brokers or other valuation techniques. Impairments of $77 million, $37 million and $43 million in 2013, 2012 and 2011, respectively, were recorded in selling, general and administrative expenses on the Consolidated Statements of Income, primarily from completed or planned store closures and software changes.

13. Other Noncurrent Assets

Other Noncurrent Assets (millions)	**February 1, 2014**	February 2, 2013
Deferred taxes	**$ 469**	$ 206
Goodwill and intangible assets	**357**	224
Company-owned life insurance investments [(a)]	**305**	269
Interest rate swaps [(b)]	**62**	85
Other	**409**	338
Total	**$ 1,602**	$ 1,122

(a) Company-owned life insurance policies on approximately 4,000 team members who have been designated highly compensated under the Internal Revenue Code and have given their consent to be insured. Amounts are presented net of loans that are secured by some of these policies.

(b) See Notes 8 and 19 for additional information relating to our interest rate swaps.

14. Goodwill and Intangible Assets

Goodwill increased to $151 million at February 1, 2014 from $59 million at February 2, 2013 due to three 2013 acquisitions. No impairments were recorded in 2013, 2012 or 2011 as a result of the goodwill impairment tests performed.

Intangible Assets	Leasehold Acquisition Costs		Other [(a)]		Total	
(millions)	**February 1, 2014**	February 2, 2013	**February 1, 2014**	February 2, 2013	**February 1, 2014**	February 2, 2013
Gross asset	**$ 241**	$ 237	**$ 212**	$ 149	**$ 453**	$ 386
Accumulated amortization	**(130)**	(120)	**(117)**	(101)	**(247)**	(221)
Net intangible assets	**$ 111**	$ 117	**$ 95**	$ 48	**$ 206**	$ 165

(a) Other intangible assets relate primarily to acquired customer lists and trademarks.

We use the straight-line method to amortize leasehold acquisition costs primarily over 9 to 39 years and other definite-lived intangibles over 3 to 15 years. The weighted average life of leasehold acquisition costs and other intangible assets was 26 years and 7 years, respectively, at February 1, 2014. Amortization expense was $25 million, $22 million, and $24 million in 2013, 2012 and 2011, respectively.

Estimated Amortization Expense (millions)	2014	2015	2016	2017	2018
Amortization expense	$ 27	$ 25	$ 22	$ 16	$ 11

15. Accounts Payable

At February 1, 2014 and February 2, 2013, we reclassified book overdrafts of $733 million and $564 million, respectively, to accounts payable and $81 million and $82 million to accrued and other current liabilities.

16. Accrued and Other Current Liabilities

Accrued and Other Current Liabilities (millions)	**February 1, 2014**	February 2, 2013
Wages and benefits	**$ 887**	$ 938
Real estate, sales and other taxes payable	**669**	624
Gift card liability [(a)]	**521**	503
Dividends payable	**272**	232
Project costs accrual	**256**	347
Straight-line rent accrual [(b)]	**248**	235
Income tax payable	**221**	272
Workers' compensation and general liability [(c)]	**152**	160
Interest payable	**85**	91
Other	**623**	579
Total	**$ 3,934**	$ 3,981

(a) Gift card liability represents the amount of unredeemed gift cards, net of estimated breakage.

(b) Straight-line rent accrual represents the amount of rent expense recorded that exceeds cash payments remitted in connection with operating leases.

(c) See footnote (a) to the Other Noncurrent Liabilities table in Note 22 for additional detail.

17. Commitments and Contingencies

Data Breach

In the fourth quarter of 2013, we experienced a data breach in which an intruder stole certain payment card and other guest information from our network (the Data Breach). Based on our investigation to date, we believe that the intruder accessed and stole payment card data from approximately 40 million credit and debit card accounts of guests who shopped at our U.S. stores between November 27 and December 15, 2013, through malware installed on our point-of-sale system in our U.S. stores. On December 15, we removed the malware from virtually all registers in our U.S. stores. Payment card data used in transactions made by 56 additional guests in the period between December 16 and December 17 was stolen prior to our disabling malware on one additional register that was disconnected from our system when we completed the initial malware removal on December 15. In addition, the intruder stole certain guest information, including names, mailing addresses, phone numbers or email addresses, for up to 70 million individuals. Our investigation of the matter is ongoing, and we are supporting law enforcement efforts to identify the responsible parties.

Expenses Incurred and Amounts Accrued

In the fourth quarter of 2013, we recorded $61 million of pretax Data Breach-related expenses, and expected insurance proceeds of $44 million, for net expenses of $17 million ($11 million after tax), or $0.02 per diluted share. These expenses were included in our Consolidated Statements of Operations as Selling, General and Administrative Expenses

(SG&A), but were not part of our segment results. Expenses include costs to investigate the Data Breach, provide credit-monitoring services to our guests, increase staffing in our call centers, and procure legal and other professional services.

The $61 million of fourth quarter expenses also include an accrual for the estimated probable loss related to the expected payment card networks' claims by reason of the Data Breach. The ultimate amount of these claims will likely include amounts for incremental counterfeit fraud losses and non-ordinary course operating expenses (such as card reissuance costs) that the payment card networks believe they or their issuing banks have incurred. In order for us to have liability for such claims, we believe that a court would have to find among other things that (1) at the time of the Data Breach the portion of our network that handles payment card data was noncompliant with applicable data security standards in a manner that contributed to the Data Breach, and (2) the network operating rules around reimbursement of operating costs and counterfeit fraud losses are enforceable. While an independent third-party assessor found the portion of our network that handles payment card data to be compliant with applicable data security standards in the fall of 2013, we expect the forensic investigator working on behalf of the payment card networks nonetheless to claim that we were not in compliance with those standards at the time of the Data Breach. We base that expectation on our understanding that, in cases like ours where prior to a data breach the entity suffering the breach had been found by an independent third-party assessor to be fully compliant with those standards, the network-approved forensic investigator nonetheless regularly claims that the breached entity was not in fact compliant with those standards. As a result, we believe it is probable that the payment card networks will make claims against us. We expect to dispute the payment card networks' anticipated claims, and we think it is probable that our disputes would lead to settlement negotiations consistent with the experience of other entities that have suffered similar payment card breaches. We believe such negotiations would effect a combined settlement of both the payment card networks' counterfeit fraud loss allegations and their non-ordinary course operating expense allegations. We based our year-end accrual on the expectation of reaching negotiated settlements of the payment card networks' anticipated claims and not on any determination that it is probable we would be found liable on these claims were they to be litigated. Currently, we can only reasonably estimate a loss associated with settlements of the networks' expected claims for non-ordinary course operating expenses. The year-end accrual does not include any amounts associated with the networks' expected claims for alleged incremental counterfeit fraud losses because the loss associated with settling such claims, while probable in our judgment, is not reasonably estimable, in part because we have not yet received third-party fraud reporting from the payment card networks. We are not able to reasonably estimate a range of possible losses in excess of the year-end accrual related to the expected settlement of the payment card networks' claims because the investigation into the matter is ongoing and there are significant factual and legal issues to be resolved. We believe that it is reasonably possible that the ultimate amount paid on payment card network claims could be material to our results of operations in future periods.

Litigation and Governmental Investigations

In addition, more than 80 actions have been filed in courts in many states and other claims have been or may be asserted against us on behalf of guests, payment card issuing banks, shareholders or others seeking damages or other related relief, allegedly arising out of the Data Breach. State and federal agencies, including the State Attorneys General, the Federal Trade Commission and the SEC are investigating events related to the Data Breach, including how it occurred, its consequences and our responses. Although we are cooperating in these investigations, we may be subject to fines or other obligations. While a loss from these matters is reasonably possible, we cannot reasonably estimate a range of possible losses because our investigation into the matter is ongoing, the proceedings remain in the early stages, alleged damages have not been specified, there is uncertainty as to the likelihood of a class or classes being certified or the ultimate size of any class if certified, and there are significant factual and legal issues to be resolved. Further, we do not believe that a loss from these matters is probable; therefore, we have not recorded a loss contingency liability for litigation, claims and governmental investigations in 2013. We will continue to evaluate information as it becomes known and will record an estimate for losses at the time or times when it is both probable that a loss has been incurred and the amount of the loss is reasonably estimable.

Future Costs

We expect to incur significant investigation, legal and professional services expenses associated with the Data Breach in future periods. We will recognize these expenses as services are received. We also expect to incur additional expenses associated with incremental fraud and reissuance costs on Target REDcards.

Insurance Coverage

To limit our exposure to Data Breach losses, we maintain $100 million of network-security insurance coverage, above a $10 million deductible. This coverage and certain other insurance coverage may reduce our exposure. We will pursue recoveries to the maximum extent available under the policies. As of February 1, 2014, we have recorded a $44 million receivable for costs we believe are reimbursable and probable of recovery under our insurance coverage, which partially offsets the $61 million of expense relating to the Data Breach.

Other Contingencies

We are exposed to other claims and litigation arising in the ordinary course of business and use various methods to resolve these matters in a manner that we believe serves the best interest of our shareholders and other constituents. We believe the recorded reserves in our consolidated financial statements are adequate in light of the probable and estimable liabilities. We do not believe that any of these identified claims or litigation will be material to our results of operations, cash flows or financial condition.

Commitments

Purchase obligations, which include all legally binding contracts such as firm commitments for inventory purchases, merchandise royalties, equipment purchases, marketing-related contracts, software acquisition/license commitments and service contracts, were $1,317 million and $1,472 million at February 1, 2014 and February 2, 2013, respectively. These purchase obligations are primarily due within three years and recorded as liabilities when inventory is received. We issue inventory purchase orders, which represent authorizations to purchase that are cancelable by their terms. We do not consider purchase orders to be firm inventory commitments. If we choose to cancel a purchase order, we may be obligated to reimburse the vendor for unrecoverable outlays incurred prior to cancellation. Real estate obligations, which include commitments for the purchase, construction or remodeling of real estate and facilities, were $449 million and $1,128 million at February 1, 2014 and February 2, 2013, respectively. These real estate obligations are primarily due within one year, a portion of which are recorded as liabilities.

We issue letters of credit and surety bonds in the ordinary course of business. Trade letters of credit totaled $1,441 million and $1,539 million at February 1, 2014 and February 2, 2013, respectively, a portion of which are reflected in accounts payable. Standby letters of credit and surety bonds, relating primarily to insurance and regulatory requirements, totaled $500 million and $486 million at February 1, 2014 and February 2, 2013, respectively.

18. Notes Payable and Long-Term Debt

At February 1, 2014, the carrying value and maturities of our debt portfolio were as follows:

Debt Maturities	**February 1, 2014**	
(dollars in millions)	**Rate** [(a)]	**Balance**
Due 2014-2018	**4.5%**	**$ 4,232**
Due 2019-2023	**4.0**	**2,215**
Due 2024-2028	**6.7**	**252**
Due 2029-2033	**6.5**	**769**
Due 2034-2038	**6.8**	**2,740**
Due 2039-2043	**4.0**	**1,470**
Total notes and debentures	**5.1**	**11,678**
Swap valuation adjustments		**53**
Capital lease obligations		**1,971**
Less: Amounts due within one year		**(1,080)**
Long-term debt		**$ 12,622**

(a) Reflects the weighted average stated interest rate as of year-end.

Required Principal Payments (millions)		2014		2015		2016		2017		2018
Total required principal payments	$	1,001	$	27	$	751	$	2,251	$	201

Concurrent with the sale of our U.S. consumer credit card receivables portfolio, we repaid $1.5 billion of nonrecourse debt collateralized by credit card receivables (the 2006/2007 Series Variable Funding Certificate). We also used $1.4 billion of proceeds from the transaction to repurchase, at market value, an additional $970 million of debt during the first quarter of 2013.

We periodically obtain short-term financing under our commercial paper program, a form of notes payable.

Commercial Paper (dollars in millions)	**2013**	2012	2011
Maximum daily amount outstanding during the year	**$ 1,465**	$ 970	$ 1,211
Average amount outstanding during the year	**408**	120	244
Amount outstanding at year-end	**80**	970	—
Weighted average interest rate	**0.13%**	0.16%	0.11%

In October 2011, we entered into a five-year $2.25 billion revolving credit facility, which was amended in 2013 to extend the expiration date to October 2018. No balances were outstanding at any time during 2013 or 2012.

In June 2012, we issued $1.5 billion of unsecured fixed rate debt at 4.0% that matures in July 2042. Proceeds from this issuance were used for general corporate purposes.

Substantially all of our outstanding borrowings are senior, unsecured obligations. Most of our long-term debt obligations contain covenants related to secured debt levels. In addition to a secured debt level covenant, our credit facility also contains a debt leverage covenant. We are, and expect to remain, in compliance with these covenants, which have no practical effect on our ability to pay dividends.

19. Derivative Financial Instruments

Our derivative instruments primarily consist of interest rate swaps, which are used to mitigate our interest rate risk. We have counterparty credit risk resulting from our derivative instruments, primarily with large global financial institutions. We monitor this concentration of counterparty credit risk on an ongoing basis. See Note 8 for a description of the fair value measurement of our derivative instruments and their classification on the Consolidated Statements of Financial Position.

As of February 1, 2014 and February 2, 2013, one swap was designated as a fair value hedge for accounting purposes, and no ineffectiveness was recognized in 2013 or 2012.

Outstanding Interest Rate Swap Summary	February 1, 2014		
	Designated	De-Designated	
(dollars in millions)	Pay Floating	Pay Floating	Pay Fixed
Weighted average rate:			
Pay	three-month LIBOR	one-month LIBOR	3.8%
Receive	1.0%	5.7%	one-month LIBOR
Weighted average maturity	0.5 years	2.5 years	2.5 years
Notional	$ 350	$ 500	$ 500

Classification and Fair Value (millions)	Assets			Liabilities		
	Classification	**Feb 1, 2014**	Feb 2, 2013	Classification	**Feb 1, 2014**	Feb 2, 2013
Designated:	Other current assets	**$ 1**	$ —	N/A	**$ —**	$ —
	Other noncurrent assets	**—**	3	N/A	**—**	—
De-designated:	Other current assets	**—**	4	Other current liabilities	**—**	2
	Other noncurrent assets	**62**	82	Other noncurrent liabilities	**39**	54
Total		**$ 63**	$ 89		**$ 39**	$ 56

Periodic payments, valuation adjustments and amortization of gains or losses on our derivative contracts had the following impact on our Consolidated Statements of Operations:

Derivative Contracts – Effect on Results of Operations (millions)				
Type of Contract	Classification of Income/(Expense)	**2013**	2012	2011
Interest rate swaps	Net interest expense	**$ 29**	$ 44	$ 41

The amount remaining on unamortized hedged debt valuation gains from terminated or de-designated interest rate swaps that will be amortized into earnings over the remaining lives of the underlying debt totaled $52 million, $75 million and $111 million, at the end of 2013, 2012 and 2011, respectively.

20. Leases

We lease certain retail locations, warehouses, distribution centers, office space, land, equipment and software. Assets held under capital leases are included in property and equipment. Operating lease rentals are expensed on a straight-line basis over the life of the lease beginning on the date we take possession of the property. At lease inception, we determine the lease term by assuming the exercise of those renewal options that are reasonably assured. The exercise of lease renewal options is at our sole discretion. The lease term is used to determine whether a lease is capital or operating and is used to calculate straight-line rent expense. Additionally, the depreciable life of leased assets and leasehold improvements is limited by the expected lease term.

Rent expense is included in SG&A expenses. Some of our lease agreements include rental payments based on a percentage of retail sales over contractual levels and others include rental payments adjusted periodically for inflation. Certain leases require us to pay real estate taxes, insurance, maintenance and other operating expenses associated with the leased premises. These expenses are classified in SG&A, consistent with similar costs for owned locations. Rent income received from tenants who rent properties is recorded as a reduction to SG&A expense.

Rent Expense (millions)	**2013**	2012	2011
Property and equipment	**$ 194**	$ 194	$ 193
Software	**33**	33	33
Rent income [(a)]	**(12)**	(85)	(61)
Total rent expense	**$ 215**	$ 142	$ 165

[(a)] Rent income in 2013, 2012, and 2011 includes $4 million, $75 million and $51 million, respectively, related to sites acquired in our Canadian leasehold acquisition that were being subleased back to Zellers for various terms, which all ended by March 31, 2013.

Total capital lease interest expense was $116 million, $109 million and $69 million in 2013, 2012 and 2011, respectively, including interest expense on Canadian capitalized leases of $77 million, $78 million and $44 million, respectively, and is included within net interest expense on the Consolidated Statements of Operations.

Most leases include one or more options to renew, with renewal terms that can extend the lease term from one to 50 years. Certain leases also include options to purchase the leased property. Assets recorded under capital leases as of February 1, 2014 and February 2, 2013 were $2,106 million and $2,038 million, respectively.

Future Minimum Lease Payments (millions)	Operating Leases [a]	Capital Leases [b]	Rent Income	Total
2014	$ 187	$ 204	$ (6)	$ 385
2015	185	198	(5)	378
2016	174	192	(4)	362
2017	168	157	(4)	321
2018	162	150	(3)	309
After 2018	3,227	4,412	(14)	7,625
Total future minimum lease payments	$ 4,103	$ 5,313	$ (36)	$ 9,380
Less: Interest [c]		(3,342)		
Present value of future minimum capital lease payments [d]		$ 1,971		

[a] Total contractual lease payments include $2,105 million related to options to extend lease terms that are reasonably assured of being exercised and also includes $135 million of legally binding minimum lease payments for stores that are expected to open in 2014 or later.

[b] Capital lease payments include $3,740 million related to options to extend lease terms that are reasonably assured of being exercised and also includes $80 million of legally binding minimum payments for stores opening in 2014 or later.

[c] Calculated using the interest rate at inception for each lease.

[d] Includes the current portion of $77 million.

21. Income Taxes

Earnings before income taxes were $3,103 million, $4,609 million and $4,456 million during 2013, 2012 and 2011, respectively, including losses incurred by our foreign entities of ($881) million, ($309) million, and ($11) million. Our foreign entities are subject to tax outside of the U.S.

Tax Rate Reconciliation	**2013**	2012	2011
Federal statutory rate	**35.0%**	35.0%	35.0%
State income taxes, net of the federal tax benefit	**3.1**	2.0	1.0
International	**0.3**	(0.6)	(0.7)
Other	**(1.9)**	(1.5)	(1.0)
Effective tax rate	**36.5%**	34.9%	34.3%

Certain discrete state income tax items reduced our effective tax rate by 0.5 percentage points, 1.0 percentage points, and 2.0 percentage points in 2013, 2012 and 2011, respectively.

Provision for Income Taxes (millions)	**2013**	2012	2011
Current:			
Federal	**$ 1,213**	$ 1,471	$ 1,069
State	**148**	135	74
International	**25**	18	13
Total current	**1,386**	1,624	1,156
Deferred:			
Federal	**66**	124	427
State	**2**	14	—
International	**(322)**	(152)	(56)
Total deferred	**(254)**	(14)	371
Total provision	**$ 1,132**	$ 1,610	$ 1,527

Net Deferred Tax Asset/(Liability) (millions)	February 1, 2014	February 2, 2013
Gross deferred tax assets:		
Accrued and deferred compensation	$ 509	$ 537
Foreign operating loss carryforward	394	189
Accruals and reserves not currently deductible	348	352
Self-insured benefits	231	249
Other	193	123
Allowance for doubtful accounts and lower of cost or fair value adjustment on credit card receivables held for sale	—	67
Total gross deferred tax assets	1,675	1,517
Gross deferred tax liabilities:		
Property and equipment	(2,062)	(1,995)
Inventory	(270)	(210)
Other	(130)	(133)
Deferred credit card income	—	(91)
Total gross deferred tax liabilities	(2,462)	(2,429)
Total net deferred tax asset/(liability)	$ (787)	$ (912)

Deferred tax assets and liabilities are recognized for the future tax consequences attributable to temporary differences between financial statement carrying amounts of existing assets and liabilities and their respective tax bases. Deferred tax assets and liabilities are measured using enacted income tax rates in effect for the year the temporary differences are expected to be recovered or settled. Tax rate changes affecting deferred tax assets and liabilities are recognized in income at the enactment date.

At February 1, 2014, we had foreign net operating loss carryforwards of $1,466 million which are available to offset future income. These carryforwards are primarily related to the start-up operations of the Canadian Segment and expire between 2031 and 2033. We have evaluated the positive and negative evidence and consider it more likely than not that these carryforwards will be fully utilized prior to expiration.

We have not recorded deferred taxes when earnings from foreign operations are considered to be indefinitely invested outside the U.S. These accumulated net earnings relate to certain ongoing operations and were $77 million at February 1, 2014 and $52 million at February 2, 2013. It is not practicable to determine the income tax liability that would be payable if such earnings were repatriated.

We file a U.S. federal income tax return and income tax returns in various states and foreign jurisdictions. The U.S. Internal Revenue Service has completed exams on the U.S. federal income tax returns for years 2010 and prior. With few exceptions, we are no longer subject to state and local or non-U.S. income tax examinations by tax authorities for years before 2003.

Reconciliation of Liability for Unrecognized Tax Benefits (millions)	2013	2012	2011
Balance at beginning of period	$ 216	$ 236	$ 302
Additions based on tax positions related to the current year	15	10	12
Additions for tax positions of prior years	28	19	31
Reductions for tax positions of prior years	(57)	(42)	(101)
Settlements	(19)	(7)	(8)
Balance at end of period	$ 183	$ 216	$ 236

If we were to prevail on all unrecognized tax benefits recorded, $120 million of the $183 million reserve would benefit the effective tax rate. In addition, the reversal of accrued penalties and interest would also benefit the effective tax rate. Interest and penalties associated with unrecognized tax benefits are recorded within income tax expense. During the years ended February 1, 2014, February 2, 2013 and January 28, 2012, we recorded a net benefit from the reversal of accrued penalties and interest of $1 million, $16 million and $12 million, respectively. As of February 1, 2014, February 2, 2013 and January 28, 2012 total accrued interest and penalties were $58 million, $64 million and $82 million, respectively.

It is reasonably possible that the amount of the unrecognized tax benefits with respect to our other unrecognized tax positions will increase or decrease during the next twelve months; however, an estimate of the amount or range of the change cannot be made at this time.

22. Other Noncurrent Liabilities

Other Noncurrent Liabilities (millions)	**February 1, 2014**	February 2, 2013
Deferred compensation	**$ 491**	$ 479
Workers' compensation and general liability [(a)]	**424**	467
Income tax	**174**	180
Pension and postretirement health care benefits	**115**	170
Other	**286**	313
Total	**$ 1,490**	$ 1,609

(a) We retain a substantial portion of the risk related to general liability and workers' compensation claims. Liabilities associated with these losses include estimates of both claims filed and losses incurred but not yet reported. We estimate our ultimate cost based on analysis of historical data and actuarial estimates. General liability and workers' compensation liabilities are recorded at our estimate of their net present value.

23. Share Repurchase

We repurchase shares primarily through open market transactions under a $5 billion share repurchase program authorized by our Board of Directors in January 2012. During the first quarter of 2012, we completed a $10 billion share repurchase program that was authorized by our Board of Directors in November 2007.

Share Repurchases (millions, except per share data)	**2013**	2012	2011
Total number of shares purchased	**21.9**	32.2	37.2
Average price paid per share	**$ 67.41**	$ 58.96	$ 50.89
Total investment	**$ 1,474**	$ 1,900	$ 1,894

Of the shares reacquired, a portion was delivered upon settlement of prepaid forward contracts as follows:

Settlement of Prepaid Forward Contracts [(a)] (millions)	**2013**	2012	2011
Total number of shares purchased	**0.2**	0.5	1.0
Total cash investment	**$ 14**	$ 25	$ 52
Aggregate market value [(b)]	**$ 17**	$ 29	$ 52

(a) These contracts are among the investment vehicles used to reduce our economic exposure related to our nonqualified deferred compensation plans. The details of our positions in prepaid forward contracts have been provided in Note 25.

(b) At their respective settlement dates.

24. Share-Based Compensation

We maintain a long-term incentive plan (the Plan) for key team members and non-employee members of our Board of Directors. The Plan allows us to grant equity-based compensation awards, including stock options, stock appreciation rights, performance share units, restricted stock units, restricted stock awards or a combination of awards (collectively, share-based awards). The number of unissued common shares reserved for future grants under the Plan was 18.7 million and 24.9 million at February 1, 2014 and February 2, 2013, respectively.

Compensation expense associated with share-based awards is recognized on a straight-line basis over the shorter of the vesting period or the minimum required service period. Total share-based compensation expense recognized in the Consolidated Statements of Operations was $110 million, $105 million and $90 million in 2013, 2012 and 2011, respectively. The related income tax benefit was $43 million, $42 million and $35 million in 2013, 2012 and 2011, respectively.

Stock Options

Through 2013, we granted nonqualified stock options to certain team members that generally vest and become exercisable annually in equal amounts over a four-year period and expire 10 years after the grant date. We previously granted options with a ten-year term to the non-employee members of our Board of Directors that vest immediately, but are not exercisable until one year after the grant date. We used a Black-Scholes valuation model to estimate the fair value of the options at the grant date.

Stock Option Activity	Stock Options					
	Total Outstanding			Exercisable		
	Number of Options [(a)]	Exercise Price [(b)]	Intrinsic Value [(c)]	Number of Options [(a)]	Exercise Price [(b)]	Intrinsic Value [(c)]
February 2, 2013	34,458	$ 50.60	$ 366	21,060	$ 48.25	$ 273
Granted	226	69.56				
Expired/forfeited	(745)	53.14				
Exercised/issued	(9,085)	46.51				
February 1, 2014	**24,854**	**$ 52.19**	**$ 136**	**16,824**	**$ 50.64**	**$ 109**

(a) In thousands.
(b) Weighted average per share.
(c) Represents stock price appreciation subsequent to the grant date, in millions.

Black-Scholes Model Valuation Assumptions	**2013**	2012	2011
Dividend yield	**2.4%**	2.4%	2.5%
Volatility [(a)]	**22%**	23%	27%
Risk-free interest rate [(b)]	**1.4%**	1.0%	1.0%
Expected life in years [(c)]	**5.5**	5.5	5.5
Stock options grant date fair value	**$ 11.14**	$ 9.70	$ 9.20

(a) Volatility represents an average of market estimates for implied volatility of Target common stock.
(b) The risk-free interest rate is an interpolation of the relevant U.S. Treasury security maturities as of each applicable grant date.
(c) The expected life is estimated based on an analysis of options already exercised and any foreseeable trends or changes in recipients' behavior.

Stock Option Exercises (millions)	**2013**	2012	2011
Cash received for exercise price	**$ 422**	$ 331	$ 93
Intrinsic value	**197**	139	27
Income tax benefit	**77**	55	11

At February 1, 2014, there was $37 million of total unrecognized compensation expense related to nonvested stock options, which is expected to be recognized over a weighted average period of 1.1 years. The weighted average remaining life of exercisable options is 5.3 years, and the weighted average remaining life of all outstanding options is 6.2 years. The total fair value of options vested was $53 million, $68 million and $75 million in 2013, 2012 and 2011, respectively.

Performance Share Units

We issue performance share units to certain team members that represent shares potentially issuable in the future. Issuance is based upon our performance relative to a retail peer group over a three-year performance period on certain measures including domestic market share change, return on invested capital and EPS growth. The fair value of performance share units is calculated based on the stock price on the date of grant. The weighted average grant date fair value for performance share units was $57.22, $58.61 and $48.63 in 2013, 2012 and 2011, respectively.

Performance Share Unit Activity	Total Nonvested Units	
	Performance Share Units [(a)]	Grant Date Fair Value [(b)]
February 2, 2013	1,256	$ 51.53
Granted	2,036	57.22
Forfeited	(145)	56.42
Vested	(277)	51.49
February 1, 2014	**2,870**	**$ 55.37**

(a) Assumes attainment of maximum payout rates as set forth in the performance criteria based in thousands of share units. Applying actual or expected payout rates, the number of outstanding units at February 1, 2014 was 1,515 thousand.

(b) Weighted average per unit.

The expense recognized each period is dependent upon our estimate of the number of shares that will ultimately be issued. Future compensation expense for unvested awards could reach a maximum of $127 million assuming payout of all unvested awards. The unrecognized expense is expected to be recognized over a weighted average period of 1.2 years. The fair value of performance share units vested and converted was $14 million in 2013, $16 million in 2012 and was not significant in 2011.

Restricted Stock

We issue restricted stock units and performance-based restricted stock units with three-year cliff vesting from the grant date (collectively restricted stock) to certain team members. The final number of shares issued under performance-based restricted stock units will be based on our total shareholder return relative to a retail peer group over a three-year performance period. We also regularly issue restricted stock units to our Board of Directors, which vest quarterly over a one-year period and are settled in shares of Target common stock upon departure from the Board. The fair value for restricted stock is calculated based on the stock price on the date of grant, incorporating an analysis of the total shareholder return performance measure where applicable. The weighted average grant date fair value for restricted stock was $62.76, $60.44 and $49.42 in 2013, 2012 and 2011, respectively.

Restricted Stock Activity	Total Nonvested Units	
	Restricted Stock [(a)]	Grant Date Fair Value [(b)]
February 2, 2013	2,895	$ 56.12
Granted	1,686	62.76
Forfeited	(130)	57.19
Vested	(516)	54.26
February 1, 2014	**3,935**	**$ 58.98**

(a) Represents the number of restricted stock units, in thousands. For performance-based restricted stock units, assumes attainment of maximum payout rates as set forth in the performance criteria based in thousands of share units. Applying actual or expected payout rates, the number of outstanding restricted stock units at February 1, 2014 was 3,551 thousand.

(b) Weighted average per unit.

The expense recognized each period is partially dependent upon our estimate of the number of shares that will ultimately be issued. At February 1, 2014, there was $139 million of total unrecognized compensation expense related to restricted stock, which is expected to be recognized over a weighted average period of 1.3 years. The fair value of restricted stock vested and converted to shares of Target common stock was $28 million, $11 million and $9 million in 2013, 2012 and 2011, respectively.

25. Defined Contribution Plans

Team members who meet eligibility requirements can participate in a defined contribution 401(k) plan by investing up to 80 percent of their compensation, as limited by statute or regulation. Generally, we match 100 percent of each team member's contribution up to 5 percent of total compensation. Company match contributions are made to funds designated by the participant.

In addition, we maintain a nonqualified, unfunded deferred compensation plan for approximately 3,000 current and retired team members whose participation in our 401(k) plan is limited by statute or regulation. These team members choose from a menu of crediting rate alternatives that are the same as the investment choices in our 401(k) plan, including Target common stock. We credit an additional 2 percent per year to the accounts of all active participants, excluding members of our management executive committee, in part to recognize the risks inherent to their participation in this plan. We also maintain a nonqualified, unfunded deferred compensation plan that was frozen during 1996, covering approximately 60 participants, most of whom are retired. In this plan, deferred compensation earns returns tied to market levels of interest rates plus an additional 6 percent return, with a minimum of 12 percent and a maximum of 20 percent, as determined by the plan's terms. Our total liability under these plans was $520 million and $505 million at February 1, 2014 and February 2, 2013, respectively.

We mitigate some of our risk of offering the nonqualified plans through investing in vehicles, including company-owned life insurance and prepaid forward contracts in our own common stock, that offset a substantial portion of our economic exposure to the returns of these plans. These investment vehicles are general corporate assets and are marked to market with the related gains and losses recognized in the Consolidated Statements of Operations in the period they occur.

The total change in fair value for contracts indexed to our own common stock recognized in earnings was pretax income/(loss) of $(5) million, $14 million and $(4) million in 2013, 2012 and 2011, respectively. During 2013 and 2012, we invested $23 million and $19 million, respectively, in such investment instruments, and this activity is included in the Consolidated Statements of Cash Flows within other investing activities. Adjusting our position in these investment vehicles may involve repurchasing shares of Target common stock when settling the forward contracts as described in Note 23. The settlement dates of these instruments are regularly renegotiated with the counterparty.

Prepaid Forward Contracts on Target Common Stock (millions, except per share data)	Number of Shares	Contractual Price Paid per Share	Contractual Fair Value	Total Cash Investment
February 2, 2013	1.2	$ 45.46	$ 73	$ 54
February 1, 2014	**1.3**	**$ 48.81**	**$ 73**	**$ 63**

Plan Expenses (millions)	**2013**	2012	2011
401(k) plan matching contributions expense	**$ 229**	$ 218	$ 197
Nonqualified deferred compensation plans			
Benefits expense [(a)]	**41**	78	38
Related investment income [(b)]	**(23)**	(43)	(10)
Nonqualified plan net expense	**$ 18**	$ 35	$ 28

(a) Includes market-performance credits on accumulated participant account balances and annual crediting for additional benefits earned during the year.

(b) Includes investment returns and life-insurance proceeds received from company-owned life insurance policies and other investments used to economically hedge the cost of these plans.

26. Pension and Postretirement Health Care Plans

We have qualified defined benefit pension plans covering team members who meet age and service requirements, including in certain circumstances, date of hire. Effective January 1, 2009, our U.S. qualified defined benefit pension plan was closed to new participants, with limited exceptions. We also have unfunded nonqualified pension plans for team members with qualified plan compensation restrictions. Eligibility for, and the level of, these benefits varies depending on each team members' date of hire, length of service and/or team member compensation. Upon early retirement and prior to Medicare eligibility, team members also become eligible for certain health care benefits if they meet minimum age and service requirements and agree to contribute a portion of the cost.

Change in Projected Benefit Obligation	Pension Benefits				Postretirement Health Care Benefits	
	Qualified Plans		Nonqualified Plans			
(millions)	**2013**	2012	**2013**	2012	**2013**	2012
Benefit obligation at beginning of period	**$ 3,164**	$ 3,015	**$ 37**	$ 38	**$ 121**	$ 100
Service cost	**117**	120	**1**	1	**6**	10
Interest cost	**136**	137	**1**	2	**2**	3
Actuarial (gain)/loss	**(125)**	107	**—**	—	**(3)**	18
Participant contributions	**1**	1	**—**	—	**5**	5
Benefits paid	**(122)**	(126)	**(4)**	(3)	**(14)**	(12)
Plan amendments	**2**	(90)	**—**	(1)	**(44)**	(3)
Benefit obligation at end of period	**$ 3,173**	$ 3,164	**$ 35**	$ 37	**$ 73**	$ 121

Change in Plan Assets	Pension Benefits				Postretirement Health Care Benefits	
	Qualified Plans		Nonqualified Plans			
(millions)	**2013**	2012	**2013**	2012	**2013**	2012
Fair value of plan assets at beginning of period	**$ 3,223**	$ 2,921	**$ —**	$ —	**$ —**	$ —
Actual return on plan assets	**161**	305	**—**	—	**—**	—
Employer contributions	**4**	122	**4**	3	**9**	7
Participant contributions	**1**	1	**—**	—	**5**	5
Benefits paid	**(122)**	(126)	**(4)**	(3)	**(14)**	(12)
Fair value of plan assets at end of period	**3,267**	3,223	**—**	—	**—**	—
Benefit obligation at end of period	**3,173**	3,164	**35**	37	**73**	121
Funded/(underfunded) status	**$ 94**	$ 59	**$ (35)**	$ (37)	**$ (73)**	$ (121)

Recognition of Funded/(Underfunded) Status	Qualified Plans		Nonqualified Plans [(a)]	
(millions)	**2013**	2012	**2013**	2012
Other noncurrent assets	**$ 112**	$ 81	**$ —**	$ —
Accrued and other current liabilities	**(2)**	(1)	**(9)**	(9)
Other noncurrent liabilities	**(16)**	(21)	**(99)**	(149)
Net amounts recognized	**$ 94**	$ 59	**$ (108)**	$ (158)

(a) Includes postretirement health care benefits.

The following table summarizes the amounts recorded in accumulated other comprehensive income, which have not yet been recognized as a component of net periodic benefit expense:

Amounts in Accumulated Other Comprehensive Income	Pension Plans		Postretirement Health Care Plans	
(millions)	**2013**	2012	**2013**	2012
Net actuarial loss	**$ 792**	$ 947	**$ 49**	$ 58
Prior service credits	**(80)**	(91)	**(62)**	(34)
Amounts in accumulated other comprehensive income	**$ 712**	$ 856	**$ (13)**	$ 24

The following table summarizes the changes in accumulated other comprehensive income for the years ended February 1, 2014 and February 2, 2013, related to our pension and postretirement health care plans:

Change in Accumulated Other Comprehensive Income	Pension Benefits		Postretirement Health Care Benefits	
(millions)	Pretax	Net of Tax	Pretax	Net of Tax
January 28, 2012	$ 1,027	$ 623	$ 3	$ 2
Net actuarial loss	23	13	18	11
Amortization of net actuarial losses	(103)	(63)	(4)	(2)
Amortization of prior service costs and transition	—	—	10	6
Plan amendments	(91)	(56)	(3)	(2)
February 2, 2013	**856**	**517**	**24**	**15**
Net actuarial gain	**(52)**	**(32)**	**(3)**	**(2)**
Amortization of net actuarial losses	**(103)**	**(62)**	**(6)**	**(4)**
Amortization of prior service costs and transition	**11**	**7**	**16**	**10**
Plan amendment	**—**	**—**	**(44)**	**(27)**
February 1, 2014	**$ 712**	**$ 430**	**$ (13)**	**$ (8)**

The following table summarizes the amounts in accumulated other comprehensive income expected to be amortized and recognized as a component of net periodic benefit expense in 2014:

Expected Amortization of Amounts in Accumulated Other Comprehensive Income (millions)	Pretax	Net of Tax
Net actuarial loss	$ 70	$ 43
Prior service credits	(27)	(16)
Total amortization expense	**$ 43**	**$ 27**

The following table summarizes our net pension and postretirement health care benefits expense for the years 2013, 2012 and 2011:

Net Pension and Postretirement Health Care Benefits Expense	Pension Benefits			Postretirement Health Care Benefits		
(millions)	**2013**	2012	2011	**2013**	2012	2011
Service cost benefits earned during the period	**$ 118**	$ 121	$ 117	**$ 6**	$ 10	$ 10
Interest cost on projected benefit obligation	**137**	139	137	**2**	3	4
Expected return on assets	**(235)**	(220)	(206)	**—**	—	—
Amortization of losses	**103**	103	67	**6**	3	4
Amortization of prior service cost	**(11)**	—	(2)	**(16)**	(10)	(10)
Settlement and Special Termination Charges	**3**	—	—	**—**	—	—
Total	**$ 115**	$ 143	$ 113	**$ (2)**	$ 6	$ 8

Prior service cost amortization is determined using the straight-line method over the average remaining service period of team members expected to receive benefits under the plan.

Defined Benefit Pension Plan Information (millions)	2013	2012
Accumulated benefit obligation (ABO) for all plans [(a)]	**$ 3,149**	$ 3,140
Projected benefit obligation for pension plans with an ABO in excess of plan assets [(b)]	**54**	59
Total ABO for pension plans with an ABO in excess of plan assets	**48**	53

(a) The present value of benefits earned to date assuming no future salary growth.
(b) The present value of benefits earned to date by plan participants, including the effect of assumed future salary increases.

Assumptions

Benefit Obligation Weighted Average Assumptions	Pension Benefits		Postretirement Health Care Benefits	
	2013	2012	2013	2012
Discount rate	**4.77%**	4.40%	**3.30%**	2.75%
Average assumed rate of compensation increase	**3.00**	3.00	**n/a**	n/a

Net Periodic Benefit Expense Weighted Average Assumptions	Pension Benefits			Postretirement Health Care Benefits		
	2013	2012	2011	2013	2012	2011
Discount rate	**4.40%**	4.65%	5.50%	**2.75%**	3.60%	4.35%
Expected long-term rate of return on plan assets	**8.00**	8.00	8.00	**n/a**	n/a	n/a
Average assumed rate of compensation increase	**3.00**	3.50	4.00	**n/a**	n/a	n/a

The weighted average assumptions used to measure net periodic benefit expense each year are the rates as of the beginning of the year (i.e., the prior measurement date). Based on a stable asset allocation, our most recent compound annual rate of return on qualified plans' assets was 10.4 percent, 8.3 percent, 7.2 percent, and 9.2 percent for the 5-year, 10-year, 15-year and 20-year time periods, respectively.

The market-related value of plan assets, which is used in calculating expected return on assets in net periodic benefit cost, is determined each year by adjusting the previous year's value by expected return, benefit payments and cash contributions. The market-related value is adjusted for asset gains and losses in equal 20 percent adjustments over a five-year period.

We review the expected long-term rate of return on an annual basis, and revise it as appropriate. Additionally, we monitor the mix of investments in our portfolio to ensure alignment with our long-term strategy to manage pension cost and reduce volatility in our assets. Our expected annualized long-term rate of return assumptions as of February 1, 2014 were 8.0 percent for domestic and international equity securities, 5.0 percent for long-duration debt securities, 8.0 percent for balanced funds and 9.5 percent for other investments. These estimates are a judgmental matter in which we consider the composition of our asset portfolio, our historical long-term investment performance and current market conditions.

An increase in the cost of covered health care benefits of 7.5 percent was assumed for 2013 and 7.0 percent is assumed for 2014. The rate will be reduced to 5.0 percent in 2019 and thereafter.

Health Care Cost Trend Rates – 1% Change (millions)	1% Increase	1% Decrease
Effect on total of service and interest cost components of net periodic postretirement health care benefit expense	$ 1	$ (1)
Effect on the health care component of the accumulated postretirement benefit obligation	5	(5)

Plan Assets

Our asset allocation policy is designed to reduce the long-term cost of funding our pension obligations. The plan invests with both passive and active investment managers depending on the investment's asset class. The plan also seeks to reduce the risk associated with adverse movements in interest rates by employing an interest rate hedging program, which may include the use of interest rate swaps, total return swaps and other instruments.

Asset Category	Current Targeted Allocation	Actual Allocation 2013	Actual Allocation 2012
Domestic equity securities [(a)]	19%	21%	20%
International equity securities	12	12	11
Debt securities	25	26	27
Balanced funds	30	28	29
Other [(b)]	14	13	13
Total	100%	100%	100%

(a) Equity securities include our common stock in amounts substantially less than 1 percent of total plan assets as of February 1, 2014 and February 2, 2013.

(b) Other assets include private equity, mezzanine and high-yield debt, natural resources and timberland funds, multi-strategy hedge funds, derivative instruments and a 5 percent allocation to real estate.

Fair Value Measurements		Fair Value at February 1, 2014				Fair Value at February 2, 2013		
(millions)	Total	Level 1	Level 2	Level 3	Total	Level 1	Level 2	Level 3
Cash and cash equivalents	$ 150	$ 6	$ 144	$ —	$ 174	$ 5	$ 169	$ —
Common collective trusts [(a)]	1,000	—	1,000	—	878	—	878	—
Government securities [(b)]	282	—	282	—	296	—	296	—
Fixed income [(c)]	541	—	541	—	560	—	560	—
Balanced funds [(d)]	903	—	903	—	925	—	925	—
Private equity funds [(e)]	221	—	—	221	236	—	—	236
Other [(f)]	170	—	43	127	154	—	32	122
Total plan assets	$ 3,267	$ 6	$ 2,913	$ 348	$ 3,223	$ 5	$ 2,860	$ 358

(a) Passively managed index funds with holdings in domestic and international equities.

(b) Investments in government securities and passively managed index funds with holdings in long-term government bonds.

(c) Investments in corporate bonds, mortgage-backed securities and passively managed index funds with holdings in long-term corporate bonds.

(d) Investments in equities, nominal and inflation-linked fixed income securities, commodities and public real estate.

(e) Includes investments in venture capital, mezzanine and high-yield debt, natural resources and timberland funds.

(f) Investments in multi-strategy hedge funds (including domestic and international equity securities, convertible bonds and other alternative investments), real estate and derivative investments.

Level 3 Reconciliation		Actual Return on Plan Assets [(a)]				
(millions)	Balance at Beginning of Period	Relating to Assets Still Held at the Reporting Date	Relating to Assets Sold During the Period	Purchases, Sales and Settlements	Transfer in and/or out of Level 3	Balance at End of Period
2012						
Private equity funds	$ 283	$ 17	$ 25	$ (89)	$ —	$ 236
Other	115	4	—	3	—	122
2013						
Private equity funds	$ 236	$ 7	$ 26	$ (48)	$ —	$ 221
Other	122	14	1	(10)	—	127

(a) Represents realized and unrealized gains (losses) from changes in values of those financial instruments only for the period in which the instruments were classified as Level 3.

Position	Valuation Technique
Cash and cash equivalents	These investments are cash holdings and investment vehicles valued using the Net Asset Value (NAV) provided by the administrator of the fund. The NAV for the investment vehicles is based on the value of the underlying assets owned by the fund minus applicable costs and liabilities, and then divided by the number of shares outstanding.
Equity securities	Valued at the closing price reported on the major market on which the individual securities are traded.
Common collective trusts/ balanced funds/ certain multi-strategy hedge funds	Valued using the NAV provided by the administrator of the fund. The NAV is a quoted transactional price for participants in the fund, which do not represent an active market.
Fixed income and government securities	Valued using matrix pricing models and quoted prices of securities with similar characteristics.
Private equity/ real estate/ certain multi-strategy hedge funds/ other	Valued by deriving Target's proportionate share of equity investment from audited financial statements. Private equity and real estate investments require significant judgment on the part of the fund manager due to the absence of quoted market prices, inherent lack of liquidity, and the long term of such investments. Certain multi-strategy hedge funds represent funds of funds that include liquidity restrictions and for which timely valuation information is not available.

Contributions

Our obligations to plan participants can be met over time through a combination of company contributions to these plans and earnings on plan assets. In 2013 we made no contributions to our qualified defined benefit pension plans. In 2012, we made discretionary contributions of $122 million. We are not required to make any contributions in 2014. However, depending on investment performance and plan funded status, we may elect to make a contribution. We expect to make contributions in the range of $5 million to $6 million to our postretirement health care benefit plan in 2014.

Estimated Future Benefit Payments

Benefit payments by the plans, which reflect expected future service as appropriate, are expected to be paid as follows:

Estimated Future Benefit Payments (millions)	Pension Benefits	Postretirement Health Care Benefits
2014	$ 152	$ 6
2015	159	6
2016	169	7
2017	178	8
2018	188	8
2019-2023	1,058	45

27. Accumulated Other Comprehensive Income

(millions)	Cash Flow Hedges	Currency Translation Adjustment	Pension and Other Benefit	Total
February 2, 2013	$ (29)	$ (15)	$ (532)	$ (576)
Other comprehensive (loss)/income before reclassifications	—	(429)	60	(369)
Amounts reclassified from AOCI	4 [(a)]	—	50 [(b)]	54
February 1, 2014	$ (25)	$ (444)	$ (422)	$ (891)

(a) Represents gains and losses on cash flow hedges, net of $2 million of taxes, which are recorded in net interest expense on the Consolidated Statements of Operations.

(b) Represents amortization of pension and other benefit liabilities, net of $32 million of taxes, which is recorded in SG&A expenses on the Consolidated Statements of Operations. See Note 26 for additional information.

28. Segment Reporting

Our segment measure of profit is used by management to evaluate the return on our investment and to make operating decisions.

Business Segment Results	**2013**			2012 [(a)]			2011		
(millions)	**U.S.**	**Canadian**	**Total**	U.S.	Canadian	Total	U.S.	Canadian	Total
Sales	**$ 71,279**	**$ 1,317**	**$ 72,596**	$ 71,960	$ —	$ 71,960	$ 68,466	$ —	$ 68,466
Cost of sales	**50,039**	**1,121**	**51,160**	50,568	—	50,568	47,860	—	47,860
Selling, general and administrative expenses [(b)]	**14,285**	**910**	**15,196**	13,759	272	14,031	13,079	74	13,153
Depreciation and amortization	**1,996**	**227**	**2,223**	2,044	97	2,142	2,084	48	2,131
Segment profit	**$ 4,959**	**$ (941)**	**$ 4,017**	$ 5,589	$ (369)	$ 5,219	$ 5,443	$ (122)	$ 5,322
Gain on receivables transaction [(c)]			**391**			152			—
Reduction of beneficial interest asset [(b)]			**(98)**			—			—
Other [(d)]			**(64)**			—			—
Data Breach related costs, net of insurance receivable [(e)]			**(17)**			—			—
Earnings before interest expense and income taxes			**4,229**			5,371			5,322
Net interest expense			**1,126**			762			866
Earnings before income taxes			**$ 3,103**			$ 4,609			$ 4,456

Note: The sum of the segment amounts may not equal the total amounts due to rounding.

Note: Certain operating expenses are incurred on behalf of our Canadian Segment, but are included in our U.S. Segment because those costs are not allocated internally and generally come under the responsibility of our U.S. management team.

Note: Through fiscal 2012, we operated as three business segments: U.S. Retail, U.S. Credit Card and Canadian. Following the sale of our credit card receivables portfolio described in Note 6, we operate as two segments: U.S. and Canadian. Prior period segment results have been revised to reflect the combination of our historical U.S. Retail Segment and U.S. Credit Card Segment into one U.S. Segment.

(a) Consisted of 53 weeks.

(b) Our U.S. Segment includes all TD profit-sharing amounts in segment profit; however, under GAAP, some amounts received from TD reduce the beneficial interest asset and are not recorded in consolidated earnings. Segment SG&A expenses plus these amounts equal consolidated SG&A expenses.

(c) Represents the gain on receivables transaction recorded in our Consolidated Statements of Operations, plus, for 2012, the difference between bad debt expense and net write-offs for the fourth quarter. Refer to Note 6 for more information on our credit card receivables transaction.

(d) Includes a $23 million workforce-reduction charge primarily related to severance and benefits costs, a $22 million charge related to part-time team member health benefit changes, and $19 million in impairment charges related to certain parcels of undeveloped land.

(e) Refer to Note 17 for more information on Data Breach related costs.

Total Assets by Segment (millions)	February 1, 2014	February 2, 2013
U.S.	$ 38,128	$ 43,289
Canadian	6,254	4,722
Total segment assets	$ 44,382	$ 48,011
Unallocated assets [(a)]	171	152
Total assets	$ 44,553	$ 48,163

(a) At February 1, 2014, represents the beneficial interest asset of $127 million and insurance receivable related to the Data Breach of $44 million. At February 2, 2013, represents the net adjustment to eliminate our allowance for doubtful accounts and record our credit card receivables at lower of cost (par) or fair value.

Capital Expenditures by Segment (millions)	2013	2012[(a)]	2011
U.S.	$ 1,886	$ 2,345	$ 2,476
Canadian	1,567	932	1,892
Total	$ 3,453	$ 3,277	$ 4,368

(a) Consisted of 53 weeks.

29. Quarterly Results (Unaudited)

Due to the seasonal nature of our business, fourth quarter operating results typically represent a substantially larger share of total year revenues and earnings because they include our peak sales period from Thanksgiving through the end of December. We follow the same accounting policies for preparing quarterly and annual financial data. The table below summarizes quarterly results for 2013 and 2012:

Quarterly Results	First Quarter		Second Quarter		Third Quarter		Fourth Quarter		Total Year	
(millions, except per share data)	2013	2012	2013	2012	2013	2012	2013	2012 [(a)]	2013	2012 [(a)]
Sales	$ 16,706	$ 16,537	$ 17,117	$ 16,451	$ 17,258	$ 16,601	$ 21,516	$ 22,370	$ 72,596	$ 71,960
Credit card revenues	—	330	—	328	—	328	—	356	—	1,341
Total revenues	16,706	16,867	17,117	16,779	17,258	16,929	21,516	22,726	72,596	73,301
Cost of sales	11,563	11,541	11,745	11,297	12,133	11,569	15,719	16,160	51,160	50,568
Selling, general and administrative expenses	3,590	3,392	3,698	3,588	3,853	3,704	4,235	4,229	15,375	14,914
Credit card expenses	—	120	—	108	—	106	—	135	—	467
Depreciation and amortization	536	529	542	531	569	542	576	539	2,223	2,142
Gain on receivables transaction	(391)	—	—	—	—	(156)	—	(5)	(391)	(161)
Earnings before interest expense and income taxes	1,408	1,285	1,132	1,255	703	1,164	986	1,668	4,229	5,371
Net interest expense	629	184	171	184	165	192	161	204	1,126	762
Earnings before income taxes	779	1,101	961	1,071	538	972	825	1,464	3,103	4,609
Provision for income taxes	281	404	350	367	197	335	305	503	1,132	1,610
Net earnings	$ 498	$ 697	$ 611	$ 704	$ 341	$ 637	$ 520	$ 961	$ 1,971	$ 2,999
Basic earnings per share	$ 0.78	$ 1.05	$ 0.96	$ 1.07	$ 0.54	$ 0.97	$ 0.82	$ 1.48	$ 3.10	$ 4.57
Diluted earnings per share	0.77	1.04	0.95	1.06	0.54	0.96	0.81	1.47	3.07	4.52
Dividends declared per share	0.36	0.30	0.43	0.36	0.43	0.36	0.43	0.36	1.65	1.38
Closing common stock price:										
High	70.67	58.86	73.32	61.95	71.99	65.44	66.89	64.48	73.32	65.44
Low	60.85	50.33	68.29	54.81	62.13	60.62	56.64	58.57	56.64	50.33

Note: Per share amounts are computed independently for each of the quarters presented. The sum of the quarters may not equal the total year amount due to the impact of changes in average quarterly shares outstanding and all other quarterly amounts may not equal the total year due to rounding.

(a) The fourth quarter and total year 2013 consisted of 13 weeks and 52 weeks, respectively, compared with 14 weeks and 53 weeks in the comparable prior-year periods.

U.S. Sales by Product Category [a]	First Quarter		Second Quarter		Third Quarter		Fourth Quarter		Total Year	
	2013	2012	**2013**	2012	**2013**	2012	**2013**	2012	**2013**	2012
Household essentials	**27%**	26%	**27%**	27%	**26%**	26%	**22%**	21%	**25%**	25%
Hardlines	**15**	16	**15**	15	**15**	14	**24**	24	**18**	18
Apparel and accessories	**20**	20	**20**	20	**20**	20	**17**	18	**19**	19
Food and pet supplies	**22**	21	**20**	20	**21**	21	**19**	18	**21**	20
Home furnishings and décor	**16**	17	**18**	18	**18**	19	**18**	19	**17**	18
Total	**100%**	100%	**100%**	100%	**100%**	100%	**100%**	100%	**100%**	100%

(a) As a percentage of sales.

APPENDIX C

SUMMARY OF FINANCIAL RATIOS

CHAPTER 3

Debt to Assets Ratio

The debt to assets ratio reveals the percentage of a company's assets that is financed with borrowed money. The higher the debt to assets ratio is, the greater its financial risk, other things being equal. The debt to assets ratio is defined as

$$\frac{\text{Total debt}}{\text{Total assets}}$$

Return on Assets Ratio

The return on assets ratio (ROA) helps measure how well a company is using the assets available to it. The greater the amount of earnings that can be obtained for a given amount of assets, the better a company is doing at utilizing its assets. So, in general, the higher a company's ROA, the better. The ROA ratio is defined as

$$\frac{\text{Net income}}{\text{Total assets}}$$

Return on Equity Ratio

The return on equity ratio (ROE) helps to measure how much the owners of a company are earning on the money they have invested in the business. The higher a company's ROE, the better. The ROE is defined as

$$\frac{\text{Net income}}{\text{Stockholders' equity}}$$

CHAPTER 4

Gross Margin Percentage

The gross margin percentage helps explain a company's pricing strategy. It compares the amount a company pays for the goods it sells to the price the company is able to charge for those goods. The more a company marks up its goods, the higher the gross margin percentage will be. Specialty shops tend to have higher gross margin percentages while discount stores tend to have lower percentages. This ratio is sometimes called the gross profit percentage. The gross margin percentage is defined as

$$\frac{\text{Gross margin}}{\text{Net sales}}$$

Return on Sales Ratio

The return on sales ratio, expressed as a percentage, indicates how much of each dollar of sales remains as profit after all expenses have been deducted. Discount stores do not necessarily have lower return on sales percentages than specialty shops. The higher the return on sales ratio percentage, the better. The return on sales ratio is defined as

$$\frac{\text{Net income}}{\text{Net sales}}$$

CHAPTER 5

Inventory Turnover Ratio and Average Days to Sell Inventory

The inventory turnover ratio and the average days to sell inventory ratio indicate how long a company takes to sell the goods it has in merchandise inventory. The first ratio, inventory turnover, explains how many times per year a company's inventory is sold, or "turned over"; generally, the *higher* this ratio is, the better. Because the inventory turnover ratio is not easily understood by everyone, the second ratio, average days to sell inventory, is often used. However, the average days to sell inventory ratio cannot be computed without first computing the inventory turnover ratio. Generally, the *lower* the average days to sell inventory ratio is, the better. The inventory turnover ratio is defined as

$$\frac{\text{Cost of goods sold}}{\text{Inventory}}$$

The average days to sell inventory ratio is defined as

$$\frac{\text{365 days}}{\text{Inventory turnover}}$$

A company's operating cycle is the time it takes it to convert cash into inventory, sell the inventory, and collect the cash from accounts receivable that resulted from the sale of the inventory. The time it takes a business to do this can be computed by adding the *average days to sell inventory* and the *average days to collect accounts receivable.*

CHAPTER 7

Accounts Receivable Turnover Ratio and Average Days to Collect Receivables

The accounts receivable turnover ratio and the average days to collect receivables ratio indicate how long a company takes to collect its accounts receivable. The first ratio, accounts receivable turnover, explains how many times per year a company's receivables are collected, or "turned over"; generally, the *higher* this ratio is, the better. Because the accounts receivable turnover ratios are not easily understood by everyone, the second ratio, average days to collect receivables, is often used. However, the average days to collect receivables ratio cannot be computed without first computing the accounts receivable turnover ratio. Generally, the *lower* the average days to collect receivables ratio is, the better. The accounts receivable turnover ratio is defined as

$$\frac{\text{Sales}}{\text{Accounts receivable}}$$

The average days to collect receivables ratio is defined as

$$\frac{\text{365 days}}{\text{Accounts receivable turnover ratio}}$$

CHAPTER 9

Current Ratio

Liquidity refers to how quickly noncash assets can be converted into cash. The more quickly assets can be converted into cash, the more liquid they are and the more useful they are for paying liabilities that must be paid in the near future. The current ratio provides a measure of how much liquidity a company has. Specifically, it compares a company's more liquid assets (current assets) to its current liabilities. Other things being equal, the higher a company's current ratio, the easier it can pay its currently maturing debts. The current ratio is defined as

$$\frac{\text{Current assets}}{\text{Current liabilities}}$$

CHAPTER 10

Times Interest Earned Ratio

The times interest earned ratio helps assess a company's ability to make interest payments on its debt. Failure to make interest (or principal) payments can cause a company to be forced into bankruptcy. Other things being equal, a company with a higher times interest earned ratio is considered to have lower financial risk than a company with a lower ratio.

EBIT is an acronym for "earnings before interest and taxes." In other words, it is what net earnings would have been if the company had had no interest expense or income tax expense. Because net earnings are calculated after interest has been subtracted, a company might have $0 of earnings and still have been able to make its interest payments. Thus, the times interest earned ratio is based on EBIT and is defined as

$$\frac{\text{EBIT}}{\text{Interest expense}}$$

Return on Assets Ratio (refined)

As discussed in detail in Chapter 3, the return on assets ratio (ROA) helps measure how well a company is using the assets available to it. The greater the amount of earnings that can be obtained for a given amount of assets, the better a company is doing at utilizing its assets, so the higher this ratio is, the better. Throughout most of this textbook, ROA has been based on net earnings. However, the use of net earnings creates an ROA that is biased against companies with relatively more debt versus equity financing. Since the ROA ratio is intended to help assess how efficiently a company is using its assets, not how it is financed, the ROA that is used in the business world is often defined as

$$\frac{\text{EBIT}}{\text{Total assets}}$$

CHAPTER 11

Price-Earnings Ratio

The price-earnings ratio (P/E ratio) gives an indication of how optimistic the financial markets are about a company's future earnings. The higher a company's P/E ratio is, the more investors are willing to pay for each dollar of earnings that the company generates. Typically investors are willing to pay this higher price because they think the company will grow in the future. Lower P/E ratios indicate investors are less optimistic about the company's future growth. The price-earnings ratio is defined as

$$\frac{\text{Market price of one share of stock}}{\text{Earnings per share}}$$

Earnings per Share Ratio

The earnings per share ratio (EPS) provides an indication of the amount of a company's earnings that are attributable to each share of common stock outstanding. Obviously, the higher this ratio is, the better. In companies that have complex equity structures, such as convertible preferred stock and stock option plans, the computation of EPS can be very complex, but in its simplest form, EPS is defined as

$$\frac{\text{Net earnings}}{\text{Outstanding shares of common stock}}$$

APPENDIX D

ANNUAL REPORT AND FINANCIAL STATEMENT ANALYSIS PROJECTS

Authored By: Linda Bell, Park University

ANNUAL REPORT PROJECT FOR THE TARGET CORPORATION (SEE APPENDIX B FOR THE TARGET ANNUAL REPORT)

Target's 2011, 2012, and 2013 financial statements have been loaded in an Excel spreadsheet which is available in the *Connect* library. The income statement in the spreadsheet has been revised to better reflect the income statement format and wording used in the course textbook. The revision moves credit card revenues (interest income) to the non-operating section and enables the project solution for gross margin percentages to agree with those identified in the Management Discussion & Analysis section of the annual report. This Excel spreadsheet provides an excellent starting point for the vertical and horizontal analysis required in the project.

Please note: All references to the company's year-end data pertain to the fiscal year-end. For example, the company's 2013 financial statements are dated February 1, 2014, which is the company's fiscal closing date. Likewise, the 2012 financial statements apply to the fiscal year-ending February 2, 2013.

Company Overview and Management's Discussion and Analysis

The annual report for Target Corporation opens with a general description of business operations, risk factors, stock market registration, and selected financial data. This is followed by Management's Discussion and Analysis of Financial Condition, in which management talks about financial results, including segment results, liquidity, and other matters deemed necessary to provide adequate disclosure to users of the report. Refer to these items to answer Questions 1–6.

1. What are the company's two reportable operating segments?
2. Identify at least five risk factors for Target.
3. On what stock market exchange is the company's stock traded? What is Target's symbol?
4. Describe the data breach that occurred during the fourth quarter of 2013 and its effect on profits.
5. According to the Consolidated Statements of Operations, sales increased from \$71,960 million in 2012 to \$72,596 million in 2013. However, according to the U.S. Segment information, sales in the U.S. declined during that same time period. Identify the contributing factors for the declining 2013 U.S. sales and also explain how overall sales increased during 2013.
6. When discussing its liquidity, management indicated that cash provided by operations in 2013 was \$6,520 million. How did the company utilize these funds? The same section reports that Target sold its U.S. credit card portfolio. How did the company utilize these funds?

Report of Independent Registered Public Accounting Firm on Consolidated Financial Statements (Auditors)

7. What is the name of the company's independent auditors?
8. Who is responsible for the financial statements?
9. What is the outside auditors' responsibility?
10. What type of opinion did the independent auditors issue on the financial statements (unqualified, qualified, adverse, or disclaimer)? What does this opinion mean?
11. The auditors' report indicates the audit was concerned with material misstatements rather than absolute accuracy in the financial statements. What does "material" mean?

Income Statement—Vertical Analysis

12. Using Excel, compute common-size income statements for all three fiscal years. In common-size income statements, net sales is 100 percent and every other number is a percentage of sales. Attach the spreadsheet to the end of this project. (To help you get started, you can find Target's financial statements in Excel format in the *Connect* library. The financial statements have been slightly reformatted to conform to the multi-step income statement format utilized throughout the textbook.)
13. Using the common-size income statements, identify the significant trends.
14. What was the gross margin (gross profit) and the gross margin percentage for fiscal years 2013, 2012, and 2011?
15. If the gross margin percentage changed over the three-year period, what caused the change? (*Hint*: Changes in either the numerator or denominator reveal what caused the change in the gross margin percentage.)
16. What was the percentage return on sales for fiscal years 2013, 2012, and 2011? What do these ratios indicate about Target?

Income Statement—Horizontal Analysis

17. Using Excel, compute annual changes for each line item on the income statement. For each of the two most recent years, insert a column for changes in absolute dollars and insert another column for the percentage changes. Attach the spreadsheet to the end of this project. (You can find Target's financial statements in Excel format in the *Connect* library.)
18. What were the absolute dollar and the percentage changes in revenues between fiscal years 2013 and 2012 and between 2012 and 2011?
19. Describe the trend in revenues. Be specific (e.g., slight/steady/drastic increase or decrease each year, or fluctuating with an initial modest/significant increase or decrease followed by a modest/significant increase or decrease, etc.) to precisely describe the company's situation.
20. What were the absolute dollar and the percentage changes in cost of sales (cost of goods sold) between fiscal years 2013 and 2012 and between 2012 and 2011?
21. Describe the trend in cost of sales (cost of goods sold). Be specific (e.g., slight/steady/drastic increase or decrease each year, or fluctuating with an initial modest/significant increase or decrease followed by a modest/significant increase or decrease, etc.) to precisely describe the company's situation.
22. What were the absolute dollar and the percentage changes in selling, general, and administrative expenses (operating expenses) between fiscal years 2013 and 2012 and between 2012 and 2011?
23. Describe the trend in selling, general, and administrative expenses. Be specific (e.g., slight/steady/drastic increase or decrease each year, or fluctuating with an initial

modest/significant increase or decrease followed by a modest/significant increase or decrease, etc.) to precisely describe the company's situation.

24. What were the absolute dollar and the percentage changes in net income between fiscal years 2012 to 2013 and 2011 to 2012?
25. How would you describe the trend for net income? Be specific (e.g., slight/steady/drastic increase or decrease each year, or fluctuating with an initial modest/significant increase or decrease followed by a modest/significant increase or decrease, etc.) to precisely describe the company's situation. Do you expect the trend to continue?
26. Which items had the largest percentage change from 2011 through 2013, revenues or expenses (such as selling, general, and administrative expenses or cost of sales)?
27. Summarize what is causing the changes in net income from fiscal year 2011 to 2012 and 2012 to 2013 based on the percentages computed in Questions 18 through 26. Do you expect the trend to continue?

Balance Sheet—Vertical Analysis

28. Using Excel, compute common-size balance sheets for the years ended February 1, 2014, and February 2, 2013. In common-size balance sheets, total assets is 100 percent and every other number is a percentage of total assets. Attach the spreadsheet to the end of this project. (You can find Target's financial statements in Excel format in the *Connect* library.)
29. Current assets constituted what percentage of total assets at February 1, 2014, and February 2, 2013? Which current asset had the largest balance at each fiscal year-end?
30. Long-term assets constituted what percentage of total assets at February 1, 2014, and February 2, 2013? (Note: solutions for percentages calculated for items 29 and 30 should total 100 percent.) Which long-term asset had the largest balance at each fiscal year-end?
31. Current liabilities constituted what percentage of total assets at February 1, 2014, and February 2, 2013? Which current liability had the largest balance at each fiscal year-end?
32. Long-term liabilities constituted what percentage of total assets at February 1, 2014, and February 2, 2013? Which long-term liability had the largest balance at each fiscal year-end?
33. Calculate the ratio of total liabilities to total assets on February 1, 2014, and February 2, 2013.
34. Calculate the ratio of stockholders' equity to total assets on February 1, 2014, and February 2, 2013. (Recall percentages for items 33 and 34 should total 100 percent.) Identify whether Target finances its assets mostly with debt or equity.

Balance Sheet—Horizontal Analysis

35. Using Excel, compute annual changes for each line item on the balance sheet. Insert a column for changes in absolute dollars and insert another column for the percentage changes. Attach the spreadsheet to the end of this project. (You can find Target's financial statements in Excel format in the *Connect* library.)
36. What was the absolute dollar and the percentage change between the February 1, 2014, and February 2, 2013, credit card receivables balances? Was the change an increase or decrease? What line item (account) on the income statement is normally directly related to accounts receivable? What happened to Target's credit card receivables? How was this event reported on the 2013 income statement?
37. What was the absolute dollar and the percentage change between the February 1, 2014, and February 2, 2013, balances for inventory? Was the change an increase or

decrease? What line item (account) on the income statement is directly related to inventory? Did this account change in a similar direction as inventory?

38. Compared to the February 2, 2013, balances, did the amounts reported for the following long-term assets increase or decrease? By how much? Include dollar amounts for each item.

	Year Ended February 1, 2014	
	Dollar Amount	Increase or Decrease
Property, plant, and equipment, net		
Other noncurrent assets		
Total long-term assets		

What line item on the income statement is directly related to long-term assets? Did this account change in a similar direction as long-term assets?

39. What were the absolute dollar and the percentage change between the February 1, 2014, and February 2, 2013, amounts for total liabilities? Was the change an increase or decrease? What line item (account) on the income statement is directly related to the largest of these liabilities? Did this account change in a similar direction as total liabilities?

40. What was the amount of the change in the balance in retained earnings between February 1, 2014, and February 2, 2013? What caused this change?

Balance Sheet—Ratio Analysis

41. Compute the current ratio at February 1, 2014, and February 2, 2013. What does this ratio indicate about Target?

42. Calculate the accounts receivable turnover and the average number of days to collect accounts receivable for the years ended February 1, 2014, and February 2, 2013. In which year was the turnover and days to collect receivables more favorable?

43. Calculate the inventory turnover ratios and the average number of days to sell inventory for the years ended February 1, 2014, and February 2, 2013. In which year was the turnover and days to sell inventory more favorable?

Balance Sheet—Stockholders' Equity Section

44. Does the company's common stock have a par value? If so, how much was the par value per share?

45. How many shares of common stock were issued as of February 1, 2014, and February 2, 2013?

46. How many shares of treasury stock did the company have as of February 1, 2014, and February 2, 2013? How were the treasury stock purchases reflected on the statement of cash flows? Include the type of cash flow activity.

47. What percentage of stockholders' equity do the following items represent at each year-end (February 1, 2014, and February 2, 2013)?

	2014	2013
Total paid-in capital	%	%
Retained earnings		
Other items		
	100%	100%

Statement of Cash Flows

48. Does Target report cash flows from operating activities using the direct or the indirect method? Describe how you can tell.

49. What was the dollar amount of the increase or decrease in cash and cash equivalents for the fiscal years 2013, 2012, and 2011?

50. Does the ending balance of cash and cash equivalents agree with the amount reported on the balance sheet for years ended February 1, 2014, and February 2, 2013?

	2014	2013
Balance sheet	$	$
Statement of cash flows		

51. Target reported a $6,520 million cash flow provided by operations in 2013. Identify the four largest cash flows for that year. Does this agree with management's comments identified in Question 6?

52. On what statement(s) would you expect to find information regarding the declaration and payment of dividends? Did the company declare or pay dividends in 2013?

Notes to the Financial Statements

53. In your own words, briefly summarize two significant accounting policies.

54. How much is the estimated allowance for discounts and doubtful accounts for the years ending February 1, 2014, and February 2, 2013?

55. Normally accounts receivable are reported at net realizable value. However, Target reported its credit card receivables at the lower of cost or fair value. Why?

56. Complete the following schedule, contrasting the effect that the three inventory cost flow assumptions have on dollar amounts reported on the balance sheet and income statement. Identify the account in each financial statement that is affected by the sale of merchandise. Insert the most appropriate term (high, middle, or low) to indicate how the specified account would be affected by each of the given cost flow assumptions. Assume an inflationary environment.

	Cost Flow Assumptions		
Account Affected	**FIFO**	**AVG**	**LIFO**
1. Balance Sheet:			
2. Income Statement:			

57. What inventory cost flow method does Target use?

58. What are the estimated useful lives of the company's depreciable assets?

59. Complete the following schedule contrasting the effect the two types of depreciation methods have on dollar amounts reported on the balance sheet and income statement. Identify the account in each financial statement that is affected by depreciation expense. Designate with an X the method (accelerated or straight-line) that would result in a higher balance for the specified account during the early years of the asset's life.

	Depreciation Methods	
Account Affected	**Accelerated**	**Straight-Line**
1. Balance Sheet:		
2. Income Statement:		
	(X = Higher balance early in asset's life)	

60. What method of depreciation does Target use?

61. Did the balance in the goodwill account increase or decrease? Speculate as to what caused this change.

62. In addition to goodwill, what kinds of intangible assets does the company have? What are their estimated lives?

63. Identify three different accrued expenses.

64. Identify two kinds of commitments and contingencies.

65. What is the amount of available unsecured revolving credit? What was the balance outstanding at the end of each fiscal year?

66. What is the amount of total long-term borrowings at February 1, 2014? Are these obligations secured or unsecured? The amount reported in the notes does not agree with total long-term debt reported on the balance sheet. What are the two additional long-term items reported on the balance sheet?

Performance Measures

67. Compute the return on assets ratio (use net income rather than EBIT in the numerator) for the years ended February 1, 2014, and February 2, 2013.

68. Compute the return on equity ratio for the years ended February 1, 2014, and February 2, 2013.

69. For the year ended February 1, 2014, was the return on equity ratio greater than the return on assets ratio? Explain why.

70. What were Target's basic earnings per share (EPS) for the years ended February 1, 2014, and February 2, 2013? Identify what caused the ratio to change.

FINANCIAL STATEMENTS PROJECT (SELECTION OF COMPANY TO BE DECIDED BY INSTRUCTOR)

Date Due: ______________

Required

Based on the annual report of the company you are reviewing, answer the following questions. If you cannot answer a particular question, briefly explain why. If the question is not applicable to your company's financial statements, answer "N/A."

Show all necessary computations in good form. Label all numbers in your computations. If relevant, reference your answers to page(s) in the annual report.

"Current year" means the most recent fiscal year in the company's annual report. "Prior year" means the fiscal year immediately preceding the current year.

1. What products or services does the company sell? Be specific.

2. What do you think the outlook is for these products or services? Why do you think so?

3. By what percentage have sales increased or decreased in each of the last two fiscal years?

4. If the company reported sales by segments, which segment had the largest percentage of total sales? Which segment had the smallest percentage of total sales? **Show computations of the relevant percentages.**
   Largest segment ______________ Percentage of total sales ______________
   Smallest segment ______________ Percentage of total sales ______________
5. What is net income for the current year? ______________
6. Did the current year's net income increase or decrease since the prior year? By how much? What caused the change?
7. If the company reported earnings by segments, which segment had the largest percentage of total earnings? Which segment had the smallest percentage of total earnings? **Show computations of the relevant percentages.**
   Largest segment ______________ Percentage of total earnings ______________
   Smallest segment ______________ Percentage of total earnings ______________
8. Did the company report any special, unusual, or otherwise nonroutine items in either current or prior year net income? If so, explain the item(s).
9. For the current year, how does net income compare to net cash provided (used) by operating activities?
10. For the current year, what one or two items were most responsible for the difference between net income and net cash provided (used) by operating activities?
11. Did the company pay cash dividends during the current year? If so, how much were they?
12. If the company paid cash dividends, what percentage of net income were the cash dividends? If the company did not pay cash dividends, why do you think it did not?
13. Which of the following is the company's largest asset category: accounts receivable, inventory, or land? What is the amount of that asset category?
14. If the company reported assets by segments, which segment had the largest percentage of total assets? Which segment had the smallest percentage of total assets? **Show computations of the relevant percentages.**
   Largest segment ______________ Percentage of total assets ______________
   Smallest segment ______________ Percentage of total assets ______________
15. How much **cash** did the company invest in property, plant, and equipment during the current year?
16. Which inventory method(s) did the company use?
17. Which depreciation method(s) did the company use?
18. If the company has any intangible assets, what kind are they?
19. Did the company report any contingent liabilities ("contingencies")? If so, briefly explain.
20. Does the company have any preferred stock authorized? If so, how many shares were authorized?
21. Does the company's common stock have a par value? If so, what was it?
22. In what price range was the company's common stock trading during the last quarter of the current year?
23. What was the market price of the company's common stock on DD/MM/Year?
24. Where (on what stock exchange) is the company's stock traded?
25. Who was the company's independent auditor?
26. Develop one question about the company's financial report that you do not know how to answer.
27. Compute the following ratios for the current year and the prior year. Show the appropriate formulas in the first column. Show all supporting computations in the second and third columns.

Ratio	Current Year	Prior Year
Gross Profit Formula:		
Inventory Turnover Formula:		
Current Ratio Formula:		
Debt to Equity Formula:		
Return on Assets Formula:		
Return on Equity Formula:		

APPENDIX E

ACCOUNTING FOR INVESTMENT SECURITIES

TYPES OF INVESTMENT SECURITIES

A financial investment occurs when one entity provides assets or services to another entity in exchange for a certificate known as a *security*. The entity that provides the assets and receives the security certificate is called the **investor.** The entity that receives the assets or services and gives the security certificate is called the **investee.** This appendix discusses accounting practices that apply to securities held by investors.

There are two primary types of investment securities: debt securities and equity securities. An investor receives a **debt security** when assets *are loaned* to the investee. In general, a debt security describes the investee's obligation to return the assets and to pay interest for the use of the assets. Common types of debt securities include bonds, notes, certificates of deposit, and commercial paper.

An **equity security** is obtained when an investor acquires an *ownership interest* in the investee. An equity security usually describes the rights of ownership, including the right to influence the operations of the investee and to share in profits or losses that accrue from those operations. The most common types of equity securities are common stock and preferred stock. In summary, **investment securities** are certificates that describe the rights and privileges that investors receive when they loan or give assets or services to investees.

Transactions between the investor and the investee constitute the **primary securities market.** There is a **secondary securities market** in which investors exchange (buy and sell) investment securities with other investors. Securities that regularly trade in established secondary markets are called **marketable securities.** Investee companies are affected by secondary-market transactions only to the extent that their obligations are transferred to a different party. For example, assume that Tom Williams (investor) loans assets to American Can Company (investee). Williams receives a bond (investment security) from American Can that describes American Can's obligation to return assets and pay interest to Williams. This exchange represents a primary securities market transaction. Now assume that in a secondary-market transaction Williams sells his investment security (bond) to Tina Tucker. American Can Company is affected by this transaction only to the extent that the company's obligation transfers from Williams to Tucker. In other words, American Can's obligation to repay principal and interest does not change. The only thing that changes is the party to whom American Can makes payments. *An investee's financial statements are not affected when the securities it has issued to an investor are traded in the secondary market.*

The **fair value,** also called **market value,** is the amount that the investor would receive if the securities were sold in an orderly transaction. More specifically, the fair value is based on the amount that would be collected (an exit value) from the sale of an asset as opposed to the cost necessary to acquire a comparable asset. For a more detailed definition of fair value, see *FASB Accounting Standards Codification Topic 820,* "Fair Value Measurements and Disclosures." Whether securities are reported at fair value or historical cost depends on whether the investor intends to sell or hold the securities. Generally accepted accounting principles require companies to classify their investment securities into one of three categories: (1) held-to-maturity securities, (2) trading securities, and (3) available-for-sale securities.

Held-to-Maturity Securities

Since equity securities representing ownership interests have no maturity date, the held-to-maturity classification applies only to debt securities. Debt securities should be classified as held-to-maturity securities if the investor has a *positive intent* and the *ability* to hold the securities until the maturity date. **Held-to-maturity securities** are reported on the balance sheet at *amortized historical cost.*[1]

Trading Securities

Both debt and equity securities can be classified as *trading securities.* **Trading securities** are bought and sold for the purpose of generating profits on the short-term appreciation of stock or bond prices. They are usually traded frequently and within short time spans from the time when they are acquired. Trading securities are reported on the investor's balance sheet at their fair value on the investor's fiscal closing date.

Available-for-Sale Securities

All marketable securities that are not classified as held-to-maturity or trading securities must be classified as **available-for-sale securities.** These securities are also reported on the investor's balance sheet at fair value as of the investor's fiscal closing date.

Two of the three classifications, therefore, must be reported at fair value, which is a clear exception to the historical cost concept. Other exceptions to the use of historical cost measures for asset valuation are discussed in later sections of this appendix.

REPORTING EVENTS THAT AFFECT INVESTMENT SECURITIES

The effects on the investor's financial statements of four distinct accounting events involving marketable investment securities are illustrated in the following section. The illustration assumes that the investor, Arapaho Company, started the accounting period with cash of $10,000 and common stock of $10,000.

EVENT 1 Arapaho paid $9,000 cash to purchase marketable investment securities.

This event is an asset exchange. One asset (cash) decreases, and another asset (investment securities) increases. The income statement is not affected. The $9,000 cash outflow is reported as either an operating activity or an investing activity, depending on how the securities are classified. Since *trading securities* are short-term assets that are regularly traded for the purpose of producing income, cash flows from the purchase or sale of trading securities are reported in the operating activities section of the statement of cash flows. In contrast, cash flows involving the purchase or sale of securities classified as *held to maturity* or *available for sale* are reported in the investing activities section of the statement of cash flows. The only difference among the three alternatives

[1]Debt securities are frequently purchased for amounts that are more or less than their face value (the amount of principal due at the maturity date). If the purchase price is above the face value, the difference between the face value and the purchase price is called a *premium.* If the purchase price is below the face value, the difference is called a *discount.* Premiums and discounts increase or decrease the amount of interest revenue earned and affect the carrying value of the bond investment reported on the balance sheet. The presentation in this appendix makes the simplifying assumption that the bonds are purchased at a price equal to their face value. Accounting for discounts and premiums is discussed in Chapter 10.

lies in the classification of the cash outflow reported on the statement of cash flows, as shown in the following statements model:

Event No.	Type	Assets			=	Liab.	+	Equity	Rev.	−	Exp.	=	Net Inc.	Cash Flow
		Cash	+	Inv. Sec.										
1	Held	(9,000)	+	9,000	=	NA	+	NA	NA	−	NA	=	NA	(9,000) IA
1	Trading	(9,000)	+	9,000	=	NA	+	NA	NA	−	NA	=	NA	(9,000) OA
1	Available	(9,000)	+	9,000	=	NA	+	NA	NA	−	NA	=	NA	(9,000) IA

EVENT 2 **Arapaho earned $1,600 of cash investment revenue.**

Investment revenue is reported the same way regardless of whether the investment securities are classified as held to maturity, trading, or available for sale. Investment revenue comes in two forms. Earnings from equity investments are called **dividends.** Revenue from debt securities is called **interest.** Both forms have the same impact on the financial statements. Recognizing the investment revenue increases both assets and stockholders' equity. Revenue and net income increase. The cash inflow from investment revenue is reported in the operating activities section of the statement of cash flows regardless of how the investment securities are classified.

Event No.	Assets	=	Liab.	+	Equity	Rev.	−	Exp.	=	Net Inc.	Cash Flow
	Cash	=			Ret. Earn.						
2	1,600	=	NA	+	1,600	1,600	−	NA	=	1,600	1,600 OA

EVENT 3 **Arapaho sold securities that cost $2,000 for $2,600 cash.**

This event results in recognizing a $600 realized (actual) gain that increases both total assets and stockholders' equity. The asset cash increases by $2,600 and the asset investment securities decreases by $2,000, resulting in a $600 increase in total assets. The $600 realized gain is reported on the income statement, increasing net income and retained earnings. The $600 gain does not appear on the statement of cash flows. Instead, the entire $2,600 cash inflow is reported in one section of the statement of cash flows. Cash inflows from the sale of held-to-maturity and available-for-sale securities are reported as investing activities. Cash flows involving trading securities are reported as operating activities. These effects are shown below:

Event No.	Type	Assets			=	Liab.	+	Equity	Rev. or Gain	−	Exp. or Loss	=	Net Inc.	Cash Flow
		Cash	+	Inv. Sec.										
3	Held	2,600	+	(2,000)	=	NA	+	600	600	−	NA	=	600	2,600 IA
3	Trading	2,600	+	(2,000)	=	NA	+	600	600	−	NA	=	600	2,600 OA
3	Available	2,600	+	(2,000)	=	NA	+	600	600	−	NA	=	600	2,600 IA

EVENT 4 **Arapaho recognized a $700 unrealized gain.**

After Event 3, the historical cost of Arapaho's portfolio of remaining investment securities is $7,000 ($9,000 purchased less $2,000 sold). Assume that at Arapaho's fiscal closing date, these securities have a fair value of $7,700, giving Arapaho a $700 unrealized gain on its investment. This type of gain (sometimes called a *paper profit*) is classified as *unrealized* because the securities have not been sold. The treatment of **unrealized gains or losses** in the financial statements depends on whether the securities are classified as held to maturity, trading, or available for sale. Unrealized gains or losses on securities classified as *held to maturity* are not recognized in the financial statements; they have no effect on the balance sheet, income statement, and statement of cash flows. Even so, many companies choose to disclose the market value of the securities as part of the narrative description or in the notes that accompany the financial statements. Whether or not the market value is disclosed, held-to-maturity securities are reported on the balance sheet at amortized cost.

Investments classified as trading securities are reported in the financial statements at fair value. Unrealized gains or losses on *trading securities* are recognized in net income even though the securities have not been sold. In Arapaho's case, the $700 gain increases the carrying value of the investment securities. The gain increases net income, which in turn increases retained earnings. Unrealized gains and losses have no effect on cash flows.

Investments classified as available-for-sale securities are also reported in the financial statements at fair value. However, an important distinction exists with respect to how the unrealized gains and losses affect the financial statements. Even though unrealized gains or losses on available-for-sale securities are included in the assets on the balance sheet, they *are not* recognized in determining net income.[2] On Arapaho's balance sheet, the $700 gain increases the carrying value of the investment securities. A corresponding increase is reported in a separate equity account called Unrealized Gain or Loss on Available-for-Sale Securities. The statement of cash flows is not affected by recognizing unrealized gains and losses on available-for-sale securities.

The effects of these alternative treatments of unrealized gains and losses on Arapaho's financial statements are shown here:

Event No.	Type	Assets	=	Liab.	+	Equity			Rev. or Gain	−	Exp. or Loss	=	Net Inc.	Cash Flow
		Inv. Sec.	=			Ret. Earn.	+	Unreal. Gain						
4	Held	NA	=	NA	+	NA	+	NA	NA	−	NA	=	NA	NA
4	Trading	700	=	NA	+	700	+	NA	700	−	NA	=	700	NA
4	Available	700	=	NA	+	NA	+	700	NA	−	NA	=	NA	NA

FINANCIAL STATEMENTS

As the preceding discussion implies, the financial statements of Arapaho Company are affected by not only the business events relating to its security transactions but also the accounting treatment used to report those events. In other words, the same economic events are reflected differently in the financial statements depending on whether the securities are classified as held to maturity, trading, or available for sale. Exhibit E.1 displays the financial statements for Arapaho under each investment classification alternative.

The net income reported under the trading securities alternative is $700 higher than that reported under the held-to-maturity and available-for-sale alternatives

[2]GAAP permits companies to report unrealized gains and losses on available-for-sale securities as additions to or subtractions from net income with the result being titled *comprehensive income.* Alternatively, the unrealized gains and losses can be reported on a separate statement of net income and other comprehensive income.

EXHIBIT E.1

ARAPAHO COMPANY
Comparative Financial Statements

Income Statements

Investment Securities Classified as	Held	Trading	Available
Investment revenue	$1,600	$1,600	$1,600
Realized gain	600	600	600
Unrealized gain		700	
Net income	$2,200	$2,900	$2,200

Balance Sheets

	Held	Trading	Available
Assets			
Cash	$ 5,200	$ 5,200	$ 5,200
Investment securities, at cost (market value $7,700)	7,000		
Investment securities, at market (cost $7,000)		7,700	7,700
Total assets	$12,200	$12,900	$12,900
Stockholders' equity			
Common stock	$10,000	$10,000	$10,000
Retained earnings	2,200	2,900	2,200
Unrealized gain on investment securities			700
Total stockholders' equity	$12,200	$12,900	$12,900

Statements of Cash Flows

	Held	Trading	Available
Operating Activities			
Cash inflow from investment revenue	$ 1,600	$ 1,600	$ 1,600
Outflow to purchase securities		(9,000)	
Inflow from sale of securities		2,600	
Investing Activities			
Outflow to purchase securities	(9,000)		(9,000)
Inflow from sale of securities	2,600		2,600
Financing Activities*	0	0	0
Net decrease in cash	(4,800)	(4,800)	(4,800)
Beginning cash balance	10,000	10,000	10,000
Ending cash balance	$ 5,200	$ 5,200	$ 5,200

*The $10,000 of common stock is assumed to have been issued prior to the start of the accounting period.

because unrealized gains and losses on trading securities are recognized on the income statement. Similarly, total assets and total stockholders' equity are $700 higher under the trading and available-for-sale alternatives than they are under the held-to-maturity category because the $700 unrealized gain is recognized on the balance sheet for those two classifications. The gain is not reported on the income statement for available-for-sale securities; it is reported on the balance sheet in a special equity account called Unrealized Gain on Investment Securities. The statements of cash flows report purchases and sales of trading securities as operating activities while purchases and sales of available-for-sale and held-to-maturity securities are investing activities. Exhibit E.2 summarizes the reporting differences among the three classifications of investment securities.

EXHIBIT E.2

Investment Category	Types of Securities	Types of Revenue Recognized	Reported on Balance Sheet at	Recognition of Unrealized Gains and Losses on the Income Statement	Cash Flow from Purchase or Sale of Securities Classified as
Held to maturity	Debt	Interest	Amortized cost	No	Investing activity
Trading	Debt and equity	Interest and dividends	Market value	Yes	Operating activity
Available for sale	Debt and equity	Interest and dividends	Market value	No	Investing activity

Alternative Reporting Practices for Equity Securities

If an investor owns 20 percent or more of an investee's equity securities, the investor is presumed able, unless there is evidence to the contrary, to exercise *significant influence* over the investee company. Investors owning more than 50 percent of the stock of an investee company are assumed to have control over the investee. The previous discussion of accounting rules for equity securities assumed the investor did not significantly influence or control the investee. Alternative accounting rules apply to securities owned by investors who exercise significant influence or control over an investee company. Accounting for equity investment securities differs depending on the level of the investor's ability to influence or control the operating, investing, and financing activities of the investee.

As previously demonstrated, investors who do not have significant influence (they own less than 20 percent of the stock of the investee) account for their investments in equity securities at fair value. Investors exercising significant influence (they own 20 to 50 percent of the investee's stock) must account for their investments using the **equity method.** A detailed discussion of the equity method is beyond the scope of this text. However, *be aware that investments reported using the equity method represent a measure of the book value of the investee rather than the cost or fair value of the equity securities owned.*

Investors that have a controlling interest (they own more than 50 percent of the investee's stock) in an investee company are required to issue **consolidated financial statements.** The company that holds the controlling interest is referred to as the **parent company,** and the company that is controlled is called the **subsidiary company.** Usually, the parent and subsidiary companies maintain separate accounting records. However, a parent company is also required to report to the public its accounting data along with that of its subsidiaries in a single set of combined financial statements. These consolidated statements represent a separate accounting entity consisting of the parent and its subsidiaries. A parent company that owns one subsidiary will produce three sets of financial statements: statements for the parent company, statements for the subsidiary company, and statements for the consolidated entity.

KEY TERMS

Available-for-sale securities 777
Consolidated financial statements 781
Debt security 776
Dividends 778
Equity method 781
Equity security 776
Fair value 776
Held-to-maturity securities 777
Interest 778
Investee 776
Investment securities 776
Investor 776
Market value 776
Marketable securities 776
Parent company 781
Primary securities market 776
Secondary securities market 776
Subsidiary company 781
Trading securities 777
Unrealized gains or losses 779

EXERCISES

All applicable Exercises are available with McGraw-Hill's Connect Plus Accounting.

Exercise E1 *Identifying asset values for financial statements*

Required

Indicate whether each of the following assets should be valued at fair market value (FMV), lower of cost or market (LCM), or historical cost (HC) on the balance sheet. For certain assets, historical cost may be called amortized cost (AC).

Asset	FMV	LCM	HC/AC
Buildings			
Available-for-sale securities			
Office equipment			
Inventory			
Supplies			
Land			
Trading securities			
Cash			
Held-to-maturity securities			

Exercise E2 *Accounting for investment securities*

Norris Co. purchased $36,000 of marketable securities on March 1, 2016. On the company's fiscal year closing date, December 31, 2016, the securities had a market value of $27,000. During 2016, Norris Co. recognized $10,000 of revenue and $2,000 of expenses.

Required

a. Record a +, −, or NA in a horizontal statements model to show how the purchase of the securities affects the financial statements, assuming that the securities are classified as (1) held to maturity, (2) trading, or (3) available for sale. In the Cash Flow column, indicate whether the event is an operating activity (OA), investing activity (IA), or financing activity (FA). Record only the effects of the purchase event.

Event No.	Type	Cash	+	Inv. Sec.	=	Liab.	+	Equity	Rev.	−	Exp.	=	Net Inc.	Cash Flow
1	Held													
2	Trading													
3	Available													

b. Determine the amount of net income that would be reported on the 2016 income statement, assuming that the marketable securities are classified as (1) held to maturity, (2) trading, or (3) available for sale.

Exercise E3 *Effect of investment securities transactions on financial statements*

The following information pertains to Botter Supply Co. for 2016:

1. Purchased $100,000 of marketable investment securities.
2. Earned $10,000 of cash investment revenue.
3. Sold for $30,000 securities that cost $25,000.
4. The fair value of the remaining securities at December 31, 2016, was $89,000.

Required

a. Record the four events in a statements model like the following one. Use a separate model for each classification: (1) held to maturity, (2) trading, and (3) available for sale. The first event for the first classification is shown as an example.

Held to Maturity

Event No.	Cash	+	Inv. Sec.	=	Liab.	+	Ret. Earn.	+	Unreal. Gain.	Rev. or Gains	−	Exp. or Loss	=	Net Inc.	Cash Flow
1	(100,000)	+	100,000	=	NA	+	NA	+	NA	NA	−	NA	=	NA	(100,000) IA

b. What is the amount of net income under each of the three classifications?

c. What is the change in cash from operating activities under each of the three classifications?

d. Are the answers to Requirements *b* and *c* different for each of the classifications? Why or why not?

Exercise E4 *Preparing financial statements for investment securities*

Molten, Inc., began 2016 with $100,000 in both cash and common stock. The company engaged in the following investment transactions during 2016:

1. Purchased $20,000 of marketable investment securities.
2. Earned $600 cash from investment revenue.
3. Sold investment securities for $14,000 that cost $10,000.
4. Purchased $7,000 of additional marketable investment securities.
5. Determined that the investment securities had a fair value of $22,000 at the end of 2016.

Required

Use a vertical statements model to prepare income statements, balance sheets, and statements of cash flow for Molten, Inc., assuming the securities were (*a*) held to maturity, (*b*) trading, and (*c*) available for sale.

Exercise E5 *Differences among marketable investment securities classifications*

Complete the following table for the three categories of marketable investment securities:

Investment Category	Types of Securities	Types of Revenue Recognized	Value Reported on Balance Sheet	Recognition of Unrealized Gains and Losses on the Income Statement	Cash Flow from Purchase or Sale of Securities Is Classified as
Held to maturity	Debt	Interest	Amortized cost	No	Investing activity
Trading					
Available for sale					

Exercise E6 *Effect of marketable investment securities transactions on financial statements*

The following transactions pertain to Harrison Imports for 2016:

1. Started business by acquiring $30,000 cash from the issue of common stock.
2. Provided $90,000 of services for cash.
3. Invested $35,000 in marketable investment securities.
4. Paid $18,000 of operating expense.
5. Received $500 of investment income from the securities.

6. Invested an additional $16,000 in marketable investment securities.
7. Paid a $2,000 cash dividend to the stockholders.
8. Sold investment securities that cost $8,000 for $14,000.
9. Received another $1,000 in investment income.
10. Determined the market value of the investment securities at the end of the year was $42,000.

Required

Use a vertical statements model to prepare a 2016 income statement, balance sheet, and statement of cash flows, assuming that the marketable investment securities were classified as (a) held to maturity, (b) trading, and (c) available for sale. (*Hint:* Record the events in T-accounts prior to preparing the financial statements.)

Exercise E7 *Comprehensive horizontal statements model*

Woody's Catering experienced the following independent events:

1. Acquired cash from issuing common stock.
2. Purchased inventory on account.
3. Paid cash to purchase marketable securities classified as trading securities.
4. Recorded unrealized loss on marketable securities that were classified as available-for-sale securities.
5. Recorded unrealized loss on marketable securities that were classified as trading securities.
6. Recorded unrealized loss on marketable securities that were classified as held-to-maturity securities.
7. Wrote down inventory to comply with lower-of-cost-or-market rule. (Assume that the company uses the perpetual inventory system.)
8. Recognized cost of goods sold under the weighted-average method.
9. Recognized cost of goods sold under FIFO.

Required

a. Show the effect of each event on the elements of the financial statements using a horizontal statements model like the following one. Use + for increase, − for decrease, and NA for not affected. In the Cash Flow column, indicate whether the item is an operating activity (OA), investing activity (IA), or financing activity (FA). The first transaction is entered as an example.

Event No.	Assets	=	Liab.	+	Equity	Rev. or Gain	−	Exp. or Loss	=	Net Inc.	Cash Flow
1	+		NA		+	NA		NA		NA	+ FA

b. Explain why there is or is not a difference in the way Events 8 and 9 affect the financial statements model.

APPENDIX F

TIME VALUE OF MONEY

FUTURE VALUE

Suppose you recently won $10,000 cash in a local lottery. You save the money to have funds available to obtain a masters of business administration (MBA) degree. You plan to enter the program three years from today. Assuming you invest the money in an account that earns 8 percent annual interest, how much money will you have available in three years? The answer depends on whether your investment will earn *simple* or *compound* interest.

To determine the amount of funds available assuming you earn 8 percent **simple interest,** multiply the principal balance by the interest rate to determine the amount of interest earned per year ($10,000 × 0.08 = $800). Next, multiply the amount of annual interest by the number of years the funds will be invested ($800 × 3 = $2,400). Finally, add the interest earned to the principal balance to determine the total amount of funds available at the end of the three-year term ($10,000 principal + $2,400 interest = $12,400 cash available at the end of three years).

Investors can increase their returns by reinvesting the income earned from their investments. For example, at the beginning of the second year, you will have available for investment not only the original $10,000 principal balance but also $800 of interest earned during the first year. In other words, you will be able to earn interest on the interest that you previously earned. Earning interest on interest is called **compounding.** Assuming you earn 8 percent compound interest, the amount of funds available to you at the end of three years can be computed as shown in Exhibit F.1.

EXHIBIT F.1

Year	Amount Invested	×	Interest Rate	=	Interest Earned	+	Amount Invested	=	New Balance
1	$10,000.00	×	0.08	=	$ 800.00	+	$10,000.00	=	$10,800.00
2	10,800.00	×	0.08	=	864.00	+	10,800.00	=	11,664.00
3	11,664.00	×	0.08	=	933.12	+	11,664.00	=	12,597.12
Total interest earned				=	$2,597.12				

Obviously, you earn more with compound interest ($2,597.12 compound versus $2,400 simple). The computations required for **compound interest** can become cumbersome when the investment term is long. Fortunately, there are mathematical formulas, interest tables, and computer programs that reduce the computational burden. For example, a compound interest factor can be developed from the formula

$$(1 + i)^n$$

where i = interest

n = number of periods

The value of the investment is determined by multiplying the compound interest factor by the principal balance. The compound interest factor for a three-year term and an 8 percent interest rate is 1.259712 (1.08 × 1.08 × 1.08 = 1.259712). Assuming a $10,000 original investment, the value of the investment at the end of three years is

\$12,597.12 (\$10,000 × 1.259712). This is, of course, the same amount that was computed in the previous illustration (see the final figure in the New Balance column of Exhibit F.1).

The mathematical formulas have been used to develop tables of interest factors that can be used to determine the **future value** of an investment for a variety of interest rates and time periods. For example, Table I on page 790 contains the interest factor for an investment with a three-year term earning 8 percent compound interest. To confirm this point, move down the column marked n to the third period. Next move across to the column marked 8 percent, where you will find the value 1.259712. This is identical to the amount computed using the mathematical formula in the preceding paragraph. Here also, the value of the investment at the end of three years can be determined by multiplying the principal balance by the compound interest factor (\$10,000 × 1.259712 = \$12,597.12). These same factors and amounts can be determined using computer programs in calculators and spreadsheet software.

Clearly, a variety of ways can be used to determine the future value of an investment, given a principal balance, interest rate, and term to maturity. In our case, we showed that your original investment of \$10,000 would be worth \$12,597 in three years, assuming an 8 percent compound interest rate. Suppose you determine this amount is insufficient to get you through the MBA program you want to complete. Assume you believe you will need \$18,000 three years from today to sustain yourself while you finish the degree. Suppose your parents agree to cover the shortfall. They ask how much money you need today in order to have \$18,000 three years from now.

PRESENT VALUE

The mathematical formula required to convert the future value of a dollar to its **present value** equivalent is

$$\frac{1}{(1+i)^n}$$

where i = interest

n = number of periods

For easy conversion, the formula has been used to develop Table II, Present Value of \$1, on page 790. At an 8 percent annual compound interest rate, the present value equivalent of \$18,000 to be received three years from today is computed as follows: Move down the far left column to where $n = 3$. Next, move right to the column marked 8 percent. At this point, you should see the interest factor 0.793832. Multiplying this factor by the desired future value of \$18,000 yields the present value of \$14,288.98 (\$18,000 × 0.793832). This means if you invest \$14,288.98 (present value) today at an annual compound interest rate of 8 percent, you will have the \$18,000 (future value) you need to enter the MBA program three years from now.

If you currently have \$10,000, you will need an additional \$4,288.98 from your parents to make the required \$14,288.98 investment that will yield the future value of \$18,000 you need. Having \$14,288.98 today is the same as having \$18,000 three years from today, assuming you can earn 8 percent compound interest. To validate this conclusion, use Table I to determine the future value of \$14,288.98, given a three-year term and 8 percent annual compound interest. As previously indicated, the future-value conversion factor under these conditions is 1.259712. Multiplying this factor by the \$14,288.98 present value produces the expected future value of \$18,000 (\$14,288.98 × 1.259712 = \$18,000). The factors in Table I can be used to convert present values to future values, and the corresponding factors in Table II are used to convert future values to present values.

FUTURE VALUE ANNUITIES

The previous examples described present and future values of a single lump-sum payment. Many financial transactions involve a series of payments. To illustrate, we return to the example in which you want to have \$18,000 available three years from today. We continue the assumption that you can earn 8 percent compound interest. However, now we assume that you do not have $14,288.98 to invest today. Instead, you decide to save part of the money during each of the next three years. How much money must you save each year to have $18,000 at the end of three years? *The series of equal payments made over a number of periods in order to acquire a future value is called an* **annuity.** The factors in Table III, Future Value of an Annuity of $1, on page 791 can be used to determine the amount of the annuity needed to produce the desired $18,000 future value. The table is constructed so that future values can be determined by multiplying the conversion factor by the amount of the annuity. These relationships can be expressed algebraically as follows:

Amount of annuity payment × Table conversion factor = Future value

To determine the amount of the required annuity payment in our example, first locate the future value conversion factor. In Table III, move down the first column on the left-hand side until you locate period 3. Next move to the right until you locate the 8 percent column. At this location you will see a conversion factor of 3.2464. This factor can be used to determine the amount of the annuity payment as indicated here:

Amount of annuity payment × Table conversion factor = Future value

Amount of annuity payment = Future value ÷ Table conversion factor

Amount of annuity payment = $18,000.00 ÷ 3.2464

Amount of annuity payment = $5,544.60

If you deposit $5,544.60 in an investment account at the end of each of the next three years,[1] the investment account balance will be $18,000, assuming your investment earns 8 percent interest compounded annually. This conclusion is confirmed by the following schedule:

End of Year	Beg. Acct. Bal.	+	Interest Computation	+	Payment	=	End. Acct. Bal.
1	NA	+	NA	+	$5,544.60	=	$ 5,544.60
2	$ 5,544.60	+	$ 5,544.60 × 0.08 = $443.57	+	5,544.60	=	11,532.77
3	11,532.77	+	11,532.77 × 0.08 = 922.62	+	5,544.60	=	18,000.00*

*Total does not add exactly due to rounding.

PRESENT VALUE ANNUITIES

We previously demonstrated that a future value of $18,000 is equivalent to a present value of $14,288.98, given annual compound interest of 8 percent for a three-year period. If the future value of a $5,544.60 annuity for three years is equivalent to $18,000, that same annuity should have a present value of $14,288.98. We can test this conclusion by using the conversion factors in Table IV, Present Value of an Annuity of $1, on page 791. The present value annuity table is constructed so that present values can be determined by multiplying the conversion factor by the amount of the annuity. These relationships can be expressed algebraically as follows:

Amount of annuity payment × Table conversion factor = Present value

To determine the present value of the annuity payment in our example, first locate the present value conversion factor. In Table IV, move down the first column on the left-hand side until you locate period 3. Next move to the right until you locate the column

[1]A payment made at the end of a period is known as an *ordinary annuity.* A payment made at the beginning of a period is called an *annuity due.* Tables are generally set up to assume ordinary annuities. Minor adjustments must be made when dealing with an annuity due. For the purposes of this text, we consider all annuities to be ordinary.

for the 8 percent interest rate. At this location you will see a conversion factor of 2.577097. This factor can be used to determine the amount of the present value of the annuity payment, as indicated:

Amount of annuity payment	×	Table conversion factor	=	Present value
\$5,544.60	×	2.577097	=	\$14,288.97*

*The 1 cent difference between this value and the expected value of \$14,288.98 is due to rounding.

In summary, Tables III and IV can be used to convert annuities to future or present values for a variety of different assumptions regarding interest rates and time periods.

BUSINESS APPLICATIONS

Long-Term Notes Payable

In Chapter 10, we considered a case in which Blair Company borrowed \$100,000 from National Bank. We indicated that Blair agreed to repay the bank through a series of annual payments (an *annuity*) of \$25,709 each. How was this amount determined? Recall that Blair agreed to pay the bank 9 percent interest over a five-year term. Under these circumstances, we are trying to find the annuity equivalent to the \$100,000 present value that the bank is loaning Blair. The first step in determining the annuity (annual payment) is to locate the appropriate present value conversion factor from Table IV. At the fifth row under the 9 percent column, you will find the value 3.889651. This factor can be used to determine the amount of the annuity payment as indicated here:

Amount of annuity payment × Table conversion factor = Present value

Amount of annuity payment = Present value ÷ Table conversion factor

Amount of annuity payment = \$100,000 ÷ 3.889651

Amount of annuity payment = \$25,709

There are many applications in which debt repayment occurs through annuities. Common examples with which you are probably familiar include auto loans and home mortgages. Payment schedules for such loans may be determined from the interest tables, as demonstrated here. However, most real-world businesses have further refined the computational process through the use of sophisticated computer programs. The software program prompts the user to provide the relevant information regarding the present value of the amount borrowed, number of payments, and interest rate. Given this information and a few keystrokes, the computer program produces the amount of the amortization payment along with an amortization schedule showing the amounts of principal and interest payments over the life of the loan. Similar results can be obtained with a spreadsheet software application such as Excel. Even many handheld calculators have present and future value functions that enable users to quickly compute annuity payments for an infinite number of interest rate and time period assumptions.

Bond Liabilities: Determine Price

In Chapter 10, we discussed the use of discounts and premiums as a means of producing an effective rate of interest that is higher or lower than the stated rate of interest. For example, if the stated rate of interest is lower than the market rate of interest at the time the bonds are issued, the issuer can increase the effective interest rate by selling the bonds for a price lower than their face value. At maturity, the issuer will settle the obligation by paying the face value of the bond. The difference between the discounted bond price and the face value of the bond is additional interest. To illustrate, assume that Tower Company issues \$100,000 face value bonds with a 20-year term and a 9 percent stated rate of annual interest. At the time the bonds are issued, the market rate of interest for bonds of comparable risk is 10 percent annual interest. For what amount would Tower Company be required to sell the bonds in order to move its 9 percent stated rate of interest to an effective rate of 10 percent?

Information from present value Tables II and IV is required to determine the amount of the discount required to produce a 10 percent effective rate of interest. First, we identify the future cash flows that will be generated by the bonds. Based on the stated interest rate, the bonds will pay \$9,000 (\$100,000 face value × 0.09 interest) interest per year. This constitutes a 20-year annuity that should be discounted back to its present value equivalent. Also, at the end of 20 years, the bonds will require a single \$100,000 lump-sum payment to settle the principal obligation. This amount must also be discounted back to its present value in order to determine the bond price. The computations required to determine the discounted bond price are shown here:

Present value of principal	\$100,000 × 0.148644 (Table II, n = 20, i = 10%)	=	\$14,864.40
Present value of interest	\$9,000 × 8.513564 (Table IV, n = 20, i = 10%)	=	76,622.08
Bond price (proceeds received)			\$91,486.48

Tower Company bonds sell at an \$8,513.52 discount (\$100,000 − \$91,486.48) to produce a 10 percent effective interest rate. Note that in these computations, the stated rate of interest was used to determine the amount of cash flow, and the effective rate of interest was used to determine the table conversion factors.

TABLE I Future Value of $1

n	4%	5%	6%	7%	8%	9%	10%	12%	14%	16%	20%
1	1.040000	1.050000	1.060000	1.070000	1.080000	1.090000	1.100000	1.120000	1.140000	1.160000	1.200000
2	1.081600	1.102500	1.123600	1.144900	1.166400	1.188100	1.210000	1.254400	1.299600	1.345600	1.440000
3	1.124864	1.157625	1.191016	1.225043	1.259712	1.295029	1.331000	1.404928	1.481544	1.560896	1.728000
4	1.169859	1.215506	1.262477	1.310796	1.360489	1.411582	1.464100	1.573519	1.688960	1.810639	2.073600
5	1.216653	1.276282	1.338226	1.402552	1.469328	1.538624	1.610510	1.762342	1.925415	2.100342	2.488320
6	1.265319	1.340096	1.418519	1.500730	1.586874	1.677100	1.771561	1.973823	2.194973	2.436396	2.985984
7	1.315932	1.407100	1.503630	1.605781	1.713824	1.828039	1.948717	2.210681	2.502269	2.826220	3.583181
8	1.368569	1.477455	1.593848	1.718186	1.850930	1.992563	2.143589	2.475963	2.852586	3.278415	4.299817
9	1.423312	1.551328	1.689479	1.838459	1.999005	2.171893	2.357948	2.773079	3.251949	3.802961	5.159780
10	1.480244	1.628895	1.790848	1.967151	2.158925	2.367364	2.593742	3.105848	3.707221	4.411435	6.191736
11	1.539454	1.710339	1.898299	2.104852	2.331639	2.580426	2.853117	3.478550	4.226232	5.117265	7.430084
12	1.601032	1.795856	2.012196	2.252192	2.518170	2.812665	3.138428	3.895976	4.817905	5.936027	8.916100
13	1.665074	1.885649	2.132928	2.409845	2.719624	3.065805	3.452271	4.363493	5.492411	6.885791	10.699321
14	1.731676	1.979932	2.260904	2.578534	2.937194	3.341727	3.797498	4.887112	6.261349	7.987518	12.839185
15	1.800944	2.078928	2.396558	2.759032	3.172169	3.642482	4.177248	5.473566	7.137938	9.265521	15.407022
16	1.872981	2.182875	2.540352	2.952164	3.425943	3.970306	4.594973	6.130394	8.137249	10.748004	18.488426
17	1.947900	2.292018	2.692773	3.158815	3.700018	4.327633	5.054470	6.866041	9.276464	12.467685	22.186111
18	2.025817	2.406619	2.854339	3.379932	3.996019	4.717120	5.559917	7.689966	10.575169	14.462514	26.623333
19	2.106849	2.526950	3.025600	3.616528	4.315701	5.141661	6.115909	8.612762	12.055693	16.776517	31.948000
20	2.191123	2.653298	3.207135	3.869684	4.660957	5.604411	6.727500	9.646293	13.743490	19.460759	38.337600

TABLE II Present Value of $1

n	4%	5%	6%	7%	8%	9%	10%	12%	14%	16%	20%
1	0.961538	0.952381	0.943396	0.934579	0.925926	0.917431	0.909091	0.892857	0.877193	0.862069	0.833333
2	0.924556	0.907029	0.889996	0.873439	0.857339	0.841680	0.826446	0.797194	0.769468	0.743163	0.694444
3	0.888996	0.863838	0.839619	0.816298	0.793832	0.772183	0.751315	0.711780	0.674972	0.640658	0.578704
4	0.854804	0.822702	0.792094	0.762895	0.735030	0.708425	0.683013	0.635518	0.592080	0.552291	0.482253
5	0.821927	0.783526	0.747258	0.712986	0.680583	0.649931	0.620921	0.567427	0.519369	0.476113	0.401878
6	0.790315	0.746215	0.704961	0.666342	0.630170	0.596267	0.564474	0.506631	0.455587	0.410442	0.334898
7	0.759918	0.710681	0.665057	0.622750	0.583490	0.547034	0.513158	0.452349	0.399637	0.353830	0.279082
8	0.730690	0.676839	0.627412	0.582009	0.540269	0.501866	0.466507	0.403883	0.350559	0.305025	0.232568
9	0.702587	0.644609	0.591898	0.543934	0.500249	0.460428	0.424098	0.360610	0.307508	0.262953	0.193807
10	0.675564	0.613913	0.558395	0.508349	0.463193	0.422411	0.385543	0.321973	0.269744	0.226684	0.161506
11	0.649581	0.584679	0.526788	0.475093	0.428883	0.387533	0.350494	0.287476	0.236617	0.195417	0.134588
12	0.624597	0.556837	0.496969	0.444012	0.397114	0.355535	0.318631	0.256675	0.207559	0.168463	0.112157
13	0.600574	0.530321	0.468839	0.414964	0.367698	0.326179	0.289664	0.229174	0.182069	0.145227	0.093464
14	0.577475	0.505068	0.442301	0.387817	0.340461	0.299246	0.263331	0.204620	0.159710	0.125195	0.077887
15	0.555265	0.481017	0.417265	0.362446	0.315242	0.274538	0.239392	0.182696	0.140096	0.107927	0.064905
16	0.533908	0.458112	0.393646	0.338735	0.291890	0.251870	0.217629	0.163122	0.122892	0.093041	0.054088
17	0.513373	0.436297	0.371364	0.316574	0.270269	0.231073	0.197845	0.145644	0.107800	0.080207	0.045073
18	0.493628	0.415521	0.350344	0.295864	0.250249	0.211994	0.179859	0.130040	0.094561	0.069144	0.037561
19	0.474642	0.395734	0.330513	0.276508	0.231712	0.194490	0.163508	0.116107	0.082948	0.059607	0.031301
20	0.456387	0.376889	0.311805	0.258419	0.214548	0.178431	0.148644	0.103667	0.072762	0.051385	0.026084

TABLE III Future Value of an Annuity of $1

n	4%	5%	6%	7%	8%	9%	10%	12%	14%	16%	20%
1	1.000000	1.000000	1.000000	1.000000	1.000000	1.000000	1.000000	1.000000	1.000000	1.000000	1.000000
2	2.040000	2.050000	2.060000	2.070000	2.080000	2.090000	2.100000	2.120000	2.140000	2.160000	2.200000
3	3.121600	3.152500	3.183600	3.214900	3.246400	3.278100	3.310000	3.374400	3.439600	3.505600	3.640000
4	4.246464	4.310125	4.374616	4.439943	4.506112	4.573129	4.641000	4.779328	4.921144	5.066496	5.368000
5	5.416323	5.525631	5.637093	5.750739	5.866601	5.984711	6.105100	6.352847	6.610104	6.877135	7.441600
6	6.632975	6.801913	6.975319	7.153291	7.335929	7.523335	7.715610	8.115189	8.535519	8.977477	9.929920
7	7.898294	8.142008	8.393838	8.654021	8.922803	9.200435	9.487171	10.089012	10.730491	11.413873	12.915904
8	9.214226	9.549109	9.897468	10.259803	10.636628	11.028474	11.435888	12.299693	13.232760	14.240093	16.499085
9	10.582795	11.026564	11.491316	11.977989	12.487558	13.021036	13.579477	14.775656	16.085347	17.518508	20.798902
10	12.006107	12.577893	13.180795	13.816448	14.486562	15.192930	15.937425	17.548735	19.337295	21.321469	25.958682
11	13.486351	14.206787	14.971643	15.783599	16.645487	17.560293	18.531167	20.654583	23.044516	25.732904	32.150419
12	15.025805	15.917127	16.869941	17.888451	18.977126	20.140720	21.384284	24.133133	27.270749	30.850169	39.580502
13	16.626838	17.712983	18.882138	20.140643	21.495297	22.953385	24.522712	28.029109	32.088654	36.786196	48.496603
14	18.291911	19.598632	21.015066	22.550488	24.214920	26.019189	27.974983	32.392602	37.581065	43.671987	59.195923
15	20.023588	21.578564	23.275970	25.129022	27.152114	29.360916	31.772482	37.279715	43.842414	51.659505	72.035108
16	21.824531	23.657492	25.672528	27.888054	30.324283	33.003399	35.949730	42.753280	50.980352	60.925026	87.442129
17	23.697512	25.840366	28.212880	30.840217	33.750226	36.973705	40.544703	48.883674	59.117601	71.673030	105.930555
18	25.645413	28.132385	30.905653	33.999033	37.450244	41.301338	45.599173	55.749715	68.394066	84.140715	128.116666
19	27.671229	30.539004	33.759992	37.378965	41.446263	46.018458	51.159090	63.439681	78.969235	98.603230	154.740000
20	29.778079	33.065954	36.785591	40.995492	45.761964	51.160120	57.274999	72.052442	91.024928	115.379747	186.688000

TABLE IV Present Value of an Annuity of $1

n	4%	5%	6%	7%	8%	9%	10%	12%	14%	16%	20%
1	0.961538	0.952381	0.943396	0.934579	0.925926	0.917431	0.909091	0.892857	0.877193	0.862069	0.833333
2	1.886095	1.859410	1.833393	1.808018	1.783265	1.759111	1.735537	1.690051	1.646661	1.605232	1.527778
3	2.775091	2.723248	2.673012	2.624316	2.577097	2.531295	2.486852	2.401831	2.321632	2.245890	2.106481
4	3.629895	3.545951	3.465106	3.387211	3.312127	3.239720	3.169865	3.037349	2.913712	2.798181	2.588735
5	4.451822	4.329477	4.212364	4.100197	3.992710	3.889651	3.790787	3.604776	3.433081	3.274294	2.990612
6	5.242137	5.075692	4.917324	4.766540	4.622880	4.485919	4.355261	4.111407	3.888668	3.684736	3.325510
7	6.002055	5.786373	5.582381	5.389289	5.206370	5.032953	4.868419	4.563757	4.288305	4.038565	3.604592
8	6.732745	6.463213	6.209794	5.971299	5.746639	5.534819	5.334926	4.967640	4.638864	4.343591	3.837160
9	7.435332	7.107822	6.801692	6.515232	6.246888	5.995247	5.759024	5.328250	4.946372	4.606544	4.030967
10	8.110896	7.721735	7.360087	7.023582	6.710081	6.417658	6.144567	5.650223	5.216116	4.833227	4.192472
11	8.760477	8.306414	7.886875	7.498674	7.138964	6.805191	6.495061	5.937699	5.452733	5.028644	4.327060
12	9.385074	8.863252	8.383844	7.942686	7.536078	7.160725	6.813692	6.194374	5.660292	5.197107	4.439217
13	9.985648	9.393573	8.852683	8.357651	7.903776	7.486904	7.103356	6.423548	5.842362	5.342334	4.532681
14	10.563123	9.898641	9.294984	8.745468	8.244237	7.786150	7.366687	6.628168	6.002072	5.467529	4.610567
15	11.118387	10.379658	9.712249	9.107914	8.559479	8.060688	7.606080	6.810864	6.142168	5.575456	4.675473
16	11.652296	10.837770	10.105895	9.446649	8.851369	8.312558	7.823709	6.973986	6.265060	5.668497	4.729561
17	12.165669	11.274066	10.477260	9.763223	9.121638	8.543631	8.021553	7.119630	6.372859	5.748704	4.774634
18	12.659297	11.689587	10.827603	10.059087	9.371887	8.755625	8.201412	7.249670	6.467420	5.817848	4.812195
19	13.133939	12.085321	11.158116	10.335595	9.603599	8.905115	8.364920	7.365777	6.550369	5.877455	4.843496
20	13.590326	12.462210	11.469921	10.594014	9.818147	9.128546	8.513564	7.469444	6.623131	5.928841	4.869580

KEY TERMS

Annuity 787
Compound interest 785
Compounding 785
Future value 786
Present value 786
Simple interest 785

EXERCISES

All applicable Exercises are available with McGraw-Hill's Connect Plus Accounting.

Exercise F1 *Future value and present value*

Required

Using Tables I, II, III, or IV in this appendix, calculate the following:

a. The future value of $30,000 invested at 8 percent for 10 years.

b. The future value of eight annual payments of $2,000 at 9 percent interest.

c. The amount that must be deposited today (present value) at 8 percent to accumulate $60,000 in five years.

d. The annual payment on a 10-year, 6 percent, $50,000 note payable.

Exercise F2 *Computing the payment amount*

Barry Rich is a business major at State U. He will be graduating this year and is planning to start a consulting business. He will need to purchase computer equipment that costs $25,000. He can borrow the money from the local bank but will have to make annual payments of principal and interest.

Required

a. Compute the annual payment Barry will be required to make on a $25,000, four-year, 8 percent loan.

b. If Barry can afford to make annual payments of $8,000, how much can he borrow?

Exercise F3 *Saving for a future value*

Billy Dan and Betty Lou were recently married and want to start saving for their dream home. They expect the house they want will cost approximately $325,000. They hope to be able to purchase the house for cash in 10 years.

Required

a. How much will Billy Dan and Betty Lou have to invest each year to purchase their dream home at the end of 10 years? Assume an interest rate of 9 percent.

b. Billy Dan's parents want to give the couple a substantial wedding gift for the purchase of their future home. How much must Billy Dan's parents give them now if they are to reach the desired amount of $325,000 in 12 years? Assume an interest rate of 9 percent.

Exercise F4 *Sale of bonds at a discount using present value*

Carr Corporation issued $50,000 of 6 percent, 10-year bonds on January 1, 2016, for a price that reflected a 7 percent market rate of interest. Interest is payable annually on December 31.

Required

a. What was the selling price of the bonds?

b. Prepare the journal entry to record issuing the bonds.

c. Prepare the journal entry for the first interest payment on December 31, 2016, using the effective interest rate method.

GLOSSARY

absolute amounts Dollar totals reported in accounts on financial reports that can be misleading because they make no reference to the relative size of the company being analyzed. *p. 13-3*

accelerated depreciation method Depreciation method that recognizes more depreciation expense in the early stages of an asset's life than the straight-line method and less later in the asset's life. *p. 428*

account Record of classified and summarized transaction data; component of financial statement elements. *p. 10*

account balance Difference between total debit and total credit amounts in an account. *p. 148*

accounting Service-based profession developed to provide reliable and relevant financial information useful in making decisions. *p. 3*

accounting controls Procedures companies implement to safeguard assets and to ensure accurate and reliable accounting records and reports. *p. 318*

accounting cycle For a given time period, the cycle of recording accounting data, adjusting the accounts, preparing the financial statements, and closing the temporary accounts; when one accounting cycle ends, a new one begins.

accounting equation Algebraic relationship between a company's assets and the claims on those assets, represented as Assets = Liabilities + Equity. *p. 12*

accounting event Economic occurrence that changes a company's assets, liabilities, or equity. *p. 13*

accounting period Time span covered by the financial statements; normally one year, but may be a quarter, a month, or some other time interval. *p. 21*

accounts payable A liability account that represents the business's obligation to pay cash for operating expenses sometime in the future.

accounts receivable Expected future cash receipts arising from permitting customers to *buy now and pay later;* typically relatively small balances due within a short time period. *pp. 73, 364*

accounts receivable turnover Financial ratio that measures how fast accounts receivable are collected in cash; computed by dividing sales by accounts receivable. *pp. 385, 13-9*

accrual Accounting recognition of revenue or expense in a period before cash is exchanged. *p. 71*

accrual accounting Accounting system which recognizes revenues when earned and expenses when incurred regardless of when the related cash is exchanged. *p. 71*

accrued expenses Expenses that are recognized before cash is paid. An example is accrued salaries expense. *p. 75*

accrued interest Interest revenue or expense that is recognized before cash has been exchanged. *p. 380*

Accumulated Depreciation Contra asset account that shows the sum of all depreciation expense recognized for an asset since the date of acquisition. *p. 426*

acid-test ratio Measure of immediate debt-paying ability; calculated by dividing very liquid assets (cash, receivables, and marketable securities) by current liabilities. *p. 13-8*

adjusting entry Entry that updates account balances prior to preparing financial statements; a bookkeeping tool. Adjusting entries never affect the Cash account. *pp. 75, 380*

administrative controls Procedures companies implement to evaluate performance and monitor compliance with company policies and public laws. *p. 318*

adverse opinion Opinion issued by a certified public accountant that means one or more departures from GAAP in a company's financial statements are so very material the auditors believe the financial statements do not fairly represent the company's status; contrast with *unqualified opinion. p. 336*

aging of accounts receivable Classifying each account receivable by the number of days it has been outstanding. The purpose of the aging schedule is to develop a more accurate estimate of the amount of uncollectible accounts. *p. 375*

allocation Recognizing expense by systematically assigning the cost of an asset to periods of use.

Allowance for Doubtful Accounts Contra asset account used to record the amount of accounts receivable estimated to be uncollectible. *p. 366*

allowance method of accounting for uncollectible accounts An accounting practice that recognizes an estimated rather than the actual amount of uncollectible accounts expense. Estimated expenses are used to improve matching of revenues and expenses and/or to more accurately reflect the net realizable value of accounts receivable. *p. 366*

allowances Reductions in the selling price of goods extended to buyers because the goods are defective or of lower quality than the buyer ordered to encourage a buyer to keep merchandise that would otherwise be returned.

American Institute of Certified Public Accountants (AICPA) National association that serves the educational and professional interests of members of the public accounting profession; membership is voluntary. See also *Code of Professional Conduct. p. 94*

amortization (1) Systematic and periodic allocation of the costs of intangible assets to expense over their useful lives; (2) periodically transferring the discount on a note or a bond to interest expense. *pp. 422, 539*

amortization (of loan) Systematic repayment of principal and interest over the life of a loan. *p. 539*

amortizing Systematically allocating the cost of intangible assets to expense over their useful lives; also a term for converting the discount on a note or a bond to interest expense over a designated period. *p. 503*

annual report Document companies publish to provide information, including financial statements, to stockholders. *p. 30*

annuity Series of equal cash flows received or paid over equal time intervals at a constant rate of return. *p. 787*

appropriated retained earnings Retained earnings restricted by the board of directors for a specific purpose (e.g., to repay debt or for future expansion); part of total retained earnings, but not available for distribution as dividends. *p. 612*

articles of incorporation Information about a proposed corporation, such as its name, purpose, location, expected life, proposed capital stock, and a list of the members of its board of directors, filed with a state agency when applying for the legal formation of the corporation. *p. 598*

articulation Characteristic of financial statements that means they are interrelated. For example, the amount of net income reported on the income statement is added to beginning retained earnings as a component in calculating the ending retained earnings balance reported on the statement of changes in stockholders' equity. *p. 25*

asset Economic resource used to produce revenue which is expected to provide future benefit to the business. *p. 11*

asset exchange transaction A transaction, such as the purchase of land with cash, that decreases one asset and increases another asset; total assets remain unchanged. *pp. 14, 73*

asset source transaction A transaction that increases both an asset and a claim on assets; the three types of asset source transactions are acquisitions from owners (equity), borrowings from creditors (liabilities), or earnings from operations (revenues). *pp. 13, 72*

asset turnover ratio The amount of net sales divided by average total assets. *p. 13-13*

asset use transaction A transaction that decreases both an asset and a claim on assets; the three types of asset use transactions are distributions (transfers to owners), liability payments (to creditors), or expenses (costs incurred to operate the business). *pp. 15, 74*

audit Detailed examination of some aspect of a company's accounting records or operating procedures in order to report the results to interested parties. See *financial statements audit*. *p. 335*

authority manual Written documentation outlining levels of authority and responsibility. The authority manual provides specific guidelines, such as those for a personnel officer, as well as general guidelines, such as giving all vice presidents authorization to approve up to a designated spending limit. *p. 322*

authorized stock Number of shares of stock a corporation has state approval to issue. *p. 603*

available-for-sale securities Classification for marketable securities that are not considered held-to-maturity or trading securities. *p. 777*

average days to collect accounts receivable (average collection period) Measure of how quickly, on average, a business collects its accounts receivable; calculated as 365 divided by the accounts receivable turnover. *pp. 385, 13-9*

average days to sell inventory (average days in inventory) Financial ratio that measures the average number of days that inventory stays in stock before it is sold. *pp. 290, 13-10*

balance sheet Financial statement that reports a company's assets and the corresponding claims (liabilities and equity) on those assets as of a specific date (usually as of the end of the accounting period). *p. 23*

bank reconciliation Schedule that identifies and explains differences between the cash balance reported by the bank and the cash balance in the company's accounting records. *p. 327*

bank statement Record issued by a bank (usually monthly) of all activity in the bank account for that period. *p. 326*

bank statement credit memo Bank statement enclosure that describes an increase in the account balance. *p. 326*

bank statement debit memo Bank statement enclosure that describes a decrease in the account balance. *p. 326*

basket purchase Acquiring several assets at once for a single purchase price; no specific cost is attributed to the individual assets. *p. 423*

board of directors Group of individuals elected by the stockholders of a corporation to oversee its operations. *p. 600*

bond certificate Debt security used to obtain long-term financing in which a company borrows funds from a number of lenders, called *bondholders;* usually issued in denominations of $1,000. *p. 544*

bond discount Difference between the selling price and the face amount of a bond sold for less than the face amount. *p. 551*

bondholder The party buying a bond (the lender or creditor). *p. 544*

bond premium Difference between the selling price and the face amount of a bond that is sold for more than the face amount. *p. 555*

book of original entry A journal in which a transaction is first recorded. *p. 158*

book value Historical (original) cost of an asset minus accumulated depreciation to date. *p. 426*

book value per share An accounting measure of a share of common stock, computed by dividing total stockholders' equity less preferred rights by the number of common shares outstanding. *pp. 603, 13-16*

call premium Difference between the call price (the price that must be paid for a called bond) and the face amount of the bond. *p. 546*

call price Specified price an issuer must pay to call bonds; usually higher than the face amount of the bonds. *p. 546*

callable bonds Bonds which the issuer, at its option, may pay off prior to maturity. *p. 546*

capital expenditures (for an existing asset) Substantial amounts spent to improve an asset's quality or to extend its life. *p. 436*

capitalized Initially recorded an expenditure in an asset account for subsequent transfer to expense as the asset is used to produce revenue.

carrying value Face amount of a bond liability less any unamortized bond discount or plus any unamortized bond premium. *pp. 100, 426, 551*

cash Coins, currency, checks, balances in checking and certain savings accounts, money orders, bank drafts, certificates of deposit, and other items that are payable on demand. *p. 323*

cash discount Price reduction on merchandise sold offered by sellers to encourage prompt payment; when taken, represents a sales discount to the seller and a purchase discount to the buyer of the merchandise. *p. 222*

cash inflows Sources of cash. *p. 644*

cash outflows Uses of cash. *p. 644*

Cash Short and Over Account used to record the amount of cash shortages or overages; shortages represent expenses and overages represent revenues. *p. 331*

certified check Check guaranteed by a bank to be drawn on an account with sufficient funds to pay the check. *p. 328*

certified public accountant (CPA) Accountant who, by meeting certain educational and experiential requirements, is licensed by the state government to provide audit services to the public. *p. 335*

chart of accounts List of all ledger accounts and their corresponding account numbers. *p. 159*

checks Prenumbered forms, sometimes multicopy, preprinted on the face with the name of the business issuing them, authorizing the bank to disburse funds from the issuer's account. The issuer enters the transaction date, the desired payee, and the amount in the appropriate places on the check form. *p. 325*

claims Owners' and creditors' interests in a business's assets. *p. 12*

claims exchange transaction A transaction that decreases one claim and increases another claim; total claims remain unchanged. For example, accruing interest expense is a claims exchange transaction; liabilities increase, and the expense recognition decreases retained earnings. *p. 75*

classified balance sheet Balance sheet that distinguishes between current and noncurrent items. *p. 498*

closely held corporation Corporation whose stock is exchanged among a limited number of individuals. *p. 598*

closing the books or **closing** Bookkeeping technique of transferring balances from the temporary accounts (Revenue, Expense, and Dividends) to the permanent account (Retained Earnings). *p. 26*

closing entries Entries that transfer the balances in the temporary accounts (Revenue, Expense, and Dividends accounts) to the Retained Earnings account at the end of the accounting period. *p. 163*

Code of Professional Conduct Guidelines established by the American Institute of Certified Public Accountants (AICPA) to promote ethical conduct among certified public accountants; AICPA members agree to adhere to this code, which goes beyond legal requirements. *p. 94*

collateral Assets pledged as security for a loan. *pp. 379, 547*

common size financial statements Financial statements in which dollar amounts are converted to percentages to aid in comparing financial data among periods and among companies. *p. 234*

common stock Basic class of corporate stock that has no preferential claim on assets or dividends; certificates that evidence ownership in a company. *pp. 12, 603*

compound interest Interest earned on interest by reinvesting interest so that it is added to the initial principal. Contrast with *simple interest*. *p. 785*

compounding Earning interest on interest. *p. 785*

confidentiality Code of ethics requirement that prohibits CPAs from voluntarily disclosing information they acquire as a result of accountant-client relationships. *p. 337*

conservatism A principle that guides accountants in uncertain circumstances to select the alternative that produces the lowest amount of net income. *p. 81*

consistency The generally accepted accounting principle that a company should, in most circumstances, continually use the same accounting method(s) so that its financial statements are comparable across time. *p. 281*

consolidated financial statements Financial statements that represent the combined operations of a parent company and its subsidiaries. *p. 781*

contingent liability Obligations with amounts due that depend on events that will be resolved in the future. *p. 485*

continuity Presumption that a corporation's existence may extend well beyond the time at which any particular shareholder retires or sells his or her stock. *p. 600*

contra account Account with a normal balance opposite that of other accounts in the same category (e.g., Accumulated Depreciation is classified as an asset, but it normally has a credit balance).

contra asset account Account used to reduce the reported value of the asset to which it relates; e.g., subtracting the contra asset Allowance for Bad Debts from Accounts Receivable reduces receivables to their net realizable value. *pp. 368, 426*

contra liability account Account used to reduce the reported value of the liability to which it relates; e.g., subtracting the contra liability Discount on Note Payable from Notes Payable reduces the amount of liabilities on the balance sheet. *p. 502*

contributed capital The claim on assets resulting from asset contributions to a business by its owners.

convertible bonds Bonds which bondholders can convert (exchange) to ownership interests (stock) in the corporation. *p. 546*

copyright Legal protection of writings, musical compositions, and other intellectual property for the exclusive use of the creator or persons assigned the right by the creator. *p. 440*

corporation Legal entity separate from its owners, created by the state pursuant to an application submitted according to state laws by a group of individuals with a common purpose. *p. 598*

cost An amount paid to acquire a resource (asset) or to pay for a resource that has been consumed. Incurring a cost results in an asset exchange or expense recognition. *p. 83*

cost method of accounting for treasury stock Method of accounting for treasury stock in which treasury stock purchases are recorded in the Treasury Stock account at their cost to the company without regard to the original issue price or par value. *p. 609*

cost of goods available for sale Total costs paid to obtain goods and ready them for sale, including the cost of beginning inventory plus purchases and transportation-in costs, less purchase returns and allowances and purchase discounts. *p. 216*

cost of goods sold Total cost incurred for the goods sold during a specific accounting period. *p. 216*

credit Entry on the right side of an account; increases liability and equity accounts or decreases asset accounts. *p. 148*

creditor Individual or organization that has loaned goods or services to a business. *p. 4*

cumulative dividends Preferred dividends that accumulate from year to year until paid. *p. 604*

current (short-term) asset Asset that will be converted to cash or consumed within one year or an operating cycle, whichever is longer. *pp. 420, 497*

current (short-term) liability Obligation due within one year or an operating cycle, whichever is longer. *p. 497*

current ratio (working capital ratio) Measure of liquidity; calculated by dividing current assets by current liabilities. *pp. 499, 13-8*

date of record Date that establishes who will receive the dividend payment: shareholders who actually own the stock on the record date will receive the dividend even if they sell the stock before the dividend is paid. *p. 610*

debenture Unsecured bond backed by the general credit of the issuing company. *p. 545*

debit Entry on the left side of an account; increases asset accounts or decreases liability and equity accounts. *p. 148*

debt security Type of financial instrument that represents a liability to the investee company. *p. 776*

debt to assets ratio Financial measure of a company's level of risk, calculated as total debt divided by total assets. *pp. 166, 13-11*

debt to equity ratio Financial ratio that compares creditor financing to owner financing, expressed as the dollar amount of liabilities for each dollar of stockholder's equity. *p. 13-11*

declaration date Date on which the board of directors declares a dividend. *p. 610*

deferral Accounting recognition of revenue or expense in a period after cash is exchanged. *p. 71*

deferred tax liability Income tax payment postponed until future years because of the difference in accounting methods selected for financial reporting and methods required for tax purposes (e.g., a company may use straight-line depreciation in financial statements but use MACRS for tax reporting). *p. 435*

depletion The removal of natural resources from the land; the depletion costs of the natural resources are systematically transferred to expense as the resources are removed. *p. 422*

deposit ticket Bank form submitted along with funds that identifies the account number, account name, and a record of the checks and cash being put in the account. *p. 325*

deposits in transit Deposits added to a depositor's books but not received and recorded by the bank prior to the date of the bank statement. *p. 327*

depreciable cost Original cost minus salvage value (of a long-term depreciable asset). *p. 424*

depreciation Decline in value of long-term tangible assets such as buildings, furniture, or equipment. It is systematically recognized by accountants as depreciation expense over the useful lives of the affected assets. *p. 422*

depreciation expense Portion of the original cost of a long-term tangible asset allocated to an expense account in a given period. *pp. 99, 424*

direct method Method of reporting cash flows from operating activities on the statement of cash flows that shows individual categories of cash receipts from and cash payments for major activities (collections from customers, payments to suppliers, etc.). *p. 646*

direct write-off method Accounting practice of recognizing uncollectible accounts expense when accounts are determined to be uncollectible, regardless of the period in which the related sale occurred. *p. 377*

disclaimer of opinion Report on financial statements issued when the auditor is unable to obtain enough information to determine if the statements conform to GAAP; is neither positive nor negative. *p. 336*

discount Amount of interest included in the face of a discount note; the discount (interest) is subtracted from the face amount of the note to determine the amount of cash borrowed (principal). *p. 501*

discount note Note with interest included in its face value, which is also the maturity value. *p. 501*

Discount on Bonds Payable Contra liability account used to record the amount of discount on a bond issue. *p. 551*

Discount on Notes Payable Contra liability account subtracted from the Notes Payable account to determine the carrying value of the liability. *p. 502*

dividend Transfer of wealth from a business to its owners. *pp. 15, 778*

dividend yield Ratio for comparing stock dividends paid in relation to the market price; calculated as dividends per share divided by market price per share. *p. 13-17*

dividends in arrears Cumulative dividends on preferred stock that were not paid in prior periods; must be paid before paying any dividends to holders of common stock. *p. 604*

double taxation Recognition that corporate profits distributed to owners are taxed twice, once when the income is reported on the corporation's income tax return and again when the dividends are reported on the individual's return. *p. 599*

double-declining-balance depreciation Depreciation computations that produce larger amounts of depreciation in the early years of an asset's life and progressively smaller amounts as the asset ages. *p. 428*

double-entry accounting (double-entry bookkeeping) Recordkeeping system that provides checks and balances by recording two sides for every transaction. *pp. 13, 149*

earnings (net income) The difference between revenues and expenses. Sometimes called *profit*. *p. 4*

earnings per share Measure of the value of a share of common stock in terms of company earnings; calculated as net income available to common stockholders divided by the average number of outstanding common shares. *p. 13-15*

effective interest rate Yield rate of bonds, equal to the market rate of interest on the day the bonds are sold. *p. 551*

effective interest rate method Method of amortizing bond discounts and premiums that bases interest computations on the carrying value of the liability. As the liability increases or decreases, the amount of interest expense also increases or decreases. *p. 558*

elements The primary financial statement categories: assets, liabilities, equity, contributed capital, revenue, expenses, gains, losses, distributions, and net income. *p. 10*

employee An individual whose labor is supervised, directed, and controlled by a business. *p. 489*

Employee's Withholding Allowance Certificate, Form W-4 A form used by an employee to report the number of withholding allowances claimed by the employee. Each withholding allowance reduces the amount of income tax withheld from the employee's pay. *p. 491*

Employer's Quarterly Federal Tax Return, Form 941 The form used to show the amounts due and paid to the government for federal tax withholdings. *p. 492*

entity Economic unit (individual, business, or other organization) for which accounting records are separately maintained; it is distinct from its owners, creditors, managers, and employees.

equity method Method of accounting for investments in marketable equity securities required when the investor company owns 20 percent or more of the investee company. Under the equity method, the amount of the investment asset represents a measure of the book value of the investee rather than the cost or market value of the investment security. *p. 781*

equity security Type of financial instrument that evidences an ownership interest in a company, such as a common stock certificate. *p. 776*

estimated useful life Time period for which a business expects to use an asset. *p. 424*

ex-dividend Stock traded after the date of record but before the payment date; does not receive the benefit of the upcoming dividend. *p. 610*

expense An economic sacrifice (decrease in assets or increase in liabilities) that is incurred in the process of generating revenue. *pp. 15, 75*

expense transactions Business events that decrease assets or increase liabilities in order to produce revenue in the course of operating a business.

face value (of bond) Amount to be paid to the bondholder at bond maturity; base for computing periodic cash interest payments. *p. 544*

fair value The price at which securities or other assets sell in free markets. Also called *market value*. *p. 776*

Federal Unemployment Tax Act (FUTA) The act that requires employers to pay unemployment tax for the establishment of a fund that is used to provide temporary relief to qualified unemployed persons. *p. 495*

fidelity bond Insurance policy that a company buys to insure itself against loss due to employee dishonesty. *p. 321*

financial accounting Branch of accounting focused on the business information needs of external users (creditors, investors, governmental agencies, financial analysts, etc.); its objective is to classify and record business events and transactions to produce external financial reports (income statement, balance sheet, statement of cash flows, and statement of changes in equity). *p. 6*

Financial Accounting Standards Board (FASB) Private, independent standard-setting body established by the accounting profession that has been delegated the authority by the SEC to establish most of the accounting rules and regulations for public financial reporting. *p. 8*

financial leverage Principle of increasing earnings through debt financing by investing money at a higher rate than the rate paid on the borrowed money. *pp. 166, 561*

financial resources Money or credit supplied to a business by investors (owners) and creditors. *p. 4*

financial statements Reports used to communicate a company's financial information to interested external parties. The four general-purpose financial statements are the income statement, statement of changes in equity, balance sheet, and statement of cash flows. *p. 10*

financial statements audit Detailed examination of a company's accounting records and the documents that support the information reported in the financial statements; includes testing the reliability of the underlying accounting system used to produce the financial reports. *p. 335*

financing activities Cash inflows and outflows from transactions with investors and creditors (except interest), including cash receipts from issuing stock, borrowing activities, and cash disbursements to pay dividends; one of the three categories of cash inflows and outflows reported on the statement of cash flows. This category shows the amount of cash supplied by these resource providers and the amount of cash that is returned to them. *pp. 24, 647*

first-in, first-out (FIFO) cost flow method Inventory cost flow method in which cost of goods sold is computed as if the earliest items purchased are the first items sold. *p. 276*

fiscal year The annual time period for which a company provides financial statements. *p. 147*

fixed interest rate Interest rate (charge for borrowing money) that remains constant over the life of the loan. *p. 538*

FOB (free on board) destination Shipping term that means the seller bears the freight (transportation-in) costs. *p. 223*

FOB (free on board) shipping point Shipping term that means the buyer bears the freight (transportation-in) costs. *p. 223*

franchise Exclusive right to sell products or perform services in certain geographic areas. *p. 441*

fraud triangle A graphic that shows the common features of criminal and ethical misconduct with *opportunity* shown at the head of a triangle and *pressure* and *rationalization* shown at the base.

full disclosure The accounting principle that financial statements should include all information relevant to an entity's operations and financial condition. Full disclosure frequently requires adding footnotes to the financial statements. *p. 281*

future value Amount an investment will be worth at some point in the future, assuming a specified interest rate and the reinvestment of interest each period that it is earned. *p. 786*

gains Increases in assets or decreases in liabilities that result from peripheral or incidental transactions. *p. 227*

general authority Company guidelines that apply to various levels of a company's management, such as requiring everyone at that level to fly coach class. *p. 322*

general journal Book of original entry in which any accounting transaction could be recorded, though commonly limited to adjusting and closing entries and unusual transactions. *p. 158*

general ledger The set of all accounts used in a given accounting system, typically organized in financial statement order. *pp. 16, 159*

general uncertainties Uncertainties such as competition and damage from storms. These uncertainties are distinguished from contingent liabilities because they arise from future rather than past events. *p. 485*

generally accepted accounting principles (GAAP) Rules and practices that accountants agree to follow in financial reports prepared for public distribution. *p. 8*

going concern assumption Accounting presumption that a company will continue to operate indefinitely, benefiting from its assets and paying its obligations in full; justifies reporting assets and liabilities in the financial statements. *pp. 19, 480*

goodwill Intangible added value of a successful business attributable to such factors as reputation, location, and superior products that enables the business to earn above-average profits; measured by an entity acquiring the business as the excess paid over the appraised value of the net assets. *p. 441*

gross earnings The total amount of employee wages or salaries before any deductions or withholdings. Gross earnings include the total of regular pay plus any bonuses, overtime, or other additions. *p. 490*

gross margin (gross profit) Difference between sales revenue and cost of goods sold; the amount a company makes from selling goods before subtracting operating expenses. *p. 216*

gross margin method Technique for estimating the ending inventory amount without a physical count; useful when the percentage of gross margin to sales remains relatively stable from one accounting period to the next. *p. 287*

gross margin percentage Expressing gross margin as a percentage of sales by dividing gross margin by net sales; the amount of each dollar of sales that is profit before deducting any operating expenses. *p. 234*

gross profit See *gross margin.*

half-year convention Tax rule that requires recognizing six months of depreciation expense on an asset both in the year of purchase and in the year of disposal regardless of the actual purchase date. *p. 434*

held-to-maturity securities Classification for marketable debt securities the purchasing company intends to hold (rather than sell) until the securities mature. *p. 777*

historical cost concept Accounting practice of reporting assets at the actual price paid for them when purchased regardless of estimated changes in market value. *pp. 16, 423*

horizontal analysis Analysis technique that compares amounts of the same item over several time periods. *p. 13-3*

horizontal statements model Concurrent representation of several financial statements horizontally across a page. *p. 28*

impress basis Maintaining an account at a specified fixed amount, such as periodically replenishing a petty cash fund to its impress amount. *p. 332*

income Increase in value created by providing goods and services through resource transformation. *p. 4*

income statement Financial report of profitability; measures the difference between revenues and expenses for the accounting period (whether or not cash has been exchanged). *p. 21*

independent auditor Licensed certified public accountant engaged to audit a company's financial statements; not an employee of the audited company. *p. 335*

independent contractor An individual who is paid by a business but retains individual control and supervisory authority over the work performed. *p. 489*

indirect method Method of reporting cash flows from operating activities on the statement of cash flows that starts with the net income from the income statement, followed by adjustments necessary to convert accrual-based net income to a cash-basis equivalent. *p. 646*

information overload Situation in which the presentation of too much information confuses the user of the information. *p. 13-2*

installment notes Obligations that require regular payments of principal and interest over the life of the loan. *p. 540*

intangible assets Long-term assets having no physical substance that benefit their owners through providing rights and privileges, such as a trademark. *p. 422*

interest Fee paid for the use of funds; represents expense to the borrower and revenue to the lender. *pp. 4, 379, 778*

interest-bearing notes Notes that require face value plus accrued interest to be paid at maturity. *p. 501*

internal controls Policies and procedures companies establish to provide reasonable assurance of reducing fraud, providing reliable accounting records, and accomplishing organization objectives. *pp. 95, 318*

International Accounting Standards Board (IASB) Private, independent body that establishes International Financial Reporting Standards (IFRS). The IASB's authority is established by various governmental institutions that require or permit companies in their jurisdiction to use IFRS. To date, over 100 countries require or permit companies to prepare their financial statements using IFRS. One notable exception is the United States of America. *p. 9*

International Financial Reporting Standards (IFRS) Pronouncements established by the International Accounting Standards Board that provide guidance for the preparation of financial statements. *p. 9*

inventory Goods under production or finished and ready for sale; also stockpiles of supplies used in the business (office supplies, cleaning supplies).

inventory cost flow methods Alternative ways to allocate the cost of goods available for sale between cost of goods sold and ending inventory. *p. 278*

inventory turnover A measure of sales volume relative to inventory levels; calculated as the cost of goods sold divided by average inventory; indicates how many times a year, on average, the inventory is sold (turned over). *pp. 290, 13-10*

investee Company that receives assets or services in exchange for a debt or equity security. *p. 776*

investing activities Cash inflows and outflows associated with buying or selling long-term assets and cash inflows and outflows associated with lending activities and investments in the debt and equity of other companies; one of the three categories of cash inflows and outflows reported on the statement of cash flows. *pp. 24, 647*

investment Commitment of assets (usually cash) by a business to acquire other assets that will be used to produce revenue.

investment securities Certificates that describe the rights and privileges that investors receive when they loan or give assets or services to investees. *p. 776*

investor Company or individual who gives assets or services in exchange for security certificates representing ownership interests. *pp. 4, 776*

issued stock Stock a company has sold to the public. *p. 603*

issuer (of a bond) Party that issues the bond (the borrower). *p. 544*

issuer of the note Individual or business borrowing funds (the party receiving the cash when a note is issued). *p. 482*

journal Book (or electronic record) of original entry in which accounting data are entered chronologically before posting to the ledger accounts. *p. 158*

labor resources The intellectual and physical efforts of individuals used in the process of providing goods and services to customers. *p. 5*

last-in, first-out (LIFO) cost flow method Inventory cost flow method in which cost of goods sold is computed as if the most recently purchased items are the first items sold. *p. 276*

legal capital Amount of assets that should be maintained as protection for creditors; the number of shares multiplied by the par value. *p. 603*

liabilities Obligations of a business to relinquish assets, provide services, or accept other obligations. *p. 11*

limited liability Concept that investors in a corporation may not be held personally liable for the actions or debts of the corporation; stockholders' liability is limited to the amount they paid for their stock. *p. 600*

limited liability company (LLC) Organizational form that offers many of the favorable characteristics and legal benefits of a corporation (e.g., limited liability and centralized management) but is permitted by federal law to be taxed as a partnership, thereby avoiding double taxation of profits. *p. 599*

line of credit Preapproved financing arrangement with a lending institution in which a business can borrow money up to the approved limit by simply writing a check. *p. 543*

liquidation Process of dividing up an organization's assets and returning them to the resource providers. In business liquidations, creditors normally have first priority; after creditor claims have been satisfied, any remaining assets are distributed to the company's owners (investors). *p. 18*

liquidity Ability to convert assets to cash quickly and meet short-term obligations. *pp. 23, 382, 499*

liquidity ratios Measures of short-term debt-paying ability. *p. 13-7*

long-term liabilities Liabilities with maturity dates beyond one year or the company's operating cycle, whichever is longer; noncurrent liabilities. *p. 538*

long-term operational assets Assets used by a business, normally over multiple accounting periods, to generate revenue; contrast with assets that are sold (inventory) or held (investments) to generate revenue; also called *productive assets. p. 420*

losses Decreases in assets or increases in liabilities that result from peripheral or incidental transactions. *p. 227*

lower-of-cost-or-market rule Accounting principle of reporting inventory at its replacement cost (market) if replacement cost has declined below the inventory's original cost, regardless of the cause. *p. 284*

maker The party issuing a note (the borrower). *p. 379*

management's discussion and analysis (MD&A) Section of a company's annual report in which management explains many different aspects of the company's past performance and future plans. *p. 335*

managerial accounting Branch of accounting focused on the information needs of managers and others working within the business; its objective is to gather and report information that adds value to the business. Managerial accounting information is not regulated or reported to the public. *p. 6*

manufacturing businesses Companies that make the goods they sell customers. *p. 29*

market Group of people or entities organized to buy and sell resources. *p. 4*

market interest rate Interest rate currently available on a wide range of alternative investments with similar levels of risk. *p. 556*

market value The price at which securities sell in the secondary market; also called *fair value. pp. 603, 776*

marketable securities Securities that are readily traded in the secondary securities market. *p. 776*

matching concept Accounting principle of recognizing expenses in the same accounting period as the revenues they produce, using one of three methods: match expenses directly with revenues (e.g., cost of goods sold); match expenses to the period in which they are incurred (e.g., rent expense), and match expenses systematically with revenues (e.g., depreciation expense). *pp. 21, 80, 380*

material error Error or other reporting problem that, if known, would influence the decision of an average prudent investor. *p. 336*

materiality The point at which knowledge of information would influence a user's decision; can be measured in absolute, percentage, quantitative, or qualitative terms. The concept allows nonmaterial matters to be handled in any convenient way, such as charging a pencil sharpener to expense rather than recording periodic depreciation over its useful life. *p. 13-3*

maturity date The date that a liability is due to be settled (the date the borrower is expected to repay a debt). *p. 379*

Medicare Health insurance provided by the government primarily for retired workers. *p. 492*

merchandise inventory Finished goods held for resale to customers. *p. 213*

merchandising businesses Companies that buy and resell merchandise inventory. *pp. 39, 212*

modified accelerated cost recovery system (MACRS) Prescribed method of depreciation for tax purposes that provides the maximum depreciation expense deduction permitted under tax law. *p. 433*

mortgage bond Type of secured debt that conditionally transfers title of designated property to the bondholder until the bond is paid. *p. 545*

multistep income statement Income statement format that matches various revenues with related expenses in order to present subtotals (steps) such as gross margin and operating income; distinguishes between routine operating items and nonoperating items such as gains, losses, and interest. Contrast with *single-step income statement. p. 230*

natural resources Wasting assets originally attached to land such as mineral deposits, oil and gas reserves, and reserves of timber, mines, and quarries; the land value declines as the resources are removed. *p. 422*

net assets See *equity.*

net income Increase in equity resulting from operating the business. *p. 21*

net income percentage See *return on sales. p. 234*

net loss Decrease in equity resulting from operating the business. *p. 21*

net margin Profitability measurement that indicates the percentage of each sales dollar resulting in profit; calculated as net income divided by net sales. *p. 13-13*

net pay Employee's gross pay less all deductions (withholdings). *p. 494*

net realizable value The amount of accounts receivable a company expects to actually collect in cash; the face amount of receivables less an allowance for estimated uncollectible accounts. *p. 366*

net sales Sales less returns from customers and allowances or cash discounts granted to customers. *p. 234*

noncash investing and financing activities Certain business transactions, usually long-term, that do not involve cash, such as exchanging stock for land or purchasing property by using debt; reported separately on the statement of cash flows. *p. 648*

non-sufficient-funds (NSF) check Customer's check deposited but returned by the bank on which it was drawn because the customer did not have enough money in its account to pay the check. *p. 328*

note payable Liability represented by a legal document called a *note* that describes pertinent details such as principal amount, interest charges, maturity date, and collateral. *p. 482*

notes to financial statements Written explanations accompanying the financial statements that provide information about such items as estimates used and accounting methods chosen when GAAP permits alternatives. *p. 335*

notes receivable Notes that evidence rights to receive cash in the future; usually specify the maturity date, rate of interest, and other credit terms. *p. 365*

not-for-profit entities Organizations (also called *nonprofit* or *nonbusiness entities*) established primarily for motives other than making a profit, such as providing goods and services for the social good. Examples include state-supported universities and colleges, hospitals, public libraries, and public charities. *p. 6*

operating activities Cash inflows from and outflows for routine, everyday business operations, normally resulting from revenue and expense transactions including interest; one of the three categories of cash inflows and outflows reported on the statement of cash flows. *pp. 24, 646*

operating cycle Process of converting cash into inventory, inventory into receivables, and receivables back to cash; its length can be measured in days using financial statement data. *pp. 386, 497*

operating income (or loss) Income after subtracting operating expenses from operating revenues. Gains and losses and other peripheral activities are added to or subtracted from operating income to determine net income or loss. *p. 229*

opportunity An element of the fraud triangle that recognizes weaknesses in internal controls that enable the occurrence of fraudulent or unethical behavior. *p. 95*

outstanding checks Checks the depositor company has written and deducted from its cash account balance that have not yet been presented to its bank for payment. *p. 327*

outstanding stock Shares of stock a corporation has issued that are still owned by outside parties, i.e., all stock that has been issued less any treasury stock the corporation has repurchased. *p. 603*

Paid-In Capital in Excess of Par (or Stated) Value The account in which a company records any amount received above the par or stated value of stock when stock is issued. *p. 605*

par value Arbitrary value assigned to stock by the board of directors; like *stated value*, designates *legal capital. p. 602*

parent company Company that holds a controlling interest (more than 50 percent ownership) in another company. *p. 781*

partnership Business entity owned by at least two people who share talents, capital, and the risks of the business. *p. 598*

partnership agreement Legal document that defines the rights and responsibilities of each partner and describes how income and losses are to be divided. *p. 598*

patent Legal right granted by the U.S. Patent Office ensuring a company or an individual the exclusive right to a product or process. *p. 440*

payables Obligations to make future economic sacrifices, usually cash payments.

payee The party collecting cash. *p. 379*

payment date Date on which a dividend is actually paid. *p. 610*

percentage analysis Analysis of relationships between two different items to draw conclusions or make decisions. *p. 13-4*

percent of receivables method A method of estimating the amount of uncollectible accounts by taking a percent of the outstanding receivables balance. The percentage is frequently based on a combination of factors such as historical experience, conditions of the economy, and the company's credit policies. *p. 374*

percent of revenue method A method of estimating the amount of uncollectible accounts by taking a percent of revenue that was earned on account during the accounting period. The percentage is frequently based on a combination of factors such as historical experience, condition of the economy, and the company's credit policies. *p. 368*

period costs Expenses recognized in the period in which they are incurred regardless of when cash payments for them are made; costs that cannot be directly traced to products. *pp. 80, 215*

periodic inventory system Method of accounting for inventory that requires a physical count of goods on hand at the end of the accounting period in order to determine the amount of cost of goods sold and to update the Inventory account. *p. 239*

permanent accounts Balance sheet accounts; contain information carried forward from one accounting period to the next (ending account balance one period becomes beginning account balance next period). *p. 26*

perpetual inventory system Method of accounting for inventory in which the amount of cost of goods sold is recorded for each sale of inventory; the Inventory account is increased and decreased with each purchase and sale of merchandise. *p. 216*

petty cash fund Small amount of currency kept on company premises to pay for minor items when writing checks is not practical. *p. 332*

petty cash voucher Document that verifies a petty cash disbursement, signed by the person who received the money. Supporting documents, such as an invoice, restaurant bill, or parking fee receipt, should be attached to the petty cash voucher. *p. 333*

physical flow of goods Physical movement of goods through a business, normally on a FIFO basis so that the first goods purchased are the first goods delivered to customers, reducing the likelihood of inventory obsolescence. *p. 276*

physical resources Natural resources businesses transform to create more valuable resources. *p. 5*

posting Copying transaction data from journals to ledger accounts. *p. 159*

preferred stock Class of stock, usually nonvoting, that has preferential claims (usually to dividends) over common stock. *p. 603*

Premium on Bonds Payable A liability account that represents reductions in the stated rate of interest. *p. 556*

prepaid items Deferred expenses. An example is prepaid insurance. *p. 83*

present value A measure of the value today of an amount of money expected to be exchanged on a specified future date. *p. 786*

pressure An element of the fraud triangle that recognizes conditions that motivate fraudulent or unethical behavior. *p. 96*

price-earnings (P/E) ratio Measure that reflects the values of different stocks in terms of earnings; calculated as market price per share divided by earnings (net income) per share; a higher P/E ratio generally indicates that investors are optimistic about a company's future. *pp. 615, 13-16*

primary securities market Market in which investee companies issue debt and equity securities to investors in exchange for assets; contrast with *secondary securities market*. *p. 776*

principal Amount of cash actually borrowed, to be repaid in the future with interest. *pp. 379, 501*

procedures manual Written documentation of a company's accounting policies and procedures. *p. 321*

proceeds The amount of cash received. An example is the principal amount borrowed on a discount note payable. *p. 501*

product costs All costs directly traceable to acquiring inventory and getting it ready for sale, including transportation-in. Contrast with *selling and administrative costs*. *p. 215*

productive assets See *long-term operational assets*.

profit Value added by transforming resources into products or services desired by customers. *p. 4*

profitability ratios Measurements of a firm's ability to generate earnings. *p. 13-13*

promissory note A legal document representing a credit agreement between a lender and a borrower. The note specifies technical details such as the maker, payee, interest rate, maturity date, payment terms, and any collateral. *p. 378*

property, plant, and equipment Assets such as machinery and equipment, buildings, and land, used to produce products or to carry on the administrative and selling functions of a business; sometimes called *plant assets*. *p. 422*

purchase discount Reduction in the gross price of merchandise offered to a buyer if the buyer pays cash for the merchandise within a stated time (usually within 10 days of the date of the sale). *p. 222*

purchase returns and allowances A reduction in the cost of purchases resulting from dissatisfaction with merchandise purchased. *p. 221*

qualified opinion Opinion issued by a certified public accountant that means the company's financial statements are, for the most part, in compliance with GAAP, but there is some circumstance (explained in the auditor's report) about which the auditor has reservations; contrast with *unqualified opinion*. *p. 336*

quick ratio Measure of immediate debt-paying ability; calculated by dividing very liquid assets (cash, receivables, and marketable securities) by current liabilities. *p. 13-8*

ratio analysis Analysis of relationships between two different items to draw conclusions or make decisions. *p. 13-6*

rationalization An element of the fraud triangle that recognizes a human tendency to justify fraudulent or unethical behavior. *p. 96*

realization Accounting term that usually refers to actual cash collection (e.g., collecting accounts receivable). *p. 71*

recognition Reporting an accounting event in the financial statements. *p. 71*

reinstate Recording an account receivable previously written off back into the accounting records, generally when cash is collected long after the original due date. *p. 371*

relative fair market value method Method of allocating the purchase price among individual assets acquired in a basket purchase; each asset is assigned a percentage of the total price paid for all assets. The percentage assigned equals the market value of a particular asset divided by the total of the market values of all assets acquired in the basket purchase. *p. 423*

reliability concept The accounting principle that supports reporting most assets at historical cost, because historical cost, unlike the market value of many assets, can be independently verified. Reliable information is not subjective.

reporting entities Businesses or other organizations for which financial statements are prepared. *p. 8*

restrictive covenants Provisions specified in a loan agreement that are designed to reduce creditor risk, such as limiting additional borrowing or dividend payments. *p. 547*

retail companies Businesses that sell merchandise directly to consumers. *p. 213*

retained earnings Portion of stockholders' equity that includes all earnings retained in the business since inception (revenues minus expenses and distributions for all accounting periods). *p. 12*

return on assets Profitability measure based on earnings a company generates relative to its asset base; calculated as net income divided by average total assets. *pp. 165, 13-14*

return on equity Profitability measure based on earnings a company generates relative to its stockholders' equity; calculated as net income divided by average stockholders' equity. *pp. 166, 13-15*

return on investment Measure of profitability based on the asset base of the firm; calculated as net income divided by average total assets. ROI is a product of net margin and asset turnover. *p. 13-14*

return on sales Profitability measure that reflects the percent of net income each sales dollar generates; computed by dividing net income by net sales. Also called *net income percentage*. *p. 235*

revenue The economic benefit (increase in assets or decrease in liabilities) gained by providing goods or services to customers. *pp. 14, 86*

revenue expenditures Costs incurred for repair or maintenance of long-term assets: recorded as expense and subtracted from revenue in the accounting period in which incurred. *p. 436*

salaries A term used to describe the amount due employees who are paid a set amount per week, month, or other earnings period regardless of how many hours they work during the period. *p. 490*

salaries payable Amounts owed but not yet paid to employees for services they have already performed. *p. 75*

sales discount Cash discount offered by the seller of merchandise to encourage a customer to pay promptly. When the customer takes the discount and pays less than the original selling price, the difference between the selling price and the cash collected is the sales discount. *p. 231*

sales returns and allowances A reduction in sales revenue resulting from dissatisfaction with merchandise sold. *p. 234*

salvage value Expected selling price of an asset at the end of its useful life. *pp. 98, 424*

Sarbanes-Oxley Act of 2002 Federal legislation enacted to promote ethical corporate governance and fair financial reporting. The act requires a company's chief executive officer (CEO) and chief financial officer (CFO) to certify in writing that the financial reports being issued present fairly the company's financial status. An executive who falsely certifies the company's financial reports is subject to significant fines and imprisonment. The act also establishes the Public Company Accounting Oversight Board (PCAOB), which has the primary responsibility for developing and enforcing auditing standards for CPAs who audit SEC companies. The Sarbanes-Oxley Act also prohibits auditors from providing most types of nonaudit services to companies they audit. *p. 599*

schedule of cost of goods sold Internal report used with the periodic inventory system that reflects the computation of cost of goods sold. *p. 240*

secondary securities market Market in which investors exchange securities with each other; contrast with *primary securities market*. *p. 776*

secured bonds Bonds secured by specific identifiable assets. *p. 545*

Securities Act of 1933 Federal legislation passed after the stock market crash of 1929 to regulate the issuance and subsequent trading of public company stocks and bonds; created the Securities and Exchange Commission (SEC). *p. 598*

Securities and Exchange Commission (SEC) Federal agency authorized by Congress to establish financial reporting practices of public companies; requires companies that issue securities to the public to file audited financial statements with the government annually. *p. 337*

Securities Exchange Act of 1934 See *Securities Act of 1933.*

selling and administrative costs Costs such as advertising expense and rent expense that cannot be directly traced to inventory; recognized as expenses in the period in which they are incurred. Contrast with *product costs. p. 215*

segregation of duties Internal control feature of assigning the functions of authorization, recording, and custody to different individuals. *p. 321*

serial bonds Bonds that mature at specified intervals throughout the life of the total issue. *p. 545*

service businesses Organizations such as accounting and legal firms, dry cleaners, and insurance companies that provide services to consumers. *p. 29*

service charges Fees charged by a bank for such things as services performed or penalties for overdrawn accounts or failure to maintain a specified minimum cash balance. *p. 328*

shrinkage Decreases in inventory for reasons other than sales to customers. *p. 226*

signature card Bank form that documents the bank account number and signatures of persons authorized to write checks on an account. *p. 325*

simple interest Interest computed by multiplying the principal by the interest rate by the number of periods. Previously earned interest is not added to the principal, so no interest is earned on the interest of past periods. Contrast with *compound interest. p. 785*

single-step income statement Income statement format which presents net income in one step, the difference between total revenues and total expenses. Contrast with *multistep income statement. p. 230*

sinking fund Fund to which the bond issuer contributes cash annually to ensure sufficient funds will be available to pay the face amount on the maturity date. *p. 546*

Social Security Insurance provided by the federal government to qualified individuals. Also called old age, survivors, and disability insurance (OASDI). *p. 492*

sole proprietorship Business (usually small) owned by one person. *p. 598*

solvency Ability of a business to pay liabilities in the long run. *p. 499*

solvency ratios Measures of a firm's long-term debt-paying ability. *p. 13-10*

source document Record such as a cash register tape, invoice, time card, or check stub that provides accounting information to be recorded in the accounting journals and ledgers. *p. 157*

special journals Journals designed to improve recording efficiency for specific routine, high-volume transactions such as credit sales. *p. 158*

specific authorizations Policies and procedures that apply to designated levels of management, such as the policy that only the plant manager can authorize overtime pay. *p. 322*

specific identification Inventory costing method in which cost of goods sold and ending inventory are computed using the actual costs of the specific goods sold or those on hand at the end of the period. *p. 276*

spread Difference between the rate a bank pays to obtain money (e.g., interest paid on savings accounts) and the rate the bank earns on money it lends to borrowers. *p. 561*

stakeholders Parties interested in the operations of a business, including owners, lenders, employees, suppliers, customers, and government agencies. *p. 5*

stated interest rate Rate of interest specified in the bond contract that is the percentage of face value used to calculate the amount of interest paid in cash at specified intervals over the life of the bond. *p. 544*

stated value Arbitrary value assigned to stock by the board of directors; like *par value*, designates *legal capital. p. 603*

statement of cash flows The financial statement that reports a company's cash inflows and outflows for an accounting period, classifying them as operating, investing, or financing activities. *p. 24*

statement of changes in stockholders' equity Statement that summarizes the transactions that affected the owners' equity during the accounting period. *p. 23*

stewardship Refers to a business's duty to protect and use the assets of the company for the benefit of the owners (the firm's stockholders). *p. 19*

stock certificate Document showing ownership interest issued to an investor in exchange for contributing assets to a corporation; describes ownership rights and privileges. *p. 598*

stock dividend Proportionate distribution of additional shares of the declaring corporation's stock. *p. 611*

stockholders Owners of a corporation. *pp. 12, 600*

stockholders' equity The interest in a corporation's assets that is owned by the stockholders. *p. 12*

stock split Corporate action that proportionately reduces the par value and increases the number of outstanding shares; designed to reduce the market value of the split stock. *p. 612*

straight-line amortization Method of amortization in which equal amounts of the account being reduced (e.g., Bond Discount, Bond Premium, Patent) are transferred to the appropriate expense account over the relevant time period. *p. 552*

straight-line depreciation Depreciation computations that produce equal amounts of depreciation to allocate to expense each period over an asset's life; computed by subtracting the salvage value from the asset's cost and then dividing by the number of years of useful life. *pp. 99, 425*

subordinated debentures Unsecured bonds with a lower claim on assets than general creditors; in the case of liquidation, holders are paid off after the general creditors are paid. *p. 545*

subsidiary company Company controlled (more than 50 percent owned) by another company. *p. 781*

systematic allocation of cost Process of allocating the cost of an asset to expense over several accounting periods in an orderly manner.

T-account Simple account representation, using two bars arranged in the form of the letter "T"; the account title is written across the top on the horizontal bar, debit entries are recorded on the left side of the vertical bar, and credit entries on the right side. *p. 148*

tangible assets Assets that have physical form, such as equipment, machinery, natural resources, and land. *p. 422*

temporary accounts Accounts used to collect retained earnings data applicable to only the current accounting period (revenues, expenses and distributions); sometimes called *nominal accounts. p. 26*

term bonds Bonds in an issue that mature on a specified date in the future. *p. 545*

time value of money The concept that the present value of one dollar to be exchanged in the future is less than one dollar because of interest, risk, and inflation factors. For example, a person may be willing to pay $0.90 today for the right to receive $1.00 one year from today.

times interest earned Ratio that measures a company's ability to make its interest payments; calculated by dividing the amount of earnings available for interest payments (net income before interest and income taxes) by the amount of the interest payments. *pp. 563, 13-11*

trademark Name or symbol that identifies a company or an individual product. *p. 440*

trading securities Classification for marketable securities companies plan to buy and sell quickly to generate profits from short-term appreciation in stock and bond prices. *p. 777*

transaction Business event that involves transferring something of value between two entities. *p. 13*

transferability Characteristic of corporations referring to the ease of exchanging ownership interests since ownership is divided into small, readily traded ownership units (shares of stock). *p. 600*

transportation-in (freight-in) Cost of freight on goods purchased under FOB shipping point terms; a product cost usually added to the cost of inventory. *p. 224*

transportation-out (freight-out) Freight cost for goods delivered to customers under FOB destination terms; a period cost expensed when incurred. *p. 224*

treasury stock Stock previously issued to the public that the issuing corporation has bought back. Contrast with *outstanding stock*. *p. 603*

trend analysis Study of the performance of a business over a period of time. *p. 13-3*

trial balance Schedule listing the balances of all ledger accounts; verifies mathematical accuracy of the accounting records and provides a convenient reference of current account balances. *p. 161*

true cash balance Actual amount of cash owned by a company at the close of business on the date of the bank statement. *p. 327*

2/10, n/30 Common payment terms indicating the seller is offering the purchaser a 2 percent discount off the gross invoice price if the purchaser pays the reduced amount in cash within 10 days from the merchandise purchase date.

unadjusted bank balance Depositor's cash balance reported by the bank as of the date of the bank statement. *p. 327*

unadjusted book balance Cash account balance in the depositor's accounting records as of the date of the bank reconciliation before making any adjustments. *p. 327*

uncollectible accounts expense Expense associated with uncollectible accounts receivable; amount recognized may be estimated using the allowance method, or actual losses may be recorded using the direct write-off method. *p. 368*

unearned revenue Liability arising when customers pay cash in advance for services a business will perform in the future. *p. 85*

units-of-production depreciation Depreciation computations that produce varying amounts of depreciation based on the level of an asset's usage each period rather than a measure of time; for example, automobile depreciation may be based on total estimated miles to be driven rather than total estimated years to be used. *p. 430*

unqualified opinion Opinion issued by a certified public accountant that means the company's financial statements are, in all material respects, in compliance with GAAP; the auditor has no reservations. Contrast with *qualified opinion*. *p. 336*

unrealized gains or losses Paper gains or losses on investment securities the company still owns; not realized until the securities are sold or otherwise disposed of. *p. 779*

unsecured bonds (debentures) Bonds backed by the general credit of the organization. *p. 545*

unsubordinated debentures Unsecured bonds with claims on assets equal to those of general creditors. *p. 545*

users Individuals or organizations that use financial information for decision making. *p. 5*

useful life The period of time over which an asset is expected to be used in the normal operation of a business. *p. 98*

variable interest rate Interest rate that fluctuates (changes) from period to period over the life of the loan. *p. 538*

vertical analysis Analysis technique that compares items on financial statements to significant totals. *p. 13-5*

vertical statements model Concurrent representation of several financial statements shown vertically on a page. *p. 90*

voluntarily disclosing Professional responsibility to clients that prohibits CPAs, in most circumstances, from revealing information obtained as a result of their client–accountant relationships.

Wage and Tax Statement, Form W-2 Form used by employers to notify each employee of the amount of his or her gross earnings for the year and the amounts withheld by the employer. *p. 491*

wages A term used to describe amounts due employees who are paid according to the number of hours they actually work. *p. 490*

warranties Promises to correct deficiencies or dissatisfactions in quality, quantity, or performance of products or services sold. *p. 486*

weighted-average cost flow method Inventory cost flow method in which the cost allocated between inventory and cost of goods sold is based on the weighted average cost per unit, which is determined by dividing the total cost of goods available for sale during the accounting period by the total units available for sale during the period. If the weighted average is recomputed with each successive purchase, the result is a moving average. *p. 276*

wholesale companies Companies that sell goods to other businesses. *p. 213*

withdrawals Distributions of assets to the owners of proprietorships and partnerships. *p. 601*

working capital Current assets minus current liabilities. *p. 13-7*

working capital ratio Another term for the current ratio: calculated by dividing current assets by current liabilities. *p. 13-8*

PHOTO CREDITS

CHAPTER 1

p. 2 © The McGraw-Hill Companies, Inc./John Flournoy; p. 4 © David Buffington/Getty Images; p. 8 © Lars Niki; p. 9 © Denny Henry/epa/Corbis; p. 20 © Jeff Greenberg 4 of 6 /Alamy; p. 31 top © PRNewsFoto/Gogo; p. 31 bottom left © Digital Vision/Punchstock; p. 31 bottom center © The McGraw-Hill Companies, Inc./Andrew Resek; p. 31 bottom right © Monty Rakusen/Getty Images.

CHAPTER 2

p. 72 © B. O'Kane/Alamy; p. 81 © Getty Images/Stockbyte; p. 91 © AP Photo/Daniel Hushizer.

CHAPTER 3

p. 147 © Robert Clay/Alamy; p. 159 © AP Photo/Paul Sakuma; p. 167 © Corbis/Punch Stock; p. 168 © Comstock Images/Alamy.

CHAPTER 4

p. 213 © Jim West/Alamy; p. 216 © BananaStock/PunchStock; p. 220 © Steve Allen/Brand X Pictures; p. 230 © Roberts Publishing Services—All rights reserved; p. 234 © Lars A. Niki; p. 237 © AP Photo/Daniel Hulshizer.

CHAPTER 5

p. 275 © AP Photo/Michael Conroy; p. 276 © Andersen Ross/Brand X/Corbis; p. 281 © Michel Kemp/Alamy; p. 284 © Imaginechina via AP Images; p. 285 © Martial Colomb/Getty Images; p. 287 © 2007 Getty Images, Inc.; p. 291 © AP Photo/Steve Pope.

CHAPTER 6

p. 319 © AP Photo/Paul Sakuma; p. 320 © AP Photo/Charles Bennett; p. 324 © B. O'Kane/Alamy; p. 325 © Royalty-Free/Corbis; p. 328 © Ryan McVay/Getty Images; p. 338 © ZUMA Press, Inc./Alamy.

CHAPTER 7

p. 365 © idp geneva collection/Alamy; p. 372 © Jack Star/PhotoLink/Getty Images; p. 383 © AP Photo/PayPal, Kim White; p. 387 top © Karen Bleier/AFP/Getty Images; p. 387 bottom left © Press Association via AP Images PA Wire URN: 10078629; p. 387 bottom center © Press Association via AP Images PA Wire URN: 10078629; p. 387 bottom right © Press Association via AP Images PA Wire URN: 10078629.

CHAPTER 8

p. 421 © AP Photo/Environmental Ministry/Rasio Ridhosani, Ho; p. 428 © iStock RF; p. 434 © Skip Nall/Getty Images; p. 440 © Adam Gault/Getty Images; p. 441 © The McGraw-Hill Companies, Inc./Christopher Kerrigan; p. 445 © iStock RF.

CHAPTER 9

p. 481 © Ingram Publishing; p. 485 © AP Photo/Ed Reinke; p. 490 © The McGraw-Hill Companies, Inc./Andrew Resek, photographer; p. 492 © C. Sherburne/PhotoLink/Getty Images; p. 499 © david pearson/Alamy.

CHAPTER 10

p. 539 © imageBROKER/Alamy; p. 545 © Falkenstein/Bildagentur-online Historical Collect./Alamy; p. 546 © Jacob Andrzejczak/Getty Images.

CHAPTER 11

p. 597 © Stockbyte/Getty Images; p. 601 © The McGraw-Hill Companies, Inc./John Flournoy, photographer; p. 608 © PRNewsFoto/Marriott International, Inc.; p. 611 © Hannelore Foerster/Bloomberg via Getty Images; p. 614 © Caro/Alamy.

CHAPTER 12

p. 645 © Zoonar GMBH/Alamy; p. 647 © Ryan McVay/Getty Images; p. 662 © Royalty-Free/Corbis; p. 666 © AP Photo/Mel Evans; p. 667 © iStock RF; p. 668 © 2007 Keith Eng.

CHAPTER 13

p. 13-1 top © Brent Lewin/Bloomberg via Getty Images; p. 13-1 bottom © Justin Sullivan/Getty Images; p. 13-2 © Susan Van Etten/PhotoEdit; p. 13-13 © AP Photo/Paul Sakuma.

INDEX

C

D